SCOTTISH LITERATURE

This volume, *Scottish Literature*, gives basic introductions to the great periods of Scottish literature; the medieval, the eighteenth century, the neglected nineteenth century, the 'Scottish Renaissance' of the twentieth century, and the contemporary and prolific revival of fiction, poetry and drama today. It gives in-depth treatment of major texts from such authors as Henryson and Scott to MacDiarmid, Gunn and Gibbon, contemporary poets like MacCaig, Morgan and Lochhead, as well as many others. Recognising that general readers, teachers and students will focus more closely on later periods, the content of discussion is greater in the post-1800 period; and for similar reasons fiction is foregrounded, aiming to meet the needs and interests of a general readership. Throughout, the aim is to present Scottish writing and writers in accessible and stimulating discussion which provokes questions as well as suggesting further authors, texts and possible comparisons. The second volume, *Language and Scottish Literature*, explores varieties of Scots and links them with literary studies; investigating questions of vocabulary and metaphor, it looks at language in use, examining sounds and structures, narrative and issues going beyond the text. In keeping with the aim of the series to look at Scottish culture of older periods, the volume ends with a discussion of the language of older Scottish texts. The third volume, *Teaching Scottish Literature: Curriculum and Classroom Applications*, engages with current debates concerning what constitutes a Scottish text, the place of Scottish texts in an English course, the theoretical issues in teaching such texts, and the use of varieties of Scots in courses and writing. The volume gives extensive and varied exemplars while suggesting models for interdisciplinary use and how to use writing workshops.

Scottish Literature
In English and Scots

Edited by
Douglas Gifford, Sarah Dunnigan and Alan MacGillivray

Editorial Assistants
*Beth Dickson, Jackie Fairgrieve, Gordon Gibson,
Hazel Hynd, Helen Lloyd and Lyndsay Lunan*

Edinburgh University Press

© The Contributors, 2002

Edinburgh University Press Ltd
22 George Square, Edinburgh

Typeset in by Baskerville by Hewer Text Ltd, Edinburgh,
and printed and bound in Great Britain by
The Bath Press Limited, Bath

A CIP record for this book is
available from the British Library

ISBN 0 7486 0825 7 (paperback)

Contents

CONTENTS

How to use this book

This is not a history of Scottish literature; nor is it a series of chronological entries. What this volume tries to do is steer between a thorough-going literary history and an itemised companion, bearing in mind a readership ranging from undergraduate university and higher school to the generally interested reader and the arts and media professional. There already exist some excellent one-volume histories, such as those by Maurice Lindsay, Roderick Watson and Marshall Walker, as well as the ambitious four-volume series of 1987–8 from Aberdeen University Press. The companion guides of Daiches and Royle have proven their worth to countless readers. That said, with new curricula in schools and colleges giving greater emphasis to Scottish culture, and the return of a Scottish parliament, the necessity for this volume and the series of which it is a part became clear. What was needed in addition to the two kinds of literary guide available was a balanced mixture of historical and cultural context on one hand, and appropriate depth of discussion of some key texts and authors on the other. It is to be hoped that this volume achieves such balance. We believe that constant reference to identification and connection with other literary and cultural traditions, from the medieval to the modern period, comes over as a clear and healthy sign of a literature only sometimes inward-looking and doubtful of its identity, which frequently turns its ambivalences and dualisms into positive strengths, and increasingly and unapologetically articulates existential contradictions and pluralities.

The volume is in six main sections with an extensive bibliography as Section 7. We have tried to recognise the importance of students – and general readers – gaining some understanding of different periods and the very different mindsets of their creative writers by defining periods which seem to us to have internal justification and patterning, and yet to suggest a flow of culture and ideas which give validity to the assertion of a broad and recognisably different tradition, with several derivative traditions, of Scottish literature. Each section begins with an overview of the period, suggesting main currents and developments. Thereafter the section chooses around six or so major authors or topics, so that general concepts and outlines are given some detailed exemplification. Where a single text of a major author is dealt with in depth, we try also to give some indication of other significant achievements. Each section then finishes with suggestions for the reader to widen the range of reference, by suggesting other important writers and texts to explore, and comparisons, authorial and thematic, which can fruitfully be made. The reader will note that we departed somewhat from this pattern in Section 6. Given the proliferation of fiction, poetry and drama in the last few decades it seemed invidious to single out individual texts, although we did realise that there had to be some foregrounding of major events such as Alasdair Gray's *Lanark* or Liz Lochhead's *Mary Queen of Scots Got Her Head Chopped Off*. But contemporary works need time to settle into their place, and for this period we decided to make the essays general, with local specific emphasis. Thus Widening the Range for Section 6 becomes more of a series of suggestions for ways of making connections than the usual recommendation for further reading.

The editors value all periods of Scottish literature; but recognising the fact that the majority of general readers and students will be interested in the later periods, and particularly in fiction, there is some weighting towards post-1800 literature, and towards the sustained achievement of Scottish fiction. That said, we very much hope that the topics and discussions here will lead readers towards a range of periods and genres.

This material covers what is essentially Lowland Scottish literature. For virtually all the readership and purposes we envisage, Gaelic language and culture is available only in translation, and we have tried at points (as with the chapter on Sorley MacLean) to recognise the impact of Gaelic culture, through translation, for a wider audience. Volume 3 in the series, *Teaching Scottish Literature* (ed. Alan MacGillivray), contains a chapter on 'Gaelic–the Senior Partner', which we recommend to those interested, together with our regret that, quite simply, the limits of space in a volume already hard-pressed to cover its remit, could not allow us to expand in that direction.

Since the book is not primarily aimed at an advanced academic audience, an early decision was taken to avoid footnotes, merely supplying sufficient context information, such as chapter location. Likewise, medieval orthography has been modified. We have supplied extensive reading lists in Section 7, balancing selected major works with selected critical reading. The interested reader can easily find primary texts in an abundance of sources, such as those already mentioned and in specific bibliographies. Our procedure has been to give primary help where we feel it is not so readily available, and to supply what is much more difficult to find; the help in discussion and criticism which enables readers to make their own interpretations and evaluations. The same considerations lie behind the suggestions for resources and connections.

The volume is part of the Edinburgh University Press series on Scottish language and literature; the other volumes are *Language and Scottish Literature*, by John Corbett, and *Teaching Scottish Literature*, edited by Alan MacGillivray. The series general editor is Douglas Gifford.

Douglas Gifford
Sarah Dunnigan
Alan MacGillivray
The University of Glasgow, 2002

SECTION 1
Early Scottish Literature

CHAPTER 1

LITERARY ROOTS: MEDIEVAL POETRY

RETURNING TO THE ORIGINS

A contemporaneous study of Scotland's early literature is needed in order to throw light on an age in history which has been unfairly neglected – an age overshadowed by the dramatic peaks of the Wars of Independence and the Reformation. And from this dark period of history emerges a literature significant for its intrinsic qualities of narrative strength and poetic sophistication.

With the loss and deliberate destruction of manuscripts and libraries during the seemingly endless incursions of invading forces (and later, during the crisis of the Reformation), scholars of medieval literature are faced with the problem of defining what materials are Scottish in origin in any works predating 1400. The earliest surviving poetry in Older Scots is this fragment which recounts the sorry state of the kingdom in the interregnum after the death of Alexander III in 1286. This version was recorded a century and a half after it was supposedly written and can be found in Clancy's *The Triumph Tree*, 1998:

Qwhen Alexander our kynge was dede,	*When; dead*
That Scotlande lede in lauche and le,	*led in law and peace*
Away was sons of alle and brede,	*abundance; bread*
Off wyne and wax, of gamyn and gle.	*merriment*
Christ, born in virgynyte,	*virginity*
Succoure Scotlande, and ramede,	*help*
That stade is in perplexite.	*is placed*

It is interesting, not just for the picture it gives us of the times, but for its literary form: its use of alliteration, metre and rhyme, which suggest an already flourishing literary culture of considerable sophistication.

THE LANGUAGE OF OLDER SCOTS

The kingdom of the Scots in the fourteenth century was a place of elaborate social and political allegiances and the linguistic situation was no less complex. The language of poetry, called *Inglis* at that time, was called *Scottis* to distinguish it from the southern tongue from which it was rapidly diverging and which political imperatives made it necessary to label differently. The poet Gavin Douglas, writing in 1513, was the first to name the language he used as *Scottis*.

Older Scots was one of the various linguistic descendants of the Teutonic invaders who began to fill the gap left by the withdrawal of Roman power in 410 AD. The Saxon tongue developed in the south; the Anglian tongue, similar, but not identical, developed in the north. By the time records of both had been written, they had taken on numerous variations and peculiarities, and while mutually comprehensible, they had diverged into distinct forms of the original. At roughly the same time as the Teutonic settlements, the Scots, from Ireland, had begun to arrive in the west. They brought with them their Celtic tongue, which would later develop into Scots Gaelic. Add to this the Norman French used by the feudal overlords, the universal Latin of education and the church, and no doubt the surviving remnants of the languages of the overrun Pictish inhabitants, and it can easily be seen that the linguistic culture of fourteenth-century Scotland was both rich and complex. (An excellent summary of the history of the Scots language is to be found in the introduction to the *Concise Scots Dictionary*, 1985.)

The language of Older and Middle Scots must inevitably have a strange appearance to those unfamiliar with it (which is all of us at one stage or another) just as the language of Chaucer, Barbour's contemporary, once appeared peculiar. However, familiarity is easily attained: basic items of vocabulary can be learnt, and certain spelling and phonetic conventions – such as the common initial prefix '*quh-*' which is equivalent to modern 'wh-' (e.g. *quhat*/what, *quho*/who) – can be quickly recognised. Reading with an ear for the sound of the text will greatly assist recognition and understanding.

Barbour's Brus

It is fitting that the first substantial masterpiece of Scots literature should deal with the successful struggle for the very survival of the nation. In any country with a history less given to irony than that of Scotland, *The Brus* by John Barbour (c. 1320–95) would be the universally known national poem, taught in schools to all children and its lines familiarly used as a reference point by its citizens. Here the quotes are from Duncan's *John Barbour, The Bruce* (2000).

Barbour's huge poem (c. 14,000 lines) covers the period of the Wars of Independence from the Competitors for the crown to the death of Robert I and tells the stirring tale of James Douglas's attempt to take Bruce's heart to the Holy Land. It is, however, principally neither journalism nor history, but a work of literature. *The Brus* crosses many generic boundaries, encompassing features of epic, romance and chronicle.

The work seems, at first glance, to be performing the role of a straightforward history in recounting the tumultuous events of the years 1286–1332. Barbour begins by expressing the wish that he should have the skill 'To put in wryt a suthfast [*truthful*] story' (I, 13), and declares 'That I say nocht but suthfast thing' (I, 36). When the narrative proper begins, there is what seems to be a conscious echo of the fragment mentioned above (I, 37–8):

> Quhen Alexander the king wes deid   *dead*
> That Scotland haid to steyr and leid . . .   *had to guide and lead*

but no sooner has he outlined the 'perplexitie' which the Scots found themselves in when they turned to Edward for advice, than he calls them 'A! Blind folk full off all foly . . .' (I, 91) for giving Edward his opportunity. This is a clear indication that the events are not merely being relayed to us, but being interpreted for us too.

THE ROMANCE OF THE HERO-KING

Although historians reckon that Barbour is fairly accurate in his depiction of events, and quite remarkably accurate by the prevailing standards of medieval historiography, nonetheless, his project was not to write history as we today would understand it. Instead, as he plainly states, he is to recount the noble deeds of arms and chivalry performed by heroic individuals, in particular the hero-king – Robert I and his loyal liegeman James Douglas. Barbour himself is open about his purposes and his methods. After a picture of the miseries of occupation under the English and the famous apostrophe to freedom (I, 225):

> A! Fredome is a noble thing!

He makes explicit what he is about (I, 445–6):

> Lordingis, quha likis for till her,   *My lords, who cares to listen*
> The romanys now begynnys her.   *The romance now begins here*

5

Using the traditional invocation to listeners to gather round, he declares that the romance will now begin, and it is through this artistic filter that we must decipher the events which he relates throughout the following twenty books. (The division of the poem into books was the work of an eighteenth-century editor and it is important to consider how this retrospective adaptation affects the reading of Barbour's narrative.) However accurate Barbour may be, he is, like any narrator, selective in the choice of incident, but is also writing with the primary purpose of extolling the king and his lieutenant, and is consequently partial in his presentation of events.

The king suffers greatly (to expiate the crime of killing Comyn) but prevails; in the face of brutality he is magnanimous; against overwhelming odds he is victorious; his own physical prowess exceeds that of his enemies; he is ever gentle to the weak and powerless. Whatever basis these elements might have in reality, they are nonetheless the stuff of romance heroes. The foregrounding of the king is paralleled only by the doughty deeds of Douglas, whilst he is contrasted against the unrelenting brutality of the first Edward, the vacillating incompetence of the second and the rashness of Edward Bruce.

As a final point, it is surely significant that a poem of 14,000 lines purporting to tell the story of the Wars of Independence makes no mention of William Wallace. Furthermore, even Bruce's crossing of his personal Rubicon by the killing of Comyn at Dumfries is dealt with in a throwaway dozen lines or so, which conclude with the author expressing his sympathy for the killer and incidentally comparing him to a romance hero (II, 45–7):

Tharfor sa hard myscheiff him fell	*In this way such great misfortune afflicted him*
That Ik herd never in romanys tell	*of a kind that I have never heard told in a romance*
Off man sa hard frayit as wes he . . .	*about a man who was so long suffering as he was*

The Brus is a work of literature, therefore, and is to be judged by the standards of artistic endeavour, rather than of historical accuracy. First and foremost, it is a rattling good tale, crammed from beginning to end with exciting incidents which could well belong to the realm of myth or romance, were they not verified from other factual sources: Bruce's escape from Edward's control, the murder of Comyn, Bruce's coronation, the rout of Methven, the escape to Rathlin, the death of the implacable Edward, the attempt to retake Carrick, the Douglas Larder, the ambush in Glen Trool, the fray at Loudoun Hill, the king's illness at Inverurie, the harrying of Buchan, the siege of Perth, the battle in the Pass of Brander, the taking of Roxburgh Castle, the capture of Edinburgh Castle, the siege of Stirling and the highlight of Bannockburn, the Irish campaigns, the capture of Berwick, the raids into England, the Treaty of Northampton, the preparation for the succession, the death of the king, Douglas's death in Spain on his way to the Holy Land with the king's heart. Even such a derisory synopsis conveys something of the breathless excitement of the tale.

These historical events are marshalled and organised by Barbour in such a way as to present his hero in the most flattering light. There are frequent apostrophes where he breaks away from the action to comment or present an analogy, often linking the deeds of the king with those performed by historical or mythical heroes, such as when he causes the king to speak of Julius Caesar (III, 277ff.) or when he expatiates on some quality, like prophecy (IV, 668ff.) or valour (VI, 323) or leadership (IX, 63ff.). The romance element is reinforced at the occasion of the crossing of Loch Lomond when the king entertains his men while they wait for the others to join them by reading to them the romance of Ferumbras (III, 435–9):

The king the quhilis meryly	*meantime*
Red to thaim that war him by	*read to them that were nearby him*
Romanys of worthi Ferambrace	*a romance about worthy Ferumbras*
That worthily our-cummyn was	*that was defeated*
Throu the rycht doughty Olyver . . .	*worthy*

There are many little incidents which are designed to illustrate aspects of character such as the king's astonishing a French knight who watches him participate personally in the siege of Perth by wading neck-deep in a ditch (IX, 387–410), or when the king causes his army to wait until a laundrywoman has her baby. Barbour takes care to underline the point (XVI, 293–6):

This wes a full gret curtasy	
That swilk a kyng and sa mychty	*such*
Gert his men dwell on this maner	*made*
Bot for a pouer lauender.	*poor laundrywoman*

One of the most attractive features running through the poem is what we might call in our own time the 'democratic' element (however anachronistic the term might be in a medieval context). For example, the senior commanders of the Scottish army are forthright in their condemnation of what they see as the king's foolhardiness in risking all in his tryst with Henry de Bohun before Bannockburn (XII, 89–92):

> The lordis off his cumpany
> Blamyt him as thai durst gretumly   *blamed him as they dared*
> That he him put in aventur   *that he put himself at risk*
> To mete sa syth a knycht and sture . . .   *to fight such a valiant and unyielding knight*

Similarly, Barbour gives credit to the many ordinary folk who contributed to the common cause, often naming individuals whose bravery or cunning have assisted in achieving the aims of war, such as Tom Dickson (V, 279ff.), or William Bunnock, who conveyed troops into Linlithgow hidden in his cart (X, 153ff.), or the delightfully romantic William Francis (X, 535ff.) who knew of a way up the rock of Edinburgh Castle because he had been accustomed to go that way to meet his sweetheart (X, 535ff.), or Sym Spalding (XVII, 23ff.).

As well as these named individuals, Barbour on one occasion names an eyewitness, Sir Alan Cathcart, from whom he claims to have heard an account of an action (IX, 580–1):

> Schyr Alane off Catkert be name
> Tauld me this taile as I sall tell . . .   *told*

Here, Barbour's purpose in naming a witness presents more than one narrative intention. It is possible that he has utilised the character primarily for artistic purpose, to lend verisimilitude to his narrative whilst also strengthening his historical presentation by external validation.

THE VERSE FORM

If *The Brus* is outstanding as a stirring tale, one of the main factors which makes its narrative so effective and fast-moving is the verse form which Barbour has chosen. Just as the 'Qwhen Alexander . . .' fragment indicates something of the cultural environment from which it arose, a huge, carefully organised work like *The Brus* could not have sprung up without progenitors. Barbour's many references to romance literature in the poem demonstrate his easy familiarity with French literature of the period, where tales of knightly daring and chivalrous adventure abound, for example, in the works of his contemporary, Froissart, the most celebrated chronicler of valorous enterprise. The metre, that fast-moving tetrameter couplet which Burns adopted for 'Tam o' Shanter', he took from English models, imparting speed when required by repeated initial use of 'And . . .' or other conjunctions, as when Sir Henry de Bohun (XII, 33–40):

Come on a sted a bow-schote ner	*came on a horse a bow-shot in front of*
Befor all other that thar wer,	*that were there*
And knew the king for that he saw	
Him sua rang his men on raw	*arranged his men in line*
And by the croune that wes set	
Alsua apon his bassynet,	*also; basinet*
And towart him he went in hy.	*with speed*
And quhen the king.	

The form is also capable of considerable dignity, as in Sir Giles d'Argentan's restrained rebuke to his monarch, the fleeing Edward II (XIII, 299–308):

And quhen Schyr Gylis the Argenté	
Saw the king thus and his menye	*men*
Schap thaim to fley sa spedyly,	*made*
He come rycht to the king in hy	
And said, 'Schyr, sen it is sua	*since it is so*
That ye thusgat your gat will ga	
Havys gud day for agayne will I,	
Yeit fled I never sekyrly	*yet; certainly*
And I cheys her to bid and dey	*choose*
Than for to lyve schamly and fley.'	*in shame*

Barbour tells us himself that the poem was written in 1375 (XIII, 709ff.) and there is record of his being paid for its completion, along with another (now lost) work based on the Stewart dynasty. The fact that the poem seems to have been commissioned, presumably by King Robert II, Robert Bruce's grandson and the son of Walter Stewart (who appears on several occasions), casts considerable light on how the poem was intended to be read.

The Kingis Quair

After this rousing tale of derring-do, chivalry and knightly virtues, medieval literature steps into a new age, opening with the first pages of *The Kingis Quair* (c. 1420s–30s). The poem has traditionally been attributed to James I, and he seems as likely a candidate as any other given the opportunities he had to familiarise himself with the models on which it is based, as well as the circumstances of his life, which appear to be referred to a number of times in the text. In 1406 the young Prince James was sent to France for safety by his father, but with ironic inevitability was captured by the English on his way and imprisoned. He succeeded to the throne only months later and spent the next eighteen years in relatively comfortable confinement before his return to Scotland in 1424 with his English queen, Joan Beaufort.

Just as *The Brus*, if considered as 'history', is not to be read from a modern perspective, *The Kingis Quair*, if biography, is something other than a mere recounting of a few incidents in the life of James I. To which genre can we assign it? Is it allegory, dream-vision or a sampler of contemporary poetic techniques, themes and concerns?

The poem shows its provenance by employing much of the machinery available to the fashionable English and French poets of the fourteenth century. The centre is in the form of an allegorical dream vision, later much exploited by Scottish poets such as Henryson, Dunbar and Douglas. It is populated by the classical pagan personages, such as the Muses, Venus, Cupid and Minerva, while still postulating a Christian view of human life. Rhetorical devices abound, like the complaint to Venus, the formal catalogue of animals, or the description of the loved one. The courtly love conventions of the desolate lover pining till granted grace by his lady, the garden setting and the chorus of the birds all appear in the poem. The range and sophistication of these poetic techniques mark a powerful new direction in Scottish poetry, as does the appearance of the elegant Rhyme Royal stanza, later much favoured by Henryson.

The quotes here are from Jack and Rozendaal's *The Mercat Anthology of Early Scottish Literature* (2000).

NARRATIVE STRUCTURE AND SUMMARY

The narrator, lying in bed on a cold winter night, entertains thoughts inspired by contemplation of Boethius, which introduces the major theme in the poem: the vicissitudes of fortune, and its expression in the form of Fortune's 'tolter quhele' (st. 9). After considering how Fortune treated Boethius, the narrator turns to how she treats himself (st. 10):

> Among thir thoughtis rolling to and fro,   *these*
> Fell me to mynd of my Fortune and ure: *luck*
> In tender youth how sche was first my fo
> And eft my frende, and how I gat recure   *made recovery*
> Off my distresse . . .

At this point he thinks he hears a bell ring, which inspires him 'Sum newe thing to write' (st. 13):

> And furthwithall my pen in hand I tuke   *straightaway*
> And made a croce, and thus begouth my buke.   *the sign of the cross; began*

and it would appear that a second start is made, in which life is likened to a ship's voyage, with all its attendant perils, and applied to the narrator himself (st. 17):

> With doutfull hert, amang the rokkis blake,   *heart; black rocks*
> My feble bote full fast to stere and rowe,   *steer*
> Helples, allone, the wynter nyght I wake,   *night*
> To wayte the wind that furthward suld me throwe.   *awaiting the wind that will guide me forwards*

After a traditional invocation to the poetic Muses, a third beginning is made, with a conventional opening in spring (st. 20):

> In Vere, that full of vertu is and gude . . .   *in spring*

Insofar as the poem is in any way autobiographical, it would seem that this introductory section does relate to the circumstances of the writer's life, and tallies rather well with what is known of the life of the young James (st. 22):

> . . . out of my contree,   *country*
> By thaire avise that had of me the cure,   *advice that took care of me*
> Be see to pas, tuke I myn aventure.   *by sea I set out on my destiny*

but (st. 24):

> quhethir we wold or no,   *whether we would or not*
> With strong hand, by forse, schortly to say,
> Of inymyis takin and led away   *enemies*
> We weren all, and broght in thaire contree.

though this is attributed to Fortune (fate) (st. 24):

> Fortune it schupe noe othir wayis to be.   *Fortune decreed it could be no other way*

A further theme is introduced and expanded: the relationship between freedom and slavery, literal or metaphorical (st. 27):

The bird, the beste, the fisch eke in the see,   *also*
They lyve in fredome, everich in his kynd;   *according to its nature*
And I, a man, and lakkith libertee.   *lack*

Then, while imprisoned, the narrator overlooks 'a gardyn fair', where the birds are singing, and in that garden he has his first sight of (st. 40):

The fairest or the freschest yong floure
That ever I sawe, me thoght, before that houre . . .

This sighting continues the freedom/slavery theme with the declaration (st. 41):

. . . sudaynly, my hert became hir thrall
For ever, of free wyll, for of manace   *threat*
There was no takyn in hir swete face.   *sign*

This provokes a lengthy rhetorical examination of the lover's reaction with an appropriately hyperbolic litany of praise for the beloved: is she a 'hevinly thing . . . Cupidis owin princesse . . . verray Nature the goddesse' (st. 42–3)? She represents 'Beautee eneuch to mak a world to dote' (st. 47). The nightingale and other birds sing as a kind of accompaniment to his new-found devotion, while the plight of the ungratified lover is signalled by the vocabulary of unacknowledged love: 'peyne', 'turment', 'wepe and waile', 'teris'. In this sorry state he falls into a reverie, and experiences a kind of dream or vision (st. 73):

Half sleping and half swoun, in swich a wise;   *fainting in such a way*
And quhat I met, I will yow now devise . . .   *describe*

Medieval writers often used the dream as a means of entry to a world otherwise unapproachable, a world of imagination where human action and motivation could be symbolically analysed, the normal rules of reality being suspended. Indeed, a similar state of deeper vision is often attained in later Scottish literature through forms of intoxication, as with Stevenson's *Dr Jekyll*, Burns's 'Tam o' Shanter,' or MacDiarmid's *A Drunk Man Looks at the Thistle*.

The dream vision occupies about half of the entire poem; as an indication of its significance, Cresseid's dream takes up about one-third of Henryson's *Testament*. In his heightened state of awareness he travels through the spheres until he finds himself (st. 77):

> Within a chamber large, rowm, and faire: *roomy*
> And there I fand of peple grete repaire.   *I found a large number of people gathered*

The people are, in fact, lovers of various kinds, old and young, happy and unfulfilled, and so his journey is an allegorical exploration of the experience of love, which is explicitly linked to the overriding theme of fortune (st. 93):

> And othir also I sawe compleynyng there
> Upon Fortune and hir grete variance . . .

Among the throng he finds Cupid with his arrows, and then Venus herself, to whom he presents his case and asks for access to the lady. Venus replies that because of his special circumstances (st. 108):

> Thy persone standis noght in libertee.

and because he is so unworthy of the lady, he needs the advice of other deities; and she refers him to Minerva (st. 126):

> And straught unto the presence sodeynly
> Of Dame Minerve, the pacient goddesse,
> Gude Hope, my gyde, led me redily . . .

Minerva tells him that if lust, rather than love, is his object, his quest is in vain. He presses to assure her that his intentions are honourable, and it is a measure of the complex machinery in such a poem that the pagan goddess Minerva cautions the lover (st. 142):

> 'Desire,' quod sche, 'I nyl it noght deny,   *will not deny it*
> So thou it ground and set in Christin wise' . . .   *in a Christian way*

Even Minerva's power seems, however, to be subject to that of Fortune, since she offers as assistance (st. 144):

> 'I will pray hir full faire   *earnestly pray*
> That Fortune be no more there to contraire.'

Minerva works her way through a familiar medieval process of argument, by citing 'sum clerkis', opposing to them what is said by 'othir clerkis', but concluding by making what is ultimately a moral observation; that fortune is at its strongest when the individual is ignorant or unprepared, and that consequently it is our duty to inform ourselves as much as we may, in order to limit the influence Fortune has in our lives (st. 149):

And therefore thus I say to this sentence:	*I conclude*
Fortune is most and strangest evermore	*greatest and strongest*
Quhare lest foreknawing or intelligence	*least knowledge*
Is in the man; and, sone, of wit and lore	*knowledge and learning*
Sen thou art wayke and feble – lo, therefore,	*since*
The more thou art in dangere and commune	*engage*
With hir that clerkis clepen so, 'Fortune.'	*scholars call*

The narrator's return to earth lands him in a pleasant place, underlined by descriptive alliteration (st. 152):

Quhare – throu the gravel bryght as ony gold –	*where*
The cristall water ran so clere and cold,	
That in myn ere maid contynualy	*ear*
A maner soune, mellit with armony . . .	*a kind of sound mixed with harmony*

A further set-piece of medieval writing is included in the list of animals (similar to that in Henryson's 'The Trial of the Fox' in the *Fables*) until he finds himself at last in front of 'Fortune the goddesse' and her wheel, on which a multitude of folk are clambering. Fortune puts him on the wheel and the dream comes to a sudden and unexpected end (st. 172):

'Fare wele,' quod sche, and by the ere me toke	*she said, and took me by the ear*
So ernestly that therewithall I woke.	*because of that*

Awake, he is uncertain of the meaning of the advice he has been given in his dream, until a turtle dove appears holding a spray of flowers with a written message of comfort and good cheer which so heartens him that he reads it over a hundred times (st. 180):

And at my beddis hed with gud entent	*bedhead; intention*
I have it fair pynnit up: and this	*pinned it up*
First takyne was of all my help and blisse.	*sign*

The first token causes him to see the situation clearly at last and to resolve the conflict between freedom and thraldom (st. 193):

14

In lufis yok that esy is and sure.   *love's yoke that is sure and certain.*

The poet's *envoi* is a conventional device. Its first words (st. 194, 1353):

Go, litill tretise, nakit of eloquence,   *treatise; naked*

recall Chaucer's *Troilus and Criseyde*, V, 1786:

Go, litil bok, go litil myn tragedye

and indeed has predecessors back as far as Roman times, with its *excusatio*, and its consciousness of launching the book on an unknown and lengthy voyage. A reverential acknowledgement of the power of God ends with a repetition of the first line of the poem, again displaying the author's awareness of structural organisation. With a final conventional invocation of the English poets Chaucer and Gower by name, 'my maisteris dere', he ends with a particularly neat double commendation, of his Rhyme Royal verses, and the souls of the poets to God (st. 197):

I recommend my buk in lynis sevin –   *book in [stanzas of] seven lines*
And eke thair saulis unto the blisse of hevin.   *also; souls*

Even if no more remained of early and medieval Scottish literature than *The Brus* and *The Kingis Quair*, the extensive contrasts in subject matter, genre, format, vocabulary, range of reference, characterisation and purpose clearly indicate a rich, varied, and thriving literary culture.

CHAPTER 2

ROBERT HENRYSON
AND WILLIAM DUNBAR

REDISCOVERING HENRYSON (c. 1450–c. 1505)

The fifteenth century was a period of great change in Scotland which saw a remarkable literary creativity. Writers were experimenting with new themes and new styles with an expertise and bravura which demonstrated the confidence they felt in their handling of their materials. The Scots word 'makar' stresses and makes explicit the craftsmanship expected of a poet. For many reasons, more historical than literary, this period of astonishing artistic achievement has been sadly overlooked and needs to be restored to its important place within the outstanding achievements of Scottish and European literature.

It is therefore gratifying to observe in recent years the rapidly growing interest in the work of Robert Henryson. The continuing rediscovery and re-evaluation of Scotland's past is enabling us to see Henryson's achievement in a more satisfactory perspective and so to give him his place as a writer with whose name and work all students of literature should be familiar. In recent years excellent editions of his work have been published; he has been recommended for study in the syllabus of the Scottish Certificate of Sixth Year Studies; and in 1993 the Robert Henryson Society was founded in Dunfermline to serve as a focus for activities connected with his works.

We know very little for certain about Henryson's life and career, but it is likely that the poet is the Robert Henryson recorded as being in attendance at the then newly founded University of Glasgow in 1462, and that he was master of the school connected to the great Benedictine Abbey at Dunfermline. The abbey was one of the wealthiest institutions in medieval Scotland and Henryson (maybe) was also responsible for the transaction of some of its legal matters. He probably lived from about 1450 to 1505.

THE MORALL FABILLIS: THE FABLE TRADITION

A glance at Henryson's work shows clearly how firmly he was embedded in the European tradition, all his major works having as their starting points stories and themes which had fascinated Europe's writers for centuries. Most readers will first encounter Henryson through his fables; an ancient and familiar method of story telling which Henryson brought to the highest level of artistic sophistication. The degree of complexity and sophistication in Henryson's *Fables* (c. 1480s) is not often realised when contrasted with his sources: most people are aware of the *Fables* of Aesop, which (in the form that Henryson read them) generally run to a dozen or so lines of Latin. French schoolchildren are familiar with the work of Jean de la Fontaine, the great seventeenth-century fabulist, each of whose fables run to thirty or forty lines on average. It should be obvious that when we look at the 2,975 lines of Henryson's thirteen fables, we are considering a work of another order of artistic ambition and complexity altogether.

Henryson's conscious shaping of his materials is evident throughout the work, as much in the choice and arrangement of stories as in the poetic expression. The fund of animal stories would have been as widespread in the Middle Ages as at any other time, but it seems likely that Henryson took his inspiration from two main sources: he himself explicitly mentions his debt to Aesop, but he also found material from the more boisterous, violent stories which centred around wolves and foxes in the early medieval period, mainly assembled under the generic name *Le Roman de Renard* (the Book of the Fox). The tales which come from a Reynardian source have quite a different feel to them: we are in a world where foxes use their brains to outwit dim but brutal wolves, or gullible human beings, a world of knockabout farce, violent incidents, plausible villains and condign retribution.

The Prologue: the art of poetry

Henryson's Prologue to his *Fables* comprises nine stanzas which utilise his favourite narrative stanza form; the seven-line decasyllabic unit rhyming ababbcc, and known as 'Rhyme Royal'. These quotes are taken from Fox's *Robert Henryson: The Poems* (1987). The Prologue is his declaration of the principles underlying the entire work, and deserves close reading. He begins by raising a problem concerning the purpose of art which has perplexed thinking people for centuries: how can what is not true have value? The first words admit the difficulty:

feinyeit fabils of ald poetre *feigned/fictional; old poetry*
Be not al grunded upon truth . . . *are not all founded on truth*

Henryson, however, goes on to justify what he is doing by thrice metaphorically making the point that the pleasure we experience from poetry can help us to absorb a moral message, which he takes to be the ultimate justification of his enterprise.

He then sets to work to establish a relationship with his reader and deals with his reason for undertaking the work, indicating his own unworthiness for the task (which we need not take too seriously) and hinting that the work had been written as a commission (29–35):

Of this poete, my maisteris, with your leif,
Submitting me to your correctioun,
In mother toung, of Latyng, I wald preif *Latin; try*
To mak ane maner of translatioun
Nocht of my self, for vane presumptioun, *not from my own desire*
Bot be requeist and precept of ane lord,
Of quhome the name it neidis not record. *it is not necessary to give his name*

Finally, he gets to the central analogy of the entire work by referring to Aesop's use of talking animals to express truths about human behaviour, which shows (48–9):

How mony men in operatioun *action*
Ar like to beistis in conditioun . . . *by their nature*

This statement would have had a far more profound significance for a medieval audience than for ourselves, since it would be taken as a reference to the intermediate position which human beings held in the great scheme of things. Whilst sharing our finer qualities (courage, selflessness, magnanimity) with the angels, and aspiring to that deific condition, we are constantly being dragged back by the carnality which we share with the animals and which explains our baser qualities (lust, avarice, self-interest). Human life was seen as a battleground in which humankind had to employ free will in order to make the choice to eschew the carnal and attain the spiritual state, and ultimately fit us for heaven.

STRUCTURE
Within the context of serious purpose, Henryson begins the delightful series of tales which form the *Fabillis*. The fables vary greatly in length, in profundity

and in seriousness, though the *moralitates* usually apply a corrective dose of gravity where Henryson felt it to be lacking in the tale itself. What follows is a summary of each tale's narrative (story) and *moralitas* (moral meaning).

1. 'The Cock and the Jasp': A cock looking for food finds a precious stone, but decides it is of no value to him. Moral: in the *moralitas* the cock is berated for lacking discernment.

2. 'The Two Mice': The country mouse goes to visit her sister in the town; while impressed by her material wealth, she is severely frightened by the constant danger in which she lives. Moral: don't try to get above your station in life.

3. 'The Cock and the Fox': This tale is based on Chaucer's version, 'The Nonne's Priest's Tale', and tells of the complacent and vain cock who is inveigled by the flattery of the hungry fox into dropping his guard, whereupon he is seized and taken away. After a chase he escapes with only his pride hurt. Moral: avoid pride and flattery.

4. 'The Fox and the Wolf': The fox realises that he is heading for a bad end and decides to reform. When the wolf appears in the form of a friar, the fox asks him to hear his confession, but the temptation of putting one over on the slow-witted wolf is too much for the devious fox, and he negotiates a fairly easy penance. He captures a kid, and since he is forbidden to eat meat, he rebaptises it, calling it a salmon! While resting after his meal he is shot by the keeper's arrow. Moral: put an end to sinning and make a proper confession.

5. 'The Trial of the Fox': This poem is Henryson's version of one of the set-pieces of medieval poetry: in this case the elaborate list of animals in attendance at the court of the lion king. The son of the fox in the previous fable finds his father's body and is glad of his death, since he will inherit his territory. All the animals are summoned to the lion's court, where, after setting up a wolf to be injured and laughed at, the fox is found guilty of killing a lamb, and is hanged. Moral: the lion represents the world with all its sensual attractions, which we should shun.

6. 'The Sheep and the Dog': This is a powerful exposure of corruption in the law. In the tale, a sheep is summoned by a dog to appear in a court packed with the sheep's enemies. The case, not surprisingly, goes against the sheep who is compelled to sell her fleece to pay her dues. Moral: unusually, the sheep appears as a character in the *moralitas*, eloquently expressing her plight. The analogy is made immediately (1258–9):

> This selie scheip may present the figure   *innocent sheep*
> Of pure commounis, that daylie ar opprest . . .   *poor commoners*

7. 'The Lion and the Mouse': This fable is particularly interesting. It is placed as the central fable, having its own prologue, and involving the arrival of Aesop himself, who is invited by the narrator to deliver the *moralitas*! The story is the well-known tale of the lion who is merciful to a little mouse and later is freed from human nets by it, illustrating the theme of the relationship of power and mercy. In the fable the forest represents the wider world; the lion is the king and the mouse the common people, who need to be taught their place. Moral: rulers must temper justice with mercy.

8. 'The Preaching of the Swallow': This profound and complex fable begins with a lengthy preamble praising the wisdom of God, particularly as evident through his creature world, and the seasons. The narrator overhears a swallow chiding the other birds for their lack of foresight they have not prepared for the winter while the fowler is making nets and laying traps for them. Winter comes and all the birds are killed except the swallow. Moral: prudence and foresight are necessary if we are to avoid damnation.

9. 'The Fox, the Wolf and the Cadger': Based upon the Reynardian world of violence and trickery, the fox, unwillingly helping a wolf, plans to cheat a cadger (a pedlar) of his fish by playing dead. The trick works, and the wolf tries it for himself, but the cadger this time is alert to the deception and beats the wolf savagely. Moral: the fish represents the attractions of the world, which we must all eschew or suffer the consequences.

10. 'The Fox, the Wolf and the Husbandman': A fox manipulates both a wolf and a farmer. The story ends with the fox convincing the wolf that a cheese can be found at the bottom of a well. Inevitably, the wolf ends up stuck down the well while the fox makes his escape. In this case, Henryson seems to have been caught up in the boisterousness of the tale, so that the *moralitas* equates the cheese with covetousness, and the well with hell.

11. 'The Wolf and the Wether': When his master's dog dies, leaving the flock unprotected, a wether (ram) offers to take over the job with the dog's skin sewn on his back. He has considerable success until his covering is accidentally torn off while he is chasing a wolf, who, enraged at the humiliation he has suffered, breaks his neck. Moral: as with 'The Two Mice', stay in your place!

12. 'The Wolf and the Lamb': A wolf, wishing to eat a lamb, tries to drum up a justification by asserting that the lamb has dirtied the water he was drinking. Painstaking, reasoned argument from the lamb makes no

difference, and the wolf takes him and kills him mercilessly. Moral: those in authority must be considerate and merciful to the ordinary people.

13. 'The Paddock and the Mouse': A mouse, wishing to cross a river, is reluctant to accept the offer of help from a paddock (frog). As they cross, the mouse's suspicions are proved correct when the paddock tries to drown her. While they struggle in the water, they are watched by a kite who swoops down, takes them both to the bank and kills them. Moral: Death comes when we least expect, always be prepared.

THE UNITY OF THE FABLES

The thirteen fables vary greatly in tone, from farce to pathos, from brutality to piety. Aesthetic shape is imposed on the disparate sections in a number of ways. Henryson seems to have organised the Aesopic and Reynardian sources in a symmetrical pattern; also, there is clearly a darkening of the tone as the series progresses, so that the earlier fables involve the characters in suffering little more than a fright, but as they progress, the 'guilty' are punished by death (the two foxes, the little birds) till eventually the 'innocent' are also killed (the lamb), and in the final fable, perhaps the bleakest of all, both characters are killed, irrespective of their innocence or guilt.

Another device by which Henryson confers stylistic unity on the fables is through his narrator. A relationship with the reader is established in the Prologue, and thereafter the narrator assures the reader of his presence and control by familiar asides or tags (614, 2203–4):

Leif we this vedow glaid, I yow assure . . .   *I assure you, we leave this widow glad*

This taill is myngit with moralitie,   *mixed*
As I sall schaw sumquhat, or that I ceis.   *as I will show to a degree before I end*

He also takes a role as an observer, and even a participant, in three of the fables ('The Sheep and the Dog', 'The Lion and the Mouse' and 'The Preaching of the Swallow').

THE MORAL FRAMEWORK

By far the most important factor unifying the fables is, at least from Henryson's point of view, their moral intent; not just in the sense of general exhortation to behave in a godly manner, but explicitly in their purpose of promoting individual salvation. It is difficult in a secular age to see that this is, in fact, the underlying motive for the entire work. The fables offer examples,

21

amusing, thought-provoking and sometimes tragic, of individuals faced with the dilemma of free will. While the fox cannot give up his life of crime, the little birds ignore the warning and the wether gets above his station; on the other hand, the lion shows mercy, the cock learns to ignore flattery, and the country mouse (362–4):

Quhen euer scho list scho had aneuch to eit,	*whenever she wanted, she had enough to eat*
In quyet and eis withoutin ony dreid,	*in peace and quiet without fear*
Bot to hir sisteris feist na mair scho ȝeid.	*yet she did not go to her sister's feast any more*

From these examples we are expected to learn that carnal desire is merely a temptation away from the spiritual imperative of preparing ourselves for the afterlife.

The Testament of Cresseid

Henryson's skilful use of the narrator to guide the reader reaches its apogee in his most sophisticated and ambitious poem: *The Testament of Cresseid,* probably written some time before 1492. This great poem is based on a supposed event during the Trojan War, when Cresseid, a widow and lover of Troilus, goes to join her father in the Greek camp, promising to return to Troilus shortly. But she becomes involved with Diomede and forgets her promise to Troilus, thereby becoming an embodiment of the supposed fickleness of women. Geoffrey Chaucer's version of the story, *Troilus and Criseyde* (probably late 1380s), ends with Troilus reluctantly accepting her desertion, and his own death in battle. Henryson is the first writer to explore the fate of the wretched Cresseid.

The first seventy lines of this poem of betrayal and disappointed love vividly establish the character of the narrator of the story. It is a bitterly cold night in springtime, when (19–21):

The froist freisit, the blastis bitterly	*gales*
Fra Pole Artick come quhisling loud and schill,	*whistling*
And causit me remufe aganis my will.	*depart*

The elderly narrator, who had been a lover in his youth, had intended to pray to Venus, the goddess of love (27–8),

Bot for greit cald as than I lattit was,	*prevented*
And in my chalmer to the fyre can pas.	*chamber; went*

22

Unable to bear the cold, he fixes the fire, gets himself comfortable, takes a drink and then opens Chaucer's volume. However much he praises Chaucer, as all writers did, he suggests that there may be more to the story of Troilus and Criseyde, issuing the defiant line: 'Quha wait [*knows*] gif all that Chaucer wrait was trew?' (64), and he claims to have found another book which tells Cresseid's story. This 'other book' he then relates to us, beginning with Cresseid's desolation when she is turned out by Diomede. The two stanzas, lines 78–91, are formally different from those around them as Henryson (or his narrator) attempts to manipulate our reactions to Cresseid's plight.

After she returns to her father, Cresseid makes the mistake of blaming her misfortunes on Cupid and Venus (134–5):

'O fals Cupide, is nane to wyte bot thow   *blame*
And thy mother, of lufe the blind goddes!'

Henryson raises subtle questions for the reader to ponder: Is Cresseid right to put the blame on Cupid and Venus? To what extent is she responsible for her own situation? Lines 78–91 are worth consideration; although the narrator is trying to excuse her ('als far furth as I may'; *as far as I can*) he has to admit some culpability on her part but the reader has to decide just what Cresseid is being accused of.

The great set-piece of Cresseid's dream then begins, fully one-third of the entire poem, and therefore a measure of its significance. The planetary gods appear in a great procession in their presumed order from Earth in the geocentric system: Saturn, Jupiter, Mars, Phoebus (the sun), Venus, Mercury and the Moon (Cynthia). Each receives at least two stanzas of description which, in typically rumbustious and vivid alliterative style, characterises the disposition and potential (whether negative or positive) of each planet.

Cresseid is condemned for her blasphemy in accusing Venus and Cupid of being the cause of her misfortunes. Judgement is pronounced (306–8):

In all her lyfe with pane to be opprest,   *pain to be oppressed*
And torment sair with seiknes incurabill,   *sore; sickness*
And to all louers be abhominabill.   *lovers; abominable/contemptible*

Saturn puts this awful sentence into practice by depriving her of her beauty (313–15):

Thy greit fairnes and all thy bewtie gay,
Thy wantoun blude, and eik thy goldin hair,   *wanton blood (euphemism for sexual desire)*
Heir I exclude fra the for euermair.   *banish*

Cynthia continues the sentence, and her detailed description of Cresseid's bloodshot eyes, hoarse voice and face covered with black spots and lumps makes explicit the nature of her infliction (342–3):

This sall thow go begging fra hous to hous   *Thus will you go begging from house to house*
With cop and clapper lyke ane lazarous . . .   *With cup and rattle like a leper.*

Her leprosy serves as a powerful and frightening symbol of moral decay.

Cresseid awakes from the dream, but with the starkly ironic discovery that she has indeed been inflicted with leprosy. A touching section showing the closeness between father and daughter follows (372–5):

He luikit on hir uglye lipper face,   *looked; leper*
The quhylk befor was quhite as lillie flour;   *which; white as the lily*
Wringand his handis, oftymes said allace   *often*
That he had leuit to se that wofull hour.   *lived*

Cresseid is taken by her father to the town leper house, where she gives vent to her feelings in the set-piece section 'The Complaint of Cresseid' (407–69), marked by a change in stanza form. In following the burden of her complaint, the reader must weigh her argument and decide how far Cresseid has come in accepting responsibility for her plight, and how far she merely complains that 'Fortoun is fikkill'. In the closing passages of the poem, and while Cresseid is among the lepers, the victorious garrison of Troy rides by, led by Troilus, to whom they cry for alms. Cresseid looks at Troilus, but her sight is dimmed by her illness, and although he looks at her, she is so altered that he does not recognise her, though with cruel irony, she reminds him of his Cresseid (498–504):

Than upon him scho kest up baith hir ene,   *cast up both her eyes*
And with ane blenk it come into his thocht   *blink*
That he sumtime hir face befoir had sene,
Bot scho was in sic plyte he knew hir nocht;   *despair*
Yit than hir luik into his mynd it brocht   *look*
The sweit visage and amorous blenking
Of fair Cresseid, sumtyme his awin darling.

It is worth reflecting on why Henryson resorts to simple language in these last lines, with his repeated use of monosyllables, and how the vocabulary of the last two lines differs from the simplicity of the lines that precede them.

Troilus throws some money to them and departs. When Cresseid is told who he was, her grief is complete, as is her arduous journey to self-knowledge. There appears to be a final moment of recognition for Cresseid, in the refrain she uses (546, 553, 560). The title of the poem refers to the testament Cresseid makes once she has reached the depths of despair. Her bequests, which are not just to her fellow-lepers and to Troilus, are significant and intriguing; they are perhaps the final indications of how she perceives herself and her tragedy before she dies – and Henryson again leaves it to the reader to arrive at a judgement.

In the concluding three verses, Henryson seems keen to finish off the poem quickly, and to disengage the reader from the emotional impact of the situation, firstly by Troilus's reaction to the news of her death: 'Siching full sadlie, said, "I can no moir / Scho was untrew and wo is me thairfoir."' (601– 2), then by the deliberately vague 'Sum said . . .', and finally by the dismissive last line: 'Sen scho [*since she*] is deid I speik of hir no moir' (616). Again, the reader is left to decide why he makes such a rapid conclusion, and to answer some outstanding questions. Does Henryson's narrator consign Cresseid after all to the Chaucerian archetype of female infidelity and moral corruption? What happened to his earlier avowal of 'pitie' and tenderness? The *Testament* is ultimately an enigmatic and perhaps ironic poem, but it is a work of intense beauty, pathos and imaginative intelligence.

Henryson's range

A dozen or so poems are normally attributed to Henryson in addition to the *Fables* and the *Testament.* Two in particular that should be known are his versions of the well-known tale of 'Orpheus and Eurydice', a poem full of narrative and rhetorical splendour, and 'Robene and Makyne', a delightful ballad-like poem recounting with terse wit the changes in the relationship between two lovers, and a masterpiece of formal perfection.

REDISCOVERING DUNBAR (c. 1460–c. 1513)

As with Henryson, little is known of his younger contemporary, William Dunbar. Possibly he was related to the Earls of Dunbar and March; possibly he was a graduate of the University of St Andrews in the late 1470s. The poems suggest that he may have been a Franciscan friar who travelled in the service of James IV, and helped arrange the King's marriage in 1503 to Margaret Tudor. He seems to have been a favourite at court with the Queen, but a constantly unsuccessful petitioner of the King for church preference. As a poet, he has long been recognised as a virtuoso verbal stylist. He has at his fingertips a dazzling battery of techniques, of subject matter, of genre, of register, all centred on his own complex and prickly personality, which was that of one who felt his worth inadequately acknowledged at court. Superficially, Dunbar's poetry might be regarded as more immediately accessible than that of Henryson: most of his poetic output consists of short, occasional lyrics, often focused quite precisely on one idea or situation, expressing one clearly defined emotion on the part of the poet, whether scorn or rapture, indignation or reverence. Much of the attraction of Dunbar's work lies in the variety of subject matter he adopts, which seems to give a cross-section of contemporary social and political life (there are also geographically specific poems on Aberdeen and Edinburgh, and the royal visit to Dunfermline) and he covers a range of more conventional moral and religious themes. The psychological and emotional immediacy of Dunbar's lyrics is often striking: he composes a lyric on the pain of migraine and gives sensitive expression to the nature of what we would nowadays term depression. From this mass of disparate topics it is possible, however, to establish certain distinct categories of interest.

Quotes are taken from Bawcutt's *The Poems of William Dunbar* (1998).

Dunbar and the court

Many of Dunbar's poems deal with court life. A poem may be offered as a New Year's gift to the king, real and fictional court characters form poetic subjects, and the extended allegorical poem, 'The Thrissill and the Rois', celebrates the political and symbolic marriage of Margaret Tudor and James IV. In particular, his own ambiguous position there is treated, as in: 'Schir, I complane off iniuris', 'Complane I wald, wist I quhome till', 'Now lufferis [*lovers*] cummis with larges lowd [*great largesse*]' (in which Dunbar assumes the persona of 'this gray hors, Auld Dumbar' to persuade the king of his supposed poverty and obsolescence compared to other courtly and 'gentill palfrayis' [*courtly tournament horses*]), and many more, in which he bewails his sorry condition, lacking both money and prestige while all kinds of less worthy individuals, as he sees them, are promoted beyond him ('Schir, yit remember as befoir', 66–9):

> Jok, that wes wont to keip the stirkis,   *keep cattle*
> Can now draw him ane cleik of kirkis,   *clutch, patch*
> With ane fals cairt in to his sleif,
> Worthe all my ballattis under the birkis.   *birches*

It is entertaining to watch him try virtually anything to get the king to act on his behalf, from flattering and cajoling to irony, insult, and indignation even to the extent of an elaborate parody of the Office for the Dead ('We that ar heir in hevynnis glorie') in which he compares life in Edinburgh to the paradisal consolations of heaven, in contrast with life in Stirling, which is purgatory (45–6):

> Out of distres of Stirling town
> To Edinburgh blys God mak yow bown.

A witty, often sardonic, humour is one of Dunbar's most obvious accomplishments, ranging from outrageous raillery to quiet self-deprecation. The former is at its most flamboyant in his various poems of diatribe or invective, such as *The Flyting of Dunbar and Kennedie*, 'A Ballat of the Abbot of Tungland', and 'Quhy will ye, merchantis of renoun', whom he decries for their selfishness and blindness with the eight-times repeated: 'Think ye not schame.'

Dunbar and the church

Of all the poets of the fifteenth century in Scotland, Dunbar is the most closely involved with the life of the church, partly because of his ceaseless quest for a benefice, partly in his familiarity with the ceremonies and the liturgy of the church portrayed throughout his works in the form of quotation or parody. His interest in philosophical or theological matters is demonstrated in various moral lyrics: 'In to thir dirk and drublie dayis' (the famous 'Meditatioun In Wyntir'), 'To speik of science, craft, or sapience', and 'I that in heill wes and gladnes' (commonly known as 'Lament for the Makaris'), with its sonorous litany of the names of the dead poets, among whom he is conscious he must himself soon be numbered (93–6):

> Sen he hes all my brether tane   *since; taken*
> He will naught let me lif alane.   *me alone live*
> On forse I man his nyxt pray be: *by necessity, I must be his next victim*
> *Timor mortis conturbat me.*   *the fear of death haunts me*

More specifically religious works, occasional or celebratory, include 'Rorate, coeli, desuper' (on the Nativity of Christ), 'Hale, sterne superne, hale, in eterne' ('Ane Ballat of Our Lady') and 'Done is a battell on the dragon blak', the great poem on the resurrection of Christ structured entirely in statements of apocalyptic certainty (1–4):

Done is a battell on the dragon black.	
Our campioun Chryst confoundit hes his force,	champion; defeated
The yettis of hell ar brokin with a crak,	gates
The signe trivmphall rasit is of the croce . . .	triumphant sign of the cross is raised

Dunbar's secular poetry

It is, however, in the two major secular poems, *The Goldyn Targe*, probably written in the 1490s and *The Tretis of the Tua Mariit Wemen and the Wedo*, first printed c. 1507, that one is most conscious of the dazzling array of technical skills and resources he displays and which represent in completely contrasting ways the highest reaches of Dunbar's art. *The Goldyn Targe* is a masterpiece of formal perfection, thirty-one stanzas in the difficult rhyme scheme aabaabbab, employing the full panoply of medieval allegorical verse: highly elaborate description with what is termed 'aureate language' as well as classical reference (10–18):

Full angellike thir birdis sang thair houris	like angels; church hours
Within thair courtyns grene in to thair bouris;	curtains; bowers
Apparalit quhite and red wyth blomes suete;	decorated; fragrant flowers
Anamalit was the felde wyth all colouris.	enamelled
The perly droppis schake in silvir schouris,	shook in silver showers
Quhill all in balme did branch and leuis flete:	until in a fragrant moisture
	branches and leaves flowed
Depart fra Phebus did Aurora grete,	from; weep
Hir cristall teris I saw hyng on the flouris,	hang
Quhilk he for lufe all drank up wyth his hete.	heat

The creative process of nature ornamenting the garden is made analogous to the creative process of the poet ornamenting his language. This is the highest of the high styles, known as the 'aureate style' (aureate is the adjective coined from the Latin *aureus*, meaning 'golden'). Dunbar uses the term himself at the very end of the *Targe* in relation to the rhetorical style of the English writers Chaucer, Gower, and Lydgate when he praises their 'tongis aureate' (263). The aureate style is intensely descriptive: adjectives qualify nearly every observation. In the first stanza, the phrase 'golden candill matutyne' serves as a euphemism for the sun or the dawn; 'matutyne' is a Latinate term (i.e. coined from an original Latin word, *matutinus*, meaning 'dawn'). The sun's beams are portrayed as 'clere depurit bemyes crystallyne' (5, a nice chiming rhyme, and itself derived from the Latin *crystallus*). Precise verbs are used in the description of the garden: 'Apparalit quhite and rede . . . / Anamalit' (11–12). This is a kind of painterly grafting of colour and texture into the description. It is a highly pictorial language which seemingly fixes or stills nature into objects of precious beauty: dew on roses are 'hevinly beriall droppis' (23); sun beams are 'ruby sperkis' (24); stanza five sustains these notions of the material, jewelled beauty of nature. This notion seems to go against the grain of our contemporary conceptions of nature: it is non-naturalistic. The landscape is 'ourgilt' (27): this means 'gilded' or 'like gold', resembling a precious medieval manuscript inscribed in gold.

The setting of the *Targe* is the conventional *locus amoenus*, literally 'a pleasant place', on a May morning (traditionally the time of love). Its dream vision (a medieval genre seen already in the *Quair* and the *Testament* to a degree) involves various classical and mythic protagonists such as Venus and Flora, with personified abstractions like 'dame Beautee' and 'tender Youth'. The narrator sees 'in to my dremes fantasy' (49) a ship arriving, bearing 'Ane hundreth ladyes' (58), too beautiful, he claims, to be described even by Homer or Cicero. The allegorical nature of the experience is made clear in various ways (82–4):

> There saw I May, of myrthfull monethis quene,   *queen of joyful months*
> Betuix Aprile and Iune her sistir schene,   *bright, beautiful*
> Within the gardyng walking up and doun . . .   *garden*

While watching the convocation of mythical protagonists and abstractions, the narrator is suddenly brought into the poem by being seen himself (136–8):

> And schortly for to speke, be lufis quene   *love's queen*
> I was aspyit. Scho bad hir archearis kene   *caught sight of; fierce archers*
> Go me arrest, and thay no time delayit.

An allegorical battle takes place, in which Reason bears the targe or shield (199–201):

Thik was the schote of grundyn dartis kene,   *sharpened darts*
Bot Reson, with the scheld of gold so schene   *shield; bright*
Warly defendit, quho so ewir assayit.   *prudently defended*

In the ensuing conflict the narrator is blinded (perhaps signifying blinded love). The vision vanishes in an instant: 'Thare was no more bot birdis, bank and bruke' (234), and the protagonists of the vision depart with the noise of gunfire (240–1):

The rochis all resownyt wyth the rak,   *The rocks all echoed with the shock*
For rede it semyt that the raynbow brak . . .   *Because of the noise it seemed that the*
                                                  rainbow shattered

Dunbar's narrator awakes from the dream, invokes Chaucer and other poets and, in an *envoi* or 'farewell' to the poem, apologises (with mock modesty) for its imperfections. The reader is left to consider the poem's possible allegorical meaning and the question as to how far Dunbar's success in pursuing the traditional conflict between the opposing powers of reason and sensuality is realised. Some critics have, however, denied the possibility of a moral 'kernel' of meaning (to borrow Henryson's metaphor from the Prologue), and insist that Dunbar is simply displaying or 'showing off' his verbal skills. But the two positions are not necessarily conflicting and the reader must be careful not to reduce the brilliance and complexity of Dunbar's lyric to the conventional debate which pits style against substance.

THE TRETIS OF THE TUA MARIIT WEMEN AND THE WEDO

This *tour de force* in 530 lines is an example of a very different kind of secular poetry which effectively undermines all the assumptions of fashionable courtly love. Its verse form, the long alliterative unrhymed line, gives the poem a demotic power which matches admirably the scurrilous conversation of the three women faithfully reported by the eavesdropping narrator. The first forty lines set up the customary expectations of a poem of courtly love: the setting in June, the beautiful garden (3–4):

Besyd ane gudlie grein garth, full of gay flouris,   *Beside a pleasant green garden full of*
                                                       beautiful flowers
Hegeit of ane huge hicht with hawthorne treis   *surrounded [lit. 'hedged in'] by a great*
                                                   height of hawthorn trees

with three beautiful ladies (27):

All full of flurist fairheid as flouris in Iune . . . *All full of flourishing beauty as flowers in Iune.*

When they begin to talk, however, their feelings about men, their scorn for their husbands and their interest in other lovers, is vented with a vicious wit (134–5, 270–1):

Yit leit I neuer that larbar my leggis ga betuene,   *yet I never let that impotent chap go between my legs*

To fyle my flesche na fummyll me without a fee gret   *to defile my flesh nor fumble with me unless for a sizeable fee*

Twa husbandis haif I had, thai held me baith deir.   *I have had two husbands who both held me dear*

Thought I dispytit thaim agane, thai spyit it na thing.   *though I despised them back, they never noticed a thing*

At the end of this shocking and remarkable account, an 'uncouth aventur', the narrator neatly turns the tables by leaving the (presumably male) reader with the question: 'Quhilk wald ye waill to your wif, gif ye suld wed one?' *Who would you choose for your wife, if you could marry one?* (530). Just as Henryson left his reader to decide between the two opposing impulses of the *Testament,* so here the reader is left to decide between sympathy or condemnation for these belligerent women, and to decide who wins in the end: the misogynist male narrator, afraid of powerful female sexual identities, or the women who deceive and betray their husbands and lovers in revenge for their own suffering and mistreatment?

CHAPTER 3

EARLY SCOTTISH DRAMA: *ANE SATYRE* AND *PHILOTUS*

SCOTTISH DRAMA – A HERITAGE LOST?

This chapter examines the most important surviving drama of early Scottish literature, *Ane Satyre of the Thrie Estaitis* (first performed c. 1540) by Sir David Lyndsay, and introduces the far less familiar Renaissance play, *Philotus*, published in 1603 and written possibly as early as the 1560s, though its author is unknown. Our knowledge of early Scottish drama is limited by the lack of surviving play texts. As Bill Findlay shows in *A History of Scottish Theatre* (1997), however, there are early medieval records of dramatic May festivities, Pasche or Peace plays, religious dramas, together with *ludi* or folk ceremonies (which often incurred church hostility), and Robin Hood plays. All these drama-based forms attest a rich popular culture of performative expression. The royal court throughout the medieval and Renaissance periods supported dramatic activity of various kinds: pageant-like entertainments, ballets, masques, farces. Poetry itself, of course, was frequently orally recited at court: Dunbar's poetry has an obviously dramatic or performative quality. *Philotus* in many ways reflects courtly dramatic fashions, as does the later *Pamphilus* (c. 1590), with its complex and controversial sexual machinations.

Dr Jamie Reid Baxter has recently drawn attention to the work of the little-known Edinburgh poet, John Burel (fl. 1590), and his translation into *ballat royal* (one of the verse forms advocated by James VI in his rhetorical treatise, *The Reulis and Cautelis* (1584)) of the anonymous late twelfth-century French play or *comoedia* entitled *Pamphilus de amore*. Although it is almost certain that Burel did not seek to have his translation staged, or converted into a complete theatrical text, *Pamphilus speakand of lufe*, printed by the Edinburgh printer Robert Charteris, still attests an enduring interest in earlier European neo-Latin dramatic literature by the cultural élite in high Renaissance Scotland. Indeed, it was dedicated to Ludovic Stuart, Duke of Lennox, son of the late Esmé Stewart, the French cousin to whom the young King James had become close politically and emotionally in the previous decade, intolerably so for the Scottish Protestant nobility. Lyndsay's play, with which we begin, is dramatically ambitious, all-encompassing in its political, comic and satirical scope.

Sir David Lyndsay

Sir David Lyndsay of the Mount (1486–1555) was a courtier serving James IV and James V, rising to the position of Lyon King of Arms (Scotland's chief heraldic officer) in the latter reign. His responsibilities included the production of regal festivities and pageants, an experience which he clearly put to good personal use in *Ane Satyre* which has a staging very reminiscent of court pageant. Lyndsay's writings were popular with contemporary readers, as is witnessed by the ten editions of his work which were published in Scotland between his death in 1555 and the end of the century. Even four and a half centuries later, readers can still derive great enjoyment from his satirical humour and down-to-earth diction. Although most of Lyndsay's poems were written for the court, there is textual evidence in many of his later writings that suggest that he was hoping for a wider readership. It is this breadth of address which allows the sixteenth-century courtier to speak to us today, as many of the issues and abuses he describes in *Ane Satyre* can be detected now in the doings of our political leaders and in our contemporary monarchy.

THE RELEVANCE OF *ANE SATYRE*

Ane Satyre is the only major dramatic text extant in Scots from the mid-sixteenth century Renaissance, yet far too often the modern reader who might enjoy the drama of Shakespeare is either ignorant of, or unwilling to approach Lyndsay's great play. Why should this be? Shakespeare's plays are not short and compact; the language of Shakespeare has difficulties of its own to present; there are, dare one say it, *longueurs* and even boring sequences in Shakespeare. How should the reader deal with the challenge of the difficult older text? Judicious editing helps, as witness the excellent Heinemann Dramascript versions, which, while using only Shakespeare's words, add stage directions and edit long speeches to make the whole more manageable. The language can be glossed, notes can be added page by page or in blocks at the end of the text. Changes in meaning, idioms peculiar to their time, jokes which are no longer topical and therefore no longer amusing can be explained. Whole scenes can simply be cut. It is rare to see a full-length performance of a Shakespeare play nowadays, which is one reason Kenneth Branagh's full text filming of *Hamlet* (1998) caused such a flurry of critical attention.

This kind of helpful editing has been given to *Ane Satyre of the Thrie Estaitis*.

The Robert Kemp acting edition of 1948, for Tyrone Guthrie's Edinburgh Festival production of 1949, contains an 'Englished' version of the play, heavily cut, and with explanatory stage directions added. Although, as an acting version, this should not be used as the text for final study, it gives a useful and manageable introduction to the full text, and suggests angles for exploration. In 1967 Matthew MacDiarmid published a more scholarly version with an introduction; and the excellent and user-friendly Canongate text of 1989 (quoted below) edited by R. J. Lyall has a great deal of useful and pertinent introductory, glossary and explanatory material, yet presents the text cleanly on the page without obtrusive academic apparatus. Being the full text, it includes the sections which were thought too indecent for the 1948 Edinburgh Festival audience, and the student who reads these will find that comedy arising from sexually explicit references and jokes about the lower bodily functions is not something invented by today's 'alternative' comedians.

From this arises a debate as to the relative value of abridged or otherwise shortened versions of classic texts and the question as to whether the opening up of the text to a new audience is a good enough reason for cutting the original work.

APPROACHING THE PLAY: A SUMMARY OF THE ACTION

The play is presented in two unequal Parts, divided by an Interlude, which is an integral part of the action, rather than the rest-break it apparently implies. The first Part concerns the court of the young Rex Humanitas, who is beset by ignorant and sensually-driven 'advisers'; Wantonnes, Placebo and Solace, their names clearly indicating their function, in the convention of morality plays. These three introduce Dame Sensualitie to the court, who is to lure the king into sensuality and luxury. While the king is thus engaged, three far more serious vices, Flatterie, Falset and Dissait, arrive disguised as clerics and prevent Gude-Counsall speaking to the king. It is now that Lindsay's wider intent is becoming clear, as the king's devotion to Sensualitie leaves his country exposed to vice and evil, with Veritie and Chastitie consigned by the vices to the stocks. Only the arrival of Divyne Correctioun, the emissary of God, saves the king and the country from perdition, the ignorance of the courtiers is rebuked and pardoned, the vices are exposed, and the process of reform begins, ending this section.

(During the Interlude, which will be discussed in more detail below, there is a comic encounter between a Puir Man and a Pardoner, which exposes the duplicity of those who are supposed to be saving souls.)

The second Part of the play is concerned with the reform of the three estates of the realm; Spiritualitie, Temporalitie and Marchands (or, in a simplified modern shorthand, Bishops, Barons, and Burgesses). While the latter two eagerly embrace the example of their king and ask for advice on how they can change their ways, Spiritualitie holds out against any kind of reform, illustrating Lyndsay's premise that the church is the most corrupt establishment of the realm. Lyndsay leavens his heavy but very serious moral and political message with a number of comic incidents, and the play ends with a sermon preached by Foly, to remind the audience that although reform may have been achieved in the play, disorder is always ready to break out.

BRINGING THE ACTION UP TO DATE

The play shows that human nature does not change much even over four and a half centuries. Its action can justly be compared to contemporary events; for example the behaviour of the king could readily be compared with concerns about the contemporary monarchy and aristocracy in our own time. Likewise the use of advisers to present the nature of kingship is akin to modern political spin-doctoring; and for Spiritualitie's obsession with Sensualitie and demands of payments for offices carried out, there are abundant modern examples of sleaze and scandal in government circles. 'The poor are with ye always' goes the old saying, echoing timelessly the complaints of the Pauper against his oppressors. Such comparisons make clear Lyndsay's relevance to modern readers. If Shakespeare is still considered relevant and worth studying today, how much more important is it that Scottish readers are aware of their country's vernacular drama of the same period?

DRAMATIC STYLE: THE PLAY IN PERFORMANCE

Lyndsay's stagecraft is very different from Shakespeare's, coming as it does from a tradition of morality plays with a strongly didactic content. This is made clear to the audience in Diligence's first speech, where, after an invocation to God the Father, Son and Holy Ghost, he demands attention (14–18, 29):

Tak tent to me, my friends, and hald yow coy!	*pay attention; keep quiet.*
For I am sent to yow as messingeir	
From ane nobill and rycht redoubtit roy,	*formidable*
The quhilk has bene absent this monie yeir:	
Humanitie, give ye his name wald speir . . .	*assured*
Be now assurit of reformatioun.	

He then goes on to ask the audience, referred to as 'yow all that I sie seasit [seated] in this place', '[t]o be patient the space of certaine houris / Till ye have hard [*heard*] our short narratioun' (56–7), and tells them they will hear '[t]he Commoun-weill richt pitiouslie complaine' (61); 'the verteous ladie Veritie . . . mak ane pitious lamentatioun' (62–3); 'Chastitie . . . mak narra-tioun / How sho can get na ludging [*lodging*] in this land' (66–7). The reader recreating Lyndsay's play might consider what is the playwright's purpose in outlining the events to come in this opening address.

Lyndsay makes it clear also that this is a play which involves the audience as participants rather than simply as watchers, and this aspect of the structure should be further examined to show how the audience is used in various ways, very much as is the practice with modern playwrights and directors. It is clear from their words: 'Mak roume, sirs . . .' (602); 'Stand by the gait . . .' (658); 'Out of my gait . . .' (2424), that characters sometimes emerge from the audience, most strikingly perhaps in the case of the Pauper in the Interlude, which, in a good production, can look like a 'real' interruption of events. Lyndsay's stagecraft could be the focus for a wider discussion on the way the various characters and situations are presented to the audience. His char-acterisation is not psychological, as Shakespeare's is, but is based on the medieval notion of vices and virtues, a tradition which is carried on in the plays of Ben Jonson (who leaves no one in any doubt as to the characters of Littlewit, Everill and Sir Epicure Mammon) and in the novels of Charles Dickens (with Uriah Heep, Magwitch and Dotheboys Hall). Alternatively, a reader familiar with the work of Bertolt Brecht could usefully examine *Ane Satyre* as a very early example of political stagecraft and a device for social commentary. It can thus be seen that in addition to its thematic relevance, Lyndsay's play can be scrutinised under a number of modern critical head-ings. A historicist reading would put the play in its social, political, religious and cultural context to examine Lyndsay's dramatic use of contemporary events; a Marxist reading could examine the attention paid to the lower ranks of society, and their oppression by the powerful; a feminist reading would have a wealth of material to examine, not only in the attitude to women expressed through the characters of Dame Sensualitie and the Sowtar's and Taylour's wives (and Diligence's rude remarks to female members of the audience at the end of Part One), but in the personifications of Veritie and Chastitie as opposed to those of Divyne Correctioun and Gude Counsall.

PART ONE: STRUCTURE AND CHARACTERISATION
Part One should ideally be looked at as a whole, and various threads drawn from it for deeper study. The obvious starting-point is the depiction of Rex

Humanitas as the epitome of the young king in need of guidance and correction, and the two groups of three, with varying degrees of self-interest, who endeavour to provide this. The number symbolism is significant here in that there are three comic vices, three real vices, three followers of Dame Sensualitie, three virtues (Gude Counsall, Veritie, Chastitie), three estates, but only two representatives of the craftsmen (Sowtar and Taylour), two representatives of the common people (Pauper and Johne the Common-weill), two causes of poverty (Thift [*theft*] and Oppressioun), and two preachers (Doctor and Foly). An examination of this patterning can help the reader understand Lyndsay's moral and satiric implications.

Wantonnes, Placebo and Solace are comic vices, concerned with the lighter or less serious venal sins of the flesh, unlike Flatterie, Falset and Dissait, who are the full-blown versions, encouraging their followers into mortal sin. Humanitas is presented as a young man who wants to rule well, and is aware of what is required (78, 83–4, 88–9):

> O Lord of Lords and King of Kingis all, ...
> Send me Thy grace with peace perpetuall,
> That I may rewll my realme to Thy pleaseir, . . .
> Be I nocht rewlit be counsall and ressoun,
> In dignitie I may nocht lang indure.

The characters of Wantonnes, Placebo and Solace are revealed clearly in their words, particularly those of the latter, who introduces Dame Sensualitie into the court. Solace says of his mother that '[o]f twelf yeir auld sho learnit to swyfe' (162) and introduces one of the running themes of the first part of the play: that women are naturally sexually rapacious, and that no man is safe from them. It is Wantonnes who produces the argument that lechery cannot be sin because all the priests indulge in it ('To luif ladies thay think ane pleasand sport', 240) which will be one of the main thrusts of Divyne Correctioun's process in the second Part. Such a misogynist attitude is clearly out of place today, raising the question as to how far a modern reading can impose contemporary values on such a work.

It is useful and revealing to make a comparison between the description that Dame Sensualitie gives of herself (271ff.), followed by that of Placebo (337ff.) and then the descriptions of the beloved lady in contemporary poetry, such as those found in the works of William Dunbar or Alexander Scott. Poetry contemporary with the play also shows how widespread was the convention of referring to bodily functions in poems of invective, and the use of alliterative terms of abuse, as found in later sections of the play.

That sex is the main interest of Dame Sensualitie and her ladies is made manifest in the words of Fund-Jonet, one of Dame Sensualitie's attendants, who seems little better than a brothel-keeper ('You knaw I [leird] yow baith to swyfe', 318). And Rex Humanitas's reaction shows very clearly that even a verbal description of this lady causes him to fall into a state of excitement which is again commonplace in the poetry of the time. Sensualitie's devotion to 'Queene Venus' (499ff.) can be compared to that of Rex Humanitas's to God in terms of content, language and tone, giving an interesting comparison of the sacred and temporal concerns of the 'ruler'. Similarly, Rex Humanitas's and Dame Sensualitie's courtly exchanges are paralleled in lower style by the conversation between Wantonnes and Hamelines, which is sexually explicit, but uses euphemism. The reader could speculate as to why Lyndsay is so explicit about sexual matters, and whether he has a deeper purpose than simple audience amusement.

THE PATTERN EMERGES: THE PERSONIFICATION OF VICE

Once Rex Humanitas is safely ensconced in the arms of Dame Sensualitie, the real vices appear, with Flatterie arrayed as a Fool (perhaps having just disembarked from a Ship of Fools). This could be compared with the Foly episode at the end of the play, which is omitted entirely from the Kemp text. Flatterie addresses the audience directly and introduces himself as 'Flatterie, your awin fuill [own fool]' (629), perhaps suggesting a much more pointed message. This is where the patterning begins to become more evident, as Dissait, the third vice, has, like Solace, been left getting drunk. The speeches of Dissait and Solace, in which they introduce themselves, are revealingly similar, although whereas Solace was entranced by Dame Sensualitie, Dissait amused himself 'in a bawburd's [prostitute's] bed' (690). Similarly, although the three comic vices denied good counsel in advising Rex Humanitas that he could take a mistress with impunity, citing the actions of the clergy to support this, Dissait has actually encountered the character Gude Counsall, and is very aware of the consequences to the three of them if they are discovered. Wantonnes, Placebo and Solace entertain the king in their own names and guises, but the true vices disguise themselves. The audience is left wondering why concealment is unnecessary in the first case, but not in the second.

The actions of the three vices are the beginning of the main thrust of the play, which is concerned with the reforming of the clergy, as their actions and words reveal why the reputation of the contemporary church orders was so low. Their words, similarly, are indicative of the deceptions that are practised by them and their masters, as is shown in the language: 'Appeirandlie [*apparently, by appearance*] ye seime sum men of gude' (851); 'Sapience suld be ane man of gude' (878); 'Ye seime to be thrie men of gude' (937); and Gude Counsall's 'The Lord mot mak yow men of gude!' (967). And Lyndsay makes effective dramatic contrast between the vices' manner towards Rex Humanitas and that employed when they are speaking to their intimates in the Estates.

THE PERSONIFICATION OF VIRTUE: VERITIE AND CHASTITIE

Although Veritie and Chastitie are clearly linked in the text through the similar treatment meted out to them, their dramatic purposes are very different. Whereas Veritie speaks generally about the need for truth in government, Chastitie has very much more pointed and directed targets among the Spiritualitie. Chastitie is also the source of some of the knock-about humour involving the Sowtar and Taylor. These were stock comic characters of the time, and were made the butts of sexual innuendo. The conversation between the two wives, totally omitted from the Kemp text, picks up points originally made about the sexual desires of women. These women seem to have a case to make, though, in that their husbands, from whom they have a right to expect sexual favours, are ignoring them and apparently spending all their time with whores. Presumably the women in the audience would sympathise with their actions, whereas the men watching would concur with the Sowtar's heartfelt (1370–1):

Bischops ar blist	*blessed,*
howbeit that thay be waryit	*even if they are cursed*
For they may fuck their fill and be unmaryit!	*unmarried*

Surprisingly, these scenes were not included in the Kemp acting text, since they work in exactly the same way as the low-life scenes in Shakespeare, where the main themes are seen to apply to all ranks of society, with their application to the lowest ranks allowing opportunities for comic relief.

THE IMPORTANCE OF CHASTITIE

The structure is now becoming more complex, in that Chastitie is involved with members of all three estates, all of whom reject her, and is finally banished by Dame Sensualitie with the full agreement of the besotted Rex Humanitas. It is true, as she says, that 'Ladie Sensualitie/Sensyne [*since then*] hes gydit this cuntrie' (1464–5) and that until her sway is overthrown, nothing will change. It is at this point that Divyne Correctioun's Varlet enters to herald the approach of his master, an event which precipitates much panic among the vices. They will seek shelter with the appropriately sympathetic Estate: Flatterie goes to Spiritualitie, Dissait to the merchand-men and Falset to the men of craft, where they will next be seen when the Estates are called to convocation. The audience is left to come to its own conclusions about their choices of sanctuary, and to ponder the significance of Chastitie, both in the sense of its personification and as a moral state.

A CLOSER LOOK AT THE LANGUAGE OF THE PLAY
Lyndsay's versification clearly uses verse form to signal allegiances and their obverse. For instance, when Divyne Correctioun announces his mission (1580) he does so in *ballade* stanzas, this form being picked up by Gude Counsall and Veritie in their replies. Such consonance of versification is an indication of spiritual allegiance, underscored by the fact that sometimes different speakers share the same stanza (1653–60):

Gude Counsall: Flatterie hes taine the habite of ane freir,	*taken; friar*
Thinkand to begyll Spiritualitie.	*thinking; deceive*
Correctioun: But dout, my freind, and I live half any yeir,	*without doubt*
I sall search out that great iniquitie.	
Quhair lyis yon ladyes in captivitie?	
How now, sisters? Quha hes yow sa disgysit?	*who has disguised you in this way?*
Veritie: Unfaithfull members of iniquitie	
Dispytfullie, my Lord, hes us supprysit.	*maliciously*

It is Wantonnes who breaks the pattern by introducing an aaab rhyme which Placebo and Solace share with Sensualitie, although in this instance there is no sharing of stanzas among characters: each character speaks in complete stanzas. Correctioun reverts to the *ballade* stanza after the inter-ruption of the minor vices. The rhyme is shared by Rex Humanitas, but just as the audience thinks that they follow Lyndsay's intentions, Sensualitie spoils the interpretation by continuing and developing Correctioun's *ballade* stanza for 13 lines (1729–40) before reverting to the tail-rhyme form in her address to Spiritualitie, who replies to her in alternate rhyme. Correctioun, now turning to Rex, begins his correction in *ballade* stanza, then modulates into the simpler tail-rhyme for his more straightforward instructions (1761–8):

Now, sir, tak tent quhat I will say:	*pay attention*
Observe thir same baith nicht and day,	*these same ones*
And let them never part yow fray;	*from you*
Or els withoutin doubt,	*without*

Turn ye to Sensualitie,
To vicious lyfe and rebaldrie,   *corruption*
Out of your realme richt shamefullie
Ye sall be ruttit out . . .   *rooted out*

Although Shakespeare in his plays moves from blank verse to prose and frequently to rhyming couplets, and on occasion to sonnet form, there is considerably less variety than is seen in Lyndsay's versification, which has a much more self-consciously poetic structure, together with the wide range of dramatic effect gained by the audience in hearing characters speak in this way.

THE INTERLUDE

The actual overthrow of the vices and acceptance of the virtues is accomplished very easily – which makes some telling points regarding the character of Rex Humanitas and his three advisers. The real battle, with the Estates, is left for the Second Part. Before that begins, however, Lyndsay has inserted a section called an Interlude, which merits careful study. It is introduced in a rather ribald fashion by Diligence, who makes plain that he is a dramatic character by drawing attention to the fact that he is in a play ('Sen ye haif heard the first pairt of our play' (1919)). This is clearly intended as an interval, as he instructs the audience: 'Go tak ane drink and mak collatioun' (1920). He acknowledges, taking the opportunity of making a crude joke at their expense, that the ladies of the audience at least be in need of what is now known as a 'comfort break' (1926–31). Appetites are whetted by his assertion that '[t]he best pairt of our play' (1933) is yet to come. Once again, Lyndsay is very deliberately drawing attention to the fact that the play is an artefact to be attended to critically, and not a piece of drama in which the audience can lose themselves. This is highly didactic writing, and it is useful to examine the ways in which Lyndsay maintains his audience's interest and attention. In any event, the Interlude is clearly an integral part of the play which emerges out of Part One and introduces the themes and narrative of Part Two. The Pauper, despite his irreverent attitude, has a vital part to play in that his complaints against the clergy reveal a tangible piece of clerical corruption, authorised by the church rules on tithes. He is clearly not simply a comic character like the Sowtar and Taylour, but is far more a representative of those who suffer under the church and the king's misgovernance. And it is the church and the king who are, in this play, being reminded of their duties to the people of the country.

Lyndsay's Sir Robert Rome-raker appears to lodge with all the vices 'with gude kynde Christiane Anderson' (2212), which is presumably Lindsay's point, and which may be exemplified by his use of the six-line tail-rhyme stanza form associated with the vices. Without going into the minutiae of the underlying theological debate, it would not be difficult to show the comic aspects of the relics he describes in lines 2087–107, the blasphemous divorce he grants to the Sowtar and his wife in lines 2129–86, and his boy's finding a new relic '[u]pon Dame Fleschers midding [*midden*]' (2192) which can be given out to be 'ane bane [*bone*] of Sanct Bryds cow' (2194). The Pauper's hope in religion triumphs over his experience of clergymen as he approaches the Pardoner for aid, ironically calling 'Sanct Bryd, Sanct Bryd, send me my ky againe!' (2230).

PART TWO: DEEPENING THE ISSUES

Diligence introduces this Part very differently from the way he closed the first Part, now using the formal *ballade* stanza identified with the forces of right, while Wantonnes, Placebo and Solace maintain the six-line tail-rhyme. The 'Estaitis' themselves display the different styles of language that would be expected at the time: Spiritualitie using an aureate, Latinate vocabulary characteristic of the high style (2359–65), while Temporalitie adopts a more natural style with fewer Latinate words and only 'superexcellent' for aureation (2366–72); in contrast, the Merchands speak in a middle style comprising a native vocabulary and diction (2373–9).

This chapter cannot examine the whole of Part Two in detail, but the complaints of Johne the Common-weill deserve to be looked at (2424ff.). His entrance on the stage is dramatic, and should look like a real irruption from the audience (2424–5):

> Out of my gait! For Gods saik, let me ga!
> Tell me againe, gude maister, quhat ye say.

Although there are similarities between Johne the Common-weill and the Pauper, it is the differences between them that are more worthy of note, and which are brought out strongly in this section of the play. Johne brings into the open many more vices and locates them directly – Covetice and Sensualitie with Spiritualitie; Publick Oppressioun with Temporalitie; Falset and Dissait with the Merchands and Craftsmen respectively (2451–9). Flatterie is described as 'guyder [*leader*] of the court' (2467). Although Spiritualitie is determined to have nothing to do with any kind of correction not directly sanctioned by the Pope, Temporalitie and the Merchands are seen as much more ready to be reformed, even to the extent of asking for the advice of Gude Counsall and Johne the Common-weill. The latter brings in the Pauper to help him illustrate the difficulties experienced by the common people, thereby showing the close relationship between them. Gude Counsall's rehearsal of the complaints of the farming community (2560–82) repeat the Pauper's complaints (1980–2027) in more general form, thus reinforcing his experience as a commonplace. Finally, his story is repeated by Johne the Common-weill (2728–42) and supported by the Pauper (2745–9), showing the central importance of this episode. (At this juncture it is worth considering why Lyndsay gives three different accounts of this story, with language and effect changing with each telling.)

THE CHARACTERISATION OF SPIRITUALITIE
The characterisation of Spiritualitie could also be examined throughout Part Two. Johne the Common-weill is, once given leave, particularly scathing of the clergy's practices, but what is clearer still is that Spiritualitie has little connection with true religion. The contradictory lines (2359–65) reveal the complacent assumption that the spiritual realm will not be reformed; but (2406–13) they realise the truth; and (2498–519) are deprived of Covetice and Sensualitie. Johne's and the Pauper's tirades (2728–803) and Spiritualitie's angry replies to their accusations are interesting not just in content but in the different uses of language and attitudes towards the clergy. There are detailed arguments about bribes, benefices and preaching (2842–960), and then individual members of the clergy justifying their offices: Spiritualitie (3375–408), the Abbot (3423–38), the Persoun (3440–6) and the Priores (3453–5). Lyndsay has all these individuals condemn themselves out of their own mouths.

THE TWO SERMONS: DOCTRINE REPEATED AS DISORDER?
A fascinating final comparison towards the end of the play can be made between the sermons of the Doctor and Foly. The Doctor's sermon is absolutely predictable, following the established pattern of elaboration on a textual theme, that of 'If thou wilt enter into life, keep the commandments', which is developed into the specific instruction 'Love the Lord thy God with all thy heart . . . love thy neighbour as thyself' and ending on the formulaic 'I say na mair' (3586) to indicate that the sermon is finished. Before Foly enters, the unholy members of Spiritualitie are removed, the Acts of Divyne Correctioun and King Humanitie read to the gathering and the miscreants are hanged (but only after long speeches). Everything seems to be on course for a new beginning. Foly most closely resembles the licensed fool found at many kings' courts, as he talks anything but nonsense in his sermon. His

oration follows the established pattern and can therefore be directly compared to that of the Doctor, but he is talking about the real world where the Doctor was talking only about the ideal Christian society. Lyndsay's intention in having Foly intervene at this point may be to show that however well established the laws and ground-rules of a reformed kingdom, it is still populated by real people who may be too self-interested to follow the proclamations without objections. There is a great deal of nonsense spoken by Foly, mostly at the expense of his wife, but the only part of the sermon which is foolish is the prophecy at the end: the rest makes perfect sense.

Philotus: *a very different kind of Renaissance play*

Philotus differs from *Ane Satyre* in purpose as well as style. *Ane Satyre* is a political morality play and an allegorical drama; its style is non-naturalistic and directly involves the audience; it was performed publicly and served as a potent political and propaganda weapon. *Philotus* reflects the Italian fashion for comedies based on ancient classical drama which focus on love intrigues, disguises and confusions. It was clearly written to be performed, and seems likely to have been written to entertain guests at a very grand wedding. From the text, with all its stress on the true nature of the divine institution of marriage, it seems obvious that it is a celebration of the nuptial link. The striking thing about *Philotus* is that, despite being described as 'Ane verie excellent and delectabill Treatise intitulit PHILOTUS . . .' in the Robert Charteris imprint in 1603 (its first recorded publication), it is a highly dramatic text, written by a skilled dramatist. As R. D. S. Jack comments in *The Italian Influence on Scottish Literature* (1972), it is guaranteed to 'produce laughter when performed'.

THE PLOT

The play, first published in 1603, has been re-edited by Jamie Reid Baxter (1995), and by R. D. S. Jack and P. A. T. Rozendaal (1997). In the Baxter edition, it has been revised with a clear eye to performance and includes act and scene divisions as well as stage directions, which were not in the original. This was produced for amateur performance in 1998 at Biggar for its first time in several hundred years. The text begins with 'The Argument' which sets out the story of the play. Unlike the prologue in Shakespeare's *Romeo and Juliet*, this does not form an integral part of the play's action, but serves to clarify the complicated relationships which the story depicts. The tale concerns Philotus, a rich old man of eighty who is enamoured with Emilie, the 14-year-old daughter of his friend Alberto. He proposes to her, using as inducement his wealth and possessions. In an impressive display of self-confidence, Emilie rejects his suit out of hand and Philotus resorts to employing the Macrell (from the French term, *maquerelle*, meaning a bawd or procuress) to persuade Emilie to marry him. The Macrell promises success, but, despite detailed descriptions of the life of ease Emilie might expect with Philotus, the joys of married life with this ancient seem to escape the young heroine. Not even the suggestions that she could be a wealthy widow fairly soon, or that she could take a young lover after she is married, are enough to change Emilie's mind.

Reluctantly, the Macrell has to admit defeat to Philotus. Disappointed but not despairing, he approaches Emilie's father, his friend Alberto, and expresses his desire to marry Emilie. He outlines all the benefits she may expect, and, more importantly, all the financial rewards Alberto will receive. Unlike his daughter, Alberto accepts the proposal with alacrity. However, both men underestimate Emilie herself who continues to resist the marriage so vehemently that her father says he will imprison her on bread and water for a year and a day. While Emilie looks out from her prison, Flavius, the handsome young hero, sees her and falls instantly and madly in love with her. He addresses her in extravagant terms and declares his undying love for her. Emilie is not so easily convinced. She enjoys the declaration of love but questions the speed of it all and, in a rather cynical way for one so young, dismisses his emotions thus (537–40):

And this conceate is common to yow all!	*conceit, language*
For your awin lust, ye set not by our schame:	
Your sweitest word ar seasonit all with gall,	*seasoned*
Your fairest phrase disfigures bot defame.	*disgraces*

Stung by this response, and wishing to vindicate the sincerity of his love, Flavius immediately proposes marriage, and is accepted – but there is a problem. Emilie is still imprisoned. She devises a plan of escape disguised as a boy in page's clothes. This is achieved but she is spotted by Stephano, one of her father's servants, who has been leering at her while she was changing. He immediately reports her disappearance to her father and Philotus. They set off to look for her. Enter Philerno, Emilie's long-lost, look-alike, forgotten, brother! Mistaking him for the disguised Emilie, Alberto launches himself at Philerno ready to punish him/her for the escape. Philerno, thinking the two old men are mad, decides to play along with the charade. He changes into Emilie's clothes and agrees to stay at Philotus's house, sleeping with Brisilla, Philotus's daughter, until the wedding can take place.

This, as might be expected, is a recipe for disaster. Philerno falls for Brisilla, who is attracted to 'Emily' – if only she was a man! The situation has been complicated still further by the suggestion that Brisilla should be married to Alberto. Philerno suggests a possible solution. He will pray to the gods to turn him into a man so that he and Brisilla can be married. A 'miracle' is effected, much to Brisilla's delight. Philerno, still posing as Emily, continues the central thread of misunderstanding by submitting to a mock marriage to the lecherous Philotus. Flavius upon witnessing this nuptial 'deceit' imagines he is married to some evil spirit in the shape of Emily. He denounces her, and Emily, listening to his farcical exorcisms, believes he has gone mad. Flavius throws her out of his house. Meanwhile, Philotus and Philerno/Emily settle, by a fierce fistfight, who shall wield the power in the marriage; Philotus loses! Philerno/Emily now further dupes Philotus by arranging for him to spend his wedding night with a whore who has been paid to make him believe she is a maid. The real Emily decides to return to her father, whereupon she finds a battered and bruised Philotus. Emily's complaint against her husband for having driven her out is followed by a complaint on the same lines from Philotus against his sham 'wife'.

The complaints present a sharp ironic contrast, and centre the humour on poor, baffled Alberto, who is unaware that he and Philotus are talking at cross-purposes. All is finally resolved when Flavius explains why he has treated Emily so harshly and Philerno confesses the tricks he has played on them all. The latter confession is particularly difficult for Philotus who realises he was cuckolded before he was married. Finally, Alberto consents to Philerno and Brisilla's marriage and Emily and Flavius are reunited. The play ends with a song by the four lovers, after which Philotus addresses the audience and admits that all his misfortunes have stemmed from his own folly, concluding that men should be the masters of their own passions.

The play uses sharply defined stock characters and situations, pitting love against avarice, youth against age and celebrating the triumph of young love. In the traditional figure of the Macrell and the cynically observing Plesant, the author has created characters with powerful stage presence. The Macrell makes the story far more dramatic, while the Plesant comments on the 'freeze-framed' action in a knowing, bawdy and comic way. A wide variety of comic methods, from obscene ribaldry to parodies of high-flown oratory, physical farce to complex misunderstandings are used. The plot moves at a brisk pace and the comic situations are diverse. The playwright shows considerable ability in treating all levels of style: the elevated high-style rhetoric co-exists with feisty colloquial rhetoric.

QUESTIONS OF PERFORMANCE AND PROVENANCE

There is no record of the play's performance and no precise indication of how close to the publication date of 1603 it was written. From references in the text, studies of language and style and examination of possible sources, the play has been dated as early as 1565 or as late as the 1590s. This leads to interesting speculation as to which monarch is referred to in the closing stanzas of the play and at which court it may have performed. Much of the subject matter, language and style of the piece is more consistent with the drama of the court of Mary, Queen of Scots. Yet specific mention is made to the king and at least one scholar has attributed authorship of the play to James VI himself. In an attempt to solve the mystery of the authorship of the play, scholars have identified the stylistic markers of a number of authors. Among those suggested are Alexander Montgomerie, Stewart of Baldynneis, George Steill, Robert Sempill and John Burel. In the absence of absolute proof the author remains anonymous.

PHILOTUS TODAY

Whoever wrote *Philotus* was an excellent dramatist with a keen eye for comic detail and farce. The play has been performed by amateur companies; in 1953 at the Edinburgh Festival and more recently in Biggar by another amateur company using the most recently edited version of the text (*The Mercat Anthology*, 1997). The vigorous and earthy writing along with the hilariously complicated plot results in a highly entertaining evening, although the play has not been without its share of controversy. Its language has been described as coarse, even for an outspoken age, one eighteenth-century critic remarking that 'This delectabill treatise is by far the most offensive drama ever produced . . . sufficient proof of the barbarous state in which Scotland remained till civilised by its intercourse with England.' Without doubt, such description will intrigue modern readers, directors, and actors!

CHAPTER 4

RENAISSANCE POETRY: THE JACOBEAN PERIOD

NEW BEGINNINGS

For the purposes of this chapter, 'Renaissance' is defined as that short period from the mid-1580s to the end of the first decade of the seventeenth century, during which Scottish court poetry underwent fascinating transformations in the reign of King James VI and I (1566–1625). Despite the wealth of vernacular literature which had survived the Reformation (see Chapter 6), King James VI was determined that Scottish literature be remade in a more European style under his guidance and patronage. James's *Ane Schort Treatise Conteining Some Reulis and Cautelis to be Observit and Eschewit in Scottis Poesie*, published in 1584, can be seen as the signal for a new poetics, a kind of literary revolution, in Scotland.

The *Treatise* is a manual of versifying for apprentice poets, described as 'docile bairns of knawledge', in Scots; this linguistic feature makes a natio-nalistic as well as a literary point. James ensures that apprentice poets have the best models to follow by giving examples, in most cases, from the work of the already-established Alexander Montgomerie (see below). Typically Scot-tish forms such as 'flyting' and alliteration are singled out for special mention and commendation, as is the sound of the verse: 'the verie tuichestane quhairof is musique'. The production of an 'instruction manual' might perhaps make this Scottish Renaissance sound artificial; on the other hand, it could be a signal that poets needed to be guided, or even that the young James felt that he had to play an appropriately kingly or magisterial role!

The development of a distinctive Scottish poetic voice

It was a self-interested desire for court position, as well as an urge to regenerate the Scottish literary scene, which drew Alexander Montgomerie, John Stewart of Baldynneis, William Fowler, Alexander Hume and the Hudson brothers to form a courtly band of poets, with James at their head as patron. The two oldest, Stewart and Montgomerie, were from the minor aristocracy, as was Hume, while Fowler's family background was the Edinburgh merchant class, and the Hudson brothers had come from England, primarily as court musicians. This was a heterogeneous grouping, whose writing covered a very wide range of themes, styles and dictions, and while it lasted it produced much that is of interest, beauty and depth.

One of the notable features of sixteenth-century poetry in Scotland is its variety of styles and forms. Towards the end of the century in England, poets developed a craze for sonnets and sonnet sequences. The main model was the *Canzoniere* sonnet sequence, a succession of 365 love lyrics written by Francesco Petrarcha (known as Petrarch), the medieval Italian poet (1304–74). This sequence told the story of the poet's chaste love for the beautiful Laura, and its appeal lay chiefly in the cultivation of intensely vivid images and universal themes. While in England, the Petrarchan sonnet was the most popular form, in Scotland variety remained, and the sonnet was only one of a range of forms that could be chosen. Unfortunately, it is very difficult for the interested reader to find much of this early material, as it has only been printed in the scholarly editions of The Scottish Text Society. All that is possible here is to give a brief introduction to these writers, discussing in detail only those poems which are readily available, primarily in *The Mercat Anthology*, edited by R. D. S. Jack and P. A. T. Rozendaal (2000) and in *The New Oxford Book of Seventeenth Century Verse*, edited by Alastair Fowler (1991). It is slowly being acknowledged that there is a body of work which is well worth popularising, and it is hoped that these editions will open up the period to a wider readership.

The court group

As would be expected from the doyen of the courtly grouping, the poetry of Alexander Montgomerie (?1555–97) is, in its variety, reminiscent of that of Dunbar. Montgomerie was musical, and at least thirty of his original lyrics were set to music by Scottish, English and French composers. The poem for which Montgomerie is best known is the long and allegorical *The Cherrie and the Slae*, impossible to date, but first printed in 1597, a courtly entertainment on the difficulties of choosing the true spiritual path in life. It was evidently a popular work, set to virtuosic music on 'dance-song', which attracted much interest both within the poet's lifetime and posthumously. However, it is his lyrical works which impress the present-day reader, such as 'The Solsequium', a lovely lyric which compares the lover to a sunflower, living only through the light of his lady-sun, and which is as metaphysical as any of John Donne's

English poems. 'Evin dead behold I breath!', 'In throu the windoes of myn ees', 'A bony "No," with smyling looks agane', and many others, have been set to music and can be obtained in recorded form. Montgomerie's graceful lines and persuasive rhetoric can be seen as the natural development of earlier sixteenth-century Scottish verse. (The poet's wide range of sonnets in different styles will be discussed in more detail below.)

In the poetry of the group's patron, James VI, can be seen an attraction to the medieval, despite his stated aim to create a new poetics for Scots. But although the early sixteenth-century tradition has a tight hold, James always appears to be trying to remake the conventions in a new way, as can be seen in 'Complaint of his mistressis absence from court'. The final stanza incorporates a series of images used by the famous French Renaissance poet, Pierre de Ronsard, in his poem to Mary, Queen of Scots when she left France, which shows James's ability to incorporate the newer developments from continental literature into the existing tradition. Drawing attention to these literary allusions reveals a much more sophisticated poetic consciousness than James is often credited with.

The predominantly stanzaic poetry of John Stewart of Baldynneis (c. 1550– c. 1605) is similar to that of King James, probably in deliberate imitation. Stewart was clearly happiest with the more copious or extravagant forms of stanzaic verse, following James's strictures. While he frequently used the same images as Montgomerie, it was the King's rules on form and style he followed. Stewart was one of the oldest members of the courtly group, but he was clearly no staid traditionalist. He took on board James's instructions to enrich the Scots language, inventing words with verve and enthusiasm. Stylistically, his poems are innovative, experimental and rhetorically exciting, often written to create interesting shapes on the page. He composed a very lively version of Ariosto's *Orlando Furioso* (1532), entitled *Roland Furious* (c. 1582–4). Such flexibility in style and tone is the trademark of the best poets of the group.

Among the court group, William Fowler (1560–1612) was the only one to show a consistent allegiance to Italian verse rather than to the French which was preferred by James and others. In *The Tarantula of Love* (?1587) Fowler adapted to his own purposes Petrarch's sonnet sequence. This is a thoroughly Scottish sequence which shows a mastery of the native tropes of alliteration, localised setting and imagery, allied to a virtuoso employment of Middle Scots rhetorical devices. Representative sonnets from this sequence will be discussed later.

The last members of the group, Alexander Hume, Robert and Thomas Hudson, have not left as much to posterity. Hume destroyed what he described as his 'vane ballatis of luve' in favour of much more serious moralising verse, the best example of which is the frequently anthologised 'Of the Day Estivall', a beautifully lyrical description of a Scottish summer's day in which all the pleasures of God's creation are celebrated and praised. The Hudson brothers contributed most strongly to the court group through their musical expertise.

The Scottish Sonnet

The Scottish employment of the sonnet, begun at the Jacobean court in the 1580s, is much wider and more flexible than the English Petrarchan love sonnet. The sonnets in *The Mercat Anthology* are used as the basis for the following discussion.

The selection from Montgomerie's work is fairly representative of the poet's range, from complaint about the state of the times, through the flyting mode (inherited from Dunbar), to translation from the French poet Pierre de Ronsard, indirect address, celebration of male friendship and playful dream-vision. The second sonnet, 'The Flyting', is the last of a group of four on his advocate John Sharpe, which changes from supreme confidence in the lawyer's ability to win his case, where the lawyer is first praised for his 'sharpness', to allegations of miscegenation, bestiality and disease. Heavy alliteration underscores the invective (1–4):

A Baxters bird, a bluiter beggar-borne,	*beggar-born babbler*
Ane ill heud huirsone lyk a barkit hyde,	*badly-formed bastard; tanned hide*
A saulles swinger, sevintie tymes mensworne,	*soulless scrounger; perjured*
A peltrie pultron poyson'd up with pryde . . .	*useless coward*

The accusations continue for thirteen lines of the sonnet, piling on the loathsome qualities until the final line: 'Quha reids this riddill, he is Sharpe forsuith' / *Whoever reads [solves] this riddle is sharp*, a pun on the lawyer's name (14). The contrasting juxtaposition of the satirical sonnets shows the poet's mastery of rhetoric and serves to counterpoint the amatory sonnets, here represented by an adaptation from Ronsard. In 'So swete a kis yistrene fra thee I reft', Montgomerie has compressed the Frenchman's twenty lines into the fourteen of the sonnet and has heightened the sensuality even of the original, implying that this kiss was stolen as part of love-making 'In bouing doun [*bowing down*] thy body on the bed') (2), and seeming to contradict the literal interpretation of 'reft' as 'stolen' since the love is clearly requited. Although the imagery is basically conventional, it is literalised: the kiss transfers the poet-lover's 'lyfe' along with his breath; hence his 'spreits wald never shed' (4) from the lady which leaves '[*his*] corps als cold as ony kie [*key*]' (6). He pictures his heart sent to find his spirit (9–10):

> Bot it wes so inamored with thyn ee,   *enamoured*
> With thee it myndit lykwyse to remane.

Bereft of breath, spirit and heart, he is in danger of death (13–14):

> Except thy breath thare places had suppleit.
> Even in thyn armes thair, doutles, had I deit.   *doubtless had I died*

which suggests rather ambiguously that he had 'died' in her arms after all. She has exchanged breath, spirit and heart with him in perfect concord when she returns the kiss.

It has been suggested that many of the poems written ostensibly as love lyrics are in fact pleas for patronage, using Petrarchan rhetoric. A group of three sonnets (the first is given in *The Mercat Anthology*) describe the poet's exile from court in terms more commonly used for the unrequited lover. Added to the image is the idea that the nightingale sings while piercing her breast on thorns, dying on her song. This is the image that Montgomerie uses in this first sonnet, where 'Thy chivring chirlis, whilks changinglie thou chants' [*tremulous trills which you sing by turns*] (3) echo the poet's feelings. The bird (7–8):

> . . . sees not, sillie, saikles thing,   *simple, innocent*
> The peircing pykis brods at thy bony breist.   *piercing thorns prick*

unlike the poet, who is very conscious of the cause of his pain. The vision of the nightingale makes him reconsider his first thoughts of giving up (12–14):

> Suld feble I, for feir, my conqueis quyt?   *give up*
> Na, na, I love the – freshest Phoenix fair –
> In beuty, birth, in bounty but compair!   *without comparison*

The references here to 'Phoenix', and 'bounty', the first a common image for James and the second the kingly prerogative of generosity, would seem to indicate that this is a veiled plea for reinstatement. Certainly the 'Evin so am I' is a clear verbal clue pointing the reader to the parallels between the bird's situation and that of the poet-lover. This kind of ambiguity adds another level of interest to study of these poems, and also encourages an examination of the cultural milieu within which they were created.

Lest one think that the life of a court poet is all lyric and literature, the next sonnet selected from *The Mercat Anthology* is a celebration of friendship, good living and the inevitable consequences of excess, revealing another facet of sixteenth-century life.

The final sonnet is an unconventional dream vision, which plays with the paradox that the devoted lover should not be able to close his eyes in sleep, so tormented is he by his feelings (as the lady reminds him: ' "Art ye on sleip?" quod sche. "O, fy for schame!/Have ye nocht tauld that luifaris [*lovers*] takis no rest?" ', 5–6) while without sleep there would be no possibility of the erotic dream. The repeated 'me thocht' maintains the tension between the wished-for and the real, with reality closing the poem as he awakens: 'alace, sche was away!' (14). It is difficult in any anthology to find representative poems to show all Montgomerie's various facets, but *The Mercat Anthology* gives readers an idea of the range of this very important poet, and shows Montgomerie's expert handling of the peculiarly Scottish form of the sonnet, with its interlaced rhymes ababbcbccdcdee.

Sovereign poetry

James's poems are rather easier to select, as he had very mixed success with sonnets, and clearly preferred the more copious form of stanzaic poetry. When he does succeed, he can produce a very effective poem, as in 'To the Queene, Anonimos' (the first of James's poems in *The Mercat Anthology*), where the trick is that the subject of the poem is in fact James himself. The poem opens with an echo of Petrarch in 'That blessed houre when first was broght to light' (1), but with more of an echo of the classical Judgement of Paris, where three goddesses are pictured vying for the chance to protect Anne. Before naming the three goddesses, James, showing the usual egotism of the sonneteer, proclaims himself king of the gods and 'happie Monarch sprung of Ferguse race' (9). Only in the sestet are the Queen's attributes mentioned. She is 'wise Minerve when pleaseth the' (10), 'chaste Diana' (12) when occupied in sporting pursuits, and finally (13–14):

> Then, when to bed thou gladlie does repaire,
> Clasps in thine armes thy Cytherea faire.

This is a successful closure, the use of 'Cytherea' creating a line which scans beautifully.

James's competence as a poet is also seen in the second sonnet, which conflates classical and natural images rather effectively. '[T]hat crooked, crawling Vulcan', becomes synonymous with the fire that he uses in his forge, buried under ashes (3–4):

> . . . whill, by his heate, he drie   *till*
> The greene and fizzing faggots made of tree.

This is a natural image of sap-filled wood burning, the onomatopoeic 'fizzing' being highly effective in the context. It is the native diction and idiom which give this poem its appeal as when the spark of love is described as 'that litle sponke and flaming eye' (5), which, once given oxygen, will 'bleaze bravelie forth and, sparkling all abreed [*abroad*]' (6), despite being 'smor'd under coales of shame' (10). This is clearly a remembered sight of the reviving of the fire which has been 'smored' [*smothered*] under peats or coals during the night.

Where James's true feelings are aroused, he uses the medium of poetry to work out his troubles. This is seen in the fourth of the anthologised sonnets, which is one of three known as 'the Bothwell sonnets'. Bothwell's challenge to the King in 1591 was a terrifying episode from which the king was lucky to escape, and the language of the sonnets reflects this. Similarly, in playful flyting with one of the younger members of his retinue, William Alexander, James shows his strengths in lively, punning lines, using alliteration and onomatopoeia effectively.

Stewart of Baldynneis: formal invention

Stewart of Baldynneis took the use of alliteration to considerable lengths, as is seen in his final sonnet in *The Mercat Anthology*, 'Ane Literall Sonnet', where every word in each line alliterates on a single letter. Although rather a catalogue, the wealth of the Scottish alliterative vocabulary, some of it borrowed from medieval tradition, as in 'peirles, proper, plesand, perll preclair' (6) and '[r]yche rubie – rycht renownit, royall, rair' (8), is impressive.

More successfully poetic is 'Of Ane Fontane', which is a translation of Philippe Desportes's 'Cette fontaine est froide'. Here the apparently effortless combination of classical deities, medieval imagery and alliteration with localised detail creates a sonnet which is as fresh as the fountain it depicts. The description of the 'fontane fair' (1) 'with bonie birkis [*birches*] all ubumbrat round [*shaded round*]' (5) could be any Scottish spring, as is attested further by the 'doucest souching' [*softest moaning*] (8) of the wind. As was seen in James's sonnet on Vulcan, the Scots were very capable of reoccupying any territory, whatever the original language.

Taking the moral high ground, or moralising generally, is Stewart's forte, and some of his most successful short poems take this form. 'Of Ambitious Men' compares social climbers to the 'dryest dust winddrift in drouthie day' [*wind-driven on a dry day*] (1), which lands on the faces and clothes of 'lords and ladies of renoune' (2), and thus for a moment becomes part of their world until the sweepers brush it away. The aspirants manage for a short time to 'volt with waltring wind' (10) before being dashed to the ground, the greatest fall being reserved for those who try to climb to the very top (13–14):

> Bot ay the swyfter and moir hich thay brall,   *high; soar*
> Moir low and suddane cums thair feirfull fall.

Perhaps the most surprising example of Stewart's work, showing the exuberance of which he was capable, is the pair of sonnets addressed from a 'hostess'. The first is superficially a poem of thanks to a woman who has given him a room for the night, but it is actually a bawdy *aubade* (a lover's dawn-song of parting) addressed to a prostitute. The disappointments of the experience are all the hostess's fault, in the view of the speaker, as he has no experience of consorting with whores.

The hostess replies in such a way that the subtext has to be carefully extracted from what is apparently a rejection of an ungrateful and over-demanding guest (5–8):

> None sutche as yow sould to my palice speir   *such; inquire*
> Quho may be eisit soon in smallest hall,   *eased, accommodated*
> Your sthomack servith bot for sempill cheir,   *stomach; fare*
> I yow againe sall not to banket call . . .   *banquet*

The antithesis between what she is offering (the 'palice' and 'banket') and what the guest is capable of receiving and appreciating ('smallest hall' and 'sempill cheir'), and between the ostensible fare (food for the stomach) and the actual provision (sexual favours as the word 'eisit' hints at) is resolved in the devastating couplet (13–14):

> Heirfoir, your pithles person to repois,
> Tak my bak chalmer for your guckit nois.

55

This woman, most definitely, has the upper hand over the hapless male. Is it not refreshing to see that the court poets were capable of real-life, and low-life depiction? It appears to be characteristic of Scots rather than English poets that the high-flown and idealised should be cut down to size and made part of the real world.

Fowler: the Petrarchan paradox

William Fowler's sequence *The Tarantula of Love* (?1587) shows a wide variety of styles, tones and dictions in a single form; that of the Scottish sonnet. The first sonnet in *The Mercat Anthology*, 'The day is done, the sunn doth eells declyne' is one of Fowler's most successful sonnets, creating as it does a simply imagined but particularly effective and affective picture of the onset of night and sleep. In the first quatrain, the poet-lover states the fact that the day is over and night approaches. The picture of the night is calm and beautiful (1–4):

> The day is done, the sunn dothe ells declyne,
> Night now approches and the moone appeares,
> The twinkling starrs in firmament dois schyne,
> Decoring with the poolles there circled spheres . . . *decorating; pole stars*

The language is simple, with a high percentage of monosyllables, and no unexpected or unusual epithets. The description is in fact highly predictable, even to the nursery-rhyme sound of 'the twinkling starrs', which is entirely in keeping with the poet's purposes. The alliteration is lightly handled, creating an overall feeling of harmony. God is clearly in his heaven and all is right with the world in this account. In the second quatrain, the writer has his world go to sleep, again expressed very simply (5–8):

> The birds to nests, wyld beasts to denns reteirs,   *retire*
> The moving leafs unmoved now repose,
> Dew dropps dois fall, the portraicts of my teares;   *do*
> The waves within the seas theme calmlye close.   *them*

This is deceptively simple writing, as it is so compressed and economical. Line 6 develops an element of wordplay, in that 'unmoved' suggests the emotional response in the following line. That the dew drops are described as the 'portraicts' of his tears, suggest that he is seeking natural correspondences with his feelings without expecting the world to weep in sympathy with him.

Fowler, in the sestet, makes much more use of the imagery of disorder, pain and the torment of love, characteristic of *The Tarantula of Love* as a whole, but here, there is a deeper level of subtlety (9–14):

To all things, Nature ordour dois impose–	*order*
Bot not to love, that proudlye doith me thrall,	*enslaves me*
Quha all the dayes and night but chainge or choyse,	
Steirs up the coales of fyre unto my fall	*stirs up*
And sawes his breirs and thornes within my hart,	*sows*
The fruits quhairoff ar duile, greiff, grones, and smart.	*whereof; misery; pain*

While the octave had been based on the ordered replacement of natural things (the sun by the moon, for instance), this section of the poem is based on antitheses, introduced by the 'bot' (but). The poet-lover's case is opposed to the ordered universe, implying that love is not under the control of nature but is in fact opposed to nature, for love does not sleep. Now the mono-syllabic words of the final line have the effect, not of simplicity as at the beginning of the poem, but of the agonising throb of a perpetual pain, the final 'smart' representing the continual pricking of the thorns of love.

'O nights, no nights bot ay a daylye payne!' is perhaps rather effusive for modern tastes, but this is a highly stylised poem showing the poet's control of rhetorical features. Such outpourings of grief and pain were typical of the Petrarchan vein. The comparison of the lover with the moth, or in Fowler's version 'that poure, foolisch fliee', which flies to the flame and is instantly killed, comes straight from Petrarch, and is perhaps one of the most vivid images of the Italian poet.

In the last poem in the collection, the constancy of the lover in the face of the ever-changing world, and, here specifically, of the erratic seas, is a sign of his worthiness to win the lady after all his trials. This poem is one of a shorter sequence, entitled 'Orknay', which seems to relate to a journey which the poet made to the outer fringes of the realm, but it is also based on the Latin proverb 'Caelum non animum mutant qui trans mare currunt' [*He who travels across the sea changes the sky but not his mind*].

These poems have sufficient substance to make them worth studying as an alternative to the English poems that are established in the canon. Because of the general tendency of the period towards anglicisation, the language is not really a problem, and most modern editions, like *The Mercat Anthology*, gloss obscure words.

AFTER THE UNION OF THE CROWNS

After the Union of the Crowns in 1603, assimilation rather than distinctiveness was the aim of most Scottish writers. Following the decision of King James himself to adapt to the dominant linguistic and cultural form, Scots writers anglicised their work, and it becomes much more difficult to distinguish Scottish writing from mainstream English. A number of writers, however, can be seen to maintain a very Scottish tone and attitude, if not language. William Alexander (1567–1640), Sir David Murray of Gorthy (1567–1629), Robert Ayton (1569–1638) and Alexander Craig of Rosecraig (?1568–1627) were almost exact contemporaries of King James, although only Alexander found favour with James as a courtier, Murray being attached to Prince Henry's court and Ayton later to Queen Anne's. Craig stayed in London long enough to petition James successfully for a pension, then took himself back to Scotland for the rest of his life.

Two other notable poets remained in Scotland, but only one of them, William Drummond of Hawthornden (1585–1649) achieved recognition from English contemporaries and later editors. Sir William Mure of Rowallan (1594–1657) was Alexander Montgomerie's nephew, and makes clear in his poems that he wishes to take up his illustrious forebear's poetic mantle. Many of his stanzaic poems, clear imitations of Montgomerie, are interesting and successful in their way, but once again are available only to the scholar.

Seventeenth-century Scottish writings are, however, rather more available to the general reader, as in, for instance, *The New Oxford Book of Seventeenth-Century Verse* which contains two poems by Alexander, fourteen by Ayton, and no fewer than twenty-seven by Drummond, in addition to one late sonnet by King James.

Anglo-Scots sonnet sequences

Alexander, Murray, Craig and Drummond all composed Petrarchan sonnet sequences, in imitation of the English vogue of the 1590s, but each sequence has its individuality. In *Aurora* of 1604, Alexander shows a desire to continue the Scottish tradition of experimentation in verse, and echoes from his contemporaries' poems can be found throughout the sequence. One of his most successful poems is the sixth sonnet of Aurora, the first in *The Mercat Anthology*, with its reference to Cadmus and the 'earthborne troupes, at jarres' representing the '[h]uge hosts of thoughts imbattled in [his] brest' (1). Read superficially, this is simply a hyperbolic description of a mind buzzing with conflicting ideas, but this battle is between earthly and heavenly love. His thoughts are forcing him to reconsider his state, which he describes with awkward syntax as (9–11):

O neither life nor death! Ô both, but bad;
Imparadiz'd whiles, in mine owne conceit,   *sometimes imparadised (a word coinage*
                                                  meaning the state of being in paradise)
My fancies straight againe imbroyle my state . . . *confuse*

The word 'imparadiz'd' here refers both to the state of the poet-lover being given some cause to hope and that of the Christian soul in a state of bliss. The mingling of secular and sacred imagery is typical of the sequence.

While embroiled in the vicissitudes of love, it was very important for the Petrarchan poet-lover to assert his constancy. In the second anthologised sonnet, Alexander declares that his love is of such strength that it holds him, no matter what happens to the world outside. There may even be a deliberate echo of Fowler in the final couplet:

That who to see strange countries were inclin'd,
Might change the aire, but never change the mind.

Sir David Murray shows an ability to pick the best of Scottish and English models and to amalgamate the current styles into an eclectic and mannered sequence of twenty-two sonnets, employing virtually every image and convention found in Petrarchan sequences. In *Caelia* 'Sonet' Ten, the first in *The Mercat Anthology*, he conflates two conventions, the river image and the impossibility trope, into a very successful, highly mannered sonnet. As Caelia 'sat once by a christal brooke' (1), the waters not only absorbed her reflection, but became animated and 'with amazement they did on her looke' (4), and having seen her, they fell into the same state as the poet-lover (6–8):

Desirous stil for to behold her beauty,
Neglecting to the ocean their duty,
In thousand strange meanders made returne . . .

This is cleverer than it might appear, for of course Meander was himself a river god enamoured of a nymph, the winding course of his pursuit giving rise to the description of the winding of a river.

Murray often gives a subtle twist to the established trope by means of ironic counterpoint, or by the literalising of the conventional metaphor, as in 'Gazing from out the windowes of mine eyes', which immediately evokes the Montgomerie lyric 'In throu the windoes of myn ees'. Montgomerie's poet-lover had been contemptuous of Cupid's power until wounded through his eye and suffering all the fiery pains of love, and had finally sent his 'longsome looks' to find the lady and his 'sighs and teirs' to intreat for him. In Murray's version, the lack of the lady is described as a physical deprivation, the metaphor of the lover starved of the sight of his lady is literalised into 'wandring troupes' of 'famish'd lookes' (3) flying out through the windows of his eyes on a foraging expedition. Like eagles they soar heavenward in search of the absent lady, and because of their lofty aspirations, and in reminiscence of Montgomerie's image of the lizard that feeds by gazing on the human face, they '[s]corn . . . to feed on any other face' (7) and return unsatisfied to their source. The poet-lover does not seem in control of his own senses as his soul, deprived of its food (the sight of the lady), has blinded him, '[s]hadowing my face with sable cloudes of griefe' (10), denying the natural daylight also and sinking the lover into artificial night.

In the same way that Petrarch used topical or classical allusions in the course of his sequence to underscore the universality of his theme, Murray appears to present the figure of Bellisarius, lieutenant to the Emperor Justinian, who was cast aside after he had outlived his usefulness, as mirroring his own situation. Murray, who lost his place at court following the death of Prince Henry, may well be referring to his court position. The passer-by is asked to witness the actions of 'never-constant fortune, changing aye' which (5–7):

> . . . in a moment tooke
> Mee from the hight of an imperiall sway,
> And plac'd me heere – blind, begging by this way . . .

Murray is a fascinating example of the dilettante poet who showed the kind of *sprezzatura* (a natural-seeming artless grace in writing) which writers of courtesy manuals of the time demanded as invaluable in a courtier, but his achievement pales into insignificance when compared with that of Alexander Craig.

Craig was breaking new ground in the sense that he addressed his *Amorose Songes* of 1606 to eight different ladies – Idea, Cynthia, Lithocardia, Kala, Erantina, Lais, Pandora and Penelope – each symbolising a different aspect of love. The sonnet in *The Mercat Anthology* addressed to Pandora, who may be identified with the wife of the courtier Sir James Hay, takes as its theme the sleeplessness of the lover. He derives no rest from the night as he is deprived of his love, and is thus out of harmony with the natural workings of the world, as in Fowler's 'The day is done . . .'

The sonnets to Penelope, Lady Rich, give Craig the possibility of punning on the lady's name. Her sonnet in *The Mercat Anthology* uses the story of Xerxes giving with one hand and immediately taking back with the other, which seems to show the ambivalence of the patron (9–10, 13–14):

> My ladie faire a Xerxes proud doth prove.
> My worthless verse she doth reward with gold . . .
> As Xerxes crownd and kild his man, right so
> Shee seemes a friend and proves a mortall foe.

Craig delighted in showing off his classical knowledge, and although this analogy is apt, frequently he employs what appear to be very obscure comparisons for his situation.

It has been suggested that Lais is named after a fabulously expensive whore of Corinth. She is 'a facill Dame' resembling Shakespeare's Dark Lady, and has no real sense of loyalty. The sonnet to Lais in *The Mercat Anthology* shows, by its introduction of the 'echo' motif, that she has only said what he wants her to say (6–8):

> 'Be true to mee, deare to my soule,' said I;
> Then sweetly quhespering, would thou say, 'I shall,'   *whispering*
> And, echo-like, 'Deare to my soule,' replie.

His knowledge of her character does not stop him loving her, and suffering from her betrayal.

There is clearly sufficient evidence here that the Scottish poetry of the early seventeenth century deserves a great deal more study than it has had up to the present, and has indeed much more to reveal.

The alternative Scottish route

While Alexander, Murray and Craig concentrated, at least while it was fashionable, on the sonnet sequence, Robert Ayton took a different path. He started out with conventional pastoral themes, examples of which can be found in *The Mercat Anthology*, but his association with John Donne and the wits of the Inns of Court encouraged a move to a more epigrammatic, harder-lined style, as is seen in many of the later poems and sonnets. Desire for a place at court was the impetus for the sonnet 'Upone King James', which uses the trope of identification; in this poem James, as leader of the court group of poets, is compared with Apollo in order to praise James's stabilising of Scotland.

However, he was not at all sure that the move to London would be beneficial for Scots and Scotland, as his sonnet on the River Tweed clearly shows in its lamenting the King's departure for London. This is the most concise yet fully formulated expression of this fear. The Tweed, that '[f]aire famous flood' (1) was the traditional boundary between the two countries, but is now seen as the link, joining 'two diadems in one' (2). However, this is no cause for celebration, but rather the river, appointed 'trinchman of our mone' (4), seems formed from the tears of Scotsmen lamenting their loss, as well as simply carrying the tale of their lament out to sea. The uneasiness of the sight-rhyme 'one/mone', which would not rhyme at all when read out in Scots underlines the unhappiness of the poet's position.

The river, once it reaches the sea, becomes part of the ocean, paralleling Scotland's becoming part of the greater British union. But in Ayton's mind the Tweed retains its integrity even in the waters of the sea, remaining identifiably itself. Because James has crossed the river to go south, the river retains a remembrance of 'our captaines last farewell' (6), the adjective intensifying the feeling that this is a finished kingdom, that will never see its 'captaine' again. Here again, the rhyme intensifies the meaning of the words. The apparently unrhyming 'farewell/reveale' rhyme perfectly when spoken in Scots, echoing the plea for Scottish integrity and identity amidst the waters of the sea.

Ayton's use of the Scottish interlaced rhyming form of the sonnet further intensifies the sense, as it mirrors the sliding and interlacing movement of the waters, and allows him to highlight the rhymes with significant words. At the end of the octave (1–8), where a conventional English sonnet form would begin the sestet (9–14), the Scottish or 'Castalian' sonnet rhyme-scheme to which Ayton's poem interestingly conforms, retains the rhyme of the previous quatrain. The use of the 'interlacing' scheme creates a rhyming couplet of lines 8 and 9 which places the verbs 'reveale' and 'conceale' in suggestive juxtaposition.

> Perhapps your lord the sea will it reveale,
> And you againe the same will not conceale,
> But straight proclaim't through all his bremish bounds,   *raging*
> Till his high tydes these flowing tydeings tell . . .

The river will maintain its message ('our mone'?) which will spread and slow out on its journey, until, in a lovely pun on 'tyde' and 'tydeing', it is finally made articulate. The use of enjambment here hastens the pace and echoes the flow of the water to the high tide mark. The river has now clearly become the Thames, replacing the English water with the Scottish, washing up to 'that religious place'.

Although he pleaded for a court position, Ayton did not appear to have much time for court ladies, if his poems are any guide. His 'Sonnet Left in a Gentlewoman's Looking Glasse' plays ironically with a conventional Petrarchan theme; that of the lady's portrait engraved in a lover's heart. That the whole poem is an artifice, is made clear in the closure (13–14):

> Or if to none of those thou'l daigne to come,
> Weepe eyes, breake heart, and you my verse be dumbe.

The commonplaces of Petrarchanism are rehearsed but without any real feeling behind them: they are merely the vehicles for a display of wit. This does not necessarily devalue the status of the poetry. Rather, it is the tendency of modern post-Romantic thought to expect that poetry must always be the expression of sincere emotion.

A more sardonic jibe against court women is found in 'Upone a Gentlewoman That painted'. Ayton has wittily confused the natural with the contrived in the same way that the gentlewoman hoped to do with her face-painting (6–8):

> Sho'le sweare sho doth not know what paintinge is,   *she'll*
> But straight will blush with such a pretie grace
> That one wold think vermelion dyed hir face.   *vermilion*

Even her natural blush has an artificial appearance. The use of cosmetics to improve on nature, and to follow fashion, is seen to be very much the same as playing the fashionable courtier, in both senses of the word.

In the section of pastoral verse in *The Mercat Anthology*, Ayton is equally well represented. Although the early pastorals are pleasing, the later 'The Shiphird Thirsis' is a comic triumph in the parodic vein. Thirsis 'longed to die' (1), a death which can only be described as *le petit mort* but at the command of his sheperdess – mistress, 'whom no less passion moved (4), so that they can simultaneously experience that 'Sweet and deathles death' (20). Ayton's poem, a wittily elegant celebration of erotic postponement, is a metaphorical rendering of the corresponding scene in Tasso's *Aminta*, where the hard-hearted shepherdess only discovers love when she believes her faithful swain is dead. Ayton is playing with the metaphor of death as sexual orgasm. The language of the lovelorn poet and the traditional pastoral imagery are beautifully combined here into a poem which one can easily imagine being recited aloud to heighten the comic effect.

In case any obtuse readers or hearers did not manage to follow the poem, Ayton makes the point clearer in the final four lines:

> Thus spent these happie two there breath
> In such a sweet and deathles death,
> That they returned to lyf againe,
> Againe to try deathes pleasant paine.

Here the 'spending' of breath is not the 'expense of spirit' deplored by Shakespeare, but rather 'expending' as the two lovers gasp orgasmically, the quasi-repetition of 'deathles death . . . deathes' and actual repetition of 'againe / Againe' allied with the assonance and alliteration of 'deathes pleasant paine', suggesting that there will be multiple deaths to come before this relationship dies.

Ayton's lyric verse shows the distance Scottish poetics have travelled from the idealistic Petrarchan vein which was *de rigueur* at the end of the previous century, to a much more realistic, robust examination of the nature of life and love as experienced in the contemporary world of the early seventeenth century. There is often a great sense of enjoyment about Ayton's verse, and the same kind of *sprezzatura* which is found in Murray's exuberant sonnets. There is also, in the manuscripts used by *The Mercat Anthology* editors, a determined Scottishness in the language used. Perhaps there is also something recognisably Scottish in the sceptical attitude and the mocking tone which refuses to take idealism in love too seriously.

William Drummond of Hawthornden

When one comes to the poetry of William Drummond of Hawthornden from a poet such as Ayton, one is struck by the rather old-fashioned style, and the almost complete absence of any Scottish markers in the language. His is the most anglicised of all the post-1603 poetry. Perhaps this is why he is the one Scottish poet who has received the attention of (predominantly English) editors: his language and style melds perfectly with that of the English Petrarchan school to which he attached himself. Yet perhaps Drummond is the best Scottish poet of the period to introduce to students, as his language is immediately accessible. He is also, as the most generously anthologised, the easiest Scottish poet of the period to illustrate.

Drummond's themes in *Poems* (1616) are profoundly melancholic, dealing with mortality and mutability, most often seen in the changing seasons of the natural world. His poetry is mellifluous, imparting a sensuous pleasure to the reader which draws him gently into the melancholic 'Romantic' world the poet inhabits. In his sensuousness of description, Drummond is both a follower of Petrarchan verse and a precursor of Keats.

The first of Drummond's sonnets in *The Mercat Anthology* is, in fact, the second of the sequence which develops the mutability/mortality theme underlying every description of the natural world from this point on (1–4):

> I know that all beneath the moone decayes,
> And what by mortalles in this world is brought,
> In Times great periods shall returne to nought;
> That fairest states have fatall nights and dayes . . .

The quiet, resigned melancholy is only relieved by the note of hope in the close, which prevents the poem from being entirely morbid (13–14):

> Know what I list, this all can not mee move,
> But that (ô mee!) I both must write, and love.

While the lady of his sonnets, Auristella, is alive, Drummond's poet-lover sees the entire world responding to her beauty and animated by her spirit, as is seen in the second poem in *The Mercat Anthology*, where the River Forth is imagined 'embrac[ing] / The boat that earths perfections doth containe' (3–4). The speaker's terror at the idea of the boat being capsized is assuaged by the thought that the 'hudge waves' are only rising because '[t]he ocean strives with Forth the boate to kiss' (14). This is characteristic of the sequence as a whole, in that the poet-lover cannot see any aspect of the natural world other than as a projection of the beloved.

When Auristella dies, the sense of desolation in the poems is tangible, as can be seen in the third of the sonnets collected in *The Mercat Anthology*. Once again, the death of a single lady is depicted as a world-shattering event, the death of beauty and love (9–12):

> Who more shall vaunt true beautie heere to see?
> What hope doth more in any heart remaine,

> That such perfections shall his reason raine,
> If beautie with thee borne, too died with thee?

This despair, which is depicted at length in 'Songe 1', in the section on Pastoral Verse in *The Mercat Anthology* is only assuaged by the ghost of the lady who leads the poet-lover to a different and higher kind of love seen in the religious sonnets of *Flowres of Sion* (1623).

Death was a familiar theme for Drummond, and a subject that he treated with a delicacy and beauty of language. Like the Romantic poets of the following century, Drummond found meditation on mortality inspiring, especially in a natural setting. The death of Prince Henry, commemorated in 'Teares on the Death of Moeliades', involves the entire world, woodlands, rivers, mountains and oceans mourning and paying their respects (27–30):

> Astonish'd Nature, sullen, stands to see
> The life of all this All, so chang'd to bee.
> In gloomie gownes, the starres about deplore,
> The sea with murmuring mountaines beates the shore . . .

Both these deaths were tragic, unexpected and untimely, but there is little detectable difference between the fictional death of Auristella and the historical death of Prince Henry; both inspire the poet to melancholy meditation which is resolved in an acceptance of Christian providence.

This is only a very small taste of the wealth of material that remains from a relatively short period of creative endeavour. It is hoped that this brief introduction inspires readers to investigate that wealth for themselves.

CHAPTER 5

THE BALLADS

Sum speiks of lords, sum speiks of lairds,
    And siclike men of hie degrie;
Of a gentleman I sing a sang,
    Sumtyme calld Laird of Gilnockie.
                'Johnie Armstrang'

READING BALLADS

Scotland has a great wealth of traditional balladry. On first consideration the 'ballad' genre seems readily identifiable: at the very least readers may be familiar with one or two examples from early education. As songs and poems in print, pieces such as 'The Bonny Earl of Moray', 'The Dowie Dens of Yarrow', 'Lord Randal' and 'Barbara Allan' remain widely known today. They have been part of the educational canon for at least a hundred years and persist with remarkable tenacity in popular performance. They are popularly acknowledged as ballads, so presumably the ballad is generally considered as a distinct enough literary category. However, while no one has ever seriously disputed the imaginative and aesthetic power of individual masterpieces such as 'Lord Randal', the more closely we scrutinise the notion of the ballad genre, the more slippery the concept becomes. It is not even clear, for example, whether these works should be regarded as products of the sixteenth and seventeenth centuries or of the eighteenth and nineteenth centuries. In what follows, we shall explore some features of the tantalising phenomenon of the ballad.

Definitions and materials

The word 'ballad' entered English from Norman French as *balade* and Scots *ballat* in the sense of a dancing song. Over the centuries the term developed many applications but the idea of a sung story remained central to most of them. The poetic form varied as did its themes, including religious, historical, heroic, scurrilous and erotic topics. By the sixteenth century, songs labelled as ballads had their place both in courtly and folk traditions – and among Dunbar's mythological gods in *The Goldyn Targe* (128–30):

> On harp or lute full merily thai playit,
> And sang ballettis with michty notis clere.
> Ladyes to dancc full sobirly assayit . . .

Of the vagrant Autolycus in Shakespeare's *The Winter's Tale*, a servant says (IV, iv, 182–7):

> O, master, if you did but hear the pedlar at the door, you would never dance again after a tabor and pipe. No, the bagpipe could not move you. He sings several tunes faster than you'll tell money. He utters them as he had eaten ballads, and all men's ears grew to his tunes.

One of Shakespeare's contemporaries, Sir Philip Sidney, also responded to the potent musical impact of ballad poetry in *The Apologie for Poetrie* (1595):

> I never heard the old song of Percy and Douglas that I found not my heart moved more than with a trumpet; and yet is it sung but by some blind crowder, with no rougher voice than rude style . . .

By the seventeenth century, commentators were recognising that these songs had a cultural function in transmitting popular history. In his *Letters by Eminent Persons* (or *Brief Lives*, 1813) the seventeenth-century antiquary John Aubrey recalled that:

> in the old ignorant times before women were Readers, the history was handed down from Mother to daughter . . . my Nurse had the History from the Conquests down . . .

Of the power of such folk history, the Scottish political thinker Andrew Fletcher of Saltoun remarked, 'I knew a very wise man . . . that . . . believed that if man were permitted to make all the ballads, he need not care who should make the Laws of a Nation.' And in a critical judgement of 1711 which was to be seen as a landmark, the essayist Joseph Addison, in comparing Virgil with the heroic appeal of that 'antiquated song' of the Percy and Douglas feud, 'Chevy Chase', demonstrated that ballads were worthy of genteel literary attention.

As these early references suggest, the world 'ballad' has, historically, covered a whole range of popular, mostly anonymous, folksongs: street songs, children's songs, work songs, execution ballads and music hall songs. Many of these made their first appearance in print via chapbooks and broadsides, cheap handbills often hawked by the singers themselves. The term has also been used in a very different sense to describe romantic lyrics in courtly and later bourgeois traditions ('ballattis of luve' and drawing room ballads).

The present chapter concentrates on the works categorised as Scottish traditional ballads, the 'muckle sangs' as they are described by singers in the travellers' tradition. These oral compositions first began to appear as printed texts early in the eighteenth century, when resurgent cultural nationalism inspired an interest in the nation's folkloric history. They were assumed even then to be old songs: their historical and social references suggest that they mostly had their origins across the fifteenth and sixteenth centuries. They have also variously been called 'minstrel', 'popular', 'border', 'classic' and 'folk' ballads.

The corpus of the traditional ballads was most fully defined a hundred years ago by the US scholar Francis J. Child in *English and Scottish Popular Ballads* (1882–98). However, this magnificent five-volume collection of some 300 'Child' ballads with all their variant forms must now be supplemented by reference to the *Greig-Duncan Folk Song Collection* of materials from north-east Scotland whose publication is now nearing completion.

Since neither of these works is readily accessible at present, this chapter uses for reference Dr Emily Lyle's valuable representative selection of eighty-three 'Child' items, *Scottish Ballads* (1994). For that reason, individual ballads are referred to by Lyle's numbering rather than Child's. Additionally helpful is James Kinsley's *The Oxford Book of Ballads* (1969), which supplies melodies where these are available, and includes English items such as 'Chevy Chase', and the long outlaw ballad 'A Geste of Robyne Hode'. Kinsley also gives a good selection of the 'riding' ballads of the Anglo-Scottish border. To date, the best introductory selection of the ballads in performance has been provided by the School of Scottish Studies at the University of Edinburgh in the album *The Muckle Sangs* (for fuller details, see the bibliographies for this section).

The ballad texts and their collectors

No literary genre is ever a clear-cut category, but the ballad is undoubtedly fuzzier than most. Its enigmatic status offers great scope for literary theorists to consider issues of textuality and authorship. When we speak of a ballad such as 'Johnny Faa the Gypsie Laddie' (Lyle 13) we need to keep reminding ourselves how complex the textual situation is. In Child's collection there are eleven variants of the basic story of runaway *glamourie*, and in Greig-Duncan's there are thirteen variants. Several very popular sung versions are available, for example Jeannie Robertson's 'The Gypsy Laddies'. Moreover, this ballad has its US, Irish and English forms. Which, if any, of these is the essential ballad? Throughout his magisterial collection, Child deployed his own ill-defined criteria of authenticity and literary quality in order to privilege certain forms among his variants, but there is really no convincing way of promoting one particular form to the rank of the definitive text. Within the family of the 'Gypsie Laddie' versions, as with most other ballads, what we have is a general motif or type which has expressed itself over time in a number of equally valid versions. The situation is further complicated by the fact that early collectors such as Sir Walter Scott felt free to recreate or collate their own preferred version out of the available variants. In some instances, there are grounds for surmising that a nominally traditional ballad is in fact largely an original creative work by Scott or some other collector. This may well be true, for example, of 'Kinmont Willie' (Lyle 2) and 'Sir Patrick Spens' (Lyle 6).

We owe the existence of ballads in their printed form to the activities of several waves of collectors from the eighteenth century to the present day. The word 'collector' may give misleading impressions of scientific objectivity. The great Oriental plant collectors in their field expeditions hunted down species such as poppies, primulas, rhododendrons and rowans and supplied them to the botanical collections of Edinburgh and London; but they did not manipulate the plant materials which they discovered. The reward of such Scottish plantsmen as Robert Fortune and George Forrest was to have their names attached to the new varieties they had discovered; their efforts were scientific in ways which ballad collectors could not be. Those who hunted ballads had no reliable taxonomies to guide them and inevitably they were actively involved in processing and altering what they found.

The first group of collectors contained a number of bourgeois professionals with antiquarian literary tastes: churchmen, lawyers and the like, prominent among whom were Bishop Percy (*Reliques of Ancient English Poetry*, 1765), David Herd (*Ancient and Modern Scottish Songs*, 1776), Sir Walter Scott (*The Minstrelsy of the Scottish Border*, 1802–3), Andrew Crawfurd (MS. collection, *The Cairn of Lochunyoch* [Lochwinnoch], 1826–8) and William Motherwell (*Minstrelsy: Ancient and Modern*, 1827). The youthful Scott engaged in something akin to fieldwork on a small scale in Liddesdale but for the most part he depended for materials on his agents, John Leyden and James Hogg, and on numerous literary contacts and correspondents. The early collectors dealt mainly through middle men, and seldom acknowledged by name the identities of the actual performers who had supplied the texts. If mentioned at all, they would be characterised vaguely in phrases such as 'from the recitation of an old woman in Kilbarchan' or 'from the recitation of a woman eighty years of age, mother of one of the miners on Alston Moor'. Though the early collectors often acquired variants, they tended to print only one version. This could either be the text which they preferred on their own criteria, or a freshly compounded version.

Child's achievement, while extraordinary, was, in effect, a compilation of the work of the preceding collectors. Working from Harvard between 1882 and his death in 1896, he assembled all the variant forms of all the ballad materials he could find in published and manuscript collections and from his network of correspondents in the UK. His methods and theoretical assumptions have been subjected to much recent criticism but more than any other scholar he deserves the credit for assembling and displaying the riches of the ballad corpus. His system of numbering and lettering ballads is still universally used. Browsing through these five massive volumes with all their variants and occasionally pedantic annotations will make the reader familiar with his system, and reveals some of the strengths and weaknesses of the collection process.

In the years before the First World War, two Aberdeenshire men, Gavin Greig, a teacher, and James Duncan, a minister, were stimulated by Child's work to undertake the project of collecting the 'older popular minstrelsy' of north-east Scotland. The outcome, a vast folk song resource of 3,500 texts and 3,300 tunes, lay largely unpublished until 1981 when the first of what will finally be eight volumes was issued. This collection goes far beyond what Child would have classified as ballads, but it invaluably supplements his work with new versions from the culturally rich north-east and with the collectors' explanatory notes. Unlike the original Child volumes, moreover, *Greig-Duncan* supplies musical notation.

With the development of electromagnetic recording during the Second World War, new techniques of collection evolved in the 1950s and, with these, unsuspected resources of traditional song were uncovered. The work of Hamish Henderson and his colleagues in Edinburgh's School of Scottish Studies brought to light ballad versions which had been carried orally for generations in the travelling and agricultural communities of Perthshire, Angus and north-east Scotland. The School's recordings also exemplified a

71

distinctive singing style which cast light on how traditional materials might have been performed over the centuries.

The ballad melodies

Throughout eighteenth-century Britain there was immense popular interest in 'Scotch tunes' as the success of John Gay's *The Beggar's Opera* (1728) demonstrated. The early collectors were certainly well aware of the musical power of the ballads. Credit has to go to Robert Burns in his role of folksong collector for insisting on the integral relationship of text and tune, but for various reasons he had few dealings with the great narrative ballads. Scott, though heartily disliking the fashionable art music of the time, encouraged his daughters to learn the old songs. In *The Domestic Manners and Private Life of Sir Walter Scott* (1834) and elsewhere, James Hogg recalled how Scott loved to hear his daughter, Sophia singing his favourite old Scottish and Border ballads. In their published work, however, these same collectors gave primacy to the printed text. They included few melodies, partly because of the cost and difficulty in getting music transcribed and printed but more fundamentally because they were mainly interested in the ballads as a literary form. This was probably also the position of Child, who included in his final volume only a meagre appendix of fifty-five ballad airs. It was not until 1987 that Bertrand Bronson was able to complete a comprehensive collection of *The Traditional Tunes of the Child Ballads*. Working in Buchan at the beginning of the twentieth century, Greig and Duncan may have been influenced towards a more musical emphasis by their English contemporary Cecil Sharp. Both could transcribe melodies and they were very active in collecting tunes for their texts. Above all, however, it was the arrival of good quality audio recording in the 1950s which caught and broadcast the skills of the surviving traditional singers and promoted a popular revival in performance among younger enthusiasts.

The interrelationship of ballad tunes turns out to be every bit as problematic as that of the texts. There is seldom a single definitive tune that can confidently be assigned to a text: the tunes, like the texts, survived in constellations and individual singers had their own preferred combinations of these. Singers, moreover, could modify their versions with each performance. The melodies are usually cast in one of the modes of the pentatonic scales common to folksong across the world. They are brief, matching the metre of the ballad stanza, and run unswervingly through the course of the narrative. With good reason the ballads have been called 'the muckle sangs'. They certainly tend to be long: for instance, half of the pieces in Lyle are eighteen or more stanzas in length and roughly a quarter exceed thirty stanzas. Over many generations singing styles must have evolved to suit these formal features.

Though we have no direct evidence of how ballad singing sounded in the eighteenth century and earlier, we do know that some observers regarded it as excitingly primitive, 'wild and monotonous' and described the style as 'chaunting'. Happily, the living tradition of the singers who have been recorded by Edinburgh's School of Scottish Studies may well preserve the essential features of the earlier styles. The musicologist, John Purser, identifies these as 'the flexibility of rhythm, the clarity of enunciation, the unaffected directness, the superb focusing of the voice by the use of a more nasal tone (a vocal timbre which can be sustained over long periods of singing), the unwavering control of pitch and intonation' (*Scotland's Music*, 1997). With Purser's criteria in mind, the listener can hear the rich variety of pieces to be found in *The Muckle Sangs* album and perhaps seek out also the late Jeannie Robertson's outstanding renderings of 'The Battle of Harlaw' (Lyle 40) and 'Son David' (Lyle 66). Recent singers have absorbed these influences in developing their own distinctive approaches to ballad materials. These include performers of the quality of Jean Redpath, Andy Hunter, Dick Gaughan and Gordeanna McCulloch. Four traditional ballads from the Greig-Duncan collection are given strong performances in the Edinburgh Festival album *Folk Songs of North-East Scotland*.

Authorship and transmission

As with the nature of the text, the authorship of the Scottish traditional ballads offers a further challenge to critical theory. Hardly any single person can be named as the only begetter of a ballad or its melodies. As pointed out above, there are some instances where a 'collector' is believed to have composed a new text or version and passed it off as traditional. Robert Burns may have contributed massively to the long and powerful version of the enchantment ballad 'Tam Lin' (Lyle 35) with its intriguing faint parallels to that other perilous ride, 'Tam o' Shanter'; we know also that 'Hardyknute', a heroic tale of the Battle of Largs, is pastiche work by Lady Elizabeth Wardlaw (*Longer Scottish Poems*, 1987); and that 'Edward, Edward' (*The Oxford Book of Ballads*, 1969, 40), a frighteningly grim version of 'Son David' (Lyle 66), owes much of its power to Bishop Percy's contact, Lord Hailes. For the most part, however, no individual authors are known. Hence the ballads are usually indexed in anthologies as anonymous. Theories and discussions on ballad authorship are often based on ideological assumptions about society and culture, and on observation of other societies such as Greece and Yugoslavia where similar traditional materials exist. Sir Walter Scott in his *Introductory Remarks on Popular Poetry* (added to the 1830 edition of his *Poetical Works*) assumed that the ballads were the work of individual makers, courtly bards or minstrels, and that their compositions had been corrupted in oral transmission to 'a vulgar audience' over the centuries: 'It is nothing surprising that it should reach us in a mutilated and degraded state.' Others have taken the view that from the first the songs were spontaneous communal productions which cannot be said to have a single author. It is now generally accepted that many of the ballads originated in a pre-literate culture and that the processes of composing and transmitting were both oral, at least in their early stages.

One influential model of transmission favoured by David Buchan in his groundbreaking *The Ballad and the Folk* (1972) is that of 'recreation'. The performer, having absorbed the basic story formula, realised the detail of each performance by drawing and even improvising on a common stock of devices of structure, imagery and language; 'He [or she] had learned both a method of composition and a number of stories from which each time he created an original oral text' (*The Ballad and the Folk*). Buchan based his argument on the texts which came indirectly to Scott and others from the gifted Anna Gordon (Mrs Brown of Falkland). Gordon, daughter of a professor at Aberdeen and wife of a minister of the Kirk, belonged to the academic bourgeoisie of late eighteenth-century Scotland, according to Hamish Henderson, 'a bookish lady who read Ossian and wrote verses'. Her distinction was that, as a young child in the 1750s, she had learned many traditional songs from a favourite aunt who had previously lived in a remote household on upper Deeside. These songs Gordon seemed to be able to recall or 'recreate' fluently. On several occasions she had performed parts of her repertoire for the purposes of transcription and it was three manuscript collections of these transcripts which reached the early collectors. The imaginative force of her versions of ballads such as 'Young Bicham' (Lyle 22), 'The Twa Sisters' (Lyle 29), 'Willie's Lady' (Lyle 71) and 'Lamkin' (Lyle 72) is worth considering closely. They present stark episodes of loss and treachery lit by gleams of domestic and exotic violence. The interested reader might examine other qualities in these pieces and consider whether there is any sense in which Anna Gordon might be thought of as their 'real' author.

The contribution of women

Although the early collectors were mostly men, their sources and the informants who transmitted the ballad texts were often women, as John

Aubrey had previously spotted. Anna Gordon is one outstanding example, but among the others who made crucial contributions were Agnes Lyle (for Motherwell's collection, Lyle 54); Mary Macqueen (for Crawfurd, Lyle 27); Bell Robertson (for Greig and Duncan) and Jeannie Robertson (for The Edinburgh School of Scottish Studies, Lyle 66). A good range of Mary Macqueen's ballads has recently been recorded by J. Millar. In singing or recitation (for not all were singers), women such as these appear to have had a crucial influence in shaping the pieces in their repertories. It has been suggested that the ballads were mostly learned and transmitted through mothers, grandmothers, nurses, governesses and servants; and that their themes and stances reflect both the diversity and the limitations of the experiences of women in the seventeenth to nineteenth centuries. The preoccupation of many ballads with the complications of love and courtship; family conflicts; upstairs – downstairs relationships; incest, sexual jealousy and revenge might, arguably, be taken to support this idea. Robert Burns certainly acknowledges the influence of his mother, an old servant and his wife in alerting him to the power of popular stories and songs. Arguing that the ballads constitute a 'vital and sustained women's tradition', Catherine Kerrigan in *An Anthology of Scottish Women Poets* (1991) has controversially staked claims of authorship for nine women on the grounds that they had in some sense created their own distinctive ballad versions (e.g. Anna Gordon's 'Lamkin' and Jeannie Robertson's 'The Twa Brothers'); and in their essays on women and song in *A History of Scottish Women's Writing* (1997), Mary Ellen Brown and Elaine Petrie acknowledge the significant contributions of several of these women.

Distinctive features of the ballad

Despite all the difficulties of pinning down ballad texts, some distinctive features of the genre can be grasped. These characteristics partly reflect how the original songs would have been composed, performed and passed on orally. They also constitute touchstones for some of the aesthetic strengths of the ballad form. The caveat needs to be made, however, that we cannot naively regard them as definitive criteria for the ballad genre. After all, collectors from Percy to Child had their own literary and historical pre-conceptions of what constituted a ballad and they preferred to admit items which best met these expectations. Moreover, we have already noted that the earlier collectors did not scruple to alter texts to fit their model. As a result, the canon tends, not surprisingly, to embody the preferences of its guardians. The nature of this self-fulfilling process is explored in Harker's *Fakesong*

(1985) which gives a fascinating Marxist critique of the circularity of the collectors' attempts to establish quintessential criteria for the ballad genre. Here is an illustration of the problem:

> Late at e'en, drinking the wine,
>   And ere they paid the lawing
>   They set a compact them between
>   to fight it in the dawing.

This is the first stanza of the best known version of the 'Dowie Dens of Yarrow' and it seems to demonstrate the ballad form at its most powerful (it can be found in Scott's *Minstrelsy*). The language is mostly monosyllabic; pronouns veil the protagonists and the nature of the quarrel; the location in an inn is merely implied; the passage of time is tersely suggested. The tragic situation has been introduced with the laconic force which we have come to see as typical of the ballad tradition. When, however, we look closely at the origins of this ballad, we find that the only version which has this concise beginning is Scott's own, and that other versions begin more explicitly but less cogently, as comparison of versions below shows.

> There were three lords birling at the wine,
>   On the Dowie dens o Yarrow.
>   They made a compact them between
>   They would go fecht tomorrow. (Motherwell, in *Child*)

or

> There was a layde lived in the North,
>   Her name it was called Sara,
>   She was courted by nine noblemen,
>   And a plooman lad frae Yarrow. (Greig-Duncan, Lyle 60)

or

> I dreamed a dream a dreary dream this night,
>   That fills my heart wi sorrow;
>   I dreamed I was pouing the heather green
>   upon the braes of Yarrow. (Principal Robertson, in *Child*)

In his *Minstrelsy* Scott himself confesses ruefully about the 'Dowie Dens of

Yarrow': 'I found it easy to collect a variety of copies; but very difficult indeed to select from them such a collated edition, as might, in any degree, suit the taste of these more light and giddy times.' In other words, we may suspect that we owe the precise form of the superb first stanza at least partly to the craft and sensitivity of Scott himself, working on materials supplied by his friends Hogg and Laidlaw. From a study of Hogg's manuscripts Valentina Bold has recently demonstrated how adeptly Scott refashioned this ballad. The paradox is that, despite the prolixity of some of his fiction and his woeful inability to write full-scale drama, he could flawlessly crystallise dramatic moments within the conventions of the traditional ballad. In *The Heart of Midlothian*, Madge Wildefire's death song, 'Proud Maisie', is another example of his genius for imitation. However, having sounded this note of caution about the lurking presence of Scott, we can nonetheless assert that however the canon came to be compiled, its texts demonstrably reveal important similarities in structure, style and theme.

The following commentary on these features is illustrated where possible by reference to 'Lamkin' in the version supplied by Anna Gordon (Lyle 72). A mason, Lamkin, who has been denied payment for building a castle, joins with a disgruntled nurse to wreak bloody vengeance on the laird's family. Of the twenty-six variants in *Child* and three in *Greig-Duncan* many stress the prowling demonic nature of Lamkin, 'wha bides in the wood', and a few work his apparent nickname into the motivation of the story. No version, however, employs both of these motifs. Otherwise the differences are secondary matters such as the names of laird, mason and castle. The mason appears variously as Lamkin, Lambkin, Lammikin, Lamerlinkin, Long Lankyn, Rankin, Balankin and so on. A melody is given in the *Oxford Book of Ballads* but no recorded version seems to be currently available.

Ballad structure

Many ballads have a taut construction that focuses on a single dramatic situation. There is little by way of scene setting, character description or contextualising. The story, as has been said, starts 'in the fifth act', right at the heart of the episode. Longer ballads sometimes use the stages of a voyage, journey or other travelling to and fro as a narrative device with abrupt filmic cutting while stories sometimes advance via a mixture of immediacy and delay which has been described as 'leaping and lingering'. Frequently the progress of the narrative depends heavily on dialogue. Much is left allusive and implicit. Typically the first and last stanzas are particularly strong with the internal ballad structure featuring some quite intricate patternings, for example 'Lamkin' (Lyle 242), as has been demonstrated by David Buchan.

In 'Lamkin' the narrative starts from a position of unironic approval for Lamkin's skills as a master craftsman (st. 1):

> It's Lamkin was a mason good
>> As ever built wi stane;

and moves relentlessly in twenty-seven stanzas through murder to its brutal consequences (st. 27):

> But sairer grat the nourice,
>> When she was tied to the stake.

A few functional references to a little shot window, the 'ha', the bower, the 'chamer' and the 'stane steps' of the stair hint at the setting of a typical sixteenth-century tower featuring a system of defence to which illicit entry was difficult. Some two-thirds of the ballad is dialogue, and patterns of phrasing recur with obsessive intensity, as in Lamkin's challenge (sts 8, 9, 10, 11):

> O where's a' the men o' this hoose
>> That ca' me Lamkin?

> An' where's the women o' this hoose . . .'

> An' where's the bairns o' this hoose . . .

> O where's the lady o' this hoose . . .

and the lady's repeated plea, 'O still ma bairn, nourice.'

Motivation is mostly implied, and the reader left to wonder whether Lord Wearie is the spendthrift who causes the tragedy of Lamkin's revenge. Seemingly, Lamkin is mortally offended by the wimpish associations of his nickname, little lamb. What harm are we left to imagine that the lady has done the nurse, in the nurse's cryptic comment 'for she neer was good to me' (st. 20)? Could class hatred be a factor in the tragedy (st. 22)?

> What better is the heart's blood
>> O the rich than o the poor?

Having looked at these structural features of 'Lamkin', the reader should consider the different ways in which narrative is handled in the shorter ballads such as 'The Wife of Usher's Well' (Lyle 31), 'The Great Silkie of Sule Skerry' (Lyle 34) and 'The Twa Corbies' (Lyle 82); and in long items such as 'Johnie Armstrong' (Lyle 3), 'Tam Lin' (Lyle 35) and 'Lang Johnny Moir' (Lyle 55).

Ballad style

The distinctive style of the traditional ballads was largely determined by the demands of oral performance. Singers needed devices which would assist them to recall, organise and interpret their materials. The most frequent metre was 'common measure', a simple form which was much used in popular song and also appeared in the Scottish metrical psalms. It consists of a quatrain in which four-stress and three-stress lines alternate, rhyming either abab or aabb. It is useful to compare 'Edom of Gordon' and 'The Earl of Rosslyn's Daughter' (Lyle 8 and 16). A less frequent alternative was the rhyming four-stress couplet accompanied usually by a refrain which might be riddling, nonsensical or formulaic. An illustration of this would be, for example, 'The Unco Knicht's Wouing', 'The Farmer's Cursed Wife' and 'King Orpheus' (Lyle 17, 51 and 37). These refrain types are thought to have had early connections with dance. In some ballad variants it seems that sense was sorely tried by the needs of rhythm and rhyme; for example, in the need to find words to rhyme with Yarrow in 'the Dowie Dens of Yarrow' (Lyle 60).

The ballads place no premium upon original imagery. The singers had to be able to call on an easily accessible word hoard of stock expressions. Hair is 'yellow' or 'gowden'; the night is 'mirk'; silk is 'green'; water is 'wan'; steeds are 'milk-white' and 'bonny'; and ships, like Lord Wearie's in 'Lamkin', sail 'the saut see faim'. The environment of the ballads is heraldic in its formality and there is virtually no realistic description of landscape, townscape, flora or fauna. Even Lady Wearie's heart's blood is 'clear as the lamer' [*amber*].

For similar reasons of performance the choice of language in the ballad often provides the singer with the support of what has been called 'incremental repetition'. Expressions are repeated two or three times with successive modifications which advance the narrative (Lyle 72, sts 24–5):

'O wha's blood is this,' he says,
'That lies in the chamer?'
'It is your lady's heart's blood;
'Tis as clear as the lamer.'

79

'And wha's blood is this?' he says,
'that lies in my ha?'
'It is your young son's heart's blood;
'T is the clearest ava.'

As already indicated, dialogue plays an important part in shaping the ballad narrative. This frequently takes the form of an unadorned sequence of question-and-answer stanzas, usually in a very direct, though seldom dense, Scots syntax and idiom. A few ballads are composed entirely in this pattern. This is 'The Fause Knicht', Lyle 18, sts 1–2):

O whar are ye gaun?
Quo the fause knicht upon the road.
I'm gawn to the skeul.
Quo the wee boy and still he stood.

This abrupt questioning can have the effect of heightening pace and tension in the narrative, particularly when, as in 'Lamkin', the identity of the speakers is left implicit.

Hamish Henderson has praised the mix of English and Scots idiom in the ballads as 'supple and sinewy ballad-language'. This view can be considered with reference to the use of language in a varied grouping such as 'Johnie Armstrong', The Battle of Harlaw', 'The Baron of Brackley', 'King Orpheus', 'Son David' and 'Lord Ronald' (Lyle 3, 4, 10, 37 and 78).

Ballad themes

Scott crudely divided the ballads in his *Minstrelsy* into two broad classes, historical and romantic, the latter being much the more numerous. It is worth scanning the contents of Lyle's collection of ballads and trying to do better than Scott by sorting them by their dominant themes. The attempt will yield a summary view of the preoccupations of the ballad singers and their audiences; and, bearing in mind that categories are bound to overlap, will reveal that there are several major themes.

The ballads deal in tragic incidents of many kinds involving murder; accident; outlawry; ill-fated love; feuds; battles; supernatural visitations; family jealousies; bad blood among brothers, mothers, sisters; loyalty to kinsmen. Within these episodes the tragedies and mischances of love bulk large. As suggested earlier, this may point to the major contribution made by women to the genre. Some ballads such as 'Tam Lin' and 'Wee Messgrove' have a distinctly erotic charge, but the self-censoring processes of the ballad editors up to and including Child ensured that no obscene or scatological texts were admitted to the canon. Comic incidents do not figure prominently in the traditional corpus but a few ballads do deal robustly with husband-and-wife strife, night-visiting and related goings-on.

In some of the most moving ballads, the world of 'fairies' interfaces with humankind. Mortals and fairies seem to live parallel lives but perilous crossings-over can occur. No marked Christian ethic is detectable in the ballads but some warning emerges of Heaven, Hell and the presence of demonic forces, all vaguely linked to the fairy kingdom. The prevailing ethos seems to be fatalism tinged with a sense of the vulnerable grace of human love.

In their own way, a significant number of ballads deal with known events in Scottish history (e.g. 'The Battle of Harlaw' and 'The Bonny Earl of Moray', Lyle 4 and 7), and others seem to have some, as yet, unidentified historical basis e.g. 'Sir Patrick Spens' and 'The Douglas Tragedy' (Lyle 6 and 61). While the power of the great historical ballads has always been acknowledged, scholars have also recently been asserting their value as historical evidence, both social and political. With their acute sensitivity to 'degree' they can be seen as a history from the stance of the common folk, 'the people who never get mentioned'. It is also productive to analyse how differences of rank are handled in ballads such as 'Johnie Armstrong', 'Johny Faa, the Gypsy Laddie', 'The Laird of Drum', 'Marie Hamilton' and 'Glenlogie' (Lyle 3, 13, 47, 75 and 81).

The Scottishness of the ballads?

A current of romantic and reactionary cultural nationalism flows strongly in the early ballad collections. Motherwell, for example, claimed that Scott's *Minstrelsy* was 'truly a patriot's legacy to posterity'. But how Scottish are the ballads? Having tried to identify some of their distinctive features, we can now ask if there is anything *essentially* Scottish about the examples we have been discussing. Undeniably there are obvious ways in which these texts can be regarded as Scottish. Mostly they were collected in Scotland and were, indeed still are, sung by Scottish singers. They use Scots language forms, though seldom dense Scots. They have Scottish backgrounds, contexts, and references. However obliquely handled, Scottish historical topics, events, persons, places occur frequently. More contentiously, it could be argued that the ballads tackle distinctively Scottish themes such as the influence of the supernatural. By these criteria, the great bulk of Child's *English and Scottish*

Popular Ballads qualifies as Scottish.

But we need also to bear in mind that cultural origins are complex matters. These same ballads are often only the local representatives of international folk types and motifs. 'Lord Randal' for example ('Lord Ronald', Lyle 78) has a well documented Italian pedigree, and 'The Maid of Coldingham' (Lyle 32) is linked to Scandinavia. Some of Child's variants were found in England, Ireland and the USA: it seems that what are now regarded as Scottish ballads had sometimes found their way up from England, examples being 'The Jew's Daughter' (Lyle 73) which is based on notorious persecutions of Jews in Lincoln in the thirteenth century, or 'The Daemon Lover' (Lyle 19) and 'Young Bicham' (Lyle 22). There is also evidence of a rich traffic in versions and tunes across the Irish Sea, particularly in the comic ballads such as 'Our Goodman' (Lyle 50), and 'The Keach i' the Creel' (Lyle 56). That seminal group of texts dealing with cattle raiding and outlawry, the 'border ballads', has deep Celtic roots, but it belongs on both sides of a debateable land where national affiliations meant less than family loyalties. For an example, see 'Jamie Telfer of the Fair Dodhead', in *The Oxford Book of Ballads*.

There is, therefore, a real sense in which the ballads, like some of their traditional singers, are 'travellers'. Historically, they contribute a precious multi-ethnic ingredient to the canons of Scottish literature. They have, moreover, exerted a marked influence on later non-Scottish writers as diverse as Coleridge, Keats, Tennyson, Morris, Kipling and Auden. In the end, we can perhaps look on all of the ballads as 'border' ballads. Not only have they migrated across political boundaries; they have also populated the border-lands of song and poetry, of history and literature. Tantalisingly, they continue to issue their intertextual challenge to contemporary writers, as can be seen in this shrewd response by Liz Lochhead in 'Tam Lin's Lady' from *Dreaming Frankenstein* (1984):

> So we're all supposed to be happy?
> but how about you, my fallen fair maiden?
> now the drama's over, tell me
> how goes the glamourie?
> After the twelve casks of good claret wine
> and the twelve and twelve of muscadine,
> tell me
> What about you?
> How do you think Tam Lin will take
> all the changes you go through?

CHAPTER 6

WIDENING THE RANGE 1

LANGUAGES, RANGE, DIVERSITY

Dunbar and Henryson, perhaps the two most prolific and brilliant writers of medieval Scottish literature, have deservedly received special attention in this volume, but it would be wholly unjust and misleading to suggest that it is only their work which is worthy of discovery. Arguably, the pleasure of medieval literature is proportional to one's experience of it: wider reading makes key literary concepts, such as allegory (here first encountered in the *Kingis Quair*) more familiar as tools of interpretation, while linguistically, further literary exploration makes us fluent readers of an initially daunting language. The medieval 'world-view', which in its literary, artistic, religious and political aspects may seem remote and strange, can be rendered surprisingly intimate and significant. The later sixteenth and early seventeenth centuries, as Chapter 4 in this section amply demonstrates, are beginning to reclaim literary and cultural importance in the history of Scottish literature when too often conventional literary histories have cordoned them off from the familiar post-1750 territory.

The period is not only characterised by its diversity of genre, mode, and subject but also by a linguistic range which cannot be justly explored here. The seventeenth century, for example, produces a sophisticated body of Latin verse. Of profound cultural and literary significance is the Gaelic literature of medieval and Renaissance Scotland. This opens up a very different poetic world from that created in Lowland royal and courtly circles. From its earliest inception, Gaelic society had its own distinct system of professional patronage for poets. There is a substantial amount of bardic poetry surviving from the period 1450–1650. The sixteenth-century *Book of the Dean of Lismore*, which belongs to the Perthshire and Argyllshire region, offers an extraordinary window onto a poetic culture embracing religious, political, heroic, satirical and amatory verse. This culture offers a very different perspective on the literary role of women in Lowland Scotland (see below): women composed poetry of praise, elegy and lament, as well as exquisite lyrics, such as those by Aithbhreac Inghean Corcadail (*fl.* 1460) or Iseabail ní Mheic Cailéin (*fl.* 1500), of *dánta grádha* or courtly love, which anticipate the much better known role of eighteenth-century women song-writers. Appreciation of the Scottish ballad tradition (discussed in Chapter 6) can be deepened by awareness of sixteenth-century Gaelic song, for example. While medieval and Renaissance literature in Scots itself remains in many ways uncharted land, its Gaelic counterpart with Irish influences (as early as the Celtic Christian poetry of Iona), should not be forgotten.

The rest of this chapter draws out other writers and works from this rich period, as well as further themes and ideas which might be explored in order to broaden our readings of, for example, Dunbar or Henryson.

COMPARISONS, CONTRASTS, PARALLELS

Throughout this time, Scottish writing derives much of its creative vigour from interaction with other European literatures. Chapter 4 shows how important French and Italian models were to the self-consciously comparative writers of James VI's court. At the same time, this literature also portrays a self-sufficient and unified or homogeneous literary culture. This, in part, stems from the distinctive artistic environment: poets such as Dunbar and David Lyndsay were among professional writers at the courts of James IV and V. In a way unfamiliar to us, writers were members of a literary community (Dunbar's 'Lament for the Makaris' suggests in a different way that he regarded himself as heir to literary traditions) which encouraged the lively exchange of ideas and styles, not least the fierce and comic rivalry of the *Flyting* of Dunbar and Kennedy (and later that between Montgomerie and Polwarth). This also accounts for the recurrence of certain styles and themes: think how often we encounter the 'aureate style' or descriptions of nature in the period's poetry. There were certain literary ideals or standards to which these poets deferred, such as the distinctively Scottish popularity of alliteration. But while they provided a repository of images and metaphors, such styles were not used in a tedious or static way. It would be interesting to pursue, for example, how Dunbar varies the aureate nature opening in *The Goldyn Targe*, 'The Thrissill and the Rois', and *The Tretis of the Tua Mariit Wemen and the Wedo* for different effects of irony, symbolism and humour.

HISTORY AND PROSE

As already suggested, the comparative approach works well for this literature. It is valuable to compare aspects of Barbour's *Brus* with those of another national epic (also largely written in couplets) based on a Scottish hero and legend, the *Actis and Deidis of William Wallace* (1476–8) by a writer known only to us as 'Hary' (or 'Blind Hary'). Both these works share the desire to reconstruct, and to an extent recreate or reinvent, the past. Though both purport to be historical chronicle, their literary and ideological textures prevent them from being simply that. What exactly does the concept of history mean to these writers (with their shared ideals of heroism, chivalry, martyrdom) who have created such immensely readable poems which resurrect in exciting ways the iconic figures of Scottish history?

Blind Hary's Wallace

Since the release of the film, *Braveheart*, Hary's *Wallace* has regained something of its status as an essential contribution to the construction of Scottish national identity. The iconic status of Wallace, the freedom fighter, is first fully realised in this fifteenth-century poem. From the time of its composition (c. 1480), *Wallace* found an audience, for it was one of the works printed by the earliest Scottish press, and it continued to be reprinted throughout the sixteenth and into the seventeenth century. William Hamilton of Gilbertfield rediscovered it in the eighteenth century, and updated it to meet the sensibilities of his own time, in language and in content; this updating was the version Burns knew and loved. But for horror and for passion, however, Hary's *Wallace* cannot be improved.

Little is known about the author, or even if he was always blind. Hary lived in the second half of the fifteenth century, and seems to have been on the fringes of the court, for the name appears in some royal records around the right time. The poem itself was complete by 1488, which is the date of the sole surviving manuscript. Its detailed sight-based accounts of events suggest that Hary was not blind from birth, and the poem's allusiveness undermines the romanticised picture of a blind bard, and instead indicates that the poet was well read and acutely conscious of literary tradition. As only one example, Wallace's first sight of his love in church is consciously reminiscent of Chaucer's Troilus seeing Criseyde, and that evocation instantly indicates the doomed nature of Wallace's love.

Clearly Hary's greatest influence was Barbour's *Brus*, from which he was not above borrowing the occasional incident. Hary's poem, however, is also strikingly different from Barbour's, since it questions some of the basic assumptions of the letter's text. Where Barbour often treats the war between the Scots and the English as a contest 'between gentlemen', for Hary it is a bloodthirsty combat in which the entire nation is involved. The enemy is demonised, and slaughter can be meted out to the English without compunction. Whereas Barbour presents Bruce always as the rightful king, through the fact of Wallace's nobility, Hary challenges Bruce's previously unassailable right to the throne. Bruce as king gains nearly as much through his struggle as does his realm, but Wallace as a man loses love, liberty, and ultimately life to defend his people. The poem is both patriotically stirring and nationalistically alarming, both chivalric and horrifyingly soaked in blood. In a world rent by nationalist passion, *Wallace* remains just as relevant as it was five hundred years ago. Unfortunately, the fifteenth-century text remains comparatively inaccessible. There is an edition from the Scottish Text Society, but it is more for scholars than general readers. What is needed is a paperback on the model of Canongate's edition of *The Bruce*, to renew wide acquaintance with this exceptional poem.

The reader could extend the theme of how historical 'characters' are represented by looking at some of the period's prose: for example, the chronicles of Hector Boece, which were translated from Latin into the vernacular by John Bellenden (c. 1495–c. 1547). The chronicles trace the origin and history of the Scots, and in Book 12 the tale of Macbeth's rise to the Scottish throne is told, provoking an interesting Scottish comparison to Shakespeare's famous play. And, however much a thorn in the Scottish psyche, the arch-polemicist Knox writes a highly sophisticated rhetorical prose. His *magnum opus, The History of the Reformation* (1559–67) reveals the conflicts and crises of the Reformation, but is artfully skewed to persuade us of the justice of the Protestant cause (especially his vivid account of the return of Mary Stewart to Scotland, his interviews with and denunciations of her). For sheer provocation, readers should try *The First Blast of the Trumpet against the Monstrous Regiment of Women* (1559). Thereafter, the later prose of Thomas Urquhart (1611–60) represents the culmination of Renaissance Scottish prose in its ornately brilliant and extravagant style: the extract in *The Mercat Anthology* shows Urquhart's dazzling and witty virtuosity at its best.

Other fables

Though Henryson's *Fables* are the most well-known animal fable in medieval Scottish literature, they are not the only representative of this popular genre. *The Buke of the Howlat* [*the owl*], written by Richard Holland around 1448, brilliantly exemplifies a specific type of fable where the allegorical world is entirely inhabited by avian characters. An owl is overheard complaining to the goddess Nature of the unjustness of his unattractive shape ('Quhy is my fax . . . fassonit so foule?' [*Why is my face . . . made so ugly?*]: in this period, the owl rarely symbolised wisdom as now but, associated with darkness, could signify the vices of folly, drunkenness, and lechery). Such is the gravity of the owl's case, a parliament of the spiritual and secular estates is summoned (each bird beautifully matched to its clerical status: swans, for example, are bishops 'in quhyte rocatis [*white vestments*] arrayed') to present the case before Nature. Nature decrees that the owl be transformed by receiving the gift of a feather from each species present, whereupon he becomes insufferably arrogant ('All birdis he rebalkit [*rebuked*] that wald him nocht bowe'). The council is resummoned, the owl is deprived of his 'new clothes', and is returned to his former state, suitably humbled.

Such an outline does not do justice to a narrative studded with lively incident (not least a visit to the peacock Pope, and a riotous feast interrupted by a flyting Irish bard). Reflecting Henryson's concept of the fable, which has a beautiful shell (the external narrative) encasing the moral kernel (what the poem means), the howlat's rise and fall has a more serious interpretation. Near the poem's conclusion, the newly 'defeathered' owl mourns that through his misfortune he has been transformed into a 'sampill' or moral *exemplum*, illustrating the proverbial wisdom that 'pryde never yit left/His feir but a fall [His companion without a fall, st. 74].

Such a many-layered poem is obviously rich in meaning but should also be enjoyed purely at the verbal or linguistic level for the joyful extravagances of its alliterative stanza. Holland's poem is the first Scottish example of this fashionable thirteen-line stanza with its four-line tail rhyme (the rhyme scheme is ababababcdddc). The following example of the poem's second stanza shows how alliteration works as a structural as well as a poetic device (each line is divided into two halves, as it were, by alliteration – the repetition of this letter acts as the bridge and places stress on the first syllable of words) (53–7):

He grat grysly grym and gaif a gret yowle	*he wept hideously; howl*
Cheverand and chydand with churliche cheir	*shivering and complaining with a churlish expression*
'Quhy is my fax,' quod the fyle, 'fassonit so foule,	
My forme and my fetherem unfrely, but feir?	*feathers ugly; without doubt*
My neb is netherit as a nok, I am bot ane owle!	*beak is turned down like a hook*

The alliterative style is especially apt in this poem as the bird characters offer ample opportunity for onomatopoeia. The reader of *The Howlat* may well be struck by the unlikely resemblance between the owl, chastised for pride and brought to a form of self-knowledge, and the fate of Henryson's Cresseid: this could be a rich source of comparison.

Comic romance

Another semi-comic poem written in this alliterative stanza is the anonymous romance *The Taill of Rauf Coilyear*, dating from the late fifteenth century and set in the time of Charlemagne ('the gentill king Charlis of micht'). An example of the popular king-in-disguise motif, the poem opens as the disguised Charlemagne seeks refuge 'harberie' [*shelter*], an important term) in the house of the humble collier Rauf. The gulf in status between each makes for an immediate source of comic contrast and irony. Charlemagne conceals his identity; rural and royal, or courtly, *mores* collide, and dramatic irony is realised to comic effect as mistaken assumptions are made: 'Thow semis ane nobill fallow' (st. 5) presumes the king (noble status being, of course, precisely what Rauf lacks). Charlemagne's deference to Rauf before entering the house provokes from Rauf the charge of discourtesy and a blow to the neck (Rauf's comic resort to violence in the name of good manners) but the king is touched by the essence of his hospitality (st. 14). At the end, Rauf is knighted for his courteousness (st. 59), and achieves the conversion of an 'infidel' Saracen to the Christian faith. In mock-heroic style the poem celebrates the code of chivalry, another of these key medieval concepts familiar from *Brus*, comparing the values of natural courtesy and those cultivated at court. The idea of nobility, therefore, is intrinsically moral.

The Fabliau

Both of the poems discussed above illustrate a very different side to medieval literature, contradicting the frequent assumption of unrelieved serious moral writing. The medieval genre which most obviously demonstrates the unexpected is the *fabliau*: French in origin, this poetic form is narrative-based (a 'good story' is its requirement), usually rendered in a plain or realistic style (the setting often domestic), and frequently deriving its bawdy (and bodily!) comedy from the themes of money, food and sex. The anonymous *Freiris of Berwik* is a particularly ebullient *fabliau* about three friars and their relationship with the innkeeper's wife Alesoune, and her husband. This erotic triangle is farcically complicated (friars were a common comic and satirical butt in the Middle Ages through their supposed failure to live up to vows of poverty, chastity and self-discipline). Berwick – the 'nobill toune' – is a particularly appropriate setting as the leading burgh in medieval Scotland with an unusually large monastic presence.

The poem deftly weaves comic strands of verbal puns or jokes: note all the references to gates; to food and feasting (in *fabliau* the desires of the body are always foregrounded); to the frequently profane use of religious language (such as Friar Rob's so-called necromancy or black magic), and the comic variations spun on 'herbery'. In this genre, we witness the comic lifting of culturally and religiously imposed taboos (this is the artistic function of euphemism, the pleasure in knowing what is *not* being said). There may be a sympathy perceptible for Alesoune comparable to that which the reader might just feel for the young wives in Dunbar's *Tretis*. The nature of the 'moral' ending deserves consideration ('This is the story that hapnit of that freir; / No moir thair is, bot Chryst us help most deir' (565–6)): is it dutifully added to protect the poem from any charge of immorality so that, in the end, we have both 'sentence' [*moral meaning*] and 'solas' [*delight*], the two ideals of medieval artistic thought?

Translation

By 1513, the year of Flodden, Gavin Douglas (1476–1522), Bishop of Dunkeld, had translated the classical epic, the *Aeneid* of Virgil. *The Eneados*, Douglas's humanist endeavour reflecting the Renaissance rediscovery of classical texts, was a monumental achievement. It was also arguably a nationalist enterprise promoting the literary and intellectual significance of Scots. In this work the language of the 'Scottis natioun' is newly proclaimed, despite Douglas's duly reverential humility about his 'ignorant blabryng [*chattering*] imperfyte / Besyde thy polyst [*polished*] termys redymyte' (Prologue I, 33–4). As Douglas himself acknowledges, translation is a skilful art which involves the challenge of adaptation and expansion, raising the question of how faithful to the original ('myne author Virgile, poete dyvyne') the translation should be. This issue might be pursued by comparing a modern translation of the original Latin with a manageable extract from Douglas such as Book IV which relates the tragic love of Dido for the epic hero Aeneas; or Book X with its rhetorically energetic portrayal of battle and conflict. The twelve Prologues stand as independent poems in their own right: sampling could include the fourth or the sixth where Douglas prefaces the account of Aeneas's journey to the Underworld by debating with his reader the status of 'gaistis and elrich fantastyis/of browneis and of bogillis' while remaining mindful of Christianity which has intervened between himself and the suspiciously pagan Virgil. Or the seventh Prologue, where the 'brym blastis' of the northern winter are beautifully recreated, could be compared with the similarly onomatopoeic, alliterative and phonaesthetic resources of Henryson's and Dunbar's nature evocations. Douglas's work is a massive and complex achievement but the power and brilliance of his 'celebration' of *Scottis* – this 'wlgar [*vulgar* or *vernacular*] Virgill' intended to be read by 'eu[er]y gentill Scot . . . / onletterit [*unlettered*] folk' – is communicated even in short extracts.

These richly diverse poems are worth studying in their own right, or in excerpted form, and many revealing parallels and comparisons can be drawn between them. There are endless possibilities for comparative topics, but particular consideration might well be given to the representation of women: are the female characters stereotyped or well-defined, do they conform to the binary representation of woman as 'fallen Eve' or 'the redemptive Virgin Mary'? What unites and makes different Cresseid, Dunbar's garrulous wives, or the *Freiris*'s Alesoune? What about different attitudes portrayed towards poetic language itself? It is useful to compare Douglas's first Prologue, Henryson's *Fabillis* Prologue, and Dunbar's *Goldyn Targe*, and the function of the narrator in each poem.

The poetry of Sir David Lyndsay

In the late sixteenth, seventeenth and eighteenth centuries, a literate household in Scotland was likely to own two books, the Bible and the works of Sir David Lyndsay. Today, while a performance of *Ane Satyre of the Thrie Estaitis* can draw the crowds, whether at the Edinburgh Festival or in a small country town, very little is known about the rest of Lyndsay's work. This is a pity: the richness and diversity contained within *Ane Satyre* is only a fraction of the variety which Lyndsay's works offer. [The volume from The Association for Scottish Literary Studies, edited by Janet Hadley Williams, is designed to introduce some of Lyndsay's best poems to a new audience.]

One of Lyndsay's greatest strengths is his skill with comic verse, and in particular a sense of the ridiculous. This is most evident in *The Jousting betwix James Watsoun and Jhone Barbour* (c. 1538–40), the description of a contest allegedly staged before James V and his queen. Instead of the usual knights, the two combatants are 'ane medicinar' and 'ane leche', and whatever their skills in treating illness, they are useless on the jousting field. Both break their spears, one discovers his sword rusted into its hilt, another swoons when about to strike, and eventually they are reduced to hitting each other with their gloves. The poem is a parody of the joust, and by visual jokes pokes fun at both the combatants we see and the formal nature of serious jousting.

Despite his distinguished career as a herald, finishing as Lord Lyon King of Arms, in *The Jousting*, Lyndsay may also be questioning the value of chivalric practices. Not only is the poem a parody, but at the very end, Lyndsay thanks God that 'that day was sched na blude'. Real jousts could kill, as happened to

King Henry II of France in Lyndsay's own lifetime. Lyndsay's longer poems, 'Squyer Meldrum' and 'The Testament of Squyer Meldrum' also interrogate notions of chivalry. 'Squyer Meldrum' is a romance and it celebrates the life of one of Lyndsay's Fife friends, William Meldrum of Cleish and Binns. While praising Meldrum, however, the poem also seems to mock the conventions of high romance as well as the knight. For while the squire is compared to Lancelot, after rescuing a noble woman from rape, he runs away from her suggestions. Lyndsay thus implies that the heroes of romance may not be so easy to find, even among the truly worthy, and these poems, which seem to have been written for family and friends, offer some gentle humour at the discrepancy between the expectations of a romance hero and Meldrum's actions.

The romance as a genre was still very much in fashion in sixteenth-century Scotland, and there is plenty of evidence to show that Lindsay saw himself as very much in a Scottish tradition. His early work, 'The Testament of the Papyngo', is a beast fable, comparable to Henryson's best, in humour and dark comment. The papyngo, a parrot, has used her time as a courtier to grow fat; despite her shape, she persists in climbing a tree. She falls, and dies, but uses her passing to deliver two homilies of advice, to king and to courtier. Like Henryson, Lyndsay uses the humour of the bird's silliness to seduce his audience, before evoking pathos to strengthen her moral points.

As well as beast fable and romance, Lyndsay also participates in a peculiarly Scottish tradition in his 'Response to the King's Flyting'. Such a poem is obviously more circumspect than the scatalogical offerings of Dunbar, but it nevertheless scores a few points against the king's sexual activities. That Lyndsay was able to do this at all demonstrates his closeness to James V. As the early poems show, especially 'The Complaynt' and 'The Dreme', Lyndsay had been an important figure in the household of the baby king. According to Lyndsay, the boy (88–92):

> bure thy grace upon my bak,
> And, sumtymes, strydlingis on my nek
> Dansand with mony bend and bek.
> The first sillabis that thow did mute

was 'Pa, Da Lyn'. This closeness permitted Lyndsay to offer advice to the king freely, suggesting moral restraint, probity, and the reform both of the church and of the nobility for the benefit of the rest of his realm; these themes of course are among the key ideas of the *Thrie Estaitis*.

As Lyndsay grew older, his poetry grew darker, and his concern for good government and church reform became more urgent. There is no clear evidence that Lyndsay himself was ever a confessed Protestant, but there is no doubt that he supported some of the aims of the Protestant movement, such as putting the Bible into the vernacular, and reforming the clergy. These concerns surface again in 'The Tragedie of the Cardinall' and 'Ane Dialogue betwix Experience and ane Courteour'. 'The Tragedie' presents the life and fate of Cardinal Beaton from the cardinal's own mouth. Since Beaton had been murdered by Protestant lairds in revenge for his burning of a Protestant martyr George Wishart, to make the wraith of the cardinal speak allows Lyndsay subtle irony in the development of the character; it also makes the warnings to other priests and princes more telling.

'Ane Dialogue' is Lyndsay's most serious work, and it castigates the state of the church, the state of the court and the state of the world. The poem presents a courtier-narrator discussing his situation with the figure Experience; as the young courtier accompanying the papyngo seems to represent the younger Lyndsay, full of hope and enthusiasm for the new king's rule, so it is tempting to read the older courtier in 'Ane Dialogue' as speaking Lyndsay's own disappointments and regrets. Lyndsay's strength here as in the rest of his poetry is his combination of a plain register with literary complexity. He is happy to take earlier forms, such as the dream vision or the romance, and rewrite them for his own ends. He is also not afraid to state his mind on government, on religious practice and spirituality, and to give due attention to those not perhaps intellectual or powerful. Such are the features that made Lyndsay a popular writer in his own time; explored again, he may regain some of that status in ours.

The Renaissance: political and religious poetry

Perhaps the most immediately appealing literature of the Scottish Renaissance is the beautiful, complex and verbally brilliant poetry of James VI's court. Yet there also exists a strikingly different body of poetry which is still potentially fascinating both in its own right, and as an unusual literary testament of the historical and political conflicts of the Scottish Reformation. This is the poetry which shows the alliance of literature and politics during the reign of Mary, Queen of Scots in the 1560s. Such poetry can be defined as a response to two crises. One is religious, embodied in the Reformation, which was tearing sixteenth-century Europe into Catholic and Protestant factions from the 1520s onwards; the other is political, arising specifically from the situation in Scotland in the 1560s and the turmoil and controversy of Mary's brief reign. The devoutly Catholic Mary antagonised the Calvinist

John Knox and the Protestant nobility. The supposed decadence and idolatry of the Catholic church (for Mary 'the trew kirk') was thought to be mirrored in the supposed decadence of her court. And her alleged complicity in the murder of her second husband, Henry Stuart, Lord Darnley, and consequent marriage to James Hepburn, Earl of Bothwell, prompted the publication of numerous pamphlets in Edinburgh. Political protest took the form of highly skilful poetry, used as a powerful medium for speaking to an increasingly literate public. The contrast between Scott's 'Ane New Yeir Gift to the Quene Mary, quhen scho come first name' (1562) and the *Lamentatioun of Lady Scotland*, written exactly ten years later, aptly reflects the change in Mary's political fortunes. Scott's courtly, ceremonial rhetoric full of hope, promise and good advice for the young queen is later supplanted by the *Complaynt* for a lapsed 'daughter' (*The Mercat Antohology*, 10–13):

> Bot, at the last, throw filthie speiche and counsell,
> That scho did heir of sum curst Kittie unsell,
> Fra scho gaif eir to sic vyle bawderie   *when she*
> God, schame, and honour, scho foryet all thre.

Yet should these texts be considered as literature, or simply as crude satire and religious propaganda? One can argue that they do indeed have wider repercussions beyond their immediate historical moment, yielding more if they are interpreted as literary texts or rhetorical structures. The problem becomes one of definition: whether they can be classified as satire, parody, or sheer invective. 'A Satire on the Age' by Sir Richard Maitland (1496–1586), a prolific writer of moral poetry shaped by social critique, is the sharpest depiction of secular and religious society in the post-Reformation period of the 1570s. The 'Satire' is a reflective moral lyric or complaint (beginning with nostalgic regret for the decay of institutions, prefaced by the elegiac question, 'Quhair is the blythnes that hes bein?') which points to a specific crisis in society: the decline of civic responsibility and the failure of the collective ideal of a harmonious Christian society. The poem offers a good comparison with Lyndsay's *Satyre* which also protests at poverty, legal and economic injustices and uses the key term 'commoun weill' [*the common good*]. Maitland's poem ends by offering specific terms of reform: 'Put our awin lawis to executioun!' (st. 15). The lyric is written in what is usually termed the 'plain style', defined by a conscious verbal simplicity which helps to communicate the moral point. This also reflects the belief that language itself has moral force and the correspondence between moral and linguistic purity which the Reformer's Bible imitates in offering 'plain and certain' truths.

The *Gude and Godlie Ballatis* is probably the first 'literary' product of the Reformation in Scotland, some of its texts perhaps written as early as the 1540s, although not actually published until 1567. Containing psalms, religious lyrics, and anti-Catholic satires, it served as a work of popular instruction and a devotional aid. As the Prologue states, it is 'ane plane text' which conveys 'the word of God' by the 'singing of the Psalmes and hymnis and spirituall sangis and that speciallie amang young personis' (who will comprehend 'the trew word' when sung in the vernacular as opposed to Latin). These songs are sacred reworkings of popular secular songs (the technical term is *contrafactum*) as evidenced by the use of incongruous refrains taken from popular forms and often characterised by a curious sensuality. How should one respond to 'The Paip that pagane full of pryde'? Can its controversially dogmatic invective be related to Reformation doctrine and ideas encountered elsewhere (in the *Satyre*, for example)? Again the purity of language is ironically urged: 'go tell thame plaine' (st. 10). The poem suddenly draws itself up, remembering that it is, at heart, a work of instruction for the Reformed populace. With its curious fusion of plain style and flyting, the 'Paip' is a startlingly diverse work.

Interested readers might also like to look at the poem entitled 'Maddeis Proclamatioun' by Robert Sempill (c. 1530–95). A devoutly Protestant poem in its linguistic ethos (praising 'sacred Scripture plaine', st. 17), it makes striking use of a rhetorical voice and framework. The speaking voice is that of Maddie, a working woman (st. 3):

For I, a wyfe with sempill lyfe,	*simple life*
Dois wyn my meit ilk day,	*earn my meat every day*
For small availl ay selling caill,	
The best fassoun I may.	*fashion; way*
Besyde the throne, I walt upone	*weighing machine; throw onto*
My mercat but delay;	*merchandise*
Gif men thair walk, I heir thair talk	
And beiris it weill away.	

The feminine voice is conventionally thought to be a marginalised one in Renaissance culture. The 'real-life' counterpart of Maddie was probably illiterate; but here we have dramatised an ordinary woman entering public discourse. Ironically, subversive power is given to the supposedly marginalised position. Maddie is a democratic figure, a female version of Lyndsay's 'Johne the Commoun-weill'.

The Bannatyne manuscript

One of the largest sources of early Scottish literature is the extraordinary but little known Bannatyne manuscript, a vast anthology or compendium of poetry (containing writing by Dunbar, Douglas and Henryson), allegedly compiled or transcribed into 'ane ballat buik' by George Bannatyne, a merchant in Edinburgh, in the 1560s. He claims to be the sole copyist, transcribing (he tells his 'reidaris') from 'copeis awld mankit and mutillait'. Bannatyne divides his 'ballat buik' into five 'pairts' or sections, each of varying length: the first is devoted to religious poetry, concerning 'godis gloir and ouir salvatioun'; the second contains poems which are 'morale' and 'grave' in nature; the third provides a contrast, 'blyith and glaid', which Bannatyne refuses gleefully to 'hyd' [hide]; the fourth explores 'luve' [love] in all its manifestations, including consideration of the moral conduct of women and men where erotic desire is concerned (which gives vent to an extraordinarily vituperative antifeminism); last but by no means least, the fifth 'pairt' contains a wealthy diversity of 'tailis and stories'. As a monument of Renaissance literary endeavour, and as a testament of enduring faith in the literature of the medieval past and the sixteenth-century present, Bannatyne's 'buik' is a joy and a revelation (there is an excellent facsimile edition available which reproduces the handwritten manuscript in its original size).

Some of its religious poetry could well be compared with Dunbar's devotional lyrics. Then there are the obvious attractions of the 'blyith' comic poetry, such as the gloriously topsy-turvy world of Lichtoun's 'Dreme'. The manuscript's fourth section contains short 'ballattis of luve'. Its principal lyricist is Alexander Scott but many are anonymous. The Renaissance love lyric (especially when found here so copiously) is often dismissed for being artificial or insincere, criticised as too stylised to communicate true feeling. But we must redefine our expectations and interpretations. Post-Romantic precepts of sincerity or 'authenticity' should not be imposed on lyrics which cultivate a rhetorical construct or voice (what we might term a *persona*, a kind of poetic mask). These lyrics were designed for performance: in the sense of being musical texts (music survives for several Scott lyrics) but also through the possibility that they were recited or declaimed within the court environment. Their nature is social and public, their expression part of the witty and elegant rituals of court life. Many of these lyrics seek novel and interesting ways to rewrite and re-express the idea of love:

So many ar thair ladyis treitis
With triumphand amowres balleitis
That I find not but daft consaitis   *trite expressions*
to say of love Bot lat it be . . .

The lyrics are generally written in the male voice (i.e. to a woman by a man) but there are exceptions which reverse the conventional hierarchy of desire and make women (or the female voice) articulate the paradoxes of love.

Women's writing

In recent years feminist critics have vigorously sought to reverse the exclusion of women from the traditional canon. Through such work, the significance of women's roles in the shaping of nineteenth- and twentieth-century Scottish literature has emerged, while the origin and history of the ballad is confirmed as a largely female creation which persisted into eighteenth-century tradi- tions of songwriting. In the medieval and Renaissance periods, however, female voices seem silent. Traditional literary history is the culprit. If we accept a definition of 'the Scottish writer' which acknowledges a diversity of linguistic expression, then Mary, Queen of Scots, who wrote predominantly in French, can be classified as the earliest known Scottish woman writer outside the Gaelic tradition. Research reveals the existence of women who appear to have belonged to a coterie of male poets but whose work regrettably survives in mere fragments. But that Anna Hume and Elizabeth Melville, authors of substantial published works, have been denied critical attention is a serious omission. The restoration of these neglected voices to the early Scottish canon is not a case of special pleading. Collectively, their works illuminate our understanding of religious and amatory poetry, and the nature of translation in the period spanning 1560–1650.

Mary's poetry offers us the largest and most diverse body of work. Little of it was published in her lifetime except for the alleged 'Casket Sonnets'. (In 1992 Robin Bell edited and translated Mary's poems in *Bittersweet Within My Heart: The Collected Poems of Mary, Queen of Scots.*) Mary's authorship of the secular love sonnets has been disputed, but in earlier periods, largely on grounds that it would amount to the moral incrimination of Mary were they to be accepted, and more recently, on the assumption that they were forged to incriminate Mary politically. How might we read poetry written by a sovereign in the first instance? Is Mary writing 'personally', or is she playing a literary game, writing not as 'Mary, Queen of Scots', but as a poetic *persona* or invented self? Her poetry can be read with translations in order to gain a sense of this relatively unknown and under-appreciated body of work, beginning with elegy. This is a beautiful, simple poem composed upon the death of her first husband, François II, when she was only sixteen. The poem is ostensibly an act of mourning but it is notable how grief is transmuted into a celebration of joyful love that survives death. The poem is the negation of death: absence is contradicted by presence, as the beloved makes several sensual returns.

The controversial erotic sonnets do not enact the traditional dialogue between lover and beloved but now include a third 'protagonist': the rival for affection, the beloved's wife. The effect of this new 'triad' is ambiguous for does it not serve to identify the lover as an adulterer? And perhaps it even calls into question the institution of married love. The sonnets ostensibly provide a definition of perfect love by indicting the inadequacies of the 'wife' who has only a legal claim to the beloved. The Marian poet-lover is highly conscious of her status as a woman, and the bearing that her gender has on the perception of her love. As the speaker implores her virtue and intellect (a woman precisely in possession of her 'iugement' [*mind*]), we paradoxically perceive the female lover as superior to the male beloved who cannot distinguish between the feigned the true:

> You mistrust my heart without evidence,
> And your suspicion does great wrong to me.

In sexual and psychological terms, Mary's sequence offers a number of provocations. The contradictions and paradoxes which inform her sonnets constantly challenge our critical preconceptions, and arise from the simplest yet most essential paradox of all: a woman's radical rewriting of poetic love tradition.

There is also a body of religious poetry by Mary. The 'Meditation' at exactly 100 lines is Mary's longest poem, divided into a general moral disquisition, and an analysis of the speaker's own inward spiritual state. Her own religion, what her letters call 'the true Catholic faith', is defined as a place of vital yet gentle sanctuary (79–81). The poem's final movement (83–100) is characterised by an emotional poise that suggests anxiously desired grace will be forthcoming: 'grant that it be my due / That at the last I draw near unto you.'

The three religious sonnets are entwined with the rhetoric and concerns of the longer 'Meditation'. Issues raised in the above discussion of the latter poem can be pursued in a reading of the sonnets. For example how does the sonnet, 'The wrath of God is not appeased by blood' (*Bittersweet*, 78–9) sustain and develop the critique of Calvinist theology intimated in the 'Meditation'? How does this relate to Mary's own poetic concept of true faith? How do we rhetorically define the last two sonnets? As an act of supplication, the plea, 'O Lord my God, receive my prayer' (*Bittersweet*, 98–9) renounces the penitent's humility by forcefully commanding God to 'Come then . . . make me your redoubt.' To what extent are the sonnets imbued with the actual language of Scripture and prayer? In the last sonnet (*Bittersweet*, 108–9), consolation is postponed until the tenuous wish of the final couplet to attain '[her] portion in eternal bliss'; note how the poetic 'I' is depicted as a mere 'object'. This sense of self-renunciation contrasts with the assertiveness of the other religious sonnets in which the speaker summons the will and confidence to make demands of her God.

The two poems addressed to Queen Elizabeth (*Bittersweet*, 21–5, 62–5) illustrate Mary's propensity for highly figurative language, and the subtle ramifications of the single conceit. In 'The Diamond Speaks', the precious stone cut in the form of a heart signifies the purity of its intended recipient, Elizabeth. The ring also aptly represents the possibility of union between Queens, 'two great jewels in one setting bound'. The poem was allegedly sent to Elizabeth with 'a ring of excellent workmanship, in which a remarkable diamond was conspicuous'.

How do we assess Mary's work within the wider context of Renaissance Scottish poetry? It is illuminating, for example, to compare the religious poems with those of Montgomerie: in both, the poetic voice conveys the anguish of the fragile Catholic penitent. Her love poetry precedes the late sixteenth-century canon of 'Castalian' or Jacobean love sequences, and may justly be considered the first Scottish sonnet sequence, albeit in French. Certain themes bridge the periods of her secular and religious writings: for example, faith is offered as the moral absolute of both secular and spiritual love; and self-renunciation appears to be the consequence of true devotion to either the beloved or God.

Elizabeth Melville's (fl. 1603) most significant work was first published in 1603. The daughter of Sir James Melville of Halhill (himself a writer who published his own memoirs), she became known as Lady Colville of Culross on her marriage to John Colville. Records attest the devotion and piety of 'the lady Culross'. *Ane Godlie Dreame* belongs to a tradition of female spiritual 'autobiography'. It is a simple enough narrative: after mourning fallen humankind, the narrator sleeps and receives an angelic vision revealed as Christ. Led by him through a variety of physical trials, the dreamer is tempted to cease the journey at a 'Castell fair', but is shown and ultimately rescued from the supposed horror of purgatory beneath. On wakening, the dreamer expounds the allegorical significances of the journey which culminate in the final stanza's hymn to divine creation and mercy.

The poem conforms to the traditional medieval genre of the dream vision. (*The Kingis Quair* is the archetypal Scottish exemplar of the mode.) From stanza forty-two to the end, the dreamer provides an explicit commentary on the meaning of the 'dream' or vision, enlarging on a generous selection of interpretative 'hints' in the narrative itself. We begin to see that the poem is founded on one central premise: the notion of the virtuous life, consecrated to faith, as an arduous pilgrimage. Melville's text is a complex weave of scriptural quotations. Many of these possess an intrinsic 'poetic' or figurative quality. The text gives no explicit clue as to the gender of the dreamer but the title includes a reference to '*hir* friends'. One commentator on medieval narrative has noted that the framing 'I' of the story is rarely feminine because the 'weight of cultural authority' lay with male writers. Is Melville deliberately reversing the tradition two centuries later? If so, Melville's poem grants the female writer a startling intellectual authority, and spiritual status.

We might feel in many ways a sense of estrangement from the *Dreame*. Clearly rooted in its own religious era, and expressive of a particularly dogmatic faith, we may feel its tone too proselytising, and the allegory too 'explicit'. Other readers might perceive it as an intensely moving spiritual drama which ultimately transcends doctrinal constraints.

Anna Hume (fl. 1644) belongs to an auspicious line of women who translated classical, medieval and contemporary works of significance. In taking as her text the *Trionfi* of the medieval Italian writer, Petrarch, Hume chose to translate a work of vast intellectual and imaginative scope. Conceived in six 'movements' or chapters, the narratives of love, chastity, death, fame, time and eternity together constituted an allegorical, religious and moral meditation on the human soul. Though there had been several sixteenth-century translations of the *Trionfi* (including William Fowler's), none produced a commentary as she did. She was to publish only the first three *Triumphs* but at the end of the work, she states her intention to translate the remaining three. Hume presents her work as a risky and brash enterprise but chose to dedicate the work to Princess Elizabeth of Bohemia, the daughter of Queen Elizabeth of Bohemia (1596–1662), who was herself the daughter of Anne of Denmark and James VI.

Hume's wholly anglified vocabulary is formally contained by the iambic pentameter couplet. This taut and rigorous metrical form requires skilful manipulation in order to avoid tedious regularity. One of the poem's most interesting features is perhaps the commentaries. Hume's annotations follow a medieval and Renaissance tradition of learned exposition. The range of 'explanations' given by Hume range from the simple identification of mythological figures to semantic interpretation. Frequently, she alludes to the 'Italian Commentary' (this can be traced to two particular editions of Petrarch published in Italy in 1543 and 1549 by two different scholars). Yet Hume is only dependent on these for the more obscure of historical or mythological references. When these sources are not cited, we see a piquant humorist at work, and a critical intelligence which takes issue with some exegetical points of the commentaries. The female wit thus opposes masculine convention to revise received notions of the infamous female characters of legend. We can perhaps interpret Hume's facetiousness as evidence that she was aware of the vast historical and cultural gulf between her poem and Petrarch's. Perhaps then, there is a tone of collusion in her wry comments which could be interpreted as an implicit address to a female readership.

The 'Castalian' sister?

One can be forgiven for regarding James VI's so-called 'Castalian band', which produced the body of Jacobean poetry explored in Chapter 4, and formed the courtly circle of intellectual and literary fervour in late sixteenth-century Scotland, as an 'old boys' network', Renaissance fashion. Many of the sonnets which circulated amongst its members evoke male intimacy and conviviality by their term of address, 'brother'. Literally, what we have is a 'brotherhood'. Yet just as the nineteenth-century self-declared Pre-Raphaelite Brotherhood actually depended on several 'sisters', so did James's possibly include a female presence, Christian Lindsay. Her nominal identity is revealed in the King's wry piece of poetic advice to Alexander Montgomerie; the 'she' in the third line is emphatic:

> Nor yett woulde ye not call to memorie
> What grounde ye gave to Christian Lindsay by it
> For now she sayes which makes us all full sorie
> Your craft to lie . . .

The sole surviving poem composed in the name of Lindsay is addressed to one of James's pre-eminent poet-musicians, Robert Hudson, commenting on Montgomerie's expulsion from the king's favour with typically manneristic rhetorical bravura.

The medieval and Renaissance influence

Scotland's medieval and Renaissance literature stands as a distinct and brilliant achievement. Its influence is witnessed in the eighteenth-century vernacular revival of Burns, Ramsay and Fergusson, not just in its recovery of the 'Habbie Simson' and 'Christis Kirk' stanzas, but in a whole variety of literary, cultural and political ways that make clear a continuity which deserves to be re-examined. And it was Hugh MacDiarmid, of course, who, for the creation of his twentieth-century 'Renaissance', loudly proclaimed 'Not Burns – Dunbar!'

SECTION 2
Eighteenth-Century Scottish Literature

CHAPTER 7

ENLIGHTENMENT AND VERNACULAR

THE HISTORICAL BACKGROUND

Any account of eighteenth-century Scottish literature must recognise the importance of the 1707 Act of Union between England and Scotland. After the Glorious Revolution of 1689, it seemed that Scotland had begun to settle its damaging religious controversies, with Presbyterianism secure as Scotland's established church. Very quickly, however, new problems arose to try the nation once more. England's hostility to Scottish colonial expansion once again made Scots resentful and envious of their old enemy. England, however, had no desire to see Scotland continue as a northern thorn in its flesh. In 1707, through a combination of bribery and the seductive prospect of entry into English colonial expansion, the Act of Union was brought about – though not without strong popular protest throughout Scotland.

The unique Union settlement had very serious implications for Scotland's national identity. After 1707, the institutions of Scotland retained their autonomy; the Presbyterian church controlled the parishes of Scotland; the Scottish legal system, based on Roman and Dutch law, was maintained and the separate traditions of Scottish education, established during the Reformation of 1560, were preserved. Regal and parliamentary power, however, were now firmly rooted in London. (In 1603 Scotland lost its monarchy to the South when James VI became James I of England.) So while Scotland retained significant institutional authority, effectively, the outcome of the Union was to bring Scotland under the political headship of 'Great Britain' and, by implication, the centralised powers of London and the South. In literature, the feeling of having 'sold out' to southern powers provoked a kind of sentimental Jacobitism. There was a desire in Scotland to look back to the vanquished Stuart cause. And from Allan Ramsay to Robert Burns, popular vernacular Scots poetry, charged with a feeling of nostalgic longing, served to fuel the sense of cheated national identity. In 1746 the last cry of Jacobite rebellion was choked in the Battle of Culloden.

Yet while popular national feeling supported Jacobitism and the integrity of Scottish identity, the work of the Scottish *literati*, the educated upper and middle classes of Scotland, tended in the opposite direction; towards 'self improvement' in anglicised language and literature. By the middle of the eighteenth century, Edinburgh in particular was leading a Scottish Enlightenment which seemed to have its primary values located in a 'North British' sensibility. Polite society tried hard to divest itself of Scotticisms and vulgar native expression, at times seeming to out-English the English in its attempts to show that it was no mere northern country cousin.

By the 1770s it could literally be seen that Edinburgh had redefined itself in the building of the New Town. An observer could now see two Edinburghs. First, the old city running down the spine of the Royal Mile, with the castle at the top and the palace of Holyrood at the bottom, which has been described as home to an organic, if ancient and insanitary society. In its huge 'lands' or tenements lived the humblest and the highest; nobles with their coats of arms over the front entrance, lawyers, shopkeepers, water-carriers and sedan chair bearers. This was a tavern-based culture where aristocracy and ordinary city folk rubbed shoulders, where Scots had been spoken for hundreds of years by both, and where a sense of community still remained. Now, adjacent to the Old Town, stood the Augustan, geometrically planned streets and rectangles of the New Town. Built on English and classical models, with its stately and symmetrical squares, its august new tenements for lawyers and the respectable classes, and its mews lanes for servants, it clearly separated classes, and emphasised that a new North British culture was in the ascendancy now. The street names (with the obvious exception of St Andrew Square) were hardly Scottish, referring deferentially to the princes, queens and places of South Britain – with the most dramatic change of political attitudes being seen perhaps in the decision to allow Cumberland Street to carry the name of the Hanoverian general who sanctioned the worst excesses of the British Army after Culloden.

Eighteenth-century Scotland is characterised by polarisation and division. In religion the insurmountable theological divisions of the moderate and extremist parties culminated in the Disruption of the Church of Scotland in 1843. The tragedy of the '45 ended the long-standing undercurrent of nationalistic rebellion. Even in intellectual circles, philosophy was divided between the 'Sceptical School' of David Hume who took an inductive and realist view of humanity and the school of 'Common Sense' which advocated a common, innate moral faculty and which sympathised with ideas of community and mutual help.

Divisions in eighteenth-century Scottish literature

These fundamental divisions were to manifest themselves in eighteenth-century Scottish literature. Traditionally the period has been seen as one divided between the vernacular poets and the anglicised *literati*. The work of the major trio of poets, Allan Ramsay, Robert Fergusson and Robert Burns, represents verse filled with the vigour of popular speech and song, with grotesque and reductive humour which mocks English pretension and political domination, and which extols the virtues of the homely, the communal and the native. In contrast, works such as Henry Mackenzie's *The Man of Feeling* (1771) stands as an example of the sentimental movement in British literature taken to its final excess. In John Hume's *Douglas* (1757), a shepherd's son who turns out to be the missing heir to a great noble house, declaims his tragedy in high-flown language most implausible for such a shepherd. James Macpherson's *Ossian* (1765) pretended to present versions of translated poems of the ancient Celtic bard Ossian; but these were later proved by Dr Johnson and others to be Macpherson's own creations, loosely based on old Celtic oral poetry. Indeed the success of Macpherson in creating a pseudo-Celtic poetry, accepted by polite society as expressing the innate nobility of a lost Celtic society, contrasts sharply with the fact that one of the greatest of Gaelic oral poets, Duncan Ban Macintyre, was, at the time of Macpherson, unrecognised and unsung by the new age of polite literature.

The *literati*, however, should not be dismissed. For all their desire for linguistic and social improvement, they continued to have democratic ideals in education and in their philosophy of Common Sense, which argued vigorously that all levels of society were equally endowed with the faculty of moral perception and evaluation. They managed to come to an accommodation with the moderates in the Scottish church which lasted for almost a century, and thus laid the ground for the flourishing of the Scottish Enlightenment. Their success in lowering the temperature of Scotland's religious divisions should not be undervalued especially in comparison with the negative effects of revived church wrangling on Scottish cultural achievement after the Disruption of 1843. And it would be totally unfair to ignore the great achievements, especially in the sciences and philosophy, of thinkers like David Hume, Adam Smith, Adam Ferguson, James Hutton, Joseph Black (these four last hailed as the 'fathers' of political economy, sociology, geology and chemistry respectively), James Watt in practical physics, or the great dynasties of medicine at Edinburgh University, to name but a few. The accomplishments of the great thinkers and doers of the Scottish Enlightenment are now well known. What is perhaps unrecognised is how this great efflorescence of rational intelligence took place without a comparable blossoming in expressions of the creative imagination. True, Scotland had its great biographers like Boswell and Lockhart, giving unrivalled pictures of Dr Johnson and Walter Scott respectively; true, too, that great portrait painting came from Ramsay and Raeburn, the finest in Britain of their generation. But the fiction and poetry of the *literati*, for all that it is increasingly explored in terms of philosophy, sociology and gender studies, have not maintained interest and pleasure for the modern reader. Rather, for some time now their literary output has been generally regarded as stultified and pretentious, and lacking in the energy which should arise from identification with or reaction to one's indigenous tradition. That said, modern critics are now exploring the extent to which we should revalue their achievement; how far there was a fruitful interchange between their modes and values and the vernacular writers, and the extent to which poets like Fergusson and Burns crossed what has for too long been seen as an impassable divide. Later in this section, some of these alternative readings of the century's culture are discussed.

Later in the eighteenth century, world events were to affect Scotland just as profoundly as events within. The American Revolution of the 1770s and the French Revolution of 1789 polarised Scottish politics and society even further, so that Tory and Whig camps opposed each other with a new virulence. Once again, as the eighteenth gave way to the nineteenth century, Scotland would polarise its loyalties into diametrically opposite camps, through its great new periodicals, the pioneering models for British literature. The Whig *Edinburgh Review,* begun in 1802 by Jeffrey and Cockburn, was opposed in all its opinions by *Blackwood's Edinburgh Magazine* (from 1817), the mouthpiece for the Tory ascendancy of Scott, Lockhart and Wilson. The nineteenth century and the age of Scott would continue this persistent pattern of dualism in politics and literature.

Thus the eighteenth century can be seen as perhaps the most enigmatic period in Scottish cultural history. At its beginning, Scotland surrendered its indigenous parliament, and through much of the rest of the century seemed to be on a course which increasingly aimed at defining the country as 'British'. Yet by the time the nineteenth century dawned, Scotland would have a stronger and more widely accepted set of national identity-images than it ever had before – although these would come in for increasing criticism as irrelevant and romanticised as the nineteenth century wore on. The apparent inconsistency here can perhaps be explained by understanding the immediate and powerful popular reaction against the loss of national identity felt after 1707. This provoked a revival in national consciousness, expression and creativity. The literature of the period thus occupies a fascinating position in the debates surrounding the direction of Scottish culture and identity in the eighteenth century.

The revival of Scots poetry

The most explicit expression in the eighteenth century of cultural nationalism is to be found in the revival of Scots-language poetry. This emerged from a complex interaction of anti-unionism, Jacobitism and antiquarianism. Following the Union of the Parliaments in 1707, important complaints were made by the Scots about both the fiscal and cultural exploitation of Scotland by its larger sister-kingdom. Even prior to the Union, Andrew Fletcher of Saltoun (1653–1716) and George Lockhart of Carnwath (1681–1731) complained that Scotland would be weakened by the Union and that political marriage would be undertaken by a selfish and minority ruling class who would benefit personally from the new arrangement while paying scant regard to the wider national interest. The most famous embodiment of such sentiments much later in the century was in Burns's bitter complaint, blaming both Scots and English, that 'We're bought and sold for English gold' ('Such a parcel of rogues in a nation' (1792)). Republican Presbyterians like Fletcher made similar complaints during the century, but it was the Jacobites (to whom Lockhart owed allegiance) who made most capital out of feelings of injustice. Indeed, from early on in the century, it was Jacobitism that lay behind the revival of Scots poetry.

The Scots poetry revival began with the editorial labours of Jacobites like James Watson (d. 1722) and Thomas Ruddiman (1674–1757). Watson's *Choice Collection of Comic and Serious Scots Poems* (1706–11) was a particularly influential volume, bringing together a sprinkling of Scotland's medieval poetic heritage, and a great deal of sixteenth- and seventeenth-century Scottish poetry. It included the carnivalesque 'Christis Kirk on the Grene' and Robert Sempill's hugely popular folk-piece, 'The Life and Death of Habbie Simson, the Piper of Kilbarchan'. The chaotic, celebratory subject-matter of the first of these poems and the jaunty rhythms in the stanzaic forms of both (the second, in particular, making the 'Standard Habbie stanza', later known as the 'Burns stanza', the most popular verse form in Scottish literature) inform the riotous and satirical form and focus of much of the eighteenth-century poetic tradition in Scots.

The impetus of anti-Unionism and of Jacobitism was to coincide with a wide revival in Scottish antiquarian activities which engaged both anti-unionists and pro-unionists, such as John Clerk of Penicuik (1676–1755), all of whom wanted to safeguard some sense of native Scottish cultural tradition. Formally, the revivalists drew on the traditions of the Scots language, on the harsh, combative alliterative and assonantal energies of the Scottish medieval 'flyting' mode and the systems of time-honoured folk-poetry to create a poetry which was both authentic and inventive.

Ramsay and literary antiquarianism

The first of the great creative users of the Scots language in the eighteenth century was Allan Ramsay (1684–1758). Ramsay was encouraged by the Jacobite, Thomas Ruddiman, who outstandingly championed both the Scots vernacular tradition and the Scottish Latinist literary tradition. It is probably the case that many Scottish Jacobites at the beginning of the century saw the appeal to a Latinist rather than a Scots tradition as marking the nationalist aspiration in literature, but Ramsay, with an uncertain knowledge of Latin, seized instead on the pioneering editorial work of Ruddiman in medieval Scots poetry and Scottish folk-poetry traditions. Ramsay's championing of both a 'high-style' and a 'low-style' Scots poetic heritage is particularly evident in his poetry anthologies. *The Ever Green* (1724) and *The Tea-Table Miscellany* (1724–37). They echo the attempts at poetic archaeology undertaken by Watson and Ruddiman while including the insertion of editorial 'improvements' and elaboration so as to assert the existence of strong and indigenous Scots poetic and nationalist historic traditions. (Some of Ramsay's work displays Jacobite undertones; paradoxically, however, it is not really until after the collapse of Jacobitism in 1746 that Scots poets such as Fergusson and Burns are more explicit in lamenting the cultural and political loss of the Stuarts.) Ramsay's antiquarianism was informed by his own poetic practice as a highly original Scots versifier writing in the 1710s. His most brutal satire, 'Lucky Spence's Last Advice' (1718), is not only a piece of demotically-charged fantasy – the area in which critics have traditionally taken its main interest to lie – but is, in its topsy-turvy vision of a dying brothel-keeper dispensing good-advice to her 'girls', a very contemporary British, Tory satire of the increasing dehumanisation being brought into society by the rules of the market-place.

Ramsay's most celebrated work, *The Gentle Shepherd* (1725), is a pastoral drama celebrating the brief restoration of the Stuarts in 1660 (revealing something of Ramsay's closet Jacobitism), and features folksongs and vernacular Scots set in a peasant location. *The Gentle Shepherd* exemplifies the paradox at the heart of the Scots language revival in the eighteenth century. Prior to the success of Burns, the Scots language was most widely brought into cultural vogue by the success of this play. Yet Scots is seen in the play to belong to a regional, rather than a national realm; a rural, rather than a metropolitan location; and to belong solely to the peasant class (whose use of the 'Doric' might, however, sometimes entertain those of a socially higher caste).

It is in this light we see the increasing popularity of Scottish ballads and folksongs in the genteel country-houses of Scotland and salons of Edinburgh as the century progresses. In the eighteenth century some of the most celebrated singers and composers of such material were to be found among the women of the landed gentry class, including Jean Elliot of Minto (1727–1805), restorer and populiser of 'The Flowers of the Forest'. As well as helping to popularise Scots-language usage, Ramsay's *The Gentle Shepherd* also indicates the tendency towards 'pastoralisation', where Scots is used to express Graeco-Romanised tales of the Scottish countryside. Good examples of this tendency are in *Helenore, or the Fortunate Shepherdess* (1768) by Alexander Ross (1699–1784), and in more ambitious poems such as Ramsay's *Tartana, or The Plaid* (1721), and later in his pastorals.

The predicament of Robert Fergusson

One poet, Robert Fergusson (1750–74), stands out between the period of Ramsay and Burns for his inventive use of the Scots language to create poetry that was not mere song or pastoral. Dying tragically young and seemingly ignored by most of the Edinburgh *literati* of the day (his main encourager was the publisher, Walter, nephew of Thomas, Ruddiman), Fergusson is often taken as an emblem of how hostile Establishment Scotland was becoming towards Scots-language literature at the end of the century. He complains, with a gravity not found in Scots poetry since Ramsay, about cultural and political corruption in Scotland. In poems such as 'Elegy, On the Death of Scots Music' (1772), Fergusson explicitly attacks the erosion of Scottish language and culture by the imported modes of fashion and gentility which were sweeping Europe at the height of the Enlightenment. In 'The Ghaists' (1773), he revitalises the pastoral mode, which was becoming increasingly tired in Scots, with the anti-Unionist argument that Scotland was being exploited economically by England due to the lack of any effective local regulation of Scottish affairs. In 'The Farmer's Ingle' (1773), Fergusson can be seen employing long-standing anti-Unionist mythology which held that the true strength of the Scottish nation lay in the virtue and physical strength of its peasantry. Fergusson's best work, perhaps, is to be found in his 'Auld Reikie' (1773), with its use of the Scots language for vivid social (and

111

philosophical) observation of Edinburgh; and 'Ode to the Gowdspink' (1773) where Scots is the vehicle for a late-Augustan lyricism as fine as found anywhere in Britain at this time. As in the case of Ramsay, Fergusson is a fierce and successful comic satirist, but he combines levity with a serious note of censure on Calvinist Puritanism and British Hanoverianism in such pieces as 'The Daft-Days' (1772) and 'The King's Birth-day in Edinburgh' (1772).

The eclecticism of Robert Burns

Perhaps the most fascinating example of eighteenth-century Scottish creative expression is contained in the work of Robert Burns (1759–96). Clearly, Burns builds on the Scots poetry of Ramsay and Fergusson – and it is an irony that Scottish Enlightenment intellectuals, when they lionised Burns in the capital in 1787, failed to recognise his place within an eighteenth-century Scottish literary tradition, preferring to see him as a 'heaven-taught plough-man', and thus a unique version of 'the noble savage', whose presence in European literature was then so fashionable. Burns's achievement, however, was far more cosmopolitan and eclectic. His role as a song-collector and writer and his imaginative utilisation of the folk-culture of peasant Ayrshire in his poetry reflect a European and Enlightenment fascination with 'primitive' materials. His masterpiece of epic Anglo-Scots language, 'Tam o' Shanter' (1790), draws on the literary traditions of Scotland, England and Europe, at the same time as exploiting the supernatural legends of Ayrshire; and another great work, 'Holy Willie's Prayer' (1785), contributes to the enquiry into the psychology of human character debated during the Scottish Enlight-enment. Burns's first collection, *Poems, Chiefly in the Scottish Dialect* (the 'Kilmarnock' edition, 1786), is both a consummation of many of the themes and formal apparatus of Ramsay and Fergusson as well as a product of the Scottish Enlightenment, in its sociological observation, political disputation and cultural enquiry.

Scottish Enlightenment

From the 1720s, the early roots of the Scottish Enlightenment can be seen in the twin exponents of a new Scottish philosophical and cultural liberalism: Francis Hutcheson (1694–1746) and David Hume (1711–76). Hutcheson, an Ulster Scot, became Professor of Moral Philosophy at Glasgow University in 1729, disseminating his interests in aesthetic enquiry and 'moral sense' philosophy. Hutcheson's arguments for scientific yet God-designed origins of aesthetic pleasure, and the innate moral sensibility of humankind, mark him out as an early Presbyterian moderate in Scotland – or a 'new licht', setting his face against the stern, puritanical, revelation and grace-centred 'auld licht' brand of Calvinism which had hitherto largely predominated. David Hume, by contrast, was an atheist, a philosopher whose sceptical opinions extended not only to God but also, in many ways, to the empirical and rational basis of human perception. At the same time, his intellectual rigour combined with the work of Hutcheson to create an increasingly open environment of intellectual and cultural debate in Scotland, particularly from the 1740s. Hume's *Treatise of Human Nature* (1739–40) scandalised much of the received religious opinion of Britain. But his various essays on literature, economics, politics and a number of other topics met with popular success throughout the country. In particular, as Hume planned, these essays, in both their stylistic panache and their intellectual vigour, demonstrated to Britain and the rest of Europe that the supposedly backward Scottish nation could produce penetrating, challenging writing.

It is clear that Hume wanted to extend that reputation further, and promote a Scottish literature of artistic sophistication and cultural integrity. Along with a number of other first-generation Scottish Enlightenment *literati*, Hume promoted the attempts of John Home (1722–1808) to produce Scottish tragic and epic drama, seen most famously in the play *Douglas* (1756). The play deals with the ancient wars between the Scots and the Norse and was written in a neo-classic style, while at the same time relying on the old ballad 'Gil Morrice' as a source-material and inspiration. Hume and a number of colleagues (comprising largely the growing moderate faction of the Scottish church) also championed the notorious *Ossian* poems. These poems, supposedly translated and published by James Macpherson (1736–96) from the work of a third- or fourth-century Scottish bard, became a matter of Anglo-Scottish literary conflict. If Hume and the *literati* were initially too sure of their authenticity, that great baiter of the Scots, Samuel Johnson (1709–84), was quick to denounce them as counterfeit. The truth would seem to be that Macpherson did unearth some traditional Gaelic materials, but embellished and arranged them to fit with the aesthetic predilections of eighteenth-century neo-classicism and the growing European Enlightenment vogue for discovering exemplars of 'noble savagery'.

Hume's role in the promotion of these literary figures may not perhaps demonstrate an especially discerning critical eye, but they reveal his desire, and that of other Scottish intellectual figures, to orchestrate and articulate a canon of Scottish literature which would vindicate the nation's cultural maturity to the outside world.

A 'crisis of identity' in eighteenth-century Scotland?

National identity, expressed in cultural terms, was a complex issue in eighteenth-century Scotland. Some modern critics argue that the period is characterised by a cultural anxiety which led many Scottish writers hastily and artificially to mimic the dominant forms of English and French neo-classical culture. Many of the Enlightenment writers strove to rid their written work of 'Scotticisms', Scots words and language forms. The paradox is that while the Scottish drive to be British is thought to have been stimulated by the European Enlightenment programme to promote progress and civilisation, such a programme ironically included a fashionable emphasis on primitivism. Furthermore, the influence of Scottish Presbyterianism is often cited as making for a politically conservative and genteel Scottish cultural expression which was to prove useful in the formation of the new centralised British state. It is these conflicting aspirations of British civility and Scottish integrity which compounded the Scottish 'crisis of identity' in the eighteenth century. Even poets writing in Scots such as Ramsay, Fergusson and Burns betray the tensions inherent in this transitional period of Scottish culture. Some critics in particular have attacked Enlightenment authors for 'selling out' their nation's identity for a share in the new Britain. (Those who adopted and promulgated the term 'North Britain' are seen to be particularly suspect in this regard.) In the accounts of these commentators, the English-writing Scots of the century who stayed at home often emerge as the villains of the period. Yet such critics tend to entrench the problem of cultural division by promoting particular writers; James Thomson (1700–48), Tobias Smollett (1721–71) and James Boswell (1740–95) who lived and wrote in England, and congratulating them for their choice to 'fall on one side of the fence' as it were (even as they berate the implications of this choice) whilst condemning those writers who chose to remain in Scotland but produced English-orientated literary works.

A new and valid cosmopolitanism?

However, the tendencies of Enlightenment Scotland towards British *mores* in the eighteenth century may be read more positively, as part of a new and genuine cosmopolitanism in Scottish culture. The intellectual ferment of eighteenth-century Scotland ('a hot-bed of genius' as Smollett memorably described Edinburgh at the height of the Enlightenment) contributed many works of history, philosophy, economics, sociology, and science which were seminal in the European debates of the time, and which mark the beginnings of western modernity. If the narrow literary critical principles of many Scottish Enlightenment thinkers are to be censured, it should be remembered too that the Enlightenment was responsible for significantly advancing the psychological approach to literature. If some of the literary creativity sponsored by the Enlightenment can seem rarefied and synthetic, some of it, such as the Ossianic poetry, should also be seen as an important part of the development of Romantic sensibility, contributing to the emancipation of European art from the arid restrictions of neo-classical principles.

An even more radical re-orientation?

The past is constantly in need of revision given that it is the progenitor of our present, and this is no less true of literary than of other narratives. We need to find new or, at any rate, alternative ways of explaining and ordering our cultural past, not least because new narratives will allow us to examine a different, and frequently a wider, range of texts.

During the time when Scottish literature was being established as a discipline and a tentative canon was evolving, the dominant cultural narrative was one of defeat and diminishment, of a movement from independence to integration and even subjugation within a larger British unit. While pro-Union narratives characterised the eighteenth century as a period of peace and prosperity, in which Scotland was laid open to the civilising influence of its southern neighbour after the civil wars, regicide and religious divisions of the seventeenth century, those engaged in reconstructing a lost or interrupted Scottish tradition saw it, as often as not, as a time of submersion and adulteration. English gradually replaced Scots and Latin as the language of debate and intellectual discourse. In increasing numbers, Scottish writers sought integration and success in a larger British/English culture based in London. Many of them removed themselves physically to the southern capital. James Thomson wrote the words for 'Rule Britannia' and James Boswell completed the most monumental biography in the English language, dedicated to a man who made no secret of his contempt for Scotland and all things Scottish, Samuel Johnson.

Why then has the so-called Vernacular Revival, associated with the names of Ramsay, Fergusson and Burns, come to dominate narratives of Scottish literature in the eighteenth century? Their poetry was seen, and most probably intended, as a rearguard action, a reaction to the loss of Scottish political sovereignty and the consequent threat to a Scottish identity (the status of which remains problematic for many commentators nearly three centuries later). It is becoming harder and harder to ignore the distortions of this perspective. Scottish writers who chose to write in English and went to London were branded as 'Anglo-Scots' and subjected to a kind of retrospective apartheid, which meant that they effectively belonged to neither literature. The fact that a sizeable portion of the work of all three of the Vernacular Revival poets was in English was conveniently overlooked. It was even implied that, when Scottish poets wrote in Scots, they wrote well, while when they wrote in English, their work sank beneath any level worthy of consideration. Edwin Muir's arguments in *Scott and Scotland* (1936), although his own positions were explicitly Unionist and pro-English, reinforced this view. But the contention that Scots were unable to write well in English because they had not been given enough time to learn the language properly is both profoundly demeaning and demonstrably untrue. As a result, a whole rich harvest of Scottish writing, and a mesh of fascinating continuities, such as those which link James Thomson's 'The Castle of Indolence', James Beattie's *The Minstrel* and Byron's *Childe Harold's Pilgrimage*, were lost to view. Paradoxically, an approach which claimed to champion Scottish interests made no serious attempt to integrate the golden age of Gaelic poetry into the overall picture, and the crucial, if endlessly controversial figure, of James Macpherson was branded as a renegade and a falsifier. The situation is all the more puzzling when one reflects that, almost certainly, the Gaelic poet Duncan Ban MacIntyre marched with the Edinburgh City Guard at the very time Fergusson was lambasting its members in the anti-Highland sections of his poetry of city revelry.

Nationalist literary criticism failed to heal divisions of this kind. The seventeenth century continues to be a largely unexplored area where Scottish literature is concerned. The paradoxes become most painful in the evaluation of the Scottish Protestant Reformation. On the one hand, with the adoption of an English Bible, the Calvinist reform movement promoted anglicisation and inhibited the full-scale development of one of Scotland's national languages, Gaelic. Yet Calvinism became, and continues to be, a core element in the debate as to what constitutes Scottish identity. Indeed, the eventual victory of Calvinism over Episcopalianism, and the establishment of a national church, which has been seen as a bulwark of Scottish distinctiveness, were in many ways a consequence of, or at any rate dependent upon, the expulsion of the Stuarts and the securing of a Protestant succession in London. Did the Union of the Crowns in fact make it possible for Scotland to preserve its own characteristic theological tradition? This is a perplexing question but its answer involves an important disentanglement of the strands of Scottish history, its literature and the response of criticism.

Alternative narratives

What alternative narratives can we now offer for consideration? It is perfectly logical to argue that the effect of the Union of the Crowns and later, the parliaments, was to make Scottish culture *more* different from English culture, rather than to bring the two into line with one another. Instead of a process of assimilation, the formation of the United Kingdom may have brought about one of dissimilation. Typologically, there is no phenomenon within English eighteenth-century poetry which parallels a Scottish poet's option to choose between, or blend two (or even three) languages. It can be argued that, from at least 1707 onwards, Scottish writing belonged to two distinct, if interlocking literary systems, one Scottish and the other British, and that no text can be adequately grasped unless viewed from both perspectives. Indeed, one has at times the impression that eighteenth-century Scottish writing is British in a way the work of English writers never was and perhaps never aspired, in the same way, to be.

It is logical and inevitable that, as the overall political trend in Scotland moves towards autonomy and away from integration in a larger British unit, Scottish critics will look for different things in Scotland's cultural past, finding and framing new narratives of it. It should then be possible to admit that the Vernacular Revival, even in its Scottish language products, drew upon a dual inheritance: that of the Scots poetry of the fifteenth and sixteenth centuries, and that of the Latin poets from the time of Augustus, in particular Horace and Virgil. The second debt is hardly less important than the first, especially in the development of a native pastoral, yet it is hard to imagine how the Scottish poets could have established this connection without the mediation of English Augustanism, with Dryden and Pope in the vanguard.

Failure to devote sufficient attention to the seventeenth century has established a kind of *cordon sanitaire* between Early Modern and Modern Scottish literature on the one hand, and the literature of an independent Scotland before 1603 on the other, preventing the cross-fertilisation which must surely result once lines of continuity have been developed between these two major areas of study. Surprisingly, cultural nationalism has colluded in the Unionist project of portraying the seventeenth century as a kind of barren age, even though this period saw the publication of the first Scottish novel (Sir George Mackenzie's *Aretina*, 1660) and of the most significant single collection of Latin verse by Scottish poets.

The development of philosophy and of cultural studies throughout the post-modern period, particularly in continental Europe, has caused the

117

achievements of the Enlightenment thinkers, both French and Scottish, to be viewed in a more critical fashion. The concept of subjectivity which informed them is now being reassessed in terms of gender, language group and ethnicity. How will the Scottish eighteenth century look once Hume and Smith have been suitably redimensioned? There is no way of telling until the necessary task of interrogation and revaluation has been undertaken.

Last of all, it may prove necessary to redefine, or to replace, the discourse of Romanticism which has been inherited from English studies. At present, Scottish literature appears to have a surprisingly rich crop of pre-Romantic writers, but a Romantic movement of an anomalous nature. Insofar as the meaning of Romanticism on British soil is still fixed primarily from an English viewpoint, Scott and Byron are depicted as rather peculiar outsiders. Paradoxically, while Scottish works such as James Macpherson's *Ossian*, which has been identified as one of the early progenitors of the Romantic movement, made a huge impact outside Scotland, Scotland itself served merely as the location of Romantic conception without appearing to originate a distinctive Scottish Romanticism free from distorting external projection. Perhaps it will be necessary to shift the timing of the Romantic movement, where Scotland is concerned, firmly back into the middle years of the eighteenth century, and to find a new framework within which to account for the work of Scott and Byron which gives full value to their enormous influence upon the European stage.

These are only some of the challenges which await scholars and students of the Scottish eighteenth century at the start of a new century. The questions surrounding eighteenth-century Scottish literature and culture remain numerous and vexed. Did the period represent one of confusion of identity and expression? Does it represent an irresponsible casting-off of Scottish tradition and the composition of new, perhaps spurious, dishonest cultural vehicles? Does it represent a new plural and modern approach to Scottish culture and identity? Might the answer lie in a qualified 'yes' to all of these questions as we survey the protean achievements of eighteenth-century Scotland?

CHAPTER 8

ALLAN RAMSAY, ROBERT FERGUSSON AND THE VERNACULAR TRADITION

THE VERNACULAR TRADITION

From the sixteenth century, the Scots vernacular tradition has been resilient in the face of hostile and capricious political, religious, and cultural movements: *The Guid and Godlie Ballatis*, for example, retained their popularity down to the eighteenth century. The vigour of pre-eighteenth-century verse in Scots has already been noted, in poems like 'The Life and Death of Habbie Simson, the Piper of Kilbarchan' and 'The Last Dying Words of Bonnie Heck, a Famous Greyhound in the Shire of Fife' by William Hamilton of Gilbertfield (1665–1751). To a great extent, the story of eighteenth-century Scots poetry is one of rediscovery, with the revival drawing on older medieval models and a diverse range of pre-Reformation poetic topics. It was not a totally successful endeavour – the revival poets never recovered the full humanistic consciousness and confidence of their medieval forerunners, yet there is a constant improvement and development in range; from Sempill's one-dimensional celebration of rustic conviviality to Burns's sophisticated satire.

Perhaps the first example of the new poetic spirit is to be found in the publications of James Watson (d. 1722). His *Choice Collection of Comic and Serious Scots Poems both Ancient and Modern* appeared in 1706, with further volumes following in 1709 and 1711. Politics were close to Watson's heart; as a printer in 1700 of *The People of Scotland's Groans and Lamentable Complaints Poured out before the High Court of Parliament* (a Darien Scheme protest) he was actually jailed as a Jacobite but set free by popular protest. And it is the strong interconnection between poetry and political life during this period which separates Scottish poetry from parallel developments in Augustan England.

Ramsay's *Tea-Table Miscellany* (4 vols; 1724–37), followed by *The Ever Green: A Collection of Scots Poems* (1724) continued the important work of rediscovering older poetry and traditions begun by Watson. *The Ever Green*, however, with its commitment to reviving the medieval poetry of the Bannatyne Manuscript, was particularly significant in the development of Ramsay's poetry. The tone of Ramsay's nationalism can be heard clearly in his preface to *The Ever Green*, and stands as a declaration of intent for the vernacular poets of the century:

> When these good old *Bards* wrote, we had not yet made Use of imported Trimming upon our Cloaths, nor of foreign Embroidery in our Writings. Their Poetry is the Product of their own Country, not pilfered and spoiled in the Transportation from abroad: Their *Images* are native, and their Landskips [*landscapes*] domestick; copied from those Fields and Meadows we every Day behold.

> The *morning* rises (in the Poets Description) as she does in the *Scottish* Horizon. We are not carried to *Greece* or *Italy* for a Shade, a Stream or a Breeze. The *Groves* rise in our own Valleys; the *Rivers* flow from our own Fountains, and the *Winds* blow upon our own Hills. I find not Fault with those Things, as they are in *Greece* or *Italy*: but with a *Northern* Poet for fetching his Materials from these Places, in a Poem, of which his own Country is the scene, as our *Hymners* to the *Spring* and *Makers* of *Pastorals* frequently do.

Ramsay's early work established a kind of manifesto for his vernacular successors, for Fergusson and Burns in particular.

Women and vernacular poetry

An interesting development in this period, which reflected the desire to revive and imitate older Scots literature, especially folk 'literature', manifested itself in the unusual number of well-born ladies of leisure who began to write poems in Scots in the style of the older folk lyrics or of the ballads. Lady Elizabeth Wardlaw (1677–1727) produced 'Hardyknute', the most successful imitation ballad of the eighteenth century; Lady Grizel Baillie (1665–1746) wrote 'Werena my Heart Licht I wud Dee', a lyric written in the folk tradition; Jean Elliot (1727–1805) produced one of the two famous versions of 'The Flowers of the Forest', the other one being written by Alison Cockburn (c. 1712–94). This is a tradition culminating in the impressive work, later in the century, of Caroline Oliphant, Lady Nairne (1766–1845), who wrote such popular Scottish songs as 'The Auld Hoose', 'Will ye no come back again?', 'Rowan Tree', 'Caller Herring' and 'The Land o' the Leal'.

Vernacular verse stanza forms:
'Habbie Simson', 'Christis Kirk' and 'The Cherrie and the Slae'

One manifestation of the renewed interest in older Scottish medieval and Renaissance poetry was the revival of a number of particular verse forms. The collection of large numbers of poems in a variety of forms presented the vernacular poets with models that they were quick to imitate. Three of the stanza forms that were most used were: the 'Habbie Simson' stanza, later called 'Standard Habbie' by Ramsay; the 'Christis Kirk' stanza; and the 'Cherrie and the Slae' stanza.

'STANDARD HABBIE'

The 'Habbie Simson' stanza takes its name from the poem mentioned earlier, 'The Life and Death of Habbie Simson, the Piper of Kilbarchan', by Robert Sempill of Beltrees. It can be traced back to the work of the Provençal troubadours of the twelfth and thirteenth centuries and is found in the work of Alexander Scott in the sixteenth century. The 'Habbie Simpson' was the commonest stanzaic form in Scots, before the work of Burns, with its six-line structure (four rhyming tetrameters in lines 1, 2, 3 and 5, and two rhyming dimeters in lines 4 and 6):

> Kilbarchan now may say alas!
>   For she has lost her game and grace,
> Both Trixie and the Maiden Trace:
>   But what remead?
> For no man can supply his place,
>   Hab Simson's dead.

James Watson printed this, along with Hamilton of Gilbertfield's 'The Last Dying Words of Bonnie Heck' in his *Choice Collection*:

> Alas, alas, quo' bonny Heck,
> On former Days when I refleck!
> I was a Dog much in Respeck
>   For doughty Deed:
> But now I must hing by the Neck
>   Without Remeed.

These two poems establish the elegiac format of the stanza with its repeated rhyme ('deid'/'remeid') in the short lines. Ramsay and Fergusson

121

also use this pattern, importing the trope of the comic or mock elegy, which deflated sentimentality with burlesque and leavened seriousness with mockery. This is Ramsay's 'Elegy on John Cowper':

> I wairn ye a' to greet and drone,
>   John Cowper's dead, Ohon! Ohon!
>   To fill his post, alake there's none,
>   That with sic speed
>   Could sa'r sculdudry out like John,
>   But now he's dead.

and Fergusson's 'Elegy: On the Death of Mr David Gregory':

> Now mourn, ye college masters a'!
> And frae your ein a tear let fa',
> Fam'd Gregory death has taen awa'
>   Without remeid;
> That skaith *harm* ye've met wi's nae that sma',
>   Sin Gregory's dead.

When Burns came to write his famous poetry he had a long-established verse form ready to his hand. He used the 'Habbie Simpson' in the mock-elegy mode for two or three poems, for example, 'Poor Mailie's Elegy':

> Lament in rhyme, lament in prose
>   Wi' saut tears trickling down your nose;
>   Our Bardie's fate is at a close,
>   Past a' remead;
>   The last, sad cap-stane of his woes;
>   Poor Mailie's dead!

This poem has the conventional blend of affection with mockery and utilises traditional rhymes, but the poem develops a much more sophisticated and subtle expression than its predecessors. For Burns, the 'Standard Habbie' came to be an infinitely more flexible and varied form than ever before. A long list of poems – 'Scotch Drink', 'The Author's Earnest Cry', 'Address to the Deil', 'Holy Willie's Prayer', 'To a Mouse', 'To a Louse' and many verse epistles like 'To John Smith', 'To John Lapraik', 'To William Simson' – all testify to Burns's supreme command of one of the oldest and richest forms in Scottish poetry.

THE 'CHRISTIS KIRK' STANZA

The anonymous poem 'Christis Kirk on the Green' was formerly, and wrongly, attributed to James I. It is a poem close in spirit to the eighteenth-century rural poets, describing the knockabout revelry at a rustic gathering with a topsy-turvy riotous conclusion. Here is the first stanza illustrating the original ten-line structure:

> Wes nevir in Scotland hard nor sene,
>   Sic dansing nor deray,
> Nouthir at Falkland on the grene,
>   Nor Pebillis at the play;
> As wes of wowaris as I wene,
>   At Christis Kirk on ane day:
> Thair came out Kitties washen clene,
>   In thair new Kirtillis of gray,
>   Full gay,
> At Christis Kirk of the grene that day.

The transmission of this form is exceptionally interesting, since James Watson slightly modernised it, shortening the stanza by doing away with the 'bob and wheel' of the last two lines and adding the words 'that day' to the ninth line as a refrain – so that the above stanza appears in his collection thus:

> Was ne'er in Scotland heard nor seen
>   Such dancing and deray;
> Neither at Falkland on the green,
>   Nor Peebles at the Play,
> As was of Wooers as I ween
>   At Christ's Kirk on a day:
> For there came Katie washen clean
>   With her new Gown of Gray
>   Full gay that day.

It is significant that when Allan Ramsay produced another version of 'Christis Kirk' and added two lively additional cantos, in which he carries on the story of the village farce, more in the manner of 'The Ball of Kirriemuir' than the original, he opts for James Watson's regular metrical version (four rhyming tetrameters alternating with four rhyming trimeters and a final dimeter with refrain). Later Fergusson uses it for his poem 'Hallow Fair':

At Hallowmass, when nights grow lang,
  An' starnies shine fu' clear,
Whan fock, the nippin' cauld to bang,
  Their winter hapwarms wear;
Near Edinburgh a fair there hads,
  I wat there's nane whase name is,
For strappin' dames and sturdy lads
  An Cap and stoup *flagon*, mair famous
    Than it that day.

And Burns later used it for one of his finest religious satires, 'The Holy Fair':

Upon a simmer Sunday morn,
  When Nature's face is fair.
I walked forth to view the corn,
  An' snuff the caller air.
The rising sun owre Galston muirs
  Wi glorious light was glintin';
The hares were hirplin' down the furs,
  The lav'rocks they were chantin'
    Fu' sweet that day.

Thus we can clearly see the line of transmission and the thematic development of this stanza down through several hundred years.

THE CHERRIE AND THE SLAE STANZA

The most complex verse form used by the vernacular poets was that of Alexander Montgomerie's *The Cherrie and the Slae*, which first appeared in printed form in 1597, and was reprinted by both Watson and Ramsay. This allegorical poem has an ancient pedigree containing all the features of the 'Romance of the Rose' allegory which dates back to thirteenth-century France. It tells of a mystic quest for some ideal good represented by the cherry (the converse being the bitter sloe berry) and contains a long argumentation between allegorical figures like Reason, Will, Experience and Danger. Montgomerie took over the stanza form from the song tradition (it was known in the sixteenth century as 'the tune of "The Bankis of Helicon"'), and he uses it with great skill. Here the poet is describing the river by which he has his vision. It illustrates the complex fourteen-line form with its opening section of six lines with three rhymes plus two four-line sections rhyming on alternate lines:

To pen the pleasures of that park,
  How every blossom, branch and bark,
    Against the sun did shine,
  I pass to poets to compile
  In high, heroic, stately style
    Whose muse surmatches mine.
But as I looked me alone,
  I saw a river rin,
Out o'er a steepy rock of stone
  Syne lighted in a linn;
With tumbling and rumbling
  Among the roches round,
Devalling and falling
  Into a pit profound.

It was Ramsay this time who included the poem in his *Ever Green* collection, and he was to use its stanza form himself in 'The Vision', a poem of strongly nationalist tone which he disguised behind a dense imitation of Older Scots and with the signature pseudonym 'A. R. Scot' – Ramsay's own nationalist sentiments were not particularly acceptable nine years after the 1715 Jacobite Rising. Here the poet is warned by William Wallace, the guardian of the nation, that the condition of Scotland will worsen and suffer greater persecution before she will finally revolt:

Quhen all your trade is at a stand,
And counzie clene forsaicks the land,   *coinage; completely*
  Quhilk will be very sune;
Will priests without their stypands preich?
For nocht will lawyers causes streich?   *plead*
  Faith that is nae easy done!
All this and mair maun come to pass
  To cleir your glamourit sicht;   *enchanted*
And Scotland maun be made an ass,
  To set her judgment richt;
They'll jade her, and blad hir,   *abuse; beat*
  Untill she brak hir tether,
Thoch auld she's, yit bauld she's,
  And teuch like barkit leather.   *hardened*

Fergusson does not appear to have used this complex metre, but it later developed into something richer and of greater substance in the opening to

Burns's Brechtian vision in 'Life and Liberty' ('The Jolly Beggars') of the riff-raff and dregs of society in Poosie Nansie's tavern:

When lyart leaves bestrew the yird,	*fallen*
Or, wavering like the bauckie-bird,	*bat*
Bedim cauld Boreas' blast;	
When hailstanes drive wi' bitter skyte,	*slap*
And infant frosts begin to bite,	
In hoary cranreuch drest;	*hoar foost*
Ae nicht at e'en a merry core	*lawless wasted*
O' randie, gangrel bodies	
In Poosie Nansie's held the splore,	*carouse*
To drink their orra dudies:	*rugged clothes*
Wi' quaffing and laughing,	
They ranted and they sang;	
Wi' jumping and thumping,	
The vera girdle rang.	

These three verse forms illustrate the collective, traditional and communal achievement of the eighteenth-century poets. The rhythms of song and dance have been imported into their work, imbuing their poetry with a sustaining vitality. Compared with the wide-ranging and confident expression of the medieval and Renaissance poets, Ramsay, Fergusson and Burns are more constrained and narrow in theme, treatment and intellectual power, but, especially in the satiric vein, they are a formidable force and their poetry constitutes the most substantial literary achievement of eighteenth-century Scotland.

Allan Ramsay (1684–1758)

Allan Ramsay was born in Leadhills, Lanarkshire and died in Edinburgh after a busy career as wigmaker, poet and man of letters. He exemplifies the characteristic 'crisis of identity' which arguably afflicted every Scottish writer of note during the period from 1707 onwards in varying degrees of intensity. 'Crisis of identity', a term coined by David Daiches to express the post-Union dilemma, refers to the conflict encountered by the dialect-speaking Scottish writer whose literary loyalties were torn between native Scottish expression or the emulation of polite English models which were thought to possess greater status and authority. Even Ramsay's accounts of his own birth were equivocal, and he often, like Robert Burns, alludes to his lower class status in terms which suggest defiant pride – or at other times betray a nervous insecurity.

LITERARY INHERITANCES

In literary terms, it is interesting to consider the Janus-faced portrait of Ramsay. On the one hand, he belongs to an older Scotland in which, still valuing the Scots language, it was possible for the Scots poet to rise to a position of some social eminence, unimpeded by the class connotations of linguistic division. To this extent, Ramsay is the last of a long tradition of poets who belong to a vernacular Scotland relatively unaffected by the attitudes of class snobbery, anglocentric deference, and cultural uncertainty which were to develop later in the century. The life and death of Robert Fergusson later that century illustrate very clearly these developing pressures on Scottish writers.

On the other hand, however, it is possible to see that already Ramsay is being affected by growing 'Augustan' notions of politeness and cultural 'improvement'. In many ways, Ramsay's career anticipated those of both Fergusson and Burns. Like them he 'improved' himself through the social clubs of the day. What Burns found in the Tarbolton Bachelors' Club and Fergusson in the Cape Club, Ramsay found in the Easy Club – a Tory and suspected Jacobite organisation, made up of people well above his own social rank, including notable early members of the *literati* like Thomas Ruddiman, the scholar and printer, Professor Pitcairne and Dr Abercrombie. Shrewdly, Ramsay combined poetry with prudence, deliberately planning his social ascension in a way very unlike Fergusson and Burns. This points to a significant difference between Ramsay and the later vernacular poets. Ramsay alone managed to achieve a strong vernacular voice, not set aside as the 'rural songster' or 'defiant nationalist', but a poetic voice fully integrated with his social status. In this he is perhaps closer to a writer like John Galt and his creations of Provost Pawkie and the Reverend Micah Balwhidder than to any romantic or peasant persona. In his Chapter 1, 'The cultural consequences of the Union', in *The Paradox of Scottish Culture* (1964), David Daiches comments on the deep-seated divisions in Ramsay's loyalties and attitudes in:

> Isaac Bickerstaff and Gavin Douglas [Ramsay's two pseudonyms in the Easy Club]; a gentleman of the Augustan Age and an ardent Scottish patriot; an admirer of Pope and Gay and Matthew Prior and a devoted champion of the older Scottish makars and of the use of vernacular Scots by contemporary Scottish poets; . . . he could defend the coarsest and frankest language in poetry and yet dress up a Scottish song in intolerable false elegancies . . .

Yet Daiches perhaps over-emphasises Ramsay's dualism. There is a voice of integrity in Ramsay's poetry which suggests a kind of Scottish Augustan – a canny and prudent Scots merchant looking from his northern eyrie at the extravagances of the world, cutting them down to size and insisting on balance and order in society. It is a genuine attitude of simultaneous ideological involvement and artistic detachment and it exemplifies a position found later in Scott and Galt. Ramsay's problem was that he had to struggle through several different stances, or several different authorial *personae* in order to find a consistent and authentic voice. It is worth looking at the range of these *personae*, since they act as a map or guide to subsequent positions adopted by Scottish poets struggling to find a whole voice.

Ramsay's life and work compose a portrait of a kindly, prudent and liberal tradesman poet, possessed with immense energy, who helped advance Puritan Edinburgh, though not without losing a battle or two. His circulating library was the first in Britain. His proposed theatre in Carrubber's Close would have been the first established place for drama in Scotland in 1737, after almost two centuries of neglect, if the magistrates of Edinburgh had not used their powers of licensing to shut it, almost ruining him. Despite this, he was able to recover with characteristic resilience and soundness of judgement, and retire a wealthy man.

RAMSAY'S POETIC PERSONAE

Ramsay's poetry reveals certain categories or poetic roles, and within these there are, broadly speaking, four poetic *personae* which he varyingly adopted throughout his poetry. A first role is that of 'Edinburgh Citizen', a man at home in a city of clubs, taverns and huggermugger street life. This *persona* conveys an intense sense of place, expressed in a tone halfway between the comic and the sentimental. Another role is that of the 'Scottish Patriot', the stance of the younger sentimental nationalist and Jacobite Ramsay; it follows after the role of the 'Scottish Augustan', a man of the world based in Scotland, looking out on Britain and Europe with a critical eye for excess and a genuine respect for the golden mean in both life and poetry. And beneath all these is his fall-back fourth role, that of the 'Natural Songster', evading the problems of politics, commerce, satire and the like, who retreats to the simplicities of the countryside, celebrating nature's beauties in sentimental vernacular Scots.

As 'Edinburgh Citizen': The extra cantos that Ramsay added to the traditional celebration poem, 'Christis Kirk on the Green', show his capacity to write with an 'ungenteel' honesty about physical detail – a form that was to act as a model for poets later in the century. This tone is echoed in others of Ramsay's poems, notably those that deal with Edinburgh life and characters. In his comic elegy, 'On Lucky Wood in the Canongate', the city is observed with an acute eye for gritty detail. While the poem is a simple and good-humoured lament for the keeper of a hostelry, it gains force from its involvement with the real issues of the day. The setting of the Canongate is quickly established; aspects of city life are referred to – the clubs, the lawyers, the porters (such as Aikenhead), the London competitors – and Ramsay relishes his descriptions of the plentiful and varied food and drink served in the Canongate inns. The burlesque of classical elegiac forms is deftly handled, as in the parallel elegy, 'On Maggy Johnston'. Both these elegies gain force from the uncompromising base realism adopted within the façade of a classical poetic convention. The 'mourners' are Edinburgh's young men-about-town deprived of their favourite drinking place with its familiar landlady. The women whose catering skills Ramsay celebrates were real characters on the Edinburgh scene, as were John Cowper, the Kirk Treasurer's Man and Lucky Spence, the brothel-keeper, the subjects of two more poems by Ramsay. These satirical poems criticise the operation of religious authoritarianism and hypocrisy in 'John Cowper', and sexual habits and social hypocrisy in 'Lucky Spence's Last Advice', where the mistress of a brothel gives kindly advice to her 'dearies' in a way which shows up pious moralising. These two poems foreshadow in their different ways the later devastating exposure of religious and sexual hypocrisy by Burns in 'Holy Willie's Prayer'. 'Lucky Spence's Last Advice' is the first in the line of great dramatic monologues written by Ramsay, Fergusson and Burns. While the other poems mentioned describe the layers of Edinburgh society in a comparatively gentle way, Ramsay's 'Lucky Spence' is a marvellous and savage ironical parody which explores the seamy underside of city life and stretches the formal possibilities of later Scottish poetry.

As 'Scottish Augustan': Ramsay's role as 'Scottish Augustan' is best conceived in the charming autobiographical 'Epistle to Arbuckle', in which Ramsay tells us how his mind is 'mair to mirth than grief inclined'; how he hates drunkards or gluttons yet is no enemy of wine or mutton; how he feels it is quite legitimate to be ambitious of 'fair fame' as a comic poet; how he is neither Whig nor Tory, nor gives credit to purgatory or transubstantiation, but is no extreme Calvinist either. What is expressed is a passionate conviction in compromise and rational moderation. This can be traced through several important poems – from the depiction of the Lothian farmers' common-sense prudence and its contrast with the reckless merchants' gambling in 'To the Earl of Dalhousie', to his insistence on moderation in social behaviour in 'To R. H. B.', and most of all in the repeated emphasis on restraint in 'To Robert Yarde'.

After reading these poems, one begins to feel that this may be the real Ramsay speaking. It would at first sight appear to be a creed that could kill poetic inspiration, but some of Ramsay's finest poetry is indeed more Augustan than traditionally Scots, drawing from Horace and the Augustan sense of order just as much as from the riotous 'Christis Kirk', Sempill of Beltrees and Hamilton of Gilbertfield. He develops this strain in a series of moral fables, many of them inspired by Henryson and French sources; indeed the fusion of the Augustan strain with the makars' tradition is the hallmark of most. The most notable are 'The Twa Books', 'The Chameleon', 'The Ape and the Leopard', 'The Twa Cats and the Cheese' and 'The Ass and the Brock'. All these express the *persona* of the Scottish Augustan; there is no affectation or pretence and they are racy, well-told, colourful and unaffected. It is, however, obvious that Ramsay is at his best when dealing with the world of commercial and legal Edinburgh, and the fables, however universal, take their life from the Edinburgh-inspired location, as in 'The Man with Twa Wives', where Edinburgh's divided society is reconciled in fable form.

Ramsay is not consistently successful in this Augustan mode. 'On Content' is a clumsy poem, taking its theme from John Dryden, with a heavily derivative opening in an English Augustan style. He is better in 'On the Prospect of Plenty', where the use of Scots, in contrast to the previous example, gives bite to the visionary comment: a dream of Scotland, rather than Britain at large, in a state of economic harmony and peace.

The greatest achievement of Ramsay in this Augustan and satirical mode lies in the poem, 'Wealth, or the Woody' [*Wealth, or the Gallows*]. Why this magnificent epic satire, perhaps fuller in range than anything Fergusson or Burns later achieved, has been consistently ignored by critics, is difficult to understand. It is startlingly prophetic of the evils of financial speculation and the new commerce, and stands as one of the very few substantial Scottish poems which combine a reductive and ironic view of life from a canny mercantile Scottish point of view with a British and Augustan perspective on universal issues. Its success is dependent on the way Ramsay plays the role of a North British or Edinburgh merchant, at first apparently vastly impressed by the English mania for colonial speculation of 1711–20 (the all too real episode known as 'the South Sea Bubble' which caused wide-spread ruin when investment schemes collapsed), then proceeding to reveal (as did Swift later in *A Modest Proposal* (1729) that behind his ironic pretence lies a deeply serious and caustic comment on human folly. As with so many great satires, the method adopted by Ramsay is of pretended favour, so that the poet wonders naïvely at this glorious tide in the economic affairs of men. Yet all through this superficial wonder runs a grim note, a hint that the position is a disingenuous one:

> See from yon bank, where South Sea ebbs and flows,
> How sand-blind Chance woodies and wealth bestows . . .

After sustaining an unusual symbolic imagery of boundless seas overflowing with wealth and golden possibility, Ramsay in closing brings the poem to the grim reality, symbolised by the solid earth with its gallows from which hang the financial manipulators and the confidence tricksters who have fooled so many:

> This I foresee, and time shall prove I'm right,
> For he's nae poet wants the second sight;
> When autumn's stores are ruck'd up in the yard
> And sleet and snaw dreeps down cauld winter's beard;
> When bleak November winds make forests bare,
> And with splenetic vapours fill the air;
> Then, then in gardens, parks and silent glen,
> When trees bear naething else, they'll carry men,
> Who shall like paughty Romans greatly swing
> Aboon earth's disappointments in a string . . .

Ramsay never wrote better poetry than this, although 'The Miser's Last Words' (with its central image of gold) had something of its power.

As 'Scottish Patriot': The third role is that of the patriot and nationalist. It is a moot point whether Ramsay genuinely held these values, or simply acted a fashionable part. There are fragments of national prickliness and concern in 'The Epistle to William Hamilton' and 'The Vision of Plenty', but not so heartfelt as those expressed in 'Wealth or the Woody'. It may well be that given the complex claims and differing loyalties in the first half of the century there was a very real but submerged part of Ramsay which felt strongly about the loss of Scottish identity but could only rarely express it in successful poetic conception. There are inferior poems that seem to hint or strive for an expression of national feeling, but only one outstanding example. The inferior poems are 'Tartana, or the Plaid' and 'The Three Bonnets', in which lapses of taste and indistinct allegory prevent success. The outstanding poem in this group is the epic, 'The Vision'.

'The Vision' appeared under the pseudonym of 'A. R. Scott' in *The Ever*

Green (1724) edited by Ramsay. In it, Ramsay skilfully uses the dream-vision device, so beloved by the makars and medieval poets, in which a symbolic figure appears to speak to the poet. In an unseasonable storm, symbolic of the troubled political times, the poet retires to a cave and falls asleep. In the dream, William Wallace, the Guardian of Scotland, appears to him and gives warnings and predictions which parallel the Wars of Independence in the time of Wallace with the Jacobite unrest in Ramsay's lifetime. The figure of Wallace, as warden of the ancient nation, becomes a symbol of Scotland's suffering, its nationalism, and its resistance. The poet thus achieves a kind of *persona*, not necessarily tied to either period, but a vision of a timeless Scottish identity conceived in heroic terms. The ideology expressed in this genre would become increasingly frequent in Scottish literature, in Fergusson's or Burns' visionary poetry, and, admittedly with less fire, in the later poetry of William Tennant and James Hogg, or in the fiction of Walter Scott, George MacDonald, and later, Lewis Grassic Gibbon and Neil Gunn. It culminates in Hugh MacDiarmid's epic, satirical yet visionary poetry, outstandingly in *A Drunk Man Looks at the Thistle* (1926). In many ways, Ramsay was the pioneer of this slow-burning impulse. In the twenty-seven verses of 'The Vision', using the 'Cherrie and the Slae' stanza form, he demonstrates a recovery of poetic confidence drawing on Scotland's past in a way which was to be highly significant for the future of Scottish poetry.

As 'Natural Songster': Ramsay's fourth role is that of the 'natural songster', anticipating Burns's role-play as the 'heaven-taught ploughman'. It is a common part for Scottish poets, although to his credit Fergusson avoided it assiduously. For many poets of the eighteenth and the nineteenth centuries, it appears as the role of retreat when the complexities of upholding other positions, satirical or serious or philosophical, become too burdened with the tensions and loyalties of the age. For Ramsay it produces a few poems worth reading, like 'Pentland's Towering Tap' or 'Up in the Air', but as with so many of his other roles, it is not surprising to find one outstanding piece of work where this position is deepened and developed to achieve something more perceptive and significant. In the pastoral drama *The Gentle Shepherd*, produced in 1724, three years before John Gay's *The Beggar's Opera*, Ramsay demonstrates surprising originality in his attempt to find a distinctive voice within the traditional convention of classical pastoral drama. Despite the acknowledged debt to older Italian models Ramsay's play struck out in a new direction. Hitherto, the Scottish pastorals which he wrote on the deaths of Addison and Prior were incongruous and grotesque, since the Scottish folk tradition could not be accommodated within the strictures of classical conventions. *The Gentle Shepherd*, however, differs from all previous types of pastoral at almost every point. In his story, for example, there is neither ethereal timelessness nor idealisation but instead a distinct historical setting in the period of Cromwell's intrusion into Scotland. It tells of the simple shepherd, Patie, who is revealed to be the lost son of Sir William Worthy, a Royalist sympathiser forced to flee. Thus, although fairly traditional and hackneyed in theme, it is a plot rooted in actual history and society. Nor are the other characters abstract nymphs, satyrs and gods, with a bucolic chorus in the background, but in fact real country folk set in a realistic natural setting. *The Gentle Shepherd* is not great heroic or naturalistic drama, but it has real value on two counts. The first is that it has song passages of natural lyricism and of a sustained quality not found again until Burns. The second is that it has a literary significance in that it leads not only to John Home's melodramatic Shakespearian imitation play *Douglas* (1757), so prized by the *literati*, but more importantly to the vigour and earthy zest of Burns's 'Love and Liberty' ('The Jolly Beggars'). Ramsay's poetry asserts both the validity of peasant experience as a poetic subject and affirms native expression as a medium for serious literature. Once again Ramsay can be seen as a highly talented originator, with his example being taken up by Fergusson and Burns. It is lamentable that Ramsay's Edinburgh lacked the sufficient cross-fertilisation of culture and confidence in its native abilities to support his radical literary initiatives.

In conclusion, Ramsay should be seen as an important Scottish poet, whose exploration of new areas in Scottish writing opened up new ground in form and content for later Scottish poets. However, for each of the roles he adopted, Ramsay produced a good deal that was banal and immature before he could find a sure voice that suited his purpose. Significantly, like Fergusson and Burns later, Ramsay finds his real maturity in sustained satirical attack on the real social and economic aspects of his genteel, Kirk-ridden, and too often divided society. With his poetry we are at the beginning of the tradition that will lead through Fergusson's 'Braid Claith', and 'Auld Reekie', Burns's 'The Holy Fair' and 'Holy Willie's Prayer', and to great satirical novels in the next century like *The Confessions of a Justified Sinner* (1824), *The Entail* (1823) and *The House with the Green Shutters* (1901).

Robert Fergusson (1750–74)

Although Fergusson has an intrinsic connection with the city of Edinburgh, as Dickens has with London, Joyce with Dublin, or Villon with Paris, and although Edinburgh is almost the sole subject and focus of his poetry, we must not confine our view of Fergusson to his obsession with Edinburgh low life, or his resentment of the Edinburgh Enlightenment authors. Hugh MacDiarmid's claim in Sydney Smith's *Robert Fergusson* (1952) that Fergusson wrote 'Gross-stadtpoesie' – poetry concerned solely with the functioning of a city – is superficially appealing, but Fergusson belongs to an older Humanist and academic tradition that has a wider set of concerns, and his poetry draws no strict line between urban and rural matter or imagery. It is nevertheless true that his greatest achievement lies in his lively and satirical pictures of Edinburgh and its people, seen from the point of view of the humble burgher, sceptical of snobbery and affectation, and raising the actual speech patterns, vocabulary and proverbs of ordinary Scots to the level of great poetry, attaining (long before Wordsworth desired it at the end of the century) 'the real language of men'.

FERGUSSON'S SHORT LIFE

Fergusson was born in Edinburgh, but spent his childhood in Aberdeenshire and Dundee before studying at St Andrews University. Although he did not graduate, there is nothing to suggest that he did not complete his academic and classical curriculum. Together with his earlier classical education at school, Fergusson's situation was thus, from childhood, very different from either Ramsay's or Burns's. On one hand his upbringing places him more in the situation of one of the *literati* than of one of the exponents of the native Scots tradition; yet on the other, his poorly-paid and arduous work as a copy-clerk in the Commissary Office in Edinburgh denied him the possibility of full entry into the genteel circles of Edinburgh society. For all that, he gained a wide circle of friends and acquaintances – lawyers, actors, tradesmen, journalists – and while, like Ramsay and Burns, his poetry makes great play of drink and drunkenness, there is no reason to suppose Fergusson himself was more excessive than his peers in a tavern age. A more realistic picture reveals an inhumanely overworked young man of poor health who lived beyond his physical means until his debilitating illness deepened into a manic depression finally exacerbated by concussion, causing his tragically early death in 1774.

Whatever else, it is possible to view the death of Fergusson in a straw-filled cell of the Edinburgh Madhouse at Bristo as a kind of symbolic representation of the fate of vernacular and traditional verse and culture in Edinburgh, an Edinburgh more concerned with the building of its New Town, with lionising the fake Gaelic effusions of James Macpherson and congratulating itself on the productions of Robert Blair, John Home and Henry Mackenzie. Fergusson's is the achievement that has stood the test of time; while the creative achievements of the *literati* who despised Fergusson have been relegated to a position of mainly documentary and historical interest.

THE RANGE OF FERGUSSON'S POETRY

Finding a principle of organisation or a running theme for Fergusson's poetry is more difficult than with Ramsay's. Fergusson died very young and his poetry is that of a young man who had only four or five years of a writing career. Arguably the tendency to poetic role-playing, as found before and after in Ramsay and Burns, would eventually have emerged, since much of Fergusson's English poetry also tends to be imitative and conventional in its use of Augustan English pastoral. That said, (and in keeping with recent critical opinion that the English and Scottish poetry of eighteenth-century poets should not be viewed as separate categories, with the first condemned and the second highly valued), critics have begun to assert the importance of Fergusson's English poetry, as much for socio-historical and cultural reasons as for literary quality. However, in Fergusson's case his Humanist background, discussed below, can give some of his English poetry an unusual distinction, as in 'Ode to the Gowdspink'; while some of the satirical poems show a playful and grotesque fantasy which can bite. 'The Bugs' 'sings of reptiles yet in song unknown', mocking Edinburgh's snobberies in high-flown style, just as 'The Sow of Feeling' explicitly mocks the sentimental excesses of Mackenzie's *The Man of Feeling* (1771) (for which he was not to be forgiven!), and his marvellous send-up of pretentious polysyllabic verbosity in 'To Dr Samuel Johnson: Food for a New Edition of His Dictionary' mocks linguistic affectation.

It is clear too that Fergusson's Scots vernacular poetry is a nationalistic response against the adoption of artificial foreign modes. Yet Fergusson's position is fundamentally different from Ramsay's. Fergusson was poor but well-educated; the opposite is true of Ramsay. Fergusson is close to the middle classes, yet conscious of a profound distance from them, which makes him antagonistic towards them. Ramsay aspired to the middle classes, and much of his poetry is about the importance of a stable middle-class order and moderation in society. Fergusson (in this respect like Stevenson a hundred years later) appears more often to be in revolt against the stifling orthodoxy of bourgeois society, and particularly against the overwhelming monotony of his white collar work in the Commissary Clerk's office.

There is a quality here that Fergusson seems to share with Burns and James Hogg; and later Leslie Mitchell ('Lewis Grassic Gibbon') who knew the intolerable strain and tedium of peasant labour. Fergusson's office work had the same tedious repetitiveness and tying drudgery, without the ferocious physical labour. In Fergusson, Burns and Hogg, the escape is both physical and literary; physically into drink and celebration for emotional and social release; and, in literary terms, into poetry and song that exults in freedom and rounds

135

fiercely on the forces that repress and deny the satisfactions of body and mind. This hedonistic escapism, emphasising the value of holiday, drink and release, is part of a larger tradition in Scottish literature from the Middle Ages through to the poets of the eighteenth century, and later in the Bacchanalian qualities of MacDiarmid's *A Drunk Man Looks at the Thistle* (1926), Linklater's *Magnus Merriman* (1934) and Neil Gunn's study, *Whisky and Scotland* (1935). For Fergusson, it leads to a poetry charged with release from mundanity; to a fantastic and perhaps nightmarish world involving very basic responses to the pleasures of food, drink, social conviviality, and even sexuality. Although there is much shrewd Humanist reflection to be found throughout his poetry, this celebratory escapism is perhaps his major theme, and the narrative of that release provides the organising principle of much of his work.

THE HOLIDAY-DRINK-RELEASE MOVEMENT IN FERGUSSON'S POETRY

Fergusson's poetry is not often 'made' poetry, fashioned in pensive solitude, amended and deliberate. Like Burns, he did not move – nor did he have sufficient life-time to move – very far towards becoming the 'makar'. In the predicament of poverty with a lack of reflective time, the work of Fergusson is therefore much more direct. His is poetry written in the gaps of time available; poetry that catches a mood of conviviality and unusual high spirits. And since it is a poetry which identified itself with the vernacular tradition, opposed to affectation, anglicisation, and the power of the Establishment, it is a poetry that takes its vital energy from popular speech. But while we find energy and ferocity in the popular response to hunger, poverty and the greyness of life, we find little approaching a considered poetic statement from an evenhanded poet reflecting on a whole society. His poetry is not, therefore, to be analysed as a conventional development or unity. What we find instead are the same themes, settings and preoccupations, recast again and again. The bulk of Fergusson's Scots poetry can broadly be seen as a long fragmented poem which has Edinburgh as its main subject. Yet it is not a rounded view of the Edinburgh city experience. For all that these poems have lawyers and councillors and fisherfolk as their ostensible topic, Fergusson does not often explore the actualities of the law or city or the characteristics of fisherfolk. Instead, he uses them as points of departure, pegs on which to hang his real subjects; his Edinburgh burghers and their diversions and release from drudgery. What skews this view, making it, like the satires of Burns, powerfully effective but very subjective, is the reductive holiday-drink-release factor, and the way in which so much of the poetry looks at Edinburgh and its society through the bottom of a glass, from the point of view of the critical celebrant observing Edinburgh on holiday.

AN EDINBURGH CALENDAR OF HOLIDAYS?

Fergusson wrote many poems, of course, which focus on topics and situations other than holiday, but many of them fit within a composite perspective which views Edinburgh in terms of a matrix of holiday, drink, release, and the defiant, maudlin indulgence which follows. Edinburgh with its classes, its pretensions, and its politics, viewed by the inebriated drinker, is refracted through an eye which changes as the drink-aided release takes the observer from ease to anger. Few Scottish poets within the tradition of drunken celebratory escape have managed to synthesise so completely his own and his lower-class fellow citizens' drink-aided responses to their predicament.

The themes and stages of holiday-drink-release can be fairly clearly distinguished. A great many of Fergusson's poems celebrate local holidays or seasonal festivities – to the extent that they can be seen almost to comprise an Edinburgh calendar of public holidays, from 'The Daft Days' (the holidays at New Year) to the important dates of the sitting and rising of the Court of Session (the Court sat for two sessions, November–March and June–August), the King's Birthday in June, the Leith Races in July, Hallow-Fair in November, and annual events like the election of the magistrates. Even poems not explicitly linked to a holiday often carry its mood, like 'Caller Oysters', celebrating the arrival of the Musselburgh fishwives with their sea-fare. Throughout many of these poems runs the sentiment expressed in 'The Election' – that after extended deprivation and dull monotony, ordinary burghers should rejoice, since 'lang-look'd-for's come at last!'. What emerges from these holiday poems is a kind of 'meta-poem', never formally planned, but constituting an overall gathering of statements which add up to a grand Edinburgh poem of holiday release, expressing the moods of the ordinary Edinburgh citizen (cobblers, coopers, and the lower orders with whom Fergusson, as a sorely-worked clerk, could identify) who endures long spells of hard work, but escapes occasionally into riotous self-indulgence, in ways which are archetypically Scottish in their mood-changes and expression. (Something like this can be seen in the work of the later Edinburgh poet, Sydney Goodsir Smith, who admired Fergusson. In two of his poetic works, *Under the Eildon Tree* (1948) and *Kynd Kittok's Land* (1965), Smith brought together separate poems, elegies on aspects of love set in Edinburgh in the former, and affectionate meditations on Edinburgh in the latter, in such a way that they could be regarded either as distinct poems or as elements in a larger whole.)

The holiday-drink-release corpus of poems apparently celebrate several calendar events, but their underlying and recurrent theme is quickly revealed. They are about the response of ordinary folk to the opportunity to escape everyday toil and inhibition, and from them emerges a kind of template for an Edinburgh day – or night – which has distinct stages of development.

The first stage involves an acute physical response to food and drink, with the poems emphasising and relishing the details of chewing and swallowing rather than just referring to the acts of drinking and eating. Poems like 'Caller Oysters' and 'The Daft Days' exemplify this explicitly. 'The Daft Days' is a good starting point, with its subversion of pastoral conventions. Instead of Pan presiding, it is 'mirk December's dowie face' glowering over the fields, and 'frae naked groves nae birdie sings', nor do shepherds pipe. The *literati* may celebrate this spurious world, Fergusson implies, but for ordinary mortals it is 'the big-arsed bicker' [*large-bottomed beaker!*] which cheers ordinary mortals in the dark of the year. And holiday is important because:

When merry Yule-day comes, I trow	*believe*
You'll scantlins find a hungry mou;	*scarcely; mouth*
Sma' are our cares, our stamacks fou	
O gusty gear,	*savoury good things*
And kickshaws, stranger to our view	*novelties*
Sin fairn-year.	*last year*

Whether it be the September fish-fair of the Leith Races, the arrival of the lawyers or the election of magistrates, the real theme is that of the contrast between haves and have-nots, play and work, the changes of the economic seasons which affect the lowly citizen. For example, 'The Sitting of the Session' shows how lawyers' business is loved because it wets many a thirsty mouth, gaping like an empty barrel, and puts 'ilk chiel's whittle in the pye' [*every fellow's knife in the pie*]. 'The Sitting' and 'The Rising' of the courts also allow Fergusson to remark wryly how:

> The wily writers, rich as Croesus,
> Hurl frae the toon in hackney chaises
> For country cheer . . .

Lawyers, provosts, and even farmers can rise above economic seasons, but not those who have to endure the city deprivation.

The first stage of the drink movement ends in good humour, and 'stappit wame' [*a full belly*]; a transformation now takes place, exemplified again in 'The Election', as an ordinary fellow *now* (Fergusson emphasises the change!) becomes 'a pow of wit and law', an armchair philosopher, for the evening. With crude realism, the poem portrays how the guests jostle for seats at their banquet, slavering with hunger, their teeth working faster than their tongues as they gratify pent-up appetites.

The second stage is marked by the wild humour which follows corporal satisfaction, a mood which is satirical, self-mocking and fantastic, in sharp contrast to the values and structures of respectable sobriety. There are grotesque, colourful metaphors, and cartoon-like depictions such as 'the bleer-eyed sun' sourly grimacing at the opening of vividly comic images in 'The Daft Days'. Burns derived two of his finest comic personifications, those of Fun and Superstition in 'The Holy Fair' from Fergusson's fun-loving peasant girl personification in 'Leith Races'; cheerful Mirth starts off the day which ends up with drunkenness and the violence of 'the black banditti', the town guard. Burns borrowed another of Fergusson's vivid and humorous personifications, this time the clever play on proverb which makes 'Langlook'd for' the name of an old friend returning in 'The Election', and which re-appears in the opening of 'The Ordination'. The poems develop grotesque and extraordinary images, transforming the grey city. This fanciful mood will change the contents of the chamber-pots of Edinburgh into 'Edina's roses', just as the 'plouky noses' of the drunkards in 'Caller Oysters' are transformed into 'simmer roses', while in 'The King's Birthday' the great cannon of Edinburgh castle, Mons Meg, is transformed into an unfortunate Edinburgh lady whose children are the cannonballs.

Predictably the third stage is that of aggression and social defiance, expressing itself through the 'canker'd snarl' of 'The Daft Days', or the violence of the town guard towards Jock Bell in 'Hallow Fair', and the way that argument becomes bloody confrontation in 'Leith Races'. This kind of disputative quarrel can also be seen in 'A Drink Eclogue', where Brandy and Whisky battle out their class merits, with Whisky the 'cottar loun' and Brandy the affected *literatus*. Their quarrel is ended – like many a drunken debate by the intercession of the landlady. It is clear that Fergusson's sympathies in these poems lie with the underdogs and the social outcasts. In 'The Mutual Complaint of Plainstanes and Causey' (where 'Plainstanes' is the verge of the road, used by ladies and better classes, while 'Causey' is the hard-worked middle of the road, of sterner stone and honest labour), Causey tells Plainstanes defiantly to:

> tak your beaux and macaronies
> Gie me trades fock and country Johnies . . .

and they decide to take their quarrel to the Robin Hood Club, well-known for the vigour and sometimes violence of its debates. Frequently such quarrels and class confrontations end in a fall, as in 'The King's Birthday', when the hated city guard get their 'clarty unctions' from the mob, or the aristocracy get their come-uppance, in ways which anticipate the similar twentieth-century reductive scenes of the later Edinburgh poet, Robert Garioch, who felt such kinship with Fergusson:

> Dead pussy, dragled thro' the pond
> Taks him a lounder
> Which lays his honour on the ground
> As flat's a flounder . . .

This reduction of pretentious show runs all through Fergusson's poetry, from the proud but drunk Deacon of 'The Election' who refuses a sedan chair but 'arslins kiss'd the causey / Wi' bir that nicht', to the splendid picture of the showy *beaux* or *macaronis* and their bruiser bodyguards reduced to the gutter at the end of a wild evening. Related to this mood of class-antagonism is, of course, Fergusson's attack on the importation of foreign music and 'vile Italian tricks' in place of Scottish heritage in 'Elegy on the Death of Scots Music'. This phase is characteristically Scottish; a mood of aggressive defiance towards all incomers, a retreat in the end into a 'wha's like us' gut nationalism that finds expression in physical violence. This is a more belligerent nationalism than that of Ramsay's 'The Vision', and it reveals itself in the ending of a great number of the holiday poems.

The concluding stage manifests itself in maudlin affection for people or places, irrespective of their merits. Since these ordinary folk cannot change their city and its systems, a virtue is made of necessity, and even the city guard are made into comic figures who can be accepted. 'Auld Reikie' [*Old Smelly*] is a name for Edinburgh which, like Fergusson's great poem of that title, makes an affectionate yet critical synthesis. Fergusson's address 'to My Auld Breeks' does the same thing, in its derogatory yet fond farewell to his useless garments. This oxymoronic conclusion, making the best of bad things or situations, is outstandingly represented in 'The Election'. Arriving home from the celebrations, Will finds his wife in bed with Soutar Jock. Fergusson spares none of the sordid details, with Will beating them 'wi a souple leathern whang'. This is the predictable end to the holiday-drink-release movement, typical of the poetry; but there is a final twist which not even Burns could have bettered, and which makes very clear Fergusson's final respect, despite his recognition of their drunken failings, for his very ordinary and human fellows:

Now, had some laird his lady fand,	*found*
In sic unseemly courses,	
It might hae loos'd the haly band,	*holy band, wedding ring*
Wi law-suits and divorces.	
But the niest day they a' shook hands,	*next*
And ilka crack did sowder,	*made up their differences*
While Meg for drink her apron pawns	
For a' the gudeman cow'd her	*frightened*
Whan fu' last nicht.	*drunk*

These poems may embody a sometimes shocking picture of the poorer side of Edinburgh, but they have at their heart, and at the heart of the matrix of holiday and drink, a warm and realistic humanity which mocks the pretensions of the gentry and shows that, however low life may get, people retain astonishing energy and resilience. The third last line of the verse quoted shows that the drink cycle will start all over again – with its humour, fantasy, snarling quarrel and violence – but this perpetual recurrence by no means reveals the whole of the story.

MAJOR SCOTS SATIRES AND CELEBRATIONS

Fergusson's Scots poetry is not, however, limited to this inebriated movement, and the few more ambitious poems he has left indicate his huge talent and promise. Burns's 'Address to the Unco Guid' is brilliantly anticipated in 'Braid Claith', where Fergusson doubts whether polite Edinburgh would take anyone seriously unless they *looked* the middle-class part. His reductive idiom is nowhere put to better effect than in the high and low images he juxtaposes in his conclusion:

For thof ye had as wise a snout on	*wore as wise a nose*
As Shakespeare or Sir Isaac Newton	
Your judgement fouk wou'd hae a doubt on	*would doubt*
I'll tak my aith,	
Till they cou'd see ye wi' a suit on	
O' guid braid claith.	

Perhaps Fergusson's greatest political poem, in which he followed the epic national complaint of Ramsay's 'The Vision', is 'The Ghaists', in which the poet raises the ghosts of two great Edinburghers, George Watson and George Heriot, philanthropic merchants who endowed hospitals and schools for the poor, from Greyfriar's graveyard. The poem implies disillusionment with the

141

Act of Union and its economic results, and focuses on the infamous Mortmain Bill of 1773; Westminster's decision to force charitable institutions to invest in government stock at a low rate of interest – leaving the poor of Scotland 'starving for England's weel at *three per cent*'. Savagely, Fergusson attacks the corrupt King George III, shockingly concluding the poem with old Heriot determined, since all else has failed, to seek help for Scotland from Auld Nick (the Devil) as his instrument of justice in these unnatural times. Nick will send 'fireflaught and hail' and make the Tweed overrun its banks till Scotland is separated from England. The poem's distinction lies in its *gravitas*; it ends with an invocation to Sir George Mackenzie (1636–91), founder of the Advocates' Library and opposer of Charles II in his efforts to unite the kingdoms, in which he is asked to awaken, like Finn McCoull or Arthur, and to 'fleg the schemers o' the *mortmain bill*'.

Beyond his satirical poetry, Fergusson could celebrate Scottish life as successfully as Burns. Indeed, in 'The Farmer's Ingle' he arguably succeeds in his depiction of simple country people and rusticity where Burns, in 'The Cottar's Saturday Night', failed. In *Robert Burns* (1966), David Daiches considers Fergusson's poem to be 'one of the finest descriptions of rural life in either English or Scottish poetry', and finds his treatment 'unforced', where Burns self-consciously moralises. Fergusson does not adopt Burns's false (and, for Burns, hypocritical?) stances towards the 'wretch, the villain, lost to love and truth' who might seduce fair Jenny, but instead accepts the illegitimate children and the gossip as simple facts of life, just as he accepts his fallen townspeople. Where Burns has his 'lisping infant, prattling', Fergusson has 'simple bairnies', tired and listening to night-time stories. His unassuming poem ends with a benediction on 'the husbandman and a' his tribe'. Once again, one can only speculate as to how this young poet might have gone on to celebrate Scotland.

His greatest poem combines satire and celebration. 'Auld Reikie' is the most vivid and vital picture we have of old Edinburgh, in its portrayal of a Saturday and Sunday in the city, with the contrast of the worldly day and the holy day anticipating Burns's contrasts of secular release and religious repression in 'The Holy Fair'. This poem, like 'The Ghaists' or 'Ode to the Gowdspink', transcends the limitations of Scots-English categorising. Next we shall consider the poem in a different context; as a triumphant synthesis of vernacular energy with Humanist reflection.

ROBERT FERGUSSON AND HUMANISM

A different, but equally valid, perspective on Fergusson's attitudes and achievement is taken by F. W. Freeman in his study, *Robert Fergusson and the Scots Humanist Compromise* (1984). He views Fergusson within the context of the great intellectual movement of Humanism, to which Fergusson had access through his classical and philosophically orientated university education. Broadly speaking, Humanism was a European Renaissance intellectual movement, dating from the late fifteenth century and focusing on a man-centred rather than a God-centred universe, embracing particularly those studies relevant to such a universe: rhetoric, history, poetry, ethics and political thought. These ideas were explored through the reading of classical culture which provided models and values for imitation. Freeman sees Fergusson as the culmination of a great Humanist tradition, his use of vernacular Scots and identification with rustics being an expression of European primitivism. Much of Fergusson's poetry is concerned with the absence of order in the society he depicts and with the poet's desire to 'remake the world through his art'. Such disorder was perceived by Scots Humanists as the consequence of a growing money-grabbing Whig mercantile class and the collapse of the traditional laird-gudeman relationship. Consequently, much of their poetry is, as Freeman describes it, 'elegiac action' – a call to reassert the national heritage.

The need for continuity, in the face of change, was an important aspect of Humanist ideology. Freeman claims that Fergusson's technique and form mirror these Humanist concepts of order and continuity: in his use of appropriate language for his subject matter, his imitation of classical forms (eclogue, ode, pastoral) as well as old Scots stanzaic forms and traditional genres (town poems, satire). Equally, according to Freeman, there is a symbolic Humanist rhetoric pervading Fergusson's poetry: concepts of Nature as a mirror of God's art, *Prudentia* or the moral vision, the law of natural harmony, metaphors of the city of chaos, the social battle, the reduction of humans to insects as an expression of moral contempt, winter as social insecurity, dirt and foulness for disorder and stagnation. Viewed in this light, many of Fergusson's poems take on a more consciously symbolic and didactic quality. This perspective does not reduce the pleasure of reading them as poems of release; it reminds us that beyond the surface levels of colour, energy and vibrancy, there is a strong intellectual and philosophical underpinning to his poetry, which might have deepened and developed into a great poetry to rival the achievement of Burns had Fergusson lived beyond his twenty-four years.

'AULD REIKIE' AND 'ODE TO THE GOWDSPINK':
SOCIETY, NATURE AND POLITICS
Thus the concept of the holiday-drink-release movement and even that of the composite 'Edinburgh Poem', cannot embrace every poem by Fergusson.

There is no doubt Fergusson's long celebration of Edinburgh life, 'Auld Reikie', his greatest extended achievement, has within it many aspects of Fergusson's Humanist and nationalist heritage Here is a city set within a double frame of classical tradition and of native Scottish; on one hand fending off 'cauld Boreas blowing snell', and on the other 'noonday Phoebus with warmer ray'. The portrait of Edinburgh dwellers from provost to prostitutes depicting timeless customs and habits, celebrating the inner lives of the taverns, clubs, and city buildings, deprecating municipal corruption and new-fangled changes, all rendered in a successful balance of Scots-English, is ample evidence that Fergusson was moving towards mature and major poetic expression.

The larger poetic vision embodied in 'Auld Reikie' manifests itself in two ways: firstly, in Fergusson's attempt to shape a whole experience in time as well as place and secondly, in his commentary on the social and moral issues of the day. In his description of a complete weekend observing a full social panorama, from the Sunday kirk-going scene to family trips to Holyrood and Arthur's Seat, to considerations of town policy, we have Fergusson trying to shape a compehensive comment on Edinburgh life. It is true that he dwells disproportionately on the night-time scenes in Edinburgh (as with his holiday poems), these being the scenes in which his imagination works best. It is also true that 'Auld Reikie' can give the impression of being a series of linked poems (which lends weight to the notion that most of Fergusson's poems seem to be part of a long unplanned 'Edinburgh Poem'). But the overall effect of 'Auld Reikie' is one of unified, chiding yet affectionate celebration, and Freeman describes 'Auld Reikie' as 'Fergusson's most elaborate exposition of the Scots Humanist city' citing the poem's pervasive Humanist rhetoric of mock heroism, false light and dirt; the 'imprints of the Whig in Humanist literature'. In balancing every fair image with a dark counter-image, Fergusson is implementing the Humanist principle of 'concordia discors', the creation of harmony through opposites. The poet's Humanist vision reconciles all chaos into order.

Although they can be seen as being within the Edinburgh scene, poems such as 'Braid Claith', 'On Seeing a Butterfly in the Street' and 'Ode to the Gowdspink' are worth looking at in detail for their universalising tendency. The first two owe their success to their shrewd and humorous observation of human vanity and universal satire. The third, 'Ode to the Gowdspink', is satisfying for different reasons, and unusual in its deeper intellectual striving and its capacity to operate on a number of different levels with a darker vision of humanity. This poem is conceived in classical terms, in the form of the Horatian ode. As it develops in English and Scots, it addresses a serious, perhaps abstract subject, sometimes symbolised by a physical object or creature (as in later odes by Keats or Shelley addressing a Grecian urn or a nightingale or skylark).

The conventional pastoral opening of the poem associates the subject of the gowdspink [*goldfinch*] with spring and summer blessings. The treatment of the gowdspink is lighthearted, viewing it as a representative of Nature's art, with a pleasing exaggeration of the colour and beauty of its feathers. There is a subtle modulation between the conventionalities of Augustan poetic diction and tropes such as abstract personification and references to classical mythology and a vigorous Scots vocabulary. A change of tone in the second verse-paragraph, however, focuses on the inhumane practice of trapping the gowdspink in a cage. The dark vision of the imprisoned bird leads to the vision of Liberty and the blessing she bestows on all living beings. Love flourishes in natural freedom, not in the inhibited and confined setting of the court and city. The ode ends with the dark conclusion that life, beauty and material prosperity are as nothing without Liberty.

It has been argued that this poem shows Fergusson reflecting on European and American revolutionary movements. A poem in 1773 by an intelligent well-read man like Fergusson might well reveal an awareness of the French 'philosophes' and other political theorists, and of French and American grievances. Closer to home, while anti-Union and Jacobite sentiments may have been placated by improved material conditions of living for most Scots, talk of political freedom and greater representation could stir chords of nationalist sentiment. The personification of Liberty may well be more than an inheritance from medieval and Renaissance allegory; it may well anticipate the radical poetry of Burns. Do we now find Fergusson grappling with new and radical ideas and emotions? While we may argue as to whether the sentiments are simply those of general musing on the human condition, or whether they have a political meaning, it is Fergusson's innovative poetic treatment which makes this a fitting – and sadly prophetic – final statement for the poet who was to die confined in the Edinburgh madhouse. Once again we recognise the tragedy of this great Scottish poet of the late Enlightenment who, had he lived, could have become the contemporary and equal of Burns.

CHAPTER 9

ROBERT BURNS

The most controversial writers in Scottish literature must be Robert Burns, Walter Scott and Hugh MacDiarmid. Of the three, Burns is probably the writer who has been interpreted in the most contradictory and variable ways. Once again, the difficulty of discovering the 'real' Burns may be traced back to David Daiches's 'crisis of identity' in the self-expression of eighteenth-century Scots writers. And we are not aided in our search for the real Burns by the fact that his life and attitudes are surrounded by a mythology which can at points radically distort the reality. As an example, Burns was frequently upheld as the indisputable 'poet of the people' but the lie to this is given by the fact that, on the major issue of the day, the Patronage controversy, he took the part of the heritors. He thus supported the anglicising habit, against Reformation principles, of taking the claim to appoint parish ministers as a land-owning right and followed this by arguing in his poetry that to allow popular election of ministers was to give the 'brutes' the power to elect their own 'herds'.

This chapter considers some of the Burns mythology, and attempts to find the reality beneath it. But in the last consideration, independent of the distorting factors of biography and legend, this chapter aims to convey the importance of Burns's poetic achievement and his significance in Scottish literature.

Poetic debts

The formal links from Ramsay to Fergusson to Burns have already been shown. The preceding chapter sought to illustrate the tendency towards an ironic and satirical critique of Scottish society and life amongst vernacular poets through their use of an idiom which is savagely and mockingly reductive. The sense of the poets' identification with the non-Establishment stratum of society both in their stance towards their subjects and also their assumed readers, suggests a notion of vernacular community which disappears in the nineteenth century. Scott, Hogg, Galt and the later novelists, however much they employ the vernacular or spoken dialogue, are very much in the position of sharing a *superior* position with their readers, whom they assume to be of a different and higher class, with correspondingly different values, broadly viewing the speech patterns and ideas of the vernacular speakers as inferior, if intriguingly entertaining. Burns in one sense (and perhaps to some extent Hogg) stands at the end of a community of vernacular speakers and writers. The other common feature of the vernacular poets, that of the 'holiday' or 'release' strain, will too be found in Burns. Yet a final shared trait – and perhaps weakness of these poets – is that outside the realm of satire their work can be somewhat simplistic in social and political thought, in a sense represented by Burns himself when he says in 'Epistle to William Simson':

> The *Muse*, nae *Poet* ever fand her
> Till by himsel' he learn'd to wander
> A-down some trottin burn's meander
>   An' no think lang . . .

Burns certainly acknowledges his debt to Fergusson explicitly and frequently. There are references to Fergusson in the first 'Epistle to John Lapraik' and in the 'Epistle to William Simson' (especially the second stanza). Burns saw Fergusson as 'my elder brother in misfortune, / By far my elder brother in the muse', and castigated the 'Edinburgh gentry' for refusing to recognise his progenitor's genius; and it was Burns, not the Edinburgh *literati*, who erected a headstone for Fergusson in Canongate kirkyard.

Burnsian myth and cultural identity

The identification with Fergusson is only one of the many *personae* which Burns adopted in the course of his poetic career. One of the main roles he played was that of the 'heaven-taught ploughman', after it was foisted on him by Henry Mackenzie and others like him. Yet Burns, far from being 'heaven-taught' or an autodidact, had a tutor in John Murdoch, who taught him, his brother and the children of the adjoining farm, and introduced him to the work of polite writers of the day, such as Shenstone, Gay and Prior. Murdoch was to become the local schoolmaster, and then schoolmaster at Ayr Academy. The style in prose that he passed on to Robert Burns is heavy and affected, but very far from illiterate. Murdoch introduced Burns to the best of English writing and grammar at the time, but nothing at all of the medieval makars or Ramsay or Fergusson. Burns had in a sense to 'unlearn' this anglicised education in order to rediscover authentic Scottish tradition. James Hogg was to acquire this tradition from his astonishing mother, a tradition-bearer of her area and time; Burns seems to have gathered this from his mother's maid, who had a huge collection of stories of devils, brownies, witches, warlocks, kelpies, wraiths and apparitions, and this informal but genuine cultural education went on alongside his formal education.

At the root of much of Burns's 'crisis of identity' is a great uncertainty and prickliness concerning his social position. There is pride and integrity about his own statements regarding his humble origins; but also, frequently, an assertion of social sophistication upheld on the terms of the very aristocratic ideals he so often claims to despise. Burns was a farmer's son in a time when the days of the small, self-sufficient farmer were passing in Scotland; in addition, Burns and his family suffered from bad harvests and the poor land of a succession of farms. These were to cause his father's death, and indirectly his own. Another myth can be disposed of here. In an age of heavy drinking and conviviality, it was not drink which destroyed Burns, but rheumatic heart disease, accelerated by the fact that Burns did a man's heavy work on his father's farm from boyhood until he became an exciseman. Even then he had to ride more than 200 miles a week in the course of his duties. For a sensitive and creative boy it is little wonder that life often appeared in dark and melodramatic terms, and that Henry Mackenzie's *The Man of Feeling* (1771) with its overdrawn sentimentality and melodramatic style, should prove initially so attractive. Ironically, the very *literati* whom Burns was later to scorn, were supplying his earliest model of literature. Burns's autobiographical letter to Dr Moore of August 1787 can be found in the Ross Roy / De Lancey Ferguson *The Letters of Robert Burns* (1985), telling of the death of his father's generous master, the ruinous bargain of the farm, the villainous factor (who is described in 'The Twa Dogs'), and the breaking of his father's spirit. It is couched in Mackenzie-like terms. He may contrast his situation with those of fiction, but his style is exactly that of *The Man of Feeling*:

> A Novel Writer might perhaps have viewed these scenes with some satisfaction, but so did not I: my indignation yet boils at the recollection of the scoundrel tyrant's insolent threatening epistles, which used to set us all in tears . . .

This is not to dispute the truth of Burn's account; but the style he used to express himself to Moore at the age of twenty-eight is very different from the style of the vernacular and satirical poems. His very first poetry reflects this division of style.

In a sense Burns strove for the rest of his life to attain a position where he could unite his reflective, philosophical and ironic view of the Establishment and the oppression he perceived in society with his local and genuine vernacular voice. Importance has been attached by critics to the influence of Burns's father, William Burnes, and his *Manual of Religious Belief in the Form of a Dialogue between Father and Son* (which may have been transcribed by John Murdoch). Thomas Crawford argues (in *Burns*, 1960) that this manual, far from being extremely Calvinist or 'Auld Licht' in its religious tone, was unusually liberal and stressed the value of subjective experience and reason; and, most importantly, the recognition of an eternal conflict between the animal instincts of man's nature and controlling reason. Crawford argues that this last preoccupation of the manual profoundly affected Burns.

Burns's personae

Crawford's diagnosis of his father's religious influence on Burns leads to consideration of Burns's ever-changing responses, and style of response, to experience. It is this chameleon alteration of opinion which leads to Burns being so frequently cited as a proponent of every conceivable belief from communism to Toryism, from atheism to Christianity. He will tailor his attitudes and alter his *persona* according to the audience he is addressing in poem or letter. For example, in his description of his formative years for Dr Moore, a member of Edinburgh polite society, Burns slants his autobiography away from tavern jollity and peasant identification and instead couches it in the terms and style of Mackenzie's fashionable hero, the 'Man of Feeling' – or his anti-hero, as portrayed in *The Man of the World* (1773). He distorts his adolescence for Moore, bringing forward his introduction to dancing lessons to the age of seventeen, when in reality he was more than twenty, so that his propensity to self-improvement in manners and sensibility is exaggerated; and he plays the 'Man of the World' when he tells Moore that the great misfortune of his life was 'never to have an AIM'. This dubiety as to his projected identity stayed with him all his life.

From early on, then, Burns had several poses at his poetic disposal. He had, in the simple and 'artless' love songs, the *persona* of the 'heaven-taught ploughman'; he had in his more ambitious fragments and attitudes the pose of the 'Man of Feeling'; when it suited him, he had the more wordly and sceptical voice of the 'Man of the World'. He also drew on elements of Macpherson's depictions of the 'noble savage' when required. He developed another pose as 'The Ranting Dog, the Daddy O't', in which he shed his 'Man of Feeling' sensibility and asserted his right to be a passionate peasant,

149

contemptuous of sophisticated criticism. And in addition to these roles, in his letters of the period, he can be seen cultivating the pose of the sardonic observer of men and affairs, telling Thomas Orr in 1782 that he was 'studying men, their manners & their ways, as well as I can. Believe me, Tom, it is the only study in this world will yield solid satisfaction.' His *Commonplace Book* of 1784 reveals all these *personae* jostling for ascendancy, with the 'sardonic observer' summed up in the opening flourish.

It has to be recognised that Burns was complicit in formulating the 'heaven-taught ploughman' mystique (just as, a generation later, Hogg was to be complicit in the creation of his role as 'The Ettrick Shepherd'). His friendships at this point reflect his split loyalties: some are expressed in his apparently frank, encouraging and down-to-earth verse-epistles to fellow peasant poets, like Davy Sillar and John Lapraik, local popular poets working in the vernacular; but he also maintained friendships with his landlord, the local lawyer Gavin Hamilton, and later many other upper-class figures in Ayrshire and Edinburgh like Dr Moore and Mrs Dunlop, and notably Mrs McLehose with whom he had a hyper-affected and pretentious love affair ('Clarinda', to whom he played the affected 'Sylvander').

The truth about Burns's character is still elusive. Gilbert, his brother, claimed that in his Ayrshire period Burns never spent over seven pounds per annum on himself, and that 'his temperance and frugality were everything that could be wished'. It is true that his relationships became ever more complex, culminating in the extreme problems which he had with his common-law marriage to Jean Armour, with his unwilling father-in-law and the Kirk Session, as well as his various relationships with several other women. Early biographers began to look for reasons beyond simple self-indulgence; and two perceptive critics, R. L. Stevenson in his pioneeering essay, 'Some Aspects of Robert Burns' (in *Familiar Studies of Men and Books* 1882), and Catherine Carswell in her ground-breaking biography, *The Life of Robert Burns* (1930), explore Burns's need for affairs with different classes and kinds of women, perceptively suggesting that he had a deep-seated insecurity which required reassurance and self-recognition from them in a world which often seemed unstable and hostile. The question as to how much he had to live up to his local reputation as a peasant Don Juan and how much he was genuinely, passionately caught up in each of his affairs will never be satisfactorily answered. Yet it is interesting to compare the extremes in his sexual identity, from the boastful assertions of male superiority of the 'ranting dog, the daddy o't' where Burns expresses himself through the pathetically vulnerable *persona* of the exploited woman, to the totally different tone of 'thou's welcome wean, mishanter fa' me', his tender and delightful apology for, and celebration of, the birth of his first illegitimate daughter Elizabeth in 1785.

Perhaps it was his visit to Edinburgh in 1786, when he was lionised by polite society, which helped Burns gain the perspective which would allow him to rediscover the integrity of his native past, as well as to see the creative limitations of the Edinburgh *literati* themselves. When Burns visited Ramsay in Ochtertyre in 1787, he was asked whether the *literati* had improved his poems with their comments. He replied, 'these gentlemen remind me of some spinsters in my country, who spin their thread so fine that it is neither fit for weft nor woof', and that he had not changed a word. By this time he had certainly decided to which tradition he belonged.

The songs

Any consideration of Burns's literary significance must recognise his immense achievements in song, both in creation and collection. It is impossible here to do credit to this, since proper consideration of its many aspects go beyond literary concerns; indeed, the degree to which songs can be regarded within a literary context is limited, since a study of the words alone is obviously an unsatisfactory enterprise; with different aesthetic criteria, crossing many borders, necessary for assessing song. (For those wishing a detailed treatment of Burns's lyrical skills, an outstanding analysis of the metrical, formal and other sound pattern devices of the songs of Burns can be found in Thomas Crawford's *Burns*, 1960.)

It is hard to estimate just how directly Burns drew from inherited tradition for the material for his songs. Furthermore, Burns was working first from a recognisable tune and then fitting his words. The achievement of great songs like 'Mary Morison' or 'O My Luve's like a red, red rose' is not that of made poems like 'The Holy Fair' or 'The Twa Dogs'. In a song like 'O My Luve's like a red, red rose', the creative process seems to be partly one of elimination, in that the words are reduced to only those which simply state the essence of a feeling or observation. The patterns and arrangements are often those of a folksong and balladry (such as David Buchan has categorised in *The Ballad and the Folk*, 1972). To what extent Burns innovates within these rules is almost impossible to ascertain. That process of winnowing down, so that the bare bones of folk statement remain in an elemental and archetypal essence, separates Burns's song achievement from his crafted poetry, which this chapter will mainly consider. This is not to belittle his achievement as a song writer and collector; his contributions in the later stages of his life to Johnson's *Musical Museum* (1707–1803) are inestimable, Burns undertaking the lion's share of collection for that hugely important repository of traditional Scottish music.

Social poetry

The term 'social poetry' covers a variety of types of verse: epistles and addresses to individuals; occasional verse; highly personalised (and often relatively uncrafted) poems for a specific one-off situation; and explicitly 'made' poetry, such as narrative poems like 'Hallowe' en', a cantata like 'The Jolly Beggars', the supernatural extravaganza 'Tam o' Shanter', as well as specific social satires like 'The Address of Beelzebub' or 'The Twa Dogs'.

Epistles and addresses

The verse epistle 'To William Simson, Ochiltree', is one of the most representative examples in this genre. Here is rambling, genial, constantly-changing subject matter, with all the virtues of a natural, strong epistolary style, and with a leavening of the simplistic 'heaven-taught ploughman' strain running all through, along with a nationalistic prickliness. After the opening stanzas, in which Burns adopts a pose of modesty in the face of Willie's flattery, he moves into a specific statement about his stance towards vernacular poetry; referring to Allan Ramsay, Hamilton of Gilbertfield, and, outstandingly, Fergusson, with the famous curse on the 'Edinburgh gentry' in stanza four. Stanza five typically changes the topic, to bring in the 'spontaneity' of his writing, and its cause – the lassies, inspiration and 'sad disease'. His muse, he says, 'gies me ease', and in the epistles indeed it does seem as though he is relaxing. It is this spontaneous quality which gives them their strength but also their weakness. A familiar strain follows, in which, as with Ramsay and Fergusson, Burns condemns the lack of Scotland's and particularly Ayrshire's or Kyle's ('Coila's') bards. Scotland is seen as having lost confidence in herself, and while the East has been celebrated by Ramsay and Fergusson, and the Borders have their great ballads, Burns deplores the lack of poetry about his native Ayrshire. This leads to a semi-visionary invocation of William Wallace. But the difference between this and Ramsay's greater intensity, ambition and power in 'The Vision' is easily seen, as Burns's two enthusiastic nationalist verses are quickly followed up by a celebration of nature's charms in the second half of the poem. Perhaps most controversially, in the second half, Burns makes his assertion that nature speaks directly to the sensitive and humble heart, and that no poet can find inspiration until he has learned to be in tune with that nature, forgetting the intellect in favour of intuitive, heartfelt inspiration. Clearly, some disingenuous role-playing is being indulged in here, in light of what we know of his actual educational background. It is clearly a role to which he is happy to resort, but which can lead to what might be considered cliché, for example, in the second last stanza about the 'warly race' [*the wordly folk*], and their worlds apart from the simplicities of the ploughman poet. The Standard Habbie stanza is perfectly mastered here; the pattern and sounds of this specific metre are so familiar to Burns that he can write it almost without effort, perhaps with too easy an ability.

Other epistles, such as 'Epistle to Davie', 'Epistle to a Young Friend', 'Dedication to Gavin Hamilton', and 'To James Smith', reveal a similar tendency to adopt the simple poet pose, but other notes come in: an increased bitterness and satirical edge in 'Epistle to Davie', a moralising tendency in 'Epistle to a Young Friend', a satirical reflection on Calvinist morality in the 'Dedication', and an awareness of the temporary nature of life and poetic fame in 'To James Smith'. It seems to be the case that when Burns moves away from addressing a real person, to address instead an idealised figure or issue, he can reflect more seriously and exercise more control over his movement of ideas.

'The Address to the Unco Guid, or the Rigidly Righteous' shows how effective Burns can be when he has a generalised satirical target in his sights. In this poem, Burns takes his theme from Solomon (in *Ecclesiastes* vii:16): the folly of the assumption of moral rectitude. In eight controlled verses, he makes a heartfelt plea for the understanding of frailty. This poem verges on religious satire; he is attacking those 'sae pious and sae holy' who are the products of the centuries following the Reformation. They are to be found in all walks of life and Burns cleverly changes the dominant metaphor in virtually every verse, so that a strikingly different image and symbolism rules over each stanza.

This rapid change of idea and topic, which was a self-indulgent feature of the epistles, becomes, in the more deliberate poetry, an asset rather than a defect. With astonishing fertility of imagination, Burns evokes different social contexts in rapid succession. Verse one uses the image of a miller watching his produce, verse two couches the argument in legal terms, verse three presents it in terms of a merchant assessing his profits, verse four changes to use the metaphors of sailors, verse five personifies 'Social Life' and 'Glee', verse six culminates in the case of the 'high, exalted, virtuous dames', given a fantastic if unlikely possibility – with a fine example of reductive idiom concluding – and the last two verses refer all these worldly states to God's judgement.

There is a further subtlety in his homogenising of all his sustained metaphors, which progressively intermingles them with larger notions of accountancy and judgement. In the penultimate verse, Burns drops his various metaphors for a simple and effective plea for tolerance since 'the moving Why' of human actions can never be fathomed; and in the final verse he transcends the world of human affairs by raising the appeal for under-standing to an omniscient God who alone can have complete empathy. A very sophisticated couplet ends the poem, in which Burns effectively conveys the complex idea that we can partially understand why and what people do, but we can never understand the fight they put up before they actually make their mistakes. The poem has a tight and well contrived structure, the verses follow a definite sequence, and it moves to a succinct and worthy conclusion.

One final important observation on the poem's language remains. It moves effortlessly between Scots and assured Augustan English, demonstrating completely that any estimation of Burns's poetry which separates 'Scots' poems from 'English', valuing the first above the second, is misleading. As in 'Tam o' Shanter' and many other of his poems, Burns uses Scots and English in effective juxtaposition, gaining effects unavailable to the simple use of one alone.

'Address to the Deil'

At first sight, Burns's 'Address to the Deil', with its Standard Habbie stanzas and its easy transition over twenty-one verses, looks to be more like the rambling verse epistles than the tightly organised 'Address to the Unco Guid'. But Burns is actually reflecting on popular mythology about the Devil; the prevailing legends and the strange relationship he holds with the peasantry. Indeed, Burns's tone towards the Devil is affectionate rather than denunciatory or satirical. The form of the poem comprises, like the longer 'Hallowe'en', a set of theories or linked reflections on the Devil's activities. It has often been remarked how Burns humanises 'Auld Hornie, Satan, Nick, or Clootie', by making him a cartoon figure, and somebody, for all his power, to be pitied, or indeed admired because of his courage. Burns's reflections summarise the world of superstition, legend and credulous invention which people have created just as much to frighten as to entertain themselves. From Burns's own experience of his story-telling granny to his self-mocking frights, Burns gives a spectrum of the ways in which the Devil is perceived throughout the country by 'countra wives' and 'young guidmen'. In the second half of the poem, Burns deliberately goes back to 'lang syne in Eden's bonie yard' and points out how, since this mythical first event, the Devil is ubiquitous. We have remarked on how Burns's tone and style change according to his recipient or audience; perhaps the most fascinating thing about this poem is the way in which he almost identifies *with* the Devil. When the poem concludes with a kind of pity for the Devil's suffering, it would appear that the poet has recognised a kindred spirit. Similarly in 'Death and Dr Hornbook. A True Story', Burns performs the feat of reducing an omnipresent supernatural figure to manageable proportions. There is perhaps something of William Blake's characteristic reversal of moral values here, together with a deliberate mockery of traditional morality, in the way the poems reject the poet's taught values (and especially the values of his father's *Manual*).

The 'Dr Hornbook' of the poem was in reality John Wilson, schoolmaster and apothecary at Tarbolton, sacked for neglecting his duties in 1791, but here associated with Death. Many of Burns's poems deal with local worthies and unworthies which is perhaps one of the ways in which the poet humanises abstract and philosophical subjects. Some critics, however, suggest that there is a danger that the poem is overloaded with too much local reference (in others, as well as here), so that the serious and general satirical point is trivialised.

'Address of Beelzebub'

Burns arouses no such doubts in this astonishing poem. Here, there is a very different orientation and a serious satirical attack is launched in a ferocious critique of John, Earl of Breadalbane, President of the Royal Highland Society, which had united in 1785 to frustrate the design of several hundred Highlanders to emigrate to Canada. For modern readers there is an unintentional added irony, in that the Scottish aristocracy are seen here trying to stop Highland clearance, when in a few decades they would do everything possible to bring it about. In this poem Burns does not use traditional vernacular form, but instead a 'Scottish Augustan' couplet, to produce a poem of only sixty-two lines with a compacted terseness and ferocity almost unrivalled in Scottish poetry. Taking a leaf out his own religious satires, Burns adopts a *persona* diametrically opposed to his own beliefs, making this one of his first dramatic monologues and foreshadowing the later 'Holy Willie's Prayer'.

Beelzebub, dating his poem 5790 (since the Creation was believed to have occurred in 4004 BC), toasts the Earl – the most successful of his catches – with a flattery of the type that, in Hogg's *Confessions of a Justified Sinner* (1824), would be applied by Gil-Martin to Robert Wringhim. The pointed satire needs little comment; it speaks for itself. What does deserve comment is

Burns's easy reference to British politics and economics, his topical references, such as to Drury Lane, as well as his assured intermingling of Scots and English, just as in the 'Address to the Unco Guid'. Here, with an absolutely clear target, Burns fashions one of his most effective satires. The uncertainty in role playing, characteristic of the epistle, has gone; the *persona* adopted is sure and skilful. Burns shows himself to be a master of sophisticated ideas. Where 'the Unco Guid' showed an awareness of the indivisible rise of religion and capitalism, this shows an equally perceptive appreciation of the ever-increasing tensions between landowners and peasantry in Scotland in 'The Age of Improvement'.

'The Twa Dogs'

On a number of occasions Burns makes use of animals as the subject or inspiration for some of his best work. In a dramatic monologue like 'The Death and Dying Words of Poor Mailie' and its companion poem, 'Poor Mailie's Elegy', Burns handles the genre of beast fable with great skill. 'The Auld Farmer's Salutation to his Auld Mare Maggie', 'To a Mouse' and 'To a Louse' show equally effective use of country metaphor and animal reference. It is worth considering whether Burns is writing in the continued tradition of Henryson's *Fables*, or whether he was merely picking up inspiration from individual poems by predecessors like Hamilton of Gilbertfield or Fergusson.

'The Twa Dogs' was the opening poem of *Poems, Chiefly in the Scottish Dialect,* published in Kilmarnock in 1786. In his poetic dialogue, or eclogue, Burns produced undoubtedly his finest exercise in the beast fable genre. It belongs to a series of dialogues used in his poetry, like 'The Brigs of Ayr', which follows in the tradition of dialogues between humble worth and 'sophisticated' pretension adopted by Ramsay and Fergusson. Luath is the collie dog of the peasant and Caesar, the Newfoundland dog of the aristocrat. Yet where 'The Brigs of Ayr' has a basic opposition of traditional peasant integrity against newfangled affectation, an added level of sophistication is provided here by the fact that these dogs of Kyle and Scotland (Burns's comic vision makes the dogs archetypal, representative of timeless national qualities) are superior to their men, having none of the defects of their owners. They also, of course, stand for simple and heroic humanity; Luath is a ploughman's collie, but the associations of his master are with Burns himself in his simple carefree poet *persona*, and Luath's name links him with the heroic figure of Cuchulain in Macpherson's Ossianic poem *Fingal.* Despite his haughty imperial name, Caesar has no false pride and will mix with dogs of any class. Detached from the class war that rages around them, the two dogs are the best of friends, and Burns sketches with a countryman's eye for detail the way in which in play they hunt, mock-fight and amicably worry each other. There is a delightful sense of irony in the way in which, after their social ploys, they grow weary and sit down to talk about 'the lords o' the creation'. The poem thus becomes a reflection on the difference between wealth and poverty, aristocracy and peasantry. What separates this poem from so many of the epistles is Burns's considered and perceptive account of the discontent of the aristocracy, despite their wealth, and the surprising resilience of the peasantry. Cleverly too, Burns makes Caesar the sympathetic spokesman for the peasants' grievances, so that it is Luath who has to insist on the overall happiness of the peasantry and to point out that it is their weariness after work and their lack of time to invent problems that makes them take such delight in the immediate satisfactions of rest and family. It is Luath too who puts in a plea for the aristocracy and their essential humanity and good-heartedness.

The reductive idiom that Burns employs to express his 'country wit' has been regarded by some critics of Scottish poetry as a limiting mode. In particlar, David Craig (in *Scottish Literature and the Scottish People*, 1961) argues convincingly with regard to this poem that the very strengths of vernacular poetry's reductive idiom, in cutting pretension down to size, can become a weakness, in that its negative manner disallows generous recognition of the richness of human art and achievement. In a sustained and perceptive comparison between Burns's savage portrayal of a young nobleman wasting his father's entailed property on a self-indulgent grand tour of Europe and Pope's treatment of the same theme in *The Dunciad* (1728), Craig points to the fact that where Pope indicates how his foppish young man misses the rich opportunities in culture and art which Europe has to offer for self-improve-ment, Burns sneers at Europe as a pointless place for his noble waster to visit; Europe's culture and aristocracy are condemned together. It is certainly true that much of the vigorous reduction of pretension in Scottish poetry comes from its assumption of a peasant or working-class community of values, and a moral fundamentalism which reaches its apotheosis in Burns's 'For a' that and a' that' (or 'A Man's a Man for a' that'), in the devastating reduction of the 'birkie ca'd a lord' to 'but a coof for a' that'. Yet it could be argued that Craig's analysis misses Burns's subtlety in putting his criticism into the mouths of beasts, and that part of the reduction is attributable to the dramatic monologues and perceptions of simpler beings. Caesar is adopting the stance of the foreign observer looking at British manners and society, and should perhaps be read in the light of Swift's *Gulliver's Travels* (1726), or Goldsmith's *The Citizen of the World* (1762). Luath, moreover, is no revolutionary; his solutions for the social division that causes the distress of the peasantry and the discontent of the gentry merely prescribe moderation of aristocratic excess and more involvement with 'countra sports'. Only a few years before the French Revolution, Burns is suggesting the rediscovery of a pyramidal social model, a kind of Tory paternalism of the kind that appealed to Matthew Bramble in *The Expedition of Humphry Clinker*. Comparison of this with another early poem, 'The Jolly Beggars' (which Burns was persuaded not to publish in the Edinburgh edition of 1787), shows yet again how Burns could represent very different values in different poems.

'Love and Liberty – a Cantata' ('The Jolly Beggars')

It is tempting to argue that Burns, both in his personal and poetic values, was moving towards the position of identification with the common man, the stance his admirers most frequently demand of him. One of the greatest of all his social satires, 'The Jolly Beggars', seems to vindicate this claim completely; and yet the evidence of his religious satires will give an entirely different perspective to this claim. We remember that Burns kept different kinds of friendships. The Sylvander-Clarinda relationship with respectable Mrs McLehose of Edinburgh produced some of his most affected style and posturing (and yet surprisingly could also produce 'Ae Fond Kiss'). The *literati* of Edinburgh, we will recall, persuaded Burns not to include 'The Jolly Beggars' in the 1787 edition – even more appropriate advice after 1789 and the French Revolution – containing as it did the poet's sentiments that 'courts for cowards were erected / churches built to please the priest.' In this poem Burns takes up the sentiments expressed in the 'Epistle to Davie' where he looked beggary in the face, contemplating the possibility that when 'banes are crazed and bluid is thin', he would have to seek shelter in barns and kilns as a bankrupt. Beggary was a very real fear for Burns in his imagination; and in 'The Jolly Beggars' he moves to an anticipation of Brecht's treatment of the underprivileged in the way that he creates a microcosm of the world in which the poor are but the shadow images of respectable society.

Alternatively entitled 'Love and Liberty – a Cantata', the poem makes use of that most traditional of riotous and holiday forms, the 'Cherry and the Slae' stanza. In manner reminiscent of Fergusson's 'The Daft Days' and his own 'Tam o' Shanter', Burns begins by contrasting the hostile weather, magnificently evoked, with the warmth and cheerfulness of the 'merry core / o' randie, gangrel bodies' who drink the proceeds of their pawned clothes in Poosie Nansie's tavern in Mauchline. Here Burns combines his genius for traditional folksong and personal invention. The poem echoes Chaucer's

Canterbury Tales, in that each character tells his or her story, with a linking recitativo – indeed there is a sense in which this is a parody of Chaucer's bigger work. The *dramatis personae* comprise the soldier ('I am a son of Mars . . .'), the prostitute ('I once was a maid . . .'), the clown or Merry Andrew ('Sir Wisdom's fool . . .'), the woman pickpocket ('A Highland lad my love was born . . .'), the dwarf fiddler ('I am a fiddler to my trade . . .'), a tinker ('My bonie lass, I work in brass . . .'), and significantly, a poet ('I am a Bard of no regard . . .'). Burns – as with Luath in 'The Twa Dogs' – seems to identify strongly with his subjects. For all the poem's apparently casual and loose structure, with its intervening songs, it has a very definite shape and contains an extremely radical criticism of contemporary politics and society. The central characters are society's cast-offs who have suffered at the hands of authority, the gentry and so-called 'civilised' British society. In the different experiences and fates of the beggars, graphically described in their own songs, a scathing comment is made on civilised society, all the more devastating for its robustly cheerful form. These randy gangrels have more love in them than in high society. Burns draws his beggar theme to its triumphant conclusion, discovering in these social outcasts, an irreducible foundation of human affection, dignity and decency. There is much here, in the mixture of polemic and song, that anticipates the ways in which in the twentieth century, Bertold Brecht would identify with suffering and impoverished humanity in plays like *The Threepenny Opera* (1928) and *Mother Courage* (1941). The bard's concluding statement (with the echo of 'for a' that and a' that' in its chorus) is clearly an amalgam of the defiant roles adopted by Burns in previous poems. But the statement works in this context, because it is articulated confidently from a distinct *persona,* who acts as a kind of shepherd for his ragged flock of squalid social misfits and outsiders.

The religious satires: Burns and religion

There was to be no simple resolution of the paradoxes arising from Burns's uncertainty about his creative identity. An account of the roles he adopts in his writing would have to include a rich and complex assortment – 'the man of feeling', the frustrated poet, the moralist, the 'roaring boy' and 'ranting dog', the bragging amorist, 'the jolly beggar', the armchair radical, the political firebrand. Integration of these various *personae* within one literary personality was difficult for Burns, especially when he wished to make positive and affirmative social or ideological comment. It was only in taking on the religious establishment of Scotland, and its excesses, that Burns found an intellectually challenging institution and controvertible creed which could provide him with the provocation that would tax his mind fully, to the extent that role-playing could be abandoned. Out of this challenge came Burns's great religious satires.

Although he was not called upon in these satires to make a full profession of faith, it is clear where he stood in religious matters at different points in his life. (An excellent account of Burns's confused stance on religious matters is given in Thomas Crawford's *Burns*, 1960.) With occasional variations, he was a moderate 'low flier' in religion, sympathetic to that civilising and common-sense school of philosophy in which religion was seen as abetting man's more liberal social urges. There was certainly a rebellious streak in him as an adolescent; as he told Dr Moore in 1787:

> polemical divinity about this time was putting the country half-mad; and I, ambitious of shining in conversation parties on Sundays, between sermon, funerals, etc. used in a few years more to puzzle Calvinism with so much heat and indiscretion that I raised a hue and cry of heresy against me which has not ceased to this hour.

The *Manual* written by William Burnes for his sons shows that he was a thoughtful and ultimately moderate man in religion. It gave Robert Burns a solid base of tolerance, and his fundamental sense that all moral life was a battle between the animal and the rational. There is some evidence that in his youth Burns was attracted by deism and even atheism, since he boasted early of walking in 'the daring path Spinoza trod'; but he also qualified this by saying that 'experience of the weakness, not the strength, of human powers, made me glad to grasp at revealed religion'. This was in 1787; at the age of twenty-eight Burns did not wish to count himself as an infidel. Nevertheless, he was always against Calvinist doctrine, and would have no truck with its central doctrines of the elect and predestination.

By that time he had completed the bulk of his religious satires, and after 1789 seems to have written no more of them. There is a basic paradox visible within them. It is that Burns, in most things the advocate of natural emotions and the common man, in this area attacked two of the values which he held most dear in his social poetry. Firstly, he turned against powerful and excessive feeling – that is, enthusiasm in religious matters; and secondly, he attacked democratic expression in church organisation – namely, popular control of the Kirk. This was to some extent focused on the issue of patronage. The question of whether a minister should be appointed by the congregation, according to the principle established after the Reforma-tion, or by the local landlords (or 'heritors') as laid down in the Government's Patronage Act, vexed the Scottish religious and political scene through most of the eighteenth century and well into the nineteenth, only to be settled by the Disruption of 1843. Surprisingly, Burns was on the side of the landowners in believing that moderation and tolerance would be best served by letting them select the minister rather than a congregation swayed by Calvinistic zeal and bigotry. In supporting patronage and the heritors, Burns was supporting religious tolerance and intellectual freedom; one instance of Burns being on the same side as the Enlightenment *literati*.

Burns of course, was opposed to the extreme doctrines of Calvinism, the main tenets of which are at the root of his religious satire. Specifically, he attacked six Calvinist beliefs: the doctrine of original sin – that as a result of Adam's transgression, all people are born sinners and liable to damnation; the idea of eternal damnation – that there is an absolute divide between salvation and damnation with no remission of the latter; the idea of a very real physical hell, a medieval notion coming out of pre-Copernican cosmology; the central notion of predestination, removing all hope of salvation being earned by good works; the doctrine of the elect, the belief that a small predestined few will enter heaven to the exclusion of all others; and justification by faith, that is, worthiness for heaven judged solely on the grounds of absolute belief.

The reality of the religious situation in Burns's time was, however, more moderate than this doctrine suggests, and the extreme believers were a minority ripe for satire without severe repercussions on the satirist. Despite the doubts and guilt complexes afflicting religious-minded people, Burns's satire found ready acceptance from most readers, as Thomas Crawford summarised in Chapter 2 of his *Burns* (1960):

> Although Burns did not by his own unaided efforts bring about the collapse of Calvinism, yet neither was he fighting battles long since won, nor kicking at a completely open door. His work was in accord with the spirit of the age, and he had many precursors; but its main value does not lie in its direct historical effects so much as in the enduring creations of universal hypocrisy he was able to fashion from a particular Scottish dilemma. Burns used a local religious situation as the raw materials of *poems*; and it is as poems, not as polemics, that the ecclesiastical satires must be judged today.

Satirical methods

It is worth beginning the survey of Burns's religious satires with a brief examination of two poems which show Burns experimenting with satiric technique. The 'Epistle to John Goldie in Kilmarnock' and 'The Twa Herds' (or 'The Holy Tulzie') show Burns adopting the *persona* of the extreme 'high-flying' sympathiser in order to express a mock approval of their religious stance, and an apparent condemnation of the local moderate ministers.

In the 'Epistle' the *persona* is not sustained, perhaps through a lack of confidence, but also because in an epistle there has to be the personal note in the speaker's address to his correspondent; in this case a moderate minister. Burns also uses personified abstractions, as he does later in 'The Holy Fair', in order to universalise the qualities of the extreme Calvinists, who have been distressed by Goldie's moderate writings. The poem is rather a hybrid, being partly satirical and partly personal and social, as Burns moves into the role of the convivial author who will use his alcohol-assisted inspiration to aid the good cause. It is in 'The Twa Herds' that Burns achieves a unified effect, by sustaining a *persona* who represents beliefs opposite to those of Burns throughout the poem. The affected pose here is that of the hard-line Calvinist sypathiser who is disturbed by the quarrel between two of the main preachers in the Kilmarnock area, John Moodie of Riccarton and 'Black Jock' Russell of Kilmarnock. In this pose Burns calls for the other extreme ministers of the region to help patch up the quarrel so that, united, they will be able to outface and drive out the moderates. Another unifying technique is employed in Burns's use of extended metaphor. The ministers are presented as shepherds of the flock, protecting them from predators, treating their ailments and resisting the incursions of the 'new-light' herds. The poem identifies the affiliations of the local ministers but Burns makes clear his own stance in the patronage question as he refers ironically (and with implied hostility) to the desire of the 'auld-lights':

> To cowe the lairds,
>   An' get the brutes the power themsels
>   To chuse their herds.

Postscript to 'Epistle to William Simson'

A more genial satirical treatment of religious polarities is found in Burns's Postscript to his 1785 verse epistle to William Simson, the schoolmaster at Ochiltree. After the rather rambling and sentimental celebration of Scots poetry in the pose of the 'heaven-taught ploughman', Burns directs a forceful, yet whimsical and fantastic, attack on the 'auld-lichts' *and* 'new-lichts' portrayed as shepherd-scholars disputing about the nature of the moon. The conflicting theories echo the Renaissance conflict between the old Copernican theory of the universe and the observations of Galileo. Burns presents the auld-lichts as dogmatic medievalists contrasted with the rational Renaissance new-lichts, with the lairds taking the role of the humane authorities putting an end to the violence of persecution and oppressyon. The satire ends in a fantastic vision of auld-lichts setting off to the moon in balloons to obtain evidence for their old-fashioned views – a humorous reduction of the whole controversy to a 'moonshine matter' unworthy of the serious attention of poets. Burns's own intellectual position is clear; the new-lichts have science and rationality on their side, as against the irrational mumbo-jumbo of the auld-lichts. The satire shows Burns handling a different technique from those already discussed. Although there is a nod in the direction of a mock-Calvinist narrative *persona*, the overall tone is that of the amused and sceptical observer. The link between moderate theology and common-sense philosophy is established in the second last verse when, from the ironic standpoint of Burns's Calvinist, Commonsense is condemned as 'that fell cur' belonging in France – a reference to Burns's own identification with the liberal ideas of the 'philosophes' in pre-Revolutionary France.

'Holy Willie's Prayer'

If these poems reveal a Burns who is still tentative in his use of satirical techniques, his dramatic monologue 'Holy Willie's Prayer' shows him in complete and assured control of his material and methods. Long before Browning's 'My Last Duchess' (1864) Burns demonstrates a mastery of the dramatic monologue (derived from the dramatic soliloquy but importing an extra level of ambiguity) in which the burden of interpretation is placed on the reader, with the true values of the poem requiring to be read in a very different way from the apparent meaning. Allan Ramsay had used the form in his 'Lucky Spence's Last Advice', and the self-revelatory voice was to become a strong feature of later Scottish fiction through Hogg and Galt to Stevenson. There are perhaps significant reasons, involving an uncertainty towards conclusive morality and fixed social value, which prompt so many Scottish writers to conceal their authorial position behind the *persona* of a character who is so often antithetical in values and identity. It is natural, therefore, to link 'Holy Willie's Prayer' with James Hogg's *Confessions of a Justified Sinner* (1824), and it has been argued that Hogg must have known Burns's satire in order to write his own powerful indictment of religious bigotry and hypocrisy.

The situation behind 'Holy Willie's Prayer' is well known; how Burns's friend and patron, Gavin Hamilton, had been tried by the Sessions in Mauchline, but had won his appeal to the Presbytery of Ayr, where he

163

was defended by the 'glib tongued' Robert Aitken. This is what inspires the supposed prayer (in reality a curse?) of Holy Willie (William Fisher, a bachelor elder of Mauchline). The power of this comparatively short poem lies in the acute perception and economical skill with which Burns has managed to convey the universal, almost epic nature of the underlying issue: how people, like Holy Willie, whatever their fundamentalist creed, are the bane of society with their self-justification and self-approbation, together with their blindness to their own personal spectrum of sin, and their effective fusion of spiritual exaltation with personal material profit. The theme is one of the most persistent in Scottish literature; Scott shows it in his portrait of David Deans in *Old Mortality* (1816), and John Galt later produced outstanding studies of this deployment of spiritual superiority for secular gain in novels like *Annals of the Parish* (1821) and *The Provost* (1822). George Macdonald and John Davidson present it in their fiction and poetry respectively, and the theme survives as late as the fiction of Robin Jenkins and Iain Crichton Smith, for example in *The Awakening of George Darroch* (1985) and *Consider the Lilies* (1968).

The poem can be regarded as having four movements. The first five stanzas contain a succinct attack on all the tenets of Calvinism that Burns abhorred. The next four stanzas present Willie's 'confession' of his own sins coupled with his application of Calvinistic 'logic' to disclaim responsibility and emerge as humbly compliant with God's will. Stanzas ten to fifteen comprise the curse proper, devoid of any sense of Christian forbearance or forgiveness, rising to a climactic scream of hatred in the words 'An' dinna spare!'. The final stanza carries a deceptively quiet conclusion, placing the emphasis on the mingled spiritual and material benefit that Willie knows he deserves. The poem moves with flawless pace and control of tone; the blend of Hebraic pulpit oratory, which captures exactly the voice of the Calvinist demagogue and his dialect vituperation, together with the underlying subtlety of its implied arguments, create a concise but epic satire that can stand with the greatest in the genre.

'The Ordination'

'The Ordination' projects the rabid intolerance of Holy Willie onto an entire community, with a supposed hard-line Calvinist narrator denouncing the moderate new-licht faction as heretics and allies of Satan, who are discomfited and driven out of the churches of the orthodox and godly by the triumphant forces of the auld-lichts. The poem was entirely topical, its occasion being the appointment in 1785 of a high-flying minister, the Reverend McKinlay, to the Kilmarnock Laigh Kirk by the heritor, the Earl of Glencairn – in this case bowing to the will of the congregation. The methods are familiar from other satires: there is a running metaphor of the minsters and congregations as shepherds and flocks of sheep; there is great play with the names of both extreme and moderate local ministers, giving a sense of reality and immediacy; there is personification of abstractions to dramatise the issues behind the local events; and there is the gloating, vengeful superiority of the Calvinistic narrator which carries an implied criticism of the speaker and his party. However, there are additional features in this religious satire worth isolating for particular examination. First, there is a consistent use of animal references and metaphors which invest the human figures in the events with a bestial quality which diminishes and degrades their humanity. Second, there is the mock-serious appearance of the Devil himself as a figure in the action, a forceful twist to the pseudo-demonism used by Burns in other poems. Most importantly, however, are the images of violence and cruelty throughout, which evoke the bad old days of religious persecution and the sadistic psychology of the religious fundamentalist glorying in the medieval apparatus of damnation and the tortures of hell. All in all, 'The Ordination' is a savage denunciation of extreme Calvinism in which the irony is perceptibly harsher than in most of Burns's other satires.

An aspect of the poem that deserves special attention is the use by Burns of a different verse form from his favoured Standard Habbie stanza. Here the form is that of the 'Christis Kirk on the Green' stanza. Why did Burns choose this form, traditionally associated with poems of social celebration? In a surprising and shocking sense, the poem is indeed about a celebration, a Calvinist 'feast' or holiday (giving a bitter twist to the idea of 'holy day'), in which the persecutions and holy exercises grimly parody the innocent high jinks and merrymaking of the 'fete champetre'. There is a disturbing point being made in the poem's theme of drunken release about the terrible unholy joy that emanates from the repressed Calvinist psyche of the Kilmarnock weavers and auld-licht preachers. The verse form ironically underscores this unholy paradox.

'The Holy Fair'

Burns's greatest achievement in religious satire ('Holy Willie's Prayer' notwithstanding) is 'The Holy Fair'. The very title is an oxymoron; that is to say, it implies a clash between the spiritual and the earthly, between holiness and earthy festivity. The occasion described is that of a sacramental gathering, a field preaching, which in the event usually became something of a holiday. Several ministers of the district got together and set up their 'tent' or pulpit, and for the day or two days that this happened the local peasantry were compelled to foregather to listen to the extended sermons. They had, of course, to refresh themselves in between these sermons with the ale and food provided. Thus what had been intended by their pastors as a holy and devout occasion instead cloaked earthly matters, reunions, love assignations, and ultimately, instead of religious enlightenment, what Burns calls 'houghma-gandie', an untranslatable word denoting holiday high spirits and fornica-tion. In this poem Burns obviously draws upon Robert Fergusson's poem 'Leith Races'. Yet, where Fergusson had Mirth as his day's companion but quickly abandoned the personification, Burns elaborates and develops the idea in a much more sophisticated way. It is also one of Burns's most highly crafted and shaped poems. Once again, as in 'The Ordination', the verse form is the 'Christis Kirk on the Green' stanza with its implications of a poem concerned with rural celebration. It has a flawless structure, with seven movements; three leading to the central movement itself, and then, as it were, a reverse set of three mirroring the first half until the poet's exit from the scene.

The first movement of six stanzas shows the poet meeting the delightful high-spirited country girl, Fun, and contrasts the poet and Fun on the one hand and the two doleful black-clad hussies, Superstition and Hypocrisy, coming behind. The second movement, verses seven to eleven, then takes the poet and Fun into the Fair itself, introducing them to the whole spectrum of country people. Again in contrast to the earthy joviality of the secular audience, Burns shows the dolefulness of the 'black bonnets'; the elders who are preparing for the ministers. Here are gentry and whores, elders and weavers, some thinking upon their sins and some upon their clothes. This section ends with the success of the ordinary peasant in finding his own dear lass, so that while the preaching commences he can sit with his arm around her. The third movement, running from verses twelve to seventeen, is Burns's central satire on the preachings of Moodie and Smith and other moderate or evangelical preachers. These three movements take us into the central fourth movement; Burns's celebration of Drink in stanzas eighteen to twenty establishes a Bacchic deity presiding like a comic pagan genius at the heart of the poem, overturning the would-be piety of the occasion. Then Burns comes out of his central position in a fifth movement (verses twenty-one and twenty-two) to revisit the preaching, this time that of Black Jock Russell. The sixth movement, from stanza twenty-three to twenty-six, shows how, after all the moral edification, the ordinary peasantry come to the most enjoyable part of the day, with guid wives and guidmen chattering together, the lads and lasses pairing off, the songs and laughter and gossip coming to a head as the day draws to its conclusion. The last movement is a single verse, twenty-seven, making a final oxymoronic and gently satirical comment and speculation summing up the poem, suggesting that the effect of the day upon the hearts of the people is very different from its official purpose. In 'The Holy Fair', Burns's satire is gentler than in, say, 'The Ordination' by dropping the pose of the Calvinist narrator, he achieves a more humane and direct tone presenting the events and characters more naturally, undistorted by caricature, and revealing their real humanity. Even the auld-licht ministers come through as men to be understood and tolerated because ultimately they cannot prevail against the tide of ordinary humanity and its timeless and irresistible natural impulses.

'Tam o' Shanter'

There is only one other poem that can compare with 'The Holy Fair' for subtlety and craft – and it is not usually considered to be a religious satire. 'Tam o' Shanter' is the most comic and fast-moving of Burns's narrative poems, and it has a clear set of secular readings: the celebration of drink and social pleasures as allies against the darker aspects of life; the dominance of the masculine spirit over the feminine; the transience of the bloom or snowflake of pleasure compared with the storm and darkness outside the bubble of the present; and the continuing power of the irrational and supernatural over the fragility of reason. Yet an interpretation of the poem in terms of *carpe diem* [*seize the day*] philosophy is to miss what can be seen as Burns's deployment of some of his most sophisticated quasi-religious ironies. Any secular moral of the poem is a trivial and humorous one – the penalties for drinking and lustfulness are insignificant. There is a more significant subtext to be analysed, which has to do with the effects, over generations, of repressive religious conditioning.

If we allow that Burns sees so much of the society around him as over-gloomy, bigoted and pleasure-denying, the theme of 'Tam o' Shanter' may be seen as a lament for the oft-remarked Scottish habit of denying pleasure; if a day is brilliantly sunny, then a price must later be paid. The poem does not merely argue that as the flower of pleasure is seized, its bloom is shed, it argues also that sad Scots do not seek the flower enough, or that when it is plucked, guilt and self-torment are its bouquet. At the beginning of the poem Tam surrounds himself defensively with warmth, sociality, affection; he is defiantly shutting out the memory of his 'sulky sullen dame'. Threatening all this conviviality is the knowledge that the hour approaches in which he must

167

depart on his long journey back to the harsh realities of his mundane life. On this journey he crosses over two key-stones, or two arches. The first is midnight, the traditional witching hour, beyond which he enters a territory of demonic apparition and topsy-turvy horror. He stays in this territory until he crosses the second arch, the Brig of Doon, beyond which lie his home and reality. Burns emphasises these two arches; they can indeed differentiate the real from the supernatural – but perhaps we can also allow that what happens between the arches can be read in a different sense from the usual traditional and supernatural interpretation.

Tam is riding home in darkness. In a dwam he lapses into dreamlike and subliminal reflection on all the things he enjoyed and desired in the pub. His mind is full of fading desires – colour, the warm fire, song and story, the friendliness of the landlady and the desire for much more. Yet, as an average Scottish Presbyterian, Tam, with his wife waiting at home, knows well that all these are taboo pleasures. After the pleasures of the pub, there must be a reckoning. In another interpretation of Burns's poetic vision, and one which anticipates much of the creative ambiguity of the fiction of Scott, Hogg, Stevenson, and the fiction and poetry of the writers of the Scottish Renaissance of the twentieth century, Burns allows a psychological reading to co-exist with an older supernatural interpretation. There is buried religious satire here, as Tam's repressed imagination creates tormented and meta-morphosed images of the things he desires, twisted into nightmare shapes attended by punishment and guilt. The conviviality of the inn becomes the wild riot of witches in Alloway Kirk; the sexual promise and camaraderie of the landlady becomes the blatant sexual temptation of the young witch Nannie, the 'Cutty Sark' of Tam's libido; and all the repressed desires for song and dance and sexuality are presided over by the monstrous black dog form of Auld Nick himself, who calls the tune and plays the pipes. By articulating his desire in calling out 'Weel done, Cutty Sark!', Tam admits his sinful human lust and brings his nightmare to a head. His conscience's need for correction – and punishment – is imminent until Tam crosses the second arch back into normality, leaving his dream fantasy behind him. What Burns implies is that Tam has morbidly fastened upon his own guilty desires and created his own hell. The closing *moralitas* stresses Burns's ironic point, that pleasure is too highly priced; he has reminded us throughout that Tam is drunk (and hallucinating, with the aid of 'bold John Barleycorn'?); and he clinches his point by 'warning' his readers that they may buy the pleasures to which their thoughts incline at too high a price – that price being exemplified in Tam's case as the tail of his horse, the end of the tale, the tale of pleasure-seeking which has in fact no sting in it.

This reading of the poem suggests that 'Tam o' Shanter' could be subtitled 'The Presbyterian's Nightmare', a sophisticated and concealed religious satire, where the target is not the institution of the Presbyterian church and its extreme supporters but the psychological condition which it induces in its victims. In that sense the poem is a parallel in some respects to James Hogg's *Confessions of a Justified Sinner* (1824), in which Robert Wringhim undergoes a similar torment of images of sinful self-indulgence when he enters into his Dalcastle inheritance. There is also a parallel with the much later satirical poem by Hugh MacDiarmid, *A Drunk Man Looks at the Thistle* (1926). It is important, however, to realise that such a reading of the poem does not cancel out other readings, but presents an extra perspective on it. With this poem, Burns leaves his reader with the height of his achievement – apparently effortless and traditionally influenced poetic utterance, but with total control of content and form, with hidden contemporary satire and social reflection lying, like Shakepeare's, beneath a hugely entertaining surface narrative drama – and more; with Scots and English deployed with equally impressive facility, each heightening and working with the other, in as great an exhibition of deceptively simple art as English or Scottish literature can offer.

CHAPTER 10

TOBIAS SMOLLETT: *THE EXPEDITION OF HUMPHRY CLINKER*

TOBIAS SMOLLETT (1721–71)

Tobias Smollett was born in Dumbarton, son of a judge and Scottish Member of Parliament; and educated locally and at Glasgow University, and then apprenticed as a doctor-apothecary. His apprenticeship over, he tried his hand at literature in London with *The Regicide* (published in 1749), a tragedy on the assassination of James I of Scotland. Failing to find a stage for this, he studied medicine which enabled him to serve as a ship's surgeon on the West Indian Carthagena expedition of 1741 and to attempt to practise as a doctor in London. Soon, however, he devoted himself completely to literature, publishing his first novel, *Roderick Random*, in 1748. Other novels followed, along with translations of Lesage, Cervantes and Voltaire, *A Complete History of England*, and *Travels through France and Italy* (1776). He was involved in political journalism in support of Lord Bute's administration, but his health began to decline and he settled in Italy for the last few years of his life, where he wrote his final novel, *The Expedition of Humphry Clinker* (1771), published just before his death.

In spite of his talents, however, his life was one of continual financial and personal struggle, with bitter quarrels with other writers like Fielding, Churchill, and Wilkes – and some of these, like his attacks on Admiral Knowles (of the disastrous Carthagena expedition) and on Lord Bute, saw him in serious trouble, in prison or virtual exile. His travel writings, while filled with insight (such as foretelling revolution in France) are marked by his cantankerous subjectivism, finding in France and Italy dirt and discomfort, and mocking many of Europe's finest treasures, from the Venus de Milo to the Pantheon. His literary output was huge but his reputation is founded largely on his novels, placing him firmly alongside Defoe, Fielding, Richardson and Sterne as one of the pioneers of the novel form in English.

Smollett's fiction

Smollett wrote five novels. In addition to *Humphry Clinker*, they are: *The Adventures of Roderick Random* (1748), *The Adventures of Peregrine Pickle* (1751), *The Adventures of Ferdinand Count Fathom* (1753) and *The Life and Adventures of Sir Launcelot Greaves* (1762).

Roderick Random was written when he was twenty-seven, and includes much of his own experience, especially of the Carthagena expedition. Roderick tells his own story; he is the classic *picaresque* or rascal hero, a bold, raw-boned and red-haired young Scotsman whose surname suggests his character. Fast-moving (and somewhat haphazardly planned) adventures take him first as a needy Scots surgeon, and then as a fortune-hunter, to the heights and depths, in a world of cardsharps, wits, courtiers and courtesans. He is often unlikeable, a libertine in his treatment of women (where he seems to represent Smollett's views), and shameless towards his humble Sancho Panza, Strap. But despite shallowness of characterisation and ramshackle structure, Smollett's energy in caricature and broad humour is undeniable, and his picture of the smells, filth and degradation of eighteenth-century social and navy life are unrivalled in their almost obsessive and subjective intensity.

Peregrine Pickle followed the pattern, on a bigger scale, with what has been termed Smollett's 'neurotic quality' in describing riotous and brutal behaviour in caricature, a feature that comes close to fantasy. Although the story shifts to a third-person point of view, the central characters are similar; both Roderick and Peregrine are outcasts from families of the gentry, and both, despite unscrupulous behaviour in love and war, end up with a fortune and a beautiful wife. Scott called Peregrine 'the savage and ferocious Pickle', disliking the novel's 'low tone', but Peregrine has pride, passion, tenacity, and occasional redeeming humanity; his idiosyncrasies are what make him live for the reader. Smollett's gift for caricature shows clearly in the one-eyed naval veteran, Commodore Trunnion, whose house is run like a ship, his servants sleeping in hammocks, and who tacks about country, naval fashion, when making land journeys and won't get married when the wind is wrong. Trunnion is, surprisingly, disposed of mid-way, suggesting again Smollet's haphazard approach to structure and unity. The novel moves to the continent and back to London in rambling tour fashion, with more new grotesques like Welshman Sir Cadwallader Crabtree, misanthrope and confidence-trickster. The happy ending is simply pasted on when Smollet feels it should happen.

Ferdinand Count Fathom takes Smollett's protagonist even further into amorality; he is a rogue who gambles his way through Europe, cunningly seducing women and robbing his benefactors. There is, however, a dark poetry in the novel – and the description of the exiled Scottish Jacobites in Boulogne, ruined through their adherence to their doomed cause, who go every day to gaze across the sea at the land to which they can never return, has a power similar to that of Neil Munro's treatment of these same exiles in *The Shoes of Fortune* (1901).

Sir Launcelot Greaves has been described as a poor travesty of *Don Quixote* (1605–15), since Launcelot's chivalry is made ridiculous. The reader is asked to accept an eighteenth-century knight in full medieval armour rescuing good men and maidens from debtors' prisons and madhouses. Smollett himself poses the question of the validity of this anachronistic chivalry at the beginning, and answers it by admitting that what was humorous in Spain 200 years ago must now be a sorry jest, insipid, absurd, and affected. Perhaps at this stage the reader might wonder why, given this admission, Smollett persists in this portrayal, and whether perhaps the novel is deliberately parodic and self-mocking, with its surface narrative hardly to be taken seriously. (Scott would play something of the same trick later, when he 'admitted' that he recurrently created insipid heroes who nobody but himself would have any time for. Scott clearly meant his fictions to have alternative meanings from what this implied and one must wonder could the same be true of Smollett?) The novel is nevertheless full of Smollett's gifts for extravagant caricature, but these are shown to best effect in his last and most considered fiction, *The Expedition of Humphry Clinker*.

Mode, content and structure

Humphry Clinker was published in 1771, the same year as Henry Mackenzie's *The Man of Feeling*. It was a time when the epistolary novel was in great vogue, the last sixty years of the century producing over 500 such novels. What makes Smollett's novel less usual is that it features such a diverse range of letter-writers.

The epistles of the novel operate as monologues which dramatise the five main writers in a way that is both direct and subjective. If the history of the novel has demonstrated a generic tendency toward focusing on the subjective impressions of the individual character, then Smollett, in his use of the epistolary form in *Humphry Clinker*, can be seen as a pioneer in the 'psycho-logising' of the novel. In Smollett's novel, characters are allowed to speak (or write) for themselves without any privileged narrative voice framing a judgement around them. Yet the views of the letter-writers are in a subtle way mediated to the reader: for one thing, there is a great deal of dramatic irony in the novel and, for another, the different characters provide a multiple perspective both on life generally and on specific episodes or experiences, so that the characters question and qualify one another in their views.

The novel deals with an extended tour made through England and Scotland by a family group – a Welsh country squire, Matthew Bramble, his sister Tabitha and his nephew and niece, Jery and Lydia Melford, with Tabitha's maid Win Jenkins. This group of people constitute the letter-writers of the novel (with one very minor addition), who communicate all that happens to their individual correspondents from their own very different points of view. The content of the novel is the sum of the impressions and events of the journey, clustering around a number of main topics: Matt Bramble's concern about the health (physical, moral, psychological, etc.) of British society; Tabitha's desperate search for a husband; Lydia Melford's romantic involvement with a mysterious actor, Wilson, who follows her on her travels; Jery Melford's observation of his uncle and the fashionable scene in different places en route; and the effects produced on the party's attitudes and fortunes by two additions to their number – the destitute young man Humphry Clinker, who becomes one of their servants, and the Scottish soldier, Lieutenant Obadiah Lismahago.

STRUCTURE

As the narrative method and the subject suggest, the novel is very loosely structured. There is a physical movement involved, as would befit a travel book (such as Defoe's *Tour through the Whole Island of Great Britain* (1724–26) or what Smollett himself wrote about France and Italy), so the action falls into natural sections based on the places where the party linger en route: Gloucester, Bath, London, Harrogate, and thence to Scotland. There is initially a journey outwards, where the emphasis is on learning, receiving impressions, meeting new companions and situations; a journey to the North, into Scotland. Then, there is the tour of the unknown land of Scotland, during which there is both geographical and social enlightenment. Finally there is a return, during which the emphasis is more on action and resolution. To some degree, this structure can be seen as symbolic and related to Smollett's underlying themes, which will be analysed later.

PERSPECTIVE IN THE NOVEL

An important concern (it may be an implicit theme) of *Humphry Clinker* is the question of human perception. This was a problem that was much discussed

173

in eighteenth-century philosophy – especially in Scottish philosophical circles – and so *Humphry Clinker,* coming from the pen of a writer educated under the cultural influence of Scottish philosophy and who knew personally some of the Scottish philosophers, might be seen as a particularly Scottish product. With unconscious irony, Win Jenkins in her letter of 26 April complements the views of Matt, Lydia and Jery, emphasising their subjectivity of vision when she informs her fellow servant back in Wales that she can 'have no deception of our doings at Bath'.

Smollett's use of the epistolary technique allows him to explore the psychology of perception – thus rendering incidents in the novel all the more intriguing and dynamic. The first few letters of the novel are a good illustration of this. As we learn about Lydia's romantic attachment to 'Wilson' and the attitudes towards it of others, notably her uncle and guardian, Matthew Bramble, we perceive that Smollett has made a far from original novelistic situation energetic and dynamic by drawing attention to the different fields of perception of the characters observing and experiencing the episode – relative interpretations informed by the predispositions of age, sex, social status, and character.

THE LETTER-WRITERS: MATTHEW BRAMBLE

Even from Bramble's very first letter, ill-natured though it is, we have a clue to his essential benevolence and community spirit. Through his planned course of action for the 'bad neighbour', Bramble is revealed as a natural (as well as an actual) justice of the peace. It is such a character who observes the disorder of urban living and the mistakes of other country squires and who advocates commercial schemes in the Highlands. Bramble must tend towards the health of the community as he sees it. Although he is conceived of as a Welshman (necessarily distanced from the English and Scottish communities which he travels through), Bramble may be read as a product of Scottish Enlightenment forces, in tune with the idea of the 'Scottish moral community' with a fear that economic liberalism, if taken too far, attacks the fabric of community. Smollett's creation of Bramble is perhaps then a peculiarly Scottish response which prioritises 'community' above money. Jery points to the root of Bramble's community feeling when he says in his letter to Sir Watkin Phillips, 18 April:

> I was once apt to believe him a complete Cynic; and that nothing but the necessity of his occasions could compel him to get within the pale of society – I am now of another opinion. I think his peevishness arises from bodily pain, and partly from a natural excess of mental sensibility; for I

suppose, the mind as well as the body, is in some cases endued with a morbid excess of sensation.

This credibly sets up the two-sided misanthropic/philanthropic nature of Bramble. It is the misanthrope who makes scathing attacks on the poor standards of hygiene encountered in different watering-places and in the capital (in which we hear Smollett, the medical man, anticipating the great Victorian public health movement). It is the benevolent philanthrope who dispenses *largesse* to the widow with the sick child. This kindness is set against both the natural injustice of the dying child and the manufactured injustice of the social system which tolerates poverty, discrimination and the ruining of innocent and worthy people. As Jery sees it, Bramble has a heart 'tender even to a degree of weakness' and the temperament of the man of feeling from whom 'the recital of a generous, humane or grateful action, never fails to draw tears of approbation.'

Yet Matthew Bramble is equally the man of reason with a sceptical turn of mind. As such, he is a robust instrument of Smollett's satirical purpose. He is the solidly respectable man with no particular religious or political axe to grind. So he is an unimpeachable observer seeing both the literal and metaphorical excrement of society and possessed of an ability to pass satirical judgement on the disordered world that springs from his utter common sense. Within the general Horatian satire of the novel, with its entertaining portrayal of human folly, Bramble seems to come out of a satire by Juvenal, expressing moral condemnation in the most contemptuous tones.

JERY MELFORD

Matthew Bramble's nephew, Jery Melford, the Oxford-educated man of fashion, is a self-conscious observer of the party on its tour. He remains largely on the periphery of the events that befall the group, having the least element of sub-plot of any of the main characters. His letters to his college tutor represent the main counterbalancing viewpoint to Bramble. In his observations and in the modification and undermining of his English prejudices, he is one of Smollett's devices for winning over the readers to his way of thinking about the state of Britain and the significance of Scotland. By the end, he has supposedly realised 'what flagrant injustice we everyday commit, and what absurd judgment we form, in viewing objects through the falsifying medium of prejudice and passion'. Yet Jery is himself observed and shown to be, not simply a recorder, but someone with his own personal foibles. Again Smollett is highlighting the subjectivity of the individual viewpoint.

LYDIA MELFORD

For several reasons, such as the lack of educational opportunities for women and an almost exclusive reading diet of romances, the three women letter-writers in *Humphry Clinker* are less penetrating and observant in their impressions than either Matt Bramble or Jery Melford. Lydia tends towards an over-romantic view of her situation and Tabitha Bramble and Win Jenkins have noticeable educational and/or intellectual shortcomings.

According to her uncle and guardian, Lydia is 'deficient in spirit, and so susceptible – and so tender forsooth! – truly she has got a languishing eye and reads romances'. Whether or not her spirit is really as weak as her uncle believes, Lydia certainly has all the attributes of the romantic heroine and her affair with Wilson/Dennison is the longest and most hackneyed plot-thread in the novel. There are hints that Smollett is presenting her as a person trapped in a limiting role within life itself. Amid so many other vividly realised individualists in the action, Lydia appears pallid and unfulfilled until we note the sharpness and liveliness of some of her observations. Perhaps her role in the novel is a didactic one, to demonstrate that social location can be a barrier to perception. If indeed this is the end to which the stereotypical romantic heroine is being used, then we see yet another aspect of Smollett's re-energising of the clichéd romantic plot.

TABITHA BRAMBLE

Matthew Bramble's sister reveals little about her own adventures in her letters, which are most fully treated in the letters of others. She is primarily concerned with sending instructions regarding domestic economy home to Wales. In this, as in her attempts to secure a husband, she is often a figure of ridicule. She reveals her ignorance or misunderstanding in most situations, and is a constant embarrassment and torment to her sensitive brother. Nevertheless, Matt's ambiguous feelings towards her are well executed and she cannot be seen as merely an object of comic diversion. In her sexual obsession, or wilful isolation, as she concerns herself only with men or domestic management, she illustrates another blocking of perception. The deeper nature of the group's tour and the serious concerns of her companions are things beyond her conception.

WIN JENKINS

Win is clearly also a character of comic function, her letters featuring in greater measure the same features of mis-spelling, malapropism and mis-understanding as her mistress's; but affording more gossipy observation due to her impressionable nature, which makes her more liable to meet her experiences on their own terms. She may be wiser than she knows. Her sense of bewilderment in the face of a strange world beyond her home territory is often not without some real substance. One aspect of this is seen in her puzzlement about naming procedures, as in Bramble's use of the name 'Lloyd' earlier in his life. So much of the complication that Win fails to cope with relates to the overlaying of what is natural and clear with artificial social complexities. The linguistic confusions of Win's letters and her social bewilderment are in the same spectrum as the greater social ills and corruptions that Bramble lashes with his scorn.

THE CRITIQUE OF GREAT BRITAIN

Through *Humphry Clinker* there is an examination being conducted of the socio-economic state of eighteenth-century Britain. The device of the journey facilitates this enquiry, creating a *modus operandi* in a kind of social and commercial geography as the environmental experiences of the party give rise to reflections on community values, luxury, town life and urbanisation, country life and agriculture. For example, the observation of Bath provides the pretext for a keynote outburst by Bramble on what is going wrong in Britain. The noise, confusion and even the badly-planned architecture have their root-cause identified: 'All these absurdities arise from the general tide of luxury, which hath over-spread the nation, and swept away all, even the very dregs of the people.' Here we have a complaint against surplus wealth (and the identification of its dubious origins, in colonial exploitation and war-profiteering). What are being registered, then, are the beginnings of the purely materialistic society and so Bramble's observations are of historical relevance.

The modern reader will, however, take less seriously Bramble's idealistic belief in the existing class system, dismissing it as an unworthy snobbery. Bramble's perception of the breakdown of social distinctions is confirmed by Jery, who observes 'a broken-winded Wapping landlady squeeze through a circle of peers, to salute her brandy-merchant, who stood by the window prop'd upon crutches'. Yet what Jery also does is undermine the essential snobbery of his uncle as he interprets Bramble's perceptions in another letter to Phillip, 30 April:

> He sees them in their natural attitudes and true colours; descended from their pedestals, and divested of their formal draperies, undisguised by art and affectation – Here we have ministers of state, judges, generals, bishops, projectors, philosophers, wits, poets, players, chemists, fiddlers and buffoons.

Bramble is horrified because in front of him are the 'respectable in their natural attitudes and true colours' both physically and behaviourally, and in these aspects the 'respectable' are no less base than their social inferiors. That is to say, Bramble's vision of a hierarchy of worth signalled by social degree or caste has broken down into a nightmare of equality in degeneracy, an anticipation of the fear of Jacobin democracy felt by a later generation after the French Revolution.

The critique extends to include the large-scale socio-cultural changes brought about by urbanisation. London 'is literally new to me', says Bramble, seeing the vast expansion of housing in the Westminster area. The causes of this lie in the Agrarian Revolution and the growth of luxury, which provoked a flight from the land into the cities. The country Tory feels his rural order threatened by the new liberal urban environment, and the reaction is to elevate an idealised pastoral vision of country life as the desirable alternative (See Bramble's letter of 8 June). One may speculate about where Smollett stands in this, being from a rural land-owning family himself. It is interesting to note that when Burns treats a similar topic in his poem, 'The Twa Dogs', some years later and still before the French Revolution, his solution to the problem of luxury and corruption is a similar return to the country life with its traditional pyramidal social structure.

There are a number of specific cases in *Humphry Clinker* that show the traditional country landowning life being corrupted and broken down under the pressures of greed, extravagance, arrogance and conceit. The main example is of Bramble's old friend Baynard, whom the party have to rescue and restore to a sensible mode of living. The marriage of Lydia with the son of a good, loving and prosperous landowner, Dennison, may be making a symbolic affirmation of the value of the traditional rural pattern of life. In this, Smollett appears not to have any particularly penetrating observations to make on the state of Britain in his time. It is not until John Galt, with the benefit of hindsight, turns his detached satirical gaze on the same period, that we find a Scottish novelist producing a convincing critique of the social changes of the eighteenth and early nineteenth centuries.

SCOTLAND AND THE SCOTS IN THE NOVEL

The depiction of Scotland in *Humphry Clinker* is a continuation of the concern with the socio-economic situation in Britain but it is also an attempt to inform a southern reading public largely ignorant of the realities of Scotland. This ignorance is registered in the novel in Tabitha's belief, as she is about to enter Scotland, that there is nothing to eat except oatmeal and sheep's heads and later in Win's conflation of the town she has just been in (Haddington) with the Scottish capital so as to locate herself in 'Haddingborough'. Matt Bramble, early on in the novel, registers both that Scotland must be considered as part of the British reality if one is to have a comprehensive picture of the nation, and his own ignorance of the country when, as he projects his trip north, he states 'I think it is a reproach upon me as a British freeholder, to have lived so long without making an excursion to the other side of the Tweed.' If Bramble is pointing out that Scotland is a part of Britain, Jery notes the cultural differentiation of the Scots: 'their looks, their language and their customs are so different from ours, that I can hardly believe myself in Great Britain.' Thus Jery adds to his uncle's enunciation of 'Britishness' by simultaneously affirming 'Scottishness' and 'Englishness' and in the ironic conclusion to his statement he identifies 'Great Britain' primarily as belonging to the area south of the Tweed. What Smollett is doing quite brilliantly is posing the question he has been asking from the beginning of the novel: what is Great Britain?

There is no doubt that Smollett intends the matter of Scotland and the Scots to occupy the heart of the novel. Among all the varied events and details of the early part of the novel, he plants a succession of references to Scots which serve to remind the readers of their unexamined prejudices about Scotland and its people: the Scotch apothecary, the Scotch baronet, the Scotsman met by Jery at Smollett's own house, and, most important of all, the Scotch lawyer Micklewhimmen, who is given the stereotypical Scottish qualities of caution, canny craftiness and attachment to money. Thus the way is prepared for the introduction of the main Scottish character, Lieutenant Obadiah Lismahago, who at first sight is a Scotch caricature in the most extreme degree, an impression that is then significantly but not entirely broken down and revealed to be a mistaken reading of his appearance and personality. In the same way, the first impressions that the travellers receive of Scotland as they cross the Border are progressively undermined and dispelled by their later more congenial experiences.

As the Bramble party moves through Scotland, experiencing Edinburgh society, Glasgow, Loch Lomondside and the nearer Highlands, they become both more knowledgeable and more tolerant in their view of the country and the people. There is an intellectual underpinning of the sensory and psychological experience through the discussions between Matt Bramble and Lismahago about the potential significance of Scotland within the Union and the ways in which Scots can come to be more accepted and understood by the English. In asserting the positive qualities of Scotland, Smollett is simultaneously asserting the positive contribution that Scotland can make to the political and economic union of which it has hitherto been a neglected part. The healthy traditional Scotland as seen in Edinburgh is balanced by the progressive element as seen in a Glasgow on the point of economic take-off. Despite the poor state of the agriculture elsewhere and the problem of a patriarchal system in the Highlands, there are, as Bramble sees, significant possibilities of sound commercial operations that will bring socio-political and environmental benefits for the future.

Lismahago, despite appearing to be 'a self-conceited pedant, awkward, rude and disputacious', turns out to be very modern (in the eighteenth-century sense) in his outlook, balancing a measured critical stance towards his own country and countrymen with a capacity for subtle reductive satire of English attitudes towards Scots. More explicitly than Bramble, with whom he often disagrees, he speaks with the full authority of the Scottish Enlightenment tempered with a note of scepticism about the supposed benefits of the Union.

Smollett's discussion of Scotland, both concrete and conceptual in the novel, continues to be developed after the travellers have left the country. Bramble and his group, now including Lismahago and Bramble's natural son Humphry Clinker, act with more resolution and effect (as in the rescuing of Baynard), and the marriages of Lydia and Wilson/Dennison and of Tabitha and Lismahago are a symbolic uniting of English, Scottish and Welsh elements in a larger family structure. The moral, despite the continuing comic tone and novelistic conventions, is clearly concerned with the benefit of a harmonious mutually-respecting Union within the traditional social patterns of Great Britain as a whole.

GAMES WITH THE READER

Alongside the 'serious' themes of perception and socio-politico-economic exploration in *Humphry Clinker*, there can also be found a literary playfulness, characteristic of Smollett's prose. Examples of this are easily found. There is the framing device of the letters between Jonathan Dustwich and the bookseller Henry Davis – reminding us of Henry Mackenzie's framing of the narrative in *The Man of Feeling*, and the later use by Scott and Hogg of the device of a tedious or morally suspect Editor figure. There is the intertextual use of characters from another Smollett novel; Ferdinand, Count Fathom, and the De Melvilles – a device later used extensively by Galt. And there is the self-reflexive device of Smollett, the author, introducing himself into his own fiction just as Hogg and Alasdair Gray do in later generations.

More than all these, however, there is the teasing title of the novel, which implies an irreverent attitude by Smollett to his own text. Humphry Clinker is the titular character but only a minor protagonist in the action and themes.

180

Thus there is a mocking deflection of attention away from the main characters, with a corresponding de-centring and deprioritisation of their perspectives and preoccupations. In one sense, the changing fortunes of Clinker might be thought to be the most dramatic circumstance of the novel. However, on examination, it turns out to be yet another instance of a particularly hackneyed plot-line, as Smollett was very well aware. It may be that Smollett is signalling, by means of ironic elevation of a creaking novelistic situation, that *Humphry Clinker* is more than a novel and is, in fact, a fiction that transcends the novel genre as it was then perceived and does something much more complex than 'telling a story'. It could be argued that Smollett is anticipating what Galt does later in his 'theoretical histories' and what Disraeli does in *Sybil, or The Two Nations* (1845), that is, using fiction with its existing techniques and sets of expectations, as the vehicle for making an examination and critique of society and the medium for a political and social message.

However, the final impression left on the reader by *Humphry Clinker* is of a rich, infinitely varied and diverse fiction that both instructs and entertains on a number of levels. If Smollett had written nothing else, he would still deserve to be remembered as a highly successful and innovative writer who pushed the possibilities of the novel form to new frontiers.

CHAPTER 11

WIDENING THE RANGE 2

WAYS OF READING

As suggested in Chapter 12, there has long been a critical tendency to read eighteenth-century Scottish literature as bifurcated between 'native' and 'alien', or 'natural' and 'synthetic', or 'Scottish' and 'Un-Scottish' categories. In relation to such perceptions, the Scottish Enlightenment sometimes emerges as the second biggest villain in Scottish literary history after the Reformation. Since powerful forces of anglicisation and neo-classical narrowness are associated with the Scottish Enlightenment, not only do many critics see the literature produced under the influence of the Enlightenment as often diseased, but the poetry of the Scots vernacular revival is also held to be ghettoised and interfered with under such hostile impulses. Scottish criticism has collated a formidable case in support of these ideas, but more recently there have arisen the beginnings of revisionist approaches to eighteenth-century Scottish literature. Broadly, such approaches point out, for instance, that the dualisms in the period, previously read as cultural handicap and division, might sometimes be read as cultural facility and bilingualism; or that such impetuses as cultural nationalism or the neo-classical urge or Enlightenment philosophical ideas are pervasive across and through the strains of Enlightenment and Scots-language creativity.

Other cultural movements

Leaving aside the grand debates about the state of eighteenth-century Scottish culture, the simple fact is that literature in the period remains seriously underexplored. The dearth of examination is particularly apparent in the early years of the century when the Scoto-Latinist or Scottish Humanist influence in literature, particularly to be associated with the culture of the North-East of Scotland, is very influential. This strain is associated with royalism (particularly with regard to the Stuart dynasty), Episcopalianism and Catholicism. At the same time as Scottish Humanism in the early eighteenth century venerates the likes of Latinist poets such as Arthur Johnston (1587–1641), it also celebrates the classical achievement of that staunch Presbyterian George Buchanan (1506–82). The eighteenth-century Scottish Humanist activists included Archibald Pitcairne (1652–1713), author of a satirical play against the Church of Scotland, *The Assembly* (1692), James Watson (d. 1722) publisher of the famous *Choice Collection of Comic and Serious Scots Poems* (1706–11), and Thomas Ruddiman (1674–1757), who published work by Buchanan, an edition of Gavin Douglas's *Eneados* (1710) and the poetry of William Drummond of Hawthornden (1585–1649). Among these men we see some of the energies which were to become increasingly prominent through the eighteenth century: anti-Calvinism, a revival of Scotland's literary past, especially the medieval, Renaissance and seventeenth-century 'Scottish Cavalier' poetic heritage, leanings toward Jacobitism, and a revival of folk-culture. If the tendency, apparent to some extent in all of these men, to see Latin as the primary language of literature does not feature or endure in the same way that their orientation of Scottish literature towards creativity in the Scots language does, the Latinist tendency is not so negligible as is sometimes thought. Especially in poets of Aberdeenshire origins, the writing of accomplished poetry in Latin endures down to the nineteenth century. One of the best of these poets was Alexander Geddes (1737–1802), a Catholic priest, a pioneer of the literary criticism of the Bible and the author of poems such as his three pieces in praise of the French Revolution, *Carmen Seculare* (1790–2), one of which was read to the French Assembly of Deputies in French translation as a morale-booster at a time when the nerve of the revolutionaries was rather fragile. Geddes also produced various Scots-language translations of Greek and Latin pastoral and satirical poetry, some of which was appended to his *Dissertation on the Scoto-Saxon Dialect* (1789), a treatise still of huge interest to language specialists today. Aside from the serious lack of studies of the Scoto-Latinist milieu and its particular texts, there is also much work to be done on the way it encourages the Scots vernacular revival in poetry. Allan Ramsay's first published work, lost for over 200 years until recovered in 1979, was his 'A Poem to the Memory of the Famous Archibald Pitcairn' (1713), which demonstrates his immersion in the Scottish Humanist cultural grouping. To take one of a number of examples of the strong Scoto-Latinist influence in Scots poetry, the Horatian odes produced by Ramsay and Robert Fergusson and others have been inadequately explored by critics.

Re-reading Ramsay, Fergusson and Burns

Although the work of Ramsay, Fergusson and Robert Burns has been much lauded in Scottish criticism, there are other impulses in their poetry which remain unsatisfactorily underregarded. In the case of all three poets, their work in English – even sometimes in Scots-English – and in the Augustan idiom wants more attention. To take simply an example from each, Ramsay's 'Clyde's Welcome to His Prince', (or even his very fine Scots-English production, 'Wealth, or the Woody'), 'Fergusson's' 'The Rivers of Scotland' and Burns's 'The Cotter's Saturday Night' are all much better poems than is often thought. No serious study of the English productions of these poets has been undertaken since the predilection of Scottish criticism has long been to see such work as *a priori* second-rate. Similarly, although the epistolary verse by all three is often recognised in its quality, what is frequently under-read is the way in which this mode is fed by the influence of English Augustan and neo-classical poets such as Alexander Pope. To take a final example of the way in which modern, overarching critical pronouncement has tended to delimit the field, the democratising, Presbyterian outlook in Burns has tended to be inadequately seen in its positive aspects.

Beyond the triumvirate

Widening the range in Scots poetry beyond the canonised triumvirate of Ramsay, Fergusson and Burns would take account of numerous other writers furth of Edinburgh and Alloway. William Hamilton of Gilbertfield (1665–1751) produces entertaining verse-epistles in Scots and a very readable translation into English of Blind Harry's epic-poem, *Wallace* (1722). Alexander Ross (1699–1784) is the author of *Helenore, or the Fortunate Shepherdess* (1768), a pastoral drama which is highly conventional in plot but often vigorous in its Scots language usage. Three poets who deserve to be better-known for their work in Scots are the aforementioned Alexander Geddes, like Burns the writer of some fine songs in Scots; Charles Keith (d. 1807), author of a very vivid portrait of Scottish country life, 'Farmer's Ha': A Scots Poem' (1776); and John Mayne (1759–1836), whose most famous work, 'The Siller Gun', a fine performance in the Scots comic tradition, appears in 1808. Women poets and songwriters who ought to have greater recognition include Elizabeth Halkett, or Lady Wardlaw (1677–1727), who produced 'Hardyknute, A Fragment' (1719), a poem which is important in setting the trend for heroic and ballad materials during the century; Lady Grizel Baillie (1665–1746), someone who influenced both Allan Ramsay and James Thomson; and Jean Elliot of Minto (1727–1805), author of 'The Flowers of the Forest'. There are signs that the work of these, a host of other female writers and Joanna Baillie (1762–1851), a poet and playwright active from the 1790s and admired greatly by Scott and by Lord Byron, are now coming in for some serious reassessment, particularly in that modern critical context which scrutinises issues of gender.

The many Scots-language poets of the eighteenth century have never been collated into anything remotely approaching a comprehensive study (although brave efforts were made in this respect by T. F. Henderson in his *Scottish Vernacular Literature*, 1898, J. H. Millar in his pioneering *A Literary History of Scotland*, 1903, and Lauchlan McLean Watt in his sentimentalising but informative *Scottish Life and Poetry*, 1912). An excellent selection of longer Scottish poems of the period, in both Scots and English, can be found in the second of the two-volume series of *Longer Scottish Poems* edited by Thomas Crawford, David Hewitt, and Alexander Law (1987), and which, beyond the poets mentioned here, contains selections from James Thomson (from *The Seasons*), David Mallet, William Hamilton, Adam Skirving, John Skinner, James Beattie, and looks forward to Scott, Hogg and Tennant. This is a field of Scottish literature which is beginning to receive its proper critical and editorial attention; for far too long the neglected work of these significant poets has lain untouched in rich collections held pre-eminently by the National Library of Scotland and the Mitchell Library, Scotland. Future scholars have a potentially huge and exciting task in properly exploring this material.

Alongside the literary strains of Latinism and the Scots vernacular revival in verse, two other broad impetuses might be identified as emerging in the early eighteenth century: Calvinist poetry and Scottish literature which takes its cue from English Augustan culture. The first of these strains is remarkable mainly for its weight. There is a huge corpus of poetry written mainly by Presbyterian clergymen from the start of the eighteenth century and running the full gamut of the emotions from the lachrymose to the morbid while enjoining piety in the reader. Representative examples are Samuel Arnot's *Eternity, a Poem* (1711) and James Craig's *Spiritual Life, Poems* (1727). There certainly seems to have been a market and a readership for this poetry (some of Burns's early morbidly pietistic productions demonstrate its influence), but no one has yet analysed the phenomenon. Scottish literature in the eighteenth century apart from poetry of Calvinist pietism or the likes of Hamilton of Gilbertfield's *Wallace*, is very often written in English.

James Thomson

Having said this we ought to be careful in too simply ascribing anglocentricity to poets like James Thomson (1700–48), a man who is often seen as marking a sharply alternative set of literary and cultural preferences to Allan Ramsay during the first part of the century. At its worst, marginalisation of Thomson (a man who is often seen as highly important as a literary innovator in European and English terms), takes the form of the ascription to him of being one of the first 'Scots on the make' who take advantage of the new post-1707 opportunities in the British political and cultural scene. There has been a tendency to make too little of Thomson's cultural roots which include writing in a rather 'Latinate' style, which speaks of his influence by Scottish Humanism, the markers of influence in his work of the poetry of Edmund Spenser and John Milton (which are part of Thomson's heritage as a sincere Scottish Presbyterian) and a strong sense of morality (which again derives from his Presbyterianism). When read with these things in mind, Thomson's phenomenally successful *The Seasons* (1726–30) might be seen to be more Scottish in its signature than is sometimes thought. As it is, this sequence of poetry tends to be too appropriated in too facile a fashion by the 'English' tradition and surrendered from the Scottish canon. Thomson is also sometimes seen as being an apostle of British imperialism (his most famous work in this respect being 'Rule Britannia' a song which he wrote for *The Masque of Alfred* (1740)). What should be pointed out, however, is that the rhetoric of xenophobic British nationalism from later in the century which Thomson certainly inspires, is largely absent from his own work. Thomson's biggest rhetorical concern in the political sense, in fact, is with the notion of 'liberty', something which inspires British Whigs and, later, radicals in favour of the French Revolution such as Robert Burns. Thomson's frequent depiction by Scottish critics, then, as an anglocentric apostle of British imperialism, is very far from the being the whole story. (A very under-researched and under-read area, though potentially one of the most fruitful in eighteenth-century Scottish literary studies, relates to radical literature of the 1790s in response to the upheavals in France and the political ferment which ensued in Britain. Tom Leonard's anthology, *Radical Renfrew: Poetry from the French Revolution to the First World War* (1990), provides some starting points in a vast field that will only properly be viewed when detailed work is undertaken on poetry and prose productions appearing in the Scottish and English radical press.)

Anglo-Scots

There are other 'Anglo-Scots' who have never had much serious critical treatment. These include Thomson's collaborator as a playwright, David Malloch (or Mallet after he had anglicised his name) (c. 1705–65), whose dislike of Alexander Pope, if not any of his poems or plays, would make for an interesting site in the examination of Anglo-Scottish cultural relations.

Similarly, John Arbuthnott (1667–1735) is involved in southern literary circles, particularly in his friendship with Pope and Jonathan Swift, and his input into the *Memoirs of Martin Scriblerus* (1741) has not been properly looked at in the light of Arbuthnott's nationality. Another writer whose work deserves some critical attention is William Falconer (1732–69), a man who served for the greater part of his adult life in the Royal Navy. His 'The Shipwreck' (1762) is marked by a serious contemplation of the power of the sea in a manner which looks forward to Herman Melville. Of all the Anglo-Scots, the most successful, of course, is Tobias Smollett. Smollett's novels have been fairly well treated though there is still much work to be done on the way in which he interprets traditions of the European novel from a Scotsman's point of view, his journalistic activities, and his ideas on identity. From London he edited *The Briton* from 1762 and contributed to other periodicals where he essayed notions of post-Union identity. A promising field for contemporary criticism would be exploration of the notion of being 'North British' as formulated by Smollett and others.

Philosophy and poetry

There is also a serious dearth of detailed commentary on the works of writers associated with the Scottish Enlightenment. The ideas and style of David Hume (1711–76) in his numerous essays from 1741 to 1756 are high in philosophical and literary merit but fail to gain admission to the Scottish canon for their supposed anglocentricity. This view has been too readily accepted in the past and warrants fresh investigation. Long overdue reassessment might also be applied to work in aesthetic and literary criticism by the likes of Henry Home (1696–1782), Thomas Reid (1710–96), James Burnett (1714–99), Hugh Blair (1718–1800), Adam Smith (1723–90) and Alexander Gerard (1728–95); and to the historiography of Hume, Smollett and William Robertson (1721–93). Such thinkers provide part of the rich, wider textual fabric of eighteenth-century Scotland which literary criticism has been slow to acknowledge except in the most cursory of fashions.

It is often stated that Scotland produces strong precursors of the Romantic movement in the likes of James Thomson, Robert Blair (1699–1746), John Home (1722–1808), James Beattie (1735–1803), James Macpherson (1736–96) and Henry Mackenzie (1745–1831). Generally, however, these writers tend to be seen as blind alleyways in Scottish terms. Blair's 'The Grave' (1743), which was admired by William Blake, represents a transformation of the strain of Scottish Calvinist poetry toward something much more genuinely meditative on the human condition. Home's best drama *Douglas* (1757) assembles native historic and ballad materials in a way that looks toward the work of Walter Scott. Beattie's *The Minstrel* (1771 & 1774), a poem that influenced William Wordsworth, is much more readable than some dismissive Scottish critics would allow. Macpherson's 'Ossianic' poetry (1760–62), part imaginative remoulding, part collection of genuine Gaelic materials, shows some signs of serious scholarly reappraisal. Macpherson's work still awaits a full re-examination, however, as a contributor to the Romantic landscape that came to be utilised by some of the greatest practitioners of European literature in the late eighteenth and early nineteenth centuries. Mackenzie has long been ridiculed for producing one of the great mistakes of Scottish literature, the over-sentimental *The Man of Feeling* (1771). There is perhaps more irony in this novel than is sometimes thought, however, something which is apparent in chapter-titles like 'The Man of Feeling in a Brothel', and there perhaps also too easily overlooked is a critique of British colonialism and the harmful social dislocation engendered by aggressively profiteering landlords during the late eighteenth century. Also of interest is Mackenzie's editing of and writing for the periodicals, *The Mirror* (from 1777) and *The Lounger* (from 1785). The greatest Scottish 'journalist' of the age, of course, is James Boswell (1740–95) whose large output is still today being properly edited. His work in various periodicals, his London diary and his *Journal of a Tour to the Hebrides with Samuel Johnson* (1785) are well-known to students of the eighteenth century generally, but the likes of his novella, *Dorando* (1767), a number of essays addressing the constitutional state of Scotland, and his *An Account of Corsica* (1768) all deserve to be better known.

Gaelic poetry

This guide attends to literature in English and Scots; but it would be unfair not to mention here the work of some of the greatest of Gaelic poets of the time, whose poetry has greatly influenced Scottish culture and poetry beyond their own language. Mainstream Scottish criticism is too little aware of the flowering of Gaelic poetry during the century. In the work of Alasdair Mac Mhaigstir Alasdair or Alexander Macdonald (c. mid: 1690s–c. 1770), author of *Galick and English Vocabulary* (1741) and a very fine collection of poems, *Ais-Eiridh na Sean-Chanoin Albannaich* (1751); and Donnchadh Ban Mac an t-saoir or Duncan Ban Macintyre (1724–1812), the famous author of the wonderful meditation on the animals and landscape of the Highlands 'Moladh Beinn Do bhrain' ('The Praise of Ben Dorain'), the Highlands boast two poets who at their best are of the quality of Ramsay or Fergusson. As in so many other cases, these poets complicate and challenge the old assumptions about an eighteenth-century Scottish culture simply divided between Scots and English language tendencies; their influence increases with time, an outstanding example of this being their impact on the work of Hugh MacDiarmid in the twentieth century.

SECTION 3

Scottish Literature
in the Age of Scott

CHAPTER 12

THE AGE OF WALTER SCOTT

THE LATER ENLIGHTENMENT

This brief introduction to one of the most significant, complex and constantly changing periods of Scottish history examines some of the major historical, social and cultural changes, with especial reference to the work of the major writers treated in the chapters of this section. At the end of the section, in 'Widening the Range', some of the other important writers of the period are introduced, with suggestions as to what texts and issues might best be explored.

When approaching the achievement of writers such as Walter Scott, James Hogg, John Galt and Susan Ferrier, it is worth remembering that their roots lie in the eighteenth century, and that the great events and ideas of the last years of the century, inside and outside of Scotland, profoundly influenced their development. Beyond Scotland, the war with the American colonies which ended in 1783 with American independence, the French Revolution of 1789 with its spread of egalitarian ideals and the growth of Romanticism in the arts and in social ideas; all these powerfully affected the thinking of writers like Scott, Galt and Hogg, as well as encouraging the radical tradition of Burns in poetry – often to the horror of the Establishment.

Within Scotland, the effects of these international changes, combined with dramatic events and pioneering new ideas developed by the philosophers and thinkers of the Scottish Enlightenment, moved Scottish culture and society to a watershed. Behind lay the older Scotland, with the vernacular poetry of Ramsay, Fergusson, Burns and its pseudo-Celtic inheritance from Macpherson's *Ossian*. At the point of watershed lay the work of the *literati*, the evolving middle class, educated and professional men of letters and science of Edinburgh, Glasgow and Aberdeen, with lawyers and ministers at their head. Beyond 1800 lay the new work of the nineteenth-century Unionists, Scott and his contemporaries, fashioning – or trying to fashion – narratives of Scotland that would diagnose Scotland's historical and internecine divisions and try to heal these self-inflicted wounds, by showing protagonists representing Scotland struggling with issues of Scottish history and politics, religion and social change. These protagonists – Henry Morton of Scott's *Old Mortality* (1816) and Jeanie Deans of *The Heart of Midlothian* (1818), Robert Wringhim of Hogg's *The Justified Sinner* (1824), the Reverend Micah Balwhidder of John Galt's *Annals of the Parish* (1821), or his Covenanting rebel in the novel named after him, *Ringan Gilhaize* (1823), Mary Douglas in Susan Ferrier's *Marriage* (1818) – initiate a tradition or school of Scottish fiction which lasted for a hundred years, until the enormous changes brought about by the First World War broke the moulds of nineteenth-century Scotland and ushered in the 'Scottish Renaissance'.

The age of Scott thus overlaps with the great period of the Scottish Enlightenment; and it would be fair to say that the death of Scott in 1832, and shortly after of James Hogg and John Galt (in 1835 and 1839 respectively), coincide with the end of that Enlightenment. Several other disastrous events followed which further disturbed the coherence of Scottish cultural life – the aftermath of the French Revolution, increasing that political unrest which Scott so feared; Whig and radical pressure which was left unsatisfied by Burgh Reform in 1832; the Disruption in the Church of Scotland in 1843; the great potato famines of Scotland and Ireland in the 1840s; the massive effects of Highland clearance and industrialisation on what had been traditionally an essentially rural society; the coming of the railways. All these rapidly produced dramatic changes Scott himself was never fully to see. His was the in-between Scotland, in a ferment of change, captured in *Rob Roy* (1818), with its linked but mutually opposed symbols of Rob Roy, the outlaw whose loyalties are to the past, to disorderly Scotland, to older and dying languages and tribal systems; and Bailie Nicol Jarvie, the Glasgow merchant, identifying with the future and trade with the colonies which have been opened to Scotland by Union with England. The old Scotland and the new are well presented by the Bailie in the novel, when he argues vigorously that Scotland has been changed for the better by the 1707 Act of Union (Chapter 27):

> Whisht, sir! – Whisht! It's ill-scraped tongues like yours that make mischief between neighbourhoods and nations. There's naething sae gude on this side o' time but it might have been better, and that may be said o' the Union. Nane were keener against it than the Glasgow folk, wi' their rabblings and their risings, and their mobs, as they ca' them nowadays. But it's an ill wind that blaws naebody gude . . . Now, since Saint Mungo catched herrings in the Clyde, what was ever like to gar us flourish like the sugar and tobacco trade? Will anybody tell me that, and grumble at a treaty that opened us a road west awa yonder?

The Bailie may oppose everything that Rob Roy stands for; but we must remember that he is, in the end, Rob's loyal cousin. Older, rural, tribal Scotland and the new, urban and commercial Scotland meet in darkness around the ancient cathedral of Glasgow, showing how these two sides to Scotland, for all their antagonism, are linked inextricably beneath their surface hostility.

And it is in the time of Scott that the literature shows this enormous transition from a backward, impoverished Scotland, resentful still of Union and loss of national identity, or confused and sometimes pathetic in its efforts to prove its ability to be more British than the English, to a country which by the mid-nineteenth century was at the head of industrialisation in its exploitation of iron and steel for shipping and railways, in the vanguard of British imperial expansion, a country increasingly romanticised by the rest of Britain and Europe in literature and painting. This occurred not least because its Highlands became the beloved retreat of Queen Victoria, whose residences at Balmoral on Deeside began a cult of Highland idealisation and nostalgia by increasingly urbanised and industrialised societies seeking a simpler rural past; a nineteenth-century distortion of reality far beyond anything Scott has been blamed for.

In this welter of change the student of the period can be forgiven for frequently being confused; there are many paradoxes and contradictions. All too often assessments of writers and their achievements have been over-simplified in the desire to impose convenient labels. Scott has for too long been seen as an arch-Tory; or, in the immensely damaging assessment of Edwin Muir, Burns and Scott in his poem 'Scotland 1941' are 'Sham bards of a sham nation', while Muir's *Scott and Scotland* (1936) views Scott as the creator, in poetry and fiction, of an 'escape to Scotland'. Too often twentieth-century critics have regarded Scott as the originator of what became tourist stereotypes of Scotland, when the truth is that such stereo-typing was not his, and had begun long before, with the reception given by the *literati* to Burns and James Macpherson's *Ossian* (1765), and the Eur-opean Romantic vogue for discovering 'noble savages'. Burns (as 'the heaven-taught ploughman') and Hogg (as the unschooled 'Ettrick Shep-herd') were both conveniently stereotyped in this way. The reality exempli-fies some of the many paradoxes of the period – Burns had to unlearn much of the genteel English-orientated reading on which he was reared before he could rediscover and refashion vernacular traditions; and Hogg, far from being the simple poet of 'the mountain and the fairy school' and the whisky-quaffing buffoon as presented in *Blackwood's Magazine,* had an immensely rich background of Border and oral Ballad and story tradition and, astonishingly, was arguably the first great psychological novelist of Europe, as the French critic André Gide has suggested in his 1947 preface to Hogg's *The Justified Sinner.*

Before, however, we too readily turn to blame the *literati* for their initiation of a process of falsification of native Scottish achievement, and their correspondingly high estimation of their anglicised and overly-mannered and sentimental achievement, we should remember that Scott, Galt and Ferrier belonged to this very class yet managed to balance their views of the old and new Scotlands, of the vernacular traditions and the new thinking. One of the most subtle of the many paradoxes of the age of Scott lies in the way in which, beneath its disdain for older Scots language and manners, the underlying philosophy and literature of the Enlightenment period nevertheless (like Bailie Nicol Jarvie?) expresses a fundamental respect for older Scottish values. We need to make the effort to understand what motivated the *literati* in their anglicisation and antipathy to vernacular expression – and to recognise that they could be inconsistent. Eighteenth-century Scotland was tired of religious and civil war, tired of its tribal barbarities, and tired of its poverty. 'Improvement' in commerce, agriculture and manners seemed all-important as the way forward. The Enlightenment had, however, to come to some sort of compromise with the established Church of Scotland, itself torn in two over the Patronage Controversy, that centuries-old running argument as to whether, as the Reformation had decreed, the congregation should have final say in the choice of minister, or whether the patrons or landowners should, as in England, have the right to appoint their nominee. Working with the moderates in the church, the great moral and social philosophers of the Enlightenment, following Francis Hutcheson, the courageous and liberal Professor of Moral Philosophy at the University of Glasgow from 1729 to 1746 (who continually risked trial for blasphemy), developed the school of 'common-sense' philosophy – which, paradoxically, is not, as its name might suggest, a hard-headed and pragmatic system of thinking, but rather the opposite. Thinkers like Thomas Reid, Adam Smith, and Thomas Brown, following Hutcheson, argued – against English and Scottish philosophers such as Locke and David Hume, who had sceptically reduced the mind and thinking to mere associations of ideas and prejudices – that all human beings, however nobly or humbly born, possess an instinctive faculty, a sense common to all, which guides them in matters of Good and Evil. The fact that this faculty has obvious connections with religious ideas of 'conscience' helped build bridges with the moderates in the church; and this informal compact between secular philosophy and church, lasting until 1843 and the Disruption, underpins the great achievements of Scott's age.

More importantly still for literature in the age of Scott, however, were the implications of common-sense philosophy. The *literati* may have been snobbish in their desire to rid themselves of Scotticisms in their speech, and hostile to vernacular traditions, but insofar as they were philosophers they stressed the moral integrity of Everyman (and Everywoman, as Scott's Jeanie Deans in *The Heart of Midlothian* nobly illustrates). Thus they laid the ground in which Scottish novelists and poets developed a tradition of the kind of humble protagonists we identified earlier as typical of the Scottish novel in the nineteenth century. Jeanie Deans is Scott's final choice as exemplar of fundamental Scottish worth; it is her absolute reliance on that common sense, 'nature's voice' as she calls it, which takes her triumphantly through her moral and social trials. Galt exemplified the same ideology in the progress of his minister, the none-too-intelligent Micah Balwhidder, whose instinctive humanity makes up for his intellectual shortcomings, converting even his enemies, just as Jeanie's simple warmth does, and just as later versions of the type, like David Balfour, Malcolm or Johnnie Gibb would do also.

This emphasis on the transcendental importance of moral imperatives, and the ultimately irrational nature of human morality, was to have a massive European influence, contributing to the thinking of Immanuel Kant and the German transcendental philosophers of the Romantic movement. And, within a Scottish context, it is arguable that the emphasis on the significance of the ordinary man and woman in ordinary community, which persists till the present day in the Scottish novel, in the work of James Kelman, Alasdair Gray, and so many of our contemporary novelists, poets and dramatists, has its roots in this fictional conception of 'the democratic intellect'. It is revealing, however, to note that the other main strand of Scottish philosophy was that of David Hume, whose scepticism regarding the validity of any religious or transcendental human experience, is essentially opposed to common sense. Paradoxically, for many Scottish writers, this sceptical counter-influence can work in tension with common sense; if Galt's minister is essentially an illustration of natural goodness in action, his provost Pawkie of Gudetown in *The Provost* (1822) is canny and utilitarian shrewdness in action, and, for all Galt's sly revelation of his merchant's selfish weakness, it is a portrait which approves his actions for their ultimate benefit to his community.

Scotland in the age of Scott seemed caught in a struggle between its past and its future, split at almost every level in its own sense of identity, divided in religion, divided in philosophy and divided in politics. It is perhaps hard nowadays for us to understand why the Scottish Tory establishment reacted so fiercely against the principles of the 1789 French Revolution since so many of these radical ideas are now accepted as fair and sensible. Before we condemn that outlook too readily, however – and it included Scott, as lawyer, sheriff of Selkirkshire, and important Border landowner – we should remember the widespread horror felt among even those initially sympathetic to the Revolution as they witnessed the bloody sequel to revolt. We should understand their very real fear as they envisaged all order, all social structure, being swept away in the French tide of levelling and lust for revenge. Scotland, with its centuries of internecine struggle, its wars of independence and religion and Jacobitism, seemed to be in real danger of losing all the benefits which the later eighteenth century had brought about in land and urban improvement. It was predictable that this precarious new society and economy would be deeply divided as to how to handle political issues such as extension of the franchise, burgh reform, and patronage.

The ferocity and scale of debate can be seen in the great new periodicals of the day which grew up out of Scotland's active intellectual arena, presenting opposing views on everything from politics to poetry. The Whig *Edinburgh Review* began in 1802 and, largely in response, the Tory review *Blackwood's Edinburgh Magazine* (1817) was begun by one of the many new entrepreneurial Edinburgh publishers, William Blackwood, and edited by Scott's son-in-law, John Gibson Lockhart, and later over a long period by John Wilson ('Christopher North'). It is yet another paradox of the time that publishing, with great names such as Constable, Nelson, Chambers, Collins, Oliver and Boyd, should make Edinburgh so eminent in literature, rivalling London, while within Scottish literature and culture there should be such polarisation of opinion and values. Constable's financial crash in 1826 brought bankruptcy to Walter Scott, whose finances were interwoven with his thoroughly concealed partnership with the Ballantynes. But it also proved a damaging blow to publishing in Edinburgh, and thus contributed to the decline of Scottish culture after the 1830s.

Perhaps then, the greatest damage to Scottish culture and society came not so much with the death of Scott, followed so soon by the deaths of Galt and Hogg, but with the disintegration of that relatively small community of thinkers and writers who had managed precariously to balance the claims of religion and sceptical thinking, together with the claims of the old and new Scotlands, and who had, through this balance and fruitful interchange of ideas, created the Enlightenment. Its decline was brought about by several negative events occurring simultaneously. Anglicisation and snobbery in values, which increasingly affected all levels of society, from lawyers and ministers to the universities and the reviews; the inexorable movement away from a rural traditional culture, which had managed to combine oral and literary traditions in a vigorous last phase, with the poetry of Ramsay, Fergusson, Burns, and Hogg; and the breakdown, brought about by the Disruption of the Church of Scotland in 1843, of that unstated compromise between the church and the philosophers which persisted during the Enlightenment. All these saw a Scottish sense of separate identity in culture and literature decline in the mid-nineteenth century to such a state of moribundity that by mid-century it could quite possibly have lapsed into acquiescence with a shared British and imperial destiny. The explanation of why this did not happen must wait until the introduction to the next section; the final contributor to the decline of the Enlightenment during Scott's age must be the Disruption of the Church of Scotland in 1843.

The Disruption was seen by Henry Cockburn as a last heroic act of the old Scotland. It was he who helped found *The Edinburgh Review* and whose *Memorials of His Time* (1856) vividly recall the times of Scott. Cockburn, an advocate, argued that, whatever the rights and wrongs of the Patronage controversy, for nearly half of the ministers of the Church of Scotland to walk out of the General Assembly, leaving safe stipends and manses, taking their families into the unknown, represented a stand for principle on a scale not seen for decades, and probably not to be seen again. 'It is the most honourable fact for Scotland that its whole history supplies,' he wrote. These men were standing up, at whatever cost, for their belief in older Scottish rights established by the Reformation. But the rebellion of the older against the new Scottish Establishment was to end the power of the General Assembly as the centre of Scottish affairs, and for several decades Scotland was to be an annexe of and willing accomplice to imperial Britain.

Evidence of the schisms and divisions in the age of Scott can be felt even now. The uncertainty regarding the future paths of Scottish identity and culture are still to be heard in debates about what should be taught in our schools and universities, and arguments as to how far progress should be resisted by tradition. And for an understanding of this dualism of Scottish thinking, it is worth walking round Edinburgh's Old and New Towns today, remembering that the New Town was built in Scott's childhood, and that he lived in both Old and New. In the building of the New Town, which ended that closely-knit community as yet relatively unaware of class divisions, not only was Fergusson's 'Auld Reikie' physically separated from New Edinburgh, but the city was ideologically split also.

Keeping in mind the vivid dualism of imagery of 'Auld Reikie', the history-haunted Old Town of Edinburgh, and the elegant, geometrically laid-out New Town, the student of the age of Scott is aware of the dominating forces of the time. Scotland is in transition, and loyalties are deeply divided. It is the success of the greatest literature of this time to capture such divisions – between Scotland's heart and its head, and between its adherence to older language, custom and belief and its desire to move away from its murky and uncultivated past.

Change was everywhere, and the major writers exploit the tensions it brought. Scott, above all, captured this conflict, torn as he was personally between his love and fascination for Scotland's vivid and passionate past and his sensible recognition that prudence regarding the present meant rebuilding, railways, gas lighting. Scott's fiction, it can be noted, did not, in the main, romanticise Scotland; instead of celebrating Macbeth, Wallace, Bruce, the tragic Stewarts and Mary, Queen of Scots, Scott worked almost obsessively with the main periods of civil war in Scotland, finding in them his extended metaphors for Scotland's abiding dualisms of politics, religion and culture. James Hogg captured an even older Border Scotland, but still a Scotland deeply divided in religion and political change; John Galt, dealing with more recent social changes in the West, nevertheless has as his main theme the clash of the old ways of church and state with the new; so too, in her own more sly and domestic fashion, does Susan Ferrier, in her contrast of the homely, if grotesque manners of yesteryear with the snobbish affectations of the new, polite Scotland.

At the end of this section, in 'Widening the Range', some of the writing beyond Scott, Hogg and Galt is briefly discussed. But these are the great representatives of the age, and they are dealt with now.

CHAPTER 13

SCOTT AND SCOTLAND

WALTER SCOTT (1771–1832)

Scott was born in the Old Town of Edinburgh. His father was a successful lawyer, his mother the daughter of John Rutherford, Professor of Medicine in Edinburgh University. In addition to this strong Edinburgh background, Scott was, on both sides, descended from some of the oldest families of the Scottish Border country. In childhood Scott suffered infantile paralysis which left him permanently lame in one leg. He was educated both at the High School in Edinburgh (1779–83) and at the Grammar School in Kelso. At Edinburgh University he studied Classics, before, in 1786, being apprenticed to his father. In 1789 he resumed studies at university in Scots Law and Moral Philosophy, and remained there until called to the Bar in 1792. In addition to the study of law, his study of Scottish history and antiquity, and extensive walking expeditions ('raids') in the Highlands, and especially in the Border country, led to his huge knowledge of the history and local legends which went into his novels.

In 1790 he was disappointed in his love affair with Williamina Belsches. She married a banker in 1797; and, as Edwin Muir has realised, this constituted an important and traumatic event in Scott's life. In the same year Scott married Frenchwoman Charlotte Charpentier, and set up homes in Castle Street, Edinburgh, and in a cottage at Lasswade. His first important work was *The Minstrelsy of the Scottish Border* (1802). He edited the old romance *Sir Tristram* in 1804, and in 1805 came success with *The Lay of the Last Minstrel*. After this Scott decided to follow literature as his main support. In 1799 he was made sheriff of Selkirkshire, and later became Clerk of the Sessions, giving him substantial incomes from both law and writing. Scott moved from Lasswade to a cottage at Ashestiel on the Tweed where he stayed from 1804 till 1812. Here he was to write the most successful of his narrative poems, *The Lay of the Last Minstrel* (1805), *Marmion* (1808), and *The Lady of the Lake* (1810), the most popular of the long narrative poems.

In 1812 he bought land on the Tweed near Melrose where he built Abbotsford, to fulfil his dream of becoming a Border laird. (His expenditure on Abbotsford and his 'yerd-hunger' [*greed for land*], together with his complex financial involvement with his printer and later publisher James Ballantyne, was eventually to lead to his financial ruin in 1826.) In 1813 he published the less successful poem *Rokeby*, and, recognising that Byron was proving more popular in this form, he produced anonymously the first of his 'Scotch novels' with *Waverley* in 1814. This was followed by *Guy Mannering* (1815); *The Antiquary, The Black Dwarf* and *Old Mortality* (1816); *Rob Roy* (1817); *The Heart of Midlothian* (1818); *The Bride of Lammermoor*, *The Legend of Montrose* and *Ivanhoe* (1819).

Ivanhoe saw Scott at the peak of popularity and fame, although the novels were published anonymously. The identity of 'the Great Unknown' as author of the Waverley novels became an open secret; in 1820 he was created a baronet by King George IV, and in 1822 he took a leading part in arranging the King's official visit to Edinburgh – the first visit by a British monarch to Scottish soil since the ill-fated second Jacobite Rebellion of 1745. He continued to be productive, if less successful, with novels like *The Monastery* ('the first public failure') and *The Abbot* (1820); and the next few years saw novels like *Kenilworth* (1821); *The Pirate* and *The Fortunes of Nigel* (1822); and *Redgauntlet* (1824). In 1825 he began his *Journal* which he continued until shortly before his death.

In 1826 the collapse of the major publishing house of Constable ruined Ballantyne and thus Scott himself (the same year saw the death of Lady Scott). From this point on he worked for his creditors, retaining only his salary and occasional bonuses allocated to him by the trustees. Nevertheless, in his remaining six years he was to pay off most of his debts – an outstanding undertaking, given that the norm of the age would have been to accept bankruptcy and defray his own losses (although the latest and often caustically critical *Life of Walter Scott* (1995) by John Sutherland points out that creditors were extremely sympathetic to him, so that he continued to enjoy Abbotsford and a high quality of lifestyle till the end). Such outstanding literary effort, including the huge *Life of Napoleon, The Tales of a Grandfather* in four series from 1827 to 1830, and all the remaining Waverley novels, till *Castle Dangerous* in 1831, led to such stress that in 1830 Scott suffered a paralytic stroke. He declined rapidly thereafter, dying at Abbotsford in 1832.

Changing responses to Scott's novels

Scott's fiction, after its initial and colossal success – probably the first example of a world best seller – has passed through a period of critical disfavour. In the latter part of the nineteenth century and early part of the twentieth, his reputation declined to the point in 1927 where in *Aspects of the Novel* E. M. Forster could describe him as a mere story-teller who moved around historical furniture, whose methodology was simply of the 'and then . . . and then' kind. Much of the damage to his reputation came, ironically, from a Scotsman, Thomas Carlyle, who had lamented the lack of fundamental humanity and philosophical enquiry in Scott's fiction – an accusation which modern critical analysis has not upheld. But for a century the denigration continued; F. R. Leavis did not include him in his 'great tradition' of fiction; and even today, the Open University has yet to accord Scott a major place in its courses in literature.

Nevertheless the last twenty years have seen a remarkable critical revival which takes Scott's art very seriously, recognising depths of irony, symbolic meaning, and historical and psychological subtlety which even the most devout of his early readers had failed to perceive. Perhaps these early readers were too close to Scott's astonishing success to see exactly what he was achieving in fictional craft. They were understandably bemused by the sheer prolific immensity of the 'Wizard of the North' (another of Scott's nicknames) who took Europe by storm, firstly with Romantic narrative verse and secondly with Romantic and historical fiction.

We can look back with clearer perception now, and see that some striking and sometimes paradoxical new judgements are emerging. Scott now seems less of the Romantic, more of the Augustan and satirical author, who found himself having to exploit Romantic fashion and imagery in order to appear as a leader in the taste of the new age. Yet behind the creator of the great Romantic poems like *Marmion* (1808) and *The Lady of the Lake* (1810) and novels like *Guy Mannering* (1815), *Ivanhoe* (1819) and *The Talisman* (1825) there is another Scott, deeply concerned with the movement of Scottish history and society, whose themes and treatments are often decidedly unromantic, and even anti-romance.

Most modern Scott criticism recognises that Scott's most powerful creations are fundamentally Scottish. This criticism has recognised that all Scott's fiction tends to express a recurrent basic pattern or situation, in which an older, wilder, and more passionate Disorder gives way to or confronts a new rational, progressive Order. A brilliant contemporary of Scott's, Samuel Taylor Coleridge, perceived this; he thought that the Waverley novels caught the imagination, not merely because the quarrels of the house of Stuart and the great religious struggles were still in living memory, not merely because their language was different from that of the present day and therefore colourful and poignant, and not merely because Scott was profoundly humanitarian. Coleridge identified beneath all this a fundamental confrontation between what he called 'loyalists and opponents', 'the contest between the two great moving principles of social humanity; religious adherence to the past . . . the desire and admiration of permanence . . . and the Passion for greater knowledge for truth as the offspring of reason – in short the mighty instinct of progression and free agency'. Thus early, and unusually, Coleridge identified Scott's fundamental preoccupations.

There is a continuing debate which, put simply, has one side which sees a Scott who responds appropriately and varyingly to the different episodes of Scottish and world history, interpreting the individual and underlying historical forces which shape them; and another which sees a Scott who constantly finds in his subject matter echoes and correlatives for his own relationship with Scotland, which he then projects onto his fiction. The first view broadly descends from the work of the Marxist critic, George Lukacs, in his great work *The Rise of the Historical Novel* (1962). The second view has been put by the American critic Francis Hart in *The Scottish Novel* (1978). (What makes the discussion more complex is that Hart, in his early study of Scott in *Scott's Novels: The Plotting of Historic Survival* (1966), broadly followed the view of Lukacs but reshaped his reading in his study of the Scottish novel.) This raises a fundamental question for the reader. Has Scott many themes, many historic canvases which he punctiliously researches and bodies forth treating each as unique? Or has he essentially a single theme of division, and a divided imaginative landscape, which he expresses in all his fictions?

Scott's sense of division

Scott himself bore frequent witness in his *Journal*, his letters and in all his actions to this fundamental division in his own loyalties as regards Scotland. His upbringing was divided, between living in Edinburgh and the Borders; he was divided in his love of the period of John Dryden and Jonathan Swift and his love of the Romantic period in Europe and of Scottish medieval culture and folklore; divided in his feelings about the constitutional relationship of Scotland to England and the 1707 Act of Union (his head supporting the prudent and materially profitable bond with England and her trade, his heart lamenting the passing of the old languages, customs and characteristics of colourful, eccentric, proud pre-1707 Scotland). In all his Scottish fiction Scott instinctively homes in on periods of civil war, of Scotland against Scotland, as a way of expressing his own sense of tragedy for the old ways combined with (however unwilling) affirmation of belief in the new. Significantly, he has little to say in fiction about many of the outstanding personalities, and the most colourful events of Scotland's pre-

Reformation past. His fiction ignores Kenneth MacAlpin, the ravages of the Vikings, Macbeth, Malcolm Canmore, the decline of the Celts, the reigns of the Alexanders, and, outstandingly, the Golden Age of Scottish culture in the reign of James IV, the time of the great makars of the medieval period, William Dunbar, Robert Henryson and Gavin Douglas, with the tragic fall of that age at Flodden in 1513; and, although John Buchan found his treatment of one of Scotland's most tragic and romantic characters, Mary, Queen of Scots, the best of his pictures of famous women in history, it is not her tragic destiny which is foregrounded. Most surprising of all, perhaps, is his neglect of William Wallace and the Wars of Independence – in his last novel, *Castle Dangerous* (1832) Bruce appears, but again, only in a skirmish of 1306. Instead he recurrently studies a Scotland split within itself, with Covenanter set against Episcopalian, Jacobite against Hanoverian, outlaw against establishment officer. *Rob Roy* (1817) can stand as a typical example of Scott's fundamental system of symbolic patterning, in its juxtapositioning of Rob Roy, archetypal outlaw figure, emblematic of Scotland's ancient tribal loyalties and mythic identity, against Rob's blood cousin, Bailie Nicol Jarvie, prudent Glasgow merchant and defender of the benefits of the Act of Union with its introduction of the sugar, tea and tobacco trade 'west awa yonder' with America.

In an earlier section it was argued that the writers of eighteenth-century Scotland were prone to a 'crisis of identity' in their uncertainty as to their literary and political allegiances. Equally, as one studies the great nineteenth-century writers – James Hogg, John Galt, Robert Louis Stevenson, and others – one finds that virtually every major Scottish writer of the nineteenth century is described by their critics as suffering from a kind of cultural and creative schizophrenia, in the sense that their work exhibits themes of polarisation and psychological dualism. Scott stands at the heart of 200 years of Scotland's uncertain cultural identity. Who better to set forth Scotland's schizophrenic cultural state than one who felt the division so deeply and personally? Scott was at once Border Baron (or wanted desperately to be so) and sophisticated member of Edinburgh's enlightened and European *literati*, those polite and philosophical professional men who included Adam Smith and David Hume. He lamented the passing of Old Edinburgh and its buildings, yet he patronised developments in gas lighting and railways. He fought for Scotland's symbols of national identity, from its separate bank notes to its crown jewels, yet stage-managed George IV's visit to Scotland in 1822. This was a symbolic ritual of unity greater than any since the Act of Union of 1707, and Scott's promotion of this second 'coronation' represents his spirit of Unionist compromise at its most outstanding. Often criticised for his part in this great show of Scottish royalist loyalty, it should also be remembered that Scott saw this regal visit as signifying reconciliation between the nations, an end to ancient enmity and the beginning of what he hoped would be a genuine partnership.

Amidst these dualisms and divisions, Scott held to one particularly Scottish set of beliefs within which he had been schooled at university. In many ways Scott was a child of the Scottish Enlightenment; and the eighteenth-century school of Adam Smith's philosophy of common sense. Thomas Reid was at its heart, in its belief in the perception of good or evil, located in feeling and sentiment rather than in willed intelligence. Scott was to use the central beliefs of common-sense philosophy as his solid basis for the reform and regeneration of a Scotland too long divided and self-destructive. A belief in the instinctive goodness of ordinary people, allied to a lawyer's commitment to social order, planned by reason and aided by compromise along with a distrust of fanatical and anachronistic attitudes led Scott in his early fiction to look at Scotland's civil wars through the eyes of a protagonist aware of the competing claims of the heart and the head, of traditional loyalties and those of independent reason.

It is easy to attack Scott from the perspective of the twentieth century as being reactionary and high Tory. Indeed his contemporary and friend James Hogg considered that the Reform Bill of 1832 had killed Scott, so averse was he to the idea of the extension of the franchise. But Scott's politics cannot be simplified in this way. He was intensely aware of the fragility of social stability and order; not only had he seen Scotland destroy itself repeatedly in previous centuries, but he was, of course, deeply sceptical about the French Revolution of 1789, having seen its initial idealism give way to internal squabbling and butchery, together with the 'Reign of Terror' which ensued. Perhaps Scott had too high a respect, as a lawyer, for the stability of established law and order; and too little for the capabilities of democratic action; but his reading of history had clearly made him sceptical regarding the validity of radical social change.

Nevertheless, a sensitive reading of Scott's fiction discovers a surprising characteristic. Just as the later and apparently imperialist and British-worshipping twentieth-century novelist, Joseph Conrad, can be seen under the surface of his imperialism to be profoundly sceptical about the corrupting influence of power, Scott, a century before Conrad, was to work in similar paradoxical fashion on two levels. On the first and superficial level, Scott seems to support capital order and establishment tranquillity. Yet beneath the surface, at the level of the underdogs and victims of history, Scott shows a rare anger and reductive scepticism about the effects of authority upon them

– in the plight of Jeanie Deans in *The Heart of Midlothian,* in the plight of the peasant Cuddie Headrigg in *Old Mortality,* in the plight of the simple Highlander Evan Dhu in *Waverley,* condemned to execution for participation in what must have seemed to him a perfectly legitimate and principled struggle.

Scott is therefore yet another – and perhaps the most outstanding – of Scotland's many paradoxical writers. Having set the context of Scottish culture and his own personality briefly, we now look at his pioneering achievements in the novel form.

Scott and the novel

Scott's contributions to the novel form have been insufficiently credited. True, individual writers have excelled his achievements in almost every category, in their advanced use of symbolism, in their sophisticated narrative expression, in their subtlety of psychological analysis. But the great nineteenth-century authors of Europe and the USA had no doubt that it was Scott who had fundamentally reshaped the novel as a form – and perhaps here we can consider briefly some major headings under which Scott contributed to the novel. These consist of three sets of linked pairs; the development of the study and use of history in fiction, together with an insight into individual psychology; the development of the use of landscape as a participant feature in fiction, together with a crucial extension and development of the use of symbols; and the exploitation of the vivacity and colour of romance while simultaneously undermining the illusions of romance with a reductive realism which, at its best, turns his novels into antiromances, with anti-heroes at their heart.

HISTORY AND PSYCHOLOGY

Taking these in turn, and dealing with the topics of history and psychology first, we find that Scott has often been praised for his developments in historical fiction. The Marxist critic, George Lukacs, in *The Rise of the Historical Novel* (1962), accords Scott the principal place in the development of real historical fiction (as opposed to pasteboard period-set melodramas). What makes Scott different from his predecessors here? One can see Scott's importance by comparing his insights into history with those of his immediate predecessor in Scotland, David Hume, the distinguished sceptical philosopher. Hume was also a historian; and his historicising is typified in his *History of England* (1763), in which, dealing with the topic of the Covenanters of the seventeenth century, he describes them as fanatical, without allowing them legitimate grievance or analysing their predicament, and, from the standpoint of an eighteenth-century man of reason, dismissing their actions as almost wilful and irresponsible. Now we understand differently; recent Scottish historians have increasingly identified the political and social reasons underlying Scotland's recurrent religious civil wars. The Covenanters sought political expression just as much as freedom of conscience, but Hume – in keeping with the bulk of eighteenth-century historians (and indeed like many of the major nineteenth-century historians such as Henry Buckle, in his *Scotland and the Scotch Intellect*, 1861) – failed to recognise the often honour-able and valid reasons underlying revolt.

Consider then Scott's way of viewing political, social and religious antag-onisms (such as are found in miniature in his 'The Two Drovers' of 1827) in *Waverley, Old Mortality*, and *The Heart of Midlothian*. Scott, despite being anti-Jacobite and Episcopalian, tries with integrity and understanding to see the point of view of his opponents, and the rebels against Establishment. In 'The Two Drovers', Robin Oig's pride in his ancestry and race are understood; as is the difference between his sense of being 'a gentleman' and Harry Wake-field's bluff acceptance of his peasant state. And if Scott does this in microcosm here, so at the higher level he understands what motivates those characters whose views he does not share, such as Evan Dhu, the loyalist Highlander, the Highland chieftains and the Royal Stuart Pretender, as well as understanding what makes Henry Morton, the thoughtful and reasonable Protestant, rebel against the state in *Old Mortality*. In all his fiction, whether set in Scotland or not, whether to do with Anglo-Saxons versus Normans, Cavaliers versus Roundheads, or Crusaders versus Saracens, Scott works hard to find and represent the motives behind each cause – and will, for example, allocate honour or blame, sometimes surprisingly, as when he praises Saracens and decries the brutality of Crusaders. Thus Scott's historical fiction is modern and pioneering in the sense that it assumes that there is always a reason behind extreme action; and that a genuine liberal (with a small 'l') awareness will try extending understanding as far as it can. No other writer in the world at this time undertook such a noble and extensive re-reading of large-scale human action; nearly all Europe and the USA's great writers, from Flaubert, Hugo and Tolstoy to Cooper and Melville admired and followed his examples, so that, however improved on latterly, Scott initiated many of what what are now considered as hall-marks of modern fiction, and not just in the handling of history, but in the areas that follow.

INDIVIDUAL PSYCHOLOGY

If history is man written large, psychology is the intimate account of individual action. Here of course, Scott was accompanied in fictional innovation by the writer he admired immensely, Jane Austen, whose acute analyses of sensitive minds and social behaviour had begun with *Sense and Sensibility* in 1811, and whose *Emma* (1815) can be compared with *Waverley* (1814) in respect of their shared examination of dangerously excessive Romantic sensibility. It may sound odd to pair these two, but Scott with his 'big bow-wow strain' admired Austen's painstaking precision in getting human motivation exactly right, because he felt the need to do this himself. After all, an understanding of the psychology of mankind's movements on the large scale necessitates an understanding of the individual action that precipitates it. Where Henry Fielding in his preface to his novel *Joseph Andrews* (1742) offers an enquiry into 'manners, not men', Scott specifically reverses this in his introduction to *Waverley* by insisting his enquiry was into 'men, not manners'. Scott was specifically stating that he was reversing the approach of eighteenth-century fiction in order to look at the individual and his idiosyncratic psychological behaviour, rather than at the relatively undifferentiated social types so beloved of the Augustans.

If it is easier to see that Scott's handling of history is innovatory, as in *Waverley*, then a little consideration will show that the psychological motivation of the main figures – Waverley and his romantic delusions, Flora and her stern idealism, her brother Fergus with his ambitions for his earldom causing him to abandon his normal standards of decency and fair play, and even Evan Dhu, with his Highland codes of loyalty enduring till death – is such a preoccupation with Scott, that he takes great care to persuade us that these characters act in such a way because they have been brought up or conditioned in that way. Thus Scott fulfils E. M. Forster's requirements that mature fiction is a matter of 'character is action and action is character'; that is to say, people are defined by what they do, but what is done is defined by people. This sounds so obvious as to be a truism, but when one considers the eighteenth-century novel, one realises that this kind of insight was just not present. Consider, for example, Daniel Defoe's character of Moll Flanders in the novel of that name (1722). She leads a picaresque life of debauchery and sexual escapade, but at the end, with no persuasive context or study of motivation, simply decides to reform and settle down, most unconvincingly leaving us her story, as she tells us, for moral edification. We are not persuaded by her change because Defoe has taken no time nor effort to make us understand why she might reform. Similarly, central characters like Joseph Andrews and Tom Jones, simply 'reform' or change their lifestyle according to their author's rather arbitrary wishes. Along with Jane Austen, Scott represents a new development in fiction which sees the need to supply reason and psychological verisimilitude in human behaviour.

LANDSCAPE AND SYMBOLISM

In Scott's use of landscape and symbolism, the next linked pair of issues by which he changed the novel, his contribution is majestic and unique. Jane Austen rarely employs landscape in a way which organically integrates with the development of her characters and the unfolding of her plot – with the exceptions perhaps of the use of the layout of the grounds in *Mansfield Park* (1814), or the unusual episode of the simultaneity of the miserable pouring weather with Emma's shame and grief in *Emma*. In this she is typical of her predecessors in the English novel. Even more in Fielding and Smollett, landscape is used simply as paste-board, almost stage-set, background. Scenes are set in a tavern, and the journeys between these taverns are episodes of farce or danger in coaches, with robbers in woods and heroic rescues. The woods, the inns, the journeys, are in no way developed in atmosphere or character as contributive to the overall design – contrasting with the way in which William Wordsworth explores the atmosphere of Tintern Abbey or the specific settings of lake and village in *The Prelude*.

Here Scott is more in tune with the great Romantic poets, in their awareness that landscape is a living entity, complementary to human behaviour. Later novelists developed this with astonishing facility. The Brontës inextricably linked people and places, as with Heathcliff in *Wuthering Heights* (1847), who is quite literally the spirit of heath and cliff, an intrusion of natural forces into the human action of that novel; or in the novels of Thomas Hardy, where Egdon Heath, or the woodlands of Dorset, or the Roman amphitheatres and Gothic cathedrals of Christminster, played an equal and symbolic part in the story of their protagonists. Scott brought romantic landscape into fiction. The blue mountains of the Highlands in *Waverley* are not just a painted background, but almost symbols of the state of mind of young Edward Waverley and his growing delusions; and in the scenes on Arthur's Seat in *The Heart of Midlothian*, Jeanie Deans sees the darkness and the legends surrounding that Edinburgh hill as portents of something satanic and menacing. Scott identifies certain kinds of people with certain kinds of places; so that, for example, Highlanders and Covenanters are radicals and agents of Disorder, identified with wild and outlawed places, places beyond civilisation, at one with the disorderly elements of nature.

As with history and psychology, the natural extension of this use of landscape is outwards to a more general symbolism, which novelists such as Charles Dickens, the Brontë sisters, and Nathaniel Hawthorne and Herman Melville in America, were to make, if not commonplace, highly impressive and normative in novels like *Wuthering Heights* (1847), *The Scarlet*

Letter (1850), *Moby Dick* (1851) and *Bleak House* (1852). This is not the place to examine uses of symbolism in the nineteenth century; it is a complex subject, with varieties of symbolism presenting themselves such as the strict definition pertaining to French symbolist poets like Rimbaud and Verlaine, where a 'symbol' has a very precise meaning; or the more generalised idea of, for example, the symbol of the great white whale in *Moby Dick*. In the latter novel the whale represents ever more suggestive ideas – the mystery of God's creation, the mystery of life itself, the goal of Ahab's bitter and vengeful quest, and perhaps in the end God and benevolence in the world.

Scott perhaps does not go to these extreme metaphysical lengths in his symbolism but he does originate the methodology which leads in this direction, for example, and outstandingly, the symbolism of *The Heart of Midlothian*, where the heart is an ambiguous symbol. On the one hand, it represents the sick heart of the law courts of Scotland, and therefore the malign or cancerous heart of Scottish justice located at the heart of the land itself in Midlothian. On the other hand, it is the healing or regenerative heart of the peasant country of Scotland in the middle of the Lothians, in the person of Jeanie Deans, the cow-feeder's daughter who, in opposition to the corruption and expediency of Scottish law, stands as representative of 'commonsense philosophy', challenging what has gone wrong in Scotland by insisting on what is good at grass roots level. We can identify many examples of such symbolism in *Waverley*, from Waverley's increasing mental disintegration as he passes across the borderline between the Lowlands of Scotland into the blue mountains of the Highlands, where these blue mountains are as much figments of his imagination as reality; or in the 'King's cavern', that burning fire at the heart of Romance; or in the stag hunt which wounds him so grievously – a piece of symbolism which suggests simultaneously the nobility and treachery attendant in that Highland fero-city. In order to reassess Scott, we have to be responsive and alive to his poetic metaphoric imagination.

ROMANCE AND REALISM

The last linked pair in Scott's innovatory deployment of ideas is that of Romanticism and anti-Romanticism. Once again, the study of Romanticism is a huge area which it is impossible to explore here. Suffice it to say that in volume 2 of *The History of Scottish Literature 1660–1800* (1987), editor Andrew Hook argues that Scott brought Scotland into the full glare of European Romanticism. He places Scotland at the centre of that movement because of the contributions of Burns and Ossian, as well as Scott's romantic poetry and fiction. However, as volume 3 of *The History of Scottish Literature* (edited by

Douglas Gifford, 1989) argues, there are two sides to this position of Scotland in the Romantic movement. Scotland can be seen as a country which exploits Romanticism for its own ends, for instance, through the rather spurious authenticity of Macpherson's *Ossian*, and Robert Burns's constant manipulation of various registers. Scott is no exception here in that his novels simultaneously exploit the colour and variety of the Scottish Highlands and Scottish history for all they are worth, but, at a deeper level, find at the heart of this colour and history some questionable and reductive motives.

Certainly Waverley discovers magnificent variety, impressive colour and adventure in the Scottish Highlands, but Scott is at pains to point out that Waverley's stability is highly suspect, that he is in a sense a self-conceived romantic looking for a dramatic canvas, and is often guilty of painting his own reality. Scott undercuts Waverley's romantic perceptions by showing (through the figure of the idiot Davie Gellatley, or through the reader's understanding of the real motives of Fergus the Highland chieftain) that the well-springs of such human idealism are really self-advancement and greed. This is true of the Highlanders and 'noble savages', or at least their leaders, in *Waverley*; it is true of many of the leaders and extremists of the Covenanting movement in *Old Mortality*; and it is true of the magistrates, the politicians, even the ministers and the monarchy in *The Heart of Midlothian*. For a Tory, Scott is not lax in undercutting and satirising the apparent nobility and authority of his Establishment figures. For a Romantic poet, he writes a strangely anti-heroic fiction.

Scott then, was caught in the transition from the Augustan age to the Romantic age; in the changes from an older Scotland to a new, post-Union and post-Jacobite Scotland. Yet how aware was Scott of his predicament? And following this, how much did Scott succeed in objectifying his own situation into a conscious art in his fiction? There is no quick and easy answer to this; indeed, one might argue that such is the complexity of creative genius that the writer is often unaware of the extent to which he makes coherent art out of his own situation. There are numerous examples, from Dickens and Melville to modern Scottish writers like Lewis Grassic Gibbon and Neil Gunn, of writers who admit that their work often has meanings that they did not intend. But Scott was certainly aware of the peculiar nature of his fictions. D. D. Devlin, in his excellent volume of essays, *Walter Scott: Modern Judgements* (1968), argues in his introduction that Scott was well aware of the criticisms of careless planning, and, outstandingly, of his creation of 'insipid heroes', men caught up and trapped within the competition of opposing factions. Scott's anonymous review in 1817 of his early novels pretended to criticise his own work under an adopted *persona*, singling out his own slight constructions, his excessive love of vivid effect, and his recurrent trapped heroes. Devlin argues that, since Scott did nothing to change this recurrent set of characteristics in his fiction, Scott's desire was consciously to create something deeper than a well-told conventional tale. In the end, in order to measure his achievement, we have to decide what Scott's deeper purpose was, and how far he realised it.

The Scottish novels: a regenerative mythology for Scotland?

Space does not permit an overall survey of the range of Scott's fiction – or even his Scottish fiction, such is the extent of both. There is a huge amount of critical work available on Scott's achievement in the novel generally, which the interested reader can follow up. The next chapter gives extended attention to the first, and arguably the greatest, of the Waverley novels. What follows here is an attempt to assess some of the most important Scottish novels in the corpus of Scott's work and to establish their place in his noble, but perhaps unsuccessful, attempt to forge new narratives of regeneration for Scotland (in poetry as well as in fiction) – outstandingly in the period 1805–18. This was Scott's major theme.

Scott sought to create a new mythology for Scotland – new narratives of Scottish history and culture which would forgive the internecine past and allow post-Union Scotland to come to terms with its equal partnership with England. He knew, as a lawyer still working on the cases of forfeited Jacobites, just how divisive the rebellions had been. He knew how terrible had been the killing times of religious civil war, and he knew too that his forebears of the Borders had been part of a too-long history of feuding, not just with England, but amongst themselves. Add to this the old wars with England, and Scott's view was complete – that the bloody past must be changed. However much he loved the songs and stories of the disorderly past, Scotland in the present, his prudent thinking told him, had to learn to be different – not to give up its identity, but to fashion a new mythology, which would give dignity to the story and support that side of the Union arch which was Scotland. The early epic poems have their place in his noble attempt; *The Lay of the Last Minstrel* (1805) lays to rest, appropriately enough, the far-off off feuds of the Border Scotts, and sees all that as an ancient music. As with *The Lady of the Lake* (1810), with its anticipation of Scott's fictional treatment of the Highlands, and its tale of King James bringing that disorderly part of the country into harmony with his Lowlands, the central theme is reconciliation and movement towards national unity. In a different and more subtle way, *Marmion* (1808), with its very British introductory cantos mourning British politicians, seems to argue that the ancient enmity of the two countries is an old mortality, a long-forgotten hostility.

Waverley, Old Mortality and *The Heart of Midlothian* (all appearing within the years 1814–18) can be seen as a kind of trilogy in which he nobly attempts to create a regenerative mythology for Scotland. In the first two novels he worked through the greatest upheavals of the previous 200 years – crises of constitution, monarchy and religion – and then, failing to find the historical and symbolic solutions he wanted, he moved on, in *The Heart of Midlothian*, to try to find this solution within a much smaller, and apparently trivial episode of Edinburgh history.

OLD MORTALITY

Waverley is fully treated in the next chapter; its successor, *Old Mortality* (1816) turned from Scotland's political and Jacobite problems to its religious tensions – and to a Scottish protagonist, caught in the middle of the war between Covenanters and Royalist Episcopalians. Henry Morton is university-educated, and instinctively a moderate in religion and politics, but because of his Protestant lineage, and his father's noble role in older religious wars, he is duty bound to take up the old cause when the Royalists, under Claverhouse, begin once more to persecute the Presbyterians. On both sides he faces enemies, even within the Protestant cause he espouses. His father's old comrade-in-arms, the uncompromising Balfour of Burley, murderer of Archbishop Sharp, manipulates the young man as a pawn in his bigger game. Habbakuk Mucklewrath, the aptly named zealot who is placed symbolically at the heart of the Covenanting camp, would alter time itself to execute Morton; and even the noble figure of Richard Macbriar, courageous martyr to the cause, is seen as part of the disease of religious extremism which threatens to destroy Morton and his country.

Scott has been accused, with some validity, of bias against the Covenanting side. He became Episcopalian in later life, and he disliked religious extremity, as his fine satirical portrait of canting David Deans in *The Heart of Midlothian* shows. But he demonstrates that Morton's Royalist enemies can be imbalanced and cruel too; his masterly portraits of Claverhouse, smooth, detached and ruthless, and his soldiers, like Bothwell, a brutal killer of noble lineage, show that Scott's satire could cut both ways. And it extends to the lesser characters also. Lady Margaret Bellenden, a snobbish and unthinking Royalist, and her unlikely counterpart in shrewish and bigoted old Mause Headrigg, who offers her son to martyrdom, are the most extreme of the lesser characters, rounding out the familiar Scott patterning of division, in this case between fanatical rebellion and insensitive Establishment. In these oppositions of past and present, disorder and order, heart and head are echoed the divisions of *Waverley*.

In the middle are caught the suffering ordinary people like Morton, the decent peasant-servant Cuddie Headrigg, and most poetically powerful of all, blind Bessie McLure, sitting symbolically at the crossroads where Morton is forced to choose; up into the mist and danger of the hills with the Covenanters, or back to the lusher valleys of privilege and Establishment. The figure of Bessie McLure, sightlessly enduring the loss of her sons, is a striking symbol for suffering Scotland – just as Old Mortality himself, the almost mythical figure who cleaned the graves of the martyrs, but has now passed into history, represents the long memory of fanaticism, as well as the fact that such fanaticism will eventually die through the passage of time.

All Scott's great features are here – his psychological probing and analysis of bigotry on both sides; his sense of a history which coerces ordinary people; his symbolism in figures like Morton and Bessie, and his contrasting landscapes, embodying on one hand the austerity of the heights of mind as well as territory, and on the other the power of authority. Romance, as always, is tempered with acute realism, as seen in the sketch of the wily innkeeper Neil Blane, who has learned to protect his interests by speaking with two voices, one for Covenanters, and one for Royalists. But somehow the novel fails in its aim of creating a regenerative narrative, perhaps because Morton is not, for all his heroic qualities, Scotland's hero; he has to flee to Holland, and must return by the back door, in disguise, to gain Edith, with his exile only finally resolved when the Bloodless Revolution of 1689 brings William of Orange from Holland to England's throne. Although William is King of both countries, it is the English solution to England's problems which, as it were, in passing, gives Scotland's Presbyterian solution to its religious wars. History has not allowed Scott's mythical story to work as a representation of Scotland solving its own problems; and brave, decent Morton, a fictional hero, cannot function as, say, did Blind Harry's Wallace, as a real figure becoming myth and example.

ROB ROY

If it is history which defeats Morton and Scott in *Old Mortality*, what then of *Rob Roy* and *The Heart of Midlothian*, both appearing in 1817–18? Rob Roy was perhaps Scott's attempt at a Wallace-style figure from history fitting for mythology; but there is a strange vacillation in Scott's presentation. On one hand Rob is indeed a tower of strength, adaptable to English, Scottish Lowland, and Highland settings, such is his acute intelligence, his confidence, and resolve. In any other period and setting he would shine as the complete man; decent to enemies, loyal to all manner of friends, and most of all, true in an almost chivalric honour to his cause. Beside him all other characters – young Frank Osbaldistone, whose Waverley-like story of Scottish adventuring this is, his evil cousin Rashleigh and his outlandish Northumbrian tribe, spirited Diana Vernon, and even the kenspeckle Bailie Nicol Jarvie of Glasgow – shrink in comparison. But the old oppositions are still there – passionate and devious rebels, prudent and established merchants, with their respective causes of the ferocious past and the prosaic present. Nowhere does Scott symbolise his 'unified design', as it has been termed, better than in the opposition of Rob and the Bailie. Highland wildness and passion are set against Lowland douceness and order. Yet these blood-cousins will meet in darkness to help each other, even although each despises the other's life-choices. Thus Scott symbolises the blood-loyalties of a divided Scotland, and the ancient quarrels which separate at every level, economic, social, and religious.

Rob Roy, however, is in the end revealed, not as a representative of the Highland or Jacobite cause, but once again the man in the middle, since he is of the proscribed 'children of the mist' – the MacGregors, against whom all men's hands are turned, Highlander or Sassenach. In the end he is a man alone, and thus Scott's search for his redemptive Scottish symbol again fails (although he has, in the attempt, marvellously caught figures representative of Scotland's internecine character, from the surprisingly adaptable Bailie and bigoted Andrew Fairservice to Rob's horrific wife Helen, who symbolises the worst of Highland savagery). Rob Roy cannot be Scotland's Robin Hood; Scottish history once more does not allow it.

THE HEART OF MIDLOTHIAN

Faced with the facts of history, Scott as historian was too honest to continue attempting to mould it to his own wishes. Instead, in *The Heart of Midlothian* (1818) (the title indicating that this is a novel about the essence of Middle Scotland) Scott moves out of the circumstances of mainstream history to minor events and minor figures – outstandingly, Jeanie Deans, the 'cow-feeder's daughter', who will, surprisingly, come to symbolise Scottish resilience, decency and redemptive goodness. Indeed, there is a running symbolic reference throughout the novel to Bunyan's *Pilgrim's Progress* (1678) which parallels the journey and tribulations of Jeanie and her sometime companion, the natural Madge Wildfire, with that of Mercy and Christiana. Scott clearly envisioned Jeanie's epic quest for justice, her astonishing walk to London to gain a pardon for her sister Effie from the king, as representing the essential integrity and goodness of the Scottish people, as Jeanie takes on a wide range of Scottish and British corruption. The law has incarcerated her sister Effie on the presumption that she has murdered her missing child and again abuses her through the devious lawyer Sharpitlaw, who tempts her to lie to save her sister. The church's failings are manifested in her devout but self-interested father's canting religiosity and hypocrisy, and his refusal to lie himself to save his daughter Effie, despite his willingness to allow Jeanie to do so. And even at the heart of Britain, in London's Royal court, Jeanie discovers that corruption thrives. Nowhere better is the lie given to accusations against Scott that he was the Establishment's man than in his exposure of rottenness at the very heart of monarchy. History knows that Queen Caroline was no paragon of virtue, yet it was her zeal which forced the harsh laws in Scotland against child murder and concealment. She becomes, however, almost a figure of virtue as Jeanie turns her coldness to pity. But Caroline has to send Jeanie to Arabella, the mistress of the king, for Effie's pardon. Scott makes the irony clear to the attentive reader. And Jeanie's ability to convert her enemies and gain powerful allies, from the Laird of Dumbiedykes and his monstrous housekeeper, Mrs Balchristie, to the Duke of Argyll and the queen herself, is symbolic of Scotland's natural goodness in action. When Jeanie asks her father what she must do, cruelly trapped as she is between the laws of God and the laws of man, he cannot answer; she appeals to nature's voice, and to that 'common sense' which Scottish philosophy argues all of humanity possesses. Her reward, the Duke of Argyll's gift of the church living of Roseneath to her and her minister husband, is not as irrelevant as some critics have made out. Roseneath is not an island, as Scott made it, but a peninsula in the Clyde estuary, poised between Lowland and Highlands. Scott was trying to show a Scotland in miniature, which Reuben Butler and Jeanie would civilise from its old Highland – Lowland feuding. Her 'island' will become a new country, the old Scotland regenerated, abandoning ancient divisions, and Jeanie is Scotland's redemptive spirit. Thus Scott tried to fashion his most potent symbol for Scottish regeneration; but for all her symbolic role, and for all that Scott could elsewhere show acute psychological understanding, in the end Jeanie perhaps fails to convince as a human being, carrying as she does such excessively heavy symbolic meaning, and called on, as a simple peasant girl, to express excessively profound ideas of morality and philosophy.

The Heart of Midlothian may not succeed in this respect, but it shows all the strength and subtlety of Scott's 'unified design'. It has a long, apparently unrelated first movement, telling of the eighteenth-century Porteous riots, when the captain of the city guard, Porteous, fired on a mob who were protesting at the hanging of two smugglers. This will link to Jeanie's story later; but the account gives Scott the chance to contrast older, wilder Scotland, in which smuggling is seen as permissible, with the new, post-Union Scotland which will not tolerate it. In the introduction, Scotland's old propensity to crimes of passion is contrasted with new manners; and throughout, Scott makes play of an older age giving way to a new and more orderly society. Figures like Madge Wildfire and her witch-like mother, together with the wild smugglers Wilson and Robertson, responsible for the hanging of Porteous, sharply contrast with lawyers like Sharpitlaw and sly advocate Nicol Novit at Effie's trial, and the self-seeking and cowardly Edinburgh magistrates.

Scott's symbolism is nowhere more obvious than in this novel, with Jeanie herself the healing Heart of Midlothian, in contrast with the sick heart, the hated Tolbooth jail, in the middle of Edinburgh's High Street; and Jeanie's journey to London acting as a symbolic quest for justice and mercy. What is not perhaps so well realised is how subtly Scott weaves an ironic and anti-Establishment pattern of pardons in this novel. Two pardonable crimes are unpardoned; those of Effie, for long wrongly accused of child-murder, and Wilson and Robertson, admittedly criminals, but in the eyes of the populace romantic figures who should be pardoned. Conversely, two unpardonable crimes are pardoned; Porteous, a multiple killer, is pardoned (and wined and dined on the floor above Effie's cell); and 'daddie Rat', Ratcliffe the Border footpad and thief, is pardoned – and made keeper of the Tolbooth jail!

And it continues; for Robertson, who escapes, turns out to be the father of Effie's child, and son of a respectable English clergyman; and long after Effie is pardoned and has married him, Robertson becomes the King's Commissioner to the General Assembly of the Church of Scotland. The reader is left with the wonderfully ironic sight of Sir George and Lady Effie leading the procession of Edinburgh's worthiest down the High Street past the cells in which Effie lay – and past the place where George hanged Porteous. And in a final display of symbolic irony, Scott has their son (who had been stolen by Madge Wildfire's mother, and grown up as an outlaw) re-appear on Rose-neath, and, in ignorance, kill his own father.

This produces one outstanding theme for the novel, which Scott never before or after attempted so insistently. It is that of Integrity versus Expediency, with virtually all the *dramatis personae*, with the possible exceptions of humble Reuben Butler and the Duke of Argyll, representing Expediency – the end justifying the means, and the adjustment of personal morality for gain; and with Jeanie, of course, unwavering in her alliance of duty with love, as Integrity. Lawyers tempt Jeanie to lie; Porteous is pardoned because it is not expedient to hang a state officer; Ratcliffe is set as a thief to catch a thief;

Jeanie's uncle, the pedantic law-obsessed Bartholomew Saddletrees, is more interested in court formalities than his niece's life, falling asleep during Effie's defence; and, in passages of Scott's most psychologically acute analysis, and in some of his most trenchant religious satire, douce David Deans is seen in the end adjusting his strict religious beliefs – which he would not alter to save his daughter from the gallows – to allow her to marry Butler, a minister whose brand of faith he decries. Deans prohibited Jeanie's marriage before; now, given the Duke's preferment, with the prospect of comfortable retirement ahead, David finds that it is not so hard after all to make faith suit circumstances.

This is why Scott turned in the last part of his 'trilogy' to humbler issues. In Jeanie Deans he could present someone untrammelled by historical involvement, working on a scale more that of local legend than myth or history, someone whose worth lay *outside* history, in the timeless and humble world of Scottish peasantry. What Scott did here is crucial for the later Scottish novel. If Scottish involvement with the major events of history is doomed to failure, some other source of mythic worth must be found. Later Scottish novelists – Galt, Hogg, Stevenson, Macdonald, Oliphant, Alexander, Neil Gunn and, outstandingly, Grassic Gibbon, with his central figure of Chris Guthrie representing Scotland's essential worth in *A Scots Quair* (1932–4) – will all follow him in locating essential Scottish identity and value in just such relatively anonymous, humble and peasant protagonists. For all that Scott could elsewhere show acute psychological understanding, the novel falls short in Jeanie's overburdened symbolic characterisation. With her ends Scott's attempt to create a positive mythology for Scotland. Rob Roy came as close as any of his male protagonists to being the redemptive hero, but again, he is doomed by his history and his clan's predicament. The bathetic fate of his successor, the giant Jacobite of *Redgauntlet* (1824), created ten years later, shows how far behind Scott has left any idea of again attempting to write regenerative fiction. The novel is fine historical romance, with a linked pair of heroes in Alan Fairford and Darsie Latimer which looks forward to David Balfour and Alan Breck in *Kidnapped* (1886); but its anti-climactic ending, in which the British Army courteously escort Redgauntlet and Prince Charles to the boat which will take them for good to France, shows that thus, with a whimper, ends the Jacobite dream. The age of Scottish heroes is over.

Scott's fiction after 1818

Critics generally now agree that Scott's earlier and Scottish fiction is his best. But Scott's best is of the highest quality, and many of the novels we have not discussed deserve to be rediscovered. Broadly, there are three main strands after 1818; the later Scottish novels; the novels, beginning with *Ivanhoe* (1820) which exploit English history; and his 'foreign' novels, from *Quentin Durward* (1823) to *Count Robert of Paris* (1832). These strands interweave; Scott rarely fails to place a Scottish protagonist in the English and foreign novels, so that impoverished young aristocrat Quentin is the romantic centre of his novel, but overall there is a reversal of the perspective of the earlier novels – where English interests and characters intruded into Scotland, Scottish issues and characters intrude abroad – with varying success. Scott maintains his dual vision outside Scotland, recurrently setting older and ultimately doomed cultures against new, progressive and ruthless antagonists – in *Quentin Durward*, for example, with violently impetuous Charles The Bold of Burgundy against wily and prudent Louis XI of France; and in *Ivanhoe*'s Saxons against Normans, or *The Talisman*'s Saracens against Crusaders. Arguably, however, the balanced and fair arguments put forward for old and new causes move away, as Scott's fortunes darken in the mid-1820s, from their earlier fairness and understanding to perspectives more hostile to change. Scott in his last years, plagued with ill-health, increasingly disliked what he saw as the political empowerment of the masses, fearing social destabilisation. Increasingly his novels include reclusive and warped protagonists, and contexts noticeably more bloodthirsty and grotesque; or older and wiser counsellors who see their societies in decline.

Later Scottish fiction

It would be wrong to think that Scott had exhausted his Scottish inspiration by 1818; and wrong to think also that the earlier Scottish novels were of consistently high quality – *The Black Dwarf* (1816) is striking in its portrait of its hideously deformed hero, Elshender the Recluse, but absurdly ill-judged in its ludicrous ending. Nineteen of twenty-seven novels are Scottish-set; the quality of many is decidedly uneven. Scott continued with novels like *A Legend of Montrose* (1819), using the wars, and contrasts of style and belief between Montrose and Argyle as background for his Highland-Gothic tale of clan murder, mistaken birth, and triumphant love. It is perhaps significant that a prominent character here is Dugald Dalgetty, a soldier of fortune who fights for the side which pays him – he and Hal o'the Wynd of *The Fair Maid of Perth* (1828), who similarly fights without regard to moral justification, suggest a growing moral scepticism in Scott. *The Monastery* and *The Abbot* (its sequel, both 1820) use the monastery of Kennaquhair ('know-not-where', but recognisably Melrose) as a link, and the reigns of Elizabeth and Mary, Queen of Scots as their focus respectively, to tell their tales of crossed lovers and mistaken birth. The first relies, to an unusual extent for Scott at this time, on supernatural agencies (The White Lady of Avenal); the second, while the character of Mary may be strongly presented, shares its predecessor's conventionality and slightness of plot. Some of this later Scottish fiction suggests that Scott was casting about for inspiration – with varying degrees of success. His next, *The Pirate* (1822), has some strength in its intriguing treatment of the Northern Isles, which shows Scott typically combining travel experience (he had been on a voyage to the Isles in 1814 as a guest of Robert Stevenson (grandfather of R.L.S.) and the Scottish Lighthouse Commission), local lore and history, and family romance, within the context of ancient Shetland life and superstition in conflict with new ways from outside. *St Ronan's Well* (1824) is the only fiction set in Scott's own time, and is a surprisingly successful and caustic mixture of manners and the familiar tangle of family loves and hates – here expressed through the enmity of two brothers. The novel's deliberately depressing marriage of the unusually modern and mundane world of new tourism, vulgar new money, and drones with Gothic family tragedy is redeemed in Meg Dods, the vigorous Border landlady of the old St Ronan's inn, whose Scots setpieces are some of Scott's finest. And his last, written amidst illness and strokes, *Castle Dangerous* (1832), is remarkably close in plot and character to Hogg's *The Three Perils of Man* (1822), in its story of Border chivalry, castle siege and its heroine disguised as a man.

Critics agree, however, that even in decline Scott could surprise with novels of dark poetry and narrative power; and the greatest of these later Scottish novels are surely the *The Bride of Lammermoor* (1819), *Redgauntlet* (1824) and *The Fair Maid of Perth* (1828). The first, the writing of which Scott claimed to remember little, as he was drugged with laudanum during illness, is ballad-like in its stark settings and its gloomy evocation of a tragic Border feud; the second, with its last great Jacobite, the giant Laird of Redgauntlet, combines the story of an apocryphal last tragic flicker of rebellion with the delightful John Buchan-like adventures of student friends Darsie Latimer and Alan Fairford; while the third, which can be read as Scott's farewell to arms, sets itself in the fourteenth century to enable Scott both to indulge his later fascination for the dark beauty of violence together with his sense of its futility. The final battle of the two feuding clans Quele and Chattan in Perth, arranged by gentle King Robert III, ending in the death of virtually all but the disgraced Highland chief Conachar and the redoubtable Perth armourer Henry Gow, is horrific and bloody, but can be read as symbolic. Scott now clearly sets authority and hierarchical order, as exemplified in his utopian descriptions of Perth and its guilds of glovers and smiths, above the ruffian violence of Highland clans and Lowland intrigue.

Scott's shorter fiction of this period contains at least two works as fine as anything he ever wrote. 'The Two Drovers' and 'The Highland Widow' (both 1827) are tragedies, with some of the anti-English feeling which had entered into his later work from *The Letters of Malachi Malagrowther* (1826: Scott's successful articles against English proposals to stop Scottish banks printing their own paper money). 'The Two Drovers' is probably Scott's finest piece of cultural relativism, in its splendid comparison of Highland, Lowland Scottish, and English attitudes to class and breeding. Its insights into Highland character, pride and superstition are as perceptive as anything written before the twentieth century; yet these cultural assessments are combined with a swiftly moving story of friendship between Highlander and Englishman gone tragically wrong, and a use of settings and dialogue which is virtually flawless in its contribution to Scott's majestic theme, that of the need for different cultures to rise above prejudice to understand one another. That said, Scott shows anti-English prejudice more strongly than Scottish – although his English judge who concludes the tragedy speaks with a nobility which fittingly rounds off what is arguably Scott's greatest single piece of writing. 'The Highland Widow' has much of its economy and tragic power, in its account of the anachronistic mother, embittered against the redcoats who killed her husband after Culloden, who tries to mould her son in the old, savage Highland way. He accepts change where she does not; he joins one of the new Highland regiments, bound for the Americas. Her wiles to stop him lead to his dishonour and execution, and leave her, symbolically, alone, broken, and in the end disappearing like a wounded animal.

The English novels

Scott was well aware, even in the early Scottish novels, of the importance of using English scenes and characters as links with his British audience. Robert Crawford (in *The Devolution of English Literature*, 1992), has rightly pointed out that Scott was trying to create a British consciousness through his explanatory portrayals of peripheral people and places hitherto unfamiliar to an English audience. Such a link can be seen in the eponymous and English protagonist of *Guy Mannering* (1815), but it is noticeable that this early novel reveals how from the beginning Scott was drawn to other fictional modes, those of manners and family romance. Arguably, as here and in *The Antiquary* (1816), with their convoluted stories of missing heirs and mannered love, he is less creatively successful in these modes. This propensity would develop in later work – novels (often immensely popular at the time) like *Woodstock* (1826), *Kenilworth* (1821), *Peveril of the Peak* (1822) and *The Fortunes of Nigel* (1822), for all their passages of vivid historical action, undoubtedly suffer from what now appear as laboured and tortuous interweavings of aristocratic family relations and stilted pseudo-chivalric love interests. It would appear that, whether in English or Scottish fiction, Scott's best writing came when his profoundest feelings for the dualisms of history were involved, so that *Ivanhoe* (which followed just after the greatest Scottish novels in 1820) stands as his finest achievement in English fiction, based as it is on the tension between older Saxon England and the new Norman overlords.

Ivanhoe

Scott's introduction to *Ivanhoe* (written long after the novel itself) describes how he felt that he might 'wear out the public favour' with 'Scottish manners, Scottish dialect, and Scottish characters of note'; and goes lengthily into why he made 'an experiment on a subject purely English'. Does he perhaps protest too much? Is the real reason for the change to the matter of Normans and Saxons and the periods of the Crusades and Robin Hood bound up with the comparative failure of *Old Mortality* and *The Heart of Midlothian* to embody his desire to portray a Scotland renewed, at ease in Union, and with its internecine wars behind it? The dark feelings which assailed Scott in 1818 and 1819, during which he was often painfully and acutely ill, show themselves in *The Bride of Lammermoor*'s sense of the tragic destiny of Scotland; and in the later ironic and reductive Scottish novels which avoid the central issues which the more hopeful Scott had tackled in the earlier novels.

IVANHOE AND SCOTT'S FAMILIAR PATTERNING

Much, however, of the basic patterning of the early Scottish fiction has survived. Scott's tendency to work within a structure of civil war is as strong as ever. England is presented as torn in two by internecine conflict, its problems centring on a basic Norman-Saxon hostility which has survived since 1066. The recurrent 'insipid hero' of the earlier novels has become Wilfred, who may do many (and rather unconvincing) acts of 'derring-do', but spends, like Waverley, much of the novel as a pawn and invalid, perhaps reflecting Scott's own feelings of powerlessness in the face of history. The idea of a deeper but impossible love emerges yet again in the triangle of Rebecca (the young Jewess) – Ivanhoe – Rowena (the Saxon princess). But most significant of all is the way in which that tragic-ironic note of *Old Mortality*, whereby all the action of the novel is put into the perspective of *sic transit gloria mundi*, with the final image of the decaying grave stones of the martyrs and their cause, is also in *Ivanhoe*. At the heart of the romantic description of the chivalry at the tournament at Ashby-de-la-Zouche is Scott's quote from Coleridge: 'The knights are dust / and their good swords are rust . . .'. This is arguably a sign of the increasing disillusion which lies at the heart of his fictional popularity. He goes on (Chapter 8):

> Their escutcheons have long mouldered from the walls of their castles. Their castles themselves are but green mounds and shattered ruins – the place that once knew them knows them no more – nay, many a race since theirs has died out and been forgotten in the very land which they occupied . . . what, then, would it avail the reader to know their names, or the evanescent symbols of their martial rank!

Note how the quotation reveals his creative split. On the one hand his deepest feelings are ironic and tragic; on the other, his desire for money to support his Border dreams of baronial Abbotsford demand he tell the reader these very details of evanescent unimportance in order to perpetuate his popularity – and, in terms of the public, it has been the most popular of all the Waverley novels.

Like *Old Mortality*, it should be read on two levels – firstly, as a well-crafted and highly entertaining romance of chivalry, and secondly, as consistently, if less obviously, a romance presented by an omniscient narrator whose attitude to his creations is frequently and paradoxically ironic and satirical.

THE TRAPPED 'HERO'

Ivanhoe's shield carries the device of 'a young oak-tree pulled up by the roots'. His name is Desdichado, the 'Disinherited Knight'. He is the English oak, denied by his father, and in a sense usurped by the Normans, Front-de-Boeuf in particular. It is a symbolic expression of a familiar theme in Scott, and one touching his essential character more significantly than might at first appear. Recurrently in Scott's fiction the sensitive young hero, from Waverley to Morton and Bertram of *Guy Mannering* and Ravenswood of *Lammermoor*, is disinherited, temporarily or permanently, by the civil antagonisms of the time. *Ivanhoe* translates the patterning of opposites and symbolic polarities Scott had established in his previous Scottish novels into a classic English historical setting, making the warp and woof of the novel the essential difference between the arrogant, and fashionable French-speaking Normans and the rustic, solid, yeoman stock of Saxon Cedric and Athelstane. Scott projects his own internal sense of past against present onto the English scene, but with marvellously convincing weight of circumstantial detail to back up the projection, while the contrasting languages of old English and French are juxtaposed throughout, in much the same way as English and Scots are juxtaposed in the Scottish novels.

OUTLAW SAXONS AND ESTABLISHMENT NORMANS

From the opening discussion of Wamba, Cedric's fool, and Gurth Beowulph (the surname establishing his heroic Saxon pedigree, just as details such as the name of Cedric's dog, Balder, firmly places his master in the same tradition) the tension between Saxon and Norman is firmly entrenched. Defiantly Cedric argues with his Norman guest that he cares not for their 'civilised' refinements: 'I can wind my horn, though I call not the blast either a recheate or a morte . . . I can slay and quarter the animal when it is brought down, without using the new-fangled jargon of curee, arbor, nombles, and all the babble of the fabulous Sir Tristrem.'

LANGUAGE AS SYMBOLIC

When the disguised King Richard wishes to find out more about his host, Friar Tuck, in his country cell, he does so by asking Tuck if he wants as song a *sirvente*, a *lai* (foreign and therefore Norman preferences), or 'a ballad in the vulgar English'. Tuck chooses the ballad: 'downright English am I, Sir Knight'. Even more revealing are the different styles of the letters of the outlaws under Robin Hood to Front-de-Boeuf; of Aymer, the fashionable prior; and of Front-de-Boeuf and Bois-Guilbert, the Knight Templar, back to Robin. Scott uses plain old English for the first; a compromise mixture, typical of Aymer, for the second; and chivalric excess for the third. Thus, as in the Scottish novels, language approaches symbolism, representing the essence of the contending parties, just as, in the Scottish novels, the protagonists carry a symbolic role as well as existing for their own romantic character.

ROWENA AND ENGLISH IDENTITY: REGENERATING ENGLAND?

Chief amongst the protagonists is, of course, Rowena. Like Disraeli's Sybil in the novel of that name, she symbolises the roots of English identity. Scott explicitly sees her in a role reminiscent of Jeanie Deans's regenerative agency when he has Cedric lament that 'the regeneration of England should turn on a hinge so imperfect' – the hinge being Athelstane, the hope being that 'her noble and more generous soul may yet awake the better nature' Athelstane possesses. When Ivanhoe chooses her as queen of the tournament against Prince John's urging of a Norman selection, he symbolically elevates the ancient stock above the new ruling Norman blood. Their final union is meant to suggest the survival in Britain of that pure breed and yeoman worth, that middle-class worth which Scott values so highly in Morton or Guy Mannering, to which Jeanie Deans and Reuben Butler are elevated. A darker side to this blood is suggested in Urfried/Ulrica, the poisoned, embittered daughter of the Wolfgangers, who dies wreaking vengeance on her family's Norman killers, just as a lighter symbolic representation is found in the Robin Hood – Friar Tuck band of outlaws, their green costume and their woodland hiding places representing (like Rob Roy's garb and provenance in Scotland) their legendary and traditional association with England's green and rural oak-strong past. De Bracy and Bois-Guilbert also stand for more than themselves – but their symbolic role belongs to that darker, satirical strain which is the other *Ivanhoe*, just as does that of Rebecca the Jewess.

SCOTT'S IRONY AT IVANHOE'S EXPENSE

It must be admitted that the quality of Scott's creations in this novel is uneven. While Prior Aymer carries on that tradition of worldly expediency represented by Neil Blane in *Old Mortality* or Donald Bean Lean, the Highland con-man in *Waverley*, the two main characters, Ivanhoe himself and Athelstane, are less impressive. Ivanhoe's feats are unconvincing since he lacks the power and ferocity of a Richard, let alone a Bois-Guilbert, and cannot match Front-de-Boeuf's triumphs of brutal energy. Like Scott's previous 'heroes', his love-talk and his philosophising are respectively un-impassioned melodrama and shallow rhetoric, as his debate with Rebecca concerning chivalry, which is dominated by the Jewess, clearly demonstrates. Ivanhoe is a bore, and symbolises a milk-and-water compromise with the very Norman values Scott so clearly dislikes. So too is Athelstane, that wooden comic figure so laboriously put into predictable situations by Scott. This last assertion is easily tested. If one reads literally any of the scenes involving him, one finds the mechanical 'flat' characteristics arising repeatedly – his slothful dullness, his essential but uninspired good nature, and, worst of all, his appetite for food. This last is so ludicrously repetitive and over-played that, when, beyond all suitability to the plot or credibility, he arises from the grave at the end, Scott piles offence on offence and has his main concern manifest itself as hunger and hatred of the priests who imprisoned him because they did not feed him enough! Something of the same tired and flat character-isation goes into Prince John, with his watchword of 'levity' over-used. Scott commits the cardinal sin of telling rather than showing, explaining his character's nature rather than letting it speak for itself in action.

THE STRUCTURE OF *IVANHOE*

There is, however, no denying Scott's control of overall structure in theme, even if this is subject to unfortunate local lapses – such as the clumsy retracing of steps in the plot to keep three or four groups of antagonists abreast of each other. For example, in Chapters 23 to 25, Scott no fewer than four times refers to Robin Hood's sounding the trumpet outside Torquilstone Castle, each time laboriously pulling together four simultaneous strands of the plot. Overall the shape of Ivanhoe is marked out by three great events: the tournament of Ashby-de-la-Zouche, the siege of Torquilstone, and the clash of champions for and against Rebecca at Templestowe, arranged by the Knights Templar. These events of apparent high chivalry are carefully placed as high points, with undercover dealings and negotiations for each of them providing their preambles. In this way Scott's structure assists his overt theme of Saxon against Norman, since each of these high points serves as crisis to the confrontation.

DISGUISES AND PRETENCES

Like *Waverley*, *Ivanhoe* can be read on a second level, where romance is seen from a critical and often ironical standpoint. A most odd feature lies in the plotting – namely, the extent to which disguise is used in the novel, and not just by the villains, but by the heroes of the story. Ivanhoe first appears disguised as a palmer returning from the Crusades; he fights as a disguised knight under the banner 'Desdichado'; King Richard goes through most of the novel disguised as the Black Knight; Friar Tuck pretends to be the holy man of piety, asceticism and celibacy, which he most definitely is not; his master Locksley is in fact Robin Hood; Ulrica Wolfganger appears for long periods under the assumed name of Urfried, hiding her greed for vengeance on the cruel Normans; Cedric escapes disguised as a priest from Torquilstone; even Athelstane's death turns out to be a kind of disguise. All the worthwhile characters have to pretend or hide at some point in the story, while it is the scheming and corrupt *personae* who appear for what they are, with the single exception of De Bracy's short-lived pretence at being a Saxon outlaw in order to capture Rowena and lay the blame on Robin Hood and his kind.

MORAL HYPOCRISIES

Scott's irony here is obvious – or at least its primary function is obvious. It is the riff-raff, the vulgar, the disinherited, and mainly the Saxons, who, despite their apparent outlawry and badges of crime, maintain real order and moral value. The representatives of monarchy, church and august spiritual bodies, like the Knights Templars, the established points of order in the State and Christendom, continually cheat and lie to each other, betraying each other again and again; as King John schemes by placing De Bracy against Fitzurse; as Malvoisin tries to ride with his fanatical Templar masters and his political hope for the future, Bois-Guilbert. Scott has much bitter comment to make on the question of the state of England. Just as in his indirect critique of modern Scottish society in the earlier Waverley novels, it seems that Scott projects yet again his instinctive misgivings about the nature of established power and authority, and his heart-felt attraction towards old traditions of apparent disorder and colourful egalitarianism onto a medieval English backcloth.

SATIRE ON 'MERRY ENGLAND'

This view of England belies his opening comments about the 'pleasant district of Merry England' which opens his tale and consistently undercuts such nostalgic pictures of the past. It is a view which offers a more subtle symbolism, too, in which representatives of the church in the opening chapters are seen to be sadly mixed – 'he is half a monk, half a soldier', says Aymer of Bois-Guilbert. Nevertheless, Rebecca alone carries authority and represents true goodness, and it is striking that Scott's underlying satirical comment on so-called 'chivalry' and England, is that the most penetrating criticism of British and English lifestyles is given to an outsider, an unacceptable and almost untouchable reject of so-called Christendom.

This is most clearly seen when she is compared with the apparent bastion of western Christian and civilised values, the Knights Templar. Can we fail to see Scott's irony here, as he labours the point about honour and chivalry being counted in dead Saracens? A monk blesses his luck on arriving amongst them. The Knight De Bracy assures him of his safety, since 'for Christianity, here is the stout Baron Reginald Front de Boeuf, whose utter abomination is a Jew; and the good Knight Templar, Brian de Bois-Guilbert, whose trade is to slay Saracens – if these are not good marks of Christianity, I know no other . . .'

REBECCA'S LAST WORD ON ENGLAND

Against this 'chivalry' Scott places, alone, Rebecca. Even Ivanhoe is worsted by her in the debate about chivalry in Chapter 29 she having the last word when she censures the 'fantastic chivalry of the word Nazarenes' as cruelty and intolerance in disguise. In the end the imagery of disguise signifies discredit even to Ivanhoe and Richard, since they are unquestioning adherents of the values of chivalry. Scott has Bois-Guilbert express Rebecca's stand in clear symbolic imagery when he refers to her 'thin and light of glove' challenge against the 'heavy steel gauntlets' of the Templars – and of chivalry itself. Admittedly, Ivanhoe serves her well; but again she has the last word when she reveals that she and her father will seek refuge and a better society amongst the Moors of Spain. She voices Scott's deepest purpose in the novel when she sums up all the deaths and deceitful intolerance of England. Rowena has pleaded that she stay with her and Ivanhoe, arguing (without seeing his faults) that King Richard is just and generous (Chapter 44):

> 'Lady,' said Rebecca, 'I doubt it not – but the people of England are a fierce race, quarrelling ever with their neighbours, or among themselves, and ready to plunge the sword into the bowels of each other. Such is no safe abode for the children of my people . . . in a land of war and blood, surrounded by hostile neighbours, and distracted by internal factions . . .'

Thus we are shown that the combination of worldly and ascetic is untenable and that the Templars have become an example of decaying spiritual values. Similarly, Aymer bodies forth a gluttonous denial of the claims of the ideal; and significantly, given directions by the acute and ironic peasant Wamba, he is guided to 'a sunken cross, of which scarce a cubit's length remains above ground'. Unlike this image of degraded Christianity even Tuck's 'chapel perilous' has more genuine value residing in it, for all its love of eating and drinking. Scott distinguishes thus between worldly unacceptable and worldly acceptable; Tuck has at bottom an essential loyalty and instinctive goodness that the official clerics lack. Government, too, is shown as corrupt. Even King Richard receives Scott's ironic and caustic commentary on his triviality and irresponsibility – and Richard is supposed to be one of the chivalric heroes! If one considers, too, that all the sound and fury of the novel is wasted since Richard betrays his own inheritance and duty, going on to ruin the future of Ivanhoe and the yeomanry of England, then something of Scott's paradoxical distrust of 'Merrie England' will be seen.

REBECCA THE JEWESS: SCOTT'S ULTIMATE OUTLAW?
This explains the inclusion of the strand of plot involving Rebecca the Jewess and Isaac her father. For all that Robin Hood or Ivanhoe or Richard are better than John and his Norman minions, it is clear that Scott cannot allow them total authority. Cedric and Athelstane are, in his view, pedantic or slothful anachronisms; and the strange and impressive order that Richard finds in the outlaw camp is not so impressive that Scott means us to see Tuck

and the Merry Men as saviours of true spiritual values; Robin Hood is hardly a figure of mythic redemption of the stature of a Morton or a Jeanie Deans. Even Rowena is not permitted this role and several times Scott alludes to her flaw of having too much of her own regal way. She crumbles in strength when under pressure at the siege of Torquilstone, where Rebecca does not; in addition it is the Jewess Rebecca who triumphantly impresses Bois-Guilbert with her absolute unwillingness to betray her ideals for expediency. Is Rebecca is a descendant of Jeanie Deans in this respect, with a similar function in the novel? Scott has changed his vision, in that Jeanie was central to her society where Rebecca is on the fringe observing as outsider the sickness at the heart of 'Merrie England'.

SCOTT'S FINAL SCEPTICISM

Here yet again is Scott's almost obsessive concern with civil war, with the divisions which are internal to the people and thus to a person. Yet again he has imaged forth his own fundamental scepticism about the survival of essential goodness and sensitivity, in a world where the evils of mob rule are only exceeded by the evils of absolute power wielded without true conscience. This is a very different Scott from that usually purveyed, as great celebrant and historian of Scotland and Britain; underlying his apparent Unionist and Tory attitudes is a buried lack of faith in the possibilities of any political fairness. Certainly, in turning from his early grand theme of a myth of Scottish regeneration, in 1818, he criticised in similar terms the broader society of England, and beyond that the broader societies of the world.

The 'foreign' novels

Scott's ambitions in fiction appeared to know no bounds, as he moved from Scottish and English history to take on (as he did in non-fiction, in his huge *Life of Napoleon*, 1827) challenges from the histories of central Europe and even further afield. *Quentin Durward* draws inspiration from Smollett's novels of picaresque soldiers of fortune, combining Scottish character and history with that of France via its Scottish hero and his fellow Scots guards at the court of Louis XI in the fifteenth century. And like *Waverley* and *Ivanhoe*, it succeeds in simultaneously presenting what John Buchan described as the archetypal folk-tale of the hero seeking his fortune, in scenes and settings of vivid romance together with their subversion; Louis, the spider at the heart of his web, is utterly corrupt, chivalry is on its last legs, and Quentin, for all his valour, an innocent abroad who ends the novel, as John Sutherland vividly summarises it, as 'a childless old aristocrat, in a dilapidated chateau, ruined by revolution'. Was Scott of Abbotsford anticipating something of his own later depression and fears?

The Betrothed and *The Talisman* appeared in the same year (1825). They are both 'Tales of the Crusaders', but very different in execution and success. The first is 'foreign' in being set around 1100 in Wales, which Scott hardly knew – and this shows. The Welsh are savage, but hardly allowed other distinctive cultural or linguistic features – and there are no crusades. *The Talisman* retrieves some of *Ivanhoe*'s satirical effectiveness in contrasting corrupt Knights Templar with chivlaric Saracens; and for all Scott knew about as little of the East as he did of Wales, he creates a highly entertaining if dubious picture of Saracen customs, emphasising their fundamental decency as opposed to the malicious, petty and xenophobic dissensions in the Crusader camp of Richard Lionheart.

Scott was now declining fast through age and illness; yet recent criticism is reassessing upwards *Anne of Geierstein* (1829) and *Count Robert of Paris* (1832), recognising in their unusual *grotesquerie* and sense of imperial moral decline parallels with Tory Britain in Scott's time, and seeing them as inspirations for later visions of English renewal for writers like Carlyle, Kingsley and Disraeli. The first is once again set in a country Scott had never seen, fifteenth-century Switzerland, with the Swiss resisting the cruelties of Charles the Bold of Burgundy. Scott thought the novel trash; it was hugely successful. The second is set in Constantinople around 1100; the waning Holy Roman Empire is judged against the ideals of chivalry of the Saxon imperial guards and the Crusaders who have come to the city – and found wanting. Thus Scott bequeathed to Victorian Britain his ideals of rediscovery of national virtue through a return to medieval – and fictitious? – values, a legacy perhaps less sound than those given by his earlier, home-based, more thoughtful, and less prejudiced fiction.

Conclusions: forgiving the past

The way in which the divisions in Scott's own loyalties and mind mirror the division of loyalties in Scotland and its history can sometimes make it appear uncannily as though he was destined to articulate national dichotomy. From his early 'raids' in the Borders as he collected for *The Minstrelsy of the Scottish Border*, he shows, like Waverley, a predisposition to causes of the imagination, of passion and romance (telling later that had he been alive at the time of Jacobite rebellion he would probably have joined the Jacobite side). Conversely, however, the early novels clearly show his prudent acceptance of the Union. The practical Scott shows in little things – his pioneering of gas lighting at Abbotsford; his sensible policies in matters such as forestry; his interest in the coming railways. His divided values and loyalties run deep. It is difficult, but not impossible, to understand what caused this massive divergence between the promptings of heart and head.

Scott, the reluctant Unionist, like so many of his fellow-Scots, was profoundly influenced by the American and the French Revolutions. The great historian Henry Meikle showed in his classic *Scotland and the French Revolution* (1912) just how shocked the Scottish Establishment was by these colossal upheavals. By the beginning of the nineteenth century it must have appeared to many observers as though all social order was in danger of disintegrating, with no prospect of a clear new order to take its place. What Scott tried to convey to Scotland was his sense that the bloody past, however attractive to him as a poet, must be laid to rest, even if the price was the Union. The early novels are all about the end of Scotland's romance, and Scott's recognition of the modern irrelevance of his own tartan fever. They nearly all end in sadder but saner compromise. Waverley recognises that the days of romance in his life are over; Henry Morton returns to Scotland to settle to a quiet life; prosperous but backwater Roseneath is held up as the model for the new Scotland; and Rob Roy is pushed out of history, as the Union and Bailie Nicol Jarvie take over.

Scott, for all his final inability to achieve a totally affirmative, coherent and persuasive new narrative for Scotland (could – and should – such a holistic account ever be achieved?) presented Scotland's deepest concerns, her cultural polarisation, with a richness and awareness of complexity such as no other writer has approached. He understood, within himself and in his society, that binary divide in Scottish identity. Merely to articulate this dilemma is most surely a positive achievement, even if the diagnosis is of a series of negations – of older Highland culture, of extreme religious authoritarianism, of traditional causes and manners doomed by progress to extinction.

Conclusions: Scott, Scottish fiction and re-assessing Scotland

There is another huge literary legacy of Scott's mixture of positive and negative perspectives on Scotland. Later Scottish writers have been inspired by his assessments of Scotland, and reworked them in ways which continue even now to show how his portrayal of Scottish dualism mapped out what became something of a school of Scottish fiction. From 1814 to 1914 most serious Scottish novelists showed their debt to Scott. We have not always appreciated just how different is this tradition from the great central English tradition, and it is only recently we have recovered novels like Hogg's *The Brownie of Bodsbeck* (1818) and *The Justified Sinner* (1824), or Galt's *The Entail* (1823) and *Ringan Gilhaize* (1823) – all of which show the influence of Scott's dualism and patterning. And Stevenson's *Master of Ballantrae* (1889), Douglas Brown's *The House with the Green Shutters* (1901) and MacDougall Hay's *Gillespie* (1914) have not always been appreciated as the great Scottish novels they are, too frequently being assessed in terms of that English tradition which views them as peripheral fiction, on the edges of the more central achievement of writers like the Brontës, Eliot and Hardy. When the great central figures, and the polarised communities, of these Scottish novels are re-read remembering Scott's archetypal protagonists and thematic internal divisions, then their pedigree and their particularly Scottish purpose become clear.

After the deaths of Scott, Hogg, and Galt in the 1830s Scottish literature was in the doldrums, under the baleful influence of Professor John Wilson ('Christopher North'), with his high Tory agenda for Scottish culture, and his anti-radical propaganda novels. It can be argued that Scottish culture generally came close to terminal decline with the increasing anglicisation of the period 1840–80. The revival, which began with Stevenson, owes its success to awareness of the immense value of Scott's fiction as the base on which to rebuild – and we are still rediscovering the greatness of writers who followed Scott's 'positive negativism'. Clearly Stevenson's Ballantrae brothers owe much to Scott's orderly and disorderly opposites. Less well appreciated is the huge achievement of Neil Munro – arguably one of our three greatest Scottish historical novelists – whose magnificent satirical novels ruthlessly undercut Highland romance, to reveal in novels like *John Splendid* (1898), *Gilian the Dreamer* (1899) and *The New Road* (1914) the reality beneath the glamour of the clans and their chiefs. Munro's satires on Highland braggadacio, on the male-dominated ethic which sees killing of fellow High-landers as 'man's work', which relies on fawning flattery of the chief disguised as blood-kinship, and which demeans women and dismissively patronises genuine creativity, are comparable with Scott's ironic reductions of old – and new – Scottish society. We will see, in the end, that the revival of the late nineteenth century was predicated on Scott's willingness to face social and cultural realities, however unflattering to Scotland. We are still in the process of re-assessing Munro's contemporaries, like Crockett and Barrie in fiction, or John Davidson in poetry. Their embittered irony regarding Scotland is another stage in a stock-taking process, whose apparent negativity is in reality a necessary satirical re-assessment of Scottish stereotypes and clichés with a view towards a positive clearing away of what these writers perceive as spurious Scottish ideologies. And as we revalue the best of Buchan, or Violet Jacob's *Flemington* (1911), and other historical novelists of the early twentieth century, we will discover just how long Scott's influence has persisted.

Conclusions: egalitarian Scott?

One final inheritance from Scott remains worthy of consideration. We have seen how the democratic ideology of the Scottish Enlightenment as expressed in the central school of 'common-sense' philosophy of Francis Hutcheson and Thomas Reid was passed on to Scott by Dugald Stewart, ultimately producing Scott's exemplars of best moral conduct in characters such as Henry Morton and Jeanie Deans. This egalitarian ideology is arguably a tap-root of Scottish fiction. From Scott its influence goes on to contribute what is probably the defining element in Scottish fiction's distinctiveness from other national fictional traditions. From this root comes the Reverend Micah Balwhidder, the apparently simple but good man at the heart of his community in *Annals of the Parish* (1821); from it comes William Alexander's marvellously realised peasant-farmer of the north-east, the sturdily independent heart of his community in *Johnnie Gibb of Gushetneuk* (1871). It is where David Balfour comes from, and Chris Guthrie, and Finn MacHamish of Gunn's *The Silver Darlings* (1941), and all the unpretentious and unglamorous protagonists whose role in countless Scottish novels is to be the ordinary member of community, revealing the importance of Everyman and Everywoman, and expressing what has been termed 'the Democratic Intellect'. It is a tradition which persists to the present day, in the Holy Fools of Robin Jenkins, in Friel's *Mr Alfred MA* (1972), in Alasdair Gray's *Lanark* (1981), and outstandingly in the work of Booker Prize-winner James Kelman, who studied Scottish philosophy at university. Unlikely as it might seem, the very ordinary people that Kelman focuses on are descendants of Jeanie Deans, and strange though it may appear to link Scott and Kelman, they share many of the same concerns. Jeanie Deans for Scott, and Rab Hines the bus conductor for Kelman, are the kind of people who matter, as they struggle to make sense of the confusions in Scottish community. The Scott of *Old Mortality* or *Ivanhoe* would approve of present-day Scotland's ability to hold a plurality of cultures, languages, and beliefs. And for all that his earlier fairness in presenting the understandable motivations of ordinary (and extraordinary) people turned increasingly towards a distrust of democracy, we owe him much for working towards the reconciliation of our ancient discords, and for re-examining more thoroughly and effectively than any other Scottish writer the legacies of Scotland's history and its older cultures.

CHAPTER 14

SCOTT'S *WAVERLEY*

Waverley (1814) was almost an eighteenth-century novel. It was begun just after the turn of the century, probably thought of and conceived in the last decade of the previous century. After seven chapters Scott put it away, and only resumed it after his great poetic narratives had been overtaken by Byron's successes. The connections with the great fictions of Fielding and Smollett are outstanding.

In its opening chapters, it was clearly designed to present Edward Waverley in the picaresque tradition, a novel of the simple adventures of a lively and rascally hero like Fielding's Joseph Andrews or Smollett's Roderick Random. Thus Scott's early methods of characterisation are clearly drawn from the 'flat' characterisation identified by E. M. Forster as typical of the early novel in English. Edward is comparable to the kind of protagonist used by Fielding in works like *Tom Jones* (1749); hardly a full hero, the prey to temptations on his own part and the deceits of others. Similarly the characterisation of the surrounding figures is typical of the eighteenth-century novel. Dr Pembroke is reminiscent of Parson Adams in *Joseph Andrews* (1742) with his kindliness, his absent-mindedness, and his prolix sermons; the figure of Cosmo Bradwardine of Tully-Veolan resembles the pedantic lieutenant Lismahago of Smollett's *Humphry Clinker* (1771); while the device of using the names of minor characters to indicate their qualities, such as the Laird of Killancureit, is drawn from the similar eighteen-century practice, as exemplified in Henry Fielding's Lady Booby (*Joseph Andrews*). Here too is the direct authorial address to the 'gentle reader'; the 'reader of fashion' is addressed in footnotes; and many of the early episodes (like the story of Sir Everard's unhappy wooing, or Waverley's dalliance with the lower class Cecilia) are reminiscent of the typical world of manners and marriages of the earlier fiction. Fielding's *Jonathan Wild* (1741) is explicitly mentioned, as is the even earlier work of Cervantes, *Don Quixote* (1605). (*Don Quixote* had been translated into English by Smollett in 1755.) But the introduction, with the usual eighteenth-century preference for the study of 'manners, not men' (preface to *Joseph Andrews*) being replaced by Scott's new focus on 'men, not manners' (preface to *Waverley*), should warn us that even from the beginning

Scott was finding the mould of the earlier style of novel too circumscribing. It is fascinating to compare the first chapters with the style and content of eighteenth-century fiction, and to see exactly where Scott begins to break the mould of his predecessors.

Is *Waverley* marred by the fact that its first seven chapters belong to a different tradition of fiction? Or was Scott already conscious of his larger themes in these chapters? Certainly there are signs that Scott only gets over his early orientation towards the eighteenth century by Chapter 16, with the introduction of the Highlands and Evan Dhu. But it is to Scott's credit that, in his resumption of the novel, his only visible slip-up is at the very end of Chapter 14, when he is forced to say that 'I ought to have said that Edward, when he sent to Dundee for the books before mentioned, had applied for, and received permission, extending his leave of absence . . .'

Generally the connections between first start and resumption are well-made. Pembroke, the tutor, is not just in the novel as a 'Parson Adams' sketch, but is a necessary part of the net which will close around Waverley. Pembroke puts his Jacobitical sermons in Edward's baggage, which gets stolen by Donald Bean Lean, so that by Chapter 32 they are a major part of the evidence against Waverley. Similarly in the matter of the seal of Waverley-Honour; it is a part of the necessary machinery which will cause the defection of the English servants under Houghton at Dundee, since they will accept only the seal's authority as representing Waverley. These early chapters capably establish not just sound mechanical links, but in addition introduce the novel's historical orientations and oppositions, with its central theme of Tory-Whig, Jacobite-Hanoverian opposition. In this text we are given the necessary contrasts of the rich and noble home of Waverley-Honour in England with the poorer homes of the aristocracy in Scotland. And, most of all, it provides an introductory and leisurely basis for the complex and, for Scott, pioneering study of the non-hero, Edward Waverley himself. With his doting uncle, his kindly and neglectful tutor Pembroke and his cold and impersonally shrewd father, we are not just being given eighteenth-century sketches, but necessary information for understanding why Waverley is excessively romantic. Here is the seedbed of Waverley's later psychological obsessions and delusions.

History and psychology

Waverley can be looked at on three distinct levels – namely, in terms of the 'linked pairs' which were discussed in the previous chapter. The first of these is Scott's handling of history and psychology.

Scott's power and skill in dealing with the background of the ill-fated Jacobite Rebellion of 1745 can clearly be seen. The novel is set within a British as well as Scottish context; and the motivation of the Jacobites, their loyalty to the Stuarts, and their cherished grievances, are sympathetically presented, just as Scott tries elsewhere to understand Covenanters and rebels of whatever cause. History is always presented in its effects on human beings – Edward's uncle Everard, withdrawn from his lost causes, like Cosmo Bradwardine; Colonel Gardiner and Major Talbot, simply enacting the loyalties to which they have been bred; Fergus and Flora committed from birth and race to their tragic cause. History moulds people, and people in turn mould history, Scott believes, and even Prince Charles is seen simultaneously as mover and victim of history. Above all, Scott shows a new and significant understanding of why and how loyalties are forged, to the extent that the reasons for commitment are now understood.

History is people writ large; individual mindsets and actions make history. The counterpart to Scott's large view of human events is his detailed and pioneering analysis of particular agents. And here his characterisation of Edward Waverley broke new ground. Waverley is not a hero, but neither is he 'insipid'. Nor is he an 'anti-hero', but a man, an individual caught up by the forces of history. It is interesting at this point to compare Scott's psychological observation with that of Jane Austen, in looking at the heroine of her *Emma* (1815). Both Waverley and Emma have been left untended by irresponsible parents; both have too much of their own way in connection with their private tutor; both prefer manufacturing a world of personal 'reality', as opposed to accepting the actuality around them. The scheme of both novels is the movement towards a sadder but wiser realisation of self, with condemnation of the risks involved in creating a personal world of delusive imagination.

Scott emphasises the dislocation between Waverley and his father Richard, the cold, politicking Whig who spends his time in London rather than with his son. Old Sir Everard and his sister are indulgent, as is Pembroke, Waverley's tutor. Waverley, from the very beginning, is thus allowed within the estate of Waverley-Honour to turn in upon his own imagination, to develop his own dream and fantasy world. We will look at this again in considering the metaphorical significance of the house and the estate in these early stages; but the damage to Waverley's psyche begins here. Danger signs for Waverley's psychological development can be seen in plot elements like his relationship with Cecilia Stubbs, his education and choice of reading, his relationship to his family and ancestors, especially Sir Wilibert the crusader, and his choice of a military career.

Waverley finds himself posted to Dundee, an unromantic centre of trade which is hardly what his romantic dreams have led him to expect from the army. A European role is unavailable to him, due to the state of British-European politics, and the blockade of France. Scott makes Waverley's disillusionment with mercantile Dundee part of his motivation towards taking up the invitation to Tully-Veolan from his Uncle Everard's Jacobite friend of the 1715 rebellion, Baron Cosmo Bradwardine. Scott subtly devlops Waverley's increasingly confused and culture-shocked psyche in his period at Tully-Veolan, in particular, through the curious relationship he develops with Cosmo Bradwardine, and his embarrassment at his own inauspicious behaviour in 'affairs of honour'. Waverley is not portrayed as a forceful controller of his own destiny.

Waverley's dream-state

Until now, however, Waverley has simply exhibited 'normal' predilections towards romantic and colourful notions of chivalry and manners. By the end of Chapter 15 Scott has stepped up the variety of cultural pressures on Waverley, by taking him beyond the already unsettling experience of the Lowlands, through fascinated discussion of blackmail and the levying of tribute by the local Highlanders, into the north, and the world of 'lawless thieves, limmers, and broken men of the Highlands'. So impressed and astonished is Waverley to be introduced to this exotic world that Scott ends the chapter with a highly significant emphasis on Waverley's state of mind. He introduces the notion of 'dream' in a sense that will become highly important as a motif or recurrent metaphor throughout the novel:

> It seemed like a dream to Waverley that these deeds of violence should be familiar to men's minds, and currently talked of, as falling within the common order of things, and happening daily in the immediate vicinity, without his having crossed the seas, and while he was yet in the otherwise well-ordered island of Great Britain.

Chapter 16 shows Waverley literally being beguiled by Fergus Vich Iain Vohr, the Highland chieftain, into the 'dusky barrier of mountains' which separates Tully-Veolan from the true tribal territories. Fergus seems indeed to have planned Waverley's itinerary more effectively than that of any modern tourist bus trip to the Trossachs, in that he deliberately takes Waverley by the scenic route, so that he is physically fatigued and thus prey to all the excessive impressions of the Highlands that Fergus can contrive. By the end of this chapter, Waverley has given himself up to the full romance of his situation, sitting 'on the banks of an unknown lake, under the guidance of a wild native', whose language is unknown to him, visiting the den of 'a second Robin Hood' at 'deep midnight, through scenes of difficulty and toil'. Scott concludes in Chapter 16: 'What a variety of incidents for the exercise of a romantic imagination, and all enhanced by the solemn feeling of uncertainty, at least, if not of danger?'

Typically, Scott qualifies the end of this exotic portrayal of the internal state of Waverley's mind: 'the only circumstance which assorted ill with the rest, was the cause of the journey – the Baron's milk-cows! This degrading incident he kept in the background.' Scott again emphasises Waverley's state of being 'wrapt in these dreams of imagination'; and takes him to the burning centre of his imagination by linking him explicitly with the small speck of light which flickers on the verge of the horizon, and which, while watched by Edward, grows, until, by the opening of the next chapter, it has 'a broader, redder, and more irregular splendour. It appeared plainly to be a large fire . . .' To emphasise to us that this 'red glaring orb' is inextricably connected with the essence of romance and imagination itself, it seems to Waverley to be like the fiery vehicle in which the Evil Genius of an Oriental tale traverses land and sea. We are seeing this 'King's Cavern' through Waverley's eyes; and Scott magnificently couches his description in terms which diagnose Waverley's overheated imagination. Fergus arranges his trap with considerable skill. After 'softening up' Waverley with the journey to the King's Cavern, he introduces him to his sister, Flora. She, of course, shares nothing of Fergus's warped ambition, being an entirely reasonable Jacobite, dedicated through ancestry and belief to her cause. But Chapter 22, 'Highland Minstrelsy', shows how, while Flora does not in the least deliberately manipulate the situation, Fergus in a sense does, knowing that Waverley will be acutely vulnerable to Flora's beauty, the enchanting glen where she plays her harp, and the remote and almost unreal beauty of the scene. There is something peculiar in the way that Scott describes Waverley's sensations; 'peculiar' in that Scott's description of his response is hardly that of a chivalrous knight:

> Indeed, the wild feeling of romantic delight with which he heard the first few notes she drew from her instrument, amounted almost to a sense of pain. He would not for worlds have quitted his place . . . yet he almost longed for solitude, that he might decipher and examine at leisure the complication of emotions which now agitated his bosom.

Shortly after this Fergus arranges a stag hunt, at which many of the local Highland chieftains are present; and of course the event is again inordinately impressive on Waverley's mind. Skilfully, Scott makes Waverley's conversion to the Jacobite cause seem a mixture of manipulation and intrinsic flaws of imagination in Waverley himself – the results of lack of discipline and training in rational judgement – so much so that even Flora reproaches him for this lack!

Much of the manipulation of Waverley is brought about by Fergus and his henchman, the much more devious and pragmatic Donald Bean Lean. Donald intercepts Waverley's letters from his commanding officer Gardiner, so that only the last communication demanding his return to Dundee reaches him, this last of course being couched in officious and – to Waverley – offensive terms. Waverley's 'honour' is hurt, and, antagonised by the Hanoverian cause, he is susceptible to the Jacobites. Likewise, by Donald's exploitation of the seal of Waverley-Honour and the baggage with the sermons in it, together with intimations of his father's fall from grace in London, Waverley is demoralised and destabilised. All this on its own would not be enough to gain Waverley for the Jacobite cause were it not for the flaws of his imagination, which Scott portrays cleverly and with deliberate irony. Chapter 25 traces Waverley's injured sensibility to the point where – hardly the response of a mature hero – he breaks down and throws himself into Fergus Vich Iain Vohr's arms, giving vent to tears of shame and indignation.

In all this the 'dream state' is a crucial device of Scott's. That is to say, Scott regularly punctuates his narrative by insisting on the close relationship of Waverley and dream. This use of dream metaphor is a very early example of the exploration of psychology in fiction.

The end of dreams

Waverley's romantic dreams are to be brought devastatingly to an end. The elaborate edifices which his imagination has conjured up crumble with much greater speed than they took to build; his capture in the Lowlands, and his agonies of mind in his cell, mark the beginning of the dawning of a new realism. But the most significant stage of revulsion against his dreams occurs in Chapter 46 when quite literally he 'sees through' his dream before the Battle of Prestonpans, while camping in Tranent:

> It was at that instant, that, looking around him, he saw the wild dress and appearance of his Highland associates, heard their whispers in an uncouth and unknown language, looked upon his own dress, so unlike that which he had worn from his infancy, and wished to awake from what seemed at the moment a dream, strange, horrible, and unnatural. 'Good God!' he

muttered, 'Am I then a traitor to my country, a renegade to my standard, and a foe, as that poor dying wretch expressed himself, to my native England?'

Already by Chapter 43 and the scenes of the ball at Holyrood, Waverley has seen the end of his 'day-dream' of gaining Flora; the failure of his dreams of love and chivalry in war bring him to the Borders of England and Scotland. There, at Ullswater, but not in scenes of Lakeland splendour, rather in the desolation of winter walks by the shores of the lake, Waverley:

acquired a more complete mastery . . . than his former experience had given him; . . . he felt himself entitled to say firmly, though perhaps with a sigh, that the romance of his life was ended, and that its real history had now commenced.

In a sense he has been suffering from 'tartan fever' – it is one of Scott's wry jokes at the end that he infects Colonel Talbot's nephew, Frank Stanley, with the same fever, so that the last we see of that romantic young man is his disappearance into the Highlands in search of romance.

Scott is studying a state of mind in which fantasy replaces reality. The novel's presentation of linked episodes parallels Waverley's growing obsessions, which continually reach a head, only to subside into anti-climax. Indeed Waverley is twice invalided with fever and injury, and frequently he is literally 'carried along', not just by his romantic imagination but by those who take his initiative from him. Probably the high point of Scott's satire on this diseased romance and distorted state of mind is when in Chapter 44 Waverley (dreaming again) is awakened to prepare himself for battle. Dressed as a full Highlander, Waverley asks how he looks; Evan Dhu's answer is perhaps unselfconsciously and unintentionally ironic: 'Like the bra' Highlander tat's painted on the board afore the mickle change-house they ca' Lucky Middlemass's'. Scott certainly means the response to be read ironically – Waverley has reached the point where his deluded mind has reinvented his personality entirely, to the point where his clothes are the ridiculous measure of this.

In all this, Scott has been heavily ironic at Waverley's expense. By the end of the novel, all his brave dreams have amounted to nothing more than the fact that he saves his enemies, acts ineffectually in the Jacobite cause, and is rescued from the gallows by the efforts of the two women in his life, Flora and Rose. It is arguable that it is the loss of Flora's interest in him, rather than a genuine loss of idealism, that induces his rejection of the Jacobite cause;

Scott's entire picture of Waverley is one of inflated irony, with attendant deflation reducing him to a figure, if not of actual mockery, certainly of anti-romantic significance.

The symbolic patterning of opposites: past and present

Now the novel can be looked at on the level of its symbolic patterning and its symbolic use of landscape. David Daiches (*Literary Essays*, 1956) sees Scott's landscape fiction in terms of a recurrent patterning of opposites – the past versus the present; present order versus past disorder; imagination and warmth set against materialism and coldness; romance set against realism. For example, in his patterning of the past against the present, Scott introduces in his very first chapter a contrast of the habits of the past and of his own day:

> The wrath of our ancestors, for example, was coloured *gules*; it broke forth in acts of open and sanguinary violence against the objects of its fury. Our malignant feelings, which must seek gratification through more indirect channels, and undermine the obstacles which they cannot openly bear down, may be rather said to be tinctured *sable*.

Similarly, Scott contrasts the older rebellion of 1715 and Sir Everard's activities therein with the 'modern' rebellion of 1745; or the cause of Wilibert and his crusades specifically with the trivialised modern behaviour of Cecilia Stubbs. This constant accretion of small points (for example, Sir Everard's regret, in Chapter 6, that his lavish retinue of the past is not to be maintained in the impoverished present), becomes Scott's typical way of presenting the gulf between the richer, more colourful, and vivid past compared to the necessarily more prosaic present. Cosmo Bradwardine and Fergus Vich Iain Vohr (Paris-educated, but nevertheless believing in second-sight or super-natural incantations) are yesterday's men, but to Scott infinitely more attractive and vivid than Major Talbot or Colonel Gardiner, prosaic modern militarists. Scott operated a continual kind of 'dual vision' this way, so that even when dealing with events in the present, there is a continual reminder of older and more vivid predecessors. For example, in Chapter 24, when Waverley is being transported by litter in the Highlands, Scott reminds us that it is 'borne by his people with such caution and dexterity as renders it not improbable that they may have been the ancestors of some of those sturdy Gaels, who have now the happiness to transport the belles of Edinburgh, in their sedan-chairs, to ten routs in one evening'. Thus Scott casually but effectively shows, through an accumulation of symbols, that habits of the past have had to give way to the present. Two symbolic figures can sum up his juxtapositioning: Flora, with her passionate and idealistic commitment, of the doomed past, where meek and prosaic Rose, no dreamer or visionary, is of the present.

Order and disorder

Clearly associated with this is Scott's thematic opposition of order and disorder. The figures of Fergus and Colonel Gardiner are polar opposites in these terms. In all Scott's work, contrast is made between figures of passion and disorder, as opposed to men of prudence and self-control. There is no more disorderly figure than that of Fergus Vich Iain Vohr (Chapter 18):

> The eyebrow and upper lip bespoke something of the habit of peremptory command and decisive superiority. Even his courtesy, though open, frank, and unconstrained, seemed to indicate a sense of personal importance; and, upon any check or accidental excitation, a sudden though transient lour of the eye, showed a hasty, haughty, and vindictive temper, not less to be dreaded because it seemed much under its owner's command . . .

In contrast, Colonel Gardiner and Major Talbot are almost Augustan to Fergus's Romantic. The officers, with their meticulous drilling, military organisation, and control of themselves and their men, are specifically set against the sprawling dependants, the casual banquets, the struggling and ill-equipped armies of Fergus. Fergus's swings in mood, his wild enthusiasm and friendships, his unnatural despairs and hatred are all representative of ancient, proud disorder. In Chapter 16 Cosmo Bradwardine explicitly contrasts the disorderly basis of Highland landownership and the more orderly, 'legal' landownership of the South.

Scott works this contrast in microcosm as well as macrocosm. For example, there is the scene in Chapter 29 where the boy Callum Beg offers to kill Cruickshanks the Lowlands innkeeper:

> 'Her ain sell,' replied Callum, 'could wait for him a wee bit frae the toun, and kittle his quarters wi' her skene-occle.'
> 'Skene-occle! What's that?'
> Callum unbuttoned his coat, raised his left arm, and with an emphatic nod, pointed to the hilt of a small dirk, snugly deposited under it, in the lining of his jacket. Waverley thought he had understood his meaning; he

gazed in his face, and discovered in Callum's very handsome, though embrowned features, just the degree of roguish malice with which a lad of the same age in England would have brought forward a plan for robbing an orchard.

This exchange is clearly meant to exemplify in microcosm the chaotic characteristics of Highland society, especially when compared with the Lowland stolidity of Alec Polwarth, or the orderly dutifulness which leads to tragedy for Houghton and Waverley's men. In macrocosm, the contrast of the disorderly Highlands and the more ordered Lowlands can be seen in Chapters 44 and 46. Firstly, Scott emphasises the bizarre and grotesque appearance of the Highlanders to the Lowlanders:

So little was the condition of the Highlands known at that late period, that the character and appearance of their population, while thus sallying forth as military adventurers, conveyed to the south-country Lowlanders as much surprise as if an invasion of African negroes or Esquimaux Indians had issued forth from the northern mountains of their own native country.

The eve of the Battle of Prestonpans allows Scott to present a very important symbolic contrast of the two forces in Chapter 46:

Here, then, was a military spectacle of no ordinary interest, or usual occurrence. The two armies, so different in aspect and discipline, yet each admirably trained in its own peculiar mode of war, upon whose conflict the temporary fate at least of Scotland appeared to depend, now faced each other like two gladiators in the arena, each meditating upon the mode of attacking their enemy.

Thereafter Scott emphasises the wild and haphazard ferocity of the Highlands. Indeed, on this occasion it is precisely this unusual conduct which enables them to win the day against the disciplined English, unused to and surprised by the attack. A further subtlety of Scott's should be noted, however; Fergus and Prince Charles, far from standing for mere anarchy, do represent a kind of anti-order. Had the Stuart movement won the rebellion, their 'disorder' would have become 'order'. We see Charles creating a new 'order' at his court of Holyrood in Chapter 19, and we realise that this disorderly structure is in its own sense quite orderly, just as the clan structure has its own idiosyncratic logic and order. We have already noted that Flora is abundantly sensible and self-disciplined – only to the outsider's eye is she in any sense 'disorderly' or romantic. Scott is making the point that one period's order is another's disorder; and that 'order', like history, is made by winners. Readers might also wish to consider a further, and psychological, subtlety; that each of these opposing groups has within it a version of its opposite, so that, for example, Colonel Gardiner wills himself to be 'orderly' precisely because his nature is prone to disorder; or Charles runs his court at Holyrood in Edinburgh like any other European and 'orderly' court, with its petty hierarchies. The extremes shown on both sides, Scott implies, result from destructive divisions in history and society; once again, history makes – and mars – psychology.

Feeling imagination and prudent reason

Yet another part of Scott's symbolic patterning involves the setting of the excesses of warm feeling and imagination against aridly prudent reasoning and materialism. This can be seen in Scott's contrast of Waverley's uncle Everard with his father Richard. The one is self-indulgently sentimental and warm in his prejudices; the other cold, shrewd and calculating. Scott thus shows that the older Tories are biased where the Hanoverians, however cold, are 'prudent'. But nevertheless Scott's sympathies, as opposed to his reasoning, obviously favour the old Tory side. After all, the constituency that Whig Richard Waverley acquires is called 'Barterfaith'. Scott casually, but deliberately, builds up this opposition in the same way that he built up the previous oppositions. For example, at the end of Chapter 3, Waverley compares the Hanseatic League with the Huguenot party:

> The splendid pages of Froissart, with his heart-stirring and eye-dazzling descriptions of war and of tournaments, were among his chief favourites; and from those of Brantome and De la Noue he learned to compare the wild and loose yet superstitious character of the nobles of the League, with the stern, rigid, and sometimes turbulent disposition of the Huguenot party . . .

Later (in Chapter 25) Colonel Gardiner will be referred to as 'a precise Huguenot'; while frequently Edward Waverley himself is contrasted with other characters of the book in order to show the continual clash between his irresponsible imagination and feeling and the arid rationalism and discipline of others. For example, in Chapter 13, Edward is explicitly contrasted with Cosmo Bradwardine:

> Edward . . . was warm in his feelings, wild and romantic in his ideas, and in his taste of reading, with a strong disposition towards poetry. Mr Bradwardine was the reverse of all this, and piqued himself upon stalking through life with the same upright, starched, stoical gravity which distinguished his evening promenade upon the terrace of Tully-Veolan . . .

All this builds up the novel's fundamental opposition between the exotic scenes of the blue mountains, the Highland waterfalls, the Holyrood gatherings, places of the imagination; and places of mercantile materialism in a Britain which Scott does not even have to elaborate on, so well would it be known to his readers. Arguably, instead of the exotic detail of his portrayal of the Highlands, all he needs to convey the opposite end of the country to his readers is a slight sketching of mercantile Dundee, the dreariness of the Lowlands, or references to the political chicanery of London. All fill in for the reader that drab and mundane world which Scott means to contrast with the apparently romantic Highlands. This is exemplified by the very full picture we have of Charles at Holyrood as a 'Prince Charming', set against the nonentity of the unseen king whom he seeks to replace. And indeed, the lesser figures of the Lowlands and England corroborate this sense of a debased mundane society; the hostess at Tully-Veolan who stops the battle in her inn because of the threat of damage to her property rather than from ethical considerations; inglorious and mean Lowlanders like Bailie Macwheeble or the Laird of Killancureit; or the blacksmith in the Lowlands who is willing to shoe horses on Sunday – at a higher price; or even the picture of Waverley's father, Richard Waverley, with his dominating and obsessive self-interest and expediency.

What is Scott trying to achieve with this opposition of apparently imaginative and feeling characters to those who are repressed and unimaginative? As with the opposition of apparent disorder and order, can the opposition finally be sustained? After all, when one looks at characters on the positive side of the opposition, characters supposedly romantic and imaginative, they reveal oppositions beneath their superficial characteristics – they are often the opposite of what they appear. This is seen with Fergus and his very real greed, as opposed to his official idealism, and similarly with his apparent 'warmth', his affection for Rose – when he realises that she is to inherit Tully-Veolan. The ultimate symbol of someone who apparently acts out of spontaneous feeling, and who represents imaginative warmth, is the figure of Donald Bean, who, occupying a place at the very heart of the novel's imaginative colour, identified with the burning centre of Romance, reveals himself to be nothing but a sordid con-man, an inglorious and cheap operator who is just as much at home in Dundee or London, manipulating the press and stealing for his ends, rather than pursuing an idealistic goal. The heart of romance and imagination has proved to be as sordid, if not more so, than any of its opposites. Scott is warning us once again that these excessive opposites mirror each other, and that – as this chapter will conclude – 'romance' is in the end as phoney or as suspect as its apparent impoverished cousin 'realism'.

Symbolic houses

More specific and clear examples of Scott's symbolic skill can be found, for example, in the way Scott patterns the novel in terms of its great houses: Waverley-Honour in the south, Glennaquoich in the remote north, with Tully-Veolan very much as the house in the middle. Once again what is revealed is that Scott is thinking in terms of extreme opposites, with a point of balance wavering, like Waverley himself, in the middle. It is fruitful to consider the symbolism associated with these three houses and their environments. To take Waverley-Honour first; its library and estates represent in microcosm an anticipation of much of the action of the novel. As a youth Waverley sees, hears, and feels the dramatic events of his ideal world; and the 'savage character' and 'untended deer forests' of Waverley-Honour, with its hidden lakes and ruined towers, become almost an expression of the undisciplined and free imagination of the adolescent. Even his love-affair with Cecilia Stubbs is prophetic of his very different love-affair with Flora; in both cases he will invest the loved ones with the qualities he wishes them to have. And at the heart of these early chapters lies Waverley's highly symbolic relationship with Mirkwood-Mere, like the later King's Cavern, his private sanctuary of romance itself. Scott is anticipating the changes which will happen to Waverley himself by using the metaphor of place.

Tully-Veolan similarly offers a range of symbolic implications. It is extremely odd in architecture, neither military nor domestic, caught between the style of an old disorderly society and that of the new more orderly dispensation. To the north it is fortified, but to the south it has a more open architecture, with a garden at its heart – it has its softer places. However, like Baron Bradwardine himself, it has a prickly profile towards the dangerous north. Its very crest, that of the bear, shambling, dangerous, but slightly comic, is a metaphor (for Cosmo Bradwardine?) for qualities lying somewhere between the domestic and the savage. What happens to Tully-Veolan (Scott based this on a typical Borders house, that of Traquair near Innerleithen) represents what happens to the Lowlands of Scotland during the contentions between the Highlands and the South of Britain.

Finally there is Glennaquoich, home of Fergus Vich Iain Vohr. There is no mistaking the disorderly remoteness of this place and its associated and highly symbolic scenes. The description of Flora's retreat, in Chapter 22, is very much in the style of later nineteenth-century epic landscape painting, such as that of Turner, or Landseer, or Scotland's own Horatio McCulloch. With its dizzying heights, its vast expanses of sky, Waverley sees this as unearthly, with Flora, typically, an unworldly inhabitant.

In all this, Scott is using symbolism in a poetic sense as the very warp and woof of his story telling. A character like Davie Gellatley is used for more than comic relief or as a necessary subsidiary servant functionary. And in the link Scott makes between Davie and Waverley, Davie emerges as Waverley's doppelgänger, as well as his Sancho Panza. There is something of the Shakespearian Fool in Davie, but Scott has developed the figure much further, so that Davie becomes the sign of Waverley's imaginative folly, unintentionally mocking and reducing his worst excesses of romantic dream, and revealing Waverley's psychological deterioration.

Symbolic landscape

Scott is particularly innovative in the ways in which uses landscape and landscape-related images and situations to advance his symbolic commentary. Scott's technique lies somewhere between that of Wordsworth, in his investiture of place with spiritual meaning, and that of the later great nineteenth-century landscape painters, exploiting what Ruskin termed 'the pathetic fallacy', the tendency for humanity to project its feelings into landscape. He paints scenes with great richness and texture, and slowly his symbolic purpose emerges – through the repetition of ideas which echo each other, through the emphasis on the shadings of colour and light, and through his conveying of local atmosphere, so that the overall mood he intends is reinforced and enhanced. A prime example lies in the transition from Lowlands to Highlands in Chapter 16. 'This,' said Evan, 'is the pass of Bally-Brough . . .' Bally-Brough is the gateway which the Highland tribes defend against the South. The key words in the description include 'beguiled', 'huge', 'tremendous', 'steep and rugged', 'tremendous' (repeated), 'brawled', 'darksome', 'chafed', 'broken' 'a hundred falls', 'precipice', 'scathed', 'warped', 'twisted', 'shroud'. There is a sense in which the key images of the landscape are also the key ideas of the dark and dangerous history of the Highlanders themselves, with a menacing undertone of future danger always present which anticipates the tragic destiny of the Highlands. Chapter 17 continues this kind of imagery; the great fire that burns at the King's Cavern comes close to representing the burning heart of romance, all the more potent in that it is perceived from Waverley's point of view, in whose own mind such a fire already burns. There is even, in a way appropriate to Waverley's love of legends and stories, an evil genius, in the figure of Donald Bean Lean, the albino Machiavelli of the region.

Scott was notably fascinated by the possibilities in water, lakes, rivers, waterfalls. Chapter 9 presented the large brook which ran by Tully-Veolan; Scott specifically divided the character of the brook into 'temporary tranquillity', and then let it assume 'its natural rapid and fierce character', so that his depiction mirrored the divided character of the Baron of Tully-Veolan himself – peaceful, ordered, but ever-ready (as in the 1715 Rebellion) to reassume his old character. It is significant that the brook escapes down 'a deep and wooded dell, from the copse of which arose a massive, but ruinous tower, the former habitation of the Barons of Bradwardine'. Scott is quite specifically reminding us that there is an older and darker side to the Bradwardines, and is doing this through the medium of landscape and features of landscape. One of Scott's outstanding presentations in this respect is in Chapter 22, which develops the symbolism of the divided character of the river valley in familiar manner.

In his description of Flora's retreat, Scott contrasts 'two brooks'. He separates them into the larger stream, 'placid and even sullen in its course, wheeling in deep eddies, or sleeping in dark blue pools'; and the smaller, 'the motions of the lesser brook were rapid and furious, issuing from between precipices, like a maniac from his confinement, all foam and uproar.' This description is not merely background noise or 'wallpaper'; it has a more active reference to Waverley's involvement in the civil war. The reader might consider some questions regarding Scott's symbolic landscape. Why does Scott separate Flora's 'narrow glen' from Glennaquoich, so that it 'seemed to open into the land of romance'? Why is he at such pains to 'elevate' or distinguish her from all about her? Why does Scott so specifically show her 'on the heights', or the dizzyingly high bridge over which she has to cross into her almost 'fairy kingdom'? At this point, clearly, Scott is making Flora into something other than a psychologically credible representative of Jacobitism. Waverely has never seen anything like her 'even in his wildest dreams'. Scott likens her to 'a fair enchantress of Boiardo or Ariosto'; and it would seem as though at this point she is to be seen, and not just by Waverley alone, as being at 'the seat of the Celtic muse'; indeed in some way, as the 'Celtic Muse' personified.

Other symbolism

By now Scott's complex and rich ways of mingling setting and action should be clear enough. Central to the novel is the examination of Waverley in the Lowland village of Cairnvreckan. The very name is deliberately chosen; it is similar to the name of the most famous of West Highland whirlpools, Corryvreckan, and it does indeed show Waverley caught in the boiling centre of the novel, where he is at the vortex of swirling forces which threaten to destroy him, as Major Melville and the minister Morton explicitly recognise. Chapter 31 is called 'An Examination', and it serves the purpose of providing a still point at the heart of the action whereby we, as well as Melville and Morton, 'take stock' of the stage Waverley his reached in his psychological development, and to what point the civil tension in Scotland has grown. Yet, beyond this psychological assessment of Waverley, there is a more important symbolic purpose. Melville and Morton are in their own ways the worldly and the spiritual, the head and the heart; between them they represent a sound vantage point from which Waverley's extreme and dream-like progress can be assessed, so several important metaphors are being deployed here – the motif of Waverley's dream, Waverley's progress of romance, Waverley as 'wavering' in his allegiances to England and Scotland. Lowland Scotland presents itself in the forms of Melville and Morton.

Finally, in the magnificent, solemn and moving execution scenes we get a glimpse into Scott's own tragic dilemma – a dilemma he never conclusively resolved. Nowhere do Fergus and Flora seem more symbolic or more tragic in their national implications than here. Flora refers to herself and Fergus as 'two poor orphans', and there is no doubt that this is the way Scott sees the entire independent, bloody, but doomed Highland society of Scotland. The execution itself is the end of an era and a way of life. Scott has Fergus recognise this; and part of Scott clearly laments this tragedy. Fergus's death takes on the entire weight of the symbolic regal 'death' of the missing Charles, Fergus being his surrogate. And the even more moving commitment of Evan Dhu to his own death is symbolic of the doomed loyalty of the Highland followers of the cause. Flora herself, just as perhaps she was the Celtic Muse itself at points, becomes the mourning spirit of that movement, tragically wondering if her enthusiasm was the cause of the executions. Scott himself is caught between two allegiances here; his emotions seem very involved with Scotland's tragic loss. A last point to consider is the symbolic significance of the very names of 'Flora' and 'Rose'. Do they represent a vision of two sides of Scotland, the wild northern flower of the Highlands, and the more anglicised rose of the South?

Realism and romance

A final level at which we can read the novel lies in the conflict between 'romance' and 'realism'. The best starting point for considering this might be with some questions. Why did Scott centre his novel on such an insipid hero, and why was this 'hero' really a trapped and captured spectator? Why was Cosmo Bradwardine placed in such an ambiguous position? And, outstandingly, why, at the heart of all his romance, does Scott find it necessary to burst its bubble so emphatically at Holyrood and at Prestonpans, and follow this disappointment or reduction with a drawn-out anti-climax?

There is an uneasy tension continually present in the central figures, as they waver between a romantic status, and subsequent reduction or even mockery. Cosmo Bradwardine is an outstanding example. He is explicitly made out to be a complete contrast to Waverley in Chapter 13; and yet he is made almost 'a man of feeling' in the consequent duel episode. He constantly moves from being a Don Quixote figure in his pedantry and self-delusion, to being a figure of some substance and nobility at other times. (It is interesting that Scott admitted kinship with both Waverley and Cosmo; and that his next novel was to be called *The Antiquary*, a study of another and Cosmo-like version of himself in Jonathan Oldbuck.)

Scott's commentary, as in the realistic and reductive descriptions in Chapters 7 and 8 of the filth, dirt, and backwardness of the village of Tully-Veolan, is often very far from being romantic or exotic. There is much shared here with the contemporary realism of Elizabeth Hamilton in her reductive *The Cottagers of Glenburnie* (1808), or Susan Ferrier's description of the Highlands in *Marriage* (1818).

In the main characters one continually detects this propensity for contradictory undercutting. Flora, for all that at one level she is the Celtic Muse and the heart of Waverley's dreams in her purple-heathered mountain retreat, is actually the most reasonable person in the book. She argues against Waverley joining the Jacobite cause realising that he is a disturbed and impetuous romantic. She hates Donald Bean Lean and quite rightly suspects his motives. Finally, she has the realism and genuine altruism to succeed in her plan of curing Waverley of his romantic moon-calf love for her. (This is perhaps the more tragic in that Scott implies that she actually does love Waverley.) She is the outstanding realist of the novel, with the exception of the evil and cynical Donald Bean Lean; and Scott clearly suggests that it is only in Waverley's mind that she is the spirit of romance.

The same contradiction exists within Fergus, just as motivated by greed as by genuine vision. Throughout the novel his actions are to be read as sordidly anti-romantic in contrast with the idealism of his sister, whose far finer sentiments – and even singing – he continually mocks. His values are not to be trusted; even his prince, Charles, turns out to be a man of self-seeking calculation. Charles and Donald Bean Lean are Scott's masterstrokes in this pattern of romance reduced to realism. In our introduction to glorious Highland scenery, and at the heart of the romantic Highland cave, after the journey through the blue mountains and all its noble scenery, behind the fire and the water, below the eagles and the splendid landscape, there lurks, not a romantic robber-baron, but a petty and sordid con-man, who would be as at home in the modern world as the most unreliable of used-car salesmen or small town crooks. This first exemplary reduction, and the many which follow, are brought to their climax at the sordid and suspicious court of Holyrood, with Charles seen at the heart of his cause as something between romantic martyr-to-be and spider at the centre of his web.

The method has run throughout, from Waverley's idealisation of Cecilia Stubbs, deflated by her preference for Jonas the factor's son, to his great dreams which end in accidents that cause him to be bundled ingloriously over the countryside and used unwittingly as a pawn in a political game. All Waverley's grand ambitions are at the end reduced to the haphazard saving of his 'enemies' – the main one luckily turning out to be the very man who can save his life.

Scott is often praised for his great gallery of characters, for his diversity of human creation. Yet, upon serious study of this novel, we see that most of his characters, including the protagonists, have feet of clay. Waverley's father, Richard, is always seen as an arid comment on political chicanery. Davie Gellately with his songs is a vehicle for mocking romance and heroism. Jonas and Cecilia represent the comfortable sound marriage of financial convenience rather than the fulfilment of romantic dreams. Even the landlady who stops the sword-play in the Tully-Veolan inn does it not because of altruism, but because she has a keen eye towards the risk to her property. Bailie Macwheeble and Jamie Jinker are caught in rebellion for the sake of reward, and, like the Laird of Balmawhapple and Davie, they are an ironic and reductive comment on the visionary enthusiasts above them. Characters like Cruikshanks at Cairnvreckan, Mucklewrath and Gifted Gilfillan are enthusiasts for a cause, but not at all averse to making money at the same time, like the blacksmith who won't shoe on Sundays unless he gets paid hugely above the normal rate. The implication of all these taken together is that their superiors, like Fergus and Donald, are no better, if not worse; and that the bulk of the Jacobite army, and its cause, is moved by irresponsible passion and greed. The rabble army, the sly Donald, Gilfillan and company, therefore, are symbols to Scott, not of romance, but of unreason and social sickness, symptoms of an unhealthy lack of integration of feelings and thoughts in Scotland – a Scotland all too often torn by internecine political causes. It is only in the mind of the deluded and immature Edward Waverley that these realistic and sordid affairs take on romantic qualities.

It is arguable whether, in the end, anything was either totally romantic or realistic to Scott. Indeed it is tempting to consider whether Scott's final position is not in fact a kind of detached withdrawal from life, since involvement (as Edwin Muir argued in discussing his tragic love affair with Williamina Stuart Belsches) leads to tragedy and divided loyalties which tear apart. A reading of *Waverley* seems to suggest that Scott prefers to stand aside from his material, to look at Scotland's problems of dissociation and history from a distance; commenting on the ways in which Scotland has lost a wholeness of imagination, feeling, and reasonable analysis of its own condition. Scotland to Scott has been dangerously filled with those who cannot see life objectively, but must impose their own extreme views upon it, and to this extent his novel does focus on examples of dislocations or divisions of sensibility, and not just on Waverley alone. Scott sees Waverley as the extreme example of a world in which virtually everyone, from the obsessively self-interested Fergus to his altruistic sister Flora, from the anachronistic and choleric Baron Bradwardine to the apparently conventional and self-possessed Major Talbot, are trapped in their distorted perceptions of the world. It is Scott's greatest achievement to reveal such relative and prejudiced perception as fundamental to history and society, and we should now recognise his deceptively ironic yet sympathetic view of human action as an important part of a crucial nineteenth-century shift towards Modernism in Western thought and culture.

CHAPTER 15

SUSAN FERRIER: *MARRIAGE*

SUSAN FERRIER (1782–1854) AND THE WRITING OF *MARRIAGE*

Susan Ferrier was born and grew up in Edinburgh, the youngest of ten children. Her mother was a famous beauty, and her father a lawyer and friend of Sir Walter Scott; the family knew many literary figures of the time. When her father became manager of the Duke of Argyll's estates, frequently visiting Inveraray Castle, Susan often went too, gaining experience which probably contributed to the making of *Marriage*. She became friendly with Charlotte Clavering, the duke's niece, and began *Marriage* in collaboration with Charlotte in 1809. 'The History of Mrs Douglas' was written by Charlotte, but she dropped out and Susan continued work on the novel alone. *Marriage* was published anonymously in 1818 and in London was attributed to Walter Scott, who admired Ferrier and her work. She published two more novels, *The Inheritance* (1824) and *Destiny* (1831), both out of print but worth finding, as is the *Memoir and Correspondence of Susan Ferrier* (1898). In later life she became extremely pious and worked for good causes, including temperance and the emancipation of slaves, until her death (almost blind from cataracts) in 1854.

Marriage was published four years after Scott's *Waverley*. Ferrier tackled the same situation as Scott, attempting to write fiction attractive to both Scottish and English readers. However, in his wake, Ferrier was writing with an added self-consciousness, entering a tradition already distinctively fashioned by an influential writer. This generated both advantages and problems for her. For example, her descriptions of landscape in Chapter 2 often seem to comment, in parodic fashion, on the Scott tradition and its presentation of Scotland:

> A small-sullen looking lake was in front, on whose banks grew neither tree nor shrub. Behind, rose a chain of rugged cloud-capped hills, on the declivities of which were some faint attempts at young plantations; and the only level ground, consisted of a few dingy turnip fields, enclosed with rude stone walls, or dykes, as the post-boy called them.

Scott, in his introduction to *St Ronan's Well*, in 1832, commenting on the type of novel being written by Ferrier, suggested it belonged to a 'female' tradition, and linked Ferrier with Fanny Burney, Edgeworth, Austen, and Charlotte Smith as possessing particular qualities, especially of observation and light satire. *Marriage* is sometimes described as a 'novel of manners' – characteristically treating matters of social conduct in polite society, and closely related to 'Conduct Books'. Such works were important for readers at the time as guides to changing social standards and values.

Fiction by women was distinctive, as was the position of the woman writer in this period. Ferrier, as a woman, was facing a different set of circumstances from those faced by male contemporaries. It has been suggested that Ferrier was unwilling to disclose her authorial identity because the people on which she based her fictional characters might be offended by her work. However, as Elaine Showalter has shown in *A Literature of their Own: British Women Novelists from Brontë to Lessing* (1973), for women at the turn of the eighteenth century, publishing anonymously was also a way of avoiding unwanted fame.

Ferrier can therefore be viewed from various perspectives: as a Scottish writer, dealing with what F. R. Hart in *The Scottish Novel* (1978) calls 'the adjustment of provincial perspectives' (there have been comparisons with Galt, for instance); as a writer of her time, in the tradition of 'the novel of manners' and other writing, particularly by women; and as both a Scot and a woman writer. In her study, *Susan Ferrier* (1984), Mary Cullinan emphasised that while comparisons with male authors are possible, Ferrier's perspectives and sympathies are those of a woman.

The structure of the novel

Marriage first appeared in three volumes, a practice common at the time, and the modern OUP edition (1977) retains the original structure. A third edition of *Marriage* in 1826 split the novel into two parts instead of three.

The structure makes use of the principles of antithesis. We are invited to compare characters, notably Juliana and Alicia Malcolm (Mrs Douglas), Mary and Adelaide, Alicia and Mary; and also various marriages contemplated or made: in the first volume, those made by Juliana and Alicia; in volume 3, those of Mary and Adelaide. The danger is that this approach can seem too schematic, tending to produce polarisation without flexibility. On the other hand, other critics have complained of a lack of organising principle in Ferrier's work implying a failure to maintain consistency of genre and tone, or to hold together comic-satiric and didactic strands. However, this assumes that consistency in these terms is the only valid critical criterion. Perhaps

Ferrier's novel has, as well as a remarkable fertile energy, another kind of unity.

Marriage as a unifying theme?

The title signals a unifying idea. The opening outlines the significance of marriage for a young woman of 'good birth' but no great fortune. Juliana, at 17, is expected to think of marriage in practical terms, as her father, Lord Courtland, bluntly explains. Marriage here, for women of this class, is a matter of social expediency, and bound up with economic factors. This view is later confirmed by the outspoken Mrs Macshake, who asks Mary in Chapter 11 of the second volume:

> 'An' nae word o' ony o' your sisters gawn to get husbands yet? They tell me they're but coorse lasses: an wha'll tak ill-farred tocherless queans, when there's walth o' bonny faces an' lang purses i' the market – He, he!'

Women do not have many choices; the relationship between marriage, money and social position puts pressure on them to marry 'wisely'. The consequent stress on the 'duty' of young women to obey their parents creates a conflict between 'duty' and 'desire'. Juliana disobeys her father, marries for 'love', and suffers her fate. Alicia Malcolm, on the other hand, dutiful to her aunt, Lady Audley, gives up Edmund. She marries not for passion but for 'good sense', and the narrator comments at the end of 'History of Mrs Douglas' (Chapter 14):

> Alas! how imperfect is human wisdom! Even in seeking to do right, how many are the errors we commit! Alicia judged wrong in thus sacrificing the happiness of Sir Edmund to the pride and injustice of his mother; – but her error was that of a noble, self-denying spirit, entitled to respect, even though it cannot claim approbation. . . . If Alicia lost the buoyant spirit of youth, the bright and quick play of fancy, yet a placid contentment crowned her days; and, at the end of two years, she would have been astonished had any one marked her as an object of compassion.

Contrasting values: Mary and Adelaide

There is a contrast between the values on which Mary and Adelaide base their choices in marriage. Mary's meditation on duty to parents and duty to God is especially significant. She is unable to obey her mother by marrying Mr

Downe-Wright. In volume 3, Adelaide, on the other hand, weighs the issues less seriously. Other couples provide further contrasts: Lady Maclaughlan and Sir Sampson; Mr and Mrs Gawffaw; Mr and Mrs Pullen: none of these is ideal or admirable unions. Moral and didactic purposes are evident in *Marriage*. Mary Cullinan's study suggests that the novel conveys a double message, revealing 'the ideal qualities a woman should possess and the ideal type of marriage into which she should enter'. To this it might be added – and the type of marriage she should avoid.

Didacticism in the novel

The didactic aspect of the novel was discussed by Ferrier in a letter of c. 1809–10 to Charlotte Clavering (in Ferrier's *Memoir and Correspondence*, 1898):

I do not recollect ever to have seen the sudden transition of a high-bred English beauty, who thinks she can sacrifice all for love, to an uncomfortable solitary Highland dwelling among tall red-haired sisters and grim-faced aunts. Don't you think this would make a good opening of the piece? Suppose each of us try our hands on it; the moral to be deduced from that is to warn all young ladies against runaway matches, and the character and fate of the two sisters would be unexceptionable. I expect it will be the first book every wise matron will put into the hand of her daughter, and even then the reviewers will relax of their severity in favor of the morality of this little work.

Ferrier was aware of the need for moral approval of her work. In the context of the time, when women were not only writing more, but also forming a large part of the reading public, moral content was often offered by women novelists as justification for the worth of their novels. However, it should also be noted that Ferrier's letter has a light, ironic tone. She knows her novel 'should' have a moral, but her attitude does not seem entirely serious. Yet she did subscribe to the notion that fiction should 'teach', and another passage from her *Memoir and Correspondence* is often quoted to this effect: 'The only good purpose of a book is to inculcate morality, and convey some lesson of instruction as well as delight'. In her later years this view grew stronger; eventually, becoming intensely pious, she gave up writing altogether. Nevertheless, the light-hearted quality is there, in the letters and in the fiction. Charlotte Clavering thought Lady Maclaughlan a marvellous comic creation. Many subsequent readers have responded to Ferrier's comic imagination, and her novels have been compared with those of Austen and Galt.

The conflict between didacticism and satire

There is, however, a conflict in Ferrier's work between didacticism and her satirical gifts. To understand this, it is useful to look at the position of the woman writer at this time. In *The Rise of the Woman Novelist* (1986) Jane Spencer discusses how women writers responded to women's position in society and to the role permitted the female author, showing how they could either accept the didactic tradition, or escape from it, or protest against the roles imposed upon women, including that expected of the woman writer. Whether or not Ferrier protests is uncertain. It might be that, through wit, humour and satire, Ferrier was indeed questioning the role of the woman writer, without entirely rejecting it, and thus working from within its confines. According to Nancy L. Paxton (in *Women and Literature* 4, 1976), Ferrier's 'frank humour' signifies the less conventional side of the author, more in keeping with early English feminist writing than with Victorian Christian moralists.

Ferrier records, in a satirical spirit, the limitations built into the lives of women, for example, in this introductory description of Juliana in Chapter 1:

> Educated for the sole purpose of forming a brilliant establishment, of catching the eye and captivating the senses, the cultivation of her mind, or the correction of her temper, had formed no part of the system by which that aim was to be accomplished.

Ferrier asks us to reflect on the importance of education for women, and the type of education women should have, a subject revisited several times: in the laird's speech on education for women (in the first volume); in Mrs Douglas's views on education (in the first chapter of volume 2); in the descriptions of the Glenfern aunts; and in Mary and Emily's conversations in the novel's last volume. Another scene in the third volume, presenting Mrs Bluemits and her circle of 'literary' ladies, while seeming to satirise so-called 'Bluestocking' women, in the last paragraph indicates the real point of the satire (volume 3, Chapter 8):

> Next to goodness, Mary most ardently admired talents. She knew there were many of her own sex who were justly entitled to the distinction of literary fame. Her introduction to the circle at Mrs Bluemits had disappointed her; but they were pretenders to the name.

This episode demonstrates the complexity of Ferrier's view, admiring 'intellectual' women (the epigraphs throughout Ferrier's novel show she was herself extremely well-read), and yet still accepting traditional ideas of a woman's role and purpose.

Finally, there is Mary's cousin Emily, who does not fully fit the bill of 'well-regulated' heroine; yet most readers today find her an attractive character. It is illuminating to set Emily's speeches alongside Ferrier's own frequently lively letters. Not surprisingly, some critics see Emily and Mary as 'opposing' sides of Ferrier herself; the more dutiful and morally aware Mary complemented by the witty and spirited Emily.

This chapter has looked at didactic and comic aspects of the novel, and their relation to the tradition of writing by women, and has considered how Ferrier, in the first part of the novel in particular, dealt self-consciously with Scottish material. These aspects are not separate. Like other writers of the period, Ferrier used the principle of antithesis to present a moral message; her 'novel of manners' contrasts the mores of Scotland and England in order to suggest relative worth, as does her presentation of women and marriage. At the same time, the treatment of the two cultures is a main source of comic effects.

Scottish culture and English culture

The reader first glimpses Scotland through the eyes of Juliana, who is seeing it for the first time. She is English, like Scott's Waverley, but in other respects this spoilt aristocrat is very different, and her view of the Highlands far from sympathetic. However, her jaundiced view may not wholly account for the negative picture of Scottish (specifically Highland) culture which emerges in the novel. The main characters at Glenfern include 'three long-chinned spinsters and . . . five awkward purple girls'. The aunts are caricature figures; they are naïve and ignorant, and we are invited to laugh at them. Although slightly differentiated from one another, the aunts work as a single 'comic unit'. Mary's cousins, named Bella, Babby, Betsy, Becky and Beenie, are never properly distinguished from one another. The laird, too, is narrowly provincial, and is a 'caricature Scot', particularly in his meanness. More positively, Scottish culture is seen also to possess kindliness, genuineness, and generosity, as exemplified in Aunt Grizzy. When Juliana arrives at Glenfern, the laird articulates these ideas: 'What! not frightened for our Highland hills, my leddy? Come, cheer up – trust me, ye'll find as warm hearts among them, as ony ye hae left in your fine English Policies.' Ferrier records Scottish speech in two ways, in 'Highland' English, and in a form of Lowland Scots, as can be seen in the following exchange between Sir Sampson of Lochmarlie Castle and his Highland servant (Chapter 16):

'Where are all my people?' demanded his incensed master.

'Hurs aw awa tull ta Sandy Mor's.'

'Where is my lady?'

'Hurs i' ta teach tap.' [*house-top*]

'Where is Murdoch?'

'Hur's helpin' ta leddie i' ta teach tap.'

Later Mrs Macshake, a Scotswoman of the old school, remarks to Mary (Chapter 11 in volume 2):

'Impruvements!' turning sharply round upon her, 'What ken ye about impruvements, bairn? A bonny impruvement or else no, to see tyleyors and sclaters leavin', whar I mind Jewks an' Yearls'.

In Chapter 2 of her study of Scots language in nineteenth-century fiction, *From Galt to Douglas Brown* (1988) Emma Letley notes that:

The novel makes conventional use of Scots in association with eccentricity and ridicule. Those people who speak the broadest Scots represent a dying generation and an outmoded way of life; that is the old laird, and his spinster sisters; and the topics expressed in Scots relate frequently to meanness, sordid questions of *tocher* and squalor.

English culture, however, is also satirised quite ruthlessly, particularly upper-class society. Juliana, who marries the anglicised Henry Douglas, and their daughter Adelaide, are among the key examples of fashionable English society. In contrast are Alicia Malcolm's thoughts on London and her return to Scotland (Chapter 14):

Alicia had long since sickened in the metropolis at the frivolity of beauty, the heartlessness of fashion, and the insipidity of elegance; and it was a relief to her to turn to the variety of character she found beneath the cloke of simple, eccentric, and sometimes coarse manners.

English society is further criticised in Chapter 21, when Mr Brittle shows Juliana his wares, and Juliana offends General Cameron; and in volume 2, Chapter 11, where Mrs Fox manipulates kind-hearted Aunt Grizzy.

Mrs Douglas, a 'model' character, puts a balanced view of the aunts at Glenfern to Juliana: 'No doubt they are often tiresome and ridiculous; but they are always kind and well meaning.' We are also told, in the early chapters that she 'had too much taste to murder Scotch songs with her English accent. She therefore compromised the matter as well as she could, by selecting a Highland ditty clothed in her own native tongue.' However, Mrs Douglas balances good aspects of Highland life against its limitations, deciding that Mary should also have the benefits of English 'civilisation' and contact with the wider world. Mrs Douglas, part-Scottish, part-English, has lived in both countries. (This balanced viewpoint perhaps derives from Ferrier's awareness of the fiction and cultural values of her friend, Walter Scott.) Mary goes south; but declares her commitment to Scotland (volume 2, Chapter 7):

> 'I shall come back to you, your own "Highland Mary". No Englishman, with his round face and trim meadows, shall ever captivate me. Heath-covered hills, and high cheek bones, are the charms that must win my heart.'

In the later part of the novel, in London, her allegiances are to people like Mrs Lennox, also of Scottish background and when going to church, against her mother's wishes, Mary finds herself homesick as she contrasts the wild of her beloved Lochmarlie with the civilised beauty of the English landscape.

Romanticism or realism?

To some extent Romantic ideas do underlie the presentation in this novel particularly of Scottish landscape and culture (and in *The Inheritance* and *Destiny*, too). Highland landscape inspires the more perceptive characters in Ferrier's work. The Highlander may also have particularly appealing qualities; Scotland is poorer than England, and the peasants are barefoot, but the female Scottish peasant (as in Wordsworth's 'The Solitary Reaper') is associated in young Mary's mind (the novel's latter stages) with energy, freedom and colour, in contrast to the duller representative of English culture ('a well dressed English rustic'). Scotland does well out of this, but the comparison in this particular incident is problematic, avoiding deeper awareness of the lives of Scottish peasants, or more questioning analysis of the cultures concerned.

Marriage also records historical changes, however. The gulf between Juliana's husband, Henry Douglas, and his father, is symptomatic of the decline of Highland culture and the growing anglicisation of landowning families. As a counterbalance, 'improvements' in the Highlands are mentioned. The problems of Highland isolation for women are strongly suggested. Thus there are some 'realistic' elements, and some sharp remarks such as Mr Douglas's 'it is only in romantic minds that fine scenery inspires romantic ideas.' The presentation of Scotland has Romantic elements, but is also robustly satirical. Interestingly, Dr Johnson's negative views of the Scottish Highlands are mocked and refuted in both *Marriage* (through the character of Dr Redgill) and at the start of her last novel, *Destiny*.

Critical opinion is divided as to how even-handed Ferrier's art is towards her two countries, some feeling that she manages to balance the claims of Scotland and England, others arguing that she is patronising in her presentation of Scotland, intending her readers to compare their own implied superiority with the inferiority of many of the Scottish characters displayed. It should be remembered, though, that satire is not intended to be 'balanced'; it characteristically employs strategies of exaggeration, caricature, parody and so on, for its own ends.

Drawing conclusions

The treatment of 'marriage', and of English and Scottish culture in *Marriage*, echoes the author's larger purposes: entertainment, and the exploration of moral and social values. Such values are perhaps explored with most clarity in volumes 2 and 3, when the reader enters with Mary into the world of fashionable English society, in some of the novel's most obviously satirical sections. For these characters, appearance is all. Artifice in Adelaide is echoed in other minor characters: ' "I go very much by outward actions," said Mrs Downe Wright; "they are all we have to judge by." '

In contrast, Mrs Douglas is reticent, concealing her emotions; she does not mention her worldly experience to Juliana until it is appropriate (volume 1, Chapter 14). Like Cordelia in *King Lear*, she chooses silence rather than ostentation. Similarly, blind Mrs Lennox attaches no importance to appearances, but has the 'vision' to see beyond her fellow creatures, and foresees the relationship between Mary and her son. Even Emily, for all her wit and spirit, has little concern with externals, declaring, 'If a person speaks sense and truth, what does it signify how it is spoken?'

As part of the theme of 'appearances', two groups of characters are set in opposition: those linked with 'artifice' and those linked with 'nature'. Juliana is comically unsympathetic to nature; when faced with the beauties of Lochmarlie Castle in volume 1, Chapter 8, she is unimpressed:

> But in vain were creation's charms spread before Lady Juliana's eyes. Woods, and mountains, and lakes, and rivers, were odious things; and her heart panted for dusty squares, and suffocating drawing-rooms.

Adelaide, too, is associated with physical interiors rather than the 'natural world'; and with 'art' (and artifice) as opposed to 'nature' (and that which is natural). Her ability – or inability – to feel, revealed in her response to Mary's weeping, suggests she lacks 'heart'. 'The heart' is associated with the 'natural' characters, Mary and Mrs Lennox (volume 2, Chapter 17):

> The language of sympathy is soon understood. Mrs Lennox seemed to feel the tribute of pity and respect that flowed from Mary's warm heart, and from that moment they felt toward each other that indefinite attraction, which, however it may be ridiculed, certainly does sometimes influence our affections.

Charles Lennox, too, has 'heart', and Emily explicitly contrasts herself with superficial people around her, telling Mary, 'mine are natural feelings, and theirs are artificial.'

The reader is invited to draw evaluative conclusions. The exposé of 'artificial' characters reveals them to be weak or foolish, but these criticisms are also applied to 'good' characters; Mary's aunts, for example, are 'weak vulgar relations' with Juliana 'indeed than folly more a fool'. All are open to criticism. Nevertheless, distinction is made between small weaknesses and major flaws. The Glenfern aunts may be flawed, but they have virtues compared to the artificial, shallow creatures of fashionable society: ' "They are, to be sure, something like brambles," thought [Mary]; "they fasten upon one in every possible way, but still they are better than the faded exotics of fashionable life." ' The 'artificial' characters like Juliana and Adelaide lack true feeling; they also fail to develop in response to experience. Mary's response to her uncle's death is intrinsically different from Juliana's response to the death of her father. Mary matures emotionally, but Juliana remains the same.

Finally, both Juliana and Adelaide fail to consider their decisions and judgements, and thus lack 'balance'. Like Austen, Ferrier seems to suggest that balance and rational moderation are desirable as a temper to passionate emotion.

In his introduction to an Oxford edition of *Marriage* (published in 1971 and reissued in 1986), Herbert Foltinek comments: 'Susan Ferrier may have lacked the all-comprehending energy of the great authors, but she was able to employ the structural principles of contrast and analogy . . .'. Such praise is faint, and there is still relatively little written about Ferrier, and the body of work that exists includes some rather 'apologetic' or even denigratory criticism. In his introductory essay to the National Library of Scotland

Exhibition Catalogue of 1982 Ian Campbell pointed to the difficulty of finding critical assessment of her work, but concluded that 'no celebratory exhibition will raise her to the rank of a Scott or a Galt, for the limitations we have tried to define are still limitations. She remains a Scottish novelist of the second rank.'

One reason why Ferrier has been either ignored or considered 'second rate' may be that she has been insufficiently 'placed' in terms of literary tradition. Consideration of her relationship to the tradition of women's writing, as well as to a Scottish tradition, might lead to deeper understanding and appreciation of her work. Efforts have been made to contextualise her; Campbell, for instance, compares Ferrier favourably with Elizabeth Hamilton, whose novel *The Cottagers of Glenburnie* (1808) Ferrier enjoyed. In his essay 'Myth, Parody and Dissociation: Scottish Fiction 1814–1914', on nineteenth-century Scottish fiction in volume 3 of *The History of Scottish Literature* (1988), Douglas Gifford points out that Scottish women writers in the nineteenth century can usefully be considered separately from the male authors. He mentions not only Elizabeth Hamilton and Mary Brunton, but also Catherine Sinclair's *Modern Accomplishments* (1836), as well as Ferrier's three novels, although, like other critics, he remains critical of these writers, commenting that:

> There is an acidic voice and a respectable voice; and the author reveals in the discrepancy between them the unsureness of moral and social values so typical of the century. These women may be detached; but they lack a consistent point of view, so that their work is no real and coherent social critique, and all that remains is the nostalgic love of old Scots songs and of old-fashioned couthiness.

There are two issues here. One is that nineteenth-century Scottish fiction in general is troubled by problems of 'unsureness' and inconsistency. The second point, expanded in Gifford's essay, is that women writers had difficulties in reconciling didactic modes with their interest in a Scotland which they regarded as backward. Women writers' work is flawed, in his view, because, being both female and Scottish, they had special difficulties of mode and tone which they were unable fully to resolve.

Yet there are signs that critics may increasingly be able to offer more positive commentary on Ferrier. In 1989 (in *Scottish Literary Journal* 16) Loraine Fletcher demonstrated the way in which Ferrier offers a radical critique of aristocratic society; and in 1997, Oxford University Press issued an edition of the novel with a new, sympathetic introduction by Kathryn

Kirkpatrick. Significant re-assessments are offered in Carol Anderson and Aileen M. Riddell's study of 'The Other Great Unknowns: Women Fiction Writers of the Early Nineteenth Century', in *A History of Scottish Women's Writing* (1997). The re-publication of Ferrier's other work would assist scholarly and critical study. With their comic vigour (there are some memorable characters like the prattling but astute Miss Pratt in *The Inheritance*), and often incisive depiction of society (Ferrier is highly critical of the carelessly wealthy, and of patronage in the church, in *Destiny*, for instance), both her other novels are of considerable interest. Her *Memoir and Correspondence* is both revealing and entertaining.

Happily, a more inclusive view of the Romantic period is now developing, with useful work by critics like Gary Kelly (1989) and Katy Trumpener helping to offer a broad context in which to read novelists such as Ferrier. There is, too, a growing interest in women writers in Scotland, following the development of women's studies, which is beginning to produce deeper insights into the achievement, not only of Susan Ferrier but of other significant female authors who have hitherto been mistakenly neglected.

CHAPTER 16

JOHN GALT: *THE ENTAIL*

JOHN GALT (1779–1839):
SOCIAL HISTORY AND FAMILY TRAGEDY

In his somewhat obsequious dedication of *The Entail* (1823) to King George IV, Galt self-deprecatingly describes his novel as one of 'a series of sketches, in which he has attempted to describe characters and manners peculiar to (Scotland)', and embracing a great part of the eighteenth century. This appears to place *The Entail* on the same footing as his other 'Tales of the West', like *Annals of the Parish* (1821) and *The Provost* (1822), thus making it one of Galt's 'theoretical histories' in which he traces social changes within a particular small locality over one or two generations. Pressures were, however, put on Galt by his publisher Blackwood, to expand his intentions to a full three-decker novel instead of his preferred single volume. The result is that *The Entail*, originally conceived as the rather rambling narrative of *The Lairds of Grippy* has a fully developed plot. It was a work which was highly admired when it first appeared, which pleased Galt himself both in the writing and the result, and which has been described as Galt's masterpiece.

In his essay, 'Mind-Forg'd Manacles: John Galt's The Entail as Romantic Tragi-Comedy' (in *The History of Scottish Literature: The Nineteenth Century*, vol. 3, 1987), Keith Costain explores this view of the novel. He suggests that Galt was seeking to write 'a novel which displays the destructive influence of passion and which belongs "to no age or country, but to general human nature"'. He defines Claud Walkinshaw as 'a character fit for tragedy who finds himself in a world that distinctly belongs to the realm of comedy, as is the case with other tragi-comic figures'. In this world Claud is at odds with the largely moral and benevolent values of the people around him, since he has become the victim of his own sour self-interest. It is only at the end of his life that he is able to turn away from his own selfishmess and try to join the moral and forgiving community. However, it turns out that he is too late to undo his actions.

It may seem to the reader that the comic world of action in the novel derives its force from the particularly Scottish quality of the characters, their actions and speech, and the local environment created by the author. If so, it is possible to modify Costain's claim that the tragedy belongs only to *general* human nature. Claud's self-interest and obsessive pursuit of the lost lands of Kittlestonheugh might be seen as a blend of the traditional Scots caution towards money intensified by a narrow fixation about family pride and property and allied to a pedantic desire for legalistic certainty, all qualities that might be seen as peculiarly Scottish. The novels of Scott furnish us with both comic and tragic examples of these character traits. If Claud's tragedy, and the tragedy of his family, is general in its relevance to human nature, it is so only in a superficial way. More specifically, it is a tragedy of a bourgeois/feudal kind that has its origins in a particular kind of social development. The extent to which this analysis applies also to the second half of the novel may be more doubtful. The third element of Costain's title must also be considered, the notion of the novel as 'Romantic', as interpreted in the particular terms of the fashionable novels of the early nineteenth century. Galt may be playing with his readers, or perhaps conspiring with them and their expectations, in his certainly self-conscious and ironic attempt to meet his publisher's wishes for a fully-plotted three-volume novel.

Some bearings on John Galt

When Galt came to write *The Entail*, he had already tasted much success with other 'theoretical histories'. *The Ayrshire Legatees, Annals of the Parish, The Steamboat, The Provost, Sir Andrew Wylie* and *The Gathering of the West* had all appeared between 1820 and the end of 1822, when *The Entail* was published – a remarkable output for such a short time. In *Annals of the Parish* (1821) Galt's presentation of the apparently simple minister of Dalmailing in Ayrshire is a masterpiece of detailed concision, combining social history with acute human observation, covering the fifty years (1760–1810) of the Reverend Balwhidder's ministry, from his intrusion by the lairds into a hostile parish till his retirement, blessed by all. What raises the account well above mere recording of change in country manners and conditions is its delightfully ambiguous treatment of its pious protagonist – who may well be less simple than he seems, since he becomes wealthy through no fewer than three marriages, and generally manages to bring about beneficial changes, for himself as well as his community, through a manipulation of lairds and commoners alike. A sensitive reading of the novel will reveal an astonishing amount of information about Balwhidder's community, presented in a way which effortlessly combines history and a unique brand of fiction.

Galt repeated the genre in *The Provost* (1822), again covering the same fifty years of change, this time in Gudetown (a version of early Irvine), seen through the eyes of an even more ambiguous protagonist, Bailie and Provost Pawkie – who, as his name suggests, has an eye to the main chance, and in more ways than one anticipates Hogg's Sinner and Edinburgh Bailie of a year or so later. In a mild and secular way, the Provost is a self-justified manipulator of social change, illustrating Galt's beliefs as a business man that self-advancement and social benefaction go hand in hand.

These are Galt's greatest 'theoretical histories', although he came close in his other studies, long and short, of Scottish worthies, which covered a wide spectrum, from schoolmistress and midwife ('the howdie') to laird and member of parliament. Perhaps his greatest novel and most imaginative creation after *Annals, The Provost,* and *The Entail,* is his magnificient evocation of the religious struggles of Scotland in *Ringan Gilhaize* (1823). This, together with Scott's *Old Mortality* (1816) and Hogg's *The Brownie of Bodsbeck* (1817), is the greatest of Scotland's fictional treatments of the Covenanters and 'the killing time' – again, significantly, presented through the *persona* of a justified agent of the Lord, the much persecuted and enduringly resilient Ringan, who seeks revenge over many years after the murder of his wife and children by Royalist troops. And revenge he gains, in a wondrous moment of divine retribution which allows him to turn the tide of history by killing Claverhouse at the Battle of Killiecrankie. Once again, the hallmark of Galt's treatment, as with so much of nineteenth-century Scottish fiction, is that of authorial ambiguity as to the moral legitimacy of the central protagonists' actions. Only in *The Entail* does Galt attempt to work on such a large Scottish canvas, and only in these two novels does he portray central Scottish characters of such gravity and cultural significance.

Galt was never again to match the speed and quality of writing which he attained in the period 1820–4. It seems that the topic of West of Scotland life, manners and social change had fired him up to a height of inspiration and fluency. Part of his success, of course, was due to the friendship and encouragement of William Blackwood and the ready publication he found in the columns of 'Maga' (*Blackwood's Magazine*). When Galt fell out with Blackwood and transferred his writings to Oliver and Boyd, he lost a lot of the impetus and power of these years.

The writing of the novel

The Entail was written in a matter of six months between June and November, 1822, with the remarkable alacrity that was characteristic of Galt, who had developed the habit of rapid writing over years of earning a living by the pen in the intervals of more uncertain business and political ventures. Started in London, the novel was continued in Edinburgh and completed in Greenock. Galt had felt it necessary to return to his home ground in the West of Scotland to brush up his familiarity with the local vernacular vocabulary, in order to make *The Entail* the most Scots (in the linguistic sense) of all his novels so far. The success of this strategy can be seen in the variety and flexibility of the Scots speech used by different characters in the novel.

As Ian Gordon recounts, in his *John Galt: The Life of a Writer* (1972), the completion of the novel was rather fraught with disagreement between Galt and Blackwood, and Galt was conscious that it did not materialise quite as he intended. 'The main fault of *The Entail* was owing to my being over-persuaded . . . I cannot proceed if I am interfered with.' How different the third volume would have been without Blackwood's pressure is impossible to say with certainty, but it would clearly have lacked the 'striking' or contrived episodes of the visit to the Highlands and the shipwreck in Caithness, remaining firmly rooted in Galt's home territory of the south bank of the Clyde. What the reader needs to decide is whether what results is flawed because it is known to be different from the author's original conception, or whether it has nevertheless a unity and textual rationality that makes it a successful literary artefact.

The central symbol

The idea of *The Entail* is at first sight abstract and colourless; a legal device for ensuring that a landed estate will not be broken up through being inherited by different and competing heirs does not seem to be a likely originator of gripping and colourful fiction. But, of course, this is a misconception about what constitutes a good plot idea; both Scott and Dickens a little later based substantial and exciting novels upon points of law and the ramifications of the legal system. Just as Galt made a significant contribution to the development of the political novel in English, so too he is an innovator in the use of legal technicalities as the mainspring for both comic and tragic fiction. The immediate inspiration may have come from his own experience. In 1817, Galt's father, a prosperous ship-owner, died and, on returning from London to Greenock, Galt found that, through a flaw in the will, he was, as surviving son, the sole heir to his father's estate, excluding his mother and sister from any share. He had to have a deed drawn up to give his mother a life-rent and to ensure that his sister shared in the estate along with him after their mother's death. This brush with legal injustice and incompetence must have played some part in deciding the details of *The Entail*, and in colouring his treatment of the members of the legal profession in the novel.

CHARTING THE ACTION: FAMILY TREE AND LEGAL TANGLE

THE WALKINSHAWS OF KITTLESTONHEUGH

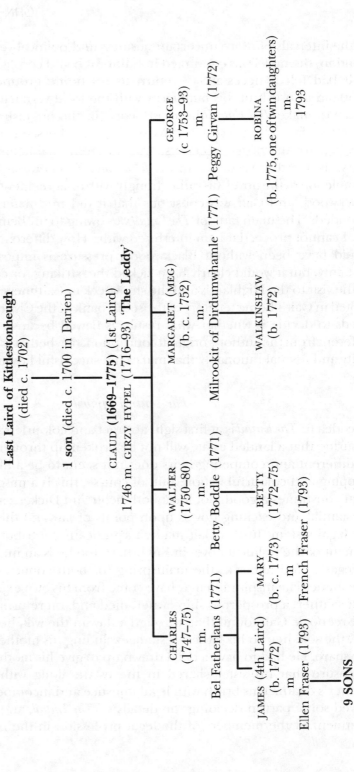

Walkinshaws of Kittlestonheugh (unrecorded)

Last Laird of Kittlestonheugh
(died c. 1702)

1 son (died c. 1700 in Darien)

CLAUD (1669–1775) (1st Laird)
1746 m. GIRZY HYPEL (1716–93) 'The Leddy'

CHARLES   WALTER   MARGARET (MEG)   GEORGE
(1747–75)   (1750–80)   (b. c. 1752)   (c 1753–93)
m.   m.   m.   m.
Bel Fatherlans (1771) Betty Boddle (1771) Milrookit of Dirdumwhamle (1771) Peggy Girvan (1772)

JAMES (4th Laird)   MARY   BETTY   WALKINSHAW   ROBINA
(b. 1772)   (b. c. 1773)   (1772–75)   (b. 1772)   (b. 1775, one of twin daughters)
m   m   m.
Ellen Fraser (1793) French Fraser (1793)   1793

9 SONS

The Walkinshaw family tree gives a picture of the main character relationships in *The Entail*. The dates are derived from textual evidence in the narrative, but must, in some cases, be only approximate. It may seem, looking at the tree and the information about marriages and births, that Galt has artificially clustered the characters into clearly separated generations – older, middle and younger – in a way that suits the direction of the fiction and the time-separation of the different episodes. This may conflict with the notion of realism in the novel, and perhaps highlight the artifice of the plotting.

The entail

It may be argued that Galt has over-developed the possibilities and possible conflicts of the entail beyond the bounds of realistic probability; but, having set up the conditions of the entail in the narrative, he may have felt bound as a novelist to work them out fully for the sake of the novel, allowing each possible heir to have the prize for a time before restoring natural justice in the form of James Walkinshaw's inheritance and the securing of Kittleston-heugh in his family through his nine sons? This raises a question of authorial manipulation of our sympathies by making Charles and his family so amiable in comparison to his brother George and his sister Meg and their families. Could the novel have been so satisfying as a fiction if George had been likeable and Charles a 'grippy' man like his father? Galt is clearly operating within established novel conventions of the right and virtuous versus the wrong and malicious. Yet to a great extent, he mitigates this by making Claud and George feel generous impulses and pangs of conscience, and keeping the family on terms of mutual courtesy and speaking terms even in the midst of the legal conflicts. Surrounding the tragedy or romance, therefore, there is an atmosphere of the ordinary and prosaic, the realistic and credible, and perhaps the comic episodes enhance and support this so that the novel is realised finally as a domestic tragi-comedy rather than the romantic tragi-comedy of Keith Costain's view.

Structure of the novel

At first sight the novel appears to be built up of three books, which might be supposed to be indicative of some plan in the plot structure whereby each book deals with a unified part of the action. This indeed appears to have been part of Galt's original intention: each volume of the novel was to have begun with the commencement of a new act in the story. This certainly worked with the beginning of volume 2, but the plan went astray by the end of that volume

LANDS OF KITTLESTONHEUGH

(Sold off by Claud Walkinshaw's grandfather, Laird of Kittlestonheugh, after the failure of the Darien Scheme, 1700)

GRIPPY	KITTLESTON	DIVETHILL	PLEALANDS
(bought and reassembled in 1740s by CLAUD WALKINSHAW and entailed upon WALTER)	(owned by Mr Auchincloss, later exchanged for the for Plealands)		(entailed upon WALTER and heirs, later exchanged Divethill and Kittleston)

THE LANDS OF KITTLESTONHEUGH, when reunited were jointed in entail as follows:

CHARLES (excluded)
WALTER
WALTER's male heirs
GEORGE
GEORGE's male heirs
CHARLES's male heirs
MARGARET's general heirs

and volume 3 shows no new beginning. In order to identify the structure of *The Entail* as a whole, the reader must ignore the volume divisions and look for another set of markers within the narrative sequence.

If the details and the working out of the entail of Kittlestonheugh are the core of the action, perhaps the development of that plot element is the determining factor in the structure. Another significant element is the alternating nature of the narrative, whereby stretches of many years are passed over in a generalised narrative before there is a concentration of narrative relating to a short period of time, including detailed episodes of dialogue, description and action. The variable pace that this technique produces in the narrative has implications for the basic structure. This is confirmed by the references that Galt made to his original wish to write a novel on the lines of *Annals of the Parish* or *The Provost* dealing with episodes in the history of the Lairds of Grippy.

Accordingly, the structure of *The Entail* may be best represented in the following way:

Preamble: ruin of Kittlestonheugh; beginning of Claud Walkinshaw's career.

First main section: Claud's wooing and marriage; first thoughts of the entail.

Linking section: Claud's family grows up.

Second main section: marriages of the children; the making of the entail. [end of vol. 1]

Third main section: tragic consequences of the entail for Claud, Charles and Walter.

Linking section: events leading to the problems of next generation. [end of vol. 2]

Fourth main section: the resolution of the entail.

Epilogue

(The dividing line between the second and third main sections is the end of volume 1; no such easy division occurs anywhere else and volume 2 ends in the course of the fourth main section.)

FIRST SECTION: PREAMBLE

The opening chapter serves the clear purpose of establishing the influences that play upon the young Claud Walkinshaw, especially the influence of Maudge Dobbie, the faithful family retainer who takes care of Claud after the deaths of his parents and grandfather. There is a contrast established between Claud and his father, who was also attended by Maudge in his youth. Whereas the father was imbued with a spirit of adventure and a sense of Scotland's turbulent history from Maudge's traditional lore (a spirit that led him to embrace the doom laid on him by his own greedy-spirited father), Claud is obviously more attracted to the material concerns of money and wordly success. William Wallace's heroism and the tragedy of Flodden leave him unmoved.

However, one aspect of tradition that clearly makes a big impression on him is the memory of his family's past wealth and the lost estate of Kittlestonheugh, constantly placed before his child's gaze by Maudge Dobbie. The lesson is taught that civic pomp and mercantile income are not fit to be mentioned beside the grandeur of an inherited landed position and pedigree. The introduction of Provost and Mrs Gorbals, with the account of what happens to them in Chapter 2, tends to confirm this lesson for Claud. The references to Miss Christiana Heritage in Chapters 2 and 3 add to the view being built up of the superiority of landed wealth and a secure inheritance over transient income from trade.

The impression given of Claud once he becomes an independent agent is not a favourable one. Set against his undoubted skill at selling, with the help of his persuasive tongue and sharp practice, there is his meanness with money exemplified by his neglect of Maudge in her last years of infirmity and poverty. Maudge correctly diagnoses that Claud's main concern is to gather the money that will help him back to his rightful patrimony. The signs of Claud's future actions towards his own family can already be read.

Two more points in the preamble need to be considered. The narrator is introduced in the first person plural, 'we'; Galt clearly separates himself from this role. Few clues are given about the identity and character of the narrator, nor are there any indications about how he stands in relation to Claud Walkinshaw, for example in age and social position. The style of the main narrative is the only indication of the type of person he is. Secondly, the city of Glasgow and its surroundings are presented as the setting for the action. It is clearly a small pre-industrial community. The strongly Scots speech of the characters helps in identifying the style and manners of the place at that moment as about 1705. Going by what Galt had already done in other novels, it is a reasonable inference that both narrator and setting are going to be significantly treated in the novel as it develops.

FIRST MAIN SECTION

After the preamble, which covers events in Claud's life up to about 1720, there is a very concise transition to the period when Claud is an established cloth-merchant in Glasgow. This can be dated to 1746. He has already owned his shop for a number of years and has been so successful that he has bought the farm of Grippy, a part of his ancestral estate. Now at the age of forty seven, he needs a wife to give him heirs so that the inheritance may be secured by entail from being dispersed again to the winds.

In this section, up to the end of Chapter 12, the action divides itself between a concentration on the calculating acts of Claud to further his obsession and the diversion of comic episodes that can almost be enjoyed as set-pieces of writing in their own right. The episodes to look at particularly are Claud's disastrous ride to Plealands (Chapter 5) and the funeral of Malachi Hypel (Chapter 9).

The crucial chapters for the formation of the entail by Claud are 7 and 8. The conditions of the future entail depend on the determination of the Laird of Plealands to have the name of Hypel perpetuated, if not through the eldest son, then certainly through the second. The first entail of Grippy is settled on Charles by Claud, while Plealands is reserved for Walter, and then for George, by Malachi Hypel. The complication introduced in Chapter 8 is that, while Charles is a normal boy in activity and development, Walter already shows signs of simple-mindedness. The irony surrounding the laird's death, comic though the funeral is, is that Walter inherits as a minor and Claud cannot then disinherit or pass him over in any future settlement.

In Chapters 10, 11 and 12, Claud's thoughts about an entail joining all the family lands and settled on Walter rather than Charles are contested by both legal and clerical opinion. Both the lawyer, Gilbert Omit, and the minister, Mr Kilfuddy, have things to say about the morality of such an action, but Claud is not at all swayed by Mr Kilfuddy's Calvinist denunciations; greed and legality are his only concerns.

Clearly, the depth of Claud's obsession with the estate of Kittlestonheugh is here being displayed by setting it against the strong claims of paternal love and the pious fears of everlasting damnation. It is clear from the end of Chapter 12 that, despite his expression of contrition, Claud is set on his course for the entail and, in the fullness of time, will implement it. The direction of the plot has been established.

LINKING

In Chapter 13 of volume 1, the characters of Claud's children are only beginning to be clearly differentiated for their later parts in the narrative. Little is said about Walter, other than that he is his mother's darling and has as little sense as she has. Considering what develops in the later stages of the novel, this seems an inadequate treatment of both characters. The emphasis in this short section is, however, on Charles. Galt, or his narrator, is notably at pains to indicate how little Charles owes in manners or education to his parents. The limited affection from Claud, the antipathy of 'the Leddy', the cultivated influence of his maternal grandmother and his city education combine to make Charles a different kind of product from his brothers and sister, more refined and sensitive in all aspects, and inclined to elevate love above baser sentiments. In a fashionable novel, we would see Charles as being groomed to occupy the position of romantic hero; in the context of *The Entail*, given the declared intentions of Claud, this upbringing looks like a recipe for damaging conflict and possible tragedy.

SECOND MAIN SECTION

Nevertheless, the grooming of Charles for a romantic role is given its appropriate outlet very quickly in terms of the novel structure. The opening of the next extended section (in Chapter 14) takes up the story from about 1765, when Charles is eighteen, and rapidly moves the reader through his developing love affair with Isabella Fatherlans to his impulsive marriage to her in 1772. There are obvious echoes of Claud's own family disaster in the bride's family background. The name – Fatherlans/father's lands; the old pedigree (Fatherlans of that Ilk); the unlucky commercial venture that ruins the father (the Ayr Bank); the need for the child to go into a menial job in retailing (with a dress-maker in Glasgow), all these provide a timely reminder of the situation that Claud is dedicated to recouping with his plans for an entail.

The main business of this section is the legal enactment of the entail by Claud. The marriage of Charles to the penniless Bel Fatherlans puts a spoke in the wheel of Claud's plans. Claud had worked out a parallel strategy for Charles so that he would be compensated for the loss of the Grippy when it was entailed to Walter. The advice to Charles to wait a year before marrying, the references to Betty Bodle's tocher from her uncle, the Laird of Kilmarkeckle and Claud's negotiations about Betty's marrying Charles, make it clear that Claud is not intending that Charles will suffer financially. It is Charles's romantic nature that leads him unwittingly into the course of action that will end in loss and arouse his father's anger. Claud goes in angry determination to visit Mr Keelevin.

The character of Keelevin deserves some consideration. He fulfils the same function as moral commentator that Mr Kilfuddy occupied in the first main section, but with more natural humanity and benevolence. He attempts to confront Claud with the injustice of his proposal for the entail towards his eldest son Charles. He represents more the spirit of humane and rational feeling, rather than the flaming Presbyterian retribution articulated by Kilfuddy. Yet in this purely human and social compassion, he is no match for Claud's worldliness and is deceived easily about Claud's intentions towards Charles. It is a pessimistic section in that Claud's obsession is shown to have grown to the point where it overcomes any opposition and hardens him against his natural paternal sympathies. The most vivid demonstration of this comes in Chapter 19 where Claud untypically calls for family worship and finds himself confronted by the big ha' Bible with a text concerning the father Isaac and his first-born Esau; the unexpected and uncanny reproach in this text certainly throws Claud into a state of alarm, but it lasts only a moment. The voice of religion is a silent one here; the minister, Mr Denholm, is given no role in the argument. So the seeds of the tragedy are sown to grow to fruition in the next section.

As in the first main section, the seriousness of the entail theme is lightened by comic episodes. In contrast to the romantic theme of Charles's love and marriage, the wooing and marriage of Walter are treated in lighter vein. It is here that Walter's mixture of innocent simple-mindedness and obstinacy is fully revealed. He is being established not merely as the usurper of Charles's rightful inheritance but as a potential victim in the way he is manipulated by his father into signing documents and into his marriage. Walter's words in Chapter 25 express the spirit of this manipulation:

'Weel, if ever I saw the like o' that. There was a Jenny Langlegs bumming at the corner o' the window, when down came a spider wabster as big as a puddock, and claught it in his arms; and he' off and awa wi' her intil his nest; – I ne'er saw the like o't.'

Certainly the tragedy strikes at Walter first. After a marriage to a girl who looks like being the best thing that could have happened to him, death takes Betty away from him and leaves behind a sickly infant substitute to whom he clings as obsessively as Claud does to his dream of the family estate. The prevailing note of this passage relating to Walter is far from comic. The snuff-obsessed Laird of Kilmarkeckle is a major comic creation, however, whose passion for making pictures on his walls with snuff ironically comments on Claud's obsession from an unexpected angle. Walter's wooing (Chapters 24–6) and the episodes preceding the wedding, involving the bulls and the feet-washing of the bride (Chapter 28) are played humorously. This may diminish the power of the entail episodes in this section and it could be argued that this is one place where the comedy is a distraction.

The narrator, who made the briefest of appearances in the preamble and the first main section, now turns up as an invited guest to Walter's wedding (Chapter 30). The purpose of this intermittent intrusion of an anonymous observer is not clear. He is apparently a sedate young man of twenty-three in 1772, which means he must have been only a boy of twelve when he was observed copying a codicil to Miss Heritage's will in Gilbert Omit's office. He is seen walking alone towards Blantyre on the fine evening of Walter's wedding day and joins the party just at the close of the service. He contributes nothing to the events but merely becomes an explicit participant instead of an implicit omniscient narrator. The reader must decide whether Galt has some hidden reason for this.

THIRD MAIN SECTION

With the break between volume 1 and volume 2, the third main section begins without any linking material. Volume 1 ended with the latest developments in the lives of the two younger children of Claud and the Leddy: George had married and become a business partner; and Meg had given birth to a son. The lines of the next generation were beginning to be spun. However, volume 2 addresses itself immediately to the question of Charles's place in the entail situation. By 1775, more than three years of being kept in the dark about his father's disinheritance of him have enabled Charles to go on with his married life with some peace of mind, despite his worsening financial position. Galt uses the beginning of volume 2 to strike an immediate tragic note with the briefest of indications that Charles is in need of money, which he thinks he can raise against the security of his prospects of inheriting the Grippy, before the 'heart-withering communication' from Mr Keelevin that he has been passed over by his father in favour of Walter.

The reader may wonder whether Galt has judged this effectively. Up to this point, the pace of events has not been hurried, incidents have unfolded themselves with a lot of dialogue, and action has not been violent in any way. Now suddenly the reader is plunged into the extreme emotions and reactions of the romantic novel. Charles rushes through the suddenly Gothicised landscape near Glasgow Cathedral, and reacts like the totally betrayed and undone hero of a melodrama. Physical fever succeeds mental and spiritual anguish, and Charles disappears as an active character from the novel. Could this sudden change of tone, raising the stakes, have been intended to make it more of a commercial winner with the bulk of the novel-reading public? Or has the action been deceptively leading up to this tragedy, laying trails in the account of Charles's upbringing, in the undeviating intention of Claud to subordinate all humane and paternal concerns to the security of the landed inheritance? In other words, has *The Entail* now revealed itself as a work of passion as well as a picture of domestic and social manners?

After a reading of the succeeding chapters, up to the death of Claud before he can undo his wrong (2–11), this view may gain credibility. The sequence of events in which Claud begins to realise the consequences of his legal actions, and his reactions to these constitute the stuff of tragedy, not as of a Lear or Macbeth, but certainly on a domestic scale, as of Lear of the Steppes or a Shylock.

After the tragedy of Charles and the tragedy of Claud comes the tragedy of Walter. Now precipitated into the lairdship after Claud's death, the spotlight falls on this simple-minded obstinate second son, shattered by the death of his beloved Betty Bodle and fixated on his infant daughter. Galt succeeds in arousing our sympathies for Walter, though he has played his part, even unwittingly, in the exclusion of his elder brother. Yet it is an ironic justice that he should fall in turn to the ambitions of his own younger brother, George, who has been established as having the same 'grippy' and mercantile outlook on life as Claud Walkinshaw.

So we have a new pair of ill-matched antagonists: the calculating and devious George, who now sees only an idiot between himself and the lairdship, and the innocent Walter, who has alienated his only ally, the Leddy his mother (Chapter 13). The unfolding of the legal process that results in the declaration of Walter as incapable through fatuity, strengthens the legal dimension of the novel and shows us how George, like Claud, finds his main ally in the supposed impartiality and objectivity of the law. The final act of Walter's tragedy does not see him suddenly struck down by fever or stroke, as with Charles and Claud, but is rather the long fading into useless neglect and obscurity to the extent that his eventual death goes almost unnoticed in the novel.

The treatment meted out to Walter and the tone in which it is rendered raises a further question about the changeable nature of the novel. The purely comic episodes seem to have been left behind. There is still the richness of Scots dialogue to differing degrees depending on the characters. Yet there is a new, sentimental, note. In Walter's grief at the deaths of his wife and daughter, in his abduction of Charles's daughter Mary as a substitute for his own Betty, in his demeanour before the court, there is pathos, an invitation to shed a sympathetic tear even as we smile. A harsh critic might see this as signalling a downward turn in the vigour of the narrative. Yet it could instead be an indication that Galt is prepared to switch tones to suit a changing purpose in the novel. This is a point that may need to be left until it is possible to view the novel as a whole.

Another new turn in the novel, that seems to become visible in this section, is the growing importance of the female characters. This is particularly the case with the Leddy of Grippy, who earlier in the action was Girzy Hypel, Claud's wife, subordinated to her husband Claud in speech, action and textual reference. Now she emerges as a strong character, influencing the action in significant ways. There is a foreshadowing of her in the way in which Galt treats her mother, Lady Plealands, the main influence on the young Charles and the protector for a time of Charles's widow and children – dominated and overshadowed in her husband's lifetime and blossoming as a widow. There are now also signs that other women are emerging into the spotlight of the action: Bell Fatherlans, Meg Milrookit, Robina Walkinshaw and Mrs Eadie.

LINKING SECTION

The third main section reaches its end in Chapter 22 with the removal of the Leddy and Walter to a flat in Glasgow, as George takes over the big house of Kittlestonheugh for himself, his ailing wife and surviving daughter Robina. With the beginning of Chapter 23, a new turn occurs in the narrative. Just as in the earlier linking section we saw Charles being removed from the main Walkinshaw influence and receiving a different upbringing, here we see his widow removing to a new environment, the manse of Camrachle (based on Pollokshaws) where the Eadies provide a more congenial home for her children. This is to be of particular importance to Charles's son James, who is to figure prominently in the rest of the novel. The parallelism has a clear structural purpose: to confirm the line of Charles Walkinshaw as different in spirit and outlook from the other offshoots of Claud, and to keep them distinct in readers' minds as more worthy of the inheritance. It is a strategy for directing readers' sympathies.

The character of Mrs Eadie has been criticised as introducing an un-necessarily melodramatic and mystical element into the plot. The way that she is treated certainly shows that when he strays away from Ayrshire or the West of Scotland, Galt's characterisation and settings are of dubious authen-ticity. The warning was sounded earlier in the novel with the reference to 'Glengrowlmaghallochan'. The comic but inaccurate stereotyping of a Gaelic name gives clear indication that Galt regarded the Highlands and their people with the typical ignorance and superiority of the urban Enlight-enment. Thus, when Mrs Eadie emerges as a character, she is given all the trappings of the Celtic Fringe: the long pedigree, the melancholy, the tragically lost Jacobite lover, the gift of second sight. It could be a deliberate ploy by Galt to change the tone and atmosphere of the novel, extra evidence of a changing purpose in the latter part of *The Entail.*

This linking section, however, is mainly centered on the attempts of George in the years after 1780 to cement good relations with Charles's family as he comes to realise that the chances of his fathering a male heir are slight and that James Walkinshaw is the next living heir to Kittlestonheugh. Thus we find the first attempts to promote a future marriage between James and George's daughter Robina. The entail continues to exercise its baleful influence on Claud's successors. Yet the atmosphere has changed. From being a living curse on the very lives of the senior members of the family, it has faded into merely a cause for concern about the future in George's mind, a factor in his calculations. To some extent this explains why *The Entail* cannot continue to be a tragedy, or even a tragi-comedy of the lives of the next generation; it must rely on other sources of interest in the action.

FOURTH MAIN SECTION

From the beginning of Chapter 28 in volume 2 to the final page of volume 3, we have the longest section of *The Entail*, covering events in 1793 that resolve the matter of the inheritance of Kittlestonheugh and work the provisions of Claud's entail through to their conclusion. One view of the novel is that, at this point, the whole becomes unbalanced and that this section, by its length and other characteristics, is an inadequate counterweight to the power of volume 1 and most of volume 2.

The section is concerned with three topics: George's wish that James should marry his daughter Robina, and the frustration of that wish by the girl marrying Walkinshaw Milrookit; the decision by George Walkinshaw to get married again (possibly to James's own love, Ellen Fraser) after the death of his wife, and to father his own male heir – a possibility ended by his dramatic death in a storm off the Caithness coast; and finally, the settlement of the rightful inheritance of Kittlestonheugh in favour of James over the pre-emptive claim of Walkinshaw and Robina Milrookit. The key figure in much of the action is the Leddy, who, in pursuing her own self-interest, largely brings about both the resolution of the entail as Claud created it and the restoration of justice to her eldest son's heirs. It could be argued that it is the Leddy who gives the greatest sense of continuity between this section and the previous ones, through her ongoing presence as a reminder of the previous generations; her Scots speech, reminiscent of Claud and the older Glasgow; and her concern about the law, one of the binding themes of the narrative.

Legal concerns bulk large in this section. Just as the earlier sections had legal business at the core of their main action, so here in Chapters 22–7 of volume 3 there is the manoeuvring of lawyers to settle the inheritance of Kittlestonheugh after George's death. It is ironical that the crucial clause respecting the entitlement of Charles's male heirs was one thrown into the entail casually by Claud to mollify Mr Keelevin (Chapter 18):

> 'first, ye'll entail it on Walter and his heirs-male, syne on Geordie and his heirs-male, and failing them, ye may gang back, to please yoursel, to the heirs-male o' Charlie, and failing them, to Meg's heirs-general.'

It is his knowledge of this clause that motivates George in his cultivation of Bell Fatherlans and her children; it is their ignorance of this clause that causes Walkinshaw and Robina to claim and occupy the house of Kittle-stonheugh until the Leddy gets moving after learning the truth from Mr Pilledge.

The various tones of this section make it clear to readers that they are experiencing a different world from the earlier parts of the novel. A number of different features deserve consideration. For example, there has been a significant change in the degree to which Scots is spoken. It is revealing to establish who are the Scots speakers and who are using English and to consider what this reveals about the social habits of late eighteenth-century Glasgow and Edinburgh. One effect that this decline in the use of Scots has on the general tone of the novel is to make it appear more like a fashionable literary product.

In addition, the settings in this latter part of *The Entail* are very different from those of the beginning. Glasgow has changed from the small-town location of the earliest episodes in the book and become a developing industrial city. Galt heightens the effect of the furnaces and factories that James Walkinshaw observes by stressing the beauty of the city's natural surroundings in one or two vivid passages. The descriptions of Highland and Caithness scenery in Chapters 16 and 17 and the storm scene in Chapter 20 of volume 3 seem more set-pieces out of Romantic 'Gothick' than the more typically Galtian descriptions earlier in the novel. To a considerable degree, they create mood independent of action and indeed are at considerable variance with the general tenor of the narrative. Criticism of the later part of *The Entail* has tended to focus on these episodes as contrived and awkward. Yet again, can these be seen as fulfilling Galt's authorial purpose in the overall conception of the novel?

This section once more raises questions about the role of the narrator, who puts in another of his fleeting appearances, this time at the very end of the novel as a witness to the reading of the Leddy's will. He almost disgraces himself: 'we confess that our emotions were almost too great for our fortitude, and that . . . our sensibility was so affected that we could, with the utmost difficulty, repress our hysterical sobbings. . . .' This narrator is beginning to appear as if he has escaped from the pages of *The Man of Feeling*, the great sentimental novel of the Scottish Enlightenment. Yet in another way, he seems different in this section. He is more obtrusive as a voice in the narrative, often ending a chapter with some sententious or prim or consciously humorous comment, often referring to the chapters that he is writing and deliberately calling attention to his role as writer of the fiction. Once again we wonder what Galt is doing with this anonymous figure. In one sense he is the 'Editor', that fictional device so beloved by Scott in his novels and used also by Hogg in *Confessions of a Justified Sinner*. In another sense he is a sympathetic friend and kinsman; it is worth comparing him in this role with the narrator that Galt created some years later for his ironic novel *The Last of the Lairds*. Yet why does Galt feel he is needed?

Perhaps a clue to the puzzle of the narrator lies in the letters that Galt received from Blackwood about *The Entail* while he was planning and writing it. Blackwood states his preference for having the main character narrate the action in his own voice, as happens in *Annals of the Parish* and *The Provost*:

> I hope you will be able to manage it so as that the hero tells the story himself for you may depend upon it, that it is always the most effective way, and it is particularly your forte. You more than any one almost I know, identify the individual, and the Author never himself appears, it is the very being telling his story himself. This is greatly lost when given in the third person. But of all this you must judge, and regulate yourself entirely by your own plan and conception of the story.

Galt received the same advice again eleven days later in another letter. From the structure and time-scale of *The Entail* it is obvious that no single character within the action could be the narrator in the first person of everything that happens. It is clear that Galt intended that the narration should be in an 'authorial' voice. The shadowy figure of the narrator, as he has been identified, seems to be a deliberate piece of fun by Galt, intended to nod in the direction of Blackwood's wishes but not allowed to interfere with Galt's 'plan and conception of the story'.

Whatever the truth about the narrator, there is no doubt that Galt uses him consciously to create a 'voice' for much of the narrative, a voice that is not Galt's own which is at times elevated, at times censorious or amused or neutral, at times irritating, a Balwhidder voice more than a Pawkie voice; and to this voice Galt gives only as much flesh and visibility as will bring him onto the fringe of the action on a few public occasions, without ever revealing why he is fulfilling this task of recording the story of Claud Walkinshaw's entail or how he has obtained his information.

EPILOGUE

This is very brief, and yet there are points of interest worth noting in it. The fact that James Walkinshaw has nine sons from his marriage, whereas the Milrookit heirs of Margaret and George have only daughters, finally exorcises the entail from the future pattern of the Kittlestonheugh inheritance and puts an end to the purposes of Claud Walkinshaw. The distinguished career of James Walkinshaw in the Napoleonic Wars marks a new orientation of the Scottish landed and mercantile classes out towards the wider world; in a way, it is the vindication of Claud's unlucky father who died in the swamps of Darien more than a century earlier, emphasising that the time of inward-looking parochialism is over, and that Scots of spirit had to look out to wider horizons. It is the beginning of the nineteenth-century expansion.

The final note of the novel, however, is clearly ironic. When our narrator speaks of the Provost and Magistrates treating Walkinshaw 'with all that distinction for which, as a corporation, they are so deservedly celebrated' and says that 'there are few communities where there is less of the spirit of ostracism, or where a man of public merit is more honoured by his fellow-citizens', we must suspect that the tongue is firmly in the cheek.

So *The Entail* ends where it began, in Scotland's western rival to Edinburgh, making it the finest novel about Glasgow in the nineteenth century.

Disunity or unity?

It can be argued that the novel has not been helped by being artificially expanded into a three-volume novel beyond Galt's own previous successes in a one-volume format, and that it would have been more artistically satisfying as a series of episodes in the history of the Lairds of Grippy, as Galt apparently initially wished. Moreover, the reader has to decide whether it is flawed by its shift in tone from a concentrated study in tragic obsession, counterpointed by comedy, to a more popular and modish story of family rivalry heightened by contrived romantic and melodramatic incidents, or whether there is a way of looking at the novel that will bring the different tones and types of incident, if not into a harmonious entity, at least into a more unified literary text than most critics are so far willing to recognise.

The problem, however, with arguments suggesting *The Entail*'s disunity is that they are based on the idea that Galt was in some way inept or careless in his writing, and not fully in control of his plot material. Under pressure to produce the manuscript for Blackwood quickly, because the novel had already been advertised, to write a three-decker novel instead of his usual shorter product, with his relationship with Blackwood beginning to come under strain, and no doubt tired after a very intensive period of writing that had already seen five novels produced in less than two years, it has been postulated that Galt let things slip in the effort to complete the assignment and produced a work which, though masterly in its opening and development, was yet below his recent standard in its conclusion.

Perhaps, however, we should look at the matter differently. If we make the initial assumption that a writer generally knows what he/she is doing, particularly after gaining experience over a number of successful publications of his/her own strengths and weaknesses, we are obliged, when faced with something that seems unusual or radically different in that writer's work, to look carefully for a positive explanation of the anomaly or discordant element before concluding that the writer is less than competent. It is a considerable discourtesy to the writer of *Annals of the Parish, The Provost, The Ayrshire Legatees,* and so many subtle fictions to say that Galt did not know what he was doing in the last third of *The Entail,* when he had already shown in the first two volumes that he was on his best form. Perhaps we have not grasped what Galt is trying to do. We have already seen that, in his treatment of the narrator, he may be experimenting rather cheekily with the notion of an elusive character on the edge of the action with a distinctive authorial voice. *The Man of Feeling* by Henry Mackenzie, a vastly successful novel in the later eighteenth century when Galt was a young boy coming to love reading, provides us with a possible antecedent for such a narrative strategy. It may indeed give us another kind of clue. As a novel illustrating a certain vogue for sentimentalism that came to a wave-crest before breaking and declining, it was part of the social history of the eighteenth century, no less so than features of economic, domestic and linguistic change.

So if we take seriously what Galt says about his intention to write 'theoretical histories', and the tendency now is to take this more seriously than Galt's own contemporaries and immediate successors did, then we may have to face the idea that such a theoretical history will deal not only with the social changes in a district or small community, but with the artistic influences on the developing sensibilities of a highly literate society. What better way to demonstrate this set of cultural changes within a novel that is a theoretical history than to build up a literary text which presents some of these as form and style instead of content?

How would this work in *The Entail,* which covers the whole of the eighteenth century, a time of great changes in literary taste and novel development? The early pages of the novel look back to the seventeenth century and an oral tradition that is passed on by Maudge Dobbie to Claud Walkinshaw and, earlier, to his father; a tradition of 'goblin lore and romantic stories', including tales of Scotland's history. From then on, the novel follows the classical lines of the mainstream English and Scottish novel, that of the 'comic epic in prose', with a serious theme based on human frailties and emotions, lightened by comic episodes. We are not far from the world of *Roderick Random* (1748) and *Tom Jones* (1749). As we have seen, the beginning of volume 2 introduces a new note, that of the melodramatic and the Romantic, a world of dramatic landscapes and natural effects serving to heighten emotions and reactions. The tragedies of Charles's death from fever and Claud's stroke fit this kind of intense fiction. Walter's plight, in his successive losses of wife and daughter and his pathos before the law, suits a more sentimental kind of narrative, a vogue into which the anonymous narrator fits equally well; whereas the family manoeuvrings and conversation pieces of volume 3 have something of the mood of the novel of social manners, of which Jane Austen was the supreme exponent. The Highland and storm scenes of the same volume extend the melodramatic elements of the previous volume into the area of fiction that Walter Scott was currently shaping into a romantic Scottish kingdom of his own.

One way of looking at *The Entail*, therefore, may be as an imaginative and conscious exercise in the shaping of a varied fiction in which tone and atmosphere capture the changing fashions of the novel in eighteenth and early nineteenth-century writing. Galt suits the climate of the novel to the matter and period being considered in the developing story of the Walkinshaw entail through three generations of family and social change in the west of Scotland. A view of the novel in these terms may help us to see that Galt's purpose could be more subtle and complex than some critics have suspected and *The Entail* might be, in its diversity, a more unified literary text than it appears at first sight.

John Galt's literary achievement

In an age of prolific writers, John Galt was amazingly productive and industrious. He turned his hand to almost every type of writing from poetry and plays to biography, history and travel writing. His reputation, however, rests surely and supremely on his prose fiction, within which he was one of the originators of the political novel in *The Member* (1832) and *The Radical* (1832), a form later taken up by Disraeli and Trollope in England, and more importantly the novel of social documentation and observation, 'le roman fleuve' which writers like Balzac later developed into one of the great nineteenth-century novel formats. As mentioned earlier, Galt termed it the 'theoretical history' and his 'Tales of the West', of which *The Entail* is the most ambitious, present a varied and absorbing picture of social life and development in the west of Scotland in the later eighteenth and early nineteenth centuries. *Annals of the Parish* (1821), *The Ayrshire Legatees* (1821), *The Provost* (1822), *The Steamboat* (1822), *Sir Andrew Wylie* (1822), *The Entail* (1822), *Ringan Gilhaize* (1823) with the late addition of *The Last of the Lairds* (1826) represent one of the truly great publishing records of any Scottish novelist. By any reckoning, Galt is one of the great novelists of his age, unfairly overshadowed for many years by the reputation of, first, Sir Walter Scott and, more recently, of James Hogg. Now he is receiving his just due.

CHAPTER 17

JAMES HOGG: *THE PRIVATE MEMOIRS AND CONFESSIONS OF A JUSTIFIED SINNER*

JAMES HOGG, THE ETTRICK SHEPHERD (c. 1770–1835)

James Hogg was born in the Borders. He inherited an awareness of rigorous Presbyterianism from his shepherd father; and from his mother he inherited his fascination for the supernatural and the folk-traditional. Until he was forty, he worked on the land, and never lost this contact, returning in 1815, after five years in Edinburgh, to farm at Altrive and Mount Benger.

He was a frank, simple man, often straightforward to the point of embarrassment with his friends, who included Walter Scott, his son-in-law, John Gibson Lockhart and the other originators of *Blackwood's Magazine* – Blackwood himself and John Wilson ('Christopher North'). He trusted, loved, and partly feared them; they helped, tolerated, and exploited him.

Hogg came from a world that had created the Border ballads, a world in contact with 'the other landscape' of enchantment. Scotland's legendary medieval seer, Thomas the Rhymer, came from this country; Hogg's grandfather, the celebrated Will O' Phaup, was believed to have conversed with the people of the other world. Hogg's background was thus rooted in oral tradition, and centuries away from the culture of Enlightenment Edinburgh, where he came in 1810 to make his way as a man of letters.

To Edinburgh intellectuals, Hogg was an anachronism; lovable, quaintly fascinating and a version of 'the noble savage'. Hogg perhaps encouraged them to regard him as successor to Burns, claiming a birthdate the same as Burns's, and playing up his 'heaven-taught' credentials. Though he had little formal schooling, and had taught himself to read and write, he had an informal education which went a long way to compensate for this.

Hogg and oral tradition

The oral tradition underlying Hogg's work was sophisticated; his mother was a 'tradition bearer', who gave many great songs to Walter Scott when he was collecting for his *Minstrelsy of the Scottish Border*. She told Scott that these songs 'were made for singin' an' no for readin', but ye hae broken the charm noo, an' they'll never be sung mair'. She clearly felt that her son was moving into a literary world. Hogg's whole creative identity can be seen as held in tension between these oral and written traditions. His craftsmanship was developed by imitating old ballads and songs, and in 1800 he published *Scottish Pastorals* followed in 1810 by *The Forest Minstrel*. Until 1810 Hogg was very much the 'Ettrick Shepherd', combining farming and poetry (albeit in the end unsuccessfully).

Hogg and Edinburgh

In Edinburgh, Hogg fell victim to snobbery. We have already noted the 'crisis of identity' faced by the eighteenth-century poets, arising from their unsureness about their audience and critics; Hogg certainly found his peasant origins clashing with the values of the so-called 'Enlightenment'. Edinburgh in 1810 was deeply divided politically, socially and culturally, with even Walter Scott split in his responses to the nature of Scotland's destiny.

The Whig *Edinburgh Review* was a leading periodical of its time; in 1817 the Tory *Blackwood's Edinburgh Magazine* came out in direct reaction against it. Quarrels were serious, sometimes becoming duels to the death. In the wake of great European crises like the French Revolution, there was a complete polarisation of response. Scotland broadly endorsed Unionism and Toryism, and in standards of taste and politeness, the genteel aped the English.

Hogg came to Edinburgh to run his weekly magazine, *The Spy*. His reception from the literary establishment sums up the whole complex picture of social attitudes of the time. Hogg's honesty at first attracted patrons like Scott, Lockhart and John Wilson ('Christopher North'), and then embarrassed them. Later, many of them exploited him, pretending friendship while patronising him and distorting his image to that of a drunken, rural buffoon with occasional lyric talent.

Scott helped Hogg, but condescendingly. His letters call Hogg 'the great Caledonian Boar', and he refers to Hogg's novel *The Three Perils of Women* (1823) as the 'Hogg's Pearls'. He tried to control Hogg's manners in public, and even offered help on the condition that Hogg abandoned poetry. What emerges is that Scott would help as feudal superior; but rarely gave support as an equal in exchange of ideas, which would have benefited Hogg immensely. Hogg described this snobbish streak in Scott in his *Domestic Manners of Sir Walter Scott* (1834), which alienated him further from polite Edinburgh society and from Scott's son-in-law, John Gibson Lockhart.

For all his disappointments, Hogg remained down-to-earth. He refused to attend the coronation of George IV with Scott because it clashed with the Melrose Fair. At fifty-eight, he won prizes in field events in Border Games. He belonged to an older, tougher culture than that of Edinburgh. His auto-biography notes that he never knew anyone happier than himself and his wife. But it is also tragic to think that, as with Fergusson and Burns, and many later writers, Scotland's bourgeois and anglicised literary values forced a talented native writer into a state of alienation.

Hogg's fiction

Space does not allow a full discussion of Hogg's fiction, but many themes and techniques found in *The Justified Sinner* are present in other works. *The Brownie of Bodsbeck* (1817), a historical novel about the atrocities committed by Claverhouse as he attacked the Covenanters in the Borders, is technically innovative, using flashbacks and sudden cuts between incidents and times, and allowing supernatural with rational readings until the very end. *Winter Evening Tales* (1820) and *The Shepherd's Calendar* (1828–9) are vividly told, and contain some of the finest of Scottish short stories, full of the influence of the oral tradition. 'The Brownie of the Black Haggs' draws on Hogg's ballad background and folk culture, with the ambiguity of interpretation which is the hallmark of *The Justified Sinner. Basil Lee* (1820), a *Spy* story enlarged into a novel, is also remarkable and innovative in the way Hogg links abnormal psychology with an anti-romantic account of how the rascally Basil continu-ally dreams of new romantic roles in love and war, but is incapable of settling to any one vocation, and instead moves from disgrace to disgrace. The story mocks polite convention by having the anti-hero eventually redeemed by a prostitute.

The Three Perils of Man (1822) comes out of Hogg's storehouse of Border lore, history, and humour. Two worlds are played off against each other; that of courtly games and knightly jousting of Scots and English at the siege of the castle at Roxburgh, and that of the appalling suffering and the earthy cynicism of the Border peasantry. Hogg shows how aristocratic and dynastic power politics affect ordinary people. Behind the surface world of Anglo-Scottish battles, Hogg creates a wonderful supernatural and comic romance which involves a motley embassy of strange comrades undertaking a marvellous journey to learn the future from the great Border wizard of the Middle Ages, Sir Michael Scott. This allowed Hogg to bring in vivid and hilarious material from the treasure-house of Border tales which he had inherited from his mother and others, with astonishing and poetic scenes of the supernatural involving devils, sprites, ghouls, and many tour-de-force scenes of wizardry and war, culminating in an epic struggle between Michael Scott and the Devil himself, in which the single great Eildon hill is torn into three hills, and the great prophecy which will win the day for the Scots is given. Despite its brilliance, Walter Scott disliked *The Three Perils* intensely. He who had himself used goblins, astrologers and the Devil in his tales and poems, accused Hogg of ruining 'one of the best tales in the world' with extravagance and demonology. Sadly, influenced by the criticism of his literary and social superior, Hogg lessened his original achievement, by later reworking the novel as *The Siege of Roxburgh*, leaving the central tale which he thought Scott had liked without the supernatural elements.

In an important review of John Galt's *The Omen*, in *Blackwood's Magazine* in 1826, Scott made clear his distinction between two kinds of belief in the supernatural. He condemned, as unworthy of a man of breeding and education, any belief in: 'the superstition of the olden time, which believed in spectres, fairies, and other supernatural apparitions. These airy squadrons have long been routed, and are banished to the cottage and the nursery'. This view had profound implications for the development, not just of Hogg's work, but of Scottish literature for the next hundred years or so, and for the use of the supernatural in Western literature for the rest of the century. Hogg had grown up hearing about such 'supernatural apparitions' from his mother; this living connection was now condemned by Scott. It was a watershed in Scottish and European literature; and Hogg was on the wrong side. The kind of supernatural which Scott decided was permissible was that which allowed gentlemen of breeding to have premonitions, much as the later Gothic fiction of Edgar Allan Poe, in *The Fall of the House of Usher* (1839), allowed a sophisticated and decadent supernatural to exist, while abandoning any connection with the folk-supernatural.

The Three Perils of Women (1823), Hogg's last novel before *The Justified Sinner*, aroused considerable controversy and continues to do so. What starts out as a light-hearted study of the relationship of two girls, Gatty and Cherry, becomes something horrible. Cherry, betrayed, dies of grief, and, as punishment for her betrayal, Gatty falls into a coma of demonic possession lasting three years, in the course of which she gives birth to a healthy boy and lies uncorrupted until she awakes, abandoned by whatever demon had possessed her. Critics howled it down; Wilson was particularly vicious. Hogg lost all self-confidence.

Nevertheless, novels like *An Edinburgh Bailie*, written about this time, show an unusual parodic sense of Scottish history. Hogg develops in this novel his sceptical view of war, politics and religion, irreverently viewing them through the eyes of a self-seeking and cowardly figure who resembles his earlier Basil Lee, and who anticipates the similar figure of Robert Wringhim in *The Justified Sinner* of 1824. Hogg brilliantly fused together in this work all his previous kinds of fiction, yet deliberately avoided falling into any single category that critics had hitherto attacked. To the critic who assailed the novel for 'diablerie and nonsense', Hogg enabled the reply that the story was rather a psychological study of a religious fanatic. Conversely, if the critic were to see the novel as the distasteful study of a lunatic, Hogg could reply that his work was a supernatural fable. Hogg thus created a situation whereby, having been hurt by criticism of his two major kinds of fiction too often, he could have his cake and eat it.

Lockhart and Hogg were close at this time, and Lockhart's fiction shows an overlap with Hogg's in its interest in morbid psychological states. However, it is unlikely, as has been suggested, that Lockhart wrote this astonishing book. Douglas Gifford argues in his study *James Hogg: A Reassessment* (1976) that it is just as likely that Hogg helped Lockhart with his *Adam Blair* (1822), and that in any case there is abundant evidence in Hogg's previous fiction of similarity of situation and character to those in *The Justified Sinner*. Hogg's attempt to break free of the criticisms that constrained him did not work. Few reviews of his novel were complimentary, *The Westminster Review* regretting that the author did not employ himself better than in uselessly and disgustingly abusing his imagination, to invent wicked tricks for a mongrel devil, and blasphemous lucubrations for an insane fanatic'.

Hogg did not develop further after this. While there are novels later in their date of publication, like *An Edinburgh Bailie*, written in the early 1820s but not published until 1835 as part of his 'Tales of the Wars of Montrose', it is most probable that this and other novellas like *The Adventures of Captain John Lochie* and *The Surpassing Adventures of Allan Gordon* were all part of a series, 'The Lives of Eminent Men', which Hogg had written about the same time as *The Justified Sinner*. He was encouraged in 1832 to put together his collected works. This is when he savaged *The Three Perils of Man*, cutting it to a third of its original length. Latterly, Hogg was content to be something like Backwood's tame 'shepherd' in the Borders, sending up occasional articles. In this sense, he joined Fergusson and Burns as examples of outstanding talent reduced by the limitations of society.

The Private Memoirs and Confessions of a Justified Sinner

A good way to approach the uncanny and extraordinary world of *The Justified Sinner* is to read Burns's 'Holy Willie's Prayer'. Hogg knew the poetry of Burns very well and it is arguable that Burns's great satire on religious hypocrisy is one of the main points of departure for Hogg's novel. In a way, the poem is the story of Robert Wringhim in miniature, and raises many of the basic tenets which underlie *The Justified Sinner*.

Burns's first verse introduces 'the Doctrine of the Elect'. God chooses his people for heaven on a whim. Holy Willie sees him as a God:

> O Thous that in the heavens does dwell!
> Wha, as it pleases best thysel
> Sends ane to heaven and ten to hell,
> A' for thy glory!
> And no for ony gude or ill
> They've done afore thee.

Burns also raises the idea of predestination, whereby omnipotent God knows, from the beginning of time, who is damned and who is saved. Willie also boasts, implicitly, that he is perfect, gifted, and full of grace – and Hogg will show that 'grace' is a term distorted by extreme Calvinism. Where other Christians mean by the term a charitable spirit derived from God, surrounding the Christian as a result of his being in harmony with God through good works, Holy Willie and his friends mean something rather different, which separates them from the others and elevates them. As Willie says, there are thousands in darkness except the few, including himself, whom God has chosen, so that he and his friends may shine out. Willie clearly believes in the idea of original sin; and yet somehow manages to include and exclude himself from that category at the same time.

Not only the beliefs in 'Holy Willie's Prayer', important though they are, impressed Hogg. As well as the conveyance of these religious values, which he had encountered in his own relatives, he was influenced by the dramatic monologue through which Burns expressed his satire. Burns's frequent habit of pretending to occupy the position of those he most scorned probably gave impetus to Hogg's methodology. Thus from Burns he inherits both the dominating idea of a 'justified sinner', and the oblique presentation which is the hallmark of the novel.

With both Burns's poem and Hogg's novel the reader has to decipher the fact that both Willie and Robert Wringhim are far from saintly. They are in fact guilty of virtually all the seven deadly sins; they have been lecherous, angry, selfish, greedy, amazingly proud, and envious. All this is revealed without Willie or Robert Wringhim ever believing for a moment that they give this impression. Burns's great poem is not really a prayer but a curse; and much of the action of the novel is brought about by its two principal curses.

In Scotland, Hogg found rich and stimulating precedents suggesting themes for this novel. Scott's *The Heart of Midlothian* had come out some six years before, offering a study of bigoted Presbyterianism, in an Edinburgh setting. Jeanie Deans's encounter with George Staunton at Arthur's Seat, near Nicol Muschet's Cairn, is echoed and transformed in Hogg's novel. Equally, John Galt's novel *The Provost*, two years before, could have suggested to Hogg possibilities in handling a self-interested, self-justifying and unheroic central figure.

The critic Lewis Simpson argues brilliantly in his study of Hogg (*James Hogg*, 1962) that Hogg was also working with records of real life. For example, *The Confession, Etc. of Nicol Muschet of Boghal* (1721) tells of a real murderer, who was hanged in the Grassmarket in Edinburgh, and has much of the tone of Hogg's account. And the work of Presbyterian ministers like Robert Wodrow in his *Analecta*, memoirs published over a century after his death in 1734, and George Sinclair's *Satan's Invisible World Discovered* (1685) were also rich sources.

Gothic novels had become fashionable in the previous half-century, since Horace Walpole's *Castle of Otranto* (1764). Hogg had read many such novels, with their love-hate relationships, demonic visitations, and fanatical religiosities. But it is important to recognise Hogg's factual and economical presentation of grotesque horrors. Lewis Simpson has remarked on his concrete way of treating the melodramatic and supernatural, in contrast to self-indulgent and loquacious Gothic novels.

The predicament of the anti-hero

In previous stories, like 'The Long Pack', 'The Baron St Gio' and the novella *Basil Lee*, dark forces had surrounded and trapped a central, pathetic and sometimes anti-heroic, protagonist who was unable to understand the mysterious depths in which he was drowning. The critic, Barbara Bloedé, has observed that Hogg's own situation, from childhood onwards, involved a sense of persecution and incomprehension as to proper behaviour, which intensified in his Edinburgh days through his inability to understand the standards and practice of so-called 'polite' society. She argues that *Confessions* is an 'exteriorisation' of Hogg's own conflicts and feelings of guilt and unworthiness (*Études Anglaises*, 1973). Influences and stimuli are perhaps secondary to the achievement itself; French critic André Gide called this 'Europe's first great psychological novel'. But traditional Scotland also endowed Hogg with precedents. In another sense, it is precisely because of Hogg's background as a shepherd with a rich awareness of folk-tradition and oral folk-tale, together with his equally deep knowledge of the Bible and religious interpretation, that he had the resources he needed to produce *The Justified Sinner*.

In resolving his predicament with critics in this subtle and carefully crafted novel, Hogg exploited ambiguity and ambivalence. Always he allows two possibilities: that supernatural manifestations may be the products of a diseased imagination; or that the supernatural is real, and that Robert Wringhim is being punished and damned for real evil. In the epilogue, Hogg's Editor examines the justified sinner's account and speculates concerning its status: either Robert was a great fool who awakened God's wrath and an all too real Devil; or he was 'a religious maniac' who was so obsessed that he eventually became totally mad.

The patterning of the novel

Hogg structures his novel in three parts: Editor's narrative; Memoirs and Confessions of the Sinner, and Editor's concluding narrative or epilogue. The parts fit an overall pattern of rational and objective experience set against supernatural and subjective experience. This is not to say that the first part is totally rational and the second totally supernatural, but broadly one can argue that the Editor's presentation strives for rational explanation, while the Sinner's account indulges in a subjective and unquestioning acceptance of supernatural events. Yet Hogg's story does not simply finish at the end of the second part. The third part introduces new evidence – and trickery – through which Hogg is brought into his own novel, via the article which he did indeed write for *Blackwood's Magazine* several months before the novel appeared.

Part One and Part Two contrast in tone; the first part has a common-sense manner, citing traditions and records in court debate, from a point of view which asserts its own rationality and humanity. The second part replaces this with abnormal, anti-heroic, and avowedly mean and petty attitudes, so that the perspective is totally polarised. Natural becomes unnatural, light becomes dark.

This patterning of opposites is pervasive. From the outset there are contrasting familial patterns, in which George Colwan, the Laird of Dalcastle, a rough Scot of the old school, tolerant, hard-drinking and garrulous, is set against the joyless, arid Reverend Robert Wringhim (the first 'justified sinner' we meet). The laird's treatment of his wife is, from a modern perspective, unpleasant; but it contrasts, in its frank crudity, with the false piety of the minister which leads to sexual liaison and the conception of Robert. There is a contrast between the narrow and intolerant Lady Dalcastle, who has overstrained the principles of the Reformation 'till nature can no longer bear it', and Arabella Logan, the Laird's mistress, more affectionate and loyal to the laird out of wedlock, who loves George more than does his mother. Hogg reverses usual moral judgments, by having the mistress, and the prostitute Bell Calvert, as his agents for Good.

But the main opposition is between the natural, outward-going son George, and the dour and introspective Robert. Robert is the unnatural scholar of arid disciplines, while George, poor at school, has a social ease and grace that his brother lacks. This contrast is symbolic. Hogg is depicting archetypes of timeless Scottish oppositions, and is also developing traditional figures, to the point that the Dalcastle-Wringhim division symbolises not just a healthy tradition of wholeness set against a spiritual deformation, the negative result of the Reformation, but a universal statement of natural goodness set against self-destructive dogmatism. Furthermore, Hogg establishes an opposition between a 'normal' and rational interpretation of human events, and an interpretation, derived from religious experience, in which the supernatural is seen as a living force. This gives the novel its unique duality of interpretations – each of the opposing readings being exclusive of the other.

Inevitably the reader wonders how to respond to the narrative. Sometimes it will be in preference for a rational interpretation; sometimes there is too much evidence for any other interpretation than a supernatural one. Hogg clearly intended readers to be bewildered – indeed it is very much the success of the novel that it confounds the reader's desire for a single coherent interpretation. The novel can be treated as two narratives or sets of possibilities, psychological and supernatural. Artificial though such analysis may be, it has the advantage of revealing Hogg's craft in juxtaposing two sets of possibilities, as well as allowing two distinct, coherent interpretations.

THE EDITOR'S NARRATIVE: A RATIONAL READING

The Editor's narrative, viewed rationally, shows Robert as the son of a bigoted minister, who fulfils his sexual desires through the guise of religious fervour. Robert resembles some of Hogg's previous creations, except that he is mentally unstable to a greater degree because of the deforming influences of his background. His encounters with his brother George at the tennis matches show him to be a masochist and a martyr, determined to push events to unnatural conclusions, and willing to join his father in cursing his enemies. The Editor shows them both deteriorating into mental illness – with the added irony that Robert and his father take pride in all aspects of their sickness. Yet Hogg safeguards the possibility of a rational interpretation. There need be no devils at the tennis matches; Robert's looks are 'black', but this may be acceptable colloquialism. All the sinister and demonic imagery of these early meetings may simply be literary metaphor.

The murder attempt at Arthur's Seat strains credulity; but Hogg introduces a significant discussion on the nature of the refraction of light. Scientific words like 'phenomenon', 'refracted', 'science', 'sublunary' and 'terrestrial' contrast with the straightforward style of the Editor. Hogg thus creates an impression which suggests that there are logical answers, despite the bizarre and apparently inexplicable events he is describing. In the language of Enlightenment, Hogg suggests that the phenomena, examined closely, may be explained as the result of refraction.

There have been critical objections to this rational interpretation on grounds that there are too many witnesses to the unnatural episodes. Bell Calvert, for example, identifies an accomplice of Robert's who takes part in George's murder – certainly not the man eventually blamed. The two ladies later see this accomplice, who resembles the murdered George. Critics have claimed that this gives objective evidence of a companion to Robert who is not just a figment of his imagination, but is endowed with supernatural abilities in changing his appearance. How are such objections to be answered?

L. L. Lee suggested Hogg used an 'envelope' of tradition at the beginning and end of the Editor's account (*Studies in Scottish Literature* 1971–2). Lee argued that the Editor was relaying information derived from the folk tradition, which, being legendary, is questionable in its veracity. This is a valid way out, but throughout the Editor's narrative the emphasis on court evidence and matter-of-fact detail is so circumstantially compelling that the reader cannot feel justified in abandoning it wholesale so quickly. Besides, there is another and more reasonable and psychologically satisfying way of reading such events. After all, Bell Calvert, by her own account, has been under pressure and had been drinking; she saw the murder attempts in moonlight – so a court would have reservations about her evidence. Hogg further suggests that Arabella Logan, grief-crazed and brooding over George's murder, in alliance with the demented and pathetically grateful Calvert, would construct an interpretation of events to suit their imaginations and feelings. Certainly, when they discuss what they have seen, in the lodging house, they quickly move from confusion to certainty. The ladies pass a nightmarish evening thinking about these events. Their grief becomes infectious hysteria. Legend would surely embellish this, so that the landlady would retell the story in a way which would be passed down, just as this story has been passed down to the Editor.

History, legal records and tradition all inform the Editor, who is looking back from 1823 to events between 1687 and 1712. Readers can never really know what happened, but it seems that these terrible events, through bigotry, envy and hatred, destroyed not only the lives, but the mental stability of all who had been privy to them. It is the Edinburgh Hogg who presents this rational version of his story, the Hogg who was fascinated by morbid psychology and with part of his mind set in the post-Enlightenment world, evolving out of the credulous Middle Ages towards Industrial Revolution and scientific materialism.

A supernatural reading: demonic possession

But there is an older Hogg, of Ettrick and the oral tradition. Viewed with the 'willing suspension of disbelief' necessary for full enjoyment of works like Goethe's *Faust* (1808, 1832), *The Pilgrim's Progress* (1678), as well as the Border ballads and the great folk tales and legends of Scotland, the entire novel becomes a 'game of souls', in an ancient European folk tradition.

Readers must wait for Robert's account to understand much of what is happening in this evil nightmare, but the Editor stresses the prayer-curses against the laird's side of the family. As in ballads and legends, this summons a figure of judgement. Read this way, it is indeed the Devil who appears at the earlier tennis matches. Hogg's language is sly and ingenious. On one level, his references to 'devils', and to 'sinister' or 'infernal' or 'damnable' events, are simply colloquial and racy metaphor. On another level, they become menacing, so that mention of the 'devilish looking youth' of 'malignant' eye who keeps steadfastly to his 'joke of damnation' is Hogg's way of indicating the Devil's presence.

Robert always appears at his brother's right hand, 'within a few yards of him', 'darting looks at him that chilled his soul'. His position is important, in terms of the folk-rules of demonic manifestation. The emphasis reminds readers that the curse which Robert and his father pronounced on George specifically located the Devil on the right hand.

Robert's recollection of being at only one of the tennis matches seems to contradict evidence elsewhere that the Devil appears at several. Hogg is careful in his presentation, using the folk-concept of possession which allows that the Devil can share Robert's conscious mind. This gives four possibilities: Robert can act on his own; Robert can act while possessed by the Devil and conscious of possession (even while not conscious that it is the Devil who possesses him); the Devil can appear in the likeness of Robert; and the Devil can be doing all this and yet also be somewhere else staging diversions. So the Devil can appear as Drummond or as George, at the same time as he is inside Robert. This subtlety must be appreciated to grasp the implications of the 'stranger' who told George about Robert's presence at the tennis match. 'Strangers' and 'someones' are Hogg's way of indicating supernatural resonances. 'Someone' happens to cry out about the plot at the Black Bull against George; the same 'someone' creates the mysterious madness which grips Wringhim senior and his Whig friends. When the riot is examined, no mob can be found, and 'the Devil an enemy had they to pursue'. While it may simply be colloquial to say that the mob has vanished like phantoms, it may be more sinister; the phantoms may be infernal realities.

The murder attempt at Arthur's Seat and the actual murder of George need to be considered in the light of such ambiguities. On Arthur's Seat, George first sees the horrifying apparition of his brother to his right. The discrepancy between the arrogant, striding apparition, giant and ghastly, in front of George, with the cringing and sneaky Robert behind suggests that the Devil ceased to possess Robert immediately before the attempt to kill George. This then leaves him free, unpossessed, when attempting murder. Indeed, he tells George that his friend came with him to the hill foot, but left him there (presumably to appear in apparition to George).

When presenting the murder of George, Hogg uses a device which will become much more important in Part Two, where the Devil speaks truth in a way which achieves the effects of lies. Insults which are apparently directed at George, concerning his unnatural character and the Devil's desire for his soul, are in fact more relevant to Robert. When the Devil crows over the murder, he rejoices because he has gained Robert's soul. Hogg emphasises at this point Robert's 'very peculiar gait'. ('He walked as if he had been flat-soled, and his legs made of steel, without any joints in his feet or ankles'.) Robert is almost the Devil – but not quite, because he can still repent. Thus the Devil must push him to commit suicide, an act for which 'there was no remission'. In the later stages of the Editor's narrative, the Devil hardly hides at all, seeming to betray Robert at every turn, signalling to Bell and Arabella that he is present and they should listen to his conversation. Indeed Arabella remarks that Robert is possessed, and that his very breath is that of the 'charnel house'. She sees that the strange figure with Robert is imitating George in order to deepen Robert's guilt.

The Sinner's account clarifies many of the more enigmatic facts. But there is a pattern to the powers of good and evil in the Editor's account. Hogg observes his own rules and the rules of folk tradition – the Devil's ability waxes and wanes according to how well or badly his victims behave. When George insults Robert, the first curse against him is allowed to take effect. Similarly, when George watches girls in church, he finds himself beset by 'fiendish glances'. His ultimate downfall comes as a result of being in a brothel. On the other hand, when George 'behaves' and vows to defend Robert, 'it was a good while before his gratuitous attendant appeared at his side again'.

The events on Arthur's Seat provide an outstanding example of this; George is unwilling to deface the 'fairy web of dew which nature had garnished his hat with as he walked on that serene morning past St Anthony's Chapel, light of heart'. George is in a state of grace, in tune with nature; he has acted generously, and the powers of Good work on his behalf. By the end of the Editor's account, it is clear that George and Robert have been locked in the ancient battle between God and the Devil.

The Sinner's confessions: a rational reading

The second part can also be considered from a broadly psychological perspective, and from one which allows the supernatural to be a valid force. There are three stages in Robert's account – stages valid in both the psychological and the supernatural interpretation, although signifying very different developments in each.

Robert's boyhood is the first stage, which explains how he has been warped by his upbringing. He has suffered enormous pressures growing up with doubt about his paternity; he has been reared in a loveless and bigoted way. From the beginning he admits that he is 'an outcast in the world'. He is in a constant state of terror, when he thinks of 'being still . . . in a state of reprobation'; and he is kept in a state of anguish and doubt by his 'father', whose constant message to the boy is that the struggle for his soul has been unsuccessful.

Apart from the cleverness of the language here (ambivalent, carrying within it alternative implications that the struggle has been with a serpent-like figure, or Satan), the warping effect of such speeches on the lonely boy can be imagined. He is, in effect, brainwashed and in great confusion about his sins and repentances, unsure where to begin or how to proceed. With his burden of original sin and his knowledge that only a few attain the status of the Elect, Robert displays a child's mind in anguish.

The second stage begins when, finally assured by his 'father' that he is one of God's Elect, the tension in Robert is suddenly released, leaving him unbalanced:

I wept for joy to be thus assured of my freedom from all sin, and of the impossibility of my ever again falling away from my new state. I bounded away into the fields and the woods, to pour out my spirit in prayer before the Almighty for his kindness to me: my whole frame seemed to be renewed; every nerve was buoyant with new life; I felt as if I could have flown in the air, or leaped over the tops of the trees.

Robert, alone and insecure, finds solace in the recesses of his own mind. He reaches inside and creates a figure who offers him release from his own straitjacket of repression. He gives this figure the name Gil-Martin, with echoes of his feared arch-rival at school, McGill.

The personified objectification of Robert's repression allows outlets for greed, hate, lust, to the point ultimately of self-destruction. By suggesting suspect courses of action, Gil-Martin relieves Robert of moral responsibility. He resembles Robert, because he is Robert, and strange feelings of 'enchantment', anger, excitement, and unnatural enthusiasm are simply the accompaniments of his madness. Since Robert has created this figure, it follows that he will (at first) profess that he is a disciple of Robert's, flattering his neglected ego. Later, Robert must admit that he and his friend have committed atrocities, although Robert will claim that these further God's purposes. He eventually transfers the burden of responsibility to Gil-Martin, as having suggested the dubious courses of action. Consistently with all this, Gil-Martin knows Robert's mind – because he actually exists within the mind being read.

Wringhim Senior dedicates the demented boy to God as his 'sword and scourge'. This urges him on his psychologically disastrous course; his physical health begins to deteriorate as his honesty lessens. The dramatic monologue masks the real nature of his 'disciple', his 'guide and director'. Once again, several objective witnesses see his strange friend; but here they all describe him differently. Robert may simply be keeping bad company.

Robert slowly changes the descriptions of his 'friend', perhaps because the 'friend' has become the tempter. It may even be that (with astonishing irony and complexity) Hogg has Robert actually begin to hint that this 'friend' may be very sinister indeed (without ever daring to name the figure as the Devil).

The murder of the kindly minister, Blanchard, is bizarre. The truth is not knowable, but it is significant that, as the minister, who believes in justification by good works rather than by faith alone, argues with Gil-Martin/Robert, Gil-Martin begins to waver, his features dissolving as his arguments dissolve against the superior strength of Blanchard. Naturally, such a threat must be removed.

Robert is now seriously ill, and having auxiliary hallucinations, as when golden weapons are let down from the sky with their points towards him. This is symbolism which embodies his guilt, representing in its golden imagery his avarice, pride and desire for the Dalcastle fortunes. It also points towards future murder. Illness is also visible in the confused and subjective account Robert gives of the tennis matches. He projects all sorts of successful outcomes and impressions onto his activities, contrary to the reality of his public disgrace. He even imagines the watchers and players to be so confounded by his appearance that they abandon their 'sinful pastime' and flee to their houses. When Robert is imprisoned after the riot, the comments of the old gaoler reveal that he is still just a poor silly boy, however sick and dangerous he may be. Typically, Robert cannot appreciate the gaoler's kindness.

The third stage of Robert's illness arrives with his disintegration into the 'strange distemper' where he thinks that he is at least two people:

> Immediately after this I was seized with a strange distemper, which neither my friends nor physicians could comprehend, and it confined me to my chamber for many days; but I knew, myself, that I was bewitched, and suspected my father's reputed concubine of the deed . . . I generally conceived myself to be two people. When I lay in bed, I deemed there were two of us in it; when I sat up, I always beheld another person, and always in the same position from the place where I sat or stood, which was about three paces off me towards my left side.

The two characters who have come to dominate his life, Gil-Martin and George, are taking over his identity; his time-sense collapses, and his imagined sequences with Gil-Martin and others become increasingly bizarre. His account of the murder attempt on Arthur's Seat is at odds with that in part one. Robert claims that he vigorously attacked George. He admits that he cannot remember clearly, but insists that he vanquished his brother, and forced him to ask him for pardon. The 'White Lady' apparition and his wild swinging from hysteria to inertia, as he runs to St Anthony's Chapel and then stops indecisively, indicate his confusion. When Robert kills George, the circumstances surrounding the murder suggest that he has 'chosen' the situation to fit his repressed envy.

Finally, amnesia and mental disintegration overtake Robert. He no longer hides his guilt, wearing gaudy clothes, indulging in sexual excesses, drinking and murder. André Gide did not like these closing stages with their monstrous apparitions – but such apparitions are the appropriate end for Robert's mind. He projects his own guilt onto the features of Gil-Martin, making Gil-Martin a hideous tempter, sometimes distorting his face to look like George's.

Perhaps the most perplexing episode concerns Penpunt, the Cameronian. Robert derives consolation from his story about the Auchtermuchty people's relish for their own damnation. Penpunt can be seen as yet another healthy yardstick, like Old Barnet the gaoler and the good old woman, who impresses Robert with the 'simplicity of human nature'.

The end sequences merely reflect the final collapse of Robert's mind, in a stream-of-consciousness composed of all his fears and nightmares. The death probably appears to Robert as entirely different from what is seen by an onlooker, in the sense that his last agonies are completely internal.

THE SINNER'S CONFESSIONS: A SUPERNATURAL READING

In some ways the supernatural reading is richer, since Hogg was so deeply steeped in traditional lore. Rather than showing mental instability, deterioration here indicates palpable evil. In this reading, Robert is a sinner, which explains why the Devil chose him. In folklore, bastards are always suspect; and Robert is 'third in a direct line who had all been children of adultery'. Such people were, to Hogg, at least half-devil, and he shows in all his work that there are very strict rules and conditions for the treatment of them. The Devil can only gain entrance where an opening has been left for him; he will only trouble 'good fowk'. Though Robert seems an insubstantial fellow for such significant persecution, in Hogg's view, significance is judged by the amount of hypocrisy and evil attributable to the protagonist. In spiritual pride, sin, and lies Robert is quite outstanding. Moreover, he is hypocritical, mean, sadistic, ungrateful and cowardly. His torments about his sins are ultimately selfish, since when he stops worrying about them he is completely amoral.

The rules for the 'game of souls' are clear. The Devil must not actually lie to Robert; Robert must become his victim within a framework of 'truth'. These rules come from ancient tradition, in ballads and folklore, where the Devil as 'Black Man' has worked thus, since time began.

Robert develops in wickedness, eventually killing father, mother, brother and Blanchard. He lies about this, cheats the widow Keeler through the corrupt lawyer Linkum (who is also the wicked Ridsley, Bell Calvert's pimp), and ruins and murders her daughter. Thus he qualifies for the Devil's attendance.

303

At the beginning of stage two, Robert has only awakened the Devil, who has to manoeuvre him into freely choosing his own damnation. Robert must be the agent of his own destruction and the Devil scrupulously observes the 'rules'. However often Robert is possessed, and in whatever way, this must never be at a moment of moral choice. The Devil may be allowed to possess him as a result of his sins, but not at the point of their commission.

At the first meeting of Robert with the Devil, Hogg emphasises their being drawn together as if linked by an 'invisible power'. Hogg signals a partial demonic possession taking place, and uses ambivalent descriptions so that this can be interpreted in different ways. Robert's parents recognise him as 'transformed' and Hogg generates irony at the Reverend Wringhim's expense in his response to his son's news about Gil-Martin, first fearing then discounting a meeting with Satan.

The Devil is artfully truthful in his answers to Robert, who fails to grasp the significance of Gil-Martin's sinister appearance, and of his Bible with red characters (a traditional sign in folklore and Hogg's work that the book is a manual of evil). Gil-Martin says he is his brother, sharing belief in the same 'truths' and in the 'same mode of redemption'. Gil-Martin is ironical about 'Christianity', commenting that prayer is selfish, since true humility insists that we accept our lot. It is part of his skill in playing on Robert's inflated pride that he does not expect Robert to notice the implications of his having only one parent whom he does not acknowledge, and that he will not use his Christian name to Robert – implying that it is his non-Christian name which is best suited for Robert's use.

The height of Robert's folly comes when he decides that Gil-Martin must be Tsar Peter of Russia (although Tsar Peter was indeed travelling in Western Europe at this time, and is reputed to have visited shipyards in Leith). But Gil-Martin has said nothing to make Robert think this. He gives Robert a fair account of his expulsion from heaven, when not a Christian, stressing that he is now a Christian, 'converted to its truths by passing the fire', and miserable in the extreme. Hogg's irony on the possibilities of distorting Christianity is displayed in Gil-Martin's arguments justifying murdering Blanchard: ' "If the man Blanchard is worthy, he is only changing his situation for a better one; and if unworthy, it is better that one fall, than that a thousand souls perish. Let us be up and doing." ' Hogg attacks the very texture of Christian belief, showing its ideals to be dangerously misconstruable. He identifies the profound weakness in the theology of the reformers, that leaves room for people like the Wringhims to derive conclusions so manifestly absurd. In this context, the novel is an extended satire on the formalisation of religion.

There are other clues to Gil-Martin's demonic nature. Hogg, in other writings, often cited the traditional folk name for the Devil, 'Gil-Moules' or 'Gil-Mouly', particularly applied when he came in by the keyhole or under the door. Once again Hogg's Devil is linked with folk tradition. There may be further irony in that the name Gil-Martin broken down can mean the 'servant of Martin', i.e. Martin Luther; thus he is a 'Protestant' devil. The analogy is with Gaelic names like Gilchrist, the 'servant of Christ', or Gillanders, the 'servant of St Andrew'.

Whenever Wringhim senior speaks, evil results; the dedication of the boy to the Lord as sword and scourge extends the Devil's writ to include violence and murder. But Robert still has reservations about murder at this stage, and is far from suicide and complete damnation. It is in the murder of Blanchard that we see exactly the rules governing the Devil's right to control and possess Robert.

Robert is 'free' to choose and looks to heaven for guidance. Heaven shows the points of golden weapons – perhaps a warning that Heaven is offended and antagonistic. Robert freely chooses to take this sign as encouragement, which causes Satan to rejoice. Robert's mind is 'exalted', he is 'inflamed' in his intentions, and he becomes 'as one beside himself', so clearly unnatural that his parents try to confine him in his room. He is now both himself and Satan. He describes himself as 'greatly strengthened and encouraged that night'. Free thought results in a moral decision, usually evil, and the Devil is permitted possession. Robert is led to the next threshold, whereupon the Devil dispossesses him so that the evil action is committed while he is free. Then, having sinned, Robert is again possessed, and the Devil assists him to escape. The cycle begins all over again. Heaven also plays its part in this cycle, sending warnings like the 'sweet voice' which whispers to Robert to beware just before he murders Blanchard. Similarly, Gil-Martin's pistol has no effect at close range on the minister; it has to be Robert's gun which does the deed.

Robert, 'broken in' by the murder of Blanchard, is now ready for the murder of his opponents, particularly his brother. The Arthur's Seat scene is a kind of rehearsal which exaggerates Robert's feelings of hatred against his brother, and his failure leads to the second curse, in which Robert gives up his father and brother to Satan, welcoming their destruction at anyone's hands.

The tennis match scenes, considered in the light of this supernatural reading, show now-familiar signs of demonic possession. There are ambivalent descriptions which can be taken colloquially, or literally and supernaturally, and, following the curse, Robert is seized with that 'strange distemper' which suggests total possession.

The previous relationship of 'love' between Robert and Gil-Martin moves inexorably towards one of 'hate'. The Devil allows this relationship to become one in which Robert is driven to desperation, for he needs nothing less than Robert's suicide to be sure of gaining his soul. Robert's decision to kill George, the curse and the mysterious 'distemper' which follows, mark the turning point in the 'game' of souls. There is a mirroring of situations whereby the first curse set Satan on George's right; now 'another person' appears to Robert 'always in the same position from the place where I sat or stood, which was about three paces of me towards my left'.

In the extended description of his meeting with 'the great personage' Robert's coded language may imply that he recognises that the Devil has tempted him all along. Hogg may be merely prolonging his story, dragging out a struggle long-since lost; but it is more likely that, since heaven's mercy is infinite, Gil-Martin must play out his game around Robert till the bitter end.

From this viewpoint, Penpunt may be heaven's last attempt to save Robert. There have been previous warnings of earthly and heavenly agents, from Barnet and the jailer to the mysterious voices and the White Lady on Arthur's Seat. Criticism has been indecisive about the role of the stories of Penpunt in the novel, but he reveals to Robert the true nature of his predicament and tries to get through to him, his Auchtermuchty tale expressing in allegory the entire action of the novel. Auchtermuchty represents Robert, suggesting that damned souls are in love with their damnation. This is perhaps the darkest point of the entire novel, suggesting that Robert in his heart of hearts, knowing that the chances of being amongst the Elect are slight, chooses a peculiar and morbid dignity in being damned. The opposite is also possible. Penpunt (a religious enthusiast) may be yet another manifestation of the Devil. The White Lady may indeed have been heaven's last warning, and Penpunt may be just another way of driving Robert towards suicide.

In this supernatural interpretation, the diabolic sequences at the end are the logical outcome to the story, as the Devil reveals himself in his totality, mocking Robert with grotesque parodies of attempts to save him. The trapping of Robert in the weaver's web is a symbolic way of revealing how Robert has been trapped in Gil-Martin's net. Robert is cut off totally from humanity, from the world of the weaver and the good-natured old woman, and is driven to that final act of which, by his own beliefs, there is no remission.

THE EDITOR'S SUMMATION

The third part brings back rationalism – to a degree. The Editor asks whether this work is an allegory of religious parable – but then admits that he does not know. His ambiguity of response re-introduces the dilemma between the consistent rational world of the Edinburgh Enlightenment and scientific materialism which is balanced against the claims of an older and traditional supernatural world.

The character involved in the last sequence ('L . . . t' is John Gibson Lockhart, Scott's son-in-law and friend of Hogg) represents reason. He is brought into the novel as one of those seeking the grave of the Sinner, and he is confounded by what he discovers when he examines the corpse. Hogg's inclusion of his own letter to *Blackwood's Magazine* brings further urban associations; yet by having the voice of Hogg himself, as the voice of an older past, together with the names of well-known people like 'L . . . w' (William Laidlaw, a farmer friend), the reader is forced to acknowledge the claims of an older society and value-structure. Thus, to the very end, Hogg re-emphasises the tension between a traditional and dark Scotland, and a present and future rational Scotland.

Such analysis reduces Hogg's marvellous sense of nightmare and bewildering complexity – but also serves to show how Hogg assembled the interweaving of these two strands of interpretation. The central issue of the novel may simply be satire on excessive Scottish Presbyterianism; or it may be a much wider satirical attack on dogmatism and fundamentalism of any kind. Hogg's warmest characters are the most worldly – the old laird, Arabella Logan and Bell Calvert – thus challenging the rigid and narrow value structure of an older Scotland.

Hogg also anticipates the fundamental and modern tension between understanding social offenders, by taking into account upbringing and influences which have led them to their actions, and, on the other hand, condemning them as evil. Hogg put his finger on a discrepancy in modern man's value structure, where he does not know whether to exercise reason and empathy or to judge according to moral absolutes. Thus his novel about eighteenth-century Scottish history and tradition becomes universal and timeless.

CHAPTER 18

WIDENING THE RANGE 3

WHY SHOULD WE LOOK BEYOND SCOTT
AND THE MAJOR SCOTTISH FICTION?

While the student of Scottish literature of this period cannot ignore the massive accomplishment of Scott and his contemporaries in fiction, Ferrier, Galt and Hogg, and while it is true that other fiction, poetry and drama rarely measure up to their achievements, it would be wrong, for several reasons, to ignore other work of the period. Firstly, the work of the major writers in other genres such as poetry and nonfiction prose is often original, vividly tragic or comic, and of outstanding quality. Secondly, there are a large number of writers in different genres producing occasional works which stand out as pioneering or unique ventures and as important cultural records of the time. Thirdly, there are the poets who tried to carry on the traditions of Burns, in radical and satirical poetry, but were increasingly pushed to the edge or indeed out of their country and its accepted culture. And finally, there are a small number of 'Anglo-Scots', like Jane Porter, Joanna Baillie and Lord Byron, whose work either contributes hugely to the development of Scottish writing or continues, despite the fact that the writer works away from Scotland, to exhibit very significant characteristics derived from Scottish upbringing and experience.

The poetry of Scott

Scott's grandparents had a farm in the heart of the Borders, and the first poetry and song he heard as a child came from living ballad tradition, which underpins all his later work. He was collecting ballads even as a teenager, and by 1792 he was making the 'raids' into Liddesdale which resulted in his great collection of *Minstrelsy of the Scottish Border* (1802). A very different impulse came from his translations of German Romantic poetry, leading to the Gothic and Romantic elements that fuse with ballad tradition in the epics which transformed Western literature in the first decade of the nineteenth century: *The Lay of the Last Minstrel* (1805), *Marmion* (1808), *The Lady of the*

Lake (1810). His later long poems – with the possible exception of *The Lord of the Isles* (1815) – were less original and more coolly received, as Byron's even more exotic settings and tortured heroes captured the market. Realising this, Scott had turned to fiction in 1814, but not before establishing himself as one of the most influential figures in poetry in Europe.

For the last century it has been fashionable among critics to downplay Scott as an epic poet – a view helped by Scott's own self-dismissal in this role, whereby he frequently suggested that he rushed his composition, and that such poetry was hardly to be counted as real literature. We can now see, however, that this self-denigration belies the fact that he planned his epics carefully, with two main objectives; one self-interested, practical and economic, and the other creative and altruistic, in that it urged reconciliation within Britain of Scotland's internecine past in Lowlands and Highlands.

Fulfilling the first motivation, *The Lay* was a subtle compliment to the great Border house of Buccleuch, firmly identifying Scott as a worthy family descendant. Thereafter, *Marmion*, with its introductions to six cantos praising great British politicians (and celebrating the greatest-ever Scottish defeat?) entrenched Scott as a favourite of the British establishment. And *The Lady of the Lake*, for all its revelation of Highland landscape to a delighted public and to painters like Landseer and the later Horatio McCulloch, who made Scott's way of seeing Scotland their own, was also by implication extolling the virtues of the Britain for which the Highlanders were fighting so fiercely in the Napoleonic wars. (Is it for this British cause that Scott has his disguised king of Scotland call himself Fitz-James, a knight of Snowdonia?)

There was another side to Scott and this self-advancing Unionism, however. For each of these long poems, anticipating the novels to follow, genuinely seeks reconciliation with the past, burying its ancient Border, Anglo-Scottish, and Highland – Lowland feuds and wars, by achieving peace for the main protagonists in the romantic tale, and by distancing the events so that they are seen as unrelated to the present.

Are these epics still worth studying now, however, apart from the light they shed on Scott's shrewdly managed literary ambitions, and then on his more idealistic visions of Scotland coming to terms with its past? Their heroes and heroines are laughably mannered by today's standards, Scott's galloping octosyllabic couplets can frequently descend to the level of McGonagall, and history is often subverted to suit Scott's Unionist purpose – as in his ennobling of King James and his treatment of his arch enemy, the Douglas, in *The Lady of the Lake*. (James was far more ruthless in sexuality and politics than this picture of an easy-going and forgiving adventurer king suggests.) The poems are structurally dubious, while the mixture of family feuds and goblin supernatural in *The Lay* was criticised at the time. The introductions in *Marmion* were originally meant to be for a separate volume of poems, and brought in because Scott could not get a publisher for them. Scott could be careless; the attentive reader of *The Lady of the Lake* will find several unresolved questions as to the fate of Scott's clans and characters.

Nevertheless, these poems are well worth reading. They would not have changed the face of poetry if they had not deeply affected major writers, so it is worth the imaginative effort of placing our reading in Scott's time. What so captured his audience was firstly their complete freshness of style and setting, and then the way that they tuned in to the age – military valour was crucial in the long period of nearly thirty years of war with France. Scott also, together with Byron, produced a new kind of 'hero' – more complex, less predictable – particularly in Marmion, a protagonist perhaps modelled on Byron himself, the loved-and-hated icon of the age. Add to this the fact that Scott also caught the public's sense of lament for the passing of noble savagery in the Borders and Highlands, with Border tribal feuds and romance only slightly less colourful than those of the Highlanders. The Highland clearances were biting hard by 1810, and, while Scott did not deal directly with this issue, his own Highlanders are seen as a doomed race, and their passing described in noble terms. There is, moreover, magnificent poetry of landscape, of passion for country, of the historical political leaders of Britain, utilising eighteenth-century models in the manner of Dryden in order to make powerful statements about a new Great Britain. Taken with the early novels, Scott's overwhelming desire to be at once Scottish and British, to love the past with his imagination and heart, and to deal with the present with a shrewd head, is clearly revealed.

Beyond these epics lie a great number of occasional poems and ballads he wrote as part of the novels, more than enough to show that Scott was indeed a great poet. To ignore this side of Scott is to ignore half of his huge achievement.

The poetry of James Hogg

While the long poems of Scott were well known in schools up till the 1960s, the same could not be said about the poetry of James Hogg. Apart from occasional anthologised pieces like 'A Boy's Song' or 'Lock the Door, Lariston, Lion of Liddesdale', the astonishing and varied achievement of Hogg in poetry (and fiction) was unrecognised, such had been the effectiveness of stereotyping him as 'The Ettrick Shepherd' and as a merely curious and eccentric version of the 'noble savage' adopted by the Scott and

Blackwood circle. In recent years, however, world-wide re-evaluation has discovered again the deeper layers of parody and fantastic playfulness in Hogg's poetry, as well as in his fiction, and has found in him a unique genius which anticipates the formal and intertextual trickery and subtlety of post-modernism.

While nothing in his poetry matches the narrative complexities and ambiguities of *The Justified Sinner*, there is nevertheless a huge range of songs, ballads and epic poems which at their best (as with his sprawling and Tolkien-like saga of sword and sorcery, *The Three Perils of Man*, 1822) are rich in their exploitation of the folklore and traditional poetry of the Borders, combining this use of tradition with Hogg's marvellously fantastic imagination and his unparalleled reductive and whimsical humour.

He began as a poet, with *Scottish Pastorals, Poems, Songs, Etc.* in 1801, imitating Allan Ramsay; his second collection, *The Mountain Bard* (1807) was inspired by Scott's *Minstrelsy of the Scottish Border*. Hogg's lack of formal education was compensated for by a wealth of oral story and ballad, as well as a thorough knowledge of the Bible and the subtleties of religious debate. This led to an unusual tension in his work, whereby he felt sure of his composition when he worked within his own tradition, but when venturing into the world of the *literati*, the world of modern and written literature, he felt a need to imitate – which could be both blessing and curse. Imitation made Hogg one of the finest parodists of the age (witness his imitations of poets like Scott, Wordsworth and Southey in his volume of parodies *The Poetic Mirror* (1816)). It too often also brought him close to a pursuit of models which, while not plagiarism, could distort and weaken his Border voice. It was perhaps just this sense of creative insecurity which made Hogg resort to the tricks and ambiguities of meaning which characterise his best work, since elusive authorial intention offered protection against final condemnation by critics.

Given the enormous range of poetry he produced, what should the student turn to first in order to find Hogg at his best? The ballad imitations of *The Mountain Bard* like 'Sir Davie Graeme' or 'Gilmanscleuch' are better than much of his later work simply because they work within the oral tradition to which Hogg and his mother belonged. There are fast-moving stories of the 'fierce wars and tender loves' of the Border clans, and on the other hand stories based on Border legends, of wraiths and unnatural death. Already, Hogg was discovering that reductive and comic voice which he would use to great effect later. In 'The Fray of Elibank' he tells the old story of Meg of the Muckle Mou', in which the noble young captive of a rival clan is given the choice of gallows or marriage to the fierce old chief's ugly daughter. When the young hero's realism wins over any notions of romantic integrity, Hogg is surely thumbing his nose at the world of the *literati* and Romantic idealism.

The best and worst of his poetry was to appear in 1813, with his ambitious *The Queen's Wake*. This collection of seventeen long poems celebrated the arrival of Mary, Queen of Scots in Scotland. It was also a competitive piece, and here again Hogg exemplifies his multiplicity – and perhaps his unsureness – of voice as he moves impressively from Scots to English, from Gothic melodrama ('Young Kennedy' wins the prize) to hilarious fantasy, from the reductive to the sublime. The epic cannot be called a success; but two of its long poems are superb, and illustrate perfectly the two very different sides to Hogg's genius. 'The Witch of Fife' is a riotous supernatural narrative which comes close to 'Tam o' Shanter' in its pace and inventiveness, if lacking the deeper levels of meaning in Burns; and 'Kilmeny', while working with the supernatural again, has a very different spiritual and contemplative beauty in its haunting account of the disappearance from earth of the innocent girl, too good for this world. Here there is allegorical depth, and Hogg comes close to Scott and his Jeanie Deans in identifying the humble maid as representative of the essence of spiritual Scotland.

And it is useful to follow these two strands as they develop in Hogg's poetry. We still need a selection which gives a properly representative example of them. It would include as examples of Hogg's fantastic muse 'May of the Moril Glen', 'The Guid Grey Katte', 'Connel of Dee', and 'The Russiade'. The first comically tells of how a witch's daughter bewitches the king of Scotland and all his knights till they kill their wives and go mad for love (she herself disappearing at the height of her damage on a magical ship); the second has the queen of fairies disguised as a cat flying over Scotland with a wicked bishop in her clutches, finally dropping him into Mount Etna; the third is a more sinister and disturbing, yet comic tale of cruel women and a hapless lover (or has he dreamed all?); and the fourth is the account of the amazing feats of the giant, Russell, which is sheer delightful fantasy.

On the other hand, there are Hogg's more spiritual and reflective pieces, stemming from his belief that the world of 'the other landscape' next to this world, the world of the brownies and the little people of green and gold who used to haunt the Borders, was disappearing in a rational and sceptical age. Long poems like 'Old David', in which the old knight meets with a procession of elfin knights (and slaughters them), 'Superstition', or 'Verses Addressed to . . . Lady Anne Scott of Buccleuch', follow 'Kilmeny', and justify his claim to Scott to be 'the King of the Mountain and Fairy School'. Hogg's fairies are not to be dismissed lightly; he genuinely believed and felt their amoral and often sinister presence, while conveying his sense of sadness that they are vanishing. But he expresses also, as he does so well in his short stories and in *The Justified Sinner,* his awareness that old belief and supernatural activity could move with shocking speed from harmless mischief to intense evil.

Hogg's poetry deserves to be much better known. Above all, he is stimulating and experimental in an age when too much Romantic poetry conformed to a rhetoric of affected spirituality and sentiment. Whether he is imitating Holy Willie as in his fake denunciation of the wickedness of 'The Great Muckle Village of Balmaquhapple', or whether he is more simply lyrical as in 'A Boy's Song', he shows a willingness to try new voices at every turn. He succeeds in so many – not just in imitation Border ballads, but also imitations of Highland songs (stemming from his knowledge of the originals, which he collected as *Jacobite Relics* in 1819), and of course his splendid parodies of other great poets of the day. Critics are still re-assessing his poetry; two of his epics, *The Pilgrims of the Sun* (1815) and *Queen Hynde* (1825), hugely ambitious in their account of interplanetary quest and the origins of Scotland respectively, are coming to be seen as subtle, original and powerful allegories.

Other writers, other genres

Of necessity this brief survey must grossly oversimplify – but perhaps two main tensions can be observed in the Scottish writing of the period. Firstly, and typically, Scottish writers are torn in their response to the Romanticism of the age. Secondly, and predictably, Scottish writers are pulled south, merging their voices with those of England and Europe. Edwin Muir argued in *Scott and Scotland* (1936) that these confusions of identity and allegiance meant that Scotland in this period had no cultural centre or indigenous values. Later twentieth-century critics have argued, however, that today's vocal pluralism has its own integrity in reflecting the fragmented nature of modern society. And arguably the variety of literature in Scotland and Edinburgh at that time marks the beginning of a polyphony which we have come to see as a valid characteristic of modernity.

Jane Porter's *The Scottish Chiefs* (1810) predates Scott's fiction, and is worth noting as the first romantic epic in fiction on the scale of Scott. Scott's romantic epic poetry doubtless inspired her, but it is still the case that the vogue for 'Scotch novels' and Scottish romantic fiction owes much to an Englishwoman. For all its hackneyed disguises, overblown rhetoric, and heroic posturing, it is still an important novel and historical document. It is melodrama in the grand manner, telling how William Wallace avenged the murder of his wife by the English governor of Lanark in 1296. It is as casual with the events of history as its predecessor, the medieval *Wallace* of Blind

Harry, and the modern film *Braveheart*. Wallace here is loved by the Lady Macbeth-like Countess of Mar and her virtuous daughter Helen, the one finally his betrayer and the other becoming his secret wife. In addition, he plans with Bruce throughout to save the nation. He is never less than the perfect knight, generous to enemies and putting country before all. But the novel has breadth and energy, like Scott's epic poems, and makes fascinating comparison with other treatments of the same theme. With its heroines disguised as pages and its Anglo-Scottish chivalry, James Hogg appears to have borrowed much inspiration from it for *The Three Perils of Man* (1822).

Modern critics are also rediscovering writers like Christian Johnstone, who in the 1820s and 1830s produced many novels in her running series of *Edinburgh Tales*; these and her romances, *Clan-Albin* (1815) and *Elizabeth de Bruce* (1827) are striking in their early treatment of contemporary issues, such as industrialisation, the Highland Clearances, and the degrading conditions in the new Highland regiments.

And beyond the historical fiction of Scott, Galt, Hogg, and Porter, there are others, like Sir Thomas Dick Lauder's *The Wolf of Badenoch* (1825), and his story of the Earl of Buchan and son of Robert II – the ferocious Alexander Stewart who tyrannised the north-east in the fourteenth century. (Lauder's non-fiction *Account of the Great Moray Floods* (1830) still stands as a powerful and realistic record of one of the north-east's greatest disasters.) This kind of romance; straightforward, vigorous .and without any of Scott's qualifying ironies and sub-texts, begins a long tradition which includes the novels of James Grant, G. J. Whyte-Melville and S. R. Crockett, and continues down to John Buchan and the present-day work of Nigel Tranter and Dorothy Dunnett. Grant's *The Romance of War* (1845) stands just after the age of Scott as an example of the strengths of this tradition – but also as a measure of how the historical novel declined after the death of Scott and his great contemporaries. Grant wrote many entertaining romances. *The Romance of War*, with its splendid rendering of the spirit of Highland regiments abroad during the Peninsular Wars, their loyalty, carousing, and quasi-mercenary approach to war, and its awareness of their dislocation from their own culture and history, shows how completely Scottish literature had fused with British imperialism in a way Scott had never envisaged.

A different kind of Romanticism appears in the novels of John Gibson Lockhart, Scott's son-in-law and editor of *Blackwood's Magazine*, especially in *Adam Blair* (1822), still worth reading for its early psychological analysis of the guilt of a minister who sins sexually (and worth comparing with the American Nathaniel Hawthorne's *The Scarlet Letter* (1850) for its pioneering treatment of religious mania in a small community). This and *Matthew Wald: The Story of a Lunatic* (1824) undoubtedly intrigued James Hogg, helping him to produce *The Justified Sinner*. Lockhart's semi-fictional *Peter's Letters to his Kinsfolk* (1819) is, on the other hand, probably the most vivid, valuable and unromanticised picture we have of Edinburgh and the Lowlands of Scotland in the age of Scott, for all its Tory bias. Read with the more balanced and liberal memoirs of Henry Cockburn, a clear and balanced picture of the time can be seen. Romanticism and realistic description of the age are successfully fused in Thomas Hamilton's *The Youth and Manhood of Cyril Thornton* (1824), a later variant on Smollett's *Humphry Clinker* (1771).

Galt, Hogg and Hamilton were not the only annalists of community life. D. M. Moir captured the life and character of Dalkeith in his charming pre-Kailyard novel *Mansie Waugh, the Tailor of Dalkeith* (1828); while more effectively Elizabeth Hamilton satirised the needless self-neglect and dirty habits of the poor in the *Cottagers of Glenburnie* (1808), balancing her condemnation of her clarty peasants with sympathy for their poverty and respect for their mutual affection, if controlling all with a heavy didacticism. Another talented woman writer was Mary Brunton, whose titles like *Self-Control* and *Discipline* (1810 and 1815) indicate their preaching tendency, but fail to do justice to their real wit and humour. In this respect the outstanding figure is undoubtedly Susan Ferrier, whose three novels, *Marriage, Inheritance* and *Destiny* (1818, 1824, and 1831) deserve to be much more widely known. She has been called 'the Scottish Jane Austen', but this does no justice to her very distinct sense of humour, her love of grotesque description, and her ability to cut down the apparently romantic, be it Highland scenery and castles or sophisticated London society, to show the too-frequent grim or corrupt reality beneath. Add to this her devastating accuracy in capturing Edinburgh middle- and upper-class affectation, from greedy ministers to pompous aristocrats, and her relish for bizarre eccentricity, and she stands out as one of Scotland's greatest satirists, flawed, unfortunately, by that tendency of the age, and especially of the women writers, to teach proper Christian piety and decent morality. Her plots are mechanical stories of persecuted young girls, resisting being forced into unwanted marriages; it is her surrounding satires of character and society which lift these to great comedy.

The decline of the Burns tradition

For all the new snobbery and changing literary values of the time, the vigour and focus of the Burns tradition did not die out immediately. Several poets deserve to be read for their valiant attempts to maintain what they saw as the essence of Burns, in radical political and social criticism and the mockery of affectation, expressed in Scots in the classic forms of the vernacular tradition, outstandingly in the use of the 'Habbie Simson' stanza. (A seminal representation of some of these poets, together with a provocative challenge to the usual critical assessment, is given in Tom Leonard's *Radical Renfrew*, 1990, indicating how rich just one region of Scotland could be in maintaining this engaging popular, socially aggressive tradition.)

Examples of poets and poems worth finding and comparing include Alexander Wilson of Paisley with his ferocious attack on loan sharks of the time, in 'Shark', or his earthy and hilarious reduction of an irate landowner who finds a pedlar defecating on his land in 'The Insulted Pedlar'; Alexander Rodger, with his mockery of Scott's welcome to Edinburgh of King George IV in 1822 ('Kneel and kiss his glorious bum') in 'Sawney now the King's come', and his hatred of exploitation of the poor in his savage 'Shavings Banks'; Paisley shoemaker John Mitchell with his scorn for both sides of the patronage controversy in 'A Braid Glow'r at the Clergy; by Ane *Not* of Themsel's'; weaver Edward Polin's bitter diagnosis that radicalism is dead, in his 'In the Days when we were Radicals'; William Finlayson's 'The Weaver's Lament' on the failure of the 1812 weavers' strike; David Webster's Holy Fair derivation, 'Paisley Fair'; the self-taught Dundee poet William Thom, who could be sentimental, then deeply critical, as in his depiction of an industrial town awakening to misery in 'Whisperings for the Unwashed'; and Alex McGilvray's remarkably comprehensive review for the issues of the day in 'An Address . . . to the Conservative Electors of Paisley'.

Yet these poets were to be displaced, or forced to amend their own work, in favour of a less controversial and socially more conformant poetry. A more sentimental tradition, exemplified by poems like Robert Tannahill's 'Jessie, the flower o'Dunblane', took over, and it was Tannahill, not any of the radical weaver poets, who became accepted as Paisley's civic bard. The stronger traditions of Scottish poetry gave way to the weaker. Where there once had been great national epics like Barbour's *Brus*, visionary poems like Ramsay's 'The Vision' or Fergusson's 'The Ghaists', ambitious long poems – even with Burns and Hogg – increasingly turned to comic, non-political subjects. Burns's 'The Vision' confines itself to Ayrshire and the West, retreating from full Scottish national comment; Hogg's spiritual epics avoid contemporary politics; William Tennant's epic, *Anster Fair* (1812), while great fun, is about a competition in Anstruther for the hand of local beauty Maggie Lauder, and his other epic, in Scots, *Papistry Storm'd* (1827), is a vigorous but nasty piece of anachronistic sectarianism.

Comic poetry came to rule: Hogg, Lockhart, William Nicholson ('The Brownie of Blednoch'), Lord Neaves (who could be biting as well as funny),

W. E. Aytoun. (Edwin Morgan's anthology of *Scottish Satirical Verse*, 1980, has an excellent and representative selection.) As with fiction, it seemed that by mid-century, Scottish poetry's willingness to deal seriously with Scottish issues had dissipated.

Anglo-Scots?

A great part of the answer of the question as to why Scottish literature loses direction after Scott must lie in the decision of so many writers to leave Scotland. In the nineteenth century Carlyle, Stevenson, Oliphant, MacDonald, Brown, Davidson – almost all the major writers, in fact – do so.

Previous to 1800 several Scots had gone south, Thomson, Boswell and Smollett amongst them. But whether *literati*, or vernacular, more than enough writers interested in dealing with Scottish issues remained, until the 1830s. Then, with the Tory *Blackwood's Magazine* under John Wilson, unhealthily dominating Scottish culture, writers like Carlyle felt they had to leave. Carlyle's achievement will be summarised in the next section; here we should simply note the work of Joanna Baillie, who worked in London, but was considered by Scott to be a major Scottish dramatist and poet.

In conclusion, more controversially, we suggest that Lord Byron, who spent his early childhood in the north-east of Scotland, and who himself recognised the strong Scottish strain in his character and work, despite his quarrels with 'Scotch Reviewers', should be considered a Scottish as well as an English writer. The qualities in his work of romance tempered with realism, of fantastic imagination and satiric reduction, together with the sense of his protagonists being outsiders to Establishment society, have often been noted as deriving from his Scottish origins and identity.

SECTION 4
Victorian and Edwardian Scottish Literature

CHAPTER 19

SCOTTISH LITERATURE IN THE VICTORIAN AND EDWARDIAN ERA

DECLINE AND REVIVAL 1832–1918

It was the German critic Kurt Wittig who suggested that the 1880s produced 'Another Spring' in Scottish literature (*The Scottish Tradition in Literature* 1958). This was a bold assessment, since many critics before and since Wittig have tended to write off the period between Scott and the 'Scottish Renaissance' of the 1920s as a kind of wasteland. A few writers, like Stevenson, Douglas Brown, and John Davidson, are recognised as enlivening the period with their poetry and fiction; but even now their work tends too often to be regarded as exceptional, and seen as belonging to English literature. Rather, they were writers who rebelled against stuffy Scottish Victorianism, satirists who had chosen, like so many, to exile themselves from the land which the English historian Henry Buckle (*On Scotland and the Scotch Intellect*, 1861) had all too persuasively described in this later nineteenth century as hag-ridden with religious authoritarianism, a country obsessed with pointless religious controversy. Conversely, the modern historian, T. C. Smout, argued throughout *A Century of the Scottish People 1830–1950* (1986) that the transformation of Scotland from an essentially rural to a predominantly urban and industrial society at the end of the century had been so horrific in its effects on the population in terms of slum conditions and human misery, that, weighed against this, artistic achievement deserved very little consideration.

So how could Wittig argue for a revival, given such powerful consensus that Victorian and Edwardian Scotland was trapped between narrow religiosity and industrial materialism; between, as so many writers argue, God and Mammon? Historical accounts certainly support this negative view. But we must also take into consideration other major forces which helped erode indigenous Scottish Lowland and Highland cultures: the ongoing clearances of the native Gaelic population from the Highlands; the co-operation of Scotland in British imperialism and militarism; and the increasing anglicisation of education in schools and universities, with its hostility (which lasted till after the Second World War) to Scots and Gaelic. Often, too, it seems as though major Scottish writers were content to regard themselves as English; Carlyle, Stevenson, Davidson and Buchan – to name but a few – throughout their work shift their self-identification from Scottish to English and back when it suits their argument or emotion, sometimes through an implied sense of shame and embarrassment in being seen as parochial or bigoted, sometimes through ambition for identification with a bigger and more impressive cultural centre. And certainly, from the 1880s on the major Scottish writers are deeply ironic and critical in their attitudes towards their country. And perhaps as a result, the period produced some of the most impressive and provocative work in Scottish writing

Scottish literature 1880–1918

Recent critical attention to Scottish writing has shown that we have simply failed to appreciate the high quality and large amount of work produced. A major re-evaluation of the late Victorian and Edwardian period is long overdue. It is true that there was a cultural dearth in the 1840s and '50s, and that there was then a risk that Scottish writing, as a literature examining Scottish issues and ideas in an indigenous and mature way, could have disappeared, leaving the field to romanticisation and sentimentalisation – an external distortion and internal escapism which certainly continued to flourish. There were, however, signs that a new national awareness was stirring. With the repeal of the Stamp Act in 1855 a huge number of new presses and papers appeared across the country. As William Donaldson has shown in *Popular Literature and Victorian Scotland* (1986), current political, cultural and linguistic affairs began now to be much more openly discussed. In the 1850s several associations and societies grew up, concerned with asserting Scottish rights in politics, education and the like, and by the '80s there existed a strong Scottish Home Rule movement. Scotland was still firmly tied to Britain and the Empire, the source of its prosperity, but there were new currents, colder towards anglicisation and imperialism.

These changes in Scottish attitudes took time, but already by the 1850s there were signs that new Scottish writers like Margaret Oliphant and William Alexander were beginning to offer frank and sincere examinations of the changes in Scottish rural life. Alexander's substantial fictional representation of the north-east appears in several fine novels, beginning with *Peter Grundie* as early as 1855, and including *Johnnie Gibb of Gushetneuk* (1871), Alexander's greatest novel. George Macdonald's *Phantastes* (1858) revealed a new and exciting mixture of European fantasy and traditional folklore, with later stories revealing the integration of Scottish themes; evidence of a new and confident eclecticism. Thomson's *The City of Dreadful Night* (1874) and Stevenson's *Dr Jekyll and Mr Hyde* (1886), clearly aware of Scottish origins (Thomson's city set amidst dark northern plains and seas, Stevenson's London setting betraying its Edinburgh origins), speak of Scottish upbringing and values and were to become classic statements of Victorian loss of faith and moral hypocrisy. And if we add recent positive re-evaluation of the work of poets like Robert Buchanan, John Davidson, the radical Dundonian James Young Geddes, Marion Angus and the young poets of the Great War, together with novelists like Neil Munro, James Barrie (whose fiction and drama frequently transcend the Kailyard), the Findlater sisters, John Buchan, Violet Jacob, and MacDougall Hay, and remember that Scottish art, from the 'Glasgow Boys' and the Scottish Colourists to the Rennie Mackintosh circle, had attained European fame, then we can begin to understand Neil Munro's assessment in the 1890s that Scotland was undergoing a revival of genuine integrity far from the populist escapism of the so-called 'Kailyard' or 'Celtic Twilight'. Perhaps later leaders of 'Scottish Renaissance' like MacDiarmid were too quick to dismiss the previous achievements of Scottish culture as stultified and out of touch with the rest of the world. Munro was the most famous novelist and journalist of his day, immensely respected as the senior commentator in Scotland on the arts (as well as for his huge amount of comment on everything from technological advance and industrial change to Highland decline and European war), and the friend of great writers and artists like Conrad and Whistler. From his perspective, looking out at the world from Glasgow in its great sea-going and industrial days, with its fine architecture and respected institutions, Scotland at the turn of the century was hardly lacking in energy. This was not to deny the existence of real cultural decline, in his beloved Highlands especially. He would anatomise the history of that tragedy in his fiction. In doing so, he used the weapons of his contemporaries, from Stevenson to Douglas Brown, Young Geddes to Davidson and Barrie; parody, satire, and mature diagnosis of divided loyalties and failure of native vision. So while it is fair to note the failure of most of the major writers to look squarely at the slums and excesses of industrial change, it is fair also to note that they were preoccupied with history, and what history had done to fragment and divide the Scottish psyche and character. At best, they used their disillusion with romanticised history and rural life as a way of clearing away much of the mid-century dead wood found in fiction like John Wilson's pious misrepresentation of Scotland in *Lights and Shadows of Scottish Life* (1822), or the rural rhapsodising of Norman Macleod, chaplain to Queen Victoria, and the melodramatic exploitation of Scottish stereotypes of the 'darlings of the lending libraries', William Black and Whyte Melville. Perhaps Scottish writing had to go through this odd revival, often rooted in bitterness and animosity towards Scotland, to create fresh soil for a different kind of renaissance – though it is worth bearing in mind that that later renaissance movement in its turn also moved towards disillusion and fell short of its visions with the onset of the Second World War.

Kailyard, Celtic Twilight and Celtic revival

We can now see that the tendency to sentimentalism in Lowland literature, described in 1903 by J. H. Millar's *A Literary History of Scotland* as 'Kailyard' ('cabbage patch' or parochial) is related to late-nineteenth-century depictions of Celtic culture which saw the plight of the western Celts as unavoidable, the result of racial decline and tragic flaws of character which had once been strengths. The promotion of these images had political connotations; it was acceptable to Establishment Britain to have the actualities of social change and urbanisation disguised by the success of Kailyard representations of timeless Scottish villages with gruff, eccentric, but ultimately worthy and devout peasants, just as it suited governments not unfriendly to forced emigration to have peripheral Gaels represented by the writers of the Celtic fringe as anachronisms, fated to decline unless relocated in a brave new world. Besides, both Kailyard simplification and Celtic romanticisation were hardly new. In their occasional willingness to give the *literati* what they wanted, Burns, Galt and Hogg had all at times given in to the temptation of bucolic misrepresentation, in, for example, 'The Cottar's Saturday Night' (1784), *Sir Andrew Wylie* (1822) and the first part of *The Three Perils of Women* (1823) respectively. That said, if any single person can be held responsible for the success of the Kailyard tendency in Scottish literature, it could well be John Wilson, whose enormous influence in the second quarter of the century came from his many public roles – as editor and major contributor of the influential *Blackwood's Edinburgh Magazine* from 1817, as the famous if controversial Professor of Moral Philosophy at Edinburgh University from 1820, and as a poet and friend of Wordsworth and the Lake poets. His writings for *Blackwood's*, and his sentimental and unashamedly Tory propagandist stories in *Lights and Shadows of Scottish Life* (1822) and novels such as *The Trials of Margaret Lyndsay* (1823), did as much as any other writer's to establish the unhealthy and anachronistic movement towards evasive ruralism in literature throughout the nineteenth century. An abundance of popular fiction, together with innumerable collections of sentimental poetry like *Whistle-Binkie* (which first appeared in 1832, with new series in 1853, 1878, and 1890) reveal endless imitators of Burns, Hogg and Wilson who preferred to freeze Scotland as they liked to think it had been in their time, preserving an anachronistic discourse which suggested that they were farmer-shepherds rather than the factory workers, weavers and tradesmen of the industrial revolution. This is not to argue that all Scottish literature of the nineteenth century was escapist and rural centred. Donaldson points out that in the rise of the enormous number of new local newspapers after the repeal of stamp duties in the 1850s, a great deal of good writing in Scots and English appeared, on topics which included the realities of urbanisation and the political issues of the times. Nevertheless, there is no denying that a huge amount of literary production in the century was tainted with distortion or avoidance of the real social and political conditions and issues, from Highland clearance and ghastly urbanisation to imperial expansion and home politics.

Literary – as opposed to political and cultural – misrepresentation of the Highlands had of course begun as early as 1760 with James Macpherson and his success in claiming that his works were authentic translations and reproduction of the poems of Ossian, the ancient Celtic bard. It suited the *literati* and government then to accept this view of a once noble but now inevitably doomed race. Moreover, while Scott and others saw great dignity in Highland tragedy, Scott especially trying with creditable fairness to analyse the reasons for this, nineteenth-century writers tended to indulge Macpherson's vanquished lament, if from a different perspective, with later influential British and European writers like Matthew Arnold, Ernest Renan and Grant Allen further romanticising the Celtic Fringe as moving through a last and tragic efflorescence. And while, inspired by the example of the Irish Revival and the poetry of Yeats, there was an attempt at a more positive Celtic Revival in the 1890s under Patrick Geddes, the Edinburgh polymath and town-planner, with its magazine *The Evergreen* (1895–96) bringing together poets, novelists, painters and thinkers, by 1914 it was clear that this movement, with its essentially rural and retrospective orientation, had failed to embrace the Celts as part of modern society. With its nostalgia, its love of songs of exile and loss, and its impossible spiritual quest for the ideal and infinite, it simply reinforced the misrepresentation of the Gael as a mystical, ocean-and-island orientated dreamer, largely irrelevant to the imminent twentieth century.

The work of Neil Munro is of great significance here, although his importance as a Scottish writer has not yet been fully appreciated. Munro know Gaeldom intimately, and it is important to dissociate him from Celtic Twilight and the Kailyard movement, for which he had nothing but contempt. He did, however, perceive a great weakness at the heart of Highland history, character and culture, a weakness he found to be rooted in the development of clan hierarchy, with its profound sycophancy towards the chief, and in the warrior and male-dominated value system which saw the killing of fellow Highlanders and strangers alike for chief and clan as noble, and women's place and work as inferior. *The Lost Pibroch* (1896), *John Splendid* (1898), *Gilian the Dreamer* (1899) and *The New Road* (1914), while working with the same subject-matter as the Twilight writers such as 'Fiona MacLeod' (William Sharp), utilise parody and ironic reduction, mocking Twilight protagonists and their pseudo-culture, while still lamenting the real historical loss of an older, more worthwhile simplicity of community and value. These great and tragic stories feed directly into the post-war Scottish Renaissance, so that Gunn, Gibbon, MacColla and Mitchison to a great extent follow Munro's view of Highland decline from a Golden Age, extrapolating their fictions from where he left off. Without Munro's subtle amendments to the historical perspectives of Scott and Stevenson, significant revision of the way we read the Highlands could have taken much longer. The misty ground of false Highland mythology had begun to be cleared – a necessary first step towards refashioning an indigenous Scottish literature.

'Positive negativism' or cultural escapism?

To appreciate the achievement of the major, and neglected, writers of this period it is helpful to remember that, while celebrating and satirising society, writers also embody its uncertainties and unease. We accept this function of writing readily enough with regard to contemporary writing and society, but perhaps less readily when we have to deal with it in terms of older writing and past societies. More simply put, it can be argued that it is the success of much of the significant writing of this period that it tells of the anger and contempt of the major Scottish writers for the state of their society, its communities and culture, as well as their own deep-seated dualism of identity, with its division of loyalties between Scottish and English language and culture. The fiction of Barrie, Brown, Munro, the Findlater sisters, Davidson, MacDougall Hay and Jacob can all read in this context, as can the poetry of Geddes and Davidson, together with a great deal of neglected writing by local poets. One way of viewing this writing is to see it as the necessary prelude to a more affirmative movement in Scottish writing; irony, satire and disillusion with romantic misrepresentation of Scotland, even when unsure of its loyalties and aims, cleared the way for the Scottish Renaissance in the 1920s. Much of the failure to see the strengths of this writing can be attributed to the British-orientated criticism of the time which either failed to understand the preoccupations of the writing, or refused to take it seriously. There were, moreover, highly successful and competing discourses of Scotland which, in their romanticisation of Highlands and Lowlands, and their arguments for Celtic Twilight or Kailyard sentimentality, effectively drew a veil over the rest of the world's view of the nightmare reality of industrialisation.

It has to be admitted that the major writers did not meet this urbanisation head on. While allowing Donaldson's argument that we have failed to realise the amount of work in Scots and English on topics which include the new cities and factories, it has to be said that much of this writing can be described as 'urban Kailyard'; the melodramatic and stereotypical treatment of the new areas. Why did the major novelists and poets not choose to write of the drastic changes going on around them? In many cases they had in fact removed themselves from the site of these changes. More simply, however, many of them saw the central problems of Scotland in different ways and as dealing with fundamental dualisms in Scottish thought. In the best work, this presentation of dualism does indeed relate to some of the most significant and central tensions in Scottish culture and society, and powerfully, if obliquely, comments on how these tensions are ultimately personally and socially destructive. Novels like *The Master of Ballantrae* (1888), *Kirsteen* (1890), *Gilian the Dreamer* (1899), *The House with the Green Shutters* (1901) and *Gillespie* (1914) all identify such tensions as a root cause of personal, family, community and national disintegration. These novels are arguably the high point of a school of Scottish fiction which has its own particular and almost obsessive preoccupation with divided self and divided family within divided community and nation.

A school of Scottish fiction 1814–1914

The beginnings of this school lie, of course with Scott, Galt and Hogg and their fictional juxtaposing of past and present, disorder and order, romance and realism. Moreover, in *Rob Roy* (1818), *Redgauntlet* (1824), Galt's *The Entail* (1823) and Hogg's *The Justified Sinner* (1824), many of what were to become the recurrent symbols and patternings of opposites were laid down. In this earlier period, as writers struggled to articulate their deepest responses to their divided Scotlands, the fundamental oppositions were those of older Scotland in tension with the new, especially when linked with civil wars of religion and Jacobitism. *Rob Roy* represented outlaw Scotland set against mercantile Scotland; Rob Roy and his clan against his cousin, the Glasgow merchant trader, Bailie Nicol Jarvie. What emerges frequently and powerfully in all these novels are central figures torn in conscience and loyalty; Scott's 'men in the middle', trapped in uncertainty between contending claims of conscience in politics and religion; Hogg's Sinner, torn between the claims of fanatical religion and of his 'common-sense' conscience and nature's voice; Galt's tormented fanatic in *Ringan Gilhaize* (1823), driven beyond his essential decency by the atrocities of an intolerant government towards his family and community to the point where he himself becomes a fanatical 'justified sinner'. Brutal authority, often expressed in father-figures (who can be of the Establishment or of the anti-Establishment) is recurrently seen as repressing moderation and sensitivity, this side of the polarisation frequently being symbolically represented by rebellious sons.

The later fiction moves away from the domestic location of division within history, focusing more closely on the psychological antagonisms within self and family. It is true that *Kidnapped* (1886) and *Catriona* (1893) are set within historical periods reminiscent of Scott, but the emphasis is on the psychological contrast in the opposing qualities of David Balfour and Alan Breck, Lowlander and Highlander, just as in *The Master of Ballantrae* the emphasis is on the two fundamentally different kinds of Scot to be found in the homely, frugal Henry Durie and his earth-wandering, prodigal and demonic brother James. It is worth considering how often – and why – a demonic metaphor is employed in describing one side of the central opposition in these novels, and how this metaphor can be deployed on either side of the divide; Stevenson changes his placing of it frequently, so that sometimes he will locate his demonic simile in his romantic and rebellious protagonists, and at other times in their repressive and materialistic opposites – for example, in the authoritarian father-figure of Weir of Hermiston. These two types, inextricably linked yet diametrically opposed, are to Stevenson and his successors representative of a Scotland divided between realism and romance, rational prudence and imaginative release, and unable to bring together its head and its heart. Neither side of the opposition is good or bad; both represent extreme tendencies in Scottish history and culture.

This recurrent structuring and symbolism is to be found (as the following discussions of texts will show) in most of the great fiction from Scott's *Waverley* (1814) to *Gillespie* in 1914. Its hold is particularly strong during the Victorian and Edwardian periods; and while it was to weaken after the Great War, novels like Gibbon's *Sunset Song* (1932), A. J. Cronin's *Hatter's Castle* (1931) and James Barke's *The Land of the Leal* (1939) show that this recurrent symbolic patterning of opposites clearly expressed dualisms deeply felt and long-lasting in Scottish culture, with echoes in work as late as that of Robin Jenkins from the 1950s on, Crichton Smith's *Consider the Lilies* (1968) and Alasdair Gray's *Lanark* (1981). 'Widening the Range', at the end of this section, will discuss some of the writers beyond Stevenson, Oliphant and Brown who exploited this patterning.

Victorian and Edwardian Scottish poetry: rediscovering lost voices

In the past decade nineteenth-century Scottish poetry has been the subject of ongoing reassessment. There are many lesser poets of the later nineteenth and early twentieth century whose work, popular in its time but since relatively forgotten, deserves attention; from William Edmonstoune Aytoun, George MacDonald and Alexander Smith, to later poets whose work in Scots anticipates and enables the so-called 'renaissance' of Scots poetry in Mac-Diarmid's early lyrics and the work of his followers.

That said, there is no doubt that nineteenth-century Scottish poetry, compared to work of great periods such as that of Dunbar and Henryson, or Ramsay, Fergusson and Burns, is limited in the range and quality of its achievement. It could be argued that the hallmark of poetry in the first half of the century is national escapism – in Hogg's comic fantasies, in Scott's romantic epics, in William Tennant's *Anster Fair* (1812), which reduces national epic to hilarious local and supernatural farce, or Aytoun in comic ballads like 'The Ballad of Sir Launcelot Bogle' or his mockery in *Firmilian: A Tragedy* (1854) of Alexander Smith's inflatedly heroic or 'Spasmodic' poetry, like *A Life Drama and Other Poems* (1853). The mood changed after the Disruption of 1843, becoming darker as religious belief was challenged in an increasingly materialist and sceptical society. All Victorian writing took this challenge seriously, but the Scots especially so. The church in Scotland had long been the bedrock of national cultural identity and to see it split in this way was deeply disturbing to the foundations of Victorian Scotland. Intellectuals of the time struggled to make sense of new matrices of meaning. Robert Chambers anticipated Darwinism in his *Vestiges of Creation* (1844); Hugh Miller, the great self-taught geologist, writer, and editor of the influential Free Church magazine *The Witness*, was to find the clash between his rational and religious beliefs deeply stressful, arguably contributing to his suicide in 1856. The most ambitious and serious Scottish poets of the later half of the century take this crisis of faith as their theme, agonising with an intensity which goes beyond that of English poets like Browning, Tennyson and Hopkins.

Seeking new voices

If the crisis of faith becomes the obsessive seminal theme of the major Scottish poets of the period, the problem and preoccupation with finding a personal voice is perhaps the other. Finding a personal voice was particularly hard for all poets in the English language after the Romantic period; the welter of new beliefs, the speed of social change, the new scientific and materialist facts which crowded in, all tended to anachronise the themes, and even the rhythms and imagery, of Romantic poetry. Very broadly, two strains can be detected in English poetry in the century: a line of descent from the Romantics which runs down through Tennyson and Arnold to Swinburne; and a line – perhaps not so fully recognised – which seeks an 'alternative voice', whether it be that of the neglected Dorset dialect poet William Barnes, or the innovative and unorthodox rhythms and colloquial, if complex arguments of the poetry of Browning. The search for new voices for new worlds is outstandingly exemplified in the poetry of the American Walt Whitman, whose *Leaves of Grass*, with its astonishing attempt to capture the immense variety of US life in what seemed to many to be rhythmic and incantatory prose, first appeared to shock the world in 1854. And Arthur Hugh Clough, whose iconoclastic poetry refused to conform to English cultural *mores* made friends like Matthew Arnold despair of him, and whose *The Bothy of Tobor-na-Vuolich* (1848) (set in the Scottish Highlands) mocked British social pretentiousness and concluded that the future lay in the new worlds of the colonies.

These last two poets were deeply influential on several Scottish poets who followed their nonconformist approach towards traditional form and content. Along with the new kind of intense poetic prose of Carlyle and his repeated challenges to religious and social orthodoxy in *Sartor Resartus* (1833), *Heroes and Hero-Worship* (1841) and *Past and Present* (1844), poets like James Thomson, Robert Buchanan, James Young Geddes and John Davidson sought, in radically different kinds of language and attitude, to develop the revolt against religious orthodoxy and conventional formal expression.

In re-evaluating Scottish poetry of the period, we need, however, to add a further level of consideration. There is certainly a need to re-assess poets whose once-great reputations sank in the early twentieth century; but beyond them, we must explore the boundaries between accepted 'literary' culture and the achievements of broader popular culture which have hitherto been excluded. Contemporary criticism recognises a neglect of Scottish popular culture, together with a great deal of its poetry, fiction and periodical writing and argues that much important literary material has been ignored or misinterpreted, and consequently undervalued. In addition, it is argued that a bias in critical perspective has denied regional writers their significance, while too often those who left their native country have had their relevance misappropriated or confined within an Anglo-British frame of reference. The nineteenth century in Scottish writing can no longer be simplistically regarded as a stagnant period fostering regional and Kailyard insularity or sceptical detachment. Rather, it is an era of considerable literary production in which writers engaged in complex ways with their Scottish cultural context and endeavoured to formulate new identities and roles within it. There are many forgotten local and national voices, from the poetic and fictional narratives (in Scots and English) on community to the assertive and prose-lytising voices of the secular prophets, who made a distinctive contribution to Scottish culture and literature which deserves to be retrieved.

Locally published writers

William Donaldson in *Popular Literature in Victorian Scotland* (1986) identified what he describes as 'a new type of professional writer' represented by W. D. Latto and William Alexander, moving freely between the newspaper and the popular publishing worlds, as well as a new generation of popular publishing houses based on the newspaper network and reflecting the identity of the areas they served. Writers such as William Alexander, involved with the Aberdeen Free Press, and the poet, James Young Geddes, who contributed to the radical *Dundee Advertiser*, and whose work was locally published, have suffered from critical perspectives, which too readily expect regional literature to be of inferior quality. Yet these writers are far from being 'parochial' in the negative sense of idealistic, nostalgic literature. Both men contributed to the revival of popular periodical writing and engaged with issues of political, economic and social change, as well as showing considerable technical and stylistic skill in their work. Donaldson's sifting of serialised publications has brought to light Alexander's neglected novels, uncompromising in their cultural integrity and their rich and intensely localised Aberdeenshire dialect, which, even more than Galt, allowed characters their own identity and expression – and which of course, in turn, limited its appreciation and influence. In addition to the difficulties of regional isolation from the literary capital and local writers' reliance on local publishing, many nineteenth-century poets like Lanarkshire's Janet Hamilton and Aberdeenshire's William Thom were un-schooled and self-educated. According to Tom Leonard, such autodidacts were by definition excluded from mainstream literary culture. Since they did not fit into the framework of English literary analysis, their thematic interests and phraseology has been prejudged as trite and sentimental by the misapplication of a literary criticism which functions within an alternative frame of reference.

Prejudice: MacDiarmid and Young

Prejudicial criticism has arisen not only from the external perspectives of Anglo-British cultural priorities, but also from the politics of literary criticism within Scotland. Even Hugh MacDiarmid, eager to establish himself at the forefront of a new and dynamic literary movement, presented the previous century as a creative vacuum, a negative situation against which the Scottish Renaissance reacted, rather than as a productive context from which it evolved. In an essay in *John Davidson: A Selection of his Poems* (1961) MacDiarmid suggested that, with the exception of a few poets like Alexander Smith and John Davidson, Scotland's writers had largely failed, and were still failing, to engage with realistic urban poetry, and argued that 'most of our versifiers continued to write nostalgic, pseudo-pastoral rubbish about an Arcadian life, which had no relation to the facts at all'. In his opening comments MacDiarmid had gone even further, baldly asserting that 'there is scarcely any Scottish poet in these three or four centuries [since the Makars] of any technical or theoretical interest whatever.'

MacDiarmid was also antipathetic towards folk culture, and this is reflected in the work of Douglas Young, a poet within MacDiarmid's renaissance movement, and the only critic before Leonard and Donaldson to examine popular literature, in producing his anthology *Scottish Verse 1851–1951* (1952). Young's associations with the Scottish Renaissance and the prevailing critical orthodoxy clearly influenced his opinion that in the Victorian period 'Scottish verse making was mainly backward-looking and sentimental'. Like MacDiarmid, Young claimed that the realities of the industrial revolution and urbanisation had had little or no place in the country's verse. Though he identifies lesser-known poetry, his overall assessment is sweeping and dismissive. Consequently, Victorian verse anthologies like the endless *Whistle-Binkie* series have been accepted by critics as being representative of nineteenth-century Scottish literature in general. This ignores the prejudice and politics which influenced both the criteria of editorial selections as well as the function for which such anthologies were designed, since much of the material was intended to be sung or recited at social gatherings and, therefore, tended toward the comic, sentimental, inoffensive and intellectually undemanding. Such anthologies do not, however, represent fairly the achievement of many of the lost voices of Victorian Scotland.

CHAPTER 20

GEORGE MacDONALD: *PHANTASTES*

GEORGE MACDONALD (1824–1905)

It is remarkable how little is known of the work of George MacDonald, even among educated literary Scots. Yet he was a prolific and well-recognised writer of the middle and later years of the nineteenth century, and his writing career spanned five decades with more than fifty books to his credit. Forty years after his death, in the introduction to *George MacDonald: An Anthology* (1946), C. S. Lewis wrote of him: 'I have never concealed the fact that I regarded him as my master; indeed I fancy I have never written a book in which I did not quote from him.' It is clear that Lewis's own fantastic fiction, and that of the later J. R. R. Tolkien, as well as that of the neglected Scottish fantasist David Lindsay (particularly in *A Voyage to Arcturus*, 1920) were profoundly affected by MacDonald's work in the genre, making it all the more surprising that his fiction, fantastic and realistic, should be so little known to twenty-first-century readers.

George MacDonald's early life in Huntly provided much material for his best Scottish novels. The Highland Jacobite origins, the stern Calvinist leanings of his grandmother that took her to the Missionar Kirk (more extreme than the Established Church), the immersion in strong local dialect and traditions, the sense in which the 'lad o' pairts' had to get education before getting out and getting on in the world – all these seem typical ingredients of the nineteenth-century Scottish ethos, an ethos that in literature became sentimentalised and softened in the Kailyard genre. MacDonald's name has been coupled with the Kailyard novelists; this assessment is being challenged in the current rediscovery and revaluation of his work.

MacDonald had a distinctive education: first in the 'adventure' school of Huntly (supported by the dissenters) rather than the parish school; then at King's College, Aberdeen, where he studied chemistry and natural philosophy in addition to the humanities and moral philosophy, developing also a passionate interest in literature, including the German Romantics; and finally at the Highbury Theological College in London, where he trained for the Congregational ministry. This variety of interests and specialisms produced a scholar of a particular stamp. The blend of scientific knowledge, romantic artistic tastes and theology was bound to produce a kind of thinking quite different from the main strand of Scottish Presbyterianism, moderate or evangelical. On the one hand, MacDonald was pious and devout in his Christian beliefs to a degree that has certainly alienated more sceptical twentieth-century readers than C. S. Lewis. On the other hand, he was profoundly out of step with orthodox Victorian religious opinion, to such a degree that he had to resign after only two years from his first and only charge as a minister (in Arundel, Sussex) having been accused of heresy. Thereafter, he never found a lucrative job, partly because in England, where he lived, non-Anglicans were excluded from most official and academic posts, and so he had to depend on his own writing and lecturing for most of his life.

After going south to London, following his graduation from King's College in 1845, MacDonald only returned to Scotland for occasional family visits and lecture tours. His absence from Scotland was partly dictated by health reasons, but mainly it was because his wife, her family and his growing circle of friends and helpers were English and his chosen life as a writer, lecturer and preacher required him to be based in the South. He and his wife Louisa had houses successively in Manchester, Hastings and London. In later years, from 1878 onwards, with an established reputation as a writer and literary figure, he and his large family lived in Bordighera in Italy for much of each year right up until 1905, the last year of his life. In thinking of MacDonald's writings, it may be relevant to see him as one of the many voluntary exiles who give an exotic flavour to the literature of the nineteenth century. Doubly exiled from Scotland, first in England and then in Italy, his writings about his home country have both the sharpness of the detached appraisal and the sentiment of the man who is generally thinking back to the Scotland of his childhood.

Throughout his long life George MacDonald had constant reminders of how fleeting and uncertain life was. In his childhood he lost two brothers and a sister; his mother died when he was eight years old; and between 1853 and 1858 he lost two more brothers and a sister, as well as his father. Between 1849 and 1857, his wife Louisa had similar losses of close relatives. He himself suffered a severe illness in 1850, which nearly killed him, something that was to recur with varying degrees of severity again and again. Four of his own eleven children predeceased him. It is small wonder that death is a common topic in his writing, and that he developed, perhaps out of necessity, a philosophy of death that entailed looking on it as a friend, as something to be welcomed, a 'great good' that is coming. It was an intimate part of his religious faith, in tune with the Christian belief that one must die in order that one may live eternally, but at the same time it was part of his integrating myth involving nature, love and death in a combined conquest of humanity's deepest psychological fears. This strong mystical and imaginative faith underpins MacDonald's success as a writer of fantastic romance, in which *Phantastes* (1858) stands as the finest example, and which arguably began with MacDonald's interest in children and the child-like imagination. The MacDonalds had eleven children between 1852 and 1867. Visitors remarked how involved the parents were with their children, a feature remarkable for the times, at least where Victorian fathers were concerned. For about twenty-five years the MacDonald family contained at least one child who was of an age to appreciate fairytales and children's stories. MacDonald's period as editor of *Good Words for the Young* gave him the opportunity to have this kind of writing published and widely read. But the appeal of these stories, like that of all good children's books, is not only to children. The themes and preoccupations, their symbols and recurring motifs, are frequently those of his 'adult' fiction. His children's novels, *At the Back of the North Wind* (1871), *The Princess and the Goblin* (1872) and *The Princess and Curdie* (1883) are classics of their kind, but are also important parts of his achievement in mature fantasy. It may be that in writing for a specific childish or childlike audience, MacDonald was able to present both his beliefs and his anxieties, his joys and his despairs, in a more direct way than other genres of writing allowed him. If at times he is heavy-handed in his explanations and moralisings, as if forgetting the age and lack of experience of his readers, he very rarely appears to be talking down to young readers. There is certainly no argument for considering his children's stories apart from his other fiction. Conversely, when he describes *Phantastes* as 'a Faerie Romance for grown men and women', he is not intending to exclude children from enjoyment of it.

Apart from his fantasies and children's books, MacDonald was also a poet, and a prolific and popular Victorian novelist. In novels like *David Elginbrod* (1863), *Alec Forbes of Howglen* (1865), *Robert Falconer* (1868), *Malcolm* (1875), *The Marquis of Lossie* (1877), fiction set in his native north-east, MacDonald combined autobiographical elements, a basically Christian message, a commitment to the use of the Scots of the north east, and a strange mixture of conventional and melodramatic plotting. His vivid Romantic imagination created grotesque situations and imagery bordering on the fantastic, as in *Sir Gibbie* (1879). These naturalistic Scottish novels, with their strange sub-texts and situations, should in the end be considered with his fantasies and seen as integral with them in many of their themes and intentions. MacDonald's overall achievement, including his poetry, is now being re-assessed; it is probable that he will in time be seen again as a major British and Scottish Victorian writer.

From poetry to fiction

Phantastes was MacDonald's first major published prose work. He worked on it in the last two months of 1857, finishing it by the New Year and immediately finding a publisher, who paid him a much-needed advance of £50. Prior to writing it, MacDonald had published a long narrative poem, *Within and Without* (1855), written during his convalescence from serious illness, and a volume of *Poems* (1857). Undoubtedly his first literary ambitions were to be a poet, yet the compulsion to provide materially for a growing family pushed him towards more lucrative prose writing and eventually into the publication of conventional novels aimed at the popular tastes of his time. *Phantastes* marks a stage towards the full-blown novel form, which he attained in 1863 with *David Elginbrod*, a novel that is partly a tribute to his father, who had died in 1858. Thereafter, his writing career was largely dictated by commercial considerations, although there is evidence that he was drawn to the writing of fantasy and children's tales as his preferred genre whenever the financial pressure eased. Nearly forty years after *Phantastes*, MacDonald turned again to the full-length adult fantasy in his bleaker and stranger work *Lilith* (1895). This was met by an even more puzzled and hostile public response than was *Phantastes*, although recent critical opinion recognises it as a work of considerable subtlety and depth.

Phantastes can be seen, therefore, as a transitional work between MacDonald's poetry, where imagination is supreme, and his novels, which are controlled by considerations of plot and readers' perceived tastes. Equally, it is the first example of the genre that MacDonald returned to again and again when circumstances permitted, in which he obviously found the greatest satisfaction and freedom.

FANTASY AND *PHANTASTES*

It is all too easy to look at *Phantastes* from our twenty-first-century standpoint and see it as just another fantasy in which a vivid alternative world is presented for our wonderment and pleasure as a means of escape from the mundane uglinesses of the real world. This viewpoint would have been conditioned by long exposure, perhaps over-exposure, to fantasies in literature aimed at us as children, adolescents and as adults. C. S. Lewis, J. R. R. Tolkien, Mervyn Peake and their more recent imitators, like Stephen Donaldson, Julian May and Tad Williams, have created world upon world of the imagination in a whole genre of fantasy fiction that has fed the jaded palates of post-industrial Western society, occasionally purporting to provide moral and spiritual messages for a materialistic age, but more often retaining any moral stances about good and evil within the borders of the fantasy world.

Such a view of *Phantastes* would be extremely unjust. MacDonald was not following an established fashion for fantasy like many modern writers of the time, but initiating much of what was to become a separate genre, providing models of imagery and episode that would inspire later writers. It would be difficult, prior to MacDonald, to find any similar works in English, or even in the German Romantic literature that so captured him. He was, however, profoundly influenced by the medieval and Renaissance tradition of allegorical chivalric romance, including the work of Malory and Spenser, and the moral and spiritual allegorising of human life developed in English by Phineas Fletcher and John Bunyan. We need to consider the main differences between these purposeful symbolic narratives, capable of being decoded in simple terms of the virtuous Christian life, and MacDonald's more complex and ambiguous fantasy. It may be worthwhile applying to *Phantastes* the definition of fantasy in literature used by Colin Manlove in the introduction to his *Modern Fantasy* (1975):

> [A fantasy is] a fiction evoking wonder and containing a substantial and irreducible element of the supernatural with which the mortal characters in the story or the readers become on at least partly familiar terms.

The story of *Phantastes* has often been likened to a dream, influenced by MacDonald's favourite quotation from the German Romantic poet, Novalis: 'Unser Leben ist kein Traum, aber es soll und wird vielleicht einer werden.' [*Our life is no dream, but it should and will perhaps become one.*] MacDonald attached this quotation to both *Phantastes* and *Lilith*. However, at the end of *Lilith*, MacDonald adds:

> Man desires and dreams; God broods and wills and quickens. When a man dreams his own dream, he is the sport of his dream; when Another gives it him, that Other is able to fulfil it.

This creates an opposition between the type of dream that we usually think of, in which our own unconscious shapes and fuels the sequence of images and events, and a different kind of religious or mystical 'dream' that is the creation of some external agency, which MacDonald would identify as God. There is certainly a dreamlike quality about *Phantastes*, which would lend validity to attempts to interpret it in terms of Freudian or Jungian psycho-analysis. Equally it is possible to discern a religious dimension to it, enabling the reader to see it as a kind of religious experience with similarities to *The Pilgrim's Progress* (1678), which is presented in a dream format, on the model of Dante's *Divine Comedy* (c. 1300). The dream model provides one valid way of understanding the unusual structure and ethereal quality of *Phantastes*.

DREAM AND BALLAD

It is important, however, to consider *Phantastes* in the terms by which it presents *itself* to the reader. The first words of the story are: 'I awoke . . .', thus apparently denying a dream interpretation. Anodos, who has had an en-counter with a mysterious woman who identifies herself as his fairy grand-mother and has been told that he will find a route into Fairy Land, goes as usual to bed and sleeps. It is when he awakes the next morning that he is transferred to Fairy Land via the transformation of his bedchamber into the fringe of the Fairy Wood. Of course it could be argued that this awakening is really the entry into a deeper dream, and that he is asleep all the time. Yet his return, after his experiences, is to a hilltop near his home, and he discovers that he has, in reality, been away for twenty-one days. The narrative implies that Anodos's strange adventure has not been dream but he has been spirited away by supernatural agencies to Fairy Land. On his return, his sisters notice he has changed, and he himself longs to leave this world for the blessedness that had been revealed to him.

There are significant literary precedents for this story within Scottish literature, without having to look to foreign influences. The ballad of 'Thomas the Rhymer', for instance, also presents a meeting with a mysterious woman of power, the protagonist's sexual attraction to her, his transfer to Fairyland, the wonderful experiences there and the eventual return to the world of men with the sense of a mission of truth. More importantly, perhaps, the experiences of the heroine of James Hogg's great tradition-inspired poem, 'Kilmeny', not only echo the Thomas the Rhymer motifs, but add the sense of a mystical vision of Paradise, which renders Kilmeny incapable of settling again in the mortal world through her longing for the great good that she has been shown. What we seem to have in *Phantastes* is the traditional story of the mortal man who crosses the divide to the world of Faerie and is forever marked by it. The story is not a dream but a ballad, yet it is a ballad embellished by the imaginative resources of dream, romance and spiritual allegory.

NARRATIVE AND DREAM REALISM

Much of the criticism of MacDonald's 'realistic' novels has concentrated on the conventionality and lack of originality in his plots. It has been suggested that his didactic purpose, coupled with his speed of writing, led him to skimp the business of plot construction in favour of those elements of imagination and instruction that most interested him and in which he displayed his real talents. Perhaps for this reason, MacDonald, in *Phantastes*, chose to reduce the potential restrictiveness of plot and structure to a minimum. The narrative follows the pattern of a dream, with Anodos, the protagonist, undergoing a succession of dream-like experiences. His easy acceptance of strange occurrences, so different from those of the waking world, exemplifies the phenomenon of 'dream-realism', in that while one is 'dreaming' events are accepted unconditionally; it is only after waking from the dream that they are scrutinised. Given that Anodos is actually removed from his own world into another, this dream-realism is clearly transferred from the dream situation to the 'real' other world of Fairy Land. MacDonald has created a fantasy realm that strikes the inhabitant with its absolute authenticity and realism, and so Anodos makes no comparison between the laws of his own world and the different laws of Fairy Land. He asks questions and learns from different sources about the nature of the place, but he does not marvel or rationally resist what he hears. Not only does Anodos accept the reality of Fairy Land but he keeps finding purposes for continuing his journey through a strange and often frightening place. Different motives are produced by Anodos to keep him moving ever deeper into the forest and then, as Fairy Land widens out, from one kind of landscape to another.

There is always a strong temptation to begin to interpret the narrative in symbolic or allegorical terms. MacDonald's main models and sources of inspiration, particularly Spenser's *Faerie Queene* (1589–96) and John Bunyan's *Pilgrim's Progress*, raise overt Christian interpretations. It would be natural to expect that MacDonald, with his theological training and his strong Christian principles in so much of his life's work, would be using *Phantastes* for the purpose of moral and religious enlightenment, making the book, however indirectly, into a kind of sermon. Yet one should try to resist the impulse to find meanings too early; some may make themselves noticeable early on, but over-exhaustive scrutiny may have the effect of reducing the imaginative power of the story and its images to something secondary; the sweet coating of a moral pill. MacDonald himself was quoted (in a letter from Louisa MacDonald to a woman who had written expressing admiration of *Phantastes*) as saying that 'he has no key to his little work but he is sure that in your appreciation of it, you must have felt some meaning and he has always told his friends to take any meaning they themselves see in it.'

UNIFYING ELEMENTS IN THE NOVEL

Although the narrative has a very episodic quality, there are a number of unifying elements, the most significant of which is the figure of Anodos himself, who serves to bind the succession of events into one narrative thread. His progress through various states of place and mind direct the course of the story and Anodos's development towards some kind of maturity or state of wisdom is one of the central themes of the narrative. But the final conclusion as to the ultimate effect of Anodos's adventure is left ambiguous, with only the comment that his sisters notice 'a great change' in him when he returns.

This focus on the central protagonist gives the story something of the quality of the picaresque novel, in which the hero progresses from one adventure to another. Or in another sense, the mental and/or psychological development of the hero lends to the story the frame of 'bildungsroman' (the account of the formative development of an individual often from a state of childhood ignorance and innocence into maturity) since Anodos has been away for twenty-one days in Fairy Land, and he has just turned twenty-one years in age. A final reading might be to think of the story as a symbolic autobiography of MacDonald himself. However, this again takes us into an early attempt to 'interpret' the story and 'fix' its meaning within one scheme of logic; a rationalisation which the very construction of the story challenges.

Other unifying features in the narrative include the recurrence of significant characters. Anodos meets an Arthurian knight (initially with his rusty armour), keeps company with him for some time, and becomes his squire. He releases a white lady from a block of alabaster, tries to follow her and, after meeting a false white lady, the Alder-Maiden, finds his ideal again as a statue in the Fairy palace; after releasing her again, he finds her finally as the wife of the knight. In the ogre's cottage, he finds a dark shadow, which he cannot shake off permanently until the end of the story. A little girl with a bright globe, whom he meets quite early in his adventures, returns as a grown woman and releases him from imprisonment in a dark tower. The use of these characters in the narrative, along with the constant presence of Anodos, provide a patterning and symbolic unity to the adventure enabling us to see the story as operating within one narrative scheme.

Apart from the introduction, part of the brief after-death episode and the epilogue when Anodos is back home, the setting for *Phantastes* is within Fairy Land. At first Fairy Land is envisioned merely as 'woodland'; the strange forest of so many North European fairytales like the greenwood of the

Scottish and English ballads. Later, it widens out to become a land with rivers and a palace, a sea, other kingdoms, an underground world, and even a religious institution. In the books found in Fairy Land there is an awareness of the real world, its society and its stories. Is this fantasy world itself conceived as an organised system? Or is it an organic invention growing as MacDonald feels the need to widen Anodos's range of experiences, as if the growing personality discovers that the world is always bigger than was thought at an earlier stage of existence?

Perhaps the most noticeable unifying factor in the novel is thematic continuity. Certain motifs and images recur throughout, as indeed they seem to do within MacDonald's fiction as a whole. It is useful to examine some of these and to consider their significance as either personal metaphors, psychological archetypes or religious symbols.

FAIRY LAND

The basic plot device of Anodos's transportation to Fairy Land suggests that it is a land akin to the Other World of ballads, into which mortals can be transported and from which they will later return, having been greatly changed in some perceptible way. And, just as it has been suggested that Fairy Land may be an evolving conception within the fiction, developing from a basic forest location to a larger world that is needed to provide more complex experiences for Anodos than a folk-legend or fairytale setting can provide, it is also a place of moral ambiguity and mutable realities. In Chapter 23 of the book, the knight of the soiled armour says:

> Somehow or other . . . notwithstanding the beauty of this country of Faerie, in which we are, there is much that is wrong in it. If there are great splendours, there are corresponding horrors; heights and depths; beautiful women and awful fiends; noble men and weaklings. All a man has to do, is to better what he can. And if he will settle it with himself, that even renown and success are in themselves of no great value, and be content to be defeated, if so be that the fault is not his; and so go to his work with a cool brain and a strong will, he will get it done; and fare none the worse in the end, that he was not burdened with provision and precaution . . . this fairyland is full of oddities and all sorts of incredibly ridiculous things, which a man is compelled to meet and treat as real existences, although all the time he feels foolish for doing so . . .

In the end, Macdonald leaves his readers to make their own interpretations concerning the nature of Fairy Land in *Phantastes*. There are constant and tantalising implications that it is somehow involved with our world, suggesting either a correspondence or a contrast – but the reader is never sure whether Fairy Land is supposed to mirror this world in its essential nature or to be free of its laws of existence. Is it a world that gives guidance about how to live consciously in our own world, or is its contact with our own confined to the levels of our subconscious or unconscious minds?

IDEAL(ISED) WOMEN

It is revealing to list the characters according to their male or female components. Apart from Anodos (and his doppelganger), the knight of the soiled armour, the brothers preparing to fight the giants, Cosmo in the story read by Anodos, and perhaps the Ash Tree, all the main characters are women or girls. Consideration of their role reveals some interesting parallels and contrasts – notably, in regard to the Fairy Grandmother (Chapter 1), the White Lady who recurs as a character almost throughout the book, and the woman in the island cottage (Chapter 19).

The fairy grandmother (significantly, not godmother) is a character whom MacDonald used again later in *The Princess and the Goblin* (1872). Indeed characters like her, with their fairy ancestry, their ageless appearance, their kindness and their wisdom recur throughout MacDonald's writing. Douglas Gifford, commenting on this character in the story 'The Golden Key', in his introduction to his anthology, *Scottish Short Stories 1800–1900* (1971) sees her as 'Charity in its broadest sense – a mixture . . . of love, imagination and all the other humane qualities lacking in the Scottish scene.' This suggests that MacDonald has turned away from the very masculine Calvinist concept of the stern and just father-figure to set up the more sympathetic and feminine ideal of the wise and loving mother-figure. Yet, interestingly, the fairy grandmother in *Phantastes* is also sexually attractive, although she rebuffs Anodos's incipient advances. And when Anodos looks deep into her eyes, he remembers his mother who died when he was young. So the fairy grandmother combines attributes of the wise old woman, the mother, and the potential lover – the three archetypes of woman so beloved of students of the occult and witchcraft. She is like the Elfin Queen as found in ballads, yet she is also related to Anodos and he shares in the fairy blood. Could this be a suggestion that he shares a similar inheritance of charity, imagination and the gentler graces of life?

The White Lady of *Phantastes* undergoes a number of modifications of a different kind from the fairy grandmother. When first she is seen by Anodos, she is entombed in alabaster. Anodos releases her from this imprisonment or enchantment by scraping away the moss in her 'antenatal tomb' (once again reminding us of MacDonald's fundamental belief that death is the precursor of life) and singing to her. The explicit comparisons are with the story of the Sleeping Beauty and with Orpheus; yet there may be an implicit metaphor of sexual awakening, something that becomes much more explicit later.

From this point, the wanderings of Anodos ('the pathless one') become a quest for the White Lady. The description of the forest and the night in Chapter 6, after Anodos receives his warning from the humbled and tarnished knight, seem to convey a sense of sexual awakening and longing that become focused on the White Lady. It is not surprising that Anodos is beguiled by an imitation of her, the Alder Maiden. There are parallels to the first encounter with the White Lady: the dimly-perceived figure, the sense of coldness, the similarity of the caves, the story (like a song?) that acts like a charm, the separation. But there are also the suspicious details: the distance kept by the lady, the refusal to turn away, the pinkness of the eye. The seduction of Anodos is clear, although not described in detail; there is a clear parallel with the situation of the knight, whose experience was similar. The dual appearance of the Alder Maiden, beautiful from the front yet repulsive and inhuman from the rear, may be a vivid metaphor for the sense of degradation and self-disgust that accompanies a substitution of lust for the ideal of love. The literary parallel of Keats's 'La Belle Dame Sans Merci' is very noticeable. Could there be a link between this episode and the meeting with the shadow, recounted in Chapter 8.

The White Lady herself does not reappear until Anodos has spent some time in the Fairy Palace. She is foreshadowed in the story of Cosmo and his mirror; Anodos then dreams of her, again turned into marble, standing as a statue on a pedestal in one of the halls of mysterious dancing but gradually enveloped in shadow until she disappears. Later, when awake, he finds a vacant pedestal with the imprint of white feet on the black marble, and he is able to sing her back into view, revealing her gradually from the feet up until she is finally freed from the shadow and glows momentarily with life. Anodos's impulsive grasping of her as she sinks back into the marble state breaks a charm and she flees, pursued by him, out of the palace and into a bare wilderness. This episode is rich with symbolic suggestion – and once again readers are left to create their own meanings for MacDonald's enigmatic events. How does one interpret the song sung by Anodos, so exalted in praise of the physical body and so full of sexual associations? Or the White Lady's words, 'You should not have touched me!' and, later, 'Ah! you should have sung to me; you should have sung to me!'? Does this represent a reversal of the previous Alder Maiden episode, with a sexually aggressive Anodos frightening a sensitive virgin?

Anodos is told by the ugly woman he meets in his underground journeying (Chapter 17) that he will see his White Lady again. However, when he does see her, she has changed to become 'altogether of the daughters of men' and is the wife of the knight of the soiled armour. Anodos, who has become invisible, hears them talking sympathetically about him. With jealousy he sees them go together to their bedchamber out of his sight. He does not see the White Lady again until he is dead and conscious of her grieving for him. His last sight of her is when his spirit infuses a primrose, which the lady plucks, kisses and wears in her bosom until it withers. The outcome of Anodos's quest is to lose his White Lady to another in life and gain her only spiritually in death.

In his search for his ideal woman or ideal love, Anodos seems to pass through a number of stages: the discovery of the ideal and the awakening of sexual desires; the falling prey to a degrading love or lust, which tarnishes him and helps to bring the shadow upon him; the aggressive pursuit of his love, which results in his losing her; the observation of her happy and fulfilled with another, though not now in an idealised form; and the union with her on a spiritual plane after shedding his mortal body and its weaknesses. Does this require an interpretation in general terms of the progress of a developing personality through sexual experience, or does it suggest a more personal interpretation related to the author's sense of disappointment with romantic love and the finding of fulfilment in a less idealised married love?

Another main female character deserves consideration; the woman in the island cottage. Again, the reader is left to interpret MacDonald's meaning behind her old, yet unwrinkled face and her young eyes; her windowless cottage with its four doors that lead to different passages of experience; the way that she mothers Anodos; the ballads that she sings; her mission to keep the fire burning in order to preserve the day and to prevent the waters from rising; and her parting words to Anodos that he will come back to her some day and that she knows of something that would satisfy him in any sorrow.

There is a wide range of other female characters: the first cottage woman met by Anodos (Chapter 3); the beech tree (Chapter 4); the woman in the ogre's cottage (Chapter 8); the maiden with the globe (Chapter 9) who returns later as a grown woman to release Anodos from the tower (Chapter 22); the Princess von Hohenweiss in the story of Cosmo and the mirror (Chapter 13); the little ugly woman who can suddenly seem amazingly beautiful (Chapter 17). Given the extent to which women seem to dominate the action of *Phantastes*, it is tempting to conclude that the meanings of the symbolic narrative can be located by reference to MacDonald himself. It is worth remembering that his own mother died when he was a small boy, that his grandmother was a dominating figure in the family embodying some stern Calvinistic attitudes, and that his wife Louisa had been the focus of his devotion since their marriage in 1851, although prior to meeting her he had had some romantic feelings about his cousin Helen Mackay, who had married Louisa's brother in 1844.

THE SHADOW

Anodos is joined by the shadow when he looks into a closet in the ogre's cottage and sees a long tunnel leading to a land of night with stars in the dark sky. The shadow comes running down this tunnel to be united with him, and he has it with him on and off until he dies in Fairy Land and returns to his own home. The shadow's properties are described in Chapters 8 and 9. Different meanings have been suggested for this potent symbol of darkness. Is it guilt, connected with Anodos's sexual fall? Is it despair that blights our perception of the world and its beauty? Is it pessimistic and cynical disillusionment, the worldliness that destroys beauty, childish and naïve pleasures, the delights of friendship and love? All these, and other possible meanings, have been suggested by critics as interpretations of the shadow. Does it need to have one meaning? Or is it most potent as an image when left elusive and unexplained?

JOURNEYS

Although Anodos is engaged in one course through Fairy Land, he nevertheless undertakes a number of different journeys, with different destinations through different landscapes and by different modes of transport. These are worth considering in regard to the changing pace and motivation of Anodos's spiritual progress. It has been suggested that when Anodos is on the move, he experiences good fortune, and he is free of his shadow as long as he is travelling in an eastward direction. There does not seem to be any clear evidence for this. There are one or two indications of direction, but they are not conclusive. Such an interpretation would impose an overtly explicit and fundamentally religious orientation in the journey, and make it more unequivocally a pilgrimage, like that of Christian to the City of God.

What may be more significant are the different *kinds* of journeying that Anodos experiences. He wanders through the forest on foot; he travels by boat on two occasions; he explores a large and complex building, the Fairy Palace; he makes an underground transition between the palace and a desolate beach; he rides as a knight himself and follows a knight as a squire; he finally flies as a spirit after death before finding himself back home. There could be particular associations with each kind of journey. For instance, his travels by boat are experiences of fulfilment and reflection as he is taken, by a purpose not his own, to a destination chosen for him such as the palace or the island cottage, and each follows a kind of death-experience – a deep sleep and an apparent drowning. Following this line of analysis with the other journeys might suggest that they have symbolic qualities that add to the depth of the narrative.

Each stage of Anodos's wanderings leads him to a new kind of experience. The end of his travels in Fairy Land comes after following the path to a temple in the forest, where he is confronted by a ritual that he knows to be evil. His last journey is in the robe of a worshipper; he approaches the high altar and at the throne grapples with a false image and dies fighting a wolf-monster that comes up from the depths. If the aim of Anodos's pilgrimage is to overthrow the symbols and forces of an oppressive religious establishment, then the book may be read in retrospect as a vindication of natural impulses and virtues in the face of theology and organised religion. This would make the book an expression of heresy by George MacDonald; it would also diminish it as a fantasy and a work of imagination. Yet the didactic purpose seems to be there. Anodos ultimately sacrifices himself so that his friend may have his eyes opened to the truth. The journey that started from curiosity and longing to enter Fairy Land and developed as a quest for love has been realised as the assumption of responsibility for the well-being of others.

PALACE AND LIBRARY

The recurrent image of the library in MacDonald's writing is well-documented. The year that MacDonald spent as a tutor in a great castle in the north of Scotland, possibly Thurso Castle, also cataloguing the library and reading deeply in German Romantic literature, left a deep impression on his imagination and provided a symbol of great power for both *Phantastes* and *Lilith*. Just as Jorge Luis Borgés in the twentieth century used the library as an image for an immense storehouse of knowledge, so in *Phantastes* MacDonald utilises the library symbol as the focus of Anodos's stay in the palace, a place where he enters and absorbs the experiences within books as if he were living them. The stories that he recounts, of a distant planet where the women have angelic wings, and of Cosmo and the Mirror, have resonances with and make references to other parts of *Phantastes*. Is the library a symbol of education in the widest and most ideal sense, an education of imagination and feeling? The library chapters are placed centrally within the palace episode, which is itself central within *Phantastes* as a whole (seven chapters between Chapters 1 and 9 and Chapters 17 and 25). There seems to be a deliberate highlighting of this section as pivotal to Anodos's story.

The palace has a number of interesting features: it stands by a river in great gardens like a stately country house; it has a complicated inner geography that Anodos never works out, as if its internal space is in a different dimension from its external appearance; its halls, pillars, courtyards and fountains suggest a Moorish building, such as MacDonald would have known in Algiers where he and his family spent the winter of 1856–7 (there may also be memories of King's College in Aberdeen); its statues of classical marble perhaps derive from his many visits to the British Museum, where he would frequently go to read as a poor new arrival in London a dozen years earlier. The palace is, however, more than the sum of its parts and possible inspirations. It is the great symbol of Fairy power; whoever ruled or ordained the whole of that fantasy world intended it as the capital. It sits like a classical Rome or Byzantium within the Arthurian Gothic world of the rest of *Phantastes*. Yet its inhabitants are elusive; invisible or only glimpsed. It almost seems to hold a greater story than Anodos ever reads or lives through. MacDonald has probably created his greatest symbol here, a powerful imaginative black hole that Anodos is drawn into and eventually escapes from without ever really discovering its meaning.

ENTRANCES AND EXITS

Entrances and exits are of immense significance in MacDonald's fantastic fiction. Consideration of the different ways in which Anodos moves from one place or state to another reveals that the basic concept is of the door or doorway to the unexpected or the different. In *Phantastes*, they can give imaginative satisfaction but, to a considerable extent, they are also plot devices to allow a swift move to another stage of the narrative and a change of tone or atmosphere. The range of 'doors' is striking: the flexible portcullis in the desk; the transformation of Anodos's bedroom into the verge of Fairy Land; the broom closet in the ogre's cottage; the surface of the pool in the palace; the books in the palace library; the exit from the palace; the four doors inside the island cottage; the door of the prison tower; and possibly others. Do they possess any kind of symbolic unity within the imaginative conception of *Phantastes*?

MacDonald as writer and myth-maker

If we define literature as an art whose medium is words, then certainly MacDonald has no place in its first rank – perhaps not even in its second. There are indeed passages where the wisdom and (I would dare to call it) the holiness that are in him triumph over and even burn away the baser elements in his style: the expression becomes precise, weighty, economic;

347

acquires a cutting edge. But he does not maintain this level for long. The texture of his writing is undistinguished, at times fumbling. Bad pulpit traditions cling to it; there is sometimes a nonconformist verbosity, sometimes an old Scotch weakness for florid ornament, sometimes an oversweetness picked up from Novalis.

This comment on George MacDonald's prose style by C. S. Lewis in his introduction to the 1962 edition of *Phantastes and Lilith* may serve as a guide to the examination of the quality of the prose writing in *Phantastes*. There are good and bad qualities to look for: on the one hand, the precise, grave, economical; on the other, the fumbling, the verbose, the over-flowery, the sickly sweet. Yet there are other qualities to be found in MacDonald's writing which the reader should assess, for example, his handling of dialogue; the ways in which he seeks to convey a mood or an atmosphere. If we regard Lewis's comment as pertaining to the whole of MacDonald's work, including a large number of conventional novels written quickly, does it apply significantly to *Phantastes*? Lewis's Introduction also commented on MacDonald's quality as a myth-maker, and it is worth allowing him the final say on this unique writer:

What he does best is fantasy – fantasy that hovers between the allegorical and the mythopoeic. And this, in my opinion, he does better than any man . . . Most myths were made in prehistoric times, and, I suppose, not consciously made by individuals at all. But every now and then there occurs in the modern world a genius – a Kafka or a Novalis – who can make such a story. MacDonald is the greatest genius of this kind whom I know. But I do not know how to classify such genius . . . It may even be one of the greatest arts; for it produces works which give us (at the first meeting) as much delight and (on prolonged acquaintance) as much wisdom and strength as the works of the greatest poets. It is in some ways more akin to music than to poetry – or at least to most poetry . . . It was in this mythopoeic art that MacDonald excelled.

CHAPTER 21

JAMES YOUNG GEDDES, JOHN DAVIDSON AND SCOTTISH POETRY

Reassessing nineteenth-century Scottish poetry

William Donaldson and Tom Leonard have made considerable advances in discovering and reclaiming hitherto neglected literary sources, and in identifying a history of critical bias. Donaldson's *Popular Literature in Victorian Scotland* (1986), and its companion volume of prose excerpts, *The Language of the People: Scots Prose from the Victorian Revival* (1989), together with Leonard's *Radical Renfrew: Poetry from the French Revolution to the First World War* (1990), provide a new appreciation of the cultural climate of the nineteenth century. Donaldson's study of Scotland's regional working-class and lower middle-class literary market has led him to a startling conclusion (Chapter 5):

> On the whole popular fiction in Victorian Scotland is not overwhelmingly backward-looking; it is not obsessed by rural themes; it does not shrink from urbanisation or its problems; it is not idyllic in its approach; it does not treat the common people as comic or quaint. The second half of the nineteenth century is not a period of creative trauma or linguistic decline; it is one of the richest and most vital episodes in the history of Scottish popular culture.

Such a study of popular literature may sometimes seem guilty of making quantitative rather than qualitative assessments; Victorian melodrama and sentimentality frequently occur in the material which forms Donaldson and Leonard's reclamation of a radical tradition. Nonetheless, they successfully highlight a productive and regionally based literary culture, and many undervalued locally-published writers. Leonard and Donaldson establish a context in which the nature of nineteenth-century Scottish literature remains open to debate and revision. They reveal the need for modern literary historians to explore neglected sources of local poetry, especially the work of the many self-taught 'autodidact' poets who remained within their localities

349

and wrote for their local newspapers. Poets like Alexander Wilson, Alexander Rodger, William Thom and Janet Hamilton indicate the existence of an enduring and defiant chorus of regional voices who continued the radical, satirical and vernacular tradition of Fergusson and Burns. In exploring these sources, Donaldson identifies a neglect or partiality within standard literary criticism, and issues of theoretical and critical bias, raising questions as to what standards of criticism are appropriate and applicable. Leonard suggests that it is necessary to examine local poetry outwith the usual criteria of sophistication and style applied to major writers.

Reassessment

In his essay 'Reclaiming Local Literature: William Thom and Janet Hamilton' in *The History of Scottish Literature: Nineteenth Century* (1989), William Findlay urged the reclamation of nineteenth-century local literature from the negative critical orthodoxy which condemned it as nostalgic, sentimental and mediocre. This orthodoxy has been identified by Findlay as developing from J. H. Millar's *A Literary History of Scotland* (1903), which condemned the sickly sentimentality of the Kailyard writers ('the triumph of sugar over diabetes') in ways continued by subsequent literary historians such as William Power, George Blake, Kurt Wittig, David Craig, Maurice Lindsay and Roderick Watson. Findlay notes that, unlike Donaldson and Leonard, these critics focus almost entirely on material to be found in book form or, as with Douglas Young, continue to give predominance to mainstream publications. This ignores both popular newspaper publications and regionally published books of local poetry. The anthologies produced by Leonard and Donaldson, in contrast to their predecessors, indicate the existence of a radical, anti-clerical, realist, urban literature. Findlay suggests that, while much has yet to be ascertained, the existence of such work must qualify the prevailing view of nineteenth-century Scottish literature as uniformly nostalgic and sentimental. Findlay illustrates his point with an analysis of two self-taught, working-class poets, William Thom from Aberdeen and Janet Hamilton from Coatbridge. Their examples, together with Donaldson and Leonard's anthologies, indicate the existence of writers who merit greater attention.

Autodidacts and lonely voices: some neglected Victorian poets

So who are these lost poets? Only a few can be briefly indicated here; readers wishing to explore this intriguing area should begin with the essays by

Donaldson and Findlay, together with Edwin Morgan's 'Scottish Poetry in the Nineteenth Century' in *The History of Scottish Literature: Nineteenth Century*, going on thereafter to the longer studies and anthologies of Donaldson and Leonard, and Catherine Kerrigan's pioneering *Anthology of Scottish Women Poets* (1991).

The poetry of William Thom (1798–1848) shows clearly how Kailyard sentimentality could co-exist with harsh realism and innovative technique and expression. His 'The Mitherless Bairn' and 'Jeanie's Grave', while undoubtedly sincere and deserving to be read within their contexts of poverty and loss, fit easily with their partners in *Whistle-Binkie*, but many of the poems in his *Rhymes and Recollections of a Handloom Weaver*, published after his death in 1880, are bitter in their condemnation of social injustice and church sectarianism. 'Whisperings for the Unwashed' is a long and successful diatribe describing the grim working conditions of weavers, even unto death; it concludes that even then;

> the session saints begrudge ye
> The twa-three deals in death to lodge ye   *boards; coffin*
> They grudge the grave wherein tae drap ye,
> An grudge the very *muck* to hap ye . . .

Thom even had the temerity to mock Queen Victoria in 'A Chieftain Unknown to the Queen'; on her visit to Edinburgh in 1843 the streets were cleared of the poor lest they disturbed her. Thom's 'unknown chieftain' who will not join the adulation has echoes of sixteenth-century Lyndsay's Johne the Common-weill; he is sullen Scottish Want, 'wi' his gathering gaunt, / An' his millions of mourners unseen'.

Janet Hamilton (1795–1873) remained all her life in industrial Lanarkshire, the daughter of a shoemaker who taught herself to read a range of poets from Ramsay to Milton. Her interests went far beyond Scotland – a supporter of Italian freedom, she wrote and was written to by Garibaldi, and she observed in her area the changes transforming rural into industrial Britain. Her poems move from 'A Wheen Aul' Memories' of the past country beauty and characters of her village to sudden contrasts of 'big lums spewin' reek' in the new town of Coatbridge; 'the sweetness is gane, noo it's black Simmerlee'. Like Thom, she is at her best finding new ways to express contemporary wasteland, in a Scots which has adapted to the new social conditions, and a rhythm which echoes the relentless march of industry, as in 'Oor Location':

A hunner funnels bleezin', reekin',
Coal an' ironstane charrin', smeekin';
Navvies, miners, keepers, fillers,
Peddlers, rollers, iron millers;
reestit, reekit, ragged laddies,
Firemen, enginemen and Paddies . . .
Sweatin', swearin', fechtin', drinkin' . . .

Hamilton was bitterly opposed to the evils of drink and its attendant vices, and it is easy to smile at her moral earnestness, as at other women poets with powerful voices like those of the almost unknown Glasgow poets Marion Bernstein (b. 1876) (in poems like 'Women's Rights and Wrongs', and 'Wanted A Husband'), and Jessie Russell (b. 1850) (in 'Women's Rights *Versus* Women's Wrongs' and that most desolate of accounts of child-tragedy, 'The Mother's Story'). Their work should be read in full realisation of its sincerity, and the reality of the conditions in which the poets lived, rather than with regard to how well or clumsily they achieve the rhetoric of established Victorian poets.

And many more poets deserve re-assessment, by no means all of them working-class autodidacts. William Edmonstoune Ayton (1813–65), Professor of Rhetoric at Edinburgh University, could be much more than a comic poet, for example in his ambitious satire on Victorian industrial money begetting money in 'The Golden Age'. Much is genuinely satirical, if lighthearted, like the attacks by Charles, Lord Neaves (1800–76) against the pompous piety of the Scottish Sabbath in 'Let Us All Be Unhappy on Sunday' or his clever deconstruction of philosophical nonsense in 'Stuart Mill on Mind and Matter'; or George Outram's (1805–56) plaintive attack on the long wait for inheritance in 'The Annuity'. And an intriguing voice is heard in 'Moses Peerie' (Principal Storey: b. 1835) and his rattling social and religious satire on 'The Goodly Ironmaster; A Ballad of the Iron Age', which, drawing as it does from 'Glendale and Co', arguably the finest extended satirical poem of one of the greatest and most neglected radical poets of the nineteenth-century, leads into our next discussion.

AUTODIDACT AND LOCAL POET: JAMES YOUNG GEDDES (1850–1913)

An outstanding example of the failure of literary historicism to recognise the contribution which local and self-taught poets can make is to be found in the work of James Young Geddes, now virtually unknown, but arguably one of the greatest of nineteenth-century radical poets, who belongs to a distinguished line of Scottish autodidacts, from James Hogg and John Leyden to Hugh Miller. He was the son of a Dundee tailor and by the age of sixteen he was in charge of the family business. All his life he was an active member of debating groups, religious and secular, and he was one of the most industrious members of the Dundee and Alyth Burns societies; his 'The Memory of Burns' clearly shows his line of literary descent, while 'The Second Advent' shows Christ returned and leading ordinary people out of city and savings banks, in a direct echo of the radical Alexander Rodger's 'Shavings Banks'.

Although in business and public life Geddes prospered, his personal life was unhappy; three of his children died before him, while two sisters died young – perhaps part of the reason why he published no more after his third volume in 1891. Another reason can perhaps be found in his busy community life. He became Bailie of Alyth in the 1880s, and was a founder-member of the local Liberal association. And like Hugh Miller, he took a keen and effective interest in local disputes over issues like land access and sanitation, and played his part on police and school boards. He wrote for *The Dundee Advertiser*, that Whig-and-radical paper founded by Henry Cockburn. All his contributions show him as defender of the people, interested in international debates about labour and public health, contemptuous of the Kailyard – and urging a Scottish cultural renaissance.

He published three volumes of poetry: *The New Jerusalem* (1879); *The Spectre Clock of Alyth* (1886); and *In the Valhalla* (1891). His achievement comprises four radical strands, which weave together to make him the strongest – and last – great autodidact radical poet, in Scotland, and possibly in Britain.

Geddes's Protestant background, with its strong work ethic, doubtless helps – and hinders – his poetry. Like so many Scottish writers (and especially the autodidacts) his attitude towards religion is ambivalent, on one hand willing something in which to believe, on the other sceptical of anything reason will not substantiate. Yet Geddes's innate optimism regarding humanity achieves a rare balance. Despairing anti-religious outpouring was not for him; but as we will see, he admired the honesty of those dark prophets who did agonise, although he turned their epic angst to a new mood of stoic realism, accepting the risks of industry as worth taking for human benefit, if not at all accepting the dehumanisation which machine monotony would bring. Some of Geddes's greatest – and ironically good-humoured – poetry succeeds because it exploits the work of these nihilistic predecessors, turning their religious negation to human affirmation.

The first of these was Arthur Hugh Clough, whose *The Bothy of Tober-na-*

Vuolich of 1848 had a special Scottish and radical resonance; the second was Walt Whitman, who claimed in his introduction to *Leaves of Grass* (1855) that his poetry was 'saturated with the vehemence of pride and the audacity of freedom necessary to loosen the mind of still-to-be-formed America from the folds, the superstitions and all the long, tenacious and stifling anti-democratic authorities of Asiatic and European past'. Geddes sought to emulate him in Scotland, often using Whitman's style and syntax. His poetry remembers the radicalism of Burns, but realises that Scotland in the later half of the nineteenth century needs a different kind of radical voice, one which speaks in a modern, international, and iconoclastic way about the changed faces of community and the rural scene, religion, industrialisation and commerce, manners and society. Geddes did not therefore turn his back on local community; far from doing so, he sought to fuse the strength of local tradition and topic with a universal statement, so that his reflections on Alyth and Dundee grow out of native Scottish experience but speak to the world.

Radical Dundee

If the radicalism of Burns grew out of western Scotland, then the radicalism of Geddes grew out of radical Dundee. In 1793 Thomas Palmer had printed a Reform address which landed him in chains in the Thames hulks with Thomas Muir of Glasgow, and ultimately in Botany Bay. Several other Dundonians suffered this fate. When reform came, Dundee – and many other Angus towns – celebrated by renaming the main throroughfare 'Reform Street'. And in Dundee's Reform Street stand the statues of two of Scotland's greatest political radicals – George Kinloch, the 'radical laird', put to the horn and only escaping transportation by fleeing to France in 1820; and Robert Rintoul, the free-thinking editor of the *Dundee Advertiser*, and later *The Spectator*. These men were all disciples and martyrs to the cause of Tom Paine and his *The Rights of Man* (1791).

Geddes deeply admired their courage and integrity, and the radicalism of older Dundee informs all his work. But equally he deplored the way in which Dundee had given in to Scotland's late nineteenth-century political apathy. One of his finest satirical, prophetic and personal poems, 'The Glory has Departed' is on the subject of Dundee's new and bourgeois snobbery, as its vainglorious city fathers parade to celebrate their newly gained status as a city.

Geddes and radical poetry

It is of course impossible to survey here the whole and mainly unknown work of this neglected writer. All that follows is the briefest of introductions to the four strands of his radicalism, mainly through single exemplars of each. This chapter, moreover, argues the case that Geddes demonstrates the need for Scottish literature to ask how unique was his lonely, compassionate, and undeservedly forgotten voice in Kailyard-dominated Scotland – a voice which, fifty years before MacDiarmid, refused to be dictated to by the Burns tradition, or to restrict itself to the out-moded and eighteenth-century-rooted cult of sentiment. Geddes stands the traditions of radical autodidacticism on their head, eliminating the personal and sentimental in order to focus on contemporary issues of politics, religion, the changing rural economy, the industrial city, and the new materialism and its bourgeois respectability.

RADICALISM AND RELIGION

Scotland was, after the Disruption of 1843, a hotbed of religious debate, as the Established Church contended with the Free Church, and with many other sects and evangelical movements urging the people to greater devotion. Historians like T. C. Smout (*A Century of the Scottish People*, 1986) and Michael Lynch (*Scotland: A New History*, 1991) have pointed to the fact that this atmosphere of religious piety was centred in the upper and middle classes, with much of the new working class in the cities beyond the reach of church ministry. But for those who were part of Scotland's dominant religious culture, Sunday, with its two long church attendances and the rest of the day devoted to uplifting activities, could be a dreary time. It was also an authoritarian time; several ministers were expelled from their ministries for heresy, by church command, during the period. And certainly much of the poetry gloomily dedicates itself to religious moralising and sabbatarian monotony in post-Miltonic epic fashion. What has not yet been appreciated, however, is how such an illiberal and morally conventional society, far from eradicating challenge, led some Scottish writers to make the most radical, satirical and outrageous assaults on established beliefs. Robert Buchanan's poetry shocked his contemporaries by out-cloughing Clough in its reversals of Christian dogma and belief; James Thomson's *The City of Dreadful Night* (1874) (dealt with separately in the following chapter), sometimes wrongly interpreted as an attack on Victorian urban industrialisation, is in fact a sustained attack on religious faith, in the bleakest possible terms of European and Italian scepticism; Douglas Brown's *House with the Green Shutters* began the twentieth century by apparently ignoring the church, but by insinuation, mocking its dead hand in the community; and John Davidson went further than any other British poet in his ferocious repudiation of traditional religious belief.

If Robert Pollock (*The Course of Time*, 1827) and James Thomson represent the opposite poles of morbid belief and unbelief in nineteenth-century Scotland, Geddes refused both, and in extended poems of bracing ironical good humour, turned the debate on its head. The long poem *The New Jerusalem* (1879) mocks, in Byronic style, the boring conventional piety of clockwork church-going in its account of pious Sir Peter's death, remembered for his five pounds donation to repair the church's heating. And beyond wholesome irony at what Willa Muir called 'McGrundyism', or the suffocating Scottish show of respectable piety, Geddes mocks the idea of heaven itself. Its scenery may be gorgeous, its lawns and centrally heated houses flawlessly comfortable, but it quickly reveals itself as monotonously self-righteous in its bureaucratic perfection. All heaven now needs to do is check the ledgers to see if would-be entrants are in their transcripts of kirk-session records, and the rest is quality-assured. Any sane angel has long since gone below.

Its partner-poem *The New Inferno*, the mock-epic sequel, goes further, taking the now bored Peter on a day-ticket trip out of heaven, and then finding an exciting and noise-filled city behind the great portal whose broken sign simply states 'Hope'. The 'Abandon' of Dante has long since fallen off, and Satan has been convinced by Milton that torturing the Damned is useless. And now, with enterprise abounding, in this glorious parody of a city of dreadful night, industry, invention and enterprise have made a heaven of human ingenuity from hell, and Satan can only ask tearfully why he should be reduced to the tour guide. The two poems work with and against each other; the energy and industry of the hell of *The New Inferno* clearly meant to symbolise acceptance of progress and science, in contrast to the sluggish *anomie* of *The New Jerusalem*, its rural torpor akin to the backwater inaction of clocks and town fathers in 'The Spectre Clock of Alyth'.

This thumbnail sketch does no justice to the sophistication of the satire, nor does it capture the wit and the rhetorical innovation of style, fusing as it does the relaxed wit of Byron with the dialectic of Browning and the terse unorthodoxy of Clough. Prefacing his epics with Carlyle's great question to humanity as to why any 'despicable biped' should have the right to be happy, Geddes, alone in his time, invigoratingly sweeps aside the dreary preoccupations of most of Scotland, and instead of monotonously decrying the Mechanical Age, suggests that in it lies our salvation.

A more contemplative poem retains the same spirited optimism. 'The Shoreless Sea' expresses religious doubt akin to that of Arnold's 'Dover

Beach' or MacDiarmid's 'On A Raised Beach', in which conventional faith retreats with the ebbing tide. Unlike in these poems and the great, dark sea that surrounds Thomson's *City of Dreadful Night*, however, Geddes's shoreless sea is neither dangerous nor pessimistic. Like the later Hopkins, Geddes concludes that though God remains unfathomable there is no need to despair; rather than submissive inertia, the dynamic principle is the only way forward. In 'Help Thou Mine Unbelief' he defends the restless, speculative intellect and in 'Calvin' he condemns the lack of compassion in religious dogma, asking 'Where shall we comfort find in system builders?'

All his religious poetry – much of it deeply faithful in a non-dogmatic way – continues this assault on conventional and intolerant belief. Much of it has the iconoclasm of Clough, but with a tempering Humanism which is effective in its constant plea for understanding of other faiths and even unbelief. When he wishes, however, he can be devastating, as in the long poem *The Second Advent*, an extended satire on the return of Christ to Dundee (Grassic Gibbon was to use the theme in an uncannily similar way in the short story 'Forsaken' fifty years later). Christ is judged blasphemous and ostracised by the established church. It opens tersely and ominously:

> The mandate came; 'Prepare the way. The Christ
> Is coming once again to visit earth.'
> His heralds everywhere were visible.
> The minds of men were ill at ease . . .

Wickedly, Geddes describes the preparations – 'admission tickets (not transferable)', reports of missionary work, jostling amongst sects for the right-hand place, and church dignitaries:

> pregnant with expectancy of proud Politico-ecclesiastic place.

Christ of course comes without show, but with stern reproach; and the poem describes the mounting indignation:

> that one hath come among the sons of men / Pretending higher claims than those of earth.

Geddes all too convincingly traces the path to the inevitable decision to:

> denounce this dangerous pestilent / And cry, 'Away with him! away with him!'

357

RADICALISM AND RURALISM

Like his north-east contemporary in prose and fiction, William Alexander (today rediscovered and republished), Geddes had no time for the romanticisation of nature or rural activities. Among many, three extended poems illustrate his wide and highly original range of approach and style. 'The Glenisla Gathering' models itself on Clough's *Bothy*, deploying to great effect his English hexameters to create a pseudo-Ossianic (no mean feat!) mock-celebration of Highland games, inflating caber-tossing and dancing and races to the point of hilarious defamiliarisation. But the Englishman who foolishly questions the ancient resident ends with more than he bargained for, as the author's overblown parody of the heroic turns sour, and the exposure of native ritual for tourists' sake turns to genuinely tragic lament:

> Ah, stranger, thou hast viewed the disgrace and the glory,
> The pride and the shame of the sons of the mountain . . .
> But what availeth their power and their prowess
> When the Saxon is lord of them everywhere, always.
> As Samson made sport in the house of his bondage
> To make merry the hearts of his Philistine masters,
> So now the Gael maketh sport for the hosts of the Sassenach . . .

'The Spectre Clock of Alyth' shows the town's provost gently savaging his peers for their ludicrous backwardness. He parodies the records of the town council to reveal the pettifogging arguments against restoring time to Alyth – for this is the real meaning of the poem. Kailyard village preoccupations are transformed into almost surreal satire, for the motion is eventually carried that if the guano which generations of starlings have dropped on the clock workings, causing them to seize and rust – and taking Alyth out of the world and into a Brigadoon time-lock – should be estimated at the same value as repairs, then Alyth will rise from its ordure into renaissance. The parochial becomes universal; ostrich conservatism is mocked into modernity.

Probably Geddes's most moving satire on rural dream lies in his slow-moving portrait of the vanity of human wishes in 'The Farm'. And now the crucial influence of Whitman can plainly be seen – but Whitman deployed for altogether different effect from the life-affirming, sensuous celebration of an awakening America of thriving ports and cities and plains and races. Geddes realises the enormous potential of the huge variety of line-lengths and rhythms for opposite effects, enabling a complete break with the pastorals of Burns and the *Whistle-Binkie* tradition. Now the long-drawn-out agony of the decent man and wife who dream of the idyllic farm they will gain through their alehouse profits is captured in a way no previous Scottish verse forms such as 'Standard Habbie' or 'Christis Kirk' could achieve, since meditation, surges of false hope, womanly and tragic sympathy, and final graveyard burial of dream, can all be accommodated by Whitman's lyrical suspension between poetry and prose. The theme is indeed that of poetic vision becoming prosaic reality, and the form, utterly new in Scottish literature, is perfect for it. This is a poem which does not lend itself to selective quoting, since its subtleties are interlinked and its Whitmanesque verses cumulative. It is one of the great tragic and ironic elegies of Scottish literature.

RADICALISM, INDUSTRY AND THE CITY

The long poem *Glendale & Co* is quite simply Geddes's masterpiece, his poetic equivalent of Douglas Brown's *Green Shutters*, but written several years before. Here, in its glory, is the Scottish adaptation of Whitman, again directed at targets at which Whitman never aimed. It is Scottish literature's greatest attack on capitalism unhindered by conscience, with a specific target of a kind which even Carlyle never managed to bring into such focus. Like Whitman, whose influence is acknowledged in an epigraph, Geddes catalogues the formidable dynamics of industrial growth. The poem begins in a confident, commanding and even celebratory tone that parodies its subject with an abrupt listing, like company reports or a statistical survey, of Glendale's achievements which reflect the unsettling extent of the firm's power: its factories 'cover acres'; they amount to 'a city in themselves'; the buildings are 'palatial and mammoth'; the firm 'dominates the town . . . it pervades it'. Workers all over the world serve its Victorian captain of industry. Then Geddes begins his real interrogation and undermining of Glendale. This is all the more effective as he allows Glendale an essential decency to family and family servants, but makes him exemplify the fundamental alienation between owner and worker:

> Glendale is a man of domestic habits.
> His home apart from the town, standing secure from observation, in the quiet of the suburbs;
> Round it high walls and tall ancestral trees –
> The latter the abode of colonies or rooks
> (Rooks, true conservatives – no lovers of newness).
> Din of the town not heard here, or only heard in a far-off subdued hum,
> adding to the prevailing sense of repose.
> Seen the tall chimneys, the spires of the churches and hospitals,

359

Between them the haze; over them the glamour of distance;
Not seen the dingy alleys, the filthy closes . . .

No one in nineteenth-century Scotland saw more clearly the slums, the poverty, and its horrific consequences, than Geddes here in his vivid and extended description of the homes of Dundee's workers. His tone changes to a Carlylean admonitory peroration, as he tells Glendale that savage chiefs were better men than him, and that an inexorable law will find him out on earth – let alone in heaven. The unique rhythms of the poem mirror the pace of productivity which de-humanises workers – and Glendale, who has become part of the machine. In this poem, Geddes evokes a sense of fragmentation and dislocation which has affinities with the work of T. S. Eliot and John Davidson.

RADICALISM AND POLITICS

All Geddes's work has political implications – urging reform, decent relations between employer and employee, and the involvement of all people in society. In subtle and symbolic poems like 'Man and the Engine', he enlarges on Carlyle's warning in 'Signs of the Times' (1829) that the foam of industrial and mechanical change will harden into shell, imprisoning the organic being in the systems Man has created. This monologue of a factory worker to his loved-and-hated servant-lord slowly shifts sentience from Man to machine, till the glowing eyes of the machine hypnotise its operative. The symbolism is powerful and clear – and what is even more effective is the way in which, like Hogg's presentation of Scotland's damned, the condemned operative embraces his servitude.

Poem after poem satirically insists on the survival of the human in the politics and the economics of the new world; 'Died on the Street' uses a casual death and a casual crowd to ask, searchingly, what just another life – or death – means; 'In the Valhalla' rejects the glorification in Westminister Cathedral of so-called 'Glorious Great Ones' of politics and war as 'colossal, adamantine sculptured slanders on the race', insisting that 'Man is only great in common, man is never great alone.' 'I will shun thee, O Valhalla', he concludes, this time rejecting Carlyle in preferring the ordinary human to hero-worship.

It is fitting to leave him with one of his finest political poems, a lament for the lost radicalism of Dundee. 'The Glory has Departed' uses Whitman one last time to deplore what has happened to the old radical town of Kinloch, Rintoul and Palmer, now that the bourgeois, burgesses and bailies are concerned about where they will be placed in the procession celebrating

Dundee's formal ascension to the status of a cathedral city. ('Shall we now claim precedence of Liverpool, Glasgow, Perth (especially Perth)? / Perth will be brought low: . . .'):

> Mine own town,
> Dear old town!
> Town with the unbroken Radical history
> Town that ever stood first for reform and independence;
> Town where Wallace declared the national freedom;
> Town that stood for Knox and the Reformation;
> Town where the Tree of Liberty was planted;
> Town where Kinloch stands, menacing even yet in bronze unjust governments
> Dear old town!
> Other men are sending thee letters of gratulation.
> I will send thee no letter of gratulation
> I will send thee rather a note of condolence bordered with black round the edges . . .

The work of Geddes is ripe for reassessment as the outstanding radical poetry between Burns and MacDiarmid.

Poets against religion:
James Thomson, Robert Buchanan and John Davidson

In contrast to the affirmative material dynamism and humanity of Geddes is the work of Thomson, Buchanan and Davidson, who may be grouped together as poets of negative religious revolt. Thomson's great epic of spiritual pessimism is discussed in the next chapter; we shall consider the other two briefly here.

In histories of English literature Robert Williams Buchanan (1841–1901) rarely receives more than passing comment. In accounts of nineteenth-century Scottish poetry he is either ignored or dismissed. In 1903, J. H. Millar set the tenor of critical comment by accusing Buchanan of insincerity, claiming 'scarce a line he has written bears the true stamp of emotion'. In his essay on 'Scottish Poetry in the Later Nineteenth Century' (in *Scottish Poetry: A Critical Survey*, 1955) Douglas Young found that 'in 534 double-column pages of *Poetical Works* (1884) I found hardly five readable' while more recent critics have found his poetry derivative, repetitive, swaggering and insincere. Yet Buchanan's technical skill and his sincerity in his social and philosophical thinking are considerable, and a forceful part of the Scottish religious revolt.

Buchanan's father was a follower of Robert Owen, the founder of New Lanark, and from him Buchanan inherited his materialist socialist standpoint. Like Geddes, he was deeply concerned with social issues; and he shared both the sense of alienation and a preoccupation with religion common to Davidson and Thomson. Buchanan experienced a lonely childhood, as his family were considered to be 'heathens'. He deeply resented the 'dismal superstition' that persecuted himself and his family – and yet religious imagery and a prophetic tone haunt his work. His sense of being the alienated outsider is reflected in poems such as 'The Ballad of Judas Iscariot', 'The Outcast', and 'The Wandering Jew', poems which reverse conventional piety in ways comparable with the treatment of outcasts in Davidson's poetry. The idea that religion restrained intellectuality is also shared with Davidson. But while Buchanan could neither believe in God nor accept Thomson's presentation of life as a meaningless experience, his poetry is nevertheless deeply contemplative and absorbed in spiritual quest. Poetry such as 'The Strange Country' reveals the mystic, searching emphasis of his thought. In 'The Outcast', 'The Devil's Case' and 'The Book of Orm' he, like Geddes, presents Satan as a dynamic figure, interested in man's political and social welfare and his intellectual advancement, for which he incurs God's wrath. Buchanan draws extensively upon Christian imagery and delivers his secular Humanism in the style of a prophet. Placed within a Scottish context, and compared with the other writers considered here, Buchanan's sincerity becomes evident, inviting reappraisal.

JOHN DAVIDSON (1857–1909)

Davidson was born in Barrhead, in Renfrewshire. He was the son of a minister of the Evangelical Union and his father's stern creed had a profound effect on him and all his work. Little is know about his earliest years; he was schooled in Greenock till 1870, then he worked for Walker's Sugar Company, later as assistant to the Greenock Public Analyst, and as a pupil-teacher in Greenock Academy from 1872 to 1876. He studied for a year at Edinburgh University after this, but finding academic life not to his taste, began instead his life-long habit of wandering the countryside. Leaving university early, he held a succession of unhappy teaching posts from Glasgow to Perth, in Glasgow again and then on to Paisley. He married in 1884, at the end of this teaching stint, and worked for a Paisley thread firm, experiencing the comparative poverty which feeds into poems like 'Thirty Bob a Week'. He had two sons, and family demands forced him back to his unhappy profession of teaching (1885–8) at Morrison's Academy in Crieff. This 'shameful pedagogy' and 'hellish drudgery' occupied his years at a private school in Greenock, his last spell as a teacher.

In his Glasgow years Davidson made friends with John Nichol, the University's Professor of English Literature, and was introduced by him to the work of Thomas Carlyle, as well as developing his interest in mainstream English writers like Spenser, Shakespeare, Milton and Bunyan and the Romantic poets, Tennyson and Browning, although less fortunate perhaps was the post-Romantic influence of Swinburne. From the Scottish tradition Scott, Carlyle and the poetry of Alexander Smith made a deep impression on Davidson. He began writing very early; his first major works are the play *Bruce* (1886) (considered by some to be a substantial contribution towards Scottish historical drama), *Diabolus Amans* (1885), *Smith* (1888) and *Scaramouch in Naxos* (1890) – all drama; novels, from *The North Wall* (1885) to *Perfervid* (1890), as well as short stories; and the poems which made up *In a Music Hall* (1891).

The move to London, journalism and the Rhymer's Club

With the '90s Davidson decided to break with what he felt to be the parochial limitations, dreich religiosity and social conformity of Scotland. Encouragement from writers like George Meredith pushed him to try for success in the London literary world as a full-time writer. Arguably, the decision to repudiate his cultural roots and to seek an identity in the mainstream of southern English writing was to lead directly to his suicide in 1909. For Davidson swapped one kind of drudgery for another, that of monotonous teaching for hack journalism, contributing to the *Glasgow Herald* and English papers in order to survive from day to day. At first things looked bright. As a member of the Rhymer's Club from its beginning in 1891, he became friends with major writers like Beerbohm and Gissing; his lyrics were appearing in the fashionable *Yellow Book* and while *In a Music Hall* had failed, his *Fleet Street Eclogues* (1893) and *Ballads and Songs* (1894) were very successful. Yeats considered him one of the most promising of the new poets, and at the same time his adaptation of François Coppée's *Pour la Couronne* (*For the Crown*) (1896) fitted perfectly with the fashionable movement in modern drama. The success, however, did not last. Davidson's poems and plays steadily proved less popular and towards the end of the century he found himself increasingly in financial difficulties. On the death of his father in 1893, he was forced to assume financial responsibility for his mother and sister, as well as provide for an alcoholic and psychopathic brother.

Withdrawal and suicide, 1909

The records of Davidson's closing years are obscure. His friends tried to help him but despite Davidson's apparent love of Bohemian sociability they recognised in him a thrawn Scottish individualism which led him away from London's social life to his habitual and lonely traversing on foot across the countryside, and to the life of a comparative recluse in Shoreham from 1896, and later in Penzance. He did get a Civil List pension of £100 in 1906, but by then it was too late and too little. From the turn of the century on, Davidson was moving into unsaleable, if impressive, epic poetry and philosophical dramas which had no hope of immediate popularity or theatrical production. Ahead of his time and behind his time, desperate to be part of the modern movement of fashionable London, yet repudiating all condescension and retreating to his unfashionable southern coastal suburbs, he grew bitter. His increasingly bleak philosophical materialism rejected all creeds and all literary and social contact. Recurrent in his poetry is the theme of the wounded animal or 'Man Forbid', seeking peace through self-destruction – more explicitly even, through drowning. All the evidence suggests that Davidson committed suicide; though, in keeping with his strange life, the final facts remain unknown.

Four poetic strands

There are, broadly, four interweaving strands or categories within Davidson's poetry. While never in love with the idea of a separate Scotland and a separate cultural tradition, there is firstly a strong 'Scottish' strand, especially in his earlier poetry. Secondly, and from the very beginning, there is a contrary strain which loves the exotic and romantic. In this strain he outdoes the Romantics themselves, following in the line of Byron in his audacious attacks on conventional morality. Thirdly, there is the poetry of the under-dog, perhaps Davidson's most appealing side, in which he identifies with individuals – or even animals – isolated and threatened by an adverse, post-Darwinian and materialistic world. And fourthly, there are the great *Testaments* and autobiographical examinations, in which Davidson, in the last ten years of his life, develops his highly personal and esoteric doctrine of pure materialism. In addition to these, there is a series of strangely imperialist poems which, by the standards of today, are unattractive, but which emerge not so much from latent fascism as from Davidson's materialist philosophy. In these poems, it can be argued, he is not so much praising English domination as postulating the inevitable triumph of English constitutionalism and ideology – wrong headed, perhaps, but in an eccentric rather than wilfully imperialist way.

Critics have tended to categorise Davidson's poetry differently; for example, in terms of his attempts to work in an immense variety of technical and thematic types – from ballad to eclogue, from Browning-like dramatic monologue to personal confession. Davidson's major critics, Townsend, Turnbull, and O'Connor, all point to his original treatment of older genres or verse forms, so that when Davidson writes a villanelle or a ballad, he is knowingly exploiting or even parodying the form in order to force it into a new era, to adapt it to a modern world. Davidson's work is so varied, and indeed so complex in its ironic approaches, that no single classification system will completely suffice.

Mocking the Burns cult: Davidson and MacDiarmid

'Ayrshire Jock' is one of Davidson's finest 'Scottish' poems. Immediately it reveals Davidson's difference in approach from that of previous Scottish poets. There is no one in the nineteenth century who consciously parodies the tradition of Burns with anything like the sophistication of Davidson. John Auld, scribbling in his Sauchiehall Street garret, is simultaneously both parody of the *Whistle-Binkie* tradition and of Davidson himself. In a sense Davidson is describing the plight of the late nineteenth-century Scottish poet – doomed to give the public what it wants, betraying his own native instincts, and yet still unsuccessful because Scotland itself is unsupportive of poetry and the arts. The poet remembers his 'roughcast cottage' with its 'sea-green shutters'; he is identifying himself, Jock Auld, with 'many another lad from Ayr', and as he drinks, he claims that 'whisky and Burns made me a poet'. There is a clear anticipation of MacDiarmid's parody of Burns Suppers, and the Burns cult, in the opening of *A Drunk Man Looks at the Thistle* (1926):

Just as the penny dreadfuls make
The 'prentice rob his master's till,
Ploughboys their honest work forsake
Inspired by Robert Burns. They swill
Whisky like him, and rhyme; but still
Success attends on imitation of faults alone:
To drink a gill is easier than to stir a nation.
They drink, and write their senseless rhymes,
Tagged echoes of the lad of Kyle,
In mongrel Scotch:

> Didactic times in Englishing our Scottish style
> Have yet but scotched it:
> In a while our bonnie dialects fade hence . . .

The 'mongrel Scotch' is remembered by MacDiarmid in his 'pigeon English and in wild fowl Scots'; and the 'lad of Kyle' is a direct predecessor of MacDiarmid's ironic comments on the tradition of Burns.

Davidson, Green Shutters and Douglas Brown?

But Jock Auld is caught in a predicament. He refuses, seeing, like MacDiarmid after him, the debasement of the Burns tradition, to write in Scots – just like the early Christopher Grieve:

> But I am of a stronger wing
> and never racked my brains or bones.
> I rhymed in English, catching tones
> from Shelley and his great successors . . .

Jock is between a rock and a hard place; he has the curse of his pedigree and whisky, which has brought him to the garret; but he has his thrawn independence and his desire to evade the parochial. Note the disgust in the vision of his boyhood – seen now as nightmare. It would be pleasing to think that the 'sea-green shutters' of the fifth verse contributed to George Douglas Brown's adoption of a title for his equally scathing treatment of Ayrshire parochialism. The poem ends, just as with young John Gourlay in *Green Shutters*, with a return to the glass of whisky toddy – and oblivion for the Scottish poetic tradition. Davidson, while repudiating the vernacular, is continuing another old Scottish tradition of dramatic monologue, which runs from Allan Ramsay and Burns's 'Holy Willie's Prayer' to the prose monologues of Galt's Micah Balwhidder, Hogg's Robert Wringhim and Ephraim MacKellar of *The Master of Ballantrae*.

Davidson has two more fine monologues, that of 'The Reverend Habakkuk McGruther of Cape Wrath, in 1879' and 'The Rev. E. Kirk, B. D.'. The first is an explicitly savage satire, the second more subtle; and both show that Burns has left his mark, as have the similar, but less effective religious satires of Stevenson in *Underwoods*, published a few years before. These poems may not be in Scots, but, like 'Ayrshire Jock', they must be read with a Scottish accent. Davidson rejects any possibility of writing a poetry which is enthusiastic or celebratory about Scotland's present or future, instead presenting Scotland through his satires as an inbred, narrow-minded fools' paradise – an extreme view, but one which he unfortunately accepted, perhaps as a result of his narrow and unhappy upbringing. It is no accident that both of these speakers are ministers, like his father, and that in each of them a complacency and self-centred egotism is revealed. As with Galt's ministers and provost, these small-minded men see themselves as the centre of the universe. There is also something, in the second verse of the Reverend Habakkuk's monologue, of James Hogg's revelation in *The Justified Sinner* that Scots love their own damnation, in which the minister says that to take from Scotland its 'dear damnation' would be like taking from space the 'law of gravitation'. Scotland must, 'for Heaven's sake, have Hell'. This is clever, in a distorted way; if Scotland is distorted, then this reaction to it is equally so.

More subtle is the way in which the Reverend Kirk, in a manner which can't help but remind us of Galt's Micah Balwhidder, eschews melodramatic overstatement and instead reveals himself inadvertently through a much more complacent love of the things of this world. McGruther is all nightmare theology; Kirk (the name symbolic of how Davidson views the comforts of the Established Scottish church) is all property, with fifty acres of glebe, his thriving corn and poultry and cattle, his 'solid steeple' which he counts amongst his 'other earthly prizes'. Here is a fit companion for Holy Willie's love of 'grace and gear'. Kirk has faith, but it is faith in his stipend, his harvest, his salmon fishing. The poem is probably unfair as regards the workload of the Scottish minister, but is effective in its caricature of Kirk's once-a-week sermon, which he writes while sipping his toddy. Presiding over births and marriages, fishing and shooting, perhaps taking a wife after he has sown his wild oats, all reveal the intense worldliness of this satirical caricature of Scotland's religious leaders. It is even hinted in the poem that, rather than an omnipotent God, it is the stars that have given him his fate – this would certainly chime with his cynical tone, which implies that he has manoeuvred himself deftly into a fine sinecure, which will benefit his children when he dies.

These are perhaps Davidson's most successful Scottish satires; when he tries to work in different modes, as in the descriptive pieces 'Winter in Strathearn' and 'Kinnoull Hill', he is perhaps less successful. Compared with the dramatic monologues, there is an immediate loss of power, in that the speaking voice behind the poems is no longer dramatically envisaged, and the voice which speaks in these two poems is constrained by an over-elaborate romantic and non-Scottish diction. Words like 'greaves', or the low hills 'scalloped' against the higher hills behind, or, in 'Kinnoull Hill', 'coign', and 'daws' for jackdaws work in opposition to the Scottish situation. There is something of the folk-ballad manner in 'she crumbled the brown bread, she crumbled the white'; but the introductory line has little narrative function within the poem. Both poems lack any development beyond mere atmospheric and scenic evocation, as though Davidson is having difficulty in finding an appropriate voice for his subject.

Davidson's development of traditional ballad

Davidson did try to write in the traditional ballad manner of Scotland, as in 'The Queen of Thule'. ('Thule' is traditionally used to indicate a far-off northern part of Scotland, and the prince in the poem is from the Orkneys.) But his aim seems less to be that of developing the classic ballad tradition, than imbuing it with a new kind of ghastly, morbid and desolate thrill. Indeed, in many of his ballads (particularly the horrific extended ballad amongst the later testaments called 'The Ordeal' in which he completely travesties the traditional romance of the Crusades, and piles sadistic horror upon horror) Davidson seems to have as his main intent an adjustment of the old form to prove the point that nature and life are malignant and are a mockery of man's hopes. Here, he is still enough in touch with the old ballads like 'The Great Silkie of Sule Skerrie' or 'Edward' to keep the basic situation of lovers, crossed and doomed, dying for one another. It is worth making a comparison, however, between a traditional ballad like 'Thomas the Rhymer' and Davidson's version. Here is the traditional topic of the great seer of the Borders, so common to oral literature and to the work of Scott, Hogg, and Cunningham; but in Davidson's poem Thomas has been reduced to a mere ironical observer, while his treatment of the central situation, his rendering of Thomas's prophecy and the description of the 'scornful Earl', are presented in an ornate diction and an extended verse which abandons the terse minimalism of traditional balladry.

Negative attitudes to Scotland: Davidson and John Baliol

Davidson's treatment of Scottish themes is manifestly negative. His presentation of Thomas the Rhymer's visions of the desolation of Scotland on the death of Alexander III, his attitudes towards Scottish culture and religion, even his rather passive and disembodied scenes of natural description, all leave an impression of Scotland as a benighted, remote and anachronistic place. It is significant that his longest and most ambitious Scottish poem (leaving aside his very ambitious verse play *Bruce*) is 'John Baliol at Strathcathro'. What Davidson creates is a kind of Scottish poetic version of Shakespeare's *Richard II*, in his picture of an ineffectual, weak but ultimately honest man trying to clutch at the rags of his dignity in the face of a much more forceful and dynamic power. Davidson seems to intend John Baliol to stand as a representation of Scotland and the Scottish situation throughout history, and he concludes his derogatory depiction with an unflattering portrait of the sycophantic Annandale/Bruce trying to wheedle the future throne of Scotland from Edward. Davidson seems to go so far in this poem as to imply that Edward's role has a legitimacy – at least of leadership and power. The poem is fascinating in its post-Shakespearean language and style; the matter of Scotland is treated through the language of the English literary tradition. Davidson works here with language not just from Shakespeare but from Tennyson's *Idylls of the King* and pre-Raphaelite poetry with its love of pseudo-medievalism. Again, one is tempted to see in the figure of John Baliol something of a reflection of Davidson's own situation – stranded somewhere between respect for a dominant external culture, and a sense of his own Scottish identity reluctantly asserting itself.

There are few Scottish poems after this, unless one counts the autobio-graphical poems like 'A Ballad in Blank Verse', 'A Woman and her Son' and *The Testament of John Davidson* (1908), which essentially belong with later poetry as attempts to express his increasingly complex materialist philosophy. Their 'Scottishness' is merely a basic premise on which, for Davidson, much more important issues then build themselves.

Non-Scottish 'exotic' poetry: Davidson and Nietzsche

A brief survey like this cannot do justice to Davidson's range and achieve-ments. His second strand of poetry, arbitrarily identified here, illustrates just how wide that range could be, as he moves as far as possible in the opposite direction from Scotland. A poem like 'The Mahdi' is both an early example of this desire to present dramatic monologues through a *persona* completely different from the small-town Scot, and an interesting revelation early on of Davidson's Messianic tendencies.

If Carlyle influenced him greatly, perhaps the other single most important influence on his work is the poet-philosopher Nietzsche, whose theories of the *Ubermensch* and The Will to Power proved most attractive for late nine-teenth-century disbelievers seeking some other kind of credo, but one which located itself amidst humans rather than gods. The title refers to the religious leader Mohammed Ahmed ibn Seyyid Abdullah (1843–85) who had declared a holy war against the corrupt Sudanese in 1881. He was the opponent of General Gordon at Khartoum; and Davidson reveals his respect for men of ruthless power (on either side) in his praise or celebration of the ruthless will of this historic leader. The imagery is apocalyptic, and although the religious zeal described here dwarfs anything Calvinism can offer, there is something of a Doctrine of the Elect running through the poem, in the Mahdi's complete sense of his own right and authority. Such a man appealed to Davidson because, in a world of compromise and materialism, of corrupt placemen, whether British or African, this *Ubermensch* took destiny into his own hands – as Edward had done with Scotland, and as Davidson willed Britain to do at the turn of the century, at whatever cost.

Hatred of religion and love of the superman

There is an interesting paradox revealed in Davidson's attitude to religion; he is at once condemnatory of all earthly creeds and illusions, but here, as elsewhere, and in his own attempts to set himself up as a Carlyle-like leader in his testaments, there is a typical Victorian prophetic urge which, ironically, devalues his own protestation that religion is an empty creed. The poem 'Cheops' takes this theme to its absurd conclusion. The speaker is the King of Egypt of 2900 BC, and the builder of the great pyramid of Gizah. His legendary cruelty to men – and his own family, since he prostituted his daughter to get money to build – identifies him again as one above mortal laws; and again, like the Mahdi, he is someone who repudiates all controls, but asserts himself as a new god. And a new tone for Davidson has emerged (though it may be implied in 'The Mahdi') which is found in his almost Swiftian disgust with human beings. 'Methinks I'd sooner be a beast or bird / Than enter once again a human frame . . .' 'says Cheops; yet his overweening cruelty is nevertheless allied by Davidson to a grandeur of savage yet admirable wilfulness. Once again a contradiction operates. Here, in Cheops, is a man who represents the enslavement of mortals by false gods and beliefs – yet Davidson clearly admires the embodiment of the power that saw the building of the pyramids.

A quieter poem in this category is 'Thoreau'. This American writer and naturalist of the nineteenth century was attractive to many who lost their faith, because of his calm assertion of pantheistic and incarnate religion. Once again, however, for all that the poem is quiet, this is a man who stands alone. It is the testament of an isolated figure who has been mocked and called a hermit, but who in scandalising the world is bringing a vision for the future. This and other dramatic monologues illustrate how categories blend into each other. 'Thirty Bob a Week' is a dramatic monologue, but its ideas come from very different directions. The sense of human beings in isolation will carry over into poems of the underdog and the recluse, as in 'The Ballad of a Nun'. Indeed, the culmination of this trend of exotic *personas* will come full circle to the great *Testaments* themselves, with their intense imaginings of the Vivisector or the Man Forbid.

'Thirty Bob a Week' and poetry of the underdog

The third strand of poetry can be described as a poetry of the underdog, of the social recluse, or even of the animal isolated from the herd. Outstanding here is Davidson's most famous poem, 'Thirty Bob A Week'. It appears to identify with the wage-slave as the typical representative of the clerking thousands who helped make possible the industrial revolution and nine-teenth-century imperialist expansion. It should be remembered that David-son himself shared much experience with the clerk, if not with the actual working-class idiom and language. He had clerked himself at various points in his life, and knew poverty, and the worry of feeding a family. The *persona* very clearly identifies with an underclass which speaks defiantly to its employ-ers. The poem has been identified as heralding Modernism in English poetry and is consistently praised for its mastery of ordinary language, signalling a new idiom in poetry. It is often seen as remarkable, too, in its courageous defiance represented in the clerk's resistance to self-pity and his willingness to fall 'face forward, fighting, on the deck'.

Is this really the meaning of the poem? In verse two, it appears that, far from resisting, the clerk accepts the class hierarchy and dispensation, in his 'It's just the power of some to be a boss / And the bally power of others to be bossed . . .'. He faces the music, accepts his mole-like journeyings in the underground, accepts that his 'missis stitches towels for a hunks', and in the end has no fundamental criticisms to make of 'Mr Silver-Tongue' at all. But the clerk eventually asserts to us, the readers, as well as his employers, that he is 'saying things a bit beyond your art' – that is, he alleges that he has insights into life beyond that of the bourgeois employer or the sophisticated reader of poetry? Isn't there an extremely unusual and 'non-underdog' representation here at the heart of the poem, when, from verse eight onwards, the clerk looks into his heart and finds demonic id-like elements ('a god-almighty devil singing small') who would, like Mr Hyde, like to crush and destroy his enemies, but for the 'sort of simpleton beside', that goes alongside the Devil? The clerk goes far beyond popular idiom in his description of 'my good and evil angels' that walk along the High Street with him, and as the poem develops, there is an increasing implausibility in his deep and eccentric ideas. Colloquial idiom becomes stretched to breaking-point in the clerk's attempts to express what is in effect Davidson's materialist philosophy – 'But I have a high old hot 'un in my mind', followed rather improbably by 'A most engrugious notion of the world / That leaves your lightning 'rithmetic behind . . .'.

'Thirty Bob A Week' has deeper meanings beneath the simple defence of the underdog. It is an early attempt of Davidson's to fuse the ideas of Darwinian evolution and the *Ubermensch* theory which later composed his theory of scientific materialism. What the clerk is incongruously trying to say is that it is right that he works himself to death as part of the inevitable evolution of man, fulfilling a destiny laid down 'A million years before the blooming sun'. He must accept his lot because all predestined (scientifically predestined rather than God predestined) life has led him to be in the predicament he is in now, ever since the time of 'mollusc or of ape'. It is significant that the clerk concludes by saying that 'it's just the very same with a difference in the name / As "Thy will be done" . . .'.

'The Runnable Stag'; English rural poetry?

If this argument is valid, then we must look more closely at the apparent 'underdog' nature of these poems. Indeed, there is a sense of doom about them which is explained perhaps by their close approximation to Davidson's own psychological and financial situation. Taking this further, another of his popular poems, 'The Runnable Stag', can be seen (although in a totally different idiom) as something of a gloss upon the previous poem. It's typical of the range of Davidson's poetry that he moves from the suburbs and urban poverty to such images of rural beauty and traditional English activity as in this Tennyson-like poem. But this is no 'D'ye Ken John Peel?'; we are not long in the poem before we realise that the 'we' voice, which presents the poem in a vigorous galloping rhythm, has a very different ambience in mind than that of bucolic and cheerful English folksong. This stag will indeed run contrary to this popular and traditional voice; the narrative 'we' is a deliberately misleading reference, in that it tricks us into a sportive and festive celebration, but (like so many of Davidson's parodies of accepted forms) goes slyly in a different direction. The stag may be 'runnable', that is, it is a superb physical specimen, leading them a merry dance, a fit prize for such brave endeavour, and so on; but it becomes heroic in a different sense – a metaphor for Davidson's own defiance of society, prouder and more heroic than the squalid human context within which it is found. Four verses from the end the stag is still running and baffling the lore of the hunstmen and the hounds; and escape can only lie in death:

When he turned at bay in the leafy gloom
In the emerald gloom where the brook ran deep
He heard in the distance the rollers boom
And he saw in a vision of peaceful sleep . . .
A runnable stag in a jewelled bed
Under the sheltering ocean dead
A stag, a runnable stag . . .

The 'fateful hope' which lights up the stag's eye is now suspiciously human, imposing Davidson's own dislike of the herd upon the human society in pursuit. The poem is all the more poignant in that it so early anticipates Davidson's own death in 1909, almost as though deep in his own fascination with the predicament of the recluse is an inkling that this fascination has but one inevitable destination.

'The Ballad of a Nun': pain as the principle of the universe

One of Davidson's most famous poems was 'The Ballad of a Nun'. He was deeply offended by imputations that it was about debauchery and nympho-mania, a kind of release from repression of prim Victorian morality. True, the nun in repudiating her convent finds herself 'a grave youth nobly dressed', and confesses her 'great desire' to him, and loses her virginity. But Davidson is surely right to claim that the complete meaning of the poem, as with 'A Woman and her Son', is a much more important symbolic movement to a fierce recognition that all beliefs of afterlife, of divinities, of divine solace, are empty promises; and that life is simple material experience. Davidson develops the emphasis in this poem on the nun's recognition of pain as a basic human state into the great theme of the *Testament of a Vivisector* (1901) where pain becomes the active dynamic principle of his materialist universe. 'A Woman and her Son' and 'The Wastrel' both stem from Davidson's feelings of guilt in rejecting the love and beliefs of his parents. There is something extremely personal in 'The Wastrel' and its revelation of the way in which the preacher condemns his own son amidst the congregation when the son is on a visit home; in the way that the poem wriggles with embarrass-ment in this public condemnation; and in the heartfelt cry of the son at the end, horrified by the shame of his mother and sisters – 'Oho, for London town again, where folk in peace can die, / And the thunder-and-lightning devil of a train that takes me there!' Isn't this a passionate cry by Davidson for the right to be the 'wastrel' or the defiant rebel, the man alone?

Davidson's jingoism

There is a corollary to these apparently sympathetic poems. They are not as deeply humane as they might at first seem, but are indeed extended metaphors of Davidson's own personal agony. It might be salutary here to look at an unattractive jingoistic strain in Davidson's poetry in order to see how far he really did appreciate the plight of the ordinary man. Poems like 'Merrie England', 'A Song of Change', the 'Ode on the Coronation of Edward VII, of Britain and Greater Britain, King', and the 'Song for the 24th May' are revealing in their blatant English and British assertion; and, taken in conjunction with his notorious *Letter to the House of Lords*, placed as the Dedication to *The Testament of John Davidson* (1908) (the *Letter* can be found as an appendix in the second volume of *The Poems of John Davidson* (1973)), they demonstrate how far Davidson's thinking had gone in seeing the Ango-Saxon race as the fittest to survive in an Godless world. Can Davidson really mean the things he says in this 'long, grave and pertinent letter' to the peers of the House of Lords? Was he entirely balanced at the time of writing this letter? Is there perhaps an explanation to be found in some kind of ironical tone which accompanies the letter? If, as it seems, it is meant to be taken seriously, how can one accept his astonishing views on the relegation of women, the Irish, and the colonies to positions of subservience to the 'English ideal'? There can be few more dangerous and belligerently patriotic utterances of this period. What may help the reader to understand is the way in which towards the conclusion he makes his despairing plea to the Lords to see that English triumph represents survival of the fittest:

> there is no Other World; there never was anything that man has meant by Other World; neither spirit, no mystical behind-the-veil; nothing not-ourselves that makes for righteousness, no metaphysical abstraction . . . there is only matter, which is the infinite, which is space, which is eternity which we are . . .

Testaments

A fourth category in Davidson's poetry is that of the great *Testaments* and longer poems, post 1900. 'A Ballad in Blank Verse' is directly autobiographical, Davidson following Alexander Smith's 'Glasgow' in celebrating the beauty of the industrial Firth of Clyde. Davidson could have chosen to develop his unique juxtaposing of rural beauty and industrial activity. But the poem is about how 'a youth whose sultry eyes . . . were not all lust' becomes disenchanted in his love for this wide firth, which is at first world enough for him, but which, because of his father's 'pinch-beck' beliefs and narrow-mindedness, are barred to him for ever. The interrogation of the son by the father and the emotional blackmail of the mother is an exaggerated, if broadly valid account of Davidson's relationship with his parents. It does seem, however, that as he grew older his tendency towards the melodramatic indulgence of this agonising predicament began to take the exaggeration to dangerous levels. The ballad has real power; notice that once again Davidson has taken the genre of the conventional ballad and made it into something completely different. Instead of anonymous folk-poetry of regular metre and stanza we have free verse and deeply personal narrative. Similarly in 'A Woman and Her Son' we are presented with yet another cameo of Davidson in relation to his parents; but surely even Davidson was never as vicious as to force his mother to such a nihilistic acceptance? There is certainly no record of anything like this in his life; so once again the poem becomes a kind of idealisation in later life of his hated adolescence.

Between 1901 and 1908 Davidson wrote six long *Testaments* – of *The Vivisector*, *The Man Forbid*, *The Empire Builder*, *The Prime Minister*, *John Davidson*, and *Sir Simon Simplex*. *The Testament of a Vivisector* shows just how unbalanced and pathologically unsound Davidson became towards the end of his life. The central sections of the poem, where the old hack horse has its vertebrae exposed in order that the vivisector may practise unrelenting and horrific pain upon it, so that he can discover the materialist secrets of the universe, has a morbid fascination which most readers will find repellent. The vivisector has lost his family and his humanity in his scientific monism; but this is increasingly Davidson's own inhuman creed in these poems, a creed which sees humanity as merely a stage in matter's evolution upwards. This argument is presented through the testimony of each protagonist telling of the tension between his ego and humanity on one hand, and the will of the universe working through him on the other. The path to knowledge means pain, and repudiation of all Mankind's consolatory or admonitory delusions of God, heaven and hell.

Davidson took these iconoclastic ideas to grandiose and melodramatic conclusion in a series of plays written between 1905 and 1908, under the running title of *God and Mammon*, in which colossal stage effects and Shakespearian blank verse express his proto-fascist disgust for modern society and his vision of the overthrow of church and state. Unsurprisingly, his contemporaries were unimpressed with such didactic poetry and drama, for all that it contains passages of enormous power and originality.

Davidson's last – and greatest? – poems

Ironically, following the excesses of the jingoistic poetry and the obsessive heaviness of the *Testaments,* and in the closing years of his tormented life, Davidson seems to have found a voice suited to his situation as the misfit and outsider who tramped the countryside simply to escape people and problems. Among the last work is a group of long poems which observe humanity and its antics, contemplating its ant-like bustle and its random movement. 'Fleet Street' shows the transition from materialist philosophising to detached observation (it is as good a poem as any for coming to grips with Davidson's evolutionary thinking, and his necessity to believe in imperial aspiration). Wondering at the human variety, the history, and the technological marvels of 'the world's most famous street' takes Davidson back through history much as Virginia Woolf would do in contemplating the city in *Mrs Dalloway* (1925).

Davidson's hindsight takes him aeons back in time and into cosmic space in ways which would inspire MacDiarmid's cosmic settings for human predicaments in his early lyrics of the 1920s. But it was the city streets, the railway stations, and places where the masses gather, which increasingly fascinated Davidson now. The extended poems of 'Railway Stations' survey the stations of London Bridge, Liverpool Street, Southampton and many more, with their bewildering variety of travellers and hangers-on, age and youth, and mysteries of purpose, and with their vast and nightmare atmosphere making them appear like industrial cathedrals. All this Davidson explored in a way which left himself on the outside, increasingly the detached observer, released from agonising about his unhappy, alienated life, and anticipating T. S. Eliot's observation of unknowable faces in the city passages of *The Waste Land* (1922).

Perhaps Davidson's greatest poem, 'The Crystal Palace', belongs to this grouping. The Crystal Palace was the edifice of glass and iron which was the centre of the Great Exhibition of 1851, but was then moved to Sydenham as a permanent exhibition in a pleasure-garden, with flying carousels, polo-grounds, cycle tracks, dance-floors outside. In the 'colossal ugliness' of the palace itself, sculpture, paintings, billiards, grill-rooms, bars, Davidson exploits this symbol of imperial pride to make his most cutting comment on the human ant-heap:

> For this is Mob, unhappy locust swarm,
> Instinctive, apathetic, ravenous . . .
> Some scores of thousands searching up and down
> The north nave and the south nave hungrily

For space to sit and rest to eat and drink:
Or captives in a labyrinth or herds
Imprisoned in a vast arena, here
A moment clustered; there entangled; now
In reaches sped and there in whirlpools spun
With noises like the wind and like the sea,
But silent vocally: they hate to speak;
Crowd; Mob; a blur of faces featureless,
Of forms inane; a stranded shoal of folk.

The voice of this great poem comes from the man who drifts, like the outcast, eliminating self, and whose poetry operates as a sort of detached perspective on the world beneath, scrutinising the human comedy in its search for the spectacular and its aimless indulgence. The reference to the 'nave' suggests that the unhappy Mob have unthinkingly sought refuge in this latter-day cathedral to Mammon; here is humanity with its new material gods, satiating the corporeal desires for comfort, food and drink, and here before us, is the chaos of modernity. Davidson is ironic and yet fascinated, mainly content to capture the eddy and flow of the day in vivid impressionist scenes, the rhythms of his verse fitting perfectly the abrupt movements of people and situation. Here there is none of the tendency towards philosophical melodrama which vitiates so much of his later poetry.

Finding the real John Davidson

Davidson is an elusive and complex figure, often antagonistic to the reader, never easy to follow in his gloomy self-torment. Yet, in many ways, he represents the predicament of many Scottish writers at the end of the nineteenth century, as he desperately seeks a voice which will eschew the vernacular, but which is neither imitative of Swinburne nor derived from Hopkins nor even alike to the Scottish English of James Thomson in *The City of Dreadful Night* (1874). Should we see him as a Scottish poet at all? If he has characteristics that are Scottish, they are hardly those of poets like Ramsay, Fergusson, and Burns in the preceding century, who utilised forms and content which were recognisably of a Scottish tradition. Several Scottish writers of the later nineteenth century seem to inhabit an unhappy half-way house between the narrow culture from which they attempt to depart, and a larger culture within which they can never be entirely happy; from Carlyle to George MacDonald, from Stevenson to George Douglas Brown. Davidson is perhaps the outstanding example.

377

His achievement may be allied to this incertitude, since his unwillingness to follow slavishly any one of the types or forms of Victorian verse, related to his dubiety as to where he belonged, physically and creatively, led to great variety and originality. There is also something admirable in his self-scrutiny and defiant honesty, even when his philosophical conclusions dismay. In poems like 'Romney Marsh' there is a bleak recognition of the basics and essentials of place, a willingness to see that rural landscapes are not entirely beautiful, as the telegraph wires ring over Romney Marsh in the wind. Increasingly his poetry confronts the scenery of industrial and technological Britain, with its concomitant spiritual alienation. Later poets like Eliot and MacDiarmid admit their immense debt to the range of possibilities and the explorations shown and undertaken by Davidson; it is fair to conclude that his achievement still awaits proper assessment.

CHAPTER 22

JAMES THOMSON:
THE CITY OF DREADFUL NIGHT

JAMES ('B. V.') THOMSON (1834–82)

In some senses James Thomson can be considered more of a British than a Scottish poet. He was born in Port Glasgow, his parents were both Scottish (his father, an officer in merchant shipping, his mother from Galloway). When his father suffered a stroke the family moved to London, where his mother supported them by dressmaking. After his mother died, James was placed in the Royal Caledonian Asylum in Islington, while his baby brother was sent to an aunt in Scotland. James later became an army schoolmaster in Ireland and England, until 1862. As a journalist in London, or secretary to the Silver Mines Company of Colorado, or war correspondent in Spain, his experience was all outwith Scotland, until his death through alcoholism in 1882.

His creative work was all published in England, mainly in his friend Charles Bradlaugh's *National Reformer*, a magazine speaking for radicalism and free thought. Thomson's problems as an unsuccessful businessman and a disenchanted war correspondent in Spain were hardly the problems of nineteenth-century Scotland. He is included here, however, because his cultural and religious orientation, inherited from his parents, was profoundly Scottish. His mother was a disciple of the Secessionist movement of the famous, controversial Scottish preacher Edward Irving, follower of Thomas Chalmers, and, from 1822, the charismatic and apocalyptic minister for Hatton Cross congregation in London. (By the time Thomson was born, the Church of Scotland, who regarded his 'gift of tongues' preaching as heretical, had deprived Irving of his ministry.)

Thomson was, from the beginning, deeply imbued with Christian and Calvinist principles, and his upbringing in the Royal Caledonian Asylum, after the death of his parents, provided a religious training very much along Scottish lines. Thus, in a way comparable to the Irish writer James Joyce, all his work was to be a tension between his earliest and dominant religious indoctrination and his attempts to repudiate and rebel against it. Unlike the similar quest for personal freedom of his predecessor Thomas Carlyle, however, Thomson was not to move from 'an everlasting No' to 'an everlasting Yea' (*Sartor Resartus*, 1836). Rather, like his fellow-Scot John Davidson, he was to be trapped in a kind of reverse Calvinism, a predicament resembling the relationship of Joyce to Irish Catholicism, where zealous commitment to religious belief, structure and symbolism is converted to a commitment to undermine those beliefs, but utilising much of their structure and symbolism to express antagonism and counter-argument.

The City and Victorian materialism

In view of the fact that Thomson's other poetry neither matches the quality of *The City of Dreadful Night* nor operates within a Scottish cultural framework, we concentrate here on his one great poem, which has for long been accepted as a most powerful extended statement of Victorian loss of faith, and the dilemma of emotionally yearning for what reason cannot supply. Before discussing the poem, however, it is worth considering one aspect of its reception. Several critics have found within the poem a running reference to Victorian industrialisation and class alienation. In this respect, David Daiches, in *Some Late Victorian Attitudes* (1969), has stressed that Thomson's frame of reference is altogether wider. In his disenchantment with Calvinism, Thomson's scepticism is drawn very much from the eighteenth century, particularly from the Italian Giacomo Leopardi, whose *Dialogues* he brilliantly translated. Although he admired Romantic poetry (Shelley and the German poet Novalis particularly: the 'B.V.' which he prefixes to his name is shorthand for 'Bysshe', Shelley's middle name, and 'Vanolis' an anagram, in tribute to these two writers) his ideological orientation is broadly based on thinkers like Schopenhauer and the earlier sceptics of the Enlightenment. Daiches points out that to identify Thomson as a critic of specific Victorian targets in the manner of, say, Dickens or Mary Gaskell, or Tennyson and Clough, is to misread the very broad and essentially timeless metaphorical reference of Thomson's work. If we clear the ground of the fallacious belief that Thomson is referring to immediate Victorian problems of physical and social degradation, then, argues Daiches, we see the poem much more distinctly within a tradition of European and Scottish metaphysical debate.

Thomson may be doing two different things, however; drawing on the older scepticism of previous centuries, and simultaneously (and perhaps even subconsciously) embodying his dislike of Victorian monumentalism and stuffy social petrification in his sterile imagery of the marmoreal suburbs of his city. But the reader has to acknowledge the absence of comment in the poem on the contemporary political and social problems of Thomson's day, raising the question as to whether this lack of contemporary relevance diminishes his achievement.

The discussion of the poem which follows is an attempt to follow the development of Thomson's sophisticated and often profoundly symbolic argument, while recognising throughout his essentially triadic and cyclic structure. It takes the poem section by section, but allows, the circular movement of ideas to remain in the reader's mind.

Tradition and Modernism

The three introductory quotations from Dante and Leopardi are a significant part of the poem. Thomson taught himself Italian so that he could read Dante in the original: the first is from Dante's *Inferno* (written circa 1300, printed 1472), translated in Edwin Morgan's Canongate Classic edition of 1993 as 'through me is the way into the city of pain'; and the second, from Leopardi's work of 1831, *Canti*, 'then out of such endless working, so many movements of everything in heaven and hell, revolving incessantly, only to return to the point from which they were moved; from all this can imagine neither purpose or gain.' The third epigraph, from Leopardi's *Operette Morali* of 1827, is translated as 'Eternal alone in the world, receiver of all created things, in you, death, our naked being comes to rest; joyful, no, but safe from the age-old pain . . . happiness is denied by fate to the living and denied to the dead'. Thus the three quotations combine the visionary qualities of medieval apocalyptic poetry with eighteenth-century scepticism – a fair summary of the dualism of Thomson's nightmare vision, tensioned as it is between a religious cast of mind of a very traditional kind and a modern rational materialism.

Dead Faith, Dead Hope, Dead Love

It is also important to realise from the beginning that the poem is structured after the manner of Dante and of Milton. The twenty-one sections are not unrelated meditations on mortality, but a systematic exploration through an overall ternary composition, echoing the themes of Dead Faith, Dead Hope, and Dead Love. Thomson gives a somewhat opaque explanation of the underlying rationale of his poem, in which he argues that the seventy years of life divided by the 'persistent three', Dead Faith, Dead Hope, Dead Love, comes to a result of ·210, 'the perpetual recurrence', which keeps returning in the poem itself. Reminiscent though this may be of the famous answer to the riddle of the universe being 42, and on the face of it, equally obscure, there is no doubt that the poem is organised in a repetitive series of cyclical movements through the three recurrent and pessimistically viewed concepts of Faith, Love and Hope.

The Proem: 'Why I write'

The sections do not have titles. The summary titles given here are merely suggestions indicating thematic topics, as an initial guide towards holding the overall movement of the poem in mind – readers will very probably wish to substitute their own mental headings. (Line number references are to lines within sections.) Thus the 'Proem' can be taken as expressing Thomson's understanding of what moved him to write at all. That is to say, it is Thomson's explanation of why, given his mental state of despair and alienation from life, he bothers to make such an ambitious, reflective expression of terminal spiritual pessimism. As he asks, 'why evoke the spectres of black night / To blot the sunshine of exultant years', he explains that his answer is a kind of cold rage, a desire (related to that of several of his contemporaries in Victorian poetry, especially Arthur Hugh Clough and the later John Davidson) to strip away the hypocrisy and false dreams of his age. In that sense he is a kind of 'anti-prophet', mocking perhaps the 'sages' of line 21, like Joseph Priestley, Thomas Macauley, John Stuart Mill, and the scientific rationalists of the period who thought all that remained for their century to do was to improve the material condition of humanity and Utopia would arrive. He allows that such optimists could not understand his poem, since their discourse is so utterly different. Mockingly, he wishes them well on their 'sweet earth' and in their 'unplaced sky' – 'unplaced' in the sense that, for the disenchanted Thomson, our world has no spiritual location in a God-created cosmos, but is spinning in a random universe. Ultimately he speaks only to 'a sad fraternity' – and, for them, he knows that the message will not be new or consolatory, unless perhaps it helps them to know that there are other 'weary wanderers' in the city of unbelief. Thus Thomson, from the very beginning, identifies the city as an abstract state of mind, mocks the idea of any epiphany or prophetic message (so beloved of the mainstream tradition of poetry in English from Milton to Tennyson), and simply admits the petty significance of his poem's recognition of spiritual gloom.

SECTION 1: WHERE AND WHAT IS THE CITY?
Readers should not ignore the extremely unusual and original features which Thomson introduces in this poem. He is not employing simple allegory, nor

typical nineteenth-century symbolism (either of the purer tradition of French poetry of the period, or as more generally used in English poetry and fiction later in the nineteenth century). Instead, Thomson is anticipating many techniques of Modernism – in particular those of T. S. Eliot's *The Waste Land* (1922) and later fictional surrealism such as found in Franz Kafka's *The Trial* (1927). The reader moves precariously from seeing the city as a real place, geographically located, to seeing it as metaphorical (it is a city of 'Night' and of 'Death' – and this night and death represents a state of mind, since he emphasises to us that 'it dissolveth in the daylight fair'). Further uncertainty is added through Thomson's description of 'a dream' of night, which remains 'in distempered gloom' and 'deadly weariness of heart' on awakening. Thomson's city is therefore a mixture of negative mind-state, nightmare, or dark hallucination – the idea and image of city used as a symbol with multiple significance, its usefulness stemming from its concrete location and its atmospheric possibilities of mausoleum gloom and stagnation.

A timeless concept of city is exploited and distorted in shifting ways which anticipate the flux of symbolic image in later writers like Eliot and Kafka, and in Scotland, MacDiarmid in *A Drunk Man Looks at the Thistle*. It was presumably the urban focus which led so many critics to educe a satirical comment on Victorian industrialisation, wrongly reading it as belonging with works such as Dickens's *Hard Times* (1854), with its exaggerated presentation of industrial nightmare in archetypal Coketown. But there is nothing archetypal or even industrial about this city, and if we read carefully, Thomson emphasises (in verse four) that far from talking about a recognisable British city, his city lies in no-man's land, in an outlandish and wasteland territory, surrounded for leagues by marshes, black moorland and mountain ridges.

At least one of Thomson's biographers has identified aspects of the city's setting as emerging from Thomson's childhood memories of Port Glasgow. While this may well be so, the use of 'broad lagoon', together with the later details of 'great piers and causeways', which connect the town and its 'islet suburbs', suggest that 'a Venice of the dark sea' haunts Thomson's mind. Similarly, the use of almost American topographical description in 'trackless wilderness' and 'savannahs', together with the eastward direction of the great sea, seems deliberately to remove London and Glasgow respectively from a list of possible correlatives (although Thomson's style and rhetoric do at times echo that of Alexander Smith's dark city celebration of 1857, 'Glasgow'). The point, of course, is that this is a city which is not meant to be any actual place, but rather a nightmare construct of an imagination within which the seas, trackless wastes, and ravines are much more landscapes of the mind than places in any recognisable world. In this, it anticipates the kind of imaginative methodology of, say, Mervyn Peake in the *Gormenghast* trilogy (1946–59) or Alasdair Gray in *Lanark* (1981).

Is Thomson consistent in his development of extended symbolism of a 'city of the mind'? Or does his use of concrete detail eventually trap him in a dilemma in which his methodologies become contradictory? Is there a tension between his use of allegory derived· from older poets, and his development of a new kind of symbolism? These are questions to which, to a great extent, readers must find answers in their own subjective inter-pretations. The poem can confuse; the people who appear within the poem – with increasing frequency – begin to take on a life of their own, yet are also meant to be aspects of mind – Thomson's or his fellow-inhabitants – of spiritual gloom. It should be remembered that all that happens in the city of night is contained within the pessimistic mentality of the poetic creator, in a kind of black dream. People and situations are thus metaphors expressing internal debates within Thomson himself, even though at times it may seem that Thomson changes the premises of his conception, so that episodes and actors in the poem become separate and free-standing phenomena, independent of the poet's internal state of gloomy self-con-sciousness.

Perhaps we must admit that, in the end, Thomson is inconsistent. He seems, for example, unsure whether to maintain the representation of the 'unweeping' inhabitants of the city (there will be weeping later); and in lines 47–9 he suggests that the inhabitants are sleeping or dead or fled from pestilence – all of which he seems later to contradict when he says that they do not sleep, that they wish to die but cannot, and that they are trapped in the city, unable to escape. How can they be dead in a city of the mind? Or is there an even more sophisticated symbolism at work here?

The reader also has to come to terms with the physical description of the city, and the implications of some of its topographical and physical details. Do the 'waste marshes' represent specific aspects of mind? Do the 'noble bridges' and 'great mansions' that fill it signify the greatness or dignity in the minds which have succumbed to the pessimism of Thomson and his forlorn fellowship? What meaning do we ascribe to 'great ruins of an unremembered past', together with other ruins of 'a few short years ago'? And the most outstanding inconsistency of this first section comes in line 64 onwards, where Thomson stresses that the individuals of the city are solip-sistically trapped, in the sense that they have turned in upon themselves, and that they pay no heed to each other in their isolated grief. In fact they speak frequently to each other in later sections, and they communicate quite sympathetically. Must this be taken as detracting significantly from Thomson's overall effect?

The final paradox is that there is a compelling and powerful suggestion that Thomson the unbeliever is portraying this city as hell. Line 78, 'They leave all hope behind who enter there,' is a deliberate parody of the famous warning from Dante's *Inferno*, 'Abandon hope all ye who enter here.' Just as later Joyce was unable to avoid reiterating a 'damned Jesuit strain' throughout his intendedly secular fiction, Thomson seems unable to avoid giving an insistently religious cast to his images throughout the poem, despite his hostility to religious belief. Is it ideologically and aesthetically valid that a poet, who is stressing the meaninglessness of existence and the lack of divinity and providence in our spiritual lives, should protest about this in terms so clearly theological?

SECTION 2: DEAD FAITH, DEAD LOVE, DEAD HOPE

Section 2 introduces us to Thomson's three 'perpetually recurring' terms of life, Dead Faith, Dead Love and Dead Hope. It also introduces us to the contrasting methodology, which Thomson uses throughout the poem, in which a meditative or reflective metaphysical stanza is followed by a gloomy narrative movement, and vice versa. Again there is a sort of mockery of convention here, in which action fails to triumph over meditation, and meditation produces no release through consequent triumphant action. This section is a parody of leadership, mocking the idea of inspiration or spiritual guidance. The poet follows (satirising the relationship between Beatrice and Dante in the *Inferno*) a shadowy walker who seems to have 'an intent'. In a world of inaction and apathy, such a leader, however 'shadow-like and frail', is attractive in his stoical persistence. What the section reveals is that he is walking in a circle – a circle which moves around the city through the three symbolic points, representing steps or stages of despair. Firstly the shadowy walker comes to a gloomy tower surrounded by graves and tombs – 'some old God's-acre', which is now 'corruption's sty'. This obvious satire on what the church has become, sub-serving British establishment and imperialism, reminiscent of Burn's 'churches built to please the priest' in *The Jolly Beggars*, is where Faith has died. The walker circles on his road once more and comes across a substantial villa. This villa, the poem will later show us, is the resting-place of the body of a beautiful woman. Some critics identify her as representing Matilda Weller, whom Thomson loved and who died tragically young. The truth is elusive; but it appears that the villa and body represent the death of the possibility of any kind of love, romantic or domestic, for the poet. The villa is placed half way between the church and the 'squalid house' which follows as the third stage of the shadowy walker's journey. Is this the end point of Thomson's own drunken and personal debilitation, the place where 'Hope died, starved out in its utmost lair'?

The circular journey gives a shape to the entire poem, since these three central concepts identify and structure the three main parts of the poem. Why should the poet bother to go on? What is the dynamic that insists that life continue to be lived and the poem to be written? The shadowy walker answers with the powerful lines 31–6, which anticipate so strongly Hugh MacDiarmid's dark vision of 'The Great Wheel' at the conclusion of *A Drunk Man Looks at the Thistle* (1926). This early and mechanistic symbolism of a piece of machinery functioning eternally and pointlessly, devoid of significance, must stand as one of the most forceful illustrations of the Victorian sages' obsession with the mechanistic mind-cast of their age, which they warned would in the end destroy itself and its society – a vision presented by many Scottish writers from Carlyle to John Davidson. The shadowy walker perpetually retraces his steps so that he is brought round again to the tower where Faith died, anticipating Sartre's idea of hell as a monotonous and endless repetition (*Huis Clos*, 1945).

SECTION 3: LEARNING TO LIVE IN THE CITY
Thomson tells us here how eye and ear learn 'a strange new vision' and way of hearing in the city. Once again, what they hear and see – empty moonlit squares and dark lanes behind sombre mansions, and the muffled throbbing and breathing which is pent up at the back of the vast and deep silence of the city – draws the reader towards different interpretations. Do these descriptions satisfactorily relate to states of mind, or do they rather suggest a tangible Victorian city? If all this is happening within the mind, what is it that the 'eye' (perhaps a pun on vision and self) is learning as 'a strange new vision'? What is the innermost mind learning to see in this darkness of mind? Again, Thomson leaves it to the reader to fathom.

SECTION 4: THE DESERT TRAVELLER
Section 4 describes a type or figure which recurs within the poem – that of the Carlylean Victorian sage. The reader has to speculate if this might be Thomson himself, in the sense that the speaker within the city must be a voice within Thomson's mind, and, like Thomson in spirit, has traversed the trackless wastes (of disillusion?) in order to bring his message here. In one reading this would be Thomson's way of expressing how he himself arrived at the City of Despair and consequently we would expect a narrative which would be allegorical in terms of Thomson's own experience. And so it

transpires. The actual journey through the desert is reminiscent of Bunyan's *The Pilgrim's Progress* (1672–8) – although it has been suggested that other sources for this grotesque landscape and its creatures are Gustav Doré's illustrations to the *Inferno* and the nightmare visions of William Blake.

Thomson leaves readers to interpret the journey's spiritual meaning for themselves. Significantly, in the early stages of the journey the traveller comes through utter darkness and horrific presences without fear. However horrific the spiritual world may appear, the faithless and hopeless traveller has the sole consolation of being fearless, since 'No Hope could have no Fear'. (The reader might wonder, however, why the previous section emphasised 'the reign of terror' in the city?) Again it is worth noting that despite the imagery of smoke and darkness, it is hardly an industrial landscape which is being presented here. This desert with its 'dusky flames' which are part of 'a Sabbath of the Serpents' has a provenance which clearly goes back to Dante and altogether older nightmares of the Western imagination.

For six verses, amidst this apocalyptic nightmare, the traveller is unafraid. He reaches that wild seashore with its giant cliffs and its burnt-out sun (the allegorical symbolism of the description of the sun as a 'bleeding eyeless socket on the left-hand cliffs, with the moon glaring on the right (54–60) is particularly challenging!) and then the poem takes a surprising turn. Why is Hope now allowed to enter? Who is this 'woman with a red lamp in her hand' who comes barefoot on that strange shore? It has been suggested that there is a visual play here on the famous Pre-Raphaelite picture by Burne-Jones, 'The Light of the World', in the sense that the woman here parallels the figure of Christ with the lamp in the painting. If so, the woman gives hope to the poem in the way that Christ gave hope to the world. But if hope is given, why does the poet then describe how he fell 'on my bier' – that is to say, on his funeral pyre? Why is he divided into two opposing selves by this apparition? Why does one of the selves swoon and one stand apart? Why should the traveller's soul grow 'mad with fear'? It is perhaps not surprising to learn that the tragic love affair with Matilda Weller has been suggested as the underlying situation that Thomson is describing here. Broadly, his loss of her inspiring affection at a crucial point in his life could be seen as the loss of Faith, Hope, and Love together, since she clearly represented, all these things to him. The poem – in very impressionistic and symbolically arbitrary terms – may well be lamenting her death ('a large black sign was on her breast', and 'that lamp she held was her own burning heart / whose blood-drops trickled step by step apart').

This still leaves open the meanings implied by the way the woman-figure tends the senseless figure of the poet, while the poet simultaneously stands 'stone bound' so near (and yet so far?). What Thomson means when his traveller describes the way in which the woman clasps one of the divided selves, the 'corpse-like' half, bearing him away into the dark ocean, is also left for the reader to decipher. What happens to each of the divided aspects of the traveller? Isn't there a powerful sense in which Thomson is saying that false Hope, Love and Faith were given to him by that temporary but tragic love; and that his intellectual or rational and sceptical self stood apart from that, only to be vindicated by their death? One side of Thomson, from this point on, is permanently dead, although, ironically, the poet wonders if the dead side is not the happier of the two.

SECTION 5: HOW ONE GETS TO THE CITY, AND HOW ONE LEAVES IT
Section 5 tells of the mystery of 'how one gets to the city, and how one leaves it' – appropriate enough, readers might think, following the graphic journey described in Section 4. But is there a discrepancy between the very clear description given of the journey by the prophet-traveller of Section 4, and the much more general 'How he arrives there none can clearly know'? Or is it simply that Thomson has described his own case, but then generalises? This section brings Thomson to the impression that to arrive in the City of Dreadful Night is 'as dying fever-stricken' – reminding us again that to come to the city is a movement within the mind, just as to leave it is a release from gloom and despondency.

One of the most moving aspects of the early stages of the poem is the way in which Thomson suggests that, as in the earlier stages of a mental condition of spiritual isolation and pessimism, escape or lucid intervals are possible. The description from line 12 onwards is very evocative of the way in which a repressed and solipsistic mind is suddenly allowed release. It anticipates Edwin Muir's descriptions (in his poems, and *Autobiography*, 1954) of how he used to break from the mental 'bell jar' within which he was contained, and how sweet the translation from the alienated dark world to the human and harmonious external world felt. Muir's poem 'The Labyrinth', with its final reminder that one is always doomed to return in dream to the dreary place, echoes Thomson's harsh insistence that the poor wretch who has once been in the 'dolent city' must return ever more frequently, despite loving wife, children and friends. (In an atypically Scottish turn of phrase the poet says that 'he must dree his weird', that is 'endure his fate'. Is there a sense here in which the theme of the poem approaches that of Stevenson's *Dr Jekyll and Mr Hyde*, 1886, as Thomson reminds us there is an inextricable connection between the explicit and extroverted human actor and his dark inverted counterpart?)

388

SECTION 6: THE SPIRIT'S RETURN FROM HELL

In keeping with the poem's oscillation between passages of metaphysical reflection and semi-narrative, Section 6 once again makes the narrator of the poem witness to activity within the city itself. At least, it seems to be in the city, although here, as with certain other passages in the poem, Thomson seems not entirely clear where the action is taking place. Could, for example, this section be located in a London of the present day, with Thomson, the poet, hearing morbid fellow sufferers complaining of their inability to break out of their spiritual predicament? What assists this confusion is the way in which certain images (the 'rough gold' of the reflection of the street lamps in the river, the 'large elm trees' along the river-walk) suggest a slightly more pleasant and acceptable environment than any we have been introduced to thus far. A London setting is unlikely, on balance, since the poet emphasises that these 'strange voices' with their 'stranger talk' come from bodiless communicants whose feet he has not heard approaching – they are 'bodiless voices in my waking dream'. Once again, we have to accept the possibility that all the speakers in the poem are protagonists created by the pessimistic mind of the poet himself. That is to say, these visitants are representative of the darker aspects of his own claustrophobic imagination. Their discussion bears this out. One of them has gone to hell to try to find, in at least active horror, a release from intolerable and inane boredom.

In a clever distortion of convention, Thomson satirises this possibility by arguing that entrance to hell demands the initial possession of hope, which must be given up at the entry. Since the hopeless aspirant to hell in this section has none to surrender, Thomson makes the point that the inertia is an ultimate despair worse than hell itself. Is this perhaps Thomson's most tendentious point? That the very boredom and disbelief of modern spiritual life is somehow worse than the older concept and nature of hell itself? Isn't there something of a wilful sleight-of-hand in his rather glib use of hell as a more positive state? Once again we are faced with the fact that the poet, who no longer believes in the existence of anything other than the mundane day-to-day, has to retreat to using concepts which he has rejected, in order to make his point. Paradoxically, the man who dismisses all but the banality of immediate existence is forced back to a discourse which presupposes spiritual alternatives. Nevertheless, Thomson is continuing to sustain his three central concepts – in this case, the concept of Dead Hope. The imaginary talkers conclude the section by vowing to grope through the dreariness of the limbo of life to find some scrap of hope which they may surrender in order to gain hell itself.

SECTION 7: THE PHANTOMS

Some of the meditative sections seem less relevant than others. Section 7 has at its centre an image very like the Shakespearean concept of the 'antic Death' (*Richard II*), in that at the heart of the city the most monstrous ghosts exhibit their skeletal and unsexed horror as a kind of mockery. Again, Thomson may be accused of inconsistency here – how can phantoms exist in what is already a phantasmagorical city? On the other hand, it could be argued that when so many conventions of imaginary creation are broken, then allegory and symbolism can merge as Thomson seems to merge them. The result approaches grotesque surrealism, so that readers have to accept layer upon layer of suggestion within the mind of the despairing poet himself. These 'phantoms', therefore, become mere nightmare dreams within dreams within the poet's own head.

SECTION 8: CURSING GOD

Section 8 is a central passage of controlled anger, which would amount to blasphemy to most Victorians (and many moderns!), and which is repeated twice more in the poem. It begins with another of Thomson's apparent inconsistencies. In verse three he has his 'inner communicants' gaze upon the river noting 'the various vessels large and small'. So what do we make of the 'shipless sea' of Section 1? This apparent inconsistency should not be seen as damaging the main thrust of the section, which is the first of three great blasphemous statements in the poem. Here, Thomson follows that other great 'heretic' of Victorian poetry, Arthur Clough, whose *The Bothy of Tober-Na-Vuolich* (1848) was an elaborate testimony to Scottish spiritual superiority in materialist Britain. Clough shocked pious Victorians with his savage mockery of their hypocrisy (in, for example, 'The Latest Decalogue', and 'To the Great Metropolis'), and poems like 'Epi-Strauss-Ium' and 'Easter Day' gave Thomson models for his parody of religious affirmation. Here is the message of 'Easter Day I: Naples 1849':

> Eat, drink, and play, and think that this is bliss!
>   There is no Heaven but this;
>   There is no Hell,
> Saver earth, which serves the purpose doubly well,
>   Seeing it visits still
>   With equallest apportionments of ill
> Both good and bad alike,
> And brings to one same dust
>   The unjust and the just
>   With Christ, who is not risen . . .

Indeed, poetry and fiction of the later nineteenth century, from Browning to John Davidson, and from Thomas Hardy to Samuel Butler, increasingly challenged Victorian confidence and jingoism with religious doubt and irony. Here, lines 21–32 must surely count as some of the fiercest and angriest protests ever penned against what is regarded as God's cheating and excluding of Mankind. And there is a desolation, powerful and prophetic, in Thomson's anticipation of a mechanistic universe, which MacDiarmid later develops in the concluding sections of *A Drunk Man Looks at the Thistle* (1926):

> The vilest thing must be less vile than Thou
> From whom it had its being, God and Lord!
> Creator of all woe and sin! abhorred,
> Malignant and implacable . . .
> As if a being God or Fiend, could reign,
> At once so wicked, foolish and insane,
> As to produce men when he might refrain . . .
> The world rolls round for ever like a mill;
> It grinds out death and life, and good and ill;
> It has no purpose, heart or mind or will . . .

Does the protester protest too much? After all, there is a crucial and significant difference between the absence of a plan or a maker and the existence of a vile being who is supposed to have created all woe and sin. Has Thomson simply recreated the Devil in his description of the God and Lord who has allowed this to happen as 'abhorred/malignant and implacable', a being ignominiously guilty?

SECTION 9: THE HEARSE
Section 9 is a successful meditative interlude, in its vivid symbolic presentation of the juggernaut, the great carriage bearing mysterious inhabitants or coffins to unknown tombs or destinations. 'Who in this Venice of the Black Sea rideth?' vividly refers back to the strange nature of the sea-girt city itself and conjures up its dark melancholy. The images of 'booming and the jar of ponderous wheels', the clash of ironshod feet, the 'rolling thunder', combined with that of the uncaring and sleeping coachman, approaches iconic definition; the coachman and his carriage take on a significance akin to that of the skeleton with the scythe or the figure of Death itself.

The open-ended inquiry in the third verse ('whence, whither, and for whom?') is the finest kind of mysterious questioning that the poem offers;

that is to say, the surreal symbolism works more powerfully than the more specific allegorising which Thomson often presents. This passage could simply be designated 'The Hearse'. It must, of course, also be noted for its skilful integration with the poem's 'Three Concepts'; that such a funeral is pointless, nameless and unmarked, in the sense that there is no healing community ritual and therefore no Hope, Faith or Love attached to it.

Taking stock: the poem's structure and patterned meaning

At this juncture it is worth taking stock of how the poem has structured itself so far. Nine sections are complete and it is not accidental that within these nine sections Thomson has already worked out a complete cycle of his 'eternal recurrence' of Dead Faith, Dead Hope and Dead Love. Section 2 showed a 'shadowy walker' moving round and round monotonously past his ever more pessimistic three points. Section 4 then re-enacted what was perhaps Thomson's own personal loss of love and hope with the death of Matilda Weller, represented in this poem by the death scene of the two lovers watched, as it were, by Thomson's 'super ego'. The mysterious speakers of Section 6 echoed and gave a final statement to the loss of Love; while the blasphemous curse of Section 8 very definitely put paid to the validity of Faith – not just in the sense that God is seen as malignant and unworthy of trust, but also in the sense that the poet has no faith in a God who can be so insane as to 'produce men when He might refrain!' Section 9 then summed up in the 'Fate-appointed hearse' the unceremonious 'burial' of all three of humanity's affirmative qualities. In the remainder of the poem Thomson repeats, in different terms, his lament for the 'recurrent Three'; Sections 10–19 will retrace the shadowy walker's movement in new narrative situations – while the climactic Sections 20 and 21 will symbolically finalise and encapsulate the entire poem's triple recurrence. Within the poem, therefore, there are three movements echoing the three themes (1–9; 10–19; 20–1). One might think that Thomson is too mechanical in his structuring – his theme is, of course, to derogate the mechanisation of man's mind through loss of Faith, and thus Thomson is perhaps succeeding intellectually in his argument that man has lost God, but is failing artistically. On the other hand, one could argue the opposite – that Thomson is fulfilling exactly and admirably his aesthetic and emotional aims by structuring his poem on the principles of mechanisation, which he identifies as the conditions of the times. (To an extent this is like Grassic Gibbon's *Grey Granite*, the final movement of *A Scots Quair*, 1932–4, which has been attacked for being too cold and literal in its pedestrian presentation of the symbolic decline of the city.)

SECTION 10: THE MANSION OF DEAD LOVE

Section 10 begins again on the dreary round of spiritual perambulation. Since the city is a metaphorical correlative for the poet's mind, this section could be read as returning to Thomson's loss of Matilda Weller. It is also an echo of the second stage of the shadowy walker's cyclic journey – we are here again at the villa where Love died 'stabbed by its own worshipped pair'. This image is made effective by Thomson's emphasis on the stifling gloom of what seems very like a Victorian middle class villa, set in its muffling shrubberies, with its dark drapes, its depressing and intimidating furnishings and dimensions, and the sense of inhumanity in the scale and details of rooms. All this seems to underscore a society which has lost intimacy and vitality and does seem to express something of the suffocating social pretension which was so often censured by novelists like Dickens and Eliot and by poets like Browning and Clough.

The section is centred on the altar and funeral bier, in which lies the body of the lost loved one. But the 'Lady of the Images' is not simply at the centre of Victorian dreariness; she lies in 'the chambers of the mansion of my heart', says Thomson. We are reminded yet again that this woman is within his mind, an archetype for Dead Love. Likewise, the young man, 'wan and worn who seemed to pray' is at once an ironic commentary on the inefficacy of prayer, and on Thomson himself, who, like the lover observed by his doppelgänger in Section 5, is being watched detachedly once again by his overseeing self, the poet. The poem is patiently stating and restating its pessimism in a way which is finally epitomised in the gigantic statue of Melencholia at the end, an image which powerfully embraces the paralysed, inert consciousness of the poem.

SECTION 11: REASON IN MADNESS

Section 11 is meditative concerning the 'Reason in Madness' of the city dwellers. Thomson testifies to the stoical rationalism of all those who have arrived at this atheistical conclusion – 'they are the most rational and yet insane.' In a parody of political poetry ranging from 'Burns's 'A Man's a Man for a'that' to Shelley's argument that poets were the unacknowledged legislators of mankind, here, a great brotherhood has been established on Earth which ranges from those great in rank and wealth to those who are poor and mean 'yet these and those are brothers / the saddest and weariest men on earth.' The tree of liberty so often dreamt of by Romantic poets has indeed been realised in an egalitarian brotherhood; but with the loss of Faith this apotheosis is a mean kind of triumph.

SECTION 12: THE CATHEDRAL AND THE PROPHET

This is one of the most impressive sections in the poem; at its centre the surreal and Escher-like representation of the great cathedral which stands in the moonlit gloom of the city. The effect of setting the cathedral in moonlight, with the shadowy pilgrims seeking some kind of authoritative consolation, but then bringing in the shrouded prophet of nihilism, is superb. Thomson captures a kind of timeless iconography in making this cowled figure an archetype of mysterious and ghostly mortality. Again, the intention is parodic. As so often throughout the poem, Thomson is mocking the fallibility of all 'prophets', represented in the nineteenth century for the Victorians by religious figures like Henry Newman, but also in secular spirituality in the work of Thomas Carlyle, John Stuart Mill, John Ruskin, William Morris and the like. Their affirmative statements, from Mill's *Utilitarianism* (1861) to Carlyle's 'Everlasting Yea' in *Sartor Resartus*, from Ruskin's *Fors Clavigera* (1871) to William Morris's teaching of Craft Ethics, sought to offer reassurance and goals to a doubting century. Thomson, like Clough, will have none of this; indeed the entire sermon of the 'Prophet' is a parody of a litany, an inversion of the conventional celebration of holy symbols. Once again, like the 'Desert Traveller' of Section 5, testimony is being given, but instead of affirmation and assurance, it is a testimony to negativism.

Before the Shrouded Prophet gives his sermon, each of his audience is accosted and asked why he has come. This is important, in the sense that Thomson now seems to be including in his poem people other than himself. No longer can he sustain the idea in this section that he is working purely within his own mind, since from line 13 to line 53 we are given ten representatives of human endeavour, most of whom cannot conceivably be Thomson. Does this matter? Can we construct a way of reading the poem which allows the interpretation of internal reflection to join with a reading which permits other minds and other human archetypes to co-exist? Or has Thomson simply – and nobly, but unsuccessfully – attempted too much? He indicates here that the city of night calls to itself senators, drug addicts, clowns, hermits, kings, preachers, drunkards, and radical politicians. Lines 41–8 even include a poet, clearly Milton and his great work 'to justify the ways of God to man'; and if Milton of all people ultimately fails in justifying the ways of God to man, then who amidst all humanity possibly can? Significantly Thomson has these speakers enter the cathedral, 'and in turn / I entered also, having given mine' – that is to say, he has given his answer, which perhaps can be read in the poem itself.

SECTION 13: TIME THE SERPENT

A meditation on time follows, focusing on the paradox whereby those who haunt the city, who should logically wish their lifespan to be at an end, fear the swiftness of time and the fleetingness of life. Yet, at the same time, 'the hours are heavy on him' and the inhabitant longs for hibernation to avoid boredom. What is particularly successful about this meditation is the way in which time is portrayed as a 'monstrous snake wounded and slow and very venomous', with its 'blindwormlike' throttling of earth and ocean in an endless recurrent circle, mirroring the cyclical movement of the shadowy walker and the poet's 'eternal recurrence', now metamorphosed into the idea of the serpent, with all its hellish significance. The meditation becomes almost an invocation, a ritual imploring for release by the 'worshippers' in the moonlit cathedral, yearning for 'dateless oblivion'.

SECTION 14: THE SERMON OF NEGATION

Now we hear the preacher. The introductory verses work by inverting the usual religious detail – 'no swelling organ-strain', 'no chant, no voice or murmuring of prayer', with no priests or censers, and the altar unlit. The prophet-like figure is given the credentials of steadfastness, burning enthusiasm, impressive and charismatic presence, almost as though Thomson finds solace in an authoritative statement of negation. We come now to the second of the blasphemous or heretical statements, and possibly for the Victorian audience, the climax of the poem's polemic:

> And now at last authentic word I bring,
> Witnessed by every dead and living thing;
>   Good tidings of great joy for you, for all:
> There is no God; no Fiend with names divine
> Made us and tortures us; if we must pine,
>   It is to satiate no Being's gall.
> It was the dark delusion of a dream,
> That living Person conscious and supreme,
>   Whom we must curse for cursing us with life,
> Whom we must curse because the life He gave
> Could not be buried in the quiet grave,
>   Could not be killed by poison or by knife.
> This little life is all we must endure,
> The grave's most holy peace is ever sure,
>   We fall asleep and never wake again . . .

> We finish thus; and all our wretched race
> Shall finish with its cycle, and give place
> To other beings, with their own time-doom:
> Infinite aeons ere our kind began;
> Infinite aeons after the last man
> Has joined the mammoth in earth's tomb and womb.

This is the finest Victorian poetry of religious disbelief. In it, almost fifty years before Eliot, and long before Sartre and existentialism, Thomson anticipates twentieth-century scientific materialism and nihilism. The despair is anchored to the intellectual thought of the time, concerning evolution and Darwin's theories of 'survival of the fittest'. Thomson is clearly setting humanity as a temporary traveller within a colossal sweep of time, and in the verses which follow, he acknowledges that man bows down to 'the universal laws / Which never had for man a special clause'. This 'sermon of negation' mocks the poetry of Blake in lines 64 and 65, and religious ideas like predestination, remaking them as natural determinism, and finding a kind of scientific necessity alone behind a universe devoid of 'good or ill, of blessing or of curse'. Significantly, the preacher ends not with a Carlylean exhortation to work, to be up and doing, an affirmation of life, but rather an exhortation or reminder to his audience that they are 'free to end it when you will' – a blasphemous invocation of suicide. Is the effect now to make the reader feel that Thomson protests too much? In lines 43–8 the miserable inhabitants are cursed because they cannot reach the grave (why not?); and the preacher's central cursing of the supreme person who first gave man life (himself 'the dark delusion of a dream') surely sits uneasily with his later statement in lines 73–5 that it is 'Necessity Supreme' that dominates ('I find no hint throughout the Universe / Of good or ill, of blessing or of curse . . .'). Thomson here seems to admit that God is a dream, then curses him nevertheless, then admits that there are no blessings or curses in the universe, but mere necessity!

SECTION 15: THE INFECTED CITY

Thomson – appropriately enough – argues that this message affects all who listen; that the 'potent evil influence' adds a poison to the air, that the effects of sermons like this and the proximity of men, and of mind to mind, creates an insufferable pall of sadness and madness; a kind of mass non-hysteria. Why must he make the atmosphere of the city 'evil' and 'poisoned'? Despair is one thing; active evil quite another.

SECTION 16: THE CRY OF DEAD LOVE

This section follows Section 14's 'sermon of negation', in its lament for Dead Faith. The 'shrill and lamentable cry' of Dead Love, which so poignantly resents the loss of 'the sweetness of the home with babes and wife', is also a general lament for the loss of all aspects of human feeling and imagination – 'social pleasures', art, the enjoyment of nature, youth, and 'all the sublime prerogatives of man'. ('Sublime'? – if we live in a godless universe, what makes these activities more special or blessed than any other?). The section mourns the loss of these things. But who is making this desolate lament? Is there significance that 'this vehement voice came from the northern aisle'? If the voice is Thomson (as it is possible all the voices in the poem are his) then the comment, however relevant to the understanding of his tragic and self-destructive life, cannot speak for the world of more ordinary mortals whose participation in family and society is unimpaired. On the other hand, if this figure is not Thomson, then he is surely speaking out of turn in claiming 'our life's a cheat, our death a black abyss' for everyone. In this respect, Thomson resembles George Orwell, and *Nineteen Eighty-Four* (1949); his vision of what can go wrong in society becomes, in the end, an excessive disenchantment, and a wallowing in nightmare for its own sake. Are we perhaps witnessing the nightmare of a neurotic and obsessional mind, which has plunged itself into depression and hallucination?

SECTION 17: THE UNCARING STARS

This is a powerful and successful expression of wonder at beholding the nature of the heavens – but it reverses the conventional poetic view of the awe-inspiring stars. Poet after poet has found a sense of divine omnipotence behind such a spectacle – not so Thomson. It is his achievement in this to exploit the usual terms of inspirational beauty, so that the section has a lyricism and grace which is traditional; but which is mocked by the implications and conclusions which lie behind these descriptions. The section is also a parody of Ruskin's idea of 'pathetic fallacy' that is to say, the fallacious way in which poets impose their own subjective feelings on what is after all alien and unknowable natural activity. Thomson parodies the idea of the glittering dark blue vault of heaven, the golden burning and the glory of the moonlight on the deep black stream. There are indeed crystal and fairy beauties in this section, but the key to the section lies in the harsh and cold qualifications which Thomson makes – turning what would have been vital to the Romantic poets into a dead imagery, 'obdurate as steel'. Man looks with 'awe and yearning' at all this and thinks that the heavens are responding to his passionate wishes that heaven *should* respond. Thomson deploys nineteenth-century astronomical discovery in this section; science's conclusion that light from the stars was reaching us long after the actuality of the stars themselves is made the turning point of the section in line 15 – 'with such a living light these dead eyes shine'. He fiercely rejects the fallacies of man in his contemptuous conclusion to this verse, stripping away all human or sympathetic aspects from these 'puppets' of the maze of heaven (although 'puppets' does imply a puppeteer). Indeed, he anticipates the twentieth century and its interstellar travel with his 'if we could near them with the flight unflown' – and is astonishingly prophetic in his description of a self-consuming and despondent Earth. Could any reports from space exploration improve on his description of the universe as 'a void abyss'?

SECTION 18: THE PILGRIM THROUGH TIME

And so the poem continues its hazy reflection of the shadowy walker's cyclical movement, keeping time with the clock mechanism, which has lost any significance. The section follows the walker's triadic movement to the final loss of Hope. It does not specifically echo the imagery of the 'squalid house', where Hope died, but its imagery follows that of the earlier movement, repeating the idea of the three stations of the cycle with the 'three close lanes' in the suburb of the north.

Once again, Thomson encounters an aspect of himself, in the wounded creature crawling and sobbing as it tries to reach its squalid lair, 'for it would die in its own den'. This is the last vestige of humanity – the last clung-to hope that there is a way out of the predicament of the godless universe. It is a 'retreat to the womb', the maddened mind of the Crawler yearning to turn Time itself back, if it can only find:

> the long-lost broken golden thread
> Which reunites my present with my past . . .

This 'thread of gold' is of course illusory, and – perhaps, like Thomson himself retreating to drink and self-destruction – the Crawler is losing his very humanity in his self-denial. He threatens the poet with 'this poisoned blade' and 'this phial' of vitriol. Are these respectively dead or poisoned Faith and Love, and thus in keeping with the well-planned and coherent imagery of the poem? Certainly the Crawler tells us that 'two lanes diverge up yonder from this lane' – his blood lies in both, and the lanes are presumably those of Dead Faith and Dead Love. The poet, Thomson himself, who knows that this yearning within himself is a delusion, brushes the thin threads of gossamer from his face like his forlorn Hope; 'The thing which has been, never is again', he concludes. It would be hard to imagine a more trenchant mockery of the Hopeful Pilgrim of Bunyan's *Pilgrim's Progress*, or a more travestied version of Everyman.

SECTION 19: THE RIVER OF SUICIDES

This section contains prime examples of Thomson's major difficulty, throughout the poem, in balancing the contending possibilities of the poem's meanings, in terms of whether it speaks for his own state of mind alone, or for many others; and in terms of whether all its situations and protagonists are internalised, or whether at times they break out into representation of reality. Once again, the reader encounters inconsistency. How does one commit suicide in a dream, or within an imaginary surrealism? In describing (in verse two) how different the ways of committing suicide are, is Thomson once again moving out from his own internal state of mind, to refer inconsistently outwards to the problems of others? Doesn't the questioning of verse four repeat the unconvincing thinking of previous parts? That is to say, Thomson realises that the reader may well be wondering why anyone would bother to stay alive in such a dreary state of mind as this – and, as in the beginning, when he asked himself why he bothers to speak at all in the poem, now he has to invent a kind of stoical justification ('To fill our so-short *roles* out right or wrong'). Again, he has told us how slowly the serpent Time drags itself along, but in verse five, he insists that it is 'but for one night after all', and asks does one night of dreary pain really matter? If it doesn't matter, he has surely been wasting his efforts. And surely the description of the state of suicide as 'sweet sleep' invests corporeal death with pathetic fallacy in just the same way that the physical stars are deplorably invested with false substance? In short, is the major defect of the poem its inconsistency in placing such concrete possibilities within the 'ideal' world of the poet's imagination?

SECTION 20: THE ANGEL AND THE SPHINX

There is no denying the bleak success, however, of the last two sections, rightly famous for including some of the most powerful images for the loss of faith and spiritual motivation of the nineteenth century. Section 20 brings the poet to the square beside the cathedral in the moonlight, to the place where the Sphinx and the Angel with a Sword confront each other across the cloistered space. The great cathedral is emphasised as 'a wave-worn rock in that calm sea of air'.

Thomson picks powerful and disturbing images of confrontation; the triumphant figure of the Angel, reminding us of the angel who expelled Adam, but also guarded Paradise – that is to say, an enigmatic but nevertheless affirmative statement of the significance of Christianity. The Sphinx, sleeping with open eyes, is the ultimate symbol of the riddle of existence. The poet is in stupor, drugged and weary – spiritually weary. His fate (reminding us of Thomson's actual downward descent) is a metaphor for his final disillusionment and anomie. And from line 22 onwards, for the third time, the poem re-enacts the triadic, cyclical movement of the poem in microcosm.

This section is both the climax of the poem and also the very effectively structured summary and repetition of its recurrent themes and movements. The crash which awakens the poet from lethargy is the Angel losing its wings – once again, Faith dies. What is left is the warrior leaning on his secular sword – and the Sphinx, the mystery of existence, unchanged. And when the next clashing noise awakens the poet, the warrior's sword has fallen and broken, leaving an unarmed man with upraised imploring hands in front of the motionless Sphinx. It would be forcing the poem to say that this is loss of Hope, since it is just as much loss of Faith and hopes for the future, or hopes of defence against the void; but we recognise Thomson's inexorable movement. The third and loudest crash shows the collapse of humanity, broken between the Sphinx's paws. Again, this isn't exactly Dead Love; but it is the fall of humanity and all that hoping and aspiring humanity had yearned for – including the love of life and community.

SECTION 21: MELENCOLIA AND NECESSITY
The final section combines both meditation and narrative in a splendid concluding symbol, that of the bronze colossus, the statue of the winged woman, Melencolia. (The source of his image, the famous engraving by Albrecht Dürer, is called *Melencolia*.) Here Thomson presents Dürer's brooding winged maternal figure, the compass and other emblems of social and domestic utility round about her, and the threatening images of the ghastly dog, the bat which holds up her title, and the strange distortion of the heavens behind. Thomson is drawing from the scepticism of previous centuries; and interpreting Dürer's engraving in a way which fittingly completes his poem. Much of his imagery has been Escher-like (especially the image of the desert-cathedral next to the sea) and his vision here adds to Dürer's surrealist symbolism in a way which is unparalleled in nineteenth-century poetry. His meaning is that some strange baleful spiritual disability has not only petrified the woman in her maternal, domestic, and socially ordering duties, but poisoned her to the point where a deep and life-denying nihilism has taken her over. Is Thomson entitled, however, to say that:

Baffled and beaten back she works on still,
Weary and sick of soul she works the more,
Sustained by her indomitable will . . .

Dürer's engraving does not seem to suggest stoical activity. What is Thomson suggesting? In *Some Late Victorian Attitudes* (1969) David Daiches has suggested that Thomson is specifically using this stoic metaphor for the purpose of representing those late Victorians who had lost their faith but still retained their sense of duty. He cites George Eliot's famous and chilling credo, that she was sure only of three things: that God did not exist; that there was no real hope of an after-life; but that one must perform one's duty in this world. Daiches uses this as an index of the Victorian intellectual dilemma – all the duties of the past still exist, but without their spiritual verification. In this respect, Melencolia is also a paradoxical necessity; a remorseless rationalism which destroys Faith, Hope and Love, but also a hard task-mistress who insists on duty, work and continuance.

Thomson's Calvinist inheritance, his being steeped in severe religious discipline and training, makes him a profoundly significant Scottish and yet British spokesman for this, since all his upbringing was bound up with a commitment to a work-and-faith ethic, which his intellect then forced him to repudiate. Is there even more to Melencolia? Is she perhaps also meant to be a play upon the idea of Victoria, Empress of so much of the world, and yet personally and emotionally insecure after the death of her consort? And is the figure of Britannia also implied, familiar as she is as matriarchal emblem of Britain's imperial achievement? If so, then once again Thomson has been astonishingly prophetic, in terms of charting the rhetoric and dogmatism which will underlie imperial ambition with increasing intensity, culminating in the work of writers like Rudyard Kipling. The perspective on British achievement has throughout the poem been bleak, northern, and sceptical, just as Thomson's cultural orientation has been peripheral and 'un-British' also. It is part of Thomson's paradoxical achievement that he finds 'sublimity' in the deconstruction of British ideological and imperial certainties.

Somehow, through his creation of the trio of summative metaphors, in the Angel-warrior, the Sphinx, and the titanic city's queen, Melencolia, Thomson has ennobled the categorical negatives of his bleak situation. To the end, his message is unrelenting, however; with Melencolia-Necessity urging her subjects 'to drink new strength of iron endurance', despite 'renewed assurance/ And confirmation of the old despair'.

CHAPTER 23

ROBERT LOUIS STEVENSON: *THE MERRY MEN, DR JEKYLL AND MR HYDE* AND *THE MASTER OF BALLANTRAE*

ROBERT LOUIS STEVENSON (1850–94): HIS BACKGROUND AND FICTION

This chapter deals with three of Stevenson's most powerful stories, which reveal his central preoccupations with the struggle between good and evil, the difficulties of setting boundaries between them, with the consequent ambiguities of interpretation and their representation through dualism of situation and character. To understand the strength of these preoccupations, we need to understand their origins in his Edinburgh background and upbringing.

Stevenson was born a child of post-Enlightenment Edinburgh, and very much one of middle-class respectability, a situation which led to his constant questioning in his fiction of bourgeois values – and probably never coming to a conclusion. His family were 'the Lighthouse Stevensons'; his father and forefathers were the great civil engineers who built Scotland's warning beacons in some of the country's wildest seascapes. His father was also a devout believer and church elder, which Stevenson was not. From being a much-loved sickly child he became a Bohemian student who rebelled against what he felt was the suffocating atmosphere of concern and disapproval at home – and to the deep unhappiness of both parents and son, against his father's religious beliefs.

Arguably, nearly all of Stevenson's Scottish fiction is an exploration of the values of, and his relations with, his family, Edinburgh society and Scotland. They mostly move between opposing poles of morality, so that up to the time of David Balfour and *Kidnapped* (1886) virtually all his protagonists are confused middle-class adolescents, like the fusionless youths who stumble through the colourfully melodramatic stories of *The New Arabian Nights* (1882) and *The Dynamiter* (1885). A comparison of two of these early adolescents is revealing in that it shows how Stevenson could present two utterly opposed sets of moral values in two different stories of 1877. Both stories present a version of the son-father relationship. In 'A Lodging for the Night', set in medieval Paris, the protagonist is François Villon, the robber-poet, who, when given refuge from pursuit by a kindly burgher, considers murdering his father-figure; in 'The Sire de Malétroit's Door', again set in old Paris, Denis de Beaulieu is a simple innocent, once again pursued, but this time by chance straying into the home of the most dangerous man in Paris, Malétroit, who, thinking that Denis is his daughter's lover, presents him with a choice; marry or die. Denis acts nobly to begin with, but since the girl is lovely and honour adjustable, he gives in – to a new, and very different, father?

These diametrically opposed presentations of youth and age are echoed throughout Stevenson's later fiction. They reflect his inability to decide whether he accepted solid middle-class respectability, or whether he rejected it as sanctimonious hypocrisy. This goes a long way to explaining why so many of his 'heroes', from the young innocents of *Arabian Nights* to Jim Hawkins of *Treasure Island* (1883), and from Charles Darnaway of *The Merry Men* (1887) to David Balfour of *Kidnapped* and *Catriona* (1893), are adrift in a complex world of intrigue and power which they cannot understand. Jim Hawkins is caught between emotional and imaginative attraction to the exotic and value-free world of Long John Silver on one hand; and sensible appreciation of the essential order and decency of Squire Trelawney and Dr Livesey on the other. *The Strange Case of Dr Jekyll and Mr Hyde* (1886) has become the literary representation of the gulf between Victorian outward respectability and inward corruption; even although this tale of the mixture of good and evil in Everyman is set in London, the reader can recognise the correspondence of the fictional setting with Stevenson's home in polite Edinburgh, adjacent to slums and vice, and recognise also that the tale is another metaphor for Stevenson's questioning of outward virtue and social status.

Story after story offers variations on the dualism of opposites, presented in paired figures of contrasting type. Often the pairings represent a version of father and son relations, with the father-figure at times seen as worthy, but just as often seen as bigoted and authoritarian, as in the relationship of the repressive religious hypocrite Gordon Darnaway and his college-educated, treasure-hunting nephew Charles Darnaway, in *The Merry Men*; or the for-giving kindly father and errant prodigal son of *The Misadventures of John Nicholson* (1888); and the unforgiving father-judge and hyper-sensitive son in the unfinished *Weir of Hermiston* (1896). Sometimes the opposite values are expressed through a version of brotherly relations where the bond can range from the attraction of opposites to something like Hogg's love-hate relationship in *The Justified Sinner*, in version like that of extrovert Alan Breck and priggish David Balfour; or Frank Cassilis and his dour opposite, Northmour, in Stevenson's *The Pavilion on the Links* (1880).

The Merry Men

Many of Stevenson's best stories were written in the early 1880s, including the marvellous 'Thrawn Janet' (1881), in which a young minister is driven close to madness by his experiences within a remote, religious, superstitious community. One of the finest works from this period is a novella, *The Merry Men*, written in 1881–2. First published serially in *Cornhill Magazine*, it appeared in book form substantially revised in 1887 in *The Merry Men and Other Tales and Fables*.

A young Lowlander tells the story of his return to Aros, 'the sea-girt farm' owned by his widowed uncle, Gordon Darnaway, an austere father-substitute to the orphaned Charles. Hoping to marry his cousin, Mary, but lacking a fortune, Charles Darnaway sets out to find the legendary wreck of a Spanish galleon. Although finding no treasure, he discovers there has recently been a shipwreck, and, stumbling on a grave, fears that his uncle, having stripped the wreck, may also have murdered one of the survivors. Another wreck occurs, when a schooner seemingly owned by Spanish treasure-hunters is driven onto the rocks. Gordon Darnaway, increasingly unstable, finally goes mad, believing that the ship's only survivor, a solitary black man, is a demonic avenger of his sins. He and the black man ultimately perish together in the sea.

One of the story's most striking qualities is its evocation of the natural world. Aros, 'not properly a part of the Ross, nor . . . quite an islet', and its surrounding sea, are evoked with immense sensuous power. The spirit of place was important to Stevenson, who wrote in 'A Gossip on Romance' (1882): 'Some places speak distinctly. Certain dank gardens cry aloud for a murder; certain old houses demand to be haunted; certain coasts are set apart for shipwreck.' The location is based on the island of Earraid, which reappears in *Kidnapped*, but *The Merry Men* had literary roots, too. Stevenson wrote to William Henley in 1881:

> It is, I fancy, my first real shoot at a story; an odd thing, Sir, but, I believe, my own, though there is a little of Scott's *Pirate* in it, as how should there not? He had the root of romance in such places.

Echoing Scott's Shetland novel, *The Merry Men* has self-consciously literary qualities. Described by Stevenson in the same letter to Henley as 'a fantastic sonata about the sea and wrecks', it has a kind of musical unity (at one point the sea itself is described as sounding 'like the combinations of orchestral music'), and a dense, poetic texture. Composed of images and symbols that recur with variations, in a formal sense it points forward to Modernist short fiction.

The 'Merry Men' themselves are breakers that crash on the rocks around Aros, rocks described in Chapter 1:

> There they stand, for all the world like their neighbours ashore; only the salt water sobbing between them instead of the quiet earth, and clots of sea-pink blooming on their sides instead of heather; and the great sea-conger to wreathe about the base of them instead of the poisonous viper of the land.

The images of the sea-conger and viper hint at evil lurking in this beautiful place. The word 'sobbing' is significant, too, for the Merry Men, as their name implies, are personified throughout; indeed many metaphors and similes suggest similarities between the natural and human worlds: the sea, for instance, is sown with rocks 'as thick as a country place with houses'. In Chapter 4, the narrator remarks on how 'human' the breakers sound: 'As when savage men have drunk away their reason, and discarding speech, bawl together in their madness by the hour; so, to my ears, these deadly breakers shouted by Aros in the night.' The story, presenting us with an actual 'drunk man' who loses his reason, conveys a strong sense of human savagery, as destructive in its own way as that of the sea with its 'dance of death'.

Besides a strong sense of place, the story creates a strong sense of cultural traditions. The narrator is 'alien' in Gaelic-speaking Aros, 'springing, as I did, from an unmixed Lowland stock'. His uncle, also a Lowlander, has married an island-woman, Mary Maclean; their daughter, another Mary, has been raised on Aros. Thus from the story's outset there is a crucial meeting of Highland and Lowland. When Charles mentions the history of the islet's name, he introduces a religious theme (Chapter 1):

> It was here that a certain saint first landed on his voyage out of Ireland to convert the Hebrideans. And, indeed, I think he had some claim to be called saint; for, with the boats of that past age, to make so rough a passage, and land on such a ticklish coast, was surely not far short of the miraculous. It was to him, to some of his monkish underlings who had a cell there, that the islet owes its holy and beautiful name, the House of God.

Thus the islet, once a refuge, has a past connection with sainthood, with (implicitly) Catholicism, with sanctity. The story shows the storm-beaten island testing the Christian faith of its inhabitants.

Aros is also a place of folklore and superstition; the non-superstitious Charles hears many legends – 'old wives' stories' – from his 'uncle's man, Rorie, an old servant of the Macleans': tales of sea-kelpies, mermaids and seals. But to Gordon Darnaway, these stories bring, increasingly, foreboding and fear, for instance, of 'a great fish' supposedly haunting the waters between Aros and the mainland. Charles believes his uncle's fears are caused by a guilty conscience, and heightened by the man's religious outlook. We learn in Chapter 1 that:

> He never laughed, that I heard; read long at the Bible; prayed much, like the Cameronians he had been brought up among; and indeed, in many ways, used to remind me of one of the hill-preachers in the killing times before the Revolution. But he never got much comfort, nor even, as I used to think, much guidance, by his piety.

Gordon Darnaway, with his increasingly disordered mind, is strongly characterised through his vivid Scots speech, as when he talks of the recent wreck of the ship he calls *Christ-Anna*: 'But troth, if it wasna prentit in the Bible, I wad whiles be temp'it to think it wasna the Lord, but the muckle, black deil that made the sea . . . But, man, they were sair wonders that God showed to the *Christ-Anna* – wonders, do I ca' them? Judgements, rather . . .' The portrait of a Calvinist personality recalls Scott's fictional Cameronians and might be compared with Stevenson's own 'Thrawn Janet'.

Darnaway exults in 'defiance', but also in his attraction to the dancing, deadly waves (Chapter 5):

> 'There's a spair spang o' the auld sin o' the warld in yon sea; it's an unchristian business at the best o't; an' whiles when it gets up . . . weel, it comes ower me like a glamour. I'm a deil, I ken't. But I think naething o' the puir sailor lads; I'm wi' the sea, I'm just like ane o' her ain Merry Men.'

Convinced of his own damnation because of his 'wild', ecstatic side and because of his 'sins', Gordon Darnaway believes the wreck's giant black survivor is the Devil come to punish him (the Devil was thought in Highland lore to appear at times in the form of a black man). This psychological aspect of the tale anticipates some of Stevenson's later fictions. Darnaway, like a number of other Stevensonian characters, a Presbyterian Lowlander, is shaped by his culture: initially repressed, he is then destructively unrestrained, and finally destroyed along with a kind of 'double'. With his vision of evil and unreason, and his outburst about 'the horror – the horror o' the sea' (in Chapter 2), Darnaway also anticipates Conrad's Kurtz in *The Heart of Darkness* (1902). (Stevenson's later, and increasingly-admired South Seas fiction also foreshadows Conrad.)

The story is narrated by Charles Darnaway, university-educated unlike his uncle, coming to Aros from Enlightenment Edinburgh, where he 'had been favourably remarked by our then Principal in Edinburgh College, the famous writer, Dr Robertson, and by him had been set to work on some papers of an ancient date to rearrange and sift of what was worthless'. This 'Dr Robertson' is most likely William Robertson (1721–93), the moderate Divine (he was a Moderator of the Church of Scotland) and influential historian, who was strongly critical of elements in the Scottish past, including what he saw as religious fanaticism and barbarism. Although soberly Presbyterian, Charles, it is thus implied, is a 'moderate'. He prays for the dead against his uncle's wishes, and despite disclaiming 'a Popish sense', shows a more tolerant outlook than his uncle. He sees beauty in his surroundings, and is moved by the island's Irish monkish past, giving up searching for gold when confronted with the evidence of men's deaths at sea. On seeing the black shipwreck-survivor, despite instinctive prejudice and fear, he extends help and compassion. Even his name, Charles, or Charlie as he is called, may be significant, given the references to Prince Charlie. Describing himself near the end of Chapter 1 as 'fellow of a mechanical turn', he seems to offer a reasonable and humane vision for the future.

This story, rich in interpretative possibilities may be read, most straightforwardly (and, probably convincingly), as a tragic 'human' story, ending with a crazed man's mistaken belief that an innocent shipwreck survivor is demonic. However it is possible to read the story in another way, if the black man, 'like a fallen king' is, as Gordon Darnaway believes, an actual supernatural presence. Folklore is woven into the tale's fabric, and superstition plays an important and ambiguous role in stories like 'Thrawn Janet'. At the same time, with its many Christian references, *The Merry Men* also appears to have parabolic significance. Some critics find the story's moral significance unclear, regarding Charles as an unsympathetic or even unreliable narrator. Edwin Eigner, in *Robert Louis Stevenson and Romantic Tradition* (1966), argues that Charles, condemning his uncle's sins and seeing his death as 'a strange judgement of God's', contributes to that death by attempting to force Darnaway's repentance, and cutting off 'the madman's last escape' at the end. Charles's belief that the final deaths enact 'the decrees of God' may be read by others, however, as the realistically-drawn outlook of a still-religious man whose judgement we need not fully accept. The ending, it may be argued, is left for the reader to interpret and judge. Whatever one's own view, such critical debates suggest that *The Merry Men* is ambiguous in its meaning – pointing towards Stevenson's profounder ambiguities in *The Master of Ballantrae.*

The story itself points to this. In Chapter 2, Charles comments on 'certain strange undecipherable marks – sea runes as we may name them – on the glassy surface of the bay . . . and many a boy must have amused himself as I did, seeking to read in them some reference to himself or those he loved'. These 'runes', interpreted differently by the central characters, suggest the subjectivity of interpretation. Charles has difficulty, too, reading the 'defaced' name of the wreck: 'I could not make out clearly whether she was called *Christiania*, after the Norwegian city, or *Christiana*, after the good woman, Christian's wife, in that old book the *Pilgrim's Progress*.' The story, like the ship, may be read as rooted in reality, or as parable. Almost like a postmodern fiction, *The Merry Men* warns of the impossibility of certainty or fixed meaning.

Life in this story generally appears as rough and uncertain, changeful, the world a place where darkness can all too quickly replace sunlight, and where death comes suddenly. Both land and sea in this story are difficult, broken terrain, 'a labyrinth' (a favourite image of Stevenson's) where maps are of little use, and where faith may falter. If perhaps in the last analysis the novella is not entirely successful, the image of Gordon Darnaway perched fearfully on a cliff is memorable, and the book's vision strikingly modern.

The Strange Case of Dr Jekyll and Mr Hyde

STEVENSON AND 'DUALITY'

The conclusion of *The Merry Men*, with the simultaneous deaths of Gordon Darnaway and the mysterious black man from the sea, suggests an interest in duality, more fully explored elsewhere, most famously in *The Strange Case of Dr Jekyll and Mr Hyde* (1886).

There are foreshadowings of the book in Stevenson's earlier work: for instance, a play, *Deacon Brodie or The Double Life*, published in 1880, dealt with the life of an apparently respectable and prosperous member of Edinburgh Town Council, a deacon of the wrights (cabinet-makers) who was hanged in 1788 for his part in a gang robbery of the excise building in Edinburgh. The same idea was used in the powerful story 'Markheim', written in 1884 and published in 1886, and 'The Travelling Companion', an earlier version of the

Jekyll and Hyde theme. Paired characters appear throughout Stevenson's fiction, of course, in *Kidnapped* and elsewhere.

Throughout the nineteenth century there was general interest in duality. In Scotland there were precedents for the kind of themes found in *Dr Jekyll and Mr Hyde*, notably Hogg's *Memoirs and Confessions of a Justified Sinner* (1824) with its many 'dualisms'. Dostoevsky's *The Double* appeared in 1846, while later, Oscar Wilde's *The Picture of Dorian Gray* (1891) shows affinities with Stevenson. Dualism is central to nineteenth-century 'Gothic' fiction, a tradition with which Stevenson has affinities. Among Gothic novels which made use of science, in particular, Mary Shelley's *Frankenstein* (1818), suggests itself as an influence. Stevenson's novella, with its labyrinthine structure, may also echo the formal qualities of some Gothic fiction. The 'fantastic' aspect of the work is echoed elsewhere in Scottish fiction, in George MacDonald's adult fantasies *Phantastes* and *Lilith*, and in the supernatural stories of Margaret Oliphant, although some elements in *Jekyll and Hyde*, including the plot of a professional man's fall, link Stevenson's work to the literary 'realism' of his day.

PSYCHOLOGY

Literary and critical interest in duality from the Romantic period onwards may reflect ideas drawn from the developing study of psychology; for example the works of E. T. A. Hoffman may draw on ideas of the times such as those of G. H. Schubert in *Die Symbolik des Traumes* (1814). Later in the nineteenth century, Taine presented the concept of 'two moral personalities in the same individual' in *On Intelligence* (1870) and similar concepts were taken up by others, including William James in the United States and T. H. Huxley in Britain. Stevenson was interested in such ideas. According to Fanny Stevenson (in a prefatory note to the Tusitala Edition), 'Deacon Brodie', 'Markheim', and *Dr Jekyll and Mr Hyde* drew on a paper on 'subconsciousness' which Stevenson had read in a French scientific journal.

PUBLICATION AND ORIGINS

Dr Jekyll and Mr Hyde is said to have originated in a dream of Stevenson's, as he himself recounts in 'A Chapter on Dreams', written in 1887 and first published in *Scribner's Magazine*, January 1888:

> I had long been trying to write a story on this subject, to find a body, a vehicle, for that strong sense of man's double being which must at times come in upon and overwhelm the mind of every thinking creature . . .
> For two days I went about racking my brains for a plot of any sort; and on

the second night I dreamed the scene at the window, and a scene afterwards split in two, in which Hyde, pursued for some crime, took the powder and underwent the change in the presence of his pursuers. All the rest was made awake, and consciously, although I think I can trace in much of it the manner of my Brownies.

According to various accounts, Stevenson's wife, Fanny, persuaded him to work up this story from being merely a 'crawler' (the 'shilling shocker' was a popular form to which Stevenson was attracted), convincing him it should be an 'allegory'. Critics were impressed. Andrew Lang (in an unsigned review in the *Saturday Review* (9 Jan 1886), commented, 'to adopt a recent definition of some of Mr Stevenson's tales, this little shilling work is like "Poe with the addition of a moral sense . . ." Yet Mr Stevenson's originality of treatment remains none the less striking and astonishing.'

It is interesting that such a remark should be made so early on, for *Jekyll and Hyde* has, like *Robinson Crusoe* and *Frankenstein*, achieved mythological status. Many films have been made of it, so that even people who have never read the book have some knowledge (often inaccurate) of the story. Many novelists have responded to *Jekyll and Hyde*, including Emma Tennant in *Two Women of London: The Strange Case of Ms Jekyll and Mrs Hyde* (1989), and Valerie Martin with *Mary Reilly* (1990), to name but two.

THE TITLE AND ITS MEANINGS

The book's full title suggests various possible interpretations. The 'case' might be a doctor's case (and of course key characters are medical doctors). It might also be a legal case (and again, there are lawyers in the story), or the kind of 'case' found in detective fiction – and detective fiction was already an established genre in the nineteenth century, with highly successful novels by writers such as Wilkie Collins. Interestingly, although the book pre-dated the murders committed by Jack the Ripper, it seems to capture the anxieties surrounding that 'case', and has often been interpreted with it in mind. The title of one chapter, 'The Carew Murder Case', draws attention to the idea of crime, inviting the reader to ponder the nature and significance of the 'crimes' enacted more generally in this text.

The adjective 'Strange' is also worthy of note. Utterson uses the word several times to Jekyll's servant Poole, when he is summoned to Jekyll's house (in the chapter titled 'The Last Night'): 'This is a very strange tale,' he remarks; also, 'This is a strange note,' and 'These are all very strange circumstances.' Throughout the book, certain words are repeated in this manner, as in poetry, drawing attention to themselves and prompting us to consider their significance. In Henry Jekyll's final statement, he describes how 'I stole through the corridors, a stranger in my own house; and coming to my room, I saw for the first time the appearance of Edward Hyde.'

In this novella, the house is closely linked to Jekyll's very self and personality, so we are encouraged to think about the ways in which Jekyll has become 'estranged' from his more usual, or public self. Often, in this book, familiar words are used in unfamiliar ways (and hence are literally 'made strange'), and unusual words are also used, creating a sense of slight 'estrangement' in the reader, too. 'Echo effects' (where words or phrases are repeated close together) mimic the concern with duality, which permeates this highly-wrought text, linguistically, thematically and, in places, structurally.

NARRATIVE STRUCTURE

Jekyll and Hyde is structured rather like a sheaf of documents or 'casebook'. It is broken up into ten chapters; within this basic structure, it can also be seen as containing various kinds of narrative:

- Opening narrative in third person by unnamed omniscient narrator;
- Enfield's first-person account to Utterson;
- Narrator's accounts with Utterson as main focus;
- Section of letter to Utterson from Jekyll, in 'Remarkable Incident of Doctor Lanyon';
- Letter to Utterson from Jekyll (in 'The Last Night');
- Account in 'The Carew Murder Case', of the maid's experience (not from Utterson's perspective); the opening recalls a newspaper account of 'notorious crimes';
- Dr Lanyon's (posthumous) narrative, including letter to Lanyon from Jekyll;
- Dr Jekyll's statement.

The apparently disconnected narrative, with its many shifts of voice and viewpoint, and Chinese-box effect (narratives within narratives) contributes powerfully to the overall effect of the work, creating not only a sense of unease in the reader, who rests his sympathy with no single narrator, but also an unsatisfied sense of curiosity. It is only near the end that Hyde's existence is explained. The technique of 'deferral' employed here shares qualities with post-modernist fiction.

The various 'objective' and 'subjective' accounts, in a structure which echoes Hogg's *Justified Sinner*, offer shifting perspectives on the central events, provoking thoughts about what constitutes 'truth'. It is, perhaps, noteworthy that it is only after having read through a variety of documents the reader comes finally to the two first-hand documents, 'Dr Lanyon's Narrative', and 'Henry Jekyll's Statement of the Case'. Even if the structure may at first seem almost random, there is a careful composition at work. The first chapter is titled 'Story of the Door'; signalling that the door will be literally important in the text. This also suggests the 'doorway' to the text itself. The last word in the book is 'end'. Within the text's framework various instances of duality can be detected; for instance, the last two sections are both first-person narratives. *Jekyll and Hyde* produces a complex effect of both chaos and order, suggestive of the chaos of Hyde, and the attempted order of Jekyll.

A WORLD OF PROFESSIONAL MEN

It is notable that the main characters are all professional men. Utterson is a lawyer, Lanyon and Jekyll are doctors, and Enfield a 'well-known man about town'. That the characters are all male, and in responsible professions, would have given the Victorian reader, especially, a sense that the story was more likely to be 'true' (and thus more horrifying). Such sober, rational men could be expected to make 'reliable' witnesses to events that would otherwise seem unlikely to say the least.

There are no major female characters, and only a few minor ones (the little girl who is trampled, the maid who sees Hyde, the old woman who keeps his house), which was noted at the time, by Henry James. This creates a stark effect, as in a fable; the small group of men is securely in the reader's focus, and the relationships between them – notably between Jekyll and Hyde – can be more readily perceived.

The absence of women, however, may have various kinds of significance. Whether intentionally or unintentionally, the text can be seen as illustrating the gendered power-structures of Victorian society, where men were dominant; Jekyll and his 'old cronies' (as they are called in 'Dr Jekyll was Quite at Ease') form a tightly-knit, exclusive group. In this period, too, there was considerable anxiety about 'the New Woman' and about homosexuality; the text may hint at fears of both (possibly on Stevenson's part, and, more certainly, on the part of the society depicted). While there are no explicit allusions to sex or sexuality, the reader may infer sexual 'irregularity' on the part of various characters. *Jekyll and Hyde* is now seen as illustrating and probing the hypocrisies and fears of Victorian society in various ways.

UTTERSON / ENFIELD / LANYON

Among the group of key characters, various pairings and dualities can be found. The first character the reader encounters is Utterson, a solitary bachelor (a stock type in Victorian fiction). He seems supremely 'rational' and restrained, like the 'public' Jekyll, who, we learn in his 'full statement' had 'an imperious desire to . . . wear a more than commonly grave countenance before the public'. In some ways, therefore, Utterson mirrors aspects of Jekyll. On the other hand, Utterson seems to repress his instincts for pleasure: 'He was austere with himself; drank gin when he was alone, to mortify a taste for vintages; and though he enjoyed the theatre, had not crossed the doors of one for twenty years', while Jekyll says 'I had not yet conquered my aversion to the dryness of a life of study' ('Henry Jekyll's Statement'), and admits to indulging but concealing his (implied licentious) pleasures. Yet again, Utterson's repression in another sense echoes Jekyll's repression of Hyde, who 'comes out roaring'.

The early paragraphs of the novella set up ideas and themes that will unfold later. We learn of Utterson: ' "I incline to Cain's heresy," he used to say quaintly, "I let my brother go to the devil in his own way," ' which foreshadows the 'going to the devil' of Jekyll. When, in the second paragraph, we learn of Utterson's relationship with his more sociable kinsman, Enfield, a second 'pair' of characters is formed, apparent opposites bound together by invisible bonds. There are similar dualities and echoes throughout, and although Dr Jekyll may be initially (as one chapter heading suggests) 'quite at ease', the reader soon is not.

The first description of Dr Lanyon, 'a hearty, healthy, dapper, red-faced gentleman, with a shock of hair prematurely white, and a boisterous and decided manner' seems superficially reassuring, but the white hair foreshadows his unhappy end (a week after announcing an irrevocable split with Dr Jekyll, 'Dr Lanyon took to his bed, and in something less than a fortnight he was dead'). Although a hint at something not quite straightforward in his manner ('theatrical') is immediately balanced by the reference to his 'genuine feeling', this kind of equivocation is echoed elsewhere in a narrative that from early on creates a profound sense of disquiet.

CREATION OF UNEASE

Enfield's story in the first chapter is disturbing:

> I was coming home from some place at the end of the world, about three
> o'clock of a black winter morning, and my way lay through a part of town
> where there was literally nothing to be seen but lamps. Street after street, and

all the folks asleep – street after street, all lighted up as if for a procession and all as empty as a church – till at last I got into that state of mind when a man listens and listens and begins to long for the sight of a policeman.

The vagueness of Enfield's comment that he was returning 'from some place at the end of the world' seems to take the story out of its 'real' context and locate it in some almost 'otherworldly' dimension, at the same time hinting that he may have been out pursuing forbidden pleasures. A sense of dread is further created by the time (late at night), darkness, and the fact that it is winter, which throws up by contrast the (unexplainedly) bright streets. There is something sinister in the image of the streets of lights, with that hint at infernal gaiety 'as if for a procession', and the repetition of 'Street after street' reinforces this. The simile 'empty as a church' is disquieting, too (why is the church empty? – suggests loss of faith?). There is a hint of inversion here (a church should be a reassuring image) that is sinister. Finally even the worldly Enfield admits that he is in an anxious state of mind (again there is striking use of verbal repetition: 'listens and listens').

The description of the 'encounter' between Hyde and the little girl is acutely disturbing, and the sinister atmosphere is repeated in the account of Mr Utterson's dream in the second chapter, 'Search for Mr Hyde'. Here, there is both specificity of detail – 'Six o'clock struck on the bells of the church that was so conveniently near to Mr Utterson's dwelling' – and vagueness of impression. Within the dream, Utterson sees 'a room in a rich house, where his friend lay asleep, dreaming and smiling at his dreams'. With a Chinese-box effect reminiscent of the larger text, this imagined sequence (which echoes a scene in Mary Shelley's *Frankenstein*) creates a greater and greater distance between the reader and 'reality'.

TOPOGRAPHY: THE CITY

In the dream Utterson traverses 'wider labyrinths of lamplighted city', the strongly visual imagery of darkness and light hinting at the moral themes to come. The nocturnal city of Utterson's dreams is London, at this time (even more than now) the centre of power and culture, so that Stevenson's text strikes at the very heart of Victorian Britain. Yet Stevenson's London also resembles his native Edinburgh, not just physically, with its foggy wynds and vennels, but in its enactment of the 'double' life he associated with that Calvinist, bourgeois city. The textual London, later in the text described as 'some city in a nightmare' (in 'The Carew Murder Case'), is suggestive, too, like James Thomson's *The City of Dreadful Night*, published in parts during 1874 and as a book in 1880, of a 'city of the mind'.

TOPOGRAPHY: THE HOUSE

The significance of locale is implied at the outset. 'Story of the Door' describes a quiet yet fairly prosperous London street which 'with its freshly painted shutters, well-polished brasses and general cleanliness and gaiety of tone, instantly caught and pleased the eye of the passenger'. In the next paragraph, we learn that 'a certain sinister block of building thrust forward its gable on the street. It was two storeys high; showed no window, nothing but a door on the lower storey and a blind forehead of discoloured wall on the upper'. The word 'forehead' is suggestive. As we soon learn, Hyde's door is in fact an entrance at the back of Jekyll's house, which with its prosperous front door and 'sordid' back door symbolises on one level the man Jekyll himself. The construction of the house itself is carefully explained (especially in 'The Last Night'), and its various parts are each significant. Bought from 'the heirs of a celebrated surgeon' the house has a dissecting room and laboratory, with echoes of *Frankenstein* or Burke and Hare. It is notable that Hyde is first observed entering 'by the old dissecting room door', and 'he mostly comes and goes by the laboratory'.

INTERIORS

It is also interesting to note the way in which cold (often wintry) streets are frequently contrasted with the warm interiors of rooms. When Utterson goes to visit Jekyll, for instance, he is admitted 'into a large, low-roofed, comfortable hall, paved with flags, warmed (after the fashion of a country house), by a bright, open fire, and furnished with costly cabinets of oak'. Yet even these warm interiors are menacing to Utterson, who sees 'a menace in the flickering of the firelight on the polished cabinets', and later, Jekyll's house is described as 'that house of voluntary bondage'. Within Jekyll's cabinet, the 'cheval glass' (a full-length mirror) is at first casually mentioned; later its significance becomes clearer, for this is where Hyde first inspects his own appearance.

Jekyll and Hyde, read carefully, reveals itself as a web of images, some of which expand symbolically to wider meanings. The wine, for instance, that the bachelors enjoy ('all judges of good wine' as they are called, in 'Dr Jekyll was Quite at Ease') is a recurrent motif; transmuted by the end to the deadly potion that Jekyll consumes in order to change his appearance. Vladimir Nabokov described *Jekyll and Hyde* as in this respect a 'phenomenon of style', in his *Lectures on Literature* (1980).

THE FIGURES OF JEKYLL AND HYDE

The names of the main characters are important in a text which uses language with such care. It has been suggested that the name Jekyll can be read as 'Je – kill', and 'Hyde' of course as 'Hide' (and there is a pun to that effect, in 'Search for Mr Hyde'). (Other names – 'Mr Utterson' of 'Gaunt' Street, for instance – are similarly suggestive.) Jekyll and Hyde, of course, are both in a sense really Jekyll, who is, like his handwriting (the 'hand' is another recurring motif), both 'upright' and 'odd', as it is described in 'Incident of the Letter'.

Dr Jekyll is not even mentioned by name in Chapter 1, but merely referred to as 'the very pink of the proprieties, celebrated too, and (what makes it worse) one of your fellows who do what they call good'. The reader is not at this stage aware that it is Jekyll being described, nor is Utterson. Jekyll is first referred to by name in Chapter 2, initially because Utterson reads 'Dr Jekyll's Will', where all his qualifications are listed, emphasising his public *persona* and professional standing, but the reader knows little more until Dr Lanyon's troubling statement: ' "But it is more than ten years since Henry Jekyll became too fanciful for me. He began to go wrong, wrong in mind . . ." '. Utterson's, and the reader's, first encounter with Hyde in fact – significantly – predate the first encounter with Jekyll.

Dr Jekyll himself only actually appears in Chapter 3, 'a large, well-made, smooth-faced man of fifty, with something of a slyish cast perhaps, but every mark of capacity and kindness.' This is a seemingly bland description, but one ominously echoed later, by that of the woman at Hyde's home, who has 'an evil face, smoothed by hypocrisy' ('The "Carew Murder Case"'). Already, much information has been deferred, and we only have hints at trouble; it is not until the last section 'Henry Jekyll's Full Statement of the Case' that we get any deeper insight into this character and his circumstances.

HYDE

Hyde first appears, in Enfield's account in the opening chapter, just as a 'little man who was stumping along', and all we learn of his appearance is Enfield's reaction to it: 'I had taken a loathing to my gentleman at first sight', an impression he elaborates only a little:

'He is not easy to describe. There is something wrong with his appearance; something displeasing, something downright detestable. I never saw a man I so disliked, and yet I scarce know why. He must be deformed somewhere; he gives a strong feeling of deformity, although I couldn't specify the point. He's an extraordinary-looking man, and yet I really can name nothing out of the way. No, sir; I can make no hand of it; I can't describe him. And it's not want of memory; for I declare I can see him this moment.'

The vagueness of this description is striking – the repetition of 'something' three times in the second sentence signals an impression reiterated throughout. The only 'visual' hint here is that the man 'must be deformed somewhere'. The description of Mr Hyde in the second chapter and others later all tend to have this indeterminate quality, although certain ideas recur.

SOCIAL THEMES

Hyde is described by several characters as dwarfish, deformed; conventionally, in melodrama and in Gothic, this suggests evil, but there are other connotations, too. On several occasions he is described as animal-like – he is 'ape-like', a 'monkey'. Such descriptions suggest that Stevenson had Darwin's theories in mind when he created Hyde. Hyde's appearance may reflect anxieties and fears of regression and degeneration in this period. He lives, too, in a poor and 'dingy' district of town; while Jekyll is a respectable 'gentleman'; Hyde is associated with 'the lower classes', suggesting anxieties about class, as well; and as his smallness is also emphasised, along with some supposedly 'feminine' characteristics, he may suggest, too, fear of the 'feminine' as it was conceived at that time.

PSYCHOLOGICAL AND PSYCHOANALYTICAL APPROACHES

The psychological interests that make *The Merry Men* so interesting are present in this text as well, which in many ways appears to anticipate the insights and ideas of Freud. In his concluding narrative Jekyll describes his relationship with Hyde as like that of father and son; 'Jekyll had more than a father's interest; Hyde had more than a son's indifference', an echo of a theme that recurs throughout Stevenson's fiction, the Oedipal drama of the father-son conflict. Jekyll fondly remembers walking with his father, but Hyde, that 'child of Hell', as Jekyll calls him, destroys the portrait of Jekyll's father. Themes of repression are explored, rather like Freud's id and ego; Jekyll tries to suppress Hyde, but cannot, and Hyde only returns more forcefully.

JEKYLL'S NARRATIVE: MORAL QUESTIONS

It is not until the end that we can really begin to assess Jekyll. It is important to note that he was not, before the creation of Hyde, a straightforwardly 'good' man although he did 'what they call good' (a hint here at hypocritical 'good works'?). He was a man ashamed of a part of his own nature (Chapter 10):

> The worst of my fault was a certain impatient gaiety of disposition, such as has made the happiness of many, but such as I found it hard to reconcile with my imperious desire to carry my head high, and wear a more than

417

commonly grave countenance before the public. Hence it came about that I concealed my pleasures; and that when I reached years of reflection, and began to look round me and take stock of my progress and position in the world, I stood already committed to a profound duplicity of life.

The 'impatient gaiety of disposition' hints at possible 'licentiousness' (this last section of the book, especially, has affinities with fin-de-siècle 'decadent texts'), although Jekyll's (and indeed Hyde's) precise wrongdoings are kept strikingly vague, so that the concept of 'evil' conveyed cannot be limited to mere sexual 'looseness'.

How is Jekyll to be judged? Earlier, Utterson reflects on his friend: 'He was wild when he was young; a long while ago to be sure; but in the law of God there is no statute of limitations', hinting at a Christian judgement. Dr Lanyon condemns Jekyll's 'moral turpitude'. The reader, by the end, has been given an opportunity to assess 'the Case', although the last chapter's title, 'Henry Jekyll's Full Statement of the Case', does beg the question, is there any such thing as a 'full statement'? In his statement Jekyll emerges as deeply troubled and confused, referring to both Jekyll and Hyde as 'external' individuals. He becomes 'removed' from Hyde although in Hyde's form, and stating 'He, I say – I cannot say, I', ends neither truly one nor the other. A close analysis of the grammatical structures used in Jekyll's statement reveals the man's self-alienation. His statement is fractured, rather than 'full'. But what are his crimes, besides the actual deaths he causes (Carew and Lanyon)? Jekyll is guilty of the hubris of the over-reaching scientist, and (although he denies this) of hypocrisy: these comprise his 'profound duplicity' of life. His own moral vision, too, is fatally flawed. Despite the concern with duality, the moral vision of the book itself is far from simple.

G. K. Chesterton wrote perceptively in his *Robert Louis Stevenson* (1927):

The point of the story is not that a man can cut himself off from his conscience, but that he cannot. The surgical operation is fatal in the story. It is an amputation of which both the parts die. Jekyll, even in dying, declares the conclusion of the matter; that the load of man's moral struggle is bound upon him and cannot be thus escaped.

There are many echoes of Hogg's *Confessions* throughout: the scene where the maid witnesses Hyde committing murder, which echoes Hogg's account of the murder of George Colwan, and in the style of 'Incident of the Letter', where Jekyll writes, 'if I am the chief of sinners, I am the chief of sufferers also.' But there are particular echoes in the final section. The moment when

Jekyll thinks a 'vainglorious' thought is when he is again overwhelmed by Hyde, just as Robert Wringhim's key moment of spiritual pride coincides with his meeting Gil-Martin. Jekyll's misery, his sense of being a 'prisoner', echoes Robert Wringhim's despair in the concluding sequences of Hogg's great novel; and in the last paragraph Jekyll describes his statement as a 'confession'.

The echoes of Hogg are telling, for just as *The Justified Sinner* undermines any single or fixed notion of truth, so too does Stevenson's novella, which, foreshadowing post-modern fiction, is hauntingly 'indeterminate'. *Jekyll and Hyde* has a fable-like quality (and Stevenson published many short moral fables), but here there is no moral coda or narrator's conclusion. The reader is left to make up his or her own mind about what Jekyll has stated, and no clear moral is drawn.

RECENT CRITICAL APPROACHES

Jekyll and Hyde has proved very popular with critics, as is apparent from the book of essays, *Dr Jekyll and Mr Hyde after One Hundred Years* (1988), and excellent articles by Stephen Heath and Ronald Thomas (1986) among others, while Elaine Showalter discusses Stevenson in her *Sexual Anarchy: Gender and Culture at the Fin de Siecle* (1990). It may be that the post-structuralist critical climate is a fruitful one for the reassessment of Stevenson's work, especially as indeterminate and teasing a book as this one.

The Master of Ballantrae

By the time he came to write his most enigmatic and ambitious novel, *The Master of Ballantrae* (1889), just after his father's death in 1887, Stevenson had established in his fiction two creative characteristics closely connected to his tortuous relations with his father and family background. The first was the pairings or opposites mentioned above. The second characteristic led him increasingly to deal with these or his other worlds with ambivalence, allowing neither of the groups and their values, or even the worlds of rationalism or the supernatural, to have a final indubitable value.

'PROVIDENCE' AND 'CHANCE'

It could be suggested that two dominating concepts in Stevenson's fiction emerged in the late 1880s in the ideas of 'providence' and 'chance'. 'Chance' had always played a significant role in his creations, as he dropped his inexperienced young men into worlds completely different from the settled, traditionally structured worlds of their parental background – amongst mad bombers, in suicide clubs, with exiled Bohemian princes of supernatural capabilities, on treasure islands and lonely Hebridean bays with sunken galleons, and into marriages with the beautiful daughters of devilish French aristocrats. Understandably this attracted Stevenson as an amoral 'way out' of his own dilemma of values, and it became a fictional device for releasing himself and his protagonists from the weight of moral choice. But to the maturing Stevenson 'chance' as a concept perhaps became something deeper, truer to the life of the later nineteenth century. By the time of *The Master of Ballantrae* (1889) it had become the sign of a way of life opposite to that represented by 'providence', the force behind the world of his father, the church elder Thomas Stevenson, and Presbyterian Edinburgh. More clearly than ever before, Stevenson bases one Master of Ballantrae, Henry Durie, in a world of 'providence', and the other Master of Ballantrae, James, in a secular, and, as one critic has called it, 'ur-existential' world of 'chance' where his making of decisions on the basis of coin-tossing reflects his 'belief' in a random universe – and his disbelief in conventional morality of 'providence'.

THE QUESTION OF RELIABILITY

It is crucial to a reconsideration of *The Master of Ballantrae* that we accept what most readers would initially agree is a fair reading of the novel. Such a reading would accept that in the narrator, Mackellar, we have a reliable witness to the fortunes of the house of Durrisdeer. He may be a somewhat pernickety, spinsterish Presbyterian of the old school, but in many ways such dry traits supply that very credibility which the reader so instinctively seeks in tracing the rights and wrongs of the various Durrisdeers. It is part of Stevenson's great skill that Mackellar supplies, effortlessly, this reader's need – in something resembling the way Nellie Dean answers the reader's need for conventional yardsticks of morality in *Wuthering Heights* (1847). Incredible and unnatural events are made palatable in both by being anchored to acceptable and reassuring figures of social certainty.

HENRY AND JAMES: GOOD AND EVIL?

In this reading Henry Durie becomes the victim of history and James. Time has placed him in an inferior role; fate has given him less obvious gifts than James, and he is less attractive to the neighbourhood and to Alison and his father, Lord Durrisdeer. And what more likely than that the quieter brother of a charismatic and subtle extrovert should retreat somewhat within himself, repressing and denying through mingled stubbornness and jealousy the qualities which might rival those of his brother? Read like this, Henry's story is a painful tracing of misunderstanding and deliberate misdirection by James, whereby Alison's, their father's, and the world's view of Henry is diminished by Henry's reticence and bad luck, and James's guileful art. In this reading the kinship of Henry to David Balfour stands out clearly, their mutual reserve actually adding to our liking for them, the underdogs of a world which prefers the superficial charm of a Breck or James Durie.

Clearly, too, in this interpretation, Stevenson presents James as a study of evil. Black is his colour in dress and in image or association, from that 'very black mark' against him in the opening pages to the night settings that surround his most mysterious episodes. The transition from this motif of blackness to the imputation of demonic traits is effortless; from his childhood exploits when he masquerades against Wullie White the Wabster as Auld Hornie; or his father cries 'I think you are a devil of a son to me'; to when he takes command of pirate Teach's ship 'little Hell'; or later, when he appears as Satan in Milton's epic, a fallen angel. (We recall that Stevenson's 'editor' in his Preface remembered that a Durrisdeer 'had some strange passages with the devil'.) Most important is James's artfulness; one recalls that the Devil himself was Father of Lies, and James is in this respect very much a disciple, since he is utter master of the lie unstated, the contrived situation where he will affect a person or company with a gesture, an argument, or a song, theatrically and consummately presented. 'I never yet failed to charm a person when I wanted', he says to Mackellar at the end of the voyage on the *Nonesuch*, when even Mackellar admits that James and he have come to live together on excellent terms. Taken this way, James can be seen as an incubus, the traditional demon who makes nightmares for unsuspecting mortals, and the descendant of Hogg's Gil-Martin, who haunts his brother as George Colwan was haunted in *The Justified Sinner*.

This entirely valid reading of the novel makes it a tragedy, where Henry, having been all but destroyed by this malevolent quasi-devil, completes his own and his family's destruction by descending to the dark levels of his brother; so much so that the running devil-motif comes in the closing stages to apply to Henry quite as much as James. Henry is finally seen to be more wicked than James, and in league with rogues darker than any of James's piratical colleagues.

TRADITIONS OF AMBIGUITY

But this reading certainly has limitations. It is difficult to understand how James, that uncannily quick athlete of cat-like reflexes and endless experience in the world's wildest scenes of action, could ever have lost the duel with his brother. For all the argument of 'contained and glowing fury', for all the

421

reader has sympathy for Henry and anger against James for what he has done to him, it seems even then too melodramatic a solution to suggest that a triumphant sense of rightness wells up in depressed, cheated, deprived Henry at just the necessary moment. Moreover, if the reading is simply to be that Henry is good and James bad, there seems little point in the way the narrators of the action, Mackellar and Chevalier Burke, change awkwardly, just as the locations change arbitrarily and suddenly from rain-gloomy Scotland to swamp-dank Albany or strange sea-voyages. If the simple good-bad reading is maintained, then in the end poetic justice has been lost by the reduction of Henry's goodness to something so inconsequential that he is allowed to share the same grave as his devil-brother. Are we to think that Stevenson committed the final artistic sin of changing his vision in midstream, having Henry reborn after the duel as a malevolent adult-child, crippled by guilt and warped into a new shape which increasingly rivalled the degradation of James?

Stevenson, it could be argued, wished only to allow this reading to exist as a possibility. With the example of Hogg's Sinner before him of 'reversible interpretation'; with indeed the tendency of the Presbyterian and Puritan traditions in poetry and fiction towards alternative meanings familiar to him from examples as diverse as Burns's 'Tam o' Shanter' to Hawthorne's 'Young Goodman Brown' and *The Scarlet Letter*, Melville's *Moby Dick* (1851), and even his friend Henry James's *The Portrait of a Lady* published some eight years earlier, there were many attractions towards a fiction of mutually exclusive interpretations. The best of Scottish fiction in the nineteenth century, from Scott's *Waverley* (1814) and the fiction of Hogg and Galt in the age of Scott to enigmatic novels at the end of the century such as Davidson's *Baptist Lake* (1894) and *Earl Lavender* (1895), Barrie's *Sentimental Tommy* (1896), Munro's *John Splendid* (1898) and *Gilian the Dreamer* (1899), consistently presents ambiguous protagonists, the question of whose moral worth is deliberately and tantalisingly left unanswered or interpretable in one of two mutually exclusive ways. And the attraction of such ambiguity for Stevenson clearly lies in the way that it would release him from his previous problems of struggling confusedly with emblems of a shifting moral consciousness, together with the constant changing of moral position in individual stories. *The Master of Ballantrae* derives its greatness from the fact that it is the only novel of Stevenson's successfully to resolve – even although it is by sidestep and sleight of creative hand – the dilemma of values so manifest in the other fiction. This is not all. In solving his own problem of values by creating a work which in effect has no definitive value structure at all, Stevenson created the classic version of the Scottish 'dissociation of sensibility' novel. This tradition of fiction had begun with Scott and developed into what virtually constituted a school of Scottish fiction, with its recurrent themes of divided self and divided community representing the tensions of past and present, disorder and order, and romance and realism, which so preoccupied Scottish writers, divided in their values and cultural loyalties.

REVERSING MORALITIES: THE OTHER READING OF THE NOVEL

All this suggests that Stevenson may have intended another reading of his novel. There are, after all, two Masters of Ballantrae. The very title poses a question similar to that of James in *The Portrait of a Lady*. It warns us, since it does not name the identity of the Master, of a struggle of brothers and opposed 'moralities'. And in this struggle, sensitive reading will show that from the very beginning Henry is not that symbol of undoubted worth of first impression. From that unnecessary 'You know very well that you are the favourite' when quarrelling with James, there is revealed something petulant and small in his personality. He is 'strangely obstinate' in silence when his true nature is misunderstood, and early we are told that he is 'neither very bad nor very able, but an honest, solid sort of lad'. Whatever else, he is certainly a dogged stay-at-home; emotionally – at least to the observer – a rather arid fellow, willing in the end to marry for the pity of the lady who loves his brother, 'by nature inclining to the parsimonious'. 'The weakness of my ground', he tells Mackellar, 'lies in myself, that I am not one who engages love'. When he is ill his instinctive preference for business emerges, 'mortifying' even Mackellar with 'affairs, cyphering figures, and holding disputation with the tenantry'.

But Stevenson is far too subtle to underdraw Henry to the point of symbolic simplicity. One of the most moving glimpses of the novel is of Henry, early on, doing the accounts of Durrisdeer with Mackellar, and falling into a deep muse, staring straight west into the sun over the long sands, where the free-traders, with a great force of men and horses, are scouring on the beach. Mackellar marvels that Henry is not blinded; Henry frowns, rubs his brow, smiles and says: 'You would not guess what I was thinking . . . I was thinking I would be a happier man if I could ride and run the danger of my life, with these lawless companions.' Like James? Henry's tragedy is deepened by the fact that he knows his own malformation, and he knows that he cannot be what he is not. His trade is far from free, as he tells Mackellar, concluding 'and with that we may get back to our accounts'.

The episode has, however, made us early aware of depths of rebellious feeling in Henry. Foreshortened emotions have their revenges, and Stevenson most effectively shows Henry's emerging in catastrophic fashion at the duel, and then, since guilt will refashion the man anew, emerging in yet more poisoned manner. After the duel – 'something of the child he exhibited; a cheerfulness quite foreign to his previous character'. This good humour is false, based as it is on brain-damaged forgetfulness, implying that Henry cannot face the reality of his actions. He beats the groom, which is 'out of all his former practice'; has 'a singular furtive smile'; and utters his black curse on James – 'I wish he was in hell' – in front of his son, which reveals how far the disease has gone in de-Christianising him. Out of dissociation of personality comes what looks very like evil, as he poisons his son's mind, and insists on his title as Master, 'the which he was punctilious in exacting'. Need we follow his further deterioration? His psychosomatic degradation, as his body grows slack, stooping, walking with a running motion? By the end, in his employment of the dregs of Albany cut-throats to do away with James, he has paralleled if not outdone James's most suspect deeds.

If further evidence is needed that Stevenson early warns us to be on our guard against too facile moral appraisal of the brothers, consider how subtly he arranges their background and support. At first only Mackellar supports Henry, with one crucial exception. In Chapter 1, beyond the family, 'there was never a good word for Mr Henry', except for Macconochie, 'an old, ill-spoken, swearing, ranting, drunken dog'. Conversely, on James's side, was John Paul, 'a little, bald, solemn, stomachy man, a great professor of piety –'; and, says Mackellar, 'I have often thought it an odd circumstance in human nature that these two serving men should each have been the champion of his contrary, and made light of their own virtues when they beheld them in a master.' Here is dissociation with a vengeance! Here is yet again Scottish fiction's warning that strange compensations must be paid when whole critical and emotional awareness is lost. For beyond this lies a pattern of similar waywardness. Countryside opinion is never reliable. James becomes a false hero after the presumption of his death in the Rebellion, Jessie Broun unnaturally swinging against her former helper, Henry, and crying up her betrayer James as a saint. Can we then trust the picture when, in mirror image, James is isolated with Secundra Dass against a hostile Albany?

PATTERN AND SHAPE

We come to the question at the heart of the discussion. And it is a question of pattern. If a visual representation could be made of the overall shape of this novel, it would resemble that of *Vanity Fair* (1848), in that the fortunes of the principal pair of characters would complete two opposed rising and falling movements. Like the opposed zeniths and nadirs of Becky and Amelia, those of Henry and James would appear with Henry uppermost in worth and respectability in the eyes of the reader in the half of the novel before the duel, and the scapegrace James seen suspiciously low; while after the duel, the pattern would be reversed, with James seen by the reader as gaining a strange dignity and worth, and Henry slouching into meanness and evil.

The comparison with Thackeray's novel, however, breaks down on closer inspection. The first movement, up to the duel, has as its theme (in this interpretation) the temporary triumph of Henry's appearance over his reality, while the second movement is not in fact a reversal of this so much as the restatement of a further riddle. And the answer to this riddle is dependent on the fulcrum of the entire novel, and the most brilliant device Stevenson ever employed. The key to this novel's meaning lies with the character of Mackellar, who has influenced its changing pattern, at times decisively, as when he translates Alison from James's camp to Henry's with his carefully prepared dossier of letters which tell against James.

MACKELLAR AND DRAMATIC MONOLOGUE

Why, virtually alone amongst his adolescent raconteurs, does Mackellar emerge as Stevenson's 'mouthpiece' now? Why does he decide to tell the tale through such an 'unrelated' *persona*? Is it simply to give him the credibility of Utterson the lawyer or Dr Lanyon of *Jekyll*, the reliability of Rankeillor in *Kidnapped*? If this is the reason, why then include so many examples of Mackellar's own prejudices and defects of character? Not only is he 'squaretoes' to the exuberant free-traders, he is an 'old maid' to Alison, who accuses him of never ceasing to meddle in the House affairs. He is a 'devil of a soldier in the steward's room at Durrisdeer', by the tenants' report, and he, like Henry, has never attracted love – far less risked marriage. He actively dislikes women.

Stevenson seems to be working in the tradition of the dramatic monologue; and this is a genre with a very strong set of Scottish roots which would be known to Stevenson. From Alan Ramsay's 'Lucky Spence's Last Advice' to Burns's 'Holy Willie's Prayer'; from Hogg's 'Sinner's Narrative' in *The Justified Sinner* to Galt's fictional monologues of minister, provost (and Covenanting Avenger in *Ringan Gilhaize*), the Scottish tradition of self-revealing, unintentionally self-satirical monologue is as strong as any Stevenson could find, say, in contemporary work like Browning's 'My Last Duchess'. Indeed, Mackellar springs into vivid black-and-white relief if one envisages him as a later Holy Willie or Robert Wringhim.

As basis then for a second interpretation the reader should consider Mackellar carefully in depth. And, as he is always insisting on chapter and verse, 'like a witness in court' (a favourite device of Mackellar's, this presentation of apparently inconfutable detail, as though he is presenting a meticulous case) the reader is entitled to examine his evidence as though it were being submitted to strict lawyerly scrutiny. For example, just what exactly is that 'very black mark' against James's name which Mackellar brings up in the opening pages? Mackellar, after mentioning the accusation, and significantly, while the reader is deciding on where to place trust, goes on, 'but the matter was hushed up at the time, and so defaced by legends before I came into these parts, that I scruple to set it down. If it was true, it was a horrid fact in one so young; and if false, it was a horrid calumny'. Indeed, Mackellar lists as one of the Master's crimes that of his treatment of Jessie Broun. Are we to hear Stevenson endorsing this? Would more liberal questioning establish a picture of wild oats and stuffy disapproval? And as to the opening wilfulness of James's insistence on going out in the Rebellion, does not the blame finally rest with the weak father, Lord Durrisdeer, who fails to act with authority? Mackellar displays his prejudice at every turn. One remembers his disapproval of James's reading matter (and his lace); 'Caesar's "Commentaries", . . . Hobbes . . . Voltaire, a book upon the Indies, one on the mathematics, far beyond where I have studied.'

But once suspected, examples of Mackellar's unreliability abound: four issues can be selected as crucial to the development of our acceptance or refusal of his word. They are the matters of the duel, of the dossier of spy papers concocted for Alison, the *Nonesuch* Voyage, and James's reception at Albany.

THE DUEL

Already noted is the feeling of unease concerning the outcome of the duel. We must remember that the most serious allegations of cowardly treachery are about to be made concerning James. All we have to go on is Mackellar's account. But if this is so, must we not take the account in all its parts, including the preparations for the duel, when Mackellar told the brothers that he would prevent it (Chapter 5)?

> And now here is a blot upon my life. At these words of mine the Master fumed his blade against my bosom; I saw the light run along the steel; and I threw up my arms and fell to my knees before him on the floor. 'No, no,' I cried, like a baby.
>
> 'We shall have no more trouble with him,' said the Master. 'It is a good thing to have a coward in the house.'

Mackellar's reliability would seem at the very least to be impaired by his emotional instability. And now we have the duel itself (Chapter 5):

I am no judge of the play; my head, besides, was gone with cold and fear and horror; but it seems that Mr Henry took and kept the upper hand from the engagement, crowding in upon his foe with a contained and glowing fury. Nearer and nearer he crept upon the man, till of a sudden the Master leaped back with a little sobbing oath; and I believe the movement brought the light once more against his eyes. To it they went again on the fresh ground; but now methought closer, Mr Henry pressing more outrageously, the Master beyond doubt with shaken confidence. For it is beyond doubt he now recognised himself for lost, and had some taste of the cold agony of fear; or he had never attempted the foul stroke. I cannot say I followed it, my untrained eye was never quick enough to seize details, but it appears he caught his brother's blade . . .

This long quotation is a superb example of Stevenson's crafty duplicity of intention. Notice especially the arrangement of 'I am no judge', 'I believe', 'it seems', 'methought' and the like in contrast to the more typical Mackellar factual terseness, 'for it is beyond doubt' (twice), 'certainly Mr Henry only saved himself by leaping'. Any defence lawyer for James would demolish the credibility of this account in very little time, on the basis that it argued first for essential limitations of subjectivity, and then proceeded to assert the validity of these subjective (and prejudiced) impressions.

THE SPY DOSSIER

Moving to the later business of the spy dossier we are yet again presented by Stevenson with duplicity of purpose. On the face of it the four types of letter submitted to Alison in 1757 appear a fair and damning 'schedule', as Mackellar imposingly calls them, especially in the fourth type, the letters between James and the British Under-Secretary of State, which most effectively show James to have run with the hare and the hounds. There are two qualifying factors, however. The first is Mackellar's unholy glee at his find in raiding the Master's papers – 'I rubbed my hands, I sang aloud in my glee. Day found me at the pleasing task.' One realises, too, that Alison, affected as she is by the dossier's toppling of James from his romantic pedestal, perceives what Mackellar does not, that the dossier is 'a sword of paper' against him. 'Papers or no papers, the door of this house stands open for him; he is the rightful heir.' Even more important is the question of James's guilt and treachery. The entire novel is, then, based on a piece of duplicity; namely, the fact that the house of Durrisdeer (like many others of the day) chose to solve the delicate problem of allegiance, by sending one son out with the Jacobites and keeping another at home as loyal to the established crown. All were privy to this; Mackellar does not censure it. The reader should now recall the date of the submission of the dossier: 1757. The 'spy' letters run from three years previously; that is, from 1754, almost ten years after the collapse of Charles's cause. By 1754 and with Charles increasingly the hopeless toper of Europe, are we to blame James for doing what his family had in 1745 condoned? It surely is a bit premature to ostracise James because Mackellar tells us he wrote to the 'English Secretary' (elsewhere 'Under-secretary') concerning what we are not in a position to know.

THE NONESUCH VOYAGE

Before drawing any definite conclusion concerning even Mackellar, the reader must be reminded that one can allow that James is a spy, and that – according to another interpretation – Mackellar is utterly reliable. But, whatever his reliability in that interpretation, there is no question that, given greater exposure to James, his entire tone and relationship with James changes. Can this not be read as showing that, when the conditions for prejudice are changed, Mackellar also changes his judgements? Once again his credibility is in doubt, and nothing so damages his case as the *Nonesuch* voyage.

Warnings reminiscent of those surrounding Melville's doomed ship, the *Pequod*, in *Moby Dick* (1851) abound; the ship is as rotten as a cheese, she is on what should be her last voyage. As these accumulate, we become aware that the ship reflects Mackellar's own strange guilty feelings. He suffers from 'a blackness of spirit'; he is poisoned as never before in soul and body, although he freely confesses that the Master shows him a fair example of forbearance. Mackellar again denounces the Master's taste and style in reading (Richardson's *Clarissa*); and excels himself when he prays during the storm for the foundering and loss of the ship and all her crew, as long as the Master should thus be destroyed. Again the language indicates the disease within Mackellar. 'The thought of the man's death . . . took possession of my mind. I hugged it, I found it sweet in my belly,' he tells us in a tone exactly like that of Hogg's Robert Wringhim. Ironically, the captain thanks him for saving the ship through prayer! Then follows his murder attempt on the Master, who (with that uncanny reflex swiftness that was his at all points but that of the duel) both escapes and pardons, in the fullest fashion, his would-be assassin.

JAMES'S RECEPTION AT ALBANY

We must return briefly to the *Nonesuch* in a moment. Let us round off the four issues concerning Mackellar by pointing out that when James does arrive in Albany, he is accused of murder. In fact James is in this case guilty of nothing more than trying to cure his 'victim', young Chew. Mackellar will later learn of his innocence in this matter from the Chevalier Burke; but Mackellar refuses to correct the record, allowing yet another 'very black mark' to be stacked against his enemy. And in the closing sequences we see Mackellar condemning the fratricidal plans of Henry, but destroying his own moral validity by refusing to separate himself from Henry's cause.

We are left, in this interpretation, with a startling thought. Allowing that Secundra Dass, the mysterious Indian, is James's personal 'familiar', must we not begin to suspect that Henry is accompanied by his? One remembers that Mackellar is 'a devil of a steward'; he too dresses in black; and goes on board the *Nonesuch* 'as the devil would have it'. Once again the Devil metaphor makes a transition, and we look upon events in a different light.

JAMES AS THE MASTER?

After all, James, as Alison pointed out, is the rightful heir. He is, indeed, always referred to as 'the Master', even by MacKellar, his enemy. What man of spirit would not identify with the romantic cause of Prince Charles? Is it so improbable that a young man (James was not yet 24 in 1745) of imagination and passion should go the way (in Paris) of the aristocratic youth Burns describes in 'The Twa Dogs' as parading at operas and stews? That is, admitting that he was indeed a wild young man, but denying that there was anything so devilish in his conduct? No one doubts his courage or resourcefulness. And it is important to distinguish between James the younger and James on his return after the duel. James the younger was a spendthrift. The greatest amount of sympathy we can accord him then relates to the fact that when he returns he finds Mackellar and Henry organised against him, and that the woman who loves him is unavailable to him. But his second return is different. Even Mackellar admits this. In contrast to Henry, fattening and bitter (Chapter 8):

> The Master still bore himself erect . . . perhaps with effort . . . He had all the gravity and something of the splendour of Satan in the 'Paradise Lost'. I could not help but see the man with admiration, and was only surprised I saw him with so little fear. But indeed . . . it seemed as if his authority were quite vanished and his teeth all drawn. We had known him a magician that controlled the elements; and here he was, transformed into an ordinary gentleman, chatting like his neighbours at the breakfast board . . .

James now wants enough of a reasonable settlement to go his own way, and it is Henry who denies this and leaves him in the intolerable position of having to answer to Mackellar for bed and board. It is outstanding how James adapts himself through a saving sardonicism to his demeaning role. He deliberately parodies himself in his relations with Mackellar, as he draws himself up in anger in the halls of his ancestors when Mackellar tells him that he has only to keep in with him for his needs to be supplied; then deflates the situation by wryly commenting that this is a pleasing return to the principles of childhood. He, not Mackellar, creates that peculiarly intimate love-hate tolerance between them, and he tries on the *Nonesuch* to explain in metaphor to Mackellar what the difference is between their values and what may be the reality of Henry's attitude towards him.

THE TALE OF THE COUNT AND THE BARON

Just as Hogg's *Justified Sinner* summed itself up in the folk tale of the Devil and the deluded peasants of Auchtermuchty, so James crystallises his case in the tale of the count and the baron. Briefly and allegorically the tale tells of long-standing enmity between the two. The cause of their hatred does not matter, says James; but in the most subtle way possible the count brings about the baron's destruction, without blame attaching to himself in any way. This story goes to the heart of the novel. Reading it for the moment in the light of an interpretation sympathetic to James, we are reminded that throughout the novel James has continuously made use of the Bible story of Jacob and Esau, with Henry always cast in the role of deceiving Jacob. Is he now trying to tell Mackellar that Henry is far more devious than Mackellar could ever realise? That he, James, has suffered from a subtlety beyond his own? This very lack of identification of either Henry or James with count or baron allows this possibility; and further, that the sequel, Mackellar's murder attempt and James's responses to it, take us as close as we are allowed to the essence of James. James tries to explain himself to Mackellar: 'Life is a singular thing . . . You suppose yourself to love my brother. I assure you, it is merely custom . . . Had you instead fallen in with me, you would today be as strong upon my side.' Mackellar has no time for this attempt, and typically casts his description of it in reductive and prejudicial terms (Chapter 9):

> But he was now fairly started in his new course of justification, with which he wearied me throughout the remainder of the passage . . . 'But now that I know you are a human being,' he would say, 'I can take the trouble to explain myself. For I assure you I am human too, and have my virtues, like my neighbours.'

And James realises that Mackellar will once more return to his former prejudices when he is again with Henry.

In all their exchanges, there gradually develops a sense that we are observing diametrically opposed human types, which are related to Stevenson's ideas of 'providence' and 'chance'. Mackellar, however black or white we read him, could speak for Stevenson and of that world of conventional and revealed religious orthodoxy. He becomes Stevenson's most subtle expression of his mingled feelings for pious respectability, family solidarity, Bible-based moral values; and conversely, James, however we decide on his lack or possession of residual morality, represents a move by Stevenson towards a modern world of disillusionment, scepticism, lack of faith in benevolent determinism. Thus James relies on chance to decide his destiny, and thus he is compelled to be the outsider, the stoic rebel, the causeless hero. Their plight, that of traditional Scottish conservatism locked in misunderstanding with rootless disbelief, is summed up in a telling exchange as they leave Durrisdeer (Chapter 9):

> 'Ah, Mackellar,' said he, 'do you think I have never a regret?'
> 'I do not think you could be so bad a man,' said I, 'if you had not all the machinery to be a good one.'
> 'No, not all,' says he: 'not all. You are there in error. The malady of not wanting, my evangelist.'

THE NOVEL AND SCOTTISH HISTORY

Finally, one can suggest that this novel is the finest expression of what Stevenson, like Scott and Hogg before him, and later writers like Douglas Brown, Davidson, Munro, MacDougall Hay and Gibbon, exemplified in his own crisis of identity, and what he successfully managed to objectify into fictional vision. The Durrisdeer family and estate represents the estate of Scotland, like Gibbon's Kinraddie in *Sunset Song* or Brown's Barbie. Their history, going back to Thomas of Ercildoune's prophecy that there would be an ill day for them when one tied and one rode (Henry tied and James rode), back to the Reformation, and back to the wise old lord, can be taken as a version of Scotland's, thus reflecting the several dark twists in the story of the nation. The fragmenting tragedy of the Jacobite Rebellion ruins the mind and the integrity of the wise Lord Durrisdeer and, leaving as he does such opposite and dissociated types as Henry and James, mirror images of each other and inheritors each of only a part of his wholeness, he himself becomes both literally and figuratively an anachronism in the novel, destroyed by the family division into 'head' and 'heart'. Henry and Mackellar are of course those forces of sober and arid 'head'; account-watching, love-repelling, feeling-repressing. James and Burke are their polar twins – romantic, self-indulgent, adept in the manipulation of feeling to the point of irresponsibility. 'Gnatique patrisque, alma, precor, miserere', says the old lord on his death-bed (echoing the plea of Aeneas to the Sibyl of Cumae, when he asked permission to go to Hades and speak to his dead father Anchises, to learn his destiny). 'Have pity on both the sons and the father', the senior Master of Ballantrae is asking; and he is weeping for his two sons, himself, his house and his country; the hostile children of a broken family in a divided country, who have as their badge the stained glass window bearing the family crest which Mackellar notices has an empty, clear lozenge of glass at its heart. The brothers' quarrel has symbolically broken the heart of their family identity, when the coin which took their destinies in opposite and mutually destructive directions was flung in anger through the window and its crest.

CONCLUSION

What makes this novel superior to others that have employed the same symbolic opposition is the way it rises above taking sides. Neither of these forces, brothers, opposing sets of qualities, have right as their monopoly. The Devil metaphor here, as opposed to Scott's usage, is flexible and destructive of either claim to rightness. The brothers, therefore, rightly and symbolically share the same grave, having symbolically exiled themselves from their native and interior land.

Thus, briefly, the changing narrators, and the changing locations can be justified. If the meaning of the novel is in polarisation of values and human qualities, then the telling and location of the novel echo that polarisation. Mackellar tells us much in his dry, domestic manner; but Burke's chevalier style reminds us that Mackellar too has his opposite, in its excessively flowery, self-indulgent apologia for the picaresque. Similarly, and echoing the theme of the brotherly opposition, there are domestic scenes and exotically placed foreign scenes. There is Henry's landscape of grey buildings and rain, and there is James's landscape of pirate deck and swamp. What is important is the final movement to a frozen wilderness, which worried Stevenson but need not at all worry the reader who has seen his instinctive skill in displacing both brothers from their humdrum or exotic backgrounds. If the results of history upon the Scottish psyche were not just polarisation, but repression within each polarised opposite, then the parts destroy each other with a mutual unrealised and sterile longing. This was Hogg's 'love-hate' relationship of Sinner and Devil; but for Stevenson the psychological fragmentation was even more complex, and more thoroughly tragic. Thus his brothers share the same grave, with balanced inscriptions which reflect the no-man's-land between them.

In this, his greatest novel, Stevenson rose above his own personal divisions, transforming what, on the whole, was a confused and immature vision into a remarkably modern and widely applicable comment on the difficulty of arriving in a godless age at moral conclusion. He thus objectifies his own troubled mind, his relations with family and Scotland, and the relations of so many creative and troubled minds with Scotland – and beyond all that, the spiritual fragmentation which is modern and universal. There is Mackellar and James in many of us, Scots or not; and their goodness or otherwise is almost impossible to ascertain.

In conclusion, it is worth revisiting one of Stevenson's most vivid and symbolic passages in the book, which sums up the changing relativity of moral positions. It is the scene on board the *Nonesuch*, where Mackellar, fascinated like a bird watching a snake, watches the Master change position, endlessly (Chapter 9):

> It was here we were sitting: our feet hanging down, the Master betwixt me and the side, and I holding on with both hands to the grating of the cabin skylight: for it struck me it was a dangerous position, the more so as I had before my eyes a measure of our evolutions in the person of the Master, which stood out in the break of the bulwarks against the sun. Now his head would be in the zenith and his shadow fall quite beyond the *Nonesuch* on the further side; and now he would swing down till he was underneath my feet, and the line of the sea leaped high above him like the ceiling of a room.

If Mackellar had reflected, he would have realised that to the Master he too would present a constantly changing position, if perhaps lacking the glory of a sunlit background. It is Stevenson's achievement in this remarkable and deceptive novel that he vividly realises the relativity of morality, anticipating well ahead of Modernism the insights of the twentieth century into the complexities of human motivation, values and behaviour.

CHAPTER 24

MARGARET OLIPHANT: *KIRSTEEN*

MARGARET OLIPHANT (1828–97)

Margaret Oliphant was a prolific author whose work was immensely popular with Victorian readers, but whose personal life was often tragic, and whose writing never gave her and her family the financial security and peace of mind she sought. Born in Wallyford near Musselburgh, just outside Edinburgh, her childhood was spent in Glasgow and Liverpool, where her father was posted as a customs officer. Her *Autobiography* (1899, the full text, edited by Elizabeth Jay, 1990) is revealing in what she does not tell of her life, given her Victorian reticence concerning family matters. Reading between her lines, and drawing from the more autobiographical of the novels, it seems that her family, with the exception of her adored mother, comprised an acidic and unlovable father, a feckless and unhealthy husband, over-dependent and wayward children, and two brothers who were drones on her unflagging industry.

In 1852 Oliphant married her cousin Francis Oliphant, an artist and a stained glass designer who died of tuberculosis in Rome in 1859. Pregnant, and with two small children to support already, Margaret was left with £1,000 of debt to clear, which forced her to write endlessly, and always kept her at the edge of necessity. Producing over a hundred novels during her lifetime as well as numerous magazine articles, she was a regular contributor to *Blackwood's Magazine*, which in earlier years had carried the fiction of great Scottish novelists such as James Hogg and John Galt, and, as Q. D. Leavis recognised in 1969 in her introduction to her edition of *Miss Marjorbanks*:

> Her novels . . . especially some of the Scottish ones, such as *Kirsteen*, help to fill the chronological gap in the tradition of the Scottish novel between *Heart of Midlothian* and *The Entail* on the one side and *Weir of Hermiston* and *The House with the Green Shutters* on the other. In these, and in the many admirable short stories with a Scottish setting, we find her continuing Sir Walter Scott's investigation into what it meant to be Scottish.

Biography and journalism

Oliphant's immense output included historical work like *Francis of Assisi* (1868), *The Makers of Venice* (1887), *Royal Edinburgh* (1890), a *Literary History of England* (1882), two volumes recording the achievements of the House of Blackwood, *Annals of a Publishing House* (1897) and several biographies, outstandingly her *Life of Edward Irving* (1862), the immensely gifted, charismatic but finally tragically obsessive Scottish preacher. These were influential in her day, and although Oliphant herself stated that she preferred writing non-fiction to fiction, this work remains relatively unexplored and undervalued. True, it suffers from enthusiasms which seem out-dated, such as Oliphant's admiration of the idea of British empire, but the best of it is full of historical insight and shrewd contemporary assessment. It is certain, however, that her main achievement lies in fiction.

Margaret Oliphant has been admired for her industry, and although the reputation of her writing has suffered as a result of her relentless output, she is now remembered for a number of outstanding novels and short stories. Contemporary criticism, in fact, as with so many Scottish writers of this period, is currently re-evaluating her achievement in fiction, which broadly falls into three main groups. Firstly, there are her novels of Scottish life and character, including *Margaret Maitland* (1849), *Harry Muir* (1853) *Katie Stewart* (1853), *Magdalene Hepburn* (1854), *A Son of the Soil* (1866), *The Ladies Lindores* (1883), *Effie Ogilvie* (1886) and *Kirsteen* (1890). Then there are her English novels, which include *The Chronicles of Carlingford* series of the 1860s, depictions of English domestic and clerical life which established her British popularity, and which are often compared to Anthony Trollope's *Barsetshire Chronicles*. From this group *Salem Chapel* (1863), *Miss Marjoribanks* (1866), and *Hester* (1883) stand out for their pungent, detached and often very 'Scottish' observation of English small-town society, their social and religious comment and ironic wit. Then, finally, come supernatural stories such as *A Beleaguered City* (1879), *A Little Pilgrim in the Unseen* (1882), *The Land of Darkness* (1888) and her stories 'of the Seen and Unseen', which include two of the finest Scottish short stories in 'The Library Window' and 'The Open Door'.

In both Scottish and English novels, Oliphant's central theme is that of the girl-woman who struggles to separate herself on one hand from Victorian notions of womanly servitude to men, and on the other from the alternative, feminine exploitation and manipulation of men through womanly wiles. The resistance of Oliphant's women is gentle in the early novels, in her Margaret, Katie and Magdalene – but by 1866 and *A Son of the Soil*, Oliphant's irony sharpens in her critical portrayal of Mrs Campbell, the Scottish Victorian icon of supportive motherhood, faithful attendant of her gifted crofter-son who is to go to Glasgow University. This novel anticipates the Kailyard mother of the brilliant yet tragic scholar of humble origins in McLaren's *Beside the Bonnie Brier Bush* (1894), though with a far more ironic perspective.

The heroines of *Miss Marjoribanks*, *Hester*, *The Ladies Lindores* and *Effie Ogilvie*, however, show Margaret Oliphant hardening in her criticism of womanly subservience to men's social, emotional and sexual demands, developing the strength of mind and character of the early Scottish protagonists, while refusing to pretend that female individualists will be allowed to be happy. Lucilla Marjoribanks, daughter of a saturnine Scottish doctor in Carlingford, brings her canniness and wit to bear on the bourgeois society around her, subtly exposing its pretentiousness, while refusing to marry conventionally. Hester longs to do 'something voluntary, even dangerous' in breaking the mould her admirers impose – and ends by perhaps discovering herself, although she is caught between impossible choices. Caroline Lindores rejoices in the death of her tyrant husband, yet, like Oliphant herself, then marries a weak man and has to support a dependent family. Effie's idealism and hopes are disillusioned by the failure of her Galloway neighbours, Englishmen especially, to understand her own vision.

Oliphant's supernatural stories emerge from very different sources. Paradoxically, although these tales were admired by religious readers, they stem from a religious scepticism which followed the death of her favourite daughter in 1864. Oliphant had been devout; after the Disruption of 1843 she was a member of the Free Church. However, following her personal tragedy in 1864, and also perhaps due to her increasing social cynicism, she turned to writing darker and more haunting fiction, strongly influenced by the work of George Macdonald in its sense of death as liberation, and similarly influenced by a faith which had been sorely tried by family and personal tragedy. These are stories of divine redemption after passing through the shadows, and although they are often immensely powerful in their conviction and humanity, they frequently leave questions of faith and belief unanswered. *A Little Pilgrim in the Unseen*, for example, may seem affirmative in its account of how the pilgrim helps the newly-dead adjust to heaven, and its writing did help Oliphant to come to terms with the loss of her daughter. Nevertheless, *The Land of Darkness*, its companion short story, has more in common with Thomson's *The City of Dreadful Night* in its presentation of the horrors of a newly-dead protagonist trapped in hell, who cannot be helped by the pilgrim. Readers interested in these could well begin with the short story 'The Open Door', in which an initially sceptical father, a brusque but loving military man, finds, contrary to his nature, the humanity and imagination to follow his dying son in his obsession that a lost spirit is crying for release in the wintry grounds of their country house. Oliphant's account of the release, brought about by the love of the spirit of the wastrel boy who calls to his dead mother, is profoundly moving, with much of the sense of strange and ultimately unknowable powers which haunts her masterpiece in the genre, *A Beleaguered City*. Here, a small French cathedral town is taken over by the dead, who try unsuccessfully to communicate with the townspeople whom they have forced outside. Only a bereaved couple, the initially sceptical mayor and his wife, respond to them, and when the visitants leave, human greed and materialism resume, suggesting a bleak view of human nature.

At their best, Oliphant's stories of the interconnection between this world and the beyond work with an understated power which comes from their ability to imply so much more than their surface events.

Kirsteen

In keeping with Oliphant's criticism of subservient women, the heroine of *Kirsteen* (1890) is simply the strongest and frankest of her many powerful yet restrained attacks on the stultifying nature of society. It is one of the strongest of Oliphant's proto-feminist novels, a mature and deeply ironic study of a complex woman whose character is developed in several societies. It begins in Argyllshire, portrayed by Oliphant as a dull social backwater at the time of the Napoleonic wars, in a way which anticipates Munro's description of Inveraray around the same period in *Gilian the Dreamer* (1899). Unlike Munro, however, Oliphant has little interest in the roots of this dull decline. Rather, the setting allows her to emphasise the autocratic and brutal nature of her version of the Scottish novel's recurrent and destructive father-figure, here a dark and decayed Highland aristocrat, Laird Douglas of Drumcarro, who has made and used a fortune gained from the slave trade, and who stands mid-way between Scott's Redgauntlet and Brown's Gourlay. Kirsteen is his rebellious child, but, as with all Oliphant's mature challengers of male authority, she is presented with qualifications which prevent her from seeming conventionally heroic or beautiful, so that the portrait is the more human and convincing. She is wilful, too convinced perhaps of her own views on morals and society. When she finally rebels against her father's insistence that she marry an elderly suitor for family gain, and decides to embark on her journey-quest for freedom, her inability to understand her sister or the Glasgow society in which she lives with her doctor husband is made clear. No great personal transformations or triumphs occur; Kirsteen will eventually come to terms

437

with her brutal (and, finally, murderous) father. Her real significance, instead, lies in her slow transition from sentimental idealist to pragmatic and successful business-woman in London, and later doyenne of dressmakers to the rich in Edinburgh. Although the novel is occasionally marred by moments of emotional cliché (Kirsteen, for all her gumption in business and family matters, unconvincingly treasures till her virgin death the blood-stained handkerchief given to her by her first love Ronald, killed in war), where it succeeds is in its presentation, unique in Victorian fiction, of a woman who manages to succeed on her own terms, independent of men.

NARRATIVE AND ANALYSIS

'Where is Kirsteen?' is the question with which the novel opens. Her family, particularly her mother, a semi-invalid, make many demands on her, and she has little time to call her own. Marg'ret, the household servant, tells Mrs Douglas that she should not take Kirsteen for granted, but Kirsteen is a Cinderella figure whose true worth is not appreciated by a family with whom she has troubled relations. Despite her mother's self-pitying complaints. Kirsteen loves her, expressing this in an old 'Scots song: 'True loves may get mony an ane, / But minnie [*mother*] ne'er anither.'

Although she is close to her brother Robbie, the opening of the novel sees him, along with his friend Ronald Drummond, leave for India to serve in the British Army, and Kirsteen realises that the boys with whom she has grown up are being given opportunities to forge a life for themselves which are denied to her. Ronald asks her to 'wait for him', until he returns to marry her, yet Kirsteen is frustrated following the boys' departure, firstly because she misses their company and secondly because the routine work she is expected to do holds little interest. Furthermore, where some women (such as Scottish writer Elizabeth Hamilton, 1758–1816) were enriched through correspondence with their menfolk who went abroad to work, no such nurturing correspondence is maintained between Robbie, Ronald and Kirsteen. Although she does indeed promise to wait for Ronald, therefore, she is not content to stagnate.

Oliphant takes care to point out that Kirsteen is not a conventional heroine. 'A daughter of the hills', her appearance is compared with 'a burst of sunshine', and her natural appeal is stressed in place of any claim to traditional beauty. Kirsteen's waist is 'round if not very small', her freckled complexion has the 'pure whiteness' of milk, and her eyes are 'full of light'. Her 'abundant' red hair, difficult to keep tidy, is in contrast with the satin smoothness required of the perfect heroine, and this symbolises her 'diffi-cult', subversive role, within the novel. In creating Kirsteen thus, Oliphant shows at the outset the difference between an actual woman and what male-dominated society (or literature?) thinks a woman should be. The further implication is that society's estimation dislikes everything which is natural and vital about Kirsteen.

Before the boys leave, Kirsteen and Ronald secretly exchange a hand-kerchief, on which Kirsteen has embroidered Ronald's initials with strands of her own hair, and a little testament in which Ronald has entwined his etched initials with Kirsteen's. As Ronald is leaving indefinitely, they are binding hemselves to an absence during which it will be almost impossible for them to communicate, and they are further pressurised by the secrecy of their 'understanding'. After this potential suitor leaves, Marg'ret takes Kirsteen's plight to heart. Marg'ret is the traditional outspoken servant of Scottish fiction who, not at all blunted by living with such an ungracious master as Drumcarro, believes in her right to speak on family and personal matters, a right which is grounded in her own self-esteem and her years of faithful service: 'I'm not to be dauntoned by words nor looks, I'm nae man's wife, the Lord be thankit.' She takes the bull by the horns, therefore, bluntly telling Drumcarro that he needs to find husbands for his daughters, and here Oliphant is subtle. Although Marg'ret knows that her own confidence stems from her singleness, she still sees marriage as a natural aim for women, and it is as a result of Marg'ret's intervention that both Mary and Kirsteen attend a ball at the Duke of Argyll's castle where Kirsteen meets Glendochart, a local landowner who seeks her father's permission to marry her. When Kirsteen herself refuses this man, however, her father becomes violent (Chapter 15):

'Dare to say a word but what I tell ye, and I'll dash ye in pieces like a potter's vessel!' cried Drumcarro . . . He shook her as he spoke, her frame, though it was well-knit and vigorous, quivering in his grasp. 'Just say a word more of your damned nonsense and I'll lay ye at my feet!' Kirsteen's heart fluttered to her throat with a sickening terror . . .

Kirsteen has a clear choice. If she wishes to stay with her family, she must marry Glendochart. Despite his controlling violence, Drumcarro has the hypocrisy to quote from the Bible in his assault on Kirsteen, referring to the image of the potter's vessel from the psalms to lend authority to his actions. If she wishes to remain true to herself and her promise to Ronald, she must leave.

Oliphant's treatment of this decision to leave both family and oppressive father is not romantic, and demonstrates the difficulty of making such a break. Marg'ret helps Kirsteen by giving her enough money for the journey.

Like most girls of her era, Kirsteen has been economically dependent on her father, and unlike her brothers who left home with a special meal in their honour, their father's blessing and a cart hired to take their luggage, Kirsteen leaves home alone, early on a cold, dark January moming. Though she receives help from a carter, and a female innkeeper on Loch Fyne, she has to deal with the unwelcome attentions of a beggar who is perhaps after more than her money, and with the novel's villain, Lord John, who in coming to her aid is also too familiar for her liking. In these situations, Kirsteen overcomes initial feelings of pity and deference respectively to discover and assert her own wishes and needs. She is tired and afraid, but her strength of character, hitherto untested, is growing stronger all the time.

When she arrives in Glasgow, Kirsteen finds her sister Anne, herself irrevocably ostracised from the family for marrying against Drumcarro's wishes, and here, Oliphant tempers our admiration for Kirsteen, as although she is fond of Anne and glad to see her happy with motherhood, she snobbishly sees her sister's marriage to someone of a lower social class as a source of dishonour to the Douglas family. Paradoxically, her disapproval of her brother-in-law is based on his use of his gifts and education to make a living, yet this is precisely what she is about to do herself. Oliphant maintains her irony at Kirsteen's expense, showing her frequently, for all her smeddum, to be applying double standards. Throughout the novel the good name of the Douglases remains extremely important to her, and she is aware that her family think that she herself has demeaned it by using it in trade; thus, she trades under her Christian name.

KIRSTEEN IN LONDON

In London, Kirsteen stays with Marg'ret's sister Jean, who owns a mantua-making business, and Oliphant's choice of profession is significant. The later Victorian period appears to have been even more restrictive to women entering work or professions than earlier periods. Elizabeth Sanderson, in *Women and Work in Eighteenth-Century Edinburgh* (1996), has shown that through the eighteenth and into the nineteenth century, society allowed women from the upper and middle classes to work in a variety of occupations including mantua-making, and not always because of necessity. By the end of the eighteenth century, however, 'mantua-making' was being replaced by the modern term 'dressmaking'; Oliphant's use of the older term 'mantua-making' is thus in danger of being anachronistic at the period during which *Kirsteen* is set, but suggests that Oliphant may have had knowledge of this earlier and freer working world into which Kirsteen could have entered. Nevertheless, by the time *Kirsteen* was published there was adverse public debate regarding women's training for the professions. Therefore while Oliphant uses her knowledge of social history to place Kirsteen credibly in employment, her family's deprecation of her move seems to reflect later nineteenth-century values rather than those of the earlier period.

Kirsteen is employed by 'Miss Jean' in London, and because of her ability and her social class, she is quickly promoted to helping with more aristocratic customers. Kirsteen so proves her innate good taste and acquaintance with fashion that the ageing Miss Jean offers her a partnership. In order to increase their business, Kirsteen – through snobbery or practicality? – suggests that they should not take any business from commoners. Miss Jean dislikes turning down orders; however, Kirsteen's shrewdness is proven and the business becomes one of the most profitable and exclusive in London – so much so that Kirsteen refuses to make a dress for her younger sister Mary, on the grounds of her not being of a sufficiently elevated rank. Again Oliphant qualifies our approval of Kirsteen, leaving the reader to assess whether her refusal is also related to the fact that Mary has accepted the proposal of Kirsteen's old suitor, Glendochart, along with the many material benefits which he has already brought to her and her family. Mary's self-righteousness is galling to Kirsteen. She assumes that by marriage she has attained a success and status which is denied to her unmarried sister, irrespective of the financial independence, wealth and respect that Kirsteen's work has brought her. Kirsteen is embroiled in a mixture of past history, her business position as a woman, and social codes which elevate marriage above all. Realising how impossible it is to explain or argue the many strands of her case, she withdraws into that stubborn silence which refused Glendochart. Kirsteen's strengths, Oliphant suggests, can also be her weaknesses, but the overall result is to deepen the reader's sense of Kirsteen as a complex and very human figure, with whom we can empathise even in her snobbery. While readers may or may not admire Kirsteen's vindictiveness in her attitude to her sister, there is no mistaking the lifetime's provocation which has led to it, and meek forgiveness of Mary's own faults would be incongruous within the make-up of such a spirited female character. As a heroine, Kirsteen may be flawed, but she is all the more real for that.

KIRSTEEN'S LOSS

Though strong, Kirsteen is a lonely figure, and loneliness is the price she must pay for remaining single. During times of difficulty she is supported by Marg'ret and Miss Jean, and at the end of the novel she is surrounded by loving family relatives. Nevertheless, throughout her life she never finds anyone whom she cares to admit to the most intimate reaches of her personality, and Oliphant movingly shows a number of instances in the novel when Kirsteen cries alone. In reading *The Times* one day, she finds a report of Ronald Drummond's death, and leaving the room in emotional turmoil, she will not explain her unhappiness, thus refusing to allow herself to be comforted. In an unusually open show of affection, Kirsteen kisses Miss Jean, appreciating her kindness, yet this episode only highlights Kirsteen's ultimate separateness from anyone – a separateness which Oliphant presents convincingly, but with implied questions as to its emotional and its social worth, questions nowhere more poignantly posed than in the central passages where Kirsteen betrays to the reader how crippled her emotional and sexual life has become, despite her economic and apparent personal victory.

She travels north in order to visit Ronald's mother and to ask her for the embroidered handkerchief which Ronald had been holding to his lips in death. Although Mrs Drummond is distraught with grief, she realises the justice of Kirsteen's claim and gives up the handkerchief. Again, the transaction shows opposing aspects of Kirsteen, positive and negative, as although she is close to Drumcarro, she does not visit but hurries back to London. By comparing this with Kirsteen's initial journey, the reader can see how much more mature and competent she now is. Meeting Agnes Drummond, who is much the same age as Kirsteen but who in the intervening years has stayed at home with her mother, the reader is shown that had Kirsteen remained at home, she would only have led a half-life. For Kirsteen, we are told, the cost of faithfulness to Ronald had been high, but that for all that she lost, life still retained its meaning and purpose, 'and thus life was over for Kirsteen; and life began'. The ambiguity of her position, and the division between the emotional and sexual on one hand, and the rational and social on the other, is made clear.

Kirsteen is no sooner in London than she is recalled to Drumcarro by the news that her mother is dying. At the last, her mother recognises in Kirsteen a strength she did not personally possess, and acknowledges that this daughter will be 'the standby' of the family. It is paradoxical yet moving that Kirsteen craves this acknowledgement of her importance to her family from such a weak woman, and it might be postulated that this is fuelled by the knowledge that she will never become mother of a family herself. In any case, the significance of Kirsteen's role as provider is emphasised in her regarding her mother's words as a 'consecration' – a strong religious word suggesting total commitment in mind, will and emotions to a particular lask or calling. Its use here is clearly deliberate and emphatic.

ISSUES OF GENDER

Kirsteen returns to London – but not before warning her brother and father to watch over her young sister Jeanie, who has confided to her that she is tempted to give in to the blandishments of her admirer, Lord John. Jeanie is naïve and does not realise that Lord John wishes to seduce rather than marry her. At this stage in the novel, the narrative leaves Kirsteen to focus on Jeanie, and it could be argued that it loses some of its imaginative coherence as a consequence. On the other hand, however, in examining the plight of this last sister Oliphant may in fact be completing the comment on gender and social class that the novel has maintained throughout.

In *Kirsteen*, Oliphant paints her central and paradoxical portrait of a complex and strong-minded woman insistent on making her own decisions, irrespective of the antagonism this causes with family and society, and yet who betrays her own unconscious acceptance of class hierarchy, protesting while trying to evade the class implications of her actions. In her unwillingness to re-enter into emotional and sexual engagement, we recognise her susceptibility to the strength of Victorian conditioning and current ideas of romance and feminine fidelity.

In Anne, Oliphant shows how marriage can – whether in reality or in the mind of Kirsteen and society – diminish a woman. Anne loses her class advantage by her marriage, and arguably exchanges one set of false values for another – although Oliphant leaves this open to final assessment. That Anne has selfish faults is evident when, for example, she uses her children as an excuse for not visiting her dying mother.

In Mary, the reader sees a woman who understands how the world works, and who makes a pragmatic bargain with it for her own comfort, improving her lot by marriage – though not without some ironic comment from Oliphant as well as Kirsteen. The reader is aware that the Douglas attitudes to class are becoming less and less relevant in a society which must increasingly recognise merit and social worth, and in which men such as Doctor David Dewar will be regarded as social leaders.

In Jeanie, Oliphant shows another kind of (potential) victim whose predicament stems from the same combination of boredom and lack of hope for personal development which characterised Kirsteen's life at Drumcarro. None of the Douglases, and few others in society apart from Kirsteen and Aunt Eelen, can entertain any doubts concerning Lord John's worth, since worth and social class are synonymous. Because of the Douglas family's outdated notions of their equality with the higher aristocracy, they can easily conceive of the possibility of a marriage between the two. However, Kirsteen, with her greater experience of the world beyond Argyllshire and her cosmopolitan knowledge of the niceties of social position, knows that such a match is impossible and that Lord John can have no honourable intentions towards her sister. As so often, Kirsteen's attitudes to social class are seen to be ambivalent. She is not able to recognise the worth of her sister Anne's husband and his new professional society, her business mind insists on snobbish discrimination, and she never relinquishes her respect for her family name; but she knows that society is changing, and she is aware that whatever was the case in the past, an unbridgeable gulf now exists between her family and Lord John's, and that for this reason, Jeanie's beauty and womanhood make her an unguarded victim to the predatory intentions of her aristocratic companion.

THE INTRUSION OF MELODRAMA?

As the novel moves its attention from Kirsteen to Jeanie, it also runs the risk of becoming melodramatic. Drumcarro overhears Lord John's attempt to seduce his daughter, and once Jeanie has run off, he pushes the young man into the waterfall. Lord John is killed, yet no one associates Drumcarro with the death, far less suspects him of murder, and Jeanie is married off to Major Gordon, a soldier who had served with her brother in India. His health failing, Drumcarro eventually confesses the murder to Kirsteen, and when she tells her father that she has money enough to buy back some of the forfeited Douglas land, she even extracts from him a grudging compliment – and perhaps some kind of recognition of his imbalanced valuation of his male and female children: 'That's the first bargain . . . ever made between father and child to the father's advantage – at least in his house. And a lass, – and all my fine lads that I sent out for honour and for gain!'

Drumcarro dies before his son Alexander returns. Old and patriarchal habits die hard; Alexander has done well in the army, but is not pleased to discover that he owes the extension of his lands to his sister because of what he describes as 'the sewing'. Despite this final illustration of family and male ingratitude, the novel leaves Kirsteen at the height of her success and fame, amid nieces, nephews and other friends and apparently accepted by the best of Edinburgh society. Leaving aside Oliphant's ironic reservations, the novel clearly and effectively approves Kirsteen's independence and economic success.

Achievement – and some reservations?

Margaret Oliphant lived during a period of industrial expansion in Britain which underpinned and paralleled colonial expansion. The majority of ordinary people lived in poor conditions in Scotland as a result of industrialisation, and many Third World countries were not allowed to regulate their own affairs but were governed by Britain. *Kirsteen* is set in the early years of the nineteenth century when these developments, though not fully established, were beginning to be noticed. Oliphant's view of national and international contexts is limited – although it should be recognised that virtually all the major Scottish novelists of the nineteenth century were similarly restricted in their recognition of the impact of industrialisation and the injustices of Empire. When Kirsteen arrives in Glasgow she sees 'visions of ugliness and dirt', though the woman she lodges with remarks that 'Glasco's no so ill as it looks', and Kirsteen is envious of the mill girls she sees going to their work with 'carefully dressed hair done up in elaborate plaits'. These women have work and the self-respect that goes with it. Kirsteen sees them as admirable workers, on whose prosperity Britain is founded, as women advantaged rather than disadvantaged by their long hours and low wages. And if this represents Oliphant's attitude to industrialisation, she is likewise uncritical of Britain's military imperialism. Kirsteen's brothers seek their fortune by joining the army and serving in the Empire. If they are to be killed, Oliphant accepts this as a contribution 'to the increase and consideration of our great Indian territory, and the greatness of Great Britain in that empire upon which the sun never sets'. Ronald, whom Kirsteen hoped to marry, was killed in a battle against 'the swarms of a warlike tribe'. Yet the reader never learns why these people were fighting, whether their attack was unprovoked or whether they had a legitimate grievance. It would seem, too, that even although the Abolition of Slavery Act had been passed in 1833, Oliphant was unconvinced of its necessity; Chapter 5 has the narrator interpolate that the outcry against slavery exaggerated the conditions in which the slaves lived.

We must accept that Mrs Oliphant was in many respects a conservative figure even in her own time, seeing the benefits rather than the horrors of industrialisation, and equating colonial expansion with the triumph of civilisation. Even concerning the feminism which was gradually becoming more assertive in the years before the turn of the century, she was suspicious of what she termed 'that mad notion of the franchise for women' (*Autobiography*), revealing her own repressed attitude toward women's potential. In another respect, however, Oliphant was frustrated by the attitudes of her time, and fought with an impressive satirical art against them. She was intensely aware that the roles offered to women by Victorian society were restrictive, and she herself had single-handedly kept an extended family together by her own efforts, during a time when it was not thought particularly seemly for middle-class women to earn their living – particularly through writing fiction. To conform to society's ideal of what was respectable, women were expected to marry and raise a family. While for many women this may indeed have been satisfying, Oliphant was deeply critical of its limitations. She knew from her own experience the benefits that work brought, not only in terms of financial gain, but also in terms of developing resourcefulness and confidence. After being paid £150 for her first novel, *Margaret Maitland,* she wrote in her *Autobiography*: 'I remember walking along the street with delightful elation, thinking that, after all, I was worth something – and not to be hustled about.' In *Kirsteen* all the strong women work and are single, while those who are married or are simply waiting to be so are feeble – less able to cope with life's difficulties. Indeed, throughout Oliphant's novels the highest value presented is that of a woman's independence of mind and body. That such valuation never denies the realities of female – and male – complexity and folly only serves to demonstrate the reality informing Oliphant's own experience, and of the historical environment in which Kirsteen and her like are placed. Oliphant's feminism is not unrealistic – independence did have its price, and her heroines' lives are imperfect. What remains impressive and highly challenging in novels such as *Kirsteen,* however, is the heroine's refusal to conform; renouncing family and friends in favour of a life of intellectual stimulation and independence.

CHAPTER 25

GEORGE DOUGLAS BROWN: *THE HOUSE WITH THE GREEN SHUTTERS*

GEORGE DOUGLAS BROWN (1869–1902)

George Douglas Brown was born in Ochiltree, Ayrshire in 1869, the illegitimate son of a local farmer who never acknowledged him – a history which helps explain some of Brown's ferocious criticism of patriarchal authoritarianism and petty-mindedness in small communities. As a bright student at Ayr Academy he moved on to study classics at Glasgow University; and thence went as Snell Scholar to Balliol College in Oxford. He was a promising student but his final examinations came just after several months of nursing his mother till her death in May 1895, and he managed to scrape only a third-class degree. He left, feeling a failure, to take up journalism and tutoring in London. Other than *The House with the Green Shutters* (1901) he wrote only one novel, a melodrama for adolescents, *Love and a Sword* (1899), under the name 'Kennedy King'. After *Green Shutters* he intended to write a historical romance set in the time of Cromwell, but he died of pneumonia. He hated the sentimental Kailyard fashion, then current in Scottish literature, for fiction and poetry celebrating the humble life of Scottish village and peasant worthies, and practised by writers such as 'Ian McLaren', S. R. Crockett, and James Barrie (although modern criticism is suggesting that several of the supposed Kailyarders, including Barrie, were in fact parodying Kailyard fiction). One critic applauded *Green Shutters* for its 'sticking the Kailyarders like pigs'. But whatever his motives, it is now recognised that this novel is an outstanding example of that tradition in Scottish fiction discussed earlier, begun by Scott in *Waverley* (1814), and in novels like *The Heart of Midlothian* (1818) and *Redgauntlet* (1826), Hogg's *The Private Memoirs and Confessions of a Justified Sinner* (1824), John Galt's *The Entail* (1823), Margaret Oliphant's *Kirsteen* (1890), Stevenson's *The Master of Ballantrae* (1889) and *Weir of Hermiston* (1896), and John MacDougall Hay's *Gillespie* (1914).

Other influences

Brown was clearly influenced by his classical training; we can see features of Greek tragedy in *Green Shutters* in elements such as the fated fall of a great family doomed through hubris (the fatal flaw of overweening pride of the tragic protagonist), and the chorus, which serves to criticise the central tragic figure. In the novel, this chorus appears as the 'nasty bodies' who assemble round the town cross. Modern drama also stimulated Brown in his radical criticism of life in a small community. In plays such as Ibsen's *Pillars of Society* (1877) and *The Master Builder* (1892), with their ironic and tragic scrutiny of small-town family tensions in Norway, there is a similar treatment of puritanical tradition to Brown's fictional Scotland. In contemporary English and Scottish fiction, Thomas Hardy's *The Mayor of Casterbridge* (1886) may well have influenced him with its similar notions of small-town patriarchy and of a dominating and tragically ironic fate, while the influence of Stevenson's fiction is clear. *Green Shutters* represents a kind of thematic completion of the novel that Stevenson was unable to achieve in *Weir of Hermiston* (1896). A dominating yet arid father figure is described in both novels; both Weir and Gourlay repress their feelings. Both are contrasted with their hypersensitive sons, so that the heart of the novels' conflict lies in their confrontation – the father destroys the son; the son destroys the father. In neither case is the pattern seen as Good versus Bad; indeed, the implication is that in the tragic dichotomy each side lacks the positive qualities of the other. And in both novels the deeper implication is that the central situation is archetypally Scottish.

WHY GREEN SHUTTERS?
Stevenson's fiction not only influenced Brown, but also helped give the novel its title. In 'A Gossip on Romance' (*Memories and Portraits*, 1887) Stevenson argues that certain places have within them an implicit potential for drama. The old inn at Burford Bridge, he says, 'seems to wait the coming of the appropriate legend. Within these ivied walls, behind these old green shutters, some further business smoulders . . . Some day, perhaps, I may try a rattle at the shutters,' he concluded. Brown took up both the challenge and the title – taking inspiration too from another and more cynical Scottish poet, John Davidson, whose satire on Scottish poetry, 'Ayrshire Jock', deals with the same territory, mocking his Ayrshire poet's cultural background and his origins in a cottage with 'old-style, sea green shutters'. Thus Brown is taking up contemporary challenges by two of the most famous writers of his time, whose work he would certainly know; and his work develops beyond theirs.

(Readers may find it interesting to read Stevenson's essay and the poem by Davidson to assess how influential they have been.)

BARBIE, GOURLAY AND HIS HOUSE

The opening of the novel repays close critical attention, because it crucially establishes the author's attitudes towards the town of Barbie. Brown contrasts Barbie's unusual beauty on that first morning with its human degradation. The reader should consider why Brown places opposites against each other – for example, the beauty of the image of the arch of falling water, set against the fact that the water is filthy, or the 'perfect stillness' of the morning contrasting with the presence of the 'frowsy chambermaid'. Gourlay is set amidst this beauty, musing at his gate as his slow-moving carts radiate out around the town. Notice that he 'was dead to the fairness of the scene'; it is his pride, which is flattered in seeing all his carts on his business, showing that he 'possessed it with his merchandise'. He is something of a spider at the heart of his web; but he will be seen as 'slow-moving', compared to his quicker neighbours, and to the speed of social change epitomised by the coming of the railways.

His house is set at the centre of the stage, dominating the town. It is significant that Brown has chosen to locate the house in this important position, rather than some other institution – a church perhaps, or a municipal building, or a school. Brown is, here, making an implicit statement by marking both the absence of more traditional landmarks and the centrality of John Gourlay within Barbie. Chapter 3 goes on to connect Gourlay and his house, suggesting that his joy in it is due to triumph over public opinion. 'Gourlay's house was a material expression of that delight . . . stood for it in stone and lime.' We learn, however, ominously, of threats to it – it is mortgaged up to the hilt, it is dependent on Gourlay retaining quarry rights, and the expanding railways are fast approaching.

THE CENTRAL FIGURE? JOHN GOURLAY, SENIOR

The House with the Green Shutters is a novel of profound and extreme contrasts, the most striking of which is found in the opposition between the brutal father and his hypersensitive son. Gourlay senior becomes a symbol of authority, materialism and brutal insensitivity. The son, on the other hand, is excessively sensitive, with an over-vivid imagination; as the dry schoolmaster tells us in Chapter 15, the trouble with young Gourlay is that he possesses a 'sensory perceptiveness in gross excess of his intellectuality'.

Yet this contrast is not simplistic. Neither father nor son is seen as superior to the other; there are good and bad qualities in both. Gourlay senior has the discipline and courage which are recognised by Brown as the better qualities of commerce and speculation. We learn from Sandy Toddle's comment that Gourlay's toolbox contains the finest tools, meticulously maintained, that he has ever seen, while one of the more perceptive bodies says that Gourlay is the only true gentleman in Barbie. The term is vague in its Victorian connotations, but there seems no doubt that Brown sincerely implies an understanding for the respect that Gourlay commands, and not just for his sheer physical bulk or his daunting black glowers. Gourlay, in the novel, is an embodiment of materialism; he is what he has built. Yet his monopoly and place are to be continually threatened: in the matter of the quarry rights; in the sinister way his monopoly in Barbie is seen; and in the news that already the railways are 'thrusting themselves among the quiet hills'.

EMOTIONAL REPRESSION

Gourlay senior may be antithetical to his son but he is not entirely devoid of feeling. Brown comments on the strangeness of seeing the dour man feeding Janet's rabbits when she is ill. And his attitude is always less brusque towards those from whom he has nothing to fear. In Chapter 22, at the forced departure of old Peter Riney, whom Gourlay has had to sack because of financial problems, Gourlay cannot manage a friendly and reluctant farewell, but – oddly – clamps his jaw and curses Peter:

> Without a word of thanks for the money, Peter knocked the mould off his heavy boots, striking one against the other clumsily, and shuffled away across the bare soil. But when he had gone twenty yards, he stopped, and came back slowly. 'Good-bye sir,' he said with a rueful smile, and held out his hand.
>
> Gourlay gripped it. 'Good-bye Peter! good-bye; damn ye, man, good-bye!'
>
> Peter wondered vaguely why he was sworn at. But he felt that it was not in anger. He still clung to his master's hand. 'I've been fifty year wi' the Gourlays,' said he. 'Ay, ay; and this, it seems, is the end o't.'
>
> 'Oh, gang away!' cried Gourlay, 'gang away, man!' And Peter went away.

Brown here manages to imply that Gourlay genuinely feels the loss of Peter's departure. In fact the novel continually suggests that Gourlay *represses* feeling and there is a pervading sense that his dammed-up feelings may burst, with terrible consequences.

There are other symbolic qualifications to the description of Gourlay's centrality within the town. Brown tells us that his house blocks a natural flow of fresh spring water from the side of the hill. When the locals come to Gourlay to ask him to release this 'fine natural supply', for the good of the town Gourlay, of course, refuses. Beyond the very real considerations of Gourlay's meanness in refusing the public good, there are then also symbolic implications for our understanding of Gourlay and the town. Gourlay unhealthily dams up more than water, he is himself a frustrated force, threatening the healthy existence of the town. And when we recall that the house is mortgaged up to the hilt, and ill-kept by Gourlay's slatternly wife, who develops cancer while his daughter contracts tuberculosis, we realise that there is something rotten at the heart of the impressive-seeming house. This contrast between outward impressive appearance and inward decay relates to a similar tension within its master, John Gourlay.

ANIMAL SYMBOLISM

Throughout the novel, animal metaphors are utilised in relation to Gourlay. This strand of imagery lends his depiction a kind of fierce brutish vigour, which is hardly that of the complete or civilised social man. He hurls Gibson through the hotel window in an act of savage ferocity and the gossips later covertly discuss Gourlay as though he were a bull in the market-place. The constant emphasis on his bull-like strength and his black power gives him at times a bestial and almost mythical quality, which echoes a recurrent usage in Scottish fiction going back beyond Stevenson's hanging judge, the awe-inspiring Weir of Hermiston, to Scott's formidable giant Jacobite laird, Redgauntlet. Scottish fiction – and Brown – thus identify a threatening power which often lies beneath the surface of figures, who can be either of the Establishment or against it, but who represent the danger of distortion through excessive or obsessive identification with a cause, whether it be that of political rebellion, the law, or in this case, excessive mercantile materialism.

A CENTRAL FIGURE? JOHN GOURLAY, JUNIOR

If Gourlay senior plays the same role in this novel as the fearsome judge Adam Weir, Lord Hermiston in *Weir of Hermiston*, then Gourlay junior has much of the character of Archie Weir in his excessive sensitivity and imagination. If Gourlay senior dams up his feelings, then Gourlay junior 'splurges' (the word most frequently used by Gourlay senior in describing the boy's self-indulgence, and the word used by Stevenson's Lord Hermiston to condemn his son's excesses). John has all the sensitivity of perception his father lacks, but has none of his father's control or discipline. Thought, in his father's case, has nothing to do with feeling. There are endless examples of

451

young John Gourlay's hyper-sensitivity. On his way to school, John is 'intensely alive' to the smell of varnish on the school desks in the joiner's yard – so much so that he turns back home. Reading in hiding in the attic, he is another of the house's trapped secrets. And his choice of shallow, melodramatic novels betrays him together with his ways of reading. His excessive responses are toward unrelated bits of books, to colours and sense impressions, since he lacks the discipline which could go on to relate the parts of the story to the whole. He gets bored. Chapter 8 tells us that 'his mind was full of perceptions of which he was unconscious, till he found one of them recorded in a book, and that was the book for him . . .'. He comes alive to vivid and immediate impressions. Brown emphasises the details that impress themselves on John's mind: the pigeons and the noise they make slithering on the slates; the 'splotch of yellow light' which 'lay, yellow and vivid, on a red clinker of coal, and a charred piece of stick'; a 'red-ended beetle' which captivates his interest; the immediate melodramatic descriptions of his penny-dreadful novels.

POSITIVE ASPECTS OF JOHN GOURLAY JUNIOR?
Brown does, however, suggest that the boy has some redeeming features. In the same chapter John reads – and responds – to the story of highwayman Dick Turpin. 'If young Gourlay had been the right kind of a boy he would have been in his glory, with books to read and a garret to read them in . . .' he comments, adding later 'perhaps he was not so far from being the right kind of boy, after all, since that was the stuff that *he* liked . . .' Oddly, Brown seems simultaneously to blame and approve. Similarly, we recall the dominie's view of John's 'sensory perceptiveness in gross excess of his intellectuality'. His judgement implies that this John Gourlay possesses great emotional depths but lacks the common sense to perceive the volatility inherent in the gift of sensitivity. Gourlay's gifts and defects are later realised in his 'successes' in Edinburgh. Brown emphasises young John's terror of the 'demoniac force of nature' and the 'vast totality of things', with their remoteness and threat and he later comes to depend on alcohol to give him 'smeddum'. It is surely significant that, at university, John listens to his professor with an unusual eagerness, because perhaps the only place in which he discovers himself is in his elder's judgement.

THE RAEBURN ESSAY COMPETITION
Young John falls into bad company in Edinburgh, and his university studies are neglected but he does enter and win the Raeburn Essay Competition. This suggests that he has real talent; but Brown is careful to stress just how

qualified was his success. The entries are poor; and Gourlay's is a lopsided, fragmentary, badly presented piece – but it is filled with vivid sense impressions. John's 'morbid fancy' has drawn on the idea of the 'lonely little town far off upon the verge of Lapland' and his poem describes drowning in the desolate and cold Arctic Sea. Thus through John's creative expression, Brown allows a glimpse into the kind of emotional destruction wrought within Gourlay junior. The poem expresses an almost metaphorical mirror of his own sense of isolation and dread of engulfment by forces more bitter and more powerful than himself.

Announcing the award, the professor discusses the different kinds of imagination, with his highest evaluation given to a kind of Shakespearian imagination which (Chapter 18):

> not only sees but hears – actually hears what a man would say on a given occasion, and entering into his blood, tells you exactly why he does it. The highest form is both creative and consecrative . . . merging in diviner thought. It irradiates the world . . .

Second to this is a still noble form of imagination which 'pictures something which you never saw, but only conceived as a possible existence'; and then lower down again is, in its lowest form, imagination which 'recalls something which the eyes have already seen, and brings it vividly before the mind'. This last is the kind of imagination which the professor finds in the winner of the Raeburn Essay competition, with its 'gaspy little sentences' and its ungrammatical structure. Significantly though, the professor detects that 'in this sketch there is a perception at the back of every sentence. It displays, indeed, too nervous a sense of the external world'. Echoing the dominie's judgement, the professor identifies John's tragic failing; and, going beyond the uninterested and irresponsible dominie, the professor delivers a stern warning to John (Chapter 18):

> 'I would strongly impress on the writer,' said the shepherd, heedless of his bleating sheep, 'I would strongly impress on the writer, to set himself down for a spell of real, hard, solid, and deliberate thought. That almost morbid perception, with philosophy to back it, might create an opulent and vivid mind. Without philosophy, it would simply be a curse. With philosophy, it would bring thought the material to work on. Without philosophy it would simply distract and irritate the mind . . .'

Significantly, John summarily dismisses the advice, preferring to drink. Brown's implication is that, lacking the discipline and willed control of his father, John is only half a person, and that his tragedy will come from this inherent weakness? Thus the central theme of the book, as expressed through the contrast between father and son, can be seen as that of (Scottish?) fragmented or dissociated personality; the father all arid calculation and insensitivity, the son excessive feeling lacking intellectual control.

NARRATIVE METHODS AND THEME

The narrative methods of the novel serve to underline this central theme. Not only does John Gourlay junior have vivid sense impressions; so too does George Douglas Brown, in his very similar emphasis on small and yet particularly vivid details – from the golden arch of the water from the chambermaid's pail, the two empty shining nails where Gourlay normally keeps his hammer, to the two red spots which flame on the deacon's cheeks, as big and round as Scots pennies. Often the emphasis is mean, as in the detail of the hair at the back of a peasant's neck, or the white lashes round small tender-lidded eyes. This tendency to express description in the same way as John Gourlay in his Raeburn essay is counterpointed by Brown's passages of metaphysical reflection on Scottish character, or his use of heavy blocks of narrative with little colour or dialogue. And this narrative effect serves to reinforce the thematic contrast between father and son.

GOURLAY SENIOR: SUPERNATURAL POWERS?

Gourlay is seen not only as a prodigiously large and brutal figure, but as embodying sinister elements, as in this description of him addressing his men in Chapter 1:

'Are ye sleeping, my pretty men?' he said, softly . . . . '*Eih?*'

The '*Eih*' leapt like a sword, with a slicing sharpness in its tone that made it a sinister contrast to the first sweet question to his 'pretty men'. '*Eih?*' he said again, and stared with open mouth and fierce dark eyes.

'Hurry up, Peter,' whispered the gaffer, 'hurry up, for God sake. He has the black glower in his een.'

Brown introduces a recurrent metaphor expressed in what could be taken as colloquially religious terms (as in 'for God sake' in the quotation above), but which, linked with 'the black glower', the descriptions of 'sinister', 'infernal', and expressions like 'damn ye', suggest that Barbie has been taken over by a malevolent spirit. Barbie is in decay; its tradesmen are drunk or lazy, the laird is a hollow drunken boaster, contracts are fiddled, dirt and meanness lie behind every front, while malice and hidden meanings lie behind every word. In this ill-fated village, Gourlay has immense power. The townspeople bow to him, hating him because he is the emblem of their corruption. With the exception of Johnnie Coe the baker, and Tam Wylie, there are virtually no decent human beings left in the village.

GOURLAY'S DEMONIC DOMINATION

It is possible to see Brown's black metaphors, not as colloquial, but as having a more sinister symbolic meaning, an assertion of Gourlay's totem-like significance. The bull is a particularly ancient pagan deity; and if Gourlay is seen as having this unnatural power, then he is, like the Devil, 'worshipped', but in reverse, by the town. Thus, instead of the church dominating the town, both physically and ideologically, it is Gourlay's house which dominates the central square. Corrupt officials like the deacon, black at the heart, have taken over from the absentee minister, Struthers, who has lost any hold he ever had over his flock. Brown emphasises that Barbie's people are lost to any beauty in their town and countryside. Greed and malice possess the place, and genuine Christianity is long gone. (Does this not highlight the significance of the reading from Corinthians as a corrective at the end of the novel?)

It is worth looking a bit more closely at Gourlay in the light of this quasi-supernatural reading. Two passages are particularly significant; the first, recounted admiringly by Johnny Coe to the bodies, concerning the birth of young John Gourlay in Chapter 6. It is spoken as though it belongs in an older, oral tradition, capturing the blunt candour of the ballads. Isn't the effect of this passage to portray Gourlay as one of the great challengers of God, exaggerating his deformed energy? Images and ideas recur which relate to hell and damnation – the thunder roaring, lightning, folk thinking that the Day of Judgement is upon them, Gourlay on his black horse riding through the elements 'like the devil o' hell'. These images have become part of the town's collective memory, eulogising his superhuman courage and skill. The story, then, acts as a key moment in establishing Gourlay's subliminal power in the community. Significantly, it is an event echoed towards the end, when Gourlay taunts his son with the recollection of his birth.

Brown's method is akin to that of Hogg's *Justified Sinner*, where 'mysterious strangers' and dark descriptions carry more sinister implication than the simply unpleasant. Gourlay's downfall holds an 'unholy' fascination for his neighbours; and the effect of Brown's casual but deliberate use of 'damn' or 'sinister', 'malevolent' or 'black' runs all through the novel. Gourlay will drive no other than a black horse; his black glower drains vitality from the most powerful of men; his corrosive sneer strikes life like a 'black frost' – Gourlay is continually linked to the powers of blackness. When Wilson indulges in some petty triumph over John Gourlay, the black glower of Gourlay's hatred makes him wish 'to all his Gods' that he had held his tongue. And if the imagery were to be taken as simply colloquial, wouldn't its significance become merely melodramatic?

There are outstanding episodes, which support such a reading – Chapter 13, for example, with its appalling climax of violence, where Gibson, taunting Gourlay, is hurled through the window of the Red Lion. Gibson is a big man, yet Gourlay (with 'fiercely gleaming' eyes and 'hard, triumphant devilry' playing round his 'black lips') throws him a considerable distance. The feat is surely one of more than realistic possibility. The next chapter develops this hellish metaphor at the heart of the book in a way which will be echoed at the conclusion. John Gourlay Junior has been playing truant and he is terrified by the lightning of the storm; he explicitly compares it to the heavens opening and shutting 'like a man's eye', and sees the eye as 'stabbing' like a dagger. This central association of lightning-eyes-violence is then firmly linked to John Gourlay senior. The boy is caught by his monstrous father; and Brown draws our attention to the way his 'widening glower' is like the lightning which has so terrified the boy. 'His eye seemed to stab – a flash shot from its centre to transfix and pierce. Gaze at a tiger through the bars of his cage and you will see the look.'

THE HELLISH CLIMAX

Chapter 25 begins the great climax to the novel, when Gourlay finds his son returned home in disgrace from the university. It unites all the spiritual implications that the novel has raised. With Gourlay's 'monstrous bulk and significance' as he stands in the doorway, and with his terrible taunting of his son, Brown now fully reveals the demonic nature of the man:

> To bring a beaten and degraded look into a man's face, rend manhood out of him in fear, is a sight that makes decent men wince in pain; for it is an outrage on the decency of life, an offence to natural religion, a violation of the human sanctities. Yet Gourlay had done it once and again. I saw him 'down' a man at the Cross once, a big man with a viking beard, dark brown, from which you would have looked for manliness. Gourlay, with stabbing eyes, threatened, and birred, and 'downed' him, till he crept away with a face like chalk, and a hunted, furtive eye.
>
> Curiously it was his manly beard that made the look such a pain, for its contrasting colour showed the white face of the coward – and a coward had no right to such a beard. A grim and cruel smile went after him as he slunk away.

'*Ha!*' barked Gourlay, in lordly and pursuing scorn, and the fellow leapt where he walked, as the cry went through him. To break a man's spirit so, take that from him which he will never recover while he lives, send him slinking away *animo castrato* – for that is what it comes to – is a sinister outrage of the world. It is as bad as the rape of a woman, and ranks with the sin against the Holy Ghost – derives from it, indeed. Yet it was this outrage that Gourlay meant to work upon his son. He would work him down and down, this son of his, till he was less than a man, a frightened, furtive animal.

Positive religious invocations are for the first time brought into the novel – from Mrs Gourlay's ghastly and intense 'God have mercy!' just after this, to young John Gourlay's temporary escape to the benignity 'of the darkened heavens', where he thanks God for being free of his father. There is a constant tension throughout this chapter between Gourlay's blasphemous remarks (Gourlay shouts in Titanic pride, 'he wasna feared; no, by God, for he never met what scaured him!') and John junior's final promise that 'by God' he will kill his father. Every second line now describes Gourlay as infernal and unnatural. His terrible mocking joviality forces his son to drink, in a parody of Burns's 'tak aff yer dram!'. All the bestial images from tiger to bull which have been applied to him throughout the novel come to a climax now. Brown explicitly tells us that 'the hell on which man is built' comes to the surface in Gourlay. And young Gourlay, escaping from this horror, carries with him one outstanding image – the memory of his father's eyes, a lightning, piercing him in a way which will take him to his death.

THE RELIGIOUS THEME: PREDESTINATION AND THE ELECT

The closing chapters of the novel, from John's loss of will after his expulsion from university, raise issues, which interrogate the inheritance of Scottish Calvinism. Throughout the novel there is a kind of parodic emphasis on predestination which goes beyond the idea of fate in Greek tragedy; from the emphasis laid on Gourlay's warning when his son plays with the great poker ('you'll be killing folk next') to the overall atmosphere of inevitability. Isn't there something of a parody of the idea of the elect, in the sense that Gourlay believes that his family – even when he actually hates them individually – are nevertheless his chosen people? Pride is probably Barbie's overweening fault; and we can see a line of descent from Burn's Holy Willie through Scott, Hogg and Galt's classic figures of hypocrisy and pride down to Barbie's modern version of a justified sinner. Justification for Gourlay has always been by a kind of faith – but a negative and bleak faith in profit and money and property. His God is Mammon, and what Brown is saying through his religious and parodic method, is that materialism and Mammon have possessed Gourlay and Barbie.

BIBLICAL ECHOES AND WARNINGS

Brown deliberately exploits biblical language. Two outstanding examples are found in the beginning of Chapter 14 ('In those days it came to pass that Wilson sent his son to the high school of Skeighan, even James, the red-haired one, with the squint in his eye. Whereupon Gourlay sent *his* son to the high school . . .') and in the biblical phrase which expresses the horror of the bodies at the end of the novel – 'their loins were loosened beneath them'. In this society, where the laird is obsessed with his quarry, the minister with his petty dignity and the dominie with Adam Smith's *The Wealth of Nations*, Brown is saying that later nineteenth-century Scotland has become hellish in its expulsion of feeling and sensitivity and decency from its society. The house is thus Gourlay's church, and he is its archpriest.

There is therefore poetic and Christian justice in the ending, in Mrs Gourlay's inspired quotation from the Bible, which can be seen as the final commentary on the spiritual collapse of community in Barbie. The reading from the thirteenth chapter of first Corinthians is arguably not truly her voice at all; Brown even suggests that God is speaking through her – 'She seemed to borrow its [the Bible's] greatness and become one with the law that punished her. Arrogating the Almighty's function to expedite her doom, she was the equal of the Most High.' The 'demoniac power' of the fate that sweeps her on suggests a terrible and superhuman justice being enacted, the message emphasising Barbie's want of charity, as well as that wholeness of mind and emotion which young John Gourlay and his father both lacked. Mrs Gourlay and Janet recognise this, and it is significant that they go to their suicide making an appeal to Christ. The ironic implication is that they can anticipate nothing worse in suicide and, perhaps hell thereafter, than staying in the nightmarish community which has treated them so savagely.

A FAIR VIEW OF SCOTLAND?

Is Brown fair to Barbie? Brown's own life was unhappy; like Lewis Grassic Gibbon in *Sunset Song* (1932) he may be charged with misrepresenting his community through a distorted lens. Brown continually punctuates his narrative with references to general Scottish attributes, for example: 'For the irony of the ignorant Scot is rarely the outcome of intellectual qualities. It depends on a falsetto voice and the use of a recognised number of catch-words . . .'; 'In every little Scotch community there is a distinct type known as "the bodie". "What does he do, that man?" you may ask, and the answer will be, "Really, I could hardly tell ye what he does – he's juist a bodie!"' The genus 'bodie' is divided into two species: the 'harmless bodies' and 'nesty bodies'. 'To go back to the beginning, the Scot, as pundits will tell you, is an individualist. His religion alone is enough to make him so. For it is a scheme of personal salvation . . .'. The statements are deliberately provocative and they force the reader to interrogate the picture of Scotland being presented. It appears that Brown allows a certain Scottish greatness in his Edinburgh University professor who, announcing the results of the Raeburn competition, distinguishes between genuine creative imagination and mere fancy, and exhorts young Gourlay to discipline his morbid talent; but the other main representation of the capital's culture, the Jock Allan circle into which John has fallen, is all too recognisable as a tavern clique, kept going through drink and trivial anecdote. And where at points in the novel Brown quotes from Burns, the choice of this emblematic poet, is, of course, significant. Burns has come to be associated with 'lazy' patriotism despite the poet's acerbic scrutiny of society and identity. Burns, is then, a double-edged tool; and the inclusion of his voice and the ambiguous associations it evokes, serves to suggest a wry provocation by Brown to our responses to Scottish pride and the foundations upon which we maintain it. From this perspective, we may view the novel as a kind of 'Scotland in allegory' and this forces us to question the very images and values which lie beneath the surface skin of Brown's portrait. However, Brown is not just derogatory of Scots, his statements suggest a disillusionment with human life in general, and the sordid, petty nature of man. This aspect of the novel perhaps qualifies the outright criticism of Scots as limited and parochial and raises more universal questions as to the condition of human nature and the politics of community.

HEAVY MACHINERY?

Brown's use of 'dramatic machinery' in the novel has been criticised by some as too obvious and laboured. For example, the paralleling of two fathers and their prospective sons, Gourlay and Wilson, is clearly meant as deliberate contrast, with the curve of the Gourlays climbing to its height with John's winning of the Raeburn and then rapidly descending, with Wilson starting at a much lower point, climbing much more slowly but then overtaking the Gourlays rapidly in the second part of the novel. This is typical of the fashion for patterning in the Victorian novel but it can lead to overly explicit narrative 'signalling'. For example, there is the heavy-footed introduction of the poker early on in the narrative leaving us in no doubt that a murder weapon has been introduced. And at these points, Brown's narrative is perhaps too obtrusive in its anticipation of the tragedy within the novel.

A SENSE OF HUMOUR?

It may seem odd, given the dark nature of this novel, to suggest that Brown is often humorous in his treatment of Scottish character. Yet he is frequently sardonic and witty regarding his countrymen and his community. Placing himself in that community as an observer, he remarks that 'ours is a nippy locality', in a tone which implies at least some affection and respect for their wit. His biblical parodies, as shown, have a grim humour within them; and consideration of this (slightly!) lighter side of Brown's novel might well suggest that yet another dualism – this time of tragedy and comedy – is operating. The effect of this wry humour is to leaven the darker aspects of the novel and by this means Brown attempts to balance the overall tone of his narrative treatment.

SCOTTISH AND ENGLISH FICTION

The novel's major themes clearly connect with themes of mainstream English fiction. In Dickens's *Hard Times* (1854) the harsh insensitivity of the business man Gradgrind crushes the imaginative sensibilities of his two children, with tragic long-term effects; in E. M. Forster's *Howard's End* (1910), there is a classic opposition of the Wilcoxs' world of mercantile materialism set against the quiet but insistent rural sensitivity of Mrs Wilcox, who in the end speaks for the superiority of an organic tradition as opposed to a destructive modern materialism. Yet there is perhaps a distinction, in that the English tradition identifies the dangers of excessive materialism, thus locating that excess as bad; while almost invariably, from Dickens to George Eliot in *Middlemarch* (1871), and from Trollope's *The Warden* (1855) to Forster, the quiet and sensitive voice is seen as indisputably good. Arguably, the Scottish tradition, from Scott, Galt and Hogg to Oliphant and Stevenson, is presenting a different dichotomy, in which a split is being identified within a family, in which the members of the split are seen as bodying forth a dissociation of wholeness of sensibility characteristic of Scottish culture after 1707. The treatment here of the novel should be read within the context of the introductions to this section, 'Scottish Literature in the Victorian and Edwardian Era', and the previous section, 'The Age of Scott', in which analysis of the Scottish tradition in fiction suggested that this and other major novels have at their heart a symbolic representation of a fundamental psychological and social split in Scottish personality and community, resulting from significant historical forces and changes.

CHAPTER 26

J. M. BARRIE AND
THE SCOTTISH THEATRE

VICTORIAN AND EDWARDIAN THEATRE IN SCOTLAND

At the end of Victoria's reign and on into the Edwardian era, Scottish theatre was dominated by London. A parallel situation existed in Ireland where theatre was similarly provided by London's touring companies. However, in 1904, the Irish National Theatre Society – better known as the Abbey Theatre – was founded. The company was to prove an important institution, in its early years run by an élite coterie of Ireland's leading cultural and political nationalists, with strong associations with both literary and nationalist drama.

The Abbey's immediate predecessors were the Irish Literary Theatre and the Irish National Dramatic Company. Begun in 1897, the founding of the Irish Literary Theatre by William Butler Yeats, Augusta, Lady Gregory and Edward Martyn, gave a distinctive and indigenous voice to Irish drama. The cultural project was, according to Douglas Hyde, 'the necessity for de-anglicising Ireland', and this was very much in line with the general social and cultural project of Hyde's Gaelic League, founded by him in 1893, for the promotion of Celtic language and culture. The new theatre company wanted to create 'a Celtic and Irish school of dramatic literature' that was distinct from the English commercial, touring theatre which dominated the theatres of Ireland and Scotland. Lady Gregory, for example, created drama based on translations of Irish heroic legend, and both she and Yeats used folk and peasant tales to provide material for drama, seeking more authentic representations to displace the caricatures of Irishness propagated by English popular theatre.

The Irish National Dramatic Company was the company run by the brothers Frank and Willie Fay, experienced amateur actors whose practice emphasised simplicity of design and clarity of vocal presentation. In addition, these two companies formed an alliance with Maud Gonne and her nascent feminist propagandist group, the Daughters of Erin.

In 1904 the Abbey Street theatre was the gift of the patron Annie Horniman, an English admirer of Yeats. The Society – the Abbey – had a particular commitment to encourage new writing. Its first great playwright was J. M. Synge. Among his plays were *In the Shadow of the Glen* (1903), *Riders to the Sea* (1904), *The Well of the Saints* (1905) and *The Playboy of the Western World* (1907). Synge's project was to produce 'work in English that is perfectly Irish in essence' and to this end he developed a distinctive, highly rhetorical theatrical language that some found offensive but is, at root, a splendid, artificial convention, poetic, lyrical and, at the same time, mocking and dynamic.

The theatre's early political difficulties focused on Synge, whose disreputable peasant characters provoked riotous nationalist demonstrations, especially against *The Playboy of the Western World* which audiences claimed defamed the purity of Irish morals and the chastity of Irish women. Yeats outfaced the demonstrators, but still, and contrary to the mythology of the Abbey, the theatre's audience seemed more satisfied with Lady Gregory's low key and undemanding folk dramas. After Synge's early death in 1909, and despite new dramas by Lady Gregory and Yeats's verse dramas, the Abbey was without a distinctive and indigenous popular playwright, until Synge's mantle passed to O'Casey, and what Maxwell and Gibbon describe in the opening pages of *The Cambridge Guide to Theatre* (1996) as 'his synthesis of poetic vernacular and urban realism'. For the first half of the twentieth century, and perhaps longer, Scottish theatre laboured under the shadow of the Abbey, of Yeats, Lady Gregory, Synge and O'Casey.

The first institutional reaction occurred in Scotland in 1909. Influenced by the Abbey and excited by the flourishing of 'new drama', the drama which dealt with social issues and current political concerns being written by George Bernard Shaw, Harley Granville Barker and others, Alfred Wareing opened the Glasgow Repertory Theatre. Wareing's purpose in founding a theatre in Glasgow had been primarily to challenge the dominance of London over the theatre in the country and to foster Scottish drama. In its four years of active operations, the company produced some thirty-five new Scottish plays in a repertoire which included continental dramatists like Gorky and Chekhov. The Glasgow Repertory Company were responsible for the first British production of Chekhov's *The Seagull* (1896), and the best of the new English drama, by, amongst others, Shaw, Galsworthy and Arnold Bennett. Their last season, in the spring of 1914, was their most successful and, had it not been for the outbreak of war, they would have continued and possibly become the first municipal theatre in Britain.

The company made significant efforts to support new Scottish writers. However, their most promising writers, Harold Chapin and George Hamlen, were killed in action during the war. Interestingly, the company also encouraged Scottish writers working in other fields to write for the theatre. In this context the most successful of the company's writers was Neil Munro who contributed *Macpherson* (1911), based on his 'Erchie' stories, a slight comedy containing much satire, directed against Dowanhill and its inhabitants' enthusiasm for *art nouveau* and heliotrope colour schemes. The play, though a success with the public, did not live up to the enormous expectations which Munro's fame had encouraged, and it remained his solitary dramatic work, if one discounts the adaptations of the *Para Handy* stories.

The influence of the new English dramatists was strong and can be seen in, for example, Anthony Rowely's play *A Weaver's Shuttle* (1910), a crypto-Galsworthian study of industrial strife, which concentrates more on the boss's family and the appealing figure of 'wee Jeannie', the patriarchal boss's granddaughter, than on the impending industrial dispute. The influence of Ibsen is also strong in the plays of Hamlen, whose work is all – with the exception of a glorious 'doon the watter' pantomime called *Colin in Fairyland* (1910) adapted from George MacDonald's story 'The Carasoyn' (from *Dealings with the Fairies*, 1867) – in the conventional naturalistic, middle-class mould.

The undoubted commercial successes of the theatre were the adaptations of John Joy Bell's *Wee Macgreegor* (1911) and *Oh! Christina* (1910), illustrating once again that Scottish theatres seldom fail if they present Scottish plays. Scots was used by several of the dramatists who wrote for the theatre, perhaps most effectively by Donald Colquhoun in his one-act play, *Jean* (1914), one of the very first plays to depict the grimness of Scottish rural life. The play is written in a vigorous, if rather eclectic Scots, with words and phrases from all over the country used to tell a tale set in Lanarkshire. It centres on the rivalry between father and son, and has a melodramatic climax, in which the father dies after a row with his son, who wants to emigrate to Canada with the farm servant, Jean. She, it transpires at the end of the play, is a 'fallen woman' with an illegitimate child. This short play, and J. A. Ferguson's *Campbell of Kilmohr* (1914), which was without doubt the best known of the plays to emerge from the Glasgow Repertory Theatre, were the prototypes for many of the plays produced by the Scottish National Players in the 1920s. The emphasis on history and on rural life was to provide material for such works as George Reston Malloch's *Soutarness Water* (1926), a gloomy and almost ridiculously melodramatic study of rural communities, and, even later, Donald Carswell's *Count Albany* (1933), a play set well after the '45 which revisits events from Prince Charlie's exile in Rome.

Of the Scottish plays premièred by the Glasgow Repertory Theatre only

Campbell of Kilmohr, which was first produced on 23 March 1914 by Lewis Casson, had a place in the repertoire of later companies. Unfortunately, Ferguson did not follow this play with anything remotely comparable. His later play on the subject of the Clearances, *The King of Morven* (1931), is only a pale shadow of *Campbell*, which Hugh MacDiarmid (writing as C. M. Grieve, in the essay 'Other Dramatists' in his controversial *Contemporary Scottish Studies: First Series*, 1926), considered 'as good as anything [John] Brandane or Malloch have produced. No anthology of the Best Contemporary Scottish Plays could omit it.' Within contemporary Scottish theatre, however, the play had been confined to the amateur one-act play festivals of the Scottish Community Drama Association.

J. M. Barrie (1860–1937): London-Scot

Although, as we have noted, Scottish theatre was dominated by London for most of the Edwardian era, and well into the 1920s, the London stage was, in turn, dominated by a Scot. J. M. Barrie wrote some of the most financially successful plays of his era, producing a body of work which shaped commercial theatre across the whole of Britain. Until recently, however, suffering under accusations of sentimental excess, Barrie's reputation has been in the critical wilderness. The standing of this most popular of Scottish playwrights has suffered and declined to a degree matched only by the parallel fall of James Bridie. However, the combination of the publication of Andrew Birkin's revisionist biography, *J. M. Barrie and the Lost Boys* in 1979, the RSC revival of *Peter Pan* in 1982 – a production that emphasised the psychological subtlety of the play, and which made Peter's cry of 'Mother', when he is deserted by the other children, the shattering experience Barrie intended it to be – and increasing interest from the academic world shows that his long-overdue rehabilitation is well under way. R. D. S. Jack's *The Road to The Never Land: A Re-assessment of J. M. Barrie's Dramatic Art* (1991) is perhaps the critical high point of an ongoing reassessment which insists that Scottish cultural studies should return to Barrie's writing and consider anew Barrie's distinctive and imaginative world. The central text in this critical and theatrical rehabilitation must be *Peter Pan* (1904) but almost all of his plays have benefited from this critical recovery – although few have won theatrical revival and revision.

THE ADMIRABLE CRICHTON

Barrie's work dissects and deconstructs the hegemonic structures of Edwardian society. His plays debate the key ideological tropes of gender roles, class, politics and education. *The Admirable Crichton* (1902), a modern fable in which a progressive but aristocratic family, and their servants, are shipwrecked on a desert island, explicitly debates ideas and ideals of gender and class. On the island, the hierarchical order of English society collapses and the butler Crichton is revealed as the most capable, practical and worthy of the group. Ironically, Crichton's recreation of the social order is just as hierarchical as the old system. Although the new order is certainly seen as a meritocracy in which the individual's abilities can flourish unhindered by convention and tradition, Barrie's eponymous hero cannot conceive of a society in which class would not shape expectations and emotions (Act I):

> Lord Loam: Can't you see, Crichton, that our divisions into classes are artificial, that if we were to return to Nature, which is the aspiration of my life, all would be equal? . . .
> Crichton: The divisions into classes, my lord, are not artificial. They are the natural outcome of a civilised society. (*To Lady Mary*) There must always be a master and servants in all civilised communities, my lady, for it is natural, and whatever is natural is right . . .

On the island the 'natural' order is recreated in a fantastical and idealised version of a civilised community. This is most evident in Crichton's assumption of authority and the experience of the family's daughter, Lady Mary, who is freed from the conventional order of her class to the extent that a match with Crichton seems possible. Her freedom, however, recreates her physical as well as social self (Act III):

> *A stalwart youth appears at the window, so handsome and tingling with vitality that, glad to dispose of Crichton, we cry thankfully, 'The hero at last.' But it is not the hero; it is the heroine. This splendid boy, clad in skins, is what Nature has done for Lady Mary. She carries bow and arrows and a blow-pipe, and over her shoulder is a fat buck, which she drops with a cry of triumph. Forgetting to enter demurely, she leaps through the window.*

This liberated and significantly active femininity suggests Barrie's explicit criticism of the abuse of women in Edwardian society: after all, *The Admirable Crichton* is a study of gender as much as of class. These strands come together in the teasing trail of sexual tension which Barrie hints at in the relationship between Crichton and Lady Mary and which anticipates a conventionally closed narrative. Such a conclusion would, however, reduce the impact of Barrie's analysis. As in Bernard Shaw's *Pygmalion* (1914), Barrie resists the obvious 'happy' ending to achieve something more provocative and political. The play concludes as a chilly and formal exchange between Crichton and Lady Mary. They have returned to London and the old social structures fall back into place (Act IV):

> Lady Mary: You are the best man among us.
> Crichton: On an island, my lady, perhaps; but in England, no.
> Lady Mary (*not inexcusably*): Then there is something wrong with England.
> Crichton: My lady, not even from you can I listen to a word against England.

But Crichton's paean to England is far from assured. There is no hint of irony in his words. It is instead a tragic exchange with both characters locked into the restricting roles dictated by the class and gender orthodoxies of their English society.

PETER PAN

Although *The Admirable Crichton* focuses on an élite and upper-class group, Barrie's more usual locus is the metropolitan middle class. His plays are set against the backdrop of the London society of Bloomsbury, Mayfair and Kensington Gardens, and yet many of the themes he focuses on parallel and repeat the key familial debates and imaginative motifs of other Scottish dramas: the family and the complications of familial relations are of repeated concern, as is an interest in the fey, the fantastical and the supernatural. Barrie develops a sustained critique of the construction of gender, played out within the conventions of family. The traditional narrative structure of his plays disguises his subtle exploration of Victorian family values. In *The Admirable Crichton*, *Peter Pan* (1904) and *What Every Woman Knows* (1908) he examines the predictable gender images assured within the idea of the family and the hedonistic and, potentially, liberating disorder that comes of violating such codings. The metaphor of the familial as social ideal, with the threat of disorder as penalty for transgression, is most clearly debated in *Peter Pan* with the correlation of Peter and the Lost Boys, existing outwith parental control, on the one hand, and the Darling children under the sway of conventional familial roles, on the other. Gender and the social constraints of gender roles are further analysed in the paralleling of the three feminine characters, Wendy, Tinker Bell and Tiger Lily.

In a world marked by a lack of hierarchical structures, Peter's identity is essentially that of a misrule character: he is both endlessly childish and fundamentally devilish, the manifestation of society's fears of the unrestrained id. The dichotomy of the unconscious and the socially restrained conscious self is dramatised in the narrative of Wendy's seduction. Within such a reading, Peter offers the temptation of transgression to the Darling children who are initially introduced in the safe, nurturing environment of their nursery. In their games and play-acting the Darlings explicitly rehearse the gender roles preferred by Edwardian society. In contrast to the figure of Lady Mary on the desert island, Wendy is a character wholly in thrall to the image of socially constructed gender roles, giving full expression to the explicit codes around the hegemonic identity of the nurturing 'mother'. No sooner is she transported to the idyllic fantasy of Neverland, a world without the cultural and economic structures which shape the limits of the conscious world available to her in Bloomsbury, than she is spring-cleaning, cooking meals and reading bedtime stories to the boys. Wendy misreads the potential liberation of Neverland and attempts to impose the structures of social organisation she has rehearsed in the nursery upon the disorder she perceives around her. The boys, including her brothers, John and Michael, enact their fantasies as hunters, buccaneers and sprites, while the limit of Wendy's imaginative engagement is to be a mother.

Wendy's cultural inhibitions are further revealed in comparison with the other feminine characters in Neverland. On one level, Wendy, Tinker Bell and Tiger Lily function as three separate characters competing in different ways for the attentions of Peter. However, they are more completely understood as distinct aspects of one female identity. In fact, it might be better argued that Tinker Bell and Tiger Lily represent different manifestations of the unconscious of unrestrained femininity (or 'female-ness'), while Wendy is contained as idealised Edwardian womanhood. So, the ideal of the nurturing mother, enacted by Wendy, is countered by Tiger Lily as the wild, sexually aggressive, untamed savage and Tinker Bell as the sensuous, free spirit liberated from all moral responsibility. Together they may reveal the prejudices and fears of Edwardian society about the sexuality of women.

With Peter as troll and cultural doppelgänger, Barrie tempts Edwardian femininity to transgress society's rules and conventions. Despite her dalliance with the fantastic, Wendy's seduction, her fall, is incomplete. Although she hints at her desire to be transformed into lover, her determined and sustained appropriation of the role of mother precludes the overt declaration, or even acknowledgement, of her own sexuality. In her criticisms of Tiger Lily and Tinker Bell she censures herself and limits her potential for expression (Act IV):

Wendy (*knowing she ought not to probe but driven to it by something within*): What are your exact feelings for me, Peter?
Peter (*in the class-room*): Those of a devoted son, Wendy.
Wendy (*turning away*): I thought so.
Peter: You are so puzzling. Tiger Lily is just the same; there is something or other she wants me to be, but she says it is not my mother.
Wendy (*with spirit*): No, indeed it isn't.
Peter: Then what is it?
Wendy: It isn't for a lady to tell.

Using the motif of a fantastic, parallel and alternative universe, Barrie holds a mirror up to his own community. The escape from everyday reality to an antic, ethereal and analogous world, Neverland in *Peter Pan*, the wood in *Dear Brutus* (1917), the desert island in *The Admirable Crichton*, is both temporally limited and psychologically constrained. The transient emancipation effected by Barrie's imagined communities is away from a problematic view of the contemporary society towards a fantastic, though not necessarily idealised, version of its supernatural parallel where characters may still assume their traditional roles.

Barrie's Neverland reorganises our understanding of Bloomsbury because it distils particular aspects of its social organisation allowing us to see more clearly the conventions and the truths of our own world. In *Peter Pan*, gender relations within the structure of the family are highlighted with humour, sympathy and accuracy: the central role in such an analysis is that of mother. Wendy's fantasy to be mother to the Lost Boys is motivated by her imaginary life in Bloomsbury and the intervention of Peter to reclaim his familial role as son. However, just as Wendy's assimilation into the role of mother is incomplete (because of her unspoken and unspeakable desire for Peter), so he too is ultimately disillusioned of his desire to return to innocence (Act IV):

'Wendy, you are wrong about mothers. I thought like you about the window, so I stayed away for moons and moons, and then I flew back, but the window was barred, for my mother had forgotten all about me and there was another little boy sleeping in my bed.'

Peter's articulation of the loss of childishness and the loss of innocence, played out as loss of the mother, resonates through Scottish drama. The family, however necessary in abstraction, is never unproblematic – the social and gender roles available within this totemic structure are often described as limited, prescriptive and constrained. It is, nonetheless, the case that a version of the family is the elusive and imagined ideal within many of Barrie's dramas and a recurrent motif throughout Scottish drama.

The figure of Peter Pan and the escape to Neverland have become classic tropes of twentieth-century culture, revised and reinterpreted across a wide range of texts (cartoons, films, novels and other plays), and referenced in contemporary phraseology. Although modern critics have warned that it is too easy to give an Oedipal reading of *Peter Pan*, it *is* intriguing to contextualise *Peter Pan* within a British society reading and interpreting Freud for the first time, as well as linking that to the period's interest with paranormal activity.

The play should also be considered in the context of West End theatre economics and the work of impresario Charles Frohman at the Duke of York's Theatre, where the play premièred on 27 December 1904 – assuring its perpetual associations with Christmas. Frohman's company of actors included Gerald Du Maurier and Irene Vanburgh, who created the roles of Hook and Peter. In her biography of her father, *Gerald: A Portrait* (1934) Daphne Du Maurier describes the effect of this first production on audiences:

> When Hook first paced the quarter-deck children were carried screaming from the stalls, and even big boys of twelve were known to reach for their mother's hand in the friendly shelter of the boxes. How he was hated, with his flourish, his poses, his dreaded diabolical smile! That ashen face, those blood-red lips, the long, dank greasy curls: the sardonic laugh, the maniacal scream, the appalling courtesy of his gestures. He was a tragic and rather ghastly creation who knew no peace, and whose soul was in torment.

While Du Maurier appreciated the full horror in a figure so commonly reduced to pantomime villain, this did not prevent the leading actresses of the time, Mrs Patrick Campbell, Ellen Terry, Fay Compton, Nina Boucicault and Lillah McCarthy, aspiring to and eventually appearing in the role of Peter.

For the first decades after its première, and before its fall into bowdlerised and superficial amusement, actors certainly took the play seriously: so too did the critics. Mark Twain was an early supporter arguing that 'It is my belief that *Peter Pan* is a great and refining and uplifting benefaction to this sordid money-mad age; and the next best play is a long way behind it.' George Bernard Shaw described it as 'ostensibly a holiday entertainment for children but really a play for grown-up people', a position confirmed by actress Gladys Cooper who argued that, 'I am inclined to hold and maintain that *Peter Pan* is really more of a play for grown-ups than for children.' This was vehemently opposed by Kenneth Tynan: 'The only adult thing about Barrie's play,' he argued, 'is its unctuous sentimentality.' Barrie's plays are often accused of mawkishness. However, one might reasonably argue that he used the idea of the sentimental (a popular aesthetic form within late Victorianism) to explore the limits of his contemporary theatre – the idea of the problem play, the escapist romance and the new fashion for children's theatre – and as a means of exposing the values, prejudices and hegemonies of his contemporary society. Such a tension can certainly be seen in both *The Admirable Crichton* and *What Every Woman Knows*, where the idea of the conventionally closed ending is a continued source of dramatic tension and narrative unease.

WHAT EVERY WOMAN KNOWS

What Every Woman Knows (1908) presents, in some degree, a more domestic scene than the explicitly escapist and fantastic milieux of *The Admirable Crichton* and *Peter Pan*. It focuses on the figure of Maggie Wylie, shrewd and intelligent, but plain and, at twenty-six or, as her brother seems to remember, twenty-seven, years old, already considered spinsterish. Barrie, a master of the use of stage directions, introduces her in Act I:

> *Here Maggie enters . . . We could describe Maggie at great length. But what is the use? What you really want to know is whether she was good-looking. No, she was not. Enter Maggie, who is not good-looking. When that is said, all is said.*

The play lays bare and dissects Maggie's relationships with men – first in the house of her father and then in that of her husband. The easy reading of the play has Maggie as the more-or-less passive object of the schemes of men, and certainly for many years the play was damned as being anti-women. However, Barrie's letters show that he intended the play to demonstrate the strength of women and to comment on the humiliation of their position in Edwardian Britain, 'in the strange days when it was considered "unwomanly" for women to have minds'. He gives Maggie great insight into the role of women within her Scottish society and again later in London. She understands fully 'her tragedy', as Barrie puts it: 'If you have [charm],' Maggie says acknowledging that she does not, 'you don't need to have anything else; and if you don't have it, it doesn't much matter what else you have.' In addition, there are many astute touches in the stage directions which make an uncomplicated reading of Maggie's role implausible; but such subtlety can be easily lost in an insensitive production. The crucial scene for most commentators occurs in Act I when Maggie seems to be bartered by her family to the young student John Shand. The Wylie menfolk, father and sons, put the offer.

> Mr Shand, we're willing, the three of us, to lay out £300 on your education . . . On condition that five years from now, Maggie Wylie, if still unmarried, can claim to marry you, should such be her wish; the thing to be perfectly open on her side, but you to be strictly tied down.

Maggie, however, is fully aware of her role within the arrangement and sees the opportunity it affords her. Shand's subsequent parliamentary success, Barrie carefully reveals, is directed and designed by Maggie. She politics for her husband but convention demands that she is careful to conceal her interventions from him. Her lack of self-worth brings her close to sacrificing her marriage for Shand's passion for a would-be mistress but, finally, her intellect and her desires come together and she admits, and he recognises, her role in his success. Barrie concludes the play with Maggie's own revelation of 'what every woman knows' – that 'Every man who is high up loves to think that he has done it all himself; and the wife smiles, and lets it go at that. It's our only joke. Every woman knows that.'

Paying close attention to his subtly detailed stage directions, full of character description and colluding asides, it is clear that Barrie presents this as a bitterly ironic comment on the lack of options which faced Edwardian women. Barrie was, after all, a strong supporter of women's suffrage and debated the 'woman question' in quite radical ways across a range of play texts. Unlike *Peter Pan*, however, *What Every Woman Knows* still awaits a revisionary theatrical production.

CHAPTER 27

WIDENING THE RANGE 4

THOMAS CARYLYE AND HUGH MILLER:
TWO PROPHETS IN THE WILDERNESS

It may seem strange now to reintroduce the figure of Thomas Carlyle, the thundering denunciator of Victorian materialism and so-called progress in economics, politics and society. After all, his first great essay, 'Signs of the Times', appeared in *Blackwood's Magazine* in 1829, just within the age of Scott, five years before he moved permanently to London, and eight years before Victoria came to the throne. Since, however, his influence was to be particularly profound on the Victorians of Britain and Scotland, and after Scott's death, we should consider him here as the greatest of a peculiarly Scottish type, who pronounced prophetically on men's morals and errors throughout the century, in a manner impossible to think of happening now. Some of the most significant pronouncements on such weighty matters came from Scots or Scottish-related thinkers: Carlyle, Thomas Macaulay, Hugh Miller and John Ruskin are just some of them, while their descendants include the poets James Thomson (*The City of Dreadful Night*, 1874) and John Davidson. What connects them all is their need to validate religion, or to find a substitute, and to preach their beliefs to a philistine world.

Sadly, many of these powerful figures and their works have been neglected and their vatic resonances have been lost to us. And yet perhaps more than ever, their voices deserve to be reheard. For they speak to us, across a breadth of ages, about the fears of a pre-millennial age – raising fundamental questions about the construction of society, our social organisation and the basis of our systems of meaning. The interrogation of old ideas that marks each new phase in man's social progress, the passing of a decade, or pertinently, the turning of a century, is mirrored in these philosophical late Victorians, who looked into the nineteenth century and responded to the incursions of industrialisation, capitalism and the mechanical age. In them we see reflected our own struggle to make sense of, and find meaning in our rapidly changing world.

Moreover, their work – especially that of Carlyle and Miller – has tremendous worth and pathos in itself in their passionate and often deeply personal struggle to negotiate the persistent dilemma between religion and reason. In this, their voices stood as powerful invectives advocating the need for faith in a world which seemed to be losing its centre as science, technology and imperial expansion began to change the appearance, and outlook, of the new Britain.

Thomas Carlyle (1795–1881)

Carlyle's work, more than that of any other writer, grapples with these changes. It is not as difficult as it first appears, with its Germanic derivations, copious punctuation and its unusual quasi-biblical oratory. Perseverance quickly reveals an almost lyrical narrative of tremendous energy and creativity. Thomas Carlyle was born in Ecclefechan in 1795 and raised in a devoutly Presbyterian family. He went to study theology at Edinburgh University but suffered fundamental doubts, and left quickly in a state of profound disillusionment. Sadly, Carlyle's biography is also notable for his departure for London in 1834, marking the steady drain of Scots writers that would choose to leave, for a life outwith their native country.

Signs of the Times, written in 1829, signals the beginning of Carlyle's secular preaching, in which he vituperatively attacked the materialist conditions of Victorian society. He condemned the contemporary politics of laissez-faire and the systematic theorising of Bentham who reduced feelings ('the passions') to the stricture of logical, intellectual patterns which so characterised 'this Mechanical Age'. Instead, Carlyle called upon the 'Dynamism' of insight, a spiritually inward eye rather than mere intellectual systematising. Carlyle's socio-political diagnosis then, advocated that true reform must come from within. He concludes his essay thus:

> To reform a world, to reform a nation, no wise man would undertake and all but foolish men know that the only solid, though a far slower reformation, is what each begins and perfects on himself.

The call to spiritual reformation that ends *Signs of the Times* can be seen to be a starting point for Carlyle's own spiritual journey in *Sartor Resartus* (1830–1). Carlyle may have lost faith in orthodox Christianity and the literal truth of the Bible, but this appears only to have increased his urgency for belief. His work betrays a deeply religious temperament severed from religion. As a result, Carlyle sought God in more than one text. If his first text was scripture (from his theological studies at Edinburgh), in *Sartor*, his second text would be nature made divine. But the text which Carlyle revered more than any other, was the text of history; a temporal scripture with the historian as the scribe of all human time, a prophet in reverse, recording the unfolding epic of the past. Truly, the God of the Victorians had not altogether disappeared, but he had been displaced; while Wordsworth would seek for him in nature and Miller for him in the stones, Carlyle sought for him in the records of history.

The narrative style of *Sartor Resartus* is deeply ambivalent, reflecting Carlyle's own divided attitude towards spiritual questions. Carlyle chose to narrate his book through the creation of the German philosopher, Professor Teufelsdrockh, himself viewed through the sceptical eyes of the editor. Teufelsdrockh is clearly a refiguration of Carlyle himself and his ideological journey, a philosophical examination of Carlyle's own spiritual crisis during his early years in Edinburgh. Yet there is much of Carlyle's own cynicism in the ironic narrator which allows Carlyle to detach at points from taking full responsibility for his own ideas. In this, we see Carlyle, perhaps subconsciously, following in a tradition of dualistic and ambivalent voices from Burns, through Scott to Hogg and Stevenson.

Teufelsdröckh ('Devil's dung'!) faces the threat of nihilism and despair. The professor must confront the 'Everlasting No', which represents a kind of spiritual paralysis in the face of an incomprehensible universe, seemingly bereft of all value. Having defied oblivion, he reaches spiritual epiphany in his recognition of the divine body of nature: 'Or what is Nature? Ha! Why do I not name thee God? Art thou not the "Living Garment of God"?' The universe itself is seen to be 'but one vast Symbol of God . . . the Volume of Nature . . . whose Author and writer is God.' Carlyle saw it as his role to revitalise that text and communicate it to the world. To attain the 'Everlasting Yea' Carlyle stressed that man must first rid himself of egocentricity. This concept of self-annihilation is perhaps the most perplexing in the body of his work for it provokes an apparent paradox. He appears to be simultaneously offering humane social analysis (as in *Past and Present*, 1843, which calls for human connection rather than materialistic division), while rejecting, outstandingly in *The French Revolution* (1837), democratic self-assertion and enfranchisement on the basis that men are fundamentally unequal and require autocratic rule. As early as 1829, Carlyle had insisted in *Signs of the Times* that:

> The plain truth . . . [is that] one man that has a higher wisdom, a hitherto unknown spiritual Truth in him, is stronger than ten men who have it not, or than ten thousand, but than all men who have it not; and stands among them with a quite ethereal, angelic power, as with a sword out of Heaven's own armoury.

This is the beginning of Carlyle's theory of hero-worship (*On Heroes and Hero-Worship*, 1841) which, in the end, would lead to the defence of tyrannical rule as a necessity for social order. To return to *Sartor*, the precursory act of self-annihilation ties man's will to the will of God, realised through the imperative to work (Book 2, Chapter 9):

> Produce! Produce! Were it but the pitifullest infinitesimal fraction of a Produce, produce it in God's name! Tis the utmost thou has in thee; out with it then, Up! Up! Whatsoever thy hand findeth to do, do it with thy whole might. Work while it is called today, for the Night cometh wherein no man can work.

Critics have indeed raised the observation that there is more than a fraction of Calvinist authoritarianism and rigour in Carlyle's spiritual solution. Yet as a spiritual resolution, it is deeply paradoxical as it offers freedom in terms of self-subjugation. An understanding of the diverse threads of Carlyle's reasoning is a complex matter, requiring many levels of interpretation. Readers interested in his philosophical conclusions are directed to Ralph Jessop's *Carlyle and Scottish Thought* (1997) and *Thomas Carlyle: Calvinist Without the Theology* (1978) by Eloise M. Behnken. In their works, the reader can see the fundamental importance of Carlyle's religious and philosophical education in Scotland. His dogmatic assertion that great men reveal themselves to the masses, argued in terms of a strangely self-justifying process, which gives them the authority to impose governance, is reminiscent of the doctrine of the elect. The reader increasingly perceives that the recurrent doppelgänger for so many of Carlyle's heroes (outstandingly Abbot Samson of *Past and Present*) is Carlyle himself, implying his own right to be the prophet-leader of Victorian Britain. Yet it is also interesting to note that Carlyle was one of the first intellectuals of his age to engage with Eastern philosophy (through Goethe's *West-Östlicher Divan*, 1819) and that perhaps a strictly Western-democratic perspective judges Carlyle unfairly. From an Islamic point of view, operating from spiritual first principles, as Carlyle clearly does in his early work, the leader or hero in Carlyle's thought may be akin to the spiritual leader; as the master to the pupil in Buddhist and Hindu traditions. Carlyle's intentions may be misinterpreted if they are understood solely as political doctrines without recognising his emphasis on spiritual reformation and the requisite of spiritual guidance.

Nevertheless, Carlyle's rejection of human equality and his increasing insistence on exalted heroes was deeply out of touch with his own times. The nineteenth century was increasingly a period of individual self-assertion and class-consciousness. The work of Engels and Thomas Paine advocated self-determination not self-annihilation; revolt, rather than repressive rule. It is perhaps for this reason that Carlyle lost credibility in his own age, as his work increasingly slid into incomprehensible and ever more dogmatic strains, most evidently in the *Latter-Day Pamphlets* (1850).

Yet Carlyle had a tremendous influence on Victorian Britain and on Western writing and thought. A return to his powerful works communicates why this was so. His writings are provocative, searching, often challenging and always engaging. And his search for a powerful system of meaning in a materialistic age is universal. It is both for the tremendous substance of his struggle and for the power and creativity, with which he communicated it, that Carlyle commands rediscovery.

Hugh Miller (1802–56)

Hugh Miller too was, in his own times, a deeply respected and influential figure, praised by the likes of Charles Dickens, Thomas Chalmers, John Ruskin and Darwin. Yet he, perhaps even more than Carlyle, has been lost to recognition. Throughout Miller's life, his diverse achievements – as journalist, geologist, historian, poet and religious commentator – betray an intensely personal struggle to come to terms with the antagonistic claims of a transitional age. And it is the profundity and integrity with which he waged that battle which gives him resonance beyond his times.

Born in Cromarty in 1802, Miller was the son of a seafaring father who died when Miller was just five years old leaving him in the care of his mother, who was reputedly fey and, like the mother of James Hogg, the bearer of a wealth of tales and legends. He was largely self-taught and, through his own endeavour, mastered the infant science of geology by scrutinising the rocks on the Cromarty shoreline during long periods of truancy from the parish school. Despite his precocious intelligence, Miller chose at the age of eighteen to become a stonemason, and his acute, perceptive analysis of Scotland and Scottish life and people is deeply rooted in his own experience as an itinerant working man in the north of Scotland.

His most famous work, *My Schools and Schoolmasters* (1854) is an autobiographical and observational analysis of his times, written just two years before Miller tragically took his own life. He is believed to have suffered, in later years, from a degenerative disease of the brain. Yet his tragic death also epitomises the implosive existential crisis suffered by so many of his contemporaries in an age of monumental, and often destabilising, change.

Indeed, much of Miller's own thinking is characterised by paradox; his radicalism and his fear of popular movements, his hatred of 'Papism' and his advocacy of Catholic emancipation, his superstition and his scientific rigour. Yet his philosophical propensity was towards concord and he responded to an age of division – the Disruption of 1843 and increasing class revolt – by seeking to create a unifying philosophy. The rhetorical construction of his work reveals countless antagonisms set in binary opposition – Scotland/ England, Highland/Lowland, Good/Evil, True/Untrue, Real/Unreal –, which are resolved by a kind of composite metaphor which equivocate seemingly disparate elements. Indeed it was Miller who, in an early essay for the *Inverness Courier*, characterised the disparate features of Highland and Lowland blood, which he himself inherited from his dual parentage:

> The Highlander is characterised by shrewdness of *observation*, the Lowlander by that of *inference*; the Highlander is delighted by the external beauty of things, the Lowlander in diving into their secret causes; . . . the Highlander is a descriptive poet, the Lowlander is a metaphysician.

'Hugh Miller was both,' George Rosie wrote in *Outrage and Order* (1981), in response to this passage, and this integration is manifest in the figurative power and incisive thinking of the best of his work. Similarly, Miller was also a romantic, patriotic Scot who approved of the pragmatic union with England. It is surely significant that it was Hugh Miller who in 1847, wrote *First Impressions of England and its People*, an observational account of the country, perhaps intended to bridge the gap created by the trend for objectified portraits of Scotland in the South (epitomised by the Victorian fashion for Highland romanticism) and offer to Scots a view of their southern neighbour. Once more, Miller is here concerned to delineate the separate parts and in doing so he makes implicit connections and associations between the two conjoined countries. Throughout his works a dualistic and yet harmonising attitude is apparent. And this integrative perspective would be epitomised in perhaps the most powerful antagonism in Miller's life – in his marriage of instinctive Christian faith and empirical science.

Miller had in his early life experimented with descriptive poetry but his real literary talent lay in prose. His writing, in essay, autobiography and even in scientific narrative, is intensely reflective, sharply perceptive and often deeply evocative. But Miller is not in any way an abstract or theoretical writer. He is profoundly concerned with the human experience, the tangible, sensory world around him. *My Schools and Schoolmasters* itself was born from contemporaneous debate – it was Miller's sardonic comment on Scotland's educational system, in which he gives a broadly Rousseau-like critique, emphasising, not Knoxian doctrine but experience: 'The only school in which I could properly be taught was that world-wide school which awaited me – the school of experience, where Toil and Hardship are the severe but noble teachers.'

The book offers itself as 'a sort of educational treatise thrown into narrative form and addressed more especially to working men'. Indeed, Miller's work persistently promotes the idea of untutored ability. He frequently makes reference to voracious readers of literature and history born of peasant stock, of layman philosophers, artists and poets living in penury and writers such as Fergusson, Burns, Crabbe, Bunyan, Blake and Hogg who rose from humble beginnings. Miller may have been self-consciously promoting an early kind of working-class canon. Yet this recurrent strain in Miller's work appears not merely as an appraisal of unnurtured talent but evolves into a kind of vindication of narrative self-possession. In 'The People Are Their Own Best Portrait Painters' (1849) Miller advocated the importance of owning one's own history, and the basis of *Scenes and Legends: A Traditional History Of Cromarty* (1835) proposes the radical idea that history must be shared between the powerful and the masses and that true wisdom is a composite between the dissemination of philosophy and the arts and the received wisdom of the traditional community. *My Schools and Schoolmasters* appears to be a kind of culmination of this belief which expresses the importance for 'working men' to communicate their wisdom to others in their position. And it seeks to vindicate the significance of a life of honest labour spent not in the pursuit of cultivated knowledge and external validation but the intrinsic lessons of a companionable and modest life.

Miller was, then, a liberal in his times, but he was not a radical. Some of his harshest words are saved for the chartists and socialists, whom he hated and feared. This paradoxical element is highlighted in George Rosie's seminal introduction to Miller. *Outrage and Order* (1981), a collection of Miller's writings, demonstrates his profound humane analysis in articles such as 'The Highlands' a bitter attack on Highland depletion, or 'Climbing Boys – Chimney Sweeping', an early defence of child protection, while 'The Strikes' reveals Miller's scathing critique of class revolt, and in 'An Unspoken Speech' in *The Witness*, December 1850 Miller offers a prescriptive narrative on the benefits of sobriety, self-reliance and, of course, self-improvement:

> You have rare opportunities of observation; you may be a butcher's boy in body, but in mind you may become an adept in . . . comparative anatomy; – think of yourself as not in a prison, but in a school, and there is no fear but you will rise.

Miller's resolution to growing class tensions was, alike to Carlyle's call to Labour, the imperative to learn. Education, he proposed, offered the means for personal advancement and this would reverberate out into the general elevation of society. Power was attained through personal growth rather than political emancipation. He was, then, conservative in his liberalism and, like many of his time, ambivalent about the nature of social progress. There is a persistent tension in his writing between the desire to preserve an older, unsophisticated way of living and simultaneously to embrace enlightened thought and modern advances. In *Scenes and Legends* he is concerned to preserve the rich vein of Scotland's traditional values, folklore and belief. Yet his 'history' is tempered by a pragmatic desire to educate beyond fallacious and credulous modes of thinking. The introductory chapter, as so often in Miller's writing, sets up a binary model:

> Extremes may meet in the intellectual, as certainly as in the moral world . . . my greatest benefactors have been the philosophic Bacon and an ignorant old woman, who, of all the books ever written, was acquainted with only the Bible.

Thus the two poles of influence – 'the old woman' (traditional wisdom) and 'the philosopher' (cultured learning) – are linked in this work by the conclusion that received wisdom has an integrity and instinctive truth from which we may learn our shared history and the antecedents of our cultural values; but art, literature and cultured learning will liberate mankind from ignorance and the bondage of outdated ideas and modes of thinking.

Nevertheless, throughout Miller's work there is a persistent fascination with these older modes of thinking. Like James Hogg, the 'Ettrick Shepherd', Miller carried the associations of an older, community workaday world into the enlightened capital, where he paraded under the badge of 'the Cromarty stonemason'. Trivialised though their rural tags perhaps were, for Hogg and Miller they were resonant of a living reality. And just as Hogg returns again and again to the oral tales of Ettrick and his mother, Miller's works abound with traditional tales. *Tales and Sketches* (1863), a posthumous collection of essays and stories, is largely an assortment of supernatural tales; and many other of his works often return to the eerie, the mysterious and the unexplained. This contention of cognisance is powerfully evoked in his description of his own father's death early in *My Schools and Schoolmasters*, where Miller recalls the ghostly apparition that appeared to him, concluding (Chapter 7):

I communicate the story, as it lies fixed in my memory, without attempting to explain it. The supposed apparition may have been merely a momentary affectation of the eye, of the nature described by Sir Walter Scott in his 'Demonology', and Sir David Brewster in his 'Natural Magic'. But if so the affectation was one of which I experienced no after-return; and its coincidence, in the case, with the probable time of my father's death, seems at least curious.

Miller is equivocal. He both attempts to make sense of the incident by reference to modern post-Enlightenment interpretations and scientific rationale and, at the same time, wishes to leave the matter indeterminate 'without explaining it'; a communication beyond the rational which is neither fathomable nor resolvable.

Such was the persistent antagonism of Miller's life and work. And this is epitomised by his dual career as a religious commentator and scientist. From 1840 to 1856, Miller wrote for and edited *The Witness*, the journalistic organ of the new Free Church. He was a powerful spokesman for the anti-patronage cause, which culminated in the Disruption of 1843. Indeed the Disruption itself is a potent symbol for the crisis of religion in the nineteenth century; the established church was literally split in two and the very foundations of Christian faith shaken by the growth of sceptical thinking in the post-Enlightenment age and the increasing politicisation of its followers who now demanded democracy in church affairs. Now religion was to face the challenges of science. Throughout his life, Miller had fought to uphold the tenets of a devout faith. Yet, as a scientist, he was inevitably and irrevocably drawn into the emerging evolutionary debate which would fundamentally challenge the very basis of Victorian faith. In response to Robert Chambers's *Vestiges of Creation* (1844) and the pre-Darwinian ideas of scientific evolution, Miller vehemently argued for the divine source of the natural world. He developed a logically rigorous defence of creationist evolution, which interpreted the seven-day genesis as a metaphor for epochal geological development. In *Footprints of the Creator* (1849) and the *Testimony of the Rocks* (1857), he argued, right up until his death, that the evidences of geology were proof of God's existence and of a divine plan. Yet he abhorred those religious defendants who attacked the works of science as heresy. In one and the other Miller found profound beauty; God was to lend science its design and science, to religion, its testimony. In *First Impressions of England and its People* (1847), Chapter 18, he enthuses:

And such is the sublime prospect presented to the geologist as he turns him towards the shoreless ocean of the upper eternity. The mere theologian views that boundless expanse from a flat, and there lies in front of him but the narrow strip of the existing creation . . . while to the eye purged and strengthened by the euphrasy of science, the many vast regions of other creations, – promontory beyond promontory – island beyond island – stretch out in sublime succession into that boundless ocean of eternity . . .

In Miller, science and religion, the sublime and the rational, stand not in opposition but in profound unity.

After the groundbreaking publication of Darwin's *Evolution of the Species* in 1871, Miller and the creationist theorists became quickly dismissed as 'unscientific' and out-of-date. However, the ongoing evolutionary debate is beginning to return to Miller some of his due. Increasingly, biologists are turning from the previously accepted conclusion that evolution is a slow and continuous progression to reconsider the catastrophic theory of evolutionary development which Miller cited as evidence of God's intervention.

The record of Miller's life has become sadly blighted by his perceived failure in the evolutionary debate and overcast by the tragic account of his suicide at the height of his career. Yet just as the scientific paradigms evolve and review, so must literary interpretation revisit Miller to discover his profound and significant place in literature. Miller was both a product and a pioneer of his times. In him, we see the profound struggles of the Victorian age enacted. Yet the rage and eloquence which characterise his search for a humane and harmonious society speak beyond the parameters of his time. What Miller had to say about the intimate bonds which link the present with its past, which bind the material to the instinctive, and regulate our establishment and endeavour, is still relevant to us now.

Variations on a theme: historical romance, Kailyard and Celtic Twilight

What do these three genres have in common? The answer must surely be that they all seem to avoid the actuality of the subject they treat. All too often the historical tales of the period, for all their focus on significant and often bloody periods of the past, offer escape from Scotland's nineteenth-century problems. Kailyard fiction and poetry, by pandering to the taste of a British and colonial market, offered nostalgic reassurance that an older, ideal Scotland survived. In this fiction, we are offered an imagined 'dear green place' which bore no relation to what was happening in real villages and small towns, of the kind described by Douglas Brown, MacDougall Hay, and Grassic Gibbon. Similarly the novels of 'Fiona MacLeod' and the poetry and art of the Celtic Twilight evaded the real problems of the crofters and a changing Highland economy to portray a romanticised notion of Celtic spirit which served to excite the jaded imaginations of a world-wide audience in a way which repeated the phenomenon of the earlier European enthusiasm for Macpherson's recreation of *Ossian*.

Does this suggest that there is therefore little here for the interested reader of the literature of the period? Certainly not: we can, by studying these evasive or distorted versions of Scotland, discover why and how these authors – and their huge audiences – preferred them to an art which dealt with historical and present actuality. Moreover, some writers have been placed within these movements too readily by historians, when they were actually trying to exploit and parody aspects of them. Stevenson in *The Master of Ballantrae* (1889) for example was working not so much with a view to retelling history as emphasising recurrent traits and divisions in Scottish character. Neil Munro uses characteristics of Celtic Twilight in *The Lost Pibroch* (1896) in order to make his sardonic reduction of them all the more effective.

HISTORICAL ROMANCE

We have already noted some of the worthwhile romantic writers beyond Scott, like Lauder and Grant. Perhaps too we should allow that historical fiction stands up to criticism better than much of the Kailyard and Celtic Twilight. Strong, uncomplicated reworkings of history retain value, if only to give us structured – if questionable – versions of the past. G. J. Whyte-Melville's *The Queen's Maries* (1862), for example, is an ambitious attempt to present the complexity of Mary, Queen of Scots (which even Scott had not attempted), and cleverly achieves this by viewing her through her hand-maids, the Maries. S. R. Crockett's reworking of Hogg's Covenanting fiction in *The Men of the Moss Haggs* (1895) is well worth setting in the company of Scott's *Old Mortality* (1816), Hogg's *The Brownie of Bodsbeck* (1818), Galt's *Ringan Gilhaize* (1823) and John Buchan's later *Witch Wood* (1927). All deal with the effect of religious bigotry and repression, and Crockett's terse, economical but effective presentation of atrocities and savage persecution is arguably as good as any of Scott's or Galt's.

Crockett was vastly productive; his best work emerges when he sets fast-moving adventure with a strong period background in his beloved south-west Scotland, as in *The Raiders* (1894) and *The Gray Man* (1896). Likewise John Buchan (whose work spans two of our periods, since he was prolific before and after the Great War); within this period his work includes *Sir Quixote of the Moors* (1895), *John Burnet of Barns* (1898), *Grey Weather* (1899), *A Lost Lady of*

Old Years (1899), *The Half-Hearted* (1900), *A Watcher by the Threshold* (1902), *Prester John* (1910) and *The Moon Endureth* (1912).

Together with Neil Munro, Crockett and Buchan form an impressive triumvirate of historical romancers, often following Scott and Stevenson's model in which a decent young protagonist finds himself out of his depth in religious and political intrigue. We should not underestimate this fiction; often it exploits (as, for example, in *Men of the Moss Haggs* or Munro's *John Splendid*, 1898) the patterning of Scott and Stevenson, in which respectability and social order are set against outlawry and social disorder, as well as their device of remembering wild adventure from the vantage point of elderly and decent retirement, so that a romantic Scottish past symbolically gives way to an inevitable new and settled Scotland.

It has already been stressed that Munro's work often, however, transcends the limitations of straightforward historical romance. Two further aspects may be emphasised. *Gilian the Dreamer* (1899) could very well be read with historical novels such as Buchan's *The Half-Hearted* and Violet Jacob's *Flemington* (1911); all three present a curiously limited but sensitive protagonist restrained, both by personality and the accidents of history, from fulfilment. Yet Munro's analysis of Inveraray after the Napoleonic wars, with its decaying military and Highland glory, its pensioned-off sergeants and generals dreaming their pointless peacetime lives away, also bears comparison with Douglas Brown's anatomisation of Lowland Barbie in *The House with the Green Shutters* (1901). Both communities are decadent. Both stifle themselves in gossip, both bear bitter witness to Scotland in nineteenth-century decline. Moreover the original title for *Gilian* was *The Paymaster's Boy*, and the bull-necked insensitive paymaster, who is probably the over-sensitive poet-boy Gilian's father, could well have been, along with *Weir of Hermiston*, Brown's model for his similarly brutal and unfeeling small-town merchant, John Gourlay. In these novels, it is clear that what is being symbolically represented is the tragic dichotomy in Scotland between the formidable and traditional powers of Scotland (judges, soldiers, merchants) and what they ignore in their over-emphasis on power, namely, finer feeling and imaginative and emotional creativity, as seen in their failed yet talented children. The theme recurs in *Flemington* and, outstandingly, in MacDougall Hay's *Gillespie* (1914) – once again demonstrating that themes can cut across genre, since the first is a Jacobite anti-romance, and the second social realism.

EMBITTERED ROMANCE

After Scott and Stevenson, Munro is without doubt the master of the ironic use of historical romance to make potent and critical comment on previously romanticised topics and periods. *The New Road* (1914) can stand as a summing-up of where Scottish literature had arrived at the end of our period. In its ambivalent representation of the effects of the great roads, which paved the wilds of the Highlands, built by General Wade to put down Jacobitism and clan depredation, Munro simultaneously approves and laments progress and the death of an ancient way of life. Once again, the main protagonists are arranged to represent the opposing forces of past and present; and once again, the Alan Breck – David Balfour pairing is exploited, with the friendly yet contrasting juxtaposition of Ninian MacGregor Campbell, a more lawful version of Rob Roy, and naïve young Aeneas Macmaster. What appears romantic in the Highlands to Aeneas, is quickly revealed to be corrupt, violent and deservedly doomed (the great symbol of Highland corruption being 'MacShimi', Simon Lovat, the treacherous spider whose web of intrigue has insidiously wrapped itself around Scotland). In his uneasy vision of the new roads of Scotland, Munro presents one of Scottish fiction's most successful and over-arching symbols of dualism and ambiguity. The novel effectively captures the death-throes of some ancient Scottish traditions; it also marks the end of a Scottish tradition in fiction.

The other great anti-romance of the period is Violet Jacob's *Flemington* (1911), this time dealing with Jacobitism in the eastern Lowlands, and with an even bleaker analysis of intrigue and double-dealing, and an engaging twist to the usual father-son symbolic order. Here, repressive authority is located in Archie Flemington's formidable and scheming grandmother, ironically named Christian. There are now no heroic causes, and only a very muted kind of heroism as Archie befriends and then betrays the man he is supposed to spy on, and finally sacrifices himself to save. Richly textured, with a interweaving plot structure, the innocents in this novel are sacrificed while the schemers remain. We remember how David Balfour failed in his would-be heroic quest in *Catriona* (1893), and how he dissociated himself forever from politics and history. This kind of anti-romance was profoundly negative, but also profoundly necessary, if Scottish writing was to rediscover maturity.

DIGGING UP THE KAILYARD: FICTION AND POETRY

We need to re-examine the Kailyard writing. Some of what has been relegated to it can be positively re-evaluated, and even when we agree with the earlier judgements we can still make very useful assessments regarding Scottish culture from doing so. In terms of positive re-assessment, we can now recognise the subtlety with which some writers exploited the conventions of Kailyard. Indeed, we perhaps need to speculate how seriously even the most dyed-in-the-wool Kailyarders took themselves. In *Beside the Bonny Brier Bush*

(1894), Ian McLaren's archetypal Kailyard novel, there is a chapter entitled 'The Cunning Speech of Drumtochty', in which McLaren, with great skill, plays upon the apparent dull-wittedness of his locals, but reveals by the end how their droll naïveté masks sharp intelligence and even cruel humour. Should this put us on our guard against dismissing his writing as purely sentimental, just as the English victim of the village gossips should have been on guard?

Certainly the classic Kailyard texts are cleverly manipulative in their ruthless arrangement of tear-jerking devices and tricks. Scholars die just as they triumph at university; gruff farmers secretly support them in their studies; loyal mothers stand as the salt of the earth; ministers and elders find that beneath arid religious debate lie community bonds far deeper than polemic. Francis Hart, the American author of the best overall account of Scottish fiction, *The Scottish Novel* (1978), has argued that Scots are too distrustful of these simple reminders of community values, and that we should re-assess the best of them. What can be agreed is that they work with definite patterns and conventions. Recurrently they are told by a narrator whose role deserves attention; he is usually a native, but somehow also of the big outside world, a go-between whose function is to explain the eccentricities of these engaging locals to a sophisticated audience. Often a teacher, sometimes hinted at as a writer, he is necessary as an interpreter and modifier of Scots language and custom, thus toning down problematic obscurity; but he is also the intermediary who can reveal the finer feelings beneath the gruff exteriors of the natives. From this it can be seen that real skill is called for in analysing these texts; it is not enough simply to dismiss them, when their collective work has probably had more international and national influence than the work of most other Scottish writers barring Burns, Macpherson, Scott and Stevenson.

The interested student might begin with *The Bonnie Brier Bush*, and thereafter move to S. R. Crockett's *The Stickit Minister* (1893) and *The Lilac Sunbonnet* (1893) (Crockett's fiction turns surprisingly easily from robust history to sentimental pastoralism) and J. M. Barrie's *Auld Licht Idylls* (1888) and *A Window in Thrums* (1889). But beware! Barrie marks the point where simple Kailyard crosses over into parody and irony; his Kirriemuir weaver families are nobody's fools, and their gossip moves close to a malicious destructiveness, tinged with a hypocritical local snobbery, akin to that of Brown in *The House with the Green Shutters*. And, to mix genres yet again, his *Sentimental Tommy* and *Tommy and Grizel* (1896 and 1900) come close to *Gilian the Dreamer* in their caustic presentation of the sensitive and talented Thrums boy who lives so much in his self-glorifying imagination that, despite the fact that he becomes a great writer and is loved by many (and hated by a perceptive few), he ultimately destroys himself, and some of those he loves. Barrie is partly anatomising himself here; and, as a psychological analysis of the Peter Pan type by the man who created *Peter Pan* (1904), this is far more than Kailyard fiction. It must take its place amongst a line of acute analyses in Scottish fiction which reveals a preference for escapist dream over reality stretching from Scott's *Waverley* in 1814 to *Gilian* and beyond to Eric Linklater's *Magnus Merriman* (1934), and which regularly features self-deceiving and over-imaginative innocents like young Archie Hermiston, John Gourlay junior, and Gillespie Strang's son Eochan. The statements these writers make regarding Scottish psyche and society in these unusually bleak stories of thwarted adolescence are worth reconsideration.

THE POETRY OF THE KAILYARD: TOPICS, DISTORTIONS, EXCLUSIONS

Just as with Kailyard fiction, there are reasons why we should not simply write off those many poets of the second half of the nineteenth century who chose to sentimentalise and distort their country. Firstly, we can legimately interest ourselves in its range of subject matter, its modes of distortion, and its exclusions. What are its topics? What does it set up as its icon? The enquiry, and answers, are fascinating.

In 1877, James Grant Wilson made what he considered to be a representative selection in his massive and typically Victorian *The Poets and Poetry of Scotland*. In the omission of several of the poets discussed above in Chapter 21 it becomes obvious that Wilson has an agenda – although so too, it must be admitted, have the majority of Scottish poets of the period. Analysing Wilson's selection from his own time, the following topics emerge as clear favourites (in descending order): mothers, fathers, grandparents, and 'the old folk'; children, in life and death; Scotia's scenery and nature, seasons, weather, rivers, mountains, animals, birds, flowers; remembered cottages and schools; orphans, the sick and the crippled; love of Jeanie, Maggie, Mary and the like; nostalgia for Highlands and Jacobites; the ballads and songs of Scotland (and Burns as Scotland's songster); heaven and the afterlife, with the Scottish Sabbath as a rock of native value. All these themes are treated in terms of nostalgia, lament and elegy, with constant moral exhortation set in the context of the rapidity of time's passing and change. Death, lost love, lost homes, lost native scenes are all-pervasive; the Scots tongue is affectionately seen as speaking of these past concerns, rather than asserted as neglected and vital for the present or future.

These topics can be seen to speak for the great regret felt towards change and the loss of tradition. What is more puzzling is why relatively few poets spoke of the actuality of change and the possible future. Perhaps it is natural that for so long they held to ever more sentimentalised memories of an idealised past, given the traumatic conditions of the urbanising present. And the omissions from their work in other areas are significant also. There are very few poems on emigration and clearance, while older traditions of subversive humour and satire, together with the relishing of drink, sexuality, and the release of holiday, seem to have vanished. More surprisingly, traditional elements such as celebration of community and the ever-present awareness of the supernatural, also disappear, along with any awareness or identification with the ancient roles of shepherd, fisherman, farmer – although, on reflection, the reason may lie in the fact that these were the themes of older, and passing, worlds, and simply no longer familiar to poets who lived in the new, modern Scotland.

Is it fair to say that this poetry distorts simply by leaving out the harsher realities? Possibly not, since deathbed scenes and poverty regularly occur. It is in fact very difficult to draw the line between sentimentality and appropriate feeling, and examination of a range of poems of this kind can lead to fascinating discussion as to what is 'valid' treatment of emotion and what is not. Tom Leonard in *Radical Renfrew* (1990), his pioneering re-examination of the local poetry of Renfrewshire and the West, explicitly and implicitly warns us not to patronise the poetry produced by humble, unliterary people. If poetry works for its reading community, what right has a 'superior' reading audience to devalue it? Poems like William Thom's 'The Mitherless Bairn' (1841) and Jessie Russell's 'The Mother's Story' (1877) can be mocked very easily, yet somehow the mockery evaporates when the poems are placed in their all too real human situation. There were thousands of motherless children in nineteenth-century Britain suffering exactly as Thom's child; the situation had not become clichéd. The subject of Russell's poem, Teenie, at six years old, was a necessary support for her mother even then (what kind of poverty finds a six-year-old's help indispensable?) and died after being nipped by a stray dog. The epigraph simply sums up: 'Wee Teenie, who died of hydrophobia, at Govan, after suffering great agony, May 15th. 1876'. Sometimes we need to shift our cultural and literary perspectives to empathise with such poetry in its historical and social context.

WHO ARE THE PROMINENT KAILYARD POETS?

Anyone interested in this area must explore; there are no contemporary collections. Tom Leonard does include several poets whose work could be described as 'Kailyard'; and collections such as Catherine Kerrigan's *An Anthology of Scottish Women Poets* (1991) have also helped greatly in restoring neglected poets to our attention. Two important essays, Edwin Morgan's 'Scottish Poetry in the Nineteenth Century', and William Findlay's 'Reclaiming Local Literature; William Thom and Janet Hamilton', both in volume 3 of *The History of Scottish Literature* (1988) are very useful; the first, for giving an overview of the field, and the second in making a case for two of the neglected (and perhaps wrongly labelled?) poets of the period. Janet Hamilton, daughter of a Lanarkshire shoe-maker was self-taught, married at fourteen with a large family, and became blind, yet often transcended the Kailyard in poems aimed at raising working-men's awareness, at changing the condition of women, and at the neglect and anglicisation of Scottish language and culture, since 'the big men of print / To Lunnon ha'e gane, to be nearer the mint' ('A Plea for the Doric', 1885). William Thom, the Aberdeenshire auto-didact weaver, contributed much in the vein of 'The Mitherless Bairn', 'Jeanie's Grave', and 'The Blind Boy's Pranks' to *Whistlebinkie*, but also succeeded at times in rising above sentiment and the parochial, in his 'Whisperings for the Unwashed', which powerfully and originally evokes the rhythms of reluctant awakening to yet more toil in an industrial village.

It is impossible here to do more than list some of the poets worth surveying in order to consider the issues raised. They include John Stuart Blackie, Robert Chambers, John Imlah, Robert Leighton, Hugh MacDonald, Norman MacLeod (novelist, moderator of the General Assembly and chaplain to Queen Victoria), Evan MacColl, Charles MacKay (who was one of the few to deal with clearance, as in his 'Lament of Cona for the Unpeopling of Scotland'), Hugh Miller (of *My Schools and Schoolmasters*), Robert Nicoll, Andrew Park, William Miller (of 'Wee Willie Winkie'), Thomas Latto, John Campbell Shairp, and the novelist George MacDonald. We should perhaps also include here Robert Louis Stevenson, whose poetry and later fiction also tended to emerge from the nostalgia of the exile, although his work in Scots had an important part to play in rediscovering its potential for serious and mature poetry and thus pointing towards the 'Scottish Renaissance' of the 1920s (see below). The issue of 'Kailyard' in poetry and fiction, and the debate as to how useful it finally is as a term, is ongoing and far from concluded.

CELTIC TWILIGHT AND 'FIONA MACLEOD'

A doomed and passing race. Yes, but not wholly so. The Celt has at last reached his horizon. There is no shore beyond. He knows it. This has been the burden of his song since Malvina led the blind Oisin to his grave beyond the sea. . . . But this apparition of a passing race is no more than the fulfilment of a glorious resurrection before our very eyes. For the genius of the Celtic race stands out now with averted torch, and the light of it is a glory before the eyes, and the flame of it is blown into the hearts of the mightier conquering people. The Celt falls, but his spirit rises in the heart and the brain of the Anglo-Celtic peoples, with whom are the destinies of the generations to come.

These are the sentiments in the preface to *The Sin-Eater* (1895) by one of the most dramatic figures of the Celtic Revival of the 1890s, 'Fiona MacLeod', in reality William Sharp, a Paisley Scot who emigrated to Australia, and returned to London (and the pre-Raphaelite circle), to become a prolific literary journalist and editor. After 1890 he was increasingly torn between male and female *personas*; 'Fiona' was the Celtic soul Sharp believed lived within him, and through her, Sharp envisioned 'the Green Life', in moments of mystical communion with the power behind landscape and nature. The Celts of Western Europe and Scotland seemed to him/her to exemplify the truest sensitivity to things of beauty and the spirit, a sensitivity made more poignant because it was doomed. From this bitter-sweet inspiration came a flow of novels, short stories, and spiritual sketches, beginning in 1894 with *Pharais, A Romance of the Isles.* Alastair and Lora are recently married and expecting children; but a doom hangs over them. Alastair is brain-sick, and hides from Lora. This is virtually the story, but filled out with portentous symbolic and mythical elements which reiterate MacLeod's essential theme – that Gaeldom is fated, in decline because of its great age, and now in its final resting places on the fringe of Europe. Ultimately Sharp/MacLeod, like John Davidson later, sees the Celts as vital to the future of an English race, and consequently is hostile to resurgent Scottish or Irish nationalism – and careless of the real problems of Highlands and Islands. *The Mountain Lovers, The Sin-Eater and Other Tales, The Washer of the Ford* (all 1895), *Green Fire* (1896), *The Dominion of Dreams* (1899) and many other volumes, saw Fiona as the priestess of Celtic doom and gloom. But for all its distortion of Gaeldom, the work should not be too readily dismissed; it is worth exploring for its socio-cultural importance – and the distinguished critic Francis Hart (*The Scottish Novel*, 1978), while disliking the underlying programme of marginalisation, finds 'legendary morality' and a stark impressiveness in the horrific family feuds and superstitions which blight the generations in *The Sin-Eater* and *The Mountain Lovers.*

Fiona MacLeod was part of a larger Celtic Revival, mainly centred in Edinburgh, and led by the polymath Patrick Geddes, with romantic Highland and Lowland novelists like William Black and S. R. Crockett working alongside artists like Macgillivray, Duncan and Hornel. It was inspired by the contemporary Irish movement in drama and poetry of Lady Gregory and the younger Yeats. These movements developed out of what Holbrook Jackson termed 'the discovery of the Celt' in his study *The Eighteen Nineties* (1913). Critics like Ernest Renan and Grant Allen had, since mid-century, argued that the Celts, in decline, were a source of inspiration in everything from arts to politics for the new world. Geddes produced four numbers of *The Evergreen* (1895–6), which tried valiantly but unsuccessfully to create a Scottish revival among writers and artists. With hindsight it can be seen that its mystical and nature-based interdisciplinarity, emphasising moody spirituality amidst the grandeur of the rural peripheries of Scotland, had more to do with the older landscape painting of Landseer and McCulloch, and even with the Romantic period's vogue for Macpherson's supposed translations of the ancient and epic Celtic poems of Ossian, than with an urban and industrial Scotland. Just as the popularity of spurious Ossianic poetry concealed the authentic Gaelic poetry of Duncan Ban Macintyre and Rob Donn in the previous century, so this movement overlaid the more genuine Gaelic poetry of John Smith and Mary Macpherson, and ignored the realities of Highland clearance and land disputes.

It may be wrong to attribute sinister motives to the marginalisation and spiritualisation of the Gael by southern writers; but certainly such acceptance of economic and political inertia must have suited imperial planning. It is also true that many Scottish writers were beginning to diagnose a malaise at the heart of Highland culture; but it is important to distinguish between, say, John Davidson's belief that England's destiny lay in the acceptance of their subsuming dominance by Scots, Irish and Welsh, and the 'positive negativism' of Neil Munro, and later, Neil Gunn, in which the diagnosis of 'feyness', ancient hierarchies and acceptance of economic and social defeat are challenged in order to rid the Highlands of their sense of being fated and their acceptance of decline, and to induce a sense of positive vision and regeneration.

The Findlater sisters: Mary (1865–1963), Jane (1866–1946)

Mary and Jane Findlater were daughters of the Free Church minister at Lochearnhead. This strong moral background, combined with aristocratic connections, furnished the main topics of their neglected fictions; morality and class pretension. They were celebrated in their day, and were befriended and admired by Henry James and Ellen Terry, as well as by Gladstone and Lord Gray of Fallodon.

Their US tour of 1905 brought home to them the difference between the new and their older world, and Mary's US diary shows the sisters as keenly interested in all levels of this new society. These intelligent, often caustic sisters deserve rediscovery, as perfect examples of sensibilities caught between the older values of their classic Victorian upbringing and their instinctive and witty dislike of stuffy respectability and claustrophobic morality, especially as expected in the conduct of women. They were virtually twins in their closeness of affection and values, and they collaborated in several major novels and collections of short stories, outstandingly in *Crossriggs* (1908), a tale of a talented girl in an obscure Lothians village forced to look after her eccentric father and her sister's children. Under its deceptively quiet surface, repressed feelings run deep, and there is real tragedy in the way conventions prohibit Alexandra Hope's sexual and artistic development. And in Dolly, the 'bad' girl who flaunts convention, the sisters created one of the finest recurrent figures in their work, who obviously both fascinates and appals them with her refusal to accept moral restrictions. *Penny Monypenny* (1911) explored similar clashes of morality, this time in middle-class Edinburgh, and with the central figure clearly modelled on Robert Louis Stevenson. The last of their collaborations, and arguably their finest, was *Beneath the Visiting Moon* (1923), a powerful, poetically symbolic, and often tragic tale of the exploitation of women, with one of their subtlest and nastiest of villains in the impoverished, vulpine Edinburgh aristocrat, Steenie Mauchlyne of That Ilk.

MARY FINDLATER

There are four novels of Mary Findlater's which deserve recognition. In *A Narrow Way* (1901) she anticipated *Crossriggs* with her sensitive picture of the suffocation of the life of a young woman by her selfish, elderly and utterly conventional Edinburgh aunt – with wicked humour at the expense of the old lady and polite Edinburgh. Probably the most famous of all the Findlater novels (along with Jane's *The Green Graves of Balgowrie*) was *The Rose of Joy* (1903), which uses Emerson's image of the rose as symbol of ideal human aspiration in emotion and thought, and then sets within the symbolism a sad tale of poisoned love. The novel is filled with the Lothian land and seascape, as background to the story of the betrayal of Susan Crawford. Her fallen lover-husband, the lovable, self-deceiving liar Darnley Stair, is no conventional villain or hero, but a complex human being (as are the surrounding *dramatis personae*), and she allows his terrible weaknesses pity and understanding. Once again, middle-class manners and weaknesses are handled with ironic affection and wit. *A Blind Bird's Nest* (1907) came out of the sisters' move to the south-west coast of England, and has echoes of Hardy in its picture of the stigmatised and blighted life of Agnes Sorel, whose father is in jail for murder. Mary's final novel returned to Scottish protagonists, in *Tents of a Night* (1914). This again revealed the half-way house in which the Findlaters found themselves, seeing the new held back by the old. Anne Hepburn travels in France with her staid Edinburgh uncle and aunt. She is following a Bulgarian lover; her upbringing and feelings will confuse the issue, and she will lose him, to discover a resigned contentment in loyalty to family, perhaps spinsterhood. Mary gives no melodramatic happy endings; but she makes Anne's discovery of the meaning of the standing stones of Brittany the centre of the story, contrasting the spiritual message of their stillness with the dust and turmoil of the traffic of tourism and endless hotels, anticipating Chris Guthrie and *Sunset Song* (1932) Anne's final perception is that the future belongs not to herself, but to her frank and outspoken cousin, Barbara. As with Jane, Mary can see the future, but cannot go there.

JANE FINDLATER

Jane's first novel made her famous. *The Green Graves of Balgowrie* (1896) is set in the eighteenth century, in a dreary mansion-house buried in Perthshire. It tells of two children, Henrietta and Lucy Marjorybanks, dragooned by their obsessive mother in bitterly cold drawing rooms to act out ancient manners and posturings. Her ruthless autocracy destroys their lives, leading to heart-break and death. In contrast, Jane has the timeless and beautiful countryside, and a constant reminder of time passing, underscored by her emphasis on graves, burial and forgotten lives. This speaks from the heart of the sisters' own predicament, and it points forward yet again to similar emphases in Renaissance fiction, especially in the work of Nancy Brysson Morrison.

As with her sister, Jane was not so successful when she wrote of places and people outwith her experience. Novels like *A Daughter of Strife* (1898) or *The Story of a Mother* (1902), the one set in London in 1710, the other in the north of Scotland almost as long ago, are more melodrama than serious fiction. But two novels dealing with essential Findlater themes stand out; *Rachel* (1899) and *The Ladder to the Stars* (1906). The first draws on the strange career of Edward Irving, the apocalyptic preacher who took Britain by storm in the early nineteenth century, but whose 'gift of tongues' angered the church who deprived him of his ministry; he died a year later. In the novel Rachel – half-friend, half-lover – is witness to the meteoric career of preacher Michael Fletcher, unable to help him avoid the destruction which lies ahead. The relationship – and indeed all Michael's relationshiops – are altruistic and unconventional, his goodness, unacceptable to society, anticipating the similarly unacceptable goodness of the impossibly saintly protagonists of so many of the novels of Robin Jenkins.

The Ladder to the Stars is the angriest and most satirical of all the Findlater novels. Set in a parochial English village, it is particularly bitter about narrow-minded respectability and religiosity, as dictated here by formidable family matriarch Aunt Pillar to her family Pillars (of the community?). Miriam Pillar, a female Jude the Obscure, refuses to obey her dictates, instead succeeding against the odds in becoming a successful writer. As always with the Findlaters, however, Miriam is only allowed partial movement into new worlds; her love affair with a foreign musician is inhibited both by herself and her society; her rebellion has bounds. Here, more clearly perhaps than anywhere else, the success and the predicament of the Findlaters can be seen, as Jane captures the turn-of-the-century sense of women's restlessness and desire for change, but also the sense of fear and guilt which restrains it.

Both sisters wrote short stories, but Jane's are outstanding, in *Seven Scots Stories* (1912) and *A Green Grass Widow* (1921). Her range of sympathy and her realism combine to make her one of the greatest of Scottish story-tellers – as Hugh MacDiarmid, no friend to women's writing, recognised in *Contemporary Scottish Studies* (1926). Her accounts of the disappearing gypsies of Scotland are grim yet wonderful, anticipating the realism of Patrick MacGill; her stories of ordinary tragedy anticipate the anti-Kailyard bleakness of Violet Jacob's tales. In other stories she spans continents, contrasting old and new ways in Scotland and America.

Stevenson and the rediscovery of Scots poetry

In the 1910 revised edition of *Scottish Vernacular Literature: A History*, T. F. Henderson pessimistically concluded that poetry in Scots was dying. He allowed little of significance after Burns, seeing what followed as overly sentimental and romanticised, and allocating later poets a mere five pages out of more than 450. He saw the death of Burns as the beginning of the end: 'The twilight deepened very quickly; and such lights as from time to time appear only serve to disclose the darkness of the all-encompassing night.' This view is of course now challenged; while it was true that Scottish poetry in English is finer overall during the nineteenth century, there was good poetry in Scots too; and well before the Great War there were many signs of the recovery which would come to fruition in the work of MacDiarmid and Soutar.

Henderson's study ignores the Scots poetry of Robert Louis Stevenson. While few would claim that Stevenson was a great poet, his *Underwoods* (1887), half in English, half in Scots, has a claim to mark the beginning of recovery. Stevenson's prefatory note anticipates the many discussions of orthography, validity, and possibilities of Scots usage:

> Among our new dialecticians, the local habitat of every dialect is given to the square mile. I could not emulate this nicety if I desired; for I simply wrote my Scots as well as I was able, not caring if it hailed from Lauderdale or Angus, from the Mearns or Galloway.

In the poem 'The Maker to Posterity' he coins the term Lallan[s] for his use of a Scots drawn from all Scotland – thus validating the term and the eclectic usage of writers in Scots ever since. For all that, Stevenson shared Henderson's view that Scots was dying. He defends his right to mix his dialects, since 'the day draws near when this illustrious and malleable tongue shall be quite forgotten, and Burns's Ayrshire, and Dr [George] MacDonald's "Aberdeen-awa", and Scott's brave, metropolitan utterance, will be all equally the ghosts of speech.' Happily, both were wrong.

How good is Stevenson's poetry? The best concise assessment is still that of David Daiches in his pioneering *Robert Louis Stevenson* (1947). He values the earliest volume, *A Child's Garden of Verses* (1885) for its vivid capturing of a child's impressions, in health and sickness, of growing up in Edinburgh, together with the bed-ridden child's yearning for other places, seen in dream or reality, on swings, on a boat, from a train. As with the work of George MacDonald, Daiches clearly distinguishes the child-like from the childish, reminding us that great poetry can be simple, and is entirely justified in taking a child's perceptions as its matter. The reader who returns to this volume will find a poetry like that written for children and adults by the later William Soutar, deceptive in its apparent artlessness, but in fact reducing the yearnings, images and situations of childhood to archetypal and poetic expression. Admitting the restriction of his poetry to childhood, Daiches nevertheless compares his achievement with that of Henryson, Dunbar, Fergusson and Burns.

Underwoods followed in 1887. Many of its English poems are pleasant enough tributes to relatives, friends like Henry James and W. E. Henley, and his many doctors, and there is a cloying and mannered artificiality in the others; but even here, in poems like 'The House Beautiful', the Scottish Stevenson appears. 'A naked house, a naked moor' may be where he lives, but the northern light and the scouring winds redeem it. Several poems on Skerryvore honour his ancestors for their triumph in lighthouse building – and Stevenson disarmingly reveals how little he values his poetry in one of

them (poem 38), when, embedding himself in his family's previous generations, he reduces his own familial place and role to that of the aftermath of
serious work:

> *A strenuous family dusted from its hands*
> *The sand of granite . . .*
> *. . . and to this childish task*
> *Around the fire addressed its evening hours.*

(The title *Underwoods* was derived from Ben Jonson's term for poems of lesser
worth and late growth.) Stevenson continued the 'childish task' of poetry in two
volumes after *Underwoods; Ballads* (1890) and *Songs of Travel* (1895). The former
combines vivid Longfellow-like long narrative poems such as 'The Slaying of
Tamatea' and 'Rahero', re-tellings of South Sea island tales dedicated to Chief
Teriitera, with similar dramatic retellings of Scottish folk-tales, the West Highland 'Ticonderoga' and the Galloway 'Heather Ale'. The latter is a scrapbook of
songs of remembrance of places and lost loves, of tributes to friends and family
(and to South Sea island chiefs and princesses) with a recurrent tone of
yearning for other places and times, rather than travel *per se*. Some became
famous as songs ('The Vagabond' 'Give to Me the Life I Love'); some, like
'Home No More Home to Me, Whither Must I Wander' (sung by James
Ballantrae on leaving Scotland forever) are poignant songs of nostalgia. There
is no doubting Stevenson's ability to reach the heights of poetic expression in
the fusion of elegy, longing and vivid lyricism of his dedication to S. R. Crockett:

> Blows the wind today, and the sun and rain are flying,
> Blows the wind on the moors today and now,
> Where about the graves of the martyrs the whaups are crying,
> My heart remembers how!

The Scots poems of *Underwoods*, sixteen in all, are different. They work within
the traditions of Ramsay and Fergusson rather than Burns, though the
opening 'From the Maker to Posterity' draws on Burns's verse epistles for
its dialogue with future readers. It uses an italicised voice to speak for
Stevenson to his imagined hearer, prophetically warning future poets, in
the cosmic manner of MacDiarmid, that posterity may be even more cruel to
them, when 'the hale planet's guts are dung / About your ears'. This gives to
Jacob, Angus and MacDiarmid a model for their counterpointing of earthly
and unearthly voices. For the most part, however, these are poems which lack
the involvement in religious, political and cultural controversy which runs

throughout the work of Ramsay, Fergusson and Burns. Stevenson's echoes of the great religious satires of his predecessors, while amusing and deft, are echoes of old quarrels, as in 'Embro High Kirk', telling of orthodoxy's horror at the installation of an organ in the High Kirk of St Giles. A sense of playing with the language and its resonances with the rural past, old customs and arguments pervades most. Stevenson's poetic recreation of his student *persona* Thomson, the kirk elder, lets him develop his satire on die-hard Calvinism. Thomson, returned from years abroad, is scunnered at the changes in the kirk – hymn-books, a lack-lustre precentor, and a poor prayer – but is consoled by the minister's sermon:

> Nae shauchlin testimony here –
> We were a' damned, and that was clear.
> I owned, wi' gratitude an' wonder
> He was a pleisure to sit under.

But Thomson is a pale shadow of Holy Willie, with his pleasure in hell-fire preaching, his sentimental pleasure at seeing the hills of home, tasting good whisky after years of deprivation, and regretting that his absence has cost him eldership. 'The Blast' and 'The Counterblast' likewise look to past glories. This pairing of poems echoes the dialogue poems of the older poets like Fergusson's 'Mutual Complaint of Plainstanes and Causey', or Burns's 'The Brigs of Ayr'; but where the flyting was kept inside these poems, Stevenson loses the flyting element by separating the two speakers into separate poems, the first being the complaint of a querulous and drunken countryman against a God who hates mankind and sends bad weather, the second being the reply of an almost equally bad-tempered countryman who dismisses such a complaint as that of a 'fractious wean', and looks forward to the complainer's death.

'A Lowden Sabbath Morn' is evocative of a sleepy rural Sunday, and in a way this, and 'Ille Terrarum', an echo of Ramsay's celebration of his Edinburgh environs, sum up the essence of Stevenson's work in their focusing on an older and time-locked Scotland. There is irony in the fact that revival in good Scots poetry should begin with poets like Stevenson who believed that its day was over. 'Hugh Haliburton' (James Logie Robertson, 1846–1922) also worked in this mode of pastoral regret in *Heroes in Homespun* (1882). One of his most ambitious long poems is his *Lament for the Language* which anticipates MacDiarmid's similar complaint nearly fifty years after in *A Drunk Man Looks at the Thistle* that loss of language, culture and identity go together. Poetry like this, together with Robertson's important work as teacher and editor of the great Scottish poets, while motivated by a sense of loss, paradoxically opened up possibilities for future writers to develop in very different ways.

Charles Murray (1864–1941), Marion Angus (1866–1946) and Violet Jacob (1863–1946)

The full extent of the influence of these three poets on the early lyric poetry of Hugh MacDiarmid has yet to be acknowledged. The originality of their treatment of their traditional subjects – herdboys, packmen, tinkers, farmers, and a rich variety of country women – in their communities and landscape, and their ability to manipulate the effects of time and age, so that their poems become a complex fusion of the traditional and the innovatory make them the inspiration and model on which so many of MacDiarmid's superb early lyrics are based. To this extent their poems deserve to be considered alongside MacDiarmid's collections, *Sangschaw* (1925) and *Penny Wheep* (1926).

Charles Murray, from Aberdeenshire, emigrated to South Africa in 1888 when he was twenty-four, yet it was in Africa that his nostalgic Scots poems about his homeland were written. He was no sentimentalist, as his most popular poem, 'The Whistle' shows. The 'wee herd' who plays such a range of traditional music is not just a typical country icon. The fact that his whistle will be destroyed by the schoolmaster after the summer symbolises the insidious and destructive effects of anglicisation in education after the Act of 1872. Like Jacob and Angus, Murray finds profound and ultimately inexplicable subtleties in the meanings and nuances of the older rural culture and music, which his poems movingly imply. His collections, especially *Hamewith* (1900), changed attitudes to dialect poetry and its potential, suggesting that such poetry might have an appeal beyond the local, reaching out to universal and deeply serious themes and issues. 'The Packman' celebrates the role of the travelling man as carrier of news in an older society, contrasting this with the new lives of his children. Murray manages to make the comparison of old and new ways of living carry a universal point, that while the old had drawbacks, the new, while more prosperous, has paid a price, as his unfortunate and discontented children discover. Like Jacob and Angus, Murray often uses tinkers and those at the edge of society as symbols of the end of an ancient oral and folk tradition.

In this revival of the creative possibilities in traditional language and culture, the north-east took the lead, with poets like David Rorie, Mary Simon, and Helen Cruickshank. Violet Jacob came from Montrose, but lived for a long period in India. Her fiction has already been noted; her poetry in

Scots, with its deceptively simple rhymes and patterns, combines the tradition of Burns (as in her version of 'Holy Willie's Prayer' in 'Pride') with a feminine intuition into the minds of her subjects. She explores their emotions, their sexuality, and their superstitions with a rare sympathy – as in 'The Cross-roads' (one of several poems of Jacob and Angus which owe a debt to Stevenson's 'The Spaewife', in *Underwoods*), where question and answer explore the mystery of a ruined house, the unnamed speakers, with questions answered in ghostly italicisation, anticipating MacDiarmid's frequent use of the same device. Above all, her work expresses the yearning of the exile for remembered scenes of home, without descending to self-indulgence.

Marion Angus came from Aberdeen and Arbroath. Her best work draws on ballad and folk tradition. She began writing after the First World War, but the themes and spirit of her work link her with the later Jacob, although she goes further than Jacob in making her poems explore deeper mysteries and subtler areas of experience, especially in her many poems of women, remembering lost love and betrayal late in life. As with so many of MacDiarmid's early lyrics, the poems work not through explicit narrative, but through atmospheric suggestion, leaving many unanswered questions. The burden of interpretation rests with the reader, who has to respond sensitively to hints and traditional cues, as in 'The Wild Lass', where the lasting impression is of the return home of a dead girl (in body? in spirit?) after hard tribulation (has she been betrayed? And died of grief, or suicide? Or even perhaps died in childbirth? The possibilities grow as the poem opens out.) In this, and poems like 'The Fiddler', and 'The Seaward Toon', the second with its eerie juxtaposition of the three ages of women, the third with its use of the symbol of the ideal place we yearn for but never reach, the imagined seaward town, Angus stands, like the Findlaters in fiction, caught between two ages; that which ended with the Great War, and modernity; between tradition and innovation.

John Davidson (1857–1909) and John MacDougall Hay (1881–1919)

John Davidson has been discussed as a major poet. What is less well known is his fiction, which deserves reassessment as complex and ironic analysis of end-of-the-century Scottish tensions and predicaments. In novels like *Ninian Jamieson* (1890), *Laura Ruthven's Widowhood* (1892), *Baptist Lake* (1894), and *The Wonderful Mission of Earl Lavender* (1895), and stories such as *The Pilgrimage of Strongsoul* (1897), Davidson showed himself to be highly original and iconoclastic. Ninian is the provost of small-town Mintern, and a lunatic; the two go naturally together, suggests Davidson, following Ninian into his ridiculous claim to the throne of Scotland. In *Laura Ruthven* Davidson presents a Scot who changes his name and accent in order to succeed in England, and *Baptist Lake* focuses on even more complex Anglo-Scottish tensions. Davidson's mockery of Scottish pretensions reaches its height in the fable of *Strongsoul,* replacing traditional Scottish epic protagonists with a boy who is knighted as 'my Lord Strongsoul of Dunmyatt', by Queen Victoria. The fable is sustained irony at heroic Scotland's expense.

John MacDougall Hay's *Gillespie* (1914) has been described as a West Highland version of *The House with the Green Shutters*. There is some truth in this; it too describes a small community dominated by an ruthless merchant, whose treatment of his family leads to their and his destruction. Here too is the patterning of brutal father set against over-sensitive son, with the son's time at university contributing more to tragedy than enlightenment. In both towns (is there an echo of Barbie in Brieston?) the merchant's house and property play a darkly symbolic role. But it would be unfair to limit Hay's achievement to mere derivation. Gillespie Strang is more complex than John Gourlay, and there are moments of greatness in his vision of the future of trade in the West Highlands, as he develops (far more cunningly than Gourlay) his great herring curing business. Greater use is made of supernatural hints, and of the idea of providence; where these were based on Lowland Calvinism and Greek tragedy in Brown's novel, Hay fuses his biblical echoes and his overwhelming notion of providence (although from Argyll, he became a minister in Glasgow) with uncanny echoes of Celtic legend and mysticism. The enduring figure of Mrs Galbraith, patiently waiting for her revenge on Gillespie Strang, who has cheated her of her land, broods like some Celtic seer, while Hay's rich range of supporting characters, set in a wonderfully evoked land-and-seascape, make this a much bigger novel than Brown's in many ways. Finally, in figures of goodness and redemption such as Topsail Janet and the town doctor, Hay gives his novel more than the tragic catharsis allowed by Brown. There is greatness, as well as greed and gossip, in Hay's humanity; and there is in the end a unity of the nobility of humanity and the grandeur of the environment. Comparison of these two novels can be fruitful, leading to sensitive awareness of subtle differences between their authors in intention, methodology, and cultural background and setting.

Three Glasgow novels

The new problems and tensions created by the rise of Glasgow as the great Scottish industrial city, with its attendant wealth and civic development, can be followed in novels which, in different ways, deal with diverse aspects of social change. Sarah Tytler's *St Mungo's City* (1885) deserves attention as the first major novel since Galt's *The Entail* (1822) to deal seriously with Glasgow manners and commerce. The classic merchant father/sensitive son patterning is here too, but tempered by 'auld Tam' Drysdale's blend of acumen and understanding, and by young Tam's discovery that his tender conscience regarding the gulf between rich and poor does not cope well with the actuality of poverty and its manners, when he tries and fails to bond with the poor in reality on a sailing excursion down the Clyde. Tytler (really Henrietta Keddie) finally accepts that inequality happens, and the real worth of her novel lies in its rich characterisation, following Galt, especially in its depiction of the older generation of formidable Scots-speaking women.

The father-son pattern is again at the centre of Frederick Niven's *The Justice of the Peace* (1914), but again handled in an even-handed manner. Its tension arises from the conflicting wishes of merchant-warehouseman Ebenezer Moir and his son Martin, who wants to paint rather than commit himself to business. But Niven again allows understanding and acceptance, and indeed the family tensions are in the end between Ebenezer and his obsessive wife. More important than familial concerns, however, is the fact that Niven sees, and persuades the reader, of the beauty to be found in commercial Glasgow. In this he initiated a new way of viewing the city, to be followed by writers like Catherine Carswell and Archie Hind. In effects of light, sunsets and smoke intermingling, Niven put into fiction what Alexander Smith had found in poetry, in his 'Glasgow' (*City Poems*, 1857).

The full extent of economic and slum degradation was not seen in these novels. It was an Irishman, Patrick MacGill, who probed deepest, in *Children of the Dead End* (1914) and its tragic sequel, *The Rat-pit* (1915). McGill worked as a young navvy in Scotland, and experienced its underworlds for himself. The main characters are Dermod Flynn and his girl, Norah Ryan, separately seeking the work which their own country cannot offer. The first novel is told by Dermod, the second by Norah, and their account of events in Ireland and Scotland overlap. Grimly realistic, bringing into the open for the first time scenes of then unimaginable squalor and violence, there is a harsh energy and authenticity to these novels which entitles them to be considered with their better-known contemporaries.

From this point on, socially realistic fiction increases, becoming especially rich in accounts of Glasgow and the West. The novels discussed could well be read alongside later fictions of Glasgow: those of Catherine Carswell, George Blake, Guy McCrone, and Gibbon's *Grey Granite* in the period between the wars, and thereafter the work of Edward Gaitens, Archie Hind, and, from the

'60s on, a host of others. This rich seam of Scottish fiction is given immensely helpful treatment, on a scale impossible here, in Moira Burgess's *Imagine a City: Glasgow in Fiction* (1998), which is highly recommended to the interested reader.

The end of an era: the poets of the First World War

In much English war poetry, the background awareness of the world is that of the public schoolboy yearning for an ideal rural England of leisured ease and affluence. There is no awareness of English suburbia or urban streets as parts of the context of the war, either as things to fight for or things to change in a better world to come. The working class, even the average middle class, has no respected voice in this poetry. In the genteel literature of the time, rougher accents and more awkward rhymes find no acceptance. Scottish readers have in the past accepted this anglocentric view of the First World War as the natural one within the context of a set of reading expectations that deny the validity of other kinds of voice within the linguistic community of the British Isles. The notion that there might have been Scottish war poets who could speak more out of their own culture with more familiar voices is one that has only recently surfaced. The pioneering collection of poetry and prose by Trevor Royle, *In Flanders Fields* (1990), clearly shows that there were indeed articulate and powerful Scottish responses to the war, very different from the English poets.

We must, of course, make a clear distinction between the First World War and the Second. In literary terms, the Second World War was a much more democratic and socially mixed set of experiences. The poetry that came out of it had much more to say to all of us, whatever social background or country of Britain it came from. And the Scottish poets, through a more fortunate publishing history and the high profile of the Scottish Renaissance movement in poetry and other genres, are clearly visible. There is a major collection still to be made of the widely respected and critically admired war poems of Sorley MacLean, Hamish Henderson and others. For the First World War, however, we have little to show in an accessible form.

So who are the Scottish poets of the First World War? There are five names in particular that are worth noting particularly for their war poems; and there are a number of other writers known more widely, who have one or two poems on the war that are incidental to their main work. The outstanding names are – in alphabetical order only – W. D. Cocker, Roderick Watson Kerr, Joseph Lee, Ewart Alan Mackintosh and Charles Hamilton Sorley. The others are John Buchan, Violet Jacob, Hugh MacDiarmid and Neil Munro.

W. D. Cocker gained some reputation after the war as a journalist and writer of humorous verse in Scots, but the poems written out of his experiences with the Highland Light Infantry and the Royal Scots and as a prisoner of war, written in English, are worth inclusion in any anthology of war poetry. Roderick Watson Kerr, who also later became a journalist, fought with gallantry in the Royal Tank Corps and was well received as a war poet to be compared with Sassoon when he published a collection just after the war. Joseph Lee, journalist and artist, fought in the Black Watch and the Royal Rifle Corps and spent a year as a prisoner of war, yet still managed to have two collections of poetry published during wartime. Born and brought up in England, Ewart Alan Mackintosh served in the Seaforth Highlanders and was killed in action in 1917; his poems have been regarded as some of the finest of the times. Charles Hamilton Sorley was another Scot brought up in England; he served in the Suffolk Regiment and was killed in 1915 after only a few months of active service with, however, some fine poems on which to base his reputation as a war poet. It was the war that gave these men their poetic voices and, apart from Cocker, their claim to be remembered as poets.

It is different for the other poets. The names of John Buchan, Violet Jacob, Hugh MacDiarmid and Neil Munro are associated with so much else in literature that their writings of the war, not being their most significant and commercial productions, could easily be overlooked. It is all the more important, therefore, that what they did produce in the stress of the war years should be remembered and given its proper place. Only MacDiarmid saw the war at first hand, as a medical orderly, and refused to publish most of what he wrote at the time. Both Buchan and Munro were older and medically unfit for service; however, Buchan acted as a special correspondent and observer in France before obtaining a government information post. Violet Jacob's only son was killed on the Somme in 1916. The war touched them all closely, as it did nearly everybody at the time, and it is a false notion of the imperatives of poetic impulse to say that only active service can produce a 'war poet'.

SECTION 5

The Twentieth-Century
Scottish Literary Renaissance

CHAPTER 28

A TWENTIETH-CENTURY SCOTTISH RENAISSANCE?

NEW MEANINGS OF 'RENAISSANCE'

The 'Scottish Renaissance' is the name which has come to signify the inter-war cultural revival in twentieth-century Scotland, a revival associated especially with literature and given impetus by the critical writings of C. M. Grieve and the Scots-language poetry of his alter ego Hugh MacDiarmid. As Section 4 has recurrently stressed, however, the literary and cultural revival of the post-1918 period should be seen in the context of literary and cultural events of the previous half-century, in the increasingly valued achievement of the Victorian and Edwardian era. There was also the flowering in the visual arts at the turn of the century, in the paintings of the 'Glasgow Boys', the achievements of the women painters and designers of the Glasgow School of Art in the pre-1914 period, and the work of architect and designer Charles Rennie Mackintosh. All of these visual artists were international in their orientation and exhibited to acclaim on the continent, thus fulfilling at least one of the aims of the post-war literary revival. The term 'renaissance' or 'renascence' had already been used at the turn of the century in relation to the Irish Celtic revival and the European-oriented work of the Edinburgh town-planner Patrick Geddes. Its reappearance in the early 1920s was due to the French scholar Denis Saurat who in an article in the *Revue Anglo-Américaine* in 1924 spoke admiringly of 'le groupe de la Renaissance Écossaise', referring to a number of writers associated with MacDiarmid's *Chapbook* and the three issues of his *Northern Numbers* anthologies published between 1920 and 1922.

Saurat's use of the 'Scottish Renaissance' designation appears to have chimed with the active, regenerative spirit present in post-First World War Scottish writing and it has persisted as the defining term for the literary period and for a group of writers whose predominant members were the poets Hugh MacDiarmid and Edwin Muir and novelists Neil M. Gunn and Lewis Grassic Gibbon. As we shall see, these writers differed from each other in their attitudes to nationalism, although all were socialist in political orientation, but all in their different ways contributed to the interrogation of Scottish history and culture and the revival in Scottish writing during this inter-war period.

The Scottish Renaissance was also a Scottish manifestation of literary modernism in the post-1918 period. MacDiarmid was the most obviously modernistic of these writers in relation to innovative literary form, but characteristic preoccupations of the Modernist period are present in all of them: the philosophical awareness of a civilisation in crisis, exploration of themes through the medium of myth and symbol and an interest in the theories of Freud and Jung in regard to the unconscious mind and the imagination.

On the other hand, however evocative the term 'Scottish Renaissance' has proved to be, when looking back on the inter-war period from the standpoint of a new millennium, one cannot but be aware that to see the literary revival of the time predominantly in terms of the work of MacDiarmid, Muir, Gunn and Gibbon is to propose a limited view of the extraordinary creative and critical activity of these years. These writers may have been the artistically outstanding male practitioners, but there were many others who made a lasting contribution to the revival: novelists such as Eric Linklater, Compton Mackenzie, James Barke; and George Blake, founder of the Porpoise Press which published the early novels of Neil M. Gunn and himself author of *The Shipbuilders* (1935) and other novels; poets Lewis Spence and especially, in the 1930s, William Soutar. Drama too made moves forward in the period with the founding of the Scottish National Theatre Society in the early '20s and the Community Drama Association in the '30s. James Bridie (O. H. Mavor) was active in the theatre at this time and Neil M. Gunn was one of a number of writers involved with the Community Drama Association. Most importantly, canonical accounts of the Scottish Renaissance period have on the whole made no mention of the strong body of work produced by women fiction writers in the 1920s and 1930s, most of whom worked contemporaneously with the MacDiarmid Renaissance, but were unrecognised as having a contribution to make to it. Yet in their different ways these women were fulfilling many of the aims which had been put forward by MacDiarmid and his associates.

It is clear therefore that, however useful, the term 'Scottish Renaissance' is an ambivalent one, being popularly seen as characterising the literary and cultural revival of the 1920s and 1930s, but in practice being most often used in relation to a small group of male writers associated with the poet Hugh MacDiarmid and his attempts to regenerate his country's life and literature. It must therefore be used advisedly, with a distinction being made between the 'MacDiarmid Renaissance Group' and the wider literary and cultural revival of the period. This introduction and the more detailed sections on individual writers which follow seeks to expand understanding of the Scottish Renaissance to include a wider range of writers who contributed to literary, cultural and social renewal in this inter-war period, while at the same time giving due value to MacDiarmid and those principally associated with him.

POLITICAL AND LITERARY NATIONALISM

The Scottish cultural and political developments of the inter-war period were to a significant extent new manifestations of earlier attempts at Scottish renewal which had not survived or had been subverted by the outbreak of the First World War. Scottish and Irish Home Rule, for example, had been on the Liberal Party's political agenda since the late nineteenth century, and in the pre-1920s period the Labour movement in Scotland had also had a strong Scottish bias, with some form of increased political self-determination as one of its primary objectives. However, with the defeat and disintegration of the Liberal party in the early 1920s, the worsening economic situation in the aftermath of the war and the Labour party's moves towards a position of internationalism, Scottish Home Rule began gradually to disappear from the Westminster political agenda, a disappearance assisted by the achievement of Irish Home Rule, which was therefore no longer an issue which provided solidarity with the Scottish campaigners. It is at this point that we begin to see the establishment of Scottish political parties with a specifically nationalist agenda: the National Party of Scotland was formed in 1928 and the Scottish National Party in 1934. Such political developments were an affirmation in changed political, social and economic conditions of a long-held sense of Scottishness and a desire to have more control in Scotland over Scottish affairs.

Literature, on the other hand, was not so confident or so outward-looking in these early years and MacDiarmid often gave the impression that he considered Scottish Renaissance activity to be a unique, new beginning that would consign the imitators of Burns and the Kailyard fiction writers to the dustbin of a false Scottish literary culture. 'Not Traditions – Precedents!' was the motto of the *Scottish Chapbook*, the literary magazine he initiated in August 1922 in the attempt to provide a platform for innovative critical writing in Scotland which would support the literary revival. Yet, even a cursory reading of his own Scots-language lyrics and *A Drunk Man Looks at the Thistle* (1926) shows how deeply involved with tradition MacDiarmid the poet (as opposed to the cultural propagandist) was – with language, history, and the awareness of what past artists of all kinds had contributed to Scotland's culture. And this was true of other writers associated with the Scottish Renaissance, even if they did not always put the same emphasis on the Scots language as did Mac-Diarmid. In addition, although Scottish writing in the early years of the century did not show the same innovative, international orientation as did the visual art of the time, the three issues of the *Northern Numbers* anthologies published in the years immediately after MacDiarmid's return from the war but drawing on the work of writers from the pre-war period, contained many contributors and contributions of quality. Writers such as Charles Murray, Violet Jacob and Helen Cruickshank used the Scots language in a traditional way that was, however, fresh and positive. Other contributors worthy of notice were Mary Symon, Pittendrigh Macgillivray and Alexander Gray who translated Heine, and German and Danish folk-song, into Scots. There are already signs in the *Northern Numbers* anthologies of a new spirit in Scottish poetry. As with the political situation in the inter-war period, therefore, the literary renaissance of the '20s and '30s can be seen as growing out of pre-war literary stirrings and also as continuing in another cultural form the forward-looking artistic achievements in the visual arts in the pre-1914 period.

What is strikingly different about the Scottish Renaissance period, on the other hand, is the way in which it interacted with the changed political climate in Scotland in the inter-war years, and, in an artistic sense, with the post-1918 phase of Modernism. The writers of the renaissance believed that lasting cultural regeneration must go hand-in-hand with social, economic and political regeneration, even if some of them were sceptical about the degree of nationalism involved in this; it was recognised that artistic life could not be seen as standing apart from the life of the country as a whole. Similarly, although MacDiarmid was the most obviously modernistic of these writers so far as literary form was concerned, the principal writers were all in their different ways aware of the Modernist agenda and committed to 'making it new' in artistic terms. So far as the women writers of the period were concerned, although, as we shall see, they did not on the whole take the 'condition of Scotland' as their theme – some, like Dot Allan, openly criticising the nationalist agenda of the male renaissance writers – these women writers were also innovators, presenting from the inside female experience in the cities, small towns and rural areas of Scotland in a way that was strikingly and confidently new in Scottish writing. Explicitly or implicitly, therefore, there is a new and comprehensive forward-looking critique of Scottish life in the literature of this inter-war period which one does not find in the 'North British' nineteenth and early twentieth centuries, however successful individual writers may have been in that earlier time. One of the reasons, therefore, for the persistence of the term 'Scottish Renaissance' in relation to the post-1918 revival may be that it appeared to characterise a movement that, unlike the 'Celtic Twilight' movement of the late nineteenth century, had a commitment to interrogate the past and to move forward into something new based on an understanding of that past.

From C. M. Grieve to Hugh MacDiarmid

C. M. Grieve, or Hugh MacDiarmid as he was to become, was the writer who provided the principal initial impetus for the Scottish Renaissance and whose polemic and poetry dominated the 1920s. He is particularly associated with the revival in Scots-language poetry in this period but at first he had been very much against any revival of the Scots language for literary purposes. As his war-time letters from Europe to his friend and former school teacher George Ogilvie show, the young Grieve was interested in modernistic writing and in the European and English-language developments of the time. Like Edwin Muir, he had educated himself culturally through his reading of the influential *New Age* periodical, edited by A. R. Orage, which gave wide coverage to European affairs, including Russian philosophy and literature. He was interested too in the Imagist poetry of Ezra Pound and in the work of French and Russian Symbolist poets such as Stephane Mallarmé and Alexander Blok. Grieve was ambitious to become a poet of standing himself after the war and to regenerate Scottish poetry so that it could take its place once again in the mainstream of European literature. At this point, the idea of writing in Scots, far less the initiation of a revival of Scots-language poetry, had no place in his plans.

On his demobilisation from the Royal Army Medical Corps in 1919, he began the series of *Northern Numbers* poetry anthologies referred to earlier, an activity inspired to some extent by the successful English *Georgian Poetry* anthologies edited by Edward Marsh. Yet although he insisted that the Scots language could no longer offer the attributes necessary for a modern poetry and that the way forward would of necessity be through English, he emphasised that it would be an English language used in a very Scottish way. Writing in the *Dunfermline Press* in August and September 1922, he insisted that while most of Scottish literature 'is, of course, and must continue to be, written in English . . . it is no more English in spirit than the literature of the Irish literary revival, most of which was written in the English language, was English in spirit.'

The Scots language debate had been initiated as a result of the Vernacular

Circle of the London Burns Club's decision in the early 1920s to promote a revival of Scots in schools and in society generally. As mentioned above, Grieve was initially extremely hostile to the idea, attacking the members of the Vernacular Circle at every opportunity and writing in the *Aberdeen Free Press* in January 1922 that 'any Doric "boom" just now . . . would be a gross disservice to Scottish life and letters.'

The existence of the controversy may itself, however, have encouraged his own experimentation with Scots, an experimentation which eventually resulted in the publication in the *Dunfermline Press* and in the *Chapbook* of the Scots-language lyric 'The Watergaw' by the new poet 'Hugh M'Diarmid' [sic]. The editorials or *causeries* of the *Scottish Chapbook* from the magazine's inception in August 1922 make interesting reading in relation to this language question, charting as they do Grieve's initial apprehension about any attempt to revitalise Scots and his eventual conversion to the necessity of any modern Scottish poetry revival being in the medium of the Scots language. The outstanding achievement of his Scots lyrics published in *Sangschaw* and *Penny Wheep* in 1925 and 1926, followed by the long dramatic monologue *A Drunk Man Looks at the Thistle* in November 1926, made it inevitable that the 1920s phase of the literary revival should be dominated by MacDiarmid's poetry and the proposal of Scots as the linguistic medium for a modern literature.

In addition to the question of the revitalisation of the Scots language for literary purposes, two other important objectives were early present in the agenda of the Scottish Renaissance: one was the European dimension of the literary revival, the other the inclusion of the Celtic Highlands in any cultural regeneration of Scotland. These objectives were consistently addressed in the periodicals edited by MacDiarmid during the 1920s and in articles he contributed to other magazines in the early 1930s. They were also addressed in the life and work of two members of the Renaissance group, the Orkney-born Edwin Muir and Highland novelist Neil M. Gunn.

Hugh MacDiarmid, Edwin Muir and Neil M. Gunn

Although they quarrelled in the mid-1930s over the question of the Scots language for literary purposes, Edwin Muir and MacDiarmid initially co-operated closely in relation to the Scottish literary revival. Muir had already made his name as a critic and the author of *We Moderns* (1918) when the *Scottish Chapbook* started in August 1922, and was living in Europe on a contract with the US *Freeman* magazine. This first-hand European experience and his contributions to the periodicals edited by MacDiarmid – his essay on the work of Hölderlin, published in the *Scottish Nation* in 1923, was the first English-language essay on the German poet – contributed much to the European dimension of the renaissance, as did the translations he and his wife Willa later made of the fiction of Kafka and other German writers. Although his *First Poems* was published by Leonard and Virginia Woolf at the Hogarth Press in 1925, the same year as MacDiarmid's *Sangschaw*, Muir was a late developer as a poet and his best poetry is to be found in the collections published during and after the Second World War. In this inter-war period, Muir's literary reputation and his contribution to the Scottish revival were founded primarily on his work as a translator and on his criticism.

Neil M. Gunn also came to prominence in the 1920s. One of his best short stories 'Down to the Sea' appeared in 1923 and his first novel *The Grey Coast* was published by the Porpoise Press in 1926. MacDiarmid acclaimed him as 'the only Scottish prose-writer of promise . . . in relation to that which is distinctively Scottish rather than tributary to the "vast engulfing sea" of English literature'. Like MacDiarmid and unlike Orkney-born Muir, who saw Scotland as his 'second country', Gunn was a strong nationalist. He had been sent away from his home in Caithness as a schoolboy to live with his sister in Galloway and had consciously chosen to return as an adult to live and work in the Highlands. What he found was not the idealised place of childhood, but an area suffering from severe decline.

Gunn's fictional investigation of Highland decline therefore came to-gether with MacDiarmid's recognition that any regeneration of Scotland must include regeneration of the previously marginalised Highlands. The revival of Gaelic had early been given as one of the objectives of the renaissance and in the poetry he wrote after *A Drunk Man*, MacDiarmid increasingly turned to the Gaelic-speaking Highlands for symbols for a revitalised Scotland. Gunn was not able to participate in the revival of Gaelic, having never learned to speak the language, but through his fiction and through the descriptive, social, economic and philosophical essays he wrote in the 1930s and early 1940s for the *Scots Magazine* under its editor J. B. Salmond, he did much to explore the contemporary condition of the Highlands and to educate Highlanders and non-Highlanders alike with regard to the values inherent in the traditions of the Highland way of life. Similarly during the difficult period of the '30s, when 'nationalism' was a term regarded with much suspicion, he argued positively for a nationalism – a 'growing and blossoming from our own roots' – that was not jingoistic but which could provide the basis for a rich and diverse internationalism.

Although the language question was still a significant factor in the cultural debate of the 1930s, as one can see from the controversy aroused by Muir's *Scott and Scotland* (1936), the economic, political and international issues of the decade gave these concerns a higher profile. After an unsuccessful brief period in London, MacDiarmid spent most of the '30s isolated on the Shetland island of Whalsay, cut off from the day-to-day involvement with Scottish events he had experienced in the previous decade, and although he continued to write much fine poetry, including ideological poetry, the dynamic of the revival movement shifted to bring Gunn and Muir into greater prominence; Gunn with his investigations of the Highlands in fiction and non-fiction articles and Muir in his Scottish books *Scottish Journey* (1935) and *Scott and Scotland* and the many review articles on Scottish affairs that he wrote for London-based periodicals. Lewis Grassic Gibbon (Leslie Mitchell) also entered the scene in the early 1930s with his trilogy of novels on the decline of small farming and the move from a rural to an urban society, *A Scots Quair* (1932–4). Although, like Muir, Gibbon was sceptical about the nationalist dimension of the renaissance, his modernistic experiments with narrative voice and the Scots language in the three books of the *Quair* added a new dimension to Scottish fiction while his collaboration with MacDiarmid in *Scottish Scene*, published in 1934, contributed significantly to the interrogation of Scottish cultural history.

Although the *Scots Magazine* and periodicals such as the *Modern Scot* and its successor *Outlook* provided a forum in Scotland for debate on Scottish cultural matters, much of the debate in the mid-1930s was in fact conducted through London-based publishers – something that might well be attributed to the high profile of the Scottish Renaissance in the previous decade. In 1934, for example, *The Spectator* initiated a series of articles on Scottish cultural and social and economic affairs and many of Muir's *Scott and Scotland* arguments can be seen in embryonic form in such review articles. Muir's reviewing also draws attention to the significant number of books about Scotland being published at the time: books such as David Cleghorn Thomson's *Scotland in Quest of her Youth* (1932), George Blake's *The Heart of Scotland* (1934), Malcolm Thomson's *Scotland: That Distressed Area* (1935), William Power's *Literature and Oatmeal: What Literature has Meant to Scotland* (1935) and many others. *Literature and Oatmeal* was in the *Voice of Scotland* series, published by Routledge, to which MacDiarmid, Muir, Gunn and Gibbon all contributed. Other contributors included Eric Linklater, Compton Mackenzie, Willa Muir and Donald and Catherine Carswell.

Women writers of the Renaissance

And what of the women writers of the period? As mentioned above, both Willa Muir and Catherine Carswell participated in the *Voice of Scotland* series and in other writing about Scotland published in the 1930s, including Carswell's *Life of Robert Burns* (1930). Carswell's two novels, *Open the Door!* and *The Camomile*, had been published earlier in 1920 and 1922 respectively, contemporaneously with MacDiarmid's *Northern Numbers* and *Scottish Chapbook*. Despite this coincidental publication, however, Carswell's fiction draws on an earlier turn-of-the-century Scotland and her preoccupation is with female sexuality, not Scottish self-determination. Willa Muir writes of women's lives in a male dominated society in *Imagined Corners* (1931) and *Mrs Ritchie* (1933) and offers also an acute critique of Scottish small-town life and the disabling influence of Scottish Calvinistic religion on the lives of both women and men. Willa was also a partner – most probably the senior partner – in the Muirs' translations of Kafka and other German writers and she translated many books herself under the pseudonym of Agnes Neill Scott. Other writers, such as Nan Shepherd and Lorna Moon (the latter operating in the late 1920s from Hollywood where she was a script writer), wrote of north-east Scotland. Nan Shepherd's *The Quarry Wood* (1928) anticipates Grassic Gibbon's story of 'the two Chrisses' (although her heroine does go to university) and her narrative is rich in Aberdeenshire Scots. Lorna Moon's short stories and her novel *Dark Star* (1929) use less Scots, but are nevertheless full of the life of the north-east. Dot Allan's *Makeshift* (1928) is set principally in the Glasgow of office typing pools and bedsits as is Catherine Gavin's later, but more upwardly-mobile *Clyde Valley* of 1938. Carswell's novels are, of course, splendid novels of middle-class Glasgow, something of a rarity in Scottish fiction, and she takes her heroines outward from Scotland to London and Europe. All these novels by women writers have at their centre the lives of women depicted from the inside, and this, together with their individual innovative approaches to language or setting or complementary themes, brings something new to Scottish fiction. They too, although overlooked for so long, can now be seen as having made an important contribution to the inter-war cultural revival.

It can be seen with hindsight, therefore, that although the term 'Scottish Renaissance' was originally coined to designate the group of writers associated with Hugh MacDiarmid and the attempt to regenerate Scottish literature in the early 1920s, its use needs to be extended beyond these writers to include the wide range of literary activity and social and historical enquiry taking place in the inter-war period.

Some deeper roots of renaissance:
Frazer, Freud, Jung and Wasteland mythology

The reader of Scottish fiction and poetry in the period immediately following the First World War may well find it fruitful to deepen enquiry into the profound psychological and spiritual concerns of many writers of the time – and to compare them with what was happening in English literature generally. It is arguable that 'Scottish Renaissance' has its roots as far back as the great anthropological work of Sir James Frazer, whose *The Golden Bough* (1890–1915) set out to discredit narrow Presbyterian religiosity and religious belief generally, but paradoxically ended up by giving material for a new kind of mysticism to Western – and perhaps particularly – Scottish writers. Essentially, Frazer's recognition of recurrent patterns in world legend and myth were to be taken up by thinkers like Freud and Jung and modified into theories of the unconscious and subconscious – a recognition that the mysterious world of the hidden mind, and of dreams, held deep significances which we ignore to our loss. Jung's development from Frazer and Freud of the concepts of archetype and of the collective unconscious or race memory were to be significant for Western literature, and particularly appealing to a range of Scottish Renaissance writers from Gunn and MacDiarmid to Muir and Mitchison. Later Western thinkers, like Jessie Weston in *From Ritual to Romance* (1920) (which profoundly influenced T. S. Eliot's great poem of Western loss of faith, *The Waste Land*, 1922), helped pass such ideas of deep mythic underpatterning to human life to them.

Underlying the work of many English and Scottish writers in the first half of the century is the notion that the way out of spiritual desolation lies in the realisation of and trust in underlying rhythms of mind and land. In the work of E. M. Forster, D. H. Lawrence, and Virginia Woolf, in novels like *Howard's End* (1910), *The Rainbow* (1915) and *To the Lighthouse* (1925) respectively, spiritual meaning is rediscovered through non-rational, organic and instinctive means. And perhaps because Scottish culture was still closer to folk tradition and legend as living forces, Scottish writers seeking regeneration of their culture found such ideas even more attractive than their English counterparts. In all the major renaissance writers, poets and novelists, we find similar use of Wasteland mythology as enunciated by Frazer and Jung; Scotland is perceived, often through dream or a version of second sight, as the spiritually barren land, and regeneration is found through acceptance of essential truth in legend and myth, discovered through varieties of epiphany which share a recurrent common situation, whereby the protagonist steps out of chronological time to discover identity with his or her ancestors of a distant past. Readers interested in this characteristic phenomenon could well explore its occurrence in the poetry of Jacob, Angus, MacDiarmid, Muir and Soutar, and in the fiction of Gunn, Gibbon, Mitchison and Linklater. Examples in fiction would include the moments of perception of ancient time at ancient places, like the holy cell or the house of peace, by the boys Kenn and Finn in Gunn's *Highland River* (1937) and *The Silver Darlings* (1941) respectively, or Gibbon's similar moments of timeless perception for Chris Guthrie at the beginning of *Sunset Song* (1932), when – awake or dreaming? – she sees the ragged man who calls 'The Ships of Pytheas', heralding the arrival of Phoenician traders in Scotland, thousands of years ago. The same kind of moment is given to Chae Strachan when he sees the warrior from the army of the ancient Pictish leader Calgacus before he goes to his own death. Like the ancient warrior, he will die in the battle to come. Similarly, with Rob Galt in the short story 'Clay', who breaks through the land to discover his ancestor in his earth-house, only to die after this moment of realisation and completion. Such examples of 'Great Memory', as Yeats called it, are characteristic of renaissance writing, and presumably were seen as romanticisation and irrational by those Scottish writers who rejected the movement. Nevertheless, the use of the mythic patterning of Wasteland imagery and symbolism in novels by Gunn, Gibbon, and Mitchison, and in poetry by MacDiarmid and Soutar (and later Mackay Brown), lends a powerful underlayer of spiritual and psychological implication, and rewards those readers who can recognise the richness of mythic reference.

CHAPTER 29

HUGH MACDIARMID, EDWIN MUIR AND POETRY IN THE INTER-WAR PERIOD

HUGH MACDIARMID (1892–1978)

C. M. Grieve – or Hugh MacDiarmid as he was to become – was born in Langholm in the Scottish Borders. His father was a postman and the family lived in the building which housed the local library, perhaps inspiring his omnivorous reading habits. The landscape and the richness of the country-side around Langholm profoundly influenced him and his poetry is full of imagery deriving from his childhood there. The essay 'Growing up in Langholm' in Millar's *Memoirs of a Modern Scotland* (1970) conveys the sense of what this Borders upbringing meant to him.

Having initially intended to become a teacher, Grieve abandoned his training in 1911 and became a journalist, working in Scotland and Wales. He joined the Royal Army Medical Corps during the First World War and served in hospitals in Salonika, Greece and Marseilles, becoming ill himself with cerebral malaria in 1918. During the 1920s he lived in Montrose, working as chief reporter for the local newspaper while at the same time writing his Scots lyrics and the extended poem, *A Drunk Man Looks at the Thistle*, as well as editing a number of cultural periodicals. After a brief period in London and Liverpool between 1929 and 1932, he spent most of the 1930s on the small Shetland island of Whalsay. His later years were spent in Brownsbank cottage at Candymill near Biggar.

The following discussion refers to MacDiarmid's *Selected Poems* (1994) which gives a wide and relevant selection from his poetry, together with a chronology, glossary and useful notes.

MacDiarmid's Scots lyrics and their context

As we have discussed in the previous introductory section, MacDiarmid is the writer who provided the principal impetus to the movement popularly known as the Scottish Renaissance and he is particularly associated with the revival in Scots-language poetry. The language he used for literary purposes was 'synthetic' Scots, or re-integrated Scots – that is, a synthesis of Scots vocabulary and expressions from different areas of the country including obsolete terms from Scots-language dictionaries. Despite the arguably artificial linguistic mode, his early lyrics sing because he had the sound of spoken Scots, from his childhood in the Borders, in his ears, and it is the convincing Scots-speaking voice of the Drunk Man which carries the reader with him through MacDiarmid's long dramatic monologue of 1926.

MacDiarmid's first poem in Scots was 'The Watergaw' which appeared in the *Scottish Chapbook* of October 1922. His first collection of Scots lyrics, *Sangschaw*, was published in 1925 and *Penny Wheep* followed in 1926. These lyric poems achieved something entirely new in Scottish writing: a creative interaction between the stylistic features of contemporary modernistic poetry and the richly allusive language, speech rhythms and supernatural dimension found in the Scottish ballads and the poetry of Dunbar and Burns.

Imagism and Symbolism

One of the contemporary poetic movements which interested MacDiarmid was Imagism. Ezra Pound defined an 'image' as 'that which presents an intellectual and emotional complex in an instant of time', a definition which emphasised economy and clarity of presentation. In addition to his interest in Pound's Imagism, however, MacDiarmid was also attracted to Symbolism, an approach to poetry which emphasised the very different qualities of suggestiveness and mysticism. He was fond of quoting the French Symbolist poet Mallarmé who said: 'Ce n'est pas avec des idées qu'on fait des vers, c'est avec des mots' [*it's not with ideas that one makes verses, but with words*], and in his own poem 'Gairmscoile', he wrote: 'It's soon' no' sense that faddoms the herts o' men'. These statements may seem paradoxical, given that MacDiarmid was very much a poet of ideas, of 'sense'. Yet they are true to his poetry in that, in these early lyrics in particular, he did begin with the sounds of his Scots words and phrases as opposed to attempting to clothe an idea in words. And the creation of an allusive and mystical context, a bringing together of the earthly and the cosmic, was as much an aim for MacDiarmid as was the achievement of the kind of economic yet emotional and intellectual image prized by Imagism.

MacDiarmid's early lyrics, therefore, brought together these two different Modernist approaches – the economical, solid image of the Imagists and the suggestive, mystical context of the Symbolists – and to these he added the resources of the Scots language with its evocative sounds and rhythms and its associations with the world of the ballads.

'THE WATERGAW'

'Watergaw' is the Scots word for rainbow and the unfamiliarity of the word allows it to be used in the poem in a fresh way. 'A watergaw wi' its chitterin' licht' presents an immediate, economical image which involves both mind and senses. In addition, the mood of the scene is set by words and phrases which evoke in a tactile, onomatopoeic way the cold, wet weather and the absence of comfort: 'ae weet forenicht' i' the yow-trummle'. Here the narrow vowels in 'weet' and the trembling of tongue and lips in 'trummle' point forward to make an imaginative connection with the 'chitterin' licht' – the adjective is a strange one to apply to the rainbow, yet it is one that catches exactly its watery, shifting quality. It is a potent image, one which appeals to our sense of the mysterious and the otherworldly and MacDiarmid draws on this effect by introducing, without preparation, the lines 'An' I thocht o' the last wild look ye gied / Afore ye deed!'. In all poetry, to a certain extent, and in modernistic poetry in particular, one finds what might be called a logic of the imagination as opposed to the kind of rational, cause-and-effect logic favoured in prose. In this unexpected collocation of images, we are being asked to make an imaginative leap between the image of the rainbow with its otherworldly connotations and the mystery of death.

In stanza two, the link between natural world setting and emotional context is continued through weather imagery, and again, as in the 'watergaw' image, we are presented with a firm visual image as well as an image which provokes allusive thought: 'nae reek i' the laverock's hoose / That nicht – and nane in mine' calls on the country symbol for stormy weather, which has doused any smoke rising to the lark's 'song-house' high in the sky; and sorrow, one infers, has allowed the fire in the speaker's house to remain unlit or to die out. The memory of that 'foolish', that strange, unearthly look has stayed with the speaker, however, causing him to return to it again and again, until in the final line of the poem he thinks he may have some inkling of its meaning. The speaker doesn't let us, the readers, into his secret. We are left with the mystery of dying and death, with the sense that there is something beyond our known lives which we cannot yet – perhaps ever – understand. This is a poem which unfolds through images and sounds and sense-impressions; yet it is a poem which speaks to our minds as well as our senses. In addition, it draws on the Scottish poetry tradition through its language, its enigmatic nature – which belongs to the ballad tradition as much as to Modernism – and its modified ballad verse form which allows the speaking voice to flow rhythmically.

'THE EEMIS STANE'

In 'The Eemis Stane' also, one finds a compelling mixture of the clear, economic images associated with Imagist poetry and the allusiveness present in Symbolist writing. In the poem one's sense of gravity and identity is immediately destabilised. The speaker appears to be standing in a field in a cold harvest night looking up at the moon – a common enough setting in literature – but then we find that it is not the moon that is moving unsteadily in the sky, but the earth itself; an image which, to our twenty-first-century imaginations, may recall the American astronauts who viewed our world spinning in space from their capsule and commented with wonder on its beauty. Wonder and beauty are not, however, the dominant emotions in this MacDiarmid poem.

As it proceeds, the initial sense of uncertainty remains, reinforced by the phrase 'eerie memories'. Then the imagery changes and now the 'stane' is not the planet Earth, but a tombstone in a graveyard. The linking image is the onomatopoeic word 'yowdendrift'; snow driven by the wind, a heavy obliterating snowfall. The sound and the falling rhythmic movement of 'yowdendrift' patterns its sense and its repetition in the second stanza makes the transition to the speaker, attempting to read the words obliterated on the tombstone. Yet, as he tries to make the words out, he is aware that they are not only obscured by the falling snow but by what he calls 'history's hazelraw', the lichen of history. History is usually thought of as important for teaching us about the past, for helping us to know who we are, both individually and from a family, community or national perspective. So, how are we to interpret this strange phrase? 'The fug o' fame' is also difficult. 'Fug' suggests 'fog', something which again obscures. Jamieson's *Scots Dictionary* – a dictionary frequently used by MacDiarmid – glosses 'fame' as either 'foam or spume' or, more usefully for our purposes, perhaps, as 'passion'. 'Fame' might also be interpreted in the sense of the Latin *fama*, meaning 'report' or 'rumour' which can obscure the truth of a situation. There is therefore in this poem, through the snow and lichen imagery and through the various suggestions aroused by 'fug o' fame', a sense of something being hidden or lost, deliberately or by the accidents of history; a loss which is significant in relation to an understanding of self or human existence or, perhaps, of country, if one brings the Scottish Renaissance context into play. One of the features of the Modernist period was the prevailing sense of a culture in crisis. MacDiarmid's *A Drunk Man Looks at the Thistle* gives expression to this sense of human crisis on an extended scale, but it is present here also in this small but powerful lyric which has a great poetic beauty in addition to the sense of loss it communicates. And like 'The Watergaw', 'The Eemis Stane' is both a poem of the Scottish tradition and a poem of the modern period.

'THE BONNIE BROUKIT BAIRN' AND 'EMPTY VESSEL'

Readers should appreciate the way in which sound engages the imagination and so leads to an understanding of the sense, the ideas in a poem; and consider also how words and images work and the way in which the basic ballad verse form can be modified and transformed to produce very different effects. In 'The Bonnie Broukit Bairn', for example, the rhyme pattern moves in a circular pattern – abccddba – so that the final 'clanjamfrie' [*the whole jing-bang; noisy, troublesome lot*] is brought up against the opening grandeur of 'Mars is braw in crammasy' in the first line, subverting the importance of these great figures and their other-worldly concerns and reinforcing the meaning that it is human life on earth – 'the bonnie broukit bairn' – which needs attention. At the same time, the circle created by the rhyme pattern, working from a back to a again, suggests both the circle of the planet and the unity which should be the marker of our human life on it.

'Empty Vessel' has both a ballad and a cosmic context. The girl's hair is 'tousie' – uncombed, wild – and the impression that something is wrong is increased by her 'Singin' till a bairnie / That was nae langer there', although the haunting iambic and trochaic rhythmic pattern is very beautiful. The second verse at first seems to have nothing to do with the first as we move in a modernistic way with no apparent logical link from earthly concerns to the cosmic winds which swing the planets and the light which lights the world. Yet the poet tells us that the power of these cosmic forces cannot compete with the power of the love this distressed girl still has for her lost child. Once again, as in 'The Bonnie Broukit Bairn', the imaginative logic of the poem points us to the human need and human love which is at its centre.

'CROWDIEKNOWE'

Not all the lyrics are so serious. Sound is at the centre of the witty, irreverent 'Crowdieknowe'. Notice the energy created through the strong consonants and the wide, 'vulgar' vowels describing the men – 'loupin', 'blaws', 'glower at God'. Notice too the contrasting way in which the women are characterised with soft consonants and narrow vowels – 'weemun-folk', 'seek' – as they fearfully try to bring their men to order. Think about the suggestions aroused by the imagery – 'gang o' angels', 'trashy, bleezin' French-like folk'. 'Crowdieknowe' is less modernistic than some of the Scots lyrics, drawing more obviously on traditional Scottish poetry, but it makes use of the same evocative and surprising interaction of sound, image and rhythm that we find in all these poems.

It is not possible to explore the Scots lyrics in detail here, but the discussion of these examples may be helpful in the reading of others.

A Drunk Man Looks at the Thistle

MacDiarmid's Scots lyrics were followed by the long dramatic monologue *A Drunk Man Looks at the Thistle* (1926). *A Drunk Man* is an exhilarating but difficult poem which cannot be satisfactorily discussed in the space available here. The best guide is the 1987 edition by Kenneth Buthlay (available from the Association for Scottish Literary Studies), which gives the poem on the left-hand page of the text with notes and elucidation of individual passages on the right-hand page. There are also several excellent discussions available, notably those of Anne Edwards Boutelle, Nancy Gish, Catherine Kerrigan, Harvey Oxenhorn and Roderick Watson (see the bibliography for this section). The following discussion may provide an introduction to the text in *Selected Poems* (1992), which can then be followed up in a more detailed way with the help of Buthlay's edition.

THE CONTEXT OF THE POEM

Letters which MacDiarmid wrote to George Ogilvie before and after the publication of the poem show us how he himself saw *A Drunk Man* – a modern poem, yet also a poem which drew sufficiently upon the Scottish tradition to be compared with Burns and Dunbar. We sense also his commitment to his country in this ambition, a commitment he shared with nineteenth-century Russian writers such as novelist Feodor Dostoevsky and Symbolist poet Alexander Blok, both of whom feature prominently in *A Drunk Man*. Adaptations of Blok's Symbolist poems are interpolated into *A Drunk Man* at significant visionary moments in the text and a long, philosophical section in the later stages is addressed to Dostoyevsky. MacDiarmid was interested in Dostoyevsky not only because of the Russian writer's involvement with nation, but also because of the 'fusion of extremes' in his fiction. For MacDiarmid, this complemented his interest in the ideas of the literary scholar G. Gregory Smith, whose book *Scottish Literature: Character and Influence* (1919) had coined the phrase 'the Caledonian Antisyzygy' to describe what he saw as the bringing together of extremes in Scottish writing. This clash of extremes was also, of course, a feature of modernistic art generally, something which

MacDiarmid had already employed in the composition of his Scots-language lyrics. It became, both philosophically and stylistically, a principal structuring device in *A Drunk Man*.

NATURE AND METHODOLOGY OF THE POEM

A Drunk Man Looks at the Thistle is a lengthy dramatic monologue in which the speaker, the Drunk Man, finds himself lying on the hillside in the moonlight beside a thistle with its jaggy leaves and beautiful purple flowers, its 'roses'. In various stages of intoxication, he muses aloud about his own condition, about the state of his country, Scotland, and about the predicament of humankind in general. The poem proceeds in a form of stream-of-consciousness, which approximates to that associated with James Joyce's fiction – and Joyce was a writer much admired by MacDiarmid. The Drunk Man says his thoughts 'circle like hobby-horses' (897) and they return him again and again to his central preoccupations, offering contradictory analyses and responses.

THE DRUNK MAN PERSONA

This is the most important of the poetic devices in the poem. It allows the author to explore many of his own ideas about life, art and Scotland through the mask of an invented *persona*, and so escape the danger of propagandist or autobiographical interpretation. It is also a very relevant *persona* in relation to the contradictory and controversial ideas explored: 'there's nocht sae sober as a man blin' drunk' (277) reminds the reader that the mythology of the philosophising drunk has a long history and that a drunk man can get away with behaviour that wouldn't be sanctioned in the sober world. In addition, the poem adopts a modernistic method; the lack of logical progression, the surrealistic imagery, the juxtaposing of extremes of image or idea, the collage-like fragments of thought and impression, the whole stream-of-consciousness process and this stylistic method is validated by the fact of the speaker of the monologue being drunk – we don't expect him to think or speak in a rational, organised way.

This Drunk Man, on the other hand, is not at all a modern Tam o' Shanter taking a night off from reality, despite MacDiarmid's references to Burns's poem in his correspondence with George Ogilvie. Neil M. Gunn talked about the 'terrible sobriety' of MacDiarmid's Drunk Man, and instead of an escape from reality through drink, this Drunk Man is freed to reach out and explore spiritual and material reality.

SYMBOLS

In addition to the important Drunk Man *persona*, the poem proceeds through a number of key symbols. These sometimes work in pairs: whisky and moonlight, each of which can delude as well as inspire; woman and sea-serpent, both creative symbols. Like the Drunk Man's moods, the meaning of these symbols can fluctuate, yet there is always a sufficient inner core of meaning to make a symbol understandable at any given time. Both whisky and sea-serpent, for example, have a connection with water, which is traditionally a symbol of rebirth. One remembers that T. S. Eliot's Waste-landers, fearing water, did not want to be reborn. In contrast, in *A Drunk Man*, whisky and sea-serpent symbols and references to water are embraced for their positive, life-giving connotations. The woman symbol is also creative and has a double presence. Sometimes the woman is the Drunk Man's wife Jean, with her 'acid tongue, vieve lauchter and hawk's e'en' and sometimes she appears as a visionary counterpart to Jean, the artist's muse: the 'silken leddy' from the adaptation of Blok in the early part of *A Drunk Man*, a symbol of inspiration who has, herself, however, a negative counterpart; the terrible goddess who fills him with fear in his moments of artistic despair and who is presented through an adaptation of Blok. Creativity is not presented as 'art for art's sake' in this poem, but as an activity which stretches the artist to his very limits.

THE THISTLE

One of the most important symbols in the poem is the thistle, and it can be interpreted in various ways. Sometimes it is just itself, an uncomfortable, jaggy plant to fall against on the hillside; sometimes the beautiful but prickly thistle symbolises the incongruent Drunk Man, described later in the poem by a similar fusion of extremes as 'this mongrel o' the fire and clay' (1365). In the thistle imagery, the ugly, jaggy leaves symbolise the Drunk Man's inadequate earth-bound parts, while his idealistic nature appears in the soft purple flowers of the thistle. In some passages, the thistle is a phallus with its flowers the creative seed – and here again we find an image where contraries are brought together, the animal aspects of human sexuality inevitably linked with creativity and beauty. Sometimes all human nature and the human condition is symbolised in the thistle, with the prickly leaves and beautiful flowers again standing in for the negatives and positives in human life. At others the thistle represents the Drunk Man's Scotland, a Presbyterian thistle which crucifies its own roses, so that the beauty of its flower in this context stands for the unrealised or lost potential of Scotland. But the dual nature of the thistle can also symbolise the oppositional nature of Scotland and England and here the flower represents England and English achievement, while the leaves are the northern and Scottish input to Great Britain, a poor country compared with the richness of the achievement of its southern neighbour.

VERSE FORM

In contrast to the sophistication of the symbolic imagery and the overall poetic method, the verse form is simple. The dominant influence is the simple ballad verse, with sections rhyming abab or abcb or sometimes unrhymed. Some passages proceed differently – for example, the jazz-like rhythms of 'O Scotland is THE barren fig' (707). But on the whole, the verse form which holds the various sections of the poem together to the end of its 2685 lines is based on the ballad form of oral tradition and this allows the Drunk Man's speaking voice to flow freely and naturally, thus giving the sense of a unified structure.

THEMES

The themes of the poem have already been hinted at in the discussion of the symbols. The *Drunk Man* is a quest poem which works on three principal levels. First of all, there is the personal quest of the Drunk Man, his exploration of his own contradictory nature as man and artist; the gap between what in imagination he would like to be or do and what is the reality of his life. Then there is the exploration of Scotland's loss of language and cultural identity; its loss of self-determination and belief in itself; and on the other hand, symbolised in the purple flowers, the potential which the poet at least believes is still there, waiting to be reawakened. And thirdly, on a wider philosophical level, the poem investigates the human condition itself. In this last thematic interpretation, we are aware of the proximity of the poem to the cataclysmic events of the 1914–18 war and the sense of crisis which was a significant part of the Modernist experience. The Drunk Man's fear that human life may ultimately be meaningless, that mankind is merely 'an atom of a twig' (1482) is one with the expression of futility and loss found in much writing of the period, most notably in Eliot's *The Waste Land* (1922), to which references are made in MacDiarmid's poem. On the other hand, the regenerative theme in relation to Scotland in *A Drunk Man*, especially in its early stages, gives the poem a positive quality which is absent from more typical Modernist writing, and this positive quality is reinforced by the mixture of witty satire, humour and even farce through which the Drunk Man explores his own and Scotland's situation.

The poem begins with the Scotland theme and the Scottish part of the Drunk Man's nature. Our attention is immediately captured by the Drunk Man's voice in the opening line with its falling rhythm and heavy, alliterated ending: 'I amna fou' sae muckle as tired – deid dune.' His exhaustion, however, is soon seen to relate not to his own condition but to his awareness of the exhausted state of his country's culture.

The Scottish theme of *Sic transit gloria Scotiae* [*thus passes the glory of Scotland*] dominates the early sections of the poem. It is given expression through satirical references to the Burns cult, where Burns is compared to Christ, as a victim of misrepresentation by those 'faitherin' Genius wi' *their* thochts'; by imagery of Scotland as a museum piece; and through allusions to Jean Elliot's 'The Floo'ers o' the Forest are a' Wede awa', the lament for the fallen at Flodden which now becomes a lament for the fallen condition of Scotland as a whole.

THE DRUNK MAN'S CREDO

In the early part of the poem the philosophical theme is related primarily to the Drunk Man's view of his mission to revitalise his country and this is expressed in a passage which might be seen as the Drunk Man's *credo* (121–60). This is a section which validates his previous didactic or moralising stance, where he had been attacking whatever he saw as degenerate in Scottish life. Now we see that he considers himself as part of the problem. He is not a critical outsider standing in judgement on what is wrong – he is warning and castigating from the inside, rebuking himself as severely as his fellow Scots. The Drunk Man's position here reminds us of the traditional role of the poet, that of the bard who recorded the genealogy of his people, who spoke what others could not, or would not, say.

In addition to this self-inclusion within the human problem and his awareness that he too must suffer if regeneration is to be attained, the significant elements in the Drunk Man's *credo* include his belief that he must be 'whaur extremes meet'. In this, he insists that he uses all his senses in his quest, not relying on rationality alone; and he accepts that there is something in the human condition and in creation as a whole which is beyond our human understanding.

Even in this brief discussion of features from the opening of the poem, we can see how the personal experience in the Drunk Man's monologue is interlinked with the interrogation of the national experience depicted in the poem and with the wider exploration of the human condition. This thematic interaction continues as the poem proceeds. These three layers of experience – personal, national and universal – are not developed separately and consecutively but, as in the opening section, are brought together in a modernistic way, fragments of each theme coming up against each other unexpectedly or one theme modulating into another in the development of any section. In grappling with the poem, readers must explore for themselves how similar patterns of personal, national and philosophical themes and imagery are communicated throughout *A Drunk Man* as a whole. When a US edition of his *Collected Poems* was published in the 1960s, MacDiarmid was persuaded to provide 'handrails' for *A Drunk Man*, thematic titles for the various sections to help readers make their way through the poem. He later regretted this, believing that it destroyed the sense of the poem as a unity, and most editions of his poetry now omit these thematic section titles. Kenneth Buthlay's edition, on the other hand, has kept them for information in the notes to the text, and they may well be useful as a guide to how the various themes and sub-themes interact with one another.

THE THEME OF SCOTLAND

The theme of Scotland is most prominent in the first half of *A Drunk Man* up to and including the section often referred to as 'The Ballad of the Crucified Rose' (1119–1218), a late addition to the poem in 1926 and called by MacDiarmid 'The Ballad of the General Strike'. This Scottish theme can be expressed directly through the poem's argument or indirectly through imagery or the stylistic associations with the Scottish poetry tradition which appear in a given passage. For example, the 'silken leddy' adaptation of Blok (169–220) brings resonances of the Scottish ballads as well as the eighteenth-century tradition of Burns and Fergusson; 'O Wha's the Bride' (612–35) from the long section on sexuality and creativity which begins about line 571 also draws on the enigmatic, other-worldly nature of the ballads while the 'Ballad of the Crucified Rose' or 'Ballad of the General Strike' again interacts with the ballad tradition in its verse form and its suspenseful narrative of an unexpected flowering which is inexplicably and tragically aborted.

What is important in the more direct Scottish-theme sections of the poem – and especially important in relation to the accusations of anglophobia which have at times been made against MacDiarmid – is that in the Drunk Man's discourse, the responsibility for the state of Scotland, for its loss of cultural identity, language and self-determination, is always placed upon the Scots themselves, as, for example, in the passage from line 751: 'I micht ha'e been contentit wi' the Rose.' Here the Drunk Man accepts the worth of English culture but insists that it cannot be a substitute for a distinctive Scottish culture. Yet he realises that the Scots have in the past often connived at this substitution. It is at this point of the monologue, too, a few lines earlier at 745, that the Drunk Man modifies Nietzsche's instruction 'to be yersel's' in a way that seems to draw on the positive features of the Scottish Presbyterian tradition. His aim is 'to be yersel's – and to mak' that worth bein' / Nae harder job to mortals has been gi'en.'

The first half of the poem comes to a climax in 'The Ballad of the Crucified Rose' (1119–1218) which tells, through its thistle imagery, the story of an unexpected flowering which is brought to an abrupt end, where the greatest bitterness is experienced by the Drunk Man as he watches the wreckers of potential stand around like connoisseurs of disaster mocking the failed attempt. Through its imagery of potentiality, loss and self-destruction, this ballad is a powerful communication of the thematic concerns of the poem – individual, national and universal – up to this point in the text.

THE MEANING OF HUMAN LIFE

From this mid-point onwards, the Scottish theme recedes and the more universal themes of the mystery and the meaning of human life come to the fore. Here we are aware of the sense of philosophical crisis, the nihilism which is present in so much of the art and intellectual life of the Modernist period, a sense of crisis which has its roots not only in the horrors of the war but even earlier in the changes which took place in the nineteenth century with the growth of industrialisation, the loss of religious faith and theories of evolution which destabilised human beings' view of themselves and their position in the universe. As mentioned previously, the regenerative theme of *A Drunk Man*, and its reminders of the potential within human life, set MacDiarmid apart from more typical Modernist explorations of the human condition. What we see in this second half of the poem, however, is the predominance of a pessimistic perspective where the positive aspects of the thistle and its flowers become less in evidence and the lack of belief in any positive outcome or significance in human life prevails. The humour and witty satire of the opening give way to a more purely philosophical register (for example 1470ff.).

It is in this second half of the poem too that we have the two sections which MacDiarmid's 'handrails' called 'Letter to Dostoyevsky' (1745–2023) and 'Farewell to Dostoyevsky' (2216–35). These point to the similarity in the struggles of the two writers, to their involvement with their native lands and to the lack of understanding which meets their efforts. Much of the imagery here and in the following sections revolves around light and darkness (1932–6):

> Men canna look on nakit licht.
> It flings them back wi' darkened sicht,
> And een that canna look at it
> Maun draw earth closer roond them yet . . .

In the 'Farewell to Dostoyevsky', the imagery is of a bleak, snow-covered universe where 'There's naebody but Oblivion and us . . . and the wund /

Rises and separates even me and you' (2218–23). The thistle here is entirely negative in its connotations.

Gradually the Scottish theme returns to the poem, culminating in the Drunk Man's vision of the Great Wheel of Life (2395–2658) and at this point the ironic humour returns. As he looks at the revolving Great Wheel, the Drunk Man sees on it the various stages and forms of human life and there among them on 'a birlin' edge' is 'Wee Scotland squattin' like a flea' (2440–1) – a reductive reward for all his struggles. His ambitions for his country are now tempered by his horror when he sees the Scottish companions he will have if he takes up his Scottish place on the Great Wheel – John Knox, Mary Queen of Scots, Rabbie Burns, Weelum Wallace, Harry Lauder – a mixed bag of the potentially heroic, the misrepresented and the suspect – and he turns once again to satire of his fellow countrymen (2614ff.).

This is an important passage, for the Drunk Man here is coming closer to the arguments which Edwin Muir was to put forward ten years later in *Scott and Scotland*. Muir claimed that the only way forward for the ambitious Scottish poet was to adopt English language and tradition as he would find no support for himself or his work if he did otherwise in Scotland – a position which earned him MacDiarmid's lasting hostility.

So far as the Drunk Man is concerned, he decides he'll 'tak' it to avizandum' – a legal phrase for taking some time to decide. He returns to his wife Jean, a mock-heroic conclusion to his adventures which re-emphasises the links with Burns's Tam o' Shanter. However, MacDiarmid's Drunk Man also returns to 'silence' – 'Yet ha'e I silence left, the croon o' a' – and this uncommitted, introspective ending might be interpreted as leaving open the possibility of the resumption of his creative search.

MacDiarmid in the 1930s

MacDiarmid's early Scots lyrics and *A Drunk Man* have justifiably attracted much attention, often to the detriment of his later poetry. Yet he wrote much fine poetry during the 1930s, in Scots and in English, which for some readers might provide a more accessible way into his work than the modernistic Scots-language poetry of the 1920s.

Many of the poems from the '30s are lyrical in nature: poems from *To Circumjack Cencrastus* (1930) such as 'North of the Tweed' and the ironic lament for Scotland's cultural winter 'Lourd on my Hert'; and 'Milk Wort and Bog-Cotton' from *Scots Unbound* (1932) where the theme of dark and light in human life is communicated through images of beauty and shadow in the natural world. A number of poems are ideological and show the same preoccupation with communist and socialist thought that we find in poetry of the '30s by English writers such as Auden, Spender and Day Lewis. Some of this directly political poetry – both MacDiarmid's and that of the English poets – can seem rather 'willed', inclining more towards propaganda than poetry as in 'First Hymn to Lenin'. Short angry poems such as 'In the Children's Hospital', 'At the Cenotaph' and 'Another Epitaph on an Army of Mercenaries' from *Second Hymn to Lenin* (1935) are more successful, but better still are poems where the message of concern for the future of the world is communicated through metaphor – poems such as the Scots-language 'With the Herring Fishers' from *Stony Limits* (1934) and the English-language 'Lo! A Child is Born' from *Second Hymn to Lenin.* The long philosophical English-language poem 'On a Raised Beach' from *Stony Limits* draws on MacDiarmid's experience of living in the remote Shetland island of Whalsay during the 1930s.

MacDiarmid's last poetry includes the experimental *The Kind of Poetry I Want* (1961) and the long visionary poem on the theme of world language *In Memoriam James Joyce* (1955). Although stimulating, both poems are very difficult and are probably best left until the reader feels at home with the earlier poetry. Nevertheless, the corpus of MacDiarmid's poetic output, spanning the '20s and '30s, in both Scots-language and English-language, is a body of work which well substantiates the claim that in MacDiarmid we have a writer to stand alongside Dunbar and Burns as a major poet of the Scottish tradition.

Edwin Muir (1887–1959)

Muir and MacDiarmid might well be seen as the 'polar twins of Scottish poetry', to adapt a phrase used by G. Gregory Smith. Unlike MacDiarmid, Muir wrote principally in English and his claim in *Scott and Scotland* (1936) that the English language and English tradition provided the only valid way forward for the Scottish writer caused a breach with MacDiarmid which was never healed. In opposition to MacDiarmid's energetic, imagistic, polemical poetry, Muir's poetical style is quiet and philosophical, drawing on biblical and Greek myth to explore twentieth-century concerns. He first came to prominence as a critic and took a long time to reach poetic maturity, his best poetry being found in collections from *The Narrow Place* (1943) onwards. His autobiography *The Story and the Fable* (1940), reprinted in a revised and extended version in 1954, and entitled *An Autobiography* is considered to be a classic of its kind.

Muir was born in the Orkney Isles and until the age of seven spent his childhood on his father's farm, The Bu, on the small Orkney island of Wyre. Wyre and The Bu made a strong impression on his childhood imagination, providing his earliest intimations of place and identity, and they were to become the inspiration behind much of his adult poetry. Muir's father was not financially successful, and having moved to a less profitable farm on Wyre and then to Mainland Orkney, the family finally gave up farming, moving to Glasgow in 1901. Their experiences in industrialised Glasgow were even more disastrous. Within four years of their arrival, both parents and two brothers had died. The remaining members of the family decided to go their own ways, and, at the age of eighteen, Edwin Muir found himself alone in Glasgow, in poor health, with little education and no prospect of satisfactory employment. These traumatic events strongly affected his psychology and imagination and his attempts to understand them were to become the impulse behind much of his future poetry. Concluding his first version of autobiography, *The Story and the Fable* (1940), he identified his life as existing in two time-periods:

> I was born before the Industrial Revolution, and am now about two hundred years old. But I have skipped a hundred and fifty of them. I was really born in 1737, and till I was fourteen no time-accidents happened to me. Then in 1751, I set out from Orkney for Glasgow. When I arrived I found that it was not 1751, but 1901, and that a hundred years had been burned up in my two days' journey. But I myself was still in 1751, and remained there for a long time.
> All my life since I have been trying to overhaul that invisible leeway.
> No wonder I am obsessed with Time.

Muir eventually 'climbed out of these years', as he described it in the second version, *An Autobiography* (1954). Like MacDiarmid, he became a contributor to A. R. Orage's European-oriented *New Age* magazine, and when he met his future wife, Willa Anderson, in 1918 he had just published his first book *We Moderns*. After marriage in 1919, he went with Willa to London where he worked as an assistant to Orage. During this period he also underwent psychoanalysis and some of the dreams he experienced are recounted in his autobiography or given new expression in his poetry. To some extent, however, Muir remained a 'displaced person' all his life. He and Willa developed a life-style of travel in Europe with periods in England and Scotland. They lived in Hampstead among a group of expatriate Scots in the early 1930s and, more unhappily, in St Andrews later in the decade. During the war years, Muir worked for the British Council in Edinburgh and after the war he went first of all to Prague with the Council, then to Rome. He became warden of Newbattle Abbey Adult Education College in 1950 and in 1955 he was invited to be Visiting Professor of Poetry at the University of Harvard. He never again lived for an extended period in the Orkney Isles, although in *Belonging* (1968) Willa Muir said that Orkney remained for him the 'north' to which his 'secret compass' always pointed. On his return to Britain from the USA, he settled in the village of Swaffham Prior, near Cambridge, and he died there in 1959.

EARLY POETRY

Muir began to write poetry during his first period of European travel in the early 1920s which 'was the first time since I was fourteen that I had known what it was to have time for thinking and daydreaming'. He commented in his Autobiography: 'I began to write poetry simply because what I wanted to say could not have gone properly into prose. I wanted so much to say it that I had no thought left to study the form in which alone it could be said.' And when he thought back to what it was that had inspired him, he could 'only think of the years of childhood which I spent on my father's farm in the little island of Wyre in Orkney, and the beauty I apprehended then, before I knew there was beauty'. Now, 'these years had come alive, after being forgotten for so long'.

'Childhood' from *First Poems* (1925) gives poetic expression to that childhood ideal while it also shows Muir's affinity with Wordsworth and Blake and the German poet Hölderlin in their belief in the visionary nature of childhood 'innocence'. Formally, the poem is very simple, with its regular abab rhyming pattern and uninterrupted iambic pentameter. This regularity of rhyme and rhythm creates a sense of peace and security and this is reinforced by the word choice and images – 'sunny hill', 'securely bound', 'still light', 'tranquil air', 'joy'. There is also in the poem an awareness of 'unseen straits', both literally and metaphorically. The boy lies watching the distant islands disappearing into the mist and the ship slowly moving through the waters into sight. His experience as a child seems timeless, but we sense that he knows that 'new shores' lie beyond his present, although this world of adult experience has not yet broken into the landscape of childhood innocence. He seems entirely at one with the natural world around him and, as evening comes, 'from the house his mother called his name', thus completing the circle of his security. Like Muir's autobiography, the simplicity of this poem has stood the test of time well and it remains with Blake's *Poems of Innocence* (1789) as a powerful symbol of the virtue within childhood experience.

Most of Muir's early poems, however, are not so resolved, thematically or formally. The search for a lost land is a consistent theme, as is the myth of the

Fall and the obsession with time. *Variations on a Time Theme* (1934), with its Wasteland opening, is full of echoes of Eliot's poetry, although its references to roads and paths and human choice were to become recognisable Muir imagery:

> How did we come here to this broken wood? . . .
> Where did the path turn like an enemy turning
> Stealthily, suddenly . . . Or did we choose . . .?

His next collection, *Journeys and Places* (1937), consists of mythical and historical journeys, haunted by betrayal: 'The Enchanted Knight' lies 'lulled by La Belle Dame Sans Merci', 'Mary Stuart' is betrayed by her half-brother. Poems in the 'Places' section tell of towns betrayed, 'the unfamiliar' and the 'solitary' place, 'the unattained place', 'the original place' and in the poem 'The Original Place':

> *. . . a hand*
> *Strange to you set you here,*
> *Ordained this liberty*
> *And gave you hope and fear*
> *And the turning maze of chance.*

In these lines one can see the philosophical tussle with determinism and free choice which was to become a hallmark of Muir's poetry in his struggle with Scottish Calvinism and its doctrine of the chosen and the damned, and the perceived consequent destruction of the worth of human activity.

THE NARROW PLACE

The title of *The Narrow Place* collection of 1943 might at first suggest a continuance of the themes of *Journeys and Places*, but it is a very different collection which marks a new maturity in Muir's poetry. Reviewing the collection, Neil Gunn commented that his poetry 'has caught a flame – from the fire that is burning the world'; and it certainly appears that the outbreak of war in Europe coincided with Muir's coming to terms with his past and being able to use that past in a new way in his poetry in order to explore what he called 'the single, disunited world'.

THEMES OF WAR

The theme of the negativity of war is present in three *Narrow Place* poems, 'The Wayside Station', 'The River' and 'The Refugees'. There is a mood of deep despondency in 'The Wayside Station' communicated through its imagery: the smoke is 'torn' from the engine, 'crawling across the field in serpent sorrow'; the clouds are 'stolid', the day 'struggling' to be born. There is menace in the 'serpent' image, arrestment in the 'furrows' black unturning waves'. In the second stanza the alienation spreads to the human figures, reluctant to face the day; even love is now an 'inaccessible land'. In the final lines of the poem, individual words such as 'bright', 'silver' and active verbal phrases such as 'leaps the gap of light' might for a moment seem to be indicating the possibility of change. These are deceptive, however, and when examined in the context of the ending as a whole, we see that the message of the poem continues to be a negative one: the light is a 'bright snare', which slips 'coil by coil' around the wood, as if imprisoning it; the stream is 'lonely' and, most importantly, its 'winding journey' is not just into the light of day, but 'through the day and time and war and history'. The little word 'war', placed unobtrusively between 'time' and 'history' in the slow-moving final line with its repeated 'and', brings out the real reason for the despondency and futility communicated by the poem – the war in Europe and the awareness that this is a re-enactment of countless previous conflicts in human time and history. This is a very effective poem where the shock of recognition in relation to the human propensity for conflict is all the greater for being delayed until that quiet yet powerful final line.

'The River' and 'The Refugees' continue the 'timeless' war theme in a more overt way. In the former, the river's 'glass' shows the 'trained terrors' and 'well-practised partings' of a recurring pattern of violence and destruction. Hillsides are split open, the debris of human life:

> Strewn on the slope as by a wrecking wave
> Among the grass and wild flowers . . .

Images like 'blackened field' and 'burning wood' and the unexpected combining of 'harvest-home' and 'Judgment Day of fire' point to the positive aspects of life which are being lost (the field which should be growing the harvest; the wood which should provide shelter) as well as pointing to current destruction. The futility of war as a means of achieving objectives is present also:

> The disciplined soldiers come to conquer nothing,
> March upon emptiness and do not know
> Why all is dead and life has hidden itself.

In 'The Refugees', the speaker looks back to find the seeds of the present nightmare in the indifference of the past, where 'we saw the homeless waiting in the street / Year after year'. The poem ends with the warning:

> For deaf and blind
> Is rejection bred by rejection
> Breeding rejection . . .
> We must shape here a new philosophy.

In *An Autobiography* Muir describes the three mysteries that have continually preoccupied human beings as 'where we came from, where we are going, and, since we are not alone, but members of a countless family, how we should live with one another'. In these poems from the Second World War, the theme of 'how we should live with one another' comes increasingly to the foreground of his poetry.

THEMES FROM GREEK MYTHOLOGY

Equally important to Muir's use of the biblical myth of the Fall in his poetry is his exploitation of Greek myth. This may seem a strange metaphorical medium for a poet born in the Norse-influenced Orkney Isles, but there is, in the stories of Greece, a deterministic context which can be seen to relate to the Calvinist belief in predestination which so troubled him. In Greek stories, wars may be won or lost not because of a warrior's skill but because one of the gods has extended or withdrawn favour. Oedipus, as in Muir's *Labyrinth* (1949) poem on the subject, treads in innocence a road that the gods have predetermined to be a road of suffering and guilt.

'The Return of the Greeks' from *The Voyage* (1946) continues the war theme of the *Narrow Place* poems discussed above, but focuses this time on the way that war distorts everyday reality, making it 'trite and strange'. These Greek warriors have come 'sleepwandering' home from the siege of Troy where their experience has been so intense yet so narrow that they are now alienated from normal life, which seems diminished. Significantly, from the point of view of Muir, who, like Neil Gunn, believed in the importance of the link between present and past, they can no longer see past and present related in a meaningful way:

> The past and the present bound
> In one oblivious round.

Words such as 'sleepwandering' and 'blundering' with their blocking consonants communicate their shut-off-from-life condition, while descriptive phrases such as 'alley steep and small' and 'tramped earth and towering stone', convey something of the obsessive, imprisoning nature of their experience at Troy. The poem ends with the warriors making tentative movements towards their wives and now grown-up children and with Penelope waiting 'alone in her tower' for the return of Odysseus – scenes which must have been patterned in many wars.

The story of Penelope and Odysseus was one to which Muir returned again and again. In 'The Return of Odysseus' from *The Narrow Place*, Penelope remains a symbol of faith in a world of disorder, weaving her cloth by day and undoing it by night, so that she will not have to fulfil the agreement to marry one of the many suitors who wish to take the place of the absent Odysseus. The poem can be interpreted in various ways: the disorder in Odysseus's house can be related to the general disorder caused by war and the breaking up of families; and Penelope seen as characteristic of the many women who waited for their men to return, often in ignorance of their fate. Philosophically, Penelope's faithfulfulness might also be seen as a symbol of human faith in trying to live good and meaningful lives without any knowledge of ultimate destiny or the purpose of human existence. And in this interpretation there lurks also the shadow of Calvinism and the idea of election and the damned which so perplexed Muir.

An interesting companion poem to 'The Return of Odysseus' is 'Telemachus Remembers' from *One Foot in Eden* (1956), where the speaker is the adult Telemachus, son of Penelope and Odysseus, who remembers his puzzlement as a child at his mother's weaving and unweaving, seeing only the weariness and emptiness of her life. Now, as an adult, he understands that:

> If she had pushed it to the end . . .
> She would have worked a matchless wrong.

Instead:

> she wove into her fears
> Pride and fidelity and love.

Other Greek myth poems to explore are 'The Battle of Hector in Hades' from *First Poems*, a poem in which Muir perhaps exorcises a childhood fear; 'Oedipus' from *The Labyrinth*, a powerful and moving exploration of the consequences of determinism in human life; 'The Labyrinth' itself, a frightening evocation of physical and spiritual entrapment; and 'Orpheus' Dream' from *One Foot in Eden* which, in contrast, emphasises human choice and human love and overturns the circumstances of the original Greek myth by bringing Orpheus and Eurydice together through the power of their love, so that Pluto is left with 'the poor ghost of Eurydice' in his 'empty hall'. This is a poem which repays careful analysis of imagery and rhythmic and sound patterns in order to bring out its message about the triumph of love, a message which is predominant in the *One Foot in Eden* collection.

THE LABYRINTH

The Labyrinth collection (1949) came out of Muir's directorship of the British Institute in Prague immediately after the end of the Second World War. This was a difficult time, when the Czechs began the move towards freedom after the departure of the Nazis only to have it suppressed by the Communist takeover. The poems in this collection, therefore, most often have a dual situation: on the one hand they continue Muir's philosophical exploration of freedom and determinism, good and evil, and his search for meaning in human life; on the other hand they either directly, or through myth and symbolic scenes, give voice to the experiences of the people of Prague in the post-war period – and by extension to the experiences of any people similarly entrapped. Poems such as 'The Interrogation', 'The Good Town' and 'The Usurpers' approach the subject more directly; in 'The Labyrinth', 'The Helmet', 'Oedipus' and 'The Combat', the method is mythical or symbolic.

'The Labyrinth' has sometimes been interpreted as relating to Muir's time in Glasgow in the early years of the century and his sense of psychological disturbance there and later in London where he felt the buildings in the streets were falling in on him. Clearly any writer draws on personal experience, but to interpret this poem so autobiographically is to diminish it. Through its starting-point in the myth of Theseus and the Minotaur, it speaks much more widely about entrapment: individual, social, philosophical; confinement which is inward and psychological or that which is imposed externally. The imagery and the blocked rhythmic movement of the poem powerfully evoke the nightmare quality of the experience; the second section, with its imagery of the gods looking down on our human world and offering a vision of peace, is undercut by the ominous recurrence of claustrophobia in the last three lines. Believing he has escaped from the labyrinth, the poet nevertheless discovers that it still lies in wait. The endless cycle of good and evil will go on:

Oh these deceits are strong almost as life.
Last night I dreamt I was in the labyrinth,
And woke far on. I did not know the place.

In contrast to the predominant pessimistic theme in the collection, 'The Combat', which took its imagery from one of Muir's early dream scenarios, suggests through its ballad-like narrative of a symbolic fight between a heraldic beast and a shabby, battered animal, the persistence of the human spirit, despite constant attacks upon it.

ONE FOOT IN EDEN AND THE THEME OF THE FALL

This, Muir's final published collection, contains poems inspired by his stay in Rome in the late 1940s and the contrast he found between what seemed to him the humanity of Catholic Rome and the harshness of Calvinist Scotland. From its earliest beginnings, Muir's poetry had been preoccupied with the biblical myth of the Fall. Through this he explored good and evil in human existence and the presence of tragedy in his own family life and in the lives of people he saw around him in the slums of Glasgow in the early years of the century and in Europe during and after the Second World War. In his early poetry, the presentation of humankind's fallen state predominated, together with the longing to return to an Eden which often appeared to have the attributes of the Orkney of his childhood.

In the collection *One Foot in Eden* (1956), this Fall theme changes significantly, validating human life on earth. The title poem is one of the best known poems in the collection and through its agrarian metaphor it offers a new insight:

But famished field and blackened tree
Bear flowers in Eden never known.
Blossoms of grief and charity
Bloom in these darkened fields alone.

The companion poem, 'The Difficult Land', is a more everyday Eden poem, more Scottish, perhaps. In it, the speaker balances against the frustrations of an existence where 'things miscarry / Whether we care, or do not care enough' the more positive fact that the people are bound by community and ancestral ties, the very attributes that the Usurpers, for example, try to deny. The positives put forward here are the values which come from Muir's upbringing in the co-operative society of Orkney, values stressed also by Gunn in his fiction: of co-operation instead of competition, of remembering the past and drawing on it to make a better present and future. Despite the difficulties of their existence, the speakers here are:

> . . . drawn back again
> By faces of goodness, faithful masks of sorrow,
> Honesty, kindness, courage, fidelity,
> The love that lasts a life's time . . .

The poem ends: 'This is a difficult country and our home' where the 'and' seems to stress the unity of the two elements as opposed to contrasting them. Similarly, 'Adam's Dream' emphasises the positive quality of the 'outside Eden' experience as he sees in his dream the faces of his descendants and turns 'in love and grief in Eve's encircling arms'.

There are many excellent poems in this final collection, as there are in *The Labyrinth* (1949). Brief discussion must suffice. As mentioned previously, 'Orpheus' Dream' uses Greek myth to point to the power of love. 'The Annunciation' similarly stresses the importance of human love through the biblical story of the Annunciation. The poem, which was inspired by a plaque featuring the Annunciation on a wall in a Rome street, focuses not on the transcendental aspects of the angel's appearance to Mary, but on the human dimension; yet it does this in such a way that the mystery of the happening is not cancelled out. 'The Incarnate One', on the other hand, contrasts the humanity which Muir found in Catholic Rome with the 'iron pen' of Calvinism. Once again Muir looks to a visual image to represent Rome's humanity – the paintings of Giotto in which 'the Word [was] made flesh' are contrasted with:

> The windless northern surge, the sea-gull's scream
> And Calvin's kirk crowning the barren brae

– an iconic picture of a Scotland in which God has been made into 'three angry letters in a book' and:

> . . . the Mystery is impaled and bent
> Into an ideological instrument.

In its references to 'abstract calamity' and to those who can 'Build their cold empire on the abstract man' one senses a comparison with the secular ideology of Communism, which Muir had previously attacked in poetry and prose essay. The ending is open but not optimistic:

The generations tell
Their personal tale: the One has far to go
Past the mirages and the murdering snow.

A final optimistic poem from this collection is 'The Horses', which must be one of the earliest poems to be written on the subject of nuclear war. Although presented as a unity, the poem divides itself into two sections; an opening section where the everyday details of the devastation and the community response to the disaster are communicated; and a more visionary and metaphorical second part where hope for a new beginning is communicated in the coming of the strange horses. There is a fine contrast here between the representative imagery for a technological age which has gone wrong in the first section – the radios and tractors, planes and warships – and the coming of the horses in the second, communicated through onomatopoeic sound and rhythm and imagery which evokes the mystery of their arrival and the 'free servitude' they bring with them from the 'Eden'. The Horses offer human beings the opportunity, not to escape from reality, but through the imaginative vision of the poem, to restore their lost relationship with the natural world and reassess their future road.

Muir and Scotland

Muir did not write many poems about Scotland, although his essays and books on Scotland written principally in the 1930s made a significant contribution to the Renaissance interrogation of Scottish history and culture. One very good poem in Scots from the 1920s is 'Ballad of the Black Douglas' published in MacDiarmid's *Chapbook* and now collected in Peter Butter's *Complete Poems* (1991). On the whole, however, early poems on Scottish themes such as 'Mary Stuart' from *Journeys and Places* and 'Robert the Bruce – To Douglas in Dying' from *The Narrow Place* remain retellings of old stories, without transformation into poetic form.

A much better Scottish poem from *The Narrow Place* is 'Scotland 1941', an angry piece which places the blame for Scotland's decline on Calvinism and on the Scots' own willingness to pay lipservice to cultural icons such as Burns and Scott – 'sham bards of a sham nation' – without any real knowledge of, or interest in, their work. A companion poem from the 1935 book *Scottish Journey* (although not collected until 1956) is 'Scotland's Winter', a lament for Scotland's situation communicated through the imagery of frozen surroundings. The poem draws on the old legend of Scotland's heroes, asleep under the Eildon Hills waiting for the call to arise to defend their country. In Muir's statement, however, the heroes cannot hear what is going on in the world above them and the people of contemporary Scotland – represented by the miller's daughter, her heels tapping on the frozen ground – do not know that they need help but 'are content / With their poor frozen life and shallow banishment'. If to these poems we add the Scottish references in 'The Incarnate One', then it seems clear that, despite the moves towards reconciliation in his late poetry, the Scottish theme in Muir's work is very much a negative one.

CHAPTER 30

OPENING THE DOORS: FICTION BY WOMEN 1911–47

WOMEN WRITERS AND THE SCOTTISH RENAISSANCE

This chapter takes its title from Catherine Carswell's pioneering novel of 1920, *Open the Door!*, and considers five very different Scottish women writing in the first decades of the present century, analysing one novel by each of them. Perhaps a justification is due: why consider this literature separately? The diverse achievements of Scottish women writers have only recently been recognised. The Scottish 'cultural renaissance' of the early twentieth century is still largely perceived as an exclusively male creation, the substantial achievements of MacDiarmid, Muir, Gibbon and Gunn. The body of work created by literary women at this time reflects themes, concerns, and literary developments with a sufficient identity of their own and shows these women to have been on the cusp of something new in Scotland. In the present context, the isolation of those achievements tries to reveal a sense of that uniqueness, and to reveal diversity among them as well as a distinctly female identity.

Arguably, just as the lyrics of Jacob and Angus can be read as anticipating and leading to the great lyrics of MacDiarmid's *Sangschaw* (1925) and *Penny Wheep* (1926), Carswell can be read as re-introducing many of the qualities which MacDiarmid considered lacking in Scottish cultural activity. Carswell's *Open the Door!* can be seen in the tradition of great nineteenth-century fiction which presented sympathetic and innovative portrayals of women, from *Madame Bovary* (1856) and Turgenev's *On The Eve* (1859) to *Middlemarch* (1871) and *Anna Karenina* (1875). As in these, Carswell fused philosophical consideration of women and society with social satire and sustaining symbolism. If MacDiarmid was right to wish for a radical, intellectual literature which refused to accept the tired clichés of Kailyard and Celtic Twilight, then Carswell was in 1920 fulfilling this desire. Following her, the characteristic blend of tradition and radicalism in the novels of Willa Muir, Nancy Brysson Morrison, Nan Shepherd and Naomi Mitchison can be seen as a major part of the twentieth-century renaissance. This chapter seeks to encourage comparisons and parallels, not only between these writers but also with the fiction of their male contemporaries with which it can be aligned, as well as contrasted and, ultimately, to encourage further exploration of novels beyond those specifically singled out for discussion.

Catherine Carswell (1879–1946)

Catherine Carswell came from a Glasgow merchant family which was strongly evangelical. Prodigiously gifted, she attended the Frankfurt Conservatory of Music before returning to Glasgow and London to pursue a prolific and controversial career as a journalist. She enjoyed a close and productive relationship with a number of notable literary personalities (famously, D. H. Lawrence), and forged a Scottish Modernist 'renaissance' sufficiently separate and distinct from MacDiarmid's through her radical biography of Burns; and her novels *Open the Door!* and *The Camomile* (1922) which challengingly portray female experience. She left a memoir in fragments of her life, published in 1950 by her son, John Carswell, as *Lying Awake*.

New literary horizons

Published in 1920, Catherine Carswell's *Open the Door!* is a novel which artistically and thematically pursues ideas of exploration and expansion. This, Carswell's first novel, crosses the divide in stylistic and structural terms between the Victorian realist novel and the type of early Modernist fiction (epitomised by Virginia Woolf) which articulates its fictive world through symbolic techniques and a 'stream-of-consciousness' narration. The emotional intensity which defines Joanna Bannerman, Carswell's heroine, and her quest for self-discovery, has echoes of the classic Brontë protagonist but also mirrors the specific literary form of the *bildungsroman*. The 'novel of development' is here given a female identity. Joanna's search for a spiritual, emotional and intellectual vocation takes shape against the changing social, economic and religious backdrop of Glasgow at the turn of the century. One of Carswell's great achievements is to create a heroine whose emotional and creative life is laid bare against a canvas rich in detail.

STRUCTURE
The novel has three books and three clear structural divisions, each of which correspond to a different 'phase' in the development of Joanna's life (spanning girlhood to early adulthood). Each phase or 'movement' of

Joanna's maturation is suggested by the epigraphs to each of the three sections; Book 1: 'Open the door and flee' (2 Kings 9:3); Book 2: 'Open a door of utterance' (Colossians 4:3); Book 3: 'Behold I make all things new' (Revelation 21:5). What do these scriptural quotations suggest? Perhaps each might respectively be described as emphasising the idea of escape; the means of articulation in the broadest sense; and the idea of renewal and fulfilment. The reader has to judge to what extent these ideas, here succinctly expressed in scriptural form, are achieved by Joanna Bannerman.

JOANNA AS DAUGHTER

From the outset, we realise that Joanna's process of self-definition (the realisation of who she is and can become) is partly determined by other lives variously impinging on her own. While her emotional and sexual relationships are paths to self-discovery, she is inextricably bound to her family. The novel's great theme of individual freedom of expression in conflict with (self) repression and constraint is first witnessed in the tense, loving and poignant relationship between mother and daughter (note how important female relationships remain throughout the novel). Joanna's perception of her mother is introduced as one of pity and embarrassment as she observes her clumsy movements in the station: 'she stared away from the imperfection facing her'.

Such 'imperfection' is expressive of other, graver limitations against which the daughter comes to rebel. The narrator's comment of Juley Bannerman at this moment – that 'she had never grown used to her body . . . sighing impatiently for wings' – is borne out by her dutiful marriage. In becoming a wife Juley 'fulfil[s] her true destiny' but has refused to give herself sexually: 'When she felt the stirrings of passion in herself she was dimly ashamed . . .' Marriage for the devoutly evangelical Juley, we learn, was a substitute for a religious vocation; but her husband Sholto fails to fulfil a 'hunger' concealed 'under self-censure'. In this desire (albeit frustrated) for self-realisation, mother does not differ from daughter; she imbues her children with 'the capacity for ecstasy'. But Juley's religiosity increasingly drives Joanna away. Distressed by what she perceives as Joanna's 'unspiritual ambitions', she tries to reclaim her unworldly daughter by attempting to instil in her the faith of her 'Low and very evangelical English church'. Joanna in turn, realising that she cannot be 'the daughter her mother so passionately wanted', symbolically seeks 'a place where her mother could not follow her'.

The incident at Eva Gedge's prayer meeting in Book 2 aptly exemplifies these conflicts between filial duty and self-determination. Joanna's horror at the vestry 'full of praying women' (instructed by Juley to ensure Joanna's spiritual salvation) is embarassingly comic, but the prayer of a young woman there, that Joanna may enter into the 'fullness of life', touches Joanna unexpectedly, confirming for us how this ideal may be differently sought but still shared by both Juley and Joanna.

The enduring parallel between mother and daughter can therefore be richly explored. To what extent in her sexual relationships does Joanna achieve the sublimation which her mother desired?: 'Dimly she realised that such a union as she desired beyond all desires was what her mother had in vain craved from her father through all the years of marriage physically fruitful . . .'. Juley's death (towards the end of Book 2) marks both an end ('the final breaking of the umbilical cord') and the beginning of Joanna's own self-renewal, grounded in a more compassionate understanding of her mother's frustrated potential: 'With all her [Juley's] struggles, her nobility, her sacrifices, she was unfulfilled. She was like the sides of an arch that fall together in a heap because the key stone is missing.' Yet, poignantly, it is through her mother that Joanna is given Duntarvie, the childhood place in the country that serves always as Joanna's 'secret lair', and in which the novel and Joanna's quest culminates.

NATURE AND SYMBOLISM

Throughout *Open the Door!* Carswell writes with a descriptive intensity which brings the physical contexts of Joanna's existence vividly to life. Her descriptions of the natural world are shot through with the urgent yet delicate beauty which we will discover in the novels of Nan Shepherd and especially Nancy Brysson Morrison. Carswell's method is always overtly (if at times didactically) symbolic. Joanna's vision, as a child, of the River Clyde framed by the 'grey granite balustrades of the Jamaica Bridge' exemplifies early on how the external world serves as a symbolic mirror for Joanna's inner states of being. The edifice of Victorian industrial enterprise that spans the Clyde is portrayed in the opening chapter in a style which evokes Impressionist painting:

> It had been raining half an hour before, but now the sun gleamed on the brown surface of the river and on the wet, grey granite balustrades of the Jamaica bridge. The bright red and yellow horse-cars flashed as they followed each other northwards and southwards along shining rails, and the passing craft on the water moved in a dun-coloured glory . . . This picture, cut into sections and made brilliant by the interposing trellis of black metal, appealed not so much to the little girl's untrained eye, as symbolically through her eye to her heart which leapt in response. The sunshine on that outgoing vessel and the great, glistening current of brown

water filled her with painful yet exquisite longings. She did not know what ailed her, nor what she desired.

Freedom, the idea of movement in both spiritual and physical senses, an unknown journey: this first epiphany (James Joyce's term for a moment of ordinary life charged with deeper insight and visionary significance) is richly suggestive though Carswell here nicely subdues its significances: 'She got no further than thinking she would like to be an air hostess when she grew up . . .'

The fusion between external and inner worlds in Joanna's life is clearly embodied in early chapters describing Duntarvie, the 'old farm-house in east Perthshire', which enduringly offers Joanna an imaginative, no less than a physical, refuge. Her bond with nature is sensually portrayed: the still, haunted serenity of Duntarvie's upper pond in particular renders this knowledge as a revelation (Book 1, Chapter 2):

> At that moment the twelve year old child entered deeply into Nature's heart, and for the first time it came to her that she might make of her rapture a place of retreat for future days. It was a discovery. Henceforth she felt that nothing, no one, would have power to harm her. For all her life now she would have within herself this hidden refuge . . .

Once secure in this knowledge, the young Joanna takes 'as remembrances of her vow . . . a small lichen-covered twig, a skeleton leaf, and the untimely fallen samara of a sycamore'. Carswell turns these natural objects into emblems (external mirrors or measurements) of Joanna's personal growth; as the samara is the seed of the ash which is blown about until it finally takes new root, so Joanna is as 'a seed, at the mercy of the winds. When would she be driven to the place where she might strike her roots and at last raise her leaf and her bud?' The fruit of the similarly air-borne sycamore has two wings. These are clearly natural extensions of Joanna's emotional being. Essentially rootless until her final return to Duntarvie, she can be conceived of as a seed which awaits fruition (in her final return to Duntarvie, she observes 'a million winged fruits, which [were] now ready with every pinion spread for the wind'). Joanna's own fulfilment is imminent. Throughout the novel there are other developments of this key imagery, for example, in Book 2's treatment of Joanna's ultimately destructive relationship with Pender, which is tellingly conceived as a 'quiet ripening . . . of the dark unregarded fruits of death'.

Joanna's desire for personal freedom is also echoed in the Italian episode in which she sets free caged birds destined for market. Carswell takes care to expound its full symbolic import. Joanna's gift of freedom to the Italian lake swallows is presaged in her dreams (Book 1, Chapter 7):

> she had dreamed she was holding her hands above her head, while hundreds of swallows passed through her widely spread fingers, brushing her skin deliciously with their feathers. At other times she was gazing into a sky thick-strewn with stars . . .

Carswell here draws two beautiful images which resonantly evoke, rather than explicitly endorse, ideas of infinite freedom and limitless possibility which Joanna seeks emotionally and intellectually. It also defines Joanna's state after the death of her Italian husband, Mario Rasponi; Joanna escapes from his destructively possessive love as a dove from outwith 'the snare of the fowlers'. In Book 3, the observation made by Lawrence Urquhart in whose love she finds proper fulfilment that obliquely defines Joanna herself – 'She looks fulfilled . . . like a web of ripe seeds that has this moment been scattered' – is the final expression of this important symbolic pattern.

LOVE AND SEXUALITY

Much of the importance of *Open the Door!* lies in its candid, enlightened exploration and expression of female sexuality at the start of the twentieth century. Yet the novel's emotional trajectory, embodied in a conventional romance structure, also confronts the (female) reader with its own dilemmas. That Carswell's protagonist should ultimately find her fulfilment in love has been felt by critics as a disappointingly bathetic resolution to a novel of psychological complexity.

Yet, with respect to the novel's feminist integrities, it is important to realise the significance which Carswell invests in Joanna's various sexual and emotional relationships. Firstly, we should take into account the historical context of the novel; a still patriarchal society where women's economic and intellectual choices are circumscribed (though in her second novel, *The Camomile*, Carswell permits her heroine to refuse the fate of bourgeois marriage in favour of her independent artistic vocation, in ways comparable with Willa Muir's *Imagined Corners* (1931), where the two principal female characters end by reclaiming authority over their own lives, rejecting the conventional narrative of women's emotional or romantic self-fulfilment). Secondly, Carswell's novel, with its fusion of realist and symbolic narrative styles, charts the interior life. What we see in the emphasis placed upon Joanna's choice of a lover, arguably, is a form of displacement: Carswell's male characters (each of Joanna's four partners) are in effect 'mirrors' of her internal flux, change, progression, each one inhibiting or nurturing the fulfilment Joanna seeks. Bob Ranken (Joanna's first relationship) represents convention (comparable to the character of Duncan Bruce in *The Camomile*, the stultifying marriage prospect whom Ellen finds the courage to reject) who can neither accept nor tolerate Joanna's emotional intensity, and (Carswell is here nicely ironic) does not feel suitably flattered or idealised in Joanna's vision.

Mario Rasponi, the Italian lecturer whom she first encounters in university classes, represents a watershed in Joanna's life: the marriage which will remove her from Scotland entails that she symbolically cast off 'the old life' ('Joanna felt all the old, accustomed moral values slipping away, and it came to her that she must put new ones in their places . . .'). Though Joanna discovers a sensual awakening in this marriage, she encounters intellectual condescension and emotional possessiveness (manifest in the physical constraints Rasponi – 'a husband and gaoler' – imposes on her). Marriage also destroys her illusions of self-fulfilment, and of Italy itself, a fabrication of 'glimpses and dreams'.

There is one important and enduring image from Italy – that of La Porziuncola (Book 1, Chapter 7):

> She looked at the yellow villas, blind and basking. She remembered one . . . which Mario had pointed out as the home of a woman celebrated for her loves. *La Porziuncola*, it had been called, and Joanna had a vivid memory of the little sunken door in the wall, where it was said the lover was wont to enter. On one of their rare walks Mario had taken her past it.

The memory of this little, secret door (with its connotations of illicit, exotic desire) is significantly evoked ('unbidden') on her first encounter when she returns to Glasgow with Louis Pender with whom she will have an adulterous affair. Much older than Joanna, and an artist, Pender represents experience, knowledge, and temptation – the biblical resonance of 'forbidden fruit' is deliberate. With Pender (unlike Rasponi), Joanna might be said to discover the meaning of sex, the revelation of consummation (what Carswell, in Lawrentian style, terms 'the secret of existence'). But destruction rather than fulfilment is at the heart of this third relationship. Joanna's desire is set in conflict with her innate sense of the sinfulness and transgessive nature of this particular kind of sexual knowledge ('For a long half-hour, Joanna lay trying with tense nerves to see wherein she was a sinner. In such an attempt it was inevitable that the religious teaching of her childhood should have a part . . .'). This crisis of conscience is given eloquent expression in Joanna's 'revelation' of Book 2, in Chapter 6. Joanna's discovery that 'evil' quite as much as 'good' had made her an individual emerges fully clarified on this sexual encounter; she has both 'dove' and 'hawk'-like aspects in her nature.

This 'revelation' anticipates the culminating crisis of Book 3 where devotion to Pender ('too old – an ebbing, dying man') is tantamount to self-sacrifice. To renounce Pender (whom Joanna equates with spiritual death) is to embrace new life, and the possibility of what we might term secular salvation. As in the portrait above of Joanna's divided self, Carswell works by simple and extreme contrast; the renewing power of Lawrence Urquhart's love counters Pender's deathliness. Joanna's emotional task in Book 3 is to shed the baleful influences of family and religion and to carve out for herself a space where she can desire in her own way yet still achieve some kind of reconciliation within herself and with the past; a harmonious balance. This is fulfilled by Lawrence Urquhart.

Accordingly, the novel ends on the union at Duntarvie between Joanna and Urquhart. Given that each of Joanna's earlier three lovers mirrored a particular emotional 'movement' or development in her life, what does Urquhart signify? From the outset, he possesses the qualities of stability and familiarity, strikingly evoked in their dance together in Book 2, Chapter 2: 'the young man . . . wholly possessed' awakens in Joanna a

> memory . . . of some far back ancestress, of whom unheedingly she had heard her mother tell . . . Beneath the candid darkness of Lawrence Urquhart's face, soon she was no more than a field of barley that swings unseen in the wind before dawn.

Such dynamism, though, is rarely expressed by Urquhart, and at this stage Joanna desires only Pender (her illicit temptation). Yet throughout the Pender affair, Urquhart corresponds with Joanna, writing letters from Europe 'out of the joy of his heart'. Though Urquhart at this stage confesses his love for Joanna, she ignores the 'rainbow gateway of escape', which he extends to her, but it is this liberating potential which is ultimately fulfilled on their reunion at Duntarvie. Duntarvie, of course, entails a reunion with the past, a return to origins (of various kinds), and the idea of familiar, intimate beginnings (reflected in the symbolic language of rebirth which Carswell deploys in the final pages). Urquhart himself (with his interest in mythology and folklore) represents such ideas. Arguably, such an ending is ideologically conservative. Joanna's final relationship is, however, entirely different from her mother's marriage. It involves not self-resignation or abnegation in love but rather an expression of self, a creative as opposed to destructive love. This is the book's final vision, and one which, in artistic terms at least, is beautifully constructed and anticipated.

RELIGIOUS SATIRE?

A recurrent criticism of revealed religion is an underlying strand in the novel, as both historical context and as a pervasive influence on Joanna's life. An inextricable part of her childhood (scriptural texts adorn the walls of their first house), she comes to rebel against the familial evangelical inheritance imposed on her at an early stage: Joanna's mother takes the children to the opening of the Free Church Assembly, urged on by the memory of 'grand-fathers' who had 'come out' at the Disruption of 1843. This paternalistic aspect of religion is embodied in Joanna's father. Joanna's desire to embrace 'life itself' conflicts with this repressive inheritance which can be witnessed in many ways. Her affair with Pender makes moral scruple and emotional desire sharply conflict. As we have already seen, sexual desire exposes to Joanna her vulnerability to 'sinfulness'. Pender is portrayed as the embodiment of worldliness (note the biblical resonance of 'Mammon'), and therefore a consciously chosen path to 'rebellion'.

All this contributes to the significance in Book 3 of Joanna's anguished refuge in Peterborough Cathedral. Seeking to renounce Pender, her break-down imminent (Book 3, Chapter 3):

> Mechanical with fear, she began to repeat the prayers of childhood . . . Suddenly then, as she cowered in the dark and lofty cathedral, it seemed to Joanna that she saw the Lord on His throne. And that He was preparing to answer her prayer for herself, not with His smile but with His sword. She could feel beforehand the stab that would destroy her. But she would not shrink. Rather she would lift up her breast to receive it. If it was God's will to slay her, then she must be slain.

Joanna, of course, is brought back from the abyss; but the reader has to wonder whether Carswell seeks, in this striking vision of a punitive Calvinist God, to criticise or condemn in any way the religion which partly destroyed Juley. Is the religious aspect of *Open the Door!* left ambiguous? The religious epigraphs which preface each book prefigure in some way the progress of Joanna's life. Are these ultimately ironic (given Joanna's desire to escape from the strictures of familiar and orthodox religion), or does religion (since the novel does reflect the narrative of spiritual renewal which the three epigraphs cumulatively imply) ultimately possess, in Carswell's fictional vision here, emancipatory power?

WOMEN AND CREATIVITY

Open the Door! addresses the idea of creativity in all kinds of ways, and is especially concerned with the subject of women and creative expression. It is interesting that Joanna briefly attends the Glasgow School of Art (reflecting the expansion of the art school in the late nineteenth century and Fra Newbery's deliberate inclusion of female students). Joanna, however, does not pursue an artistic career. Is her failure to sustain such a vocation Carswell's attempt to suggest the restricted spheres of employment for Edwardian women? Arguably, compared to *The Camomile* (where the central character Ellen, the diarist/letter writer, is defined by her aesthetic creativity first as a teacher of music, ultimately as a writer), *Open the Door!*'s vision of female creativity is at heart reactionary. Yet in Carswell's first novel, as has already been suggested, self-expression – the freedom to desire – also acts as an index of women's emotional creativity. Unlike in the poignant case of Juley Bannerman, Joanna's mother, we feel (or Carswell urges us to do so) that Joanna has succeeded in fulfilling her latent potential. Further, the novel, concerned with the general idea of female destiny at a particular historical period, alludes to the fates of its other female characters which are interesting to pursue and compare with Joanna's own: not simply her mother's, but that of Mario's sister Maddalena, or of Joanna's Aunt Perdy (compelled to write, as if ventriloquistically, with the aid of her dead father – 'I in myself am nothing') and the kind of 'escape' (bourgeois marriage) which Joanna's friend, Phemie, finds.

SOCIAL AND NATIONAL SPHERES

Throughout each of its individual books, Carswell's novel attentively and lovingly evokes place and context, whether in a domestic or national sphere. Turn of the century Glasgow (the Exhibition of 1886 is referred to in Book 1) is painted by evocations of the university, the art school, the sophistication of Mildred Lovatt's *salon* and the city's artistic coterie who frequent it. Each of these places is in turn defined against what Joanna increasingly perceives as the provinciality and constraints of the Bannerman home (note Carswell's wry humour in her contrast between Edinburgh and Glasgow social *mores* in Book 1). The gulf between city and country is not only apparent in the contrast between Glasgow and Duntarvie but in Book 3's depiction of London's degradation and pollution (though the city succeeds in offering Joanna partial freedom). Italy, 'glorious land of liberty and rebellion', ultimately contains only the fragile illusion of 'romance'. Yet its first symbolic significance is enduringly important (desire, freedom, escape, the geographical and emotional traditional contrasts of the south to Scotland). Of course, it is Scotland (or aspects of Scotland, or Scottishness, qualified or made acceptable) which Joanna, in the figure of Lawrence Urquhart, finally embraces.

Willa Muir (1890–1970)

Willa Muir has, until recently, unjustly remained in the shadow of her husband, the poet and translator, Edwin Muir. This in part is the result of how they themselves created and portrayed the relationship which Willa movingly portrays in her memoir *Belonging* (1968). Born Willa Anderson in 1890, she enjoyed a brilliant university career at St Andrews, and is now recognised as a gifted translator of German literature in her own right. She wrote *Mrs Ritchie* (1933), a compelling and darkly ironic portrayal of Calvinism embodied in one woman, and several non-fictional long essays on the state of Scotland and feminism which reveal her to be a shrewd cultural commentator.

IMAGINING WOMEN IN SOCIETY

Imagined Corners (1931) was Willa Muir's first published novel. It is an ambitious work both in its intellectual scope, analytical style, and the complexity and detail of the many different characters with which it is peopled. Carswell's preoccupation with the nature of female identity is inherited and deepened by Muir to encompass questions of women's place within different kinds of society, and the pressures which a woman may face in retaining her identity within marriage and in defining herself in relation to other women and men. The relation between self and society is thus lent a distinctly feminine (and feminist, as we shall see later) perspective as Muir's principal female characters, the two Elizabeth Shands, by turn conform and rebel against the society of Calderwick, the 'orderly – important, self-respecting trading community' on the Scottish east coast. It is also stifling in its provinciality and narrowness; conservative and constraining (peopled by douce 'Calderwick ladies' who adhere to a restricted model of female behaviour), it can be traced to other fictional towns in Scottish novels. Within Calderwick, as discovered by the second Elizabeth Shand and the sensitive, depressed Ned Murray, the individual can be exiled. The novel begins with Elizabeth Shand's entry into Calderwick and closes with her flight from it; Elise has escaped from her native town to the continent and an improper marriage through a self-imposed and voluntary exile. She returns to the place of her childhood only to make another escape.

THE TWO ELIZABETHS

Muir creates two heroines of the same name: one who assumes the name on marrying Hector Shand, and one who is originally of that name and the sister to the other's husband, Hector, and his brother John. Through a foreign marriage she has become Elise Mütze. Why this identical name? While the double name of the latter Elizabeth avoids confusion within the narrative (she is usually referred to as Elise), the sense of double identities is a deliberate creation on Muir's part. The other Elizabeth Shand, prior to marriage, possessed another self, Elizabeth Ramsay: 'Give up the old Elizabeth Ramsay, she told herself, emotion sweeping her away, and become Elizabeth Shand. She lay down again. She must learn to be a wife.'

Muir inter-relates the lives of these identically named but different women. The younger Elizabeth, anxious to be a good wife to an unfaithful husband and her loyalties divided between self-renunciation and self-preservation, learns from Elise; but in one respect she represents the Elizabeth Shand (to John Shand his sister is 'the phantom of the other Elizabeth Shand') which Elise could have become (if she had accepted the 'old tradition') until the novel's second half. Prior to their meeting Muir sketches a portrait of an emotionally ardent but naïve young woman, possessed at moments of a kind of secular mysticism or pantheistic belief in a spiritual communion between herself and nature, and linked to Hector 'by nothing less than a universal force. Their love was like the sea, the mountains, the rushing wind and the evening stars. It was drawn from the source of life itself, and would bear them up through every vicissitude'. Her idealism, as Muir's narrator comments, prompts her to create 'imaginary structures[s] not yet filled in by experience'. Hector's eventual desertion of her and Calderwick for another woman dissolves her faith. This outcome is inevitable for Muir throughout shows us a marriage riven by intellectual difference (Elizabeth is a graduate) and the expectations of it which Elizabeth herself harbours, and which entails some renunciation of herself and her beliefs: 'It pleased her to recognise that he was both stronger and heavier than she was. That helped her to be Mrs Hector Shand'.

Elizabeth's attempt to become, and her eventual rejection of the role of 'Noble Wife' occurs against the background of Muir's sharp and wry commentary which chafes against social and sexual hypocrisy (Chapter 9):

> Wives, in Calderwick, were dull, domestic commodities, and husbands, it was understood, were unfaithful . . . There was no easy drift to which Elizabeth might commit herself except the traditional stream of respectable wifehood. Both as a member of society and as an individual she was more buffeted than Hector.

Muir's candid and courageous exposure of the sexual climate of a particular place and period is well exemplified by Hector Shand, dictating how Elizabeth should behave, refusing to judge women as individuals in their own right.

Unlike Hector, Elise is an emotional and intellectual revelation to Elizabeth who feels torn between the two worlds represented by them. Previously 'a victim' of conventional thought and morality, Elise symbolises a 'world of ideas', and through her different perspective perceives Hector as he is. The relationship is mutual: Elise too finds companionship with the woman whose resumption of her initial identity and name she at first resented. The themes of memory, change and transformation are evoked by Elise's return: in church she feels 'the ghost' of her earlier self, 'that impetuous and resentful small girl'.

WIDENING THE CIRCLE

The relationship between the two Elizabeths is the book's core but, in accordance with the novel's opening metaphor of precipitation and distillation, the formation and growth of each woman has wider repercussions. Elise's relationship with the brother who fondly instigated her return (desiring her vigour and ebullience) is ultimately limited: he cannot really accept her shunning of authority and tradition, nor she his effect of 'embalming me in his affection . . . All he asks is that I should make him laugh occasionally – pipe a merry tune in my little cage'. Elizabeth's relationship with the Murrays – the severe, anguished Presbyterian John and his brother, Ned, suffering a mental breakdown – is drawn with particular sensitivity. The bond which at first gently and tenderly forms between Elizabeth and William Murray is shattered by the latter's final incarceration of Ned whom Elizabeth had known at university. William Murray is a minister whose philosophical wrestlings with the problem of evil – which he believes is manifest in the tormented (and victimised) figure of Ned – lead to self-destruction; the fate of both gives the novel a tragic but not overstated intensity, and exemplifies Muir's skilful interweaving of characters and destinies throughout the work.

Among Muir's busy canvas of characters Mabel Shand (husband of John) is interesting, exemplifying in her superficiality and flirtatiousness (at least to Hector) conventional femininity. Her liaison with Hector is never really achieved and she is ultimately a poignant character, a Madame Bovary figure trapped by stultifying and demanding small-town conventions and, lacking the intellectual and imaginative visions of either Elizabeth or Elise, unable to escape except by weakly exploiting herself sexually.

Elise returns to Calderwick only to leave again but this time with Elizabeth. The ending is enigmatic, raising unanswered questions. How significant is this new female pairing? Does this constitute a rejection of male or conventional society, and the fate of marriage which it offers to intelligent and independent-minded women? Is this the most radical of all the endings offered by these novels? The title may be important here: *Imagined Corners*. Is this an ideal and idealistic vision of female potential?

Nancy Brysson Morrison (1907–86)

Nancy Brysson Morrison's roots were highly artistic, stemming from a family known as 'the writing Morrisons'. Born in Glasgow, Morrison became a prolific and highly acclaimed novelist, and a writer of literary and historical biography. In *The Gowk Storm* (1933), her third novel, she created the compellingly beautiful and harrowing narrative of three nineteenth-century sisters, daughters of a Highland manse, who seek to grow emotionally and sexually from a socially repressive and religiously conservative soil. The interwoven stories of the sisters' frustrated desires portray the larger circumscriptions of the small, cloistered community and of dogmatic Calvinism. These enduringly Scottish fictional preoccupations are translated into exclusively female terms: that 'muffled, breathless place', the manse garden into which we first enter, speaks for the peculiar kinds of repression inflicted upon the three young women.

NARRATIVE STYLE

The sisters' fate is conveyed by the first person narrative of the youngest sister, Lisbet, both vividly and tenderly, and characterised by a gentle yet often stark lyricism. This is a narrative choice which imposes a female, perhaps naïve, point of view; and the choice of narrator (the sister who has yet to reach the troubled maturity of the elder two) perhaps intensifies the sense of helpless inevitability with which we witness events unfolding. The novel is indeed preoccupied with the idea of fate. At one moment, Julia and Emmy question the predestination which Nannie fiercely asserts (Book 3, Chapter 1):

'I sometimes think everything we do is prompted by some part of us wanting it, even unknown to ourselves. When things happen –'
    'Things dinna juist happen, Miss Julia,' Nannie put in quickly, 'there is a reason for a' things.'

The conflict between instinctive desire and what is 'fatefully' decreed (in the sense also of long-standing familial or religious authorities) is crystallised here. This notion of life's predetermined patterns is also echoed in the portents and omens which stud the narrative, and evoke the non-naturalistic worlds of ballad poetry.

SYMBOLISM

The novel's title is derived from the untimely fall of snow (a prefatory note to the novel glosses the book's title: 'Gowk Storm. A storm of several days at the end of April or the beginning of May; an evil or abstract obstruction of short duration') which symbolically prefigures Emmy's tragically early death. The narrative action unfolds within the period of a year, each of the five brief 'books' 'annotated', as it were, by the changing seasons. Like Carswell's *Open the Door!*, the novel is highly imagistic and impressionistic, laced throughout with quietly symbolic moments: for example, as Julia leaves after her wedding the narrator comments that 'the very shadows flung across the gleaming carriage were deepened into meaning'. Throughout Morrison imbues her landscape with premonitory significance.

DESIRE AND CONFLICT

Julia is compelled to enter into a loveless but dutiful marriage after her father prohibits her love for the dominie. The dominie's Catholicism clearly represents a threat not only to Julia but to the larger community, as Nannie's judgements of Roman Catholicism show. Nannie, significantly, is the only major character to speak in Scots: is Morrison attempting a portrait of small-minded, provincial bigotry?

The notion of forbidden or illicit desire dominates Emmy's personal tragedy: in loving the fiancé of a friend (who later commits suicide), she transgresses the prescribed bounds of social, sexual and moral decorum. In the character of Emmy, Morrison depicts most acutely the passion, energy and impatience with life that firstly characterised Julia: ' "I wish-I wish-oh, so many things!" '. Her dynamism and spirit vividly contrast with the religious quiescence and repression of 'papa'. This potentially tragic conflict is beautifully brought out in an early incident: Emmy disagrees with the meaning of the scriptural text, 'Be thou faithful unto death and I will give thee a crown of life,' on which her father is to deliver a sermon (Book 1, Chapter 1):

'Yes,' said Emmy, after a pause, 'I like that. What do you suppose a crown of life is?'

'Immortality, of course,' said Mamma, troubled in case an unorthodox meaning was going to be culled from it, 'it says life most distinctly.'

'It says a crown of life,' insisted Emmy, moving over to the piano, 'but who's to say that that means life? Anyway, what does the crown matter as long as you are faithful unto death?'

Emmy's words are prophetic, for she dies, having failed to be reunited with Stephen Wingate after the narrow-minded dominie, Mr Boyd, frustrates her attempts to escape the manse by locking her room. As she dies, Lisbet reads from the Bible: ' "The sacrifices of God . . . are a broken spirit: a broken and a contrite heart, O God, Thou wilt not despise." ' The reader, as well as witnesses in the novel, must ponder the meaning of 'that terrible sentence'. Are we to see Emmy's death as a punishment for her effort to place the instincts of feminine desire above repressive convention? Or does Morrison's irony not rather stand above Lisbet's reading, pointing to the failure of so many others?

The Gowk Storm is a subtle and delicately patterned novel which offers a rich mine for analysis of character, narrative structure, and the use of symbolism. It is arguably a darker work than the other novels of female development discussed here. It is apparently a pessimistic novel; but perhaps the closing scene in which Lisbet herself leaves the manse and the graveyard where her sister lies 'facing east' offers hope or the promise of renewal in the youngest daughter. It is an intensely poetical work which explores the idealism and failure of love, but its tragic perceptions also sustain an incisive and trenchant exposure of female repression.

Nan Shepherd (1893–1981)

Nan Shepherd remained all her life in Aberdeen, a fact reflected in her creative work which takes geographical and linguistic inspiration from the north-east landscapes and communities. Educated at Aberdeen University, she lectured in English at the Aberdeen Training Centre for Teachers, and contributed literary articles to *The Aberdeen University Review* of which she eventually became editor. *The Quarry Wood* (1928), Nan Shepherd's first novel, is often compared to Grassic Gibbon's *Sunset Song* in its portrayal of a young north-east girl, socially and spiritually rooted in the land and the small agricultural community, yet striving for intellectual freedom. Yet Shepherd's work preceded Gibbon's by four years, a remarkable fact given the canonicity and critical acclaim of *Sunset Song* compared to the relatively unknown *The Quarry Wood*. The portrait of Chris Guthrie among the Standing Stones recalls Martha Ironside's early love of (Chapter 1):

a great cairn of stones. They had lain there so long that no one troubled to remember their purpose or origin. Gathered from the surrounding soil, they had resumed a sort of unity with it. The cairn had settled back into the landscape, like a dark outcrop of rock. There Martha played. The stones summed up existence.

But Shepherd's novel, though it provides a fascinating analogue with Gibbon's book and both might usefully be studied in tandem, presents a far different and female-authored version of early womanhood. Arguably the story of Martha Ironside – the intellectual awakening of her arts studies at Aberdeen University, her difficult discovery of sexual passion, and the enduring influence of her courageous and unconventional Aunt Josephine – offers an optimistic and affirmative vision of female selfhood at the beginning of the twentieth century.

SETTINGS
Shepherd achieves much within a small compass. Though Martha's childhood is dealt with in three brief chapters, each is richly filled with vivid sketches of the frenetic Ironside household (Martha's intellectual isolation nicely symbolised by the Latin homework carelessly stained by her brother), and nuances, in such delicate moments as the child Martha's wonder at her father's geographical definition of Scotland – 'bounded on the south by England, on the east by the rising sun, on the north by the Arory-bory-Alice, and on the west by Eternity' – which partly mirrors her passionate dream 'of knowing all there was to know in the universe . . . She had no idea of the spaciousness of her own desires; but she knew very fervently that she was in love with school'. The fulfilment of that desire at university is then portrayed by Shepherd as a blend of eagerness, *naïveté* and real enlightenment.

DISCOVERIES
Like Carswell's Joanna Bannerman, Martha's growth into maturity and self-knowledge demands the experience of love. The relationship between Martha and the academically precocious (and married) Luke Warrender is sensitively judged, on occasions ironic: Martha discovers the sensual intensity of the passion she had believed was 'sheerly spiritual' while Luke conceives her as a paragon of sexless purity. Rory Roy Foubister, after his initial enchantment, rejects Martha as a 'fallen woman' on learning of her misconstrued liaison with Luke in the quarry wood (Shepherd shows, as does Muir, the fragility of female reputations in small comunities). By the novel's end, Martha realises that she had simply been conceived in the image of what

both Luke and Roy wanted her to be rather than accepted and so desired as she truly is. Martha in taking repossession of herself – her identity – does achieve, in Shepherd's haunting phrase, 'the evocation of a new woman'.

Yet unlike the symbolically absolute renewal granted Joanna by Carswell, Shepherd more cautiously and gently suggests Martha's future, forged by her new relationship with the young child, Robin (adopted by her mother) and her reconciliation with, and understanding of, her Aunt Josephine, 'dour, obstinate, invulnerable'. This relationship dominates the novel's later part (ending with the aunt's death), offering an interesting comparison of two female lives differently led but inextricably bound together. Like Muir, Shepherd questions the intellectual and emotional dependence of women on men. Martha demands of herself, 'Am I such a slave as that? Dependent on a man to complete me! I thought I couldn't be anything without him [Luke] – I can be my own creator.' The reader is left to decide whether Martha achieves this self-creation in her choice to remain within the community and the house bequeathed to her by Aunt Josephine in order to educate Robin, or whether, wiled back by Robin, Martha thereby assumes the traditional female role of the nurturer. On the other hand, perhaps hers is a wholly different traditionalism because it is her own choice, sustaining the strong, independent resolutions of the older woman, Josephine. The openness of interpretation is again seen in the narrator's final judgement of Martha that 'she had acquiesced in her destiny and so delivered herself from the insecurity of the adventurer'.

Violet Jacob (1863–1946)

Born Violet Kennedy-Erskine to an aristocratic north-east family associated with the house of Dun, Jacob has bequeathed a substantial, still underrated, body of writing: short fiction, poetry in Scots and English (the pervasive influence of the ballads seen in its range of musical settings), and a series of novels, the first of which appeared in 1902.

Flemington (1911), a rich and subtle 'romance adventure' intensely imagined at the period of the Jacobite risings in Scotland, is Jacob's most enduring and critically acclaimed fiction. This intelligently compassionate account of political fanaticism and emotional loyalties, while remaining Jacob's own distinctive achievement in early twentieth-century Scottish fiction, strongly echoes Scott's historical fiction (the sensitive, vulnerable Archie Flemington caught up in political turmoil particularly recalls Edward Waverley); parallels with Stevenson can also be drawn. Superficially, Jacob's novel might appear anomalous among the writing of her female contemporaries (there is only one principal female character, the dogmatic and tortured Christian Flemington). Jacob clearly has a purpose firstly in choosing a historical setting (despite her disclaimer at the novel's beginning), and secondly this particular historical moment, with its consequent readings of Scottish history. As with Naomi Mitchison, the most prolific Scottish exponent of her time of historical fiction, there is a revisionist view of history here which challenges many of the conventions of nineteenth-century Scottish fiction.

EMOTIONAL AND POLITICAL SENSITIVITIES

Archie Flemington is the son of a Jacobite French family raised in Scotland by his grandmother who has turned in her political loyalties to the Whig cause (opposing the Jacobite aim of restoring a Stuart monarch). Politically moulded by her influence, Archie becomes a government spy enlisted to inform on two Jacobite brothers, David and James Logie of the House of Balnillo. His subsequent inability to betray the newly discovered loyalty and friendship of James is at the root of the personal tragedy which enfolds Archie, and leads to his eventual death as a traitor. Archie is an unlikely political infiltrator, a painter by profession with a 'passion for beauty' and effeminate 'grace . . . [and] happy carelessness . . . more from the cheerful love of chance than from responsible feeling'. This Waverley-like imaginative sensitivity instils sympathy and affection in Archie for James on hearing of his personal suffering in political adversity. The fraternal affection which each bears the other conflicts with Archie's inherited political and familial loyalties, crystallised in the fragile yet enduring bond between Archie and Christian, grandson and grandmother.

PRIVATE CONFLICTS

Jacob portrays this in stark yet never simplistic terms: '[Christian] found her influence and her power at stake, and her slave was being wrested from her, in spite of every interest which had bound them together. She loved him with a jealous, untender love . . .'. Archie's instinctive response to place feeling before political principle violates Christian's intransigent political faith. Yet this itself, we learn, is ironically the result of her own personal sense of family betrayals, so that if Archie were to join 'those worthless Stuarts' her own past would be unexpectedly resurrected. 'Archie had never seen Madam Flemington so much disturbed . . . the power he had known always as self-dependent, aloof, unruffled, could be at the mercy of so much feeling': in *Flemington,* Jacob exposes at every level that at the heart of supposedly abstract historical conflict and political tension lies unresolved and complex feeling.

None of Jacob's main protagonists – Archie, James, Christian, David Balnillo, even the itinerant beggar musician Skirlin Wattie – acts disinterestedly. Prejudice of one kind inheres even in the positively portrayed James (his heart 'generous' but also 'bigoted').

Is Jacob's novel ultimately pessimistic? There are frequent dark references to arbitrary fate (early critics commented on this Hardyesque notion which perhaps also links it to George Douglas Brown's novel and its ideas of fated human choices), and Archie's death is felt as a tragic sacrifice as political values seem, in the end, to override the personal. Is the novel, as a whole, the 'education in pain' which Archie is made to endure? This refusal to simplify or reduce historical and emotional complexities enriches Jacob's novel which is also a work of historically imaginative sensitivity: as Carol Anderson has noted in her introduction to her edition of 1994, Jacob's evocation of time and place is shot through with a vivid symbolic intensity, and the traditional folk community (embodied in the demotically ebullient but foolishly conniving Wattie) depicted with unsentimental energy. The geographical, not least, the historical landscape is recreated as Jacob, like Carswell's chronicle of Glasgow and Shepherd's own north-east descriptions, shows her fidelity to the physical scenes of her fiction.

Naomi Mitchison (1897–1999)

The life and fiction of Naomi Mitchison are linked together by their sheer remarkableness to which this chapter cannot do proper justice; her work is also dealt with in Section 6, in Chapter 41. Chronologically, her life spans the entire twentieth century and is therefore witness, as Jenni Calder's recent biography *The Nine Lives of Naomi Mitchison* (1997) has shown, to profound historical, social and political changes.

Born in Edinburgh, she was the daughter of J. S. Haldane, the distinguished scientist, which led to a childhood in Oxford. This academic and scientific background is arguably reflected in the intellectual scope of her work, and in the analytical rigour which she brings to the writing of historical fiction (see the Notes to her Jacobite novel *The Bull Calves*, 1947). She belonged to the literary and cultural circles of early twentieth-century London (she knew, for example, Aldous Huxley); at the same time, she remained loyal to her Scottish roots and, with her husband she became an active, often controversial, political campaigner. She sought to reconcile her aristocratic family heritage with her socialist principles; all her life she was to be a tireless worker towards what she envisioned as 'the just society', working for causes such as birth control, the rights of crofters and fishermen, or for

Africans striving for education. Like her fiction which is both internationalist and distinctively Scottish, Mitchison travelled extensively and courageously (particularly in Africa, where she became a *Mmarona* or tribal mother of the Bakgatla tribe in Botswana). Her work always fully realises a geographical space, an imagined land, whether ancient Greece, eighteenth-century Scotland, Africa or Orkney.

Reimaginings and reinventions

Just as she has written not only fiction (including short stories which show Mitchison's stylistic range) but poetry, drama, literary and political journalism, so her novels encompass a kaleidoscopic expanse of themes and subjects bound together by the recurring frameworks of myth and history. In this, her fiction bears rich comparison with Gibbon and Gunn but (arguably unlike theirs) her epic reworkings of historical and mythical pasts are given a feminist slant: the return to earlier societies (frequently ancient and classical or, as in *The Bull Calves*, Scottish society post-Culloden) gives Mitchison the opportunity to explore and challenge the different roles assigned to women in clearly patriarchal communities; there is frequently an important alignment or pairing of female characters (as in *The Bull Calves*, the tender and protective relationship or 'tutelage' of Kirsty and her niece Catherine which embodies a female generation within that family). *The Corn King and the Spring Queen* (1931) is a remarkable epic historical fiction, portraying the gradual and profound clash between two cultures: the philosophical rationalism of Hellenic culture threatens to supersede the primitive, ritualistic culture of Marob society. In a sense, Mitchison holds up the mirror of the past to contemporary society to catch ironic reflections: *The Conquered* (1923), set in the Roman invasion of Gaul mirrored the Irish political situation of the period; *The Bull Calves* reflects on the strengths and fragility of Scottish national identity; *The Corn King and the Spring Queen* invents Marob, an island on the Black Sea, an independent cultural entity threatened by imperial mainland Greece for which an analogy between Scotland and England can readily be imagined. But it is the passion and brilliance of Erif Der, the Spring Queen (her name is 'red fire' backwards) who so vividly embodies the principle of the island culture, her powers of magic, witchcraft and fertility serving as Mitchison's exploration of the strengths and dangers of female power and sexuality.

THE BULL CALVES

The Bull Calves (1947) was Mitchison's first wholly Scottish historical novel, set in the period immediately after the defeat of the 1745 Jacobite rebellion, and a period in which Highland society endured significant political and economical transformations. The novel clearly owes a debt to Scott's *Waverley* which took this troubled moment in Scotland's history to reflect on the formation of Scottish identity (Highland/Lowland; Jacobite/Hanoverian); like Violet Jacob, Mitchison seizes the vast literary potential of this epoch. But as much as Mitchison's aims in this book are political and intellectual so equally are they emotional: it is an intensely personal novel, a fictionalising of the real Haldane family. The family trees given in the novel's preface show clearly the significance of the Haldanes' historical genealogy (the 'bull calves' are the resilient Haldanes), and how the roots of the past entangle and complicate present lives. The novel is also an elegy for Mitchison's daughter who tragically died virtually at birth in 1940: in 'Clemency Eala Said' she commemorates the child and her love for her in a prefatory poem:

'With only thorns left on my white rose
To jag and tear at the heart suddenly,
Hands out, I move . . .

and makes a plea for forgiveness of humanity's horrors and for regeneration.

STRUCTURE AND SOCIETY
The novel's epic scope is mirrored in its structural division into four books but the action itself is skilfully condensed into the two days of a family gathering. During this period, the past is exorcised (through the arrival of disruptive presences, and reflection on the conflicts which arise in the aftermath of rebellion), and the present is finally embraced and celebrated in the love of Kirstie and William. As Douglas Gifford has shown in his discussion of the novel (in *Studies in Scottish Fiction*, 1990) it sets up a series of oppositions in Scott's manner within this family dynamic: Black William MacIntosh of Borlum, the positive Highlander as contrasted with the destructive Jacobite traitor Lachlan MacIntosh of Kyllachy; Patrick Haldane, 'the Bear' and political lawyer is set against Duncan Forbes of Culloden, Lord Advocate of Scotland, who acts as an agent of peace at the novel's end in resolving the dangerous complications created by the duplicitous Kyllachy. Mitchison shows a society riven by the '45 rebellion and by the destruction of old loyalties: Patrick Murray of Auchintyre is a physically and emotionally scarred young Jacobite rebel.

PUBLIC AND PRIVATE LIVES: REPRESSION AND REDISCOVERY
Kirsty, the most important female character, recreates her past (her first marriage) in conversation with her young niece, Catherine: the public and

private are inextricably interwoven as she begins this account of her life in the aftermath of the very first Jacobite rebellion of 1715. She confesses how she was 'coerced' into a destructive marriage with the minister Andrew Shaw of Bargarran after the death of her sister, relating the subjection and pain of that marriage based on religious oppression. When he preached, she wondered (Part 1, Chapter 4):

> if this was my husband, or if it was a spirit that took possession of him in the pulpit, or how at all to put together the two halves of him, or if they were the same and not opposite, then maybe God and the devil were also the same person, only looking on different things. Oh, the Sabbaths I have swithered with such thoughts, Catherine, and far enough from God's love, and lonely, for the congregation was taking it one way, but I couldna, for at the solid back of it was the knowledge that I was Mistress Andrew Shaw and like to be for all the days of my life . . .

In the next part, recollections of her past with William, her second husband (whose earlier marriage in his hidden American past is unearthed by the malicious Kyllachy), reveal her belief that she brought about Shaw's death through her practice of witchcraft. This allusion to witchcraft reveals a persistent theme of Mitchison's, the subversive nature and power of female 'magic' linked with the association of sexuality. William's return is, in a sense, intended to purify and redeem Kirstie from her dark past (Part 2, Chapter 2):

> He could not bear it, the witch-word, the coven, the word that pulled at her, whether there had ever been such a thing or not! The thick, slippery way of her saying it made him feel sick. Thon time she had been alone, out of his protection, at the mercy of folk whom he could never now reach and punish. Nor even forgive. Yet he must meet this nightmare of his wife's with kindness and sense.

Kirstie's confession acquires an extraordinary psychological intensity when she conflates her imagined temptation by the Devil with recollection of William's marriage proposal (Part 2, Chapter 2):

> 'Aye,' she said. 'I will mind through all eternity. That one from whom I expected the utmost evil, on whom I could almost smell the Pit-reek, he looked at me and said: "*I am asking you to be my wife in the name of God.*" Could you have said yon, my heart, if you had known how deep in I was?'

The novel ends with various kinds of forgiveness and restoration (political, cultural, emotional) but the central reconciliation is that between Kirstie and William as the process of memory and recollection annuls the importance of their dark pasts, and commemorates the loving significance of their present union. Kirstie confesses to Catherine: 'William, my husband, he is healing me of mine. He is aye turning me towards good. Catherine, it is a kind of redemption'. Kirstie and William 'are the image and opposite and equal' of one another (Mitchison was interested in the theories of Jung and the feminine-masculine complement at the time). The novel's process of symbolic renewal culminates in the final image of the dawn 'breaking over the Ochils' and the Haldane house in which Kirstie and William and the other 'bull calves' are sleeping. In this, Mitchison's personal and political epic finds its closing affirmation.

CHAPTER 31

THE POETRY OF WILLIAM SOUTAR

WILLIAM SOUTAR (1898–1943): TRADITION AND TRAGEDY

Soutar's biography is a sad one. Born in Perth, he showed great promise as a schoolboy both mentally and physically. After war service in the navy, he graduated from Edinburgh University in 1923, having already published his first book of poems. But signs of the spondylitis which would kill him were already showing; in 1930 he was confined to bed until his death in 1943. This bald account, however, should be set against an immense achievement and an unrivalled courage in accepting and overcoming such odds.

Any re-assessment of his poetry should begin by refuting the claim that he wrote in the shadow of MacDiarmid. Soutar was no unquestioning disciple in the 'Renaissance' movement. MacDiarmid's edition of his *Collected Poems* in 1948 did him a great disservice, leaving out much of his best work, and presenting a talented but restricted poet writing escapist fantasy, or rhymes for children. Soutar's own classifications of his poetry gave readers a false sense of a qualitative hierarchy within his achievement. The impression which can wrongly be taken from his generic titles for groupings of poems, 'Bairnsangs' and 'Whigmaleeries', is that of amusement, diversion and withdrawal from MacDiarmid's agenda for radical national, social and intellectual change. If Soutar is removed from MacDiarmid's shadow, and instead placed in the wider context of all Scottish poetry, viewed as the inheritor of traditions from Dunbar and Henryson, the ballads, Ramsay and Fergusson, Hogg, Stevenson, Davidson, Angus and Jacob, then he can be perceived not so much as a disciple of MacDiarmid's 'Scottish Renaissance' as the celebrator of the entire tradition of Scottish poetry. In this tradition he worked to create a personal renaissance to set against his own imminent death, by finding a new identity at one with the timeless voices of the great poets, which he praised in his most ambitious poem, 'The Auld Tree'. MacDiarmid was among these poets; Soutar dedicated this poem to him, and the inspiration of MacDiarmid's early lyrics is everywhere in Soutar's work. Equally we should recognise that he drew inspiration from the more reflective poetry of Edwin Muir. Even more effectively than MacDiarmid,

Soutar went 'back to Dunbar', and to Henryson and the makars and the ballads. For Soutar, all Scottish poetry was alive; poems like 'The Tryst', 'Birthday', 'The Whale' and 'The Auld Tree', reveal just how many of Scotland's poets were living tradition and inspiration to him.

Tradition was not, however, his deepest source of creation. Where other writers mingled with the world, Soutar, after 1930, could not. Ten years of being semi-invalid lay behind him; thirteen years of imprisonment in bed lay ahead. Yet Soutar, as a schoolboy, was outstandingly physically active and mentally well-adjusted; later, as a sailor, and a student, a world of promise lay ahead. Loss of all this haunted him for the rest of his life, but he recognised that he should never conceal this from himself, but deal with it honestly and without self-pity – which he did, right up until his final diary entry, detached and self-deprecating, written as he faced death.

In the room in Perth which his carpenter father created for him, looking out to the garden and hills, he read and thought about the changing Scotland outside, and listened with patience to his well-meaning visitors. What release could there be for a mind in love with the physical world outside, and a body which was still alive to desire and fulfilment? His escape was to be found in the diaries, the letters, and outstandingly, in the poetry. It is deceptive poetry, its statement most often made in the short lyric, and the abundance of these lyrics with their apparent simplicity can tempt the reader to move too quickly over the surface, missing their humane and subtle nuances. Its greatest achievement lies in its transcendence of time and place, so that the poems part company with the here and now, in ways comparable with the work of Muir and Mackay Brown. The representation of nature, of events, and of human agents, takes on a detached unearthliness and humour, in voices drawn from what Soutar hears as the living voices, from past and present, of Scottish poetry – and, in later years, the voices, with their rhythms and anecdote, of his 'ain toun' and community. Above all, escape lay in the world of the great supernatural ballads, in the twilight and *glamourie* where this world and the Other Landscape meet, where – as Soutar recurrently describes it – his dreams and visions 'smool awa', 'smool' being his motif-word for the disintegration of dreams and dream visitors in daylight. This is not escapism, but a paradox which Soutar continually articulates, in which desire for the ideal and visionary co-exists with recognition of earthly limitation and loss.

Death – or life?

Suspended between death and recreation of the self, Soutar was forced in the '30s to work between oppositions, which embodied his imprisonment, but also the means of his spiritual escape. On one hand lay the world of dream, nightmare, false echoes and disillusion, the cheating world of the gowk, the delusive cuckoo; and on the other the world of vision and commitment to the pursuit of an ideal beauty or cause, so often symbolised by the elusive unicorn. Sometimes he turned to the wall; sometimes he willed himself to fight on, with a visionary assertion of the Scottish Renaissance. This oscillation was resolved only in the last years, when he turned from both to his community and his ordinary fellow-Scots; dreams and visions gave way to acceptance of a more mundane, yet richly varied world.

These final poems of acceptance were hard earned. In 1930 Soutar was facing a drastic re-assessment of himself and his personal and creative ambitions. He had been writing poetry, mainly in English, since *Gleanings by an Undergraduate* in 1923. Romantic, rebellious and English-traditional in inspiration, this was a voice which was to continue through *Conflict* in 1931, and to modify into reflective abhorrence of violence and inequity, akin to that of Muir, in later volumes like *The Solitary Way* (1934), *A Handful of Earth* (1936) and *In the Time of Tyrants* (1939). It is tempting to simplify Soutar's re-assessment of himself at this point as resulting in a decision to let English poetry give way to Scots, but he continued to write in English till he died. Scots language gave to Soutar a concision, a dry and traditional irony, and a *grotesquerie*, which he could not find in English; but these years of self-appraisal also brought the poet, raised on English literature, who had initially scorned MacDiarmid and ideas of Scottish Renaissance, to a re-discovery of the ballads of Henryson, and the Scottish tradition.

1930 AND THE WAR OF THE ROOM

The poetry written after 1930 began with a recognition of limitation. Soutar's room was at first a place of confinement; but it became a place of rebirth. The war of the room was fought over more than a decade – often the most personal and vivid accounts of confinement and solitude are tersely expressed in his English poetry, as in 'Cosmos'. 'There is a universe within this room', it begins – but it is a negative space, with its images of monotony and 'the ticking tongue of time' stuttering in silence and dust, marking descent 'from gloom to gloom'. Poem after poem of this period reiterates loneliness, as in 'Black Laughter', where the poet dreams that he has godly power to help his 'own land' but awakes, shuddering, hearing insistent, mocking laughter. 'Beyond Loveliness', opening with a dream of contentment on a hill in the noon-day sun, with Soutar 'at one, within this solitude', closes with the dream broken by the intrusion of the old man with his burden, with 'no eye for nature'. 'With him my thought went down', Soutar concludes, since a dreary death awaits them both. This world seems a cheating dream; and 'The Mood' likens the cuckoo's cry in the neighbouring wood to a delusive dream, ending with the poet's reminder to himself that he must recognise his – and humanity's – final solitude. 'Autobiography', as late as 1937, shows that these dark moods persisted for long periods, and sums up this confessional bleakness in a spiritual palindrome, its movement forward mockingly echoed in reverse, from a positive ascent through life; womb / bed / room / garden / town / country / earth / people set against the negative descent of people / earth / country / town / garden / room / bed / tomb.

Understandably however, Soutar's impression of 'The Room' underwent constant re-definition; 'Reverie' of 1933 seems to echo the sense of a shrinking world, Soutar's room-garden now seen as a world 'shrunk into a little garth / And life to phantasy' – but in the translation to 'phantasy', hope arises – in the greener grass and bluer sky of dream, which paradoxically suggests that actual life may be a lesser dream-world. These English poems of the early '30s could express a strikingly different mood from that of pessimism, as in 'The Return of the Swallow', which is placed against 'the singing sigh' of the cuckoo, and startles the blood with 'a quick pulse of joy', akin to the God-like epiphany of 'A Summer Morning' and 'At Peace', which tells us that frequently Soutar was content 'to cease / From mortal busyness and stare / Silent, alone, at peace'.

CUCKOOS AND GOWKS

Out of Soutar's dilemma, certain images and ideas began to emerge, becoming recurrent symbols, with the most outanding being those of gowk [*cuckoo*] and unicorn. They are by no means Soutar's only effective symbols; he gives allegorical significance to images of tree, bird, seeds, roots, worm, the brig, the wall, the stone and the graveyard, as well as the lion and whale. But the gowk/cuckoo and unicorn stand at the head of this rich symbolism, which is more in the manner of the timeless and heraldic imagery of Muir and Mackay Brown than the constantly changing symbolism of MacDiarmid. Soutar's diaries reveal that his use of symbolism in poems like 'The Whale' is Jungian, stemming from dream and the unconscious, an 'intuitive choosing', which makes his symbols vividly express his fluctuation between negation and affirmation.

Soutar's ideas of 'gowkishness' carry both the Scottish implications of the gowk in itself and the more generalised implications of the verb 'gowk' as Scottish foolishness in action. His earliest Scots poems, like 'The Gowk' of 1928, show that the bird held associations of false promise, betrayal and loss for him – although here it is Soutar who kills the bird. After 1930 the

568

significance of the gowk is more consistently negative. The 1932 Bairnrhyme 'Ae Summer's Day' depersonalises 'Mood', an English poem, into Scots and the timeless voice of Scottish folk poetry, so that the poet is absorbed into older poets' experience of similar pain. Once again the place is between here and another landscape, as the poet hears the gowk's elusive and mocking call by the fountain (of life?) crying above a fernie brae (a brae of ballads immemorial). And with the second of the poems entitled 'The Gowk' (1932) ('Half doun the hill . . .'), Soutar has clearly recast the deceiving bird, in a haunting poem in which memory renders his natural description archetypal and timeless, echoing both the seasons and the cycles of human life and fortune in ways which recall the poetry of Marion Angus and Violet Jacob. A casual reading will miss the subtlety of the contrast between the first and second verses. The first tells of spring and the Wordsworthian presence of the howie hill at the poet's back; the second, apparently continuing the narrative, in fact transforms the scene to winter, with the waterfall frozen, and with a ghostly echo of the gowk's call thus completing a tableau which juxtaposes youth and age, hope and disillusion, innocence and experience, in one of Soutar's finest poems – sadly, not included in the 1948 edition.

Until he died, Soutar exploited the gowk for this evocation of lost youth. It is a rich seam, and working in it, Soutar avails himself of the creative associations carried by Scots terms like 'Gowkstorm', and 'Hunt the Gowk' (which Soutar made into a poem in 1933, which looked beyond gowk-illusion to his final acceptance of the intermingling of good and evil). These poems thus embed themselves in a traditional Scottish dialectic of language and culture. The diary entry for Friday, 16 August 1940, while not explicitly using the gowk-image, sums up the forlorn yearning of the gowk poems, and adds a deeper layer of lost sexuality to the significance of gowk-illusion:

> This drifting into day-dream which is so dangerous; this ranging through unreality which is so negative; and which by the prolongation of circumscription, becomes more and more liable: bordering land into which one has wandered by a single side-step. And the phantoms which beckon most persistently are in the shapes of women – since that which we would touch and cannot becomes the more desirable. And it is here that to follow the dream is to degenerate desire; to chase the image of creative joy and to gather only the weeds of self-pity; sickly fondness, corruptive regret . . .

This mood of yearning for what cannot be held, is most poignantly expressed in the most evocatively moving, and deeply symbolic of all these gowk-related poems of transitory and delusive desire, 'The Tryst' is Soutar's ultimate example of negative – yet paradoxically haunting and moving – dreaming. This is the apotheosis of his dream poems, and it was particularly unfortunate that MacDiarmid, in 1948, left out this finest and most intense of lyrical laments for lost love. Now, in Soutar's familiar Borderland, the cheating gowk has transmogrified into a particular aspect of Soutar's yearning, sexual and emotional desire for Woman which he continually reveals in diary and poem. With apparent simplicity, Soutar captures the rise and fall of desire and loss, fused with an ambivalence which leaves the reader wondering whether the lover is real, ghost, or dream. He adapts ballad abruptness to suit his theme, softening the opening to combine lullaby with lust, idealisation with despair. There is a real and tender eroticism in the poem; but whatever else the lover may be, she is beyond reality, all his lost loves, together with an unattainable beauty; and she is also fantasy, which is why she does not speak and why he hears her heart 'gang soundin' with his own, since she is indeed bone of his bone – although the description is doubly evocative in emphasising the bodily closeness of the dream lover. The balladic cock-crow sees her 'smool awa' like so many of Soutar's dream-visions; she comes and goes with the movement of appearance and recedence, leaving, like the gowk, only the memory of lost summer days.

UNICORNS AND VISION

If the gowk was, from early on, Soutar's main symbol for false dreams and lost hopes, the unicorn later became his symbol of vision and hope, increasingly with a Scottish political and cultural association. In his diary entry of 19 May 1938 Soutar articulated what the unicorn meant to him:

> Like all profound associations I cannot date when the unicorn began to impress itself upon me, but it was no doubt deepening by my early thirties, when I was definitely turning to Scots and when I was experiencing a more limited physical life. Since then I can follow the growth of the symbol in two directions, the one towards a richer comprehensiveness and the other towards subtler privacy. Thus from a purely Scottish emblem the creature has come to represent truth, reality, life under varying aspects but all manifesting the eternal nature of man's quest; always he is but holding the image in the pool of his mind: so the arts, philosophies and religions build up their cages round an ever elusive vision. The private identification has grown out of circumstance and an element of aloofness in my own nature: perhaps also, now, from the premonition that with the years I may find myself more and more alone.

The unicorn is a willed vision, part of Soutar's personal and spiritual renaissance, the rediscovery of recreation of new self which is such a poignant movement through his last thirteen years. The beast is elusive, created from something deeply solitary in Soutar. It leads us into one of the richest veins in Soutar's poetry. By 1932, in a series called 'Symbols', the unicorn began to symbolise hope:

> Mebbe the morn ayont the morn
> A man, or bairnie, sall be born
> Wha'll win hame wi oor Unicorn–

sighs a three line poem in the series. Unlike the gowk, straddling worlds of childhood and maturity, the unicorn is most certainly not a Bairnrhyme symbol, although, astonishingly, one of Soutar's greatest and most ambitious poems, the medieval-dream-visionary ballad 'The Whale', with its triumphant use of the unicorn, began as a Bairnrhyme, but burst its childlike bounds to take its place amongst his great political poetry.

'The Whale' is a twenty-five verse epic working in a mixture of traditions, from Dunbar and medieval dream poetry and the supernatural ballads, to the great political visions of Ramsay and Fergusson in 'The Vision' and 'The Ghaists'. It fuses timeless reflection with contemporary satirical application, showing clearly that the unicorn's significance belongs, not to childhood or retrospective yearning, but to the future, and as the essence of mature human art and aspiration. It falls naturally into five sections. Verses 1–6 locate the poet beside the Forth, in darkness without companions. As in 'Birthday', Scotland is seen as benighted and bereft of common purpose. The poet is a latter-day Jonah, cut off from his fellows, but burdened with a mission. The whale which now manifests itself is, if not divinely guided, linked to the redemptive monsters of MacDiarmid's 'Sea-serpent', 'Bombinations of a Chimaera', and *A Drunk Man*; it is a manifestation of lost spirit, ancient identity, but it is the carrier of such essences rather than agent of redemption.

The first part ends with the swallowing of the poet. Verses 7–15 then describe the great whale's interior; here is a lost Scotland, with beasts and nature unknown to the present. The poet wanders within this fantastic lost land, marvelling at the grotesque and alien creatures – and principally at the blood-red unicorn. (And behind all his wonder he hears the sounding of the great heart of the whale, every strong beat bringing a visionary light to his eyes.) Verses 16–18 remind the poet of the ancient legend of how a great whale swallowed creatures before the assembly in Noah's ark, taking them from the world – and from Scotland. 'And I was wae for my ain land / Twined o' its unicorn', concludes the poet, echoing MacDiarmid's lament for the 'twining' of primeval smeddum from Scotland in *A Drunk Man*. Verses 19–22 set the poet on the back of the unicorn, while 23–5 set them free, and the unicorn is now snow-white. Poet and unicorn go their different ways, but as the unicorn 'snoov'd owre Arthur's Sate', the poet concludes his allegory with his realisation that change is at hand: 'I heard the lion roar'. As with 'Birthday', the vision is of the reawakening of Scotland, and in both the unicorn plays its crucial role in relating Scotland's past to its future.

'Birthday' belongs with 'The Whale' and 'The Auld Tree', Soutar's three most affirmative and powerful nationalist statements. It is probably one of Soutar's best known poems, but its nuances may not be so well realised, and deserve comment. Again, the setting is night, in what is seen as a Scottish Wasteland. Again, and more emphatically, there is no common purpose; there may be three riders together, but 'nae man spak to his brither', suggesting that in this benighted Scotland fraternal unison does not exist. They ride unspeaking past creatures of the night, on some lonely and mysterious journey, until, going past birk and rowan (traditionally benign harbingers) they see their vision of the unicorn with its glowing child-rider. Brilliantly Soutar fuses Wasteland mythology akin to that used by other Renaissance writers such as Gibbon and Mitchison with echoes of Christian belief – the three wise men, the adoration of Christ. The conclusion synthesises these into a message of rebirth and hope for Scotland, a dawn in which each man will look his brother in the eye and tell of what they have seen all over the nation.

These poems mark the high point of Soutar's affirmative use of the unicorn. Sadly, disillusionment with the Renaissance movement was close at hand. By 1933 the satirical 'Vision' is much more sceptical about the ability of the unicorn's horn to clean the filth from Scotland's poisoned waters; and later, in 'Myth', the unicorn takes on something of the gowk's mockery of humanity. In the same year 'Genethliac Chant', while still yearning for ideal beauty, treats unicorn vision with a new and relaxed self-mockery:

This is the day whan I was born
Tak pity on my mither:
I hae the saul o' a unicorn
Tak pity on my faither . . .

and a consolatory acceptance of his unicorn soul, in that 'The Lord has pit a sang in my mouth / That micht hae been a sechin'.

By the late '30s, with the shadows of war ahead, and what Soutar was to call 'the greatest catastrophe which has erupted in the world', the unicorn's role changes from affirmative to passive. It is still related to the ideal, but now it is less to do with Scotland's development than the world's loss. In 'Life' and 'Faith' the unicorn becomes a symbol close to that of the victim of Muir's killing beast in 'The Combat', hunted in darkness by the hungry faces hurrying by, and 'sae far awa, sae far awa'. And, illustrating the fact that both English and Scots continued as successful languages for Soutar, one of the last, saddest, and best of his unicorn poems, simply entitled 'The Unicorn', is a poem in English which combines 'Life' and 'Faith', leaving its unicorn to stand beyond Scotland and humanity:

> When from the dark the day is born
> Life's glory walks in white:
> Upon the hills the unicorn
> Glitters for mortal sight . . .

OTHER RECURRENT SYMBOLS: THE TREE OF LIFE

But Soutar's dreams and visions are not to be limited to gowks and unicorns. They are the most powerful amongst a cognate variety of symbols patterned into the poetry. Outstanding among these evocative for Soutar in their associations with fundamentals of nature, death and regeneration, are trees, roots, and, used to reductive and sardonic effect, worms. And his tree-symbolism, always ambivalently evocative in its intense fusion of pagan-Christian implications, is nowhere more powerfully expressed than in 'The Auld Tree', his epic celebration of the Makars of Scotland, their decline into political and cultural wasteland, and their release into a hopeful Scotland in the twentieth-century 'Renaissance' of MacDiarmid. Soutar's imagination fuses together a host of far-reaching implications, linking the original Tree of Paradise with its ballad echoes, as from 'The Wife of Usher's Well', and with ideas as disparate as Christ's cross as Tree, Ygdrassil, the Eildon Tree, and exotic trees of many mythologies. Here Soutar's symbolism is akin to the key-symbols of thistle and moon of MacDiarmid in *A Drunk Man*, but arguably held and sustained with greater imaginative unity, as in 'Birthday' and 'The Whale'.

The poem is 353 lines long, and Soutar structures it in three parts. Lines 1–140 set the medieval-dream context, emphasising spiritual as opposed to earthly vision, the poet's 'thowless' enervation (suspended in a negativism comparable with that of the protagonists of 'Birthday' and 'The Whale'), moving into a seer-like awareness of the Great Tree, an earthly Yggdrasil (reminiscent of MacDiarmid's sea-serpent, in that it is as old at least as God, and shares his creative intention). At the heart of this section lies the poem's refrain; 'The challanee [*challenge*] o' the singin' word / That whunners [*thunders*] like a lowin' sword'; the tree is set in an Eden-like 'saft gairthen [*garden*], but in place of the flaming sword at Eden's gate there is instead the challenge of the creative word, since this is a poets' garden. From the time of its oldest bard, that mysterious and ancient first 'carl', it has been a kind of Eden-Valhalla, and all the great company of 'leal makars' sit in the shade of the Great Tree. Somehow the narrator manages to join them; and hears Burns speak, firstly of the waywardness of reputation, and then of Scotland's parlous state, bereft of real poetry since himself, and Dunbar and Henryson. Unless someone awakens the nation, 'doun to death / She'll gang and canker a' the world'.

Lines 141–262 make up the second movement; 'a lang stillness' ensues, followed by a cold wind (the *hwyl* or 'devil's laughter' which blew round the ears of MacDiarmid's Drunk Man?), and the poet finds that the garden has gone, transformed into a bare hill of whins. This is Scotland's mythical, yet modern, Wasteland, for all that the place is the Eildon Hills; and the 'deid man wi' the muckle sword' who now appears is Wallace. (Among its several medieval and later predecessors in Scottish visionary poetry, the poem now seems yet again explicitly to echo Ramsay's 'The Vision' which also set a disenchanted poet in a beleaguered Scotland, and – in dream or vision – made Wallace the prophetic guardian of the nation.) Wallace points out the legendary significance of the location, implying its ballad ancestry, and its being a doorway between this world and the Other Landscape, as Thomas Rhymer found when he went with the queen of that other world, as well as its associations with Merlin, Douglas and Bruce. (Clearly Soutar's poet is aware also of later associations with Hogg and Scott.)

Wallace seems powerless to act, till in an agony for Scotland the poet cries out:

> but no my ain
> Spirit, in anguishment, alane,
> But Scotland's sel', wi' thorter'd pride
> Cried oot upon that cauld hillside:
> And her ain name was a' she cried . . .

Wallace, released from his enchantment, strikes, cutting away the two-headed snake which twines around the Eildon Tree (both English and, more controversially, Irish influence are thus cut away), and the challenge of the singing word is heard again in the land. He strikes again, and a bleeding sap is restored to the petrified tree, while a sigh 'Like the owrecome o' an auld-world sang' marks the stirring of new life. With Wallace's third stroke the earth is cleaved beyond the roots of the tree, 'To the livenin' lowe at the world's hert'; the poet knows that the hill 'Hings owre into the mirk o' space', and hears strange sounds:

> o' reeshlin' banes,
> And sklinterin' rocks, and brakin' chains,
> And wails o' women in their thraws,
> And the rummlin' march o'harnest raws . . .

Scotland is being reborn, with lightning crack and turmoil. The poet is blinded and his senses overcome till, symbolising the completion of renaissance, the poet concludes this movement with an effective and symbolic modulation:

> Yet, far ben in the breist o' me
> I heard the soundin o' the sea . . .

Lines 262–353, the third and final movement, awaken the poet on a moonlit and now peaceful hillside. Wallace has gone, but his sword is sheathed in the Eildon Tree (a play now on Arthurian legend?), and the 'begesserant [*sparkling*] rime' inscribed on it ('The challance [*challenge*] o' the singin' word . . .' glows supernaturally, till the blade, like 'A fiery cross a' growin' green', metamorphoses into a great thistle which replaces the ancient, withered Tree. This evocation of the meta-symbolism of *A Drunk Man* is Soutar's generous and unique tribute to MacDiarmid and his poem; and it is MacDiarmid with burning eyes, and 'word-drucken' [*word-drunk*], who sings the song which awakens the thistle and inspires Soutar's poet to believe that 'on a guidly hill was I' – and that Scotland and the Eildons are released from Wasteland:

> And that there breer'd, at ilka hand
> The braid shires o' a promised land . . .

Birds return, the Thistle-Tree is a burning bush, and a great song for Scotland is taken up by Soutar's poet rejoicing in the new dawn, and that:

> Scotland stands abüne
> Her ain deid sel'; and sterkly steers
> Into the bairntime o' her years . . .

In the last eight lines the poet awakens to this world. Although it is night, he is content carrying with him his affirmative vision, and hearing always:

> The challance o' the singin' word
> That whunners like a lowin' sword.

The *gairthen* or garden of Scottish poetry has been re-established; Scottish renaissance has begun. It is deeply ironic that this, Soutar's longest poem, and certainly his most ambitious statement regarding the need for a renaissance of Scottish tradition in poetry and politics, and arguably his finest tribute to his poetic predecessors, should be dedicated to Hugh MacDiarmid as the potential saviour of the soul of Scotland, given that MacDiarmid did not include it, or the other great poem of Scottish political and mythic regeneration, 'The Whale', in the 1948 edition.

OTHER SYMBOLS; THE WORM BENEATH THE TREE OF DEATH

'The Auld Tree' marks Soutar's maturation as a Scottish makar, simultaneously exploiting the entire Scottish tradition in poetry, and his belief in Scottish cultural renaissance. But after this great poem the connotations of the tree changed. By the late '30s the coming war began to dominate his mind, as it did for so many Scottish writers of the period like Gunn, Gibbon, and Mitchison – and, as with Gunn, Soutar responded with an emphasis on the importance of the human, the local, and the ordinary. 'Song', in English, puts forward a simpler tree, which must seasonally decline; the poet tells himself not to hoard happiness 'from the indifferent worm', but to accept death, the transitory life. The song of life is one of natural and human change, and it now has more in common with Grassic Gibbon's *Sunset Song* than MacDiarmid's song of national renaissance. In the Muir-like 'Nightmare', the bleeding tree is now the dream-symbol of man's inhumanity; the dreamer awakes, and still the tree bleeds. And with 'The Enemy' it is clear that Soutar is preoccupied with war and international hate; the enemy crucified on the tree is forgiven, and becomes a brother eating the fruit of the Tree of Life. Then, with 'Far Awa in Araby', Soutar recasts the Scottish symbolism of 'The Auld Tree' as international, reducing the core meaning of the longer poem to seven intensely lyrical verses. The tree now grows in a limbo world half-way between here and heaven; and instead of harbouring poets, it is now the place where the souls of gaunt kings and restless lovers 'maun rove, and canna come on rest'.

The tree – and increasingly, the worm – remain, however, as powerful symbols, but becoming more generally human and Muir-like symbols which focus Soutar's meditations on death, decay, earth, necessary corruption, rebirth, and growth. The focus of this cycle of meditation is not simply personal, or archetypally human, or allegorical regarding national or international culture – it is all these, grasped by Soutar holistically in an impressive one-ness. The philosophical effort is revealed in his later diaries, and it bears comparison with MacDiarmid's metaphysical explorations. It also has similarities with the later work in very different genres of Muir and Gunn in its yearning for final understanding. The long and complex allegory, 'Why the Worm Feeds on Death', is a extended meditation on human betrayal, as evinced in the story of Cain and Abel, in which rebirth is clearly set in the non-national, general context of man's inhumanity to man. The poem is perhaps over-ambitious; the link between the failure of the fundamental and essential cycle of worm-corruption and creativity, and the archetypal dualism of Cain and Abel, is never effectively revealed. It is in striking contrast to the later, succinct bleakness of 'King Worm', which cuts out such complexity of thought to replace it with stark brevity and an even starker conclusion:

> The hale world is my heapit plate
> And death the flunkey at my airm:
> Wha sae merry owre his meat?
> I am King Worm.

SOUTAR REMAKING SOUTAR

Arguably Soutar's greatest triumph was still to come, in his accommodation with tragedy and his personal renaissance, which Alexander Scott caught so well in the title of his critical biography, *Still Life* (1958). The deepest tension within Soutar concerned the nature of selfhood. The English poems obsessively asserted the idea of self, or its loss; but paradoxically about the same time Soutar began the movement towards his greatest triumph, a much more significant personal renaissance or rebirth. It wasn't just for his adopted sister Evelyn or for the children of Scotland that Soutar argued for the return of the Doric on a cock-horse – it was just as much for himself, as he had to rediscover the deepest creative part of himself within a Scottish tradition he had ignored or even scorned while an undergaduate. Soutar had read Henryson when he should have been reading Anglo-Saxon at Edinburgh University, and had discovered ballads on his dreary trip to Orkney in 1923; but in the 1920s he doubted whether Scottish literature could ever become a national literature again. Indeed, one of his longest poems, unusual in his early poetry for its extended use of Scots, the substantial satire, 'The Thistle Looks at a Drunk Man', very clearly shows Soutar's early scepticism regarding MacDiarmid's agenda for renaissance. This hilariously reductive statement of antipathy modelled itself on the previous great flytings of Dunbar and Fergusson, cleverly exploiting the 'Habbie Simson' stanza to express Soutar's dislike of what he saw as MacDiarmid's pretentious show of world-knowledge and his innovative treatment of Scots ('he wud droon / That honest Doric . . .'). Paradoxically, Soutar's invocation of older makars here anticipated his later identification with the central traditions of Scottish poetry; but for now he argued that the old Thistle cannot be taught new tricks. It is certainly easy to understand why this poem was not included in the 1948 collection.

Conversion to MacDiarmid's 'Scottish Literary Renaissance' only came – and for a short time – with increasing illness. As his physical condition deteriorated, so his need for the only possible consolation for a man of his intelligent honesty increased. That possibility lay in embedding himself and his predicament within the tradition of his peers, the makars from the distant past down to Jacob, Angus, MacDiarmid and Muir in the present, and within the folk experience of proverb, anecdote, song and legend. To do this, Soutar had to accelerate a process of growth from innocence to experience which is clearly the organising principle behind the linked categories of 'Riddles', 'Bairnrhymes', 'Whigmaleeries', and Scots poetry.

The Riddles are poetry; like so much of Soutar's work, based on an unusual, apparently fragmented, but in essence a circumnavigatory and lateral creative approach, which builds from what may seem occasional pieces for children but are the essential basis of Soutar's process of remaking himself, for all that they are apparently written for his sister Evelyn. Like George Macdonald before him, Soutar respected the significance of the childlike imagination, recognising its superiority over the merely childish. These poems are indeed charming for children; but disturbingly they include as subject-symbols rainbow, soap-bubble, beard, echo, shadow, skull, dream, cuckoo, and 'the child you were'. Turn after them to the 'Bairnrhymes', and poems like 'The Daft Tree' and 'The Wind' show how Soutar worked with the idea of Riddles reversed. Riddles grow into Bairnrhymes and similarly, among Bairnrhymes like 'Bawsy Broon' wonderfully suited to children, there regularly occur – as we saw with 'The Whale' – some extremely unchildlike and sardonic comment on human frailty. Bairnrhymes grow into Whigmaleeries. Henryson's influence is seen everywhere, as in 'The Herryin' o' Jenny Wren', a sophisticated Scots 'Who killed Cock Robin?'; and comedy and tragedy are grotesque partners in poems like 'Wish' and 'Lauch Whan Ye Can'. Is the unicorn-linked 'The Hunt' really for children?

And the Whigmaleeries likewise – at a higher level – burst their apparent bounds. Real grimness and mature ironic comment, managed with consummate craft, suggest that separation of these poems into a category which implies that the poet is indulging himself in fantasy and cantrips is to demean their achievement. The Japanese legend-poem, 'The Wood' goes far beyond mere fanciful escapism; 'The Hungry Mauchs' of the same time is a thinly-disguised and grotesque worm poem; 'The Hungry Toun' is similarly disguised social anger, akin to the English 'Symbol' with its terrible imagery of 'wizzent bairns like auld men' and there's extremely sophisticated satire on Scotland in 'Second Childhood'. And with poems of the stature of 'Far Awa in Araby' and 'King Worm' it is obvious that the distinction between Whigma-leeries and mature Scots poem has vanished. It remains for Soutar's personal and creative renaissance to go beyond vision and dream, gowks and unicorns, to discover something beyond despair or commitment to politics or pacifism. 'Scotland' shows how far Soutar has moved from the nation – affirmation of 'The Auld Tree' and 'The Whale'. Beginning with the visionary stance of the poet, who 'sees whaur he canna see', as in the earlier poems, the poet now sees a very different Scotland. Restless and unsure of itself, with 'Sauls that are sterk [*stark*] and nesh [*shivering*]' and 'Sauls that wud dree the day', Soutar's core-symbolism has gone. This difficult and ambiguous poem marks a withdrawal from the desire to be identified with the New Scotland, instead asking readers to find – whatever it turns out to be, mean or great – their own Scotland. The poet concludes:

> It is owre late for fear:
> Owre early for disclaim;
> When ye come hameless here
> And ken ye are at hame.

THE LATE POETRY OF COMMUNITY

Soutar's new selfhood was not to be found in unqualified commitment to a programme of national cultural revival. Instead, it was found, in these last years, in other people from his community and other poets from Scotland's past. Scottish tradition, oral and communal, literary and popular, in the broadest sense, with its essential characteristic of a communal voice speaking and singing in story and ballad-song (identified as 'the speak', in Gibbon's *Sunset Song*, and as the stream of consciousness of timeless community), allowed Soutar to depersonalise his tragedy; but more than this, his bed-ridden state brought him, as his diaries tell us, back to the kindliness of people who came to talk with and to tell him stories of his community. Where MacDiarmid started with such empathy for his rich variety of humanity in *Sangschaw* and *Penny Wheep*, then abandoned it for a 'poetry of facts', Soutar's recreation of himself moved in the end back to the community of Scotland, as exemplified in his 'ain toun'.

Soutar was, in these last years, to discover that he had always had an astonishing variety of character and expression, creature and landscape around him. Justice cannot be done here to the richness of the poetry which Soutar produced in this final, selfless, mature phase. Arguably it is just because there are so many accomplished short poems within this period that critical appreciation has tended to glance over them, too readily seeing them as pre-renaissance rural nostalgia, and missing their timeless lyricism or their gentle but laconic wit and irony.

The Diaries of a Dying Man reveals that in his last years Soutar was able to accept his doubts, and the mysteries of self and existence, and to relish what was happening to him day-to-day. There are many poems now which sum up his involvement with community (which he listed as projects under the titles *Yon Toun* and *Local Habitation*). At the time of his death, Soutar himself had come to accept the ageless philosophy and the quiet assurance he had captured in his poem, 'Hunt the Gowk' with its recognition that, in the end, dreams and visions, gowks and unicorns, are distractions from deeper self-hood and a final homecoming.

> What guid has it dune onie ane
> What has gaen a' roun' the airth –
> An' gowpit on the Brahmaputra
> An' the ootfa' o' the Congo;
> An' kent the graith o' the Amazon
> Lang efter the hinnermaist hicht
> Smool'd oot o' sicht – an' cam aince mair
> Tae his bairn-place: an' dee'd
> Afore he saw hoo bonnily the burn
> Gaed by his ain back-door.

CHAPTER 32

LEWIS GRASSIC GIBBON AND ERIC LINKLATER

NOVELISTS OF RENAISSANCE? GIBBON, GUNN, LINKLATER

Lewis Grassic Gibbon, Neil Miller Gunn, and Eric Linklater are three of the greatest novelists of the modern Scottish Renaissance. They stand together, clearly distinct from their English and Irish counterparts; Forster, Woolf, Lawrence and Joyce. Their three territories, while lying close to each other (Gibbon's in the hinterland south of Aberdeen and in the lee of the Cairngorm mountains, Gunn's in the north-east corner of Scotland, and Linklater's directly across the Pentland Firth) each have their own striking sense of community tradition and cultural identity. And as writers within the Scottish cultural renaissance, they each explored tradition, legend and Scottish history in a new and critical way, which to a great extent repudiated the earlier views of Scott and the nineteenth-century way of looking at Scotland. They question the value, for Scotland, of historical episodes like the Reformation and the industrial revolution. Instead Scottish Renaissance writers looked to pre-history, to legend and myth, especially the myth of a golden age of primitive, uncorrupted, non-institutional man, for a basis to their work.

For all that, they are all writers aware of international work in their field and they acknowledge debts to other traditions. For example, Gunn's favourite writer, whose influences can be seen in *Highland River* (1937) and *The Silver Darlings* (1941), was Wordsworth (of *The Prelude*, 1805–1855, especially), and he acknowledged also the significance of Freud and Proust in his thought. Gibbon, for his part, was impressed by D. H. Lawrence's *The Rainbow* (1929) and the quest for 'dark Gods' in primitive cultures, while Linklater's novels such as *The Men of Ness* (1932), *Juan in America* and *Juan in China* (1931, 1935) and *Magnus Merriman* (1934) drew on sources as wide-ranging as the Norse sagas, old and new traditions of picaresque fiction, and Byron's *Don Juan* (1819), as well as showing the influence of Evelyn Waugh in his social and political satire.

AFFIRMATION AND NEGATION: RECOGNISING DIFFERENCES

We should, however, recognise their fundamental differences. It is Gunn and Gibbon who immediately inspire comparison – firstly as individuals, responding to their Sutherland or north-east environment. Gunn was a happy man; Gibbon, overall, unhappy in his life, developing a 'love-hate' ambivalence to the Mearns and to farming. Gunn, coming from an unusually strong community background, had no such confusion, respecting his parents and forebears, where Gibbon all too frequently felt hatred for his community and the effects that hard farming labour had upon it. Gunn in his work thus bound himself with his beloved Highlands, making them his metaphor for spiritual regeneration, where Gibbon retreated, through his years in the services, to Welwyn Garden City, to write with frequent bitterness about the death of traditional community. And if we then compare the work of Linklater with theirs, it will be seen that Linklater too responded with dubiety to the idealistic claims of the Scottish Renaissance movement, much of his writing preferring an English setting and theme. In the end, his final and most personal assessment of renaissance claims, in *Magnus Merriman*, suggests that his deep-seated scepticism regarding human significance meant that he could not regard the movement without seeing it as over-blown and slightly comic.

Linklater's upbringing was different from Gibbon's and Gunn's; the son of an Orkney sea-captain, he spent his earliest childhood in Wales, went to school and university in Aberdeen and fought in the Black Watch in the First World War. His experience was much more cosmopolitan; he had studied both medicine and literature, was a journalist for *The Times of India*, and assistant lecturer in English at Aberdeen. As a scholar and writer he travelled extensively, and in the Second World War he became commander of the Northern Garrisons. For all this, he identified strongly with Orkney, allowing his Welsh childhood to fade in memory, and representing himself as 'an old peasant with a pen'. Like the division between the Scottish and non-Scottish work of James Leslie Mitchell and his alter ego Lewis Grassic Gibbon, Linklater was to develop two broad strands in his fiction, one exploiting English society and literary tradition, the other emphatically rooted in Orkney, arguably to a much greater extent than in mainland Scotland. Recognising this, the fundamental differences between Gunn's positive holistic persepective and Gibbon and Linklater's more divided, sceptical response to the claims of the renaissance, Gunn's fiction will be treated seperately in the next chapter; although readers will find constant and striking affinities amongst all three writers.

The following general discussions cannot do justice to the outstanding artistry of Gibbon's major works such as *Sunset Song* – the first part of his *Quair* trilogy. The corpus of Gibbon's work has received full treatment elsewhere – for example, there are entire chapters on *Sunset Song* in Douglas Young's *Beyond the Sunset* (1973), William Malcolm's *A Blasphemer and Reformer* (1984) and Ian Campbell's *Lewis Grassic Gibbon* (1985). Both Gibbon and Gunn are treated in Gifford's *Gunn and Gibbon* (1983) and Isobel Murray and Bob Tait's *Ten Modern Scottish Novels* (1984). Nor can we here do justice to the sheer range of Linklater's achievement; Michael Parnell's *Eric Linklater* (1984) and Julian D'Arcy's *Scottish Skalds and Sagamen* (1996) are highly recommended.

Lewis Grassic Gibbon (1901–35)

James Leslie Mitchell (who would later derive his pen-name from his mother, Lilias Grassic Gibbon) was unhappy in his family and farming background. He was discouraged in his education and his father continually threatened to make him 'tak a fee' as a hired farm worker. The boy's natural literary talents were in direct opposition to both his family wishes and his community's influence.

After an unhappy and curtailed secondary education in Stonehaven, he went to Aberdeen and later to Glasgow as a journalist where he became active in communist politics. Already there were contradictory impulses in his life. Like young Ewan in *Sunset Song* (1932), in his youth he had been interested in the standing stones and the flint artefacts, the signs of early mankind which were to be found in abundance all around the countryside in which he grew up. His sense of an ancient elemental past was now to meet political creeds which denied humans their natural inheritance, shared past and communal background.

Gibbon and the golden age

To this contradiction there were added many others. Mitchell was to be increasingly persuaded that man had lost an original state of innocence, a golden age. This belief, fostered by his reading, was strengthened when, in disgrace and despair, he joined up in the army and was posted to the Service Corps in the Middle East. It was indeed a paradox that the man who hated all imperialism and brutish authority had to turn to the military institution for a livelihood and an escape. It was in Mesopotamia and Egypt that he found his sense of the living past rekindled by the ancient remains of pyramids and burial places.

When he came across Eliot Smith's anthropological theories, known as 'diffusionism', Mitchell adopted them enthusiastically. Diffusionism suggests that Man was originally nomadic, godless, unchained; but that accidental discovery of the regular fertility of the Nile and the Euphrates caused Man to enter into a territorial agreement with river and season, which eventually enslaved him to a process in which he was tied to land, to the propitiation of river gods, and thence to a fully developed bureaucratic and property-owning institutional system. This was the rationale behind Gibbon's vision of man's lost golden age and of his hatred of centralised imperial authority which he viewed as having destroyed an original anarchic harmony and individualism.

Gibbon and religion

Some critics have portrayed Mitchell as an atheist, one whose communism seeks to destroy false gods; after all, his vision of an lawless golden age saw early Man as free from superstition. Mitchell's Presbyterian background was stronger than critics have previously recognised. Throughout much of Gibbon's work there is an ambivalence regarding religion. In the short stories, 'Forsaken' and 'Greenden', Mitchell as Lewis Grassic Gibbon employs explicit religious symbolism of a positive and affirmative kind so that Christian values and ideas are dominant. In *Spartacus* (1933), a vivid account of the slave rebellion against imperial Rome, Mitchell gives a proto-Christian vision to the rebel Greek, Kleon, at the point of death. And a similar use of Christian doctrine and symbol can be observed in the closing pages of *Cloud Howe* (1933), the second part of *A Scots Quair*.

Gibbon and 'The Land'

Finally, Gibbon displays a deeply divided attitude towards the land and his native country. Outstandingly, *Scottish Scene* (1934), which Gibbon wrote and edited in collaboration with Hugh MacDiarmid, is crucial in our attempt to understand Lewis Grassic Gibbon as a writer and thinker. Sub-titled *or the Intelligent Man's Guide to Albyn*, it is an eccentric survey of Scotland in the 1930s, extreme in its opinions and highly unconventional in its attitudes. Despite the richness of MacDiarmid's poetic input, the book is memorable because of Gibbon's contributions – five fine short stories and seven long essays, of which 'The Land' is the best known. Written after *Sunset Song*, it employs a similar structure of four sections named after the seasons from winter through to autumn, from the unfurrowed field through to the harvest, from sterility to ripe fulfilment.

In the essay, Gibbon develops two propositions that are basic to his thinking about rural Scotland, especially as he evokes it in *Sunset Song*. Firstly, he proposes the centrality to human life of the land and its cultivation. Delivered to us through a long tradition of folk culture, the notion of labouring the land is the closest to the original, and lost, golden age, of all the activities of civilisation. In Scotland the peasant stock are directly descended from the Old Pictish Folk, seen by Gibbon as the basic element in the Scottish inheritance, linked to the original hunters and food gatherers of the primitive age. There is an idealising process going on here, visible too in *Sunset Song* and clearly articulated in *Scottish Scene*. Gibbon argues that the land will be remembered, with the people who farm it, for millions of years to come, when humanity has triumphed over division and materialism. Yet rarely can we hold Gibbon to one definitive ideological statement. He concludes here that mankind's endless struggle to wrest harvest from the earth is his most noble activity, for all that Gibbon's diffusionist principles led him elsewhere, to attack servitude to the land for its demeaning cyclical drudgery. Indeed, towards the end of 'The Land', as he celebrates the end of winter and the release of animals into the fields, he suddenly changes mood. Inherent in his appreciation of the natural world is the reminder that the ultimate purpose of husbandry is to fatten the beasts for slaughter, and he concludes that humanity hides from its 'strange unthinking cruelties, the underpit of blood and suffering and intolerable horror on which the most innocent of us build our lives'.

Whatever the contradictions in his thinking, there is no doubting his regret that traditional community and its intimate connection with the land is coming to an end. The old way of life of the crofter and the small farmer is passing away as social changes – incomers working far larger farms, tractors and machinery replacing horses, battery farming – break the traditional cycle. *Sunset Song* documents this in both the Prelude and the Epilude, and in *Scottish Scene* Gibbon expresses his remorse with bitterness and deep-felt pessimism. What the Reverend Robert Colquohoun proclaims with a moving elegiac eloquence at the end of *Sunset Song*, Gibbon expresses throughout all his work as a social and economic disaster.

Gibbon and nationalism

Gibbon's attitude, in his work, to Scottish national identity is a matter of some controversy. Hugh MacDiarmid claimed that Gibbon, towards the end of his life, was becoming more and more committed to Scottish Nationalism and increasingly recognising his country's 'Renaissance'. However, Gibbon frequently speaks of nationalism, especially that of small countries, in scathing terms. In the essay 'Glasgow', in *Scottish Scene*, Gibbon expresses himself forcefully:

> What a curse to the earth are small nations! Latvia, Lithuania, Poland, Finland, San Salvador . . . The Irish Free State . . . an appalling number of disgusting little stretches of the globe, claimed, occupied and infected by groupings of babbling little morons . . . mangy little curs a-yap above their minute hoardings of shrivelled bones.

While Gibbon later modified this extreme position, it does reveal that his international socialism found little encouragement in the post-war Versailles settlement that carved up the European empires into independent small states, frequently with right-wing ruling élites. Gibbon conceives of Scotland as an entity only in terms of popular community. For him, Scottish history was an unmitigated sequence of vicious class exploitation from the arrival of the 'Kelts' onwards right down to the First World War. Insofar as he imagines any specifically Scottish future, it is as the local manifestation of the ideal anarcho-socialist haven for the remains of the Old Scots Folk. In *Cloud Howe*, nationalism is but another of the clouds that obscure the reality of the hills, to be eventually blown away with all other creeds.

A Scots Quair

Discussion of Gibbon's Scottish trilogy, *A Scots Quair* (1932–4), has tended to concentrate heavily on *Sunset Song*, the first and most popular of the novels. It is indeed an impressive artistic accomplishment and an enduringly popular novel, but the result has been to obscure Gibbon's purposes in the trilogy as a whole and to devalue his achievement in the other two novels, *Cloud Howe* and *Grey Granite* (1934). It may be of value to try to look at the trilogy here as a unified narrative and picture of traditional Scottish rural life and to avoid giving undue over-emphasis to the first section of the work. Full and informative treatments of *Sunset Song* and Gibbon's other work can be found elsewhere (see the bibliography for this section).

SUNSET SONG
Sunset Song's enduring appeal perhaps lies in its firm location within a Scottish cultural landscape. And it is a novel embracing many of the distinctive features of an on-going Scottish literary tradition. Firstly, there is the negotiation of language. Although Gibbon devises his own solution to

the problem of conveying a Scottish mode of expression to non-Scottish readers, the novel remains true to the integrity of the Scots language. (His linguistic note at the start of the novel makes this clear.) Secondly, there is a recognition of the place of the older oral folk tradition. Gibbon gives seminal significance to the story-telling pedigree of his novel, by using the oral mode through a variety of narrative voices, and by alluding to the ballad tradition through the novel's inclusion of story, anecdote and song. Thirdly, the community of Kinraddie is placed within a historical frame of reference and a particular pattern of Scottish history. Gibbon is concerned to portray Kinraddie as a typical rural community which has grown, over many generations, through the tumults of an often tragic and disruptive past. Fourthly, as in so many other Scottish novels, both before and since, there is a realisation of Kinraddie as a fictional community within the real locality of Scotland; Gibbon maintains a mutable border between the real and the imagined and draws much of his description and characterisation from actual experience. Finally, there is the dark strand of Scottish religion, in the form of Calvinist Presbyterianism, although a declining force, still portrayed as a warping and inhibiting element in community life.

Sunset Song, however, is more than just traditional in its intentions. The novel displays an innovative fictional treatment and it has status and relevance as a Modernist novel in its own time. If we are to regard *Sunset Song* as something more than a parochial story or a regional novel or indeed the limited product of a small national culture, we have to see it in terms of the significant literary movements of its time. And in order to do this properly, with full justice being done to Gibbon's purposes and achievement, we have to consider the novel in its full context as one of the elements in a larger literary work, *A Scots Quair*, published over three years (1932–4) and containing also the novels *Cloud Howe* and *Grey Granite*.

THE QUAIR

A first reading of the title, *A Scots Quair*, suggests a strongly traditional narrative. Indeed the title's origin lies in medieval Scots writing; King James I of Scotland's courtly, romantic poem is entitled *The Kingis Quair*, the King's Book. *A Scots Quair* implies 'a Scots Book'; but what does this mean? When Alasdair Gray was writing his great novel, *Lanark* (1981) in the 1960s and 70s, he conceived it as the Scottish Book, as the *Iliad* was the Greek Book, or *War and Peace* was the Russian Book. Can *A Scots Quair* be seen likewise as a great story of allegorical or symbolic significance for Scotland? Is, moreover, the title to be seen as a democratic statement; a book of the Scottish people, in the Scots language without the royal élitist associations of *The Kingis Quair*? In a sense, it is both. The content is Scottish and the language is an attempt to present Scots, in some form, to a wider readership. It has often been suggested that *A Scots Quair* should be seen as the symbolic story of Scotland, with Chris representing the nation itself, enduring the three major stages of Scotland's development, from prehistoric and peasant nation, through domination by church and war, to industrial revolution.

This sequential movement is broadly seen in the three novels, and its symbolic nature emerges when the trilogy is looked at as a whole. *Sunset Song* identifies Chris as an incomer in the rural community of Kinraddie; *Cloud Howe* takes her, as an incomer again, to the small weaving town of Segget; and *Grey Granite* takes her further into the industrial city of Duncairn. Only at the very end does she discover her roots, her first home again, in Echt. The move from countryside to burgh to city is clearly significant in symbolic terms. Chris moves through the typical social and historical environments of Scotland, so that her experience of each will evoke the development of a changing Scotland. In personal terms, Chris moves from her girlhood and marriage to the peasant Ewan, through motherhood and widowhood in *Sunset Song*, into a second marriage to a church minister, and widowhood in *Cloud Howe*, and, with the miscarriage of her second child, into a third marriage with the joiner Ake Ogilvie, without love or child and in ultimate isolation in *Grey Granite*. After the primary focus on Chris and her personal hopes in *Sunset Song*, the main focus of *Cloud Howe* is on the social and political hopes of Chris's husband Robert Colquohoun, with their final frustration and defeat. In *Grey Granite*, it moves to the development of Chris's son, Ewan, from a state of intellectual and emotional detachment to a strong political and social commitment that takes him away from his mother and her life. In all these novels, there is a close observation and analysis of the communities and their divisions, weaknesses and movement into economic decline.

Chronologically, the main period covered in *Sunset Song* is from 1911 to 1920; in *Cloud Howe* from 1920 to 1932; and in *Grey Granite* from 1932 to 1934, bringing the story of Chris up to the period of the novel's completion. So the events of *A Scots Quair* are not separated in time from the period of the writing. When Chris and Ewan part at the end of *Grey Granite*, it is a contemporary event, so the events and outcomes of *Sunset Song* are not of another world that is past, inhabiting some other time, but of the world that the readers are experiencing in their own lives, linked to the present by visible connections of the kind that link our own younger selves to the people we have become. *A Scots Quair* was a work of modern times, concerned with the contemporary world.

MODERNISM

The novel is indeed modern but is it 'Modernist'; breaking with the long established conventions of art, and breaking down the patterned structures which regulate the ordered and settled society?

The English poet Stephen Spender thought that modern art reflected awareness of an unprecedented modern situation in its form and idiom. From the first decade of the twentieth century, unprecedented developments created a new modernity, and the First World War accelerated and precipitated it into an age where art and literature were forced to seek new techniques, forms and voices to reflect changed social and cultural conditions. T. S. Eliot thought that literary Modernism was simply a way of controlling, ordering, and giving a shape and a significance to the futility and anarchy of contemporary history. If we go no further than this and apply it to the case of Lewis Grassic Gibbon, who was clearly oppressed by the futility and anarchy, not just of contemporary history, but of all history and civilisation, we might reasonably suppose the well-tried literary formulae of his predecessors would not content him. A conventionally structured novel tracing Chris's life in a chronological series of chapters would slip too easily into an existing genre of novels about fictional growth and development, success and failure, happiness and tragedy, against a realistic social backdrop. Such a novel could not make the case he wanted, against a corrupt and unjust social system. A conventional language would be a lubricant for the reader's responses rather than a stimulant, or even an abrasive. The language and structure of *Sunset Song* have usually been examined in terms of their undoubted traditional associations. But how do they also fulfil a Modernist criterion of stimulating and provoking thought?

LANGUAGE

Gibbon created a particular language for *Sunset Song*, a modification of English in a Scots idiom which conveys a strong Scottish traditional and rural atmosphere. He was aware, while writing the trilogy, that this could not be a final solution applicable to the town and city settings of the other novels. He was also aware of the experimental nature of what he was doing with language, a characteristic Modernist attitude, associated with the experimental approach of James Joyce in *Ulysses* (1922) and *Finnegan's Wake* (1939). Equally he was fully conversant with what Hugh MacDiarmid was attempting in poetry, in his synthesis of a new Scottish language out of dialect speech and the resources of the Scots Dictionary. His main criterion, however, was to evoke a voice that possessed a realism and authenticity compatible with reader's expectations. The balancing of linguistic requirements thus became very complex. There is a range of different local voices at work in *Sunset Song*. As *Cloud Howe* and *Grey Granite* develop, the community voice, the folk 'speak' of *Sunset Song*, virtually disappears in favour of different character voices (viewpoints of identifiable characters over and above Chris and young Ewan) and also anonymous individual voices (the spinner in *Cloud Howe* or the unemployed man in *Grey Granite*). The level of Scottishness also changes. The richness of the *Sunset Song* speech becomes more and more diluted, reflecting both change in Scottish speech over two decades of anglicisation and americanisation, and the difference between the countryside and small town and large cosmopolitan cities. Chris herself becomes more English in her narrative viewpoint and inner thoughts, and is increasingly aware of this change in herself. For the reader there is a constant challenge – who is speaking now? Sometimes Gibbon will explicitly identify the speaker; at other times it must be deduced from internal evidence. Thus the language remains a positive and active element in the fiction, not merely a vehicle carrying the content to the reader. Indeed, rather than a passive voice, the language is significant for its very force, expressed more and more in the later novels, articulating Gibbon's own feelings of anger, hatred, scorn, disgust. Such an abrasive idiom can have the effect of forcing the supposed speaker aside and bringing the author's own voice to the fore. In this way, the general objectivity of *Sunset Song* gives way to a more subjective style, which has been criticised, but yet represents a Modernist flouting of traditional conventions such as the imperatives of neutrality and detachment of authorial tone.

STRUCTURE

The continuity of pattern through the three parts of the trilogy is one of Gibbon's greatest achievements in the novel. The structural pattern of *Sunset Song* begins with a historical and descriptive sketch of Kinraddie. This is followed by four sections in which Chris Guthrie, seeking refuge at the Standing Stones above her home from recent dramatic events, recalls the action that has intervened. The concluding section describes the final state of Kinraddie, looking ahead to the future. The structure works well for *Sunset Song*, although, within the framework of Chris's memory, many of the events are not, in fact, derived from her own direct observation but belong to the community consciousness. The pattern is generally repeated for *Cloud Howe* and *Grey Granite*. Chris returns at periodic intervals to a removed spot overlooking the town or the city: in *Cloud Howe*, it is the Kaimes, a ruined Dark Age fortification on a hill above Segget; in *Grey Granite*, it is the Windmill Brae, a steep flight of steps going up from the city centre with a bend in the middle and a safety mirror where Chris stops to look down on the city and to observe herself in the reflection. Again there is a supposed framework of recollection, mediated through Chris's memory of intervening events, but now even less derived from the central heroine and increasingly communicated through external voices and accounts. The structure therefore, which has an element of artificiality in *Sunset Song*, becomes more deliberately unrealistic, more of an artifice than a natural communication. Although the episodes of Chris's return to these places are significant, like her first morning in Segget, or her first outing after her miscarriage or the morning of her third marriage, the effect is to create a fragmentation of Chris's experience and to suggest a movement from crisis to crisis in a specifically Modernist manner.

Other structural elements vary in the novels. *Sunset Song* has a Prelude and an Epilude; *Cloud Howe* has only a Proem (as Prelude), since Segget does have a history to be recorded; yet *Grey Granite* has neither Prelude nor Epilude, since, for Gibbon, the industrial city of Duncairn has no history and is a rootless and incoherent place. While Gibbon's thinking here seems tendentious and prejudiced, since any inhabited place, whether parish, burgh or city, has its history, there is certainly a heavily symbolic view of the superiority of the traditional locality over the modern. The titles that Gibbon gives his novel sections reveal a similar explicit symbolic view of the development. In *Sunset Song* the use of the stages of the farming year (Ploughing, Drilling, Seed-time and Harvest) symbolises the stages in Chris's emotional and sexual development (although it is arguable whether the trend of events in Chris's life in Kinraddie is towards ripeness and fulfilment since she loses her husband, Ewan, and her other lover, Long Rob of the Mill, to the war). *Cloud Howe* repeats the strategy, utilising the names of cloud formations (Cirrus, Cumulus, Stratus and Nimbus) suggesting a movement from calm to storm. In *Grey Granite*, the use of the names of crystalline formations within granite (Epidote, Sphene, Apatite and Zircon) reveal an emphasis on the movement of Ewan towards a hardened politicised nature and Chris to a 'stony' alienation. His symbolism may seem heavy and less humanised than in the two previous novels, but this is arguably because his intention is to emphasise the increasing disconnection between the land and humanity, which has turned from it.

VIOLENCE AND HORROR

Thus both in language and structure, *A Scots Quair* has an experimental quality, deliberately so, since it is not part of Gibbon's purpose to comfort or lull the reader with a fluent development and smooth expression. Allied to this deliberate intention to disrupt and discomfort, there is a clear purpose on Gibbon's part to shock and disturb. The increasingly frequent depiction of cruelty, violence and suffering reveals Gibbon's anti-romanticism and his commitment to a social realism. We have already noted Gibbon's vision of the horror beneath the rural way of life in 'The Land'. In *Sunset Song* the dark underside of life is revealed in episodes such as the death of John Guthrie's horse Nell, the suicide of Jean Guthrie and her poisoning of the twins, the sexual rampage of Andy the daftie, the marital rape of Chris by her brutalised husband Ewan Tavendale, and old Pootie's torturing of his donkey with a red-hot poker. This portrayal is intensified in the two following novels – a fascination with corporeality and mortality (the lingering death of another horse, the slaughter of a pig and a horrific practical joke with its corpse, the gnawing of a baby by rats), the rape of the Chris's housemaid Else Queen, a mounted police charge on a peaceful demonstration, the beating and sexual abuse of young Ewan by the police – all used by Gibbon to exemplify his black vision of centuries of cruelty against the poor and oppressed. Not the least part of this vision is Gibbon's creation of an all-pervading atmosphere of vindictive lying and malicious gossip in Kinraddie and Segget, which, particularly in *Cloud Howe*, will surround and sicken Chris. In keeping with the novel's realism, moreover, are Gibbon's depictions of human behaviour, particularly in his frankness on sexual matters in the trilogy, more circumspect in its language than it would be today, but strong for the early 1930s. It is no wonder that some reacted to the novels of the trilogy with outrage. To Scotland and the Mearns at the time, it seemed that Leslie Mitchell was traducing his own people and his own homeland. Today we can see the trilogy as a signal of the growing tendency, in the writing of the time, towards greater frankness, uncomforting realism and a rejection of bourgeois and genteel conventions and inhibitions.

ALIENATION AND CHRIS GUTHRIE

One of the great thematic preoccupations of Modernist writing and art is that of the alienation of the individual from society and its values. In *Sunset Song*, Chris feels herself alienated at certain moments and in situations of stress from those close to her – father, husband, community, and indeed the whole system of government and civilisation. Perceived in the context of *Sunset Song* alone, this alienation might be seen as her response to pressures, a kind of deliberate mental detachment, in the face of difficult situations of change. However, over the whole sweep of *A Scots Quair*, it appears as more than that; alienation becomes in fact the general drift of Chris's life. The sudden estrangement from a lustful paralysed father and a degraded brutal husband is followed in *Cloud Howe* by a progressive distancing from the hopes and aims of her second husband Robert and his passive, unquestioning faith following his political failure; and in *Grey Granite* by an alienation from all beliefs, ideals or philosophies and from personal ties, including love and men's desire. As her third husband leaves her, Ake Ogilvie thinks: 'Ay, a strange quean, yon. And not for him. He'd thought that glimmer in her eyes a fire that he himself could blow to a flame; and instead 'twas no more than the shine of a stone.' At the end of *Grey Granite*, Chris is beyond all human feeling, utterly isolated increasingly by choice more than by events. The fragmentation of her life, the successive losses of all family, all friends, all sources of love, all commitments and responsibilities, make her finally that most typical of modern myths – the Outsider.

SOCIETY AND ALIENATION

In modern literature, it is, of course, the city, that featureless, artificial community, that is the source of individual alienation, and the invented city of Duncairn certainly plays its part in Chris's ultimate exclusion from life. Like Segget, Duncairn is supposed to be in the Mearns, as Gibbon remarks in a cautionary note to *Grey Granite*, 'the city which the inhabitants of the Mearns (not foreseeing my requirements in completing my trilogy) have hitherto failed to build'. Chris's destiny is worked out within the compass of a few square miles, and her alienation is accomplished by the threefold influences of countryside, burgh and city, each in its own way inhospitable and inhumane. In particular, despite its placing in supposed home-territory for Chris and Ewan and despite its superficial resemblance to other Scottish cities that might evoke empathy, Duncairn, the 'stronghold of stones', is to be seen as the ultimate alienating environment of Modernist writing. An analogy may be made between the implications of the name 'Duncairn' and those of Hugh MacDiarmid's mighty poem of 1934, 'On a Raised Beach', with its bleakly eloquent statement of the utter apartness of stones. For Gibbon, the city is all the more alienating since he viewed any organised human community as hostile. Yet his view of Duncairn (and also of Kinraddie and Segget) does work within Raymond Williams's classic Modernist thesis about the city or metropolis.

Firstly, Gibbon presents the theme of the modern city as a crowd of strangers. For Chris this is true of all three communities to different degrees. In Kinraddie, there are a significant number of incomers: Chris herself is an incomer; the community spirit only manifests itself at intervals; and the trend of the action is to deprive her of all those close to her. In Segget, Chris is alienated from the community by her position as minister's wife and her reluctance to involve herself in the usual church activities. She is shown to have few friends, and as in Kinraddie, she is the target of cruel and malicious gossip. In Duncairn, of course, her position is like that of many others – not belonging, rootless, living in a place that is not a home, on the poverty line, remote from those around her except for a very few, whom characteristically she loses. The second of the themes identified by Williams is the city's isolation of the individual, who is lonely even in a crowd. Chris, as we have seen, has few close friends during her life, all of whom are taken away from her and it seems to be part of Gibbon's major purpose to make her appear excessively isolated. Williams's third theme is that of the city encouraging unrest and crime. The first is more relevant in Gibbon than the second. The unrest that develops as a major theme through the three novels is labour unrest; discontent with working conditions, angry at unemployment, retaliating with demonstrations and strikes, of which the greatest is the 1926 General Strike in *Cloud Howe*. Yet, aside from this social violence, there is, as we have seen, an underlying current of violence and cruelty on a personal, family and community level that runs through the novels, giving the lie to any comforting illusion that these communities are settled, happy and spiritually healthy.

The fourth and final theme of urban alienation in the novels is the tendency away from the city in a quest for peace or innocence or spiritual health. We see this continually at work in Chris, and at times in young Ewan, in their need to get away to quiet places, mainly in the country. For Chris, there are the Standing Stones, the Kaimes, the Windmill Brae, a visit back to Echt, her birthplace, and indeed her final retreat to her roots, buying the farm of her birth, Cairndhu (the 'black heap of stones'), and settling there. Finally and supremely, we see her mystical withdrawal from all worldly concerns and her union with the natural environment on the top of the Barmekin hill above her birthplace, becoming one with the stones around her. Critics disagree as to the nature of Gibbon's conclusion. Some interpret the ending as marking Chris's final realisation of her two great principles of existence, change and death; others read the ending as a transcendence of reality, with Chris entering into a kind of mythical one-ness with all the natural universe. Whichever reading is taken, it is fair to say that Gibbon's ideology here meets, once more, with those of Neil Gunn and the Scottish Renaissance writers.

CHRIS GUTHRIE

Gibbon, in his portrayal of Chris and other female characters, brings to bear a new and Modernist perception of the condition of women in society and presents them with new roles and status. In Chris Guthrie he created a strong female protagonist. Thea Mayven in *Stained Radiance* (1930), the first of these, is a fumbling attempt; Domina Riddoch of *The Thirteenth Disciple* (1931) and the eponymous heroine of *Gay Hunter* (1934) (these three written under his real name of Leslie Mitchell) are others, perhaps more successful. Chris Guthrie is the supreme example. There are so many positive things to be said about Chris that, to some extent, analysis of the *Quair*, especially *Sunset Song*, has been centred on the study of narrative viewpoint and her as heroine. The success of Gibbon in representing her maturing thoughts and feelings, her inner strength, especially in *Sunset Song*, in the face of so much adversity and loss; her perceptiveness and cool detachment that mark her as the intellectual and spiritual centre of the trilogy – all these positive aspects and more have been scrutinised in criticism. Less attention has been paid to one or two more questionable aspects of Chris – for example, that she never seeks to rise above the position in which she finds herself: she does not go to college; she does not take any further steps to fit herself for independent living in the society of her time; she does not plan ahead or launch herself into any positive self-redeeming action, other than marriage or physical work. She certainly cannot be seen as the New Woman in action. In a way, Chris, with her real qualities of intelligence and perceptiveness, is a disappointment, falling short of her possibilities, especially since, in each novel, she is set against other women or girls who seem to be more committed to the improvement of society. In *Sunset Song*, there is Marget Strachan, who is to be a doctor, and Maggie Jean Gordon, who organises the farm-workers' union in Kinraddie; and in *Cloud Howe* and *Gray Granite* the radical women school-teachers. It is through Chris – three times married – and many other women, many other novels, that Gibbon examines women in marriage; although it is women other than Chris who seek to find new social roles, who wish to inform about contraception and healthy sexual attitudes (in the manner of one of Gibbon's earlier idealised fictional women, Domina Riddoch, in *The Thirteenth Disciple*). Such involvement is not to be Chris's role; she stands on the sidelines, detached and often sardonic.

It seems that, instead, Chris's role is to remain passive – to observe, to reflect, to endure all kinds of displacement: environmental displacement from one location to another; class displacement from rural working class to professional middle class to urban lower middle class; role displacement from schoolgirl to housewife, from wife and mother to widow, from farmer to lady of leisure to boarding-house keeper. Primarily her business in the novels is symbolic, representative of the land with which she identifies and is identified throughout.

SYMBOL AND MYTH

Symbolism is a major feature of Modernism, more than in any previous age; with Modernism, the literary boundaries between realism, symbolism and allegory began to shift and blur. This is true throughout *A Scots Quair*. In *Sunset Song*, a realistic narrative carries the diffusionist myth of the decline of humanity from a primeval golden age through the warping influence of civilisation, and occasional episodes transgress the realistic mode into the mythical or archetypal. *Cloud Howe* and *Grey Granite* continue this technique. Chris and young Ewan are made to carry on the associations of the original golden age hunters and the old Pictish stock. They both have an unashamed attitude to their own naked bodies, Ewan has an interest in the flints of the old hunters, and their physical appearance corresponds with the idealised vision that Gibbon had of the ancient people. Another potent myth to be seen in the *Quair* is one that T. S. Eliot exploited in *The Waste Land*, the myth of the fertile land rendered sterile and unfruitful. Kinraddie becomes a waste land in a literal sense after the First World War; but in another symbolic sense, it becomes a waste land after the failure of a vital vegetation ritual. The Corn King and Spring Queen figures of John and Jean Guthrie fail in their appointed roles of guarding the fertility of the land; John Guthrie maimed by the unnatural religion he has adopted, and Jean Guthrie sacrificing herself as a result of its demands. Their natural successors, Ewan and Chris Tavendale also fail, especially in the case of Ewan, who removes himself from the land and loses his natural authority. The land falls into spiritual sterility. This myth is worked out in other Scottish fiction of the time, in different ways, by writers like Neil Gunn and Naomi Mitchison.

The major political symbolism developed is that of the hero who comes to lead the slave masses in revolt against their cruel oppressors. For Gibbon, the figures of Spartacus and, to a lesser extent, William Wallace are potent mythical figures, symbols for the leader who must come to bring the necessary socialist revolution. Disappointed in his hope that Christ might be such a leader, Robert Colquohoun calls in his final sermon for a 'stark sure creed' that will cut like a knife through the doubt and disease of society. The main political theme of *Grey Granite* is the transformation of young Ewan Tavendale from symbolic golden age hunter, superior to and detached from his surroundings, into the committed revolutionary leader, a potential Spartacus – in reality, an agitator and worker for the Communist Party, a role that separates him from his mother, Chris. Had Gibbon lived beyond 1935, it is debatable whether he could have sustained this belief and vision. It is a spiritual and political myth rooted in the conditions of his own times.

There is a powerful symbolic movement through *A Scots Quair*. Both Chris

596

and young Ewan emerge from the sunset of Kinraddie, out of tradition and a dying way of life into the modern world. In *Cloud Howe*, the valley of the mists, different political solutions are examined and found wanting; socialism, nationalism, fascism, Christianity. All are found to be merely clouds that pass over the immutable, stark mountain tops, the grey granite that is found in people like Chris and Ewan. In *Gray Granite*, the harsh reality must be faced and a new creed found to cure a sick society, applied by a solid, hardy leader. This is what Ewan finds and follows. For Chris, Ewan's solution is only another illusion. Only change is constant, and what she finds, like Meursault later in Camus's *L'Étranger* (1942) is a kind of comfort in the revelation of the insignificance of all human endeavour and the indifference of the universe.

A Scots Quair is a central product of the Scottish Renaissance, a fiction inspired by traditional elements and executed in the spirit of the modern age. Gibbon is totally at one with MacDiarmid, Gunn, Soutar and others in seeing how Scottish literature needed to join the contemporary world and reflect the spirit of a small nation in an international cultural context. As the greatest achievement of a tragically unfulfilled writer, it remains a classic of twentieth-century Scottish fiction.

Gibbon's beliefs and his other writings

Gibbon died aged thirty-four, and virtually all his work was published between September 1930 and November 1934. These four years covered an output of eleven novels, two books of short stories, three books of anthropology and exploration and (with MacDiarmid) a book of essays and short stories. It was Mitchell/Gibbon's unhappy and confused child-hood, upbringing and adolescence which resulted in his complex love-hate reaction to his native country and its rural cultures. Three powerful Mitchell novels, *Stained Radiance* (1930), *The Thirteenth Disciple* (1931), and the angriest of all, *Image and Superscription* (1933) contain a great deal of disguised, yet recognisable and painful, autobiography which testifies to the ambivalence of Gibbon's attitude towards his native country and the depth of his resentment of what he saw as crippling creeds. And the other short stories, essays, and fiction other than *A Scots Quair* bear further evidence to the antagonisms in Gibbon's mind. As he reacted against his upbringing, four 'positive' creeds emerged and can be seen throughout his writing; diffusionism, communism, Christianity and what can roughly be termed 'magic'. But typically of Gibbon/Mitchell, these 'positive', if often mutually inconsistent, reactions to life all too frequently give way to a negative and dark side which is sceptical of all such aspirations.

DIFFUSIONISM

As discussed above, the solution Gibbon committed himself to most fully was diffusionism. Some of his finest writing stems directly from it, but significantly this is to be found not in novels so much as essays like 'The Land' and 'The Antique Scene'. The most diffusionist novels, *Three Go Back* (1932), *The Lost Trumpet* (1932) and *Gay Hunter* (1934) are arguably his weakest and least imaginatively convincing works, with their bizarre time travel, implausibility of situation and their excessive theorising. Gibbon's diffusionism is most successful, as in *Sunset Song* or *Spartacus*, when it is transformed into a haunting substratum of poetic conception, never, as in these propaganda novels, appearing as clots of argument and lecture, or clumsy and improbable symbolic action. But in the essays diffusionism can become poetry. 'The Antique Scene' is a useful base for study of Gibbon. Here is his view of Scottish history; industrial revolution and modern Scottish social history are anathema to him, but he supplies pre-history with poetic description, and sets forth a clear outline of diffusionist belief. In the essay, he renders argument into a fierce invective poetry, transforming himself from social theorist to passionate representative of the people, arguing and evoking what Spartacus and Chris Guthrie feel in their bones:

I like to remember I am of peasant rearing and peasant stock . . . I feel of a strange and antique age in the company and converse of my adult peers – like an adult himself listening to the bright sayings and laughter of callow boys . . . while I, a good Venriconian Pict, harken from the shade of my sun circle and look away bored, in pride of possession at my terraced crops.

Already, amidst the poetry, are the inconsistencies. Gibbon boasts of a farming ancestry that makes him superior, when elsewhere he called it 'a beastly life'. But, honest as Gibbon in the end always is, he admits the fact in the essay; 'for once I had a very bitter detestation for all this life of the land and the folk upon it. My view was that of my distant cousin, Mr Leslie Mitchell . . .' How altered is his view of land-work now! ('The Antique Scene'):

This is our power, this the wonder of humankind, our one great victory . . . Three million years hence our descendants out on some tremendous furrowing of the Galaxy, with the Great Bear yoked to the Plough . . . will remember this little planet, if at all, for the men who conquered the land and wrung sustenance from it . . . Nothing else at all may endure in those overhuman memories; I do not think there is anything else I want to endure.

COMMUNISM

His other 'creed of the head' was communism, although he was always sceptical about commitment to any one doctrine. Storman the communist is satirised in *Stained Radiance*; while Ewen and Trease in *Grey Granite* are out to use the movement as means to anarchistic ends. Gibbon's friends seemed confused as to his allegiance, James Barke saying that he was a communist before his death, MacDiarmid claiming that he had become an out-and-out Scottish Republican. What is certain is that he cared passionately about a revolution in the state of the world's poor. Like Malcom Maudsley in *The Thirteenth Disciple*, he could rage at political movements and wash his hands of his commitment to them because of their sloth or tendency to pointless dream. The essay 'Glasgow', in its picture of the speakers on Glasgow Green, shows this, with only the communist speaker (with no audience) allowed dignified comment. All others are impatiently dismissed for their evasion of commitment to revolt.

If the diffusionist novels are too often flat and ratiocinative, the political essays and novels are flawed because Gibbon's emotion cannot be controlled. 'Glasgow' has great strengths, but its most vivid and feeling passages are its weakest, intellectually and argumentatively. Gunn criticised Gibbon's welcoming of a 'Chinese army of occupation' to Scotland as demonstrably irrelevant to the problems of Scottish economy, far less the problems of the 150,000 of the slums of Glasgow whose plight Gibbon felt so deeply. The hysteria comes in as his rage mounts and finds no immediate outlet: For example, on 'Scottish Culture' which he hears 'ad nauseam':

> the patter is as intimate on my tongue as on theirs. And relevant to the fate and being of those hundred-and-fifty thousand it is not more than the chatter and scratch of a band of apes, seated in a pit on a midden of corpses.

Presumably then the song-culture and beautiful poetry he employs at Chris's wedding in *Sunset Song* is also as irrelevant, as is his discussion of culture in 'Literary Lights'. But of course in a different mood Gibbon would not argue thus. Again, as we have seen, there is anger and dismissal in his remarks on small nations, in the same essay.

In this abrasive mood, police are seen in *The Thirteenth Disciple* as 'rat-brained clowns', servicemen 'atavistic little perverts', scholars 'apeptic pedants in the British Museum Reading Room' whom he wishes he had 'at bayonet practice'. 'Clownish' becomes the adjective for anything from the Norsemen to the councillors of *Grey Granite*, till one sees that, at his worst in

599

his politically impatient moods, the entire world is 'clownish' and insufferable to him. Whenever political argument enters Gibbon's fiction, unless it is treated with irony (as with Chae's socialism or Rob's reading of Ingersoll, the 'watchmaker' in *Sunset Song*, as with fascism and nationalism and socialism in *Cloud Howe*), it rarely succeeds. And *The Thirteenth Disciple*, the Mitchell novel with the greatest amount of political (and autobiographical) involvement, functions as a novel more successfully because the pseudo-editor looks at Malcom Maudsley's political career with a certain ironic mockery.

RELIGION

At first sight it appears redundant to examine Gibbon's religious beliefs, since as diffusionist and revolutionary, he abandoned them on principle. But Christianity played two vital roles in his work; first, as in James Joyce's 'damned Jesuit strain', as provider of imagery and poetry retrieved from a world in which Gibbon grew up. His work is littered with reference to the Bible and Christian lore, and he uses the image of Christ's crucifixion alongside the image of the trapped and maimed soldier on barbed wire as his two images of man's horrific inhumanity to man. And secondly, even more inconsistently, it evokes the notion of belief, with a commitment to respect and recognise the supernatural hand of Christ in action.

The first aspect is easily and quickly understood from a reading of his early poetry ('Dust'; 'I see the Christ, an outcast, stand forlorn / A dream, a tale, a wonderment of tears') and short stories like 'Greenden' and 'Forsaken'. The first tale takes the song of Calvary, 'There is a Green Hill', as an ambiguous but possibly satirical indication that the girl who sacrifices her reason and her life for her husband's health has done so on account of an unhealthy dream. The second story brings Christ himself to Duncairn (city of *Grey Granite*) to find that his former disciples have become realists and communists who forsake him. It should be noticed though, that the story presents a further problem – for it argues the *existence* of Christ. It's a realistic fable, with kitchen-sink surroundings and industrial unrest, and its implication is clear: that Christ is or was good incarnate, but that so fallen is this world that his dream will no longer be achieved by his methods. Christ was to Gibbon the outstanding martyr, chief of a line from Spartacus to Wallace and, in *Sunset Song* and *Cloud Howe*, Long Rob and Robert Colquhoun. It's even more important to realise that at times Gibbon used Christ and Christian imagery as a meaningful thematic framework. 'For Ten's Sake' presents – on Easter Day – an old geologist obsessed with ideas of revenge on the murderers of his son in Mevr, 'Hell-Gate of the East', city of prostitutes and thieves, at the crossroads of the Asian caravans. Gibbon vividly describes the old man's delight when he realises that earthquake will destroy the city shortly. But amidst his unholy joy, in the street of Ten, the foulest of places in Mevr, a phrase increasingly haunts him. In his mind 'an unknown voice' starts counting the episodes of courage which occur as the earthquake begins. The words are taken from the Bible: 'Peradventure there be fifty righteous men within the city. Wilt thou also destroy and not spare the place for the fifty righteous men that are therein . . . And He said, "I will not destroy it for ten's sake." ' The old man collapses, his son's killers save him, and he learns that his son has been wicked. Desperately he counts, and finds nine righteous men; then at the eleventh hour, he finds his tenth, a shadow in the corner beyond the thieves and murderers: 'he saw stand for a moment One whom he had never known, One with bleeding hands and feet and hidden face.' The vision of Christ crucified brings redemption to the old man and to the city. Beyond this, 'And the Cock Crew' relies on its characters' identification with St Peter, Simon and Judas, and *Spartacus* ends with Kleon the Greek having a vision of Christ 100 years before he is born. What this shows is not just inconsistent with the 'scientist's' diffusionist diagnosis and the communist cure; it shows us Gibbon's need for emotionally and aesthetically satisfying myth and poetry, not to be found in the conclusions of the head, but in the quests of the heart.

MAGIC

Time and again, Gibbon's tales rely on magic to achieve their deepest effects. A good example is in the short story 'Daybreak'; the Scottish heroine, with the symbolic name of Dawn, is dying in Egypt at the story's end but at the eleventh hour, the wind changes into the Delta wind, 'a green wind'. It brings, even to the narrator who has never been in Scotland, the never-before-experienced smell of heather – with objective corroboration from Dawn's husband. ' "My God!" he whispered. "Did you smell it? It was *heather!*" ' And the narrator *sees* the purple slopes of a Scottish valley. Under the alibi of emotional stress, Gibbon will always bring in magic.

The Thirteenth Disciple evokes Malcom's death-vision of the Golden City of the Mayas, and of human hope, just as on the other side of the world his wife gives birth to a son; and *Spartacus* too has its magical ending. Gibbon needed such episodes to achieve a deeper purpose than that which diffusionism or reason could provide. This is the 'tradition and magic' which Gunn so admired in his work, and lies behind *Stained Radiance, The Thirteenth Disciple* and the angriest of his disguised autobiographies, *Image and Superscription*, much finer novels than the diffusionist-dominated three. They anticipate the themes and situations of his best work, although it's obvious in the changes of style, narrator and tone (from irony to lyric enthusiasm) that Gibbon is still searching for a coherent voice. In each, there is a character or there are characters who stand very close to Mitchell's own history and attitude, tormented by a warping religious background and enthused by diffusionism – but not to the point of being taken over by it. Rather, these surrogates of Gibbon follow and hunger for a dream, a vision of something beyond golden age man or theory. For example, Malcom Maudsley all his life has explored 'beyond the Walls' even from his first pages of experience, when we see him as a sobbing child clutching a stone with which to shatter the horizon. Found at night, weary and dirty amidst the moors, 'the stone was still clutched to his chest and the conviction firm in his heart that beyond the next scaur, the next stretch of gorse, an incredible adventure awaited him'. Malcom's beginning prefigures his end. He dies in Yucatan pursuing the Golden City of this dream of magic. More important than diffusionism, the idea of quest dominates these novels, and the quest is for adventure, magic and love, in terms that are religious rather than scientific.

There is no more confusing – and frequently used – term than 'God' in Gibbon's work. He uses it to denote the false dreams Man must fight, as in Ewan's and Chris's war of Freedom against God, described by Ewan in the closing pages of *Grey Granite*, or in a totally different sense in the closing pages of *Spartacus* when the gladiator-leader, rising to height of greatness, finds 'a God' within him. In this second sense we are using the term as the mysterious force of 'Daybreak', which is neither the theology of a Robert Colquohoun or the Godlessness of Chris Guthrie, but the force which drives the instinctive Ewan or Malcom or Spartacus.

For all these hopeful creeds, Gibbon's writing moves finally towards a vision of despair. In *The Thirteenth Disciple* Domina Riddoch, the diffusionist heroine, speaks for Gibbon when she whispers yearningly, 'I'm God's man, Malcom, if you can find him for me.' Like Domina, Gibbon is bleakly honest. Beyond his four positive, if confused, ideals lies an opposing scepticism. Against the dogmatic and loving seeker-warrior is placed the doubter, who questions every dream. A moment of realisation is in the essay 'The Land', when the full depth of Gibbon's horror of existence suddenly reveals itself. Celebrating the end of winter and the release of the cattle from the byres, vividly he conveys their delight. Humorously he describes their happy mooing, their racing a grocer's cart the length of the field. Then, with no warning:

> they abandoned playfulness and took to grazing, remembering their
> mission was to provide fat carcasses for the slaughtershed . . . We balk

from such notions, in Spring especially, in especial as the evening comes with that fresh smell all about it, impregnating it, the kind of evening that has growth and youngness and kindliness in its essence – balk from the thought of our strange unthinking cruelties, the underpit of blood and suffering and intolerable horror on which the most innocent of us build our lives . . . The Horror is beyond personalism, very old and strange and terrible. Even those hunters all those millennia ago were eaters of flesh.

Critics reproved his indulgence in scenes of sadism and violence, but perhaps what this morbid preoccupation reveals is not sado-masochistic self-indulgence so much as a horrified fascination which draws him to the possibility that it may be the random, pointless norm of a pointless universe.

'Clay', 'Smeddum' and 'Greenden'

In the end Gibbon's beliefs are often at odds with each other, and confront one another with a final ironic scepticism. The real creative tension lies somewhere between the extreme poles and produces his finest work, which successfully embodies a dual vision, a presentation of the riddle of existence which permits a response of hope or despair.

'Clay', the story of Rob Galt, a decent Mearns crofter, is told by 'the speak', and much of *Sunset Song* is here in embryo – the father's servitude to the land, his daughter Rachel's wish to go to college, the hardship of the mother, the place of the croft and its people in history. But Galt is no Guthrie, loved as he is by Rachel, and 'a fine, frank childe . . . kindness itself'. Rob has asserted his independence by breaking from being foreman with his father and buying the croft of Pittaulds (the name suggesting ancient Pictish agriculture). But a 'queer-like' change comes over him and Galt becomes short-tempered towards his family and obsessive about his farm work. Cleverly Gibbon transposes the language of sexual and family love from Galt's relations with his family to his relations with the land – fields are 'women you'd to prig and pat afore they'd come on', or 'bitches', or 'on the sulk', and he caresses the soil, running it through his fingers. He's not cruel like Guthrie, but his wife, now terminally ill, and daughter, disappointed in her hopes of college because of his greed for the land, now mean hardly anything to him. The story can be read, so far, as Galt's pursuit of an obsession. But what emerges is eerie and deliberately open to supernatural interpretation. Galt begins to take in moorland, 'wild and unfed since the Flood', as locals tell him. But he sees it otherwise: 'Maybe, but they're queer-like, those braes, as though some childe had shored them tight up.' In heaving out a great root (the roots of his race?) he finds an earth-house, with the bones of a man of the antique time, and his flints and implements for tilling the soil. Rob also finds his own death. Hauntingly suggested is the notion that with Rob's vision of his ancestors a wheel has come full circle. He has linked up with his ancestors, and something greater than he has been completed. Unlike the ending of 'The Land', there is no explicit praise or blame for the generations who farmed, but an open question, asked by Rachel before she leaves the life of the land:

> And she thought of the men who had made these rigs and the windy days of their toil and years . . . was it good, was it bad? What power had that been that woke once on this brae and was gone at last from the parks of Pittaulds?

The rhythms of the close suggest, as in Chris Guthrie's end, a rule of time and Earth in which Man has little place, since whins and broom; wild, manless growths, triumph, and humanity are Earth's 'hungry bairns in her hungry breast where sleep and death are one'. But the story permits different levels of interpretation: Galt as a warped good man and farming as corrupting; or Galt as somehow noble with an ancient dream, fulfilled at the cost of family, but disturbingly epic; or finally Galt and farming as an intrusion on a nature which does not need humanity.

'Smeddum' seems at first uncomplicated humour, with its 'earth-mother' Meg Menzies as a force of nature, uncomplicated in her independence and vigour. But there are deeper considerations. Meg is the land, resilient as nature – 'Day blinked, and Meg did the same.' Her children (nine) 'couldn't but live' given her way of bringing them up by the scruff of the neck. But, like Chris in relation to her son Ewan, she is the past to her daughter Kathie, trapped in her obligations and the land for all she talks of Smeddum and freedom. Thus Kathie is Meg herself, but going on to become the new age, like Ewan, enriched by identity with the past, but accepting no necessary obligation to it.

Lack of this saving sense of self is the theme of 'Greenden', the most difficult of Gibbon's stories. The story has several levels of interpretation. This first is that it is a story of self-sacrifice, with the wife Ellen Simpson re-enacting Christ's sacrifice. Gibbon's skill in weaving the hymn together with the actual green hills of the Cairngorms, which Ellen sees through her restricting trees, is masterly; as is his ability to suggest that we may need to reverse the parable and see her sacrifice as unnecessary, as 'the distortion of Innocence by Civilisation' as Young puts it. Her husband survives in the rank growth of modern farming and the gossiping Murdochs, growing, vampire-like, 'thicker and bigger' where she is thinner, till her lonely spark of sensitivity is quenched by Murdoch's building his new barn across her life-line view of the hills. Gibbon keeps his distance through the folk-narrator, so that no single message comes through. The suffocating woods, with their beastlike presence, become, in one sense, the projection of Ellen's sense of the malice and gossip about her. Her enigmatic 'God died, but I needn't, He saved him, not I' can be taken as not merely the ramblings of a crazed woman, but as a dim realisation that she must not follow her Christian sense of duty to a self-destructive conclusion. In the end, though, the tale is confused; Gibbon puts one further and disruptive element into his story. The den is haunted by a padding beast which even Grocer Webster senses, a presence which is not merely Ellen's projection, but the ghost of the former owner, Old Grant, whispering in the uncanny stillness of the breathless and unclean place. Even the narrator feels the trees threatening and the broom whispering and the 'beast with quiet breath'. And so another reading can see an ancient evil breathing through the den woods.

'Greenden', then, is powerful – but confused, with just too many perspectives and possible interpretations. At the back of the tale is a sense of waste, of human effort unavailing in the face of the horror as in the last of these Mearns tales, 'Sim'. Sim Wilson has only enough vision to go from one shallow dream to another; golden age man gone wrong in a world which can give him none of the rewards of the ancient life. His repeated cry is the cry of sceptical Gibbon: 'Show me a thing that is worth my chave (toil) and I'll work you all off the face of the earth!' The end and reason for toil is never shown – unlike Rob Galt, Sim is not even given a private view.

There are two volumes of short stories which go far beyond Scotland – *Calends of Cairo* (1931) and *Persian Dawns, Egyptian Nights* (1932). These stem from his years in Egypt, and purport to be stories told by Colonel Anton Saloney, a White Russian dragoman. While critics have found these excessively romantic, over-exotic and mannered, there are amongst them some powerful stories like 'Daybreak' and 'For Ten's Sake' which exemplify Mitchell/Gibbon's hatred of Calvinism and his supernatural ambiguities.

Spartacus

Gibbon's great achievement of his last years was *Spartacus*. Here, all his elements are richly interwoven; and here, for once, his affirmative view of life almost triumphs over his sense of its underlying horror. The diffusionist background is subdued and ironically presented. A burning but controlled political anger makes the novel an allegory on modern inhumanity, while there is an active use of Christian symbol and the figure of Christ, with a sense of Man's traditional quest for a magical and transforming vision of life. But there is more; for so distanced is Gibbon from his creation that the sardonic and doubting vision is there too, in Kleon, the Greek intellectual, a permanent reminder of 'the Horror' with his castrated body and warped, coldly-amused mind.

If *Sunset Song* has its 'speak', *Spartacus* has its terse, detached almost inhuman narrator, who has seen legends born and die; who, the sardonic rhythm and tone implies, has no illusions left. Protagonists are reduced to dry motifs. Kleon, 'to whom life was a game'; Castus, 'who loved Spartacus'; Gershom ben Samballat, 'who loathed Gentiles'; Titus, always madly remembering the 'Men of the Western World', or Brennus and his brother, longing to hear the lowing of the aurochs, the wild ox of their lost homeland, ancient Gaul. The violence and cruelty, abundant and sickening, is delivered with a dry understatement which convinces us that indeed life was thought to be cheap. There is, however, a wild and magnificent poetry of image, and legendary moments which combine to create, as only Gibbon and Gunn can, the sense of myth. In Part 1 (*Insurrection*): 'The War Begins', there is an unforgettable scene where Spartacus, maddened and bewildered from a head wound, addresses the temperamental gladiators he has led in escape from Rome, and when he finds a horse:

> All stared, Spartacus now silent, with strange, glazed look and heaving breast. Then they turned their gaze to the giant stallion which stood shivering beside him. Its nostrils were still in the grasp of his great fingers, and as the general of the strange host groaned, his knuckles whitened and the stallion groaned beside him . . . Those near at hand cried out to Spartacus to beware, but he did not move, staring at the stallion. It heaved its head and snorted with quivering nostrils between its knees till its white knees were spattered with a bloody foam. Then it raised its head and slowly, hesitatingly, made a step towards the Gladiator.
>   The leader of the slave-horde had found a mount.

The power of this has nothing to do with argument and political belief. It is a mythic poetry, which Gibbon recurrently achieves, the highest point being the terrified and awe-struck vision which the Roman legions have of Spartacus when pursuing his army up to the Italian Alps. The legions stumble through the mist. Then, the mist clearing, they stand aghast at the figure helmeted in gold, 'armoured, immense in the spreading glow of the mist, the sun suddenly upon him. So he gleamed like a God, and the legions stared and murmured . . .'

Spartacus was written just before *Grey Granite,* and is arguably a more successful version of what Gibbon tried to do with Ewan and his workers in the unconvincing beginnings of revolt in Duncairn. Partly the success here is due to the fable-form, the actions of the century before Christ not calling for the kind of persuasive social verisimilitude that the modern novel requires. But the success is also due to the skill in staging Spartacus's development, and also to the fact that, of all Gibbon's novels, this is the quest-novel which finds Love – not sexual or the personal emotion of lovers, though that is here – but love as empathy and identification with humanity. Ewan's belief that the end justifies the means has no place in Spartacus's conduct, who turns time and again from success because he feels the rightness of giving immediate aid, even to those who, like Gannicus and Castus, betray him. He abandons Rome not on his own account, but for his troops. He finally destroys himself because there are no more ends more important than dying with his men.

All this suggests quasi-religious affirmation – and indeed affirmation is hard earned. Gibbon does not spare the reader the horrific historical ending of the slaves' revolt. The triumph comes through Kleon who has hitherto represented that side in Gibbon which saw life in *Cloud Howe* as a game, or worse, a malignant horror, a 'midge-swarm'. Kleon's maimed body causes him to retreat into the aridity of intellectual theory, and his toying with the Platonic theory of a republic is Gibbon's way of being ironic about such theorising. Kleon is the head to Spartacus's heart, and, in contrast to *A Scots Quair,* we are led to believe that the heart eventually wins this struggle. Cold Kleon is warmed, despite himself, through anger and pain to the point where he transcends his limitations of feeling, covering the retreat of the slave-horde and expecting to die in so doing. Kleon, who started by amusing himself with the idea of playing Spartacus like a puppet in a game of chess with Rome, ends by dreaming of a 'Lex Servorum', a new and better age. Spartacus continually makes inroads on his inhumanity, till the human miracle is achieved, whereby Kleon moves from scepticism ('What does it matter one way or the other, when all we do or dream are but blowings of dust?') to affirmative seeing, before he himself dies on the cross (Part 6, *The Masters*: 'The Appian Way'): 'gigantic, filling the sky, a great Cross with a figure that was crowned with thorns; and behind it, sky-towering as well, gladius in hand, his hand on the edge of the morning behind that Cross, the figure of a Gladiator. And he saw that these Two were One, and the world yet theirs; and he went into unending night and left them that shining earth.'

Gibbon had, temporarily, in this novel reasserted the dominance of his Christian vision, with Spartacus finding 'a God in men'. This vision has its limits, however. Christ is an ideal expression of an endless fight – but the God behind him, as Spartacus says, is 'an unknown God'. What has sustained this novel, more than religious vision or liberal Humanism or simple visions of endless revolutionary struggle, is love.

In the end, the reader of Gibbon/Mitchell has to weigh up the claims of his clashing beliefs and their expressions in fiction to decide whether the fate of Chris Guthrie at the end of the *Quair* represents a withdrawal from life, and Gibbon's final position; or whether, as in *Spartacus*, he sees the magic of human love possessing a redemptive potential for his fallen world.

Eric Linklater (1899–1974)

Eric Linklater went through life in quiet complicity with a popular misconception which said that he was an Orcadian, born and bred. Bred, but not born, is actually nearer the truth. It was not until 1970, with the publication of his third autobiography *Fanfare for a Tin Hat*, that the ageing novelist admitted that he had in fact been born in Penarth in South Wales in 1899, adding with characteristically evasive humour that he had certainly been conceived in Orkney. This might seem a rather unremarkable – if intentional – oversight, but for the fact that he made such efforts to stress his Orcadian connections (he lived there for part of his life, his father was an Orkneyman and a ship's master, the family maintained close links with the islands and always had a home there, he wrote many books about Orkney, the surname Linklater has been there for centuries . . .). The uncorrected error is indicative of a lifelong quest for identity which shapes much of Linklater's art.

When he was fourteen the family moved to Aberdeen. He completed his schooling there and matriculated briefly as a medical student at Aberdeen University in 1916. After two terms, however, he left and joined the army, going to war as a sniper in France. After a brief period of action, his war ended in 1918 when he was invalided out of the army with a head wound from a machine gun bullet – hence the title of the autobiography which alludes to the helmet that saved his life. He returned to Aberdeen University after the First World War, giving up medicine to take first-class honours in English literature. Between the wars he worked as a journalist in Bombay, taught at Aberdeen University, travelled in Asia and America and stood as a prospective parliamentary candidate for the SNP in Fife. He married Marjorie MacIntyre in 1933 and they lived in Orkney and in Easter Ross. Linklater returned to the army in the Second World War, reaching the rank of Lieutenant-Colonel.

The sheer variety of experience in his career, the combination of physical and intellectual pursuits and the extent of his travels are all reflected in Linklater's literary output. Indeed, the only general comment that can safely be made about his fiction is that it is infinitely wide-ranging in terms of influence, style and subject. His prose is characterised by exoticism and exuberance. Amid a huge amount of varied writing he is best remembered for the novels *White Maa's Saga* (1929), *Juan in America* (1931), *The Men of Ness* (1932), *Magnus Merriman* (1934), *Private Angelo* (1946) and the short stories such as *Sealskin Trousers and Other Stories* (1947).

WHITE MAA'S SAGA
'White Maa' is the Orkney name for the herring gull and the nickname of the hero, Peter Flett, in Linklater's début novel. The choice of the term 'saga' in the title is highly significant for here Linklater is alluding to the Norse heritage of the Northern Isles (Orkney and Shetland were under Scandinavian rule until 1469) and suggesting – in the title at least – the medieval Norse genre used to record the heroic deeds and genealogy of earls and kings. The Orkney Islands have their own saga called *Orkneyinga Saga* – literally 'the story of the men of Orkney'. Although he was later to adopt and develop the saga style more fully in *The Men of Ness*, there is clearly Norse influence at work here.

The novel is loosely autobiographical. After a magnificent opening 'Prelude' describing a pub crawl in Aberdeen (or as Linklater calls it 'Inverdoon' – real people, events and places often appear in these books and are but thinly veiled), Flett drops out of his medicine course at university to return to his native Orkney. On returning home he sails, brawls, poaches, falls in love with Norna Sabiston and eventually settles a score with a murderous rival.

In terms of achievement *White Maa's Saga* (1929) falls short of the sharper and more mature handling of similar themes in *Magnus Merriman*. Linklater's first novel has been seen as apprentice writing by some critics. *White Maa's Saga* explores some interesting areas which are more fully developed in later works. These include Linklater's adoption of the picaresque mode where we follow the adventures of a likeably roguish character: Peter Flett's Viking attributes and his insistence that he is of Norse descent and therefore significantly different in temperament and outlook from the other students at Inverdoon; the way in which the beleaguered Flett, who has been too long in the city, finds comfort and solace in the rich, fertile land of Orkney; and the eerie presence of the neolithic standing stones, so potent a symbol in the literature of the Scottish Renaissance and Gibbon's *Sunset Song* in particular. All of these themes are developed in Linklater's later work.

JUAN IN AMERICA

This was the book which established Linklater as a popular novelist, selling well in the UK with nine reprints in its first year of publication. Here the 'picaro' or rogue we follow is Juan Motley, the aristocratic English descendant of an illegitimate son of Don Juan, the eponymous hero of Byron's poem. Following Byron's model, Linklater uses Juan's journey through the USA as a vehicle for satire, with hilarious results.

For a novel set in the USA during the prohibition period of the 1920s *Juan in America* (1931) contains an overwhelming amount of alcohol. Of course this ties in with the novel's theme of social and moral hypocrisy. In fact, the recurrent pattern of drunkenness/hangover lends the book theme and structure. Linklater reveals his talent for comedy and his eye for the absurd through Juan's giddy highs and dismal lows – as in the chapter where Juan's curiosity gets the better of him and he gatecrashes a Mafia funeral only to be shot in the shoulder, or his début as a US football player where his error costs his team the game in front of a crowd of 60,000. On his first night as a cabaret singer he ruins the duet; his (female) co-star beats him up. Opportunities arise at the corner of every block and Juan consistently falls flat on his face. Symbols point up meaning very effectively throughout – Juan floating helplessly downstream in a flood river on the back of a mule, an orchestra who have never rehearsed abysmally playing Strauss's *Don Juan* . . .

This symbolic ridicule is not reserved for Juan. What suggestions are being made about the USA when a crowd observe two giant yaks copulating in an enclosure in Central Park, within 100 yards of skyscrapers and subway? (Linklater's original version of this scene had to be edited for publication.) The professors who had shown so much interest in Juan's obvious academic potential shun him after his mistake on the football field. Later, two completely indistinguishable presidential candidates spread apocryphal sleaze about each other while swagbellied senators drink a toast of bootleg whiskey to the virtues of prohibition. Juan's musings on this strange land show it with all its inconsistencies and contradictions and leave us wondering how many of these observations are Linklater's own from his time there. We begin to see a possible explanation why sales of the novel in the USA were slower than those in the UK, but this is not to say that the Old World mindset and British imperialism are let off the hook either. It is significant that, in spite of relentless bad luck, Juan never contemplates a return to England. Although we see the USA and its problems through English eyes, modern England is equally ridiculed as a quaint and irrelevant backwater, a land of cricket on quiet lawns notable only by its absence from the real world. Exile Dora Squire, despite enjoying her husband's substantial wages and having all the mod cons that are unaffordable in England, is an utter snob and unable to fit in in the USA because she cannot stand any criticism of England. With regard to the British Empire, there is supreme irony in the reference to 'redcoats rampaging . . . through the West Indies, and philosophers teaching freedom'. Historically, England has been brutal, and it is the atrocities of history which become the final, dark and disturbing theme running through *Juan in America*. In a beautiful and poignant description of the famous New England fall, Linklater shocks us: 'It was the blood of Mohawks and Tuscaroras and Cayugas, lying heavily at the roots of the Maples, that made their leaves so splendid. The sap of these trees was the blood of the red hunters who had been killed by white men.' Later, at the very centre of the presidential inauguration parade, a climax of sentimental national feeling, Juan witnesses a lone Indian in the rain, naked and on horseback, who silences the crowd, seeming to say 'I am America . . . It is my blood that paints the maples red and glorifies the crimson sumach'. These moments of calm in the midst of hilarity beg the question of whether *Juan in America* can really ultimately be considered a comic novel.

THE MEN OF NESS

After the success of *Juan in America* Linklater's publishers tried to encourage him to write a sequel, but *Juan in China* was not to appear until 1937. Instead, he wrote *The Men of Ness*, which could scarcely have been more different from its predecessor. This is the story of a family of medieval Orkney Vikings who live at the farm of Ness on the island of Rousay. Signy, Thorleif and their warrior sons, Kol and Skallagrim, are the characters who dictate events in this saga. Signy's first husband Bui is murdered and usurped by Ivar the Boneless. Ivar subsequently deserts her whereupon she marries his brother, the wise but unadventurous sage Thorleif Coalbiter (so called for his tendency to sit at home by the fire). The rest of the plot is driven by Signy's desire for revenge on Ivar for the murder of Bui. She mocks and cajoles her sons constantly to spur them to avenge Bui, but Thorleif's wise counsel against violence always prevails, until Fate – the all important force in any saga – intervenes. Kol and Skallagrim are blown off the course of an expedition and come ashore in the north of England, virtually on – Ivar's doorstep.

Linklater's main sources for *The Men of Ness* are *Orkneyinga Saga* and *Njal's Saga*. From the former he uses historical details like the death of Earl Sigurd of Orkney in Caithness; from the latter he plunders certain elements of plot: the peaceful sage with violent sons; a powerful female character manipulating her kinsmen; horsefights; children insulting grown men; cowardly braggarts and barking dogs. A contrast to the novel's terse yet vivid saga

611

action is effected through the traditional figure of Thorleif's neighbour, Gauk of Calfskin, who provides a comic foil to the bad blood and violence which saturate the story, and relief to Kol and Skallagrim's epic sea journey from the North Isles of Orkney to Northumbria. All are skilfully woven into the novel. The scene where an ox falls through the lean-to roof of Gauk's house 'Calfskin' actually happened in Orkney in the nineteenth century and is recorded in a John Firth's little known *Reminiscences of an Orkney Parish* (1920). *The Men of Ness* is meticulously well researched. The plagiarisms lend the story authenticity and are excusable because they are developed into a whole which is much more than the sum of the parts.

Perhaps more interesting than the way Linklater uses his sources for plot or events is the way he adopts the style of the medieval saga. The most apparent peculiarity of the saga to a modern reader is the way all extraneous detail is stripped away leaving a very terse, laconic narrative. Unendurable hardships are often quietly understated. This is done to great effect in the magnificent storm episode in *The Men of Ness*: 'Now the gale broke on them in all its strength and roared about them. The Skua drove before it, beating the tide and plunged into the heavy sea. It was not easy to steer it then.'

Also following Norse literary tradition is the use of skaldic 'kennings', the cryptic metaphors of the Viking poets – Linklater makes up his own, waves in the storm become 'white hooded ladies'. Saga heroes often display courage by dying with a jest on their lips, the men of Ness being no exceptions, as in the black humour in the following dialogue after Gyfli has been mortally wounded Kol knelt beside him and bade him be of good heart. ' "My heart is good enough," said Gyfli, "but my guts are falling out." '

As well as borrowing from the sagas, Linklater carefully adapts the medium for his modern readership. For instance, *Njal's Saga* and *Orkneyinga Saga* include long and cumbersome family trees of all the major characters: because the sagamen considered their works to be historical records, they liked to prove their heroes' aristocratic pedigrees. Linklater uses a minimum of genealogical detail, only giving enough to set the scene before allowing his narrative to develop. Sometimes the sagas can seem to have somewhat rambling plots, again because they mirror reality to some extent. *The Men of Ness*, however, is tightly structured providing suspense, contrast and climax.

If *The Men of Ness* seems a curious departure from Linklater's previous subjects and themes, it may help to consider it within the wider context of the Scottish Renaissance – Neil Gunn also has his 'Viking' novel, *Sun Circle* (1933), the year after *The Men of Ness*. There was a great deal of interest among Scottish writers of the time in questions of race and ancestry; it was natural that Linklater should wish to experiment with the medium used by those he considered to be his ancestors.

MAGNUS MERRIMAN

Magnus Merriman (1934) is a novel which chooses the Scottish Renaissance as its central concern and is indeed a central text of it. Here Linklater uses his experiences as a nationalist candidate in the 1933 East-Fife by-election (where he lost his deposit) to write a book which is essentially a satire on the Scottish Renaissance in both its literary and political manifestations. *Magnus Merriman* might be considered something of a daring move at a time when Scottish writers and politicians were rallying round the standard of nationalism, but for its deliberate and perplexing ambiguity. This, Linklater's masterpiece, is a novel in which the author's cultural and political loyalties are virtually impossible to pin down.

Magnus Merriman is an Orcadian who fights in the First World War, studies at Inverdoon, writes a bestselling novel and travels across Asia – the correspondences with Linklater's own career are obvious. Magnus has the same Christian name as Orkney's twelfth-century earl and saint, yet his surname, while also common in the islands, suggests something less than saintly. So the ambiguous tone is set as Magnus returns to Scotland and becomes an overnight convert to the cause of Scottish Nationalism, agreeing within days of his conversion to contest a coming by-election.

In this novel Linklater's evasive humour comes to the fore. It seems we have little option but to read *Magnus Merriman* as at least semi-autobiographical. Where, then, do Linklater's gibes at Magnus and his quick conversion, political vacillation, ballot box humiliation and return (with his tail between his legs) to Orkney, leave us? Surely Linklater believed in what he stood for in East Fife? Is there a sadness underlying the farce? Is the humour a self-defence mechanism, a diversion tactic? Or is Magnus presented simply as an empty-coat figure caught up in the tide of fanaticism? Francis Meiklejohn, who persuades Magnus to join the cause, is certainly enthusiastic: 'A renascence is on the way – political and literary – so come and be its midwife . . . We talk of liberty when we're sober and dream of it when drunk. Come to Scotland . . .' Note that 'renascence' remains in lower case letters. Hugh MacDiarmid was using the term Scottish Renaissance as early as 1923 – Linklater seems to be saying that he has his doubts whether to afford the phenomenon proper noun status ten years later. Note too the reference to alcohol. Like *Juan in America*, much of this novel is viewed through the hazy lens of beer and spirits, again placing the reader on unsteady ground. Magnus too dreams when drunk, and invariably ends up with a hangover.

Shortly after what can only be termed a semi-religious experience, where Scotland is transcendentally revealed to him in all her glory, he enters a town hall to present a speech to voters: 'Magnus rose to speak, and throwing aside all thought of Atlantic islands and sunbright lochs, recited so dull a string of facts and figures even the Calvinised Boeotians sitting in front of him were bored.' He is far too romantic to take any real interest in the nuts and bolts of politics. Time and again his lofty ideals and perhaps visionary plans are ruthlessly undercut in what seems a bitterly cruel world. However, the satire is not reserved only for Magnus as Linklater declares open season on all followers of the nationalist movement and their catholic enthusiasms for 'Communism, pacifism, vegetarianism, poetic nonconformity and economic heresy'. Magnus thinks they just might fail to present a united front. Among the various caricature portraits of eminent Scottish Renaissance figures, that of Hugh Skene (Hugh MacDiarmid) stands out: 'his eyes shone brightly. On the edge of the light that escaped from a shaded lamp his great bush of hair seemed like a burning bush. His political opinions, thought Magnus, are the waste products of his genius.' Skene is allowed an undeniable genius, but what are we to make of the utter impenetrability of his Scots poetry in 'The Flauchter Spaad'?

Following a failed love affair in Edinburgh, drunken brawls and subsequent hangovers, disaster at the ballot box and a humiliating robbery, Magnus returns to Orkney to lick his wounds. He very quickly settles down to marry Rose, a farmer's daughter, and take his own farm. These final, rural chapters of *Magnus Merriman* provide a pleasant contrast to the frenetic account of Edinburgh and the election but are not without their own troubles. Magnus's farming career is also, somewhat unsurprisingly, a non-starter. Drunk in Caithness, he squanders a vast sum on a bull which presently dies. Rose is not the quiet and passive beauty she seemed to be . . .

Linklater seems to be placing himself deliberately within the Scottish literary tradition in these closing scenes. They might be considered a jocose equivalent to the opening chapters of Edwin Muir's *An Autobiography* (1954). Magnus's return to the soil – albeit comic – is comparable to the anthropological connections suggested between Chris Guthrie and the land in Gibbon's *Sunset Song*, published two years earlier. Going further back, Scott's wavering hero Edward Waverley also settles down after a career of crests and troughs to marry his Rose. Are we really expected not to see the parallel between the drinking session Magnus and Johnny Peace the shoemaker indulge in and the similar antics of Tam o' Shanter and Souter Johnnie in Burns's Ayrshire tavern? Why satirise the Scottish Renaissance of the early part of the twentieth century only to include so many deliberate and self-conscious references to great moments of Scottish literary history? *Magnus Merriman* is ambiguous to the end.

LINKLATER'S OTHER WRITING: NOVELS, SHORT STORIES, NON-FICTION

Much of the reason for the relatively low profile of Linklater's reputation today can be attributed to two things. Firstly, his own self-mockery and refusal to take himself and his work with great seriousness ('an old peasant with a pen' was one of his typical self-descriptions; and 'life is God's tragico-romantico-comico-bawdy novel, and we are its sentences' a typical reductive remark). And secondly, the chameleon-like nature of his life and work – he had been, with varying degrees of success, a medical student, a scholar of English, a soldier (in two wars), a journalist, writer and traveller. Like his friend James Bridie, he had an equivocal attitude to the world of the arts and its high seriousness (as witnessed in his mockery of Hugh MacDiarmid and the Scottish Renaissance in *Magnus Merriman*). And both of these character-istics show themselves in the sheer range and variety of his writing, from novels and short stories to plays and polemical essays; (*The Lion and the Unicorn: Or what England Has Meant to Scotland* (1935), and serious and popular histories, such as *The Ultimate Viking* (1955), *Mary Queen of Scots* (1933) or *The Prince in the Heather* (1965). The autobiographical accounts are *The Man on my Back* (1941), *A Year of Space* (1953) and *Fanfare for a Tin Hat* (1971).

THE ENGLISH NOVELS

This chapter has mainly focused on the Scottish stories; but this Orkney writer had another side, cosmopolitan and anglo-centric, if simultaneously mocking, like Evelyn Waugh, the pretensions of Southern English society. *Poet's Pub* (1929) is typical of this side of his work, in its farcical mock-heroic improbabilities and riotous conclusion – characteristics worked far more successfully in the *Juan* novels. Linklater continued this strand, perhaps too influenced by the success of similar work by Evelyn Waugh and Compton Mackenzie, in *Ripeness is All* (1935), *The Impregnable Women* (1938) and *Position at Noon* (1958) – this last, however, for all its grotesque comedy, showing a tragi-comic view of life which emerged more fully in some disturbingly powerful later novels. An important novel in this respect, pointing towards Linklater's darkening vision, is *Mr Byculla* (1950), which, occurring almost exactly midway in his writing career, combines successfully two strands of his writing – on one hand his love of the supernatural and legendary, and on the other his satirical treatment of English society. Mr Byculla is a hybrid of nationalities and origins – McKillop is his real name, but he uses Byculla to remind himself of the vanity of human wishes. Apparently a pleasant Asian, he slowly reveals himself as a more sinister figure, steeped in ancient Thuggee tradition; yet his motives are to relieve human suffering. This disturbing dreamer is descended from Stevenson's Mr Hyde, but looks forward to Muriel Spark's grotesque narratives, ambiguous protagonists and justified sinners, as we slowly realise that he is the well-meaning murderer in London fog.

The Merry Muse (1959) is a sardonic mixture of hilarity and sad bitterness in its juxtapositioning of elegy for Scottish Renaissance and grotesque comedy. Its likeable last Makar Eachan Dhu ingloriously ends his life, knocked down on Edinburgh's Dean Bridge. Linklater seems here unsure of mode, with the novel's other narrative a middle-class romp, sitting uneasily next to a more serious and symbolic theme. *Roll of Honour* (1961) suggests that Linklater's view of life had become pessimistic and self-doubting. It is a picture of a retired schoolmaster who laments pupils killed in the war, and his own insignificance is redeemed only by his refusal to indulge in self-pity. And this led Linklater into strange new territory, which had been heralded in the novella *A Sociable Plover* (1957). This contains several perspectives on its tragic and supernatural narrative which centres around a thinly disguised version of Linklater himself, and the bizarre poetic justice visted upon him by the plover, which is no ordinary bird, but a 'fetch' or unearthly visitant – or is it? This is continued in *A Man Over Forty* (1964), and, outstandingly, in *A Terrible Freedom* (1966), in which the ageing Evan Gaffikin (who disturbingly featured in *A Sociable Plover* – another version of Linklater himself?) explores, through dreams of startling beauty, the final questions of spirituality and self in ways which share the enquiry of the last novels of Neil Gunn.

LINKLATER'S SHORT STORIES

As well as being an acclaimed novelist, Linklater is also recognised as a short story writer of great ability. There are three volumes of short stories: *God Likes Them Plain* (1935); *Sealskin Trousers* (1947); and *A Sociable Plover* – and a selection of them appeared in *The Goose Girl* (1991). They reflect his variety of writing, from his great Scottish supernatural stories to more exotic tales of restive crusaders, wives, patriotic but misguided Russian actresses, Swedish poets whose lives are better than their poetry, and assorted *fabliaux* which show off Linklater's undoubted erudition, but also his tendency to enigmatic philosophising.

Probably his best-known collection of short fiction is *Sealskin Trousers*, with its wide range of subjects and locations. All the stories are characterised by Linklater's gift for narrative economy and the style here is subtly different.

Gone is the flippant, reductive idiom of *Juan in America* and *Magnus Merriman*; in its place is a serious and sometimes disturbing tone.

'The Goose Girl' is the opening story and plunges directly into action: 'When I woke among the currant-bushes I saw her coming out of the cottage door with her fist round the gander's neck.' Such an arresting opening captures the reader's attention, raising many questions within one short sentence. The language of the piece is marvellously descriptive and subtly erotic. The story goes on to adapt a classical myth (where Zeus took the form of a bird to make Leda, wife of King Tyndarus, pregnant) to a modern and northern setting. Robert Tindall, an English infantryman, returns from war and makes his way north to Orkney; partly as an escape and partly to talk to the family of a comrade who has been killed in action. He finds himself trapped in a re-enactment of the myth of Leda and the Swan, with his daughter Helen destined to cause a third world war, echoing the destiny of Leda's daughter, Helen of Troy.

Between this and the final title story are sandwiched three international tales. 'The Dreaming Bears' and 'The Three Poets' both have Scandinavian settings, the first in Finland, the latter Sweden. 'The Dreaming Bears' continues the metamorphic theme of 'The Goose Girl' in a slightly different vein, while 'The Three Poets' postulates that poetry and engineering are functions of one another. 'Joy as it Flies' describes an extramarital flirtation which begins in Edinburgh and is – possibly – consummated in Dublin ten years later. Is there a suggestion being made here about Calvinism and the Scottish city as the couple drive through the streets under the 'intolerant sky of Edinburgh'? The book finishes with the title story, once again working in that territory, halfway between myth and reality, in which Linklater excels. The narrator (who can hardly be considered reliable) begins with the words 'I am not mad', and then tells his sinister supernatural tale of how he lost his lady to a half-man, half-seal. 'Sealskin Trousers' uses the Orkney folk myth of the selkie – a seal that comes ashore and takes human form – introducing a further variation on the theme of shape-shifting which pervades the collection. Linklater's selkie is hardly the benevolent creature of the traditional folk tale, however. Roger Fairfield (the name the selkie adopts from a drowned sailor's pay book) comes ashore to investigate the world of men, taking an MA at Edinburgh University before returning to his seaworld to tell of the 'other side'. This selkie is highly educated and familiar with modern genetic science – as well as selfish, intimidating and manipulative, persuading the girl character to leap off the clifftop to join him in what he describes as the hidden and finer world of seals. Linklater's blend of ancient folklore and modern science is beautifully balanced, drawing the reader into his narrator's ambiguous account, so that it works in the classic tradition of the ambiguous Scottish story, which can be read as a study of psychological breakdown or genuine supernatural occurrence, as in Hogg's *The Justified Sinner* (1824), Stevenson's 'Thrawn Janet' and Barrie's *Farewell Miss Julie Logan* (1932).

But Linklater could be more straightforwardly satirical and serious in his Scottish short stories than he was elsewhere; 'The Duke' is a vivid version of the famous rejection by the peasantry of the Duke of Sutherland's appeal for soldiers for the Crimean War; 'It was sheep you preferred to men, it is sheep who live on all the good land today, and sheep are all you can command.' Linklater's sense of the grotesque clearly appreciated the baa-ing off of the shamed Duke by his flock. A novella, *The Masks of Purpose*, in the collection *A Sociable Plover* (1957), explores through a dark poetry the masks worn by all those complicit in the atrocity and betrayal of Glencoe.

As these stories and the later novels show, Linklater could be a deeply serious writer. Perhaps the reasons for the modern neglect of his work lie partly in his own sceptical view of humanity and his constant deprecation of his work, and partly in his frequent willingness to write light-hearted fiction suited to a home counties readership. But whatever the reasons, the time is ripe for a re-evaluation which sees him as the major Scottish writer that he is.

CHAPTER 33

JAMES BRIDIE AND
THE SCOTTISH THEATRE

JAMES BRIDIE (1888–1951) AND MAINSTREAM THEATRE

In the inter-war period, James Bridie (in his other professional and 'real' life, respectable medical practitioner Dr Henry Osborne Mavor) dominated Scottish theatre as both a writer and a manager. His name is associated with almost every theatrical organisation in the century, from the Glasgow Repertory Theatre, for whom he wrote his first play, to the Scottish National Players (SNP), on whose board of directors he sat. After gaining a reputation as a West-End playwright, he was a founder member of the Scottish committee of the Council for the Encouragement of Music and the Arts (CEMA), the Citizens' Theatre, the Scottish Arts Council, the Edinburgh Festival Society and, just before he died, he achieved a long-held ambition by contributing to the establishment of a drama school in Glasgow.

His name is invariably linked with 'Establishment' mainstream arts. His work and his political and aesthetic project was the opposite of groups like the left-wing Glasgow Unity Theatre; they felt, with some justification, that he used his influence to thwart their attempts to gain long-term Arts Council funding. Ironically, recent Scottish theatre has been more directly influenced by the policies and the drama of Glasgow Unity than that of Bridie. Since the 1970s, the plays and playwrights promoted and premièred by Unity have been revived by theatre makers and reassessed by critics – Robert McLeish's *The Gorbals Story* (1946), Ena Lamont Stewart's *Starched Aprons* (1945) and *Men Should Weep* (1947) and Benedict Scott's *Lambs of God* (1948) have proved of lasting influence within the Scottish repertoire. In contrast, Bridie's plays are largely forgotten by theatre makers and even his reputation as a manager and policy maker is tarnished by allegations of his active opposition to Unity. 1988, the centenary of Bridie's birth, passed almost unnoticed. There was an extensive celebratory exhibition at the National Library of Scotland, the major revelation of which was Bridie's drawings, designs, paintings and sketches; and there were several productions in Scottish theatres, but none of these prompted any major critical reassessment of Bridie.

Bridie's standing as a West-End dramatist, the very role which gave him the power to be so influential within Scottish theatre, has proved to be the main stumbling block for the revaluation of his achievement by Scottish critics. As Edwin Morgan has pointed out, the perception of Bridie as a West-End, or at least an Anglo-Scottish, playwright has cost him dear, even though, he was, above all, a Scottish dramatist and one of the most innovative. (Fuller details of Bridie's controversial relationship with Scottish theatre are given later in this chapter.)

Bridie, MacDiarmid and the Scottish Renaissance

In 1928, when the young medic O. H. Mavor began writing for the SNP, under his first pseudonym of 'Mary Henderson', cultural Scotland was in the throes of a literary renaissance. In *Contemporary Scottish Studies* (1926), MacDiarmid had criticised Scottish dramatists in general, and the SNP in particular, for their failure to create a distinctively Scottish drama: 'No Scots dramatist has produced drama of the slightest note or in any way other than most superficially differentiated from English drama.' None of the plays the SNP produced, he argued, represented a distinctively Scottish form, the dramatic equivalent of the *differentia* of Scots psychology. He argued that, though they were Scottish in subject, they were all alien in form. Inspired by Gregory Smith's theories of dualism in Scottish character and culture as expounded in his notion of 'the Caledonian antisyzygy' in *Scottish Literature: Character and Influence* (1919), MacDiarmid had some constructive suggestions as to the possibilities which the SNP might explore when creating a distinctively Scottish theatre craft. He cites Smith in Chapter 1 of his *Scottish Literature*: 'There is more in the Scottish antithesis of the real and the fantastic than is to be explored by the familiar rules of rhetoric. The sudden jostling of contraries seems to preclude any relationship by literary suggestion.' This antithesis of the real and the fantastic, and the opposition of contraries, seemed to MacDiarmid to be a fruitful source for Scottish dramatists, though in fact it is the stuff of almost all drama. But it was Bridie alone, amongst MacDiarmid's contemporaries, who put these ideas into practice and who tried, wittingly or not, to fulfil some of MacDiarmid's other suggestions.

Bridie's early drama

With his first play, *The Sunlight Sonata* (1928), Bridie gave Scotland a modern version of the morality play whose last manifestation had been seen in Edinburgh in 1554 with Sir David Lyndsay's *Ane Satyre of the Thrie Estaitis*. In Bridie's play, a 'farce-morality', the Devil and the Seven Deadly Sins fight for the soul of Kelvinside and a Hollywood-style '20s vamp. The Devil speaks in a rich Ayrshire dialect; and the Sins are thwarted while the vamp is saved by Faith, Hope and Charity in the guise of maiden aunts and economical plain cooks. Bridie, unfettered by the constraints of the well-made play, created his own version of the morality play and made it distinctively Scottish. It was a form which, as *Ane Satyre* had shown, could lay bare the soul of a nation, or, at the very least, of a class.

The morality play was perhaps a strange choice of dramatic form for Bridie. A morality play requires a moral system and Bridie spent his life fighting the 'worship of dogma' of all sorts. It was a form and a politic which suited him well. He only returned to it at the end of his career with *The Baikie Charivari* (1951), but here he used the much more neutral sub-title of 'miracle' play rather than 'morality' play. It seems at least unfortunate that he did not return to this medieval form till the end of his career, as it is almost infinitely adaptable and suits the wide, discursive, dialectical scope of his dramaturgy.

Bridie's early writing was hampered both by having no professional companies with whom he could work and experiment, and by there being no Scottish equivalent of, for example, Terence Gray's Cambridge Festival Theatre, where new methods of staging based on Craig, Appia and the recent German Expressionists could be tried out. All attempts to achieve an independent Scottish stage, except that of the Glasgow Workers' Theatre Group, through whom the influence of London Unity was filtered in the late 1930s, had either been thirled to naturalism or to London's current idea of what was good dramatic technique.

Bridie and last acts

The most persistent criticism, which dogged Bridie, develops from this lack of early production experience. It was that he had no 'technique', and, in particular, that he could not write last acts. But this again was a result of his seduction by the West End. His natural inclination was for wide-ranging epic plays which have an almost novelistic structure, but, in order to make his plays commercially viable, he had to compress them. Occasionally this compres-

621

sion meant that they seemed to be constructed like short stories rather than novels, and this is especially true of his rather creaking use of prologues in, for example, *A Sleeping Clergyman* (1933) and *Mr Gillie* (1950). In them, the main dramatic action is framed by a device, used by many short story writers: two men sitting in a club, one telling and one being told the story. Those who accuse Bridie of being prolix will see the influence of the West-End compressors as no bad thing, but if the resultant scramble for the curtain is unsatisfactory, then Bridie had his own *apologia* at the end of his autobiography, *One Way of Living* (1939): 'And all this nonsense about last acts', he sighed, 'Only God can write last acts, and he seldom does. You should go out of the theatre with your head swirling with speculations . . .'. However clever this may be, it is not very convincing. The Priestleyesque detective who ends *Dr Angelus* (1947), for example, is a blatant *deus ex machina* to get the curtain down, and we are left with no notion that the events we have just seen are historical fact and not Grand Guignol fantasy.

Bridie's reaction to such criticism was to have some fun at his critics' expense, though in the plays the best jokes are, like Barrie's, often in the stage directions. The last Act of *Daphne Laureola* (1949), for example, is set in the restaurant of Act I, where '*Curiously enough, most of the people who were dining there six months ago are dining there now*'. In the preface to *Colonel Wotherspoon* (in *Colonel Wotherspoon and Other Plays*, 1934) he wrote of the reaction of the critics to his work:

> My newspaper cuttings tell me that I am an amateurish, but edifying dramatist. I hope to remedy the first by close study of the best authorities. The second, I felt, invested me with a sacred duty. I wonder, at times, whether the 5 million odd lecturers on Drama, now ravening through the country and using the word 'technique' as they use the word 'definitely', have any clear idea what it means . . . Which of us hasn't sat yawning in a theatre watching the rules being applied like postage stamps on circulars . . . The only sound evidence that an actor or a producer or a playwright possesses technique is an ability to hold an audience . . . [My plays] play well – and that is more than can be said for a good many more pretentious dramas.

This determinedly no-nonsense approach to writing for the theatre is repeated time and again: 'A play is a story told by actors' and, most notoriously, in his provocative essay, in *Tedious and Brief* (1944):

> A stage play is a method of passing an interval of time by putting an actor or actors on a platform and causing them to say or do certain things. If it is

amusing, that is to say if it succeeds in making the spectators unconscious of the passage of time, it fulfils its function and has merit. If, on the other hand, the spectators are conscious of the passage of time, of the dreadful progress of the Universe towards destruction and nothingness, the play has failed . . . Other qualities of a play – its educative, its thought-provoking, its exciting, its poetic qualities – are not basic.

It was this anti-intellectual impulse to be provocative and the unwillingness to be pinned down that led to Bridie's lifelong battle with the Scottish critics, and it often seemed that the more a play like *Daphne Laureola* was praised by London, the more hostile was its reception in Glasgow. Bridie, however, always fought back with characteristic force, as here in the Preface to *Colonel Wotherspoon and Other Plays*:

> I think of each of them [my plays], when it was performed in Scotland, it was said that the first Great Scottish Play had yet to be written. The truth is that Scotland does not yet deserve a great play. She has not yet expiated her scandalous treatment of the Theatre in the past.

In spite of his impeccable Establishment credentials, Bridie was not afraid to take on Scotland in general, though his greatest reserves of venom were spent on what he saw as the philistines of Glasgow who were killjoy enough not to support his new theatre. But it is clear that all through his life as an artist, he ran up against the mean-spirited side of Scottish life, against which artists have battled through the centuries: 'In Scotland', he wrote, 'there is only one recent tradition of persecution, and that is the persecution of artists and the light-headed and the light-hearted by the unco-guid'.

Developing a Scottish drama

Much of Bridie's drama was dedicated to the fight between good and evil, most memorably in *Mr Bolfry* (1943). Many of his plays also tackle the hypocrisy and evasion of the Scottish middle class. In Act III of *Dr Angelus*, for example, there is a point in the quagmire of murder, adultery and deceit at which the young English doctor, Johnston, having been unable to see just how seductive evil can be, at last confronts the murderer and accuses him of dispatching his wife and mother-in-law. Angelus pauses for a moment, deliberately misunderstands what Johnston is saying, and chooses to treat the outburst as an expression of sympathy: 'Poor Margaret is at peace. Her weary journey is over. She is in Abraham's bosom. And we can only hope she's comfortable. Her story is told. To me, at least, it will always be an inspiration'. The short speech encapsulates the sanctimonious humbug of the Victorian middle classes, but Bridie carefully shows us by the context of the speech that humbug is not only funny, it can be dangerous. The road to hell is paved with mottoes and platitudes. Moreover, there is something very Scottish, highly antisyzygic, about that cosy biblical reference followed by the aside which is so dry it is barely noticeable.

The question of technique, however, is more than just an academic quibble. MacDiarmid rightly saw in this play the seeds of a distinctive Scottish drama. In her study of Bridie (and, very usefully, of the Scottish theatre of his time) *James Bridie and his Theatre* (1955), Winifred Bannister tells of the rehearsals at Malvern for *A Sleeping Clergyman* (1933). The play electrified the stage-hands and cleaners with its mixture of emotional violence, murder and drunkenness, but appalled Sir Barry Jackson, the founder of the festival, who was sure that if it pleased the cleaners then it was too vulgar for his patrons. His feeling about the play was similar to that of the actor Robert Lorraine and others about *The Anatomist* that it was too raw and violent for civilised audiences.

Civilising Bridie

The process of making Bridie fit for civilised audiences began with the production of his second play by Barry Jackson at Birmingham Rep and at Malvern. Jackson had been part of the Repertory Theatre Movement of Edwardian Britain; indeed he was its only survivor. Bridie had come into contact with the movement in Glasgow at Alfred Wareing's Glasgow Repertory Theatre (1909–14), the first resident professional theatre in the city since the days of J. H. Alexander and the Glovers. At that theatre he had seen Ibsen's plays, which he reviewed for the *Glasgow University Magazine*, and, more unfortunately, he saw plays by Shaw, with whom he would be endlessly, and wrongly, compared, since there was a fundamental difference: Shaw was interested in answers, Bridie in questions.

Led by these twin gods, Bridie had written *The Switchback* in or around 1911. The play is about medical ethics and middle-class respectability versus paganism, with a sexual sub-plot and a dotty old lady thrown in. The play sounds like a *cri de coeur* from an artist being stifled by bourgeois society. Echoes of Ibsen's *An Enemy of the People* (1882) and Shaw's *The Doctor's Dilemma* (1906) abound, not always to its benefit. It was rewritten in 1929, and it remained a respectable play, but it was not the great play Helen Luyben praises in her book, *James Bridie: Clown and Philosopher* (1965). For one thing, the rich Scots and the free-form of *The Sunlight Sonata* (1928) were lost. It is only fair to point out that in his reassessment of Bridie for *Scottish Theatre News* the playwright Donald MacKenzie chose this very point in Bridie's career as the moment that Bridie accepted some discipline, and matured as a writer. But one might also argue that it was a backward step and a moment of loss for Scottish drama.

The Anatomist (1930) shows Bridie moving towards the form of the 'well-made play', with the drama played through scenes contrasting the douce but safe, English-speaking New Town and the dangerous, exciting, Scots-speaking Old Town, to the detriment of the New. The play makes one wish that Bridie had stuck with his explorations of Scotland, but he had a West-End reputation to make, and it was vital for the future of the Scottish theatre as a whole, if not for the development of his art, that he did so. Seen from Scotland, Bridie may appear a traitor – one of Barrie's 'Scotsmen on the make' – but seen from London, although the West End and critics like James Agate took him rather more seriously than his fellow Scots, he was still no more than an exotic. When histories of the London stage of the 1930s and 1940s came to be written, Bridie's work merited very few lines, and he was usually bracketed with Priestley as a dramatist of ideas, or with Emlyn Williams as a peripheral Celt.

His plays for London in the 1930s are, with few exceptions – *A Sleeping Clergyman* is one – uncomfortable, messy creations. The spirit of Mary Henderson reappears in a fitfully funny play for the SNP, *The Dancing Bear* (1931), but then was lost until the Citizens' was founded in 1943. Its opening production was his *Holy Isle* (which had played in London in 1942). This was a gentle exploration of, and satire on, Neil Gunn and Edwin Muir's vision of a lost golden age of Scotland, a pre-historic Arcadia. Whatever the dramatic shortcomings of the play, it showed a renewed interest in Scotland and the themes of its literary renaissance. This new lease of life came to maturity with *The Forrigan Reel* (1944), and it achieved a new resonance when coupled with what might be seen as West-End farce in *The Baikie Charivari*, a play about an Indian civil servant returning home to Scotland.

Bridie's reputation in British theatre

Bridie suffered more than just a hiatus in his best work by being associated with the West End. His posthumous reputation also suffered, and for many years he was joined in a post-1956 theatrical limbo by many illustrious figures, including T. S. Eliot, Christopher Fry, J. B. Priestley, Noel Coward, Somerset Maugham and Terrence Rattigan. Only Coward has been fully and critically

625

rehabilitated, although directors and critics alike have begun to reassess both Rattigan and Maugham, with some success. This is possibly because all three wrote such challenging parts for the older actresses of whom British theatre has so many distinguished examples. Bridie, on the other hand, his admiration for Flora Robson notwithstanding, wrote most of his best parts for male actors, and for very idiosyncratic actors like Alastair Sim and Duncan Macrae. Since their deaths, no one else has been able to make much of the roles created by them.

Coward, Maugham and Rattigan were also gay, setting most of their plays in the *beau monde*, where illicit and illegal behaviour would pass with little, but suitably acid, comment. Theatre since the 1970s has determinedly recovered its gay past and delighted in style, in camp and the re-examination of the sexual sub-text of plays written earlier in the century. Within this discourse, Bridie's plays are irredeemably heterosexual and middle class. But there are some more immediate reasons why Bridie has been neglected.

Perhaps the most obvious negative feature of his plays for present-day audiences and critics is Bridie's sexual politics and, in particular, his treatment of women. In the decades since Bridie's death women's role in society, especially the role of the middle-class women about whom Bridie writes, has changed beyond all recognition. Even the last female characters he created in 1951, Judy and Baby in *The Baikie Charivari*, could simply not be created today. It might be argued that they are of their period, but their period is not far enough removed in time. There is still a shock at the moment when Baby – and even her name suggests her status in the family – is given away, like something in a cornflake packet, to the first half-decent plumber's mate who happens to come through the door. When Maggie Wylie is bartered in *What Every Woman Knows* (1908) Barrie gives enough evidence in the stage directions to undercut the moment while his 'Suffrage scene' makes it clear that Maggie's plight is a metaphor for the fates of all women. In *The Baikie Charivari*, however, the 'arranged marriage' is too sudden and raw for comfort.

Though Bridie's plays have a wealth of witty dialogue and dry asides, many of his jokes rely on a humour which needs a particular audience, like the majority of theatre-goers in the 1930s and 1940s, public-schooled, male-oriented, classically educated and biblically literate.

It was probably his first profession, as much as anything in his plays, which allowed the label 'middle-class dramatist' to attach itself to him so early on. Bridie was a complete product of Glasgow's medical upper middle class but his dissection of both his class and his profession, though quiet, as in *The Golden Legend of Shultz* (1939) is usually deadly, as in *The Anatomist* and *Dr Angelus*.

Many of Bridie's plays are either rather touching, if sometimes insubstantial, character studies, like *Mr Gillie* (1950) with no message, moral or political point, or they are dramas of bewilderment, like *The Baikie Charivari*, which wither in our more robust times. The debate about ends and means in *The Anatomist* gives the drama a stronger core but, as one might expect, Bridie had little time for those who criticised his plays for having no message. Edwin Morgan suggests that this 'impishness' was his undoing but, towards the end of his career, in both *The Baikie Charivari* and *Mr Gillie*, the playfulness goes. Here, one feels, is genuine pain and bewilderment; here is someone brought up with certain social certainties, confronting a world of rationing, post-war reconstruction and socialist policies, including a National Health Service and confronting it with questions, but still with optimism.

At the end of *The Baikie Charivari*, however, Dr Mavor betrays Mr Bridie. When Dr Pothecary, the hearty lady GP, observes that, beneath seeming social stability, there lurks a hotbed of complexes, Judy Pounce-Pellot, the voice of reason, replies, with her author's full agreement, 'I don't care.' Sadly for Judy, and for Bridie, the bulk of the British theatre-going public did care, and so Bridie's plays went into eclipse.

Though *The Baikie Charivari* is Bridie's last play, it is by no means a valedictory piece and still has endless promise. Bridie was changing, developing, assimilating Scotland, making us open our eyes. The pity is he died when he did. The pity also is that he wasted so much of his life in pursuit of what MacDiarmid called 'alien theatredoms'.

It would be idle to argue that Bridie was a playwright for all Scotland, but he was the dramatist of a substantial and influential section of Scottish society. His dryness, his love of debate, his humanism, his love too of a good story, a major part of his appeal, are Scottish. But in his scrutiny of dogma, of figures of authority, and in the awkward questions he asked of the Scots, he is his own man. Viewed from Scotland, Bridie, whatever his faults and shortcomings, was a playwright of national significance whose work and the lessons of whose life, as regards the position of the dramatist in society, we ignore at our peril.

TWO BRIDIE PLAYS: *THE ANATOMIST* AND *MR BOLFRY*
The Anatomist

Since its first performance in 1930, James Bridie's *The Anatomist* has been persistently criticised for two major faults. The play has been castigated for being melodramatic or over-theatrical (particularly in the presentation of its central protagonist, Robert Knox) and, in complete contrast to this first criticism, of purveying a very limp dénouement (a fault often identified in Bridie's oeuvre). Notions of theatricality and role-playing pervade *The Anatomist*. Bridie writes in his prefatory 'Author's Note' to the published edition, that the real-life Robert Knox 'was so theatrical in his life and habit that it is possible to transfer him almost bodily to the stage'. This claim perhaps leaves Bridie open to the charge of laziness in his construction of the character of Knox. The flippant, one-eyed dandy practising experimental anatomy on dubiously acquired cadavers, is, on first appearances, all too much of a stock-villain. What we need to understand from the play, many commentators have insisted, is the interior of Knox's mind and psyche; what motivates a talented man of science to encourage the horrific, 'resurrectionist' or body-snatching scandal of early nineteenth-century Edinburgh? Instead, Bridie gives us only intermittent glimpses of the possible motivations for Knox's seemingly cavalier contempt for moral and social opinion around him. And the suspicion that the dramatist has taken an easy theatrical vehicle in the character might seem to be confirmed when Bridie acknowledges 'the mystery of Knox's attitude' in the preface, both in real-life and within the play. Knox's mysterious psychology, his cruel and flippant behaviour, however, have most light shed upon them when his character is considered within the texture of the play as a whole as opposed to being analysed in a one-dimensional mode of character-study.

Bridie's Robert Knox plays many roles. He is the archetypal nineteenth-century scientific pioneer, pursuing his work in spite of the mass distaste of the *hoi polloi* during the 1920s. He is also an outsider, in his *persona* of sinister dandy (an appearance which proved too much for Alastair Sim in his 1950s production of the play; Sim had his lead-character dispense with the usually obligatory eye-patch for the role of Knox). Knox is, moreover, a very Scottish intellectual rebel. He is a man well equipped to rattle the cage of the bourgeois and Calvinist Edinburgh of his day. We see this as he engages with *brio* in high-flown theological rhetoric with virtually everyone with whom he comes in contact. With deliberate affront to Presbyterian sensibilities, he talks of his work in biology as marking him out as 'the apostolic successor of Cuvier'; Mary Belle Dishart responds by changing the location of his religious simile as she implies that a better comparison would be with that of his great Calvinist namesake, the harsh and misogynistic John Knox. Just to unsettle audience response even more, in what could claim to be a keynote statement in the play, Bridie has Knox claim a yet higher authority for his actions as he announces, 'I have no opinions I would die for. But if I heard but once the noble patriotic cry, "Crucify him!" I would know my cause was good'. Such a claim sets the scene for Knox to be revealed as yet another of Scottish literature's many 'justified sinners', characters who believe themselves chosen or elected (by God, or by an unnamed power) so that they count themselves entitled to act beyond their society's accepted moral code. (The type is found most famously in the sanctimonious speaker of Burns's 'Holy Willie's Prayer', and in Robert Wringhim of James Hogg's *Memoirs and Confessions of a Justified Sinner* (1824); or in two post-Bridie examples, in the figures of Duror in Robin Jenkins's *The Cone-Gatherers* (1955) and the eponymous character in Muriel Spark's *The Prime of Miss Jean Brodie* (1961).) Knox frequently expresses himself in religious terms, which might appear to run counter to his just as frequent declamations in the name of reason and science, as in his dubious desire for confirmatory martyrdom, or when he demands 'Do you know that . . . much of my work is already immortal?' At other times, however, Knox seems to be playing games, either mocking himself or his audience as he takes his theatrical set pieces to the pitch of barnstorming, as instanced in his references to himself in reductive terms such as 'a monstrous fine fellow'. There is a central and unresolved ambiguity in Bridie's presentation of Knox as, on one hand, an idealistic and dedicated searcher for scientific truth and progress, and on the other as a 'justified sinner' with demonic tendencies.

At the start of the play, as he interrupts the drawing-room quarrel of his demonstrator, Walter Anderson and Anderson's fiancée, Mary Belle Dishart, Knox sarcastically enquires if he is intruding upon some 'theatricals'. Bridie often allows Knox to appear to cut through humbug to the essence; and here he seems to do so, since the young lovers' quarrel has arisen because each of them has been indulging in competing, idealised fantasies prior to his arrival – Anderson of becoming a great anatomist like his mentor, Knox; and Mary Belle of an idyllic life in Fife settled as general practitioner with wife. Knox contemptuously reduces this to a 'domestic imbroglio', and proceeds through a series of shifting roles which rupture the proprieties of the drawing room. He begins by casting the young couples' altercation in the context of theatre and poetry. He becomes a ranting visionary desiring persecution by the mob (and so mocks Anderson's idealism, expressed in his quarrel with Mary Belle, where he asserts the altruistic motives of being a man of science). He offers to be the surgeon searching for the 'hidden abscess' in the relationship of the pair. And he then becomes a presiding judge, as he demands the presentation of their emotional difficulties to be aired more calmly. Through all this protean activity we catch a glimpse of the shape-changing (and demonic?) Knox. Bridie subtly has Knox use the traditional terms of folklore as Anderson appeals to him over his dispute with Mary Belle in Act I.

> Walter: To-night I have been offered the choice between my dearest happiness and another year's work at anatomy. I have risked my happiness – I may have lost it – to work with you. Am I right? Have I been a fool? Knox: You are in the right. You have been a fool. You are in the right to be a fool, and a fool to be in the right.

What Knox suggests, at one level, is that the pursuit of truth and social conformity do not necessarily go hand in hand; though in typically elusive fashion Knox evades any real or definitive moral pronouncement. Knox is also questioning the labels the world thrusts on people and situations such as 'fool' or 'right', and this again highlights his unwillingness to accept society's normative roles. He is resentful of the way in which his own life and work are circumscribed by the descriptions of others and, up to a point, his audience can accept this attitude. The conversation in the drawing room, where Mary and Walter discuss Knox prior to his arrival, develops Knox's chameleon characterisation. To Mary, Knox is 'ogreish', but Walter, when Mary questions the extra-marital activities of Knox, argues that this is due to the fact that 'Dr Knox's domestic life has been a tragedy', to which Mary, with considerable insight, responds, 'There is no compulsion upon him to transform it into a French farce.' On one level, again, what we witness is Mary and Edinburgh's New Town drawing-room propriety condemning Knox, which in turn prompts his rebellious, riotous play-acting. To such a restricted view of manners and values Knox is a man marginalised and seen as bestial for his grisly, pioneering work in anatomy, and thus his presence in the drawing room is an uncomfortable one. His unacceptability to Mary may also stem from his grotesque physical appearance; there is additionally the much more mundane reason of having a wife who is said to be suffering from some ailment (unspecified) but whose fundamental problem, as Amelia Dishart avers, is one of class unacceptability. (Hence, Walter's 'polite' but overblown euphemism of 'tragedy' to codify Knox's home-life.) For all these reasons, we see his theatrical and role-playing responses as a complex mixture of self-protection, anger, hurt and defiance. Thus he 'over-plays' the roles he feels middle-class Edinburgh has inflicted upon him, to the extent of overloading and exploding his part. If they want a stage-scientist, a monster, or a even a Satan, Knox seems willing to give in to them; in a travesty of poetic justice we see Bridie's and Knox's awareness of Scottish Calvinist and bourgeois society creating its own devils. Bridie plays with several genre labels which complement the many roles referred to in the play and which create a texture of high artifice. He labels *The Anatomist* a 'lamentable comedy' and, in his preface, refers to the play as a 'fable'. In this way games of definition are played with the reader, just as games of character definition are played with the readership/audience.

Knox deals with a world of exteriors and surfaces because, trapped as he is in roles, he cannot engage more deeply with life – and Bridie exploits the irony of Knox's position as he attempts to lecture Mary on 'life' which he declaims to be 'not all assemblies and quadrilles, or even dressing, bathing and smacking babies'. Knox may consider Mary and her ilk as too overly absorbed with the frivolous and unimportant to recognise the hard realities of 'life'; but for all his apparent ability to deal with these hard realities, he evades a great number of the realities which underpin his idealistic activities – and can be seen as one who, however inadvertently, destroys life.

One of the lives which he has a hand in destroying is Mary Dishart's Edinburgh Old Town slum *alter ego*, Mary Paterson, who, for all her astonishing beauty, her singing, and her vivacity, is a world removed from the middle-class pretension which Knox so despises. Role-playing allows him to deny his own part in her murder as 'the man who buys the beef', choosing to view her as a common prostitute whose life is of no account other than to benefit medical science. The audience however sees deeper, contrasting his snobbish involvement with the pretentious exotic music and manners of the drawing-room-world Disharts with his disgust for the folksong and drink-sodden world of The Three Tuns tavern and its low – but authentically Scottish – life.

It is possible to see Bridie as juxtaposing this Mary with her upper-class cousin; and also possible to see Knox as possessing a morbid horror of real human life and emotion. He avoids or dresses up reality, and is seen at his most crass when he evades the tears of Amelia Dishart (a woman with whom it seems Knox might just share a human relationship) with 'You mustn't cry. It congests the conjunctival sac.' Set pieces are his forte; in them he can posture to his heart's content, sounding mighty fine but in the end revealing to the audience the sheer extent of his bombastic egotism and hyperbolic rationalisation, as here in Act III, in his response to Mary's question as to why Walter should wish to go to London:

> I should say because of some essential and ineradicable strain of vulgarity in his nature. It is this that drives many of our promising young men to these provincial towns. They shiver in the snell east wind of Modern Athens. London! Pompous Ignorance sits enthroned there and welcomes Pretentious Mediocrity with flattery and gifts. Oh, dull and witless city! Very hell for the restless, inquiring, sensitive soul. Paradise for the snob, the parasite and the prig; the pimp and the placeman and the cheap-jack. The

women chatter like parakeets, the men fawn like jackals. On my soul, vulgarity or no vulgarity, I cannot tell you why Walter Anderson is going there. Or what there is in London to awaken in a realist any feeling but loathing and contempt. Yet she entraps great men and sucks their blood. Her streets are littered with their bones.

Bridie is, of course, teasing his London West-End audience here, and also more sardonically, and with historical accuracy, acknowledging the scientific superiority of late-Enlightenment Edinburgh over London. A more important point, perhaps, is being made regarding Knox's methods of defending himself and his self-importance in Edinburgh. Is he in fact jealous of the metropolis, and therefore protesting too much? Does he create a nightmare London (where, undoubtedly, he could have been a great man of science!), so that, in the cosy *milieu* of Edinburgh, he is free to play the Devil for himself? There is certainly enough evidence in these subtleties of interpretation to counter the argument that Bridie's characterisation of Knox is flat and unconvincing.

And there is of course a final subtlety in Bridie's presentation of Knox; for all his posturing and unsureness of identity, Knox can be seen positively, as the worthwhile rationalist Bridie, as a physician himself, respects as a fellow in medical science. But which of the set pieces of philosophical self-justification do we accept as valid?

Arguably Bridie's final comment is that virtually all humans posture, knowingly or unknowingly; but their actual worth may lie beyond this. In some ways, Walter Anderson's behaviour represents a self-deception beyond that of his mentor, Knox. We first see this in The Three Tuns where the raw assistant attempts to mimic the attitudinising swagger of his master. Anderson's discovery of the murder of Mary Paterson, however, allows him the opportunity to take the moral high ground, strongly enough to lead us to think that he will duel with Knox in defence of his principles. But instead Anderson apologises and there is reconciliation between the two anatomists. Additionally, we should be aware of Anderson's ambivalent response to the discovery of Mary Paterson's body in the trunk in the laboratory. He is horrified at the sighting of a beautiful girl who has reminded him of his fiancée. He does not, however, allow this discovery to extend beyond a little trite lamentation to empathise with the human reality of Mary Paterson. Anderson's protest, then, takes the form of a genteelly chivalric (set-piece or role-playing) protest which easily crumbles in the cold light of day, as he grasps the fact that the woman (socially) is very unlike the lady to whom he is betrothed. Anderson ('Arranging churchyard raids. I disapprove of them very strongly') is a decent man, but also a hypocrite who will accept the bodies which come from the churchyard raids, in order to sustain his research. He is also a thoroughly middle-class prig whose role in society will be one of complacent conformity. Weak and conventional, he represents much of what Knox despises.

The Dishart ladies, especially Mary, are also imprisoned in their roles. The high moral tone of Mary, which has appeared normative earlier in the play, has totally dissolved by the end. She constantly invokes her woman's right to change her mind and stance. Returned from Italy with her sister, she forgives Walter for their earlier quarrel and separation as soon as she knows he is to go to London and will thus escape the influence of Knox whom he has previously and patently hero-worshipped. Her earlier disapproval, then, is revealed, in the main, as ignorance regarding the nature of medical science and a jealous peevishness against a man who has supplanted her in Anderson's attentions. Mary's sister, Amelia, is equally disappointing. She can be ironical and cutting to Knox when he offends the decorum of the drawing room. Her refusal to recognise life and passion becomes a kind of poetic justice for Knox when she beats off his desperate entreaties of love for her with the bland facility of drawing room chatter. While we might relish Knox being cut down to size by Amelia in this way, the depressing truth is that she is acting here from her upper-class social conditioning rather than out of considered choice. Clearly, there are undercurrents of reciprocated feeling in her behaviour toward Knox but she never loses sight of her firm location in polite, middle-class Edinburgh society (her reputation, particularly, as a lady). This is shown in her vacuous responses to the equally inane English student Raby, as for example when Raby suggests that Knox should give his lecture in the drawing room in Act III:

> Amelia: Oh, do, Dr Knox. And may we listen? It is on a subject to which ladies may listen?
> Knox: Eminently so, madam. It is on the Heart.
> Amelia: How charming! Do say you will.

Raby is of course deliberately overdone as a joke Englishman and Bridie, the Scottish Renaissance activist, makes hilarious mockery of his stupidity (even if the Naples joke is carried too far). He is a music-hall character with his home location of Sutton Bottom symbolising himself; but the joke of his existence ends up being on Knox. With huge irony, the anatomist is rescued from the angry mob by Raby at the head of a gang of middle-class students, now known as 'Knoxites'. Knox ends up indebted for his survival to the farcical Raby and the very students whose intelligence and class he has constantly lampooned.

No less than the middle-class characters, the lower-class characters are portrayed satirically. In Act II, scene ii, Davie Paterson, Knox's janitor, sits in the laboratory reading his Bible awaiting the arrival of a corpse, and Bridie mocks the Calvinist preoccupation with scriptural scrutiny at the expense of human observation. Burke and Hare, the providers of the body, are also presented in satirical and stereotypical terms. Their stagy Irishness is as transparently false as their account of where they have obtained the cadaver, but their spurious forelock-tugging and shallow explanations are all that are required to stop both Paterson and Walter Anderson enquiring too deeply into their story. Like Knox, if in very different ways, Burke and Hare craftily play on middle-class and Calvinist hypocrisy, cowardice and laziness.

For all her tragic destiny, Bridie also uses Mary Paterson as a satirical stereotype. She represents the timeless and faceless woman at the service of man's sexual (and more sinister) urges – and points up the contrast between herself and her more privileged version, Mary Dishart. At The Three Tuns she affects an image of femininity to attract male attention and this is her undoing. Burke and Hare engage her in a sham flirtation so as to ensnare her. The scene at The Three Tuns represents a grotesque but revealing parody of 'civilised' human behaviour. For instance, mindful of Anderson's reputation, the landlord of the howf seeks to provide him with a false name in his dalliance with Mary and when Anderson resists this attempt, he says with bitter innuendo, 'Aye. You're fine upstanding lads, you o' the Surgeons' Hall.' The implication, clearly, is that Anderson's candour is only owing to his drunkenness. Bridie allows the lower classes of the city a clear understanding of the hypocrisies which underpin eighteenth-century Scottish polite society in the play – and perhaps continue to underpin modern society.

The play ends as it began, in the Dishart's drawing room with Knox's lecture, which the mob prevent from being delivered at the university. This somewhat limp ending is appropriate; Knox has come full circle. The grand stage is denied him, and this prosaic setting is, it suggests, his fitting finale. Is he allowed an honest confession to Amelia of his inner insecurities, behind the ranting actor? Bridie surely leaves his audience to wonder if this too is a performance. He also forces his audience to recognise that Knox and bourgeois Edinburgh society deserve one another, with a satirical commentary which critics have not appreciated. In *The Modern Writer and his World* (1964) the Scottish critic and poet G. S. Fraser argued that Bridie's plays tend toward 'a smug, self-warming, self-approving quality, which has done so much to damn Scottish literature over the last hundred years'. Yet *The Anatomist* can be seen as a subtle and seriously satirical play in its anatomising of Scottish society and human hypocrisy generally, and in its diagnosis of human conventionality.

Mr Bolfry *and the problem of evil*

Bridie's *Mr Bolfry* (1943), a play in four scenes, is a less theatrically dynamic play than *The Anatomist*, but it marks the high point of its author's intellectual engagement with the problem of evil and the character of the Devil. Bolfry, a senior emissary of Satan, is summoned at a Free Church of Scotland High-land manse during the Second World War by the niece of the minister and two bored soldiers who are billeted there. Jean represents 'modern' woman-hood; she is recuperating from illness and on leave, she avows, from 'the Ministry of Interference' in London (humanity's 'dark arts' thus ironically counter-pointing the satanic dark arts we are to encounter in the play). Bolfry is a far more urbane and wily figure than Robert Knox. His clerical outfit and his theological rhetoric are identical to that of the minister, the authoritarian and commanding Mr McCrimmon, and thus Bridie manages to link these apparent polar opposites. Bolfry can quote scriptures, like Hogg's satanic Gil-Martin in *The Justified Sinner* (1824); he holds the centre of stage and play in scene iii, persuasively arguing his demonic case as valid in a modern world.

Jean: We're fighting Hitler.
Bolfry: And who is Hitler?
Cohen: Blind me, I'd've thought that if anybody knew the basket, it'd be you.
Cully: Do you mean to tell me that we've all gone to the trouble of fetching a damned medieval hypothesis out of Hell to tell us what life is all about, and now we have to tell *him?*
Jean: Mr Bolfry, dearest, Hitler is the man who started the War.
Bolfry: Is he? I thought I had done that. How is the War getting on . . . No. don't tell me. I'll try to guess. [*Bolfry helps himself to another drink.*] I should think some lunatic has been able to persuade his country that it is possible to regiment mankind. I should think the people he has persuaded are my old friends the Germans. They are sufficiently orderly and sufficiently stupid so to be persuaded. I should conjecture that mankind has risen in an intense state of indignation at the bare possibility of being regimented. I should think that the regimenters will succeed in hammering their enemies into some sort of cohesion. Mankind will then roll them in the mud for a bit and then pull them out and forget all about them.

635

> They will have much more interesting things to attend to – such as making
> money and making love . . .

Here we find Bridie's characteristic theatrical trick of bringing high-flown
disquisition into a rather mundane domestic setting (a manoeuvre, which
implicitly comments upon post-Enlightenment society's over-neat compart-
mentalisation of matters of metaphysics and practicality into separate
spheres). The melodramatic vision of the humans in the play, who see their
war in apocalyptic terms (as a deciding contest between good and evil), is
mocked. Bolfry offers an implicit critique of the teleological storytelling with
which humanity seeks to order the events of the world. The struggle between
good and evil is interlocked and seen as unending for all human time, far
beyond the ephemeral dispute of the Second World War. This was a daring
approach for Bridie to take at the time, since it flies in the face of the
necessary British propaganda about the magnitude and significance of the
events in which the country was then embroiled.

The quoted passage also points to the personalities of the three young
people. Bridie heavily accents Cohen's Cockney dialogue throughout the
play to counterpoint Cohen's notion that he represents the very epitome of
normality. The centre of his universe is the Borough Road in the East End of
London, the marvels of which he boringly boasts to the other characters.
Jewish, but atheistic, Cohen (rather than representing any anti-semitism on
Bridie's part) is a man who has forgotten the problems of his race. Cully, the
university-educated, highly secularised Anglican, is more intelligent than
Cohen, but suffers from a similar kind of modern and morally detached
sensibility. He talks of having summoned a 'damned medieval hypothesis'
and represents the cool and casually profane way in which modern man
converses unperturbed on verities which would have made his ancestors
tremble. Likewise, Jean is constantly flippant and perpetually seeks entertainment (her easy frivolity being seen in her address to 'Mr Bolfry, dearest'),
having become distanced from her Highland Calvinist upbringing. It is she
who comes up with the diverting idea of casting the spell from Reginald
Scott's *Discoverie of Witchcraft* (1584), one of her uncle's store of fearful books
(but in fact one which an educated audience would recognise as an ironic
comment by Bridie, since Scott was an Oxford-educated Englishman whose
work was designed to expose the folly of belief in witchcraft; his 'Discoverie'
thus being its essential falsity). All three characters are designed as a rebuke
to the easy assurance of the modern age.

The Reverend McCrimmon appears at first as the archetypal dour,
Sabbath-keeping Calvinist minister. Early on Jean identifies Free Church

religion thus: 'They don't worship God. They worship the Devil', and the audience's expectation is surely that a critique of the joyless, sin-centred puritan mentality is to follow. This is, however, a trick which Bridie is playing, and not at all what transpires. McCrimmon is awakened by Mr Bolfry's appearance and arrives in the parlour to debate with this agent of the Devil. From being at first scandalised by Bolfry, McCrimmon finds himself in agreement with much of his characterisation of human life and morality. Both agree that the spirituality of Mankind is the major issue, whereas the young people in the play have dismissed spiritual reality completely. The young teleological view of human progress has no room for a God-and-Devil-created metaphysical and eternal world. Bolfry and McCrimmon, on the other hand, realise the enduring imperfectability of the world and its recurrent struggle with the forces of good and evil.

Bolfry and McCrimmon cannot agree for long; eventually, with the impossibility of any resolution in their debate, McCrimmon chases Bolfry out into the night and over a cliff into the sea, which boils diabolically as it receives the malign presence. Bridie leaves his audience with many unresolved issues, in a story intended as a mirror to the unresolved issues of life itself. Has McCrimmon killed the Devil, as he believes? Or, as the play suggests, have McCrimmon, his wife, his niece, and the two soldiers shared a nightmare? This suggestion is, however, undercut with Bridie's last-minute special effect; Bolfry has left behind his umbrella, and in the middle of their breakfast agreement that it was probably a dream, the umbrella walks out. Once again Bridie takes resort in ambiguity; is McCrimmon supposed to represent a valuable morality? Has he – or Jean and her friends – been taught some ideological humility? As so often, Bridie leaves his audience to decide; they can adopt the conventional and complacent domestic dismissal by the minister's wife that the entire episode is a storm in a teacup, or they can infer a darker meaning.

THEATRE IN SCOTLAND IN THE INTER-WAR YEARS

Professional theatre

Professional theatre in Scotland in the 1920s and 1930s saw a decline. The major theatres in Scotland still hosted a variety of touring companies, which, as in the days of Alfred Wareing, ranged from the best of new productions touring on pre-London try-outs, to rehashes of old London successes. Some companies tried to breathe new life into the touring system. These included The Macdona Players, whose repertoire consisted entirely of Shaw. There were also several touring repertory companies who produced seasons of plays by well-known authors; the best known of these were the Masque Theatre run by Robert Fenemore, the Jevon Brandon-Thomas Company and, later, the Wilson Barrett Company. These groups produced a selection of classic plays and recent West-End successes, but commissioned few new writers and almost no new Scottish plays. The exceptions to this were *The Anatomist,* which was written for performance in Edinburgh by Fenemore's company, and Margot Lister's *Swords About the Cross,* a play about Mary Queen of Scots, which enjoyed a phenomenally successful run with the Brandon Thomas Company in 1936. In fact, both these new plays were amongst the most successful the companies produced, but, sadly, the message of this was not heeded. Although a few young Scottish actors and actresses trained with the companies, there was nothing essentially Scottish about them, and they would often present their repertoire with no changes at theatres in England.

The Scottish National Players

The objects of The Scottish National Theatre Society were to develop Scottish national drama through the production of plays of Scottish life and character; to encourage, in Scotland, a public taste for good drama of any type; and to found a Scottish national theatre. Because of widespread sympathy with their aims, the Scottish National Players dominated Scottish theatre throughout the 1920s; every aspiring playwright wanted to have his or her plays produced by them. From early on, inspired by the example of J. M. Synge and W. B. Yeats, they specialised in verse drama and plays about Scottish rural life. (Dates hereafter in this part are of first performances.) Their great successes were John Brandane's *The Glen is Mine* (1923), George Reston Malloch's *Soutarness Water* (1926), and the verse drama *Gruach* (1923), a study of the early life of Lady Macbeth, by the SNP's Yorkshire-born supporter, Gordon Bottomley. Unfortunately, tensions arose between the supporters of this type of drama and others in the group who felt that their drama should be more relevant to, or at least more representative of, contemporary Scotland. A continuous controversy raged over 'the kind of theatre that we want for Scotland' (with, as we have seen, Hugh MacDiarmid becoming involved, in ways which were perhaps to lead James Bridie to take inspiration from his notion of 'Caledonian antisyzygy').

The Scottish National Players were a small amateur organisation, and could produce only a very limited number of plays each year. Difficult choices had to be made; there was always a faction who felt happier with simple Scots comedies, avoiding controversy – as when this grouping tried (unsuccessfully) to prevent the production of Malloch's *Soutarness Water* because of its alleged blasphemy (a glass of whisky is compared to the Holy Ghost).

The Gunn/Corrie controversy: Highland versus Lowland?

But major controversy surrounded another decision – to produce Neil Gunn's *The Ancient Fire* (1929), rather than Joe Corrie's *In Time o' Strife* (1927). Although this was quite consistent with their 'Irish Players' policy of presenting plays of Scottish rural life and examining Scottish psyche, Corrie chose to interpret their rejection of his play as a political act. Doubtless there was very little sympathy for his politics among the selection committee, but the real storm about their decision came only when the production of Gunn's play failed – Corrie's allegations were made two years after his rejection.

However, the dispute also pointed up a genuine difference of opinion between those who felt that the 'soul' of Scotland, which a national company had to capture, lay in the Highlands, and those who felt that it lay in the industrial Lowlands. It was a difference no one involved in the Scottish Renaissance was to address satisfactorily. The SNP perhaps revered the dramatists of the Abbey Theatre too much, simultaneously adopting a patronising Glasgow-oriented approach to their potential audience. And given their criteria for choosing plays, which would be 'virile and direct', 'observed at source' and having 'the quality of direct truth', there might seem to be some substance in Corrie's claim that his play was rejected on grounds other than its dramatic merit.

Two Scotlands – Ancient Fire or Time of Strife?

Gunn's play, *The Ancient Fire* (1929), attempted to synthesise the two Scotlands, but was accused by MacDiarmid of portraying Gaelic culture as superior to that of urban Scotland. The play is a curious mixture of Ibsen-like realism with social comment and Strindbergian symbolism. Its central character is a Gorbals draper, Lachie MacDonald. He feels caged in Glasgow and takes his annual holiday back home in 'the glen' – poaching. Stalking a fine stag one day, he accidentally falls into a dream or trance, which returns him to the mysterious natural sources of his identity. As in much Scottish Renaissance fiction and poetry, Gunn presents a strong sense of a lost golden age and a celebration of the constant and natural rhythms which rule the land which, he argues, we ignore at our peril. But these theories were anathema to a Marxist materialist like Joe Corrie, for whom Utopia could only be achieved by political means. Reviewers described the play as undramatic (and there certainly are moments, such as the virtually unstageable trance scene, which indicate Gunn's inexperience in the craft of drama). In its favour, however, the play was a determined attempt to explore the roots of Scottish identity and did so more deeply than many of the SNP's productions.

Many members of the Scottish National Players went on to become the first professional actors in Scotland, with careers in Scotland, and influenced the BBC's Scottish drama. A number of them were involved in later enterprises such as the Gateway Theatre in Edinburgh; and the influence of the SNP was sustained. Two quotations from Andrew Wilson in their newsletter from the early 1920s can summarise its ethos:

> If the Scottish Theatre has anything to learn from the nationalist move-ments in European drama, it is the necessity of going far ben into the national soul . . . It has endeavoured to do that by playing two Jacobite pieces, *Campbell of Kilmhor* and *The Dawn*, not in order to propagate antiquated and foolish dynastic politics but to give Scotsmen something to dream over. We have not had anything similar to Yeats' *Kathleen ni Houlihan* . . . we need dramatisation of our lost causes; we would welcome a fine tragic play woven around William Wallace, one which will show us all the splendour of the Man of Scotland, the man who did not merely represent the Scottish nation, but who was the Scottish nation in himself.
>
> Along with the drama we will get comedy. For no country is richer in its vein of humour than Scotland. A Scottish theatre, then must show all the rich treasure of our characteristics . . . It must be a place where the intimacies of Scottish Life, the pawkyness of its people, and the whimsical nature of its events and situations are shown . . .

Surprisingly, the play which most fulfils the objectives of these quotations is Corrie's *In Time o' Strife* (1927). Corrie, who had been a miner himself, presents the economic hardships endured by striking miners in the 1920s, and the pressures which divide families and produce blacklegs. There is no doubting the power of the play, but Corrie's portrayal of character is inconsistent, and tragedy is too often undercut by facile comedy. Moreover, the play is a curious blend of propaganda and morality. It tries to convey socialist theory in an easily understandable and palatable form, but its characters often come across as stereotypical (the heroic mother, the wicked blackleg, the noble striker), and at times there is a strong sense of the play as tract rather than discussion.

Sadly, Corrie's potential was not realised; while amateur companies produced his play, the SNP, disliking its politics, would not. Corrie turned back to amateur comedy, with the occasional short, but outstanding play like *Hewers of Coal* (1927) revealing the loss to Scottish theatre – a loss which, had the radical Unity Theatre then existed, might have been avoided.

Scots or English? The amateur movement

Although Scottish Theatre in the 1930s was dominated by amateur groups, in particular the Curtain Theatre, the decade did see the beginnings of professional theatres in Perth and Dundee. In the next ten years Scottish theatre was to move from amateur to professional, with far-reaching repercussions.

The reasons for the growth in amateur theatre in the '20s and '30s are many; from the increase in leisure time, the educational and 'improvement' encouragement of drama performance, the first-time experience of drama by soldiers during the war, to the growth of organisations like the British Drama League, established to lend scripts and offer advice to amateur players. The Scottish Community Drama Association (SCDA), the umbrella organisation which ran festivals and dispensed advice, grew from twenty-seven members in 1926 to over 1,000 ten years later.

What this upsurge of interest in drama produced was a vigorous competitive streak amongst the clubs, as in the annual SCDA competitions. In Glasgow, élite clubs began to form, which attempted to improve standards of playing and to recruit and train the cream of amateur talent in the days before any specifically Scottish drama training was offered. The undisputed king of the SCDA throughout the 1930s was Joe Corrie. Every pronouncement he made on drama was reported in *The Scottish Stage*, and every new play he wrote was eagerly snapped up for the annual competition. Although he began the decade by claiming bourgeois bias in the SCDA, by 1937 the Newbattle Burns Club Dramatic Society had won the festival with his stark *Hewers of Coal*. Corrie had evolved a vision of Scottish theatre that was genuinely exciting. He saw it as amateur-led, but truly democratic: 'it is a real community drama. Ploughmen, railway-men, fishermen, miners, lawyers, schoolmasters, doctors, and ministers are all writing plays . . . Such a movement cannot fail, must not fail.'

In the cities, other, more élitist, groups were forming. The most prestigious of these groups was culled from the members of various dramatic clubs associated with the Keir Hardie Institute and R. F. Pollock, an architect and amateur theatre director who was very influenced by the theories of Stanislavsky. Pollock's group was called the Tron Theatre Company and was formed when Pollock, inspired by the Chekhov productions at Little Thea-tres in London by Komisarjevsky – a Russian emigré who ensured the place of Chekhov and John Gielgud on the London stage – wanted to bring to Scotland the same meticulously detailed productions as London enjoyed. His main aim, he wrote, was to 'make an audience believe that real things were happening to real people'. To do this he applied a form of the Stanislavskian system; that is, a series of acting exercises which would co-ordinate the physical and mental sides of the character, aiming ultimately, at artistic and psychological truth (as exemplified later in 'method' acting used by film actors like Marlon Brando and Robert de Niro). Pollock's work is worth mentioning not only because it marks the maturing of the Scottish theatre, but also because some of Scotland's best-known actors, like Molly Urquhart and Duncan Macrae, trained with him. Pollock's was the first step away from the amateur organisations that revolved around the SCDA festivals (which Bridie compared to the football league) and towards the Little Theatres with their emphasis on the art of the theatre. The step was vital, both in improving the standards of performance and in enabling groups to nurture the work of playwrights; it provided a permanent theatre and a pool of committed and skilled actors.

Little Theatre was a US invention. The features which distinguished them from other amateur organisations were an all-year-round commitment to the company and the acquisition of a permanent play-house. In the USA, the Little Theatre movement had produced the dramatist Eugene O'Neill, who had learned his craft with the Provincetown Players. This early success had led the movement to be associated with 'good' plays, and 'improvement' – a feature James Bridie was to criticise in 1949 as leading to 'coterie' art. While approving overall, he saw the problems of Little Theatre as limited budget, and dependence on originators who might leave; but he admired Glasgow's Curtain Theatre in particular, for producing the playwright Robert McLellan and the actor Duncan Macrae. His praise for The Curtain was fully justified, but his analysis of the inbuilt self-destruct mechanism in many amateur dramatic organisations was equally accurate; The Curtain later became a victim of its own success.

The Curtain Theatre

Glasgow's Curtain Theatre was founded by Grace Ballantine, Molly Urquhart and other enthusiasts, in what had been the drawing room of a Glasgow West-End Victorian residence. The auditorium seated about seventy and was opened in January 1933. Norman Bruce was its first artistic director; the house dramatist was Robert McLellan and its star actor was John Duncan Macrae. From the start, the theatre aimed at the highest standards of design, acting and direction, and to give Scottish writers and actors a platform. It worked on a subscription policy, like the Glasgow Rep before them, allowing the Curtain to work from a firm financial base and enabling them to commission and produce many new plays, while also allowing room for manoeuvre, should a good new play suddenly arrive. The organisation was amateur, there were few running costs to pay and no problems with actors' contracts, and, with the subscription system, the need to please a crowd disappeared. The highlight of the Curtain's career was their production, in 1937, of Robert McLellan's *Jamie the Saxt*, with Duncan Macrae in the title role, a play and a performance described as a 'revelation which astonished Glasgow'. But Bridie's fears were to be justified; an undisciplined administration and the outbreak of war conspired to bring the Curtain to an end, and it was superseded by The Park, founded in 1941 in the house next door, by John Stewart, who was later to found Pitlochry Festival Theatre.

Scots or English? Robert McLellan (1907–85)

All his life Robert McLellan fought to establish Scots as a legitimate vehicle for national drama and writing (his *Linmill Stories*, 1977, originally produced by BBC radio, and rightly praised as the finest short stories and prose which we have in Scots, has recently appeared in the Canongate Classics series). Scots was his mother tongue, and he saw no reason to abandon a language capable of the full range of human expression, for one in which he felt much less at ease. McLellan was an enthusiastic member of the Scottish Renaissance movement. His early dramatic mentor (as for Bridie) was John Brandane, author of the popular *The Glen is Mine* (1923). McLellan, however, did not follow Bridie on the road to London and to writing plays which would have a wide general appeal. Instead, he chose to write in Scots and to wait until there was a company who could perform his plays. This company he found at the Curtain, where a unique blend of careful production and actors, skilled in both elocution and Scots speaking, gave his plays the production they deserved. McLellan was not given to compromise, however, and his relations with theatre companies were often difficult. In the 1940s and 1950s, in the wake of the Citizens' rejection of *The Flouers o' Edinburgh* (1947), he spent a great deal of energy attacking Bridie and Scottish theatre in general, for what he saw as their betrayal of the principles of Scottish theatre and their importation of English personnel unsympathetic to Scots plays like his own.

643

Jamie the Saxt (1937) is arguably the finest play in Scots or English to emerge from Scotland in the inter-war years. In its picture of 'the wisest fool in Christendom', the apparently eccentric and hapless king of Scotland who is destined to rule both kingdoms, McLellan manages to combine psychological subtlety with almost choreographical stagecraft. James may seem a foolish adolescent, surrounded by problems familial, national and international, and out of his depth in his dealings with burghers, lords, church and English diplomats, but his Scottish glaikitness conceals a sharp mind. Evidence for this can be seen in his victory over enemies like Francis Bothwell and his balancing of contending forces to the point where he triumphantly looks forward to succeeding Elizabeth. Throughout James's travails, the movement of the *dramatis personae* on stage indicates his failure or success; he can be alone or isolated in a corner, or encompassed, as decisions as to allegiance are made, or backed up in triumph, with Bothwell in turn isolated. And beyond characterisation and stagecraft, McLellan deploys Scots as a rich national language juxtaposed with English smoothness and affectation, and as a sustained metaphor for canny and prickly Scottish character.

But beyond this, what does the play achieve? If we disregard McLellan's use of Scots, is there anything left? In other words, is there anything which would survive in a translation into another language, not necessarily English? However we answer, and however one-dimensional some of the characters may seem, like the jealous queen and the villainous Bothwell, actors themselves love this play. Tom Fleming called McLellan 'the greatest dramatist writing in Scots we have had since David Lyndsay'. The actor Ron Bain, who played James with great success in the 1982 revival, considered the role of Jamie the most fulfilling he had had in a long and distinguished career. And McLellan's use of Scots has provoked a variety of responses, from the enthusiasm of poets Alexander Scott and Donald Campbell to Alan Bold's suggestion that Scots makes a play 'a coterie piece, unable to appeal to the majority of Scots'.

The 1930s and Scots comedy

In 1936 Joe Corrie could write optimistically about the Scottish theatre in *The Scottish Stage*: 'A few years ago there was no Scots drama worth talking about. From now on there is going to be progress . . .' This optimism was challenged, however; many critics felt that Scottish audiences would rather see 'simple comedies than psychological plays which they don't understand', and that any part which smacked of political involvement or immorality would either be cut, watered down or simply not performed. Amateurs, notoriously, liked their plays bland and sanctioned by the West-End where, in the 1930s, they would of course have been subject to the censor.

It does seem true that a majority of amateurs were content to produce 'simple comedies'; 'Scots Comedy' became a derogatory term, used to insult, for example, the plays of T. M. Watson, such as *Beneath the Wee Red Lums* (1955). These comedies work within a tradition which stems from the comic scenes of Scottish Chapbooks and transferring of characters like Bailie Nicol Jarvie, from Scott's novels, to the variety stage and Scotch comic turns later in the century. The idea of short turns in dialect was also taken up by news-papers and magazines, and many Scottish amateur entertainers worked up readings from these sources. The short plays performed by amateur com-panies in the 1920s were written by amateur playwrights who chose their subject matter, tone and construction, from the short printed sketches which were readily available. Hundreds of the plays were published by Brown and Ferguson of Glasgow and by printers in Arbroath and Aberdeen. No matter how inconsequential these dramas are in literary terms, they were immensely popular and also important for introducing people who were not regular theatre-goers to drama, presenting as they did no language problem to people unused, or hostile to received pronunciation. The plays had no pretensions to art; they were recreation and entertainment, but as such still merit attention for their important cultural effects.

However, many involved in the theatre felt that an antidote was needed. In *The Scottish Stage* of May 1936, Jack House wrote an article entitled, 'Scotland needs a Left Theatre', calling for the formation of a group which would produce plays like Clifford Odets's *Waiting for Lefty* (1935). In the same year The Glasgow Workers' Theatre Group was established.

A Scottish people's theatre? The 1940s

Although this decade saw many new Scottish plays produced, and the opening of several new theatres, the most important theatrical event of the decade was neither the foundation of the Citizens' theatre in 1943, or the staging of Robert Mcleish's *The Gorbals Story* in 1946, but the start of government subsidy to the arts in general and the theatre in particular. This availability of what were very small sums of money for theatrical enterprises allowed Scottish theatre to develop from a predominantly ama-teur into an almost wholly professional organisation. This change, however, which meant excessive reliance on London and on English plays and players, was not always to the theatre's advantage, and the immense success of

Glasgow Unity Theatre in the late 1940s meant that amateur theatre in Scotland went down in a blaze of glory.

CEMA and Citizens'

Government subsidy of the arts began, as a temporary measure, to provide entertainment to boost civilian morale during the Blitz. It was administered by the Council for the Encouragement of Music and the Arts (CEMA), the forerunner of the Arts Council. In 1942, CEMA established a Scottish committee, with James Bridie responsible for drama. Bridie realised the possibilities that the new funding held for Scottish theatre and saw that his vision of an independent theatre in Glasgow was now, with the assurance of a guarantee against loss from CEMA, a distinct possibility. With George 'Cosmo' Singleton, playwright Paul Vincent Carroll, accountant Norman Duthie and T. J. Honeyman, the director of the Glasgow art galleries, Bridie very quickly raised sufficient capital to open his theatre. With difficulty they settled on the Atheneum Theatre, small and ill-equipped, but in the city centre at the top of Buchanan Street. (Other tenants of the building who were ousted to make way for the new Citizens' Theatre included the fledgling Glasgow Unity Theatre.)

There was no mention in the discussions on the policy for the Citizens' Theatre to provide a platform for specifically Scottish drama. Instead, the directors wanted to produce 'great plays, past, present and future'. With Bridie at the helm, there was a tacit assumption that many of the great plays would either be his, or at least, Scottish. Tactical policy making soon prevailed, however, and the objectives of the theatre were publicly changed to 'the presentation of plays of didactic and artistic merit [a ruse to avoid paying entertainment tax], establishing a stage for Scottish dramatists and actors and founding a Scottish drama school'.

Bridie, virtual controller of the theatre, had a low opinion of the average Glasgow theatre-goer and attempted at first to stress the connection between his theatre and those of the West End. He calculated, probably correctly, that a London producer and company would appeal more than anything native to the élitism of the middle-class playgoers who thronged theatres like the Kings and the Alhambra and the Theatre. Unfortunately, because of the war, there were still very few London producers or actors free; the first producer to come, billed as a London luminary, was Jennifer Souness, who had no experience and left after three productions.

In order to fill out his company, Bridie turned to the skilled amateur players of Glasgow and recruited Duncan Macrae and Molly Urquhart, with others like James Gibson and Eileen Herlie. The theatre opened in 1943, with a production of Bridie's *Holy Isle*; in spite of inexperience, audience discomfort, and rats backstage, the theatre was established. Popular success, however, only came with their third production, Paul Vincent Carroll's *Shadow and Substance* (1944), a play about the reaction to mysticism amongst Irish priests and peasantry.

By 1945, the Citizens' Theatre had outgrown the Atheneum and moved across the water to the Gorbals where the Royal Princess's Theatre was renamed the Citizens'. In spite of the success the theatre had on CEMA tours with his own *The Forrigan Reel*, Bridie chose to open the new building on 11 September 1945 with a non-Scottish play which had failed in London, J. B. Priestley's *Jonson over Jordan*, which explores *bardo*, the Tibetan concept of the dreamlike state after death. Such dubious choices were to become a feature of this theatre – perhaps because Bridie was determined to present plays which were, by his definition, 'great'. He argued that 'If the Citizens' Theatre is forced by its audiences into a more or less beaten track, there is no particular reason why it should continue to exist.' The Citizens', however, did establish a reputation for adventurous plays and new writing, and, as Bridie also boasted, 'Most of these plays have been by Scots.'

Apart from Bridie, in the first few years of the theatre, new plays by Joe Corrie, Eric Linklater, George Munro, Moray McLaren, Craigie Howe, Robert Kemp, Robert McLellan, Frank Carney and William Douglas Home were presented. As with Robert McLellan, Bridie was not always a good judge of other writers' work, and, apart from Eric Linklater, none of the playwrights had the close relationship with the theatre which would have allowed their talent to be nurtured. It was only after Bridie's death that other writers, like Alexander Reid and Alexander Scott, became 'house dramatists'.

Bridie, however, fulfilled his promise to put the Scottish theatre on a sound footing, not only by producing new Scottish plays, but also by commissioning Scottish versions of Molière, productions of Scots classics, and writing his own Scottish version of *A Midsummer Night's Dream* (1948), with Glasgow 'mechanicals'. The theatre, however, failed to stamp itself on the consciousness of Glasgow until the Christmas show of 1950, *The Tintock Cup*. This started life as a rather laboured Christmas play written by Bridie, George Munro and others; but by the first night a team of actors including Macrae, Molly Urquhart, James Gibson and Stanley Baxter, had produced 'Polly from the Palais', 'Battlin' Joe MaClout', 'The Hing', and the immortal 'Tatty Baccante'. These characters had emerged from the actors working on their own set pieces. Although Bridie had written a sketch for Flora MacDonald, played by Macrae to Molly Urquhart's Bonnie Prince Charlie, it was the

647

Baxter/Urquhart characterisations (such as Baccante) which stuck in the minds of the audience.

The Tintock Cup ran from December till May, and was only taken off the stage at the insistence of the Scottish Arts Council. Instead of capitalising on the new audience created by the success of *The Tintock Cup*, Bridie idiosyn-cratically replaced it with *The Top of the Ladder* (1950) by Tyrone Guthrie (who had directed for the SNP, and the 1948 Edinburgh Festival revival of *Ane Satyre*). It flopped. The Arts Council alone were pleased; its charter of 1946 stated that the concern of the council was with the 'fine arts exclusively', suggesting that there was little room for popular drama in its brief. This was a change of policy from CEMA's original encouragement of amateur drama, to one where the arts were divided into the fine and the not-so-fine; and it would have serious repercussions for Glasgow Unity Theatre, the Citizens' only serious rivals in the struggle to establish a permanent Scottish theatre. When the Arts Council withdrew Unity's small grant, Unity accused Bridie of an act of petty-minded wrecking.

Citizens' or People's?

Scottish drama had now two alternatives: a Scottish National Theatre at the Citizens', or a Scottish People's Theatre with Glasgow Unity, the first seen as middle-class and élitist, the second as identifying with Scottish working-class life.

Glasgow Unity was formed in 1941 by an amalgamation of five Glasgow amateur groups, most of whom had a left-wing commitment: the Clarion Players, the Glasgow Players, the Transport Players, the Jewish Institute Players and the Glasgow Workers' Theatre Group. Shortages of materials and manpower forced the groups to work together, and the new organisa-tion was affiliated to London Unity Theatre, begun in 1937 and with a reputation for productions of Odetts, O'Casey and political satire and pantomime.

Each group brought its different traditions. The GWTG had specialised in political agit-prop and pioneered a documentary style of production in Scotland. The Jewish Institute Players had performed several anti-fascist plays. The Clarion Players were closely identified with the Communist Party, and the Transport Players had introduced several very challenging plays, such as Joe Corrie's Audenesque satire on totalitarianism, *And So to War* (1936), into the normally sedate SCDA Festivals.

Initially, Unity's statements of aims contained no reference to the establish-ment of a distinctively Scottish drama; and even today members of the group still recall productions of Gorky and O'Casey as the highpoints of the group's achievements.

UAB Scotland: Glasgow Unity

The impetus towards Scottish drama may have come from GWTB, whose last production, in March 1940 at the Atheneum Theatre, was a mixture of agit-prop, revue and declamatory political poetry, called U [Unemployment] A [Assistance] B [Board] Scotland. This impressive piece of theatre, although written in 1939, is written in the style of a morality play, and with the developing political consciousness of a young worker. It focuses on the economic and social deprivation of Scotland, using music to highlight its message. An impressive and extended central section of the play is a poetic contemplation of Scotland's history from the clearances, through the industrial revolution, to Red Clydeside, and is addressed directly to the audience:

> Paint this picture on your brain.
> This is Scotland. YOUR Scotland.
> Sixteen houses with one common entrance.
> Worn, unlevel floors.
> Loose, unsafe window sashes.
> Cracked ceilings, rat holes.
> Bugs dropping into the food.
> Damp, decay and death.
> Half a million new houses needed.
> What do you say? When do we begin?
> Stop building. There's a war on.
> WHOSE WAR?
> There's a place in the line for a fit man.
> This means you.
> Get back to the breadline.
> This doesn't mean YOU.
> Two out of every three Scottish recruits rejected
> On the grounds of unfitness.
> Two out of three.
> One sixth of the women of Scotland suffer from anaemia.
> 93 out of every hundred children medically examined were found physically defective.
> Where? In India? In China?

What are we going to do about it?
Why must the sum of our efforts prove always a Flodden in the grim page of our history?
There must be a solution.
There is a solution.
What is it?
What is the solution?

This acute awareness of Scotland's history and wrongs was to be reflected in many of the plays written for Glasgow Unity. However, almost as if in reaction against the idea of a Scottish theatre, with its echoes of the Scottish National Players and their concentration on the Highlands and poetry, Unity identified with Glasgow and not with Scotland as a whole: 'Scotland? "It doesna mean much tae Glesca folk"', says Peggie in Robert McLeish's *The Gorbals Story* (1946); his exposure of Glasgow's appalling housing, and Unity's greatest success. This sentiment may very well have been in line with the international socialism of many of Unity members, but such a concentration on one city, whose working class was, in the main, of Irish origin and Catholic, was bound to undermine claims to be a people's theatre, despite their manifesto claims that they aimed at a theatre "indigenous to the people of Glasgow in particular, and Scotland in general . . . reflecting the lives of the ordinary people of Scotland".

At first Unity favoured an international repertoire. They performed political plays like Clifford Odets's *Awake and Sing* (1935), a Group Theatre piece with a strong political message to the oppressed everywhere. Favourite dramatists came to include Sean O'Casey and Maxim Gorky, both writers of heightened naturalism, and this affected the kind of Scottish plays which came to be written once the company was established.

Unity's directors, Avrom Greenbaum and Robert Mitchell, soon developed the company's ability to present new Scottish writing. One of their early successes was James Barke's *Major Operation* (1941), a long play of starry-eyed, socialist-realist, political correctness, which details the conversion to socialism of a Milngavie coal merchant who eventually dies under the hooves of a police-horse during a demonstration in Buchanan Street. Other early plays by Barke included *The Night of the Big Blitz* (1944), about the bombing of Clydebank, and *When the Boys Come Home* (1945), a visionary look at the possibility of a socialist Utopia after the end of the war, set in a Clydeside shipyard, but also including long speeches from Burns, Marx and Rob Roy. (It is instructive to compare Barke's treatment of the Clydebank Blitz with that of Paul Vincent Carroll in *The Strings my Lord are False*, 1942. Both deal with the same events, Barke's apparently much tougher, but only on the surface. For beneath the Hollywood surface of Carroll's portrayal, he manages to introduce many searching questions and deals with sensitive areas, such as the black market, so that finally treatment of the central issues is less glib.)

A successful visit to London with their Scottish version of Gorky's *The Lower Depths* (1903) gave Unity the courage to develop after the end of the war. The first fruit of their new-found confidence and success was a series of remarkable new Scottish plays, the first of which was Ena Lamont Stewart's *Starched Aprons* (1945). This play was a slice-of-life drama set in a Glasgow hospital, and was to provide a pattern for many more, characterised by their detailed observation of character, and their close attention to the rhythms and idioms of Glasgow speech.

These qualities were very evident in the next Unity production, *The Gorbals Story*, a play whose success was to become legendary. The first night saw a squatters' group harrangue the Lord Provost and James Bridie; it was said to have been seen by 100,000 people in its first year, and was later filmed. It became a burden for the company, who never gained great financial profit from it, even from film-rights (the West-End production lost a great deal of money), and they could never quite escape from its overpowering reputation.

In this play, the company became partners in the script, moulding it to suit their needs – a very different way of working on scripts compared to the writer-dominated Citizens'. Only in the pantomime were the Citizens' actors allowed real involvement, and, as we have seen, the results could be sensational. But McLeish was writing for an amateur company, who all wanted their turn and their chance to shine in a character with which they were specially identified. This led to a structure like that of a variety show. It gave a sense of the texture of life in an almost impressionistic way. The resulting picture of Gorbals existence appealed both to those who knew it at first hand, and to the middle classes who flocked to the show to have their eyes opened to another aspect of their native city. But the play, as one might have expected from Unity's pronouncements, was more than just a picture of Gorbals life. James Barke said that if there was a moral to *The Gorbals Story* it was 'solve the housing problem' – sentiments which, along with concern for dialect and local idioms recur throughout the plays of McLeish and Lamont Stewart.

But however serious the intentions of this play, it also underlined one of Unity's organisational problems. It was so successful that some members of the company turned professional in order to tour it as widely as possible, thus opening up a split in the company, which had been dedicated to the group ideal, with all involved in discussing plays before production; as a team without stars. It proved much more difficult to keep up this company spirit once there were two distinct theatre groups. Their idealism continued, however, and bore fruit when, following the success of *The Gorbals Story*, Ena Lamont Stewart was asked to follow with a woman's version. She moved the setting of the story to the East End, changed the decade to the 1930s and called her play *Poor Men's Riches*, changing the name to *Men Should Weep* for the 1947 première production.

Ena Lamont Stewart and social realism

Plays about slum life in the city were not new. Glasgow Repertory Theatre had produced Harold Chapin's *The Philosopher of Butterbiggins* (1915), a portrait of an old man in the Glasgow slums, which was probably written when Chapin was acting in the Glasgow Repertory Theatre. It is a moving account of age and poverty, and a companion piece to his more famous picture of life in London's East End, *It's the Poor that 'Elps the Poor*. Robin Miller's *The Shawlie* (1922) has some very sharply observed characters and dialogue, and paints a picture of life in the slums of Cowcaddens. But these tended to be lonely accounts. Even a play like George Blake's *Clydebuilt* (1922) concentrated, like Galsworthy's *Strife* (1909), on the masters rather than the men in an industrial dispute. Only Joe Corrie showed the other side.

During the 1930s and 1940s there was also a vogue for Glasgow novels, and the Gorbals, for example, had been used as a backdrop for a famous ballet, *Miracle in the Gorbals* (1944) because it was, like Glasgow itself, a by-word for urban deprivation. The setting was of the 'Christ in the slums' variety, but the designs, by Edward Burra, were a powerful evocation of the Gorbals. Paul Vincent Carroll chose the slums of the East End rather than the Gorbals as the setting for his play *Green Cars Go East* (1941). This dealt with the struggles of a young teacher to make a new life for herself and her brother, away from their feckless parents. Carroll, however, did not share Unity's more incisive social analysis of the effects of slum dwelling.

Then came Lamont Stewart's *Poor Men's Riches*, soon renamed *Men Should Weep* (1947), and one of the great Scottish plays of the century. It is the tragedy of Maggie Morrison and her feckless family: her alcoholic, unemployed husband, John; a child with tuberculosis; a son badly married; and nasty in-laws. In *Poor Men's Riches* the tragedy is complete with Maggie dying in childbirth. The play's potential was not to be recognised till its revival in the 1980s by the 7:84 company – perhaps due to its '70s rewriting of the last two acts, so that a contemporary women's perspective was included and much of the original temperance melodrama excised.

It is interesting to compare the ending of *Poor Men's Riches* with that of *Men Should Weep*. In the first, John goes back to drink, Bertie dies, Alec murders Isa, Maggie dies in childbirth and Jenny returns home after an unsuccessful career as a prostitute. The final image of the play is of Jenny trying to sober up her father, saying that they must take care of the children for Maggie's sake, and with John attacking his insensitive neighbours. This is transformed with the coruscating last scene of *Men Should Weep*, in which John is sexually humiliated by Maggie, and all sense of an irrelevant middle-class morality is swept aside. 'There'll be flowers come the spring', may seem like a sentimental phrase to a well-fed and well-housed middle-class audience, but for Maggie it is genuinely thrilling prospect. The play has become a steely and unsentimental look at relationships between the sexes and between the generations. Maggie is no faultless Madonna; she is weak in her treatment of Alec; she is maternally jealous and suspicious of Isa. Nor is she the indomitable working-class woman of spurious and patronising socialist mythology. She is a real person with appalling problems which she meets with courage and common sense, but the constant fight with life wears her down. The play has no need of a denouncement of capitalism from the footlights. There is a critique of the system in every syllable spoken on stage.

Unity also tackled other issues of sexual politics, notably in Benedict Scott's *Lambs of God* (1948), in every way as great a play as *Men Should Weep*. Scott's play takes a similarly unsentimental view, this time of working-class homosexuality, placing his discussion carefully in the context of a small Scottish town. The play, however, has a metaphysical dimension, lacking in all Unity's other plays; a struggle between good and evil for the soul of a young man. The play has real poetic intensity, and resembles a Greek tragedy more than an O'Casey-style play of heightened naturalism. The Unity actors, however, were rather embarrassed by the play's subject matter and failed to give the play the commitment it deserved – all the more sad given that the play has a power beyond most of the writers developed by Unity.

Unity's production methods were based very much on those of Stanislavsky at the Moscow Arts Theatre. In practice, this meant an emphasis on realism, which suited some plays, like *Men Should Weep*, but not others. Spectacular failures included the polished comedy required to do justice to McLellan's *The Flouers o' Edinburgh* (1948) and the sophistication needed to carry off Lillian Hellman's *The Little Foxes* (1939). For the development of Scottish drama this meant that a rigid adherence to naturalism was required, and Benedict Scott felt that some of the universal themes his play contained were left unexplored in the drive to recreate the actual life of a Scottish small-town vennel. This play showed that socialist realism could prove constricting – although, with Ena Lamont Stewart and Robert McLeish having shown how Scots plays could be written, Unity could claim to have justified itself with some honour.

Decline of Unity

Many reasons have been put forward for the demise of Unity. One of the most emotive, and one still widely believed by Unity members, is the hostility of Bridie and the Citizens'. Bridie, it is said, in order to protect his theatre, encouraged the Scottish Arts Council to cut their funding to Unity. In fact, he was not a member of the council at the time, but from some of his pronouncements, it is clear that however much he admired Unity's writers, actors and plays he thought they had gambled away both their funds and their reputation by the neglect of common-sense procedure, and that they had been misled by initial successes in Glasgow. More patronisingly, Bridie associated their audiences with club outings and Rangers supporters – and remarked that they possessed 'a deadly love of the cheap laugh'.

It does indeed seem unfair that Unity was supported as little by the Arts Council as they were. Communist links during the Cold War or not, their work obviously deserved support. However, within the company, the tensions between the amateur and professional sides, coupled with financial misman-agement and the unhelpful attitude of the Scottish Arts Council, led to Unity being disbanded in 1951. Scottish theatre after their demise would be the poorer; and its eventual recovery would owe a great deal to unity.

CHAPTER 34

THE POETRY OF SORLEY MacLEAN

MACLEAN'S GREATEST ACHIEVEMENT?

It would be hard to overstate the importance of the collection which appeared under MacLean's name in early November 1943, with the title 'Dàin do Eimhir' *agus Dàin Eile.* It consists of two parts. The first contains the 'Dàin do Eimhir' proper, a sequence of forty-eight love poems given Roman numerals from I to LX with some gaps, plus a closing 'Dimitto'. The second groups together the 'Dàin Eile'. All texts appear in Gaelic only, but there is a scattering of English prose translations at the very end of the book.

The preparation of the volume had been entrusted to others, in particular to Douglas Young, given that MacLean, who enlisted in the Signal Corps in September 1940, was seriously wounded in the battle of El Alamein in November 1942, and spent the following nine months recuperating in military hospitals. His letters to Young offer valuable insights into the form the poetic cycle eventually took. MacLean was to write, long afterwards, that, when they met in 1940, Young 'pretty well took me over aesthetically' (*O Choille gu Bearradh, From Wood to Ridge: Collected Poems,* 1999). MacLean never allowed the poems in the 1943 volume to be reprinted in their original form. The collections he published in 1978 (*Reothairt is Contraigh: Spring Tide and Neap Tide: Selected Poems 1932–72*) and 1989 both include a generous selection from the *Dàin do Eimhir* sequence, but the lyrics are given individual titles. Only in the latter book did MacLean allow the numbers showing their place in the sequence to be added, discreetly, at the foot of each poem. Yet there are grounds for arguing that it is the 'Dàin do Eimhir', rather than the extended poem 'An Cuilithionn' / 'The Cuillin', the war poetry, 'Hallaig', or the 'Elegy' on his brother Calum, that constitute MacLean's greatest achievement (this case is argued by Christopher Whyte in *Scottish Literary Journal* 17, 1990).

Song-poems, poems and songs

The translation of the title is a problem, since the Gaelic word 'dàin' means both 'poem' and 'song', and the ambiguity is significant. Of the three major

Gaelic poets of the nineteenth century, both John Smith of Iarshadar (Iain Mac a' Ghobhainn, 1848–81) and Mary Macpherson (Màiri Mhòr nan Òran, 1821–98) confined themselves to lyrics in the strict sense, that is, words intended to be sung. In doing so, they followed what remained an overwhelming trend in Gaelic verse right up until the Second World War. The concept of words ordered metrically but independent of a melody was alien to the tradition. Only the wilful and eccentric William Livingston (Uilleam MacDhunlèibhe, 1808–70) produced rambling heroic verse intended to be read, not sung, and his example encouraged few followers.

MacLean's collection broke with the tradition in a second way. Very roughly, it can be said that Gaelic verse in the preceding centuries falls into two categories. The first is public poetry, to which the adjective 'bardic' can with some justification be applied. It is preoccupied with communal and political issues and may often be addressed to a figurehead or an important leader. Trusting to his privileged position within the community, the poet can voice his concerns with relative impunity. Women, too, aspired to this role, though the example of Màiri Nighean Alasdair Ruadh suggests that such ambition was not without its dangers. (For the traditional story of this poet's banishment to Mull at the hands of her MacLeod patron, see the Introduction to *Gaelic Songs of Mary MacLeod*, 1965.) One could argue that the kind of subjectivity, the concept of the self developed in Western cultures in the course of the Enlightenment and the Romantic movement, was absorbed into Gaelic language culture only after a considerable lapse of time. The second category of Gaelic verse is made up of a rich tradition of anonymous popular verse, speaking not infrequently from a woman's standpoint, often linked to a tragic or overwhelming event in the life of an individual who is, as it were, briefly transported to the status of a poet by the strength of his or her emotion.

In MacLean's work, the two strands combine in a way which is both innovatory and transgressive. His verse is not entrusted to oral tradition. It does not rely for its survival on the lips and memories of people often unable to read or write their first language. It reaches the wider community through the chiller medium of print. Abstruse, riven by deep personal conflict, at times exasperatingly cerebral, it is the very opposite of popular poetry. With *Dàin do Eimhir agus Dàin Eile*, MacLean brought the Gaelic tradition resolutely into the contemporary world. Some inkling of the violence of this process can be gained from a terse quatrain, which is the seventeenth of the *Dàin Eile*, or 'other poems'. MacLean never chose to reprint it, but a Scots version by Douglas Young was included in *Auntran Blads* (1943):

'n e d' mhiann bhith eadar sléisdean nìghne	Wald ye be atween a lassie's houghs
's do bheul air blàth a cìochan	wi' your mou' on her breists sae
	fair and sauchin',
's an t-Arm Dearg an éiginn àraich	and the Reid Army warsslan' to daith,
air a shàrachadh 's a riasladh?	jurmummlit and forfochen?

(*Auntran Blads* glossed 'sauchin' as 'supple, tender' and 'forfochen' as 'exhausted by fighting'.)

The writing of the sequence of love poems which forms the core of the book extended over more than a decade, from August or September 1930 until late June and early July 1941. Joy Hendry gives these dates in her essay in *Sorley MacLean: Critical Essays* (1986). It may, however, be worth pointing out that, in a letter to Douglas Young dated 30 March 1942, MacLean gives August or September 1931 as the date of writing of the first lyric in the sequence, and early September 1941 for the last.

The influence of Modernism

If Modernism was becoming a spent force in English literature by the outbreak of the Second World War, MacLean's work nonetheless presents strikingly Modernist traits. As has already been pointed out, it constitutes a break with tradition rather than its continuation. Subjectivity, the idea of the self, is pushed nearly to its limits, in an exasperation that had produced, in a different medium, the 'stream-of-consciousness' or 'interior monologue' technique. The poems' speaker engages in constant debate and dialogue with himself, and the poems are permeated by images of division and fragmentation, as in these lines from XLV, 'An Sgian'/'The Knife':

Rinn sgian m' eanchainn gearradh	The knife of my brain made incision,
air cloich mo ghaoil, a luaidh,	my dear, on the stone of my love,
is sgrùd a faobhar gach aon bhearradh	and its blade examined every segment
is ghabh mo shùil a thuar.	and my eye took its colour.
Thionndaidh mi gach mìrean léige	I turned every jewel fragment
fo ghloine gheur fhuair	under a sharp cold glass
is fo mo lasair chéille,	and under the flame of my reason,
a dh'fhiach iad ceudan uair.	which tried them hundreds of times.

Through its references to other poets and poems, the cycle redefines the literary canon in an eclectic and idiosyncratic fashion, which nevertheless bears witness to the influence of the Modernists on MacLean's own tastes and reading. When a bursary from Portree High School brought him to Edinburgh University in 1929, he was 'full of nineteenth-century English poetry and Gaelic song poetry', but 'the poetry of most prestige at Edinburgh University in those days was the seventeenth-century metaphysicals' (*Studies in Scottish Literature* 14, 1979). It is not hard to detect shades of John Donne's fondness for conceit and paradox in a poem such as 'The Knife', especially when it pushes its chosen imagery almost to the limits of comprehension:

Mar a rachadh i an àireamh	As it increased in the number
nam bruan geàrrte prann	of cut and brittle fragments,
's ann a ghabhadh i aonachd	so it took unity,
'na h-aonar cruaidh teann.	alone hard and taut.
Dh'at i gu meud mìle chuantan	It swelled to the size of a thousand oceans
is chaidh gach bruan 'na bhraon,	and every fragment became a drop,
ach b' i uisge chaidh an cruadal	but it was water that went to hardness
le teannachadh at gaoil.	with the tightening swelling of love.

During his time at Edinburgh University MacLean wrote verse in both English and Gaelic. The former was strongly imitative of the work of Eliot and Pound, who played such an important part in combating the domination of Milton in the English tradition, and gave European poetry of the period before the Renaissance (particularly Dante, the *dolce stil nuovo* Italian poets, and the Provençal troubadours) a central place in their own, redefined canon.

Mingling traditions

'A' Bhuaile Gréine', 'The Sunny Fold', poem XIII in the sequence, is especially interesting for its debt to Ezra Pound and to the troubadour Bertran de Born (c. 1150–c. 1215), whose work Pound had translated and who is named in MacLean's poem. (This is discussed by Christopher Whyte, *Scottish Gaelic Studies* 17, 1996.) It opens with an extended list of women whose beauty has been celebrated in poetry and song:

Do m' shùilean-sa bu tu Deirdre	To my eyes you were Deirdre
's i bòidheach sa bhuaile ghréine:	beautiful in the sunny cattle-fold;
bu tu bean Mhic Ghille Bhrìghde	you were MacBride's wife
ann an àilleachd a lìthe.	in her shining beauty.

Bu tu nighean bhuidhe Chòrnaig	You were the yellow-haired girl of Cornaig
is Mairearad an Amadain Bhòidhich,	and the Handsome Fool's Margaret,
an Una aig Tómas Làidir,	Strong Thomas's Una,
Eimhir Chù-chulainn agus Gràinne,	Cuchulainn's Eimhir and Grainne.
bu tu té nam mìle long,	You were the one of the thousand ships,
ùidh nam bard is bàs nan sonn,	desire of poets and death of heroes,
's bu tu an té a thug an fhois	you were she who took the rest
's an t-sìth bho chridhe Uilleim Rois,	and the peace from the heart of William Ross,
an Audiart a bhuair De Born	the Audiart who plagued De Born,
agus Maebhe nan còrn.	and Maeve of the drinking horns.

In *Sorley MacLean: Critical Essays* (1986), Tomás MacSiómóin speaks of this as 'a veritable galaxy of *femmes fatales* and tragic heroines'. We have Queen Maeve from the *Táin Bó Cuailnge* (composed through the 7th and 8th centuries); Deirdre and Eimhir from the Ulster Cycle; Grainne from the Fenian Cycle; the Una whose praises Thomas Costello sang in Irish; the Cornaig girl; and Margaret from 'An t-Amadan Bòidheach', the last two immortalised in Scottish Gaelic; Mór, who rejected the love of William Ross of Gairloch (1762–90); Maud Gonne, idolised by William Butler Yeats; and, of course, the Audiart mentioned in Bertran de Born's 'Dompna pois de me no'us chal'. What matters here, as much as the range of erudition, is MacLean's determined mingling of elements from different traditions not hitherto brought together in a single poem. The strategy is an indication of what he was attempting to do aesthetically, on the larger scale of the cycle as a whole.

The same eclecticism comes to the fore at the end of XX, where he cites Yeats, Blok and William Ross as the models whose virtues he would like to combine in his own lyrics. It is almost certain that MacLean owed his familiarity with the Russian poet Aleksandr Blok (1880–1921) (whose initial enthusiasm for the revolutionary movements of 1917 eventually turned to dismay and despair) to the work of Hugh MacDiarmid. He first read MacDiarmid at the end of his university career, and subsequently wrote (see William Gillies's *Ris a' Bhruthaich: The Criticism and Prose Writings of Sorley MacLean*, 1985) that:

the lyrics of Hugh MacDiarmid might very well have destroyed any chances I ever had of writing poetry . . . To me, the best of them were, and still are, the unattainable summit of the lyric and the lyric is the summit of all poetry . . . In them I saw a timeless and 'modern' sensibility and an almost implicit 'high seriousness' and an unselfconscious perfection of rhythm that could not be an exemplar because it was so rare.

He discussed the remaining two poets at some length in a letter of 12 December 1940 from Catterick Camp to Douglas Young:

> I am afraid that I am one of those weaklings who have one love affair that upsets the whole of their lives. No doubt many a bourgeois Philistine is in the same predicament but so were Yeats and William Ross. At least Ross was. I now am come very much to doubt the depth of Yeats' feelings. . . . most of his finest poetry is just a specious camouflage for his feelings . . . I even doubt the depth of his feelings to Maud Gonne. After all he did not become a revolutionary for her sake. He just remained a crossed troubled aesthete.

The degree of self-projection in MacLean's relationship to Yeats is unmistakable. He implies that there was an element of inflation, of sham, in the Irish poet's unrequited love for Maud Gonne and that, if it had been genuine, Yeats would have had to become a revolutionary. MacLean evidently placed a great deal of value on sincerity in poetry, and also saw love and political commitment as intricately related.

'An Roghainn'/'The Choice'

His own poem on the topic comes roughly one third of the way through the *Dàin do Eimhir* sequence. It is numbered XXII and was titled later.

Choisich mi cuide ri mo thuigse	I walked with my reason
a-muigh ri taobh a' chuain;	out beside the sea.
bha sinn còmhla ach bha ise	We were together but it was
a' fuireach tiotan bhuam.	keeping a little distance from me.
An sin thionndaidh i ag ràdha:	Then it turned saying:
A bheil e fìor gun cual	Is it true you heard
thu gu bheil do ghaol geal àlainn	that your beautiful white love
a' pòsadh tràth Di-luain?	is getting married early on Monday?
Bhac mi 'n cridhe bha 'g éirigh	I checked the heart that was rising
'nam bhroilleach reubte luath	in my torn swift breast
is thubhairt mi: Tha mi cinnteach;	and I said: most likely;
carson bu bhreug e bhuam?	why should I lie about it?

Ciamar a smaoinichinn gun glacainn	How should I think that I would grab
an rionnag leugach òir,	the radiant golden star,
gum beirinn oirre 's gun cuirinn i	that I would catch it and put it
gu ciallach 'na mo phòc?	prudently in my pocket?
Cha d' ghabh mise bàs croinn-ceusaidh	I did not take a cross's death
ann an éiginn chruaidh na Spàinn	in the hard extremity of Spain
is ciamar sin bhiodh dùil agam	and how then should I expect
ri aon duais ùir an dàin?	the one new prize of fate?
Cha do lean mi ach an t-slighe chrìon	I followed only a way
bheag ìosal thioram thlàth,	that was small, mean, low, dry, lukewarm,
is ciamar sin a choinnichinn	and how then should I meet
ri beithir-theine ghràidh?	the thunderbolt of love?
Ach nan robh 'n roghainn rithist dhomh	But if I had the choice again
's mi 'm sheasamh air an àird,	and stood on that headland,
leumainn á neamh no iutharna	I would leap from heaven or hell
le spiorad 's cridhe slàn.	with a whole spirit and heart.

The lyric is written in something very close to ballad metre, alternating lines of four and three stresses. The characteristic Gaelic rhyming of stressed vowels (but not the following consonants) links words at the end of even lines ('chuain' and 'bhuam', 'òir' and 'phòic'), and occasionally the last stressed vowel in an odd line is echoed in the course of the line immediately following ('éirigh' and 'reubte' in the third stanza, 'chrìon' and 'ìosal' in the sixth). The situation has a ballad-like feeling, too. Immediately before a wedding, there is the hint of a secret love which, while not dangerous enough to threaten its interruption, will nevertheless be 'checked'. The dialogue during a walk along the sea's edge is deceptively normal, until one realises that the poet has divided into two, and is engaged in a discussion with his 'reason' which, for the time being, exists separately from the rest of him. It (in the Gaelic poem 'she') speaks accusingly, even contemptuously, and the poet's reply is full of bitterness and self-accusation. He has created for himself what would be described today as a logical double-bind. The only way to deserve the love of the woman who is about to marry another man would have been to volunteer as a soldier in the Spanish Civil War, and to meet death in that country. In other words, either choice means losing her, because by failing to enlist, the poet has lost, as it were, his claim upon her love. The closing quatrain is, and is perhaps intended to be, unconvincing, as it indicates no way out of the impasse. The poet is unsure whether his starting point is heaven or hell, and the closing word in the Gaelic text, 'slàn', is a key word throughout the cycle, combining as it does the meanings 'whole' and 'healthy', inextricably linked and equally unattainable for this deeply riven and tormented speaker.

It is possible to indicate a precise biographical background to this lyric. At a Celtic Congress in August 1937, MacLean met and fell in love with an Irishwoman who in December 1939 married a man who gave up his Jesuitical training and became a bit of a socialist. Yet it would be a mistake to establish too direct a connection between lived experience and the poetry into which it was transmuted. MacLean used the name Eimhir rather as the Provençal troubadours used a 'senyal' to disguise the identity of the woman their singing was addressed to. The poems in the cycle appear to have been inspired by at least three different women. In the interview with Angus Nicolson, MacLean admits to simplifying the circumstances of his life so as to attain a greater clarity and concision in the poetry:

> I would say myself, you see, that the Spanish Civil War, and especially 1937, was a very important year for me because certain circumstances, family circumstances, prevented me from going to fight in the International Brigade. It wasn't a woman fundamentally that kept me from going through there was one.

In real life, love took second place to more mundane considerations, as he recalls in *Ris a' Bhruthaich*:

> My mother's long illness in 1936, its recurrence in 1938, the outbreak of the Spanish Civil War in 1936, the progressive decline of my father's business in the Thirties . . . my rash leaving of Skye for Mull late in 1937, and Munich in 1938, and always the steady unbearable decline of Gaelic, made those years for me years of difficult choice, and the tensions of those years confirmed self-expression in poetry not in action.

The seeds of MacLean's rueful classification of Yeats as 'a crossed troubled aesthete', a condemnation which is also, after its fashion, an identification, lie here.

This cerebral self-torment, with its neat, imprisoning syllogisms couched in a deceptively limpid, folktale-like narrative, is only one of the strands in the 'Dàin do Eimhir'. Another is a visionary, nightmarish kind of writing which borders on the surreal. MacLean told Young (in the letter of 30 March 1942 already referred to) that two poems in the sequence (XXVIII and XXIX, which in the 1943 volume already bear the titles 'Na Samhlaidhean' and 'Còin is Madaidhean-Allaidh', or 'The Ghosts' and 'Dogs and Wolves') had been 'composed simultaneously in a troubled sleep'. He wrote that he had 'never changed one word from that first writing down'.

The second of the pair is a very remarkable poem indeed, and again is quoted in full:

Thar na sìorraidheachd, thar a sneachda,	Across eternity, across its snows
chì mi mo dhàin neo-dheachdte,	I see my unwritten poems,
chì mi lorgan an spòg a' breacadh	I see the spoor of their paws dappling
gile shuaimhneach an t-sneachda:	the untroubled whiteness of the snow:
calg air bhoile, teanga fala,	bristles raging, bloody-tongued,
gadhair chaola 's madaidhean-allaidh	lean greyhounds and wolves
a' leum thar mullaichean nan gàrradh,	leaping over the tops of the dykes,
a' ruith fo sgàil nan craobhan fàsail,	running under the shade of the trees of the wilderness,
a' gabhail cumhang nan caol-ghleann,	taking the defile of narrow glens,
a' sireadh caisead nan gaoth-bheann;	making for the steepness of windy mountains;
an langan gallanach a' sianail	their baying yell shrieking
thar loman cruaidhe nan àm cianail,	across the hard barenesses of the terrible times,
an comhartaich bhiothbhuan na mo chluasan,	their everlasting barking in my ears,
an deann-ruith a' gabhail mo bhuadhan:	their onrush seizing my mind:
réis nam madadh 's nan con iargalt	career of wolves and eerie dogs
luath air tòrachd an fhiadhaich	swift in pursuit of the quarry,
troimh na coilltean gun fhiaradh,	through the forests without veering,
thar mullaichean nam beann gun shiaradh;	over the mountain tops without sheering;
coin chiùine caothaich na bàrdachd,	the mild mad dogs of poetry,
madaidhean air tòir na h-àilleachd,	wolves in chase of beauty,
àilleachd an anama 's an aodainn,	beauty of soul and face,
fiadh geal thar bheann is raointean,	a white deer over hills and plains,
fiadh do bhòidhche ciùine gaolaich,	the deer of your gently beloved beauty,
fiadhach gun sgur gun fhaochadh.	a hunt without halt, without respite.

The versification is very different from that of 'The Choice'. All lines are rhymed on the penultimate syllable, in groups of two or four. Even the reader who has no Gaelic can observe the repeated vowel sound in the spellings: 'snEAchda', 'dhEAchdte', 'brEAcadh', 't-snEAchda'; 'cAOl-ghlEAnn', 'gAOth-bhEAnn'; 'AOdainn', 'rAOintean', 'gAOlaich', 'fhAOchadh'. The sustained use of syntactical parallelism, evident in both the original and the translation ('Across . . . across . . . I see . . . I see . . . leaping . . . running . . . taking . . . making . . .') encourages one to read very fast, as it is only necessary to pay attention to the new elements introduced into a structure with which the reader is already familiar. All the lines are effectively end-stopped. The effect is of an obsessive hammering which reflects the action of the poem, an endless hunting, a Möbius loop which will permit no escape or respite.

The landscape is recognisable. MacLean has chosen for his imagery a hunt through wild, barren country, and Gaelic is rich in descriptive vocabulary for such phenomena. Nevertheless, this is an image. He modernises the traditional theme by making it into an allegory, turning it into an expression of psychological processes and an emotional state. The pack of hounds represents the poems he has not written (and will not write?); they are dogs of poetry, both 'mild' and 'mad'. The nature of their prey is revealed only gradually. They are pursuing a beauty which is both physical and spiritual, the beauty of Eimhir, the addressee of all the poems in the cycle. The implication is that, were MacLean's poems to succeed in catching up with the woman he loves, she might well be torn to pieces by them. The situation of unrelenting frustration at the same time ensures her survival.

There is, then, a strain of ambivalence in the kind of loving expressed in the poems of the cycle. It comes powerfully to the fore in the last stanza of XIX, another poem of the 1943 collection which MacLean never reprinted:

Thog mi an calbh seo	I raised this pillar
air béinn fhalbhach na tìme	on the shifting mountain of time,
ach 's esan clach-chuimhne	but it is a memorial-stone
a bhios suim dheth gu dìlinn,	that will be heeded till the Deluge,
is ged bhios tusa aig fear-pòsda	and, though you will be married to another
is tu gun eòl air mo strì-sa,	and ignorant of my struggle,
's e do ghlòir-sa mo bhàrdachd	your glory is my poetry
an déidh cnàmhachd do lìthe.	after the slow rotting of your beauty.

The lines have an undeniable classical poise, given the reminiscence of the last ode in Horace's third book with which the stanza opens. Emotionally, there is a confusing mixture of triumph, vindictiveness and pride. The speaker acknowledges that he has lost Eimhir definitively to another man, yet it is as if the rival will be left, in the course of time, with only a wraith of what she once was, while she will live on forever, intact, in these poems. A second theme of the cycle, less often discussed, is the poet's clear awareness that, thanks to the poems Eimhir inspires in him, he is ascending to a significant place within the Gaelic tradition and, further afield, in the literature of both Scotland and Europe. If some readers might accuse MacLean of lacking modesty, one can only reply that time has proved him to be absolutely justified in the claims he made.

'An Cuilithionn' / 'The Cuillin'

The surreal, automatic quality in the writing of 'Dogs and Wolves' recurs unmistakably at the conclusion of 'An Cuilithionn' / 'The Cuillin', an extended poem which MacLean started writing in spring or early summer 1939. MacLean has said the lines in question 'came to me in sleep in the last days of December 1939' and they have a whispering, haunted quality:

Có seo, có seo oidhche dhona,	Who is this, who is this on a bad night,
có seo a' coiseachd air a' mhonadh?	who is this walking on the moorland?
Ceumannan spioraid ri mo thaobh	The steps of a spirit by my side
agus ceumannan ciùin mo ghaoil,	and the soft steps of my love:
ceumannan, ceumannan air na sléibhtean,	footsteps, footsteps on the mountains,
monmhar cheumannan ag éirigh:	murmur of footsteps rising,
ceumannan fiata, ceumannan ciùine,	quiet footsteps, gentle footsteps,
ceumannan èalaidh socair mùinte.	stealthy mild restrained footsteps.

In a way not dissimilar to what happened in 'Dogs and Wolves', the range of mountains in Skye is given a meaning, a charge, far beyond mere physical presence. They come to represent everything humanity can aspire towards in times of oppression and despair and, at the conclusion of this, the seventh and last part of the poem, they rise in the far distance, an indestructible source of hope and fortitude:

Thar lochan fala clann nan daoine,	Beyond the lochs of the blood of the children of men,
thar breòiteachd blàir is strì an aonaich,	beyond the frailty of plain and the labour of the mountain,
thar bochdainn, caithimh, fiabhrais, àmhghair,	beyond poverty, consumption, fever, agony,
thar anacothrom, eucoir, ainneart, ànraidh,	beyond hardship, wrong, tyranny, distress,

665

thar truaighe, eu-dòchas, gamhlas, cuilbheart,	beyond misery, despair, hatred, treachery,
thar ciont is truaillidheachd, gu furachair,	beyond guilt and defilement; watchful,
gu treunmhor chithear an Cuilithionn	heroic, the Cuillin is seen
's e 'g éirigh air taobh eile duilghe.	rising on the other side of sorrow.

The sight of the Cuillin, from MacLean's viewpoint, becomes a kind of alphabet for the predicament of Europe at the beginning of the Second World War, and for the sorrowful lot of humanity since the beginning of time; a lot which makes the heroic values embodied by the mountains all the more precious and indispensable. In the second extract from this section, the reader may have noticed a tendency to accumulate adjectives for a single noun, which has been a characteristic feature of Gaelic verse at least since the eighteenth century. What is good style in Gaelic might well be considered bad style in English. In 'Dogs and Wolves', MacLean revealed a fondness for abstract nouns, most notable in elements such as 'caisead' ('steepness') and 'loman' ('barenesses'). The closing paragraph of 'The Cuilithionn' presents the reader with a veritable avalanche of abstract nouns, whose harsh, intractable effect tellingly mirrors the very negative realities over which, nonetheless, the mountains tower. Stylistically, it is a fascinating effect, and not untypical of MacLean at his most experimental.

MacDiarmid and 'An Cuilithionn'

It is tempting to see MacDiarmid's influence in the plan of 'The Cuillin', for MacLean has written that the example of *A Drunk Man Looks at the Thistle* (1926), which he considered 'the greatest long poem of the century I have read', had 'converted me to the belief that the long medley with lyric peaks was the great form for our age' (*Ris a' Bhruthaich*). He broke off work on the poem in December 1939. There was some talk of publishing it in 1943, but the conduct of Stalin's army at the time of the Warsaw Uprising in 1944 destroyed any lasting idealism MacLean might have entertained as to Russian Communism, leaving him 'politically as well as aesthetically disgusted' with most of the poem. Sections of it appeared in *Chapman* magazine between 1987 and 1989, and in 1989 MacLean reprinted, as the second part of *From Wood to Ridge*, 'what I think tolerable of it'. The Sorley MacLean papers acquired in 2001 by the National Library of Scotland contain the 1939 version of the poem, over 400 lines longer than the version MacLean eventually published.

Maclean's war poems

MacLean's war poems are, not surprisingly, informed by a grim and almost resigned heroism, a respect for courage and manliness which does not make distinctions of race or class. This makes them very different from those of George Campbell Hay (Deòrsa MacIain Deòrsa, 1915–84) who, though he too saw service in North Africa, refused to view the combat as anything but a vicious and senseless torment inflicted on ordinary men and women by the leaders of both sides. 'Curaidhean' / 'Heroes' is a generous if tight-lipped tribute to an unlikely champion, an Englishman whose valour and whose death MacLean was witness to in Egypt:

Fear beag truagh le gruaidhean pluiceach	A poor little chap with chubby cheeks
is glùinean a' bleith a chéile,	and knees grinding each other,
aodann guireanach gun tlachd ann –	pimply unattractive face –
còmhdach an spioraid bu tréine.	garment of the bravest spirit.

This account of the man goes very much against the traditions of Gaelic battle poetry, where evident prowess and outstanding physical beauty are taken to be the natural and inevitable signs of the individual who will carry out heroic feats. There is little sense of glory in the Englishman's fate, more of a harsh necessity willingly accepted:

Thàinig fios dha 'san fhrois pheileir	Word came to him in the bullet shower
e bhith gu spreigearra 'na dhiùlnach:	that he should be a hero briskly,
is b' e sin e fhad 's a mhair e,	and he was that while he lasted,
ach cha b' fhada fhuair e dh'ùine.	but it wasn't much time he got.

The word used here for 'hero', 'diùlnach', is glossed in Dwelly's dictionary (under the form 'diùlannach') as 'hero, brave man', 'good man', 'handsome man' (and derives, ironically, from a Gaelic word for 'payment', 'dìol', having at one time been used for mercenary soldiers). The closing quatrain of the poem sums up the paradox of this unprepossessing creature's heroism, and sets him against the hero of the Battle of Sheriffmuir, whose death in 1721 (or possibly 1724) was lamented by Sìlis Nighean Mhic Raghnaill, more commonly known as Sìlis na Ceapaich (of Keppoch) in a celebrated song:

Chunnaic mi gaisgeach mór á Sasainn,	I saw a great warrior of England,
fearachan bochd nach laigheadh sùil air;	a poor manikin on whom no eye
	would rest;

| cha b' Alasdair á Gleanna Garadh– | no Alasdair of Glen Garry; |
| is thug e gal beag air mo shùilean. | and he took a little weeping to my eyes. |

MacLean reproduces a line from Sìlis's song, 'Thug thu 'n diugh gal air mo shùilibh', inserting the word 'beag' ('little') as if to emphasise the difference in stature between the soldier he is celebrating and the legendary figure from the Gaelic past. This can be seen in Colm O'Baoill's *Bàrdachd Shilis na Ceapaich / Poems and Songs by Sileas MacDonald c. 1660–c. 1729* (1972).

Although 'Heroes' in fact dates from 1965, it would appear that a large portion of MacLean's most significant work had been written by the end of the war. Joy Hendry's discussion in 'The Man and his Work' in *Sorley MacLean: Critical Essays* (1986) attributes this decline in output to material circumstances:

> MacLean now had a wife and three daughters to support, and the necessity of teaching meant that he had little energy left to write in the years 1943–72. Even week-ends did not provide much respite, because it would usually take until Sunday for new ideas to come and he would rarely find time to write them down before Monday morning destroyed the beginnings of creative activity and the possibility of intellectual continuity.

'Time, the deer, is in the wood of Hallaig'

A high point of the later period comes with a poem first published in the Gaelic-language quarterly *Gairm* in 1954, 'Hallaig'. The poem takes its name from a settlement on the east side of Raasay, MacLean's native island, abandoned in the course of the clearances which occurred there between 1852 and 1854. The clearances are never explicitly mentioned in 'Hallaig'. The events of the poem take place 'gun bhristeadh cridhe an sgeòil' ('without the heartbreak of the tale'). This indicates the subtlety of MacLean's approach to a topic which, having been obligatory for so many Gaelic poets over more than a century, had also become hackneyed and predictable in its treatment. The epigraph itself ('Tha tìm, am fiadh, an coille Hallaig' / 'Time, the deer, is in the wood of Hallaig') gives the reader notice that the poem should not be read in everyday, logical terms. The opening stanza confirms one's impression that a different organising principle is at work:

| Tha bùird is tàirnean air an uinneig | The window is nailed and boarded |
| troimh 'm faca mi an Aird an Iar | through which I saw the West |

's tha mo ghaol aig Allt Hallaig	and my love is at the Burn of Hallaig,
'na craoibh bheithe, 's bha i riamh . . .	a birch tree, and she has always been . . .

The opening image is a violent one. It is almost as if an eye has been nailed and boarded over. (The Gaelic word, 'uinneag', derives ultimately from the Norse 'windauga' or 'wind eye', which is also the source of the English translation, 'window'.) The stanza is phrased so as to imply a logical connection between its two elements, the boarding of the window and the presence of the speaker's loved one in the form of a tree, yet the reader struggles to establish a causal link between the two. Here, and repeatedly in the poem, MacLean exploits a syntactical feature of Gaelic by which an English sentence such as 'I am a doctor' appears in Gaelic as 'I am in-my doctor' ('Tha mi 'nam dhotair'). Where the English translation must be satisfied with a mere apposition ('my love is at the Burn . . . / a birch tree . . .'), the Gaelic says something much closer to 'she is in-her birch tree'. By identifying natural features as human presences, the speaker repopulates the deserted township thanks to a feat of the imagination which, however, is limited to the time of his own existence as a thinking subject. His beloved is a birch, a hazel and a rowan tree in turn. The sons and daughters of Norman and Big Hector 'are a wood / going up beside the stream' ('Tha 'n nigheanan 's am mic 'nan coille / a' gabhail suas ri taobh an lòin'). A clear distinction is made between the alien, invasive pines on Cnoc an Rà and the birch wood which is the object of the poet's love. Again, no explicit reference is made to the replacement of the native population by incomers or sheep. The poem is contented to remain within its own, allusive frame of reference.

Next comes 'the Sabbath of the dead', where those who have vanished return to Hallaig, with the poem's single most haunting, elliptical line: 'the dead have been seen alive' ('Chunnacas na mairbh beò', the first word in the line is an unusual verbal form which emphasises the exceptional nature of what is happening):

Na fir 'nan laighe air an lianaig	The men lying on the green
aig ceann gach taighe a bh' ann,	at the end of every house that was,
na h-igheanan 'nan coille bheithe,	the girls a wood of birches,
dìreach an druim, crom an ceann.	straight their backs, bent their heads.

The speaker lovingly reiterates a series of place-names which may now be known only to a small community of people, and which feel like part of an eternal vocabulary as the girls return 'from Clachan, / from Suishnish and the land of the living' ('as a' Chlachan / á Suidhisnis 's á tìr nam beò'), their laughter filling the surrounding landscape. At the close, a bullet from the gun of love strikes the deer, whom we know to represent time. The time which separates the speaker from the centuries when this place was alive and inhabited can be abolished in a bloodless killing which will have value 'while I live' ('ri m' bheò'). The implication seems to be that, once those like MacLean with an inherited knowledge of Raasay tradition and lore are gone, the miracle of remembering and re-evocation contained in 'Hallaig' will no longer be possible. The poem stands as a testimony that this may not prove to be so.

Following MacLean: some further reading in Gaelic poetry

While MacLean's achievement is undoubtedly outstanding, the picture of Gaelic poetry in the latter half of this century would not be complete without consideration of the work of Derick Thomson (Ruairidh MacThòmais, 1921–), a Lewisman, for many years Professor of Celtic at the Glasgow University and editor of Scotland's longest-standing literary magazine, the Gaelic quarterly *Gairm*. His work is collected in *Creachadh na Clàrsaich: Cruinneachadh de Bhàrdachd 1940–80 / Plundering the Harp: Collected Poems 1940–80* (1982), since which two further volumes, *Smeur an Dòchais / Bramble of Hope* (1991) and *Meall Garbh / The Rugged Mountain* (1995) have appeared. A new edition of the work of the unjustly neglected George Campbell Hay (son of John MacDougall Hay, author of the novel *Gillespie*, 1914) has recently appeared from Edinburgh University Press (2000). The bilingual anthology *Nua-bhàrdachd Ghàidhlig / Modern Scottish Gaelic Poems* [1976] (1995) sets MacLean's poems alongside the work of both, as well as that of Iain Crichton Smith (Iain Mac a' Ghobhainn, 1928–) and Donald MacAulay (Dòmhnall MacAmhlaigh, 1930–), who edited this collection. Eight younger poets are featured in *An Aghaidh na Sìorraid-heachd: Ochdnar Bhàrd Ghàidhlig / In the Face of Eternity: Eight Gaelic Poets* (1991), a collection edited by Christopher Whyte, and Polygon have recently published individual, bilingual collections by three poets (Meg Bateman, Rody Gorman and Aonghas MacNeacail). The signs are that the tradition is far from fading, as the twenty-first century begins. The interested reader can explore twentieth-century Scottish Gaelic verse in Ronald Black's ambitious anthology, *An Tuil* (1999). Derick Thomson gives an authoritative overview of the tradition in *An Introduction to Gaelic Poetry* (1990). An edition with commentary of the 'Dàin do Eimhir' by Christopher Whyte, including eight restored or unpublished items, will appear in early 2002 as the annual volume of the Association for Scottish Literary Studies.

CHAPTER 35

THE EPIC FICTION OF NEIL GUNN

Modern Scottish fiction reaches its highest peak in the novels of Neil M.
Gunn . . . so far the only Scottish novelist whose work in some measure
embodies all the ideals of the Scottish Renaissance. On the surface, Gunn
seems chiefly or even exclusively concerned to mirror the way of life followed
by crofting and fishing communities of Caithness and Sutherland. But . . .
he is looking for the pattern of life, the underlying ritual, the myth.

These words of Kurt Wittig in *The Scottish Tradition in Literature* (1958) provide
a perceptive starting point for examining the work of Gunn. In contrast with
the ultimately lonely and arguably negative vision of Change and Death in
Gibbon's *Quair* (1932–4) and the exuberant but finally reductive mockery of
renaissance in Linklater's finest work, *Magnus Merriman* (1934), Gunn
celebrates Highland and Scottish tradition, legend and myth with an affirmative intensity only rivalled by MacDiarmid and Soutar. But Gunn is no
inward-looking nationalist; Wittig compares his quest for ancestral roots and
values to that of Hemingway, and other critics have seen connections
between Gunn and writers as diverse as Wordsworth, Proust and Faulkner.
Gunn has, until comparatively recently, been little known by many students
of Scottish literature, indeed almost deliberately ignored in some quarters;
yet he is arguably Scotland's greatest epic and regenerative writer since
Walter Scott, with a series of historical and speculative fictions which together
form the most ambitious treatment in existence of Scottish and Highland
cultural and spiritual values.

Gunn starts from the premise that the experience of his race and
immediate forebears, the Gaelic-speaking Highlanders, was essentially one
of strong community. This may well be debatable; but it is the fundamental
premise of his art – and is a view which is common to many of the greatest
Scottish Renaissance writers. The view, however, that Gunn is arguing for a
Highland spiritual superiority or looking at northern rural life through rose-
tinted lenses, is not borne out by the savage realities of his descriptions of
Highland deprivation and poverty in his major novels, nor indeed in the facts
of his own community and family.

Gibbon and Gunn

It should be recognised that, for all their fundamental difference of response to the great changes taking place in rural Scotland, there were many shared renaissance beliefs. Both Gibbon and Gunn develop the 'golden age' myth, the belief that primitive and prehistoric man was somehow better, more in tune with his instincts and his surroundings, than so-called civilised man. Both use the device of almost supernatural experience or 'race-memories' of ancient time: Chris Guthrie and Chae Strachan have their 'visions' of the ships of Pytheas and the warrior of Calgacus; Finn has his vision of the old Druid monk. Both writers are deeply aware of the racial elements that make up Scotland's population: Pictish and Viking origins are contrasted through Ewan Tavendale and Long Rob in *Sunset Song* and Tormad and Roddie in *The Silver Darlings* (1941). Gibbon and Gunn are equally resentful of the workings of British imperial 'authority' throughout Scottish history. Both *The Silver Darlings* and *A Scots Quair* show ordinary and good people destroyed callously and thoughtlessly by a remote power system; and the statement of opposition to this is a major theme in both novelists. While Gibbon becomes at times almost hysterical in his diatribe, Gunn understates his case, perhaps thereby making it more effectively. Both writers also make use of symbolic structure in their major work; the Standing Stones and the House of Peace have basically similar roles to play, and there is at times an almost uncanny resemblance in method. Finally both Gibbon and Gunn attempt to solve the problem of regional language with similar strategies; both use English basically, but Gunn uses the rhythms and at times the syntax of Gaelic, while Gibbon uses the rhythms and syntax of the north-east (the 'speak') without the burden of dialect vocabulary. Equally, both have unusual but similar ways of entering into the consciousness of the central characters.

There are also, however, profound differences in the ideas and methods of the two novelists. They move in very different directions in terms of depicting relationships and families. *The Silver Darlings* begins with the situation of broken and dispersed Highland communities and of Catrine's broken marriage, and proceeds through struggle to union and family / community harmony. *A Scots Quair*, on the other hand, starts with a whole family and a basically intact community, but goes on to depict their break-up and destruction. For Gibbon, sacrifice and death, as in the Great War, are pointless, a harvest of no meaning. Gunn, however, shows in *The Silver Darlings* that war is not an end but that from it can develop new life. At the root of the differences between the two writers lies a contrast of vision of the 'folk'. So often in *A Scots Quair* ordinary people are herded together under disparaging animal terminology, 'swine' or 'sheep' or 'goats', whereas, by contrast, Gunn depicts a diversity of characters who are yet similar in their real human worth. Everywhere, Gunn is concerned with life, and his House of Peace is the symbol of the living past of people and their belief in a future. Gibbon chooses a similar symbol, the Standing Stones, but they are symbols of the dead or dying past, monuments to man's cruelty and sacrifice of his fellows. *The Silver Darlings* is the song of change and life; *A Scots Quair* the song of change and death.

Neil Gunn (1891–1973)

Neil Gunn was born into a fishing family at a time when the fishing industry was beginning to die out. The additional experience of the First World War intensified the effects on local communities, and it is not surprising that when Gunn looked back at this former world, which he had left at the age of twelve, it was a derelict place, stripped of its young through death (he lost three brothers in the war) or emigration. Gunn's earliest work adopts something of the negative bleak attitude to Scotland and home that is found in George Douglas Brown's *The House with the Green Shutters* (1901) and MacDougall Hay's *Gillespie* (1914). The latter, with its study of greed and fishing based on Tarbert, Loch Fyne, its sense of Gaelic 'feyness' and prevailing gloom, may well have been a dominant influence.

Gunn would have liked to believe in a Celtic revival, as it was happening in Ireland, with the work of Yeats, Synge and O'Casey and the Abbey Theatre. But hatred of the false imagery of Scottish Celticism projected by writers like William Sharp ('Fiona MacLeod') in his fashionable doom-laden misty Celtic melodramas shows very clearly in Gunn's first novel, *The Grey Coast* (1926). This is Dunbeath, but drained of colour and life: the fishermen starving or emigrating, incomers buying up the land in the wake of the clearances. It is well worth looking at this novel, or at its close relative, *The Lost Glen* (1932, but serialised in *The Scots Magazine* in 1928), to gauge the depth of despondency to which Gunn had sunk, at this point, in his view of modern Gaelic and Scottish culture and economy. All the more striking is the two-fold movement of this pessimism. This takes the form, on the one hand, of exploring the notion that 'the child is father of the man', and manifests itself before *The Silver Darlings* most strongly in *Morning Tide* (1930) and *Highland River* (1937). On the other hand, it is carried on simultaneously in a fundamental analysis of the Gaelic predicament, tackled in a clever allegorical study of whisky and its progress through the ages as a history of the 'spirit' of Scotland, *Whisky and Scotland: A Practical and Spiritual Survey* (1935). Gunn expresses these ideas most profoundly in a trilogy of novels, Tolstoyan in scope, ambition and human significance: *Sun Circle* (1933), *Butcher's Broom* (1934) and *The Silver Darlings* (1941); and in a linked pair of war-time fictions, the stories of *Young Art and Old Hector* (1942) and the dystopian vision of *The Green Isle of the Great Deep* (1944).

From Grey Coasts to Highland Rivers

The affirmative vision of these great novels did not come easily. Early novels like *The Grey Coast* (1926) and *The Lost Glen* (1932) were bleakly pessimistic. The first tells of the poverty and grimness of life for the fishermen of the north-east when the fishing failed around the turn of the nineteenth century, with its young folk having to emigrate to find a future, leaving the Highlands to sheep and incomers. The second has its embittered young Highlander Ewan destroy himself and the intruding colonel, whose hunting and fishing he has been forced to serve. *Morning Tide*, however, discovered Gunn's triumphant – and perhaps only possible – way of finding hope amidst gloom; in the child, whose dreams and vision are not to be suppressed by history. Young Hugh is the prototype for many of Gunn's regenerative protagonists after this: Kenn of *Highland River*, Finn of *Silver Darlings*, and Art in *Young Art* and *The Green Isle*. Hugh may witness his family in economic trouble, forced to emigrate or leave for service or the cities, and see friends drown in their dangerous relationship with the sea, but for him it is his morning tide of life, and the title, as so many of Gunn's, holds the key to Gunn's fictional affirmation. Likewise, *Highland River*, one of Gunn's most innovative and poetic novels, places childhood experience at the heart of redemption from the trauma of war and social change. The book juxtaposes the boy Kenn's experience with adult Kenn, returned from the trenches in France. Daringly, Gunn reverses the movement of Conrad's *Heart of Darkness* (1902). Where Conrad's movement up-river found in its origin only horror, Gunn has the adult Kenn rediscover delight and wholeness as he retraces his childhood memories and places, finding – as he never did in youth – final harmony and peace at the river's source, in a moment of wonder and epiphany. This novel came after *Sun Circle* and *Butcher's Broom*, but before *The Silver Darlings*. Readers responsive to Gunn's movement of ideas in his Highland 'trilogy' will see that it stands as a crucial stage of spiritual and psychological stock-taking, one which Gunn had to pass before tackling the final and triumphant statement of *The Silver Darlings*.

The beginnings of myth

Sun Circle (1933), like William Goldings's *The Inheritors* (1955), attempts the difficult feat of representing what is virtually a prehistoric mind. Gunn conveys an overwhelming richness and immediacy of smell, animal aware-ness, weather, light and dark – presented from an authorial perspective deliberately timeless and unidentified, so that from the very opening we don't know whose is the 'long gaze' which moves from Orcades to Western Isles, to rest on Iona. This is a view of Scotland entire, sweeping over forest and valleys and mountains like some airborne observer or collective uncon-scious, drawing the reader back through time and contemplation of pre-historic Scotland to land in Gunn's own Dunbeath, under the sea-cliffs, and wandering inland to an unnamed valley, to a woman and child. This is the beginning of Scotland's history and what is no less than Gunn's quest to summarise the history of Gaeldom and to reverse fatalistic despair and acceptance of inevitable defeat.

We are back with the Raven tribe and Drust, their chief, in the eighth century – an ancient people, Pict-Celtic, who have been in this place since time out of mind. Darkness surrounds their origins, and darkness here is seen (as by MacDiarmid) as a creative, natural element, in Manichean opposition to the light. The image of sun circle here stands for a circle of life, of ritual and song – against the dark, or in intuitive balance with it. 'In my locality . . . there did exist traces of the ancient kindness and interest of the Simple Folk. It goes far beyond the Gaelic . . .' wrote Gunn to Gibbon in 1935, reminding us that from the outset he thought of his roots as representing a Scotland far beyond the confines of an ideological Gaidhealtachd, and that, in this first part of his quest, he was recreating his vision of this simple people and the nature of their lives over thousands of years. In *Whisky and Scotland* (1935) he ties Gaelic tradition to a Pictish base like that of his 'sun circle': 'the old Gaelic poetry was sun-bred, exuberant and yet vigorous, charged with life or the wild singing of death, positive . . . There was a flame at its core. Slowly the flame died down.'

A patterning of the opposition between darkness and light substantially replaces conventional narrative. The dark girl Breeta contrasts with the golden daughter of the chief, Nessa. The disciple of the Druid Master, Aniel, is similarly set against Viking Haakon, leader of the raiders (who are one part of the destruction of the sun circle of the community of the Ravens). The Druid Gilbrude and the Grove are set against the Columban missionary, Molrua, and his house of Christian peace downriver; ancient darkness against new light. The notion of sacrifice itself provides a central contrast. Gunn avoids judgement, simply showing an ancient ritual of propitiation in which enemies are burned, virgins given to the knife, or animals offered up, as one way of coping with the darkness; as opposed to Christian self-sacrifice, as when Molrua allows himself to be butchered by the Vikings. Neither is better, although the Christian way may be the ritual of the future, as the Druid Master allows. Judgement is suspended likewise in the matter of gods. Gunn suggests that the old gods – Leu the sun god, the Dark Ones, Rhoss the moor-spirit, together with serpent and bull spirits – had a potency as valid as Christ's. The unusual authorial perspective allows – as always with Gunn – that such presences, pagan or Christian, emanate from the essential myth-making part of the human mind, and are thus to be treated with equal consideration. Ritual likewise has its place as a deeply necessary spiritual metaphor expressed in action. Here, walking sunwise in a circle around a dwelling, or the dowsing and relighting of fires symbolising regeneration are set against the new Christian practices of Molrua and his main convert, the chief's wife Silis.

The timeless authorial perspective may allow all such oppositions and tensions to be equally valid. The immediate considerations of the Ravens, caught between the demands of Christian submission and meekness, and the need for vigorous aggression against the invaders, do not. All the antagonisms between paganism and Christianity are focused in the tension between Drust and Silis. Drust has to hold to the old and potent dark ways, to lead as true chief; Silis, the archetypal civilising force, cannot understand the desperate nature of the Viking threat – although it has to be said that Aniel's father, the bard Taran, suggests a middle course of temporary withdrawal, which implies that both chief and wife are wrong. (The failure of this flicker of leadership from within the tribe itself, unusual and ignored, will later be seen as epitomising the characteristic failure of the Celts and the Scots, a lack of confidence in self or group when devoid of leadership.)

Fatally flawed from within by the loss of that 'sun-bred . . . wild singing of death, positive and challenging', Drust and the Ravens are slaughtered. Silis kills herself. As with *Butcher's Broom*, *The Silver Darlings* and *The Green Isle*, we are given a glimpse of early harmony or hope; only to have it crushed, as the promises of so much in Scottish history itself have been broken. Gunn's method is the same in all these novels. From tragedy and disruption, from the breaking of the circle, the shattered survivors have to regenerate themselves. Gunn is offering no easy answers to the problem of regeneration, but rather suggesting a need for simultaneous retreat (to dark sources of instinctive power) and progression (to absorption of Christian and Viking strengths). But the source is most important of all, since without a sense of ancient identity (through song, story and ritual), as the Master tells Aniel at the end, the folk 'feel that by going forward they leave their true riches behind'. The Grove is their primeval sun circle. There is a heart of darkness here, one in which Gunn does not avoid the horror, but one where out of horror also comes life, purged and renewed. Gilbrude is the anachronistic aspect of the Grove, the Master, the adapting consciousness who recognises that the ancient ways have come to a great turning-point, one of those turns of the cycle Yeats called 'gyres'.

The idea of sacrifice dominates this novel, through the haunting presence and threat of the Grove. With an ambivalence similar to that of Gibbon in his images of standing stones in *Sunset Song*, Gunn pursues the heart of the Grove's mystery – a mystery of complexity of mind rather than of the supernatural. What needs did the sacrifice assuage? The novel attempts to explore that alien territory in a way no other work of Scottish literature has. With the destruction by fire of the Grove, the Master recognises the finality of change: 'It is finished'. The biblical echo is intentional, the phrase highly significant throughout Gunn's work, in its profound ambiguity. It carries two oppositional meanings. First, it is tragic, signifying the doom of a way of life. But there is a deeper, and strangely affirmative meaning, signifying ending because the work, of art or of life, is complete and appropriately finished. This the Master sees; in its profundity of meaning, its implication that out of tragedy comes renewal or renaissance, lies Gunn's deepest meaning. In the heart of despair lies what *Butcher's Broom* calls 'a hostile happiness'. No lesser insight can console the tragedy of Scotland's folk in their repeated cataclysms. But the Master also identifies the legacy of such a cyclic tragedy. Gunn's most recurrent word, in all its variations, is 'fated'; as 'fey', 'fatalistic', 'fatal' or 'fatalism', becoming the motif of hopeless generations from *Sun Circle* onwards. Its hypnotic use in all these major novels should tell us what is his final diagnosis of the Scottish folk condition – that despair has taken on its own life or rhythm, locking will and character into an expectation of tragedy. Starting with *Sun Circle*, Gunn seeks to challenge that fatal rhythm, that Scottish *anomie* or *aboulia* (to borrow MacDiarmid's terms), and to show that endurance and resilience can break the black circle of defeatism.

Aniel and Breeta discover love and wild joy amidst Viking carnage; Nessa finds a kind of fulfilment even in her death; the musician Leu's pipe (taken originally from an even older tribe than the Ravens) is taken back, to make new music reflecting the turn of night to day. Leu's name is that of the ancient Celtic sun god, just as later characters are given Ossianic names like Finn, Bran, or Luath. And Leu's death symbolises the death of an older mythic cycle, which will be supplanted in *Butcher's Broom* by the Fiann legends.

So too, at the novel's end, does the death of the great white bull, in the cleansing, revolutionary fire, destroy the Grove and old ways of life; but 'It was a satisfying end for the old bull, driven out by the younger bulls . . . His prime had been too splendid . . .' Aniel's future telling of the bull's death will create legend, by contributing to mythology.

Thus, very early in his development, Gunn begins his great statement about the regenerative nature and function of art in Scottish community – and community universally. Here, as in all the epic novels we are considering, story, song and dance evolve out of life itself: from a defeat; a great natural event (like the death of the white bull); the rhythms of seasonal and regular activities, from the making of fire, to the lamenting of the dead. At the heart of the Ravens' circle is 'a cycle of stories whereby all the ways of tragedy were traced out'. A final understanding of Gunn's work will elude the reader if the magical transcendence of tragedy is not seen as emerging either from the therapeutic rituals of ceilidh and dance, or through a contact with the wholeness of natural background. It is a view which draws much from Wordsworth, but in the end argues more simply that both art and immediate consolation come from an ancient and animistic relation with the Earth itself. From the beginning of this novel, with Aniel's ever more insistent urges to carve and paint the unknown, to the final chapters of *The Silver Darlings*, Gunn shows what he sees as the essential, abiding function of art. Its luminous radiance from self to community is Gunn's most subtle variation of the metaphor of 'sun circle'.

And the relationship between the Master and Aniel shows the underlying way the meaning of art is passed on. It is no accident that the Master is described frequently as 'brown as the hazel', anticipating *Young Art* and *The Green Isle* in their use of the legend of the hazelnuts of knowledge which, falling into the river of life, are eaten by the salmon which becomes the body of wisdom itself (in its turn eaten by Finn McCoull). The Master is a part of that legend, and of the art which will change and develop the meanings, metaphors and legends constantly. He is almost the 'collective unconscious' of his race. Aniel tells Breeta 'he can sit down and think . . . back through the life before' (Aniel in turn is learning from him how to do this). Gunn leaves it open how far we read this 'thinking' as metaphor for imaginative empathy with other times, other states; or whether a variation on 'second sight' (so central to *Butcher's Broom* and *The Silver Darlings*) is being suggested. Certainly it is significant that the Master foresees fire in the strath in ages to come, just as Seumas Og in *Butcher's Broom* 'sees' the clearances. The Master predicts both the regeneration of the race after the Viking horror and the future disruption once again of the sun circle through clearance. Thus Gunn forges the links of theme and motif through his trilogy. Several times in the novel Gunn even looks forward to *Young Art and Old Hector*, as he emphasises how special the hazel tree is for youth and age. It is the tree of age because it carries 'the nuts of divination and wisdom', but 'is also a boy's tree, because no other tree sends up such straight young shoots'. And Gunn asks, 'Do age and youth meet here – the wisdom that must become as a little child? . . . between the lovely straight shoots of youth and the final nuts of wisdom, what is there, after all, but growth of wood?'. The relationship between Aniel and the Master which thus begins Gunn's epic work, is concluded in the even more essential form of the relationship between young Art and old Hector.

But much has to happen – much wood must grow between the first and last simplicities. Gunn has started on a personal quest, and the sly pun in the name of Aniel is the first of many. Thus the author will find himself at the start of a quest, like Aniel at the end of the novel, and Gunn's continuation of the quest will be shown in the variations of Gunn tribal names in later novels, and in the central role given to the Gunns thereby. Two ancient presences emerge from *Sun Circle* into future works. The ancient people of the hinterland, older by far than the Ravens, the Finlags, have a mysterious role. Are they 'the little people' (for they are wee and elusive, elflike in themselves and their houses and weapons), the originals of the 'Sidhe na Danaan', whose echoes will be heard throughout Gaelic and Irish folk-history? Within their name is future legendary naming, perhaps leading to Finn of *The Silver Darlings*, Gunn's final hero, descended from the heart of the sun circle Picts, the oldest folk of all. Finn, after all, will have his vision of the Master at the centre of the House of Peace. And, moreover, Drust has another son, enchantingly conceived in his love with the Dark Woman of the Finlags, the Black Hind. Gunn sees this as carrying future import – else why have 'Breeta and Aniel offering homage to that small dark woman of the Finlags and her small son'? There is an open face of history, but, says Gunn, there is also a mysterious hidden face, and it looks in secret down through the ages. It may even look from the Black Hind to Dark Mairi of the Shore in *Butcher's Broom*: Mairi's origins are deliberately made uncertain, but she is 'an inland woman' of the enduring kind found in the oldest places, and granddaughter of Black MacIver, a legendary Caithness smuggler. Her line of descent is very old and dark – she is, finally, Mairi Sutherland, eponymous spirit of her race.

Butcher's Broom

Butcher's Broom (1934) has an arresting title with disturbing significances. Gunn means it so. The 'butcher' is in one sense the Duke of Cumberland,

Germanic leader of the genocidal Hanoverian troops at Culloden and after; and his 'broom' swept thousands of Highlanders to death and exile, and made rubbish of their culture and identity. This is the breaking, once more, of the 'sun circle' (used as metaphor throughout this novel) of community which has regenerated itself and endured for another millennium. We are to witness yet again the intrusion of vast impersonal forces into a simple, good community; though this time the enemies will be more insidious than directly hostile Vikings or well-meaning missionaries. Gunn was now deeply involved in nationalist politics, and it is important to read (just as it is with Naomi Mitchison's *The Bull Calves* more than a decade later) a double reference throughout, to the ancient past and to modern Scotland, in two time planes simultaneously. Gunn and Gibbon were in correspondence after the book appeared. Gibbon shared Gunn's anger at the plight of the common people of Scotland. Gunn wrote to him that 'the poor seem to obsess us both', and it is in this sense, of the timeless plight of ordinary people confused in their identity and as to their survival, that the novel should be read.

The other meanings of 'Butcher's Broom' refer again to the secret face of history. Butcher's Broom is the folk-name for *Ruscus aculeatus*, or box holly – an ancient cleansing and tonic plant, unused now because the skill in handling its bitter and its poisonous aspects is lost. It would be one of Dark Mairi's regenerative herbs, such as we see her employing at the symbolic opening of the novel, when she purges the toxins from a sick man. Like Scott's Jeanie Deans, she is an archetype of regeneration; and as with Scott's novel, there is a polar opposite to her, in the authoritarian forces of centralised society which, using Cumberland as a tool, will negate her traditional society. Gunn's is the darker vision, however. Mairi will be destroyed by the sheepdogs of the Sassenach shepherds, just as her people will be. The local tacksman's wife will throw the sprig of butcher's broom (which is also to be the badge of her clan) into the fire, as formal resignation of family honour. The chief has become an absentee, who no longer identifies with his kin, preferring to allow them to be exiled, and the land cleared instead for sheep. It is a terrible story, as Gibbon said to Gunn. But is it a tragedy?

The Ravens have become the people of the Riasgan, as the Master foresaw. The first half of the book shows that – despite ominous signs – the 'sun circle' of their ceilidhs, their glen, their life, is again rich and light-filled. Gunn's descriptions subtly use the circle image again and again so that even the waulking of cloth is performed in a sunwise circle, turning like a 'mythical serpent'. Thus links with the past are woven, just as frequent storytelling recalls that old world with 'wolves and bears and boars and bears like little lions . . . and . . . beasts like hairy men'. The reader will recall the lynx which terrified Breeta, and the Ravens' mockery of the hairy Finlags. To this has been added the legends of Finn and Cuchulain and Deirdre, and a wonderful sun-poetry which blesses the little streams and the grassy hillocks. The reader will find this again in *The Silver Darlings* blended with the twenty-third psalm's green pastures and still waters, but descended and continuous from that first circle. The Ancient Bard, credited with much of this poetry, could well be a descendant of Aniel and his father Taran (and we should always remember the sly identification of Neil Gunn himself with that continuity), so that the storyteller is at once old Angus Sutherland, the voice of Sutherland itself speaking through the ages, as much as Neil Gunn, descendant of Aniel.

For the novel is about Scotland as well as Sutherland. As the danger signs of troop-raising for the Napoleonic wars grow, the tone of the book grows grimmer, and a chill enters, literally: 'a chill night wind from the south . . . searching along the backbone and between the ribs of ancient Alba, searching up . . . the game of death . . .'. When Mairi's adopted daughter, Elie, wanders through the starving Lowlands with her illegitimate son Colin (her lover Colin having answered the chief's call for volunteers for the war), Gunn is clearly calling on Hugh Miller's radical essays on the nineteenth-century blighting of Highland and Lowland Scotland. His *My Schools and Schoolmasters* (1853) portrayed a savage and sympathetic picture of vagrancy and the poverty of bonded and enslaved workers such the Lowland coalmi-ners, recorded later by T. C. Smout's pioneering and fiercely critical *A Century of the Scottish People* (1986).

Once again the key word is 'fatal', with all its variations, and now darker by far. Betrayal by the clan chief is Gunn's main target. Here, at the heart of an older, humanistic Scotland, lies the unspeakable; that the leader, who is of the tribe, should separate himself from them for a house in Bond Street, rack-rents, and a pair of overdressed showy Highlanders at his door to impress all London; and at the very time he and British law are assiduously destroying these very Highlanders. Perhaps Aniel's journey to Inverness to find a southern son of Drust was *Sun Circle*'s ultimate mistake, the final tragedy of Aniel's people being that they have no ability to lead, since they don't understand the concept of hierarchy. After all, Aniel's most instinctive and powerful vision was of Nessa and Haakon the Viking becoming an inter-married Pictish-Viking leadership, but the fatalism of his tribesmen destroyed this. Is the fatal flaw of Celt and Scot thus endemic, inherent, a genetic doom? Gunn is being savage here; Aniel's failure, Colin's acceptance of the chief's treachery (for Colin and Elie are the descendants of Aniel and Breeta), the childish bluster of the Riasgan all exemplify a Celtic and Scottish proclivity for defeat, what Gunn describes in the culminating chapters of the book as shameful, 'a recognition of some inner futility and weakness in their character, a fatal central dividing within them, paralyzing all power of decisive action'.

Gunn's contempt for those of his race who accept Celtic Twilight cliché reaches its height here (in Chapter 2, part 3) with his picture of the young Highlander Davie's vituperative 'Children of the Gael! Children of the tempest! Children!' Davie's perception of a dangerous infantilism in their debased images of themselves is also Gunn's mockery of the Celtic Twilight and the Kailyard literary school, of Fiona Macleod and even of Neil Munro's *Children of Tempest* (1903), which, while Gunn drew much inspiration from Munro, he clearly felt had evaded the real issues for its islanders. For Gunn sees this as the time of the spiritual deformation of the Highlands, when women took over the guardianship of the communities from men, since the forces which are destroying the community have drained them of men and of their essential manhood. Now is when Gaelic becomes seen by predatory outsiders as the language of feckless, devious and idle Highlanders, and the stereotypes of drunken unreliability are created. Gunn shows (outstandingly, in his portrayal of the spiritual disintegration of Rob the Miller) the grim, enervating reality of fatalism and loss of hope.

In *The Green Isle* Gunn shows that God has withdrawn from his people; and indeed Gunn suggests here that there is a curse upon them, such is their agony. Not, of course, a curse such as the church suggests, because of their pagan ways: Gunn mocks this, seeing the church's role in the clearances as collaborative with landed interest and exploitation. His motif for the land-lords' treatment of tenants and communities is that of Christ before Caiaphas. The agents' names, Falcon and Heller, show their natures (Heller echoes that of real-life agent Patrick Sellar, hated during the Clearances). Heller is the archetype of the new materialism of the Lowland Scot, with 'the hard bone in his cheek and jaw . . . the set of his mouth'. The Countess of Sutherland recognises his type, since she 'had been brought up in the Lowlands of Scotland by her grandmother, a scheming worldly woman . . . they could be harder than the bone in their faces'. As with Culloden, the destruction of the older Scotland is mainly brought about by dark forces within Scotland itself.

The Riasgan has a last golden summer before its destruction. It is all the more striking since Gunn sets it within a context of gathering greyness and ominous change. This last summer is fated and diseased. References to the 'Aged Bard' and to the great pibroch 'The Lament for the Children' by the doomed pipers, the MacCrimmons, are all shot through with bitterness and parody. The community corrodes from within, the men's ineffectuality rotting their self-respect. All this is summed up in the Riasgan's last wedding, the corrupt marriage of Elie to Rob the Miller. It is a union which should never have been, attended by sniggers and despair, and with unspoken reservations and the worst kind of fatalism: on Elie's part from the need to protect her bastard child, on Rob's because deep down he knows of the essential wrongness of the marriage. Significantly, it is the boy Davie – heir to the Finlags – who sees that in condoning the union, the community has lost its instinctive rightness: 'They had handed her over.' We are reminded of Breeta's becoming scapegoat, sacrificial victim for the ills of community, a thousand years before. It was wrong then; it is as wrong now.

There is a choric figure who serves to pass judgement, savage and embittered, on all this. Tomas MacHamish the cattle-drover has an epic role to play. A sharp observer at all times, he is enlarged through tragedy to mythical scale, becoming the frenzied daemon of his race's despair. Boldly Gunn has him cite Tacitus as comment on the atrocities of government ('where they make a desert, they call it peace') and invoking the ancient spirit of Galgacus, leader of the Picts against the Romans in ancient times. What deepens Tomas's ironical role is the realisation that such noble resistance and high ideals are now pointless and misplaced. As the bitter cripple Murdoch, symbol of the deformed modern Highlands, sees, there are no simple enemies such as Roman or Viking, but more insidious enemies mainly within their community, like the absentee chief, their own loss of hope, and the ironically misplaced trust they are conditioned to give. Similarly epic is Tomas's central vision of the cloven-footed presence, which will destroy them. Gunn fuses wild humour and deep satire in Tomas's invocation of the ram as destroyer; true, since sheep will replace humanity, and effective, since biblical and pagan echoes attend the pan-devil figure. Tomas, as the last living witness to Ossian and the ancient bardic tradition, is given the right to utter the final curse – and its savagery, coming from a gentle and chief-trusting people, will be evident. Now a veritable doubled-up rag of a man, with 'burning eyes . . . and skeleton arms', Tomas gives voice to Gunn's repeated attack on vast, impersonal, and centralised power, whether that of imperial Britain, with press-gang and law court, or later of totalitarian Russia or Hitler's Germany. It is 'law' which allows the chief to clear the people. In the face of this irony, Tomas suggests that the folk should thank chief and authorities for allowing them to rot on their sea-beaches. Then, close to the novel's end (Part 4, Chapter 2) abandoning sarcasm, Tomas deepens his satire by suggesting that at least the slave-trader 'traffics honestly in human bodies, and enlists the aid neither of Progress nor of Jesus Christ'. The

Countess of Sutherland is worse, not because she has abandoned the ways of her forefathers – many have – but:

> I am cursing her now not for dispossessing the people of their own land, not for having made the law that gave her the power to dispossess her own people, not for having burned them out of their ancient homes, not for having made them wanderers and beggars and eaters of filth, not for the angels of insanity and disease and death she sent amongst them, not even for having tried to justify herself in the eyes of the world by employing an army, by using Christ's Church, by weighting the balances of justice . . . but because in using all these things . . . she has broken the spirit of her people, she has destroyed the soul of her people; as surely as if she were Judas, she has crucified the Gael.

Is there any doubting Gunn's passion, his epic anger about his race? It is Gunn at his darkest and finest – yet, even here, it is only part of a bigger regeneration; for at the heart of darkness, Gunn regenerates the old myths, recreating them to offer hope and ancient strength to Scotland.

It is the old trick, whereby an ancient resilience reasserts itself. It was at the heart of the book, when Elie, utterly lost and hopeless, found that mysterious 'hostile happiness' amidst a wintry, bleak landscape, or where Dark Mairi, smooring the fire on the brink of clearance, finds meaning beyond tragedy in the traditional blessing of the hearth. Mairi is endurance, and a reading of her terrible death as tragic is simply wrong. 'It is finished'; the Master of *Sun Circle* recognised the finality of his work, and Mairi Sutherland is fitly his successor. It is Mairi who is seen as the real knotting of history; she herself would not recognise defeat in her own death. Thus Gunn tells his race that they are never, and have never been, truly defeated. The fire is smoored, but not out.

In all this the links with *Sun Circle* have been strongly made. Not only does Mairi follow the Master; not only are Elie and Colin latterday and fallen Breeta and Aniel; Tomas has kept lore and legend alive ('Fingal never fought a fight without offering terms'), from far before the Ravens' time. With the occasional fragmented memories of the 'nameless ones', Dark Gods of the Night Wind, or the glimpse of fairy lore, we see that these are descendants of Ravens and Finlags. Even the breaking of the circle of the Riasgan is not final. Gunn tells us that these people are endurers, greater than all the leaders who come and go, transient and irrelevant to them. And it is important to see that the links forward to *The Silver Darlings* have been made likewise. Catrine, like Elie, will be 'fey', arid and alone, yet will find her own 'hostile happiness'; and she will moreover, be married to a descendant of the MacHamishes, who have featured significantly here. Tomas the Drover was a MacHamish ('a sept of the Gunns, thoroughly godless dangerous ruffians', Gunn slyly has Mr Falcon comment); there's a 'black giant', a friend of Rob, who is also a MacHamish; and the traditional community piper is of the sept. This will be the pedigree of young Finn of *The Silver Darlings*; their energy, awareness of tradition, and centrality to community will be his. (There's even – looking beyond to the later novels – a 'young Art, who is thirteen and a leader'!)

Gunn's search for personal and spiritual renewal

Butcher's Broom held at its core the assertion of a profound natural endurance, with its central location of Dark Mairi discovering affirmation at the heart of negation. The next movement in the quest for the sources of Scottish spiritual regeneration naturally called for a shift of emphasis from the large-scale diagnosis of groups like the Ravens or the Riasgan to the analysis of private self. Gunn's location of new hope in the boy Hugh in *Morning Tide* was based on the idea that, in the awakening of the private self in the child and adolescent, tragic public history is defeated, since the child perceives and makes the world anew. Somehow, the insight of *Morning Tide* into the circle of self, with its convincing sensitivity and delicacy, had to be allied with the two epic novels' sense of the sweep of tragic community history. *The Silver Darlings* took Gunn another seven years to write; the hardest challenge of all, since it called for a triumphant and relatively contemporary conclusion to the trilogy of Pictish, Celtic and Scottish spiritual history.

As early as 1933 Gunn revealed (in a letter to MacDiarmid) his recognition of the need to base his conclusions on sound psychological theory. Hating the accusation that his work was ever 'mystical', Gunn saw the essential challenge in the need to reconcile myth, notions of 'Great Memory' or collective unconscious, and instinctive endurance, with rational and practical modern ideology:

> I recognize that where you have a given psychology, like the Scottish, you must deal with it as scientifically as possible in accordance with such rules as advanced psychologists have formulated . . . When an expert like A. S. Neill is dealing with a perverted or sub-normal child he doesn't slam educational facts into the child with the help of a rod, like the old dominie: on the contrary, he apprehends the level of the child mind and makes a point of contact . . .

Significantly, Gunn perceived Scotland as 'perverted' through history, and A. S. Neill (the radical, non-authoritarian and controversial educationist) is chosen as the fittest exemplar of modern psychological understanding. Neill's organic and sympathetic methods in relation to children strongly influenced Gunn's development now, and *Highland River* (1937) was the 'new phase' through which Gunn had to move to *The Silver Darlings*.

In *Highland River* Gunn stood aside, as it were, from his epic, exploring instead the theme of the child as father of the man in a *Prelude*-like prose-poem which was also an extended meditation on the nature of discovery of essential self. The influence of natural objects on war-scarred Kenn Sutherland has epic qualities. Kenn discovers, in his roots and in his real river's source, the origin of natural self, forgotten by modern Man when the river (of Man) took the wrong turning. The 'source' he discovers is a Scottish poise of place and community, with respect for private communion together with a sense of wider involvement. It supplies *The Silver Darlings* with the spiritual insights, which illuminate its often tragic history.

Triumph over despair

The Silver Darlings (1941) fuses all Gunn's themes heretofore. There is the satirical commentary on the warping of Scottish and Highland community. There is a continual exploration of legend and myth through song, dance and story. There is an examination of the way tragedy affects individuals: widowed Catrine, Roddie the fisherman, at sea in his emotional life since he cannot fulfil himself; a wonderful range of relationships which Gunn controls and arranges to body forth his grand symphonic design. There is, in it, a fundamental appreciation of the pragmatic issues of fishing, the rural economy, trade with the Baltic. Gunn drew from his political involvements of the 1930s, his reading of his encourager and friend Peter Anson's books on fishing like *Fishermen and Fishing Ways* (1932), and his own summer of sailing in Scottish coastal waters in 1937, when he made that impulsive leap for freedom (by leaving his employment at HM Customs and Excise) described vividly in *Off in a Boat* (1938). Or was it so impulsive? Was it perhaps Gunn's deep insistence on getting his perspectives right, asserting itself 'behind the scenes' prior to tackling *The Silver Darlings*? Certainly that novel's wonderful dualism of perspective, whereby the first movements are seen through the eye of land-based characters like Catrine, and the later movements through the sea-washed vision of Roddie and Finn, has an authenticity which surely demanded personal experience going beyond the fact that Gunn's father had been a Dunbeath skipper.

In fusing all previous themes, however, there is one which stands out – that of the central figure of the boy in his passage through initiation into community and mature self. Indeed, *Sun Circle*'s symbolism is brought triumphantly to a close in the novel's final chapter, 'Finn in the Heart of the Circle', and Finn, on the final page, is given the last of his glimpses of the Master, 'the white-haired man he had once imagined here'. Is this journey from Master to Finn not in itself proof that Gunn was – however arduous and long the quest – searching for a way of completing the broken circle, so that he could use the phrase 'it is finished' in its most positive sense? Finn, in mastering self, in reconciling himself with mother, community, and his role as husband and father, in Gunn's final and finest exemplar of Scottish spirit triumphing over forces within and without Scotland. Gunn's love and understanding of the child (here perhaps so intense because he was creating the child he and his wife never had) is only rivalled by the insights of *Young Art and Old Hector* – his next book.

Finn is not just a very real boy, however. He has a mythical doppelgänger who accompanies him throughout his childish ploys and adolescent adventures (like his fabulous climb of the Cliff of the Seven Hunters), his dreams (when he has his vision of the great war-horn of Finn, which he has to blow to awaken his sleeping people), and most of all in his art, his achievement of his place in the web of symbols and meanings captured in traditional dance, story and song.

The penultimate chapter of the novel, 'As the Rose Grows Merry in Time', draws all the novel's strands together majestically and movingly. Here, Finn, in North Uist, learns from and participates in the seamless garment of the community's own story, through its three nights of ceilidh. At last he understands his mother and his selfish desire to shun her – because of a song and a dance. He understands himself, because in telling the story of his epic voyage and by singing the song of challenge by maiden to her lover to achieve the impossible, he recognises how actions and situations like his own have become recorded and made into legend and myth, giving traditional identity to later generations. Finn, who 'came from the hills', and is laughed at by the market boys, is a Finlag. His recurrent identification with the House of Peace, relic of his race in the times of the Ravens and before, performs the same function as Chris Guthrie's link with the standing stones in *Sunset Song*. It shows that he is the apotheosis of his race, descendant and hero, whose exploits will stand like those of his namesake, the great Finn McCoull. The people create Finn; Finn creates the people – and thus the circle of action and art move inextricably around. Gunn allows the psychological elements of the novel to sit in easy co-existence with folk and supernatural elements. Incidences of second sight, of rowanberries performing their healing function, of perceptions transcending time such as Finn often experiences at the House of Peace, are left in a suspension in which Gunn provides perfectly adequate rational explanations – but suggests also that the rational and the supernatural are not so antagonistic as modern materialism insists.

The triumph of the herring fisheries around the coast of Scotland in the nineteenth century stands as Gunn's ultimate example of a model of regeneration of mythical stature. His recurrent description of the times of the silver darlings as 'fabulous', however, doesn't mean that 'magic' has brought about salvation. Far from it, since it is essential to his purpose that this Scottish myth also stands as realistic model for the nation, which he had told MacDiarmid in 1933 was failing because of 'internal warring elements'. Walter Scott had sought to reconcile these, as had others after him; but neither in Scott's main efforts, nor anywhere else in Scottish literature – not even in MacDiarmid's *Drunk Man* – does supreme art marry so fruitfully with social and historical authenticity and sensitive and persuasive psychological delineation. *The Silver Darlings* has a claim as the greatest of all Scottish novels. And the trilogy it completes, the quest for a new myth which will (to use the words of the American anthropologist Philip Wheelwright) 'explain the origins and ends of a race to itself' is a claim to mark the highest level of achievement of Scottish and Western literature.

History and fiction: telling stories of the great fishing renaissance

The Silver Darlings takes up the story of the Highlands only a few years after the events of *Butcher's Broom*. At the beginning of the novel, we are introduced to the settlement of Dale on the coast, beside Helmsdale, where the uprooted people of the inland strath are having to learn how to make a living from fishing. Tormad and Catrine MacHamish, the married couple struggling with poverty at the start, are the heirs of the characters of *Butcher's Broom*, creating a direct link with the final episodes of that novel. *The Silver Darlings* is, on one level, the history of how the Highlands and east coast found a new dynamic and economic basis in the great herring fishing industry that grew up in the early nineteenth century. The events of the novel at this level make coherent and convincing historical fiction. It is 1816 and Napoleon is in St Helena. Throughout Europe and Britain these are bad years, such have been the ravages of war, and the press-gang is still active, forcibly enlisting men for the Royal Navy. It takes (and kills) Tormad, when he is at sea fishing, leaving Catrine pregnant, ignorant of what has happened to him, though somehow she feels he is dead. She leaves Dale for Dunster (Dunbeath) and a new life with her aunt, Kirsty Mackay.

There she stays for the next twenty years, crofting, trying to keep her son Finn from the sea which 'killed' his father. Since she does not know, formally, that Tormad is dead, she is not free to marry Roddie, who is, in 1816, the youngest, and best, skipper of a fishing boat in Dunster. Roddie, and Dunster generally, take advantage of the government's bounty on every cran of herring exported, to begin the great nineteenth-century herring fishing industry, which stretched from Shetland in the far north southwards as far as Anstruther in Fife and Leith beside Edinburgh and which was to save the people of the north and east of Scotland. Its effects were felt throughout Scotland and beyond; as Gunn tells us, Dunster, a tiny village, by 1835 had seventy-three boats out, employing West Coast men, since there were not enough local men. The parish in which Dunster was situated had 305 boats out. Duplicate such figures for villages all down the East Coast and the context for Gunn's story becomes clear. The fishing was a regeneration, a rebirth of hope and prosperity, a 'fabulous time'.

In this magical atmosphere young Finn grows up, drawn inexorably towards the sea, from which he has been forbidden. How could a child ignore the bravery, the excitement of the adventures going on in the village? Finn's friends and their fathers go to sea in thirteen- to twenty-foot open boats without cover from rain and storms, far into the North Sea and, later, into the Atlantic, staying at sea for days on end, sleeping in the open and the wet, running a real risk of drowning. Finn is thus torn between his loyalty and 'duty' to his mother who wants him to be a crofter, and his own need to discover himself, his abilities and his courage. Catrine and Roddie are also torn. Catrine realises that she is smothering her boy, and though she is drawn towards Roddie, she fends him off for her own complex reasons. Roddie too, respects Catrine's sorrow for Tormad and her need to wait for confirmation of his fate, also knowing that to claim Catrine would be to hurt Finn. So all three have lonely and difficult paths to travel, and the novel is not just about one but about all of them and their delicate, powerful and complex relationships.

After Catrine has lifted her prohibition, Finn and Roddie go to sea and, for a while, Finn is content to share the comradeship of the crew of the *Seafoam* and epic adventures on cliffs and at fishing. But as Finn moves from boyhood (barely seventeen when he first goes to sea) to manhood, he increasingly feels Roddie as a rival, both in his adventures and in his relationship with his mother. Finn must come to terms with this jealousy. Through his own epic voyages, further than any Dunster fisherman has gone before and working heroically with Roddie at the wreck of three fishing boats at the end, he achieves a sense of his own separate identity. He is thus enabled to resolve his differences with Catrine and Roddie, and, taking his own thirty-four foot fishing boat, settles into a marriage with Una. These are the high points of what is of course a much deeper and subtler novel than this outline can suggest.

THREE GREAT MOVEMENTS: LAND, SEA AND SYNTHESIS

One way of responding to the novel is in terms of its three great movements or parts, each part having a different emphasis, a different music. Music is indeed an important element in Gunn's development of theme. Although the term 'symphonic' is all too often and loosely used about long novels, it is entirely appropriate to *The Silver Darlings*. Gunn has a majestic overall theme, to which the lesser parts are subtly related and subservient. Within these parts there are symbolic 'motifs', which in Gunn take the form of images like the rowan berries, or birch trees or circles of ancient stones. They remind us constantly of the large, overall theme, since they appear both surprisingly and repeatedly, even when the novel's action would seem to preclude them. For example, Gunn manages to bring the House of Peace, the ancient Druid holy place of Dunster (Dunbeath), into the setting of the Atlantic Ocean. He is never obtrusive about this, but the effect is symphonic, as two strands of the narrative combine and move towards a final unity.

Gunn did not separate his epic formally into its three parts. There are chapter headings, which are aways significant and helpful, but the great trio of movements which give the book its symphonic shape are not labelled. Gunn clearly felt that to do so would detract from the sense of time and life moving forward like the waves of the sea itself, organic and inseparable from the definition of each chapter boundary. The reader will find, however, a natural series of shifts; Part One covering Chapters 1–13, Part Two Chapters 14–18, and Part Three Chapters 19–26. The progression in most of Gunn's novels (with the arguable and understandable exception of *Butcher's Broom*) is from disruption and disharmony to unity and harmony.

In *The Silver Darlings*, Part One shows a land-based people out of their depth at sea, and throughout this section the sea is viewed from the land. Part One *is* the land, expressed through Catrine and her obsessive love for it, since the sea has ruined her life, by taking her husband away from her. This first movement, therefore, is centred around the symbolic presentation of Land and Woman, since broadly we see events predominantly from Catrine's point of view. (Gunn's presentation of Catrine's womanly protectiveness, her mothering obsessiveness, could fruitfully be considered alongside Lewis

Grassic Gibbon's presentation of Chris Guthrie in *Sunset Song*.) This part of the novel ends when Catrine is reminded that, if death can come from the sea, it can also happen on the land, since the cholera plague takes another of those most dear to her, Kirsty. Her perceptual balance is restored, and Finn, her son, is released to the comradeship of men, to sail with the *Seafoam* in Part Two.

Part Two views the land from the sea and is male-dominated, with Finn relishing the company of Roddie and the crew of the *Seafoam*, and delighting in this new element. Yet it is, like the land in the first section, only a part of life. If Catrine was obsessive about the land, then Finn is now, like Roddie, obsessive about the sea. Whereas Catrine shuts out the world of men, Finn shuts out memories of his mother and Una. The prevailing motif of this section is that of the boat in its 'wooden dream', and all the metaphors and adventures suggest a time of enhancement and heroic saga, moving from 'Thorstown' (Thurso) to the Cliff of the Seven Hunters and the perilous depths of the Atlantic.

Part Three sees Roddie settled with Catrine, thus bringing sea and land, man and woman, together. Finn still resists his fate, although his deepest self is in fact moving him steadily towards 'the heart of the circle'. Parts One and Two, then, are balanced opposites, with Part Three a resolution to their opposition, a harmonious and triumphant statement of themes treated discordantly in the earlier parts. Part Three also reveals the dominating images of the circle; for Finn is only re-enacting a struggle which Roddie, and Tormad before that, have already acted out. Life, Gunn suggests, can be both a rhythm of successive waves and a cyclical movement from tragedy to delight repeated and varied through generations.

Looking outward: Scotland and totalitarianism

Where would Gunn's epic quest take him thereafter? Later novels like *The Drinking Well* (1946) might explore the contemporary problem of rural Scotland, but could hardly be seen as a sequel, since the idea of completion, of a historical circle coming round to the totality of 'it is finished' (as Gunn knew it was, from the vanishing fishing fleets of his father's day) gave that trilogy its integral rhythms. Scott had gone 'out of history' to find Jeanie Deans and a folk model for his vision of abiding Scottish strength. Gunn had developed that model triumphantly so that the centripetal or inward dynamics of Scottish development could be seen as self-generating. But what of the value and nature of these Scottish archetypes in relation to the centrifugal, outward-looking dynamics of Scotland? In terms of modern philosophical and political materialism, in a world darkened by Stalin, Franco and Hitler, of what value could peripheral minutiae and far-flung folklore possibly be? The answer was of course implicit in all Gunn's previous work. As early as 1958 Kurt Wittig, in his *The Scottish Tradition in Literature*, argued that Gunn 'is looking for the pattern of life, the underlying ritual, the myth' – in short, the meaning of life itself. Gunn himself argued that 'if a Scot is interested in dialectical materialism or proletarian humanism . . . he should study the old system in order to find out how the new system would be likely to work amongst his kind. It might help him at least to get rid of his more idealistic wind.' Significantly, Wittig ended his account of Gunn's work with discussion of *The Green Isle of the Great Deep* and *Highland River*. *The Green Isle* is not, however, a work which stands alone. It can be read as such, just as, say, *The Silver Darlings*, but it is immeasurably enriched by being seen as part of a duality, or an archway, half of which is *Young Art and Old Hector*. It is the second part of the adventures of Art and Hector, and the culmination of their relationship. Essentially the two parts make up a single great work of art which addresses different issues from those he has handled before. We are exploring what periphery can offer centre, or how ancient values of simple community must qualify the values of modern scientific rationalism. Having demonstrated how Scots need not accept decline with self-fulfilling fatalism, Gunn presses on here to show that their enduring qualities of traditional community are the missing and essential ingredients of our brave new world.

Youth and age in community

Young Art (1942) nevertheless continues the trilogy's quest. Finn had seen himself at the end of the novel as 'a whitehaired old man, head of a tribe, sitting on this knoll in quiet thought, his sea days over'; and, daringly, Gunn forges links now which will, for the reader who has followed the quest, link and fuse the Master with Finn, with Old Hector – and God himself. How slyly Gunn hides his clues! But look closely, and Hector – at times comic and hairy – is one of the old Finlags, the last of his race, a bridge between unbroken sun circle (his village was the Clash, the Riasgan-like community lost in the clearances) and the new Highlands of young Art. Circle imagery still performs its linking function. Art's family is 'a circle of peace', blessed by his father's Grace, as were the families of the Riasgan. (Gunn has changed the locale to the west – perhaps to emphasise the archetypal role of his figures, and to avoid the charge of parochialism?) The very first story of the novel (for it is both collection of stories and novel, just as the volume itself is also part of the next novel) echoes the relationship, in *Sun Circle*, between Aniel and the

Master. It does so twice: first in the Art-Hector encounter, and, second, in the consoling story Hector tells the irate little boy about the Druid and Finn McCoull. The Master's teaching persists – and more. The Dark Ones ('who can be vindictive') are still remembered in this nineteenth-century tale, if not as vividly as in *Butcher's Broom*, as are the fairies, their dwellings and their habit of replacing children with changelings. Most of all, however, the older themes are developed towards a new statement of the concept of 'it is finished'. In 'The First and the Second Childhood', Hector finds in the pupil-Druid master and innocence-wisdom relationship he has with Art a 'vision of the circle completing itself', so that 'panic or time could no more intrude'. It will be the disgrace of modern rationalism in *The Green Isle* that it cannot accept the magical quality of their relationship, restlessly examining it for hidden motivation or even sexual exploitation.

From the outset it is worth knowing that the two novels will contain a shared pattern and movement. Taking the opening of *Young Art* and the end of *Green Isle* together, we see that the movement has been from the Hazel Pool (shades of the Master!) to the Hazel Pool; from Art's desire to find the river, to the river itself as end of his quest; from a story of a salmon, to the living salmon they bring out of the pool at the end; from the wisdom of the Druid at the beginning to that of God at the end; and, more mundanely, from Morag, Art's sister and her shepherd, Tom, to their crucial role in rescuing Art and Hector at the end. And the shared quest is, quite simply, for wisdom – the heart of the legend of the hazelnuts of knowledge and the magical movement beyond knowledge and rationalism to the mysterious territory beyond. As the imagery of pools held *Highland River* together, so the recurring, tantalising glimpse of the Hazel Pool unites this work.

The title, of course, is charged with far-reaching meaning. Art is a common name in the north, as is Hector; but seven-year-old Art (like Finn) has his other level of existence, in which he is timeless youth – and particularly Arthur, the young hero-king, who was tutored by the wise old Sir Hector. Gunn exploits the fact that the Arthurian legends are parents to the Celtic Fianns, so that the implication is that the relationship here is older and deeper even than Finn's with the old Druid. But there is another and major new aim in this quest. It is nothing less than to find the heart of the relationship between psychology and myth. In *Young Art* Gunn keeps the two separate, delicately and perceptively analysing the mutual interests of Art and Hector, while allowing myth to come in through illustrative folk tales (many taken directly from J. F. Campbell's famous collection of 1860–2, *Popular Tales of the Western Highlands*). Reality and legend move intimately, but separately. *The Green Isle* dramatically abolishes the distinction, by moving directly into the shared unconscious of Art and Hector (in their drowning dream at the bottom of the Hazel Pool) to intuit the sources of myth-making. Dream will be seen as the place where reality and myth are synthesised. This is Gunn's triumphant step beyond historical materialism.

If much of the substance of *Young Art* is drawn from legends and children's tales, there is nothing childish about Gunn's exploitation of them. Art will teach Hector (that life is divided into three parts, in 'The Knife, the Glass Ball, and the Penny'), just as much as Hector's stories will lead Art to wisdom. The role of storytelling is again crucial – even when Art, miserable at the loss of his mother, will not listen to the consoling Hector. How delicately Gunn implies that even 'unheard' stories have their subtle effect: 'though Art did not listen to him, he spoke of the hunter and the hunter's courage and of how Art had now proved himself and would one day be a grown man . . .'. And how charmingly he shows the effect of the tales on Art and Donul, his big brother. After hearing of the strange birdbeast and the twelve puppies who ate the youngest daughter's bannock: ' "I thought once or twice," said Art in a quiet voice, "that I just saw them". "I have thought that myself sometimes," answered Donul.'

Each episode is building towards the time of testing ahead in *The Green Isle*. Each will contribute to Art's (and Hector's) resources, so that a perceptive reading will show that the significance of these apparently trivial events in Young Art is crucial, unfolding into full meaning later. Each episode calls forth new growth from Art, leading him to intuitive insights, such as in 'Machinery', when, fascinated, he watches the terrible teeth of the mill-wheel's cogs and gears. 'Darkly Art suspected that this machinery had more in it than men who laughed at him believed. They had better look out or one day it would catch and drag them in . . .'. Likewise his powers of imagination are being developed. Art elaborates on details of the birdbeast and puppies to Donul, telling him, as he grips his hand, 'I thought the birdbeast was like a great raven, and the puppies were little black puppies'. Gunn lets us see the virtue of the openness of folk-tale, in allowing such individual freedom in interpretation, and Art's originality. And the episodes are not separated – they refer back and forward, and often their full meaning or subtlety will only emerge much later. For example, in the sensitive account of Art's resentment of his new brother Henry James, Gunn plants Art's jealousy without telling us what it is about – or why, much later, he goes about pale and quiet, wasted by an unnamed guilt. We learn in a later story that he has implored the fairies to take away Henry James, and thus, when he hears his mother say that Henry James 'is not like himself', being ill, he assumes the fairies have visited, and left a changeling. The notion of Art's jealousy, fairy involvement, and guilt is sustained over several episodes, and, like Finn's encounter with the serpent-conger eel in *The Silver Darlings*, is both positive and negative in his development. It shows him discovering guilt (and becoming 'fey'); but it leads him to the ruined homes of his ancestors, in a lyrical sequence in which he seeks the old gooseberry bush outside Hector's old house in the Clash, in a quest which is simultaneously for peace and knowledge (since Henry James has come from such a bush!). Hector finds him asleep within the ruins of his (Art's) grandfather's house. The past is imparting itself to him; like Finn, seeing the Master at the House of Peace, Art has achieved a kind of epiphany in which he is given communion with his ancestors. Hector is as astonished to find him as if he had 'come upon a fearful and fabulous beast, sunning itself in an unexpected place'.

This is the central epiphany of the first volume. It marks Art as special, and, like Hector, a leader of his people – as *The Green Isle* will demonstrate. But lesser and magical epiphanies surround it. Probably the next in the scale of importance are respectively 'Art Runs a Great Race' and 'Art's Wedding Present'. In the first, Art is beyond himself with excitement at the local games, and never more so than when he bursts himself to win his race. His feat will stand him in good stead in *The Green Isle*, and we will meet the 'starter from Clachdrum' again. In 'Art's Wedding Present', Art comes of age by saving Hector from prison when he discovers the excisemen sniffing up the glen for illicit distilling. Hector is an old hand in this, and has his secret den in a hillock where his 'worm' distils whisky. Art saves the wedding of his brother, the whisky for it, and Hector; and Hector concludes that all that remains ' "is for you to hold it *as secret as the grave.* "*As secret as the grave*", murmured Art, his heart like to burst with the amount of life and loyalty in it'. Gunn ends with a sly pun and Hector's delight is great: ' "I was beginning to think we had hidden the old worm too well . . ." '. But there's more than Art proving himself in his community. Hector's den is also 'Knocshee' (cnoc na sidhe) the fairy hill; and Hector its magical inhabitant, as in the astonishing moment when Art comes upon him emerging, the hairy 'oorishk' itself, the fabulous beast-human, from his den. Is this where legends are born? (And were trolls and the like, hidden humans, from smugglers to persecuted Covenanters?) For Art, magic, fable and reality combine to distil, beyond reach of the inquisitors, a fundamental goodness and strength. Everything he's heard – older discussions about the clearances, about property, about loyalty; and everything that's happened, down to his wonderful moment when he gets his first knife – will fulfil its purpose in the Green Isle.

There is one apparent drawback to this unified design. Some stories, notably 'The Little Red Cow', are not about Art or Hector. What have Donul, or the red cow he looks after in the south, to do with the totality of *Young Art* and *The Green Isle of the Great Deep*? In fact, this is one of Gunn's most subtle pieces of oblique comment on the essential spirit of his race. The small, shaggy red cow with her fiery eyes and wild unhappiness is the embodiment of the spirit of the tormented and displaced Celts; commenting on her dourness, the cattleman remarks that 'they're like that, them that come from the West.' The discussion that follows is really about Donul, Art's brother, who intuitively knows what the little cow feels, since she's like his own and Hector's cattle at home, and part of the community. Indeed, a whole way of life goes with the intimate milking and herding of her kind. And in a sense Gunn foreshadows *The Green Isle* in placing Donul in a planned, ultra-rational system where his and the cow's ways are redundant and wasteful – as perceived by the new world. Donul will write home and Art will hear and understand his predicament. Thus *The Green Isle* consists essentially of Art's drowning dream, haunted by all the things he has experienced in the earlier part, but especially moved by the sense of his brother in a strange country, far from home. *The Green Isle* opens with the comic rescue of just such a little red cow.

From community to dystopian nightmare

The Green Isle (1944) starts like another episode of *Young Art*. Here – with the fun and sensitivity of *Butcher's Broom* – is community in harmony, till the talk turns to modern totalitarian methods of brainwashing and wartime concentration camps. To these people such things are worse than the clearances, since the breaking of the mind, as Hector makes them all see, is the most appalling atrocity of all. Art is, of course, drinking all this in. When Red Dougal asks why God does not interfere, Gunn stresses the haunting provocation this leaves in their minds – and in Art's. Art and Hector fall into the Hazel Pool, and they fall into a dream, a fable, a sustained meditation – or into an enchanted world. And here, emphasis is given to their most recent and vivid experiences, both deriving from the first chapter 'The Night Before', and from the prequel, *Young Art*, the first part of the duality.

The dream is ambiguous. It is psychologically explicable, in terms of theories of one's past life flashing before one at the point of death, and stories like Golding's *Pincher Martin* (1956) or Bierce's 'An Incident at Owl Creek' in which entire extended experience is made the hallucinatory matter of the text. It is also fabulous; since Art has the hazelnuts of knowledge in his pocket, which he takes with him into the river of life, he becomes part of the legendary quest for wisdom. Gunn again poses the idea that traditional art and psychological development, 'magic' and realism, are one. And the aim of Gunn's final epic quest is to show how the apparently trivial but dogged endurance of those, such as Hector and Art – and the strength of Scottish (or any) traditional community life – can confound all Utopian totalitarianism, and expose its transition to Dystopia.

It is also much more. Gunn has given several differing accounts of the genesis of the novel. In one version it was the nephew of a friend who prompted the book, as though a type of Art himself had suggested it. In another, Naomi Mitchison's refusal to accept the plausibility of the Art-Hector relationship, or to recognise the universal importance of a Highland strath or its problems, is supposed to have provoked him to create this surrealist yet satiric fantasy. Certainly it shows him deliberately entering the territory of Huxley's *Brave New World* (1932) and the later *Nineteen Eighty-Four* (1949) of Orwell, and doing so with a success which demands that the novel be seen alongside these as modern satire on new social orders of the West. But, more simply, the novel was the natural development into speculative myth after *Young Art*; all the positive groundwork there insists on some final test, some meta-legend, set against modern negativity, to complete the epic quest.

For the Green Isle, with bluer than earthly waters and greener than earthly fields, into which Art and Hector fall, is a daring fusion of Tir-nan-Og, the Celtic paradise, with a nightmare vision of modern totalitarianism, which forbids individualism. Gunn always fused pagan and Christian elements in his work. This is the culminating example of his interweaving, so that Celtic and Christian heaven are one, but now eroded by modern materialism and scientific rationalism generally, and totalitarian social conditioning particularly. Disentangling the elements of pagan/Christian belief can be difficult. For example, there is a play on 'no room at the inn', in that Art and Hector are expected on arrival in this new land to go dutifully to the inns, and their refusal to go is precisely because there is now too much of the wrong kind of 'room at the inn', so that the arrivals who eat the treated food there become automatons, hooded and sinister 'pilgrims', processed into the new 'perfection' where a kind of authoritarian utilitarianism has come to rule. Man has taken over from God, the overseeing of order, through the establishment of Inquisitors, at the central cities of each region. The fruit on the trees of the countryside is not to be eaten. Gunn works a strange variation of the taboo placed on the Tree of Knowledge in Eden, hardly following Christian practice, but in a way which suggests that Christianity and pagan mythology have truth somewhere in both of them. But just as no single authoritarian interpretation of life's meaning is allowed to hold sway in Gunn's work, so the

697

very point here is that it is the wonder of Christian image and myth which matters, not its dogma. Gunn argues that dogma destroys, just as the dogmatic 'atomic psychology' of the Inquisitors at the seats of power destroys poetry, fun, real laughter, spontaneous delight. (Gunn will later place his analysis of *The Atom of Delight*, 1956, directly against such destructive analysis.) His picture of the 'perfect society' is chilling, with the monotonous singing of 'Three Blind Mice' by disciplined infants, the curious superficial expressions of the people of the isle, which Art hates, and the menace of officials, all the more effective since overt violence is replaced with soulless power and control. Art and Hector are indeed welcome in this centralised, categorised society. The Inquisitors and their helpers, such as ambitious young Merk and Axel, relish the idea of taking them to pieces to find out what ancient and atavistic primitivism moves them. They are a cerebral challenge, as in a game of chess, the prey of an intellectual hunt.

Art and Hector are not alone in their resistance, however. Some peasants – notably Mary and Robert – are helpful, if reluctantly, as though their instincts are at war with their calculations. Mary lost her child on earth, and Robert, protective to excess, is a failed poet. (There is the gentlest of hints that they are Mary Campbell and Robert Burns, finally united in the Green Isle, but now distorted by this fallen heaven's warping.) Besides, Mary comes from the same stock as Hector, and they are both descended from Mairi Ross of generations ago. (Could this be Dark Mairi of *Butcher's Broom*, thus giving continuity of *dramatis personae* as well as values?) Mary cannot ignore the claim of kin – or humanity. Art awakens her maternal instinct, as Hector awakens the spirit of hospitality. (It is a sign of how far basic community values and Christianity have been lost on the Green Isle, that they tell their visitors that it is 'not our business to feed the stranger here' – a cardinal sin by the lights of any traditional culture.) Hector's Grace – both formal and informal – continues the awakening. We should realise, however, that in a sense their awakening had already begun. Mary, Robert, and friends do not eat the processed food, which kills individualism.

Mary (like Mairi before her) has ancient herbal skills which she uses (in her tart green jelly) to restore the quality of the sytheticised fruit taken from the Tree of Life, even after being programmed to eat only the synthetic fodder. As in all the great heroic legends, the heroes come when their hour is right. God works, as Hector says, in strange ways. And is there perhaps the suggestion that Mary and Robert are kin to Mary and Joseph? Their roles are almost as crucial as those of Art and Hector. God's ways are even stranger when we consider that Art is art; creativity, rumour leading to legend and fable. For Art goes on to run, accompanied by the great dogs (with names from Ossianic legend), so that his elusive fleetness becomes a wonder throughout the Green Isle; and he becomes 'a fabulous youth', an archetype of freedom, energy, disorder and fun. He grows in the telling, too, so that (as well as actually appearing to become a 12- or 13-year-old in this place where time and light can play strange tricks) he becomes Cuchulain (Art's favourite, as was revealed to us in the very first story of *Young Art and Old Hector*), the epitome of all great hero-rebels.

Gunn now synthesises all previous elements of his epic fiction, so that Art becomes the elusive meaning of life itself, for everybody in the book – including the Inquisitors, since unless they can pin him down, their own meaning and authority will be invalidated. The latent cruelty of the Inquisitors is revealed as their ruthless Hunt develops. Since ultimate significance is thus invested, in defiance of all conventional modern values, in a boy and an old man, we are prepared for the breathtaking audacity of Gunn's final involvement of God himself. Art, on the run yet again, after being recaptured, stumbles on Hector, or at least a figure uncannily like him. But this old peasant is, if similarly wise, a bit faster and more resourceful. They run together – after Art has tested God's credentials against the yardstick of home, Hector and Clachdrum. For God it is. Rumour, started by Art and Hector, and Hector's final demand to see him, have called him from his meditations. What is Gunn's meaning here? And is the visualisation of God not bound to be bathetic and irrational, in that his portrayal is too human? Does this not raise the question as to why God abandoned his heaven (and, by implication by Gunn, his earth) in the first place? Well, it is after all Art's dream, which is irrational anyway. In a sense, Gunn seeks a sublime bathos, whereby he insists that if God is not made in the image of Hector, and Hector in the image of God, then all he has been arguing through his epic novels is pointless. Myth is created by the human imagination and art. In turn, that myth creates new generations of the folk who re-enact the varieties of the myth. God is man, and man is God – and Gunn sees nothing blasphemous or odd about that. It is a simpler idea than, say Coleridge's notion of the esemplastic imagination, or 'divine creativity'; and available to the simplest community. Gunn can go no further in this direction. Hector is the last of his race, he 'is finished', as he tells Art throughout their relationship; not 'finished' in hope or resilience, but rather, he is complete in his life. He knows his people's history, the straths, their streams and their living things. He teaches Art that he (and Art as human process) need look no further than the immediate human locality for beauty and meaning. This noble and wise man taught this throughout *Young Art*, and his hero-king, Art, fulfils his teaching by finding God and saving his people – a role which is, as Jessie

Weston identified in *From Ritual to Romance* (1920) the basic and abiding archetype of all religious mythology.

But Hector has a crucial role in the Green Isle too. He is caught, early on. He is tempted to give in to the endless questioning, to let his spirit fail. But the reader should not miss the fact that it is the conflict of loyalties and the fear of hurting Mary and Robert, the strangers who took them in, which primarily motivates his temporary – and conditional – surrender. Like old Jeems in *The Grey Coast*, however, there is that in Hector which is wily, elusive and primordial, which will instinctively find ways of resisting even when not appearing to resist. Only when cornered, like some hunted beast, does Hector directly insist on his right to see God. That old-fashioned and unheard-of exercise of right is the final factor in the regeneration of the Green Isle and the transformation of its Dystopia. Gunn's handling of the meeting of God and Hector is pitched perfectly. The two are mirror images of each other, though Hector's reverence for creation does not let him see that God is himself, talking in dream.

For we return to the fact that all this is Art's – and Hector's – dream. What can they find to talk about? asks Morag fondly, as she and Tom watch the pair they have saved from drowning, rapt in conversation. Gunn implies that they are comparing dreams, and that the ultimate condition of a shared 'second sight' has been achieved. And when we bear this in mind, curious aspects of their stay in the Green Isle emerge into the front of our minds: Hector's occasional dizziness throughout; the references to the fluctuations of the 'psychic barometer' (a kind of measure of the intensity of their dream?); continual pseudo-recognition or identifications of characters from the real world – so that Morag (as Mavis) and Tom are here acting under new *personae*, but are still essentially themselves. Robert and Mary are older archetypes, from 'collective unconscious' memories, but Art's use of his new knife, his discovery of the hazelnuts of knowledge in his pockets when *in extremis* with God, his references to the Clachdrum Games, and his identification of God as the Starter of the Great Race (which he won, and wins again here) – these show that 'reality' is working in their drowning minds, as they lie at the bottom of the Hazel Pool. How typical of Art's imagination and his love of Cuchulain's heroism, that God should exit from the dream and the festivities at the regeneration of the Green Isle with the most fabulous long-jump!

But 'reality' can be seen crowding in as the story begins to climax. Axel has a mouth like a pike, people look like eels, and Sweet Innocence, the horrifyingly unnatural girl guerrilla, is a haddock. The closing chapters have a green underwater tinge, together with a roaring in Hector's ears which suggests their rescue by Tom and their emergence from the Hazel Pool. Hector meets God in 'a vast sea-green cavern'. Isn't Gunn suggesting that 'heaven' is here and now, and in the mind? Hector said as much to Mary when they talked about the final good of a fruitful harvest. The distortion of man, through industrialisation and mental disintegration, is the real fall; in this Gunn is utterly at one with the poet Edwin Muir.

In the end all Gunn's meaning lies in the idea of the Fruit of the Land, and the novel's ubiquitous symbolism of living and eating naturally off the land. The hazelnuts of knowledge are thus triumphant over Eden's Tree of Knowledge; Art finds the wisdom of Finn McCoull, through finding the salmon in the Hazel Pool which has eaten the nuts and thus, swimming in the river of life, gives wisdom to man. It is also a very real salmon in a Scottish river which they bring back with them. They have been to paradise, and come back with the realisation that it can be, indeed is, Scotland; their landscape, their community – potentially. Read like this, Hector's insistence on seeing God is the end-point of Gunn's quest for essential Scotland. Art, setting out, and Hector, about to die in his remote landscape, are the meaning of their country, and its finest fruit.

Gunn goes on to explore depths of self and complexities of meaning, in profound novels like *The Other Landscape* (1954) and the spiritual autobiography *The Atom of Delight* (1956). But his great epic phase is complete; it is finished. His trilogy and duality have given his country the regenerative mythology lost for so long. Gunn's epic fiction is not overtly political. He kept his nationalistic activities by and large separate from his novels. But by asserting the great age and essential resilience of Scottish community spirit, Gunn gives back perspective to Scottish literature and culture, and urges rejection of that fatalism and apathy induced by hundreds of years of failure of will at national and local level. The enduring memory of these novels is of resilient women, strong as their land around them, like Breeta and Dark Mairi and Catrine and Mary Campbell; and forward-looking men like Aniel, Colin Sutherland, Finn and Art, standing on the threshold of their adventure, armed only with a sense of their past, and their will to make the present – and, of course, the wisdom of old Hector, the quiet Master of their country's knowledge, the wisdom and knowledge of Neil Gunn himself.

Gunn's other fiction

This chapter cannot do full justice to the huge achievement of Gunn, in the other novels he was writing alongside his great epic fiction, such as *Wild Geese Overhead* (1939), *Second Sight* (1940), *The Serpent* (1943) and *The Drinking Well*

(1946). While the latter two are fascinating in their analyses of modern Scottish/Highland issues, from religious bigotry to land economy, as with the first two, they do suggest that Gunn was less assured in his handling of contemporary Scotland, as his *deus ex machina* ending to *The Drinking Well* suggests. Indeed, after the war it seems that the quest of *Highland River* for personal meaning took precedence over the search for public and national renewal, with Gunn increasingly finding substantiation of his ideas in his reading of Eastern philosophies. The eight later novels, written between 1948 and 1954, fall into Section 6, and are briefly discussed in the first of the two fiction chapters there. But readers seeking fuller and fairer discussion of the subtle metaphysical considerations of these novels, together with their rich and subtle transcendental comedy, are referred to the studies of, amongst others, John Burns, Douglas Gifford, Francis Hart, Margery McCulloch, and Richard Price (see bibliography). Gunn was also a fine short story writer (*Hidden Doors*, 1929, *The White Hour*, 1950); and of non-fiction such as *Whisky and Scotland* (1935), *Off in a Boat* (1938), *Highland Pack* (1949) and, outstandingly, his last work which showed how far he had taken his search for spiritual identity, the ideological autobiography *The Atom of Delight* (1956).

CHAPTER 36

WIDENING THE RANGE 5

1918–45: SCOTLAND REBORN OR IN DECLINE?

One of the main arguments of this guide is that Scottish literature did not die in the nineteenth century, after Scott. In Section 4 attention was drawn to what was described as a revival of Scottish literature, even if that revival took the paradoxical form of a 'positive negativism', a perspective on Scottish life and character deeply critical and often satirical and parodic, which can be seen now as a necessary stripping away of excessive romanticisation and sentimentalisation of Scottish life and character. It should be remembered that writers like John Davidson, Neil Munro and George Douglas Brown, for all their ironic bleakness, had a positive role to play in the re-awakening of Scottish culture before the First World War. And that MacDiarmid perhaps emphasised too strongly a parochial dearth in Scottish artistic achievement and a disconnection with European cultural development, for his own ends. With this in mind, it might be useful to consider why MacDiarmid would wish to represent Victorian and Edwardian Scottish culture in the negative ways he did, and to what extent he misrepresented positive achievement.

Thus the major unanswered question, which lies behind this period, is how far MacDiarmid's 'Scottish Renaissance' can be credited with the revival of a vital Scottish literature. Or had that revival in fact started as early as the 1880s or before, with Stevenson and a whole range of significant new Scottish writers? Related to this question is another; how far does the title of 'Scottish Renaissance' adequately describe what was happening in Scottish literature in the inter-war years? In surveying the period beyond the major writers so far dealt with, three groups suggest themselves: firstly, those older writers who had seen previous revivals come and go, together with those younger yet uncommitted writers who nevertheless worked with more traditional content and form; secondly, those committed to the aims of 'renaissance'; and thirdly, those sceptical regarding the validity of notions of 'renaissance'.

Renaissance forerunners and fellow travellers

The important writers, whose work overlaps the periods before and after the First World War, and whose reputations have declined – for whatever reasons – include Robert Bontine Cunninghame Graham, John Buchan, Frederick Niven, James Barrie, Catherine Carswell, Violet Jacob, Marion Angus, Helen Cruickshank, and Will Ogilvie. Arguably they all deserve re-assessment; and indeed that work has begun for many of them, re-establishing, for example, Carswell's *Open the Door!* of 1920 as a key text which precedes MacDiarmid's 'Scottish Renaissance', and dealt with substantially in Chapter 30. Unacknowledged by MacDiarmid, this text is just one example of earlier Scottish writing fulfilling the very requirements MacDiarmid insisted on – requirements that Scottish culture and writing should work with the best of international thinking and literary innovation, symbolic and psychological representation and expression. Contemporary criticism needs to re-assess many of MacDiarmid's verdicts, and modern readers should be prepared to explore and revalue neglected areas. And while this section has foregrounded a re-assessment of Carswell and other women novelists, justice remains to be done to many more.

Carrying on older traditions

The life and work of R. B. Cunninghame Graham (1852–1936), linking two centuries, illustrates the move from Victorian into Renaissance values. An aristocrat and contemporary of Robert Louis Stevenson, he outlived Grassic Gibbon; and his adventurous life, moving between Scotland and Latin America, where he gained the nickname of 'The Gaucho', saw him involved in radical politics (and jailed) in Britain in the 1880s. Yet by the 1920s he had become a leader of the new nationalist movement, and was closely associated with Scottish Renaissance writers like MacDiarmid and Gunn. His writing reflects his astonishingly varied life, and indeed it is probably the very range and diversity of his prose and fiction on world-wide subjects which has excluded him from proper consideration as a major writer. In *The Scottish Sketches of R. B. Cunninghame Graham* (1982) some of the best of his prose and fiction has been anthologised by John Walker.

John Buchan (1875–1940), the prolific, popular yet undervalued master of many genres, from historical fiction to thrillers, short stories to serious scholarly study, also crosses over from one century to another – with huge success in his move to popular fiction like *The Thirty-Nine Steps* (1915) and *The Three Hostages* (1924). Popular novels like these have perhaps lessened

Buchan's literary reputation, although there is presently a revival of interest in his work, finding a more significant contribution in more serious fiction like *The Path of the King* (1924), and, outstandingly, *Witch Wood* (1927) and *Sick Heart River* (1941). Buchan's work can be seen in three main phases. The first, up to the First World War, saw him as the student prodigy, publishing many books while at Glasgow and Oxford (and then perhaps dividing his loyalties, as he worked on one hand with MacDiarmid and the early Renaissance movement, and on the other pursued his keen ambition within the English Establishment, which culminated in his becoming Governor-General of Canada). The second, in the inter-war years, saw him working with the thriller genre which ingeniously functioned as propaganda for Britain's imperial and anti-German role. The third, in the years before his death in 1941, saw his loyalties and imagination returning home to Scotland. *Witch Wood* looks back to the great religious satires and adventures of Galt, Hogg, and Stevenson, in its powerful account of a young minister's discovery of Devil-worship in his Border community, and his battle with that hidden evil. Buchan works here at a level he rarely achieves; this and *Sick Heart River* deserve to be considered with the best of Scottish fiction. The latter was written as he was dying; it is set amongst the frozen wastes of northern Canada, and is the story of the quest of a dying British politician to find the one man who can save the West, but who is lost in the wilderness. Buchan was perhaps writing an *apologia* for his own career in this moving account of the politician's discovery that humble Indian (or Scottish?) tribes matter more than the affairs of Great Ones. His protagonist discovers a perfect Lost World, but in the end chooses to leave it and sacrifice his own possible cure for the sake of his adopted tribe, thus becoming the mythical king who dies for his people.

As with Graham, there is a huge body of varied work for the reader to explore, from early undervalued work such as *Sir Quixote of the Moors* (1895) and *A Lost Lady of Old Years* (1899) through the numerous and immensely readable romances and thrillers like *The Thirty-Nine Steps* (1915), *Greenmantle* (1916), *John Macnab* (1925), *The Courts of the Morning* (1929) and *The House of the Four Winds* (1935). Buchan's heroic characters are endearing, from the bluffly resilient Richard Hannay to the elusive and more spiritual adventurer Sandy Arbuthnott, Scottish aristocrat and king-maker in far-flung part of the globe, or Glasgow grocer Dickson McCunn and his 'Gorbals Diehards', the street-urchins he adopts, who do great things in sport and adventure. Despite representing an older, male-dominated, imperialistic and racially incorrect British world-view, he has a satisfying ability to portray action, politics and character on a huge historical and territorial scale, together with a genuinely poetic and imaginative power in his visions of lost worlds at home and abroad, and a poignant sense of elegy for a lost Scotland.

A very different kind of inheritance from the past is found in the strange worlds created by David Lindsay (1878–1945) in *A Voyage to Arcturus* (1920), *The Haunted Woman* (1922), *Devil's Tor* (1932) and *The Violet Apple* (posthumously published in 1976). Lindsay was born in 1878, and was clearly influenced by the fantasy novels, with their parallel worlds, of George MacDonald. *A Voyage to Arcturus* is the most ambitious of these complex and disturbing allegorical works; it adds an element of science fiction to MacDonald's moral allegory, taking Maskull the earthman to the planet Tormance and portraying his surreal encounters with grotesque creatures. Lindsay's gift is to disturb the reader's unconscious as well as conscious mind and imagination, so that there is continually a sense of being on the edge of vast and dimly intuited meanings, with the suggestion of the Manichean dualities of William Blake. While unsuccessful in his lifetime, Lindsay's work undoubtedly inspired the similar allegories of C. S. Lewis in the 1940s, and thus acts as link between the nineteenth-century fantasies of MacDonald and the famous later work of Lewis and Tolkien.

It could be considered that, as with their contemporaries, the Findlater sisters, the reputations of Graham, Buchan and Lindsay suffered because they were formed as Victorians and Edwardians, and found the new world after the First World War too formless and different for them to adapt to. The drama and fiction of James Barrie is discussed in Section 4; but an astonishing tour-de-force, his novella *Farewell Miss Julie Logan* (1932), can stand here as representative of a tendency – not without power and value – to hark back to an older Scotland and traditional (and often supernatural) ideas. Here is the naïve minister of Buchan's *Witch Wood*, a protagonist familiar to us since Scott, Stevenson, Munro and Crockett, caught up in community duplicity and supersition. Yet Barrie makes his farewell to the classic Scottish supernatural story of the nineteenth century with the sly and parodic twist which has so often eluded his critics. Adam Yestreen tells his story in the classic Scottish form of a dramatic monologue, revealing more about himself than he intends; and it appears that the supernatural events which he experiences are in fact manifestations of his repressed longings for forbidden beauty, sexuality and art, encouraged in a half-mocking, half-affectionate way by the annual English visitors, whose liberal lifestyle Adam deplores and envies. But there may be other ways to read his story; the local aristocracy may be supernaturally bound by the ancient order/curse, given by the fleeing Prince Charles, to honour forever his saviour, the beautiful and wayward Julie Logan, and Adam may be her earthly – and ultimately unearthly – lover. The classic ambiguities of

Scottish texts like 'Tam o' Shanter' and *The Justified Sinner*, allowing either psychological or supernatural interpretation, are thus invoked; and the enigmatic figure of Julie Logan is allowed to remain as one of Scottish literature's eeriest and legendary figures. Yet she is more; she is in the end almost mythical, and Barrie's personification of a timeless and haunting Scottish landscape, and of the lost causes of centuries of forlorn and internecine Scottish history. She is Barrie's farewell to an older Scottish culture.

There are, of course, many other writers whose work fits none of the three categories initially suggested. Frederick Niven's (1878–1944) major and innovative study of Glasgow commerce, *The Justice of the Peace* appeared as early as 1914, but his work continued till *The Transplanted* in 1944. He was born in Chile in 1878 but returned, in childhood, to Glasgow. Like Graham and Buchan, he travelled extensively as a journalist till the war; but after this, unhappy with conditions in Scotland and Britain, he emigrated to Canada, where he continued to write many novels. Several are set in Glasgow, like *Mrs Barry* (1933) and *The Staff at Simpsons* (1937): the first anticipating the ironic yet humane Bell McShelvie of Robin Jenkins's *Guests of War* (1956) in its portrait of a widow enduring poverty with dignity; the second showing that Niven, in Canada, had lost none of his ability to portray vividly the commerce and vigour of twentieth-century Glasgow. John Cockburn's (1898–?) worthy, if overtly Zola-esque, evocation of Glasgow street life in *Tenement* (1925) initiates what will become representative of that unwillingness to subscribe to Renaissance affirmation, dealt with below. A. J. Cronin (1896–1981) is now remembered as the inspiration of the *Dr Finlay's Casebook* television series; but his impressive contribution to the tradition of *The House with the Green Shutters*, *Hatter's Castle* (1931), with its grim portrait of a tyrannical Dundee merchant-father, deserves recognition, as does his account of adolescence and tragedy in the west of Scotland in *The Green Years* (1945). Bruce Marshall's (1899–1987) *Father Malachy's Miracle* (1931) is outstanding for its hilarious supernatural transformations. John Macnair Reid's (1895–1954) *Homeward Journey* (1934) is a subtly ambiguous account of a Glasgow love affair, while his *Judy from Crown Street*, only published posthumously in 1970, bears comparison with Niven's *Mrs Barry* and the later work of Jenkins.

Unacknowledged poetic debts?
Jacob, Angus and forerunners of MacDiarmid

As we have seen in the previous section, there were poetic voices which did not succumb to the lute of Kailyard or Celtic Twilight; and succeeded in articulating a predominant ironical and critical view of Scottish culture of its period. MacDiarmid did at first pay tribute to his contemporaries. In 1920 his *Northern Numbers* poetry anthology referred to many Scottish writers 'of the highest merit' who would 'unquestionably be given a place in any future anthology of Scottish poetry', and then included as contributors, amongst others, John Buchan, Violet Jacob, Neil Munro, Will Ogilvie, the war poets Joseph Lee and Roderick Watson Kerr – and himself. A second *Northern Numbers* followed in 1921; adding, with others, Charles Murray, Alexander Gray, Mary Symon and Lewis Spence. MacDiarmid, shortly after, converted to the cause of Scots language and distanced himself from many of those, including Buchan, Munro and Spence, who had helped him. The reader of poetry in this period might find it rewarding to assess what MacDiarmid found impressive at the time of anthologising, and what he later decided was insufficient and requiring change.

Without denigrating MacDiarmid's achievement and originality in his Scots poetry of the 1920s, there is at least a case to be made that on one hand the Scots poetry of Ogilvie, Murray, Symon and, outstandingly, Angus and Jacob, gave a great deal to MacDiarmid's Scots lyrics, while on the other, the shocking contempt for war in the work of Lee and Kerr gave him much of the new, iconoclastic, and often savagely anti-social tone of *A Drunk Man* and the later English poetry.

Although Hugh MacDiarmid played a profoundly important role in the revitalisation of Scottish poetry during the inter-war years, it is essential to note that he did so in the company of other skilled poets. A complete portrait of the Scottish Renaissance would be incomplete without an examination of two poets who preceded, and in many ways influenced, MacDiarmid. We have already considered two poets from the north-east of Scotland, Violet Jacob and Marion Angus, in the context of the Victorian and Edwardian period. It is worth here revisiting them to consider the contribution they made to the poetry of the Renaissance movement. Although Grieve/MacDiarmid in *Contemporary Scottish Studies* (1926) dismissed their work as 'minor and for the most part very minor,' their poetry nevertheless set the stage for the renewed interest in Scots as a viable literary medium. Their work combines both the lyricism and verbal economy of traditional Scottish ballads with a proto-Modernist fascination with voice and the self.

Singing lyrics for MacDiarmid: Violet Jacob (1863–1946) and Marion Angus (1865–1946)

Jacob and Angus share several common attributes – north-eastern roots (the House of Dun in Montrose for Jacob, Arbroath for Angus), a love of the ballads and folklore, and similar life spans – but the differences between the poets remain far more compelling than these surface similarities. Jacob, who published *Songs of Angus*, her first volume of Scots poetry in 1915, focused upon articulating voices from the edges of conventional rural society: travellers, poor farm labourers, disenfranchised women, and children. In poems like 'The End o't' (*Bonnie Joann*, 1921), 'The Guidwife Speaks' (*Northern Lights*, 1927) and 'The Jaud' (*Northern Lights*), Jacob explores the relationship between self and community, highlighting the marginalised status of her speakers. Poems like 'Donald Maclane' (*Northern Lights*) present a profoundly sympathetic, albeit gritty vision of rural poverty – a vision largely absent from the work of her contemporaries. Exile, and its emotional implications, also emerge as important themes in her work. 'Craigo Woods,' from *Songs of Angus*, records an exile's yearning for the 'braw reid puddock-stules . . . like jewels' in his distant home. Jacob lived for most of her adult life outside Scotland – in Egypt, India, and England – and consequently in her numerous poems of exile, one discerns an earnest longing for the Angus countryside she so lyrically evokes in her poetry. Perhaps the most notable element of Jacob's poetry remains, however, her technical dexterity. Jacob masterfully combines traditional ballad metrics and diction with a complex and sophisticated rhythmic structure. For example, her poem 'The Water-Hen' (*Songs of Angus*) describes a supernatural interaction between speaker and the titular bird that is reminiscent of the ballads; the poem's sprung rhythm, however, creates a ragged and unsettling metrical speed wholly unlike the ballads. In this and other poems, Jacob's technical skills and deft use of the Scots language imbue the work with the same vitality MacDiarmid's early lyrics illustrate.

In comparison, Angus focuses less upon poetic structural complexity, turning her incisive gaze to reveal the unspoken desires and fears of her locuters. Unlike the generalised, broadly representative selves in Jacob's poetry (the wife, exile, traveller, shepherd), the selves in Angus's work possess highly individual, particular voices. More often than not, the speaker is a woman; in several poems, however, Angus deliberately conceals the speaker's gender, age, or sexuality. Nevertheless, in poems like 'Mary's Song' (*The Tinker's Road*, 1924) and 'Jean Cam'bell' (*The Singin' Lass*, 1929), Angus expresses the yearnings of distinct (however mysterious) selves. Her poems contain what have been termed 'covert narratives'; eerie, enigmatic inter-actions between the speaker and her surroundings. In many poems – 'Hogmanay' and 'At Candlemas,' for example – Angus presents an intriguing confrontation of different versions of the same self. The self in these poems becomes fragmented and exists as a series of distinct aspects contained within one identity. In other poems, however, Angus shifts her focus from an examination of the self's myriad facets to an investigation of the relationship between the speaker and an external object of desire. In 'The Eerie Hoose', 'Waater O'Dye,' and 'The Can'el,' for instance, Angus reveals the complex fusion of desire and violence underlying erotic relationships. The speaker both desires and shuns an interaction with the lover. In her characteristically elusive style, Angus in poems like 'Jealousy' and 'Barbara' refuses to explain the precise nature of the relationship between speaker and allocutor; ambiguity both conceals the poem's emotional motivation and allows for a spectrum of possible interpretations to coexist. Ultimately, Angus's poetry offers a compelling portrait of the proto-Modernist self: cryptic, questioning, ambiguous, and constructed from fragments of folk belief and Modernist uncertainty.

Jacob published five volumes of Scots poetry during her life, Angus six. Despite the enormous popularity of these works, none remains in print today. Literary tastes change over time, and for some, Jacob and Angus's apparently non-political Scots work fails to satisfy the post-Modernist appetite. Nevertheless, their influence on the young Hugh MacDiarmid – who eagerly distanced himself from them for fear, perhaps, of not appearing unique – should not be overlooked. A fascinating comparison can be made of his early, and untypically humane and community-minded, Scots lyrics and those of Angus and Jacob, which would reveal the enormous extent to which MacDiarmid exploited possibilities already opened to him.

Celebrating rural Scotland

Other poets well worth returning to include Will Ogilvie, whose long life (1869–1963) saw him move from the Borders to Australia and America, and in retirement, to the Borders again. Like so many of his contemporaries, such as Cunninghame Graham and Charles Murray, exile made his verse nostalgic, yet simple and evocative of Border life and history. Alexander Gray wrote with similar evocative power of the north-east, in English and Scots (his 'Scotland', simultaneously acknowledging the bleakness and the austere beauty of the country, is one of the most anthologised of Scottish poems); while W. D. Cocker (1882–1970), whose work successfully celebrates the Stirlingshire countryside in which he grew up, and who still enjoys a wide popularity, has been underrated by literary criticism as a poet. Andrew Young (1885–1971) was thirty-three when he left Scotland and the Free Church ministry in 1918 for Sussex and conversion to the Church of England; his poetry goes further than mere celebration of nature, as it fuses celebration and detailed observation with religious belief in ways comparable with the poetry of Hopkins and Mackay Brown.

Supporting Renaissance: poetry

While several of the poets discussed above, like Jacob, Angus and Cocker, were associated with *Northern Numbers* and the early days of MacDiarmid's 'Scottish Renaissance', a few others deserve mention here. Helen Cruick-shank (1886–1975) is remarkable both as a supporter of MacDiarmid from the very beginning, and as a poet herself. She came from Angus, and her work derives much from the earlier poets of rural Scotland discussed above, and from Angus and Jacob in particular, in volumes like *Up the Noran Water* (1934) and *The Ponnage Pool* (1968). A. D. Mackie (1904–85), whose *Poems in Two Tongues* (1928), and the later tour-de-force, the carnival celebration of a nation in *Sing a Song for Scotland* (1944), demonstrated an ease in colloquial Scots and a perceptive eye for ordinary Scottish life. The work of William Jeffrey (1896–1946), in *Prometheus Returns* (1921), showed, however, that Renaissance poetry was to be very different. Jeffrey might evoke his Lanark-shire and Scotland, but to this, in English and Scots, he added a love of classical mythology, together with a disgust at modern society and a mystical symbolism, which, if over-ambitious, signalled the new and international aims of Renaissance. (Alexander Scott, a later Renaissance poet, edited his *Selected Poems* in 1951, after Jeffrey's death in 1946.) And just before the Second World War a remarkable new wave of Renaissance poets came on the scene, whose work more rightly belongs to the post-war period, but who should be noted here as working in Scots and inspired by MacDiarmid's movement, such as Douglas Young (*Auntran Blads*, 1943), Crombie Saunders (editor of MacDiarmid's *Selected Poems* in 1944), Sydney Goodsir Smith and Robert Garioch.

Goodsir Smith came from New Zealand via Oxford to become an unlikely leader of Renaissance. He viewed himself as poet, as the enemy of Establish-ment, and regarded Scots language in poetry as 'unreal', as remote from ordinary speech as the language of *Lear*, Keats, or Gavin Douglas. Thus his Scots poetry, from *Skail Wind* in 1941 on, works within a rich context of Scottish and international literature and language, with a sonorous and self-conscious indulgence of Scots sound-effects which constantly, and positively, reminds us of the artifice of poetry. His paradoxical respect for, and reduction of, his learning can be compared with that of an Edinburgh poet whose work originates in the period, Robert Garioch. Garioch was similarly steeped in classical and European Renaissance learning, and a fine translator, especially of Italian poetry; who also enjoyed cocking a snook at pomposity and his own intellectual pretensions. Garioch's first work appeared with that of Sorley MacLean in the typically self-deprecatingly entitled *17 Poems for 6d* in 1940; his major poetry came after the war, and arguably can be seen as sceptically diverging from Renaissance aims.

Like Sorley MacLean (discussed in Chapter 34), poet of three languages (English, Gaelic and Scots) George Campbell Hay, who was son of novelist John MacDougall Hay, drew inspiration from MacDiarmid's example. Hay was already a fine Gaelic poet before becoming inspired by MacDiarmid's *Scots Unbound* (1932); this and his war experience lie behind the work which he produced after the war, like *Fuaran Sleibh* (1947) and *The Wind on Loch Fyne* (1948). And with the war itself another wave came forward: Maurice Lindsay's poetry began to appear with *The Advancing Day* in 1940, although it was to be some time before he found his best voice. Like Norman MacCaig, whose first work appeared in 1943 with *Far Cry*, he was at first unduly influenced by the 'New Apocalypse' movement. George Bruce produced his first volumes of north-east poems with *Sea Talk* in 1944, although he was to be silent for twenty years thereafter until becoming a major contemporary figure, while war had merely delayed the poetry of Aberdonian Alexander Scott. The work of these poets, however, belongs to the next section.

Supporting Renaissance: fiction

Neil Gunn was clearly the most positive of the Renaissance fiction writers, and on the most ambitious scale. Eric Linklater also celebrated Renaissance, although we have already noted how his most important novel dealing with it, *Magnus Merriman* (1934), did so ambivalently, offering a reductive and hilariously satirical view of the movement's pretensions and weaknesses. Naomi Mitchison's work during the period tended to locate itself in other countries, while at the same time – as in *The Corn King and the Spring Queen* (1931) – having clear implications for Scotland in its patterning of small and vulnerable versus large and dominant cultures. Not until after the war, with *The Bull Calves* of 1947, did she make explicit her Renaissance support, while the extent of Lewis Grassic Gibbon's commitment to the cause of Scottish cultural and national rediscovery remains questionable. Enigmatic in other ways is the contribution of the much-lauded Compton Mackenzie, whose apparently supportive role in the Renaissance has perhaps not been sufficiently questioned. Born into an English acting family in 1883, after an exotic career as law student, playwright, novelist and spy in the Dardanelles during the First World War, he settled in Scotland in 1928, befriending Hugh

MacDiarmid and supporting his political and cultural nationalism. His most ambitious series of novels is contained in the epic *The Four Winds of Love* series (1937–45). The hero, Juan Pendarves Ogilvie, owes something to Linklater's comic and grotesquely extravagant modern versions of the adventures of Byron's Don Juan in *Juan in America* (1931) and *Juan in China* (1935), although much of this Juan's progress through life follows Mackenzie's own, taking him as a young man from the horrors of public school to success as playwright and secret service in the Aegean. *The East* and *South Winds* cover his life until *The West Wind* sees Ogilvie buying his Hebridean island. But the winds of change also cover involvement in love and politics in the USA, in Cornwall and in tortured Ireland, as well as the universal predicament of small nations. It is only in *The North Wind* that Ogilvie reveals himself as a Scottish nationalist leader, but one who seeks to fuse his Celtic, communist, and by now Catholic ideals into a holistic world-view. To this end he travels restlessly to France, England, Italy, Poland, Asia Minor, and throughout his journeys observes the growing threat of Hitler's Germany – to the point where he begins to doubt his nationalist commitments. The ambition is overwhelming, the success much less so. Mackenzie's Juan lacks the psychological subtlety and self-mockery of Linklater's Juan; he takes himself incredibly seriously as he lectures to the world, and his many women are mere phases in his life, secondary to his egotistical quest for mystic fulfilment. Nevertheless, the sheer scale of achievement in this complex romantic-symbolic quest is impressive, and deserves consideration as a major text of the movement.

What is more disturbing is what this reveals about Mackenzie's view of his role in Renaissance. With such a colossal world-view, local Scottish events could never signify much, for all the lipservice he pays to the significance of small nations. Mackenzie's many volumes of memoirs (*My Life and Times*, 10 vols, 1963–71) betray his ultimately minor interest in Scottish culture; there is little discussion of Scottish Renaissance. Indeed, his contribution to it can be seen finally as profoundly negative, since he took MacDiarmid, after his marriage broke up, to London in the early '30s, a move which helped create MacDiarmid's antagonism towards other Renaissance writers like Gunn, whom Mackenzie deeply disliked. Later novels like *Whisky Galore* (1947) and *Ben Nevis Goes East* (1954) reveal a fundamentally condescending and manipulative view of Scottish people and culture – to the extent that suspicions grow as to what Mackenzie's involvement with Scotland was really about.

Mackenzie preferred the fictional version of the Highlands offered by Tom Macdonald, writing as 'Fionn MacColla' (1906–75), to that of Gunn. A disciple of MacDiarmid, Macdonald, like his mentor, was a Lowlander who changed his name to endow himself with a Celtic and messianic role. Comparison of these two writers is illuminating. Where Gunn is detached yet critical, but always humane in his analysis of Highland character and even in his anger at Highland exploitation, MacColla is angry and savage in his shrill hatred of all things English and his denunciation of the role of the reformed church in Scottish history. Where Gunn transforms historical argument into human situation and example, MacColla harangues in pseudo-Socratic manner. His best work is in two novels, *The Albannach* (1932) and *And The Cock Crew* (1945). The first is a novel of spiritual rebirth; a Free Church minister's son is regenerated from alcoholic despair and rejection of what his father stood for, healed by the influences of his natural background and by his discovery of Gaelic culture, his career thus becoming symbolic of potential Scottish Renaissance. This was MacColla in affirmative mode. Later work became heavy polemic against the Reformation's effect on Scottish culture, although there is no doubting the nightmare energy of his version of Highland clearance in *And The Cock Crew*. It is a tragic portrait of a visionary minister who tries to help his cleared flock. But he is fatally impaired by his inability to understand the ancient cultural traditions of his people – represented by the bard Fearchar who insists upon the Gaelic culture's ancient life-giving vitality – and tainted by his own negative creed.

No time for fairy tales: Renaissance sceptics

As early as *The House with the Green Shutters* (1901) there had been a reaction against Kailyard and fin-de-siècle escapism or negativity. This novel should be seen as setting a precedent for *Gillespie* (1914) and a whole run of writers who then work through the Renaissance, such as Patrick MacGill (1898–c. 1940) (*Children of the Dead End* 1914, *The Rat Pit* 1915), down to Ian Macpherson (1905–44) and John McNeillie (b. 1918) (later writing as Ian Niall). The novels of Ian Macpherson are unfairly neglected. His *Shepherd's Calendar* (1931), appeared a year before *Sunset Song*. It is a novel set in the Mearns, and bears comparison with the autobiographical novels Gibbon wrote under his real name of Leslie Mitchell, *Stained Radiance* (1930) and *The Thirteenth Disciple* (1931). These are north-east novels without the rich texture of Scots, 'the speak' of Gibbon in later work. They are imbued with a harsh realism, focused in a sensitive, unhappy protagonist. *Shepherd's Calendar* portrays young John Grant in the bleak Arn valley. And in John's father-hatred and repressed sensitivity, and his weak mother's efforts to turn him towards university and away from farming it echoes the grim *Green Shutters* tradition.

The ending leaves John – as later, the heroines of Jessie Kesson's north-east fictions – on the threshold of university and an uncertain future. This is a powerful, if crude, novel; its successors, *Land of Our Fathers* (1933) and *Pride in the Valley* (1936) move deeper into the Highlands to deal with the Clearances and, with increasing ambition and effective irony, the remnants of Highland pride in the Victorian era. Macpherson's story of the Cattanach family, shepherds around Loch Laggan, is notable for its portrait of the arrogant but penniless Highland chieftain, Cluny Macpherson, and his undeserved claim on the obeisance and loyalty of his clansmen.

Ian Macpherson was tragically killed in 1944, but his last novel, *Wild Harbour* (1936), in its strange and powerful account of a couple who seek escape from what they see as an increasingly mad world by taking to a cave in the hills, has a shockingly pessimistic conclusion, and suggests that Macpherson had perhaps come to the ends of his inspiration. McNeillie (later writing as Ian Niall) was the author of numerous documentary-like fictions of Scottish rural life and archetypes. They begin with *The Wigtown Ploughman* (1939), in which his protagonist, Andy, is no representative tiller of the soil carrying his burden of ancestral greatness in his humble labours. McNeillie's introduction to the novel – 'Would you have me tell you a fairy tale?' – suggests a specific hostility to the ideology of Gunn and Gibbon. And his harsh and at times almost bestial representation of Andy is in sharp contrast to their investing characters with profound historical, spiritual and archetypal significance.

Another unjustly neglected work of epic realism is James Barke's (1905–58) account of the impoverished and degraded existence of generations of the Ramsay family as they move all over Scotland in search of decent living. *The Land of the Leal* (1939) exposes, in its deliberate omission of land-celebration and any spiritual and mytho-poetic apparatus, what Barke sees as the lyrical excesses of the Renaissance writers. (That said, many would consider Barke guilty of another kind of idealisation in his series of bardola-trous novels on the life of Burns, which began in 1946 with *The Wind that Shakes the Barley*.)

It is arguable that the seeds of Renaissance negation were contained within the very works which seemed to assert most poetically the values of a rural and golden age past, since simultaneously such past glory was seen as lost to the new world. The dualism of land-celebration and ironic land-realism can be seen in what is often held to be the centrepiece of Renaissance fiction, *A Scots Quair*, while, in a sense, Linklater's *Magnus Merriman*, for all its paradoxical celebration of natural beauty and intimations of the unconscious mind, mocks the Renaissance in a fashion very similar to that of Stella Gibbons in

Cold Comfort Farm (1932), with its parody of English 'back-to-the-soil' writing in the work of Mary Webb and D. H. Lawrence.

And the Scottish novel was by the mid-1930s increasingly extending its perspective of ironic social realism to the city; James Barke's *Major Operation* (1936), in which a hospitalised businessman and worker argue out their differences, had no time for non-political and non-economic considerations. Edwin Muir's non-fictional classic *Scottish Journey* (1935) is a travel guide, which strips all comforting illusion away from the Scotland of his day. As the dustjacket to the first edition stated, 'No reader, thinking to find the Scotland of the tourist's delight, should open this book.' His novel *Poor Tom* (1932) anticipated this in its harrowing account of Orcadian Mansie Manson (a grimmer Magnus Merriman?) and the slow death of his brother Tom in the grey Glasgow to which their family has been forced to relocate. Much of this is the great *Autobiography* (1954) fictionalised, but made more complex through Tom, because he is the scapegoat for the family's loss of rural innocence, who must die. Both Mansie and Tom are Muir, in a fascinating objectification of Muir's deepest anxieties. Not all is bleak; Glasgow's cultural and political energy is here, alongside the condemnation of urbanisation. (Muir wrote two other novels: *The Three Brothers*, 1931, which had also dealt fictionally with Muir's tortured relations with brothers and family, but pushed back into the sixteenth century; as well as *The Marionette*, 1927, a profound and moving fable-like fiction of mentally-damaged Hans of Salzburg who prefers the world of puppets and dreams to reality.)

There are many novelists of the period who deserve to be remembered for their uncompromising commitment to portrayal of current social and political problems. Here we can only note Dot Allan, whose finest novel (*Makeshift*, 1928) is the story of a girl surviving her mother's suicide, after loneliness and tragedy. *The Deans* (1929) perhaps pushes its depiction of the problems of tenement-dwellers beyond realism into melodrama; more powerful and convincing are her later depictions of a Clyde shipbuilding family (*Deepening River*, 1932), and the march of Glasgow unemployed in the Depression (*Hunger March*, 1934). Arguably John Cockburn's *Tenement* (1925) began this move to present the lives of ordinary Glasgow folk. An excellent and detailed discussion of these novelists of Glasgow, its industry and its Depression, with other novelists such as Robert Craig (*O People!*, 1932), Catherine Gavin (*Clyde Valley*, 1938), George Woden (*Mungo*, 1932) and Edward Shiels (*Gael Over Glasgow*, 1937), is to be found in Moira Burgess's study, *Imagine a City* (1998). An outstanding example can stand as representative of many. George Blake wrote many novels based on Glasgow and Greenock, in several of which the myth of the glorious Clyde, its skilful communities and epic shipbuilding, is prefigured as doomed, in an elegiac strain which runs counter to the Clyde mythology otherwise being cele- brated. Outstanding amongst them are his chronicles of the great shipbuild- ing Oliphant family of *The Valiant Heart* (1940) and *The Constant Star* (1945) – but his most poignant account of the river's decline is in *The Shipbuilders* (1935). In this respect, later novelists like Gaitens and McColla, and later still, Jenkins, Friel and Kelman (and Welsh) come at the end of a long line of denigratory fiction.

Industrial elegy

The reader wishing to explore the underlayer of scepticism beneath the willed positivism of 'Renaissance' could well begin with *The Shipbuilders*, simultaneously a celebration and lament for the rise and fall of the great days of the Clyde. This novel spoke, in the period of the Depression, of the despair accompanying the decline of traditional heavy industries, in a manner prophetic of a major strand of modern Scottish fiction, which continues to the present. It is undoubtedly Blake's most ambitious and serious work, with an elegiac tone unmatched in any of his many others. It is Glasgow and the Clyde together which concern him, and his portrayal of the linked fortunes of Leslie Pagan, shipyard owner and manager, and Dannie Shields, shipyard worker and Pagan's war-time batman, follows and represents the decline of shipbuilding as the heart-industry of Glasgow in the years of Depression.

Pagan's yard launches its last ships as the novel opens; and the roll-call of the great but now vanished yards remembered by Pagan as he sails down the river in his last vessel, the *Estremadura*, comes close to an industrial prose-poetry, almost mythic in its recollection of epic achievement. Against this is set the slow degradation of the workers' city, and Danny, unemployed, his marriage breaking up, is a disillusioned witness to the new and sleazy city (which later writers will follow) – a city of wasteland and pubs, football violence, and cheap entertainment. Blake's account of the 'paid gladiators' of Rangers and Celtic is devastatingly and prophetically ironic; with Blake the detached observer, who neither praises or blames, but understands the release these frustrated workers crave. If the book has faults, they must lie in Blake's confused love-and-hate for his subject. He despises the system which allows Pagan to escape to the comfortable certainties of the home counties when his yard fails, but leaves Danny in hopeless squalor, one of the thousands who made these yards. But Blake's irony stops short of consistency, in his unattractive identification with middle-class values which sees 'dagos', 'pimps', and 'yids' as a curse of Glasgow, and which locks Danny in his officer-servant role, and even condones his beating of his wife. These are faults of the time, shared by writers like Buchan; and they cannot finally spoil Glasgow's greatest testament to a great tradition of shipbuilding.

SECTION 6

Scottish Literature since 1945

CHAPTER 37

DECLINE AND REVIVAL: MODERN SCOTTISH LITERATURE

FROM RURAL TO URBAN: THE DECLINE OF THE SCOTTISH RENAISSANCE

This introduction to contemporary Scottish literature begins by contrasting the ideals and values of the inter-war 'Scottish Renaissance' with those of the period following the Second World War. This section proposes that, after the failure of National Socialist ideologies in Germany, and their supportive traditionalism, a mood of social realism and sceptical materialism emerged, which was distrustful of Renaissance ideology and mythology, with its respect for the traditional and the supernatural. This movement culminates in the work of writers such as Robin Jenkins, George Friel, James Kelman, and reaches its final point of negation in the work of Irvine Welsh.

Had this been the only direction for Scottish writers after the war, we should have been left with a very bleak Scottish literature indeed. Indeed there is still much powerful writing which argues that contemporary Scotland is too often a twilight zone of run-down satellite communities like Drumchapel or Wester Hailes, or traditionless rural communities now no better, in their materialism, violence and poor quality of life, than the cities. Even the writers like MacCaig and Mackay Brown who appeared to celebrate the landscape and the natural rhythms of rural life, nevertheless seemed hostile to what they saw as false mythologies of the past and ideas of material progress.

But major changes took place throughout the 1980s, with writers like Edwin Morgan, Alasdair Gray and Liz Lochhead, in poetry, fiction and drama. Their work developed a new kind of imaginative relationship with their country and its culture, a relationship which refused to accept the elementary realism of generally bleak and economically deprived urban character. Instead, the connection of the urban with the rural, and the idea of a whole modern Scotland, linking past with present and future, began to be emphasised. And these and many other writers insisted on reintroducing, albeit in different form from Renaissance usage, elements of a new kind of magic realism and a new kind of mythology, employed for symbolic and socio-political reasons. The changes of these writers in approach and ideology, and of the contemporary writers who follow them, have radically altered the directions of Scottish literature, and fiction especially.

There were other major changes. An impressive range of women writers like Janice Galloway, Alison Kennedy, Sue Glover, Rona Munro and, outstandingly, Liz Lochhead, began to explore new areas of fiction, drama and poetry. Male writers correspondingly began to 'write women', that is, to present fiction through a female protagonist – Alasdair Gray, Ronald Frame and Alan Warner in particular. New writers from minority groups emerged, such as Jackie Kay. Much of the new talent came through the encouragement of writers' circles, emphasising that traditional link between Scottish literature and its communities. From the late '60s on, the new Scottish Arts Council sponsorship provided greater opportunity and encouragement.

All in all, the changes of the last few decades have led to confidence; a plurality of voices never heard before, have spoken of the multiple parts and situations that comprise Scotland.

New fictions, new Scotlands

The perspectives taken by the new writers on landscape, history, legend and tradition, and their essential ideas of what contemporary Scotland is, are in a sense a synthesis of the fundamentally opposing views of the two major groups of writers before them. Firstly the writers of the 'Scottish Renaissance' period extending roughly from 1920 to the Second World War; and secondly, the writers of the period from the Second World War till the early 1980s. The new Scottish writers refuse to accept former values, disagreements and polarities, and their novels especially create an interlocking and interweaving of ideas which takes what it sees as the best from both groups while denying the positive or negative extremes of either. Such writers include Iain Banks, Margaret Elphinstone, Andrew Greig, Janice Galloway, Sian Hayton, Alison Kennedy, Carl MacDougall, in fiction; as well as writers like Carol Ann Duffy, Douglas Dunn, W. N. Herbert, Jackie Kay, Edwin Morgan, Robert Crawford, in poetry; and dramatists like Sue Glover, Chris Hannan, Ian Heggie, Liz Lochhead and Rona Munro.

How are these contemporary writers so different from their twentieth-century predecessors? The essence of the Scottish Renaissance movement, whether seen as mainly a poetry revival or as a wider movement in fiction and drama as well, was a desire for roots, for Scottish identity defined in terms of traditional language and place. A shared belief in a kind of pre-historic golden age of a rural Scotland, as in Muir's 'Scotland 1941', gave common ground to otherwise very different writers. Their desire to re-unite themselves with what they saw as their origins and roots was so strong that it reached beyond reason and science to exploit folk ideas of the supernatural fused with modern psycho-mysticism such as Jung's theory of a 'collective unconscious', a racial 'great memory' transcending individual experience.

Perhaps the most disturbing aspects for the modern reader of writers such as Gunn, Gibbon, Linklater and Mitchison, is to encounter in their work moments when rationality or the rules of biology and time are set aside. Some of the most powerful episodes in *Sunset Song* happen when central characters relive events from thousands of years before, as Chris does when she 'sees' the ragged man calling 'the ships of Pytheas', or when Chae Strachan, aided perhaps by drink, 'sees' the carter/soldier from the time of the wars of Calgacus against the Romans. Similarly Gunn transcends time with Kenn in *Highland River* and Finn in *The Silver Darlings* to allow them to share in ancient pre-Christian experience. Mitchison and Linklater likewise give their protagonists awareness which is beyond that of their own time. And in poetry, MacDiarmid, Muir and Soutar, endow their poetry with this same awareness of 'other time', so that the sense of modern Scotland living in the shadow of an older, even timeless, *ur*-Scotland is constantly suggested to the reader.

These writers continually used metaphors for time, such as that of the river, to suggest the significance of tradition and continuity, with the river of time being the connecting artery to 'essential' racial origins which they felt continued to flow through, and define us in the present. This is perhaps the strongest belief and representation of the Scottish Renaissance writers; MacDiarmid's drunk man, Gibbon's Chris Guthrie, Gunn's Finn McHamish, Mitchison's Kirsty Haldane and Linklater's Magnus Merriman, are all defined by the history of their race. They are seen as knots in a web of history, tradition, and legend which shape them in ways they may resent, but which they are ultimately powerless to deny, and with which they must merge in order to fulfil their personal and national destinies. For all are bearers of their country's destinies, and all act in relation to a Scotland which is not simply a locality, but a living entity created from the region with which these writers identify – the Borders, Orkney, the Mearns, the north-east coast of Scotland. The aim is to fuse the local with the national, and even when a writer like Gibbon is negative about his Scottish communities, nevertheless the underlying emphasis is that Scotland as a whole, in history and in the present (as clearly exemplified in the opening pages of Gibbon's *Sunset Song*), is the living context.

723

Despite surface arguments about politics and language (found in the much-publicised quarrel between MacDiarmid and Muir), fundamental agreements of a potent yet questionable nature run through all the major texts of the significant Renaissance writers. Past defines present; roots are deep and tenacious; contemporary individuals are powerless to resist the effects of tradition, and they will only successfully realise themselves if they move with the grain of 'Scottish' experience. Standing stones, earthhouses, brochs and cairns, 'speak' to their human descendants; ruined castles and graveyards have still the power to communicate with the present, captivating aristocrats and peasants and insisting on the significance of their ancient ideology.

Such collective ideology manifests itself in recurrent shared imagery and symbolism. For example, serpent symbolism abounds in the work of Muir, MacDiarmid, Soutar, Gunn and Mitchison; virtually always carrying the same implication of older, pre-Christian, wisdom which significantly insists on being heard as a correcting voice or meaning within the fallen worlds of these writers. Beyond the pagan serpent, with its implied rebuke of Christian appropriation for the representation of evil, lie an impressive number of animal symbols, carrying varying degrees of the mythical and suggestive. Unicorns, white hinds, white or black bulls, salmon, horses – with their disturbing ideas of linkage between the world of wild nature and servitude to humanity – appear, as well as birds of varying sorts from swans and eagles to cuckoos as 'gowks'; and, in the work of Gunn, a host of humbler animal ideals, from green linnets to black rabbits, to the curlews equally beloved of Gibbon. All these are messengers, speakers of an underlying union of the world of nature and of man. They are embodied for example, in Gunn's concept of the strath, so much more than glen or valley, in that it contains a total organic symbiosis of creatures from the animal to the human in a growing place which is also developing in time, with the systole and diastole of its river as its heartbeat.

And beyond notions of time and symbols which create a world far beyond the human, lies the sense of the central protagonists of these works wrestling with the destiny of their nation. This destiny is revealed to them in Jungian terms through dreams and epiphanies which suggest a potent force lying beyond themselves which vouchsafes these moments of 'truth' and significance. The drunk man of MacDiarmid, or Gunn's Finn McHamish, are seen as leading millennia of Scotsmen out of ill-fated history into decisive economic and communal purposiveness, just as Mitchison's Kirsty Haldane reconciles immediate opponents in the post-Jacobite Rebellion period and also symbolically points the way for modern and timeless reconciliation in Scotland.

Breaking with the past: the war and National Socialism

These shared 'Renaissance' ideals were to be discredited during and after the Second World War. Renaissance values seemed to many to come dangerously close to many aspects of German National Socialism of the '30s and '40s. Across Europe, writers who professed to find value in the living traditions of the land and in the racial origins of their peasants were suspect, as somehow collaborating with the ideas of propagandists such as Himmler, who emphasised a rediscovery of the purity of German youth and delighted in locating that youth in an organic and historical tradition which would show racial purity. Knut Hamsun in Norway was to find himself criticised for his apparent association with just such ideas, with novels like *The Growth of the Soil* (1920); and even Gunn was to find himself questioned regarding his innocent visits to Germany before the war.

Suspicion of 'Renaissance values' persisted long after 1945, and this, together with disillusion and scepticism stemming from the prevailing drab urban greyness of the '50s, led to a rejection by writers of the values and beliefs of 'Renaissance' writers. This helps explain the falling off of interest in the work of fine writers like Alexander Reid, Alexander Scott and even Robert McLellan. Their interest in Scots language, and a continued cultural-political agenda which came out of Renaissance made them appear old-fashioned compared to the new work which in the '50s and early '60s was sceptically and savagely repudiating organic and mytho-poetic ideas of Scottish destiny. In fiction, the work of Robin Jenkins shows this disenchantment with ideas of a Scotland reborn and yet descended from illustrious ancestors. In novel after novel of that time Jenkins challenged such notions – mocking ideas of Scottish heritage in *Happy for the Child* (1953), *The Thistle and the Grail* (1954) and *The Cone-Gatherers* (1955). Outstandingly, *Guests of War* (1956) took the idea of the protagonist representative of Scotland, and parodied it in Bell McShelvie, evacuated from the Glasgow slums during the war to Langrigg, an idyllic Border community, only to find as many tensions and as much back-biting as in her fallen urban Glasgow. And by locating his exemplary Scot in an urban woman, Jenkins exploded ideas of national regeneration – substituting in typical Jenkinsian fashion the ambiguous idea of a hard-earned spiritual rediscovery which might, in the end, prove to be as hollow as the Scotland within which it was located. The dominating image of *Guests of War* is of Bell McShelvie patiently trying to climb the local mountain – failing, yet returning to Glasgow with a certain stoical acceptance. This, said Jenkins, is where the real moral and spiritual battles are to be fought, and Bell carried back to Glasgow only the fading memories of her love of landscape and rural release, luxuries not to be retained in the fallen city.

Great denigrators

The post-war disillusion began with Edward Gaitens and his tragi-comic picture of slum community and its crushing of adolescent talent and hope, *Dance of the Apprentices* (1948), and continued in novels like *Winter's Traces* (1947) by Dorothy Haynes. Her grim presentation of a typical bleak, small semi-industrial town in the Lowlands was to be repeated, shortly after, in Jenkins's *The Thistle and the Grail* (1954). Perhaps Scottish realism of the *Green Shutters* variety was re-asserting itself; certainly it continued down to the work of George Friel and James Kelman. In poetry and drama there was a similar disillusion; for example in the reductive idiom of Robert Garioch, greatest of the post-MacDiarmid writers to use Scots. His poetry reveals a continual urban insistence on the grotesque pretentiousness of Scottish and international 'culture', so that the voice of the dramatic monologues mocks its own Scottishness, albeit identifying with the traditional Scottish Humanist pedagogy of George Buchanan, and aware of the richness – and the loss – of the tradition of Ramsay and Fergusson in eighteenth-century Edinburgh. In drama, James Bridie turned from exploration of the Scottish past in *The Anatomist* (1930) and *Mr Bolfry* (1943), to the much more negative *Mr Gillie* of 1951. In the later play, foreshadowing Robin Jenkins's schoolmasters and George Friel's disappointed idealists, Mr Gillie is placed in the urban sprawl of Lowland Scotland after the war, disappointed in all his educational ideals and the urban children who destroy them. Meanwhile Ena Lamont Stewart's *Men Should Weep* (1947) presented tenement and male-dominated life with heart-breaking realism and despair. (Significantly, however, in the successful revival at the Citizen's in the 1980s, she changed the last act to allow women a more positive and redemptive role.)

Culture and politics: a paradox

For all that there is a persistent dark strand in twentieth-century Scottish writing, it remains true that the centre of energy of Scottish writing before Jenkins contrasts dramatically with the work of Jenkins and those who followed him in the '60s. And here we notice another paradox in the contrast between these two periods. The Renaissance movement, for all its ambitious and regenerative aims for Scottish political and economic life, produced a coherent body of writers who shared the same broadly socialist and nationalistic positions – and yet the achievements in terms of nationalist members of parliament was nil. In the '70s, when the main thrust of Scottish writing disavowed and repudiated any identification with an organic Scottish cultural and literary tradition, the Scottish National Party succeeded in getting eleven nationalist members to Westminster. What does this imply about the attitude of Scottish writers to Scotland at this point? Jenkins, Friel, Mackay Brown, McIlvanney, Kelman – all insisted that they were not operating within Scottish fictional or even historical parameters, but instead drew from international writing and cinema. The ideas of 'Renaissance' seemed lost. In 1981 the index to plagiarisms in Gray's *Lanark*, indicating the writing which had helped shape Gray's work, omitted acknowledgement of any of the writers of the Renaissance, with the exception of MacDiarmid, instead listing as influences local West of Scotland writers and major international writers. Scottish writing and fiction in particular seemed to have decided to repudiate all connections with a mytho-poetic culture dedicated to Scottish spiritual regeneration. Even the Anglo-Scots seemed determined to explode Scottish mythologies. Outstandingly, *Tunes of Glory* (1956) and *The Prime of Miss Jean Brodie* (1961) showed that James Kennaway and Muriel Spark preferred to present central characters who still stood as representative of Scotland and its values, but whose actions were ambiguous and whose moral value was deeply questionable.

The loss of the dear green place

The main thrust of post-war negativity was to be found in novels which specifically mocked the mytho-poetic and emphasised the discontinuity of past and present. Archie Hind's *The Dear Green Place* (1966) can be seen as a landmark in the specific targeting of Renaissance values with its deliberate mockery of the supposedly Gaelic roots of Glasgow's very name, as a beautiful and fertile place. Hind showed his Glaswegian Matt struggling to articulate his complex feelings about his city – its layers of history, its Victorian materialism, its occasional industrial beauty. Glasgow's fragmentation and discontinuity eventually led Matt to despair of his task, and to vomit up his hopes on a ferry between the two sides of the Clyde. The current of tradition has failed; Matt is adrift instead in a backwater of history which has lost its past and is going nowhere.

The full extent of the repudiation of Renaissance values can be seen in the work of Mackay Brown, so often seen as an inheritor of Renaissance ideas. In *Greenvoe* (1972) he showed how the community of his Orkney village had lost any sense of place in history and time, becoming instead the victim of a modern, centralised and alienated bureaucracy. William McIlvanney's *Docherty* (1975), for all its loving recreation of a close-knit Kilmarnock mining community, nevertheless, in the final image of Docherty's clenched fist rising from the coal fall in a gesture of stoical defiance, suggests that the day of his community is over. The entire novel is, in a sense, a lament for lost story-telling and oral traditions, where a 'speak' similar to that lamented for Kinraddie by Lewis Grassic Gibbon, has had its day. Docherty's sons move uncertainly into a fragmented and non-communal future where – as in the *Laidlaw* novels – lonely individuals search with increasing difficulty in a disconnected society (whether urban or semi-rural) for identity and integrity. And George Friel's novels of the '70s along with those of James Kelman in the '80s, are the culmination of this fictional trend. Friel's characters are lost in desolate city-peripheral places, whose old Celtic names mock what they have now become, so that the slum of Blackhill in *Mr Alfred MA* (1972) is seen nostalgically by the reminiscing older inhabitants of that benighted district as Tordhu, with its lovers' lanes and its older associations. But now the lovers' lane has become the haunt of gang battles, and the Gaelic Black Hill has become the modern urban festering blackness of a lost society.

Throughout the '60s and '70s Jenkins and Friel were critical of all romanticised or mythical representations of Scotland. Both were teachers, and sceptical about education's effect on industrial youth. Both deeply dislike what modern Scottish – and Western – society has become. Both signify the decline in society by giving noble or traditional names, redolent of a better past, to what have now become sordid places – the names of Wallace and Bruce, the titles of weavers and spinners, are applied to streets and people in a modern Scotland which has no memory of their greatness or their simpler communal values. In *Mr Alfred MA* Granny Lyons has a stucco bust of Robert Burns on her mantelpiece; the very cheapness of the artefact and its irrelevance in urban Glasgow emphasising her dislocation from a rural past.

By focusing on the run-down industrial outskirts of the city, where it meets and spoils countryside, the point is made even more forcibly that the day of Gunn and Gibbon is utterly over; that scenes like these are the fallen and dismal truth. In *From Scenes Like These* (1968) Gordon Williams's title once again emphasises the loss of the rural world of Burns; the real scenes of Scottish life are where Scotland's contemporary non-grandeur arises. In his portrayal, as in so many of these novels, the boy Dunkie moves from innocence to imitation of the aggression and brutality he sees around him. This setting is found endlessly in the shadow-land of so many of the novels of Jenkins, Friel and McIlvanney, and the role of the central characters in these works, far from representing the destiny of their nation, is to show the tragedy of lost community and identity.

Rural community, as conceived by the major writers, is not much better; for example, in Fionn MacColla's reductive portrayal of Lewis community and kirk in *The Ministers* (1979) or in the recurrently bleak Highland and island villages in the stories of Iain Crichton Smith. To the boys in his *On the Island* (1979), the great standing stones of Lewis are simply incomprehensible, bleak and devoid of poetical and mythical power, mere outcrops of an alien time past. Short stories like 'By the Sea' sum up Smith's bare environment in which landscape and seascape have become unrelated elements utterly different from those of Scott's *Waverley* or Stevenson's *The Merry Men*, and in complete opposition to the archetypal significance of land and sea in writers like Gunn, Gibbon and Linklater.

Drama and the decline of community

The picture is rounded out when drama and poetry are considered alongside fiction. The plays of Bill Bryden, Hector MacMillan, Roddy McMillan, Stewart Conn and Donald Campbell, to name a few, all subscribe to this sense of a dying notion of the communal and the historical. Outstandingly, Bill Bryden's *Willie Rough* (1972) exploited the idea of the protagonist descended from Lindsay's Johne the Common-weill of *Ane Satyre of the Thrie Estaitis* in the sixteenth-century. But Rough by name and rough by nature; Willie, the mouthpiece of his dispossessed workers on the shipbuilding Clyde, is a failed visionary, whose poetical perspectives from the heights of the hills above the Clyde give way to the acceptance of destruction and the devaluation of his community. Like Docherty, all that Willy can show at the end is defiance. In later plays like *Benny Lynch* (1974) Bryden was to deepen his sense of Lowland Scottish deterioration in his picture of the icon of macho Scotland whose reality was insecurity, fear of the dark, and an utter lack of integrity and awareness of self in time and place. Similarly, *The Bevellers* (1973) by Roddy McMillan and *Play Donkey* (1977) by Stewart Conn showed variant pictures of Scots whose hard-man mentality had taken over from any genuine sense of society. McMillan's play has its moments of pseudo-communality, when, arguments temporarily over, his *dramatis personae* show a workplace in harmony – but a harmony which disappears in the second half; the play ultimately a lament for this lost working community. Conn's hard man is the ultimate displaced and rootless Scott; the mercenary soldier now condemned to death for his part in African wars. Again and again, the stereotypical Scottish 'hard man' emerges from plays like these as the dominant representation of the period, as in Donald Campbell's *The Jesuit* (1976). This view and representation of an underlying bedrock of working-class maleness is of course ambiguous. These Docherties and Willie Roughs are anachronisms and failures. In *The Hard Man* (1977), Tom McGrath's portrayal of his convict isolated in a Peterhead cell, we see the reduction to the final, solipsistic loneliness of a Scottish experience completely disconnected from all ideas and representations of Scotland other than that of a sad, harsh and desolate sub-romanticism.

Contemporary drama has not finished with destroying Renaissance conceptions of Scotland. Outstandingly, John Byrne's *The Slab Boys Trilogy* (appearing on stage between 1978 and 1982), and his later television series, such as *Tutti Frutti* and *Your Cheating Heart,* have (despite their grotesque humour and unusual representations of working-class protagonists as highly intelligent and quick-witted, exploiting a great number of literary and social registers) insisted on immediate social interaction, without reference to Scottish or traditional contexts – although this must be qualified with recognition of Byrne's perceptive use of local Scottish detail, in terms of social groups and local places. Sue Glover's *Bondagers* (1990), or Bill Bryden's *The Ship* (1991), and drama versions of *A Scots Quair* (1993), exhibit this reforming and challenging new creative thinking about the identity of Scotland. There is an impressive new range of adaptations in drama of mytho-poetic Scottish fiction. And there are also powerful fresh versions of the ideologies of the rural and the urban, as in Liz Lochhead's *Mary Queen of Scots Got Her Head Chopped Off* (1986) and her translation into Scots of Moliere's *Tartuffe* (1990); and Edwin Morgan's translation into Scots of *Cyrano de Bergerac* (1990). Contemporary young dramatists like Chris Hannan, Ann Marie di Mambro and Rona Munro continue this revolt against traditional perspectives of the past.

Losing the landscape: the poetry of Crichton Smith and MacCaig

While post-war poetry avoided drama's ambiguous representations, it nevertheless managed, like fiction and drama, to repudiate Renaissance iconography and mythology. The work of Iain Crichton Smith is particularly revealing here. His fiction, from *Consider the Lilies* (1968) to *Thoughts of Murdo* (1993), over twenty volumes of fiction and short story, is preoccupied with the difficulty of finding a whole self within a community repressed by narrow religion and obsessed with bourgeois materialism. In his work, island and Highland tradition is viewed with deep suspicion, as devoid of the kind of spiritual intimations which were found by Gunn and Gibbon. His poetry shows this negation of Renaissance values even more emphatically. As early as the late '50s, Smith was stressing the disconnection of community from landscape and physical context. Amongst his earliest verse, 'Poem of Lewis' wonders at the dissociation between elementally magnificent environment and the lack of aesthetic expression, and, as so often in Smith's work, finds the sea 'visionless' and devoid of significance for the Gaelic islander. Regret for something lost is interwoven, however, for there is a sense that Smith laments the disconnection, and deplores the loss of a kind of grace for the islanders, a grace which would fuse people and place. Throughout his work, especially when he speaks of the eighteenth-century Gaelic poet Duncan Ban MacIntyre, there is the suggestion of a lost Eden, an older and healthier state of mind in which the animal and the human, the setting and the individual, were at one.

The poetry of Norman MacCaig is very different in tone, mood, and setting, but it shares an important characteristic with Smith, in that he too doubts whether his landscapes have anything to do with himself, even though he loves them (whatever 'love' means – an issue his poetry constantly explores). With very occasional exceptions, such as 'Celtic Cross', one looks in vain for MacCaig's exploration of Highland or Scottish history, culture, tradition. There are moments of reference to Edinburgh history or Highland battles; but MacCaig has no intention of allowing any deep contact with the past to bind us. Rather he wishes to imply the disconnectedness of past from present, as in 'Celtic Cross' or the present disconnectedness of self from experience, as in 'Centre of Centres', with its demonstration that the contemporary self has enough trouble in maintaining control over its constituent selves, in the endless present-day confusion of the senses as they struggle to construct meaning out of natural activity or personal experience, without attempting to find spiritual meanings in history. The clear implication of all his work is one of sardonic hostility to all mythologies, renaissances, labels and creeds.

Final loneliness: James Kelman

Following writers like Jenkins, Smith, MacCaig and the urban realist dramatists, much of contemporary Scottish writing continues to reject claims of territory and tradition. Indeed, arguably the culmination in the rejection of mythologies is to be found in the work of James Kelman. Since 1973, Kelman has been producing stories, novels and plays which make no concessions whatsoever to irrational ideology, but insist on limiting their human agents to immediate or immediately inherited problems which are nothing to do with literary traditions, Scottish or English. Kelman wages war on cultural imperialism and 'Eng Lit'; and implicit in this is hostility to all other cultural constructs that impose irrelevant feelings and spurious identities and inheritances on his Lowland Scottish, urban and predominantly working-class protagonists. Kelman damns the issues of landscape, race, tradition, by exclusion; they just don't enter his work, which is usually set in nameless places, vaguely recognisable as post-industrial Scotland, but signifying anywhere in the world with such economic and social deprivation. And his example has created followers; Gordon Legge (*The Shoe*, 1989), Duncan McLean (*Bucket of Tongues*, 1992) and *Blackden* (1994), and, most ferociously uncompromising of all, in his scenes of Edinburgh drug addicts and their terrible tragi-comic predicaments, Irvine Welsh and *Trainspotting* (1993), *The Acid House* (1994) and *Filth* (1998). Janice Galloway's impressive *The Trick is to Keep Breathing* (1989), which explores the post-traumatic regeneration of Joy Stone, struggling in a male-dominated West of Scotland to re-assert her sense of self, through 'stream of consciousness' narrative, must not simply be allocated to 'school of Kelman'. But it is clear from her structural patterning and her typography that both Kelman and Alasdair Gray have, in different ways, greatly impressed her (especially Kelman's *The Busconductor Hines*, 1984, and Gray's *1982, Janine*, 1984). The refusal to negotiate with any other values or modes of representation, other than those felt to be personally valid and rational, shows Galloway, at the start of her career, to belong firmly to the myth-rejecting camp. Agnes Owens likewise declared her hard sense of social realism in *Gentlemen of the West* (1984), *Like Birds in the Wilderness* (1987) and *A Working Mother* (1994). And a host of similar tough realists, many published by Polygon, have appeared in recent years, though it is significant that the most successful of these, Jeff Torrington's *Swing Hammer Swing* (1993), bends Kelman's dry mundanity towards the tradition of Irish absurd humour.

A major re-orientation: Alasdair Gray (b. 1934), Edwin Morgan (b. 1920), Liz Lochhead (b. 1947)

All this said, however, something has changed in contemporary Scottish literature. Somewhere in the '80s a new mood, and a new perspective, entered into the work of novelists, poets and dramatists. Three texts may be singled out as pivotal and deeply influential. Alasdair Gray's *Lanark* (1981), Edwin Morgan's *Sonnets from Scotland* (1984) and Liz Lochhead's *Mary Queen of Scots Got Her Head Chopped Off* (1987) helped initiate and exemplify the change which is still under way, breaking significantly with the scepticism of the urban-fixated, anti-historicism of the post-war period. Perhaps Edwin Morgan deserves pride of place in this new development. With *The Second Life* (1968), he had reorganised his perspectives on himself, Glasgow, and, arguably, the universe. 'Does every man feel like this at forty?', he asked, in an awakening which was to be of profound importance for those writers around him. When *Sonnets from Scotland* appeared, this awakening revealed itself as a rediscovered sense of the limitless imaginative possibilities of the *idea* of Scotland, or Scotlands, a matrix of myths, attitudes, possibilities, histories. In fifty-one linked sonnets, ranging to extremes different from, but every bit as mind-stretching as MacDiarmid's in *A Drunk Man Looks at the Thistle*, Morgan explored the geological formation of Scotland, its prehistoric and wolf-haunted forests, its medieval grimness and *grotesquerie*, its religious turmoil, its industrial bondage, its modern debates. And astonishingly, but on reflection not so surprisingly (given Morgan's record of fine speculative science-fiction poetry, and his concern with humanity's relations with whatever lay out there in space), Morgan went on to show post-nuclear Scotlands, Scotland as a republic, and even Scotland as a kind of time-and-space doppelgänger in an alternative universe.

All this was made the more disruptive, in traditional ways of seeing Scotland, by making the perspective that of inhuman visitors travelling in space and time. Now his poetry took on the task of creating new attitudes and new mythologies – with one important qualification. These new myths do not pretend to any other source of authority than the human imagination. Identity is not perceived as an almost magical creation of past communities and their dreams handed on through collective unconscious, nurtured by a presiding Mother Scotland. Instead, the self is a web of rational and irrational meanings consciously constructed and acknowledged as such. Morgan delicately balances the claims of Scottish and international cultures, maintaining both an international and home focus, and insisting gently on an ultimately more than rational basis for living relationships.

Liz Lochhead's poetry had also been making its mark, from *Memo for Spring* (1972) to *Dreaming Frankenstein* (1984). In poems like the early 'Revelation' to the sophisticated 'Rapunzstiltskin', she created a new kind of context – one of European folklore and archetypes, but used now as correlatives for the unconscious desires of women and men to be simultaneously victims and predators. Again, a new kind of mythology; woven with verbal and ideological punning so that apparently casual song-lyrics and jazzy statements carried dark timeless understatements, placed Scottish experience in wolf-and-vampire-haunted Europe. Like Morgan, Lochhead reached a wide audience, who responded to this rich new way of imaging and representing Scotland, in which the prevailing ways of seeing Scotland as urban wasteland were enriched with fantasy, humour, surrealism, and constant interplay with tradition and magic.

Lochhead's plays, exploring the subliminal sexuality of the Romantic poets and relishing the multiplicity of meanings inherent in Stoker's *Dracula* gave this changed perspective even greater influence. *Mary Queen of Scots Got Her Head Chopped Off* (1989) is, in this respect, of major significance, as well as being exciting in its novel, dramatic presentation and the richness of its language. La Corbie, the female crow who presides as commentator and witness to Scotland's history, has something of the presence of Lindsay's Johne the Common-weill in *Ane Satyre of the Thrie Estaitis* (1552), but simultaneously reminds us of the great modern Renaissance protagonists who represented Scotland – Chris Guthrie, the Drunk Man, Kirsty Haldane. Yet she is different; raucous, shabby, a parody of that renaissance, but still somehow suggesting a sad glory, an endless cycle of tradition and violence. The play insists on breaking the boundaries of present and past, changing queens into guttersnipes, lovers into the street urchins of present-day Scottish slums. Lochhead's perspective sees myth as protean, unfixed, a range of haunting possibilities which aren't an objective and inherited magic, but constantly recreatable by the contemporary mind, a chosen – if not always understood – landscape of the imagination and the emotions.

But it was Alasdair Gray's astonishing *Lanark* of 1981 which most dramatically changed literary creative consciousness in the '80s and '90s. Utterly different in so many ways from the work of Morgan and Lochhead, like *Sonnets* and *Mary Queen of Scots* it thrust the idea of the entirety of Scotland again to the fore, instead of asserting fragmentation. It is true that fragmentation of society in Glasgow and beyond is still a major theme, and the novel hardly approaches Gray's late-'90s position as advocate of Scottish Home Rule, when his novels carry on their covers a heraldry symbolic of Scottish regeneration. *Lanark* presents Duncan Thaw as witness to the loss of holistic awareness of Scotland. Nevertheless, Gray's panoramic illustrations of factories, oil refineries and rigs, cities and glens, bens and seascapes, together with the exploration of recognisably Scottish institutions, from art college to infirmary, from crumbling church to empty factory or shipyard, show the matter to be Scotland as it has developed through history till now. This totality of vision is different from what was happening in the '70s, despite similarities between, say, Jenkin's Fergus Lamont and Thaw, or even between Thaw and McIlvanney's Conn Docherty. All are confused about their place in their communities, or about whether community now even exists; all carry a weight of representation of an entire type of Scottish predicament – but Thaw represents the beginning of Gray's quest for a new and whole Scotland.

Gray goes beyond any previous Scottish writer in synthesising a huge and bewildering variety of literary and pictorial genres in his work. *Lanark* fuses together many varieties of Scottish storytelling and theme with endless examples of US and European literature, but, like Lochhead, doing so in order to place Scotland in the wider world context, as well as to reintroduce new layers of mythical meaning and suggestion. And yet once again, there are glimpses – fleeting, elusive, insubstantial – of dear green places, and celebrations of landscape – notably in the novel's outstanding moment of epiphany, in the vision Lanark has of his son Alexander climbing Ben Rua, both at peace for once in a day of rare beauty.

What is happening to contemporary Scottish literature?

Scottish literature of the '80s was marked by radical ground-breaking; reassessing its older texts, re-examining the place of women in town and country, exploring ways of using a recognisably Scottish perspective in viewing the world outside and simultaneously re-asserting the validity of Scottish fictional and literary tradition as source material for contemporary creativity. In every aspect of literary productivity, from financing to deciding on topic and theme, the post-war ambience of scepticism and negativism was examined and challenged. And while this challenge was tempered by the post-referendum disappointment of 1979, it can be seen now to have merely slowed. The underlying forces of insistent Scottish identity-making were moving, and are moving, inexorably in the direction of synthesis, but synthesis which permits multiple perspectives and a plurality of approaches through different genres. This new spectrum of possibility is based on a new willingness to allow a multi-faceted Scotland, no longer demanding allegiance to a single MacDiarmid agenda, but recognising other people's right to perceive Scotland differently, and to imagine it differently as well. Nevertheless – and this is possibly the crucial element in this redefinition of the new Scottish literature – there is a desire to retain, amidst the plethora of possible Scotlands, a unifying sense connection which holds together what would otherwise deconstruct into meaningless regional variants, each of them susceptible to further deconstruction, so that as 'authenticity' is lost, so also is any awareness of identity or permanence.

A main thrust of contemporary Scottish writing uses its imaginative energy to counter the all too common and international sense of a lack of place in history, and the consequent lack of identity and meaning. The prevailing

735

mood in modern Scottish writing suggests that what we make of Scotland can be what we want, since mind and reality are an interplay, and we live in worlds we ourselves create in our language and our minds. In a sense, contemporary Scottish writing is deciding that, if the ancient traditions and hidden powers of Scotland are dead, then it's necessary to reinvent them. As Scotland tackles the twenty-first century with its new parliament, and its old ways of working under a new scrutiny, the implications for Scottish social, cultural and political futures are incalculable, but profound.

CHAPTER 38

SCOTTISH POETRY AFTER 1945

PART ONE: MODERN SCOTTISH POETRY

Anthologising the Scottish Renaissance

It is a truism, but no less valid for being so, that the settled state of poetry in a society at any particular time may be judged by looking at the anthologies that are produced for the general reader. Anyone wanting to gain a sense of who have been the established writers on the Scottish poetic scene over the last half-century can hardly do better than to look at two or three key collections of contemporary Scottish poetry published between 1946 and 1994. From Maurice Lindsay's ground-breaking anthology, *Modern Scottish Poetry: An Anthology of the Scottish Renaissance, 1920–45* (1946, rev. 1966), to O'Rourke's *Dream State: The New Scottish Poets* (1994; 2001), there have at intervals of ten to fifteen years been fresh opportunities to obtain an update on the state of Scottish poetry and its main practitioners. As the years have passed, some familiar older names have disappeared, and new, now equally familiar, names have made their appearance. It is equally true, of course, that the unsettled state of poetry, its flux and swirl of new creativity and experimentation, can be observed in the pages of the small magazines and ephemeral publications, of which Scotland has had its full share (*Lines Review, Poetry Scotland, Scottish International, Akros* and, more recently, *Chapman* and *Cencrastus* and many others). From the evidence of these two kinds of publication, it is possible to see that the last half-century has been the most productive and interesting period in the long career of the Scottish poetic imagination, inseparable sister of the democratic intellect.

The appearance in 1946 of *Modern Scottish Poetry* was a significant literary event. As a *Times* review recognised, it was now possible 'to estimate and focus with some success the conscious attempt to revise a native Scottish literature'. Within the pages of this slim volume, Maurice Lindsay assembled representative short poems of thirty-six Scottish poets. There is an interesting internal division, certainly unintended but visible with the hindsight of another generation. The first seventeen poets represented, arranged by Lindsay approximately in the order in which they first came before the public, belong to what we would now recognise as the first wave of the Scottish Renaissance. They include Violet Jacob, Marion Angus, Helen B. Cruick-shank, Hugh MacDiarmid, Edwin Muir and, tragically cut down before the new post-war era, William Soutar. By and large, those who come after Soutar in the anthology belonged to the newer generation and their major poetic output was still to come. They include William Montgomerie, George Campbell Hay, Robert Garioch, Sorley MacLean, Sydney Goodsir Smith, G. S. Fraser, Norman MacCaig, Tom Scott, Maurice Lindsay and W. S. Graham. Some names that we might be looking for as well-known poets of the post-war era, such as George Mackay Brown, Edwin Morgan, or Iain Crichton Smith, are not there; their poetic voices are not yet developed or recognised.

Placing these poets into time categories is an uncertain and unreliable business. Some of those identified above as belonging to the earlier wave of the Scottish Renaissance still had many years of active life and poetic creativity after 1945. Edwin Muir had fourteen years of very fruitful writing in Europe and America ahead of him; Hugh MacDiarmid was to be the Grand (and Disreputable) Old Man of Scottish Letters for another thirty-three years.

Post-war Muir and MacDiarmid

For Muir, there were three major collections of poetry to come: *The Voyage* (1946), *The Labyrinth* (1949) and *One Foot in Eden* (1956). Yet, while these in considerable measure mark the height of Muir's poetic achievement, they continue the themes and tones of his earlier poetry both darkened by his perceptions of the post-war world and lightened by the Christian faith he had discovered during the war. They are dealt with in Section 5.

By contrast, an assessment of MacDiarmid's post-war poetic production is rendered difficult by two major features. The first is the fact that a significant proportion of what MacDiarmid published after 1945 had been written much earlier, perhaps as part of another work, and now appeared in a new revised form with new titles and contexts. The second is MacDiarmid's subordination of lyricism (perhaps because of his loss of the lyric gift) to the concept of a poetry of facts, with the associated expansion of his long-standing practice of literary borrowing, of taking and reshaping the words of other writers to incorporate into his own work. Thus it is arguable that by 1945 most of what we would value and wish to keep in MacDiarmid's poetry had already been written, and he was thereafter more of an influence on other writers than a continuing fount of original writing.

The new makars

A more fruitful and continuing strand in Scottish poetry has been the tradition of the 'Makars', particularly in the use of 'Lallans', or Lowland Scots as the preferred linguistic medium. It is debatable whether this was an indication of the strength of the MacDiarmid factor, or, as some would now convincingly argue, a sign of the awareness by poets of the continuing relevance of the Scots language as practised from the age of medieval and Renaissance Humanism through the vernacular revival of the eighteenth century to the present century. In this latter context, the poetry of MacDiarmid's immediate predecessors and his independent contemporaries such as William Soutar have a higher profile and are freed from the sometimes unjust stigma laid on them by MacDiarmid in his criticism and polemic. In the period under consideration, poets like Albert Mackie, Robert Garioch, Sydney Goodsir Smith, Tom Scott, Alexander Scott and J. K. Annand stand in no man's shadow, not even that of MacDiarmid. Their commitment to the use of Scots for a variety of poetic purposes, and the variety of kinds of Scots that they used, from the local to the specifically literary, produced one of the two strongest bodies of Scots writing in the immediate postwar years (the other being in Scottish drama).

Robert Garioch (1909–81)

Although he has often been seen as being under MacDiarmid's influence and one of his friends, Robert Garioch (full name Robert Garioch Sutherland) specifically denied such a direct influence on his poetry, claiming Albert Mackie as being more significant. Like Mackie in such a poem as 'The Molecatcher', Garioch uses a fairly dense Scots, although in his case it is generally based on Edinburgh, and not on Mackie's Lothian. Mackie and Garioch shared an interest in the medieval makars and found irony and satire congenial ways of expression. In a number of poems, such as 'Elegy' and 'Garioch's repone till George Buchanan', Garioch targets teachers and headmasters, revealing an ironical disillusionment with education and those who practise it, people such as himself. The picture widens out in what is perhaps Garioch's best-known poem, 'Sisyphus', in which the poet (in brilliantly deployed classical hexameters) humorously looks at modern attitudes to wage slavery in the context of Greek myth. The poem's protagonist is Sisyphus, the man condemned to an eternity in Hades of rolling a huge boulder up a hill without ever reaching the top and knowing the satisfaction of completing the task. In Garioch's modern reading, the toiling prisoner (a teacher? civil servant?) on succeeding in placing the stone at the hill-top, deliberately shoogles the boulder off. The sardonic implication is that the trauchle of monotonous work has its consolations, not the least being those of fulfilled habit and salary:

> Whit was he thinkin aboot, that he just gied the boulder a wee shove?
> Bumpity doon in the corrie gaed whuddran the pitiless whun stane
> Sisyphus dodderan eftir it, shair of his cheque at the month's end.

CLASSICAL INFLUENCES

Garioch's interest in the makars and his relationship with Edinburgh are vitally important in his work. In 'Fable (Twa' Mice)', he shows his affinity with Robert Henryson, with a poem that is comparable with Henryson's beast fables, particularly 'The Taill of the Uponlandis Mous and the Burges Mous'. The poem is not weighty, but Garioch has assimilated Henryson's notion of the terrible vulnerability of the human condition, and infused a satirical edge in its criticism of hypocrisy. What links Garioch even more closely with these poets are the classical elements in his background. In his book, *The Democratic Intellect* (1961), George Davie argues that, underlying the democratic tradition in Scottish education, there is a very old tradition of Scots Humanism that extends back to the Middle Ages. Because this tradition is based on classical literature (that is, Latin and Greek literature insofar as the latter was translated into Latin at that time), it is anything but parochial. The makars entered European culture through Latin; Buchanan, Dunbar and, probably, Henryson were educated and taught in Europe; and Garioch's classical background gave him literally a common language and culture with them.

GARIOCH AND FERGUSSON

Two other pieces of evidence are relevant here: Garioch's translations from the Italian sonnets of Giuseppe Belli (first in *Selected Poems*, 1966) and his admiration for Robert Fergusson, the eighteenth-century Edinburgh poet. Garioch's outward-looking European point of view led him to the work of Belli, a nineteenth-century Italian poet who wrote a series of sonnets, often satirical, in the Roman dialect against the excesses of the Vatican. Garioch translated these sonnets into Scots throughout his life, and they form a superb commentary on his abilities and interests.

As far as Scotland is concerned, the missing links between the makars and Garioch are eighteenth-century figures like Thomas Ruddiman, who published Fergusson's poems in his magazine, and Robert Fergusson himself.

Garioch returns to Fergusson often in his poetry: in his poem, 'To Robert Fergusson', he dwells on the similarities in their backgrounds:

My ain toun's makar, monie an airt
formed us in common, faur apairt
in time, but fell alike in hert; . . .
The auld High Schule (gane Royal syne)
your Alma Mater was and mine,
and whaur ye construed, line by line,
the Gallic Weirs
we ken the airt, doun by the Wynd
of the Black Friars.

Garioch seems to be attempting a fusion of the two strands of the tradition, the Humanist and the indigenous. Each is in itself inadequate, the former leading to aridity, the latter to sentimentality. The ideal fusion produces a tradition of writing in Scots which is not parochial or confined to the influences which have inspired it, but which, when successful, becomes part of a larger pool of national imaginative resources on which succeeding poets can draw.

The Edinburgh context of Garioch's work is fleshed out in a number of sonnets. 'Did Ye See Me?', 'And They were Richt' and 'Festival 1962' satirise Edinburgh occasions and attitudes, firmly establishing Garioch in the same position regarding the city in the present age as Fergusson occupied for a tragically brief period in the eighteenth century.

A DARKER POETRY

Not all of Garioch's concerns can fit neatly into poems about Edinburgh or in the makar mode. His war experiences, particularly as a prisoner of war, were treated in his autobiographical *Two Men and a Blanket* (1975), but his musings about war and the inimical forces behind it surface in poems like 'Programme Notes' and 'During a Music Festival', where thoughts about particular pieces of music lead to consideration of the bigger issues. Some poems, such as 'The Bog', 'The Wire' and 'The Muir', wrestle with the large concerns of the mid-twentieth century. The war colours them dark – 'The Wire' in particular being a surreal recollection of his time in a war prison camp. But in a strange but effective fusion of the metaphysical tone and matter of MacDiarmid in *A Drunk Man* and the claustrophobic Muir in 'The Labyrinth' they transcend any specific time and place. 'The Muir' is certainly his most ambitious – and darkest – poem; it moves in its metaphysical exploration from Fergusson through nuclear physics to Hiroshima in extended reflection of a quality and intensity not found outside MacDiarmid's best work. The ending of 'The Wire' exemplifies the way in which Garioch shifts his apparent immediate concern with prison or moorland to a timeless observation: the prison fences become all our fences, and wire becomes Wire:

> In ither airts, whaur folk are thrang,
> the Wire vibrates, clash gae the tins,
> flures blume frae bluidie marl, dugs
> yowl throu the blatter o the guns.
> I saw you planet slawlie birl;
> I saw it as ane endless muir
> in daylight, and I saw a few
> guid men bide still amang the stour.

The ending is ambiguous; has the best of humanity died, or do a few of the best survive?

Garioch's humanity asserts itself in these poems ('Jehovah by the hairt maun aye be sought'), but they are very different from his shorter, ironical and comic commentaries on Edinburgh, the brilliant fusions of Humanist and modern observer which have established his reputation as one of the greatest of modern Scottish poets.

Sydney Goodsir Smith (1915–75)

Sydney Goodsir Smith is a poet's poet; that is, he is interested in techniques of poetry, the sound of words and the patterns he can make with them. Sometimes he seems to be more interested in the special effects of the Scots language than in the subjects he writes of. Much of his poetry is lyrical and centres on the general and ancient themes of lyric poetry: love and death.

However, Smith was also much influenced by MacDiarmid, especially by some of the new or adapted Scots words MacDiarmid used. 'Crammasy', that striking word which occurs in 'The Bonnie Broukit Bairn', appealed to Smith and he uses it more than once. In particular, he agreed with MacDiarmid's arguments for the use of Lallans. Smith came to Edinburgh from New Zealand with his family when he was twelve (his father was Professor of Forensic Medicine at Edinburgh University) and it may be that his personal experience of varieties of English – the New Zealand 'speak' differs from Standard English – made him less antagonistic to Lallans as a literary alternative to Standard English. He made a deliberate choice to write in

Lallans as can be seen from the poem 'Epistle to John Guthrie', in which he argues for the use of Scots against the person who has blamed him for writing a language which no one speaks:

> We've come intil a gey queer time
> Whan scrievin Scots is near a crime
> 'There's no one speaks like that', they fleer
> – But wha the deil spoke like King Lear?

SMITH'S USE OF SCOTS

Smith forcibly makes the point in this poem that Scots is very much alive and well, 'raff and slee', as any visit to the Canongate will reveal – and more slyly, demonstrates that what is being argued about is very much to do with social class. Beyond all these considerations, however, he points out that poetic language is hardly that of any ordinary speech, Scots or English. And with this in mind his poetry uses both traditional literary Scots and modern colloquial Scots. In some poems also, he even makes up his own words – in 'King and Queen o' the fowr airts', he coins the word 'shilpiskate' to mean 'nonentity'. What is obvious about Smith's Scots is that it is a deliberate artistic construction. For those imbued with the Romantic idea that the words just 'come', and could have been no different, this self-conscious striving may seem odd. It certainly places Smith in the tradition of the original Makars, the 'makers' of poetry out of the materials that lie ready to hand. Smith was involved in drawing up the 1947 Style Sheet, designed to bring some order and system to the conventions of written Scots, and his own poetry shows a very deliberate approach to language. Yet he went much further in that as he constructed an alternative language, he also constructed an alternative identity. What is radical about Smith is not his themes or his insights, but his innate understanding that the relationship between the poet and the language is not fixed but a matter of individual human decision.

SMITH'S POETIC 'CREDO'

In his poem, 'Credo', Smith discusses how the poet ought to live and work. His statement of belief is a very traditional one. The poet must celebrate life, seek truth, find his own gift and simply 'tell what happened ye'. Death is to be confronted despite the starkness of its terrible aspect. The muse of his poetry must be awaited in all her fickleness. Equally fickle and inconstant is love, influenced by the moon, which will bring pain and betrayal into the poet's life. While Smith is to a fair extent accepting and reworking the Romantic stereotype of the debonair sensual bard, he is also working from the positions of the medieval makar and the later vernacular poets. Both Dunbar and Burns contribute to Smith's poetic *persona* – and in the epigrammatic summation of each verse there is something too of the quality of Soutar's terse riddles and whigmaleeries. 'Credo' is a concise statement of poetic belief. In other poems, this formal stance is bodied forth in more homely and local detail: 'Ma Moujik Lass', 'The Muse in Rose Street' and 'Spring in the Botanic Gardens' set the poet in characteristic sardonic and vulnerable poses within an Edinburgh setting.

DEATH AND LOVE

The themes of death and loss are never far away from Smith's poetry. He has poems arising out of the Second World War, such as 'Armageddon in Albyn', articulating the destruction it brought, expressing a hatred for war and cursing the impotence he feels in the face of it. In 'Largo', Smith mourns the loss of freedom and human community spirit as the Fife fishing industry declines to almost nothing. There is a political edge to many of his poems that toughens the general mood: 'Vox Humana' is an uncompromising vision of human brotherhood in conditions of oppression, perhaps another indication of a MacDiarmid influence.

However, it is love that is Smith's great theme. Perhaps it is his love poems that remain most with us. 'Cokkils' is a great poem about the persistence of love, captured in the memorable image of the cockle shells drifting down through the deeps of the sea to build 'their ain subaqueous Himalaya' on the ocean floor. And Smith's greatest poetic achievement is in his collection of love elegies, *Under the Eildon Tree* (1948), where individual elegies, like 'I Heard a Lassie at the Winnock Sing' and 'Slugabed', range over a wide variety of moods of love like a medieval love-allegory or Renaissance sonnet-sequence. This love has universal qualities but works itself out in Smith's own beloved Edinburgh. Like Fergusson and Garioch, he is an Edinburgh poet, and his great tribute to the city comes in the sequence, 'Kynd Kittok's Land', in which he salutes his 'auld rortie city' . . . 'for ever and ay till the World's End'.

Modern Makars

Robert Garioch and Sydney Goodsir Smith are by no means the only poets of this period who chose to write in Scots. Others who wrote extensively and successfully in Scots in the three decades after the war include Alexander Scott, Alastair Mackie, Tom Scott, Douglas Young, George Campbell Hay,

William Neill (who writes in English, Scots and Gaelic), Duncan Glen and Donald Campbell, although the initial impetus of the reforming Renaissance had dissipated. There were both negative and positive features about this practice. Negatively, it could be seen as a turning away from the more powerful and fruitful English culture and literature – though many of these poets made wide-ranging reference to English and European culture. More positively, the alignment with a rediscovered Scottish tradition, which contained a strong European and classical dimension, gave the poets all the imaginative stimulus they needed.

Alexander Scott (1920–89) was one of the most effective users of Scots after the war, his Aberdonian background and his distinguished war experience giving his poetry a hard, sardonic edge. For many years head of the only department of Scottish literature in the world, Scott's energy in teaching, critical and editorial work at Glasgow University (his *Still Life*, 1958, is the standard biography of William Soutar), and his poetry and drama, as well as his founding activities in successful ventures such as the Association for Scottish Literary Studies, greatly contributed to the rise in interest in Scottish literature at this time. His own poetic output was not huge, but it widened considerably the range of topics addressed by Scots, some of his most memorable poems being on topics such as interstellar travel, rock music, and popular icons such as Isadora Duncan, Marilyn Monroe and Jayne Mansfield. Several collections include *The Latest in Elegies* (1948), *Cantrips* (1968) and *Greek Fire* (1971). His variety of voice, style and topic have led him to be compared with William Dunbar; he can range from moods approaching anger and cynicism to moments of poignant tenderness in sexual and emotional love. His courageous and successful return to themes from Old English poetry, as in 'Seaman's Sang: Frae the West Saxon' (adapted from 'The Seafarer') showed vividly the closeness of Scots to its parent language; his frequent poems in Scandinavian vein, such as 'Steel on Stane', where he muses over the inscriber of the early graffiti in the Orkney tomb ('Ingabiorg is the brawest o wemen') show his creative spirit to have much in common with writers like Eric Linklater.

'Heart of Stone' is possibly his greatest achievement, his extended meditation on Aberdeen, 'a teuch toun, whaur even the strand maks siller'. This poem fuses the stress rhythms and alliterative patterning of Old English with modern free verse to striking effect; the old-new juxtapositioning of styles is echoed in the contrast of themes, where old strengths of land, sea and people are set against new forces of commerce and media. At best Scott's lyric gift is as fine as that of any other poet. His love of his craft is nowhere more passionately put than in his Blake-like celebration of the creative urge, 'The

Bricht Bird'. The bird flies at the sun; always dying ('in flame he hurtles doun / a fleeran star'), always recreated to attempt the impossible once more. The last verse captures well Scott's lyric voice:

> But look hou the bricht bird flees to chack at the sun!
> He's seekin fairheid there,
> And tho for the scaud o the flame he canna win,
> His sang maun daur
> The beauty and bleeze o the fire
> To faa wi death a lowe til the lichtless grun.

Scott's combination of eclecticism and insight into the north-east exemplifies a tendency amongst the poets in Scots of his time. Many of them worked like him, commenting on local issues of the day and identifying with a local area in Scotland, perhaps finding Scottish nationality in the wake of the failure of the Renaissance too difficult a subject to approach. Looking once more at Scotland whole and in itself had to await a younger generation of poets and perhaps a less loaded linguistic medium. What they achieved, nevertheless, was the maintenance of Scots as a viable medium, sustaining it until the more enlightened educational and social attitudes of the '80s and '90s recognised the entire spectrum of linguistic expression, thus confounding critics who had (over two centuries, from the Enlightenment to Edwin Muir) prophesied its death. It is clearly impossible to do justice to the achievement of the many poets of the period writing in Scots. What follows is a brief notice of some of the more prominent, introduced according to their birth-date.

Schoolteacher J. K. Annand (1908–93), who published some of the early work of MacDiarmid, continued the work of Soutar in bringing back the Doric on a cock-horse, in his Scots poems for children, as well as writing vividly about his naval experiences in the Second World War. His Scots was enriched by his scholarship, and he worked tirelessly to standardise it, outstandingly through the Scots Style sheet adopted by the Makars Club in Edinburgh in 1947, and his later editorship of the magazines *Lines Review* and *Lallans*. Douglas Young (1913–73), a professor of classics and nationalist activist, endured imprisonment for refusing conscription in the Second World War. He translated widely, from Aristophanes to Sorley MacLean, and as editor and critic contributed much to Scottish cultural revival. His own poetry has been seen as working in the manner of his mentor, MacDiarmid. Tom Scott (1918–95), like Mackay Brown, studied as a mature student with Edwin Muir at Newbattle Abbey and at Edinburgh University, where his work led eventually to his fine study *Dunbar: A Critical Exposition* (1966) and his joint editorship with Jack MacQueen of *The Oxford Book of Scottish Verse* (1966). Sorley MacLean argued (in his introduction to Scott's *The Collected Shorter Poems* (1993) that for all the striking quality of Scott's shorter poems, it was in his longer poems that his finest achievement was seen, especially in his epic allegory, *The Ship* (1963), in which the sinking of the *Titanic* is used as an extended metaphor for Western decline into war; in his great poem against war, *At the Shrine o' the Unkent Sodger* (1968), and in *Brand the Builder* (1975), which combines moving testimony to his father's unpretentious achievement with fierce satire on anglicised Scottish culture. Alastair Mackie (b. 1925) was a fellow Aberdonian who published late, encouraged by Duncan Glen and his Scottish Poetry magazine *Akros*, founded in 1965. Alexander Scott considered his collection *Clytach* (1972) to be the finest all-Scots collection since Goodsir Smith's *So Late Into the Night* (1952). William Neill (b. 1922) writes in Scots and English, and had the distinction of being a non-native speaker of Gaelic who became Bard of the National Mod in 1969. Like Tom Scott, he uses his Scots for vigorous polemic regarding national issues, together with an evocative sense of landscape at its best when working with his native south-west. Duncan Glen (b. 1933) lectured in graphic design in Yorkshire for thirty years before returning to Scotland in 1987. His *Hugh MacDiarmid and the Scottish Renaissance* (1964) was a seminal work; from 1965 to 1983 he edited *Akros*. He has tirelessly promoted Scottish writers and their work, and his poetry explores his origins, his family, and his own life in a deceptively simple and often humorous conversational Scots. Donald Campbell (b. 1940) is better known as a fine playwright (the quality of his poetry can be seen in plays such as *The Jesuit*, 1976, and *The Widows of Clyth*, 1979), but his best collection, *Rhymes 'n Reasons* (1972) has much of the easy irony of Garioch, with its view of Edinburgh up-dated to take account of social change. More recently, the vigorous Scots of Raymond Vettese (b. 1950) in *The Richt Noise and Ither Poems* (1988) demonstrates that Scots is still rich in possibilities, as in the opening of the title poem:

No words alane but the soond
tint, smeddum o' vowels foond   *energy, force*
lowpin' thegither in unco' dance –   *leaping*
an' no' there by chance.
Raxin' consonants sinnened for battle;   *sinewed*
the richt noise tae hurl at the storm's rattle!

Abandoning Renaissance? Post-war poetry in English

In 1962, Maurice Lindsay, who had written in Scots until that time, stopped doing so, arguing (in his collection, *Snow Warning*) that 'it is utterly unthinkable that this poor wasted and abandoned speech, however rich in theory its poetic potential, can possibly express what there is to be expressed of the Scottish ethos in the age of the beatnik and the hydrogen bomb.' This view is debatable, since as long as there is an awareness of a separate Scottish identity, there will always be people who find it natural to express that identity in whatever form of the language is available to them, and they will, as Scots, use the language to express whatever they want it to express. What Lindsay's change of practice did point to, however, was the passing of the Renaissance's grand conception of a Scotland culturally reborn. Compared with MacDiarmid's epic grappling with the Scottish psyche and Scottish nationhood in *A Drunk Man Looks at the Thistle*, Garioch works at a more local level, with a narrower sense of literary tradition and – with the exception of a few poems – without MacDiarmid's metaphysical complexity. And, for all his pyrotechnical virtuosity, Goodsir Smith can hardly be said to work at MacDiarmid's level either, given his personal preferences for lyricism and celebration. Scots poetry, as we have seen, most certainly survived, but singing in a lower key, and more often in local territory. And with the mature work of MacCaig, Mackay Brown and Crichton Smith, it was clear that English could be adapted and modulated to give full expression to a sense of Scottish identity and place, arguably producing the finest poetry of the last three decades. Besides, the notion of a standardised Scots had dissipated by the '60s, with the poetry of writers like Tom Leonard and Stephen Mulrine forcefully injecting another kind of non-standard, urban demotic speech, based on Scots, but repudiating the cultural baggage it carried; fiction would shortly after develop this linguistic middle territory.

One enriching way of reading the poets in English after the war is to follow and respect their coming to terms with identity in an English which increasingly and sensitively tunes itself to local and national variation. Poets like George Bruce and Maurice Lindsay evoke the north-east or the variety of the central belt in their time; and who can argue that the language they speak, with varying degrees of Scottish accent, is not the most appropriate for their experience? As with the Scots poets, it is clearly impossible to do more than give a bird's eye view of the wide range here. After the overview, which simply places poets in order of birth-date, more detailed attention is given to MacCaig, Mackay Brown, Edwin Morgan, Liz Lochhead and Iain Crichton Smith, arguably the outstanding five poets since 1945.

Post-war poetry in English:
George Bruce (b. 1909) and Maurice Lindsay (b. 1918)

George Bruce turned away from the Scots of the north-east because he wished to find a spare, terse language which would reflect the simplicity of his Fraserburgh fishing-merchant background. *Sea Talk* (1944) was minimalist in its winnowing of childhood, family and place, capturing what Bruce felt was the essence of a society threatened by cataclysmic changes of war and mechanisation. After the war, moving from teaching to work as a BBC arts producer in Edinburgh, there was a long interval till *Landscapes and Figures* appeared in 1967, with *Collected Poems* in 1970. The later poetry expands its horizons to encompass European art and culture, with a new irony informing the vision. The terseness and essential humanity is not lost, however, as his vivid realisation of the moment of death of 'Laotian Peasant Shot' from *Landscapes and Figures* shows:

> He turned momentarily,
> his eyes looking into his fear,
> seeking himself.
>
> When he fell the dust
> hung in the air
> like an empty container
> of him.

Bruce has outlived most of his great contemporaries; his contribution to Scottish and British culture, as poet, editor, critic and broadcaster, like that of his colleague and co-editor Maurice Lindsay, is immense. Impressively, in a recent volume, winner of the Saltire Book of the Year Award, *Pursuit* (1999), Bruce continues to seek 'a wider, more accommodating integrity, a wholeness which would contain opposites'.

Maurice Lindsay has been a huge figure in Scottish culture. He is a Glaswegian who trained in music; and after the war his roles as journalist and broadcaster led to his becoming controller of Border Television, and director of the Scottish Civic Trust. His critical works include a *History of Scottish Literature* (1977, rev. 1992), *Francis George Scott and the Scottish Renaissance* (1980) and major volumes on Burns. He has been an influential and controversial editor of many writers, anthologies, and magazines, outstanding being his *Modern Scottish Poetry* (1946, rev. 1966), his founder-editorship (with George Bruce and Edwin Morgan, and latterly with Alexander Scott and Roderick Watson) of the influential annual anthology *Scottish Poetry* (1966–76), and more recently, his editing of the magazine *The Scottish Review*. He has produced around twenty volumes of poetry, most critics finding his best work appearing from *This Business of Living* (1969) onwards. His *Collected Poems 1940–90* (1990) is an impressive gathering. Lindsay coined the phrase 'Calvinist deviationist' in regard to a poet he greatly admired, John Davidson (he edited a *Selection*, with essays from himself and Hugh MacDiarmid, with a Preface by T. S. Eliot, in 1961). The term implies a zeal for faith and order unaccompanied by the ability to believe, and the reader of Lindsay's poetry often feels a paradoxical tension between a yearning for form and meaning on one hand and a recognition that life is random and disordered on the other. This gives rise to a restless variety of topic, which some have criticised; but Lindsay genuinely grapples with his wide range of issues, since he is a man of immense worldly involvement. If older voices inform him, they include Byron, Davidson (of 'The Crystal Palace'), Bridie and Linklater – no bad pedigree for a writer who wishes to be detached yet involved, stylish yet honest, with a keen sense of the ridiculous. With such a prolific output, it is impossible to do justice to the poetry by brief quotation. Lindsay's is a poetry which deserves to be reflected on, in its constantly changing themes and forms.

Scottish poetry and the 'New Apocalypse' poets

An influential poetic movement which began in the 1930s and, straddling the war years, continued into the later 1940s was that of the 'New Apocalypse', and a number of Scottish poets carried its mark for at least part of their poetic careers. The poetry of the Apocalyptic Movement, as practised south of the Border by such writers as Henry Treece and, to some degree, Dylan Thomas, was marked by extreme complexity of syntax allied to a fondness for large portentous themes. The principles of the New Apocalypse embraced restatements of the need for greater human freedom and of the importance of myth as an antidote to the mechanistic thinking and denial of freedom implicit in the machine age.

J. F. Hendry (1912–86), G. S. Fraser (1915–80), W. S. Graham (1918–86) and Norman MacCaig, to very differing degrees, were associated with this movement in the earlier parts of their poetic careers, though it would be true to say that probably their best work was done when they were standing apart from the Apocalypse or shaking off its influence.

Scottish poetry in English

It is impossible to do justice to the many poets who contributed outstanding work in the next three decades after the war. (Part two of this chapter continues with discussion of the work of contemporary poets.) The roughly chronological listing which follows does not imply lesser achievement; individual volumes mentioned have been judged by many readers to be amongst the best of Scottish poetry. What it does show is the eclecticism and variety of the poetry as it grapples with new Scotlands, and the beginnings of what was to become the major impact of women's voices.

The finest poetry of Naomi Mitchison (1897–1999) appeared in her moving attempt to heal the wounds inflicted by aristocracy on ordinary people in *The Cleansing of the Knife* (1978). William Montgomerie (1904–94) and his wife Norah made substantial collections of children's songs; his own poetry appeared in *From Time to Time* (1985). The best of the sensitive nature poetry of Sidney Tremayne (1912–86) can be found in *Selected and New Poems* (1973). The early Apocalytic-metaphysical poetry of W. S. Graham caused reviewers of the time much difficulty in understanding, but later volumes like *The Nightfishing* (1955), with its use of the central vivid fishing sequences as emblem and epiphany for the poem's real subject, the poet's crisis of mental and emotional darkness in which he tries to catch meaning, and *Malcolm Mooney's Land* (1970) established him as a major, if complex and elusive, poet. Yet readers of his *Collected Poems* (1979) will find moving poems which return to his native Greenock, as in 'Loch Thom'.

Elegies for the Dead in Cyrenaica (1948, rev. 1990) by Hamish Henderson (b. 1919) is quite simply the finest volume of poems to come out of the Second World War; his *Collected Poems and Songs* (2000) now show the immense range of Henderson's talents and sympathies. The sardonic and metaphorically dazzling poetry of William Price Turner (b. 1927) is unjustly neglected, since at its best, as in the beautifully controlled, witty, moral and metaphorical punning of *The Flying Corset* (1962) and *Fables from Life* (1966), it rivals MacCaig. American-born Burns Singer (1928–64) published one volume, *Still and All* (1957) in his lifetime; a marine biologist and philosopher, his restless and sad moving across Europe gave him a unique personal voice which can be heard in *Collected Poems* (1970). George Macbeth (1932–92), London-based editor of *Poetry Now* and a prolific producer of war poetry, fiction and much more, nevertheless has a Scottish voice in *Collected Poems* (1971). The quiet, meditative, intellectual, but often sinister poetry of Robin Fulton (b. 1937) has been one of the most influential voices of the '60s and '70s; for the last twenty-five years he has lived in Norway, and is famed for his translations of that country's poetry. His *Contemporary Scottish Poetry* (1974) was a seminal study; his work belongs equally in the company of the contemporary poets of Part Two of this chapter.

A very different kind of poetry, but also moving into the contemporary period, is that of Ian Hamilton Finlay (b. 1925), whose conceptual work, identifying itself with few or no traditions of expression, crosses the boundaries of language to express itself in stone and wood. He has described 'Little Sparta', the symbolic landscaped garden around his home in Dunsyre, near Lanark (with its beautifully arranged artefacts which are commentaries on seasons and change, but also subtle plays on language and human perspectives) as a 'war zone', indicating a life-long distrust of bureaucratic materialism. Much of this work, and his typographically arranged poems, have, in the words of Alan Bold, 'to be seen to be believed'. Often considered a founder of the 'Concrete Poetry' movement, but in fact going far beyond its bounds, Finlay is world-famous for his way of combining the verbal and the visual. A stimulating sample of this multi-talented artist can be found in *The Dancers Inherit the Party* (1960).

In contrast, the all-too-brief contribution of Tom Buchan (1931–95) shone particularly vividly in *Dolphins at Cochin* (1969). Buchan was a contradictory figure, on one hand a respected teacher, on the other a rebel who sought meaning in Iona and Findhorn. His great talents were never fully realised, as he spent them in inspiring new theatrical modes (*The Great Northern Welly Boot Show*, 1973), editing *Scottish International*, and helping younger writers. His work represents a new and irreverent mood in the late '60s; *Dolphins*, with its easy ironic command of topics ranging from space travel to high-tec mountaineering expressing for the first time a new plurality of Scottish identity, at one with hip America and the beauties of Scottish landscape. 'Scotland the Wee' ('land of the millionaire draper, the whisky vomit, and the Hillman Imp') became for a while an anti-anthem, while 'The Weekend Naturalist', expressed a contemporary ironic awareness of traditional Scottish attitudes. Here was 'My humanoid friend, myself, a limited animal / in love with the planet' stumbling across Assynt in search of the something mountains are supposed to give. The tone is close to that of MacCaig's 'A Man in Assynt', wry, self-mocking, but more acutely deconstructive of society. Looking at himself on the boggy slopes he sees he is:

scared out of his wits by an equally terrified stag:
and always very conscious
of his wet socks, deaf ear, balding pate
and overfilled gut
but retaining even here persistent after-images of
his bank statement . . .

Stewart Conn (b. 1936), dramatist and BBC producer, has become a major figure; during the '60s and '70s he developed his unique way of looking at landscape and his Ayrshire farm upbringing. Owing something to Ted Hughes, his perspective on people in country and city in collections like *Stoats in the Sunlight* (1968), *An Ear to the Ground* (1972), and *In the Kibble Palace* (1987) fuses an intensely personal and loving view with disillusionment and regret, like Bruce's, with respect to the passing of an older generation and their way of life. His later poetry sensitively balances his position as a vulnerable family man with his perception of potential danger and wildness, as in 'In the Kibble Palace' (*Under the Ice*, 1978) where, reading poetry in a Glasgow West-End Botanical glasshouse, he is transported in imagination to feel whales crashing upwards into the ice-floe on which he's stranded:

> The horizon closes in, a glass
> Globe. We will admit it is there
> When it is too late; and blunder for the exits
> To find them locked. Seeing as though through ice
> Blurred forms gyrate, we will put our heads
> Together and try to batter a way out.

Stolen Light (2000) is his latest and thematic selection of his poems.

Kenneth White (b. 1936) is a distinguished graduate in modern languages of Glasgow University who has spent most of his career in France, where he is viewed as a leader of post-Modernism. In 1983 he became Professor of Twentieth-Century Poetics at the Sorbonne. His is a unique voice in Scottish and European poetry, owing something to Whitman and MacDiarmid, but essentially aiming to avoid the Western tradition, and to articulate an untrammelled, pure statement about the essentials of land-and-seascape, its weather and birdlife, its difference from the human. *The Bird Path* (1989) and *Handbook for the Diamond Country* (1990) brought his work to British recognition, and he is now seen as a major Scottish and European poet, whose bleakly pure evocations of the life, texture and light of the Brittany coastline (where he now lives) nevertheless owe much to his childhood at the edge of the Clyde, and his Scottish sense of the natural. His work has been a continual search for 'other paths', alternatives to what he perceives as academic ruts, and – as in his prose-poetry writings like *The Blue Road* (1983) and *Travels in the Drifting Dawn* (1989) – this takes him to startling juxtapositionings of familiar and esoteric places and cultures. He has in recent years worked to establish his Institute for Geopoetics, to focus his vision of new and liberating ways of relating to nature and experience which bypass the systematic hindrances of language.

Douglas Dunn (b. 1942) has developed into one of the finest of contemporary Scottish poets and short story writers. A librarian for much of his life, he moved from Glasgow after a year in America in 1964 to study at Hull University. America and his new friend and later colleague in Hull, Philip Larkin, had a profound influence on his first collection, *Terry Street* (1969), with its evocation of shabby modern Britain's back streets and tired lives. His poetry has, however, remembered its Scottish roots, and some of his most moving poems deal with a detached nostalgia with his Renfrewshire and West of Scotland background, as in the poem 'Drowning' (*Barbarians*, 1979), which captures a child's view of another boy's death. After the death of his wife in 1981 he wrote about his desolation, guilt and love in a poignant collection of *Elegies* (1985). He had already temporarily returned to Scotland as writer-in-residence at Dundee University for a year in 1981, and he returned permanently in 1984, becoming Professor of English at St Andrews University in 1991. *St Kilda's Parliament* (1981) showed that his involvement with Scotland was as strong as ever, with its use of old photographs of the islanders in 1879 as a basis for contemplating the limitations of the Western 'improvement' which led to 'the emaciated dead, the lost empires'. *Northlight* (1988) contains his extended imaginary conversation with a friend who questions his decision to live in Scotland, 'Here and There'. This poem encapsulates Dunn's craftsmanship in creating the appearance of an easy, highly intelligent, conversation in the manner of Browning, but working more rigorously than any other Scottish poet, perhaps, to declare the validity of choosing a northern Scottish identity rather than staying in the South of the supposed creative intelligentsia. His critic-friend argues that he's mad to love his East-Coast weather, that he'll become provincial, that his art will become parochial, that he'll drop out of history; Dunn's justifications range from the quality of light, even the rain, the legends, the university learning, to the gift of being alone, on 'imagination's waterfront' and 'backroads with a sense of time'. Step by step, benignly, gradually and cleverly, Dunn confutes his friend, revealing his limitations in not understanding landscape, tradition and magic, the universality of anywhere, and simple love, till, in a fine cumulative semi-flyting, he reverses the attack:

> You're wrong again, old friend. Your Englishness
> Misleads you into Albionic pride,
> Westminstered mockery and prejudice –
> *You're* the provincial, and undignified

Anachronism. The Pax Britannica's
Dismissed, a second-rate Byzantium,
Self-plundered inner Empire's Age of Brass.

His latest ambitious and moving undertaking is a sequence of poems which are in the form of letters from a Russian naval engineer to his wife, as he sails round the world towards his tragic destiny at what was to be the world's biggest sea-battle, at Tsushima in 1905.

Valerie Gillies (b. 1948) was born in Canada, brought up in Lanarkshire, and educated in Edinburgh and India. Out of this comes a richly varied poetry, which celebrates life from greyhounds (the central subject of *Bed of Stone*, 1984) to children, Afghan motorcyclists to her central love affair. Few poets are so alive to immediate experience, which is at its best in volumes like *Each Bright Eye* (1977) and *The Chanter's Tune* (1990). William McIlvanney (b. 1936) is of course famous for fiction, but has produced three volumes of poetry. *The Longships Enter the Harbour* (1970), *Weddings and After* (1984) and *In Through the Head* (1988) deserve recognition for the ways in which their honesty and toughness treat a huge range of human types and situations. These poems, unashamedly traditional in craftsmanlike mixture of free verse and rhyme, have qualities of Hardy and Larkin; they treat in poetry the worlds of the stories of *Walking Wounded* (1989). Alasdair Maclean (1926–94) wrote a non-fiction classic study of the decline of the Highland way of life in *Night Falls on Ardnamurchan: The Twilight of a Crofting Family* (1984), a mixture of autobiography and elegiac commentary which revealed a gifted man deeply unhappy with modernity. There are only two collections, *From the Wilderness* (1973) and *Waking the Dead* (1976); but the poetic eye here, at best, is as sharply metaphorical and disturbing as MacCaig's, and his uneasy relationship with his West Highland home produces a poetry which beautifully balances love and regret.

Challenging discourses and conventions

Alan Jackson (b. 1938) captured the spirit of the '60s and early '70s in poetry which danced with an epigrammatical mischief and covered biting satire ('Young Politician': 'What a lovely, lovely moon / and it's in the constituency too'). *The Worstest Beast* (1967) (humanity of course) and *The Grim Wayfarer* (1969) were socially and ecologically radical; his essay on spurious Scottishness, 'The Knitted Claymore' (*Lines Review* 37, 1971) was ahead of its time, and provoked much debate; and it is pleasing to see his return after too long an absence in *Salutations: Collected Poems* (1990). D. M. Black (b. 1941) is another fine poet whose work in the '60s and '70s was unique in its surreal fantasy and bizarre symbolic characters like the Red and Black Judges. *With Decorum* (1967) and *The Educators* (1969) mingle nightmare with biting satire – the title poem of the latter volume becoming a piece representing the destructive effects of systematised education in its shocking image of well-groomed teachers dismembering a joyous dwarf. He has been recognised as one of the few poets of today who can handle the long narrative poem; as with Jackson, his *Collected Poems* (1981) appeared after too long a silence.

From the brief descriptions of poets so far, in their varieties of language and the affirmative eccentricities of their creative positions, it will be realised that post-war Scottish poetry is remarkably polyphonic and multi-faceted, challenging conventional ideologies and discourses. No single poet does this more originally and effectively than Tom Leonard (b. 1944), a poet with strong connections with the Glasgow grouping of writers which, encouraged by Professor Philip Hobsbaum and Edwin Morgan in early years, includes Alasdair Gray, James Kelman and Liz Lochhead. All of these challenge the authority of 'English' language and Received Pronunciation in their fiction, drama and poetry; none challenges more fiercely than Leonard, who not only subverts the cultural power-claims of English, however, but in his own phonetic orthography for Glasgow and urban Scottish speech, reveals disturbing truths about the mind-sets behind that speech. On one hand his thrust is against English language's hidden assumptions of power; on the other, his poems cut into narrow-minded secular and religious parochialism and the insensitivity of dispossessed and doubly impoverished victims of Establishment power.

Leonard is a scholar, whose *Places of the Mind* (1993) is arguably the finest study of the poet James ('B.V.') Thomson, and whose *Radical Renfrew* (1990) began an on-going debate about the way in which poetic reputations are established, and the way deserving local poets are ignored for reasons other than of worth. Like Gray and Kelman, he involves himself through writing and protest with major issues of today, such as the Gulf War and the continued bombing of Iraq. He has experimented with sound poetry; but his best-known work lies in his subversions of authority and victims in his award-winning *Intimate Voices* (1984). One example, from 'The Qualification', illustrates both his unique methodology and his double-edged attack, as the speaker of whining clichés (dissatisfied parent, Glasgow) hits some real targets (anti-unionism, snobbery, chattering students) but in doing so reveals embittered self-limitation. Leonard's presentation also forces the reader into an initial sense of the alienness of such utterance, emphasising the gap between the position of most readers and the speaker; reading out loud, however, hopefully re-establishes meaning and kinship:

wurk aw yir life
nuthinty show
Pit oanthi nyuze
same awl drivl
yoonyin bashn
wurkir bashn
lord this
sir soan soa thaht
shood hearma boay
sayzwi need gunz
an armed revalooshn
nuthn else wurks
awright fur him thoa
uppit thi uni
talk aw yi like therr
thats whit its fur

Leonard's work does not confine itself to such satirical dramatic monologues. He varies the presentation; speakers also use authoritarian English; and in 'A Priest Came on at Merkland Street' it is apparently he who speaks/thinks in a stream-of-consciousness which analyses his relationship with religion in hilarious yet deeply serious fashion.

PART TWO: FIVE MODERN SCOTTISH POETS

Few would disgree that the most imaginative, innovative and often metaphysical poetry since the '60s has come from five poets: Norman MacCaig, George Mackay Brown, Iain Crichton Smith, Edwin Morgan and Liz Lochhead. Together, they represent a poetic treatment of Scotland which ranges from islands to cities, traditional to modern, religious to sceptical; and continually challenge our perspectives, in terms of our relations with nature, language and gender issues.

Norman MacCaig (1910–96)

Of the young poets influenced by the New Apocalypse, the one whose ultimate achievement was the most substantial was Norman MacCaig. His debt to the movement was perhaps greater than he was himself prepared to admit, yet he never included any of the poems from his first two volumes in his subsequent collections and virtually renounced his Apocalyptic period. For us today, MacCaig belongs more definitely to post-war poetic diversity, with his links with Garioch and Goodsir Smith (also an Edinburgh poet, a schoolmaster, friendly with MacDiarmid). Yet – perhaps because of his Highland origins? – at no point did MacCaig use Lallans Scots in his poetry. A swift creator of short 'witty' or metaphysical poems, he covered a very wide range of human experience, yet localised much of it in his own Edinburgh and the Assynt district of Sutherland that came to mean so much to him.

MACCAIG'S IMAGERY

It is in his imagery that MacCaig reveals most clearly his Apocalyptic roots. The difference between the rejected poems and those in his *Collected Poems* (1996) which were written in the '50s and '60s is more one of degree than of kind. The vivid metaphor which reveals (and requires) an imaginative leap in the manner of the best metaphysical verse is used more sparingly, as a rhetorical flourish rather than as part of a spate of bizarre and apparently unrelated images, but it is recognisably the same mind at work in 'Growing Down':

> So when I leave the antiseptic room
> Of my cold brainpan to discover where
> A star may shine you in the elsewhere gloom
> Or shadow figure you in the empty air,
> My old ancestor, dropping from his tree,
> Sidles through centuries and creeps into me.

This stanza, revealingly, is from a poem which deals directly with the nature of metaphor, taking up (as an epigraph explains) 'a theory which finds language more and more metaphorical as it is traced back in the past'. Yet, in true metaphysical manner, MacCaig uses this linguistic observation to create a love poem: his theme is the power of love to call up a primitive, non-rational level of experience. In this stanza the syntactical distortions and the vivid images embody the metaphorical capacity of language and also discuss it.

Elsewhere, MacCaig reinforces his imagery through an exploitation of the ambiguities of syntax, as in the following lines from 'By the Canal':

> The snow is trash now and the blackbirds sing
> A gold and blue day trying to be Spring.

Here, the verb 'sing' at first sight appears to be intransitive but turns out to be used transitively; the element of surprise created by this and other examples in the poem plays a genuine part in constituting the poem's whole meaning. 'By the Canal' is a poem which is almost entirely objective, depending upon the creation of an external scene to convey the poet's feeling. The speaker is wholly undramatised and transparent. As a celebrant of nature in its multi-plicity of forms, MacCaig frequently writes himself out of his poetry in this way. There is, however, another side to him, the overt striker of dramatic poses.

'SUMMER FARM'

The well-known poem 'Summer Farm' illustrates both tendencies. The first two stanzas present an objective sequence of observed details; while the second pair of stanzas give the poet's subjective metaphysical awareness of the experience. The poet 'finds himself' at the centre of a concentric universe. He is imaginatively, both outside the scene, lifting the farm as if he were God, and yet inside as well. There are two sets of receding forms, 'self under self' and 'farm within farm', and the relationship between them is intimate and mutually enclosing. There is a link with the Platonic notion that there is an ultimate reality underlying individual objects, events and experi-ence, so that all things are copies of a single paradigm. At the period around 1960, when MacCaig published the collection, *A Common Grace*, these ideas seem to have been one of his key preoccupations.

EDINBURGH POEMS

An increasing maturity in MacCaig's 'metaphysical' approach to imagery can be seen in two contrasting Edinburgh poems, 'November Night, Edinburgh' and 'Edinburgh Courtyard in July'. The imagery of the former is more densely packed, but both pieces are recognised as among MacCaig's most effective work in the descriptive mode. The techniques employed in these two poems recur in a more complex environment in 'Nude in a Fountain'. The focus here is more clearly metaphysical – that is, in the philosophical sense – but the central image of the statue screened by the play of water from the fountain is surrounded by a careful, and at times playful, picture of a summer scene in Edinburgh. Part of the point appears to be sheer pleasure in play with language, but it is important that MacCaig sees the relationship between the figure and her screen of water as 'a pose of meaning', which clearly has to do with the relationship between permanence and change. 'Nude in a Fountain' implies more than it states, hinting at an insight into reality which we must ourselves reconstruct from the pattern of language that MacCaig has built up.

759

THE IMPORTANCE OF STRUCTURE AND IMAGERY

Formal structure is an important element in MacCaig's early poetry. He uses a great variety of stanza patterns, usually with full rhyme as in 'Edinburgh Courtyard in July' and 'Nude in a Fountain', but occasionally built on assonance and slant-rhyme, as in 'November Night, Edinburgh'. By the time of his 1966 collection, *Surroundings*, however, he had largely moved away from formal devices towards free verse. A new directness of manner seems to accompany this shift, reflected in the two Italian poems, 'The Streets of Florence' and 'Assisi'. The emphasis here is on a lucid economical style in which MacCaig comments on experience directly, without relying heavily on metaphorical language. 'Assisi' makes greater use of imagery than 'The streets of Florence': the dwarf, in a telling simile, is 'like a half-filled sack / . . . from which sawdust might run', while the tourists who ignore him are dismissively seen as hens 'clucking contentedly' after a priest who 'scattered the seed of the Word'. Yet even these images are more direct than those employed by MacCaig in the earlier phases of his career; and they are carefully deployed in support of the total irony. An obvious danger in 'Assisi' is sentimentalising the dwarf, but MacCaig ensures that he wins our sympathy without introducing pathos: the first two stanzas end with an ironic twist at the expense of the St Francis cult and the priest, but the third ends delicately, continuing the positive treatment of the dwarf. There is perhaps a difference in the ways in which MacCaig approaches his Scottish and his non-Scottish subjects; such difference can be seen reflected in the group of poems written during a visit to the USA in the later '60s. In 'Hotel Room, 12th Floor', 'Brooklyn Cop' and 'Leaving the Metropolitan Museum', he appears to be more detached from his subjects (without, however, losing an emotional contact) than in his treatment of native scenes and situations.

OTHER THEMES

Close to home, in poems arising out of his engagement with the experiences of his private life, and progressively with the landscapes and people of the north-west Highlands, MacCaig can charge his generally short poems with a cool passion and controlled love that gives them a power that can far outweigh their apparent slightness. In one of his few longer poems, 'A Man in Assynt' (written for television, like Goodsir Smith's 'Kynd Kittok's Land'), MacCaig celebrates the Highland landscape which is the focus for much of his later work. There is an alteration between a lyrical voice which evokes the natural features and a more 'realistic' voice that comments, sometimes with anger, on the contemporary situation in the area. One of his central preoccupations is Highland depopulation, symbolised by the image of the receding tide. Ultimately MacCaig's personal experience, his feelings about the land and its alienation from the people, and his natural observation fuse into a complex political and philosophical statement.

MacCaig rarely attempted a poetry dealing with Scotland in terms of history, legend and myth, deeply distrusting the effects of history and myth-makers in terms of what they had done in the past through their religious and authoritarian accounts. This makes a poem like 'Celtic Cross', which unusually does deal with history and pre-history, particularly interesting for those wishing to seek out MacCaig's views behind his customary statements of distrust of myth. Here, for once, he explores the meaning of the archetypal Celtic cross: its origins as stone; its earliest carvings of doves and abstract interweaving designs; and its third phase, when Christians cut through earlier configurations to hew out the cross, with its 'unjust demands'. What makes the poem particularly interesting is MacCaig's subtle speculation regarding the 'abstract vocables' of the Celtic designs – what do they signify? Are they symbols of the 'implicated generations', interwoven through the ages, intertwined like weeds in a river? Why did the first carvers not depict the world of sea and bays, of nature, instead of this kind of stone music? MacCaig gives few answers, but typically, ends with posing the reader possibilities which are implied questions: the cross he dislikes, because it stands for authoritarian demands; the original stone he simply sees as the hard world of nature; but in between, he speculates, in the first Celtic carvings, he finds something that is the stone echo of the 'singing responses', the ancient music, of the Elder Folk – a people whose music is captured here, in an interweaving carving, and serpent and dove imagery, which 'seems like love'. Note the 'seems'; all MacCaig's poetry draws back from allowing final meaning, since we are trapped by our senses, but at last, here, he comes close to the views of Muir, Gunn and others that an ancient Scottish culture had a culture of community and tradition which was over-written by history and cruel demands of religion, leaving the finally unknowable message of the Celtic stone and cross.

MacCaig's development through his later poetry was noticeable. The emergence of a confident free-verse style; the growing objectification of imagery and complexity of viewpoint; an increasing engagement with landscape; an equally significant preoccupation with birds, animals and other natural creatures as poetic subjects – all these are observable in the prolific output of a poet who made himself into the most significant and popular Scottish poet of the post-war period. By the '70s and '80s Norman MacCaig could have fairly laid claim to be the natural successor of MacDiarmid as the Grand Old Man of Scottish poetry; his own ironic self-deprecation would have been the main obstacle to such a lofty presumption.

George Mackay Brown (1921–96)

Perhaps more than any other Scottish poet of the post-war period, George Mackay Brown focused his work (not only in poetry, but in fiction, drama and journalism also) on the community where he was born, grew up and continued to live almost without a break until his death. This community was that of the Orkney Islands, a highly individual community, where fishing and farming are of supreme importance and where the sea is a constant presence bringing both a livelihood and the possibility of sudden death to all who sail on it; a community which tends to foster a strong sense of identity with the shared values of the present and inherited traditions of the past. Mackay Brown's poetry is filled with these considerations and associations, intensified by his own particular religious outlook as a Catholic convert, not a mainstream Orkney standpoint since the time of the Scottish Reformation. Thus Mackay Brown's poetry is at one and the same time both an expression of an Orkney view of life and an individual faith-based critique of how it has developed in modern times.

'HAMNAVOE'

The result of this has been that the Orkney of his poetry has tended to be an Orkney of the past, if not actually historical, at least some distance away from the modern and contemporary community that he inhabited. A poem of some importance in seeing this tendency is 'Hamnavoe'.

It is a poem in which Mackay Brown pays tribute to his father and vividly evokes the town of Stromness ('Hamnavoe') where he grew up between the two world wars. There are glimpses of people and things that were around him in his boyhood, yet there is a carefully selected series of details which give a quality of timelessness to the poem; this is a general 'time past' that is apparently untouched by the age of mechanisation. This Hamnavoe exists in an ideal vision of 'seapink innocence', in the same way that he himself as a boy is preserved from 'the worm and black wind' of progress. In several places, such as his *An Orkney Tapestry* (1969), his classic and characteristic account of his islands in history and culture, George Mackay Brown described the purpose of the artist at work in a way that justifies this selection of images from reality to work into a harmonious ideal (Chapter 1, 'Islands and People):

> What the artist tries to create at the centre of his life and time is a place of order, a place of remembrance, a place of vision, to which he returns again and again in times of difficulty and confusion, in order to have things

made simple and meaningful once more. It is the workshop of the imagination that fills the world with beautiful shapes.

George Mackay Brown's work as a poet is inspired with this impulse to create an orderly, meaningful and therefore beautiful shape out of his memories and experiences of Orkney, his reading (especially of the Norse sagas) and his Catholic faith.

MACKAY BROWN AND 'PROGRESS'

One of Mackay Brown's major concerns was to criticise the materialistic values which threaten to destroy both his own and other island communities. He did this recurrently in *An Orkney Tapestry* (Chapter 1, 'Islands and People'):

> I think we are not interested in the past at all. There is a new religion, Progress, in which we all devoutly believe, and it is concerned only with material things in the present and in a vague golden-handed future. It is a rootless utilitarian faith, without beauty or mystery; a kind of blind unquestioning belief that men and their material circumstances will go on improving until some kind of nirvana is reached and everyone will be rich, free, fulfilled, well-informed, masterful . . . . I feel that this religion is in great part a delusion and will peter out in the marsh. A community like Orkney dare not cut itself off from its roots and sources. Places like Rackwick and Eynhallow have no meaning if you try to describe them in terms of a newspaper article. They cannot be described in that way.

Note the focus here on the past, as opposed to a vague future; on humane values rather than hollow material motives; and on roots and sources rather than evaluation. For Mackay Brown, materialism is not simply an urban phenomenon from which the islands can remain isolated and insulated. He was not so naïve as to promote his islands as a haven from materialism, nor did he condemn progress in all its forms. What he is concerned about is the erosion of moral values that comes with materialism, which is a state of mind to be found everywhere.

PATTERN AND RITUAL

In a number of his poetry collections, Mackay Brown is concerned to counter moral decay and imaginative poverty by celebrating moments in Orkney's history, clearing the historical roots of the place and reviving dying ritual. This includes the expression of the variety of personalities in a community.

763

Even when he is writing of Vikings, as in the poem, 'The Five Voyages of Arnor', for example, he presents a ship's company that includes not simply rampaging sea-farers, but 'poets, warriors, and holy men'. The poem 'Unlucky Boat' evokes a traditional Orkney that could be the present day with a range of Orkney characters – the craftsman, the fisherman, the farmer and the tinker. It is a series of vignettes, capturing the main features of events and people's varying responses and fates. In only thirteen lines, there is room and time for considerable variety of character and incident, for superstition to interact with modern medicine, for luck to operate in a context of religion, and for each event to be placed in a social context. The effect of the tight structure of the poem is to suggest that the different types in modern Orkney are helpless against malevolent forces which only those in touch with the harmonious pre-Reformation past, like the tinkers, can evade. 'Unlucky Boat' is not merely an anecdote about a boat; it is a patterned allegory of fate.

In that poem, fishing was seen as a hazardous business, but in 'Our Lady of the Waves' it is represented as a gift from God. The poem is set in a monastery; values of abstinence and devotion are the norm, and, in fact, the poem is designed as a hymn, with verses that praise 'Our Lady', 'Holy Mother', 'Sweet Virgin' and 'Queen of Heaven'. In this poem death is not cursed or feared but fitted into the scheme of things. The same attitude comes through in 'Warped Boat', in which the drowning Willag issues his last instructions with a humorous understatement that has the effect of presenting his drowning in the laconic heightened manner of the Norse sagas. The imagery and rhetoric of both traditional religion and pagan saga have the effect of ritualising everyday occupations. A similar effect is created in 'Old Fisherman with Guitar', where the title suggests a painting and a patterned visual composition: the first part of the poem emphasises the music and focuses on the man's hands that create the music; the second part evokes the experience of these same hands in dealing with both death and love. The hands are seen engaged in ritual activities that bring together the different aspects of the fisherman's life, aesthetic, practical and emotional. Brown is clearly also crafting a particular kind of utterance, or poetic voice. There is richness, but there is a risk as well of the poem coming to seem out of date in tone because of a deliberate archaism of syntax and diction.

'HAMNAVOE MARKET'

'Hamnavoe Market' is one of Mackay Brown's most anthologised poems. He arranges his characters in an order that will best illustrate their differences from each other, and these differences seem to be part of the point of the poem. The characters represent the seven varieties of Everyman, the market is life itself. The seven men who set off together ('They drove to the Market with ringing pockets') become involved in different activities; not all travel back together. The patterning of the stanzas gives the sense of a ritualised performance. Each man is carrying out his own 'rituals', according to his own tastes, personality and opportunities, so that a visit to the market becomes a series of emblems of life's varieties, with the differences between them expressed in subtle variations of style. No judgements are passed on the men and their different choices. The implication seems to be that each life and personality is valid in its own terms and finds its own particular ritual to symbolise it.

CYCLES OF NATURE AND LIFE

Brown draws almost exclusively on the history and life of Orkney for his poetry (as indeed for his prose). He has told the story of Magnus, for example, in a variety of genres at different times. Yet this local material is presented with an archetypal universality, and within a larger context which is infused with a sense of the cyclical nature of life and nature, in ways which frequently echo the formalism and traditionalism in the poetry of his great Orkney predecessor (and teacher at Newbattle Abbey in the early 1950s), Edwin Muir. His poem cycles work with subjects ranging from animals and weather to the life and death of President Kennedy and nuclear holocaust. A sense of continuity and universality lifts his poetry far above the local and regional. Brown does address some of the central issues of our time and seeks affirmation in rituals that do not depersonalise but which promote the value of ordinary and traditional human activity, as he argued in his novel *Magnus* (1973) (Chapter 7, 'The Killing'):

> There are constants in human nature, and constants in the human situation, and . . . men in similar circumstances will behave roughly in the same fashion . . . Poetry, art, music, thrive on these constants. They gather into themselves a huge scattered diversity of experience and reduce them to patterns; so that, for example, in a poem all voyages become The Voyage, and all battles The Battle, and all feasts The Feast. This is to look at those events of time which resemble one another yet are never quite the same, in a symbolic way.

'JOHN BARLEYCORN'

Brown's poetry attempts to fuse all aspects of life and tradition, and many versions of religious belief, into a cycle of meaning, so that pagan and Christian meaning synthesise. A poem which superbly exemplifies this is

765

'John Barleycorn', written in what seems a traditional and simple ballad style; yet the reader who follows Brown's allegory will discover here a rich mixture of pagan and Christian ideology. On one level Brown exploits the Corn King rituals exemplified by Frazer in *The Golden Bough* (1890–1915); Golden Barleycorn must die for the people – although Brown goes further, and makes the very crops themselves the kings who must die. This poem distils all his beliefs in earth magic; resurrection comes from the wounding of the earth, and in the miracle of annual seasonal rebirth. But John is called a 'priest', he is cut down at his 'golden prayer', and thus becomes a version of Christ, broken as he is and shorn of his glory. (Or Christ becomes John Barleycorn – such is the strangeness of Brown's Catholicism.) Just as Christ rises from death, so does the threshed corn – transformed miraculously into bread and wine, a favourite transition for Brown. An understanding of this poem sheds light on much of the difficulties in Brown's poetry and fiction.

George Mackay Brown the poet tended in his later years to be overshadowed by the writer he chose to become; George Mackay Brown the novelist and short story writer. Yet the material he created and worked on in the latter mode is of the same kind and from the same roots as his poetic work. As a creative writer, he was all of a piece, and the qualities of the poet are those that make much of his prose fiction vivid and illuminating. Orkney has to date produced no writer to rival him in imagination and inventiveness, and, although coming from the periphery of geographical Scotland, he can be seen to be central to post-1945 Scottish writing in his human and social concerns.

Iain Crichton Smith (1928–98)

Like George Mackay Brown, Iain Crichton Smith was born and brought up in an island community. As he said in Chapter 1 of *Towards the Human* (1986):

> To grow up on an island is a special experience, but it is not an experience of Eden. Newspapers arrive late, the world outside is distant, its concerns are remote. Above all there is the sound of the sea, that eternal sound that haunts the islands, and has found its commemoration in a poem which is, like so many of our poems, an elegy.

For Smith, the island was Lewis in the Western Isles, and the elegy he speaks of is a Gaelic elegy, 'An Ataireachd Ard' ('The Eternal Swelling of the Sea'). His feeling for the community seems to have been very different from that of Mackay Brown, as he records in his essay in Lindsay's collection, *As I Remember* (1979):

I had no feeling for Scotland at all as a country except through football. I didn't feel myself as belonging to Scotland. I felt myself as belonging to Lewis. I had never been out of the islands in my whole life . . . I had hardly read any Scottish writers, not even MacDiarmid. Most of the writers I read were English ones. The island was in a way self-sufficient and there were even, strange to relate, many parts of the island I had never visited . . .

In a strange sort of way too the island seemed to have no history. There were standing stones on the moor behind our house but I never found out why they were there or who had put them there . . . It was a hard bleak island which did not reverberate when one touched it with one's mind.

Iain Crichton Smith does not idealise the island of Lewis; in fact, he reveals that it gave him images not only of the permanence of the sea but also of the 'bare mind'. It also left him thinking of class and politics as a 'trivial obsession'. Consequently, his poetic statements about island life are not nostalgic, not the 'lovely cry of the transient' but the 'proved monotony of the permanent'. He presents his island not as a rural retreat from twentieth-century life, but a crucible where the individual self must struggle to create and maintain a sense of identity. Smith had a love-hate relationship with his island, critical of its pettinesses and its inherited tradition of repression, yet respecting its sense of community and enforced self-determination: 'I love it for its very bleakness, for its very absences.'

Between two cultures

When Iain Crichton Smith moved to Oban, after studying at Aberdeen University and teaching in Clydebank, he seemed to find a liminal zone between the Gaelic, rural, island culture of Lewis and the anglicised, urbanised, industrialised culture that has become more and more the mainland norm. The town seemed to balance conflicting developments in Scottish society and gave Smith a specific location for a perspective that was both part of and yet apart from that community. In a real sense, he was not far removed from the standpoint of George Mackay Brown in his awareness of the fragility of his own Gaelic culture in the face of materialistic external exploiting forces. Growing up speaking Gaelic, then switching to English at school and university – these have been the root of a dividing self, which is aware of how the Gaelic culture hovers between revival and extinction. It is remarkable how, over many years until he began to feel that he was losing touch with living Gaelic expression, Smith managed to write extensively and with great critical acceptance in both Gaelic and English using a variety of genres and modes. His Gaelic poetry, plays and stories, including a Gaelic novel, require comment elsewhere; in English he is, besides being a major poet, an accomplished novelist and short story writer. The parallel with George Mackay Brown goes beyond their island origins.

To the end of his life, however, Smith could be regarded as primarily a poet. Again and again in his poetry he analyses the predicament of being between two poles as being a condition of 'exile' or being 'in the middle' (titles of two of his poetry collections), created by separation from the community, by a decision to take a stand against the flow of the development of the community. The condition appears in Smith's work in a variety of forms, including conflicts between young and old, emigrant and resident, religious and sceptical, naïve and intellectual voices. Contrasts are often set up between different groups of people – fishermen and university students, poets and schoolboys; or between different perspectives – the place as the poet sees it, compared to how visitors or tourists see it; or the role expected of him, compared to the role he wants to play. The solution that Smith proposed – to what he saw as a serious, and recurring, problem for Scottish culture – was to avoid the divided self, to take measures against the forces which create it in childhood, as he argued in 'Real People in a Real Place', in his collection of autobiographical and critical essays *Towards the Human* (1986):

> To give such a culture the possibility of a future means that the children must grow up in a world that they recognise as being as important as any other. It means that they be not divided into two by the sudden incursion of a new language.

The artist also has a function, to take in the broader perspectives – in space and time – and not to dwell on the past and the loss: 'It requires that the artist should sense a future and not be forever imprisoned in the forms of the elegiac.'

Freedom and repression

Much of Smith's writing raises a larger question about how a condition of exile – or exclusion of any kind – is established. He provides not only descriptions of exile, but also analyses and explanations of the condition. So, in the poem 'Old Woman' ('Your thorned back . . .'), we are given both a description of her mind-set, in the first five stanzas, and an explanation of it, in the last three, with the two halves of the poem reflecting the mirror images of repression and 'instinctive' freedom. Stanza six works as a pivot, a transition from the first half, which could be taken as a series of bitter recriminations, and the second, which builds pathos and compassion into the portrait. The final effect is of a set of contrasts, of unreconciled opposites. It is arguable that in this poem Smith does not seek a reconciliation and that he enacts the very intolerance that diminishes the old woman.

On the other hand, in two of his poems about Lewis, 'Some days were Running Legs' and 'Poem of Lewis', there is a strong equation of poetry with freedom and gaiety. In the latter poem particularly, there is an outspoken critique of repressive attitudes on the island:

> Here they have no time for the fine graces
> of poetry, unless it freely grows
> in deep compulsion, like water in the well.

Poetry represents, or is aligned with, forgiveness, measured thought, lightning – swift and bright – and gaiety, while the forces which work against poetry are compulsion, a 'barren rock', 'dryness' and mourning. Both extremes meet 'in one breast', where some balance must be worked out. If the balance tips against poetry and 'grace', there is a tidal wave of anger, bringing with it a gale of destruction and a flood. This establishes one of Smith's favourite oppositions, between the 'law' and the 'grace' (the title of another of his collections), the law of repressive religion and control and the grace of poetry and freedom. One of the most explicit statements against repressive religion is 'A Note on Puritans':

> I accuse
> these men of singleness and loss of grace
> who stared so deeply into the fire's hues
> that all was fire to them.

In *From Bourgeois Land* (1969), Smith continued his analysis of mechanical thinking and repression. Here he deals with urban problems as well as rural contexts, a much wider frame of reference. In 'From Bourgeois Land (12)', for example, he brings the horror of Nazi death camps to 'Scottish towns' and their 'tidy flowering squares'. The aim is to make us question the apparent innocence and superficial serenity of the Scottish burgh; the potential for a parallel with the small towns of Nazi Germany that came to harbour the terrible secrets of the camps is lurking there – 'From such quiet places furies start.' We must not be fooled by the stereotypes of the Scottish town, and replace observation and attentiveness with complacency and passivity. In a sense, this poem takes the argument of 'Poem of Lewis' a stage further. The earlier poem condemned the blighting forces of repression on the island; it tells us how it is, whereas 'From Bourgeois Land' is more subtle, in that it demonstrates the problem, showing how we construct images of communities. Sense of place can become a cocoon, cutting us off from the outside world, or from the real place itself, and stifling our powers of observation and social action.

Themes in Smith's poetry

Iain Crichton Smith is a poet of several places. In his work, twentieth-century Oban provides a vantage point from which to view Lewis and Gaelic and Calvinistic culture objectively. Yet the island community also provides a commentary on materialism and industrialisation. Change and progress are weighed in the balance with the permanence of the land and the stability of traditional values and rituals. At some points, reluctance to view the old ways critically, the disapproval of any kind of change, is shown to be a poisonous device for avoiding the inevitable course of 'progress'. Yet at other points, the old values – of community, history, religion – are reaffirmed. Most of the time, the two are juxtaposed and held in a state of tension providing a constant commentary on each other.

Iain Crichton Smith's poetry developed steadily throughout his life, but the struggle to achieve moral vision of a valid sort dominated all of his work. Each novel he wrote was painfully honest about the stage he felt he had reached in coming to terms with the rejected Calvinism of his Lewis upbringing and in constantly, agonisedly, seeking moral and existential perspectives on experience. In his thinking, language is centrally questioned about its capability of carrying a true account of experience; the longer poems, 'Deer on the High Hills' and 'Shall Gaelic Die?', explore this issue deeply. Yet, most impressive in his work is the continual debate about what kind of values should dominate one's life; those of shared community, of the village, with all its limitations and narrowness of vision, or those of personal free development, a romantic and absolute quest for individual fulfilment.

'SHE TEACHES LEAR'

'She Teaches Lear' is arguably Smith's finest poem, and one of the finest of all modern poems. It may be appropriate to end this consideration of Smith's poetry with a brief comment on a dramatic monologue that brings together in their complexity and restless interaction the various issues that have preoccupied the writer for so much of his poetic career.

In reading the poem, the reader must decide how much the schoolteacher (who is teaching Shakespeare's *King Lear* to a senior class) is spokeswoman for Smith himself, and to what extent she is *dramatis persona*, and thus an empathetic and satirical portrayal like the responsible spinsters and old women of other poems by Smith. Beyond her are the viewpoints, respected and listened to carefully by class members like Moira (explicit) or Jean (cleverly implicit), a wide range from the quasi-Nazi ('purity of the race') to 'James Dean' romantic. Add Smith's understanding of the perspective of the old man (the teacher's father?), and the manipulative hidden control that he as poet exercises in controlling the teacher's poetic expression, and this poem begins to reveal its rich diversity of points of view. Out of several moral perspectives, Smith finally rests precariously on that of a purely social and human responsibility. What particularly impresses, however, is not the conclusion but the fundamentalism, the secularised version of a traditional and perhaps Calvinist rigour and desire for personal conviction. Smith performs the astonishing feat of setting the localised desire of the teacher (and the Western Scot) in the rich contexts of Shakespearian drama, stoicism and hedonism, and various social debates, between Utilitarianism and Romanticism, and between Victorian duty and modern existentialism. Scottish poetry here achieves a universal interaction, which not even MacDiarmid achieved, through Iain Crichton Smith's unforced and unpretentious dialogues, both internal and external.

Edwin Morgan (b. 1920)

In 1984 an international festival of sound poetry took place in Glasgow. The programme notes (presumably written by the organiser, the poet Tom Leonard) included this entry on one of the participants:

> Cultural attaché to the legendary city of Morganiana, said to exist behind a door marked 'Morgan' in an unobtrusive block of flats off Great Western Road. From here translations and original poems go out daily to magazines all over the world, while the city director converses by golden telephone with the spirits of some dead but perky Russian Futurists.

A conventional account of Edwin Morgan's life would record his birth in 1920, war-time service with the Royal Army Medical Corps in the Middle East, and an academic career teaching English literature at Glasgow University until retirement in 1980; but the above quotation takes us closer to the true nature and spirit of the poet. It is useful because it not only suggests the range and volume of the writing, but also indicates Morgan's readiness to step outside a purely Scottish tradition, allowing himself to be influenced by the poetry of other countries, particularly of the USA and Russia. For example, the Russian Futurists, alluded to in the quotation, have particularly interested Morgan, and if the verse of Mayakovsky (1894–1930) continues to be 'perky', it is partly because Morgan has translated a selection of his work into vigorous Scots (*Wi' the Haill Voice*, 1972).

MORGAN AND GLASGOW

However, the most significant detail of the notes is their indication of the most convenient point of access to Morgan's poetry, the fact that the door which leads to Morganiana is in Glasgow. Morgan grew up in the city, and its life has influenced him at least as much as any of the writers he admires. The influence of Glasgow runs throughout his work: the architecture, both the traditional buildings among which he grew up and the modern structures which have transformed the city since the 1960s; and the accompanying sense that Glasgow is an exciting city in a state of flux, suitable material for poetry. The influence of US writers such as Allen Ginsberg and Jack Kerouac was strong on Morgan, with their flouting of prevailing academic notions of literature in favour of the finding of inspiration in the paraphernalia of modern life. The Glasgow all around him played a large part in forming Morgan's outlook; indeed, its rapid change and the new phenomena of an age of change have often seemed to produce in him an almost visceral delight. 'Glasgow Sonnet, viii', for example, discovers an aesthetic pleasure in structures built for utilitarian purposes: 'the flyovers breed loops of light / in curves that would have ravished tragic Toshy'. (Even the assumption that the reader will recognise that 'Toshy' is the city's soubriquet for architect Charles Rennie Mackintosh exemplifies its Glasgow allegiances.) 'Loops of light' and 'curves' suggest that the grandeur of the motorway is modern man's equivalent of the medieval cathedral, an achievement that would have gained the approval of Mackintosh.

Yet, change, even improvement, provokes an ambiguous response, which Morgan recognises. In 'The Second Life' and 'To Joan Eardley', Morgan suggests that the changing Glasgow scene brings loss as well as renewal; the 'barefoot children' in the former poem and the children of an Eardley painting, as well as signalling a poverty that Glasgow could well get rid of, contributed a raw enduring life and were part of an 'energy that has vanished from the city'. Acknowledgement of that fact is not a repudiation of the changes, simply an honourable acceptance that a degree of loss is always part of progress.

'KING BILLY'

Attentiveness to the appearances of life in his city inevitably leads Morgan to consider the historical forces that brought them into being. In 'King Billy', a newsworthy funeral in July 1962 is the starting-point for a reappraisal of the familiar, often stereotyped, view of working-class life in Glasgow. The poem concerns the procession which takes the coffin of former gang-leader William Fullerton, 'King Billy of Brigton', from Bridgeton Cross to the cemetery. These two different renderings of the place-name, 'Brigton' and 'Bridgeton', take us to the heart of the poem. On the map, the place is Bridgeton, but to those who live there it is Brigton. One name is a simple tag applied to a district of the city, but the other evokes the historical and linguistic community and culture which exist there. An outsider can know precisely where Bridgeton is while understanding nothing at all about Brigton. So, the poem suggests, it is with many popular images of Glasgow. They may not be inaccurate, but they are totally inadequate as an account of the lives they describe.

The deliberately stereotypical account of the gang warfare of the '20s and '30s within the poem seems to come not so much from reality as from highly-coloured literary descriptions as found in such a novel as Alexander McArthur and Kingsley Long's notorious *No Mean City* (1935); there is no sensitivity to the nuances of a real situation. Morgan's poem argues that the people who lived in those times cannot be adequately represented in such a two-dimensional melodramatic manner. The poem breaks with the stereotype in the line 'No, but it isn't the violence they remember . . .' to offer a more subtle and convincing appraisal of the people who mourned Fullerton. What they remember is the 'legend' of a man who offered some kind of leadership and unity 'in the bad times'. Whatever the reality of his criminality, he stands as a symbol of their community's ability to cleave together in a crisis. Its history is more complex than we might think, more intricate than stereotypes allow; the closing lines insist on the importance of deeper understanding:

> Go from the grave. The shrill flutes
> are silent, the march dispersed.
> Deplore what is to be deplored,
> and then find out the rest.

MORGAN'S DIVERSITY

Since the 1960s Morgan has written less and less explicitly about Glasgow. A creative restlessness is a deeply rooted part of his personality. In poetry he seems to find constant means of surprising and therefore renewing himself. His work has taken a number of dazzlingly diverse directions over the last three decades.

In the 1980s he was at his most imaginatively liberated when working in set forms. In one of his most ambitious and successful works, *Sonnets from Scotland* (1984), written in the aftermath of the failed devolution referendum of the 1970s, he uses the apparently limited patterns of the sonnet while ranging widely for his subjects across the vast tract of time between Scotland's distant past and its remote future, to create surprising combinations and to project both disturbing and exhilarating possibilities that combine the real and the fantastic. The poem-sequence is in a sense one long poem, made up like a mosaic from individual pieces. Similarly, in 'Byron at 65', the poet reviews his life in a lengthy and intricate soliloquy in the Byronic 'Don Juan' stanza.

The move away from 'Glasgow poems', however, may also have been stimulated by the limitations he found in the genre as well as by a natural inclination to change poetic tack. Morgan, a Romantic poet in modern guise, is much taken by such themes as the indomitability of the human spirit, which is seemingly incapable of doing anything other than persisting, no matter what horrors it encounters, or even brings upon itself. At times, in his Glasgow poems, Morgan seems to be willing large conclusions from mundane incidents. Examples of this can be found in 'In the Snack-Bar', 'Trio' and 'Glasgow Green', where large rhetorical effects emerge rather overtly from the preceding city reality.

LOVE POEMS

It is in his love poetry that Morgan most successfully indicates how the inner emotional life and the external concrete world shape one another. The barrier between 'matter' and 'spirit' becomes permeable to the point of disappearance. In poems like 'One Cigarette' and 'At the Television Set', we are reminded that love is always love in a particular place and at a particular time; it is coloured by its setting. The images of the cigarette and the television have cultural associations; as for instance, the cigarette and the romantic movie, which emphasise the existence of the lovers and their emotion within a ever-pressing external context, the outside world, which is nevertheless used to feed and colour their private feeling.

SCIENCE FICTION THEMES

The range of styles and subjects in Morgan's work should not blind us to his essential, if implicit, didacticism. He is rarely content, even in his love poetry, simply to evoke a particular mood; his need to draw conclusions from experience is strong. As with his Glasgow poems, the love poems do not ultimately satisfy the larger purposes that struggle to be fulfilled in Morgan's writing. The best of his later poetry uncovers human truths in subjects that are at first sight out of the ordinary. In fact, the title of his 1973 collection, *From Glasgow to Saturn*, indicates the direction as well as the range of his work. His poetry is most potent and relevant when it seems to have moved furthest away from ordinary experience. In particular, the science fiction genre has served Morgan well. In his poetry, science fiction has come to serve the same purpose as myth does in the poetry of Edwin Muir. Action occurs on the kind of epic scale which allows it comfortably to carry the weight of symbolic significance. 'In Sobieski's Shield' and 'From the Domain of Arnheim' are on such a scale, producing with natural ease the large resonances that sit uncomfortably in some of his Glasgow poems and raising in a spacious context the questions about the identity and stature of humanity that clearly concern Morgan. Some of the later sonnets in *Sonnets from Scotland* also catch this larger and cosmic note.

The range and versatility of Morgan's poetry cannot adequately be summed up here. From his experiments in concrete poetry through sequences like 'From the Video Box' and 'An Alphabet of Goddesses' to his most recent public performances of poetry accompanied by a jazz group, he has covered and is still covering a vast domain of poetic expression. And this is not to mention his translations both of poetry and drama from different languages. Whatever the arguments may be about the overall quality of his poetry, and the final judgement will be a long time in the making, it is clear that Edwin Morgan has been the most versatile and experimental of poets in Scotland in the period since 1945, the closest in spirit to a true 'Makar'.

Liz Lochhead (b. 1947)

The charge is often made against the Scottish literary world that it has been excessively male-dominated. Most of the writers who have achieved publication and critical success over many generations have been men, and the place of women in the Scottish literary tradition has, until quite recently, been regarded as marginal. This is only starting to be remedied; the recent publication, *A History of Scottish Women's Writing* (1997) is an important milestone in this process. It would be easy to gain the impression that hardly any women in Scotland wrote poetry in the period after 1945 until recent decades. The standard anthologies give very little representation; *Voices of our Kind* (3rd edition, 1987) included only two women poets, a 100 per cent increase over the first edition (1971).

Liz Lochhead has been a significant figure in this issue. It would be simplistic and patronising to suggest that she has been a kind of role model for women poets since her first publication, *Memo for Spring*, in 1972; but it is undeniable that, over the last twenty-five years, there has been an upsurge in the numbers of women poets in Scotland.

MEMO FOR SPRING

Liz Lochhead was born in Motherwell and, after a Lanarkshire upbringing and education, trained at Glasgow School of Art. However, she was also writing, and many of the poems in *Memo for Spring* were completed by the time she left art college. *Memo for Spring* was a best-seller in poetic terms and established Lochhead's reputation immediately. The title suggests that the poems, and indeed the book as a whole, should be thought of as observations of particular moments rather than as final conclusions. Lochhead was widely praised for the vividness of phrase and sharpness of eye which gave these observations their freshness. The nature of her work has altered considerably with the passage of time, but those qualities have continued to be central to her success. In 1984, *Memo for Spring* was incorporated into a larger collection, *Dreaming Frankenstein*.

'GETTING BACK'

A poem such as 'Getting Back' (*Memo for Spring*) provides a good example of her vividness of phrase. It particularly highlights her gift for putting timeworn expressions into new settings that restore their power. Lochhead has a creative and deft way with a cliché. The speaker describes a phone call to a lover on their return to Scotland after having spent four months on different sides of the world. As she contemplates that separation from the apparent safety of its conclusion, she is inclined to consider it glamorous. Her descriptions embellish it: 'You/Had done with the sun by the time I got round to it.' The words 'got round' refer both to the movement of the planet and to the individual's choice to get out of bed and face the daylight. The deftness of the description is being savoured in a poem which might be poised to celebrate reunion. The last few lines, however, reveal that the couple's past lives cannot be so easily resumed. Separation has indeed killed their relationship. The last line is a tour de force, wrenching the poem away from objective description of the conversation and voicing instead the speaker's reaction: 'Don't you remember the girl I'm a dead ringer for?' The contemporary phrase 'dead ringer' puns on her roles as a telephone caller. She has 'rung' up only to discover that her significance for the man is 'dead', just as his is for her. The words also work in their conventional sense; 'dead ringer' suggests that she is physically the same as she was before while recognising that she is no longer the same person. The phrase 'dead ringer' makes a distinction even as it acknowledges a resemblance.

LATER DEVELOPMENT

Other poems like 'After a Warrant Sale' (*Memo for Spring*) and 'Laundrette' (*Islands*, 1978) show Lochhead's ability to make burnt-out language transmit meaning and, in the latter case, to create vivid dramatic description. Both of these qualities find a fuller expression and a more expansive development in later stages of her writing career. Lochhead, in a comment on a selection of her poems, noted that she turned her back on the kind of writing which made her initial reputation. Perhaps, despite the successes of individual pieces, there was something frustrating about the role of observer which she assumed in her earlier poems. There may be a dangerous degree of detachment for her in that stance, which produces a certain glibness of treatment. Sometimes it seems that the advertising slogan is the most obvious influence on her writing of that period. We should not disparage her gift for memorable phrase-making, but there are occasions in her poems when it seems to apply gloss to subjects that it should instead strip bare. Too often the love poems produce a neatly-turned poignancy or self-mocking irony as a substitute for a fuller exploration of the emotions. Lochhead herself said that she had come to suspect that irony is a way of expressing opinions without taking responsibility for them.

OLD MYTHS, NEW MEANINGS: 'TAM LIN' AND 'RAPUNZSTILTSKIN'

A fruitful new line of development was born when, like Edwin Morgan, Liz Lochhead was able to find a greater resonance by turning from simple realism towards a more stylised and genre-rooted poetry. She came to be especially attracted by 'familiar mother-tongue legendary, folk-tale oral traditions'. This has been particularly noticeable in her collections *The Grimm Sisters* (1981) and *Dreaming Frankenstein* (1984), in which she draws upon fairy tales and ballads, as well as literary sources, finding vivid psychological and sexual implications and resonances in the popular mythologies which had grown up around such sources as the Gothic horrors of Dracula and Frankenstein. 'Tam Lin's Lady' retells the traditional ballad from the female, perhaps feminist, point of view. Lochhead cleverly finds modern-day equivalents for the elements of the traditional story about the brave and resourceful girl who releases her lover from the spell cast on him by the Faerie Queen. In Lochhead's version, the girl plays truant from school and meets a man in a park. He already lives with a woman but claims to be unhappy, and the girl eventually wins him away and marries him. Lochhead's achievement is to keep the story effective on three levels. At its simplest, 'Tam Lin's Lady' is an economical piece of story-telling, in which, as in the ballads, a few telling details sketch in the characters. The poem also works as an entertaining travesty of the original. Like so much of Lochhead's later work, it seems designed as much for public performance as for the page. She derives broad bawdy humour from the original ballad's talk of imprisonment in fairyland, but what is mainly being mocked is the modern Tam Lin's spiel to his schoolgirl lover. He improbably portrays his existing lover as a monster to try and hold on to the girl's affections. This leads us to the poem's most important level, that is, as a critique of the original ballad. In that, Janet the heroine gains stature by clinging to the shifting shape of Tam in his enchanted powerlessness; in Lochhead's version, the man's transformations are those of a weak and unstable personality. In the ballad, the woman represents only salvation for the hero; in the poem, she is an individual in her own right, and the main transformations will be hers in the future as she develops beyond her unworthy lover. After Lochhead, it is impossible to read the original 'Tam Lin' without feeling that there is something unsavoury about its hero.

A poem which fully exemplifies Lochhead's ability to infuse old legends and mythologies with new and feminist meaning is 'Rapunzstiltskin'. The reader must know the folk-tales of 'Rapunzel' and 'Rumpelstiltskin' to gather the meaning and delightful ironic humour of the modernised versions – and to recognise how cleverly two archetypal human situations are being exploited and fused. The style is contemporary laconic and laid back, beginning in mid-situation (note the worldly shorthand ampersand) '& just when our maiden had got / good & used to her isolation . . .'); this, implies Lochhead, goes on all the time, it's part of our modern world-behaviour. This maiden lives in a tower which we quickly realise is high-rise; other references, modern clichés, and metaphors pull us from legendary to modern, but always maintain the underlying fairy-tale situations. Rapunzel was trapped in a tower, and had to lower her hair for her rescuing knight to reach her; Rumpelstiltskin was the goblin who seemingly rescued the maiden-to-be-princess, but tried to take away the princess's first-born, and was thwarted by her guessing the answer to the riddle of his name.

Fully enjoying the poem depends on the reader seeing that the lady whose sad tale this is begins as Rapunzel but ends up as Rapunzstiltskin, an intolerable merging with Rumpelstiltskin. Additionally, the readers have to form their own picture of who the maiden and her rescuer are – she seems to be a still-attractive spinster, getting on perhaps in years, almost happy – and he seems to be a bit stupid but 'sort of gorgeous', though he 'hollers' 'like a fireman in some soap opera' (a nice Hollywood turn of phrase which places him mid-Atlantic?). They are not of course, actually saying to each other what they appear to be saying; these clichés and questions are the unspoken messages and desires between them, made more subtle in that both are acting roles. She, being female, has to overlook his stupidity, and to present herself as trapped – so that he can release her inner self. As the poem moves on, however, and she lets down her hair, metaphorically (re-enacting Rapunzel's situation), the 'lifelines' that she throws her modern prince are designed to make him pop the important question. She is becoming not the old hag inside, but the goblin who insists on answers. And being a modern version of the legendary prince (and perhaps not as stupid as his clichés might suggest) he manages to avoid asking the right questions, for all she hints, beautifies, cuts her hair (farewell to Rapunzel?). The poem's ending, as she stamps her foot through floorboards in tantrum, and 'as finally she tore herself in two', reveals the plight of women through the ages, disallowed from frankness, exploited by the pretences of males, and finally trapped again in loneliness. Lochhead has brought us into contemporary Scotland in the contemporary world.

DRAMATIC WRITING

The simultaneous farce and seriousness of 'Tam Lin's Lady' illustrate the richness found by Liz Lochhead in a genre which allowed her to write from myth as well as from life. It is as a verse story-teller, as a public performer of her own verse and sketches, and as a dramatist that Lochhead has most fully developed. This is demonstrated in her collections, *True Confessions and New Clichés* (1985) and *Bagpipe Muzak* (1991), and most triumphantly in her plays, especially *Dracula* and *Mary Queen of Scots Got Her Head Chopped Off* first performed in 1985 and 1987 respectively, two of the most important Scottish plays of recent decades. The condition of women in society, and especially Scottish society, has emerged as a continuing motif in Liz Lochhead's writing, helping her to reach a wide and sympathetic audience on a popular, indeed populist level, largely unattained by other Scottish poets of the period.

PART THREE: CONTEMPORARY SCOTTISH POETRY

Millennial poetry

How does contemporary Scottish poetry chart the complexities and contradictions of living between one millennium and the next? This part will
provide one answer to that question, but also point towards others. The new
generation of poets will be set within the context of their mentors in the older
and middle generations of poets now writing. Reference will be made to
poems in two major anthologies of the 1990s, Douglas Dunn's *Faber Book of
Twentieth-Century Scottish Poetry* (1992) and Donny O'Rourke's *Dream State: The
New Scottish Poets* (1994), but individual writers will also be grouped in ways
which may help readers make sense of a fluid and busy scene.

Just keeping track of the sense is difficult. *Contemporary Poets* (1996), a
bibliographical guide to 'the world's most important English-language poets'
gives details of thirty Scottish poets. Not bad for a small nation? But Dunn's
anthology adds twenty more, and O'Rourke's a further seventeen. A recent
selection (*Comparative Criticism* 19, 1997) adds another five.

Scottish poets, then, swim in a crowded pool, and as in most public pools,
the atmosphere is noisy, the reflections confusing, and the swimmers of all
shapes and sizes. That some at least of the new wave of poets sport 'post-
modern' logos on their swimwear can create further problems: how seriously
or playfully are we meant to read their work?

A new generation?

There were mixed emotions (even among the winners) when Scottish poets
gained seven out of the twenty places in the 'New Generation Poets'
promotion organised in 1994 by the Poetry Society and Waterstone's Book-
sellers. On the one hand there was satisfaction that the work of John
Burnside, Robert Crawford, Carol Ann Duffy, W. N. Herbert, Mick Imlah,
Kathleen Jamie and Don Paterson, individualistic and varied as it is, constituted such a strongly accented group among the multiple voices of new
British poetry. Yet there was also an ironic self-awareness of the constructed
nature of such media/literary events, of the many excellent poets not in the
top twenty, and (particularly in the Scottish context) of the precursors of
these new poets among the older generation of writers.

Every new generation, of course, takes its bearings from earlier ones, even
if that means beginning by heading off in a different direction. The powerful
presence of parental poets must somehow be evaded, or readdressed in

different terms. Thus we might see, for example, Edwin Morgan taking the supposedly intractable technical vocabulary of the later MacDiarmid and releasing it into new worlds of science and space technology; or Robert Crawford turning from machine to information technology as a domain for poetry.

Distance is another way of finding aesthetic space. Younger Scottish poets such as Alan Riach in New Zealand or Peter McCarey in Switzerland also have their precursors in previous generations: Gael Turnbull (b. 1926) whose Migrant Press followed his medical practice through Canada, California and Cumbria, or Robin Fulton (b. 1937), teaching in Norway for more than twenty years. Nowadays travel is likely to be quicker, or even virtual, as email and the world-wide web put poets in contact with other cultural centres as well as with each other. Such rapid juxtapositions intrigue the poetic mind, and contribute to what is 'post-modern' about current writing.

Post-modernism is not a definite term, but applied to literature it is generally seen as an eclectic approach, often given to parody, pastiche or cross-references between cultures and texts. This reflects the co-existence in complex modern societies of lifestyles, images and opinions which are all electronically but powerfully present through television and computer screens. It also signals a relativistic and personal approach to social values made possible by multinational capitalism and liberal ideas in education.

British-based Modernist writing at the beginning of the twentieth century (the generation of Eliot, Pound, Lawrence, Joyce and MacDiarmid) generally reads as a journeying through the social and technological changes of a rapidly modernising world (made visible in warfare, transport, urban life, relationships between the sexes) in search of some future coherence, which might be made present in artistic terms, or at least glimpsed, through image, symbol or myth. Post-modernist writing, in contrast, has been seen as modernity without illusion: as an exhilarating surrender to living without the security of that possible coherence, and an enjoyment in experiencing the sheer number of possibilities, the excess of values available.

That such choice exists only for a tiny favoured minority in mainly Western societies, of course, leads in some cases to a more actively political post-modern concern. This is linked to the rise in the last thirty years of Marxist, feminist and psychoanalytical theories applied to literature, with the aim of exposing the contradictions inherent in some of the great 'meta-narratives' or hidden value systems which control relationships between cultures and people. The relative values of English and Scots as poetic languages, or the relative power of men and women in Scottish society, would be examples of such taken-for-granted systems which it is the post-modern poet's job to

781

challenge or subvert. And contemporary Scottish poets, like their predecessors, are rarely neutral.

The informationists

The most self-consciously avant-garde of the younger contemporary poets
write against this background of ideas. 'Informationism' is a jargon term for a
body of poetry which itself manipulates media and academic jargon for
aesthetic or satirical effect. Most of the Informationists have strong academic
backgrounds; all respond to the 'information revolution'; they establish and
exploit literary magazines and reviews (much as Eliot, Pound and MacDiarmid did earlier) to advance the cause of a 'Macavantgarde'; they co-operate,
co-edit and co-write. Here Robert Crawford (b. 1959), W. N. Herbert (b.
1961), David Kinloch (b. 1959) and Richard Price (b. 1966) are used to
exemplify key features of Informationist practice, although it is in their
individual treatments of shared themes, of course, that the real worth of their
writing resides.

The first three met when pursuing doctoral studies at Oxford University in
the 1980s. At the cultural heart of English literary life, they discovered that
the Scots language of their childhood (fuelled by MacDiarmid-like raids on
Scottish language dictionaries) enabled them to say new things about
contemporary life in an increasingly dis-United Kingdom. *Verse*, the magazine
co-founded by Crawford and Kinloch at this time, was strongly international
in outlook, and their grounding in dialect and locality enables them to play
off the intimate and familiar tune of old Scots words against the 'post-
colonial' literatures developing world-wide, as well as the new transnational
electronic systems of communication within which most of humanity is now
living.

This new technology enables Robert Crawford to re-assert the paradoxical
qualities of a modern Scotland which, like a microchip, is 'crammed with
intimate expanses', containing vast opportunities for knowledge and self-
knowledge: 'to be miniaturised is not small-minded' ('Scotland').

Knowledge of all sorts is important to him both as a subject for ironic verse
(see his 'John Logie Baird' and 'Alba Einstein') and as a way of creating an
alternative 'great tradition' of boldly encyclopaedic Scottish thinkers, who in
codifying human knowledge also open it up democratically to their fellow
citizens. Not surprisingly perhaps, there is a willed or programmatic quality
about some of Crawford's early poems, but self-knowledge has increasingly
come through exploration of family relationships and emotional needs, as his
collections *Masculinity* (1996) and *Spirit Machines* (1999) demonstrate.

W. N. Herbert's work is wilful in different ways. Fiercely intelligent and imaginative, he possesses most confidently of all the younger poets the surge and pitch of MacDiarmid's vision, and is able to challenge English readers by the sheer 'otherness' of his cultural vision, and Scottish readers by the visionary and quasi-fictional Scotland he creates. In 'The Gairfish', for instance, 1,000 left-wing radical poets come riding up the Tay estuary on the backs of porpoises, or gairfish, to shock the Scottish bourgeois out of their complacency.

As a medium of poetry, Scots language seems best suited to expressing three particular states of consciousness: satire or insult; domestic tenderness; and an awed apprehension of the mystery of the universe. Again like MacDiarmid, Herbert manages to combine these even within the compass of a single poem – often by a surprising succession of metaphors. This characterises his English language poetry too: the closing lines of one poem move from 'weed in a wave's translucence' through a pane of glass, a giant's grave, the first name of both his grandmothers, to 'all of Scotland, rolling up and down on death's yoyo' ('Dingle Dell').

Such innately anarchic creative power has its drawbacks. The title of his first major collection, *Forked Tongue* (1994), signals not only the English/Scots language choice facing Scottish speakers in different social situations, but also the duplicitous nature of much human language, including his own. *Cabaret McGonagall* (1996) and *The Laurelude* (1998) offer a remarkable concentration of Scottish Border and cross-Border obsessions, carried off with a wild energy which manages to be both utterly modern while also looking back to an older visionary ballad tradition. His magazine *Gairfish* is more polemical and self-consciously avant-garde than *Verse*, quirky with an outrageous giftedness which can both attract and also disturb the reader.

David Kinloch's is a quieter voice, but disturbing all the same. His Scots, as a socially suppressed language, is linked with the counter-culture of homosexuality through the figure of Dustie-Fute, a wandering acrobat whose queer Scots terms somehow represent what is both suspect and tender. The impact of AIDS ('love's curious virus') on individuals and relationships is recorded with compassionate concentration in his English language poems 'Envoi: Warmer Bruder' and 'The Clinic'. As a modern linguist, Kinloch sees contemporary Scottish poetry as crucially linked to translation, in its careful attempts to find words to communicate accurately and with dignity the dimensions of pleasure and loss which belong to life at the end of the twentieth century.

Slightly younger, Richard Price (b. 1966) is based in London, where his work as a curator of Modern British Collections at the British Library keeps him in touch with avant-garde and experimental poetry. He has written literary and cultural criticism as well as co-founding *Gairfish* and *Southfields* magazines and three small imprints: Vennel, Southfields and Au Quai. His Informationist anthology *Contraflow on the Super Highway* (1994) helped define that movement, and a recent collection, *Perfume and Petrol Fumes* (1999) exemplifies it in ways that are individualistic, witty and tender.

While the Informationists claim to be doing new things, however, some might argue that their play with language, meaning and politics is derived from Edwin Morgan and W. S. Graham in the older generation, and from the demotic satire of Tom Leonard in the 1960s and 1970s. Perhaps their self-conscious use of new diction and imagery even relates to a Scottish tendency for expansive verbal display that reaches back to the aureate diction of Dunbar. In their paradoxical pursuit of a poetry at once intellectual and colloquial, does the memorable expression of human experience somehow vanish? It may be interesting to try to spot already in particular poems the points where their personal interests and values are beginning to pull this group apart.

The exiles

Some poets have already pulled apart, working overseas but still defining their poetry as Scottish. For Peter McCarey (b. 1956), Alan Riach (b. 1957) and Ian Bamforth (b. 1959), distance from Scottish culture, and the simultaneous translation of the Scots linguistic experience into French, Russian, or antipodean English, gives their work a generally clear-eyed quality, with a satirical edge and a preference for open or experimental forms. Bamforth's obsession is the strictly sectarian religion of his childhood, generalised into a 'Calvinist Geography' with a richly oppressive verbal surface. Riach's is ancestry, landscape and distance: he rewinds and fast-forwards memories and connections. McCarey's is the evasions of political language, and the contrasts between hunger and plenty in different societies.

These poets also join a line of poets in exile that stretches back to the earliest poems of Scotland: the Irish Columba's 'Altus Prosator' and the *peregrinus* tradition of Celtic monks on wandering missionary journeys in Europe. This finds an odd contemporary expression in the work of Kenneth White (b. 1936), whose *The Bird Path* (1989) and *Handbook for the Diamond Country* (1990) record in a blend of Celtic and Zen mysticism his search for unity or ecstasy beyond a world of separation and distraction. Questions remain about the poetic success of any exploration of emptiness, yet the work has achieved a considerable following in a present-day Scotland perhaps hungry for new articulations of spiritual experience.

His contemporary Robin Fulton has developed a more remarkable spiritual poetry in a Nordic and Lutheran landscape. His *Coming Down to Earth and Spring is Soon* (1990) reveals how his earlier detached lyricism has deepened into a meditative poetry of real woods, lakes, light and music. He is a notable translator of Swedish poetry and has learned in particular from the intense and disturbing imagery of Tranströmer, for example, in 'Travelling Alone':

> The countless forests we pass hour after hour
> They are anonymous with such grace.
> Would we feel safer
> if all the dead came back and stood waiting?

Perhaps all such poetry of exile raises questions about whether distance diminishes or intensifies a Scottish vision. How authentic or immediate can the work continue to be (and yet, do we not also need to see ourselves as others see us, from a distance)? Exile can work both ways, of course. The New Zealand poet, Gerrie Fellows, now based in Glasgow, made an immediate impact with her exploration of the Scottish 'diaspora' of Empire in *The Powerlines* (2000) and elsewhere. There are signs, too, of an emergent Scots-Asian writing, expressing the cultural diversity, and tensions, of a new Scotland.

Urbane and Electronic Ruralists

This subtitle hints at the sort of dichotomy for which much has been perhaps too easily claimed in Scottish literary studies. Scotland's geography and history do seem to combine to sustain difference: Highland/Lowland; Gaelic/Scots; West/East; rural/urban; island/mainland; Catholic/Protestant. Electronic technology, however, holds out the potential, at least, for overleaping distance and difference, and it is interesting to note that the contemporary poet in whose work the natural world resonates most deeply was for many years a 'knowledge engineer' in computing.

The poetry of John Burnside (b. 1955) typically explores the tangled boundaries between the natural and the supernatural, suburbs and countryside, the dead and the reborn. The mysteriousness of life glimpsed from the corner of the eye or heart in warmly-lit domestic settings is as real in his work as the darkness of manipulation and abuse; different corners of the same garden. It is difficult to express in brief quotation the strange blending of threat and promise in his poetry. Here as an example is 'Urban Myths':

> networks of bone and nerve in drifted leaves
> snagging the rake; a perfume of resurrection
> filling our throats, sweeter than we expected,
> the scent of a garden surrendered to someone else . . .

The physicality of such quasi-mystical perceptions, made present here in the sound effects of consonant and vowel as well as in the air of scientific observation, is typical. Burnside's voice was immediately recognisable in *The Hoop* (1988) and a series of collections has followed: *Common Knowledge* (1991), *Feast Days* (1992), *The Myth of the Twin* (1994), *Swimming in the Flood* (1995) and *A Normal Skin* (1997). Crucial to his vision seems to have been the sense of psychological and linguistic fracture that came when his family moved from Fife to industrial middle England when he was eleven. Like Edwin Muir, this raw dislocation seems to have sensitised him to the lyrical surfaces of a mythic narrative of loss with Christian (and also mysteriously pre-Christian) echoes and signs, locked into landscape and human habitations. The ambiguities of its beauty and cruelty are deeply explored: the title of his recent collection *The Asylum Dance* (2000) catches that resonance.

Gerry Cambridge (b. 1959) edits *The Dark Horse*, a magazine with international links to the New Formalist movement in US poetry, with its commitment to metrical and rhyming poetry. Sonnets, villanelles and rondeaux do figure in *The Dark Horse*, countering expansiveness and confessional statement. This is saved from artificiality in Cambridge's own writing by the sense of a poetic self-education being intelligently undertaken, and by the accuracy of his naturalist's eye and knowledge of rural life. His work in farming communities in Ayrshire and Orkney balances art with reality in *The Shellhouse* (1995) and in his vivid photographic and poetic studies of the natural world in *Nothing but Heather!* (1999). He also practises more open forms, and his work is a useful reminder that to be 'radical' essentially means to return to the roots of the matter, not merely to follow poetical fashion.

Behind these sophisticated rural poets lie others of the middle generation born in the late 1940s and early 1950s, who have achieved much (but not a key anthology to define their achievement). John Glenday (b. 1952) has published two remarkable collections: *The Apple Ghost* (1989) and *Undark* (1995). Douglas Dunn republishes the title poem to the first of these, a numinous episode in the Scottish tradition of poetic hauntings. Andrew Greig (b. 1951) has a variation on this, in 'The Maid and I'. His recent collection *Western Swing* (1994) is an ambitious, dramatic and humorous quest poem, which deliberately mixes styles and discourses in its exploration of the human search for both spiritual and physical fulfillment.

Ron Butlin (b. 1949), Tom Pow (b. 1950) and Brian McCabe (b. 1951) also write a subtle masculine poetry, born out of concerns for inheritance, personal history and significance: the combination of sensitivity and endurance in all of these poets is exemplified perhaps in McCabe's *Body Parts* (1999), an inventive and witty series of projections into human and animal life. Stewart Conn (b. 1936) is of an older generation in the same mode, if more urbane: his exploration of the beauty of art, the passage of time, and the strength and guilt inherent in relationships is exemplary, and his background in broadcasting ensures a vivid pictorial sense of people and place: see his *Stolen Light: Selected Poems* (1999).

Reading these Electronic Ruralists raises (un)certain questions. Do they offer a clearer vision of the irredeemably mixed nature of modern Scottish life than the younger generation? Or do they represent only the insecurities of a generation caught between the great Modernists and the postmodernists? Perhaps their strength in the depiction of place and personality, and their formal skills developed over years, will prove of more lasting relevance than we (or they?) seem to suspect.

The new women

A few sentences ago the phrase 'masculine poetry' was used, although with some uncertainty. Does gender exist in poetry? If there is 'male' writing, what exactly is 'female' writing, and is it different from feminist writing? Catherine Kerrigan's *Anthology of Scottish Women Poets* (1991), and Gifford and McMillan's *A History of Scottish Women's Writing* (1997), demonstrate that the place of Scottish women writers in a tradition hitherto mainly defined by men – with a consequent absence or erasure of women's voices – has at last begun to be addressed. But questions still exist about the standards of judgement which should be applied, or suspended, when reading the work of any group of underprivileged writers. And questions even exist about the questions: is every act of reading inescapably 'gendered', or does creative writing of itself enable us to slip free of physiology and conditioning?

Because the range of women's writing has been so recently reclaimed, little more can be done here than to refer in admiration to the humanity of Elma Mitchell (b. 1919) in the older generation (for example, the multiple energies and ironies of her 'Thoughts after Ruskin'), and the intellectual subtleties of Veronica Forrest-Thomson (b. 1947), too early lost in 1975. Alison Fell (b. 1944) and Valerie Gillies (b. 1948) are others of that unanthologised generation.

Male poets bulk larger than female ones in most anthologies, but overtaking any disparity of numbers, three women poets are outstanding in the new generation. The voices of Kathleen Jamie, Carol Ann Duffy and Jackie Kay are at once radical, strong and distinctive. The sheer impact of their work relegates issues of gender and identity to a secondary level, while the poems themselves deal energetically, paradoxically, honestly, or tenderly with the realities of those very experiences.

Kathleen Jamie (b. 1962) studied philosophy and practised mountaineering. There is an intellectual toughness and a steady aspiration about her poetry, which often appears to proceed by a traversing motion, with strongly gripped images as pivots of progress: see her 'The Republic of Fife' or 'Permanent Cabaret' for examples, with the latter also revealing a tendency to use emblematic characters such as acrobats, queens or princesses to symbolise aspects of the energy of her own personality. The Queen of Sheba lends her triumphant title to Jamie's 1994 collection, and draws readers and listeners into the subversive sources of her power: but that drive has been evident from the earliest work, most obviously in 'The Way We Live', the title poem of her 1987 collection:

> Pass the tambourine, let me bash out praises
> to the Lord God of movement, to Absolute
> non-friction, flight and the scary side:
> death by avalanche, birth by failed contraception.

The experience of modern women enabled to travel, to climb, to not have to be shielded, is evoked here. The act of climbing evokes spiritual journeying also: Jamie is drawn to the human and mystical perspectives of Julian of Norwich, or the wandering Buddhist monk who appears on her Tibetan journey to *The Autonomous Region* (1993). Back home, the tone of her poems of love and domestic life is unaffected and unencumbered: she wants to sweep things clear of hypocrisy, to leave room for bliss and mixed emotions. Recent poems have seen her developing a voice in Scots to articulate messages from her own or Scotland's past (as in 'Arraheids' and 'Den of the Old Men').

Such an authentic spoken voice is also a source of strength in the writing of Carol Ann Duffy (b. 1955). Again and again her poems touch the linguistic scar of an early move to England, and the requirement to speak with a different tongue: the theme of 'Originally' and 'The Way My Mother Speaks'. Unlike John Burnside, she has learned to mimic the tones and turns of English social and commercial speech, and uses this to satirical effect in such poems as 'Translating the English, 1989'. This mimetic skill is also played off against US ('The B Movie') and Scottish working-class English ('Politico').

Coming to terms with the ambiguities of her own Scots-Irish-Catholic upbringing, she can be both antagonistic (as in 'Ash Wednesday 1984') and yet also often, here in 'Plainsong', filled with a spiritual pathos:

Listening. The words you have for things die
in your heart, but grasses are plainsong,
patiently chanting the circles you cannot repeat
or understand. This is your homeland
Lost One, Stranger who speaks with tears.

In *The Other Country* (1990) and *Mean Time* (1993) she has moved away from the earlier dramatic monologues towards a more personal, autobiographical style. Whether exploring conventional or lesbian relationships, she is dramatically direct and insightful, and the range of her poetic gifts is the equal of any British women poet now writing.

Jackie Kay (b. 1961) adds the further outsider credentials of being black and adopted, and produces a poetry which is lively, open-hearted and in no way self-pitying. Beginning like Duffy as a dramatist, she creates confident poetic monologues, or dialogues of voices at cross-purposes. Her writing on the subject of AIDS and bisexuality is gay in both senses; shot through with tenderness and a passion to be authentically accepted and self-accepting: 'Close Shave', 'Lighthouse Wall', and 'Pounding Rain' are good examples. Her recent collection *Other Lovers* (1993) has several purposefully sustained sequences, notably one on the blues singer, Bessie Smith.

This section started with questions about the nature of women's poetry. It prompts the further question, whether the existence of such a sustained body of work from these three poets makes such questions irrelevant, or even more necessary? And what of younger women writers such as Angela McSeveney (*Coming Out With It*, 1992) or Kate Clanchy (*Slattern*, 1995): does the presence of such powerful 'older sisters' make the development of their own voices as women poets easier or more difficult? Feminist awareness among Scottish women poets is gathered in *The Wild Women Anthology* (2000).

The new Gaels

The uneasy co-existence of our three languages has been suggested as one reason for the numbers of Scottish linguists and lexicographers, as well as of poets drawn to translation. One of the most interesting developments in contemporary Gaelic poetry is the amount being written by non-native speakers, possibly as a result of a growing cultural interest through the 1990s in Celtic music, art and spirituality. The convention of printing a translation (generally English but sometimes Scots) alongside the Gaelic conveys some sense of the subtleties of Gaelic verbal patterning, and may encourage further writing by non-Gaelic poets. This process is not new, as the poetry of George Campbell Hay (b. 1915) and William Neill (b. 1922) shows, but it has become more marked in the last two decades in Scotland, as it did much earlier in Ireland. Currently, Christopher Whyte (b. 1952), Roddy Gorman (b. 1960) and Meg Bateman (b. 1959) are the best known of these new Gaels.

Three recent collections stand out: Meg Bateman's subtle *Lightness and Other Poems* (1997), Rody Gorman's wirier *Fax* (1996) and Aonghas MacNeacail's prize-winning *A Proper Schooling and Other Poems* (1996). MacNeacail (b. 1942) is a native Gaelic poet of the middle generation who blends contemporary and innovative approaches with discernible elements of the older bardic rhetoric. The section from 'the great snow battle' in Dunn's anthology (*The Faber Book of Twentieth-Century Scottish Poetry*, 1992) is an excellent earlier example of this in his work.

What must writers reared among native Gaelic resonances make of this new group of Gaelic/Scots/English writers? Is it akin to reading Scots-Asian poetry, and attended by a similar sense of strange anticipation? – together with a sense, perhaps, of how any good poetry may serve as the best translation possible between individuals, clans and cultures. Rob Mackenzie's *Off Ardglass* (1997) shows the potential of combining Gaelic Scots and English in a macaronic style, and Kevin MacNeil's *Love and Zen in the Outer Hebrides* (1998) combines languages and spiritualities in attractively accessible ways. Black's *An Tuil: Twentieth-Century Scottish Gaelic Verse* (1999) is an impressive anthology of the continued inventiveness of contemporary Gaelic poetry.

East and West Coast individualists

There is a long tradition of Scottish poets who are difficult to categorise, often by choice – for example, Ivor Cutler (b. 1923), Ian Hamilton Finlay (b. 1925), George Macbeth (b. 1932) and Tom Leonard (b. 1944). They are unconformable to fashion and sometimes as awkward to try on as someone else's suit. In the younger generation, Brian Whittingham, Hugh MacMillan and Graham Fulton are examples, their live readings being sharp, and humorous. Most individualists emerge from the West Coast, but with the recent shifting of poetic emphasis to the East Coast examples surface there also.

Frank Kuppner (b. 1951) came to prominence in 1984 with *A Bad Day for the Sung Dynasty,* 500 unrhymed quatrains in which details from Chinese paintings are recorded with photographic detachment and sly humour. Their language catches the odd bathos which sometimes characterises translations of oriental poetry, and there is a refusal to accept the norms of reader expectation or, sometimes, patience. *The Intelligent Observation of Naked Women* (1987) and *Everything is Strange* (1994) continued in this post-modern mode, although the scene might shift to Prague or Glasgow: there is a quasi-scientific observation and a mannered ennui or repetitiveness, broken through occasionally, almost overwhelmingly, by sharp emotion.

Wilful disregard or deliberate disruption of reader expectation also features in the poetry of Don Paterson (b. 1963). He writes a glittering poetry of cruelty, mixing eclectic verbal brilliance, formal elegance and an amorality of stance in his *personae* which can be unsettling. His panache has won prizes, however, and praise for a jaunty nihilism. *Nil Nil* (1993) and *God's Gift to Women* (1997) reveal a knowing sophistication. Street-wise and book-wise references jostle the reader in an autodidactic manner, as the working-class childhood in Dundee and the travelling life as professional jazz musician and poet are held together by sheer willpower and intelligence. Paterson's readers can't ignore him. There is also something deeply Scottish and Calvinistic beneath the manic surface of jokey references to poetry readings as religious services, with himself the mock-minister. These poems often read like justifications of a self-confessed sinner, a new twist to an old Scottish genre. *The Eyes* (1999) is notably more meditative and sombre, however, created out of adaptations from the Spanish poetry of Antonio Machado.

Roddy Lumsden (b. 1966) is an Edinburgh-based individualist who shares Paterson's themes of wine, women and song, and an unsettled lifestyle, but little else. His collection *Yeah Yeah Yeah* (1997) reveals a *persona* as bright and self-aware as Paterson, and as given to wide-ranging reference, but there is nevertheless a humility, humour and self-deprecation about his poems which, allied with their formal elegance, makes them appealing at a human level.

Individualists of their nature resist categorisation and a history, but D. M. Black's *Collected Poems* (1991), published from the 1960s onwards, exemplify the enduring power of a peculiarly Scottish tradition of formal engagement and disturbing subject matter. The temptation is to say that the roots of this tendency reach down into some Calvinist substratum of Scottish cultural life, but there is now an increased awareness of the need to recognise the sheer diversity of Scotland at the start of this millennium. In poetic terms, such a view is exemplified in *Across the Water: Irishness in Modern Scottish Writing* (2000), an anthology which explores the literary impact of Scotland's largest 'minority culture'. Economic migration from Ireland in the nineteenth and twentieth centuries has now created a substantial number of Scottish poets writing out of a subtle sense of difference or the marginal, mainly Catholic but with some significant Scots-Irish Protestant voices too. Such poets include Gerald Mangan, Alan Spence, James McGonigal, Donny O'Rourke and Raymond Friel (as well as others mentioned above, such as Burnside, Cambridge and Whyte). Ancestry cannot and should not be used to label in any simplistic way, of course, and that is why they appear as 'individualists' in this overview. They are, however, a significantly different presence in contemporary poetry, with a sort of lyrical edginess which catches something of modern Scottish life.

Gatekeepers and activists

In conclusion, the temptation simply to list all of the poets missing from this outline has to be resisted. All overviews are doomed to partial failure. It is probably more useful to direct readers to sources of information which will enable them to construct their own anthologies, and certain publishers and places come immediately to mind.

Polygon has built up an impressive list of contemporary poets, with a focus on known writers of the new wave. Scottish Cultural Press has more recently published a growing series of newer poets and anthologies. Canongate Books and Mercat Press also publish poetry, but as part of a wider list. Joy Hendry with *Chapman* magazine and Chapman Publishing has supported a wide range of Scottish poets over many years. The Association for Scottish Literary Studies has published eighteen of its annual *New Writing Scotland* anthologies, in which new poetry in all of the languages of Scotland features strongly. And the Scottish Poetry Library founded in Edinburgh by Tessa Ransford, and now, in a new building, being further developed by Robyn Marsack, is a focal point for poetry resources and performance, with significant outreach to schools and communities all over Scotland.

While the Scottish Poetry Library is well publicised, it is less well-known that the Mitchell Library in Glasgow has the largest collection of poetry in Scotland. Hamish Whyte, who was senior librarian for arts there, is a poet and noted anthologist whose Mariscat Press has also published important collections by Edwin Morgan, such as *Sonnets for Scotland* (1984) and *Demon* (1999); and by Gael Turnbull, such as *For Whose Delight* (1995).

Such small-press activists continue the publishing tradition of Duncan

Glen's *Akros* in the 1960s and 1970s, revived on his return to Scotland in the 1990s. He publishes Price and Turnbull, among others. Those who read widely in or write Scottish poetry soon come to recognise overlapping interconnections, co-editings, co-writings, and this can at first appear too close for comfort, or honesty. And yet contemporary poetry *is* a crowded pool in which people are bound to bump into each other. Moreover, the sheer amount of (largely unpaid) energy being expended for poetry is admirable, as is the way experienced poets and editors spend time helping the less experienced to get started, and to keep afloat – not merely gatekeepers, perhaps, but lifeguards for Scottish poetry.

CHAPTER 39

MODERN SCOTTISH DRAMA

PART ONE: THE 1950s AND AFTER

Scottish theatre in the 1950s

It is difficult to escape a sense of anti-climax about the 1950s in general and about the Scottish theatre in particular. Between 1939 and 1949 at least five theatres and one major theatre company had been started in Scotland; the government had begun to fund the arts; the possibility of a Scottish acting profession had been opened up; a major international festival had begun, and Scotland's dramatic heritage had been displayed there without shame; there had also been a deluge of new plays on Scottish themes by Scottish writers.

By contrast the 1950s look thin. Instead of theatres opening, television forced many to close. The Arts Council became increasingly conservative about what it would and would not fund. The supply of Scottish plays seemed to dry up, and the Edinburgh International Festival became more international than Edinburgh. Without their pilot, the Citizens' drifted with no clear artistic vision. For the reasons already outlined, Unity ceased to exist, and many of their best actors joined the Citizens' company, so removing a useful dialectic from the Scottish theatre. Bridie was gone by 1941; promising writers like Ewan McColl went south to Theatre Workshop.

But it was not all gloom. The Edinburgh International Festival had started in 1947, opening up possibilities; Tyrone Guthrie's 1948 production of Lyndsay's *Satyre of the Thrie Estaitis* would inspire audiences, and, crucially, dramatists, with its remarkably 'modern' structure and stagecraft and its dazzling use of Scots. In 1953 the Gateway Theatre opened in Edinburgh to give a window on Scottish theatre. The professional status of Scottish actors was enhanced, and the coming of television brought new possibilities of employment. There was a mini-vogue for Scottish films, especially those based on the novels of Sir Compton Mackenzie; some fine plays were written in Scots; and the new theatres became much more firmly established in their communities.

Alexander Reid (1914–82)

The debates in the Scottish theatre, however, did not change, and one of the writers who came to prominence in this decade, Alexander Reid, re-opened the question about writing in Scots and reminded us that there was more to the country than slum-living in Glasgow. In two plays, both set in the Borders in the Middle Ages, and which have been very successfully revived by Theatre Alba, *The Lass Wi' the Muckle Mou'* (1950) and *The Warld's Wonder* (1953), he demonstrated his ability to use Scots, but took this slightly further than McLellan by making *The Warld's Wander* a kind of parable for the age of the Cold War, the fight between the two wizards having a metaphorical function. MacDiarmid's call for antisyzygy in drama is met here with the play's move-ment between rational and irrational, this world and the world of the supernatural. The play ends, however, above the clouds with the wizard Michael Scott apostrophising young love and warning the world:

> Whenever the world falls back in the weary rut
> Worship of dogma or the causal chain
> Back to the old brown earth I come again
> To break the shackles on imagination!
> Confound professors and upset the laws!
> Bell out the school and set young fancies free!

The pity is that such glorious sentiments are attached to a flimsy story, however charming the overall effect may be. *The Lass Wi' the Muckle Mou'* again charms, but is really no more than a dramatised Border ballad, with the addition of Scots as rich as any in McLellan's *Toom Byres* (1936) or *The Laird of Torwatletie* (1946).

Scots or English?

The extract quoted above is in English. In the Foreword to *Two Scots Plays* (1958) Alexander Reid explains why this is so:

> The two plays which follow, anglicised versions of plays originally written in Braid Scots with the aim of their performance by the bi-lingual players of the Glasgow Citizens' Theatre, were made by acting on a suggestion of Mr Ivor Brown [who] suggested that if my work, 'the Scots of which would baffle an English audience', could be put into 'near English', it would find an audience elsewhere . . .

795

Robert McLellan always refused to do this and consequently remained unknown south of the Border. Is it possible to say who made the correct decision? Reid goes on to defend his initial use of Scots:

Scots English – except in exceptional cases – stems not out of life but out of literature. At its best, as in R. L. Stevenson, it smells of printer's ink and the English Literature class. It is written out of our educated heads and not out of our whole personalities and it speaks to the head and not to the whole person . . . If we are to fulfil our hope that Scotland may some day make a contribution to World drama as individual and valuable as that made by Norway in the nineteenth and by Ireland in the present century, we can only do so by cherishing not repressing our national peculiarities (including our language), though whether a Scottish National Drama, if it comes to birth, will be written in Braid Scots, or the speech, redeemed for literary purposes, of Argyle Street, Glasgow, or the Kirkgate, Leith, is anyone's guess. That it will be written in some sort of Scots, however, is quite certain. A national drama cannot be created in a language foreign to the people from whom it springs, and the spoken language of Scotland, whatever name we give to it, is not standard English. The root of the Scottish literary revival is a humble recognition that we are what we are, and we must make the best of that. For myself I do not think that either what we are or the culture we belong to needs any apology.

Reid's enthusiasm for the possibilities of Scots language in drama was shared by a few others, including Alexander Scott, who worked with the Citizens' in the early '50s with plays such as *Right Royal* (1950), *Untrue Thomas* (1952) and *Shetland Yarn* (1954). And with the exception of his satire on Edinburgh manners on the love affair of Robert Burns and 'Clarinda' (Agnes Maclehose) in *The Other Dear Charmer* (1951), the plays of Robert Kemp (1908–67) like *Festival Fever* (1956) and *Penny Wedding* (1957) are slighter and less successful than his exemplary Scots translations of Molière, as in *Let Wives Tak Tent* (1948) and *The Laird o'Grippy* (1948) (originally *L'École des Femmes* and *L'Avare*), his adaptation of Lindsay for the 1947 production of *Ane Satyre*, and his radio versions of Henryson's *Fables*. His more ambitious work, like his Bruce play, *King of Scots* (1951), tends to pageantry rather than stage drama, but its treatment of crucial stages in Scottish history inspired others – for example, poet Sydney Goodsir Smith's *The Wallace* (1960) which again had much of pageant, but was more successful in its dramatic power and its rich Scots.

But these were a few, and sadly, Reid's brave words found few echoes through the decade, or indeed through the '60s, so that it might seem to an observer as if Scottish drama gradually became more dormant after 1950, to be awakened by Bill Bryden's kiss at the Lyceum in 1970.

Other 'fifties playwrights

Until the advent of the angry young men in 1956, the 1950s were also a time of theatrical slump in England; and the London stage was, so critics bitterly complained, swamped by US and continental plays. In Scotland, while there was perhaps not the stream of consistently interesting plays there had been in the previous decade, there were, however, some excellent individual plays, covering the whole spectrum of Scottish life. Writers like George Munro (1901–68) continued to produce urban plays for Unity till its demise in 1951 – *Gold in His Boots* (1947) anticipates the Jenkins novel *The Thistle and the Grail* (1954) in its combination of satire on Lowland social deprivation, in its obsession with football, and its religious bigotry. Less well received at the Citizens' was his *The Gay Landscape* (1958), a grim and quirkily written family saga set in Govan and exploring the same theme as Neil Gunn in his 1929 play *The Ancient Fire* about rediscovery of essential Gaelic virtues; the very ambiguous feelings of people from the Highlands about their spiritual incarceration in Glasgow. It serves, yet again, to remind us that there is more to Scotland than Glasgow. Unity continued to influence the theatre through the work of its now disbanded troops, and in 1954 Roddie McMillan's play *All In Good Faith*, very much in the Unity mould, opened at the Citizens' Theatre, to 'unanimous acclaim'. This play is still, in the opinion of many playgoers who remember it, considered a far superior piece to his much more successful play *The Bevellers* (1973).

The popularity of comedy

The plays of Reid, McMillan and Munro, for all their differences, are all sincere and serious attempts to write a Scottish play. The 1950s, however, also saw an upsurge in the kitchen comedy school of Scottish writing. These plays were given credence, unfortunately, by Duncan Macrae, who appeared in many of them, most notably T. M. Watson's charming picture of late-medieval Glaswegian execution techniques, *Johnny Jouk the Gibbet* (1953). This play illustrates the gulf which separates picturesque history as handled by a master – McLellan – and an apprentice – Watson. The play has, of course, brought a great deal of pleasure to many. James Scotland also called on the services of Duncan Macrae in his charming picture of late eighteenth-century Glaswegian social mores, *A Surgeon for Lucinda* (1954), loosely, as in the phrase 'the jacket hung loosely on the skeleton', based on Molière's *Le Médicin Malgré Lui*. A short extract will suffice:

> The mavis in the rowan tree
> The lintie liltin o'er the lea
> They sing a bonnie sang for me.
> Lass I loe ye dearly.
> The wind that soughs ayont the Ben
> The burnie claverin' doon the glen
> They chaunt the words I canna yen
> Lass I loo – oh alright loe – ye dearly.

The play has, of course, brought a great deal of pleasure to many, though in Duncan Macrae's defence, let it be said that when taxed with his appearance in such plays by a young colleague, he invited the young man home and introduced him to the family as 'the man who wants you all to starve'.

As better housing became available and more people moved out from the centres of the cities, so urban audiences dwindled. The only booming part of the Scottish theatre was that at which intellectuals tended to turn up their noses, until the 1970s explosion in cultural studies sent them to analyse the semiotic value of Dave Willis's moustache or Harry Gordon's frocks. Scottish popular theatre would eventually succumb to the television – but not without resistance.

The other popular theatre tradition

> What are the principal products of Scotland?
> Whisky and comedians.
> And footballers, don't forget footballers.
>
> (*U.A.B. Scotland*)

In much recent writing about the theatre, the phrase 'popular theatre' is used to describe political theatre of the 7:84 type. Like so much critical jargon, the definition of this phrase is unclear, and in a discussion of the Scottish theatre there can be some confusion between the tradition of political theatre and the type of theatre from which the companies drew so many of their techniques and so much of their inspiration: the music hall and variety stage. The confusion is all the more bizarre, because, whereas the one is avowedly socialist, the other is nakedly commercial and has never been subsidised by the Arts Council. Indeed, theatre proprietors like Harry MacKelvie or A. E. Pickard prided themselves on being absolutely free from any interference, on being totally independent. They would, one suspects, have run a mile from the idea that the State should run their theatres and they would have had no political sympathy with the proponents of socialist theatre. They provided what the people wanted, but the people paid the going rate for it.

Perhaps it would be wise here to illustrate the confusion over the word 'popular'. The historian of many Scottish working-class dramatists and theatre groups, Linda MacKenney, sees no difficulties in a concept of Scottish popular theatre. She divides Scottish theatre in the twentieth century into two camps – the popular, and the 'conventional repertory' – and argues that there was an undying blood feud between the two. Yet even the Citizens' and Unity, the two most influential representatives of each side, shared actors and dramatists; and this small point should alert us to the dangers of constructing such mutually exclusive models in theatre history, as should the political dimension in many of the early repertory companies. These would probably have regarded themselves as the people's theatres of their time – Liverpool, for example, was run for some years by a workers' co-operative, as was Perth Repertory during the Second World War. The Glasgow Repertory Theatre called itself a citizens' theatre and catered for the whole community.

Industrial revolution and popular theatre

Because of the influence it has had throughout the century, it is necessary to look more closely at the tradition of popular entertainment in Scotland. More than once it has come to the rescue of an ailing theatre of a more exclusive sort. The Glasgow Repertory Theatre, for example, kept their seasons of new Scottish plays and continental dramatists going on money made from performances of plays like J. J. Bell's *Wee MacGreegor* (1911). Bridie restored the Citizens' fortunes in 1949 with *The Tintock Cup*, a pantomime stuffed full of comic Glasgow characters. More recently Wildcat and 7:84 have used techniques from Scottish popular theatre to develop their own work. But what is popular theatre and where did it come from?

Popular theatre was born at the time of the industrial revolution, when the influx of workers into the towns and cities brought an increased demand for entertainment. The popular theatre tradition, in the sense of a commercial theatre which catered for a large, regular audience of mainly working and lower middle-class spectators, is a much earlier product of the same process of urbanisation and industrialisation which eventually gave rise to the workers' theatre movement. It too was predominantly working-class in its audience, its location and its performers. Respectable theatres providing similar entertainment, for example, the Alhambra in Glasgow, opened only long after the tradition had become established. From the early nineteenth century, when the jute workers of Dundee segregated themselves voluntarily into men in the gallery and women in the pit to watch the melodramas at the Yeaman Shore Theatre, to Mumford's 'penny geggy', to the five month runs of the pantomime at the Royal Princess's Theatre, to the quarter of a million people who saw Freddie Carpenter's production of *A Wish for Jamie* in 1962, the popular theatre tradition was the main source of entertainment for the Scottish working class. The early mainstays of this theatre were, in fact, Shakespeare, melodrama and the national drama. In Glasgow the social mix of the auditorium, even at the Theatre Royal, was more heavily working class than one might expect from both the prices and the supposed exclusivity of such theatres.

MELODRAMA AND MUSIC

The influence of melodrama was vital. First, the very name links drama with music, and if one had to point to the one element which singles out the popular theatre from other types, it would be the supreme importance of music. Melodrama also had a very clearly defined view of right and wrong; it thrived on injustice exposed. Although there was always a backbone of sentimentality, there was also great scope for bawdry in many of the farces which made up the five or six-hour long evening bill in most Victorian theatres, though these became shorter later in the century. This mixture of bawdry and sentiment is found in many popular dramas. Indeed, if we had to single out another dominant feature of popular theatre, it would be a willingness to mix genres. Humour and sadness, tragedy and comedy, co-exist. A constant juxtaposition of sentiment and comment, of fact and fantasy, is a feature of pantomime and variety. Quick changes of mood and style from one scene to the next, sometimes from one moment to the next, perhaps make popular theatre styles the theatrical equivalent of 'the Caledonian antisyzygy'.

THE SALTMARKET

Scottish popular theatre could almost be said to have originated in one street in Glasgow, the Saltmarket. Not only were the 'geggies' and booth theatres grouped round the green at the bottom of the Saltmarket, but from Mumford's Geggie at the corner of Greendyke Street to the various public houses with entertainment which lined the road, to the Britannia Music Hall, just round the corner in the Trongate, which saw the first performances by Stan Laurel and Jack Buchanan, and the Scotia Bar next door in Stockwell Street, where Harry Lauder made an early appearance, the Saltmarket area was unrivalled for the variety and concentration of its entertainments.

The area was a mecca for middle-class men and working-class men and women, who wished to see and hear popular theatre and entertainment. At the Sir Walter Scott tavern, near the Bailie Nicoll Jarvie, the Shakespeare, the Jupiter and the Odd-Fellows, you could listen to and marvel at an 'Ethiopian Serenader'. With Graham Moffatt you could have listened to a Cockney patter merchant, or joined J. J. Bell slumming it in the Scotia to see Miss Bessie Bellwood dance the can-can and sing 'Aubrey Plantagenet – can you imagine it?'. You could see a circus there at New Year or watch a bioscope picture later in the century. However, it must be added that by 1858, the Saltmarket had also become the home of Scotland's most notorious dens of thieves, shebeens and brothels – many in church-owned buildings. Perhaps it was the consequent association of popular entertainment with moral lassitude which made the whole idea of going to a music hall so exciting to a well-bred West-End boy like J. J. Bell.

The area in which so much popular theatre was concentrated obviously had an effect on the kind of performers who went on the stage. Although, towards the end of the nineteenth century, it became socially possible for a middle-class boy or girl to become an actor in the West End, it was still unthinkable for anyone respectable to 'go on the halls'. The only exception to this was the possibility of becoming an entertainer at temperance concerts. Consequently, talented working-class performers took the opportunity to leave the drudgery of their everyday occupations and perhaps become stars. Harry Lauder started working in a flax-mill at the age of eleven for 2/1d (about 10p) a week. He later became a miner and earned 10/- (50p); this had risen to £3 by the time he decided to join a concert party. To do this he had to take a pay cut to 35s (£1.75), but he felt it was worth it to escape the mines.

Although Lauder is generally felt to have sold out to the Establishment, other performers who rose from poverty, like Tommy Morgan in the '30s and '40s, not only drew most of their audience from the working class, but drew most of their material from working-class stereotypes. Morgan's creation was Big Beanie, denizen of the Steamie and destined for war-time romance with a GI. This form of character-based humour has very obvious echoes in plays of working-class life: the neighbours and Granny in *Men Should Weep* are obvious examples.

Another example of the difference in working-class attitudes to the acting and entertainment professions – music hall performers had an established profession with a strong trade union in Scotland long before their 'legitimate' fellows – was the complete lack of the censoriousness and disapproval which the middle class affected. Popular theatre then, in this other sense, really was theatre by the working class for the working class in a way that the Oxbridge Marxist 'popular theatricals' of the '60s and '70s could only pretend to be. Their contribution was in understanding the working class and their history, rather than, in the main, being working class themselves. In a country like Scotland, with a huge proportion of the population belonging to either the working or the very low middle class, it was inevitable that a form of theatre designed to appeal to this, the largest section of the people of the country, should prove a fruitful hunting ground for material and techniques to be exploited by the newly politicised theatre which emerged in the political turmoil of the Wilson and Heath years.

The 1970s and after

The background of popular entertainment, of music hall and of pantomime, is therefore essential in histories of Scottish theatre, where it attains a significance as an indigenous and alternative tradition. It is certainly a technique and an idea rediscovered and redeployed within contemporary Scottish theatre-making since the 1970s. In his essay 'Scottish Drama and the Popular Tradition' (*Scottish Theatre Since the Seventies*, 1996) Femi Folorunso observed that 'in nearly every modern Scottish play, recognisable bits and pieces of music-hall aesthetics can be found, the impact of music hall is everywhere discernible.'

Among the most significant features of popular and variety theatre is the stage craft of the performer, and the particular relationship between the performer and the spectator; an engagement that goes beyond immediacy to encompass collusion with the audience and to embody a range of performance techniques predicated on a dramaturgy – direct address, audience participation, topical referencing – which cannot permit a fourth wall. Within the context of Scottish popular theatre direct address and interrogative technique are familiar. One might argue that a Scottish dramaturgy *is* a popular one and it is certainly the case that this tradition can easily and effectively slip into another of Scottish theatre's favoured aspects, a political discourse; and Scottish theatre's quintessential politicisation of the popular is 7:84's *The Cheviot, the Stag and the Black, Black Oil* (1973) by John McGrath.

POLITICISATION OF THE POPULAR

The Cheviot was the first play to be produced by the theatre company 7:84 (Scotland). This company was formed in 1972 by John McGrath, Elizabeth MacLennan and Feri Lean. It was one of three companies – the other two were 7:84 (England) and Belt and Braces – to emerge from the split of the original 7:84 company, a company at the heart of the alternative and political theatre movement in Britain in the late 1960s, as discussed by Maria DiCenzo (*The Politics of Alternative Theatre in Britain, 1968–90: The Cause of 7:84 Scotland*, 1996). The new company, therefore, had clear and determined socialist roots. The relocation to Scotland saw the merging of an engagement with class politics with a concern for specifically national and regional problems. The company's first venture was *The Cheviot*, a production which revitalised and restructured the very idea of political theatre within Scotland, deconstructing and representing the preferred and the popular histories of Scotland using the iconography and the rhetoric of the Scottish popular theatre tradition.

The Cheviot, a collective piece which drew on the skills of all actors, writers and musicians involved, was the first widely seen play to exploit, for political reasons, Scottish traditions of popular entertainment. The play told the story of the people of Scotland, tapping a folk-memory of one of the most emotive episodes in Scottish history – the Clearances. It was seen by thousands of people, both Highlanders and Lowlanders, and for once it gave the sense of Scotland's history as being that of a divided nation. This was replayed in the formal aspects of the production, which used a broad range of techniques, elements of the folk tradition of balladry and lament, fiddle music and Gaelic song, and the slapstick and presentational style of performance drawn from the tradition of the Scotch comics and the music hall.

McGrath chose to structure his production using the form of the ceilidh – the ceilidh is principally a social event, an informal evening of entertainment among friends combining music, song, recitation and dance, predicated upon the idea of community. It is generally associated with Highland society: by interweaving indigenous music and song *The Cheviot* used the idea of ceilidh to appeal, in particular, to a Highland audience. However, by combining this structure with audience participation, comedic sketches and active use of broadly drawn stereotypes and caricatures, McGrath achieved a unique synthesis of popular entertainment forms from all parts of the country – both the traditions of the urban pantomime and those of the Highland ceilidh. In so doing, and although principally created for a Highland audience, 7:84 created a distinctive type of performance, a play which would find resonances everywhere. Indeed, perhaps the most enduring legacy of the production was its rediscovery of a Highland audience ignored by other theatre companies and the revitalisation of the touring tradition within Scottish theatre. This one production quite simply created the modern touring circuit in the Highlands and Islands.

The play linked entertainment and politics in a memorable and effective way. There was excitement and emotion at performances. Audiences felt that the company was talking about them, about their history and their experiences. If the form was rooted within Scotland, so too was the topic – the impact of capitalism on the Highlands from the time of the Clearances to the contemporary impact of North Sea oil. The play overtly links the exploitation of the past with that of the present. At last, it seemed, someone was talking publicly about class exploitation in places where this exploitation was at its most raw and obvious.

Falling into a short, episodic structure, connecting scenes through music and song, the explicit paralleling of action and character, repetition of particular stereotypes, particular dialogues and exchanges, direct address, audience participation and broad comedy, the production demands the audience's attention and involvement. Music is used as punctuating devices ending or linking segments. Different types of song are used, from the traditional ballad to the Gaelic lament to new satirical songs, often linked to particular stereotypes in the play. McGrath uses traditional songs to greet the audience and adds new and satirical lyrics to traditional melodies – the lyrics to 'Bonnie Dundee' are rewritten several times in the course of the play. The production uses music to encourage the audience to participate – an involvement developed through the use of songs with simple choruses and pantomime-style song sheets. Speech is equally various. Many lines and monologues are given in direct address to the audience. Throughout, the relationship of the audience to the performance is never settled; like the actors they shift in and out of roles, they are a congregation during a sermon, a jury being addressed by a judge, tenants being addressed by an army recruiter. The participation is active and the purpose is propagandist.

Structurally, then, the play is something of a Chinese box – a hugely complex arrangement concealing a vast repertoire of ideas, images, analysis and commentary. At root *The Cheviot* is a history play. But it is a history play reset within an overtly socialist and internationalist discourse. The company drew on extensive primary research – exploring parish records, contemporary newspaper accounts, letters and biographies – retelling that in the form of readings, re-enactments and dramatised segments. Although claiming authenticity and overtly demonstrating their use of primary sources within the production, the history was, of course, mediated for both theatrical and political purposes. The first section on the Clearances uses a range of contemporary evidence to tell a story of forced evictions and emigration. The stories are true but they also efface the voluntary nature of many of the clearances, especially on islands like Islay; they evade the true role of the church, especially the Free Church, which advocated armed resistance where necessary; and they ignore the reputedly peaceful co-existence of the High-landers and the native population in Canada.

The play's history was filtered through an agit-prop dramaturgy predicated upon socialist and internationalist principles. It is a 'recovered' history, a 'people's history', and as a result it is as partial, as prejudiced and as incomplete as was the 'legitimate' history it sought to revise. In many ways that was the point: a counter history that encompassed and celebrated the experience and the culture of ordinary people, that effaced the idea of false objectivity in favour of a politically committed and socially focused history. Quite simply *The Cheviot* told a history which had been forgotten or suppressed or ignored, and its audiences responded to that as active and as informed participants.

Revival and the city-based theatres: Lyceum, Citizens' and Traverse

At times during the early 1970s it seemed as though 7:84 alone was demonstrating the efficacy of small-scale touring companies in developing and broadening ideas of what Scottish theatre could and should be. However, simultaneously the large city-based theatres were spearheading an astonishing revival of theatre in Scotland, providing plays and new ways of staging them. It is, therefore, very important not to reduce Scottish theatre in the 1970s to the huge achievement and towering reputation of 7:84 under McGrath. Their success is to be more fully understood, more fully celebrated, in the context of widespread artistic experimentation and popular success in Scottish theatre – at the Royal Lyceum and the Traverse in Edinburgh and the Citizens' in Glasgow.

The Lyceum was established in 1965 as a municipal repertory theatre. Its first artistic director was Tom Fleming but he was quickly replaced by Clive Perry, who led the theatre into a decade of popular writing. Perry gathered around him a group of new young directors – principally Richard Eyre and Bill Bryden – and began to commission new plays. The same process was under way at the Traverse. It had been founded in 1962 as a venue for international theatre and avant-garde performance outwith Festival time. In the 1960s the new Scottish writers associated with the Traverse included C. P. Taylor, Tom Wright and Stanley Eveling. Their work was seen alongside an international repertoire of new plays by Albee, Genet and Ionesco. These two theatres' ground-breaking output included Bill Bryden's *Willie Rough* (1972) and Roddy McMillan's *The Bevellers* (1973) at the Lyceum and Tom McGrath's *The Hard Man* (1977) and John Byrne's *The Slab Boys Trilogy* (1978, 1979, 1982) at the Traverse.

Meanwhile at the Citizens' the 'triumvirate' of Giles Havergal, Philip Prowse and Robert David MacDonald quite simply reinvented what theatre in Scotland could be and reset it within an utterly contemporary and determinedly international zeitgeist. Their great achievements included a series of radical reinterpretations of plays by Shakespeare, Brecht, Coward and Wilde, and bold and inventive adaptations and original plays by Mac-Donald including *Camille* (1974), *The De Sade Show* (1975), *Chinchilla* (1977) and *A Waste of Time* (1980).

Increasingly, however, it was the Traverse which was to emerge as Scotland's leading new writing venue. This reputation was won by Chris Parr who ran the theatre from 1975 to 1980 – a period which saw premieres of new writing by Tom Gallagher, Hector MacMillan, Tom McGrath, C. P. Taylor and John Byrne. The jewel in Parr's crown was Byrne's *The Slab Boys Trilogy*. This cycle of plays – and in particular the first play, *The Slab Boys* – has been endlessly revived since the first play's production in 1978. This play, McGrath's *The Hard Man* and Hector MacMillan's *The Sash* (1974) were perhaps the three most popularly successful plays in Scottish theatre in the 1970s.

All three have certain themes in common; they are all set in working-class communities; and they are all written in a vivid urban Scots, and, like the macho plays of the Lyceum, none of them has women in central roles – they are all written round a dominant male figure, Johnny Byrne, Phil McCann and Bill McWilliam. The images, representations and reputations made by these and other contemporary plays were very male. They were written and directed by men, predominantly telling the stories of men. The plays were further associated with depictions of urban and working-class Scotland, their heroes working men or men in the dying industries of the central belt, engaging in some measure with one of the dominant myths and stereotypes of Scottish culture and feeding into the growing mythology of the 'urban Kailyard'. This very influential 'imagined community' allowed two very distinct, and one would have thought, mutually exclusive, types: the decent working craftsman, a figure like the eponymous Willie Rough, and the criminal working-class anti-hero, for example, Johnny Byrne, with a Benny Lynch falling somewhere between the two.

FOREGROUNDING HARD MEN AND BACKGROUNDING WOMEN

The figure of the 'hard man' flits through all these plays; four of them are discussed more fully in Part two of this chapter. The archetype was refined and dissected in the quintessential 1970s Scottish text, McGrath's *The Hard Man*. Through the character of Johnny Byrne, this play tells of Jimmy Boyle's life as a Glasgow gangster and his imprisonment in the then hugely controversial Barlinnie Special Unit. It is a bleak play marked by depiction of violence; a vicious and realistic account of urban brutality written in a vivid contemporary dialect.

Some of the scenes, however, especially those in which the institutionalised violence of the approved school and prison are put under scrutiny, have a power which, in the theatre, transcends literary criticisms. The scenes in Peterhead and Inverness prisons demonstrate the *reductio ad absurdum* of institutionalised violence. Byrne's resolve not to be broken, which he clung on to with an animal determination, did shock the audience. In these scenes the seeds of future violence are shown as the result of brutalisation and degradation, and, though it is suggested society condones this violence, the personalisation of this point is a far more effective device than blaming everyone.

However, what remains disturbing about the play is its representation of women and the stated but never examined premise that all women are 'whores' who in some measure 'expect' to experience physical violence in their relationships. Byrne says in prison, 'Ah ran ma hands over ma body and felt it sharp and strong'. His glorying in his physical strength is seen as positive, but the effects of this strength, the bullying and beating of Carole and fixing anyone who gets in his path are glossed over. Society is indicted for its attitude to Byrne, but Byrne's attitude to women passes without comment. McGrath's use of a chorus of women in a 'hing' also serves to reinforce the position of women as objects in the background who provide food, sex and serve as a punch-bag when necessary.

Of all the playwrights who were encouraged by the Traverse, it is the artist/writer John Byrne whose work holds its place on the contemporary Scottish stage. Byrne began drama in 1977, with a spoof Radio 3-style documentary, *Writer's Cramp*, about the Scottish poet Francis Seneca MacDade, doyen of the Nitshill Writers' Circle. It was performed by Bill Paterson, Alec Norton and John Bett, all of whom had been part of the first production of *The Cheviot*, which had been designed by Byrne. Although Byrne is described by both Alan Bold and Roderick Watson, in their histories of Scottish literature, as a product of 7:84, John McGrath has dismissed Byrne as a 'bourgeois writer', and, in fact, there is nothing in Byrne's work to link him with 7:84.

Instead he is to be associated with the Traverse and its policy of producing new writing.

THE SLAB BOYS TRILOGY

The Slab Boys was the first part in a trilogy (1978–82) completed by *Cuttin' a Rug* and *Still Life*. *The Slab Boys* has a structure and organisation very different from the formal experimentation which was part of Byrne's *Writer's Cramp* (1977). It is a tightly constructed, almost classical play set in the slab room of a Paisley carpet factory, like the one in which Byrne himself had worked. In common with many Scottish plays of the 1970s it was, if not quite 'historical', then at least set in the past. However, although it traded on nostalgia for some of its effect – the poster of James Dean and the mentions of Elvis and Radio Luxembourg help to place it in time – it has been condemned as a 'nostalgia trip for war-babies', the play managed to be funny, penetrating, and unsentimental.

Cuttin' a Rug (variously called *Threads*, or *The Loveliest Night of the Year* or *The Staffie*) again used an almost classical time-scale – the time for the drama to unfold is the actual passage of time experienced by the audience. *Cuttin' a Rug* takes place on the same night as *The Slab Boys*, but the scene has shifted to Paisley Town Hall and the firm's annual dance. The action centres first on the ladies' and gents' toilets and then on a balcony outside the hall, on which, as Byrne memorably describes it, you can 'smell the ozone coming up from Largs'. Both parts of the third play, *Still Life*, use the same setting, Hawkhead Cemetery in Paisley, with a time change, from 1967 to 1972, between the acts. The play, however, uses only Phil, Spanky, Lucille and Jack Hogg from the earlier plays, and only partially resolves the questions raised in the first two plays. Nor does it bring anyone's life, with the exception of Hector and Phil's mother, to any sort of conclusion – unless Lucille's revelation of her pregnancy suggests that, for herself and Phil, there is still life.

Of the three plays *Cuttin' a Rug* is perhaps the most dramatically developed. The characters are sharper and deeper, and there is a much greater range of emotion. The uneasy, bullying relationships of the slab boys are given a greater depth, and the female characters, especially Sadie and Miss Walkinshaw, are given a series of set-pieces which allow them to outshine the men. In a 1993 Scottish Television programme on Scottish theatre the actor and director David Hayman, who has produced and acted in the trilogy, admired *Cuttin' a Rug* in the context of the trilogy:

> I think *Cuttin' a Rug* works very well – at least in the context of the trilogy. And Byrne always intended the work to be played as a trilogy. In *Cuttin' a*

Rug there is no focal point – we just get snatches of how the various characters behave at the staff dance. It is not a 'nice' play. It's very sombre, with many dark undercurrents. The characters are, for the most part, monsters with some redeeming qualities – and they are very real. In this play, Byrne's flair for producing convincing heightened realism with his painter's eye is still evident.

This quality of work-place banter is one which *The Slab Boys* shares with McMillan's *The Bevellers*, a play with which it is often compared, though Byrne says that he never saw it and was not influenced by any other working-class play. The two plays do share both a time-scale and a setting, but little else; whereas McMillan's play is a lament for a lost craft, Byrne's play shows just how petty and futile many of the old craft jobs were, and how eagerly the opportunities of the late 1950s, for education and escape from the drudgery of factory life, were seized upon, by the very people whose working lives dramatists in the 1970s sought to sentimentalise.

Byrne's comic technique, like his sentiment, is drawn from the popular theatre tradition, and he fully exploits a richly idiomatic, vernacular speech, and delights in slapstick, farce, double-entendre and misunderstandings. Examples of all these traditional forms of humour abound: Hector being refashioned for the dance; Phil pinching cream cakes; Alan and Terry mixing up girlfriends and motor vehicles in their first conversation; Miss Walkinshaw reading the bumps on the bingo balls; the workman's conversation with Phil about his mother's grave; and the confusion in the dark at Paisley Town Hall. Seamlessly combining visual and verbal humour, these plays are both rooted in the popular tradition of Scottish comedy and are classic examples of the comedy of manners – or perhaps, more correctly, they are quintessentially comedies of lack of manners.

The rise of women's drama

If the new writing promoted by the Lyceum and the Traverse in the 1970s seemed mostly to favour male writers, it was the late 1980s and 1990s that saw a flourishing of writing by women in Scottish theatre. Although Joan Ure, Catherine Lucy Czerkawska, Marcella Evaristi and Sue Glover won some critical and production success in the late 1970s and the 1980s, it was the arrival of Liz Lochhead and, in particular, her feminist revisioning of the history play in *Mary Queen of Scots Got Her Head Chopped Off* (1987) that seemed to usher in an era of new opportunities of women writers.

Like McGrath, Lochhead uses the past to make clear political comment on the present. Her 'history play' is littered with anachronism and incongruity: she makes use of twentieth-century props (prams, telephones and bowler hats), music, rhymes and games; draws deliberate and explicit parallels with contemporary British politics (in particular in the figure of Margaret Thatcher reworked in the representation of Elizabeth I as arch-politician); and the dramaturgy itself, the structure, the language and the narrativity of the play, borrows from across the centuries to create a rich tableau of theatrical forms and to debate the ideas and representations of 'Scottishness'. To this end she makes explicit use of a tradition of Scottish balladry, for, at root, Lochhead is a story teller, the author of strongly narrative plays and dramatic monologues. The stories she recounts are often drawn from popular memory and folk culture but are reset with a distinctively feminist voice. History, myth and memory interconnect, are analysed and deconstructed in a body of work that finds reference in both literary and popular culture.

Mary Queen of Scots is typical of Lochhead's dramaturgy in its re-presentation of the cherished and even hegemonic myths of Scottish national identity, its feminist re-setting of both 'legitimate history' and 'popular culture' and its activation of metaphors of playing, acting and storytelling: 'Once upon a time', La Corbie, the play's fantastically grotesque narrator, chorus and sometime-conscience, begins, 'there were *twa queens* on the wan green island' (*Mary Queen of Scots Got her Head Chopped Off* and *Dracula*, 1989). The two queens are, of course, the Catholic Mary of Scotland and the Protestant Elizabeth of England and the play is an elaborate charade based on their stories and their mythologies, their lies and their legends. In *Mary Queen of Scots* Lochhead deconstructs the mythology associated with both Mary and Elizabeth, and again finds disturbing parallels between the demands made of the characters in the play and the prejudices that still limit women's expectations and ambitions.

Lochhead re-examines the history, mythology, legends and even the iconography of Reformation Scotland, presenting an iconoclastic version of one of the 'privileged moments' of Scotland's past. The play's beginning distils some of the key elements of Lochhead's unravelling of the shibboleths of Scottish history. It is traditional and familiar but simultaneously can be read as aggressive and unexpected; the haunting tones of fiddle music and Scots dialect are richly evocative but, even in the context of theatre-making within Scotland, strikingly unexpected. While the audience attunes to the heady mix of Lochhead's eclectic version of sixteenth-century Scots and her expert application of standard English, the 'legitimate' theatre space itself is transformed in Act I into a diabolical circus ring, with La

Corbie as ring-master and barker. The play's opening stage directions set the scene:

> *Alone,* Fiddler *charges up the space with eldritch tune, wild and sad, then goes. Enter into the ring, whip in hand, our 'chorus',* La Corbie. *An interesting, ragged, ambiguous creature in her cold spotlight.*

La Corbie's long introduction is a sardonic deconstruction of the pop semiotics of Scotland, undercutting the sentimental effect of the fiddle music and interrogating the audience's perceptions with her wild interpretations and commentaries. The other characters begin to appear as a fantastic parade rather than a royal entry: *In a strange circus our characters, gorgeous or pathetic, parade.* The audience's spectating is immediately and radically altered from theatre-goers to freak-show voyeurs. Lochhead's characters are stripped of their historical and political significance to be recast within an absurd menagerie, with the audience positioned in paradoxical uncertainty with the action. Overseeing this ambiguity, La Corbie is able to transgress narrative, theatrical and historical convention: for example, scene vi of Act II.

> La Corbie *wheels on baby, first loop of her circle – she sings a sinister wee song, which is also a familiar West-Coast lullaby.*
> La Corbie: Wee chookie burdie
> Tol-a-lol-a-lol
> Laid an egg on the windae sole
> The windae sole it began to crack
> And wee chookie burdie roared and grat.
> (La Corbie *wheels him.* Elizabeth *revealed soliliquising à la Act I. She has a letter and a Polaroid snapshot of a baby as if from proud new parents, and a hand mirror.*)
> Elizabeth: And so she has a son and heir. They do say he is perfect. (*Looks at photo.*) Well, 'James of Scotland', are you going to end up my heir for want of a better or a nearer? Surely not.

The role of La Corbie alone points to Lochhead's determination to problematise Scottish history as both subject and ideology: the repertoire of narrative techniques she employs overtly deconstructs a dominant, 'legitimate' historiography while her incongruous vocabulary of performance styles underlines her counter-hegemonic and overtly feminist dramaturgical agenda.

Sue Glover, too, has found the history play to be a particular ubiquitous genre and her play *Bondagers* has become one of Scottish theatre's most popular pieces – successfully revived by the Traverse, toured widely and produced internationally, published and anthologised, and widely studied within secondary education. As Glover explains in *Bondagers* and *The Straw Chair* (1997):

> Bondagers were the women workers of the great Border farms in the last century. Each farm worker was hired on condition that he brought a female worker to work alongside him – if not his wife or daughter, then some other girl that he himself had to hire at the Hiring Fair, and lodge and feed with his own family in his tiny cottage.

The play recounts one year – from one February hiring fair to the next – in the lives of six women working the land under this system. Told in a vivid, energetic and poetic style, it too draws on Scottish popular traditions of story-telling, song, dance and music, adding stylised physical movement and choral elements to investigate gender and history, women's work and families, social and agricultural improvement, industrialisation and emigration. Glover confronts difficult issues of class, land, ownership and belonging, and parallels the agricultural exploitation of the land with the economic and, in one brutal rape, the sexual exploitation of the women. The play is, however, more than a dramatisation or metaphor of colonialism; it is also a vibrant domestic drama of women subject to economic 'bondage' but also revelling in female 'bonding', the women finding strength and communion even within a context of subjugation, as one of them cries in the opening of Act I: 'I want a place on a big farm. Plenty lassies for the crack. Plenty ploomen for the dancing!'

The play centres on the community of women bondagers: Sara and her 'daftie' daughter, Tottie; Ellen, a former bondager now married to the master of the farm; Maggie, a woman married to one of the farm workers, with numerous young children; Jenny, a young bondager; and Liza, the play's narrator, whose independence of spirit challenges the accepted class and gender conventions of the society. The women's work is hard and laborious, described in the play through a compelling mix of poetic language and elaborate, ritualised movement sequences re-enacting the women working the fields, and paralleled by strange visionary sequences, described by Tottie, foreseeing the industrialisation of agriculture and the inevitable displacement of the people. Throughout, the play uses music and song and dance – the agricultural calendar is marked out by fiddle music and dances in the barn, by improvised and traditional songs for hoeing, sowing and harvesting.

In this the women celebrate their labour and their identity close to the land and linked to its cycles.

The play's dramatic climax sees Tottie raped by the most seductive of the ploughmen and taken away from her extended family to an asylum. The community of women is then dispersed with the end of the agricultural year: the improving master of Blackshiels is put off his farm by the laird; the farm workers lose their security and are returned to the dwindling open market of an industry in long-term decline; the bondagers are left to the uncertainty of the hiring fair and their sustaining, but increasingly desperate, friendships. These conclusions prefigure the end of a whole way of life. The metaphor is clear in Tottie's visions (in Act II, scene x) of 'ghosties', stark images of the future, with the people cleared from the land to make way for great agricultural machinery:

> She 'saw' them, she said, on the moor, in the mist.
> In a hundred years – more –
> We'll be ghosts in the fields,
> But we'll cry out in vain,
> For there'll be no one there.
> Fields without folk.
> Machines without horses.
> A whole week's harvest
> All done in one night,
> By the light of great lamps
> Not by the light of the moon,
> They won't wait for the moon, no need for the moon.

The play poetically and powerfully prefigures the inevitable changes in rural Scotland brought by industrialisation, hinting at the inevitable destruction of communities such economic shift would bring about.

One can also find such commonalities and continuities – in particular women acting together, women protesting against their invisibility and power-lessness and the use of Celtic mythology and imagery – in the diverse writings of Rona Munro. Active throughout the 1980s, when some memorable early plays were written, including *Fugue* (1983), *Piper's Cave* and *Ghost Story* (both 1985), Munro came to particular prominence with *Bold Girls* (1990), a play at the very centre of the new canon of contemporary Scottish plays.

This is an evocative and haunting piece set in Belfast and against the backdrop of the Troubles. Like Lochhead, Munro makes purposeful use of folk, traditional and popular culture to assess the roles available to women in a determinedly patriarchal environment. The play negotiates a complex path between realism and expressionism and is full of heavy portent and symbolism. It tells of a group of women facing up to and living with the emotional and practical ramifications of the violence of Northern Ireland. The play has a strong narrative core – exploring and explaining the relationships between Marie, Cassie, Nora and Deirdre, the mysterious, spirit-like figure who seems to haunt Marie – but this merely serves Munro's incisive feminist analysis of contemporary, urban, patriarchal society. Like Lochhead and Glover, Munro facilitates this through an analysis of the mythologies and images of that society, weaving a text full of references to both folk and popular culture. Munro has returned to folk mythologies and, more particularly, Celtic legend to deepen the resonances of many of her dramas and *Bold Girls* is littered with references to or engagements with the fantastic and the imagined: for example, in the naming of the characters there is explicit reference to Deirdre of the Sorrows, the tragic heroine of Celtic mythology, the inspiration of great kings and heroes. But the references are also topical and current: the women watch and provide mordant comment on both the television programme *Blind Date* and the film *The Accused*; they dance to popular music and enter a raffle in their local social club; they discuss the loss of their men folk to the violence around them. In *Laverock* 2 (1996), Douglas Gifford celebrates the play's dynamic intertextuality:

> It draws on many traditions and types of drama, from Celtic myth and legend, and plays of the Irish Revival from Synge's *The Playboy of the Western World* to O'Casey's *Juno and the Paycock*, and from modern work like Pam Gem's *Dead Fish* or Liz Lochhead's *Quelques Fleurs*, as well as evoking something of the mood of Bernard McLaverty's *Cal*. But its running references to popular culture, to game shows and horror videos, to supermarket brands and contemporary pub-and-bingo ritual, separate it from all these, and identify Munro's main theme as a satire on the way ordinary people live now – not just in Northern Ireland, but in the West, and indeed in any culture which imbalances the sexes in their social roles, encouraging stereotyping of male dominance and social privilege and female subservience to that behaviour.

Bold Girls confronts the idea of the urban hard man, but contextualises it much more widely, extending the theme so that the politically and religiously motivated violence of Northern Ireland is read as an extension of domestic violence, with women as the ultimate victims: indeed, the moral is also extended away from the Irish locus to all violent societies.

814

Unlike her other plays, the Belfast setting of *Bold Girls* removes Munro from the linguistic world of north-east Scotland which she captures so effectively in *Fugue, Piper's Cave* and *Saturday at the Commodore* (all 1989), and *The Maiden Stone* (1995). She has, in fact, set a determined example to write in the numerous dialects and ages of Scots – Alisdair in *Piper's Cave* speaks a recognisable but curiously heightened Scots; Lena, the narrator of *Saturday at the Commodore*, in a rich and evocative Aberdonian; the characters of *Your Turn to Clean the Stairs* (1992) in the vernaculars of contemporary Edinburgh; while *The Maiden Stone* is filled with a range of voices of the north-east of Scotland which, despite being set in the nineteenth century, she describes as 'the native dialect as I remember it in no sense [a] historical but a living language' (*The Maiden Stone*, 1995). She therefore demonstrates the utility of Scots to tell stories of fantastical possibilities, contemporary relevance and emotional worth. As she says in her 'Comment' in K. A. Berney's *Contemporary Dramatists* (1993): 'I am a Scottish playwright, a woman playwright, and an Aberdonian playwright, not necessarily in that order. All of these facts inform my writing but don't define it.' All these identities are discernible in the language and structures of her writing. While her plays generally deal with issues of sexual and gender politics, her engagement with issues and representations of national identity is more slippery. *Piper's Cave* is an odd two-hander with an additional 'character' of the 'landscape', named by Munro 'Helen'. In her 'Afterword' on the play (*Plays by Women* 5, 1986) Munro wrote:

I wanted to write about women making an identity for themselves rather than adapting one of the many roles provided for them; I mean: what is all this Mother Nature stuff? Who classifies landscape as female in all those poetic metaphors that have got their way inside everything and *why*? What does that say about our assumptions about male and female, active and passive? What is the nature of any empathy we feel with an environment?

Lizbeth Goodman, writing on Rona Munro (*Contemporary Dramatists*, 1994), approved of such revisionist dramatisation.

Such a statement is a welcome modifier within Scottish culture. Rather paradoxically (and despite the various representations and thematic concerns developed within Scottish culture as being dominated by a mythology of masculinity) it is common for 'Scotland' (physical Scotland as opposed to cultural Scotland) to be represented and embodied by a woman. Although Munro's landscape is ostensibly female, it is troublesome, sophisticated and much less fey than the increasingly other-worldly Jo and Alisdair; it is a representation which 'challenges ingrained essentialist notions about "Mother Nature" '.

Recent Scottish drama has indeed challenged many of our previous assumptions about writing for and in theatre in Scotland. This is not restricted to dramaturgical issues but extends to the relationship of the writer to the company. In the 1980s and 1990s new writing has continued to be supported in the established new-writing contexts of the Traverse – responsible for premières of work by Glover, Munro, Anne Marie di Mambro, Donna Franceschild, Catherine Lucy Czerkawska, Liz Lochhead, Simon Donald, David Greig, David Harrower, and others – and 7:84 – with premières of work by di Mambro, Munro, Jackie Kay, Stephen Greenhorn and Greig. However, there has also emerged a vital collection of newer, small touring companies. Many of these companies have been founded by and operate with a resident writer and/or writer/director – for example, John Binnie and Aileen Ritchie at Clyde Unity, David Greig with Suspect Culture, Nicola McCartney with Look Out – who along with energetic and innovative companies like Communicado, Wiseguise, Theatre Cryptic, KtC, NVA have combined to produce a remarkable and exciting range of text-based and non-text-based theatre being made across Scotland. This expansion of the locus of production, combined with a determined post-1990 international dynamic, has led to a healthy and distinctive diversity and eclecticism in contemporary Scottish theatre writing that Peter Zenzinger is right to celebrate (*Scottish Theatre Since the Seventies*, 1996) arguing that:

> while the new works are informed by an artistic vision that is distinctively Scottish, they have largely moved beyond the self-conscious Scottishness of the earlier dramatic tradition, which often hampered its artistic realisation and limited its appeal outside Scotland.

The range of writing evinced by Scottish writers as contemporary and as different as Peter Arnott, John Clifford, Simon Donald, Stephen Greenhorn, David Greig, Sue Glover, Chris Hannan, Iain Heggie, David Harrower, Liz Lochhead, Sharman Macdonald and Rona Munro reflects this distinctive dynamic and suggests that there exists within Scottish theatre culture a very different agenda from the fashion-victim, nihilistic 'shopping and fucking' introspection of London's theatre scene.

The foregoing overview of contemporary Scottish drama provides an introduction to dramatists, plays and forms of drama to be found in Scottish theatre since 1945. What follows in Parts Two and Three are two brief discussions: the first, of a grouping of plays which represent the direction taken by much Scottish drama in the period 1970–80, in the recurrent exploration of the figure of the 'hard man' in Scottish history and society; and the second (an extension of earlier text), of an important example of the development of Scottish theatre in the 1980s, in Liz Lochhead's *Mary Queen of Scots Got Her Head Chopped Off* (1987). The two discussions may offer a useful contrast of approach and methodology, the 'hard man' plays working through traditional theatrical realism, where Lochhead's play employs a range of non-naturalistic performance styles which foreground the role-playing nature of drama.

PART TWO: FOUR 'HARD MAN' PLAYS

Hard men and failed lives: four plays of the '70s

As Scottish drama discovered a new vitality and variety in the '70s, there was one theme above all others which preoccupied dramatists; that of the way in which Scottish male culture produced a stereotype of macho behaviour and attitude whose toughness paradoxically undermined itself, leading to social failure and self-destruction. Arguably, the plays produced on this subject were necessary parts of a national self-recognition and self criticism; equally arguably, their emphatic social realism and recurrent types left them open to criticism that they were backward-looking and failing to exploit new forms of dramatic expression. There is no doubting, however, their commitment to forcing Scottish audiences to rethink traditional attitudes, and it is worth recording here something of their message and impact at a crucial stage in the redevelopment of Scottish theatre – but, outstandingly with the play *The Hard Man*, also analysing their ambiguous ways of evaluating their protagonists.

The plays discussed are Tom McGrath's *The Hard Man* (1977), Bill Bryden's *Benny Lynch* (1974), Stewart Conn's *Play Donkey* (1977) and Donald Campbell's *The Jesuit* (1976). Those interested in this kind of drama could usefully consider them with plays which give variant versions of the theme, as in Hector MacMillan's study of inflexible religious bigotry, *The Sash* (1973) or the older *Men Should Weep*, originally produced in 1947, but revived (and revised) for 7:84 Theatre Company in 1982 by its author, Ena Lamont Stewart, to carry its message into the '70s. Hard men in the work-place feature in Roddie McMillan's *The Bevellers* (1973) and Bryden's *Willie Rough* (1972), while another work-place play, John Byrne's *The Slab Boys* (1978) carries its deeply serious message via deceptively comic set-pieces whose humour eventually betrays its savage satire. A play apparently disconnected in time and place, but which strikingly deals with the failure of so called 'hard men' by focusing on their absence is Rona Munro's *Bold Girls* (1991), which, though set in Belfast, presents a similar theme from the perspective of the deserted women.

THE HARD MAN

In a way, *The Hard Man* is two plays. Its first part comprises a vivid impression of the Gorbals and the events which surrounded the life of Johnny Byrne, a hardly-disguised version of the controversial Glasgow gangster Jimmy Boyle, as a boy. Its theme is familiar but strikingly-handled, that of the damaging effect of environment and upbringing. The play is deeply serious in its implicit social questioning; how far are we moulded by our backgrounds? Or can genuine moral character triumph over all obstacles? Part of McGrath's real achievement here is to portray the callous, bleak, emotionally stunted world of Byrne without sentiment or melodrama, using a running device whereby genuinely good community qualities go bad, becoming parodies of good qualities. The play opens (after a sharp glimpse of two wifies window-hingin' and gossiping about the most recent atrocity of Byrne's) with Byrne showing leadership: 'We're a' in it thegither!' McGrath's use of monologue for Byrne, where Byrne reveals a detached and stoical coolness, devoid of self-pity, shows us his potential greatness – a theme of all these plays, that somehow the Scottish disease is to distort character so that it becomes self-destructive.

The first half has a fierce pace, with fragmented and sharply contrasted scenes as its mode of presentation. Form thus mirrors subject matter; broken scenes reflect broken lives. Indeed, images of the broken mirror and of lives and friends being literally cut down dominate this first part. Subtly, reasons are suggested for Johnny being the way he becomes; 'Schools are shite,' says Johnny tersely. Occasional glimpses of Johnny's family life reveal more reasons for his distortion. His mother was loving but feckless, spoiling him, not wanting to take the money he brought back at first – but then taking it without too many questions. 'Ach, he wisnae a bad boy really . . . ma son . . . whit chance did he huv?', she whines, telling us that he wanted to be an altar boy, but wasn't allowed because he didn't have the right sandshoes. Another telling anecdote from Byrne's monologue, all the more impressive because it's only drily remembered long after by the adult, concerns his father who wouldn't be seen for days on end, but would come home with presents for everybody and a half-bottle in his pocket; and who lifted his son up to show him a 'brand new, shining motorcar' out of the window, telling the boy that it's his: 'The next day I got up and looked out of the window. But the car was gone. And so was my father. And I never saw him again.'

It's as much the 'poorhoose' taunts as anything that drive Johnny to stealing; as Big Danny of the local shebeen says, 'A man's forced intae thievin'.' McGrath manages to give the first half an inevitability, a sense of one thing leading to the next; from gathering protection money to handing out stitches for non-payment. The accompanying comments of victims and relatives and girlfriends build up a total picture of a society of little choice – which is strangely then undercut by McGrath in his alternative picture of Byrne as a maniac, almost demonic. He calls Johnny 'evil'; intriguing, since this counters the possible interpretation that Byrne is what he is because he's been made this way. And one of the effective horrors of the play's first part (very effectively caught by Peter Kelly in the radio version, with his sinister, malevolent, and bitter humour at the expense of his victims) is Johnny's savage, quiet irony. When he's on the run, blood-soaked, his prostitute befriender gasps at the blood. 'It's no ma blood, Ah hivnae goat a mark on me,' says Johnny drily. And when he takes up later with Carol, whom he's carved up for 'sleeping around' when he was inside, he is wickedly tender to her about the 'awfy bad mark on yer face, Carol'.

All this builds up a harsh, powerful picture of a too-familiar Glasgow type. When the police 'get' Byrne, even the wee court clerk raises his thumbs up in triumph. But from the audience's point of view, the end of the first half introduces the first false note, when Johnny laconically says that he did not do the crime for which he was convicted. This hint at social injustice, and its corollary that Byrne is a martyr at the hands of corrupt society, is to become the very different theme of the very different second half.

The second half is dominated by the symbolism of imprisonment and jail – jail repeated as image and reference till the sense of claustrophobia almost smothers. Inverness, Peterhead, Barlinnie – Johnny does not know which is which, so isolated in solitary cells and cages is he. And yet Johnny is now 'rehabilitated' – not in any sense that he is improved by prison life, rather the opposite; but in the sense that McGrath now rehabilitates him in our estimation as a sensitive human being. The audience is confused; is Byrne more sinned against than sinning?

Johnny is now seen from a different perspective; as victim – as he says disdainfully and proudly – of 'your justice'. Instead of the first half's neutrality and detachment concerning the original rights and wrongs of Gorbals and Johnny Byrne, we are clearly witnessing the struggle of one man's spirit against a power bent on crushing his individuality. This is made explicit when the old lag says to Johnny, in tones for the first time sentimental: 'It's no yer body they're tryin' tae break . . . it's yer proud spirit.'

The play is strong drama till the end, where Johnny is seen alone, evocatively so; talking to that companion of solitary prisoners, the fly. He finds out that he's become a father from muttered whispers. (Little is made now of his former violence to other children, though we know from else-where in the play that Byrne has 17 adult and 15 juvenile convictions for assault and other crimes.) By making Johnny have a suggestion of a human relationship with Johnston, the prison officer, and by making some of the stories of Johnny's 'impalings' and atrocities seem outlandish, and by even suggesting that Johnny was something of a peacemaker (!) in his territory, since violence now rules in his absence, and most of all by softening Johnny's demonic nastiness, McGrath slowly builds up sympathy for him. More and more caricatures of 'our' society are presented – the 'Commando' governor, the psychopathic bully officer, Paisley – these are used so much as black against Johnny's new white that we cheer when he downs the governor. Does McGrath now realise that he must try to recover his early detachment? Or is there a deeper subtlety in his varying perspectives? A most peculiar scene occurs half-way through the second half, when Paisley the prison officer suddenly breaks off from the particularly atrocious bit of Byrne-baiting (they semi-drown him in a sink, and he fights back, half-blinding an officer) to address us directly: 'Listen – if you excuse him on the grounds that he's a product of this shit-heap system, then you'd better excuse me on the same grounds'.

The dramatic power of the second half, with its images of cage and fear and brutality – and dignity – is considerable. But this remark forces the audience to consider two perspectives, as it moves them from condemnation to admiration of his individual spirit. And the play ends with this being done shockingly vividly – but unbelievably. Johnny covers himself with his own excrement. By forcing his captors to realise that in tormenting him they reduce themselves lower than animals, so the play argues, Johnny discovers the ultimate weapon. It might be argued that Johnny's final discovery of self is too much in the manner of enlightenment through transcendental medita-tion to carry the ring of conviction which it needs inside a prison régime.

Yet for all the play's moral ambiguities – or perhaps because of this – the play remains one of the most powerful of recent Scottish dramas – and it states with authority what is a theme of all these four plays, that of the Scottish male tendency to self-imprisonment.

BENNY LYNCH

The second play, *Benny Lynch*, lacking the overt prison sequences of the other three, is nevertheless a play about a prisoner; a Glasgow hard man locked up in his own image of himself, by himself and all his 'friends' and the Glasgow society who 'worship' him. And another aspect that these plays share relates to the fact that their tragic central figures are virtually predestined to their fates through peer pressure and weakness – as with Johnny Byrne ('Ah'm a lunatic . . . Ah'm fur the Bar-L, it's inevitable'), Benny can't escape his reputation ('Give us a drink . . . I'm Benny Lynch! . . . I take on all comers . . .'), just as with Tommy Ryden the gallus mercenary of *Play Donkey* ('It was my own doing, after all. Didnae have to. But I did, so it's only right . . . I get what's coming.'), and *The Jesuit* martyr priest ('God knows I do not want to die! I am in love with life as any man! But there is no way out of my situation . . .'). In these plays, the tragedy stems from religious constraints and prejudices, memories and images of self which destroy both the toughest – and the most vulnerable.

Another more surprising quality is that of humour. Grotesque, savage, sometimes apparently out of place – like Benny's stealing of the Spanish boxer's lucky stick, his escapades in and out of the ring, as when he and Stoorie put plaster of paris in the gormless boxer's gloves so that he wins against all the odds, the sheer quality of backchat amongst priests and trainers, promoters and punters – it is always convincing. Such vigorous and vital patter is a hallmark of this drama. From *The Cheviot and the Stag* to Byrne's *Slab Boys* trilogy; from *Willie Rough* to *The Bevellers* or *The Sash*, the dramatic talk is searingly alive, presenting like Kelman in fiction or Leonard in poetry the realities of Scottish working-class language, and paradoxically deepening the social satire. For example, *Benny Lynch* is organised to a great extent around comic oppositions. Much comic anti-foreigner prejudice about Jews, 'Eyties', and the like is combined with the fact that many of the protagonists are foreign, or of different religion – so that a smokescreen of prejudice covers a deeper social tolerance which means that speakers are always having to apologise ('Sorry Father, Ah didnae mean you . . .'). Similarly a superficial hardness of talk goes along with a maudlin sentimentality; sentimental Irish folksong and Hollywood falsity show a society which lacks a balanced, mature middle way which cannot look in proper perspective at the real social depression which underlies the economic depression of the '30s, the vividly realised setting for Benny's tragedy. For Benny represents all these opposites and he embodies the Glasgow and Scottish tragedy of his play, just as all the other protagonists represent their different Scottish tragedies. Benny reads comics, evades reality, avoids responsibility, sleeping with other women just as he gets married, playing what seem trivial enough jokes like that of the plaster of paris in the gloves – till one realises that he's feckless, childish, a product, like the hard man, of a spurious social system.

Again like *The Hard Man*, the play wavers between placing responsibility for disaster on society's shoulders or on the protagonist's. Benny is a victim; there's a particularly effective sequence towards the end when he's drunk, and mustn't be shown to press or promoters, and he's hidden in a locker. Benny had been locked in a boiler in the shipyards for twelve hours when he was fifteen. The men with him died. Now – after some comic moments when a naïve boxer puts everyone's hearts in their mouths by nearly discovering Benny – they open the locker and take Benny out at last (Act II, scene vii):

> Benny (*weeping*): I was in the dark. Hate the dark. There was a deid man
> . . . Where's ma mammy? How she no hame? Who's she wi'? Don't pit me
> in the dark . . . Keep that light on or I'll fucking do ye! Out of order, that.
> Who's on the bell?
> Dingley: The world's champion. Jesus Christ!
> Benny: Where's my maw?
> Johnny: She's ben the room, son. Ye're all right Benny.

There's enough in this fragment to make the point that the stark language, the humour, the social comment are finally deeply serious means towards an important end – that of showing the complexity of events which have led Benny to and exploited him for his world championship. Spoiled, from childhood by a neglectful slattern mother, and now by trainers and friends who are a convincing mixture of loyalty and sharp practice, Benny, like Johnny Byrne, is a shell, a creation of himself and others to both hide and exaggerate weaknesses and strengths. Thus Benny need rarely if ever face up to his real self, or his traumas concerning his loveless background, the shallowness of his tastes and ideas; instead he vastly overplays his pseudo-virility, his animal hardness – and others love him for supplying a phoney image of themselves. *Benny Lynch* is about human beings who use the only ways they know to escape the poverty trap – their fists and their shrewdness.

Arguably, *Benny Lynch* is a better play than *The Hard Man* in one respect particularly; it does not evade the implications of creating a hard, false image around Benny, the way *The Hard Man* does by discovering resources and spiritual integrities of a most unlikely order in its debased protagonist. Benny is shown – somewhat melodramatically – reeling drunk through the blitz of Clydeside during the war, without home, friends, anything, but his trophy. A strange moment of communion is given between him and a Salvation Army girl – both talking high above plausible levels, Benny almost philosophical and articulate in the extreme, the girl simply a device to show his tragedy. Benny in the end has nothing, and is nothing, except a bundle of paranoid, boastful reactions which lead him to alcoholic death at thirty-three years of age. The atmosphere in this play of depression and increasing darkness around Benny, towards the end wandering around in a moorland in the darkness with lights flickering around him as the searchers (symbolically) look for him, ends in total blackness in the blitz.

PLAY DONKEY

Stewart Conn's *Play Donkey*, like Gordon Smith's *Jock* (1971), explores the hard man theme in military terms. Tommy Ryden is a mercenary, being tried in Angola. Conn contrasts two locations: Tommy's cell, with his Scottish lawyer interviewing him with a view towards making the best case he can for Tommy against his black prosecutors; and Tommy's relatives and sweetheart at home. The bizarre nature of Tommy's predicament is brought home all the more fully through that contrast, since in Edinburgh we see the ordinary, if nasty, details which helped make Tommy the way he is – which is what got him into the red berets and then into mercenary fighting abroad.

Conn's is a slightly more gentle play than the other three – strong meat still by most standards, but restrained in its sketching in of background. There are fewer dramatic clues than those in the first two plays to Tommy's making: loneliness at school; feckless parents who mean well but hardly connect with their own lives, let alone his, spoiling him rather than giving understanding and sharing his adolescence. Tommy has turned to guns; to the more sinister camaraderie of war, where bonds of humanity are forged at the expense of any recognition of the claims of their victims, and where these 'bonds' are highly questionable in themselves. Conn sensitively shows how Tommy has ceased to relate to anybody in his Edinburgh past. His mother doesn't really know him, other than as a token figure, eliciting set responses; his father is pathetically inarticulate, a good man struggling to keep his own identity alive without having enough left over to help Tommy. Most telling of all is the sub-plot concerning Tommy's girlfriend who thinks she's pregnant. Running though the play is the dialogue with her best friend – tough, soft, stupid, occasionally bitterly perceptive. Zoe's pathetic romantic dreams about Tommy are shattered by the revelation that he was so little concerned about her that he slept with lots of other people, including Beryl herself. Conn juxtaposes these conversations with Tommy's meditations in Angola – and when these are about girls, we see that Tommy is a chancer as far as Zoe is concerned. Favourite memories of Zoe's are to him merely chauvinistic and smutty episodes amongst many over which he gloats.

For Tommy, like Byrne and Benny, has no integrity; merely conditioned – and very ill-conditioned at that – responses about coloured bastards, bits of stuff to enjoy and abandon. Only one thing saves him in our eyes at all, and that is his unwillingness to lie to his lawyer, Gibb, a well-meaning if ineffectual middle-class Edinburgh idealist, young and out of his depth, who tries to get Tommy to make a plea of diminished responsibility. Tommy rejects this; at least he will accept what his background has made him, although part of the play's provocation for our purposes is the way Tommy has to examine aspects of Scottish history and culture to discover how he got where he is: from Bonnie Prince Charlie to Gorgie Road, the Grassmarket and social deprivation. His new reactions are fierce, to say the least; now that he begins to be aware of his plight, total bitterness and a kind of stoical courage are all he has. He even sees a kind of similarity in the fate of Prince Charlie (Act II, scene xiii):

> I mean, he didn't make it, did he. And we've been trying ever since. That's where I should've been. Back there. Marching on the bloody English. Instead of out here in the Darkie Sunday School. I mean, there'd have been some point in that eh? Fighting for your freedom, after all these centuries . . .

But Tommy isn't sentimentalised; Conn doesn't pretend that sudden martyr-like internal peace or insight is going to happen to him. Tommy cannot escape the cheap fantasies which are what his deprived life have woven into his fabric. In the same scene, he continues:

> Might even have been a chance of me getting paid for it, now there's all that oil. Eh? Paid by the barrel-load. See me, the back court stacked with the stuff . . . Sheikh of the bloody Grassmarket, I could've ended up. Who knows?
> Country villa up the Braids . . . swimming pool and that . . . Bacardi on tap . . . Big darky to slice the lemons . . . naked women, . . . cutting my toenails . . . How's about that, eh? Having it away, left, right and centre . . .

Tommy is shot; Zoe and Beryl rejoice to find that Zoe's not pregnant – and to find that Tommy isn't really a powerful memory at all, but irrelevant; even his mother is numbed to find that she has no real way of expressing her grief. Conn's eye is sharp and sardonic – the newspaperman who steals family photos, the British consul who cynically writes Tommy off as dead, the system – these are the makers of Tommy's tragedy. Indeed, Tommy's visions of rats' eyes in the darkness of his cell, facing death, are remarkably similar as images to the recurrent motif, 'chasin' rats wi' a wee dug roon the back', of

McGrath's *The Hard Man* and Bryden's *Benny Lynch*, with his fear of the dark and the 'deid men' who are in his nightmares. These are the images of a Scottish subconscious which instinctively sees the darkened wasteland from which it grows, stunted and fated.

THE JESUIT

At first sight *The Jesuit*, with its picture of a Catholic martyr-priest from the seventeenth century, might seem out of place with these plays of so-called hard men. It is true that *Willie Rough* in some ways would have rounded out the group well; but *The Jesuit* in fact probes the nature of 'hardness' in a historical Scottish context more deeply than any of these others; and, by examining a moment in Scottish history when possibilities of compromise were wasted, or by showing the penalties of avoiding involvement, presents a kind of timeless analysis of the Scottish tendency to extremism or irrelevance.

In this play there are three hard men: the well-bred idealist, John Ogilvie, the historical priest who was canonised in the 1970s for his martyrdom at the hands of the Scottish Episcopalian Church in 1615; Archbishop Spottiswoode of Glasgow, the ostensible persecutor and power behind Ogilvie's torture and death; and the common soldier in the Archbishop's employ, Andrew. There are other points of view: Spottiswoode's wife; the foul-mouthed other soldiers; the young naïve boy-soldier Will who is converted by Ogilvie in jail; but the three that matter are this group of dreamer, pragmatist and agnostic.

Ogilvie is a complex figure. The play shows a likeable, if aristocratic figure who may, it is hinted, be partly motivated by sour grapes in the sense that his family have cheated him of his inheritance. But Campbell intends Ogilvie to be a complex character; and there is no doubt that his faith is strong and courageous and he himself attractive with his boyish enthusiasm, his gentle sensitivity, his charm; but to let this interpretation carry through to the exclusion of a another, more difficult reading, would be to fail to present the real and tragic theme of the play – that men's stubborn hardness is the producer of violence and death. For Ogilvie, for all his charm, is harder than Spottiswoode and Andrew.

Spottiswoode and Andrew seem very tough and abrasive; properly played, they should come over as abrupt, experienced, and at first rather heartless. But it should emerge as the play goes on that their pragmatism is based on scepticism rather than cynicism; that they have seen too many wars and deaths over 'faiths' and dreams of various sorts to have very much trust in them. Spottiswoode is an archbishop, but his 'faith' is in compromise, in tolerance of others, and his dream is of a Scotland which won't be made up of

825

hardened extremists. The play anticipates *The Sash* to the extent that Spottiswoode looks forward with horror to the kind of extremists who will result if martyrs like Ogilvie have their martyrdom, for example in Act II, scene iii:

> I'm feared that I'll be hinging him again and again and again. Owre and owre and owre and owre! Martyrs are a queer-like breed . . . they hae a way of turning into saints. Saints! Saint John Ogilvie . . . can ye no imagine it? Oh, Rachel. I look intae that young man's een and I see a dream – a dream that is a lowe with a bitter hatred . . . I want a Kirk in Scotland that will serve aa men. I want a Kirk in Scotland that will bring Catholic and Protestant thegither in the ae faith, in the ae life; I want peace and guid will amang aa men – as the Guid Lord aye intended it should be! That is *my* dream, Rachel . . . He can set the clock back twenty years! Ogilvie can change reality – and it is reality that is important. No dreams! That is the lesson we maun learn here in Scotland!

Spottiswoode is a dreamer, but his dream is of a Scotland of no spurious allegiances, but of general tolerance and charity. Andrew is a different case. Even harder physically than his master, harder probably than any of the hard men of these plays, he has lost all dreams. He is the Tommy Ryden who might have survived – hopeless, detached and drawing a circle round himself so that he's left within his enduring circle. This kind of hardness is not enough, argues Campbell – but at least it doesn't interfere with others and their liberty the way Ogilvie does. Ogilvie tries to get Andrew to admit that he is a residual Catholic; and it's a clever stroke by Campbell and a measure of Ogilvie's ultimate shallowness that he cannot perceive that Andrew's real flicker of anger – which Ogilvie thinks is guilt for betraying Catholicism – is really anger that such a man should try to invade his privacy. Andrew is agnostic to his soles – his only remaining pride is his privacy. He has compassion, though. Andrew hates the torture of Ogilvie, but hates also what Ogilvie does in torturing ordinary people like Will with his ideal claims. Indeed, the message is very close to that of Ibsen's *The Wild Duck* (1884), that life would be tolerable enough if it weren't for idealists coming around ordinary people's doors with their demands for belief and reform.

The play shows Ogilvie being tortured, and captures his courage and humour, as well as showing the relationships that develop between him and his captors. But most of all, it shows that the prison is one of Ogilvie's own making; that like Ryden and Byrne and Benny he is victim of a false image of life and self which has imprisoned him far more effectively than Spottiswoode or others ever can. Spottiswoode indeed leaves the prison door open in the end to let Ogilvie go, so that there will be no hanging, and martyrdom, and consequently no mob riots in the streets; but Ogilvie wants his martyrdom and accepts that blood may follow. There's a marvellous scene towards the end where Ogilvie finally asks the archbishop for his hand, despite their differences; and the archbishop – who has liked the young man, and tried hard to dissuade him from his extremity – finally refuses: 'No. No. This is no game, Faither; this is no game.'

In the end this is what all the hard men learn, that their hardness is self-destructive, deriving from Scottish historical and social distortion, and in turn contributing towards that distortion. These plays use drama in the way of contemporary fiction and poetry; as an examination of Scottish history, culture and society, and with an implicit message that profound change is needed.

PART THREE: LIZ LOCHHEAD'S
MARY QUEEN OF SCOTS GOT HER HEAD CHOPPED OFF

Liz Lochhead developed *Mary Queen of Scots Got Her Head Chopped Off* (1987) in association with Communicado Theatre Company under its director Gerry Mulgrew. She was attracted by Communicado's 'non "fourth wall" direct-to-the-audience style of presentation (rather than "acting")' (Perth Theatre programme notes, 1992) which influenced the formal organisation of her play. *Mary Queen of Scots* draws significantly on Brechtian theories of epic drama and especially on the *Verfremdungseffekt* or 'alienation' effect, which involves the audience in questioning what they see on the stage instead of becoming 'caught up' with the happenings and characters 'without reason and without judgement' as Brecht phrased it. As John Willett's translation of *Brecht on Theatre* (1964) reveals, Brecht instructed his actors to:

> let the audience see you are not this character, but you are an actor representing this character . . . When you go on stage as a certain character imply what does not take place as well as showing what does. Try to show that instead of moving down left – you could have moved up right. Instead of saying 'You'll pay for that', you could have said 'I forgive you'.

This foregrounding of performance, of roleplaying, of choice is very important in Lochhead's deconstruction of Scottish history and her investigation of themes relating to gender and power.

Her methodology is seen at work in the opening scene of Act I. The principal character here is the 'chorus' La Corbie, 'an interesting, ragged ambiguous creature in her cold spotlight', as the stage directions communicate. La Corbie is ambiguous not only because of her peculiar bird-like appearance, but also because she enters the stage whip in hand like a ringmaster about to set the performance in motion. The presentation of La Corbie therefore brings to our attention at the outset the non-illusion-of-reality nature of the play, while her speech leads us to think about the image of the country, Scotland, which is being presented; to recognise its plurality and diversity as well as the subjectivity which lies behind descriptions of national identity. What we notice in La Corbie's account of Scottish identity, therefore, is the variety of Scotlands which emerge: 'a bricht bere meadow or a park o' kye . . . a tenement or a merchant's ha' . . . Princes Street or Paddy's Merkit'. There is no unitary image imposed, as so often in accounts of Scottish history and culture. La Corbie's words also make us realise that we ourselves are involved in the characterisation of the Scotland we belong to: 'Ah dinna ken whit like *your* Scotland is. Here's mines.'

In the second part of the opening scene La Corbie takes up her role as ringmaster, cracking her whip for the Entrance of the Animals, the characters of the play. The historical personages are presented in a manner which subverts the expectations we bring from our knowledge of history, while once again role-playing and theatricality are foregrounded.

Within this overall approach, Lochhead's dramatic methodology calls upon a range of performance detail including symbolic mime, music, song; anachronistic detail such as Riccio's typewriter and paper aeroplanes, John Knox's bowler hat and Orange Order banners. Throughout the play the use of Scots language is rich and varied. Among the most important of the dramatic devices are the stage directions, which are not merely directions for entering, exiting or positioning, but are an intrinsic part of the text for the reader and, in performance, have to be carried out faithfully in order to communicate the dramatist's intentions. In Act I, scene i, for example, in addition to the specific, even if 'ambiguous' description of La Corbie, we have Fiddler who 'charges up the space with eldritch tune, wild and sad'. The word-choice precisely designates the kind of music wanted, a fiddle tune which will create uncertainty, even an eerie foreboding, while the phrase 'charges up the space' once again emphasises that the stage is being brought to life for this particular presentation of our history. The stage directions are similarly important throughout the play, especially so in the scenes involving the presentation of John Knox. In 'The Suitors', the second scene of Act I, the direction for a 'mad tango' to accompany the ambassadors' suits to the queens adds to the sense of confusion in the scene while at the same time ironically emphasising the unreality of the marriage 'game' being played out on stage.

Mary and Elizabeth never met in reality, although novelists, film-makers and historians have speculated as to what the outcome of any meeting might have been. In Act I, scene ii Lochhead cleverly does and does not create a meeting through the device of positioning the queens at either end of the stage and alternating the action between them as the ambassadors ply their suits. The effect of this bringing together of the queens is to make plain the difference in their temperaments; in their approaches to the role of female sovereigns in a strongly patriarchal culture. There is an emphasis placed on individual choice; on the variety of responses available in the presentation of the queens' behaviour when confronted by more or less the same marriage proposals. Elizabeth is always the politician, confident, formal in language yet with a playfulness in word-choice which demonstrates that she is well aware of the political game being played: 'Do contrive to keep the ambassadors dangling. Do dandle the odd demi-promise . . .' Mary, on the other hand, appears to be personally motivated by what she holds dear: 'At least he is a good Catholic, even if he's not a king in his own right.' She seems easily taken in by appearances, all too ready to believe in the goodwill of the ambassadors and their principals. While Elizabeth maintains a distance through the use of the royal 'we', even when she is at her most playful, Mary's register is personalised, intimate despite her status. The stage directions note that she should be presented as '*a French-woman speaking Scots, not English, with . . . quite a French accent*', an instruction which signals early in the play her cultural displacement within the politics of the British Isles. Unlike Elizabeth, who realises that to marry will destroy her authority as sovereign, Mary is a queen who attempts to rule with womanly values and she feels that she cannot truly be queen until she marries: 'I want to marry and begin my reign at last.'

Lochhead has said of her early poetry, 'my country was woman', and the focus on the two historical queens in this play offers an opportunity to continue an investigation of issues of gender and power. Elizabeth's political acuity is confirmed when Mary, having rushed emotionally into marriage with Henry, Lord Darnley, finds herself demoted when her new husband issues a commemorative coin with the order of their names reversed: 'The damnable cheek of it – *Henricus* et Maria, Deo Gratia *Rex* et Regina Scotorum! Wrang order!'. The historical John Knox also appears to have had no faith in the 'regiment [rule] of women'. As presented in Lochhead's play, he bullies Mary in an abusive way in which a sexual as well as religious motive for his anger is implied. This is apparent in Act I, scene iv, where he reduces Mary to tears and then is stirred to 'certain pity, perhaps lust'. In Act I, scene vi, 'Mary Queen of Scots's Progress and John Knox's Shame' the vulgar wee street lassies Mairn and Leezie taunt Knox, provoking an uncontrolled sexually abusive outburst which then becomes a sexual attack on the queen herself, as wee Mairn is suddenly transformed to Queen Mary in a symbolic tableau. Knox's gossip with Bothwell about the queen is also sexual in nature and Bothwell himself sees all women – commoners and queens alike – as sexual prey, as the episode with Alison Craik and the fine piece of prose poetry about 'a fine white hind dancin' afore me through the trees' in Act I, scene v, demonstrate. For all these men, it is Mary's gender and her sexual being which defines her identity and therefore her lack of authority in their eyes.

Although no man would dare to treat Elizabeth with such disrespect, she too suffers in the attempt to maintain her role as female sovereign in a world where men traditionally wield power. Her suppression of her femininity and sexuality leads to nightmares (brought to the audience through symbolic mime), to envy of Mary (who, ironically, has little happiness to envy) and to her deliberate decision to separate herself from the one man she truly loves. Elizabeth remains in control to the end of the play's action, but the psychological price is high. As the previous drama overview section indicated, there are indeed disturbing parallels to be found between the demands made on the female characters in this historical play and the prejudices in our present-day society which still limit a woman's ambition and her capacity to fulfil her potential.

Another important theme in Lochhead's play is religion, a traditional text in Scottish poetry, fiction and non-fiction. Having grown up with a Protestant family background in a Scotland where Catholicism was marginalised and Catholics discriminated against, and where John Knox had come down through history as the hero of the sixteenth-century Protestant Reformation, Lochhead in adulthood and as dramatist has turned the historical tables in order to re-examine traditional interpretations of the Scottish Reformation and the presentation of Knox. Although the play encourages us to question Mary's judgements as queen and woman and to look with some scepticism on her actions, Lochhead nevertheless inclines in sympathy towards this Catholic queen. Several of the intimate scenes involving Mary have a naturalistic as opposed to stylised manner, a mode which draws the audience's sympathies towards her. This is especially so in her interview with John Knox in Act I, scene iv, which follows immediately after the Brechtian presentation of Knox as a ranting Orangeman. Although modified somewhat from his earlier outburst against 'the papistical religion in all its pestilent manifestations in

Sodom priesthooses and poxetten nunneries', Knox's language in his address to the queen is still intolerant and abusive of her religion, dismissive in relation to herself. Mary, in contrast, seems well-versed in scripture, committed to her own religion but tolerant of the right of others to worship as they see fit. While Lochhead here shows affinities with the attacks on Scottish Calvinism by writers such as Burns and Hogg and, in our own century, Muir and Jenkins, this is also an interrogation of the kind of prejudice and bigotry which so often accompanies adherence to any single religious creed; an interrogation of the kind of 'religious' leader who believes with certainty that he knows God's mind and can speak for Him, and who believes also that his is the only possible way to worship. There is a nihilistic destructiveness in Knox's approach as presented here which is caught in the imagery of La Corbie's response to Mary's questioning (Act I, scene iv):

> La Corbie: Knox has torn the Mother of God from oot the sky o'Scotland and has trampit her celestial blue goon amang the muck and mire and has blotted oot every name by which ye praise her – Stella Maris, Star of the Sea, Holy Mother, Notre Dame, Oor lady o'Perpetual Succour.
> Mary: But if he has torn her frae the blue sky what has he left in her place?
> La Corbie: A black hole, a jaggit gash, *naethin'*.

This interrogation of a supposedly spiritual creed is continued in Act II, scene iv. Again the dramatic presentation of Knox is by means of the Brechtian technique of *Verfremdungseffekt*. Where, however, in Act I, scene iv, the 'making strange' effect was achieved largely through visual effects – '*Knox, in bowler hat, and with umbrella, stands on back pedestal, marching. Two men, stamping, sway a big sheet like a blank banner behind him, swagger in to strut with exaggerated Orangeman's gait*' – in Act II, music, and especially the effect of dynamic, the use of *crescendo*, is the outstanding element. As always, the stage directions are significant: '*And our ragged troop swagger on like an Orange Walk singing out hatred in "The Good and Godly Ballad"*'. This is a very frightening scene. Lochhead has chosen ballad 23 of the mainly Lutheran *Gude and Godlie Ballatis* popular in the sixteenth century (1940). She has cut the ballad down from the original thirteen verses to six, choosing those verses in which the storyline is most clear and transposing verses five and six so that her ballad ends with the strong message that 'the Pape is the fox, Rome is the rocks / That rubs us on the gall'. The metaphor is the hunt and the identities of hunter and hunted are clearly stated: 'Jesus our King is gane hunting' and the fox to be hunted is the Catholic church and all its adherents. The ballad begins quietly, sung by the whole company, then stanza by stanza the dynamic

831

increases alongside the increasing violence of the language. When the final stanza is reached the dynamic is '*louder than ever*' and is accompanied by stamping as in the Act I parodic parade. Heard on the stage as opposed to being read on the page, this is a terrifying experience of being taken over by the intensity of the sound and, by implication, by the hatred and intolerance, the contagion of the message being promulgated. Although Knox and the Reformed church seem the principal targets here, the laying bare of religious prejudice and hatred extends more widely to include, by implication, all religious creeds – perhaps even secular creeds held with a religious fervour – which refuse to recognise the right of other beliefs to exist and which maintain their power through violence and hatred. The dramatic methodology of the play encourages us to think about what we mean by terms such as 'religion', 'spirituality' and about what kind of God we worship if this is the way we live our lives in His image. In Act II, scene v, where the Mummers murder Riccio with great violence, we see in a secular context the effect of stirring up hatred against those who do not belong.

Act II moves swiftly through the main episodes in Mary's story until, deposed from her Scottish throne, she takes refuge in Elizabeth's England. As throughout the play, Elizabeth is presented as the wily politician in her consultations over Mary's fate. The penultimate scene ends with her repeated 'Trick me' and the stage directions suggest that '*her manic repetitions begin to sound like instructions to invisible advisers*'. At the same time, Knox is scrubbing the floor as if to erase indelible bloodstains. In the final scene, all the characters come on stage:

> *stripped of all dignity and historicity, transformed to twentieth-century children by the rolling up of trouser legs, addition of a cardigan or pair of socks . . . and one by one Knox baptises them by pouring a cup of dirty water from his pail over their heads, soaking them.*

The stage actions and street songs in this scene are violent and vulgar as Wee Mary is questioned about her religion in traditional West of Scotland manner. Wee Knoxxy, who has been described in the stage directions as '*a loner*', comes in for mockery too and he and Mary are brought together by the children forcing his head up Mary's skirt to the accompaniment of a rude chant. Wee Knoxxy is '*crying in real terror*' – which reminds one of earlier suspicions in Act I that suppression of sexuality or unhealthy attitudes towards sexuality were involved in his difficulties with Queen Mary. Mary, like all abused women, is a '*sobbing shamed victim, ignored*'.

What is one to make of this vicious, bullying scene, all the more depressing because it is played out by children – traditionally associated with innocence – and children who will be the future of Scotland? An interpretation that we have learned nothing from our history, that bigotry, inequality and the destruction of creative, caring values continue to flourish, might seem justified, especially in view of Lochhead's comment in Charles King and Iain Crichton Smith's *Twelve More Modern Scottish Poets* (1986) that 'the longer I live in Scotland the more assertively feminist – in the sense of longing for "womanly values" in both men and women in this repressed violent, colonised society – I get'.

On the other hand, such a pessimistic and deterministic interpretation of this final scene would be to ignore the dramatic methodology of the play as a whole. For this is not a play – or a scene – which attempts to present an illusion of reality. Its stylised, eclectic range of performance styles have interacted with each other to encourage us to question the implications of what we see on the stage; role-playing has been foregrounded and characters have been presented with alternative roles and choices. This methodology encourages us as audience to realise that things can be other than they are, as Brecht instructed his actors to demonstrate. Bigotry itself is diminished and mocked by the non-naturalistic method of the final scene where Knox becomes 'Wee Knoxxy' and his 'baptism' is subverted by the dirty water in his pail. Although the anachronistic imagery does indeed link past and present, making us aware that our present is not all that it could be, one could argue strongly that ultimately the dramatic method as a whole communicates an optimistic message in the way it leads us to understand that interpretations can be questioned, prejudices investigated and overturned, different choices made. Mary's ending may well point us to our new beginning.

CHAPTER 40

SCOTTISH FICTION SINCE 1945 I: CONTINUITY, DESPAIR AND CHANGE

MAPPING A WIDE FIELD

Contemporary Scottish fiction is arguably the most successful and vital genre of modern Scottish literature, and certainly the most prolific and controversial. It is also the area of literature which most attracts readers and students. The treatment here, even when extended to two long chapters, cannot hope to do more than indicate the main features of the work since the war, together with a brief discussion of the work of the most significant writers. It may help to begin with some of the most informative critical material available.

Francis Hart's *The Scottish Novel* (1978) is the only attempt at a complete history so far. The various essays on modern fiction in *The History of Scottish Literature, Twentieth Century*, vol. 4 (1988) give more recent coverage; while fiction by women is given extensive treatment both on specific authors such as Mitchison, Spark, Duncan, Kesson and Davie, and in detailed introductions to contemporary writers such as Margaret Elphinstone, Janice Galloway, Sian Hayton, Alison Kennedy, Joan Lingard, Agnes Owens and Dilys Rose in two extended accounts of contemporary women's fiction in *A History of Scottish Women's Writing* (1997). This, with the essays in *Scottish Fiction since the Seventies* (1993), and the companion volumes *Studies in Scottish Fiction: Twentieth Century* (1990) and *Scottish Fiction since 1945* (1996) come up almost to the present. Marshall Walker's *Scottish Literature since 1707* (1996) has useful contemporary coverage, while for particular novels by McColla, Kennaway, Spark, Williams, Mackay Brown, McIlvanney, Jenkins and Gray, Isobel Murray and Bob Tait's *Ten Modern Scottish Novels* (1984) is excellent. Moira Burgess's *Imagine a City* (1998) gives full coverage of Glasgow fiction, while the *Scotnotes* series of monographs from the Association for Scottish Literary Studies includes McIlvanney, Mackay Brown, Crichton Smith and Spark. Important new discussions of modern fiction are in Cairns Craig's *Out of History* (1996) and *The Modern Scottish Novel* (1999). Douglas Gifford has since

1975 covered important new Scottish fiction in extended review in the periodical *Books in Scotland* (*In Scotland* from summer 1999), and examined the novel in the West of Scotland in *The Dear Green Place?* (1985). An excellent source of both texts and introductory criticism is found in the rapidly growing Canongate Classics series, which in our period includes fiction by Friel, Gaitens, Gray, Gunn, Jenkins, Linklater, McLellan, Rush, and Crichton Smith. (See Section 5 for earlier work.) (Since so many living writers are covered in the following two sections, dates of birth are given only for writers given extensive treatment.)

Modern fiction: periods, topics and themes

Since the war there have been three distinct fiction periods: the first, traditional or pessimistic regarding the past-ridden present, running from 1945 to the mid-'60s; the second, preoccupied with transition and change, from the mid-'60s to 1980; and the third, carrying a message of qualified (and often faint) hope, from 1980 to the end of the century. Roughly speaking, the first period includes those writers who were famous as part of the affirmative movement termed the 'Scottish Renaissance', and this chapter briefly examines how their fiction developed after 1945. It then looks at writers who made post-war confusion their subject-matter, moving on to identify post-war disillusionment and scepticism as the main response of the writers of the '50s and early '60s, and presenting some examples of writers and texts. The treatment of the second period considers the way in which writers of the '60s and '70s developed this post-war disillusionment, initially maintaining its scepticism, but going beyond this to find some more positive, if ambiguous, possibilities for personal redemption in a changed Scotland. The move to a new optimism regarding self and society in Scotland after 1980 is treated in the following second chapter on contemporary fiction.

Survivors of 'renaissance'

The introduction to this section has already drawn attention to the ways in which the values and ideas of the 'Scottish Renaissance' were repudiated by disillusioned writers after the Second World War. Before, however, looking at the major periods of change and the major writers within these periods, we should be careful not to over-simplify the change. Many of the great Renaissance writers continued to work well into the post-war period, although with changed emphases and perhaps with a growing uncase regarding the new Scotland in which they found themselves. We should include amongst these Neil Gunn, Eric Linklater, and Naomi Mitchison.

Gunn's work in national epic can be said to have ended with *The Drinking Well* (1946) – and it may be significant that, for once, the ending of this attempt to portray Highland regeneration depended not on spiritual and economic renewal within Scotland, but on an outsider, a rich American, to save its hero and Highland future. Later Gunn fiction is important, but very different from what came before. Now Gunn focuses on two strands of fiction. In one, he writes a series of what can only be described as spiritual thrillers, in that the surface stories of murder, revenge and espionage are in fact haunting allegories for spiritual sickness in modern post-war society. Examples of this line – with titles indicating their double meanings – are *The Key of the Chest* (1945), *The Shadow* (1948), *The Lost Chart* (1949) and *Bloodhunt* (1952). In the other, Gunn follows a spiritual quest for ultimate meaning, fusing Eastern and classical myth with his own searching enquiry, in difficult but often richly comic novels like *The Silver Bough* (1954), *The Well at the World's End* (1951) and *The Other Landscape* (1954), and rounding off forty years of fiction with an unconventional spiritual autobiography in *The Atom of Delight* (1956), which holds the keys to an understanding of Gunn's achievement.

Something of the same move away from national epic can be seen in Linklater's later work. Linklater had always tempered visionary nationalism with sardonic wit; but after the war his humour darkened, becoming even more sceptical regarding the human condition. The superb and often supernatural stories in *Sealskin Trousers* (1947), which give ambiguous twists to traditional folklore, and his disturbing portrayal of a modern Devil-figure in *Mr Byculla* (1950), can be seen as his farewell to Renaissance themes. With *The Merry Muse* (1959) and its sardonic portrayal of the career and death of the likeable, world-weary misfit Scottish poet Hector McRae in an absurd road accident, Linklater seemed to be symbolising what he saw as the decline of an older Scotland in a new, ridiculous, and materialistic world. Later novels shared this scepticism – although in two of his last novels, *A Man Over Forty* (1963) and *A Terrible Freedom* (1966), he moved into a powerful new phase of metaphysical enquiry into dreams and the roots of identity, in ways shared by Gunn's final fictions.

Naomi Mitchison differs from Gunn and Linklater in an important respect. Prior to the war, living and working in the circles of power and culture in London, she had been celebrated as one of the new writers of historical fiction. Her autobiographies reveal however that underneath the dazzling success Mitchison was, from the mid-'20s, becoming uneasy about her sense of identity. She lost a child in 1927; she would lose another in 1940. The retracing of roots portrayed in her first novel *The Conquered* (1923), in which the Roman slave Meromic follows wolf-tracks back to Gaul and his fatherland, was to be prophetic; and through the war years Mitchison, translated from London to Kintyre, remade herself as a Scottish novelist, with *The Bull Calves* of 1947 (discussed in Section 5) as the epic culmination of this process, in which her present post-war re-affirmation of identity with Scotland was presented through her fictional eighteenth-century and post-Culloden heroine-ancestor, Kirsty Haldane. Nothing which followed – and Mitchison produced another thirty-odd novels and collections of stories as well as numerous volumes of travel, memoirs, drama and polemic from 1947 till her death in 1999 – attempted to work on this scale, but the later work is remarkably varied and positive in topic and treatment – and is therefore treated in the next chapter.

Defending the rural

For all the disillusionment of older writers with Renaissance belief in the fundamental importance for human life of the rhythms of land and season, it would be unfair not to acknowledge the continuing defence of rural strengths and traditions by a dwindling, but still impressive group of writers. They form no modern movement, but in comparative isolation have continued to maintain that there is dignity and fitness in humanity's elemental relationship with land and sea.

Oddly enough, the outstanding (and most neglected) writer of this grouping was also one of the most powerful antagonists of the Renaissance novelists. John McNeillie's *The Wigtown Ploughman* (1939) had sought to present a corrective picture of life on the land, with its protagonist drunken wife-beater Andy dead to almost all the beauties of nature. The local furore which greeted his novel may well be the reason behind his change of name and move to England. As Ian Niall he became famous for his naturalist non-fiction, in work like *The Poacher's Handbook* (1946) through the next thirty years; and while his post-war novels, set in England, like *Foxhollow* (1949), *No Resting Place* (1949) and *The Deluge* (1951), continued to expose the brutal realities of country life in apparently idyllic communities, his later fictions, several of which return to Scotland, adopt a markedly different attitude to those who work the land and live in isolated places. His *The Country Blacksmith* (1966) and *A Galloway Childhood* (1967), his autobiography, mark the change-over to a view which sees dignity and elemental simplicity in the lives of a series of archetypal country figures. In *The Galloway Shepherd* (1970), *The*

Village Policeman (1971) and *The Forester* (1972) Niall presents his figures on a landscape with the barest of fictionalisation; they are life-studies, without any surrounding apparatus of the land-myths or spiritualism of writers such as Gibbon, Gunn or Mackay Brown. In this respect Niall's work can be read as an important sign of a new way of reading landscape, devoid of sentimentalisation but introducing a new yet realistic optimism.

The work of David Toulmin has been compared to that of Lewis Grassic Gibbon, but Toulmin's vision, while absolutely focused on the lives of his north-east farmers, had more in keeping with that of James Barke and *The Land of the Leal* (1939) in its unwillingness to turn harsh reality into poetic myth. Toulmin viewed his landscape and people as one of them, without Gibbon's poetic detachment. *Hard Shining Corn* (1972), *Straw into Gold* (1973), *Harvest Home* (1978) and *A Chiel Among Them* (1982) contain the best of his wryly humorous, yet often tragic stories and sketches, while his novel, *Blown Seed* (1976), while over-consciously imitative of 'the speak', the community voice developed by Gibbon with its unmistakable sing-song rhythm, is poignant in its re-creation of the bleak lives of the MacKinnons of Bogmyrtle farm. Yet these lives are seen with love and respect too, as is their older landscape; and Toulmin's work overall is a moving testimony to the past, with an undertone of contempt for what is taking its place. So too is David Kerr Cameron's comparable novel, *A Kist of Sorrows* (1987). These novels, together with Toulmin's stories and essays and Cameron's series on the lives and traditions of the crofters in non-fiction accounts like *The Ballad and the Plough* and *Willie Gavin, Crofter Man* (1980), show how strong were the traditions of the north-east and how influential Gibbon's trilogy.

These writers can be seen to belong to older worlds, if none the less important for that. Some younger writers, however, continued to work in their tradition of lament for an organic past. In *Peace Comes Dropping Slow* (1983) Christopher Rush gives a poetic and elegiac account of Fife's sea-coast and fishing tradition, together with a profound sense of loss. Without Mackay Brown's mixture of religious and traditional belief to sustain him, he shares Brown's antipathy to material 'progress', and shares also Brown's clear and vivid imagery and poetic rhythm. *A Twelvemonth and a Day* (1985) is, if anything, even keener than Brown in its lament for his lost community, and closer to Brown in its structure – each month is a chapter, with a sustaining patterning of natural seasons in which the human stories are embedded. The difference lies in Rush's brave, if not entirely successful, attempt to embed these powerful stories in a background of English literature. With *Into the Ebb* (1989) the determination to see old and new Fife through perspectives so close to Brown's view of the Orkneys begins to seem forced, although the stories of modern Fife, setting sea and weather against cafes, transistors and teenage love, have an anger and engagement found less in the more contrived historical tales. Colin Mackay likewise celebrates ancient rhythms of land and time, outstandingly in *The Song of the Forest* (1986), written in the tradition of Gunn's *Sun Circle* and Mitchison's *The Corn King and The Spring Queen.* This timeless story of earth-magic, with its villagers, a priest and a witch symbolically joining forces to make an earth-giant, the golem Uruisg, to fight the wolf-raiders, has a dark poetry of its own; the involvement of the animal world as participant in the drama is original and deepens the sense of the active role of an ancient Scotland. The earth-giant disappears with the foundling Mairi in an ending which shares much of the valedictory poetry of the great Renaissance novels. This mythology in which human and animal intermingle with elemental and unearthly beings anticipates the contemporary movement which returns to magic and mythology, treated below – and especially the larger-than-human and mysterious earth-gods of Sian Hayton. And David Stephen's similarly symbolic evocation of the passing of Scotland's atavistic and primeval energy in *Alba: The Last Wolf* (1985) shares Mackay's awareness of earth and animal vitality; this is a powerful attempt to link the death of Scotland's last wolf, around 1740, with the loss of Scottish identity and essence.

Land and sea magic, myth and ritual: the fiction of George Mackay Brown (1921–96)

With the work of George Mackay Brown we go beyond evocation and defence of the lives of rural communities and their traditions to a deeper level of mytho-poeticism, in which the surface activity of humanity in simple communities is seen for itself, but more significantly as a symbolism for fundamental spiritual and religious truths. Since the mid-'60s the work of George Mackay Brown has ploughed a lonely furrow, in celebrating Orkney past and present in a way which seemed to continue Renaissance values, but in the end can be seen both to set limits to these values and to take its own unique direction. It would be fair to say that Brown kept the anthropomorphic and mythical alive in fiction when most others were turning from it.

Mackay Brown rarely left Orkney or indeed Stromness, the Hamnavoe of his poems and stories. (His father was a tailor and postman there; his mother a crofter-fisherman's daughter from Sutherland.) His work draws from Norse tradition and mythology, perhaps even more than from the Scottish tradition which shaped the mainland writers he met in Edinburgh in the '60s. Above all, he saw his islands as a microcosm of the human race, which underlies his

preoccupation with the eternal themes of birth, love, death – and resurrection. Edwin Muir was Brown's Orkney predecessor; and Brown owed a huge
amount to Muir's own poetry, and his teaching and encouragement when
Brown was Muir's student at Newbattle Abbey in Dalkeith in 1951. Muir had
been impressed with the 1954 short collection of poems published in Orkney,
The Storm, and helped Brown to publish his first substantial collection, *Loaves
and Fishes*, in 1959. Muir's Orkney, a place of fabulous significance, became
Brown's, a land and seascape seen timelessly, stilled into heraldic quarterings
of sea and sky, peopled by fishermen with ploughs.

That said, Brown intensified and localised Muir's mythology, his conversion to Catholicism in 1961 paradoxically fusing with his original and almost
pagan view of Orkney. In Edinburgh as a postgraduate student of literature
he was profoundly influenced too by the poetry of Gerard Manley Hopkins,
with its clarity and sureness of imagery, and its refusal (like Muir's) to work in
fashionable movements or current styles. Even more than Muir, Hopkins
stresses a central spiritual dynamic which drives all his work. And this
insistence on an essential dynamic mythology has remained throughout
every poem and story Brown has written, in several volumes of poems, eight
collections of short stories, five novels, two volumes of poem-plays, and
several studies of Orkney, as well as stories for children and occasional
journalism. Virtually everything he has written has presented Orkney life,
past and present, as archetypal, an elemental expression of the meaning of
life itself, conveyed through a consistent and overwhelming symbolism of
land and sea, of seasonal change and the rites of passage of birth, fruition and
death. While much of this ideology came from the Scottish Renaissance of
the inter-war years, his fiction and poetry has real differences of emphasis
from those earlier writers, with their dreams of a lost golden age and their
presentation of central figures who stand for an enduring Scotland. Brown's
vision is at once more and less affirmative than theirs.

His fiction opened with two magnificent volumes of short stories – *A
Calendar of Love* (1967) and *A Time to Keep* (1969). Their titles sum up a
fundamental aspect of his fiction; its preoccupation with patterning, with the
stories embedded in a structure of months, seasons, the seven ages of
humanity, stages in Catholic ritual, – such as the stations of the cross –
and the sense that all things have their time and place in an order beyond our
ken. Yet within this – as with the dark short story 'Celia' – there existed a
strand of weary doubt, suggesting a tension between scepticism and faith.
This, expressed with Brown's astonishing poetic gift of lucid image and
appropriate metaphor, created the vital theme running through all these
stories of modern Orkney and its drunken fishermen and their failed loves

and lives, and old Orkney with its Viking ferocity and its clashing religions. *Greenvoe* (1972) crystallised this early perception of Orkney. Yet while its closing scenes were affirmative, with the farmers banished by the island's nuclear project returning in their own cycle of time to their ancient service to the land (much the same message as Muir's 'The Horses'), before this Brown had painted a far from idyllic picture of fallen village community, with the reader hard put to to decide whether the village had reached the end of its cycle of meaning, or whether outside materialism had destroyed something of ancient value. Richly populated with vividly realised characters from the alcoholic, tormented minister and his guilt-ridden mother, through island visitors and local gentry to meticulously observed fishermen and farmers, with its village and island setting captured with much of the rich poetry and detail of Thomas's *Under Milk Wood* (1954), yet with an even richer and deeper symbolic pattern of landscape and spiritual darkness and light, this must be Brown's greatest work.

If *Greenvoe* worked with broadly secular material, then Brown's next novel developed his unique Christian-pagan vision of the martyrdom of Christ as emblematic of necessary sacrifice as part of the human – and inhuman – condition. His perception of Orkney as representative of all humanity in *Magnus* (1973), with the sacrifice of Earl Magnus and the twelfth-century cathedral of St Magnus in Kirkwall standing outside of time, with northern versions of the Christian sacrifice and the Christian church, is unique. *Magnus* daringly juxtaposed the ancient Orkney sacrifice with Nazi atrocities, revealing the depth of Brown's sense of the endless battle between the violent now and the ancient permanencies (again, reminiscent of Muir's poem 'The Combat').

Brown's anthropomorphic view of humans in landscape goes far beyond the ideas and aims of the Renaissance writers. Such a vision cannot allow the nationalist individualism central to the work of MacDiarmid. And the later short stories in *Hawkfall* (1974), *The Sun's Net* (1976), *Andrina* (1983), *The Golden Bird* (1987), *The Masked Fisherman* (1989), *Winter Tales* (1995) and *The Island of the Women* (1998), while deepening Brown's conviction that legend and story, and the role of the community artist, were spiritually and creatively crucial, if now neglected, continued with familiar pictures of peasants, ministers, merchants and lairds caught up in the hierarchies of season and history – or losing that history in self-destructive denial – in ways which have caused some critics to complain of repetition and didacticism. Yet here, and in the novels, Brown must be allowed his own intense convictions, which have produced tapestries of community moving in time unrivalled by any modern author. His islands are seen in these later stories, as in his great sea-poem sequence *The Wreck of the Archangel* (1989), as vessels freighted with human souls moving through mysterious and yet ultimately God-ordained storms; and the frequent tragic bleakness of the stories suggests that Brown's Catholicism has not forgotten Orkney's pagan and Calvinist inheritances.

The later novels, *Time in a Red Coat* (1984), *Vinland* (1992) and *Beside the Ocean of Time* (1994), became more complex and fabulous in their meaning. The first personified Time as a suffering princess, moving across all history to arrive at the end of a seemingly endless and violent quest all over the world, in humility, in Orkney; the second, apparently telling of the Norse settlements in North America, in reality told of the sagas and sagamen who accompanied such heroics, emphasising once again the primacy of story and myth over reality. This movement towards allegory reached its apotheosis in his last and strangest novel, *Beside the Ocean of Time* (1994). A recurrent and mysterious figure in Brown's work (outstandingly in 'Andrina') is that of the island girl, who can be real or ghostly, who brings strange epiphanies to the islands. Here Brown went far further than ever before, in allowing the girl, Sophie, and her wild horse Selkie, to move mysteriously between actuality and symbolism, a symbolism whereby Sophie harks back to MacDiarmid's figure of the silken lady with her attendant suggestions of White Goddess, inspiration, essence of creativity. This novel holds in microcosm Brown's view of his own creative development and symbolises what he sees as the essence of creativity; it was perhaps his farewell to his art.

The cumulative effect of all Brown's fiction and poetry can be read as a rich set of variations on a great theme. His central ideas are all found in his poetic study of his islands in *An Orkney Tapestry* (1969), his confessional autobiography, *For The Islands I Sing* (1997), and in the posthumously published collection of his Orkney essays, *Northern Lights* (1999), in all of which he stated his implacable opposition to so-called modern and materialistic progress, and his contempt for the fashionable and the transient. In the story 'Sealskin', from *Hawkfall* which spoke for Brown himself through the character of the composer Magnus Olafson, Brown attacked 'the new priesthood', leaders of the world of 'every tawdry miracle – the phonograph, the motor car, the machine gun, the wireless'. Brown conjectured that the task of the artist was 'to keep in repair the sacred web of creation – that cosmic harmony of God and beast and man and star and planet – in the name of humanity, against those who in the name of humanity are mindlessly and systematically destroying it'. Even more succinct was his description of the quest of Everyman, in his poem 'The Masque of Bread', as 'a pure seeking past a swarm of symbols' – surely a description of all Brown's work.

Elegies for an older Scotland

To read the later work of these writers is to realise how much they contrast with the post-war novelists – though it would be true to say that the work of both George Blake and Guy McCrone hardly belonged to 'Renaissance', and prefigured post-war disillusion, from *The Shipbuilders* (1935) and *Wax Fruit* (1947) to their nostalgic later work, reflecting on the glories of an older Glasgow before either of the world wars.

The fiction of Guy McCrone is due for re-assessment; his acid edge in presenting the Glasgow middle classes who grew rich on the profits of industry and empire is best read in his enormously successful *Wax Fruit*, his impressive trilogy on the social ambitions of the Moorhouse family. For all his ironic stance, McCrone, like John Galt before him, sees that the development of the West of Scotland depends on a mixture of vision and petty ambition in his merchants and their families. In later novels such as *Aunt Bel* (1949) (again reminiscent of Galt and his magnificently ironic portrait in *The Entail* of Leddie Grippie, most impressive and sly of Scottish matriarchs), *The Hayburn Family* (1952) and *An Independent Young Man* (1961) he continued to show a middle-class Glasgow which is comfortably insensitive to the arts and complacently illiberal in its social and political views.

Neil Paterson's *Behold Thy Daughter* (1950), with its impressive protagonist Thirza Gair, the north-east fisher-girl who helps create the herring fisheries, as a more active version of Chris Guthrie, works within the tradition of Gunn and Gibbon, if giving way finally to melodrama. His best work (although it would be fair to say that this too works in an older tradition) is his novella *The China Run* (1948), the deceptively simple story of the daughter of a small-town missionary, sold in marriage at sixteen, yet becoming at twenty-seven the formidable skipper of a sailing ship trading all over the world. And several other impressive writers produced novels which even more poignantly looked back from a sadder and disillusioned present to events in that older, pre-war Scotland, as in Hannah Aitken's *In a Shaft of Sunlight* (1947) or Nancy Brysson Morrison's *The Winnowing Years* (1949). And this post-war mood was brought to allegorical conclusion by J. D. Scott in *The End of an Old Song* (1954), a sensitive yet merciless picture of middle-class Scottish rural life, on the surface telling the sad story of three lovers, set against the backdrop of a crumbling old Scottish aristocratic house, but through all this deliberately echoing the famous words, used to end Scotland's independence in 1707, in order to lament another, later end of something very Scottish.

Perhaps too we should consider here one of the most powerful and spiritually dark of Scottish novels, Fionn MacColla's *And the Cock Crew*

843

(1945) (which can fruitfully be compared with Mitchison's *The Bull Calves* of 1947, a historical novel which tries to heal Scottish divisions). Very different in its tone and mood from his *The Albannach* (1932), written affirmatively at the height of the optimism of the Scottish Renaissance, this later novel burns with unremitting anger at the atrocities of Highland clearance, with the anger directed as fiercely at the role of the church in collaboration. This may be a historical novel, but in the death of its misguided Maighstir Sachari, the decent but dark visionary minister who sees too late how he should have led his people, MacColla creates a powerful symbol for what he sees as a fundamental rottenness at the heart of Scottish society – a perception taken up again in his unflattering and bitter portrait of the extreme Presbyterian church in *The Ministers* (1979), anticipating the similar criticisms of small-minded religious bigotry in the work of Iain Crichton Smith.

The post-war fiction of Fred Urquhart should not be forgotten in its combination of elegy for old ways with an astonishing ear for the richness and vitality of contemporary rural and urban Scottish voices. Before the war his first novel, *Time Will Knit* (1938) had captured the changes in a fishing village outside Edinburgh. Spike, the American nephew, is witness to the random flux of modernity which transforms his Scottish family, his American voice alternating with native Scottish monologues. That of the grandmother, Mirren, bears comparison with the formidable voices of her great prede-cessors in Scottish fiction, from Galt to Stevenson and Gibbon; but her Scottish children have lost her rooted presence and strength. *The Ferret was Abraham's Daughter* followed after the war in 1949, with its sequel in *Jezebel's Dust* (1951); the familiar fictional Scottish character of a fantasising dreamer recurs in both, in 'the ferret', Bessie Hopkiss, whose dreams cannot over-come the urban squalor which surrounds her, be it in Edinburgh or London – unless her move to the USA as a GI bride can be read as final escape.

His later stories anticipate the increasing scepticism of Scottish fiction, as in his fine collections of short stories, *The Dying Stallion* (1967) and *The Ploughing Match* (1968), collections of his earlier tales which bear comparison with work like Gibbon's 'Clay' and 'Smeddum' in their fusion of harsh realism and symbolic sympathy for the passing of country traditions and ways, and for the broken dreams of his innocent country and city dwellers. Urquhart's writing came into an Indian summer with his autobiographical novel, *Palace of Green Days* (1979), his re-creation of the ways (and palaces) of old Scottish aristocrats and the green days of childhood, seen through the eyes of Jenny and Andrew Lovat, children of a chauffeur who is modelled on Urquhart's father. Urquhart's blend of the affectionate and the humane, the sardonic and the shocking is his hallmark; and he used these to striking new effect in his final collections of stories, *A Diver in China Seas* (1980), *Proud Lady in a Cage* (1980) and *Seven Ghosts in Search* (1983). The first revisited the Edinburgh he knew so well, of working-class energy and dreams; some of his finest short stories are here, in his ageing self-deluding, and tragi-comic misfits. The last story in the third collection pointed forward to Urquhart's final phase, in which he refashioned the traditional Scottish supernatural story into something which fused ancient and modern. Both of these last volumes achieve the precarious balance of haunting from the past in a contemporary setting, so that a girl at the check-out in a supermarket can sense the past, and finds herself as the Countess of Buchan hanging in a cage where she has been imprisoned by Edward I; or a pair of American tourists in Galloway find themselves in the horror of witch-drownings in the seventeenth century. Urquhart's final vision of Scottish history is depressingly convincing; he leaves the reader, as so often with Scottish fiction, with the overwhelming sense that its past lives were short, brutish, and nasty. (An excellent anthology, *Full Score*, edited by Graeme Roberts, appeared in 1989.)

Post-war scepticism 1: Gaitens (1897–1966), Hendry (1912–86), Haynes (1918–87) and Kennaway (1928–68)

Several writers of the late 1940s, like J. F. Hendry, Dorothy Haynes and Robin Jenkins (treated later), share much of Urquhart's tragi-comic realism, and are likewise bleakly impressive in their mingling of affection for urban and rural community together with a sustained bitterness regarding the effects of war, industrialisation and economic depression. This grouping is best approached via Edward Gaitens's *Dance of the Apprentices* (1948). Gaitens was one of the first to exemplify the new mood of disillusionment. 'The dance' is the ironical metaphor for the movement to manhood and the reverse movement of failed idealism among the youth of the Gorbals slums of Glasgow. It is on one level a dance of misery and death for the apprentices, a group of friends growing up before the First World War, but on a deeper and more cynical level, the predestined downward movement of all doomed young dreamers everywhere. The novel focuses on the Macdonnell family, and particularly on Eddie and Francis. Eddie will end up in jail as a conscientious objector, while Francis will die young, tormented by his impossible dreams of a green place to live, and for political freedom and equality; he is a powerful symbol for Gaitens's despairing view of the industrial poverty trap. But Gaitens, like so many Scottish novelists working with this theme, also presents rich humour and insight into the humanity of his slum-dwellers, in a way which shows up the melodramatic excesses of previous attempts to portray slums like the

Gorbals, as in McArthur and Long's sensationalising *No Mean City* of 1935. Scenes of the spontaneous and epic parties of the Macdonnells, vividly capturing the wide range of urban character through each guest's mandatory 'turn', anticipate the best of William McIlvanney's sympathetic social observation, as in the hilarious party-comedy of *Remedy is None* (1966). Both writers, too, share a sense of the tragi-comedy of poverty, as well as a basic theme of youthful idealism broken by claustrophobic circumstances. Perhaps Gaitens is limited in his empathy for women – his tone, besides, moves somewhat uncertainly between pity and ridicule; and sometimes he seems unsure whether to focus simply on Gorbals or to make wider social criticism – but the novel, together with his earlier short story versions of the novel, *Growing Up and Other Stories* (1942), remains the outstanding evocation of the heart of Glasgow in the inter-war period.

A novel just as poignant in its evocation of Glasgow decline (this time describing Springburn and its change from being the Green Knowe to the great birthplace of the world's railway locomotives) is J. F. Hendry's neglected and poetic *Ferniebrae* (1947). Hendry re-creates a rural Springburn lovingly through the memories, childhood and adult, of David Macrae. Here is an echo of *Dance of the Apprentices*, and Muir's *Poor Tom* (1932), as the familiar restrictions of school and religion and authority confine his dreams, just as in another neglected novel, this time focusing on Glasgow's East End, John Lavin's *Compass of Youth* (1953). Again, a grown-up narrator looks back; again, the essence and variety of past life and place is beautifully evoked; and again, as with *Poor Tom*, there are oases of decency and culture – although shades of *The Rat Pit* (1915) by Patrick MacGill and the dark edges of Glasgow poverty always threaten.

This threatening bleakness was to dominate much of Scottish fiction in the next two decades. In 1947 Dorothy Haynes had brought to wintry life the Lowland mill town of Magbank in *Winter's Traces*, anticipating the bleak ironies of Robin Jenkins's treatment of desolate small towns (as in *The Thistle and the Grail*, 1954) in her caustic but ultimately forgiving picture of a sleazy murder in a town of trauchled women, feckless men and squalling children. Her short stories, the best collected in *Thou Shalt Not Suffer a Witch* (1949), are similar in theme and style to the later stories of Fred Urquhart.

An outstanding example of the lingering mood of denigration and deconstruction of nineteenth-century Scottish icons is found in James Kennaway's powerful account of the end of an older and glorious Scottish military tradition, *Tunes of Glory* (1956), in which Colonel Jock Sinclair represents the Scottish soldier par excellence, but qualifies praise for his heroic integrity and force of character in seeing him also as an anachronism, and part of a macho and destructive tradition which has no place in modern Scotland. Arguably Jock's breakdown at the end, in which he describes how the regiment will bury the new colonel, whose suicide has been brought about by Jock and his men's hostility, is also a kind of suicide, as Jock inters part of himself and Scotland with his former enemy. Kennaway moves the older Scottish novel's use of the protagonist who represents Scotland from a positive to a negative meaning, as Jock the Scottish soldier does indeed stand for something very old in Scottish culture and history. Kennaway went on to present more disturbing and caustic analyses of Scottish character in other novels. *Household Ghosts* (1961) examined familial and sexual betrayal among Scottish landed gentry, with the ghosts of ancient family disgraces haunting the present – and the even older ghosts of Mary, Queen of Scots and John Knox evoked in the central and destructive love – hate relationship of Mary Ferguson with the local schoolteacher David Dow. Kennaway's presentation of vivacious Mary, destroying brother and husband as she pursues her obsessive love, is a brilliant psychological exploration – as are the explorations of other obsessive, self-destructive, and at times implicitly demonic figures in non-Scottish novels like *Some Gorgeous Accident* (1967) and *The Cost of Living Like This* (1969). His own character reflected that of his protagonists; he lived hard, with complex relationships, and a fear of early death – and was killed, by coronary and car crash, at forty.

Post-war scepticism 2: Robin Jenkins (b. 1912)

THE EARLY NOVELS

It is the early work of Robin Jenkins which most effectively captures Scotland's post-war scepticism – always, however, with a mockingly ambiguous glimmer of hope for human redemption. He began with Renaissance memories, with *So Gaily Sings the Lark* (1950), which told simply of how a Lanarkshire miner found fulfilment with his Kirstie in working in a Highland forest; but this was followed by a much grimmer picture in a novel which lies midway between *The House with the Green Shutters* (1901) and the sardonic detachment of George Friel's portrayals of adolescence. *Happy for the Child* (1953), its title mocking the Kailyard sentiment of the folksong refrain 'home then was home, happy for the child', presents an unremittingly pessimistic account of Scottish urban poverty in its evocation of dreary lives – mainly those of two contrasting protagonists, the one a self-torturing but brilliant schoolboy, the other a crass guttersnipe. Between their extremes lie the many positions of self-deluding humanity which Jenkins went on to anatomise even more perceptively. Parents and sisters, teachers and middle-class employers, are shown as victims of their prejudices and guilt, in a Lowland Scotland devoid of the consolations of landscape beauty or human grace – although, as always, glimmers of human goodness fitfully illuminate the moral twilight.

The Thistle and the Grail (1954) was even more satirical about Lowland Scotland in its picture of Drumsaggart, a blighted small industrial town and its investment of all its damaged hopes in the Cup Final success of its football team, the 'thistle' of the title, in search of its and the town's holy grail. Two characteristics of modern Scotland are treated ironically here – economic depression and football worship; while the events are seen through the first of a recurrent figure in Jenkins's work, that of the team manager Rutherford, who can be read as either a suffering saint or a whining hypocrite – Jenkins leaves the reader to decide.

This began a long series of complex and morally ambiguous novels, one of the greatest of which is *The Cone-Gatherers* (1955), the harrowing account of the hatred of a gamekeeper, Duror, for the two cone-gatherers posted on his estate during the war. The two are brothers, one a simpleton dwarf with a beautiful face and natural kindness towards all created things. In his trees, Calum the simpleton is at one with birds, skies, nature – his deformity cancelled out as he climbs confidently to the highest places. Duror hates him because his mind is by now poisoned by his own deformed life. His wife is a grotesque, bloated, bed-bound doll, simpering or weeping, utterly incapable of satisfying his needs; his mother-in-law a vicious gossip. For Duror, Calum becomes a representation of all the world's deformity, and the story builds up like a Greek tragedy, expressed through tree and seed imagery which is poetic and elemental. The book is filled with trees; and the minds of its characters are shaped by them too. Duror feels a great and horrific tree of hatred growing in his mind, while the cone-gatherers, collecting their seed for the future, are servants to the trees which are good and natural. And as subplot to this stark tale there is the linked account of a well-meaning aristocratic Christian who cannot reconcile her notions of class and rank with her Christianity, Lady Runcie-Campbell, and her genuinely Christian son, Roderick, who, in his admiration and love for the cone-gatherers, constantly shames and rebukes her. This is a savage tale, filled with grotesque moments such as the end of the deerhunt, in which Duror has forced Calum, who hates all killing, to march as beater. Duror's cutting of the deer's throat is shocking, and even more so when we realise that he is going slowly mad, and that he is here cutting the throats of his wife and Calum in the deer's form. Simple, strong situations and symbolic images carry this novel forward; there is no cluttering detail, no intrusive indulgence in landscape for its own sake.

The end is typical of Jenkins's enigmatic juxtapositioning of despair and hope. As this black tale of cruelty and madness works itself out in killing and suicide, Lady Runcie-Campbell 'went down on her knees, near the blood and the spilt cones. She could not pray, but she could weep and as she wept pity, and purified hope, and joy, welled up in her heart.' The reader is left to wonder how Jenkins can produce such a redemption from such bleak evidence – and to begin to realise that virtually none of the perceptions or epiphanies of Jenkins's characters or endings can be taken at face value, but must instead be placed within the author's detached view of humanity as a spectrum of self-delusion, trapped between visions of deistic benevolence and cruelty on one hand and an unknowable and perhaps cosmically ironic universe on the other.

This was followed by *Guests of War* (1956), which perhaps of all Jenkins's novels most strongly repudiates through its ironic reversal and grotesque comedy older fictions of regeneration through links with land and its rhythms. Bell McShelvie is a middle-aged, country-born woman who is evacuated from the Gorbals district of Glasgow during the war – thus Jenkins makes the war the point of clarification for her and for us that older romantic ideologies are delusive anachronisms. Bell and her simple but innocent son Sammy go with 800 others to Langrigg, a town like Biggar or Peebles. There, Bell makes two discoveries: that her memories of green places don't stand up to the actualities of Langrigg's snobberies, gossip and inability to cope; and that, in setting up a hostel, she has the qualities of leadership which town officials lack. The novel is one of Jenkins's richest in its varieties of character and moral perspective. No one, not even Bell (or with the exception of poor Sammy?) is clear-cut in goodness or badness. The novel's main candidate for hero, the enthusiastic and idealistic teacher Edgar Roy (disliked by Bell), who seems to work hard for the incoming children, if not revealed as having feet of clay, is shown to have mixed motives, and in the end goes off to war – to kill German children or die? Jenkins mocks his romantic idealism, especially in his love affair with a local aristocrat – although, as so often with his would-be do-gooders, the reader is left torn between respect and suspicion, to wonder if the grace of true goodness can ever be found.

The novel constantly reverses Renaissance conventions. Bell turns out to be no Chris Guthrie, content beneath her standing stones; instead, she fails to climb the mountain, Brack Fell, which she's dreamed of, in a symbolic ending which implies that Langrigg, the country, and landscape cannot be enough. Sammy is killed – perhaps intentionally – in this green place; her dreams fade; and she turns down the chance to stay on as warden of the hostel she's successfully piloted. In her climb down the darkening mountain, and her return to her husband in slum Glasgow, Jenkins embodies what he sees as the real choices to be made in his post-war Scotland. And this reversal of pre-war iconography and convention is aided by an ironical usage which will be taken up by later writers, especially Friel; in that Jenkins continually uses older and glorious names and causes of Scotland, but now in a debased and mocking context, to emphasise that the glory has gone. Thus Covenanting history and martyrdom becomes modern bathos, rich folksong and Burns become hackneyed and trite, and the tradition of Jeanie Deans and Chris Guthrie is brought, if not down to earth, then back to the realities of the city.

Jenkins continued to explore and satirise traditional Scottish beliefs and values in *The Missionaries* (1957), which equally mocks the secular 'missionaries', the officials who heavy-handedly try to evict the 'real' missionaries, a fanatical sect who are squatting in a holy Hebridean island. Who are most false? Or are there perhaps real miracles and grace to be found? And the darkest of Jenkins's novels so far comes with *The Changeling* (1958), with its account of well-intentioned but ill-thought-out idealism, in which a Glasgow schoolteacher takes a slum boy with his own family on holiday down the Clyde – only to find that naïve goodness can become horrible tragedy. Again Jenkins adapts traditional ideas, here that of the changeling, from its original rural location as the substitution by the fairies of a fey weakling for a healthy human child, so that the sensitive slum boy Tom becomes a demonic intruder to the holiday family – and to himself, as he sees prospects and beauty that can never be his. This first great period of creativity ended with an even more anguished novel, *Love is a Fervent Fire* (1959). Here Jenkins examines a nasty Highland community given over to lechery, gossip, and yearning for lost innocence. Again the war marks the final decline; the protagonist is an incomer seeking to atone for his war actions, but marred by drink and disillusion, and hated by those he condescends to help. As with *The Cone-Gatherers*, the abrupt shift from despair to hope may not convince all readers. In any event, the novel suggests an author who has himself come to a point of crisis.

THE 'FOREIGN' NOVELS

Given his disillusioned view of Scotland, it comes as no surprise to find Jenkins leaving Scotland in 1957, for almost all of ten years, to teach in Afghanistan, Spain and Borneo. And while these new locations allowed Jenkins to encounter new cultures and to find release from Scottish restrictions, they did not eliminate Scotland from his fiction; instead, the move helped him create a series of novels in which he explored his own perceptions of his native country through a series of protagonists, complex, well-meaning but damaged Scots who, like himself, are forced to make comparisons of their own with the very different cultures of these three locations. The confused nature of being Scottish is just as much at the forefront of these novels as the other great theme, that of the moral hypocrisy and injustice of imperialism. And while Jenkins did return to Scotland, actually and in fiction, in three novels within this period, it is helpful to consider briefly the 'foreign' novels here, as a unique and impressive quest for some kind of personal meaning and community grace.

Some Kind of Grace (1960) fittingly opens the quest. John McLeod hunts through the mountains of Afghanistan for the tribesmen he believes have murdered his compatriots Donald Kemp and Margaret Duncan. What he discovers overturns all his preconceptions; the Scots are not dead, but living through choice among the tribesmen, and refusing to return, for religious reasons which he cannot understand. The men and their barbaric leaders are no murderers; poor and backward, they show him a dignity and grace which shames him, and inspires him far more than his compatriots. This first foreign novel exploited the thriller genre; the next, *Dust on the Paw* (1961) is one of Jenkins's greatest. He knew Afghanistan now, and its tensions arising from Russian-American imperialist ambitions. He mocks older British imperialism first, however; the perspective is initially that of the British embassy, viewing Afghan affairs with superiority and condescension. But Jenkins does not stereotype; as in so many of these novels, there are decent human beings associated with embassy, here in Howard Moffat, deeply committed to the Afghan, angry at embassy prejudice. But he has a hypocritical secret; deeply concealed is his racism, his self-denied reason for not allowing his beautiful and utterly honest Chinese wife Lan to have children. Her grace is to know his real reasons and yet to forgive. Set against this relationship is another, that of another idealist, Afghan Abdul Wahab, and his English wife-to-be, the crippled Laura, which brings Moffat's hidden racism to the surface, as he attempts to blacken Wahab in the eyes of the authorities. He fails; the poisoner is himself poisoned, yet somehow, and convincingly, through Lan's immense love and grace, a charity all the more impressive because she herself has suffered more than any of them (losing her sister in the Chinese revolution), Moffat is pulled from the brink. Lan becomes pregnant, with Moffat becoming Wahab's friend, and welcoming Laura – who shames the embassy with her quiet self-possession and dignity. And around this ironic pairing of opposites Jenkins places rich supporting patterns, with the embassy snobs contrasting vividly with Oxford-educated, liberal and coolly effective Prince Naim, or local officials like the education minister and police chief. Jenkins symbolises the finding of grace in this novel with the marvellous moment when *shaddry* (the baggy purdah garment which conceals Muslim women) is abolished; the police chief's wife is revealed as a glorious beauty, in a blaze of poetry. Thus Jenkins – for once – allows human transcendence.

Such communal affirmation is not often to be repeated. In *The Tiger of Gold* (1962) Sheila McNair journeys to self-discovery through India, following her love for Prince Chandra – who is, in his wealth and beauty and power, the tiger of the title, although the title carries other rich symbolic resonances. As India reveals its contrasting squalor, Sheila reveals to us her shame at her own mean superiority; she finds humility, and reverses her estimates of those around her, rejecting Chandra, and finding decency and humanity in the apparently crude and materialist US family with whom she travels. And throughout, as in all these novels, Jenkins manages to juxtapose Scottish and foreign experience in perceptive and liberating ways, finding both worth and defect in the national traditions and identities of Scotland, Afghanistan, India, and in his next novel, Spain. *The Sardana Dancers* (1964) reflects Jenkins's two years spent there, and his comparison of the harsh treatment of the Catalans by central government with relations between Scotland and England at home. As with the previous novel, self-discovery does not go along with personal happiness and fulfilment. Jenkins contrasts two expatriate painters, one upper-class English and the other working-class Scottish, the first merely competent, the second a genius. Their relationship, and their relationships with Catalans and Scots, ultimately lead them both to varying degrees of self-knowledge and release – but hardly to happiness, since both are too much the victim of their national backgrounds.

The later foreign novels and stories are set in Borneo. *The Holy Tree* (1969) is perhaps the most fiercely critical of empire and its patronising yet ultimately dismissive treatment of native talent. Once again, the title symbolises ambiguity; the tree is at once the poisoned tree of Western learning and culture, and the Oxford scholarship which native Michael Eking yearns to attain, and the ambition which his imperial teachers betray; but it is also the very real and sacrificial holy tree of his people, beneath which he is killed – or sacrificed? – by them, for what they perceive as his betrayal of his roots and race – or as a propitiation of their gods? Yet another innocent is sacrificed in *The Expatriates* (1971), because of the mixture of arrogance and guilt of an expatriate businessman, Ronald McDonald, who makes his former Malaysian housekeeper, give up their child, to be brought up in Scotland with his new wife. In the suicide of the girl's mother Jenkins once again controversially finds a kind of redemption and grace in the chastening of the McDonalds.

A Far Cry from Bowmore (1973) is a fine collection of stories, the enigmatic title story itself exemplifying Jenkins's unique juxtapositioning of Scottish and oriental values and settings, in a way which honours the foreign and satirises the Scottish. A pious and priggish Scot (of a kind traditional in Scottish fiction since Scott and Hogg) is persuaded to go up country in Borneo to visit a dying fellow Scot. The reader's expectations, implied in the title, of exile calling nostalgically to exile (Bowmore is a village on Islay), are typically turned around, as once again a kind of grace is discovered by Hugh Macpherson when he discovers the immense dignity and love of his fellow Scot's Asian wife, and, through her and the dying man's last words, the worth of his own wife. There is unusual affirmation in this story; Macpherson learns to allow oriental religion its place, as he re-aligns his values, guided by the simplicity and vision of Asians like Dr Lall and MacArthur's wife, and, it must be conceded, the residual goodness of some fellow Scots. But clearly it is Scots who are mainly in need of such epiphany; and clearly Jenkins locates a higher worth in his orientals, a position which separates him from so many of contemporary Western writers, and places his work well ahead of the critical and moral revisions of the post-colonial movement. Equally clearly, the story juxtaposes the ridiculous with the profound, MacArthur's trivial last words with Macpherson's vision, in ways which allow the reader to keep the possibility of some final huge irony; is the far cry, which could be seen as that of Macpherson as well as MacArthur, for human redemption, indeed a far and lonely cry of humanity into the void? Metaphysical irony will come to dominate the later work. More simply and typically, another story in the collection, 'Imelda and the Miserly Scot', reveals Jenkins's disgust with the egotism and dour rectitude of the Scot abroad, and – as Jenkins increasingly shows – the resilience and the drive of the Asian women who fascinate these Scots, and who represent the movement to independence of their colonised peoples. Andrew McAndrick from Paisley (the name clearly indicating that he represents a Scottish type) is the womanising dentist of Api in Borneo. The latest in his conquests, a beautiful Asian girl, rejects his condescending domination, and kills him – the blowpipe which she uses, and her reversion to her roots, symbolising the way in which the East will reject Western imperialism.

These recurrent themes and patterns in the foreign fiction are emphatically reiterated in two strikingly similar novels separated by twenty-one years, *A Figure of Fun* (1974) and *Leila* (1995) (which belongs to Jenkins's later work, but which can usefully be treated here as a revisiting of older experience, and demonstrating how deeply and consistently Jenkins's foreign experience marked him). As always, they show his hatred of British arrogance and complacency. Both are set in Borneo; both centre around a Scotsman with

divided loyalties – a deputy director of education, a deputy principal of a
training college – and a tendency to pomposity and an idealism laughed at by
other expatriates. Both novels make this uncertain colonialist choose between fundamentally opposite women as wife; on one hand, a practical
Scottish nurse, on the other, an exotic and politically idealistic Asian woman.
The position of both Scotsmen is compromised by their high standing in
expatriate society and their links through clubs, golf, yachting, and the like
with the powerful local leaders whom their Bornoese lovers oppose. These
similarities emphasise how deeply matters of moral choice preoccupy Jenkins, with an intensity far beyond any other modern Scottish author. In a
sense the foreign settings of these novels merely emphasise and polarise
moral issues which originate in Jenkins's Scottish experience. The basic
questions are to do with whether one chooses to accept social hypocrisy,
injustice and comfortable privilege, or whether one asserts fundamentals of
Christian-rooted morality, but with the resultant price of being regarded as a
naïve and untrusted outsider to Western values – in short, whether one is a
worldy conformist or a holy fool. As in so many novels, Jenkins leaves it to the
reader to allocate praise or blame to his would-be idealists; his men and
women of vision, for all their apparent humility and charity, may be self-
deluding and self-justifying sinners, latter-day believers in the modern versions of that older creed which so plagued Scottish writers, the doctrine of the
elect.

THE LATER FICTION
Whether set abroad or in Scotland, the work of Jenkins exemplifies the
prevailing post-war mood of disillusionment with the fundamentals of Scottish identity. And, for all his world-wide search for meaning, Jenkins had not
turned his back on Scotland; the preoccupation with Scotland's psyche and
its problems accompanied him. Moreover, three novels, *A Love of Innocence*
(1963), *A Very Scotch Affair* (1968) and *A Toast to the Lord* (1972), written
during and just after the years of self-imposed exile, show that he had lost
none of his sardonic and reductive attitude towards Lowland Scotland. The
first, one of his most ambitious and moving novels, can be seen as a return to
the themes of *Guests of War*; the theme of innocence at risk, revealed through
displaced slum children at odds in a more privileged setting, allows Jenkins to
achieve his finest effects, with a finely-crafted interweaving and contrasting of
places and symbols. John Sneddon is one of Jenkins's most compelling
innocents; he has seen his father murder his mother, and he and his wee
brother Tom are taken from a Glasgow orphanage to Calisay (clearly a
version of Colonsay) for trial adoption. Around this simple situation Jenkins

weaves one of the most complex of his patterns of idealism and betrayal, as the island, though transcendentally beautiful, is barren, in the sense that its womenfolk are childless, its economy failing. One of Jenkins's most challenging characters stands at its heart, a figure whose Viking stature and attractiveness to women seems to mark him as an archetype of West Highland manliness. But Angus McArthur has a devious Celtic rottenness of the kind which Neil Munro satirised in Sim McTaggart of *Doom Castle* (1902) and for the reason of exposing the stereotypical charm of apparent good nature; like the later Agnes Tolmie (of *A Toast to the Lord*), Fergus Lamont, and the sinister adolescent Duffy, he believes himself to be one of God's chosen, and therefore above moral law. This is arguably Jenkins's most affirmative novel, however, and for once the goodness of children and women is allowed to transfigure the disillusioned Glasgow officials and the God-fearing islanders. Even scheming Angus is allowed a second chance to transcend his bigamy and betrayal, and to find dignity in self-recognition.

Here, however, ended affirmation. With *A Very Scotch Affair* Jenkins began the negative presentation of a series of enigmatic protagonists, at best ambiguous in their worth, more usually petty and egotistical in their holier-than-thou self-deception. Mungo Niven obviously represents a Scottish type, and his affair is at once very real, as he leaves his dying wife and family for a brief Barcelona fling with a ruthless mistress who leaves him; and emblematic, in that the whole affair of his life reveals some very nasty things about Scottish psyche. He is a moralising charlatan, a variant on Angus McArthur; and Jenkins turns even nastier – and perhaps surrealist – in *A Toast to the Lord*, with its Ardhallow (Dunoon) set next to the US nuclear base in the Clyde's Holy Loch. Agnes Tolmie is the modern equivalent of Hogg's justified sinner, Robert Wringhim. She too has a father who is a religious fanatic, who has poisoned her mind. She and her father bring blight and death to those around them: her mother, worn out with repression; the American sailor, Luke, whose shallow sensitivity and moral scruples she overcomes with guile and rape; and the by now familiar innocent scapegoat, Tommy Springburn, who will die horribly and alone in the wild. With echoes of Willa Muir's *Mrs Ritchie* (1933), this is a daring fusion of traditional satire on Scottish religiosity and a modern setting which includes weapons of mass destruction, thus adding an additional layer of irony to the moral confusions of Jenkins's townspeople. *A Would-Be Saint* (1978) reversed the irony; now young Gavin Hamilton in Lanarkshire is apparently a model adolescent – a charismatic scholar and athlete – and more, in his shining goodness an impossibly Christ-like figure, but finally presenting the reader with the insoluble riddle of his motivation. Gavin gives up a brilliant football career, since football has become Scotland's false religion; he gives up his beautiful girlfriend, instead giving shelter to a prostitute; and he becomes a conscientious objector. Jenkins is at one level asking if genuine goodness could ever be acceptable among fallen humanity; Gavin gains grudging respect, even from army officers, but he forfeits any place within ordinary community. The ending is as enigmatic as his life; the last traces of him are cycle tracks into a wintry and inhuman whiteness. Jenkins leaves the reader with the responsibility of deciding; is Gavin too good for this world – or a self-destructive egotist?

In *Fergus Lamont* (1979) Jenkins next approaches a character of similar intricacy from a different angle, but with the same aim of rejecting conventional assessment for the complexity of human motivation. He now for the first time adopts a first-person mode of narration, as in the sinner's account in *The Justified Sinner*. Fergus tells his own story with a curious candour. He is a child of the slums of Gantock (Greenock?), instinctively, he believes, rejecting their violence and insensitivity. He learns that he is possibly the bastard son of a local earl's son. The knowledge, together with hatred of his grandfather's unforgiving Calvinism and his wrongs towards Fergus's mother, inspires (or corrupts?) him to manufacture himself an image – kilted, of noble bearing, eventually military – which will let him take his place with the aristocrats of this world. He succeeds, marrying money and the authoress of pious sentimental historical novels who has the morals of an alley-cat. But underneath this level of ambition, despised by many of his friends, is what only the reader knows – the ambition to be a poet of the gutter, and a martyr-complex aiming at the fulfilment of becoming scapegoat of the humble of Gantock and his street. Fergus looks back from embittered old age over the chapters of his life; the movements towards disillusioned self-knowledge take Fergus from membership of the aristocracy and rejection by his wife and the society he has prized, to an apparent humility and genuine love in the Hebrides. But this ten-year idyll passes also; and the reader is left to decide whether Fergus is the quintessential hypocritical and selfish Scottish social climber, denying his background, or whether he is redeemed in reading by our understanding of his tormented Calvinist and motherless background, and his strange, but just possibly genuine idealism. And the novel – and Fergus – operates on a deeper level still. Like Mungo in *A Very Scotch Affair*, Fergus is archetypally Scots and the novel is about Lowland Scotland, and its deforming religion, education, class prejudices. In the figure of Fergus, Jenkins initiates a tradition in Scottish fiction of holy fools, insufficient idealists, who, in the work of George Friel, Iain Crichton Smith, and Alasdair Gray, reveal an *anomie*, a personal and spiritual paralysis and confusion, at the heart of modern Scotland.

And from now on Jenkins was preoccupied with the ambiguities of human motivation in matters moral. *The Awakening of George Darroch* (1985) is Jenkins's only historical novel, set at the time of the Disruption in the Church of Scotland in 1843. His analysis of the religious politics of the time is impressive, raising the question as to why this is, so far, his only attempt at the genre. The evocation of Edinburgh and the Lanarkshire coalfields effectively emphasises the central questions of principle and privilege; and the subtle exploration of moral motivation focuses on the Reverend George Darroch, who seems blessed with good looks, charm, a handsome family, the prospect of a wealthy parish, and an apparently simple and pious worth which makes his fellows uneasy. But his wife is dying; he sleeps with (then dismisses) his housekeeper and he will shortly have to decide whether he will stay with or leave the Established Church on principle. Darroch's person and action are presented in terms which bring him close to Fergus Lamont; he knows how his golden-haired appearance impresses his listeners, especially women, and his appeal for the church to extend its hand to the new industrial workers, while at one level seeming authentic, is undercut by his vain self-awareness. Indeed, hardly anyone is left unquestioned in this novel about ministers; vanity, martyrdom, and self-interest are seen by Jenkins as being ubiquitous amongst clergymen. And when Darroch finally does choose to join the walkout of the Free Church, it is his son who decides that 'for the sake of a minute's vanity he had sentenced his family to years of poverty'. Darroch is in fact not that stupid, and has a fallback appointment; but Jenkins has successfully posed fundamental questions regarding the claims of family and morality.

Just Duffy (1988) returns to contemporary Scotland, and is in ways reminiscent of the plot and theme of George Friels's *The Boy Who Wanted Peace* (1964). Thomas Duffy – but just called Duffy – is an illegitimate and introverted adolescent in a small town outside Glasgow. He is a kind of innocent – not simply a holy fool like Callum in *The Cone-Gatherers*, but rather the holy fool turned sinister, an innocent but dangerous idealist. Human evil perplexes Duffy. If people can be good, why are they not consistently so? Whereas in *A Would-be Saint* the thought of war led Gavin to pacifism, here it provides the justification for Duffy's holy war to 'save' society. But Duffy is corrupted by his own idealism. The motley assortment of people who comprise his army demand complicated moral responses with which his undiluted idealism cannot cope. He despairs after his own act of treachery and retreats into silence. Cooley, Duffy's friend, assesses people realistically and realises that Duffy's motives are mixed and therefore because of his idealism his actions will end in tragedy. Though more realistic than Duffy she is just as ineffective in changing society – indeed it is not even something she is interested in. The novel ends with Duffy resorting to what he sees as justified murder, but the world is unchanged. The bleak setting of urban decay contains a bitter vision: although goodness exists, the evil within us all inevitably overcomes it. The surrealist tinge to Jenkins's work which had appeared in earlier fiction makes this novel disturbing in its oscillation between realism and caricature.

In a different blend of modes, *Poverty Castle* (1991) also disturbs the reader who seeks to find the meaning of the symbolism of the title image. A novelist in his seventies wishes to write 'a celebration of goodness, without any need of irony'. He will die, and his long-suffering wife will bury him in Kilmory – where his fictional characters, the (simple?) Sempills, build their dream house, Poverty Castle. They seem too good to be true, with their disregard for title, their candour, their family beauty; their neighbours, common and aristocratic, are nonplussed and charmed, and their visitor, the critical working-class friend of the lovely daughters, unable to find the flaw she expects. Jenkins manages, however, to suggest that flaws there are, in hints of selfishness and complacency: Diana's marrying into aristocracy; Edward Sempill's lifelong but futile attempt to complete a great work on Scott; his wife's self-destructive obsession with having a male heir for Edward. His final irony, the reader suspects, is that in which he satirises himself as author in his review of his fictional author's idealistic and unrealisable aims.

Yet the urge to explore simple goodness emerges again in *Willie Hogg* (1993). This is a much simpler story in presentation – that of the hospital porter Willie Hogg, retired after an uneventful life. He has been well-liked; he is a decent, ordinary Glasgow man who lives up a close with his apparently simple wife Maggie. Maggie's sister Elspeth, who always despised him, is dying of cancer. She runs a mission for Navajo Indians in the Arizona desert. And the essence of the story is again in the meeting of two worlds in a few brief weeks, in which Willie and Maggie are violently wrenched out of their retired world, because a tabloid Glasgow newspaper takes up their plight as a human interest story, organising a fund and sending them from one world to another. The strain of the situation reverses the relationship of Willie and Maggie. She, simple and almost giving the impression of being handicapped, emerges as decisive, aware, alert on the flight to the USA and in the choices thereafter; Willie stays aware, but is increasingly confused and surprised. The bleakness of the desert, the run-down settlements and Indians, the greed of Elspeth's congregation who are there for the free handouts, the sheer shabbiness of life; all these get to Willie, forcing recognition of the question which is present in all Jenkins's novels, and which concerns God – is it all colossal irony on his part, a shabby mockery in which the good like Elspeth are left to die in agony, while the opportunists of the tabloids, the pompous of the town councils and the posh hotels, and the entire garish American way of life, roll on regardless?

Lunderston Tales (1996) focuses more tightly and enigmatically than ever before on Lowland Scottish character, in thirteen stories unified by their location, a Clydeside town created, as so often in Scottish fiction, from several originals – here, Lunderston fuses Largs, Gourock, Dunoon and the American presence in the Clyde, holding them together under the name of the Arran-viewing bay. The device indicates the intention; which is to work through stereotypes of douce small-town Scotland to explore their deeper layers, their ambiguities, until essences of situation and character stand clear, becoming Scottish archetypes. The deceptive low-key simplicity of these stories of small hypocrisies and rebellions, of absurd sexual liaisons, of the parochial juxtaposed with the exotic, recalls that older historian of Clydeside manners, John Galt – the difference being that where Galt mocked the ludicrous pretensions of his provosts and pompous townspeople, Jenkins manages simultaneously to reduce and ennoble his Lunderston worthies. Jenkins's foreword – an unusual practice for him – sets these stories as representative of a Scotland and Lion unrampant, 'happier on his belly, with his paws covering his eyes', yet 'paradoxically, its individual people . . . as interesting as any in America and Russia'. His fiction usually divides its attention between novels about Scotland and novels set in far-off locations; but in these short stories, as in previous collections like *A Far Cry from Bowmore*, he juxtaposes prosaic home and glamorous away so that both emerge as overrated in their romantic respects, but undervalued in their essential virtues. But beyond all evocation of town and its characters, the rollickingly bawdy widows and the cowed menfolk who make love under wraps once every six months, and the visitors from the big outside world who at once fascinate and annoy Lunderston, lies Jenkins's final and mysterious insistence on some kind of grace – that moment which can emerge at the most unlikely time and in the most unlikely circumstances. The greengrocer who finds out the irrelevance of family respect; the young plumber who breaks through Lunderston primness to find grotesque and almost holy sexuality; the savage old lady who tempers her sarcasm to forgive badly written books and their readers at the last meeting of the Ladies Book Club; the tart who marries the American serviceman, only to find herself stranded with him in the loneliest of desert filling stations, who has the grace to laugh and endure – these and their modest epiphanies are the lasting achievement of these stories.

Matthew and Sheila (1998) has an opening of typical ironic inscrutability.

'Matthew was nine when he discovered, or more accurately, decided that he was one of the Chosen, those favourites of God who could do no wrong, or rather who, if they did what in others would be called wrong, were immediately absolved and protected from punishment.' All that consoles Matthew for his motherless, lonely, yet privileged childhood is his moment of epiphany in the Hebrides when he feels assured of this election; but this assurance is to be challenged by one of Jenkins's most striking creations. The almost childish ring to the novel's title belies the monstrous nature of Sheila, the angelic, supremely talented schoolgirl who forces a horrific intimacy on Matthew – horrific because her ugly private face is utterly opposed to her public moral and physical beauty. Manipulating all around her, she succeeds in forcing herself as homeless into Matthew's house; and then he becomes her unwilling confidante, forced to keep silent about the unbelievably wicked things she says she's done. Has she indeed murdered a baby, and then the simple slum boy Davy? Does she go on, as she tells Matthew she will, to drown her father, leaving her to grieve impressively amidst Lunderston's sympathy, but to boast to the bewildered boy of her joy in the deed? And, when Matthew's father does eventually return with a native South American wife, is it Sheila's sacrificial magic on a bleak bay in the Hebrides which kills her and her baby?

This classic juxtapositioning of apparent good and evil is of course set up to be questioned. After all, Matthew's belief in his chosen status as one of God's elect depended on killing – admittedly only a beetle – but he will eventually see himself justified in seeking Sheila's aid in his desire to eliminate the only rival for his father's affections, his stepmother. It is Matthew who commits the final act of ritual and mimic killing on the sand-statue which represents his stepmother. And if Matthew's sensitivity and quiet decency is undermined, Sheila's astonishing duplicity is rendered as tragic when Jenkins effectively suggests the terrible self-torment that this far-too-intelligent girl endures as she fails to find any decency, morality or God behind human hypocrisy. What remains enigmatic about the book is its genre. In its curious pseudo-simplicity, is it to be accepted as a moral fable, or is Jenkins close to a dangerous edge where realism gives way to improbability? He has always walked this edge, emphasising the uncertainty of interpretation which his narrative contrives. It is a measure of the continuing power and success of this great fiction-writer that these questions continue to work long after his novels have been read. His most recent novels, *Poor Angus* (2000) and *Childish Things* (2001), may be familiar in their themes, but show no loss of ironic control, or intriguing ambiguity of character.

Post war scepticism 3: Muriel Spark (b. 1918)

THE EARLY SCOTTISH NOVELS

Kennaway and Jenkins satirised Scottish icons like soldiers, ministers and teachers – but the most effective ironic and subtle deconstruction of Scottish teaching was surely Muriel Spark's *The Prime of Miss Jean Brodie* (1961). Spark's irony and ambiguity concerning her colourful but dangerous pedagogue challenged traditional educational ideas in Scotland. Jean Brodie could be read as a new and necessary energy in teaching, or almost a witch, a malign force with its origins in older Scotland and her uncanny ancestors, something reminiscent of things that Scotland did not need. But the novel was much more than simply a critique of Scotch education; it worked with an eye for Edinburgh pretension and for the grotesque details of human relations in a way previously only found in the novels of Scott's contemporary Susan Ferrier – and to that extent Spark was consciously working with some very old Edinburgh traditions and attitudes. This novel is well known; readers can usefully consider it with another of Spark's novels, set in London, but with a similarly ambiguous protagonist. In *The Ballad of Peckham Rye* (1960) Spark presents Dougal Douglas as a vivacious and charismatic figure in dull suburban London society – but seen in a different light, as having many of the sinister characteristics of Jean Brodie: charm, dangerous force of personality, a poisonous charisma. Dougal too echoes older and dark Scottish characteristics of split personality and belief in dark forces. (The first Penguin paperback portrayed him on the cover as a beguiling horned devil, while Dougal himself (jokingly?) admits to friends that his fate is to wander the earth as a demon.) But while Jean and Dougal may recall older protagonists from Hogg's Sinner to Stevenson's Master of Ballantrae, much of their behaviour is also presented by Spark as signifying modern Scottish and Western psychological and moral confusion, in the protagonists as individuals, but also in their societies.

Spark has lived long and produced over twenty novels. She has received extensive critical treatment, but perhaps not enough examination of the way her fiction implies a serious criticism of Scottish insularity and psychological complexity, in the frequent Scottish characters and characteristics of her novels. Even when set well beyond Scotland, her fiction shows a Scottish preoccupation with the grotesque and surreal, while novels like *Symposium* (1991) returned thirty years after Jean Brodie with an even stranger variant on Jean and Dougal Douglas – Margaret Damien, or Murchie, a newly-wed in fashionable London who may well be also a murderess and a witch. 'In Scotland . . . people are more capable of perpetrating good or evil than

861

anywhere else', declaims Magnus, her uncle and wizard-mentor – and this assertion of moral polarisation seems to sum up Spark's ambivalent view of her native country. (Spark's later and non-Scottish fiction is dealt with in the following chapter.)

Between the dear green place and the new wastelands 1: Alexander Trocchi (1925–84), Archie Hind (b. 1928), Alan Sharp (b. 1934), Gordon Williams (b. 1943)

The introduction to this section has looked at how Scottish fiction turned away from rural and historical idealisation, in fiction like Hind's *The Dear Green Place* (1967). Hind's novel, and the fiction of Sharp and McIlvanney, are important in themselves and as markers of social and fictional change. In many ways they mark the final point in that decline first charted by Gaitens, and Hendry, yet show significant developments from them most of all in their subtle way of making the attempt to write a Glasgow novel its subject matter. After them, the Scottish novel becomes much more self-aware, so that later work from Friel, Jenkins, Gray and the new writers makes its fictions into more complex commentary on problems of Scottish identity and development.

In a notorious clash with Hugh MacDiarmid (at the Edinburgh Festival Writer's Conference of 1962) the novelist, poet and literary *agent provocateur* Alexander Trocchi claimed to have changed Scottish literature more than MacDiarmid himself. Trocchi wanted Scottish literature to be radically international, taking account of writers such as Jean Genet, Allen Ginsberg and William Burroughs, whose *The Naked Lunch* (1959) Trocchi's own *Cain's Book* (1961) echoes in its account of drugs-drifter Joe Necchi's dark life-journey from Glasgow to New York. Trocchi may not have been justified in his claim of internationalisation, but his existential and bleak vision certainly looks forward to a generation of writers whose despairing introversion and dystopian vision viewed Scottish city experience as suffocating alienation. Trocchi's outstanding work here is *Young Adam* (first published as early as 1954, under the pseudonym of Francis Lengel, then under his own name in 1961), which tells the story of another Joe (we never know his second name); where Necchi worked on a New York river barge, this Joe works on a Forth-and-Clyde canal boat. The novel echoes Albert Camus's *L'Étranger* (*The Outsider*) (1942); its protagonist suffers from a paralysis of spirit and intelligence like that novel's Meursault, relieved only by Joe's casual lovemaking, his observations of the twilight canal-and-grimy-township landscape through which he is carried in a sort of pointless journeying, and his guilt, kept to himself, regarding the hanging of another man for a murder which didn't happen, but an accident in which Joe was very much involved. This is the territory of Kelman and Welsh; more immediately, Trocchi's gloomily powerful account of a lost soul in a twilight Scotland neither urban or rural was to be followed by a series of similar dystopian accounts of spiritual failure by later writers.

Hind was the first to turn fiction towards examination of modern Scottish creative dislocation. The phrase 'the dear green place' has taken on a currency far beyond its original post-Gaelic usage, and beyond the ambivalent meanings implied by Archie Hind. We should remind ourselves of Hind's dual notion, which suggests both a bitter-sweet lament for the loss of community, and the Glasgow that Daniel Defoe saw in 1700 as the most beautiful orchard town in Europe; and, in more complex fashion, a lament for a green place of mind, of creativity and innocence and the hopes of youth. These ideas link all three writers of this group, all of them featuring protagonists, often young and would-be creative, who move in a spiritual territory between older traditional bonds of family and community and a modern and Western existential disillusion. Hind's novel examines more deeply than ever before the plight of the struggling writer hindered by lack of cultural condition, experience and encouragement, together with his sense of loss of older and better community values and tradition. Mat Craig's family mocks his efforts to write his Glasgow novel, in which he means to capture the solidity of Victorian achievement, and its connection with Glasgow's origin as 'Gleschu'. They tell him that 'people like us' don't write novels. Hind captures the day-to-day experience of Glasgow as well, if not better, than anyone before him – but without any trace of the violence or melodrama of the publicity-seeking *No Mean City*. Anticipating McIlvanney and Kelman, instead of urban stereotypes, he presents a city with many thoughtful and well-read workers, whose drama lies not in drink and aggression, but in the slow collapse of their ambitions and ideals. In this sense the title is ironic, since the final view of Glasgow, for all its worthwhile folk, is of a cultural wasteland, whose fitting central symbol is the superbly evoked slaughterhouse; and in common with others concerned with the lack of spiritual possibility in the city, Hind is in the end ambivalent, finishing with two questions. Is Glasgow's blankness of vision particularly a problem of that city, or is it rather a general modern and Western disease, causing – as it would for McIlvanney and Kelman – an existential despair concerning the validity of writing and art, and indeed life itself? Has Mat abandoned all intentions of writing his 'Wee Glasgow Opus' by the apparently negative ending? Or, seeing that we have just read a novel very close to that which Mat was trying to write, does Hind imply that his and Glasgow's problems are surmountable? Whatever else, the image of Hind's title established itself for the next three decades as Glasgow's, and its writers', symbol for Scotland's biggest city, and beyond that, for an underlying yearning for roots and a return to innocence.

Alan Sharp's *A Green Tree in Gedde* (1965) shared much of Hind's yearning, and his disillusionment, with its similar ironic play on the 'green oak' which in legend lies behind the naming of Greenock, the Clyde industrial town, lamenting and mocking 'green' origins; Sharp (in this and the second novel of what was planned as a trilogy but never completed, *The Wind Shifts*, 1967) anticipated Hind's portrayal of failure to achieve a sense of identity in the West of Scotland, and the world at large in his picture of his main protagonists, two Scottish and two English, haunted by their obsessions with failed religion and unfulfilling sex. Only Harry Gibbon (an echo from *A Scots Quair*?), drawing on very old and almost pagan Scottish roots, finds a kind of native peace in this typical novel of simultaneous yearning for and denial of Scottish identity. And in Gordon Williams's *From Scenes Like These* (1968) a raw picture is given of the fall from innocence and hope of young Dunky Logan. Set in the twilight territory which lies between city and country, in a blighted landscape resembling that around Paisley, with an all too convincing background of crippled father, nagging mother, and foul-mouthed bullying fellow workers on the shabby farm where Dunky gets his first job, the novel shows how environment makes character, ending with Dunky transformed into yet another brute male.

Between the dear green place and the new wastelands 2:
William McIlvanney (b. 1936)

William McIlvanney's *Docherty* (1975) can be seen now as the link between older fiction like *The House with the Green Shutters* and *Grey Granite* and the work of later writers like Spence and Banks. McIlvanney has written eight novels, a volume of short stories, a collection of essays written in anger at the failure of the devolution movement in 1979, *Surviving the Shipwreck* (1991), three collections of poems (*The Longships Enter the Harbour, Weddings and After,* and *In Through the Head* in 1970, 1984 and 1988) and several plays (unpublished; although the short story 'Dreaming' became a full length BBC TV drama-musical). The fiction comprises *Remedy is None* (1966), *A Gift from Nessus* (1968), *Docherty* (1975), *Laidlaw* (1978), *The Papers of Tony Veitch* (1983), *Walking Wounded* (1989), *Strange Loyalties* (1991) and *The Kiln* (1996). Outstanding in every one, for all their local humour and rich metaphor, is anger about social injustice, and a hatred of Western materialism, its hypocrisies, and its claustrophobic conventionality, as well as a sense of the tragi-comic absurdity of the human condition.

McIlvanney's thinking is rooted in existentialist philosophy. The emphasis on individual choice and romantic agony as embodied in the fiction and non-fiction of Albert Camus (especially *L'Étranger*, 1942, and *L'Homme Révolté*, 1952) gives an intellectual and yet dramatic energy to his writing which frequently sees moral debate erupt in the novels in terrible scenes of frustrated, almost incestuous violence. Brother will attempt to destroy brother, or a son will pointlessly but persistently and symbolically try to obliterate a scapegoat for the more serious, less accessible enemy, the society which has destroyed a father or a family. 'A debt is owed' is the revolutionary McArthur's cry in his play *The Attic*, and such is the power of McIlvanney's prose that the first awed reaction to the violent energy is liable to drown the nagging voice which tentatively asks to know a bit more about the nature and validity of this 'debt'. *Remedy is None* was a clear statement of this. Charlie, university student, well-liked, involved to the point of suspected paternity with a girlfriend, gets the news that his father is dying. The death changes him: he begins to look for the reason in his father's failure, for his father died a broken husk of the man he had been. Partly – and mainly – Charlie and McIlvanney see the reason in the desertion of Charlie's mother to remarry into the middle classes, since this seems to have broken Charlie's father, the formerly vital, cocky, real father losing the nerve to be himself. Charlie becomes alienated from friends, university, girlfriend. After several harrowing and violent confrontations with 'enemies' he discovers aren't the real enemy, he kills Whitmore, his stepfather, when the mother and Whitmore try to remake the family. Charlie is last seen in jail, symbolically and actually trapped, isolated from the society which destroyed his father. Has he found, despite this, an understanding of himself and a kind of peace? The reader must decide whether the ending is a valid closure, as with *A Gift from Nessus*, in which a middle-aged business man pulls himself back from self-destruction after an affair ends in the suicide of his mistress, deciding for honest self-employment and marital status quo.

McIlvanney settled on sure ground, however, with *Docherty*, arguably his greatest novel. Docherty is head of an Irish/Scots family in Graithnock, a town like Kilmarnock with its pits and very basic working class in its High Street. Tam Docherty lives there with his wife Jennie, sons Mick, Angus and Conn, and daughter Kathleen, in clean, honest poverty. Tam is his own man; not big, but indomitable, and increasingly questioning his upbringing, religion, politics, so that although he's respected by his workmates, there's a line between him and them; and Tam smoulders throughout this novel, trying to define what he believes he really is underneath his conditioning, and where his life is going. This picture of Tam is magnificent and compassionate. Tam becomes an almost mythical figure, and McIlvanney makes us feel the history behind him, from the west of Ireland to the harder and greyer west of Scotland. And in achieving this McIlvanney shows an ability to make character emerge from background as inevitable product, in a way close to that of Gibbon in *Sunset Song* with a version of 'the speak', Gibbon's term for the community voice, evoking past memories, comic and tragic incidents and characters. The tales told by the men in the High Street are from generations of ancestors; and for the Docherty boys, Angus, Mick and young Conn they are folk tales which dissolve time and become the life-blood of rural community just as they do in the rural communities of Gibbon, Gunn and Mackay Brown. Tam's sons are real human creations; but they are also symbolic in their varied responses to life of modern community disintegration and confusion of values. Mick, crippled mentally and physically by war, turns to Communism, reminding of Ewan in *Grey Granite*; Angus, physically proud and brashly materialist, takes on the bourgeoisie on their own terms; and only Conn, neither one nor the other, takes over something of Tam's older values. The novel reaches a climax which is no climax at all, but a ferociously described, moving, yet utterly ineffectual drawn fight between Conn and Angus – a battle which only expresses, like Charlie's in *Remedy*, both Conn's and McIlvanney's confusion of ideas and guilt about compromise. There is no epiphany or peace in this early fiction: Conn will be the progenitor of protagonists in later novels who carry on his inconclusive existential search for meaning to life.

After *Docherty*, McIlvanney turned to modern Scotland, with varying success. The Laidlaw novels are more than detective thrillers; as Beth Dickson rightly emphasises in her *Scotnote* study of *Laidlaw*, the genre is used to articulate criticisms of contemporary Scottish society in ways unavailable to other fictional approaches. The philosophical, liberal yet world-weary and damaged Inspector Laidlaw is in many ways a *persona* for McIlvanney himself, wrestling with real Scottish society at all levels, facing its disgusting deviations and yet relishing its redemptive humour. McIlvanney has used the Chandler-like detective genre as a means of commenting on modern violent, confused Glasgow; but despite the often dazzling imagery and metaphor, and however entertaining and absorbing the vigorously described clashes of lovers, families, classes and cultures, McIlvanney can at times be accused of melodramatising and even glorifying violence; drawing too heavily on traditional Irish and west of Scotland male-dominated ideology to allow him to be seen as part of the new fiction opening up debate and possibility regarding new identities and new gender and group relations in future Scotlands.

Readers may feel that *The Big Man* (1985) highlights the male violence it professes to condemn, and comes close to implausibility in order to manipulate its romanticism; for example, in the three-week preparation of an untrained amateur so that he can face an Scottish ex-boxing champion. Is this Charles Bronson and *The Streetfighter* translated from Hollywood film to west of Scotland shabby post-industrial hinterland? If so, it is a derivation which betrays its underlying pseudo-romanticism, a too-slick and forced cultural paralleling which could be seen as a distortion of real Scottish issues. That said, McIlvanney has, when he cares to deploy it, an impressive tragi-comic perspective on the west of Scotland, seen at its very best in the short stories of *Walking Wounded* (1989) which appeared in the same year as James Kelman's *A Disaffection*.

Comparison is revealing of the similarities and differences between these two great writers. Both are concerned with the ways in which environment affects its inhabitants; both identify closely with their urban landscapes and their inhabitants; both see a great divide between themselves and most of the rest of modern British writing, to the extent that both adopt stances of alienation from and defiance towards dominant present-day Establishment and aspirant social values. Yet the outcome in practice of these shared attitudes is strikingly dissimilar, to the point where one could imagine real disagreement between the two as to the validity of interpretation of modern urban Scotland. The twenty short stories have far more melodrama, humour and even romance than Kelman would allow. A business man is stunned by a young employee's abrupt request for a loan of £500 and three months' leave of absence; a broke and fading small town spiv pulls off a stylish New York gangster impersonation in a tatty bar; a genteel spinster dies in gorgeous underwear; varieties of middle-aged working (or unemployed) men take lonely stock of their lives as widowers or drinkers or ex-convicts or worse, as married men serving sentences, incarcerated in loveless marriages, stale with repetition and poverty, or irremediably damaged by infidelity; a girl lies dead of an overdose in her room as her answerphone remorselessly carries on recording her complicated life; a boy insists on dreaming, triumphantly and comically, through the knock-backs of no employment and the banalities of his family's incomprehension of the ways of modern youth. All the protagonists are the walking wounded, since all are damaged and vulnerable – yet they are handled with a humanity which combines an essentially tragic view of life with a deep respect on one hand for their often terminal predicaments, and on the other with a recognition of the energy, wit and resilience of ordinary people, which can sometimes redeem hopelessness. This collection, taken with the Laidlaw story, *Strange Loyalties* (1991) and *The Kiln* (1996) reveals that McIlvanney is in fact writing one single great mosaic-like west of Scotland fiction from *Docherty* on, in which descendants of figures in the older novel interrelate with characters from other previous novels. Overall, this powerful, disturbing interconnectedness yields a sense of angry confusion on McIlvanney's part; a respectable anger, shown in his polemical essays on Scottish devolution, *Surviving the Shipwreck*. His is an older voice which survives into a contemporary Scotland, restating old loyalties and yearning for old class bonding and community and simpler solutions, a yearning which increasingly seems poignant in its despair and romantic anachronism.

The Kiln integrates the pieces of the mosaic at which McIlvanney has worked over since *Remedy is None* in 1966. In many ways the later novel is a reprise of the earlier, with its young protagonist facing uncertainties in community and education, struggling to hold together a sense of integrity against a changing world. Lesser characters from other stories and novels reappear in supporting roles. Tom Docherty and Laidlaw move across from *Strange Loyalties*, with Laidlaw as school friend of the young Tom, and Tom foregrounded, with the added inter-novel dimension that he is son of Conn Docherty, son of the eponymous Tam Docherty, who battled heroically to make sense of his coal-mining life so that he could make sense of life for his community and his children. Tom is now a middle-aged writer, peripatetic, still as unsure of life and values as his father and grandfather before him. He is alone, drinking and remembering in a borrowed flat in central Edinburgh, looking out over a Warriston graveyard. The novel is fragments of memory, incidents of import drawn from all through a life which has involved the rejection of teaching, marriage, conventional friends and assured place in society, but with continued loyalty to children and certain less conventional people from the past and present. With the irony of *Remedy is None* and *A Gift from Nessus* we are shown the repetitive rituals of middle-class Saturday night parties, the conversations which mask betrayal and complacency, pushing Tom and his wife Gill to arid after-party recriminations and eventual separation. Interwoven with this run of forty years of memories from university to the flat in which the lonely man muses over his life, is set another, even more vivid set of memories; those of adolescence, and more particularly, of the last summer before university. This is when Tom worked in the kiln of the brick factory, with Jack Laidlaw amidst some rough good-humoured company, but with the growing realisation that at some point he will have to face up to the huge, dour, hostile Cran, whose only subtlety lies in his baiting of the boy with sneering mockery of his ambitions and family. The novel thus uses the central image of the Kiln to symbolise the point at which Tom will either be hardened and tempered by the successful meeting of this central challenge, or will crumble like the ill-made brick in the heat of the Kiln's ovens. As with *The Big Man*, some readers may find here once more that confrontational moment beloved of Hollywood films, which McIlvanney has frequently admitted as a central influence in his childhood. It can also be argued that McIlvanney's fiction works within a culture in which it's simply true that such confrontation takes place. But McIlvanney tempers his 'truth' with realism; when the showdown between Tom and Cran takes place, and Cran surprisingly caves in almost immediately, it turns out that his Achilles heel lies in his haemorrhoids. Thus, with the reductive coarseness of Billy Connolly and the folk humour of the west of Scotland, the pretentiousness of what a man has got to do is undercut (although the reader is perhaps left wondering what might have happened if Cran hadn't had piles; and if he had crushed Tom – could Tom then have been the crumbling brick, traumatised in his self-respect of life?).

Within the ambiguities that surround this moment in which 'truth' is mocked lies a clue to the complexities of McIlvanney's awareness of the ridiculous and claustrophobic nature of human existence. The novel continually muses on the absurdity of our condition, yet, while accepting no God-given values or meaning, asserts simultaneously the need for dignity of self, and the need to laugh at self. This last need threatens to steal the novel; for the account of young Tom's ferocious sexual drive is hilarious. In Tom's climactic encounter with the idolised mature woman, Maddie, he undergoes another, and similarly undercut, rite of passage. There is another Kiln-like moment of development to be faced up to with this perhaps even more significant climax, and Tom discovers that emotional drama can have a weird unpredictability, as he is forced to recognise the endless complexities of male-female relations. Once again the question of whether Tom has been hardened in the kiln of experience, or whether he has crumbled, is put to the side, in a way that shows how far McIlvanney has indeed tempered *naïveté* with experience. In a sense the kiln metaphor is used for both of the central situations of work and love, as a chimerical notion, held and then abandoned through reductive actuality. It is clear that the long journey from Tam Docherty the first to his sadder, wiser, yet still metaphysically challenged grandson is very much the author's; but it is also that of so many of the disillusioned writers of the post-war period.

Blighted nation, blighted cities 1: George Friel and James Kelman

The tradition of radical criticism of urban decline in Scotland and Britain in the Glasgow novel began as early as Gibbon's *Grey Granite* (1934), James Barke's *Major Operation* (1936) and, in a more ambiguous way, George Blake's *The Shipbuilders* (1935). Gaitens's *Dance of the Apprentices* (1948) and Hendry's *Ferniebrae* (1947) made this critique more sophisticated and harsher, while the work of Robin Jenkins revealed the grim monotony and restricted opportunities of living in the post-war West. Jenkins and George Friel share a similar nightmare vision of Scottish cities, and ask the same central question, as to whether urban society is to blame for producing its decadent protagonists, or whether these protagonists are failures in themselves. Gordon Williams understood the influence of bad environment and warped peer groups on childhood in *From Scenes like These* (1968), but also qualified his sympathy for his debased central characters. And, as the 'new wave' of writing about the West developed, this central ambiguity remained – in Tom Leonard's ambivalent attitude to closed minds and Glasgow stereotypes in his hard, embittered poetic dramatic monologues, in John Byrne's equivocal attitude towards Phil McCann and Spankie Farrell, the factory layabouts of his play *The Slab Boys* (1978) and his later television plays which presented a complex mix of social conditioning and personal failure of a kind impossible to tease out in order to apportion sympathy or blame.

And, while writers like McIlvanney and Alan Spence found epiphany and self-justification in their presentations of struggle and failure, James Kelman and Alasdair Gray, in very different ways, preferred to work in the tradition of ambiguity and enigmatic treatment of the nature-nurture controversy. Both Kelman and Gray leave unanswered the question as to whether their protagonists are victims of a Scottish, deprived, post-war and grey environment and upbringing, or whether the faults lie essentially in themselves. To this extent the work of Kelman emerges from an ethos, and perhaps even a literary movement, in the west of Scotland, which includes writers like Byrne, Leonard, Gray, Lochhead, and the even 'newer-wave' writing of Iain Banks and Frank Kuppner.

The separation of the previous grouping of writers from the following might seem unnecessary, since they share many themes and approaches. But where the previous three look back with an angry nostalgia to the past, this group deal satirically and uncompromisingly with the actualities of what Scottish – and Western – society has become, each in their own way finding a new style and language strategy, together with a black humour, for what they see as possibly irreversible social decline. With slight exception, their protagonists are not allowed hope, but are seen almost as outcasts, flawed and ill-fitted for their worlds.

George Friel (1910–76)

George Friel first articulated this new kind of sardonic social scepticism, and nowhere more powerfully and intelligently than in *Mr Alfred MA* (1972). With much of Jenkins's reduction of irrelevant idealism, but with less ambivalence and perhaps more humanity he portrays Mr Alfred, a prematurely middle-aged, disillusioned, semi-alcoholic teacher in a rough comprehensive school in Tordhu, in the east of Glasgow. ('Tor dhu' is Friel's satirical Gaelic re-naming of Blackhill, notorious in reality for multiple deprivation, bad housing, drugs and hostile youth.) Gerry Provan is one of his pupils, from a broken home, with a survivor's street awareness and a hatred of teachers, rules and all authority.

Friel interweaves the lives of these two, with Gerry causing the slow downfall of Mr Alfred through his sly distortions and slander. What makes the novel so original, in its style and theme and in its treatment of Glasgow, is its unique mixture of detached and intelligent irony and its implied sympathy. Mr Alfred may be a failure, but he has much that redeems him and endears him to the reader: he is a failed but possibly genuine poet; he holds traditional but liberal views; and is instinctively a helper of weaker children and colleagues. For all the sympathy, however, Friel mercilessly shows how he helps to bring about his own ruin, through his self-indulgent and ambiguous relationship with his favourite pupil, the lovely Rose (who, far from Alfred's image of her as a gentle paragon, is in fact a foul-tongued hoyden). What were his final intentions towards her? Friel leaves this open, like so much of the final meaning of this enigmatic study of the waste of education on the young. Highly original too is Friel's recurrent ironical use of metaphors of animal innocence, with violent children seen as 'colts' and 'fillies' as though they merely indulge youthful high spirits, when they are involved in gang-fights to the death with belts and knives in the lanes around their school.

Thus Friel symbolises decline of society and standards, achieving an effect of profound and perhaps prophetic pessimism about the possibility of modern education ever really improving the raw material of modern society. Maybe this was due to Friel's own lifetime experience as a teacher in similar conditions; and perhaps his scepticism here explains why the book goes on to mock all would-be helpful social systems, from social workers to armchair do-gooders, and most of all the media who thrive on the sensational failures of these systems, as they do with Gerry Provan and the gangfights he incites.

Friel's ending is surreal and apocalyptic, in his scenes of Alfred's final descent into madness, and his meeting, real or imaginary, with a familiar demonic figure in Scottish fiction, in this case in the nightmare embodiment of all Glasgow's evils, the demonic Tod, the archetypal monster product of debased streets and bad living. The novel presents a final picture of the decline of Glasgow into surreal wasteland. Friel is unsure where to allocate blame – is it with the system which produces slums, the lack of hope amongst the children, or are there simply bad people? At the centre of the story lies the ruin of the suicide-pact pupils who had intelligence and reason to live, Graeme and Martha; and significantly, Friel shows how much of the blame lies with the neglectful teachers who so disastrously misguided them. The tragedy and the irony are made all the more chilling and effective by Friel's minimalist, elliptic and Joycean presentation, and his linguistic inventiveness and ironic paronomasia – so that, paradoxically, the novel's outstanding intelligence in the end mocks itself and the pretensions of society.

Friel had been developing his theme of failed idealism in earlier fiction. *The Bank of Time* (1959) belongs with the bleak fiction of the '50s, with its black-and-white realism (like that of filmmaker Bill Douglas in *My Childhood*) in its (autobiographical?) account of growing up in poverty in Maryhill. The theme became less personal and more subtly expressed in *The Boy who Wanted Peace* (1964), which has a group of boys finding the proceeds of a bank robbery. Their leader, Percy Finn, tries to use this loot to civilise his slum gang, and founds the cult of 'El' (the pound) to dispense the money for morally good purposes. His dream is of course fated; but Friel's ironies on so-called civilised society are inventive and rich, as they are in *Grace and Miss Partridge* (1969), with its lonely and self-tormenting old tenement lady trying to save Grace, whom she believes to be an innocent Glasgow girl, from sin – through murder. Grace is far from innocent, but there is a kind of residual grace in her survival, and her marriage to the author.

Friel's hatred of what society had become was most enigmatically and symbolically presented in *An Empty House* (1974), his last published novel. The house, a once grand villa, now decaying and surrounded by urban sprawl, is representative of an older Scotland, and older values; a feckless descendant, Adam, inherits, and lives uneasily with threatening drop-outs, the new youth of Scotland. As in *Mr Alfred MA*, the loutish materialism of youth is seen as an encroaching threat to the remnants of civilisation.

James Kelman (b. 1946)

I was born and bred in Glasgow
I have lived most of my life in Glasgow

It is the place I know best
My language is English
I write
In my writings the accent is in Glasgow
I am always from Glasgow and I speak English always
Always with this Glasgow accent
This is right enough

This, from the introduction to Kelman's contribution of six stories to *Three Glasgow Writers* (1976) (with Alex Hamilton and Tom Leonard), is probably the closest to poetry Kelman has attempted. It resembles Tom Leonard's attitude to Glasgow in important respects – the insistence on self-definition, on the legitimacy of locality and self-expression, and the right of the writer to claim English as a language which can be used to articulate Glasgow life. Kelman has a fierce hostility to all the social and aesthetic connotations of 'English Literature', based on his perception of its 'wee game going on between writer and reader', which he so witheringly described in *Edinburgh Review* 71 (1985). He sees the 'wee game' as underpinning snobbery, privilege, and outmoded political arrangements which dominate Britain today. 'Eng Lit' as taught in schools and universities is a state controlling apparatus of England and its upper classes to Kelman, and its root assumption is that 'in the average novel written about a working-class character, the assumption is that the character doesn't know as much as the writer and the reader, and often you'll get those wee things such as dialect, for instance, in phonetics. In other words, the person who speaks is not as good, or rather not as intellectually aware as the writer or reader . . . the depth of the sell-out is just so great . . .'

Implicit in this quotation is another important Kelman assertion – that he is entitled to oppose English assumption of effortless linguistic and cultural superiority through such literary condescension with whatever means of subversion of conventional literary practice he can find. Conventions of plotting, of scene-setting and atmospheric description, of 'beginning-middle-end', and most of all, of value systems in which good and evil, 'niceness' and nastiness, are shared in a 'British' way, are rejected.

One aspect of his revolt against standard English practice has aroused much controversy – namely, the uncompromising way his characters speak. From *The Busconductor Hines* (1984) on, his central characters don't 'rise above' what's generally viewed as 'slovenly' or 'working-class' or 'deprived' speech patterns; they speak with relish within such patterns, with 'debased' speech forms like 'she didni' or 'how no?' or 'Λw Christ naw' – and these are presented as utterly normal, so that the more 'literary' or 'articulate' remarks contrast with a ground normality which emphasises their alien quality. The busconductor Hines tells his driver that his behaviour towards him has become less considerate (Section 5):

> Look Reilly I mind fine when you were first out the stupid bastard driving school; couldn't do enough for your conductors. No matter what by Christ – a day like this man when here I am in a state of utter desolation, you'd have been out there dragging them in off the street just so's my head could stay as an entire entity, an entire fucking entity ya cunt, but now, no now; those days of the halcyon era have gone forever.

To which Reilly reductively and monosyllabically replies 'shite'. What is Kelman doing in such typical exchanges? Obviously Hines shows that he can articulate with 'the best' of Britain, as shown in 'utter desolation', concepts like 'entity', which many middle-class speakers wouldn't be so sure of using, and with 'literary' words like 'halcyon'. More important, however, is the ironic reduction of these in their importance, since Hines is really contrasting their affectation and unreality with the hard reality of the world in which he and Reilly work – foul weather, outraged passengers, monotony. 'High' language is used by Hines and Kelman's lonely and intelligent protagonists simultaneously for irony and defence, a ring of words around their alienated situations. The reader can become confused as to whether the defiance is motivated from solidarity with those like Reilly, the lowly-paid and assumed-to-be illiterate underclass, or whether the Kelman protagonist is rather a Camus-like outsider, destined never to belong in entirety to any value structure of any class level; but from whatever motivation, Kelman's stories refuse to acknowledge privileges or taboos attaching to registers or speech-patterns. Thus to Kelman (as to many contemporary Scottish writers, especially, interestingly enough, playwrights like Tom McGrath, John Byrne, or Chris Hannan) the use of what is conventionally regarded as foul language is not only necessary – it's just not an issue, since such categorisation of language isn't accepted as anything other than an attempt to create ghettoes of expression which will enable distancing. When Duncan McLean said to Kelman (in the *Edinburgh Review* interview) that he thought the *The Busconductor Hines* was one of the first times he'd found 'a realistic amount of swearing in a piece of literature', Kelman asked him what it was that made him think it was swearing?

> You see when you use the term 'swearing' it's a value. I don't accept that it is swearing at all . . . Obviously if I say 'Look at that sun, it's fucking

beautiful', obviously I'm not swearing, I'm doing exactly the opposite . . . So in that sense I object to taking part, for instance, in a discussion that hinges on the use of swear words in literature, because right away you've begged the question of what those words are, you know, and you're involving me again in a value system that isn't your own to deny.

One of Kelman's most telling achievements throughout his fiction is to repeat 'swear words' in casual talk in such a way as to reveal their lack of 'verbal violence' (Kelman's term for what he does regard as potentially offensive in language use). Perhaps he's not entirely convincing in arguing a purpose for repetitive use of such terms – he never really explains 'the reason' he suggests underlies usage – but he has logic in his argument that an arrangement of vowels and consonants cannot in itself amount to constitution of a separate and taboo category of utterance. It's what's done with words and sounds which matters, not the words and sounds themselves, out of context. And to establish this reveals another crucial aspect of his work. The language Kelman constantly uses takes place in reality in Glasgow and Britain. If it is heard as a kind of background noise, a rhythmic punctuation, then the more subtle things being punctuated by it can be recognised. The reader of Kelman who tunes in to this kind of listening, which no longer feels the obligation to shock-response, finds a rich and complex world of irony, self-mockery, allusion and sophistication, which argues convincingly that very ordinary people are much more self-aware, articulate and rich in redeeming humour, than is conventionally allowed.

Much of Kelman's background can be deduced from the stories. He left school at fifteen and started as an apprentice compositor. When the printing trade didn't work out he undertook several different jobs (and spells of unemployment) in different places, from Manchester to London, the Channel Islands, Wales and the USA. His return to Glasgow in 1970 coincided with poet and critic Philip Hobsbaum's arrival from Belfast to teach English at Glasgow University. Hobsbaum had a habit of drawing together writers in the places he worked – Redgrove, Porter, MacBeth in London; Heaney, Longley, MacLaverty in Belfast; and in Glasgow he brought several young writers together, from the US poet Anne Stevenson and Gaelic poets Catriona Montgomery and Aonghas MacNeacail, to dramatists Liz Lochhead and Marcella Evaristi. (They weren't always sympathetic to each other's work. Kelman was uninterested in Alasdair Gray's work towards *Lanark* while Gray records in a postscript to *Lean Tales*, 1985; short stories with Kelman, Owens, Gray, that he was 'writing a novel which used the devices of fantasy to overlook facts which were essential to Kelman's prose').

THE SHORT STORIES

It's a sad reflection on Scottish receptivity to new kinds of writing that ten years before Polygon brought out his first full-length collection in Britain, the US Puckerbrush Press brought out the collection *An Old Pub Near the Angel* in 1973. Kelman decided early on tone, perspective and style, and thereafter stuck to it. In *An Old Pub Near the Angel* it is striking how quickly Kelman moves on from the 'omniscient narrator' stance of 'The Cards', the first story, in which the gaps between dialogue are filled in with material like 'Duncan stopped and looked away' or 'he made a note then sat back on his modern chair', or 'his eyebrows arched in astonishment'. By 'A Roll for Joe', the next story, these conventional links have virtually disappeared, and the Kelman world is firmly established: of impoverished migrant workers, young men at odds with – but not estranged from – their families and background; of conversations which begin laconically in pubs or on pavements, where strangers give little away other than in agreeing that the world is a precarious place, and that the dice are loaded against them in particular. They call each other 'man' and it's not just '60s carry-over, but a neutral avoidance of 'Jimmie' or 'Mac'. The Kelman protagonist isn't socially and linguistically located in a Scottish context in the way, say, McIlvanney would firmly place a figure in a Kilmarnock pub, with Ayrshire dialect. Kelman insists that English is his, and his characters', language; by removing the coding which in other Glasgow novels would locate character in specific parts of West of Scotland culture and history, Kelman deliberately takes his underclass out of Scotland, and into an almost Kafka-type world, grey and vague around its edges.

Thus in this early volume specific place is quickly eliminated too. In 'The Cards' there is an unusual definition of place: 'Duncan knew every bump and hill on this road, he could also name every pub and betting shop between Garthill and the boundary'; or 'the journey to Killermont Street from Garthill bus depot took forty five minutes exactly'. Buchanan Street and Arnott's will disappear, like the authorial intrusions, almost immediately, so that the stories will deliberately turn their back on anything to do with sentimental associations or 'tradition' in any sense of Scottish 'urban Kailyard' or fiction of Glasgow manners.

Perhaps this rejection of traditional Scottish fictional representation contributed to the relative neglect of Kelman in the '70s. There were collections, either with others or in booklet form: *Three Glasgow Writers* (1976; with Tom Leonard and Alex Hamilton), and *Short Tales from the Nightshift* (1978). The first showed Kelman at his best; the story 'Remember Young Cecil? He Used to be a Very Big Stick Indeed' identifies with an exactness rivalled by few

British writers an area of urban life which can hardly ever have been explored at all. That's Kelman's point, of course; the story reveals the hierarchy in the billiards and snooker world of Glasgow. Kelman implies that this is as meaningful a hierarchy as anybody's; as good as the footballer's, the writer's, the lawyer's. It's significant that here and thereafter his work doesn't focus on football (or, for that matter, religion or violence). Kelman avoids Glasgow cliché and the world of snooker here widens out from Glasgow so that its context becomes international. Young Cecil meets his nemesis when Cuddihy or 'the County Durham' comes up to play him – and Cecil is revealed as 'a good handicapper and nothing else'. The voice telling the story simply accepts that his hearers will know the world he talks about; and the reader is assumed to share its values and inside knowledge. Thus Kelman turns the tables on that root assumption of privileged 'Eng Lit' by challenging middle-class readers to come out of their value-systems to explore and empathise with others.

All the short story work of the '70s culminated in the first major collection, *Not Not While the Giro* (1983). The very title sums up Kelman's paradoxical existentialism; there's sardonic humour in the idea that suicide can be postponed as long as the giro cheques keep coming from Social Security. There's a double edge; what kind of existence is it that makes its high points out of survival and drink money? These are stories about misfits – lonely, unemployed and introspective young men with cash and landlord problems in seedy digs. The high points of their lives are petty windfalls of dole money, or a cheap rent, or a new job; the low points are boredom and the realisation of the shallowness of self. Very occasionally Kelman allows a McIlvanney moment of melodrama, as in the short shocking story of the son who falls into a vat of acid, to be pushed under by his father, since he's dead already – but this will happen less and less as Kelman develops his unique, detached, vision of the human situation.

Since then Kelman has produced three more volumes of short stories, each in turn becoming more austere and detached in their observation of human loneliness. The forty-seven short stories of *Greyhound for Breakfast* (1987) bring a new perspective on his lost characters, alone or in families, which captures the random casualness and the empty rhetorics of relationships. Kelman's starting place may be Scotland, but he universalises it so that his characters speak for a modern rootlessness of language, place and morality. The US-Glasgow stream-of-consciousness reaches a new fusion of realism and surrealism in its disorientated complaint; as one Scottish drifter in the USA exemplifies in 'More Complaints From the American Correspondent':

Jesus Christ man this tramping from city to city – terrible. No pavements man just these back gardens like you got to walk right down by the edge of the road man and the big fucking doberman pinchers they're coming charging straight at you. Then the ghettos for Christ sake you got all them mothers lining the streets, hey you, gies a bit of your cheeseburger. Murder polis.

Later collections are *The Burn* (1991) and *The Good Times* (1998). These show clearly that there is an important distinction between the collections of stories and the novels, a distinction more subtle than that simply of genre. It's not a criticism that the stories in the three main collections could fit in any of the others – and that almost any of the longer stories could supply a title for a consequently re-shuffled volume. These aren't stories dependent on dominating poetic symbolism, like, say, Mackay Brown's or some of Janice Galloway's, like the title story of *Blood* (1991); nor are they normally dependent on a central striking dramatic incident. What emerges as overwhelming is the way the bulk of them are fragments of an endless, formless talking, drinking, walking, quarrelling, sitting, and petty doing and getting by of Kelman's fiercely championed underclass. Given Kelman's desire to be true to life, there can't be a poetic radiance – like, say, Alan Spence's *Its Colours they are Fine* (1977), those Joycean epiphanies of Glasgow street life, since Kelman doesn't hold with that kind of literary or religious experience. That's not to say there are not moments of communion – the end of 'A Situation' or even 'A Walk in the Park' in *The Burn* show respectively a guilt-tormented young man falling back on basic love to see him through his guilt and a girl reassuring her desperate lover that things aren't as bad as his wifeless and weanless situation might argue. But – and it's an important 'but' – the ends of these and most of Kelman's stories aren't closed: Deborah of the first story could pursue matters and find that her boyfriend has slept with her sister; the girlfriend of the Park may be offering cold comfort, mere trite cliché.

Kelman always runs a risk in such fidelity to ordinary living; that the danger is that 'reality', striven for with such integrity, may convince readers but leave them flat and preferring a literature which distorts and melodramatises life for dramatic effect. There's ultimately a paradox at the heart of Kelman's work that he should deliberately make stories whose aim is to remove the 'artistic' perspectives from ordinary lives; and in *The Good Times* Kelman is as uncompromising in this regard as any writer has been. The tendency of this latest writing is to push realism towards Pinter and Beckett-like surrealism, but in a way which suggests that the human condition is actually and observably surreal, as in the long-short story 'Comic Cuts', the most difficult and profound work he has produced so far, with its echoes of Pinter's *The Birthday Party* (1957), and its increased metaphysical pessimism. Alasdair Gray succinctly sums up Kelman's stories (in *Lean Tales*) as 'cool third-person narratives, obsessional monologues, and – the Kelman speciality – grotesque humour and real pity masked by dead-pan cliché'.

THE NOVELS

Kelman's first novel, *The Busconductor Hines* (1984) develops in depth the typical protagonist of the short stories. The study of Hines reveals a central ambiguity which runs all through Kelman's work. On one hand he can be read as a representative of a Glasgow underclass, and as such standing for the dispossessed and under-rewarded of the world. On the other, his greater intelligence, his zany irony, and his alienation from his fellow-workers shows him to be a man alone, like Camus's 'Outsider'. This duality of perception haunts the book; on one hand Hines relishes the chat of his fellow busmen, and typically bickers and socialises with them. He loves his wife Sandra and his son Paul, and resents the squalor of their tenement in Maryhill. He loves his Drumchapel parents, but doesn't see them enough; he resents the condescension and dislike of Sandra's middle-class family. And on one level this way of reading him culminates in his successful stand on a point of principle against the transport authorities. But there is another side to him, and indeed to the way in which his working mates are seen, in the opening scenes of their drunken invasion of an old men's club, and their loutish behaviour. Hines reveals strange depths; he could have gained Highers at school but chose not to – and the reader never gets to know whether he's just lazy or whether, in his disgust at Great Britishness, he stands against self-improvement on principle. Certainly he is lazy; constantly late for work, constantly making promises to Sandra and Paul which he doesn't keep. But he is also in fear of losing Sandra and Paul through his faults; and a dark thread of possible violence is hinted at in his recurrent notion of getting a gun, for unspecified but clearly criminal reasons. This portrait of a loser – for Hines will never get round to changing or even emigrating – shows a man locked in a circle of futility, trapped in his life as in the repetitive journeys of the buses he works on. Is this the fault of a social system which dehumanises able people? Or is it the fault of a wilfully intelligent individual who chooses alienation from family and community as well as the hated social system?

A Chancer (1985) continues the exploration of the same malaise, in its presentation of the aimless life of Glaswegian Tammas, who lives uneasily with his sister and her husband, spending his dole money on dogs and horses, playing with gambling in a way which suggests that it holds some metaphysical meaning for him. Here are no hard men Tam Dochertys or Willie Roughs, raging against their cage, but hard lives, in the different sense of a bleakness and hopelessness which comes from repetitive banality. Tammas wins money, even seems lucky occasionally; but, as with his grim little love affair with a criminal's separated wife, he is locked into a cycle of self-defeat. The picture is the more convincing because of the little kindnesses which happen all along, from his sister, her husband, workmates; the fault lies not in them, but in Tammas himself.

A Disaffection (1989) takes the exploration of this kind of protagonist into a different arena, into the interior monologues of Patrick Doyle, the 29-year-old disaffected schoolteacher in a Glasgow comprehensive. The mundane events of his week are detailed with prolixity: he doesn't go with colleagues for the Friday night drink; he drives pointlessly down the London Road; he goes to a football match (and misses the only goal) and guiltily visits his parents; he almost gets a relationship going with a fellow teacher, married Alison; and he has weird and oath-littered classroom sessions with his convincingly precocious pupils. He feels increasingly odd and alienated; he finds he's got a transfer to another school which he didn't want; and he visits his brother Gavin and his wife Nicola, yet again getting drunk and not quite managing to relate to them. He's left in a kind of limbo – is he or is he not in trouble with the police? Anyway, if he is, that's the least of his verge-of-early-middle-age worries. This outline, however, reveals nothing of Kelman's often hilariously funny presentation of Patrick's elaborate, tortuous, profane and always utterly credible self-examinations. The effect is to foreground the bizarre, lonely and defiant musings of a protagonist whom it would be easy to condemn for his wayward inconsistency, and his seeming irresponsibility with his classes and his impulsive leave-taking from school. The patient reader who follows Patrick with open mind discovers endless subtleties, from his first opening account of the two strange pipes he finds at the back of the local arts centre (old electrical piping? plumbing equipment? musical antiques?) to his recurrent motifs of the paintings of Goya, with their dark and tortuous suffering, or Goethe's Werther, with his adolescent *Weltschmerz*, or his personal devils who seem to writhe all around him. With patience the reader can perceive the tragedy of a deeply honest and caring teacher, who draws back from spoiling Alison's life, who wants to communicate with his friends and parents but can't tolerate the dishonesties involved. As that happens, however, the central Kelman ambiguity returns to trouble the reader. At one point of the novel the children in his classroom accuse him: 'what do ye start all these things and then ye don't finish them or even just in a way follow them through properly . . .'. Doyle maintains it's his role to start and theirs to finish; they tell him he's patronising – and he responds by drowning them in Zeno, Parmenides, Pythagoras and Plato. Is he a fraud? Jean Brodie comes to mind, and Gray's Duncan Thaw/Lanark, or Jenkins's Fergus Lamont, or his twisted idealistic schoolboy Duffy.

Kelman is working in the tradition of enigmatic idealism so prevalent in modern Scottish fiction; the other classic of the pedagogic strain being George Friel's *Mr Alfred MA*. The pedagogic novel expresses the confusions of modern Scottish value systems admirably, since the clash between the realities of the taught and the values of the teachers simply exaggerates clashes and tensions at the heart of Scottish – and British – conventional social moralities. Doyle is trapped in the mire of morality and language; his ritual 'fuck it' at the end of a typical bout of self-exploration isn't just profanity, but frustration and fatigue resulting from recognition that the attempt to find any truth in the web of words, stock phraseology, and stock morality is vain; and that he, his headmaster, his family, and society are trapped in conditioned intolerance and contempt for other people's differ- ence. The Judas motif through this novel is thus simultaneously a reference to intolerant value systems of the past and, applied by Alison to Doyle, and by Doyle himself, the raising of the possibility that Doyle is profoundly self- deceiving, a self-betrayer of what he most believes in.

How Late It Was, How Late (1994) controversially won the Booker Prize. It pushes Kelman's examination of personal and social responsibility in terms of class, language, and moral ideas further than ever before. Joe Samuels – Sammy – is an ex-convict, around forty, back in Scotland, and living with a new lady, barmaid Helen whom the reader never meets. Some break, due to his drinking, or his honesty about his crimes, has caused her to leave the flat, permanently or temporarily. Sammy has problems with this, both since she's his main hope, and since he's now blind – blind since a weekend drinking bout that has ended in violence, when the police reacted none too kindly when they caught up with him; they know his record, and he's kept some bad Irish political company while boozing. Sammy can't remember the weekend, can't work out what's happened with Helen, and, most basic of all, can't get his bearings in a darkened world. Even if he could remember, however, he wouldn't grass on his mates; and he won't whine about what's happening, however bad. Sammy is Kelman's example of human endurance at the lowest level and the lowest ebb. The novel is told through his stream-of-conscious- ness, in a Glaswegian much more basic than that of Hines or any of Kelman's protagonists so far. He is not evil. He is naïve yet shrewd, hard yet kind, weak yet very strong. His criminal convictions resulted from involvements out of his depth, and his entire life is a stumbling on through false codes and hypocritical standards with a reiterated 'fuck sake man!'.

Kelman pushes his readers to the limit here; not in the sexual and viscerally shocking way, say, of Welsh in *Trainspotting* (1993), but at a lower level of mundane boredom, frustration, bewilderment. Sammy is thwarted by DSS officials, unsympathetic doctors, 'friends' who don't want to know him after his police run-in. It's almost that his blindness isn't believed or accepted, or that he's got blind deliberately to milk the system – which retaliates by obfuscating his simple condition with jargon like 'pseudo-spontaneous band of disfunction', to describe the doubt the snooty DSS feels about him. Battered by police interrogation, by unhelpful welfare, by departure of friends and lady, Sammy takes all this as normal – a little worse than usual perhaps, but to be coped with. As his stature slowly rises, our evaluation of him turns to respect, and we see a dignity and courage which, seen in the right perspective, seem heroic. Could we cope with sudden blindness? Like an old dog, Sammy noses forward, refusing to lie down, instinct threading him around obstacles, and a deep human slyness of the right sort enabling him to handle awkward questions from 'friends' and police alike. This man is a valid human being, says Kelman; naïve and easily tempted, but perceptive and constantly thinking in metaphysical ways about sight, meaning, reasons. The reader is with Sammy in the dark, smelling and feeling; a rare empathy of sense and situation lets Kelman make the questions of how permanent? What future? Where is Helen? surround Sammy, so that suspense – not usually associated with the style or intention of a Kelman story – carries right through to the remarkably moving if ambiguous ending, where Sammy's son and his friend come through with a disarming adolescent honesty that puts the adult world to shame.

Before leaving Kelman, it should be remembered that he writes plays as well. 'Comic Cuts' has been dramatised as a full-length radio play for BBC Scotland, and a collection of plays, *Hardie and Baird*, appeared in 1991. Given the enigmatic nature of his stories, it is significant that his most ambitious play, which is set in the Edinburgh jail where the two leaders of the 1820 weavers' rebellion await execution, should reveal quite explicitly where Kelman's loyalties lie. Before the lights go out – for justice, as well as for Baird and Hardie – they conclude:

> Hardie: That's how ye know it's a cheat, the injustice, the suffering, ye'd go daft if ye sat doon and just thought aboot it aw, the wey things are.
> Baird (*quietly*): They've never gave us nothing wioot it being wrested from them, never. We've aye had to fight. Every bit o' progress, it's had to get

> tore aff them, they'd have gave us nothing if we left it to them –
> nothing . . .

Kelman's essence is, perhaps, in that exchange – the low-key intensity, the alternative syntax, the suggestion that to bring the full horror out other than indirectly would be to face the impossible to accept. Typically, the play ends without trace of the kind of dramatic gesture that, say, McIlvanney employs when he has Tam Docherty's clenched fist thrust through the coal-fall which has buried him. Kelman ends with gentle human comment about friends, and no sensational words before execution. As Baird asks 'Hey Andy . . . Andy, are ye sleeping?', the stage goes dark. To the end the final thoughts and meanings of Kelman's characters are their own.

Blighted nation, blighted cities 2:
Agnes Owens (b. 1926), Jeff Torrington (b. 1935), Irvine Welsh (b. 1958)

Gentlemen of the West (1984) was the first novel of self-taught Agnes Owens, who was encouraged by Kelman and Alasdair Gray, joining with them in the collection *Lean Tales* (1985). Her choice of protagonist for her novel was clearly influenced by Kelman; Mick, later Mac, is a sometime bricklayer who lives among winos and feckless dropouts in a down-at-heel community outside Glasgow. Cadging for drink, pub fights, and hangovers are the staple of his life; only the death of his drunken mate Paddy pushes Mick into leaving to try for a job in the north. Owens presents her blighted characters in a more rough-hewn and basic way than Kelman, with something of the style of Patrick MacGill in *Children of the Dead End* (1914); but her work grows continuously darker. In *Like Birds in the Wilderness* (1987) she continues Mick's (now Mac's) story; work in Aberdeen hasn't succeeded, and Mac reverts to drink and shady deals. He and his would-be redemptive girlfriend Nancy are the birds in the wilderness, and Mac's quest for self-respect is a wild-goose chase. Mac has become the stereotypical drink-and-blather Scot, and the story would end in mere farce if it were not also a kind of microcosm of a national tragedy.

Two bleak little novels show her vision of contemporary Lowland Scotland. *A Working Mother* (1994), and the deliberately crudely entitled *For the Love of Willie* (1998) turn her exposure of blighted character towards women. In the first, a manipulative and deceitful wife cheats and lies to husband, employer and friends, in a shameless avoidance of responsibility for her drinking and lust. Betty is so blatantly bad that she has style, resembling that of Dougal Douglas in Spark's *The Ballad of Peckham Rye*

(1960) – and, like him, becoming exemplary of a Scottish type. Owens has a direct honesty in presenting her warped protagonists, and *For the Love of Willie* presents an urban and negative version of Jessie Kesson's *The White Bird Passes* (1958) in its pathetic account of the ruining of a girl's life by the oily, lying grocer who abuses adolescents. Owens never sentimentalises; Peggy tells us her story from a mental hospital – but she also reveals herself to be moody and malicious, another representative of the nastier side of Scottish character. And her short stories, in *Lean Tales* and *People Like That* (1996), are even darker. In the latter an old woman waits in Glasgow's Central Station for her lost son, only to be raped, and to remember that her son died of an overdose years ago. Sneered at by station clerks and public, she, together with the down-and-outs and no-hopers of the other stories, is 'people like that' – the utterly dispossessed; the kind found in some of Edwin Morgan's most poignant poems.

Jeff Torrington's *Swing Hammer Swing* (1992) (which won the Whitbread Prize) and *The Devil's Carousel* (1996) also acknowledge a debt to Kelman, as well as to Runyon and O'Brien. The first is a sardonic celebration of Glasgow's Gorbals as the hammer of demolition destroys a community. Tom Clay, the teller, is very much a post-Kelman type; an unpublished writer who doesn't like regular employment, whose wife is in hospital having a baby, whose tenement is crumbling, and whose wife's relatives, like conductor Hines, despise him. The plot is deliberately aimless and bizarre; weird events and people abound, to remind us that urban truth is stranger, and often funnier, than fiction. In Torrington's second novel, however, the humour darkens as it recounts the last days of a west of Scotland car factory. As in drama like McMillan's *The Bevellers* or Byrne's *The Slab Boys*, there's no glossing of proletarian characteristics or melodramatising of factory confrontations or class conflict. Instead, there are failures of communication, quiet breakdowns under stress, trivial betrayals, and quick forgetting of former colleagues. The title captures the oxymoronic nature of the workplace – ludicrous events and people circling around in a grotesque comedy which is in the end really tragedy, a carousel of US capitalism, careless of its workers' welfare and of Scottish community – and prophetic in its description of the destruction of Scotland's industries.

In the context of the writers discussed above, it can now be seen that, far from representing a radical new wave of writing in Scotland, the work of Irvine Welsh is the end-product of post-war scepticism and a widely-felt sense of blighted urban possibilities. Drug addiction adds itself to problems of drink and poverty; and a new and ferociously black humour effectively portrays a new low of human sensibility – but it is nevertheless the culmination of a general movement in Scottish writing which dates back to the beginning of the century, with *The House with the Green Shutters* of 1901. The tradition of caustic analysis of Scottish identity and community which it began continued through writers like McNeillie/Niall, Blake and Gaitens, through Trocchi and Jenkins to Kennaway and Spark. More recently that tradition was intensified in Glasgow and Edinburgh with the work of Kelman and writers like Duncan McLean, Gordon Legge, and James Meek.

With *Trainspotting* (1993) Welsh claims that his Edinburgh and Leith and housing estate dwelling drop-outs do live like this, talk like this, and believe in absolutely nothing or nobody, like this. At first, *Trainspotting* comes over as short stories and fragmented scenes, as when desperate Sick Boy and Rents visit Mother Superior, alias Johnny Swan, drug dealer of Tollcross and Wester Hailes; or when Rents, alias Mark Renton, tries to come off drugs – on the first day of the Festival – and, failing, injects himself in the foulest of toilets; or we have an international monologue from Simon Williamson, alias Sick Boy, chatter-up of girls, and petty thief, yet articulate in whatever register he chooses to exploit; or when Nina, adolescent, more interested in going to a disco than her Uncle Kenny's funeral party, is having trouble with her period. All seems jerky and disconnected, if terribly alive and sometimes shockingly funny. Then connections begin to make themselves, and the central figure, Rents, emerges as Mark Renton, (deliberately) failed university student, junkie (but trying as we meet him to kick the habit) and member of a group which includes those already named, and mad Begbie, alias Franco, a psychopathic bully, whose 'friends' have a tortuous relationship with him – afraid yet glad to have such a mental case on their side, and using him as excuse for releasing their pent-up fears and aggressions. Welsh knows these characters are sick. But Spud, Second Prize, Sick Boy, Rents and Begbie know that too – they are what they are because where they live is the way it is, and because they are intelligent, not stupid. They know the unlikely chance they have of making it, they see the merchant bankers and the festival-goers, and they know about world politics. Underlying all the violence and visceral happenings and details, Welsh contrives to make us see that they all hate themselves, what they've become, so that drugs are as much a metaphysical escape as a temporary high.

Rents is the complex centre. He moves uneasily between trying to give up drugs and repeatedly going back, in a confused circle of attempt, some success, followed by perception of his restricted life, then relapse through guilt and disgust. He hates Begbie, and most of the others, with the exception of Spud, who is one of the world's perpetual losers. The others he cares for – some girls, a dying HIV friend – he usually treats badly because that is the done thing. Through him the reader witnesses terrible scenes: a cot death that happens while the group are high on just about everything; disgusting scenes, sexual and drug-related; betrayals and violence. Welsh's laid-back tolerance of it all, in Mark and the others, is chilling, as an authentic sign of our times. This is not just local comment; Rents and his friends work a scam which takes in London and false security claims throughout Britain, and have their extended connections. The Euston dead-beats, the bus-station desolations, the cheap hotels working other sources of income – all are here. Indeed, it's the London connection which enables Rents to get clear – as clear he can ever get by a final act of betrayal which is also revenge and the most positive thing he's ever done. He takes the £17,000 Begbie and company had scored and runs for Amsterdam, knowing he has burnt his boats, that he can never go back to Kelly, his girlfriend, his parents (sick with honest worry about his habits), his Edinburgh. Such is the moral darkness of this novel that it is possible to feel that he is right; in Edinburgh, 'he could not be anything other than he was; now, free from them all for good, he could be what he wanted to be. He'd stand or fall alone.' This is the strongest of indictments of a blighted urban Scotland, and our herd behaviour, our peer group pressures, and the society we have created.

Welsh has since written two volumes of short stories and three more novels. *The Acid House* (1994) revealed a wider range to his talents; here are very clever stories which make Hollywood stars talk in Leith language, with a coarse directness which achieves the satirical linguistic inversion of Tom Leonard's 'The Six O'clock News'; has God turn useless Boab into a bluebottle; and has Keith's (living) head put in a fish tank after his Porsche crashes. Alongside this new comic fantasy run familiar stories of the *Trainspotting* world, with even darker *grotesquerie*, as in *Marabou Stork Nightmares* (1995), a novel which can be usefully compared with the fiction discussed in the next chapter under the heading 'Emerging From Trauma'. Where these other novels allow hope, Welsh's use of the out-of-trauma mode ends in horror. In his new novel, Roy Strang is in a hospital bed, where a suicide attempt has brought him. Like the protagonist of Banks's *The Bridge* (1986), he takes refuge in his sub-conscious mind, inventing new worlds and new people to evade the horror of the places and people he has known in reality. But his *Boy's Own* fantasies, like his nightmare vision of the horrific marabou stork, reveal the underlying reality; in addition, we learn of his abnormal and violent family, his abuse at the hands of an uncle, his football casual friends, his double life, and his sexual savagery. The ending is appalling; but the novel tries to be ruthlessly honest about contemporary problems – and, paradoxically, manages to weave a grotesque humour through its nightmare realities.

The latest work, the three novellas of *Ecstasy* (1996) and the terminal account of a rogue policeman, *Filth* (1998), can be criticised as sensation-seeking in their more frenetic search for fresh horrors – necrophilia, chain-saw murders, ultimate sexual degradation. The question they must answer is what has happened to the balance of valid shock, humour, and social truth? It is of course a question to be asked of much contemporary art, including comparable versions in film such as *The Bad Lieutenant, Reservoir Dogs* and Scottish equivalents like *Shallow Grave*. The fact that the question has to be asked may cast doubt on Welsh's literary worth – but it also forces readers to confront him as a sign of Scottish and international times.

Blighted nation, blighted cities 3:
contemporary pessimism and dystopian visions

Beyond fiction which explores warped psychology through dream and hallu-cination, there are many contemporary writers who create satirical distortions of Scottish society, which move in the direction of science fiction. If anything, the tendency to speculate about Scotland's blighted present and uncertain future is increasing. The more positive use of dystopian fiction in the work of Gray and Banks is examined later; here we can simply note work which ranges from caricature of actuality to apocalyptic extrapolation. These include Ian McGinness's *Inner City* (1987) and its Border town version *Bannock* (1990), John Mackenzie's apocalyptic *City Whitelight* (1986), and later work of Paul Johnston and Terry Houston. Johnston's dystopias are set in a future Edin-burgh, and in a Scotland and Britain where all public order has broken down due to drug wars and economic depression; an even more apocalyptic post-devolution Scotland is presented in Terry Houston's *The Wounded Stone* (1998).

The later dystopias can be related to the companion genre of contem-porary *crime noir*, which since Hugh Rae's *Skinner* (1965) and *A Few Small Bones* (1968) and McIlvanney with his Laidlaw series (perhaps the orgininat-ing series of the movement), can at its best be considered as serious fiction. It is arguable that these well-written stories transcend the limitations usually associated with the detective and thriller genre – namely, the repetitive types of protagonist, and the inherited rhetoric of the US tradition. In their recurrently dark settings, cities plagued by drugs and political corruption, and in their pessimistic analyses of urban futures, they go beyond previous Scottish and British versions of the genre, using crime and the drama of urban corruption to emphasise the legacy of industrial decline and post-imperial isolation. McIlvanney was followed by Frederic Lindsay with novels like his peculiarly sinister *Brond* (1983) and later fiction involving his version of the emotionally damaged and socially sensitive policeman, Detective Inspector Jim Meldrum. The amount of fiction in this genre has recently increased dramatically. The most successful exponent now is the enormously successful Ian Rankin with his Laidlaw-like Inspector Rebus series which began with *Knots and Crosses* (1987), and now amounts to a dozen volumes, the latest being *Dead Souls* (1999); other striking new practitioners include Quintin Jardine, with Christopher Brookmyre and Tom Morton giving the genre a grotesquely comic twist, and a number of women writers like Val McDermid, Ajay Close, Manda Scott, and Denise Mina showing that the genre is by no means a male prerogative (details of these new writers are given at the end of the next chapter).

Blighted highlands and islands 1

Away from the cities, writers from islands and rural areas were equally disenchanted. The poet Alasdair Maclean wrote a non-fictional and poignant account of decline in his deeply-felt *Night Falls on Ardnamurchan: The Twilight of a Crofting Family* (1984), which in many ways can stand as the summing-up of the feelings of so many writers from the islands and Highlands. Mackay Brown himself needs to be revisited in this respect, since his sentiments regarding the impact of materialistic modernity on his Orkney communities come close to Maclean's, especially in *Greenvoe* (1972), but throughout his fiction and poetry. It is significant that these three writers are poets, whose creative imaginations are outraged by the loss of tradition and community through the anonymous spread of technology and its replacement of ancient labour with instant help and entertainment. None of them is foolish enough to deny the hardship of old toil; but all see that with it came a bonding and a mutual respect in community, together with a shared art which graced the singer, the song and the listeners.

And beyond Smith and Brown we should remember that from MacColla's *And the Cock Crew* (1945) through Gibbon, Gunn, and Barke some very negative rural representations could be found, Barke especially reminding us just how bleak that experience could be. Several later Highland and island writers continued this tonic realism; Norman Macdonald's *Calum Tod* (1976) in particular deserving attention, as it bravely tried to fuse older Gaelic tradition with the demands of modernity. Calum is the alienated islander, and Macdonald uses a series of apparently unrelated streams-of-consciousness of family and lovers to reveal his restlessness and shame in a stagnating Lewis which drives Calum into exile and alcoholism. Two powerful novels by Dominic Cooper pursued a similarly negative view, echoing the existential despair of *An Honourable Death* by Iain Crichton Smith (1992). *The Dead of Winter* (1975) told of a feud to the death between islanders, shocking in its ultimate and hopeless violence, which Cooper used to symbolise the futility of man's place in the harsh nature of the islands. *Sunrise* (1977) is as bleak in its account of the simple crofter Murdo who abandons his wife and community and Sunday sermonising to find freedom, only to find death amid majestic sunsets and a landscape of unbearable beauty. This juxtapositioning of an uncaring setting and human futility takes Cooper to the ultimate bleakness, in which little more can be said. It is not surprising that his last novel, *Men at Axlir* (1978) chose as setting eighteenth-century Iceland in time of famine, volcanic despoliation, and bloodfeud, since perhaps only here could he darken his already grim view of human irrelevance. More recently, Lorn Macintyre has sustained a satirical portrait of Highland aristocracy in his *Chronicles of Invernevis* series, beginning with *Cruel in the Shadow* (1979), and then in *The Blind Bend* (1981) and *Empty Footsteps* (1996). Macintyre effectively deconstructs the pretensions and vain-glory of the great landed Catholic family of Macdonalds as their lairds exploit and condescend, abrogating to themselves a divinely-given right to what pleases them among their people. These are well-researched period pictures, set around the turn of the century, bringing to life the Macdonalds at their height of power, in military dress, in Highland games, in their estates – and the more effective because Macintyre has an attitude towards his subjects which combines love as well as hate, regret for their inevitable anachronism and passing as well as satisfaction in their self-inflicted downfall. And more recently Shetland historian John Graham's *Shadowed Valley* (1987), with its echoes of Gunn's *Butcher's Broom*, demonstrates how pervasive and long-lived is the resentment of the forced decline of traditional community. He uses Shetland dialect extensively to give an authenticity to his sad stories. The events are seen through the eyes of young Hakki, already responsible for his family. As with the great Clearance novels, the closeness and warmth of the old community is vividly shown, as well as the church's siding with 'improvement' and the incomers' inability to understand the language of the natives. The incomers and their mixture of greed and cruelty are embodied in Da Sodger, the laird's estate manager.

With these modern fictions of Highland and island decline this topic ends. As far as they are concerned, regeneration is hardly relevant, and it is hard to see beyond their despair. Perhaps a glimmer is there in the ending to *Calum Tod*; but the reader of these novels would be hard put to imagine how and from where hope for Scottish community could emerge.

Blighted highlands and islands 2: Iain Crichton Smith (1928–98)

Iain Crichton Smith is one of Scotland's greatest poets and novelists. With Jenkins, he has proved to be the most persistent questioner of Scotland's moral and religious attitudes, within a materialistic Western world. His background (educated in staunchly Presbyterian Lewis, with a devout Free Church mother; thence to the University of Aberdeen, national service, and then teaching in Clydebank and Oban till 1977; then continuing to live as a full-time writer outside Oban) has meant that, while the Gaelic and island experience is seminal, he nevertheless shares much in Scottish cultural experience and moral questioning with Jenkins and beyond him many modern Scottish novelists who include Muriel Spark, George Friel, Elspeth Davie and Alasdair Gray. All of these, despite their differences, are profoundly concerned with the inheritance of Scottish Calvinism, together with a contrary awareness of a nightmare of flux and random amorality, in a fallen world. Smith transposes his disillusionment and religious scepticism to the islands and West Highlands (although several of his novels juxtapose this experience with passages in Glasgow and the Lowlands). This background helps place Crichton Smith's lonely and prolonged quest, sustained until his last novel, *An Honourable Death* (1992), the study of an outstanding case of Scottish and Victorian Jekyll-and-Hyde appearance and contrary reality, that of Brigadier-General Sir Hector Macdonald, 'Fighting Mac', the archetypal Scottish soldier.

Smith's poetry and fiction is that of the isolated and sensitive moralist, wrestling with deeply personal problems, and projecting them through art so that as with Jenkins, Friel, and Gray, his art becomes a therapeutic process which allows change and release. Like Gray particularly, Smith has been frank about the extent to which his personal traumas have entered his fiction. *In the Middle of the Wood* (1987), an autobiographical novel describing his mental breakdown and private nightmare, showed this especially. But the reader who has followed the career of Smith's 'holy fools' (the term used increasingly to describe the half-hero, half-victim who haunts Scottish fiction from *The Man of Feeling* and *Waverley* to Barrie's *Sentimental Tommy*, Linklater's *Magnus Merriman* and the modern fiction of Jenkins and Gray) from the simple but morally confused old woman of *Consider the Lilies* (1968) down through the succession of confused would-be writers, failed teachers, doubting ministers and dreaming lecturers of his pages will know that – with various disguises which usually involve giving anglified names to his would-be great writers and idealists, like Ralph Simmons, Trevor Grierson, or Drew Dixon – a protracted struggle of Smith's own has taken place through these pages.

Smith was a poet with an international reputation before writing any fiction, with several major volumes such as *Thistles and Roses* (1961) and *The Law and the Grace* (1965) in the thirteen years before *Consider the Lilies*. That novel was cathartic for him; and it is significant that, along with *An Honourable Death*, his first and last fictions are the only two to present their account through a character clearly not Smith himself. All the others – Mr Trill, the Reverend Murchison, Mark Simmons et al. – while clearly fictional creations, nevertheless express vital aspects of his personal and aesthetic development, reflecting his self-doubt in relations and profession, his questioning of the inherited beliefs and moral values of his youth, and his steady distancing of himself from village and island. The reader is forced to ask why, in first and last novels, he should have adopted such very different modes of presentation.

A preliminary answer can be found when *Consider the Lilies* is perceived as a novel which is about much more than the Highland Clearances in Strathnaver. It is certainly a poet's vivid and deceptively simple account of an old woman expelled by Patrick Sellar from the house for generations of her dead husband and family. Smith's vivid images of emigration, church deceit or failure, village suffering, compel sympathy. But when compared with two other great novels of Highland clearance, Gunn's *Butcher's Broom* (1934) or MacColla's *And the Cock Crew* (1945), its treatment of the drama of atrocity is peculiarly understated, as though other issues were even more important than physical deprivation and dislocation. And Smith has the main insight of the novel – presented through the free thinker stonemason who shelters Mrs Scott – clarify this. It's not the clearance of the houses that's the worst, he thinks, as he observes the painful process of reconsideration and recognition of other values in the old woman, as she revises her ideas of church and morality, but the 'internal clearances' of a black church and a repressive authoritarianism which have evicted simple love and joy from the hearts and minds of simple Highlanders. And the reader of *Consider the Lilies* quickly recognises characters and situations, which have strayed back from Smith's later fiction of contemporary Highland and island life to the clearances of the early nineteenth century. In past and present fiction Smith recurrently employs the image and symbol of the melodeon playing for the dancers under the moon at the village crossroads; and here in *Consider the Lilies* are the people of *The Village* (1976) and *The Hermit* (1977), collections of stories which anatomise the gossip, betrayals and epiphanies of modern village life, translated to Strathnaver. What is Smith trying to express through this mingling of present and past character and predicament?

The answer can be found in the way Mrs Scott is both the suffering soul of

Scotland and of Highlands, Lewis and Strathnaver, in the past. Mrs Scott is Smith's own stern and pious mother; but she is also his awareness of familial bonds in his island and mainland homes, and in the end an archetypal figure representing repressive authority, duty, and controlling love, still maintaining her hold through the guilt she induced and the confining love she gave. Her name is eponymous, reminding us that she represents a kind of traditional matriarch to be found throughout Scotland in time and place. It is worth exploring her presence throughout Smith's poetry. Poem after poem is entitled 'Old Woman' or deploys a version of that title, together with a constant re-examination of the figure in praise and blame. While it recurrently allows his mother great dignity and pathos in her simple religious faith and her acceptance of poverty, it cannot make her what she isn't, and ultimately it leaves her uncomprehending amid the modern world's social and political chaos. *Consider the Lilies*, written after many of these poems of agonised scrutiny, allows Smith to forgive and understand; to gift to memory a transfiguring catharsis and epiphany, so that at least in his ideal world the mother is given glimmerings of true perception. The movement of Mrs Scott from negativity to affirmation is seen in three phases in the novel: firstly resisting 'the demands of Patrick Sellar for her eviction (and resisting the impending break-up of all she has believed as a fixed and traditional world); secondly, having literally and metaphorically crossed a bridge to speak unrewardingly with her minister, finding herself unsettled and adrift in a limbo where nothing can be trusted; and finally, having recrossed the bridge of the past, breaking down, mentally and physically, in order that she may rebuild herself, even in her seventies, to re-create a new awareness of the dignity of other and freethinking human beings (represented here in the stonemason's integrity). In addition, she comes to recognise the significance of story-telling and art, and of how, in imprisoning her husband and her children, she was life-denying. The novel is thus a moving epiphany simultaneously acting as a transforming fable for Smith himself, and for modern Scotland, in a sense punning on the idea of clearance, since the actual and negative Highland Clearances are here followed by Mrs Scott's clearing from her mind the accumulated debris of past dictates and repressions.

After this watershed fiction Smith could begin to put this preoccupation behind him, and begin in the later novels the long exploration of the possibility and nature of identity and freedom. The quest follows two directions: on one hand there are the novels which focus on Lewis, and village community life; on the other, there are novels which, usually centred on city life, have their protagonists wrestle with issues of artistic value, often giving rise to crises of identity concerning the existence of any genuine social and aesthetic values whatsoever. That said, both sides of the quest are of course interwoven with each other. In this respect it is worth looking first at Smith's early short stories, in *Survival without Error* (1970) and *The Black and the Red* (1973), which reveal this interweaving, and which articulated clearly what had become his fundamental symbolism regarding the need for pain in vital living, and the deadness of life dictated by dogma and devoid of human involvement and change. 'You bleed to death/from all that's best, your active anima', his long poem 'Deer on the High Hills' had argued as early as 1962, discussing a theme of the intermingling of life and death which would work through all his fiction and poetry. The stories of *The Black and the Red* work with the dualisms of community and loneliness, home and exile, dogma and freedom – the black and the red. Out of these accounts of loneliness in all aspects of living – with colleagues in teaching, in love, national service, railway stations, parties, weddings and reunions after exile – emerges a choice; between taking risks and throwing oneself into life and its moral and personal struggles, or surviving in the safety of conformity and unquestioning acceptance of convention and class, without risking human error. Smith uses his poet's gift of symbolic imagery to the full in these stories, so that on one hand the drabness of blackness and greyness attach themselves to childhood and his mother and her narrow church; to unhappy adolescent and student experience in Aberdeen; to army authority; and to a huge range of human negativity. On the other hand emerges Black's inextricable opposite; the Red colour of blood and life, aggressive, ferocious, even selfish in its insistence on natural living.

These two volumes of short stories can stand apart from the novels, dealing as they do with such a range of situation and experience. They set out themes which Smith will then examine in the novels, in the two broadly different ways described. After *Consider the Lilies* came *The Last Summer* (1969), which belongs to the first strand. This examination of the crisis in 18-year-old Malcolm's final term at school in Lewis, in which he has for the first time to grapple with real moral choices arising from his village-school split loyalties, begins a line of novels which take as their central issue Smith's long-drawnout coming to terms with his island and small community background. Lewis – bleak, featureless, remote, with its elemental and, to Smith, almost historyless detachment from the rest of the world (as he describes it in his collection of essays of 1986, *Towards the Human*) – was a hard motherland; and it takes many poems on the subject of loyalty, duty and filial obligation, together with many short stories and novels, to work free from that what Smith was constantly to symbolise as a black influence. In *The Last Summer* Malcolm solves his dilemmas through exile; he leaves for college, abandoning the destructive claims upon him of rival football teams, as well as, and more importantly, the claims of his mother, his village, and of competing adolescent loves.

From now on exile, actual and psychological, is one of Smith's main subjects. In the line of fiction which studies the island inheritance, like *The Village* and *The Hermit*, 'exiles' can be found within their communities – bitter, islanded people, disappointed and repressed wives, precocious and malicious children. These stories tend to channel Smith's more negative feelings. In them, and throughout his fiction and in collections of poems like *From Bourgeois Land* (1969), Smith showed that the reality of peripheral Scotland was a mixture of council housing, cars, Chinese restaurants, television sets, and the materialistic and pseudo-religious gossip of neighbours. If anything could be rescued from this, it could only be found in the occasional moments of empathy and communion between damaged people, or the innocence of childhood. *On the Island* (1979), a novel made up of episodes of childhood experience, used the latter to find some kind of acceptance and forgiveness for the bleak experience of Lewis, as Smith recalled childhood moments of significance – the places and the people who shaped him seen with a new kindness and delightful empathy reminiscent of Neil Gunn in *Young Art and Old Hector*. And while Lewis still refused to allow any kind of spiritual bond with its bleak landscape (the boys have a confrontation with its great standing stones which significantly refuse them the kind of spatial and temporal epiphany which was found in the work of Gunn or Gibbon), these childhood memories helped Smith assess small communities in a more affirmative way. When he next focused closely on the problems of living within a close-knit and potentially malicious group, in *A Field Full of Folk* (1982), he allowed his minister protagonist to resolve his cancerous doubts through a kind of epiphany, a vision of the humbler ways in which the mean-spirited neighbours can be reviewed as redemptive and capable of great humanity. Through the theme of the prodigal returning (a favourite of Smith's) the minister glimpses the balance of the black and the red in his parishioners and, as a later collection of poetry, *The Village* (1989), shows, Smith was never again as tormented by his island inheritance.

That line of fictional exploration related to his past. What of the future, as the exiled boy left in real life for Aberdeen University just after the war? The other strand of fiction wrestled with issues of more abstract import, tackling questions relating to the place of art in real living, the importance of the novelist (and the artist in general), the question as to what kind of art really mattered, and the final question of whether anything about human life can be said to matter at all. It's as though, having resolved one set of black

894

influences in his life, Smith went on to rediscover the black in abundance elsewhere – in relationships, in aesthetics, in philosophy. The novels and stories which agonise over these new dilemmas include *My Last Duchess* (1971), *Goodbye Mr Dixon* (1974), *An End to Autumn* (1978), *The Search* (1983), *Mr Trill in Hades* (1984), *The Tenement* (1985), *In the Middle of the Wood* (1987) and, pulling together both strands of the quest, *The Dream* (1990). Recurrently, the protagonist is an English-named would-be writer/teacher. Their names are significant. Smith tells us in *The Search* that the protagonist's mother liked names like Ralph, Trevor, Mark; these exotic non-Gaelic nomenclatures reflect the false choices which their bearers can make – for an affected, anglicised, and an inhuman art without loyalty to community and native traditions. In these novels the protagonists have to find themselves behind their names, by stripping away the false social and literary aspirations and identifications which have either led them into false relationships or damaged relationships which need honesty and pain to grow. Mr Trill – a recurrent figure of self-parody throughout Smith's work – discovers in Hades that classical heroes and heroines are crueller, more selfish, and less authentic than education and books had led him to believe. Like all the protagonists of these novels, he is reborn in a red world, where people bleed from redemptive pain and emotion, where being ordinary is the only possibility of finding grace, and where – from Scotland to the USA and Australia – the risk of exile isn't so much a matter of losing one's physical homeland so much as losing one's true self through failing to see the random, lonely, and mundane quality of reality. *The Search* seeks a lost brother in Australia; in finding him, the seeker realises that he doesn't need him as much as he needs to find himself. He finds release from spiritual exile amid the vastness of Australia, as well as realising a spiritual kinship with Aboriginal poetry and dreamtime, proof again that 'community' and 'exile' are ultimately not terms to be tied to conditions of place.

In the Middle of the Wood (1987) marked Smith's resolution of this second, and more difficult, self-questioning. Owing much to the title story of Smith's most bizarre and tragi-comic fiction, *Murdo and Other Stories* (1981), it used self-parody and surreal comic perspective to come to terms with what had been Smith's most difficult period, in the early '80s. Murdo, agonisingly poised between grotesque humour and appalling pain, had anticipated Smith's personal disintegration as he wrestled ludicrously with his soul in his seaside town, donning his clownish red nose to terrify neighbours with his disturbing questions about life, death and MacBrayne's boats. Murdo didn't then save Smith from breakdown; but *In the Middle of the Wood* later uses its ferocious negativity to positive effect, cathartically enabling Smith to see the nightmare comedy of his own trauma, as his protagonist twists and turns in pathetic attempts to escape the wife, doctors and nurses whom he believes to be hired actors trying to eliminate his superior talent from the world. The ending was important for Smith, involving the recognition by the minister in *A Field Full of Folk* that it is the ordinary people of the world, the doctors, firemen and essentially human keepers of society who matter, and that no one can really live outside that community. After this Smith had but one remaining memory to transform, and in *The Dream*, his last-but-one novel, he had his Glasgow University Celtic lecturer finally dispel his life-long yearning to return to champion his island and Gaelic culture. Impressively, Smith united both strands of his work here, so that his very fear of the flux, of random chaos, was made into the reason he couldn't and shouldn't go back. His protagonist's wife knows, as a despised bastard orphan from Lewis, how bleak with repressed religiosity that background can be; and her husband has to temper his sentimentalised memories with her real distaste. The dream is shown to be any failure to see clearly; any rose-coloured view of nation, religious cult, political creed which asserts its pathetic fallacy above real people – and (with echoes of his disturbingly ambivalent summing-up of his views on the Gaelic language in his difficult but comprehensive long poem, 'Shall Gaelic Die?') Smith seems to be saying that even cultures, dreams, passionate identifications must be allowed to die, along with their adherents' passionate identification and dreams, so that the present can survive.

Consider the Lilies, it can be seen in retrospect, was for Smith unusual in not having himself as central focus (always allowing that, as in the early stories such as *Survival Without Error*, 1970, and frequently thereafter in collections like *Murdo*, his shorter fiction explored different kinds of lonely, misled, elderly, and tragic figures of assorted kinds, victims of upbringing and alienation in rural and urban Scotland). In the main, his fiction was his self-therapy, refashioning his hurtful experience and questioning.

It is surprising that he chose as subject for his last novel a figure from history distant from Smith's personal values and background; Sir Hector Macdonald, the Brigadier-General and outstanding military hero of Britain and Victorian empire. His suicide on account of his homosexuality caused shockwaves to run through Britain and the Highlands. *An Honourable Death* can be seen, however, as marking Smith's transition from an art which dealt with his own dilemmas to an art which empathised with the dilemmas and predicaments of his countrymen. In a sense all his fiction did this; Mrs Scott was an embodiment of some prevalent Scottish types, as were Smith's subsequent protagonists. Hector Macdonald may seem remote from Smith himself, but deeper consideration shows that Smith has chosen his final protagonist carefully, in a way which follows on from the ruthless evaluations of *The Dream*. For, until Macdonald's final and honourable recognition of a life of despair and falsity, in his moment of spiritual awakening, he is portrayed as being in a dream. It's a dream at times akin to Smith's; this is the basis of shared experience from which Smith measures the gulf between them. Both men are exiles, in spirit more than space, from their Gaelic background. Both seek a classical order, which will let them escape from the dull, limiting banal disorder of their rural youth. Both are victims of systems: Smith, of a British imperialism of culture and the inculcation of classical models, which moulded his early life and career as teacher, till he rejected it in 1977; Hector, as moulded by that classic escape-route for the Highlander after the Jacobite Rebellion and Culloden, the British Army. There, the likeness ends. But Smith has sensed a vulnerable pain and sensibility in this adolescent runaway from an Inverness draper's. A curious placeless emptiness surrounds Hector, becoming his hallmark, wherever he goes in Africa, the Sudan, South Africa, India, Ceylon. For Hector is neither fish nor fowl in the officers' mess, since he lacks pedigree and private funds. Likewise, he's no longer an ordinary soldier. What emerges is that he's only truly happy in the release of drill and the function of war; only truly relaxed with his foreign soldiers, especially the blue-black, skinny-legged Sudanese, who come to revere this strange white chief, much as Highlanders revered the head of the clan. Hector enacts the Highland parallel, without ever realising the cruel ironies latent in his situation – which ironies are Smith's overriding point in this analysis of why a man whose country had been despoliated by imperial Britain could give himself over to unquestioning service of that very machine, and then perpetrate the same tribal atrocities as had been visited on his own tribe earlier. Smith threads this constant analogy through the novel quietly, without bitterness, although the effect on the reader is one of embitterment that history should so quickly be allowed to pull a veil over the past. The most moving moments concern Hector's loneliness and sensitivity, and whether this has any basis in fact comes not to matter very much, as Smith persuades us that just such an archetype as he presents, whether real Hector or no, must have brought just such alienated loneliness and private efficiency to empire and conquest.

Another motif woven through the novel, placing it firmly in an old Scottish tradition going back to Hogg and Stevenson, is that of constant reference to the divided nineteenth-century soul of respectable Scotland. Hector finds a strange kinship with the stories of Major Weir and Deacon Brodie when he's billeted in Edinburgh. Again, he fails to recognise why, just as he fails to understand the bond between himself and his coloured soldiers. But the reader sees why; it's exactly his own predicament, as the respectable soldier in the eye of Victorian Britain, but secretly married, secretly unsure of his sexuality, finally secretly homosexual. Again, perhaps, Smith maintains the curious reticence he does in linking the Jekyll-Hyde motif with Hector precisely because he wishes the reader to have to strive hard to fathom the depths of motivation which Hector himself can't – until his death. For his death is honourable; Smith is stretching his empathy as far as possible to understand and forgive – as he did in *Consider the Lilies* – a man whom he could have reviled as hypocrite betrayer of Highland tradition. Instead, he posits the integrity of someone who just can't fathom the meaningless ironies of the ancient war of the black and the red, of authority and humility, power and weakness, duty and freedom. We must understand the Hectors of Scotland and life, otherwise we are still in our imagined corners, our separate dreams. The story actually began as a short tale in *Selected Stories* (1990), in which the primary element to have captured Smith seemed to be the crossing lives, at the moment immediately before Hector's suicide, of Picasso and Hector, outside the Paris hotel in which Hector died. Thus the randomness of life lies at the heart of this story – how we are led, insensibly, to our strange destinies. In describing that Macdonald died 'with an ironic smile', Smith suggests that, in recognising the final lunacy of things, he achieved existential honour in a death which paradoxically defined himself and his integrity.

If we were to assess Smith's fiction on this novel alone, we might find his vision of humanity bleak indeed. Yet for all Smith's depiction of blighted islands and the decline and narrowness of much of community, there is a saving grace. For all its dislike of modern Orkney and 'progress', the work of Mackay Brown allowed sadder but wiser ministers, lairds, writers to find self, though often after much wasted life; and similarly Smith discovers possibilities amidst negativity. Even in Smith's last bleak novel of loneliness can be found an austere redemption; and a recurrent theme of both kinds of his fiction argued the significance of redefining self, even on the edge of death. Mrs Scott will die, Hector Macdonald kills himself – but both have achieved something. And throughout Smith's fiction, grace is found in humble places, eccentric characters, while the central protagonists winnow similar lonely gains from their too often fallen backgrounds. Scottish fiction can be seen changing, and moving towards hope.

CHAPTER 41

SCOTTISH FICTION SINCE 1945 II: DESPAIR, CHANGE AND HOPE

THE PARADOX OF SCOTTISH POLITICS AND CULTURE

The previous chapter ended with a sense of pessimism regarding the future of community and culture in Scotland. Scottish politics through the '70s would serve to underline this feeling, beginning as the decade had with Scots electing eleven nationalist members of parliament, and with a sense of a nation rediscovering a sense of identity, yet ending in the referendum anticlimax of 1979, with the indecision of a third of voters revealing that a new sense of national purpose had been premature. Amongst Scottish writers there was a tangible disappointment like that recorded at the time in the essays of William McIlvanney, collected in *Surviving the Shipwreck* (1991). Perhaps, instead of regarding this as the end of hopes for devolution, more attention should have been given to history, and the rhythms of rise and fall in Scottish political expectations since the beginning of the twentieth century. Various movements for national and political renewal, from just before the First World War, to the Scottish Convention of the '30s, to the first success of the nationalists just after the war, and the success of the late '60s and '70s, had come and gone; yet always, after ever shorter intervals, these disappointed aspirations had renewed themselves, and the height of the next wave was higher than before. The revival of aspiration in the '90s should have been expected.

Something else should have been remembered. The 'Scottish Renaissance' of MacDiarmid and others in the '20s and '30s, like the vernacular revival of Scots poetry after 1707, showed that a national cultural regeneration could take place apart from political renewal. Elsewhere this volume discussed 'negative positivism' as a necessary precondition to such renewal; and the pattern of negativity followed by positive assertion repeated itself in the '80s and '90s, when arguably it was Scotland's writers and artists who kept the sense of commitment and faith regarding national identity and autonomy alive. When Scottish political nationalism was at its peak around 1970,

Scottish writers were often dubious regarding Scottish literary and cultural tradition, preferring either to denigrate such experience or look outward to the USA and elsewhere; paradoxically, when nationalism ebbed, a sense of the importance of Scottish languages and identities was reborn amongst Scottish writers.

This is the necessary context within which to view what happened to Scottish fiction around 1980. It is fair to describe the new fictions of writers like Alasdair Gray, Iain Banks, Alan Massie, Ronald Frame and many others as the most dramatic signs of change in Scottish fiction. It is however also fair to say that change was in the air in the late '70s, before their work appeared. Scottish publishers were prepared to take on new fiction, as well as increasingly reproducing neglected fiction of the nineteenth as well as the twentieth centuries. By the '80s, the various streams became a river from tributaries like Paul Harris, Macdonald, Mainstream, Richard Drew and, later, Canongate Classics – with Virago and other non-Scottish publishers joining in. The work of older writers like John Buchan, James Barrie, David Lindsay and Naomi Mitchison became available, with novels like *Witch Wood* and *Sick Heart River*, *Farewell Miss Julie Logan*, *A Voyage to Arcturus*, *The Corn King and the Spring Queen* and the late-Renaissance *The Bull Calves*. Much of the credit for this must go to the Scottish Arts Council, which in 1967 had become an autonomous council with its own devolved budget, as opposed to its previous subsidiary position as the Scottish Committee of the Arts Council of Great Britain. Immediately, Scottish writers and publishers reaped benefits: new bursaries, awards, and publisher's grants followed; a large proportion of the new writing and reprints appeared with its help, as did also the increasing body of critical material, from Francis Hart's *The Scottish Novel* (1978) and studies of writers from Gunn and Gibbon to Linklater and Compton Mackenzie, as well as the increase in discussion taking place in the magazines. *Chapman, Cencrastus, Books in Scotland* depended on Arts Council support – as did the new anthologies of the '80s like *New Writing Scotland, Scottish Women's New Writing, Original Prints,* the short story anthologies and anthologies of gay and lesbian writing. Awareness of the richness of Scottish literature and language was dawning, in the school curriculum, in universities, and in bookshops, which began to promote it on separate shelves, and most of all, amongst the writers themselves, who seemed to have gained a new confidence.

Rediscovering Scottish traditions in fiction

With so much of older Scottish writing becoming available, many Scottish writers began to explore the possibilities of exploiting a new awareness of

Scottish literary genre and fictional tradition. Alasdair Gray would do this outstandingly in *Poor Things* (1992) and *A History Maker* (1994) (exploiting Stevenson and Hogg respectively). Likewise John Herdman worked with reference back to James Hogg's *The Justified Sinner* in *Pagan's Pilgrimage* (1978) and *Imelda* (1993), and Elspeth Davie exploited her readers' awareness of the Scottish Enlightenment in *Coming to Light* (1989). Sometimes, as in the case of Stuart Hood's novels, a new internationalism accompanied the exploration of older Scottish texts, as in his *The Upper Hand* (1987), which carried clear echoes of the brother-brother love-hate relationship so characteristic of Stevenson and Scottish fiction. The traditional dualisms of Scottish fiction were now to be found, used with parodic referentiality, in the work of Gray, Herdman, and even in the later novels of Robin Jenkins, such as *Poverty Castle* (1991), with its exploitation of the fiction of Walter Scott as key to its quasi-allegory. Even amongst Anglo-Scots this derivative redeployment of Scottish fictional themes could be found: Emma Tennant's *The Bad Sister* (1978) and *Two Women of London: The Strange Case of Ms Jekyll and Mrs Hyde* (1989) refer back to Hogg and Stevenson specifically. And this use of traditional fiction continues, in work like Muriel Spark's *Symposium* (1990), Alice Thompson's *Justine* (1996) and Andrew Greig's ballad-based *When They Lay Bare* (1999).

Rediscovering regions

Another apparent reverse direction assisted rediscovery of confidence. A preoccupation with 'regional traditionalism' entered into the fiction of men, particularly. From the late '70s on, writers like Dominic Cooper, Norman Macdonald, James Shaw Grant, David Kerr Cameron, David Toulmin, Colin Mackay, Christopher Rush, Alan Jamieson and John Graham began to assert a new attitude to places and regions as diverse as Iceland, Lewis, Buchan, Aberdeenshire, the Lothians, Fife and Shetland respectively. Their work was often satirical; but its assertion of the value of the history of regions places it as a version of that 'negative positivism' which recurs before periods of growth in Scottish literature. This, taken with the urban regionalism of, say, Morgan, Gray, Lochhead and Kelman in relation to Glasgow, and the newer writers like James Meek, Irvine Welsh in Edinburgh, or Gordon Legge in Grangemouth, or Janice Galloway in Irvine, suggests a retreat to home territory in order to reassess identity.

Older writers, new perspectives: Naomi Mitchison (1897–1999), Jessie Kesson (1916–94) and the adaptability of women's writing

Before looking at the new writers of the last two decades, however, it is important to recognise that many established writers developed striking new fictions in the '80s. Women writers like Naomi Mitchison, Jessie Kesson, Elspeth Davie and Joan Lingard seemed best able to move from one age to the next; and from pessimism to positivism, more easily than men. When Mitchison wrote *The Bull Calves* (1947), her epic novel which looked at the aftermath of the Jacobite rebellions and a divided eighteenth-century Scotland in order to give examples of healing and reconstruction to Scotland after 1945, she was a lonely visionary amid the post-war gloom. Her Scottish work continued with another attempt to forgive the sins of aristocratic Scotland against the ordinary people in the magical time-quests of *The Big House* (1950), and with a fine collection of short stories working in the same area of folk-tradition as Linklater's *Sealskin Trousers* (1947) in *Five Men and a Swan* (1957); but *Lobsters on the Agenda* (1952), dealing with modern Argyllshire, showed, in its portrayal of herself failing to achieve the changes she wanted amidst deceptive and drunken locals, that for Mitchison as well as Linklater and Gunn dreams of Renaissance were over. She returned briefly to *Corn King* territory with *Travel Light* (1952), the saga-quest of Princess Halla, disgusted with the human world, who goes (like Meromic turning wolf in Michison's *The Conquered* (1923) to live with bears and dragons. The title indicates Mitchison's desire to get clear of the deceitful Western world – and shortly after, she found a new dream. She became involved with the Bakgatla tribe of Botswana, and a spate of non-fiction books on Africa. The short stories of *Images of Africa* (1980) present the predicament of a traditional Africa struggling to reconcile itself with modern internationalism. But neither Scotland nor Africa could exhaust Mitchison's range of enquiry; now she moved into science fiction to speculate even more radically on human identity, sexuality, and development, in pioneering work like *Memoirs of a Spacewoman* (1962), *Solution Three* (1975) and *Not By Bread Alone* (1983); and the surreal Scottish stories of *What Do you Think Yourself?* (1982) and *A Girl Must Live* (1990). Perhaps we should finally remember this quite outstanding Scottish, British and world writer with *Early in Orcadia* (1987), her imaginative and convincing account of how the first settlers came to the Orkneys, a fable full of the freshness of humanity setting out for new shores untrammelled with national identity or the problems of our material world.

The work of Jessie Kesson also acts as link between the concerns of older novelists and the contemporary writers, spanning as it does the period 1958 to 1985 when *Where the Apple Ripens* (1985) appears. Her first novel, *The White Bird Passes* (1958), questioned the situation of women in Scotland, refusing to accept the old allocations of roles and duties in its warm portrait of Janie, the orphaned daughter of an Elgin prostitute, who repudiates all the dreary jobs in shops or service offered to her by traditional charity, and instead makes her wonderful claim of rights: 'I don't want to dust and polish . . . and I don't want to work on a farm. I want to write poetry. Great poetry. As great as Shakespeare.' Her next novel, *Glitter of Mica* (1963) deployed her innovative time juxtapositionings and unorthodox treatment of women as well as working in the tradition of the older ruralist male writers, in particular that of Ian Macpherson in *Land of our Fathers* (1933), as though she felt the need to place herself in terms of Scottish writing. The treatment of Helen Riddell here drew on the tradition of Douglas Brown and the pessimism regarding possibilities for women which had characterised the work of older writers of the north-east like Jacob and Moon, and now threatened to dominate contemporary women's writing.

But *The White Bird* had not passed unnoticed; three years later Anne Smith's *The Magic Glass* (1961) refashioned Janie as Stella, the street urchin of the imagined Fife town of Skelf. This portrait reinforced Kesson's assertion of freedom for young women whose voices had hitherto been ignored in Scotland. Perhaps this encouraged Kesson, for she returned in *Another Time, Another Place* (1983) to her semi-autobiographical account of Janie, now away from the orphanage and married to her decent crofter, but frustrated by his dullness and lovemaking, the insensitivity of neighbours, and the eternity of mundanity which seems to lie ahead. The title indicates her yearning, and Kesson's insistence on seeing Janie's repression as that of an older era. A qualified hope for reconciliation between the older woman's values and the younger woman's shamed yet irreversible breach of community rules lies in the final image of the young woman standing in the doorway accepting dour Elspeth's, 'You'd better come on inside.' The novel can be seen as a turning point in Scottish women's writing, both thematically and formally. This, and Kesson's novella *Where the Apple Ripens* (1985), with their impressionistic mosaics of short episodes, and their fragments of tradition, in song, dance, and story-telling, capturing the sense of a break-up of older conventions, literary and social, must have suggested to many that this new kind of stream of woman's consciousness-in-community could be deployed in other and urban contexts.

Elspeth Davie (1919–95)

The work of Elspeth Davie is deliberately low-key in presentation, with an equally deliberate anonymity of setting. Slight hints suggest that Edinburgh is her location, but her characters are neutrally British in name, and her houses, shops, streets neutrally modern. Her early work includes *Providings* (1965), *The Spark and Other Stories* (1968), and *Creating a Scene* (1971). *Providings* gives the clue to her unique approach, in its picture of Peter Beck, lonely, vulnerable, classless. He and his predicament could exist anywhere in Britain. His mother's smothering love manifests itself in pots of jam which he tries to give away to church sales; and slowly the reader grasps how Davie sees things (providings?) as potentially suffocating, surreal, night-marish in their endless catalogues, which surround their human victims in a grotesque dance, demonstrating the power of inanimate objects to rule our lives. Yet her fiction is recognisably North British, and ultimately affirmative. This is a story of love – unusual in its lack of sensuality, or qualities like colour, feel and smell. Davie emphasises the mundane in order to make more vivid the spark of the human amid the prevailing grey. The stories of *The Spark* present variations on the theme, with quiet, damaged people finally rebelling against the tyranny of things – some through drastic action, in accident or suicide, some simply burning the debris which suffocates – but all at least signalling identity or life, even in death. What Davie insists is that we should recognise how ordinary people are extraordinary, and how they come to terms with their limitations. *Creating a Scene* focuses on a very ordinary school; a teacher tries to conjure up interest in art amongst bored teenagers, and here the affirmation lies in his success in moving them enough to paint walls, make relationships, and cross threshholds.

The later work is less positive, and more taken up with human eccentricity and the surreal. The stories of *The High Tide Talker* (1976) and the novel *Climbers on a Stair* (1978) increased the degree to which the lives observed were those of melancholy misfits; *Climbers on a Stair* interlinking lives in an Edinburgh tenement in ways which anticipated Iain Crichton Smith's *The Tenement* (1985). Here at least some inter-human involvement is achieved; in contrast, the title story of the collection *The Night of the Funny Hats* (1980) emphasises the aloneness of people. A bus party is crossing great wastes of Australia; their forced last-night celebration, as they wear their funny hats, turns sour with the news of their driver's death. Davie approaches Beckett in her descriptions of disorientated guests wandering through abandoned hotel kitchens. Her situations become emblems of surreal loneliness. Two more collections followed: *A Traveller's Room* (1985) and *Death of a Doctor* (1992), and a novel, *Coming to Light* (1989). The novel juxtaposes Edinburgh and Enlightenment history, on one hand, and unattractive adolescent Niall Gaffney and his violent, tender and finally unconvincing garage-owner, caretaker, dentist and tailor friends on the other. For once the setting, Edinburgh during festival, is explicit; with Davie satirising what enlightened Edinburgh has become, and with the great Enlightenment philosophers and scientists set in contrast to Niall's fallen Edinburgh. Yet the placing of her characters so precisely arguably denies Davie the displaced surrealism which is her unique territory. Comparing this with the next two fine volumes of stories reveals that she is better at short stories than sustained narratives, and right to allow her creative urge to deal in darker territory, rather than force an affirmation she cannot present persuasively.

A Traveller's Room and *Death of a Doctor* are Davie at her peak. She plays with bizarre misunderstandings through simple failures of perception or misinterpretation of words – 'bulbs' (for planting or lighting?), 'fields' (for crops or areas of expertise?) – and she reveals her protagonists in more bizarre narratives than before. Where she used the surreal as gentle flavour, she now brings it to the fore, so that in 'Green Hair' a boy grows a head of grass, and in 'Fur Coat' the coat takes control of its wearer's personality. What deepens the effect of the stories is the way in which such transformations merely cause mild embarrassment, but are otherwise accepted as odd occurrences. Her work came full circle with *Death of a Doctor*, with its original and effective emphasis on the contingency of things – in the doctor's waiting room, its health posters, the bored masks of the waiting people, the people on buses passing, looking in. She has the eye of a poet allied to the twist of the short-story teller; in the title story the doctor has just died, and the patients are being told, so that the situation is held in slow motion. Her gift is to render the ordinary strange through dwelling on it, in the same way that by looking for long on a word it can be made to dissolve into uncanny shapes and arrangements. Her characters, moreover, grow more extreme in their oddness: a customer disdains all advertising from his disillusionment with recurrent promises of 'absolute delight'; a women held up in a train develops a life-long phobia; a viewer at a gallery responds to a blank canvas's tiny invitation, 'write on me'; a banker dies in calmness, musing over the word 'stroke', and its many uses, violent, sporting, artistic. Her unique vision won her the Katherine Mansfield Award for her short stories in 1978.

Joan Lingard (b. 1933)

Joan Lingard has produced nearly twenty novels since *Liam's Daughter* in 1963. Many explore modern Scottish society, especially in Edinburgh, and the way in which women are hemmed in by conventions of class and gender. Her early novels showed much of the cloying background of propriety which surrounded Spark's Jean Brodie, in novels like *The Prevailing Wind* (1964) and *A Sort of Freedom* (1969), where the prevalent winds are those of Edinburgh's austere conventionality and their eventual triumph over the women who have dared to seek freedom. *The Second Flowering of Emily Mountjoy* (1979), marks a turning point in its reversal of defeat so that a middle-aged woman who dares to take a lover is reduced to wise, if unfulfilled, happiness. Perhaps in reaction against this repressive Edinburgh, *Greenyards* (1981) turned to the more colourful territory of the the Highlands during clearance, and the genre of historical romance worked by writers like Agnes Short and Elisabeth Sutherland. *Sisters by Rite* (1984) dealt with the troubles of Northern Ireland, where Lingard was educated. *Reasonable Doubts* (1986) returned to observe the contemporary moral dilemmas of middle-class Edinburgh. These are accomplished fictions; but Lingard's major achievements arguably lie in novels of the last ten years: *The Women's House* (1989); *After Colette* (1993); and *Dreams of Love and Modest Glory* (1995), which break into very different worlds, and develop a stronger and more affirmative stance on women's issues.

The Women's House, set in southern England, with its group of strangely assorted women set against a wealthy Italian Mafia-like male hierarchy, finds a kind of grace amidst the gender and sexual tensions, purging violence and pain through a mixture of understanding, charity and womanly solidarity, while realising the realities of male injustice and dominance. Something is born from the ashes of the women's house; Lingard manages with sensitivity and understatement to suggest that, despite apparent defeat, movement forward has been achieved by the surviving women.

In her next two novels Lingard worked on a far bigger scale and with more sophisticated techniques than ever before. *After Colette* interweaves lives in France and Scotland. Two women are born at the same time in the Burgundy village of Saint-Sauveur-en-Puisaye in 1873; one is Berthe-Amélie Grenot, the other is Sidonie-Gabrielle Colette. The novel is not about the best-loved and most famous of French women writers, the elegist of the lost country of childhood in the *Claudine* accounts, but her presence runs like a strong motif through the lives of the women whose interlinked stories over a hundred years are told here. Colette's work powerfully impresses young Berthe; and marks her descendants, Eugenie and Aimée. In several senses, they are all 'after Colette', in time, in ideas, and in pursuit of that elegant, poised life-style which continually eludes their more earth-bound, less talented natures. Poverty, war and chance deal less favourably with them than with cat-like and cat-lucky Colette, with her adoring men, her elegant rooms, her ability to edit messy things like her daughter and family out of her life. Ordinary mortals like Berthe and her children stumble through harsher marriages and lives, in France and Edinburgh, with the banal realities of squalling children and money worries. It's not that Colette is seen as guilty; rather, in the glimpses of her rooms with their blue lamps and delicate paperweights, or in her gracious reception of Berthe's descendants, that she's representative of a dream, an ideal which has haunted the generations. The 'I' who opens and closes the story is the unnamed Edinburgh cousin of Aimée/Amy Balfour, trying to trace Aimée, who in her sixties has gathered her poor possessions and disappeared, last seen as a lonely figure in the Gare de L'Est. The dream of following Colette has dominated Aimée's life; and Lingard, by presenting life from the perspectives of three very different women, and two very different cultures – the sophisticated French and reductive Scottish – deconstructs that dream. Yet the ending suggests one more meaning to 'after Colette', beyond those of dependency on suspect values. When Amy goes east, she is perhaps at last rejecting Colette for the earthier world of human intermingling and pain.

Dreams of Love and Modest Glory widened and deepened European dimensions. Lingard follows the Russian Revolution and the Latvian struggle for independence from 1913 to 1993, and from several perspectives. These are those of the Aberdeen twins, Lily and Garnet Mackenzie, and their respective husbands, Thomas Zale of Riga and Count Sergei Brunov of St Petersburg. In a sense the perspectives on European upheaval are also those of Scotland, Latvia, and Russia, since the central protagonists are effectively made to represent essential characteristics of their nationalities, with the pairing of Lily and Garnet cleverly presented as a kind of traditional polarisation of Scottish head and heart, although Lingard is far too sophisticated simply to recreate a conventional dualism of Scottish fiction.

The title is drawn from Pushkin ('Our dreams of love and modest glory/ delusive hopes now quickly sped') and the dreams are those of the two couples and their respective countries. From the meeting of the girls with the two foreign architects in Britain, and their hopes for the future, the novel moves to the crumbling of aristocratic Sergei's dreams as Russia under the Czar moves into poverty and revolution, and his self-indulgent family with it; from there, it shifts to the tensions in Latvia, caught between exploitation by Germans and by Russians, and Thomas's dreams moving from career and family to concern for his suffering country, as the huge nightmare of the First World War begins. Lingard moves on the grand scale of historical fiction here, embedding her convincing characters in richly detailed and controlled settings in several countries. Her success lies in the connection, drawn strongly and persuasively, between history and its effects on individuals – and vice versa. The novel is imbued with the tragic sense of Pushkin, as Lingard sets his grim Russian god of snowstorms, pot-holed roads, cockroaches, cripples and famine at the heart of early twentieth-century Russia and Europe – with the contrasts of the palaces of the Czar and the Burnovas set like jewels amidst trash, a striking metaphor which echoes the Colette/Grenot opposition of dream and reality in her previous novel. The novel is held together through the twins; Lily, sensitive and withdrawn, Garnet, bold and decisive. Their strong Aberdeen background, the world Lingard knows so well of Scottish middle-class homeliness, with its gossip, tea-parties, Salvation Army good works, is here used less to expose narrow convention and repressive intolerance (though these, unsurprisingly, still thrive), than to allow that, set against the darkness of central European chaos, this mundane Scottish community life has compensating virtues of understated kindliness, stability and peace.

In addition to Lingard's control of her implicated generations and her rich mirror-image patterning, the novel works through consistent and sustained imagery and motifs. And there is yet another layer to the patterning. The events are framed within the view of cousins Katrina Zale and Lydia Burnova, grandchildren of Lily and Garnet, in 1993 visiting Latvia to explore family history. The movement between modernity and past events creates effects of time and forgiveness which echo the narrative's movement to the tragic event which finally purged the disease of the generations which started in 1913. With its command of place and time, its sureness of control over vast movements of people and power, and its exploration of profound moral issues, this novel takes its place alongside the best of contemporary Scottish fiction of that internationally orientated kind produced by writers like Alan Massie, Stuart Hood, and William Boyd.

From dystopian nightmare to qualified hope

Dystopian views of city Scotland are not new, from west of Scotland memories underlying Thomson's *The City of Dreadful Night* (1875), and the nasty and dreamlike city sequences of MacGill's *The Rat Pit* (1915) and Gibbon's *Grey Granite* (1934). The previous chapter has emphasised the overwhelming tendency of much of twentieth-century Scottish fiction and literature towards urban gloom, from Edwin Muir's poetry and his novel *Poor Tom* (1932), through the Renaissance novel generally to Gaitens's *The Dance of the Apprentices* (1948) and the '50s fiction of Robin Jenkins. More recently we encountered the nightmare end-scenes of George Friel's *Mr Alfred MA*

(1972). But with *Lanark* (1981) the general bleakness became more focused; and many Scottish writers thereafter tried their hand at cityscapes designed to distort urban representation via the methods of science fiction, surrealistic colouring, and dream allegory.

And in the impressive number and quality of novels dealing with the psychological breakdown and trauma expressed through the experience of life as waking nightmare or through dream allegory, a fascinating new preoccupation of content and form emerges in contemporary Scottish fiction. Many of the most impressive new novels come out of this preoccupation with trauma and recovery. We may be too close to it to be able to see what this recurrent theme implies about the pressures of modern living in Scotland, but there is no doubting the conviction and subtlety with which many of the new writers handle what is in essence the same situation – a damaged protagonist (the damage can be physical, but it is the mental harm which matters most), unwilling or unable to face the events which caused the damage, evades reality through various diversionary strategies, these often taking the form of dream escape. These escapes, however, are never successful; either the dreams reveal to us deeper truths than the dreamer intends, or in other ways we see through the protagonist's trickery to what has really happened – and, significantly, we realise that the protagonist has subconsciously needed the dreams and apparent escapes to lead him/her back to some kind of sanity and health. Alexander Trocchi's pioneering study of the outsider reliving dystopian horror, *Young Adam* (1961), has been considered earlier. This ground-breaking novel has not been recognised as the innovative and trend-setting work it undoubtedly was, perhaps because the first version was published under a pseudonym as early as 1954, when its style and content seemed alien to current Scottish writing. Its central situation, that of a man hiding a traumatic personal experience from himself and the reader, would however, provide a model for later writers like Gray, Galloway, Banks and others, who would give an affirmative twist to the emergence of the protagonist from trauma.

Lanark

No consideration of contemporary Scottish fiction can fail to begin with Alasdair Gray's *Lanark* (1981), which will undoubtedly stand as one of the greatest of Scottish novels, as well as bearing comparison with the best of great surrealist and dystopian fiction throughout the world. Gray (b. 1934) has made his picture of Glasgow and the west of Scotland in decline his *Waste Land* – with its exaggerated images of sterility and decay thus becoming the images of the decline of the bigger West; the barren city failures of Europe and the world beyond. Gray's title is deliberately misleading; there may be intentional evocations of a 'dear green place', the country town by the Clyde where it approaches its transformation to industrial river; and certainly when the nameless protagonist searches his memory for a name, it is the picture in a railway carriage of just such a little Scottish town which prompts his choice.

The novel opens with 'Book Three'; thus plunging the reader into the confusion felt by its amnesiac protagonist. Lanark is a person, his name chosen by himself later and arbitrarily (if one can accept that 'choices' like this are ever artistically arbitrary). He is a displaced, memory-less, impoverished traveller whom we first meet in a Glasgow once-plush cinema café amongst the seedy intellectuals and their ladies. But before the atmosphere becomes too reminiscent of Sauchiehall Street and the environs of the Art College, weird glimpses that this city is *not* Glasgow disturb, increasingly, till shortly it bursts upon us that we are living in a Kafka nightmare.

This city has little or no sunlight, and its inhabitants have lost memory of or need for the sun. Its inhabitants tend to disappear suddenly, at nights, when alone – without much note being taken. Its industry has either disappeared, rotting away, or is focused on the curious cylinders of sinister but undefined function which rust on the muddy banks of a shrunken Clyde. Gray's evocation of a sterile and wasteland version of Glasgow is without parallel – harsh, bleak, yet horrifyingly and naggingly relevant and prophetic. His exaggerated description of the loss of population, the emptying inner city, the gloom and mood of sallow misery has the power of Thompson's *City of Dreadful Night*. Yet what makes it worse is that all the time the reader is enabled to make the modern connection seeing that the fictional disappearance of people is in reality disappearance in terms of unemployment, isolation in peripheral housing schemes, and consequent social unimportance – the Glasgow disease, its mood one of apathy and despair. Gray's apparent fantasy is really symbolic social satire, showing how real social problems are made to disappear from more privileged view.

This is vision of a very high order indeed – yet before we are overwhelmed by this mood, Gray moves us along in Lanark's bewildered mind which is trying to grasp where he is, who he is and where he's come from. All he knows is that he's come to the city (later named as Unthank) by railway, with some few tokens of a past life like a map, keys, a compass (all which possible clues to identity he throws away) and the odd haunting sense of an unhappy former life. Lanark's is a nightmare quest for self and meaning, an Everyman journey, which introduces him to some strange but all too convincing types; from bureaucratic social workers who don't seem greatly concerned or

910

perplexed by him, to corrupt city politicians making a killing on the misery. After a poignant but unsatisfactory affair with the enigmatic Rima (but what affair could be happy in Unthank?) Lanark discovers, in a midnight cemetery, the way through the baffling surface appearance of this 'civilisation' to the organising power behind it and other 'civilisations' – the power centre of the world, the Institute. Gray fuses the ideas of academy, university, hospital board and professional organisation in his nightmare vision of a huge, amorphous, yet disturbingly familiar body of professional people, with their meetings, theories, places of work. He is thus representing and satirising the privileged heart of modern, international society. Gray's portrayal of Lanark's discovery of the Institute, and the horrific impression he succeeds in giving of its vast but rather demented rights and powers, is amongst the astonishing achievements of the book – made all the more effective for being realised in down-to-earth harsh concrete detail, where reality and fantastic nightmare merge.

The Institute helps those it finds to be worth helping – but Lanark looks (literally) over its dark edge to the pit beyond, where the sighs, moans, and darkness of the mass of humanity are heard and seen – and discovers, to his horror, that the Institute actually feeds on this sub-stratum of humanity. He himself has come close to being such fuel-fodder; for throughout his Unthank days reference is made, in a most unpleasant and itchy way to his 'dragon-hide', his scaly patches of skin – which is the novel's way of expressing the hardening, the alienation, the sealing-off behind selfish carapace, of the lost individual. Rima is such; she is being kept now in the Institute in an advanced state of dragonhood, about to undergo some weird transformation which the Institute will use for its energy needs. Lanark, in acts of symbolic humanity pulls her back from this fate, and the two turn their back on the crazy logic and the all-too-convincing academics, administrators and dreamers of the subterranean Institute.

For Lanark is haunted by a recurrent vision, sometimes glimpsed through the high windows of the Glasgow-Infirmary-like windows of the Institute, of hills, and greenness, and most of all, sunlight. This lyrical and immensely refreshing counter-theme relieves the darkness of city and underground vault. Lanark becomes last home of the human urge for freedom and light, and Gray makes us feel the need to find the open spaces of mountain and sea. And besides, Lanark is haunted also by a memory of déja-vu; of having seen all this through other eyes; of having been before – and Part 1, which is described as Book Three, ends with Lanark finding, through the oracle, his real past life as Duncan Thaw, Glasgow child and art student.

Then follow Books One and Two, which are presented in the style of *bildungsroman.* Thus the surrealistic or fantastic dream account of Book Three precedes the naturalistic account; with Books One and Two sandwiched by the return of Book Four to Institute and Unthank. If this sounds over-complex or pretentiously obscure, it is not in reading. As we follow the traditionally told events of Duncan's life, the pattern and meaning of the telling become eminently clear. Duncan is Lanark, in an earlier life, yet still they are the same – Duncan not with dragonhide, but a skin-disease which makes him horribly shy, affecting all his relationships. Here, in 'reality', is the origin of Lanark's nightmare loneliness, and his dragonhide disease. This inner novel, so close to *Portrait of the Artist as a Young Man* (1916), is the moving description of the agonisingly sensitive and yet absurdly humour-filled life of Duncan Thaw. It is far from self-indulgent reminiscence; cruel about self, embarrassing in its revelation of private detail, hurtful in its familiarity, and very funny. But the overall movement is to an agonised realisation of Duncan's loneliness, as friends fail to be enough, as his mother 'disappears', as love doesn't work and sexual satisfaction is unattainable. Yet Duncan's misery is not over-drawn; he has a rich variety of friends who do try to reach him, and one of the book's most moving passages is when his father, in a desolation of sympathy and love, rocks the asthmatic Duncan in his arms offering his own suffering in replacement of the boy's. Indeed Gray is fairly merciless on Duncan; he is selfish, self-indulgent, but finally honest. And the honesty forces him to see that he's finally alone – as a painter, painting on walls which are going to be demolished, starving, pursuing an impossible dream. It is the very normality, humanity, and sometimes physical beauty of Duncan's surroundings that highlight his tragic dilemma – that he is not born to enjoy sexual love, that he cannot translate these hopeless feelings into an art he finds acceptable as substitute.

Does he then commit suicide? Or does he return in a state of mental breakdown to a nightmare Glasgow which his nightmare mind re-creates as Unthank? Gray leaves alternative readings all through the novel – as, for example, with the 'murder' which Duncan/Lanark believes he has committed. Whether through suicide or breakdown, Duncan returns to the limbo-land of Unthank, where as Lanark he has to work out his salvation, if such is possible. Here, after bizarre journeys and rejection of what the Institute stands for, Lanark has his family – but finds, yet again, in Rima's rejection and his separation from his son Alexander, alienation and frustration. At this point one feels the misery so much that one is about to cry why? – why and with what possible reason are we witnessing yet another failed life? – when, slowly, Gray's conflicting human struggles resolve themselves. There is a moment of communion between Alexander and Lanark on a hill, in the sunlight, when Lanark thanks life for sunlight, and that moment, if for nothing else. There is, amidst the nightmare political struggles between Unthank and the Institute at the end, acceptance by Lanark, amidst the wreckage of the cathedral and Glasgow/Unthank, of his place in what is finally seen as an upward human movement – slow, incredibly encumbered and frequently farcical, but upward.

All this deliberately leaves unclear just what Lanark has to do with Duncan Thaw – is he an afterlife, or a subconsciousness, or the stream-of-consciousness of past life which is supposed to rush through us just before death, but then, in this bewildering case, extrapolated into the future? Critics have accused Gray of wilfully clowning within the book, by having an 'Epilogue' at the beginning, as well as an index of plagiarisms. He also introduces himself, the author Nastler ('nasty Alasdair?') – who meets and talks to Lanark. But we should remember that part of the book's meaning is a satirical comment on our inability to organise memory and experience – so that, as 'authors' of our own lives, we bungle in recall, we cheat in interpretation, we glamorise or falsify just as Gray does about Thaw or Lanark. In this triumphant confusion of genres and meanings, Gray parodies his own life and ambitions, but uses them as exemplars of universal human dilemmas.

For behind the apparent transparency of Gray's elegant and classical style the reader can perceive allegories and trickeries which sustain a unified pair of themes. These are to be found throughout his work, and they are on the one hand a surface, but very powerful and Swiftian satire on the injustice and lack of empathetic imagination of the ruling organisations of Western (and all?) human society; and on the other, an underlying admission, expressed through many protagonists and situations, of a deep personal loneliness and a disarming admission of inadequacy in matters of love and art. Gray has admitted (*Glasgow Herald*, 6 December 1986) that he and his closest friend, the artist Alan Fletcher, who was killed while young, are two recurrent protagonists in his fictions. *Lanark*, with its colossal blend of fantasy, science fiction, *bildungsroman* and social satire, bears this out with its barely concealed clues that Duncan Thaw, the 'real' identity behind all the other versions in nightmare or limbo, has much in common in his Glasgow upbringing and emotional, intellectual and artistic development with the Gray who likewise grew up in years of wartime austerity and family suffering. The later great novels which juxtapose fantasy and satire, *1982, Janine* (1984) and *Poor Things* (1992), also play with this blend of personal and perhaps therapeutic exploration and impersonal commentary on repressive and excessive social authority. An essential personal shyness combined with an addiction to self-protective trickery causes Gray simultaneously to reveal and conceal himself in his novels and stories, using sleight of hand to tantalise the reader who is continually invited close, then distanced through false voices, withdrawal, and retreat to literary allusion and deception.

UNLIKELY STORIES, MOSTLY

Unlikely Stories, Mostly (1983) is the crucial volume for the reader wishing to understand Gray's work, its deepest motivation and its underlying meanings. Yet here is Gray at his most elusive, from the collection's initial bibliographical and typographical trickery to its deepest layers of personal concealment and revelation. On first publication, *Unlikely Stories* had an erratum slip which mocked pedantic correction in its ingenuous 'This slip has been inserted by mistake', and the dust jacket lampooned the ineffectuality of brief authorial biography while allowing Gray as author to slip away:

> He was
>   and educated
>   and became
>   residing
>   and   remaining
>   and intending
>   then on
>   became   in
>   and again

But alongside this refusal to fill in the personal gaps ran a more positive social message urging the reader to radical national and personal reconsideration; handsomely printed in gold on its royal blue hard binding, the first edition bore emblematic thistles, with the exhortation:

WORK AS IF YOU WERE
LIVING IN THE EARLY DAYS
OF A BETTER NATION
SCOTLAND   1983

Gray has always enjoyed such antithetical deceptions. But the reader should be aware that behind all the superficial trickery and literary camouflage lies a deeply serious, if paradoxical, agenda; the questioning of his own unstable position in an unstable world, along with a very Scottish yearning, doomed to almost complete disappointment, for spiritual value and authority.

Many of the stories in *Unlikely Stories* appeared before 1960, and most were written before 1980 – like 'The Comedy of the White Dog' or 'The Cause of Some Recent Changes', and show a love of surrealism and fantasy and the absurdly comic, but without much attempt to explore the relationship of a sick self to a sick society. But with 'The Crank Who Made the Revolution' and 'The Great Bear Cult' Gray began to move into new territory; 'The Crank' introducing the first of a series of Scottish and other eccentrics who recur in this volume, and 'The Bear Cult' opening up Gray's series of social satires. Self and society emerge here as Gray's two main preoccupations, a movement from fantasy and grotesque surrealism towards an ambitious reconciliation of the autobiographical and personally therapeutic with the socially and politically satirical; of the private with the public. Five stories from the volume stand among his best work. These satirical allegories in the second half of the book form a five-part sequence, with a different orientation from the previous tales. Now the narrator announces that he writes 'for those who know my language', signalling a new desire to communicate with readers who have taken the trouble to 'tune in', to read between the stories to see the deepening seriousness of this new Scottish blend of myth and satirical allegory.

In 'The Start of the Axletree', the axletree is Gray's symbol for the manipulation of religion and social class for its own ends by centralised imperial power. The achievement of the emperor is to transform the hub of his 'last and greatest world empire' into this axletree, creating a monstrous vertical holy city. By giving them the task of endlessly building their city ever higher, in the impossible aim of reaching the sky, he motivates his followers and descendants. To what extent does Gray mean us to recognise British imperialism in his allegory? Is he creating a timeless story-myth of all the world's capitalism and empire-building? It is the mark of Gray's development as a major writer that he is able to leave his allegory open-ended, signifying so many possible readings.

When Gray turns in these stories from social satire to focus on a central protagonist, there's a curious ambivalence in his recurrent treatment of the figure which can be found throughout his fiction, from Kelvin Walker to Lanark and Jock McLeish. The figures are wise and foolish, flawed human beings and conscientious citizens, holy fools of a kind found frequently in Scottish fiction, from Galt's *Sir Andrew Wylie* (1822) through Macdonald's *Sir Gibbie* (1879) to modern versions in Iain Crichton Smith's fiction and the later work of Robin Jenkins. This holy fool, with his confused and ambiguous feelings about the nature of secular and religious grace, illustrates a deep unease on the part of these Scottish authors towards their society's moral standards and religious heritage. In Gray's presentation, the significance of the figure lies in two directions: in being implicitly autobiographical; and in the way the biography is handled. Three of the stories illustrate this.

'Five Letters from an Eastern Empire' is one of Gray's finest allegories. Bohu is the tragic poet of the empire. Tohu is his much smaller, meaner comic counterpart. In an unplaced, timeless, vaguely Chinese background, with an apparently benign emperor organising a rigidly demarcated society of palaces, gardens, lakes, walls, and humble dwellings, organised on a chequer-board pattern, Bohu moves on huge clogs, pampered, wooden, priggish, yet naïvely honest, to his destiny. This is to be gulled by the emperor into writing a tragic poem – which the emperor then deploys to justify genocide. The parallels here with *Lanark* are clear, even in the relationship of Bohu to his parents. There is the same well-meaning concern on their part, the same sense of alienation and sad love, and in both cases the parents seem pathetically small figures, victims of a system they haven't remotely comprehended. Bohu is 'honoured' and invested with his orders, just as Lanark becomes a doctor (and as Duncan Thaw became an art student). Bohu's weird robes and rituals are his society's way of placing him above the common herd; Lanark has the institutional bruise-mark upon his brow. All this fits the theme of the five-story sequence, that of the misuse of power-centralisation, privilege and snobbery: 'Were you born outside the rim?' is the crucial question asked by those who live inside the great wheel. Just so Bohu condescends to Tohu, his servants, and lesser mortals. Is all this a mythic statement concerning the inevitable exploitation of the artist by his society, and, more locally, the Scottish artist's essentially irrelevant role in his community? Or is Gray representing the role of the creative artists in modern capitalist society, seeing them as exploited in the interests of the state? In Bohu, one discovers a familiar figure, camouflaged by his unfamiliar territory, but in the end not unlike Kelvin Walker, the innocent and wise fool. Perhaps even more, it is Lanark, self-important as ambassador of Unthank to Provan and the council, but in fact a laughing stock who is being used by more worldly operators for their own ends, exactly as the emperor uses Bohu.

Nowhere does the ambiguous holy fool appear more eccentric than in 'Logopandocy', Gray's fable about one of Scotland's most endearing eccentrics, Sir Thomas Urquhart of Cromarty, 'the mirror of perfection' in knightly attainment of the seventeenth century. It would be easy to miss Gray's concealed identification with Urquhart behind this charming, sad, bizarre account of the progress of a wise fool; easy, too, to miss the amount of Scottish satire, the detailed (but ultimately hopelessly confused) self-assessment by Thomas in the uproarious 'Pro Me / Contra Me' inventory of his assets. In this allegory a fool and his foolish countrymen are seen squandering their talents abroad, fighting on opposite sides and causes, wilfully wasting themselves. Urquhart's Logopandocy outlandishly applies Napier's logarithms 'to the grammar of an Asiatick people, thought to be the lost tribe of Israel, whose language predates the Babylonic cataclysm' with the end of 'rationally reintegering God's gift of tongues to Adam'. It is the pursuit of the goal of alchemy in language, a linguistic fool's gold, and on this and such quests the noble Urquhart destroys himself.

Or does he? A question arises which was hinted at in Bohu's final useless act of integrity, his brief tragic poem – and one which arises concerning Lanark's final achievement, and Jock McLeish's hard decisions in *Janine*. Is there, for all his posturing irrelevance, a point of self-recognition, of socially useless yet personally valid choice, which, in its final statement of truth, is the only possibility of human significance in a lunatic and power-distorted world? Thomas disintegrates in a mental breakdown which can be compared with those of Thaw and McLeish. Gray apparently redeems Thomas's tragicomedy by saving him from his historical death and allowing him to find love in a strange land.

More cleverly still, Gray makes this collection enact an over-arching journey. The non-literary material, the illustrations between stories, now reveal their thematic function, which is to link the apparently disparate narratives, making them parts of a bigger and concealed story about a meta-protagonist, shadowy behind unlikely stories, telling indirectly of his background quest for meaning and love. On the flyleaf, an eccentric looking knight sails in a silly boat, blown by a zephyr; then, sword extended, perches precariously but defiantly, at its prow as the book opens. An inscrutable wizened emperor-face (Gray? The demon-saint of 'The Start of the Axletree? Emblem of the centralised power Gray so hates?) broods over all, watching the audacious human voyager; the voyager decays (note the richly-cuffed knightly hand becoming impoverished, gnarled, enclosed by a hand of love). But, while that is the last we hear in the story of Thomas Urquhart, seventeenth-century Scot, in fact his journey isn't over. The drawings which began on the fly-leaf continue, Thomas's boat is blown on, and, transmogrified, reappears in the next story 'Prometheus', in the twin guises of Prometheus and modern French thinker and poet Monsieur Pollard, 'shy, fastidious, and arrogant'. Thomas had thought himself 'come to the edge of the greatest and happiest discovery of my life' at the end of his account; Pollard thinks that he has just encountered a lady who can be sexual partner and witness to his elevated thought and life.

Nothing could seem more distant from the world of a Glasgow Art College student of the 1950s than these grotesque stories. In fact, Parisian intellectual Pollard is yet another version of Duncan Thaw, Bohu, Kelvin Walker, McLeish, Lanark, Thomas Urquhart. Even closer to home and to Duncan Thaw is Pollard's student career: 'I depressed my professors at the Sorbonne by finally submitting no thesis. A poet need not truck with bureaucrats.' But a yet more striking identification also enters here. Gray has Pollard explicitly link his loneliness with that of God, and his proud intellectual separation from humanity with God's. 'My infancy resembled that of God, my ancestor', he tells us. Behind this 'joke' of Pollard lies a strange metaphysic of Gray's, which will extend itself in the Gray-Nastler-Lanark-Thaw manipulations of the novel, and become most sophisticated in Jock McLeish's recognition of God within himself, the inner voice which stops his suicide in *Janine*. This story marks the introduction of this final, spiritually enigmatic theme, which enables Gray to envisage a possible and positive ending to his Urquhart-like quest.

Pollard's story doesn't reach the qualified optimism of passages of *Lanark* or the stern acceptance of the self in *Janine*. Pollard (the name signifies his blighted growth) fails in his attempt to find love, since Lucie will not accept his estimate of himself as mirrored in the myth of Prometheus, nor will she surrender to the intolerable selfishness which will use her as supporting *anima*. The holy fool is often reduced in Gray's work by the ferocious female. What emerges is a profoundly personal statement of despair about the mismatch of human needs and longings. Beautiful girls love worthless men; the central figure finds increasingly that talent and intelligence are no guarantee of success in sexual and emotional relations.

Gray's carefully arranged illustrations and emblems now begin to tail off, till, after the drawing of Prometheus, naked, arms outstretched, falling, we are left with final drawings of the voyaging knight, now an old man, sailing on stoically until he is last seen in the closing pages edging past Arran, past Ailsa Craig which carries a sign (his destination?) 'Glasgow 78 miles'. Thus Gray slyly connects his allegories to home. 'Prometheus' was even more revealing of this connection; a voice spoke, as it were, from behind the story.

> This story is a poem, a wordgame. I am not a highly literate French dwarf, my lost woman is not a revolutionary writer manqué, my details are fictions, only my meaning is true and I must make that meaning clear by playing the wordgame to the bitter end.

Who is speaking? It must be the author behind Pollard. Who is that? We can't simply say 'Gray', for *Lanark* shows us there can be authors behind authors

918

behind authors. Gray's allegories express yet conceal their human situation in which a talented but eccentric and physically unattractive protagonist has to realise that his idealistic Promethean aspiration after truth and justice and beauty may finally be seen as self-interested sexual desire dressed up to look good.

The final story, 'The End of the Axletree', moves from personal analysis to public satire, completing Gray's essential dualism of theme throughout the volume. Taking up where the emperor left off the fable tells how the great vertical city finally reached the sky, which is found to be tangible, a great canopy enclosing the world. Men, of course, can't leave it alone, and (in a marvellous allegory for human greed and destructiveness from the beginning of property-holding to wars and space programmes and their place in political economy) tear it open, drowning the world in a new flood. Thus the overall story of the volume is ended; as in *Lanark*, and *Janine*, 'man is the pie that bakes and eats itself, and the recipe is separation'. We war with ourselves, with our society; full of sound and fury, we signify very little, as individuals, artists, societies. We are right to mock our pretensions, destroying ourselves and the earth we live on. And yet, and yet . . . something in the all too tragi-comic lives of Bohu, Urquhart, Pollard – and Lanark, and Kelvin Walker, and Jock McLeish – remains to suggest a glimmer of the transcendental. At the end of *Unlikely Tales* we see Sir Thomas Urquhart, sailing on through time, his little boat moving on, a glimmer of hope in a grotesque world.

1982, JANINE

1982, Janine (1984) is a very different, but equally impressive achievement. This is a novel which, like MacDiarmid's *A Drunk Man Looks at the Thistle* (1926), uses the personal and metaphysical experiences of a single night, as undergone by a protagonist who exemplifies much of the psyche and the character of the male Scot, to move towards an ambiguous series of epiphanies or self discoveries which possibly point towards a more hopeful future for the protagonist, and – if we accept him as exemplary – his country. Jock McLeish is a supervisor of security systems. He is alcoholic, neurotic about his age, his broken marriage and sexual failure, and cynically Tory. Insomniac, he lies in a hotel room in Peebles (or is it Greenock?) and to pass the night fantasises with control and imaginative intensity about Janine, and Superb, and big Momma, and the men who manipulate and degrade them – all in a stereotypical US glossy and violent setting. It's escape, of course and it has to be the USA to work, because Scotland and Britain can't give the possibility or authenticity of imaginative release. Also to imagine the USA and

Playboy ladies then takes the place of real and hurtful memories – so that the night becomes a battle between synthetic replacements for traumatised bits of Jock's mind and the real people from mother and father to friends and lovers who will insist on invading his fantasies. Note that the protagonist is 'Jock' – the *Lanark* like Epilogue tells us that the book's 'matter of Scotland refracted through alcoholic reverie' is based on MacDiarmid's *A Drunk Man Looks at the Thistle*. While there are many other and international 'sources', this first clearly places the protagonist as exemplifying significant features of Scottish character. His job with security has been chosen by Gray as saying something about Scottish playing-it-safe, steady employment, being an instrument rather than a valid entity. And in the course of the spiralling-down into Jock's real unconscious, as opposed to the superficial fancies of erotic situations (not so superficial when they indicate to us why he prefers bondage to mutual embrace, details of dress to straightforward nudity, complex and deviant foreplay to actual consummation) Gray manages to say much more explicitly about the politics and economy of Scotland than in *Lanark*.

It's a much more positive book than *Lanark*, in that Jock does manage to exorcise his ghosts – the lost hope of Scotland; Jock's brilliant and tragically short-lived friend Alan; his betrayed lover, Denny; Helen, his wife; his father. This is in many ways not an easy book to read, and a superficial appreciation will probably dislike the sick sexuality it will find. But that sexuality is in the end not employed for sick satisfaction, but rather as a deeply moral exploration of aspects of men's minds which most of us are frightened and incapable of handling. The honesty and depth of this book's analysis is challenging and disturbing. But in its condemnation of what has happened to Scotland, in its defeat of its first half's self-indulgence by its second half's hurtful autobiographical honesty, after Jock tries and fails at suicide, it stands as a new stage in Scottish culture. In this, the complex investigation of our benighted personal and public aesthetics is not dodged by recourse to British or transatlantic or parochial models such as Mackay Brown's, but confronted and, if not overcome, admitted and placed clearly in focus as the too materialistic, anglicised, snobbish and finally phoney tradition which Gray and fellow writers like Kelman and Leonard insist must be fought. Jock resigns his job, gives up ideas of suicide, and his last words in the novel to the maid who knocks on his door announcing breakfast are, 'All right'.

This is a sophisticated and complex novel. In its integration of different time sequences, its flashbacks and subtle allusions to the past, and its parallel of fantasy and fact at one and the same time, it is arguably even more ambitious than *Lanark*. Gray continues here to use fiction as a therapeutic way of handling his own past experience as much as he uses it as a post-modern art form, as in his introduction of himself as the moody author of the Edinburgh play (which sounds very like Gray's play *The Harbinger Report*, on which the novella *Ludmilla and McGrotty* is later based).

LEAN TALES AND THE FALL OF KELVIN WALKER

Lean Tales (1985), a collaboration with Agnes Owens and James Kelman, is significant in demonstrating the inter-connected values of these Glasgow writers. Gray's contribution is, however, hardly fiction; his 'Report to the Trustees' is a a non-fiction account (signed 'Alasdair' to the trustees of Glasgow's Art College) of a disastrous scholarship abroad, once again blurring the distinctions between fiction and autobiography. His discussion and finishing-off of R. L. Stevenson's unfinished 'The Story of a Recluse' points forward to the influence of Stevenson on *Poor Things*. And with *The Fall of Kelvin Walker* (1985) Gray begins to adapt his previous dramatic work for television to fictional form. This fable of the earnest young Scot who takes London by storm has been presented in various forms by writers like Galt, Barrie and Bridie; and there is a curiously old-fashioned tone to Gray's version, in which Kevin's *naïveté* and ability to ask fundamental questions which sophisticated Englishmen no longer pose, together with Scottish net-working in the media, pushes him swiftly to the top of TV presentation. Here too is Gray's version of the classic father-son opposition in Scottish fiction, as Kelvin's little black session-clerk father becomes his public destruction on television, the one person who can still intimidate his cocksure son. The novella's stereotypes of repressive Scottish character have power, but are less impressive than the more sophisticated treatments of *Lanark* and *Unlikely Stories*; but what is clear is that Gray has continued to explore Scottish literature; Kelvin's tone of pompous justification is that of Hogg's *Justified Sinner*.

McGROTTY AND LUDMILLA AND SOMETHING LEATHER

Both these novels appeared in 1990 after five years, fictional silence from Gray. He had been writing; a study, *Five Scottish Artists*, appeared in 1986, and a fine (and revealing) volume of poems, *Old Negatives*, in 1989. Perhaps this was a period in which Gray found it difficult to decide on direction, with the competing claims of painting, poetry, and politics. (The failure of the devolution referendum in 1979 to achieve a definitive result in favour of home rule concerned him greatly, as it did so many writers like Kelman and McIlvanney, and his polemical study *Why Scots Should Rule Scotland* appeared in 1992.) What is clear, however, is that Gray's next two fictions were based on the extensive body of dramatic writing for television, radio and stage which he had produced in the '60s and '70s. The novella *McGrotty and Ludmilla*, based on his play *The Harbinger Report*, resembles *The Fall of Kelvin Walker* in its presentation of the innocent Scotsman abroad in London. McGrotty differs from Kelvin in his working-class background and his even less attractive snivelling insecurity. But he is used as a pawn by power-hungry Sir Arthur Shots, and by the ultimately more dangerous Ludmilla, polished daughter of a government minister, and his own essential amorality works well with her ambition. While there is no doubting the bitterness of Gray's political satire in its hatred of what he sees as a rotten and south-of-England Establishment, the reader may once again question the validity of Gray's stereotypes. (The novel has also appeared as a play with the same title.)

Something Leather (1990) also reworked plays which Gray had written earlier into a novel. Here however there is a movement forward, showing how deeply Gray was committed to a re-evaluation of the attitudes of men towards women, and to asserting new roles for women in response. In this study of four women who have been abused in different ways, and who get together to form a leather-fashion group which is really a cover for their new agenda for sexual and psychological recovery, Gray plays quite openly with the fact that he is pushing together what used to be separate and unrelated dramas, seeing their linking as his challenge. It still reads as jointed and over-coincidental – but in such an obvious and at times surreal fashion it seems to be the effect Gray has intended. What is not in dispute is the wit and satirical bite achieved through characters like Harry, the south-of-England public-school damaged sculptress specialising in bum-shapes who comes to Scotland to condescend to its art world. Gray mocks the hype – and the sickness? – of contemporary art ferociously here; but now avoids stereotyping by exposing Harry's essential loneliness and decency and having her re-deemed by the group. And Gray joins Kelman and Leonard in their attack on the power which resides in language and accent in his clever reversal of the usual deployment of phonetic orthography, in his representation of southern English speech as quirky and at odds with Scottish received pronunciation. For example, here is Harry's mother defending public school education: 'They learn to look to themselves, not to othas fo what they need, so in laita yias they make othas do tha bidding.'

POOR THINGS

Gray returns to the territory of himself as subject in *Poor Things* (1992). This may not at first seem apparent. His role indeed appears restricted to that of editor and commentator, in the time-honoured way of Mackenzie, Hogg, Stevenson and all the other false 'editors' of Scottish fiction. He performs his trickery well, speaking in the role of the social historian who has been examining old papers found by other (and actual) social historians. Like James Hogg's 'editor' in *The Justified Sinner*, Gray finds a perfect tone for his framing introduction and endpiece; factual, yet opinionated, nicely balancing the sort of credibility an old lawyer would be given by Stevenson with a cantankerous eccentricity which reveals itself in quarrels with fellow-historians. Registry and historical facts are placed alongside subjective interpretation; by loading enough circumstantial detail in the right dry, factual way, otherwise incredible events slip through the reader's scepticism.

Gray purports to have found the papers of a nineteenth-century public health officer, Archibald McCandless MD, complete with etchings by a famous Victorian, William Strang, as well as lavish reproductions of sexual organs as drawn in Gray's *Anatomy* – the other famous Gray, a nice touch. Strang's etchings are, of course, Alasdair Gray's; but there is no serious attempt to persuade the reader that this Frankenstein-based tale of how Sir Colin Baxter, knighted by Victoria for services to medicine, actually scientifically created his monstrous son Godwin (note the typical name-play on Mary Shelley's father). Godwin in turn makes the wondrous Bella, by implanting the brain of a drowned woman's unborn child into the woman's body. Gray keeps the game up to the end – with the last paragraph of the book carrying a sting.

Dr Victoria McCandless (Bella, who became a famous pioneer of treatment for women, and married Archibald) was found dead of a cerebral stroke on 3 December 1946. Reckoning from the birth of her brain in the Humane Society Mortuary on Glasgow Green, 18 February 1880, she was exactly sixty-six years, forty weeks and four days old. Reckoning from the birth of her body in a Manchester slum in 1854, she was ninety-two. Such obvious Victorian fable-making is delightful, if transparent. As in Stevenson – to whom the content and style is massively indebted – claims of either side, the supernatural/fabulous and the rational/sceptical are apparently fairly balanced; so Bella/Victoria gets her chance to present her account, in which she dismisses her husband's claims, attributing his wild beliefs to envy and insecurity, and simultaneously reducing his wonderful love affair to a matter of pity and indulgence on her part. Her tone is rational, reductive, yet nicely calculated to allow suspicion that she herself wants to hide the 'truth' for her own reasons. Read on this level, it is a parody of the traditional Scottish Gothic fable. But what is Gray's underlying purpose?

The answer can be gained from the striking original cover illustration; brooding over his tired creations and dependants is Godwin Baxter, drawn, weary, his artificial metabolism disintegrating slowly. His massive face, unlovely yet moving in its patient, detached suffering, Victorian and patriarchal in the better sense of these qualities, in the manner of, say, a reformer like Edwin Chadwick (or an antimaterialist like Thomas Carlyle), shows much of Gray himself. There's even facial similarity, though more important is the idea that this is a later Nastler, a developed version of the Promethean failures, flawed creators and geniuses, of *Unlikely Stories*, and yet an earthier version of the quietly insistent God-voice of *Janine*. And what Godwin Baxter represents is, however complex, reducible to an essential idea of liberal and humane rationalism: Alasdair Gray's own flinty, quirky, Scottish-Enlightenment-influenced ideology. Lumbering, socially unfashionable, virtually deformed, yet noble in aim and motive, there is all that is best in what made Scotland, Britain, and Western philanthropic man; and combined with this, Gray articulates many of his feelings concerning himself and his attempts to define a position in work, art, and society.

Thus something deeply serious moves beneath the dazzling mockery of fictional genre in ways both post-modernist and derived from the misfits of fiction – Cervantes, Sterne, Joyce. McCandless's function is to act as Boswell to Baxter's Johnson, recording again and again Gray's and Baxter's Augustan irony and social belief. Throughout Chapters 2 and 3, Baxter makes withering comment on social and institutional orthodoxies:

'The public hospitals are places where doctors learn how to make money off the rich by practising on the poor. That is why poor people dread and hate them, and why those with a good income are operated upon privately . . .'

'Our nurses are now the truest practitioners of the healing art. If every Scottish, Welsh and English doctor and surgeon dropped suddenly dead, eighty per cent of those admitted to our hospitals would recover if the nursing continued . . .'

'If medical practitioners wanted to save lives . . . instead of making money out of them, they would unite to prevent diseases, not work separately to cure them. The cause of most illness has been known since at least the sixth century before Christ . . .'

'What you call *mysteries* I call *ignorances*, and nothing we do not know (whatever we call it) is more holy, sacred and wonderful than the things we know . . . The loving kindness of people is what creates and supports us, keeps our society running and lets us move freely in it.'

The 'poor things' of the title are thus Baxter's dependants; and then the rest of the sick, poor, deprived classes Victorian affluence didn't reach; and then humanity, and its impoverished spiritual condition.

Alongside this Swiftian satire runs an extension of Gray's feminist arguments in *Something Leather*. Bella, Godwin's creation, is more than a new woman; she is 'Bella Caledonia', portrayed by Gray against a backcloth of all Scotland. Hers is a Shelley-inspired and Stevenson-styled story of life created artificially, with attendant problems, presented with the wonderful and comic account by Bella of what it might have been like to be a liberated woman in a male society, and its initially funny but ultimately deeply unfunny portrayal of caricature imperialist General Blessington, with his inflexible authoritarian maleness and divine right to rule.

TEN TALES TALL AND TRUE, A HISTORY MAKER,
MAVIS BELFRAGE AND THE BOOK OF PREFACES
In Gray's last three fictions he has continued to mingle older material with ventures into radically new territory for himself and Scottish fiction. *Ten Tales* (1993) is Gray at his best in the short story – with his insistence on controlling all aspects of the book's production never seen to better effect than in the embossed inside cover, this time showing the stump of a tree (the cutting-down of devolution?) with a single shoot trying to grow, and Bruce's spider dangling below. This slight indication of hope is, however, qualified by the book's recurrent illustrations of dinosaurs, snakes and scorpions set against cats, beavers and squirrels, emblematic of the collection's themes, even darker than before, of predators and their exploitation of humbler species. Here are exploiters in sex, politics, and society contrasting with more ordinary humans, like lovers, travellers, teachers, in stories of betrayal, lack of human sympathy, aggressive, concealed or condescending power. Gray seems to have regressed in terms of social optimism here; and the concluding story is chillingly relevant to our high-tech society's deepest fears in its account of the railway journey of the future between Bundlon and Shaglow, where the super-train's computer fails at the speed of 500 kilometres an hour. Among the decent and friendly ordinary travellers the last cries heard are of 'mummy', and 'no one's in control' – and by finishing the volume with a farewell tribute to his old teacher Mr Meikle, Gray suggests that modern society is careering off the rails, while older values have disappeared.

This darker vision recurred in Gray's most enigmatic novel, the science-fiction parable *A History Maker* (1994). He describes this as 'a kilted sci-fi yarn full of poetry and porridge, courage and sex' – when in reality he is exploring a future Scotland which appears to be a Utopia. The setting is the Scottish Borders 200 years from now; matriarchies are in control of communal families which grow around organic power plants. Global media coverage has reduced war to game show status, in which clan-teams fight with swords; we witness the ferocious battle to the death between the Ettrick clan and Northumbria United, in which Ettrick are virtually wiped out. Gray recounts this bizarre satire on future society, technology and present mass-sport media obsession with a parodic boyish enthusiasm which succeeds in lightening the novel's very dark prognostications by simultaneously mocking itself. Male aggression is mocked and channelled into what is seen as permissible killing, and apparently, at last, women have gained their proper role. Readers familiar with Gray's deceptions will know that there are far deeper meanings. But what are they? The novel has been interpreted as Gray's response to Fukiyama's infamous notion of the '90s that, with the triumph of capitalism, history as a matter of ideological change had come to an end. What seems here to be Utopia is, of course, wide of the mark; Utopia, for Gray, is an impossible concept. Wat Dryhope, sole Ettrick survivor of the Ettrick – Northumbria confrontation, realises that the price of this Utopia negates its value, and sets out to do two things; to show that such killing is unnecessary, and to defeat the scientists who seek to disease the world with a virus which will destroy the organic power plants. Is Gray being too clever here, in trying to make too many satirical comments on too many issues, sexual, political and ecological? In addition to Wat's story, this is also the account of his mother, Kittock the Henwife – who appears to be a symbol of tradition and folk-continuity, and who also evokes the Border world and values of James Hogg. Moreover, there are over sixty pages of notes ranging from Border lore to world religions (including a useful definition of post-modernism). Earlier holy fools had a recognisable role in Gray's fiction; here Wat's significance is blurred, and he moves from a position of genuine worth to an ending in which he and his wife are gangrels who beat each other. This summary of what appears confusing may well be missing Gray's point. The main thrust of the novel seems to be that history does not end, that humanity continually lives in change, often violent, but that this does not mean that we should not aim at the ideal.

Gray's last collection of short stories and a novella, in *Mavis Belfrage* (1996), while returning to apparently mundane worlds (the dust jacket slyly argued that 'this book should be called *Teachers: 6 Short Tales*'), continued to show Gray less optimistic and more sceptical regarding human improvement. The clear satire of earlier fiction has gone, leaving a viewpoint which is disillusioned with the complexities of political and emotional life and relationships. Again, he deceives in his description of the title novella as 'A Romantic Novel'; far from being his 'only straight novel about love', this is reminiscent of so many earlier tales of solemn young Scots destroyed by their relationship with headstrong, introverted (or dangerously extroverted) women, in its account of a selfish woman abandoning her husband and son. The other stories either echo this theme of awkward mismatching, or present biographical pieces about Gray's friends which he relates to sad outcomes and failed ideals. All this contrasts with the book's cheerful artwork and its inside cover development of his by now expected embossment of a political message. Now the cover is emblazoned with the banner 'INDEPENDENCE'; and the child of Bella Caledonia plucks the fruits of the thistle. The reader is left wondering at the discrepancy of moods. Gray leaves us with simultaneous mockery and exploitation of post-modernism.

From 1996 on Gray turned back to a long-cherished project, culminating in 2000 in *The Book of Prefaces*. The publishers (or Gray?) described it thus: 'This book is NOT a monster created by a literary Baron Frankenstein, but a unique history of how a literature spread and developed through three British nations and most North American states.' The echo of Godwin Baxter in that description reminds us that Gray's recurrent creative role is one in which the author hides himself while simultaneously re-creating his weaknesses and dreams. This astonishing collection of 175 visionary declarations, from Bede to Barbour, Henryson to Hooker, Hobbes to Hume, Burns to Byron, Carlyle to Conrad, emerges from Gray's most affirmative self as dreamer and idealist. By involving a host of colleagues to co-operate with him Gray asserts the validity of the good community and its values against the manipulative and expediential traits of modern society, and it stands as a fitting place to leave this most thoughtful, imaginative and socially concerned of Scottish and British writers.

Lanark *and* The Bridge

Iain Banks (b. 1954) has become such an accomplished and successful novelist in so many genres that it is perhaps unfair to begin with his third novel, *The Bridge* (1986). The reason for doing so, however, comes from Banks himself, who admitted that *Lanark* had such a profound effect upon him that he wished to try working in the same vein. It would not be fair, however, to see his work as in any sense derivative. The reader of *The Wasp Factory* (1984) will realise how original, macabre and deviantly comic is Banks's imagination (as will the reader of the science fiction novels written under the name Iain M. Banks); and it is a hallmark of his work that no two novels exploit the same fictional style. Eclectic, protean, cross-generic, Banks stands as exemplar for the new spirit of Scottish fiction. From the rural *grotesquerie* of *The Wasp Factory* he turned towards city dystopia, with the strange conceiving of a surface world operated from underneath by hidden puppet-masters, the Kafka-and-Castle-like *Walking on Glass* (1985).

The Bridge outstripped anything he had written, however, in ambition and extent of social comment. This brilliant follow-up to *Lanark* – for it presents a protagonist in nightmare, caught in an institutionalised system which grows increasingly dark, and presents similar satire against class and economic systems and structures, with the same difficulty for the reader of determining how the dream-logic is to be interpreted – has a thought-out and total control of its layers which rivals the skill and achievement of Gray's work. Alexander Lennox (his name is not openly stated, but clued into the narrative) has reached a bridge or crossroads in his life; having moved across from the west of Scotland, and upwards from the working class, he has not yet consciously realised the price he has had to pay in terms of betrayal of self, origins, language, parents. His lady has gone to stay with rival Gustav, ill in Paris. Alex doesn't protest; his faith in reason and machines forbids. Is his crash on the Forth Road Bridge, scene of childhood and later romantic visits, an accident or subconscious-willed confrontation with self? For this is a study of the psyche, and how its strange healing powers can insist over our conscious minds. He awakens as patient, like Lanark, with a new identity and amnesia, in an institution; here, the great Bridge society, stupendously envisaged by Banks as a 2,000-foot high structure, packed with hundreds of layers of buildings and thoroughfares; a bridge running in endless repetitions for thousands of miles in either direction. All that is known is that the kingdom (of Fife?) and the city (of Edinburgh?) lie in opposing directions. But there's more; for interwoven with this living dream are other kinds of local dreams, of confronting the other (Gustav? self?), of the barbarian, fighting his crude and Scottish dialect-expressed way through underworld and crashing ever on to find the 'Sleeping Byooty' – who turns out to be Lennox, all the while in hospitals, the dim form of the man in the bed glimpsed at intervals throughout the novel. Lennox's unconscious knows best; the id-barbarian forces through, and the dreams become increasingly insistent on breaking out from the bridge-world where Lennox has initially preferred to hide.

Perhaps, like *Lanark*, it is in the last stages that the novel shows possible weakness, in the difficulties encountered in resolving the issues raised. A long train journey, moving off-bridge and through savage wars in strange lands, changes the focus in ways not prepared for; the sense of dislocation is unsettling. But the conclusion has more coherence and commitment than *Lanark*; and precisely here lies the significance as an example of dystopia struggling to become a more positive vision. Alex comes out from coma, months later; Andrea sits by his side; 'Welcome back', she says, and Alex, perhaps now changed, more assertive about his life and his roots, less willing to be detached, simply and laconically answers, 'Oh Yeah?'. Is this cautious optimism; will Alex find life worth living in Scotland, but now on his own more confident terms? What Banks suggests, as so often with his protagonists at the end of their stories, is that they stand on a threshold in a new Scotland; a sign of the times. *Lanark* and *The Bridge* are important markers of a move towards cautious optimism.

THE RANGE OF THE FICTION OF IAIN BANKS

The Wasp Factory (1984) was a fashionable success which immediately established Banks as one of the most promising new British writers; a novel grotesque and comic, disgusting in much of its imagery, unbelievable in its central situation, yet hilarious. Frank lives with his eccentric father on a tiny north-east island. He has suffered some horrific childhood accident; his brother has just escaped from a lunatic asylum; and he reveals that he has murdered several of his relatives by contrivances such as a snake in an artificial leg, a derelict bomb, a giant kite. His relationship with the wildlife of the island is that of *Lord of the Flies* (1954): propitiatory, pagan, chillingly atavistic. He has warning posts with rabbits heads skewered on them to guard the island; he has a shrine with an altar of horrid items watched by the skull of the dog which castrated him; and he has a Heath Robinson quintessential nightmare contrivance which is the wasp factory. Banks made this novel a deliberate exercise in the comic macabre, with the horrors so wildly vivid that the effect is intentionally hyperbolic. With the ending Banks plays tricks with gender that clearly point to future explorations in the area, as in *Canal Dreams* (1989), *Whit* (1995) and *The Business* (1999); and it is significant that even in this first novel the ending realised its protagonist's emergence from trauma into a world – and a Scotland – with promise. Banks followed this with the less successful *Walking on Glass* (1985), which tried to fuse Kafka-and-Peake derived fantasy with social realism; its three narratives relate uneasily to each other. What Banks demonstrates is his recurrently unpredictable experimentation with genre. *The Bridge* followed, likewise combining apparent fantasy (in the end revealed as dream) and social realism, and showed the experimentation suceeding.

In 1987, the same year as his first science fiction novel, *Consider Phlebas*, Banks produced *Espedair Street*, his study of a traumatised and guilt-ridden Paisley rock star hiding out in a disused Glasgow church (two powerful symbols of Scotland now?), his concealment of his identity as the surviving member of the world-famous group, Frozen Gold, and of his incredible wealth, parallels Lennox's coma, his drinking binges masking his hiding-out from painful realities, a Scotland neither can face. The novel charts his return to Paisley friendships and communal ties. Social realism prevails here, although, as always in even the most naturalistic of Banks fiction, the grotesque and other-wordly creeps in, with his bizarre settings.

Canal Dreams followed, taking Banks away from Scotland in a thriller about international terrorism, in which an improbable heroine, a Japanese cellist in her forties, exacts ferocious revenge on hijackers in the Panama Canal. Again, the female protagonist emphasises Banks's desire to undermine gender stereotyping, and again, the boundaries between science fiction, fantasy and grim modern reality are blurred in Hosaka's nightmares of blood and the surreal canal settings, the scenes of carnage evoked with a weird balletic beauty.

Banks then undertook his most ambitious examination of contemporary Scotlands in *The Crow Road* (1992). The title typically mirrors Banks's blending of romance and realism, implying the dualisms of contemporary Scotland; it is a 'kenning' or traditional symbolic shorthand for the sky, the place of flight and escape (as in MacDiarmid's 'the laverock's hoose', or the old English 'swan's way'), but it also refers to the very real Crow Road which brings the road from the Highlands into the heart of Glasgow. Here Banks tries nobly to weld urban and rural, with his characters using BMW cars to cross the Rest-and-Be-Thankful mountain pass which links Lowland and Highland Scotland. This juxtapositioning is indicative of a host of interweavings in the same manner. His protagonist, Prentice McHoan, comes from a Banks-invented, Oban-sized town placed in what is in fact Knapdale wilderness; a railway line is invented to connect it with Glasgow; teasing near-identifications (a method familiar in the modern Scottish novel in Jenkins, McIlvanney, and more recently Alan Warner) with real places and events, imply that this is about Scotlands, about possibilities. Prentice has to lose his father and to discover that Rory and his Aunt Fiona were murdered by his uncle Fergus, before the bizarre end, which involves him pushing a Rolls Royce off Lewis cliffs into the Atlantic. He, like Banks's other Scottish protagonists, can now stand ready to face the new Scotland.

Banks then explored a new area, but with echoes of older Scottish fiction's preoccupation with dualism and doppelgängers, in a bleak Scottish-based story of obsession, murder and betrayal of friendship, *Complicity* (1993). Despite its harrowing and all-too-credible modern atrocities, and with a far less likeable (but credibly modern) protagonist than *The Bridge*, *Complicity* has an underlying affirmation. Cameron Colley is a cynical, apathetic, computer games-obsessed, drug-taking journalist. The Scotland in which he lives is always seen in relation to a bigger world in which issues like the Falkland War, Thatcherite politics, capitalist exploitation are those which either induce apathy or, as in Cameron's horrific friend, murderous revenge. Cameron has to resolve his divided loyalties; the novel's movement is towards his re-awakening as an individual in a changing Scotland.

By now a pattern of production was emerging. Banks was working a programme in which thrillers, science fiction, and serious and ambitious explorations of contemporary Scotland emerged in triads. Of greatest interest to this work is the last category; although as always with Banks it must be said that his best work in the two other categories, such as *Complicity* or the hugely imaginative *Feersum Enjinn* (1994) should be treated as substantial parts of his literary achievement. That said, *Whit* (1995) is his continuation of what had emerged in *The Wasp Factory*, *The Bridge* and *Canal Dreams* as an unusually radical approach to issues of gender.

Whit (otherwise known as Beloved Isis, and born on 29 February) is the granddaughter of His Holiness The Blessed Salvador-Uranos Odin Dyaus Brahma Moses-Mohammed Mirza Whit of Luskentyre, Beloved Founder of the Luskentyrian Sect of the Select of God. Her sect lives in an oxbow of the River Forth, a hierarchical community of brothers and sisters leading Amish-style lives. Isis is heir to all this; she has the gift of healing, which may be genuine, and has been elected to future leadership and grace. The sect has corruption at its heart, however, forcing Isis on a wonderful quest; launched into the Forth in a coracle made from the converted inner tube of a lorry tyre she begins a hilarious journey that takes her in a modern pilgrim's progress from polite middle-class Edinburgh to grotty student bedsits in London. Amongst many maturing discoveries, she learns that her grandfather is in reality an army deserter and thief who was shipwrecked in Harris, and took up with two Asian ladies from an island haberdashery to cover his tracks; that he is a lustful old rogue who wants her at the Festival; that her brother Allan is conning the sect, planning on a Thatcherite takeover; and that she herself is being vilified and exploited by him towards this end, as the obstacle in his way to the leadership.

As a novel, *Whit* deliberately circles, echoing its preoccupation with serendipity, and the oxbowing Forth. Banks loves the grotesque incident and the cumulative too much to change the method of *The Crow Road*, with its similar, but male-based peregrinations. But like Alan Warner's Morvern Callar, Whit embodies radical new and Scottish ideas of gender, of behaviour, of values; she is a variant on Bella Caledonia. For Banks's great success here is to juxtapose its bizarre Luskentyrian sect with 'normal' Britain at large; and neither comes out on top in the comparison. Britain is post-Thatcherite, mobile phoney, conscienceless; the sect is almost a mirror-image, with its phoney authoritarian grandfather (is the basis of his power any different from that of hierarchical Britain?), its entrepreneurial pretender Allan, its easily-swayed membership. Whit's role in this is ambivalent, and Banks means her name to carry suggestions; firstly, of religious and social significance, whereby she can be seen as a new and holy spirit, traditionally descending in the Christian calendar seven weeks after Easter; and secondly, as questioning, literally, in the vernacular – what now? what next? She has, it seems, a magical healing gift; and she could be a new spirit for Scotland and the West, as she assumes power in the sect. It is not accidental that her kitbag contains *Paradise Lost, Pilgrim's Progress, Waverley*; we cannot rule out that she will use the Luskentyrians as fruitfully, if not more so, as do those other sects – the churches, the political parties, the multi-nationals.

Since *Whit* Banks has continued his programme of mixing genre productions – but always involving experimentation with new genres. *Excession* (1996) and *Inversions* (1998) are ambitious science fiction epics – complex and impressive in their huge scale of visual imagination and consistency of detail; while *A Song of Stone* (1997) and *The Business* (1999) demonstrate yet again Banks's restless, and perhaps creatively spendthrift insistence on trying new styles and taking on challenging new territories. *A Song of Stone* is an attempt to create an image of modernity, in a dark poetry of war and despair; and it is Banks's most pessimistic work. In an unnamed post-apocalyptic land ravaged by Bosnian-style wars, with gangs roaming, the castle stands as a place of (rather decadent) civilisation, with Abel and his lover-sister as its laconic inmates. Once again distinctions between Iain Banks and Iain M. Banks are blurred, as hints of futuristic possibility merge with Kafka-esque symbolism. And in a distortion of his unconventional presentations of leader-women, Banks now extrapolates his notion of the progress of women to bring on his lieutenant, a ruthless woman of style who leads the invading band into the castle, taking Abel prisoner and his sister as lover. All conventional thriller scenarios are reversed, as Abel muses, Hamlet-style, in passages which reflect on the contrasts of natural beauty and fallen humanity. No peasants are led in revolt, and Abel, like Shakespeare's Richard II, is reduced to apathetic if cynically courageous acceptance of his fate. All ends disastrously; the reader is left to speculate on the novel's meaning – is this the way the world ends?

Arguably Banks tries too hard to find impressive and dramatic new territories, producing at a financially rewarding pace which perhaps leaves little time to revise and deepen characterisation and meaning. His sheer energy and variety of invention must be admired, however; and with *The Business* he develops his blending of a naturalistic fiction representing the world which readers live in with surreal and satirical dimensions beyond. The Business is just that; an organisation which has built itself up through judicious and mainly ethical trading since well before the birth of Christ.

It owned the Roman Empire for sixty-six days; and since then its power and influence have extended in a vast web world-wide. There are echoes of Gray's visions of Institute and Creature in *Lanark*, but with the narrative in a much friendlier and lower key, as Kate Telman, a Glasgow-born waif who has become a key player in The Business, and who is yet another version of Banks's new woman, sorts out corruption within its ranks, and along the way becomes bride to a Himalayan prince. Here is Whit coming into her own with a vengeance; Banks leaves his healing woman on the most unusual of his many odd thresholds, this time poised to take on third world problems with the resources of contemporary technology and economics. For since *The Bridge* Banks has shown that, unlike many modern Scottish – and modern – writers, he has great respect for what human imagination, together with reason and technology, can achieve. It is the theme of his *Culture* series of science fiction epics, in which creative reason and science are seen as perhaps the only forces which can save us. In this novel and elsewhere he does not condemn capitalism or even multi-national companies, but accepts their energy and power, while insisting on their need to maintain human ethics. Banks must be seen as one of the most gifted, eclectic and promising of contemporary Scottish authors.

Qualified optimism:
from Cliff Hanley (1922–99) to Gordon Legge (b. 1961)

This chapter has so far followed the movement in Scottish fiction from its focus on social pessimism and personal trauma to its dramatic shift in perspective in the work of writers like Gray and Banks. It must now briefly turn back to take account of several important writers who in different ways made a similar shift of mood and perspective. Cliff Hanley, for example, celebrated Glasgow warmth and humour in his non-fiction *Dancing in the Streets* (1958); novels like *The Taste of Too Much* (1960), *Nothing but the Best* (1964) and his hilarious comedy of errors during that rarest of events, an idyllic Clyde-coast summer,*The Hot Month* (1967), anticipated McIlvanney's celebrations of the wit and colour in working-class Scottish life. Matt McGinn conjured humour and vitality as well as pathos out of a harsh Jesuitical childhood in *Fry the Little Fishes* (1975); and Chaim Bermant celebrated Jewish community in Glasgow in *Jericho Sleep Alone* (1964). His *Diary of an Old Man* (1966) is a rare, sensitive and unsentimental evocation of old age. All these preceded what was the finest collection of Glasgow short stories since Edward Gaitens's *Growing Up and Other Stories* (1942). Outstandingly, the work of Alan Spence in *Its Colours They Are Fine* showed that humanity and humour could be found in grimmest Glasgow;

but he was not alone in insisting that it was wrong to stereotype urban Scotland as hopelessly bleak and violent. In the last decade Gordon Legge has emerged as the antidote to Irvine Welsh's tragi-comic presentations of poisoned urban youth; novels and linked story collections like *The Shoe* (1989), *In Between Talking about the Football* (1991), *I Love Me: Who do you Love?* (1994) and *Near Neighbours* (1998) present a more genial picture of adolescents of industrial Lowland Scotland who can relate to adults, who share their music like a private language, who have no illusions about drugs and drink, handling them in the main with control, and generally treat each other with a laconic decency. Legge manages to set street realism, with its occasional violence and victimisation, accidents and anxieties, in housing estates where intelligent if foul-mouthed friendliness rules.

Qualified optimism: Alan Spence (b. 1947)

It is Spence, however, whose poet's imagery and ability to find epiphany in paradox has most successfully celebrated the vitality of city dualisms in Scotland. His much-praised first collection of stories, *Its Colours They are Fine* (1977) has something of Joyce's *Dubliners* (1914) in its beautifully evoked series of ambiguous epiphanies expressing simultaneous love for, and anger at, Glasgow character and poverty, physical and mental. In an Orange walk drinking-session, a desolate night-time hitch-hike from London to Glasgow, in the West-End Botanic Gardens or social security premises, Spence finds radiance as well as gloom. Frequently he achieves this through the perspective of children, or damaged innocents of the streets. His gift is to find the transforming moment of communication – between a Catholic prospective father-in-law with his Protestant future son-in-law, or the moment when children transcend sectarian boundaries in play, or even when winos share. In addition to this enormous human empathy he has a poet's eye for the flash of redeeming colour – in a puddle, the cheap tinsel of festivity, or a discarded red football jersey. He followed this with his massive, gentle, and lyrical novel, *The Magic Flute* (1990), which in many ways encapsulates the ways in which Scottish fiction began in the closing decades of the century to move from bleakness and trauma to regeneration.

The presentation of this ambitious novel is clearly related to Spence's earlier way of looking at life in short-story form, in which ordinary lives are seen with a poet's eye for the colourful moment which states the vividness and energy of life. Its interlocking of the four Glasgow boys' lives – Tam, George, Brian and Eddie, Protestants from Govan – is masterly, as is the sense of period, from early '60s to early '80s, from the death of Kennedy to the

934

death of Lennon, two events from Western myth deliberately chosen as markers for their development. Equally impressive is the unforced way the novel's seven parts control motif and symbols of music; the flute is their first common bond in the book, as they go along to try to join an Orange band. A profound theme develops in the recurrent speculation as to whether God is a deliberate or improvising musician; the Mozartian title-image counterpoints the earthy, sectarian folk-flute; and as the novel goes on, popular music from Dylan to Beatles, to Lou Reed and John Lennon, charts the moods of the main characters and their world.

The style is gentle, unpretentious, and true to real conversations and periods. World events are seen from the immediate, human side, as when the most unstable of the four, Eddie, is blown up in Northern Ireland. Spence sympathetically and subtly relates this to the sterility of opportunities previously offered to Eddie, coming as he does from a broken home. More subtly still he presents George, of Masonic parents, kept in Boy's Brigade line, taking no risks but sticking to the people who will help if the handshake is right. George's hell is to inherit the business world of nudge and wink, to lose genuine relationships because of his conventionality and social timidity. These two are set against Tam and Brian, who do take genuine risks, each in his own way. Tam gets to the USA, but loses his wife – or does he? Spence gently suggests that ultimately two such real people may find each other again, and again the magic flute shows its power, since Tam trusts it when he hears it, trusting it to bring him back to Scotland, and perhaps back to Ruby.

Brian is the closest perhaps to Spence himself, moving through the hippy years with a cool intelligence, not over-ambitious, finally a teacher in a deprived Edinburgh scheme. There's some of the bleak honesty of George Friel's *Mr Alfred MA* in the way Brian is surrounded by cynical, crossword-filling battle veterans. Does Brian give up teaching? Whatever his decision, Spence means us to read it as willingness to change in a qualified optimism which he has developed since *Its Colours they are Fine*. The closing pages are full of arresting ideas ('Man's function in the Universe is anti-entropic', Mozart 'is sublime *and* ridiculous'); but in the key passage where Tam listens to the spiritual teacher who plays the variety of flutes, the book is saying 'be open to all experience', and suggesting that a kind of cosmic music is played through all of us if we will listen to it. Spence has Tam actually *see* the flute player in an aura of blue light; and for many readers this is where his ideology and theirs will part. Yet there is no questioning the success with which Spence renders the modern world, with its horrors now on our doorstep, amidst the drug-taking kids of thirteen and fourteen. Only Friel and Kelman describe classroom pointlessness and banter as well, and only Gordon Legge, in *The*

Shoe (1989), has given popular music its intimate and significant place in adolescent life.

Spence's dual vision, regarding Scotland in vivid clarity of image, then juxtaposing it with the larger world, is the organising principle of his next collection, *The Stone Garden* (1995). Short, poignant stories of lonely and impoverished Glasgow childhood alternate with stories of adulthood set in the Caribbean, America, Italy, Japan. Thus innocence and experience jostle together, with Spence's recurrent discovery of delight amidst pain. There is a linking identity behind these stories, as they move towards a maturity and faith; the title story reminds the reader of Spence's commitment to the values of Eastern philosophy and religion; and its glimpse of the flashing bird of paradise in the Japanese place of designed beauty carved out from the random world stands as a fitting emblem for Spence's final optimism regarding the human condition.

That optimism is put to its most severe test in *Way to Go* (1998), with its fundamental question – what happens when you die? The recurrent *persona* of previous fiction and drama, the lonely and motherless Glasgow boy, appears again in Neil McGraw, son of a dour undertaker. Yet he is not a morbid boy, even when his father's punishments take the form of locking him at night among coffins. His lonely questioning prompts him to assertion of life and takes the youth down the well-travelled one-way road to London, never to see his father again.

There are four places which matter in Neil's story: Glasgow, London, India and Glasgow (Glasgow on Neil's return with his Indian wife is not the same place as his first grey and motherless world). London saves him from the all-too-usual fates of escaping adolescents, and introduces him to the eccentrics who show him that karma – or serendipity – works, and who will be interwoven in memory and the rest of his life. India shows him the extremes of life and death, and gives him Lila, who is the colour which makes his life fine. Glasgow becomes, on his father's death, the challenge to turn death (his father's undertaker's business) into style, grace, life, through making coffins and ceremonies which are tailored to real people and their desires, even their fantasies. Neil and the friends which life has given him reform McGraw Undertakers into a controversial new way of death; 'Way to Go' becomes the name of their company, which, denounced by the kirk, hyped by the media, and threatened with a takeover by the new undertaking conglomerates, flies in the face of tradition with its coffins shaped like boats, cars, aeroplanes, football boots. The coffins are so beautifully crafted and painted that they became fashionable art objects in exhibitions of modern art. 'Way to Go' as a business becomes a gale of fresh, liberating ideas in a dour and repressive

Scottish climate of gloom about death; and *Way to Go* as a novel celebrates life in the midst of death.

There is, however, a non-narrative meditation running through this novel which redefines it as a Book of Death, an extended reflection via famous last words, jokes, tragic and bizarre historical death-situations which recalls Frank Kuppner's blacker series of examplars of inhumane death in *Something Very Like Murder* (1994). The safety-net which Spence supplied in previous fiction, that gentle hint of faith in Eastern spiritualism, is no longer so readily present. This is a remarkably tough, courageous book, which faces real pain and death, the loss of love and light, unflinchingly, using art and humour to find grace in ways which are arguably the only valid negotiation with the ultimate fear and mystery.

Spence was not alone in his discovery of humour and colour amidst urban Scottish gloom. Beyond those already discussed, like Gordon Legge, the work of Janice Galloway, Carl MacDougall, Alison Kennedy, Andrew Greig – to name but a few – has, for all its recognition of Scotland's darker inheritances, refused to remain in a Scottish existential cul-de-sac; but their work not only repudiates pessimism, but goes on to find new and hopeful territories, in ways which considerably extend the range of Scottish fiction.

The wind shifts: the recovery of national hope in Scottish fiction

By the '90s the moods and possibilities of the fiction had changed profoundly. An eclectic restlessness was linked to the need to find a fresh starting-point, or to find different aspects of Scottish tradition as inspiration. This impulse can also be found in the work of novelists who mainly chose to set their work outside Scotland, though often using a Scottish protagonist – so that discussion here should be linked with the treatment of writers in the section below on *the new internationalism*.

Clearly the rest of this chapter cannot do justice to the output of the dozens of new and impressive writers in contemporary Scotland in the last decade of the second millennium. What follows is an attempt to acknowledge the major contributors to a new and affirmative mood in Scottish culture and society under several headings, together with a general discussion of what seem to be the major shifts in approach and perspective. This is not to suggest a new romanticism; the traditional sceptical bleakness of Scottish fiction could hardly disappear overnight, and indeed much of the impact and energy of these writers lies in the dramatic way in which harsh social realism is combined with humour and positive vision. And where at the beginning of the '80s Gray's *Lanark* marked the most dramatic post-war change in

Scottish fiction, one novel in particular may be singled out at the end of that decade as exemplifying the dominant modern theme of emergence from trauma, as well as representing an important new direction in Scottish women's writing.

The new women's writing:
Janice Galloway (b. 1956) and The Trick is to Keep Breathing

Douglas Gifford has dealt with the achievement of Scottish women fiction writers in depth in *A History of Scottish Women's Writing* (1997); the interested reader is referred to the two extensive chapters there for much fuller treatment than can be given here: 'Contemporary Fiction I: Tradition and Continuity' and 'Contemporary fiction II: Seven Writers in Scotland' (which deals in detail with the work of Elphinstone, Galloway, Hayton, Kennedy, Lingard, Owens, and Rose). 'Contemporary Fiction III: The Anglo Scots', by Flora Alexander, deals with the work of Emma Tennant, Shena Mackay, Alison Fell, Sara Maitland, and Candia McWilliam. Here, however, we attempt to gain some kind of whole view of contemporary fiction, and so this chapter has deliberately avoided treating women's writing as a category apart, although such treatment can be justified, given the way in which women's experience has been marginalised. What is true is that in the last two decades Scottish women's writing has come into its own. From the situation in the '70s and before, where a few outstanding figures like Mitchison and Davie, together with Anglo-Scots like Spark, Shena Mackay and Sheila Macleod, spoke for very different and isolated individuals, a whole range of new and mutually supportive voices were now heard – all of the previous women simultaneously developing alongside this exciting new wave, with Jessie Kesson in *Another Time, Another Place* (1983) finding a new kind of voice to express and challenge women's isolation. Thereafter Agnes Owens, Janice Galloway, Dilys Rose, Alison Kennedy, Sian Hayton, Margaret Elphinstone and many others showed that they were refusing to accept allocations of roles and perspectives made to them in the '50s and '60s.

The resurgence should be noted, however; and most readers of contemporary Scottish fiction would recognise Janice Galloway's *The Trick is to Keep Breathing* (1989) as outstanding amongst new ways of looking at women in modern Scotland. She had absorbed the fresh approaches of West of Scotland writing, particularly those of Alasdair Gray and James Kelman, and her novel exploited techniques used in *Janine* and *The Busconductor Hines* especially. Gray's moving account of a disillusioned middle-class drunk coming to terms with his traumatic memories here found a female equivalent in young teacher Joy Stone's journal of horror, in which she performed the trick of just keeping on breathing after the drowning of her lover Michael. Like *Janine*, it is a journey towards rehabilitation – or a beginning; and like *Hines*, it makes no concessions to cliché or falsely contrived narrative, taking Kelman's brave risk of incorporating the mundane along with the occasionally funny, grotesque, or moving event. Galloway finds her own voice with a more immediate sense of the absurd, and a keener eye for banal detail, than either. She allows us at first to feel only the tragic horror of Joy's return from the Spanish holiday where the drowning occurred, creating the intense feeling of unexpected tragedy with a fragmented technique whereby Joy allows the barest glimpses of what's actually happened, interrupting her day-to-day teaching, her interviews with the housing department and friends. But even through Joy's understandable self-centred grief two things force themselves through; her awareness of her own whingeing, and our awareness of things she can't yet see, like her inability to understand dead Michael's wife's position.

The novel is sometimes hilariously and embarrassingly funny, as Galloway recounts the absurd situations Joy gets into – loveless sexuality, patronising hospital treatment, dutiful visits to her best friend's smothering mother, the funeral. Joy's intensity of confession dominates, however; but just as it begins to create a sense of overdose for the reader, Galloway subtly turns its implications around, till we realise that Joy is unable to recover or begin to heal precisely because she's hiding something from herself. All her binges, anorexia, sleazy men, and the uneasy diary entries, are brought about by her buried feelings of guilt; guilt concerning Paul, the man she lived with, and left for Michael, and Michael's wife, and all the attendant social guilt. Galloway doesn't resolve the question of how deserving she is of this guilt; instead she allows that it's simply there, fair or not, and has to be got out into the open. The crucial penultimate paragraph is a kind of epiphany. Alone, drinking, Joy tells us:

The voice is still there.
I forgive you.
I hear it quite distinctly, my own voice in the empty house.
I forgive you.

Galloway followed up this ground-breaking novel with two fine volumes of short stories (*Blood*, 1991, and *Where You Find It*, 1996), which deal with issues of male-female relations, in a range of perspectives, moods and styles; from the humorously sympathetic regarding gender differences to ferocious anger and even surrealism. Her second novel, *Foreign Parts* (1994), is her gentlest, in its portrayal of the French holiday of Cassie and Rona, mature social workers. Cassie is full of a restless discontent about herself and her men; Rona competently accepts life. In their journey around Normandy cathedrals and war graves they find an accommodation which suggests ways forward for contemporary women. Not only does Galloway suggest an exit from old traumas; her use of a life-enhancing landscape (despite brilliant satire on tourist guides and package holidaying) suggests that new perspectives on Scottish urban introspection can be liberating.

Healing divisions of self and nation

Women writers like Galloway and Alison Kennedy were to the fore in what was to become a movement in fiction towards personal and national regeneration. Before them, Kesson and Lingard, and others like Alison Fell (in the aptly-named *The Bad Box*, 1987) and Una Flett (in *Revisiting Empty Houses*, 1988), had foregrounded the predicaments of women coping with rural and urban repressions; and Anne Smith and Bess Ross had presented poignant portrayals of girls growing up in small town and rural Scotland in *The Magic Glass* (1981) and *Those Other Times* (1991) respectively; their protagonists, street-wise Stella and survivor Marjie, stand with the women of Kesson and Lingard, half-way between the survivors of the older world of novelists like Gibbon and Shepherd, and the new worlds which Ross recognised in her earlier stories of *A Bit of Crack and Car Culture* (1990).

The section below on new directions in Scottish fiction suggests that one of the most rapidly burgeoning areas in contemporary Scottish writing lies in the short stories and novels of women who have taken their exploration of the situations of women at the turn of the century into even more sophisticated analysis of issues of gender and identity. An outstanding example is the work of Dilys Rose (b. 1954), who has an extraordinary range as poet, short story writer, and novelist. Again, however, it is her involvement with humanity which stands out, whether it be in stories of disillusioned Californian waitresses, of risky Turkish encounters, of London street life, or more mundane encounters in Scotland. *Our Lady of the Pickpockets* (1989) showed her work to be willing to take risks and explore varieties of short story genre, but with a recurrent emphasis on the vulnerable traveller abroad, and damaged yet defiant victims in New York, Mexico, and Scotland. *Red Tides* (1993) was more assured and impressive in the way the title symbolism held its wide range of stories together; for the tides are the movement of human emotion and passions of the blood, presented from the point of view of a sympathetic feminism which is never intolerant, if often angry at male aggression and selfishness, and ambivalent in response to the claims of sexuality and family.

War Dolls (1997) extended an already impressive range, again travelling widely and presenting a richness of place as well as a rare ability to evoke varieties of situation and pain without exploiting actual violence. *Pest Maiden* (1999) was her first novel; and once again the poet's sense of unifying image and symbol showed clearly in the way the levels of meaning come together. The pest maiden is disease, perhaps the ultimate virus, and perhaps arrived in the Edinburgh laboratory in which the shabby and lonely protagonist works as security officer. The maiden appears again as the laboratory's logo, possibly representing the greedy risk-taking of the multi-nationals, a madonna figure floating in a giant capsule outside the buildings; but she also appears in Muriel, the resilient Filipino political refugee who has seen terrible things, and who rescues the abandoned protagonist. Rose's international perspective and concern shows throughout; the pest maiden can come in many forms, from within or without, and is as likely to be the product of human folly as accident of infection. But despite Rose's ambivalence towards her fallen humanity, she allows the possibility of release from loneliness and despair – if, as in the closing words of Alexander Lennox in *The Bridge*, when welcomed back to this world ('O yeah?'), affirmation is tempered by wry realism.

For male writers the ghosts and repressions of the past were obviously different in nature. As early as 1973 John Herdman (b. 1941) had drawn on earlier Scottish fiction (notably that of Hogg) to try to portray figures haunted by inherited guilt or by mysterious doppelgängers; *A Truth Lover* (1973) and *Pagan's Pilgrimage* (1978) exemplify an increasing tendency in modern Scottish writing to link itself with traditions and genres of older Scottish writing, and to redeploy the folk supernatural and grotesque (tendencies discussed later). They are also Herdman's attempt to exemplify how Scottish psychological demons can be exorcised – later work would lessen the thrust towards redemption in favour of a grimmer *grotesquerie*. Ron Butlin (b. 1949) has shown in poetry and prose his empathy with the complexities and tensions of family and community, in the short stories of *The Tilting Room* (1983), *The Sound of My Voice* (1987), a powerful novel about exorcising the demons of alcoholism, and *Night Visits* (1997), a sensitive portrayal of the loneliness and solipsism of a boy following the death of his father, and the strange journey to release with his tormented aunt. Another fine poet and short story writer, Brian McCabe (b. 1951), used the theme of rediscovery of self with a sardonically comic twist in *The Other*

McCoy (1990), with his protagonist discovering at Hogmanay that he isn't dead, as his friends seem to think; McCabe's short stories in *The Lipstick Circus* (1985) and *In a Dark Room with a Stranger* (1993) (in which life is the dark room, and the stranger oneself as well as partners and other people) have an impressive range of empathy, and are particularly sensitive in evoking the perspective of children and the most vulnerable. More recently, a similar concern with the spectrum of humanity and a comparable skill has emerged in the short stories of James Robertson, outstandingly in *Close and Other Stories* (1991) and *The Ragged Man's Complaint* (1993).

The fictional exorcising of Scottish ghosts continues unabated, indeed if anything increasing, though growing more discriminating and focused on its scapegoats. Recent examples include poet Jackie Kay's first novel, *Trumpet* (1998), Christopher Whyte's *The Gay Decameron* (1998) and Andrew O'Hagan's *Our Fathers* (1999). Each of these works out very different problematic inheritances, but what links them is their sense of coming to terms with previous generations and older patriarchal intolerance and authoritarianism. Kay attacks prejudice against colour and lesbian love, in her vivid account of how Joss Moody, a black jazz musician, turns out to have been a woman; his/her widow and their son have to come to terms with their different traumas. Whyte portrays a range of gay males in Edinburgh, recounting the loneliness of most of them as they separate their careers and their private lives; O'Hagan brings his protagonist back to Ayrshire to confront the parents who left him to be brought up by grandparents, and to assess the achievement of his formidable dying grandfather, a legend in his lifetime for his pioneering role in the post-war years in the building of high-rise new towns. The fathers of the title are what O'Hagan perceives, rightly or wrongly, with a potent mixture of anger, love and elegy, as the archetypal patriarchs of Scotland; drunken and brutal, or self-justifying zealots. All three novelists clearly express their different sense of restrictive Scotlands; all three end their novels with a kind of healing catharsis.

It would be churlish, in considering Scottish fiction of speculative hope, not to acknowledge here the achievement of Bernard MacLaverty, the Northern Irish fiction writer long resident in Islay and Glasgow. While most recent critical guides omit his work as non-Scottish, he won a Scottish Arts Council award for his first volume of short stories, *Secrets* (1977), and his work has won major Scottish awards ever since. He published regularly in the Arts Council *Scottish Short Stories* series (1973–96); and while many of his short stories (*The Great Profundo*, 1987, *Walking the Dog*, 1994) and his novels (*Lamb*, 1980, and *Cal*, 1983) are sensitive and profound responses to his Irish background and its radical divisions, more tragic and ubiquitous than those of Scotland, his Glasgow allegiances and observations have increasingly come through in recent stories. *Grace Notes* (1997) is one of the most distinguished novels in English of recent years, and it should remind us how increasingly we live in multi-national contexts; no one can now claim absolute national identity. Catherine McKenna, from a Belfast Catholic background, is a young composer, and an unmarried mother. She has lived on a Scottish island; the father of her child is a typically attractive, feckless fisherman. She now lives in a kind of limbo, with her child in Glasgow. She is returning to attempt reconciliation with her working-class family – and, more fundamentally, with her divided worlds.

This account of divided loyalties and traumatised experiences of the deficiencies of two cultures is balanced beautifully by MacLaverty with his story of the other Catherine, who finds release through creativity. The novel explores the nature and grace of creativity in many arts, focusing on music; Catherine has composed a powerful extended orchestral piece called 'Vernicle' (the name indicating that for her it enacted a kind of pilgrimage). In the work she uses the Lambeg drums of Orangemen to powerful effect – although MacLaverty avoids the temptation to make their contribution harmonising or reconciliatory. Thus 'gracenotes' can be heard as moments in Catherine's personal life, or as epiphanies which art can offer, but, implies the novel, never final moments of rest or fulfilment, rather stages on a journey. The novel's complex, but effective, manipulation of time sequences reminds us that what may seem a time of grace will pass; life is a continual negotiation with a problematic flux of possibilities. It is a salutory paradox that this novel which transcends Scottish and Irish experience stands as one of the most impressive examples of contemporary and subtle positivism in Scottish fiction.

Synthesising city and country

MacLaverty's *Grace Notes* had shown that place – Ireland, Islay, Glasgow – whether rural or urban, was simply a background for the working out of human issues, neither good or bad in itself. Some writers went further, viewing the post-war cynicism which saw rural idealism as false as a destructive attitude which must be changed. If self is to be refashioned in Scotland, argue these writers, then it must emerge from trauma into a Scotland which can unite city and country, curing the old disillusion which mocked ideas of inspiration from the beauty of landscape or the people, events and ideas of history and folklore. Gray's *Lanark*, with its symbolic illustration of a whole Scotland of firths, cities, oilrigs and mountains, had insisted on the idea of the better nation, where dear green places met man-made institutions; his later work has reinforced this new appraisal, as has the work of Iain Banks with novels like *The Bridge*, *The Crow Road* and *Whit* disallowing traditional mutual exclusion, and, with their casual juxtapositioning of BMWs, computers, and city life with Scottish countryside, allowing easy transition from an appreciative awareness of landscape, to a zestful engagement with city for their young Scots. Since Gray and Banks set about breaking the old moulds, many have followed.

In seeking to identify the contemporary work which most successfully synthesises traditional and emerging Scottish urban-rural ideologies, many examples could be cited; a few must suffice, from some of the leading contemporary writers. Representative are Carl MacDougall's *The Lights Below* (1993), poet Andrew Greig's *Electric Brae* (1992), and Alison Kennedy's *Looking for the Possible Dance* (1993). MacDougall (b. 1941) had to work for affirmation; his short stories in *Elvis is Dead* (1986) were sharp, savagely comic and grotesque glimpses of Glasgow loneliness, amidst the paraphrenalia of modern pop culture and gear. Related to the matter and style of Spence, they are forerunners for Kennedy and Welsh. *Stone Over Water* (1989), kept at the centre of its poignant story of an orphan adopted by a suburban Glasgow family a very Scottish pessimism about the ability of love to communicate among them. Each is in a prison of his or her own conditioning. Significantly, in *The Lights Below*, MacDougall's protagonist Andy is just out of prison (he's been framed). He is slowly coming to terms with this, the greyness of his life, and the fact that his mother has married his father's murderer. The lights below are the vitality and warmth of residual community traditions under the surface, which restore him, despite the cheapened superficiality of the new Glasgow and Scotland. MacDougall is daring in his creation of Andy's Granny and her strange, classless, unplaceable yet philosophical friend Orlando; these two represent between them a traditional Scottish smeddum and a timeless and nationless humanity, and it is their peculiar magic which helps bring Andy back to humanity. Grotesque, yet convincing in its knowledge of Glasgow, its dying railway works in Springburn or its horrific social problems in Possilpark, this is a novel which exploits older fiction like *Dance of the Apprentices* (1948) or *The Dear Green Place* (1966), but adds the new dimension of possibility in Andy's dawning awareness of traditions and strengths buried in city and country which are nevertheless potent forces of renewal. As Greig and Kennedy would do, MacDougall ends his novel with a quiet, updated version of epiphany; Andy climbs the hills above Glen Lyon, and despite the Rob Roy tourist centres and the ubiquitous craft fairs, finds a perspec-

tive on himself and his place in his world not unlike, say, Gunn's presentation of Kenn's self-discovery at the end of *Highland River* (1937).

In *Electric Brae*, Andrew Greig (b. 1951) like Banks in *The Crow Road*, seeks
to unite the Scotland of oilrigs and technology with the Scotland of tradition,
with its mountains and historical relics. His protagonists can find Gunn-like
epiphany in brochs, yet exploit the hardware of modern climbing gear.
Action moves from Orkney cottage to Edinburgh flat; characters move out
and in of Scotland restlessly, echoing the contemporary unfixedness of work
and home, just as traditional and modern musical references run throughout, and illustrating the multiple identities we grow amidst our different
cultures. All this is linked by a poetic sensibility which loves Scotland, but
recognises just how intangible and changing a concept of mind lies behind
the naming of a country or an identity. Constant references to issues such as
the 1979 referendum, or to characters being 'in a state of dependence, just
like your country' show that Greig consciously seeks synthesis. (Greig's later
fiction is discussed below.)

Alison Kennedy (b. 1965) illustrates the new ways of synthesising old
ideologies and the major input of women to this change in *Looking for the
Possible Dance* (1993). The metaphor of the dance, rural traditional and
modern, unifies this first novel, from the earliest memories Margaret has of
dancing with her father to clumsy exploratory dancing and lovemaking with
Colin, to her continual and sometimes desperate search 'for the possible
dance, the step, the move to beat them all'. She is desperately unhappy, lost
without her father, unable to commit herself to Colin, uncertain in her social
work. Yet, as with MacDougall's work, it is out of the society with which she is
at odds she finds new rhythms, and a new and possible dance. The group of
social misfits she looks after begin to look after her; and when Glasgow's
terrible violence comes close to destroying Colin she finds in herself and
from unpredictable others the resources and new strength she needs. Again,
her experience of country and time past, among the ancient ruins of Argyll,
alters her perspectives, providing a modern epiphany. For Kennedy, as for
many of her contemporaries, Scottish landscape in its abundance of cairn
and burial mound, stone crosses and relics of ancient past, can stand as a
polar opposite to contemporary Scotland, whether of bourgeois town or
deprived overspill. The conclusion suggests, as in *The Lights Below*, that here
again we have survivors, who may create another kind of Scotland.

Kennedy's fiction is unpredictable. Her first volume of stories, *Night
Geometry and the Garscadden Trains* (1990) was outstanding in its range of
approaches and modes; from grim urban realism to surrealism, satire, and
sardonic humour ('Bonnie Charlie's Glasgow Cookbook' and 'Seven Cen-

turies of Scottish Slaughter' and its advice to children on 'Playing Dead'). Yet a unifying perspective emerged, which looked eccentrically at the misfits and losers of a richly diverse range of class and situation with a detached but profound sympathy. *Now That You're Back* (1994), her next collection of stories, shifted the emphasis from urban realism to surrealist comic satire, with two effective and Swiftian extended satires in her allegorical representation of human excess and disgusting self-destructiveness. These are seen in exaggerated form in the dreadful Mousebok Tribe ('The Mouseboks Family Dictionary'), and the contrasting treatment of the virtues of penguins, who don't hatch genocidal plots or besiege cities ('On Having More Sense'). Yet together with grotesque and comically horrific stories there are stories of sensitive exploration of damaged psyches and attempts at reconciliation, as in the title story, where brothers separated in youth struggle, on a caravan holiday by the sea, to regain contact. Kennedy does not try to melodramatise the reasons for the separation, leaving them unexplained. Instead, and typically, she lets the reader wonder about that, to concentrate on the immediate subtleties of their difficult relationships.

Her later fiction has proved just as surprising and varied. *So I Am Glad* (1995), perhaps her most audacious work, is a love story set in contemporary West-End Glasgow which takes magic realism to its limits (and is discussed later). Her titles seem deliberately to tease readers' expectations with their bland innocence belying the range of surreal and shocking content; as in the bitter-sweet short stories of the varieties of human love relations in *Original Bliss* (1997) and the tortured and lonely writers who push their lives to the edge on their tiny Welsh island in her hugely ambitious novel *Everything You Need* (1999). With this last novel Kennedy's fiction seems to be moving in new and more cosmopolitan directions; the most obsessive of the writer protagonists of this novel, Nathan Staples, may carry some residual Calvinist angst from his Scottish background, but his destiny is worked out between his Welsh island and fashionable London publishing parties. In this respect Kennedy's latest work joins the recent movement of Scottish fiction towards a broader and more cosmopolitan outlook, a movement discussed below under the heading of the new internationalism.

New syntheses in Scottish fiction: men writing women

One of the strongest indications of a new direction for Scottish writing lies in the way that new male writers are trying to empathise with women, and the way that both men and women writers are challenging conventions of gender difference. Signs that a shift in male fictional perceptions of women was under way can be read in Gray's *1982, Janine, Something Leather* and *Poor Things*, with their recognition of repression and maltreatment of women by men, and their awareness of the nuances involved in Scottish variants. Gray's *Something Leather* plays with predictable reader expectations and reactions, turning the tables on those who naïvely read the grouping of women in this novel as a portrayal of sexual deviation. For once, unhappy women organise together, and Gray takes comic delight in their new potency, as he does in his grotesque and ferocious re-creation of ideas of Mary Shelley and Stevenson in his provocative account of the creation of a sexual and gender-unconditioned *tabula rasa* in the man-made female Frankenstein, Bella Baxter, the girl who becomes the symbolic and potential New Woman of Scotland. She is now 'Bella Caledonia', whose social and sexual unconventionality and frankness shock all who meet her.

Working in different vein and genre, but with many of the same aims, the fiction of Iain Banks has also sought to revalue and replace the roles of women in fiction. In particular, *Canal Dreams, Whit* and *The Business* portray women stronger than men. Other male writers have shown this empathy, alongside an exploration of gender boundaries, perhaps the most important being Ronald Frame, Stuart Hood, and Alan Warner. Frame's novels are consistently presented from the perspective of middle-class women, in ways which are deeply sensitive to the particular pains and problems of women coping with the difficulties of class conventions, none the less complex and hurtful for their proximity to wealth and privilege, which so readily disappear for these straitened and mysterious people. Stuart Hood's fiction explores many issues, from the narrow-mindedness of small-town Scots to the morality of international terrorism, but always with the new emphasis on treating the dimensions of gender with empathy, and an argument for recognition of the roles of women – as to a lesser extent does Andrew Greig in *Electric Brae* and *The Return of John Macnab* (1996) (this last illustrating yet again the new habit of Scottish novelists of reshaping older models, this time reworking the values and relationships of Buchan's rural thriller, *John Macnab* 1925), allowing forceful females to take unconventional and emotional initiatives within traditionally male activities. In comparable fashion Greig's *When They Lay Bare* (1999), a story of family love, betrayal and revenge set in the present day borderland of Scotland and England, eerily recreates the themes, values and dénouements of the ancient ballads, reworking traditional gender patterns by placing powerful women in control of sexual passion, and ultimately the choice of life or death itself.

Exemplifying new Scottish writing: Alan Warner (b. 1964) and Morvern Callar

A representative example of many of the aspects of new Scottish writing we have been surveying can be found in Alan Warner's *Morvern Callar* (1994). Here is recovery from trauma, deconstruction of the boundaries of rural and urban, and presentation by a male writer of a female *persona* who challenges gender stereotypes. Set in a West Highland town which is clearly identified via railways, islands, hotels, and its hilltop folly as Oban, this novel refuses to allow greater value to either urban and rural ideologies, but balances the ugliness and vitality in both, demonstrating that both are now mutually dependent, commerce and the decline of traditional culture dragging them together. Morvern Callar works in a supermarket; she has the attitudes of any unpretentious girl of modern Britain, but with unexpected depths of character. Morvern finds that her boyfriend has cut his throat, with a disk from his PC as his suicide note. Morvern tells no one, but laconically works as normal, giving out Christmas presents and going to parties. Warner strips his West Highland town of romantic associations, so that its seedy bars, lanes, and railway cuttings are seen as hardly different from city housing estates. Oban and countryside don't disappear; but sea and hills are simply there. This unconventionality of perspective parallels the central dissociation of conventional gender patterns. Warner makes Morvern alive to physical detail, textures, weather; a contemporary Chris Guthrie, she can vividly respond to 'nature' as well, as when she goes camping outside Oban. But in another sense she is a repudiation of Chris Guthrie and her community. For Morvern, it is now which matters; one reason for the camping is to bury her lover's body.

The reader begins to see that Morvern is traumatised, but handling her grief her own way. She becomes entirely credible in her mixture of gallus shrieking laughter, mortal drink-drug sessions, warmth towards friend Lanna, strange qualified loyalty towards her foster-father and his new woman, and apparently heartless treatment – some of it dangerously hilarious – of her lover's body and his loft, filled with model trains. Grotesque surprises and situations abound; she has to abandon her promising driving test because she sees from the car that the council are fixing the roof of her flat, and will find the body. What this humour conceals, however, is Morvern's depth of character, which is slyly understated; the reader has to tune in to see why Morvern acts as she does, and to read past the extremes of 'bad taste' in which she thoughtlessly indulges to find the new woman Warner represents in her.

The story takes risks, halfway through leaving Oban for the Mediterranean. Morvern has taken her lover's credit card, which she can use, sent off his novel under her name to a publisher, and skedaddled with Lanna for sunshine. Like Janice Galloway in *Foreign Parts*, Warner shows up the sex-and-drink-drenched falsity of the cheap tours; but Warner controls the transition to this totally different scene by continuing Morvern's concealing account. The reader knows that she is concealing her responses to death and pain, that something slow to articulate itself is building up; and recognises why she has to leave Lanna and – as she did when camping – go back to sensations of weather, sea, night. Three years later she will return to the west pregnant by an unknown father, with a child of the rave scene. It's virtually impossible to know how to take Warner's ending, as she heads on down to the port, except that the reader knows that Morvern being Morvern will survive, as quarry-worker, as author (for the novel is to be published), as triumph of the new ungendered dispossessed, just as Kelman's Sammy or Galloway's Joy will survive. Warner has arguably succeeded in presenting a woman so completely that awareness of male authorship disappears. There are many other achievements – the grasp and control of Morvern's voice, with its Oban-yet-not-Oban phrases, strange syntactical turns, the ferocious, unpredictable local and Mediterranean characters, and Warner's strange, dark poetry of place; but it is the creation of Morvern herself which marks a significant reorientation in the gendering of Scottish fiction.

Warner continued Morvern's story in *These Demented Lands* (1997), shifting the point-of-view to a shadowy figure tantalisingly implied as himself, a supposed air crash investigator who is nothing of the sort, but a damaged *persona* who comes like so many other waifs and strays to the Drome Hotel, somewhere far up Scotland's West Coast. Morvern, disillusioned yet following her undefined quest, is still central; but the main thrust is to portray the Highlands as they really are, broken fragments of a romanticised past, filled with incomers who have failed elsewhere. Returning south to Oban, *The Sopranos* (1998) won the Saltire Book of the Year Award and continued Warner's audacious intrusion into the representation of the range of female experience – here, in an astonishingly vivid evocation of the characters and dilemmas of a range of girls in a Catholic girls school. This hilarious presentation of the reality of adolescent toughness, sexuality and surprising tenderness conceals a deeply serious exploration of how resilient its girls are in coping with a range of traumatic family backgrounds and a stereotypically shallow religious conditioning. However outrageously these girls act – and they can be shocking – they are sane in a world of commercial greed, narrow-minded parochialism and hypocrisy.

The magic returns

These two chapters on modern Scottish fiction have attempted to combine a summary of some of the main shifts in fictional direction with appropriate recognition of the achievement of the major writers. This huge expansion in the amount of substantial Scottish fiction is one of the most heartening features of contemporary Scotland; and the remainder of this chapter tries to show some of the many new and exciting directions the fiction is taking. One of the most interesting aspects of contemporary Scottish fiction at its best is the way in which it deliberately echoes themes and issues of older Scottish literature – but always with its insistence that these are echoes, and not rules or conventions to be adhered to. Thus tradition can be kept and exploited, but with freedom rather than restriction. And it is out of their changing but distinct sense of Scottish identities, traditions and history that contemporary writers seek to counter the pointlessness of a too-prevalent modern root-lessness.

With hindsight it can be seen that yet another effect of Gray's *Lanark* was to reintroduce the fantastic, surreal and the traditional supernatural. This was not confined to fiction. In poetry, Edwin Morgan's wonderful range of imaginative perspectives opened new vistas in *Sonnets from Scotland* (1984), with its astonishing science fiction framework containing a spectrum of supra-rational effects; and in her poetry and drama Liz Lochhead refashioned European and Scottish mythology, from *Dreaming Frankenstein* (1984) to *Mary Queen of Scots Got her Head Chopped Off* (1987), all of which imbued old imagery, symbolism and belief with a range of modern sexual and psychological implications. Other writers were quick, in very different ways, to grasp these new possibilities. What results is not so much 'magic realism', but the creation of magical and transforming visions of Scotlands, thirled to the older identities created by past writers and historians, but no longer employing their absolutes.

Reworking the traditional supernatural:
Margaret Elphinstone (b. 1948) and Sian Hayton (b. 1944)

Following the inspiration of Naomi Mitchison and Mackay Brown, Margaret Elphinstone and Sian Hayton have developed a vein of quasi-historical, speculative and magical fiction. Elphinstone and Hayton have explored the mythical and non-rational. Elphinstone has written two novels concerning the wanderings of singer-poet Naomi around Galloway and the Lake District – only a landscape changed, a region of the future after apocalypse and returned to isolated and uncertain communities. Her use of the visionary Green Light in *The Incomer* (1987), and her dark discovery of poisoned lands in *A Sparrow's Flight* (1990), were symbolic treatments of modern issues extrapolated into the future, handled with delicacy and power from a quietly feminist position. Their sense of magic and myth was heightened in the short stories of *An Apple from a Tree* (1991), with its encounters in Galloway with Pan, and its unapologetic supernatural yet clearly allegorical events. Her ambitious novel *Islanders* (1994) seemed a change of approach in its portrayal of the quiet lives of Fair Isle farmers and peasants with only the slightest hints of the magical, yet somehow still managed to embed these lives in a world view deeply aware of the rhythms of seasons, seas, and the importance of tradition. This is an impressive attempt to work partly in the Scottish Renaissance tradition of writers like Gunn, Linklater and Mitchison, yet to handle this with a quiet contemporary feminist insistence on seeing the restricted role of women in Norse culture. Its account of the hard progress of marooned Astrid from tragic girlhood to limited yet mature self-realisation marks a high point of the new synthesising. The book's maps exemplify its new perspectives; they are, in terms of conventional cartography, upside down – and this creation of alternative views of the physical world is matched by the novel's different ways of reading history and myth.

The achievement of Sian Hayton in her *Hidden Daughters* trilogy, comprising *Cells of Knowledge* (1989), *Hidden Daughters* (1992) and *The Last Flight* (1993), is also impressive, original and synthesising. These stories tell of the Celtic daughters of the giant Uthebhan, women of superhuman powers and great spiritual strength, but doomed to be distrusted and ostracised by the new male-dominated Christian era. Set around the end of the first millennium, the stories contrive to lose history in myth; places are named in ways which hint at what they are now, but suggest a very different origin and society. Again, a sense of allegory hangs over all; but quite what the allegory means Hayton refuses clearly to define, leaving meaning open to the reader's often intuitive interpretation. Is one main thrust that the old woman-led Celtic society is measured against male-Christian dominance, and found to be greatly superior? Hayton maintains a deliberately cloudy and interlinked set of narratives to move unsettlingly throughout the trilogy, but permits hints and echoes of traditional Celtic mythology and *personae* to intrude, so that her stories seem to shadow traditional legend and character. She begins in the Christian world, only gradually revealing her worlds of lost and hidden magic; then returns to the Christian, posing unanswered questions as to what will happen to the giant's daughters and their descendants – with constantly disturbing implications for our modern values and gender relations.

It is this implicatory relationship between past and present which works in the American-Scot Ellen Galford's *Queendom Come* (1990) and *The Devil and the Dybbuck* (1993); ancient traditional magic hilariously placed in modern settings helps historicise and humanise her lesbian protagonists into normality and acceptability. In *Queendom Come* Gwhyldis, arch-priestess to ancient British Queen Albanna, is awakened on Arthur's Seat (ironically, by Edinburgh lawyers indulging in Druidic-masonic male rites). When her queen is recognised by Margaret Thatcher as an important and traditional endorsement of her own iconic stature, their unholy alliance wickedly satirises some marvellous barbarisms in Thatcher's agenda. *The Devil and the Dybbuk* moves south, but again ancient magic provides an ironical comment on modernity, with a London lady taxi-driver becoming possessed by a traditional Jewish *dybbuk* or demon.

A similar and successfully ironical use of old magic is worked in Christopher Whyte's (b. 1952) *Euphemia McFarrigle and the Laughing Virgin* (1995) and *The Warlock of Strathearn* (1997). The first plays hilariously with sacred cows of Catholic religion, employing an ancient demon (in her Glasgow incarnation she is the middle-aged spinster Euphemia) to bring about magical tenements, pregnant nuns, farting archbishops and a papal emissary of alternative proclivities who grows flowers from strange parts – all to mock religious authoritarianism and to release ordinary suffering humans from joyless thralldom. Whyte's second novel was more ambitious and serious, once again deliberately echoing Hogg in its destabilising device of having an ancient manuscript whose truth is uncertain as basis for its narrative, so that its events can be read as grotesque fantasy or as a profound psychological exploration of the formation of gender. Whyte presents a seventeenth-century spirit whose kinship with animals and nature, and his uncanny powers, brings about condemnation as a warlock from family and society, as well as guilty self-condemnation when he sees how his powers wreak revenge on his vicious grandmother. Both novels thus use their magical aspects to emphasise the repressiveness of authoritarian orthodoxy towards whatever it considers alien or subversive.

Several other contemporary writers use protagonists whose magical powers set them against their societies. Echoing many of the ways in which the earlier fiction of Dorothy Haynes and Fred Urquhart used superstition and the supernatural to reveal a less than romantic older Scotland, like Whyte and Harry Tait, Alison Prince chooses the seventeenth century to show intolerance at its worst, in *The Witching Tree* (1996). Mary McGuire suffers torture, the burning of her mother, and life-long persecution until she accepts her powers as life-enhancing rather than a curse. As with Whyte and Tait (and Mackay Brown in stories such as 'Witch', from *A Calendar of Love*, 1967) conventional social values are reversed and the traditionally monstrous is perceived as misunderstood, the projection of a diseased community onto a scapegoat.

And in recent years signs of these new perspectives are widespread; for example, in Alan Massie's *The Hanging Tree* (1990), his first venture into Scottish history and legend, which draws on the legendary lore of Thomas the Rhymer and the border ballads, and the later Border tales of Hogg and Stevenson in its romance of the fifteenth century, dealing with the tortured relations of Scotland and England as a backcloth for the story of the curse which hangs over the Laidlaws of Clartyshaws. Massie seems less sure in this territory than in his haunting motif of a magical dimension to the otherwise stoical and rational life of Walter Scott in his masterly creation of an 'undiscovered journal' written and kept secret by the author in *The Ragged Lion* (1994). And Ronald Frame's novella *The Broch* (in *The Sun on the Wall*, 1994) brings its story of the break-up of a middle-class family on holiday, coming to its visionary conclusion of hope in its vision of an ancient broch-girl. There's something of the closure of Gibbon's short story 'Clay' here; a completion, a sense of the present being contemporaneous with the past, which harks back to Renaissance use of the idea of the collective uncon-scious. Like Frame's *The Lantern Bearers* (1999) (below), he continues his movement back towards older Scottish fictional themes.

And the development of this mode goes on – for example, with Alan Clews, in a modern, haunting and beautifully told Renfrewshire ghost story, *A Child of Air* (1995); and in two novels from Christopher Wallace, *The Pied Piper's Poison* (1998), a sinister reworking of the famous legend, set against the grim aftermath of the Second World War, so that the plagues and horrors of the Thirty Years War of the seventeenth century are revisited in the Hamelin of the twentieth, and *The Resurrection Club* (1999), a grotesque tale of diablerie set in contemporary Festival Edinburgh. Andrew Greig's *When They Lay Bare* (1999) has his modern Borders tragedy uncannily re-enact traditional ballads such as 'The Twa Corbies', 'Barbara Allan' and 'Edward'; an ancient magic seems to control the present.

Re-visioning Scotland in history and place

The use of the supra-rational and supernatural was to develop into something much wider and more revisionary than re-creation of traditional legendary lore, as can be seen in the sheer variety of usage in the work of Gray, Morgan and Lochhead. All three were, to a great extent, rewriting Scottish social and cultural history, in very different ways and genres. And this rewriting was occurring simultaneously in some very varied work of the period. In many ways the doyen of all modern Scottish historical novelists must be acknowledged as Nigel Tranter (1909–99) whose coverage of Scottish history has been credited with providing most Scots with their knowledge of the subject. He has covered virtually all main periods and figures; outstandingly in his epic Robert the Bruce trilogy (*The Steps to the Empty Throne* to *The Price of the King's Peace*, 1969–71), and perhaps his finest, *The Wallace* (1975) and *Macbeth* (1978). Tranter believed politics to be much the same in all ages, and this goes some way to explaining the lack of differentiation of character in his work; more important to him are the recorded facts of history, and these he serves with respect and impressive industry. His contribution is unique, not least because post-war historical fiction has been dominated by women writers, whose work has tended to blend romance (in the modern sense of love interest) with period settings. (Beside Tranter existed what was and is almost a successful industry of novelists, mainly women, using history as backcloth for their love melodramas – numerous writers like Alanna Knight, Agnes Short and Jessica Stirling have created many hundreds of tales set amidst religious wars, rebellions, clearances, and war – fuller accounts of the huge range of writers in this genre can be found in *A History of Scottish Women's Writing*, 1997.) And challenges to the orthodoxies of history increased thereafter: for example, in Harry Tait's Saltire-Award-winning *The Ballad of Sawney Bain* (1990), with its recreation of the legendary cannibal monster of Galloway as a dreamer and community-builder trapped in the barbaric historical nightmare of Scotland during its killing times of the religious wars of the sixteenth century; in David Craig's *King Cameron* (1991), a bitter account of the horrific ways in which political activism in Highlands and islands was treated in the first half of the nineteenth century; and in Simon Taylor's *Mortimer's Deep* (1992), which used Taylor's immense knowledge as a contributing editor of the huge *Scotichronicon* by Walter Bower, the fifteenth-century abbot of the Augustinian monastery of Inchcolm, to recreate the starkness of twelfth-century life for the brothers of the island, together with the complexities of European politics of church and state during the reign of William the Lion.

Such scholarly yet convincing re-creation of time past is rare, but in lighter and at times surreal vein it is achieved by Ross Laidlaw in *The Linton Porcupine* (1984), which audaciously argues that the Scots won the Battle of Ancrum Moor in 1545 because they had invented a kind of machine-gun. This, and

Laidlaw's *Dispatch'd from Athole* (1992), are games with history which nevertheless illuminate concepts and mindsets of the time through their careful contextualising. In the second novel, the early feminist and novelist Aphra Behn, who is supposed to have died in London in 1689, is daringly exhumed for the purposes of fiction to become a spy on Scots in the manner of Defoe – and more daringly still, falls in love with her enemy, Claverhouse, yet is his executioner at Killiecrankie.

George Macdonald Fraser (who was immensely successful with his *Flashman* series, begun in 1969, and his comic stories of scruffy ne'er-do-weel Private McAuslan) achieved a more serious and undervalued re-creation of a prose ballad of Border lawlessness in 1993 with *The Candlemass Road*. In its terse understatement this is more effective than more elaborate attempts to achieve this such as Massie's *The Hanging Tree* or Hunter Steele's re-working of James Hogg's *The Bridal of Polmood* (1820) into a grotesquely humorous pastiche of history and Hogg, in *Chasing the Gilded Shadow* (1986). Lorn MacIntyre's trilogy of novels, under the heading of *The Chronicles of Invernevis* (*Cruel in the Shadow*, 1979, *The Blind Bend*, 1981, and *Empty Footsteps*, 1996), follows the declining fortunes of an aristocratic West Highland family over three generations, until the Great War ends their sorry saga of arrogant exploitation of peasantry, and dispels any romance which may linger around the notions of chieftainship and Highland community.

One writer attempts and achieves more than any other in the genre. Tribute must be paid to a writer whose encyclopaedic knowledge of European history in the fifteenth and sixteenth centuries has created what are undoubtedly some of the most ambitious, richly detailed and vastly entertaining historical epics in English. Dorothy Dunnett's (1923–2001) *Game of Kings* sextet (1961–75) portrayed sixteenth-century Scottish-English and international intrigue with astonishing control of innumerable characters and stories, with its heroic history-making protagonist Francis Lymond operating as a more sophisticated and influential period James Bond. The action moved across all Europe, and beyond, with dazzling dramatic turns and plots within plots, the sheer scale of control commanding admiration. Even more challenging to received notions of Scottish history was her *King Hereafter* (1982), with its haunting refashioning of Macbeth as Earl Thorfinn and its vision of a post-Celtic Scotland. Even more impressive than the Lymond epics is her colossal eight-volume series under the heading of *The House of Niccolo*, which began with *Niccolo Rising* in 1986 and culminated in 2000 in *Gemini*. Nicholas de Fleury begins as a humble young merchant, in the fifteenth century; by the end of the first novel his intelligence and amazing combination of skills have established him not only as a prince of merchants with a team of loyal friends, but as a pioneer in New World trade. The novels take him from Bruges to Trebizond, from Cyprus to Africa, from Venice to Scotland, as he simultaneously and subtly influences the destinies of nations and explores the labyrinthine secrets of his own origins. It is little wonder that he is increasingly called to Scotland by a persistent, virtually supernatural psychic force. The riddle is magnificiently solved in *Gemini* – and there, in a final magical touch, Dunnett reveals him as an ancestor of Francis Lymond, thus linking her two great series. Praise for Dunnett has been qualified by the suggestion that her historical telling is traditional, and her heroes modern within a period setting; but no one else in this genre has her range and authorial control of such huge material.

Rediscovering locality

This revisioning of history insisted on emphasising the importance of the neglected parts of Scotland. Attempts had been made to rediscover such territories before: the Western Isles had been revisioned in the fiction and poetry of Crichton Smith, and Norman MacDonald's *Calum Tod* (1976), one of the most impressive attempts to trace the confusions and agonies in the tensions of Gaelic-Scottish identity in its portrayal of the divided worlds of its protagonist; and Charles MacLeod's *Devil in the Wind* (1976), and James Shaw Grant's *Their Children will See* (1979), are short stories which range over the history of the Hebrides with a poetic sense of love, anger and elegy. Ian Stephen's *Living at the Edge* (1982) is a group of short stories about modern Stornoway, where 'on the edge' implies not just territorial periphery, but modern islanders on the edge of a dying culture and a modern world. Elphinstone's *Islanders* (1994) is set in Fair Isle; Robert Alan Jamieson's *Soor Hearts* (1983) captures the darker side of Shetland social history in the manner of MacDougall Hay or MacColla in its timeless picture of an island mafia of landlords, preachers and shopkeepers who use innocent Magnus Doull in ancient fashion as scapegoat for their crimes. His *Thin Wealth* (1986), while focusing on the oil-boom Shetland years of 1973–83, then acknowledges the value amid the introversion of Shetland culture and history in its portrait of Linda Watt and her Chris Guthrie-like seeking for meaning in a confused world of ancient feuds and greedy incomers, whose time in the island will end with the oil. John Graham's *Shadowed Valley* (1987) went further back to the Shetland Weisdale clearances of 1843 in ways reminiscent of Gunn and MacColla, but with its own authenticism of dialect and recollection of community custom. Graham's *Strife in the Valley* (1992) focused on nineteenth-century community debates regarding the place of

Shetland dialect and culture in schools, but with a parallel narrative which seems to echo themes of *The House with the Green Shutters*. More recently, Gregor Lamb has undertaken a loving recreation of a traditional Orkney family saga of the fifteenth century in *Langskaill* (1999); for all it has echoes of Mackay Brown, the novel has a richness of detail and theme which even Brown didn't attempt – and, more importantly for placing it in terms of revisioning of Scottish history and culture, it manages simultaneously to live in the past and, in its stressing of the separate sense of Orkney identity from Dane or Scot, to imply living tradition in the present.

Rediscovery was not limited to peripheries; Gray's *Lanark* evoked an East-End Glasgow childhood; Kelman focused on localities such as Drumchapel and Maryhill; Banks and others followed in confidently setting their narratives in localised settings.

Revisioning Scotlands now: surreal perspectives

The use of surreal elements in the revisioning of Scotland was not new. Mackay Brown's fiction had from the beginning used dream, vision, and apocalyptic imagining to deliver its message of hostility to modern Scotlands, and as early as 1969 George Friel had frequently moved his fiction into nightmare surrealism, as in the spectral questioners of the lonely spinster in *Grace and Miss Partridge*; and his later fiction constantly used surreal or dream-like situations or figures to embody what he saw as some things rotten in the state of Scotland – for example, the demonic figure of Tod in *Mr Alfred MA* (1972) and the decaying Victorian villa of *An Empty House* (1974), representing increasing urban violence and decay. Other established writers like Robin Jenkins had turned towards surrealism; *Fergus Lamont* (1979) created a strange and enigmatic protagonist who represented extended and ambiguous satire on Scottish icons such as Burns and 'The Lad of Pairts', and *Poverty Castle* (1991) used its strange symbolism of the dream-house to suggest fundamental self-deception and weakness at the heart of the Scottish psyche.

But around 1980, partly stimulated by the work of Gray and Banks – and perhaps indeed having stimulated Gray and others – a rich vein of metaphysical and fantastical eccentricity was opened up by writers such as Stewart Hutchison in his highly original and disturbing *Scully's Lugs* (1979), while strange, dreamlike and unclassifiable texts appeared in increasing number, ranging from Douglas Dunn's *Secret Villages* (1985), which casts a very different kind of semi-sinister surrealism over short stories about strangely unplaceable communities and their elusive inhabitants, to the Scottish-Canadian surrealism of Eric McGoldrick's *The Paradise Motel* (1989), the

957

Scottish-Italian *grotesquerie* of David Mackenzie's *The Truth of Stone* (1991), or the weird American's-eye-view of Edinburgh and Scottish kitsch in Todd McEwan's *McX* (1990). Possibly the most successful of these new fictions was Elspeth Barker's (b. 1940) *O Caledonia* (1991); its macabre lyricism, in which young Janet passed her unhappy adolescence in Gothic Scottish Achnaseuch, an aristocratic house with its dim and vaulting hall, with selfish siblings and parents and assorted eccentrics, managed at once to celebrate the beauty of Janet's Highlands and to express, with a richly black humour the agonies of her loneliness. This was no novel allowing escape from repression; instead, its sardonic comi-tragedy disallowed any stock responses, constantly distancing and distorting its protagonists and events to the edge of surrealism. The title (beginning the famous quotation from Scott) is, as so often, ironical, and carries elusive implications – is Scotland, its grim communities, creeds and weather, being lamented, or honoured for its beauty, as meet nurse for Janet, as a poetic child failed by family? The novel does not attempt to survey Scotland entire; its villagers are seen only from the big house, reduced to stock peasantry, and its history and variety excluded, as the fictional perspective insists on its right to be subjective.

Perhaps the most extreme development of this kind of creative eccentricity, designed to destabilise conventional understanding of traditional Scotlands, can be found in the unique prose of Frank Kuppner (b. 1951) (also a fine and disturbing poet) in *A Very Quiet Street* (1989), the idiosyncratic, moody, and yet angry meditative investigation of the scandal of the Establishment's hypocritical misuse of criminal justice in the infamous case of Oscar Slater; and in *A Concussed History of Scotland* (1991), a series of 500 'chapters' which meditate on life, the universe and the youth hostel on Park Circus in Glasgow. Autobiography? Prose-poetry? Fiction? Following Gray's lead in destabilising generic classification of Glasgow and Scottish experience, Kuppner mingles his genres, outstandingly in *Something very like Murder* (1994), an apparently detached study of Scottish and international travesties of justice and man's inhumanity to man, which, combined with its account of the loss of the author's parents, manages to be simultaneously appalling, sardonic and profoundly compassionate. *Life on a Dead Planet* (1996) and *In the Beginning there was Physics* (1999) have continued Kuppner's unique, lateral and unsettling scrutiny of what he sees as the flux of random existence. Under this eye for human absurdity Scotland as place, history and tradition disintegrates, as does any human arrogance which thinks to impose categories on unknowable experience. Kuppner's work represents some of the most intelligent, poetic and exploratory writing in Scotland and Britain today.

Scottish magic realism

Alison Kennedy's *So I Am Glad* (1995) can perhaps illustrate how bold and adventurous contemporary Scottish writing had become in juxtapositioning actual worlds of modern Scotland with high fantasy and the surreal. The novel is told in the first person by lonely Jennifer Wilson, an over-stressed Glasgow radio announcer. She has turned in upon herself – until she meets the new lodger in her Glasgow flat, not the least of whose peculiarities is that his body gives off a blue glow when he sweats. He has lost all memory, and suffers from acute agoraphobia. He also happens to be Cyrano de Bergerac, somehow translated from seventeenth-century France to become Jennifer's responsibility as he struggles with his nightmare transition. And just as James Hogg kept his readers guessing as to whether his Sinner invented his loved-and-hated devil, or whether Gil-Martin actually existed, so Kennedy keeps her readers wondering whether Cyrano has been magically re-created or whether he is the product of Jennifer's psychological and emotionally damaged needs. Her flatmates, Arthur the bluffly kind, Liz the abrupt, the intermittent Peter, all recognise that 'Martin' the new lodger has problems, and help in different ways. But are her flatmates simply humouring Jennifer and her new lover, leaving her alone in her fantasy of love? And yet . . . if that's the case, what happens to Cyrano in the powerful and mysterious ending which takes them to Paris and his birthplace? Kennedy has two perspectives; on the one hand, a marvellously inventive and ambiguous reworking of the classic Scottish 'either/or' tension between the supernatural and the psychological, and on the other, that of the modern Scottish fiction exemplified in work from Trocchi to Gray, Banks to Galloway, Welsh to Warner, in the depiction of a traumatised mind using displacement and fantastic imagination simultaneously to avoid and redeem the damage from which it hides. The novel succeeds in creating a concrete, factual ambience around the grotesque and weird which convinces. Cyrano is realised tactfully and sensitively. Once he finds his feet in Glasgow he is impressive, intellectually as well as physically; his mind is disarmingly honest, his speed of reflex awesome, as his psychopathic Glasgow enemy discovers.

Does Jennifer invent this endearing superman? A psychological reading is attractive; she has been warped since childhood by her parents – perhaps not physically, but certainly mentally, abused. Her own sexuality has become deviant; with the submissive Steven, she goes to the edge of mental as well as physical tolerance, perhaps over the edge. She has revulsion for herself as a woman for her job as media liar, for the world she lives in; Kennedy constantly juxtaposes Jennifer's personal problems with glimpses through her of a sick society, a world of atrocity and sadistic exploitation, in ways which recall *Janine*, with its linking of the personal pain and amorality of Jock McLeish with the world's pain and amorality. As Gray argued, we destroy ourselves and our universe simultaneously. Jennifer needs both to avoid and atone; Cyrano answers both needs, and answers her yearning to be free of herself. And read thus, the book's progress shows her healing instead of damaging, being valued for the spiritual even more than for the physical, acquiring a personality, confidence, and a voice which had hitherto been lacking. Cyrano is her cure; since he represents her lack and need, when fulfilled she must remove him. 'So I am glad', she realises; she recognises the healing and the affirmative meaning behind her experience. This is moving, positive, and poignant; but questions remain. What about her flatmates seeing Cyrano? His presence, even as 'Martin', seems real enough. In the end the answers – or evasions – are the post-modern sleights of *Lanark*. So the novel contradicts itself? *Lanark* operated in several genres at once, none of them gaining authority. Here Kennedy teases us, knowing full well we'll ask our old-fashioned questions of how and why, when the reality is that the author can make whatever fictions and irreconcilables are wanted. This new fiction accepts few or no limitations to its scope, and is no longer contained by traditional folk-and-Gothic rules. It extends the worlds of *Poor Things*, *Dreaming Frankenstein*, *Sonnets from Scotland*, until the Scottish and mainly urban present intermingles with anything and anywhere the author cares to imagine. It also again illustrates the predominant theme of current Scottish writing, that of the emergence from a traumatised personal – and modern Scottish – past.

Challenging sacred cows and taboos of society and sexuality

If the rules of fiction are there to be broken, so too are the rules of society. Scottish fiction is increasingly confronting issues of language, of class, of political status, and the expression of sexuality. In respect of language and class James Kelman (and Tom Leonard in poetry) has clearly pioneered change. His repudiation of the society's idea of swearing as taboo language together with his insistence through his existential protagonists on a funda-mental reappraisal of notions of Scottishness and Britishness, and his un-willingness to accept any validity in class hierarchy, has influenced writing in and beyond Scotland hugely. Many novelists like Duncan McLean, Alan Warner, Irvine Welsh and Des Dillon now insist on their right to use slang and non-standard English, and not as traditionally the case through the expression of their characters, but in their authorial and narrative voice. This is no simple borrowing of US freedoms, but a revolt against British authority from localised Scottish speech communities.

And several, like Welsh throughout his fiction or McLean in *Bunker Man* (1995), or Whyte in *Euphemia McFarrigle* (1995) and *The Gay Decameron* (1998), Ellen Galford in *Queendom Come* 1990) and *The Devil and the Dybbuk* (1993), Ali Smith in the stories of *Free Love* (1995) and her novel *Like* (1997), and Jackie Kay in *Trumpet* (1998) have challenged the orthodoxies of sexual behaviour and expression. *Bunkerman* can seem gratuitously crude in its raw sexuality, but its title should remind us that McLean is exploring what is all too prevalent in Scottish male culture, a combination of repressed sexuality and violence. His small-town school janitor, whose release of obsessive desires and jealousies destroy his marriage and himself, is the real bunkerman of the novel, with his male jealousies and fantasies. McLean and others like Dillon and John Burnside insist on bringing what they see as realities into the open, however shocking; and while sometimes with Welsh and Dillon (in novels like *The Big Empty*, 1997, and *Duck*, 1998) the reader may sometimes suspect that the desire to shock precedes the urge to truth, there can be no doubting the energy behind the commitment to changing boundaries. This is especially valid in respect of the fictions of Whyte, Galford, Kay and Smith, with their unapologetic and enthusiastic depiction of gay relations, who have success-fully changed sexual perspectives in contemporary Scottish writing.

Less contentious, perhaps, but in their own ways challenging specific social issues and targets, are the novels of authors with particular affiliations – for example, the many novels of Colin Douglas, from *The Houseman's Tale* (1975) to his most ambitious denunciation of what he regards as the present undermining of the medical profession and the National Health Service in *Sickness and Health* (1991). Through the Waugh-like picaresque adventures of Doctor David Campbell Douglas, as in the sardonic *A Cure for Living* (1983), Douglas has exposed many of the shoddier sides of hospitals, drug companies, and consultants on both sides of the Atlantic. In *Last Lesson of the Afternoon* (1994), Christopher Rush delivered a virulent attack on what he saw as a similar erosion of traditional liberal education by the intrusion of management methodologies and bureaucratic meddling, while Alasdair Campsie, well-known for challenging romantic and Establishment ortho-doxies, tilted ferociously at the Edinburgh legal establishment in *By Law Protected* (1976), and then at conventional readings of the life of Burns in *The Clarinda Conspiracy* (1989) in suggesting that Burns's last years as an excise officer were part of an elaborate plan by Scottish Establishment to silence him as a political satirist. And Lorn Macintyre's *Invernevis* trilogy (1979–96) revealed its driving impulse as a hatred of the pretensions and unromantic hypocrisies of hierarchical privilege in Highland aristocracy. Taken with the many versions of re-evaluation and refusal to accept old ideologies and narratives of Scotland which these two chapters have discussed, what becomes apparent is that the overwhelming impulse in post-war Scottish writing has been one of discontentment with old versions and images of what Scotland has been and should be – not the least of this discontent arising from an aversion to accepting Scotland as some kind of sealed-off entity, with readily categorised characteristics.

A new internationalism?
William Boyd (b. 1952), Ronald Frame (b. 1953),
Stuart Hood (b. 1915), Alan Massie (b. 1938) and
Muriel Spark (b. 1918)

It is also apparent that Scottish fiction is pushing the idea of 'Scottishness' in identity, place and time, ever outward in terms of themes, settings and temporal conjunctions. New Scottish fiction can move easily from rural Scotland to Italy, the USA, Mexico, within the parameters of a single fiction. Writers like William Boyd, Stuart Hood, Ronald Frame and, outstandingly, Alan Massie and Muriel Spark, create fictions set within and outwith Scotland, with central characters who move between worlds in ways which sometimes reveal their Scottish limitations, but equally often show them adept in dealing with their new places. Just as often, this new internationalism allows these authors to choose protagonists from other countries, or, as in the case of Massie, to work impressively in periods of history quite unrelated to Scotland.

All five of these writers can be considered as major Scottish, British and international writers in English. Their achievement cannot be assessed appropriately here; but perhaps what can be indicated is their achievement insofar as they are recognisably Scottish writers and part of evolving Scottish traditions. African-born William Boyd is possibly the least tied to Scotland. His short stories and his novels such as *An Ice Cream War* (1982), *Brazzaville Beach* (1990), *Stars and Bars* (1984), *The Blue Afternoon* (1993) and *Armadillo* (1998) are mainly set abroad (in France and England in the First World War, the Phillipines, the USA, Africa and London respectively) without a Scots person in sight. Some critics have however found in his work a love of the picaresque, the tragic-comic and the grotesque, together with idiosyncratic moral viewpoints, which they recognise as coming from his native country; and it is true that his first novel, *A Good Man in Africa* (1981) measured its feckless and Waugh-like protagonist, the ineffectual foreign diplomat Morgan Leafy, against Scottish doctor Alexander Murray whose steady morality and social responsibility – and death – finally shame the shallow place-server into self-appraisal. In more recondite fashion, *The New Confessions* (1987) showed Scottish roots in its portrayal of Edinburgh born-and-influenced neo-Boswellian (with shades of Hogg's *Justified Sinner*) John James Todd making his name in the film industry; but to balance this Scottish orientation Boyd evoked another informing spirit, that of the unstable European polymath Rousseau, so that his egotistical film-maker – who, in his vain and unreliable narrations, frequently recalls the recurrent holy fools of Scottish fiction from Hogg to Friel, Crichton Smith, Gray and Jenkins – is ultimately unplaceable.

Over the decade 1984–94 Ronald Frame produced five novels and five collections of stories which established him as one of the most impressive young British writers. Frame insists on the essential Scottishness of his work, for all that it looks widely at Britain, from Bearsden and West-End Glasgow to Cornwall and fashionable London, with a detached and sceptical analysis of the sophisticated lives of the English South seen from a curious but recognisably Scottish viewpoint. No one is better at creating nuances of menace around the apparently mundane lives of selfish wives and mothers, lonely husbands, intolerant and snobbish communities with secrets of the past, set within a period atmosphere of a Britain of the '30s to the '50s, all expressed through a reflective, elegiac and fascinatingly circulocutory style which has echoes of Henry James, Proust and Hartley in its manipulation of effects of memory and time. Within this, hints of the supernatural and deliberate play with ambiguities of morality are recognisably Scottish qualities; and his eye for the subtleties of difference in English and Scottish class behaviour recalls the tradition of Ferrier, Oliphant, the Findlater sisters, Catherine Carswell and Willa Muir. *Winter Journey* (1984) established his territory as the sophisticated worlds of the upper-middle classes, the skeletons in their cupboards, revealed in dream-like remembrance or through the observation of their damaged children in the manner of Henry James's *What Maisie Knew* (1897). His most ambitious explorations of English society are found in *Sandmouth People* (1987), *Penelope's Hat* (1989) and *Bluette* (1990), long novels which richly evoke intrigues and betrayals, behind walled gardens or in fashionable restaurants. Frame's range is unusual, however; there are also evocative and convincing short stories of lonely Glasgow children and misfits in *Watching Mrs Gordon* (1985) (the short story 'Paris' is a most sympathetic study of age and loneliness), while novellas like *Prelude and Fugue* (1986), *A Long Weekend with Marcel Proust* (1986), and *Walking my Mistress in Deauville* (1992) play sensitively with the surreal and supernatural – and we have noted above how recently in his novella *The Broch* Frame has been drawn to the traditionally Scottish supernatural as used by writers like Gibbon and Gunn.

After *The Sun on the Wall* (1994) there was a silence of five years, till 1999 and *The Lantern Bearers*, which brings together all the modes and themes of his earlier fiction, but with a significant change of perspective. This is arguably his finest novel; and it echoes *Winter Journey* in that it is told by a lonely child, with the limited and dangerous understanding of complex adult relations. Here too are the secrets behind high walls, talked of in a suspicious community, and the tragedy which emerges with fated inevitability. This is a much more Scottish novel in character and setting than anything Frame has attempted, however – and, moreover, it follows that recent tendency we have noted for modern fiction to draw on older Scottish literary and traditional models and ideas. Stevenson's essay of 1887, 'The Lantern-Bearers', which describes childhood holiday in North Berwick, haunts the novel; the children's huddling of almost magical light under their great-coats becomes a metaphor for the modern child, Neil Pritchard, and his experiences in a Galloway seaside town.

Neil has been sent by his divorcing parents to his aunt. His summer is mundane enough amidst afternoon teas and seashore walks until his services as a singer are enlisted by one of Scotland's leading composers, Euan Bone, writing a work based on Stevenson's vivid evocation of childhood. The boy and composer are clearly attracted to each other; but Bone equally clearly avoids involvement. The tragedy which follows stems from what Neil cannot know; that the reasons that Bone and his musician friend Maitland are in this small Scottish town are to do with Bone's sexual offences in London, and his dangerous Scottish nationalist sympathies. Neil is far from guiltless, for all his youth, in Bone's sinister death in Glasgow, and Frame spares us none of the shame and horror he feels. What redeems the novel, in so many ways comparable to that other fine novel using music as extended metaphor, MacLaverty's *Grace Notes* (1997), is its final perception of art and music as some kind of grace among the ruins. Neil, whose discovery of fatal illness in middle-age opens the novel, will in the closing stages of novel and life redeem himself by bringing Bone's long-lost composition of 'The Lantern-Bearers' to the world.

Stuart Hood has for too long been neglected by accounts of Scottish fiction and literature. He has had a distinguished career in war (his *Pebbles From My Skull*, 1963, rev. as *Carlino*, 1985, is his own story, of living and fighting with the partisans, an account filled with action and timeless meditation regarding the cycles of life and death brought so starkly before him) and peacetime (he was head of the World Service and controller of programmes for the BBC); and his earlier work includes studies of television and radio, novels such as *In and Out the Window* (1974), and a series of translations of modern European

literature. Undoubtedly, however, his major contribution to Scottish literature came with his Indian summer of five novels from *A Storm from Paradise*
(1985) to *The Book of Judith* (1995). His work fully exemplifies the new
internationalism of Scottish writing, constantly linking Scottish protagonists
and inheritance with European politics and culture. Possibly his finest novel,
A Storm from Paradise moves continually between times; between the modern
authorial voice, purporting to be the son of a schoolmaster in one of the
small towns in the Grampian foothills, and the story of the schoolmaster,
John Scott, and his passionate affair with Russian exile Elizavyeta de Pass,
which, in the years just before the Second World War, shocks the inward-
looking Free Church community. The storm is in John Scott; the paradise he
discovers as he releases his repressed feelings for great art and frank
discussion of matters sexual, political and social in his love for Elizavyeta
cannot last. John's moment of chance and choice to break free from
trammelled Scotland fails, through subtly different reasons to do with his
own limitations, Elizavyeta, and the strength of the community in pulling him
back. She is genuinely fond of her schoolmaster, but as temporary solace in a
wasteland; she has a Russian husband – although her sophisticated control of
her life will, ironically, crumble, leaving her with neither man. Local worthies
will succeed in binding him through marriage with their own. Ghosts of great
European tragedies like *Madame Bovary* (1856) haunt this book – and haunt
the authorial voice, which sometimes reveals itself as speaking beyond Scott's
son as Hood himself, remembering his own childhood and father with
simultaneous love and detached irony. Hood's two worlds are, for a moment,
imaginatively fused in what he admits is a fantasy, but a fantasy which
expresses magnificently the yearning for other times, other places which
Gibbon and Kesson expressed with a comparable sensitivity and poetry
through their misplaced heroines.

The novels which followed all exhibit an important contemporary characteristic of Scottish fiction in their reworking of themes of writers like Hogg
and Stevenson – and in the case of *The Upper Hand* (1987), of James
Kennaway, whose themes of jealousy and betrayal in *Household Ghosts*
(1961) and *Some Gorgeous Accident* (1967) are worked out again in the
unreliable evidence of the dramatic monologue of James Melville, son of
a severe minister, whose life is interwoven with that of laird's son Colin
Elphinstone. Colin went to Fettes; James to the local school. Colin has easy
grace; James lacks it. With echoes of *The Master Ballantrae* the tragedy is set, as
Melville, possibly deliberately and obsessively, measures his life against
Elphinstone's. Melville even turns paid British spy at university, reporting
on Elphinstone's undergraduate socialism, as well as other nationalists and

communists. He manages to share Colin's friends and lovers, shadowing Colin in increasingly sleazy and self-destructive ways, until his chance to express his obsessive envy presents itself. Elphinstone has had a heroic war with the partisans experience – and Melville exploits his heroism for final betrayal.

A striking feature of the new international fiction is its preoccupation with themes of divided loyalties and the examination of the point at which they become betrayal. Hood's following novels all demonstrate his awareness of the complexities of allegiance and integrity, with a superb sense of shifting European politics. *The Brutal Heart* (1989) recounts an elderly Scot's unwitting involvement in German post-war terrorism, his affair with one of his son's friends leading to his son's murder. *A Den of Foxes* (1991) is Hood's most complex and meta-fictional work, with its intermingling of reality and fantasy, with Hood himself in his plot, in the strange but powerful memoir of Peter Sinclair. He tells us of the bizarre international and fantasy war-game in which he's now involved; but this game increasingly relates to the actual war Peter fought in, and eventually wars past, present and imagined mingle in a nightmarish world of sex and betrayal which is possibly only comprehensible by allowing it to be the reworking of past life and sins of a dying man. The den of foxes finally seems to have its origin at San Vito, in the past war; but it is also a name for the darkest place of the mind, where our cunning rationalisations betray us. All this is set against a vivid backcloth of international move and counter-move; it comes as no surprise to find *The Book of Judith* (1995) using the backcloth of Spain in Franco's dying months for its familiar story of love and betrayal. Judith is married to respected film-maker Fergus McIver. He is also an old style British Communist Party member, who agrees to work for them against the old régime in Spain, taking Judith with him. The Spanish comrades want much more complicity than he expected, and Judith is house-arrested. The novel becomes a searching examination of rights. She desires her female integrity; Fergus wrestles with his obligations. As in the biblical tale of Judith and Holofernes, so here; Judith has to kill her husband for her freedom.

There is a great deal of similarity between the work and achievement of the internationally famous Alan Massie and the much less well-known Hood, especially in their grasp of the ruthlessness of people who play the great games of politics and war. Massie's range, however, is wider than Hood's, moving from fine journalism and academic studies to three main strands of fiction; respectively, studies of the morality of twentieth-century international politics and power, sensitive accounts of Scotland in history and change, and his acclaimed Roman and related period novels.

The first strand began in 1978 with *Change and Decay in All Around I See*, a Waugh-like satirical survey of London middle classes and eccentrics. This lacked the *gravitas* and focused intensity of *The Death of Men* (1981), which, in its mature exploration of Italian politics (and based on the murder of Aldo Moro in 1978), showed Massie working in the tradition of great political fiction like Conrad's *Nostromo* (1904), teasing out complexities of ethics and political loyalties. Internationally acknowledged as his finest work in this vein are *The Sins of the Father* (1989) and *A Question of Loyalties* (1989). The first is a sophisticated account of the quest of a middle-aged Frenchman living in Geneva to find out the truth about his father, who collaborated with Marshal Pétain and Germany in the wartime Vichy government. The novel, told from many angles and sources, analyses with sensitivity and psychological depth the way in which modern political forces can twist and betray decent human beings. So too does the second; in contemporary Buenos Aires, English Rebecca and German Franz, in love, introduce their parents. Rebecca's Jewish father recognises that Franz's father is his wartime captor and a top-level German war criminal, and his exposure leads to Kestner's show-trial in Israel. The tragedy reveals depths and nuances of pain and guilt, blurring clear-cut edges, and exploring the fundamental questions of duty clashing with morality in ways as profound as any fiction of the kind. Told through the recollections of a journalist who comes from a wealthy and political Scottish family, *Shadows of Empire* (1997) examines the rise of fascism in Spain and Germany, and how other countries responded to it. Alec Allan's family, in their varying responses, mirror this; private actions in love and politics are shown as inextricably linked with public and international dealings – and here, as in all these novels, any brief affirmative moments Massie offers are lost in a prevailing sardonic weariness regarding the tortuous betrayals and deceits of humanity.

Massie's Scottish novels show an uneasy relationship with Scotland, historical and modern. The novels of modern Scotland comprise a linked pair, *The Last Peacock* (1980) and *These Enchanted Woods* (1993); and *One Night in Winter* (1984). The pair deal with the territory of James Kennaway in *Household Ghosts* (1961) – upper-class families, here in Perthshire. The symbolism of the titles suggests the death of something showy, a gilded way of life; and the two novels examine the moral and physical decline of a family, their friends, and their county class, who have too much private privilege and too little social conscience with the same tone of world-weariness as in the political novels. The success of these satires shows Massie's familiarity with this world; his grasp of people and class in his analysis of the rise and fall – through murder – of a leading Scottish nationalist politician in *One Night in Winter* seems less sure, arising perhaps from Massie's equivocal sense of his own Scottish-British identity. Massie's antipathy to nationalism is well-known; he tries to be fair in giving his nationalist charismatic qualities, but in the end his aim of discrediting the kind of modern Scotland he dislikes, and his distance from the classes he portrays, make this novel less convincing than his international or classical studies, where antipathy and distance disappear. His two Scottish historical novels are very different. *The Hanging Tree* (1990), an attempt at a Borders romance set in the fifteenth century, works uneasily between melodrama and pastiche of ballads, Hogg and Stevenson; but *The Ragged Lion* (1994) brings Massie onto his own ground, being a marvellous re-creation of the life of Walter Scott, told from an unknown discovered Scott manuscript. Massie knows and empathises with Scott superlatively, and creates a Scott who tells his own sombre, rich, and impressive story in a way which echoes Scott's own deeply personal *Journal* of the last seven years of his life, and successfully marries biography with fiction.

His Roman series began with *Augustus* (1986), and has continued through *Tiberius* (1990), *Caesar* (1993) and *Antony* (1997). The novels don't follow chronologically; Augustus was the golden boy who emerged as the ruthless victor following the murder of Caesar by Brutus and accomplices, and Tiberius was Augustus's stepson. The central theme is that of Rome's transition from republic to empire, in the dramatic decades just before and after the birth of Christ, each novel focusing on one of the great figures of the period, and each refashioning the conventional view of them, derived from Plutarch and Shakespeare. Pompey defeated, Caesar emerges as charming and ruthless showman, the conspirators as cynics, roués and pompous asses, Augustus as the arch-manipulator, and Antony as indecisive. Tiberius is the noblest of the lot, his decent efforts foiled and reputation warped by his inheritance from Augustus, the first Emperor, of a police state based on bribery and corruption. Once again, Massie's world-view of human affairs as generally disgusting emerges; and once again his ability to handle monumental historical events and a huge cast of historical characters is vastly impressive. And the quartet has become a quintet with *Nero's Heirs* (1999) telling of the aftermath of Nero's suicide in AD 68. Now the Flavian dynasty begins with Vespasian, Titus and Domitian; and the double-dealing and betrayal goes on; and Massie's reinterpretation continues. In *King David* (1995), outside of the quartet, he has produced a vivid account of the wars of Israel – small compared to Rome's great affairs, but huge in mythical and religious significance – in his re-creation of the life of the man who sang to Saul and slew Goliath, uniting Israel against the Philistines. This is a more poetic novel than usual, with its moving account of David's rise and fall into final loneliness. Massie has inspired followers, Ross Leckie and David Wishart outstanding amongst them.

The 'non-Scottish' and later work of Muriel Spark

The earlier and Scottish-based work of Muriel Spark was discussed in the previous chapter under the heading of 'post-war scepticism'. Since *The Prime of Miss Jean Brodie* (1961), with more than fifteen novels and story collections (and autobiography, in *Curriculum Vitae*, 1992) she has become recognised internationally as one of the greatest of modern fiction writers; but, with the exception of *Symposium* (1990) and some of her short stories, there is little explicitly Scottish about the later work. This of course does not mean she is no longer a Scottish novelist. Spark has acknowledged her experience of Scotland as having had a formative effect on all her art; her abandoned Calvinism figures as both thematic undercurrent and narrative method throughout all her fiction. Her 'non-Scottish' novels constantly weave in references to the ballads, Scott, Hogg and Stevenson in ways which show her sophisticated understanding and use of them. For instance, earlier work such as *The Comforters* (1957) and *Memento Mori* (1959) showed her preoccupation with the supernatural and her awareness of older Scottish writers' usage of it, and her pleasure in developing a kind of grimly comic metaphysical *grotesquerie* in a modern London setting. Her first novels had simultaneously showed Spark's cleverness in playing narrative tricks which constantly destablised her characters' (and the reader's) identity, and her early unsureness as to her moral basis. Her increased sureness in handling theological satire is obvious in *The Ballad of Peckham Rye* (1960); but at this point she produced a trio of novels which clearly relate to an exploration of her own unsettled background and values, in *Jean Brodie* (1961) (discussed in the previous chapter), *The Girls of Slender Means* (1963), and her most straightforward and perhaps personal of narratives, *The Mandelbaum Gate* (1965). Edinburgh background and values, wartime disillusionment, and a quest for self-knowledge amongst the claims of Judaism, Protestantism and Catholicism are their subjects, respectively.

After this exploration of herself through fiction, five very different short novels followed. *The Public Image* (1968) examines the spurious and destructive nature of fame through its portrait of a shallow actress. The protagonist of *The Driver's Seat* (1970), Lise, is brutally murdered at the end, but only then does the reader realise she has been the driver, and has with grotesque stylishness planned her own death all along, as her final act of self-determination, thus challenging conventional notions of the female as victim. This is arguably Spark's finest work to date in terms of its tight narrative control, its concealment of motive, its feminist agenda and its bleak vision of the emptiness of modern consumer life. *Not to Disturb* (1971) saw Spark's textual trickery reach new heights; echoes of Sartre's *Huis Clos* (1943) emphasise the hellish entrapment in shoddy morality of victims and destroyers. Such textual trickery could overplay itself, however; *The Hothouse by the East River* (1973) and its ghostly protagonists hover between moral satire and fictional confusion – although this is recovered from in *The Abbess of Crewe* (1974), where Catholicism, theatricality and artifice come together most potently in one of Spark's most successful satirical novels, which astonishingly transplants the events of the Watergate scandal to a North of England nunnery. Perhaps the novel's success stems from the scheming abbess of the title being a descendant of Jean Brodie; unconventional (reciting English poetry in place of the standard liturgy), devious (bugging the nunnery) and tragically, dramatically attractive. In the end, and having apparently circumvented the scandal that threatens the abbey, the abbess orders the transcription of her tape-recordings, albeit heavily edited: 'Remove the verses that I have uttered. They are proper to myself alone and should not be cast before the public. Put "Poetry deleted".'

One of Spark's most ambitious, if more traditionally told, novels followed; *The Takeover* (1976) exploits Frazer's *The Golden Bough* (1890–1915) and his location of mythical kingship at Lake Nemi in Italy – now polluted, surrounded by houses of the internationally famous rich, a modern mockery of the ancient mysteries of religion. Here con-men, charlatans and betrayers abound, and shallow Christianity and Diana-worship vie for the heights of bad taste. Rarely has Spark been so condemnatory – and after the Italian-set complex blackmail-and-espionage thriller games of *Territorial Rights* (1979), her fiction has focused on less dramatic, if more complex characters, usually set among the hangers-on of privileged London and southern England, as in *Loitering with Intent* (1981). In Spark's fiction violent death and grisly events occur suddenly and with laconic understatement in the narrative. *Loitering with Intent* typically juxtaposes its dark subject-matter of blackmail, drugging, and suicide with self-referential game-playing, all the more disturbing for its location in upper-class London, treated here and in *A Far Cry from Kensington* (1988) in her most acidic manner.

The following three novels have concerned themselves with more serious issues. *The Only Problem* (1984) treats human suffering in a different way. Focusing on the traumas of a scholar of the Book of Job, Harvey Gotham, like his biblical object of study visited with trials and taunted by supposed comforters, the 'only problem' is that of reconciling a beneficent creator with a world of pain, disease and starvation. This question recurs throughout

Spark's work; what is the relationship between the artistic mind and the dystopian universe it oversees? Spark's narrators are, perhaps, closest to the Calvinist God of Brodie, who, for Sandy, implants in certain people 'an erroneous sense of joy and salvation, so that their surprise at the end might be the nastier'. If Harvey Gotham emerges relatively unscathed from his sufferings, he is forced to conclude that the Book of Job, a text in which God is more a limited character than an omnipotent force, could never supply any clear-cut answers in the first place.

Symposium (1990) resuscitates Scottish themes in its demonic pairing of Margaret Murchie, cursed with the evil eye, and her scripture- and ballad-quoting mad uncle Magnus. Here, Calvinism, the ballads, Hogg and Stevenson bring us back to the world of Jean Brodie; although ill-starred Margaret takes her right to interfere in others' lives far further than Jean Brodie; as far, in fact, as Hogg's Robert Wringhim, the justified sinner. The reader is never quite sure, however, whether those who die or disappear are her victims, or if random fate foils – or carries out – the murderous plans of her mad uncle and herself. Spark is open to the accusation that old subjects and tricks are being replayed excessively, as in her recent novel, *Reality and Dreams* (1996), where the subject matter of novels like *The Public Image* is reworked, in its reduction of the god-like role of the film-maker Tom Richards, who lies on a hospital bed, having fallen from a crane while attempting to gain a degree of directorial omnipotence on the set of one of his films. The implication seems to be that the maker of movies, limited as he is by budget, space and (often belligerent) human resources, can never achieve the control and vision of the novelist.

Spark remains one of the most complex and challenging of contemporary writers in English. There is no doubting her astonishing ability to fictionalise fiction, and to reveal through a wealth of narrative strategies the shortcomings of modern society. But for many readers the principal question regarding her work is one of final and moral meaning. She has converted to Catholicism; yet finding where that faith shapes and informs her work is almost impossible, other than to say that her characters overpoweringly illustrate how humanity goes wrong, and the ubiquitous lack of transforming moral belief. Is this exactly the point? That we must all find our own way through the modern morass?

Problems of placing

Once again, we must remind ourselves that categories overlap. These chapters have tried to group writers in broad categories, but it is obvious that categories can falsify or conceal. In placing discussion of these writers under the 'international' heading it should not be overlooked that much of the work of the 'new internationalist' Scottish writers can be read as exemplifying that preoccupation with emergence from trauma discussed above with particular reference to home Scottish writers. Likewise, William Boyd might have been included with writers who will briefly be discussed below as Anglo-Scottish. And many of the Anglo-Scottish writers can be seen as sharing to varying degrees in the exploitation of the irrational and supernatural. Their 'magic' may not be that of a George Mackay Brown or a Sian Hayton, but they exploit new dimensions of the wonderful. And we noted amongst the new magical fictions a distinctly original internationalism of theme in writers like McEwan and McGoldrick. We must add to this 'new internationalism' the recent work of writers like Galloway and Kennedy, with their movements beyond Scotland, and the recent work of Joan Lingard (*After Colette, Dreams of Love* and *Modest Glory,* discussed above), while many younger writers use the settings of other countries and periods as context for post-modern fictions whose main thrust is exploration of the nature of fiction, narrative, and authorship. Their work is discussed briefly at the end of this chapter.

Anglo-Scottish or Scoto-English?

Spark is but one of a remarkably high number of contemporary Scottish women writers who base themselves and the focus of their work outside Scotland; yet significantly, like Spark, they often share the interest of the home Scots in the possibilities of the supernatural, and in older Scottish fiction, but with a powerful feminist deployment. For example, Emma Tennant's *The Bad Sister* (1978) reworked Hogg's *Justified Sinner;* and exploited Stevenson in *Two Women of London; The Strange Case of Ms Jekyll and Mrs Hyde* (1988). Tennant moved into a bold mixture of myth, magic and modernity in her fable of men and women in *Sisters and Strangers* (1990). Alison Fell's *The Bad Box* (1987) used traditional Scottish lore, while her *Mistress of Lilliput* (1999) magically retraced Gulliver's travels – this time with Gulliver's wife travelling in search of her lost husband. And Sara Maitland has used magic realism to explore boundaries of gender and sexuality in work like *Arky Types* (1987) and *Women Fly when Men aren't Watching* (1993). Arguably the outstanding Scottish writer to work out of England is Shena Mackay, whose fiction from *Old Crow* (1967) to *Dunedin* (1992) has established her as one of the finest novelists in English. Her work retains Scottish characteristics, using Scottish characters and situations, and *Dunedin,* for example, satirises the legacy in modern Britain of Scottish Calvinism and the Scottish colonisation of New Zealand. Later work includes *The Laughing Academy* (1993), *The Orchard on Fire* (1996) and *The Artist's Widow* (1998). In *Debatable Land* (1994), Candia McWilliam has moved from English society-based fiction to explore the boundaries of Scottish, English and foreign identity in *Debatable Land* (1994); the stories in *Wait Till I Tell You* (1997) juxtapose groupings of 'North' and 'South'. In the same year as Elspeth Barker's darkly sensitive and rural Gothic evocation of a childhood in the Highlands, *O Caledonia*, Carol Morin's *Lampshades* (1991) ushered in a new Anglo-Scottish Gothic punk, with another girl misfit in its Scottish Big House. The theme is varied again in Emma Tennant's blend of fictional presentation and fact, her creative autobiography, (*Strangers*, 1998, *Girlitude*, 1999, *Burnt Diaries*, 2000), while Helena McEwen's *The Big House* (2000) draws on these and the tradition of Nancy Brysson Morrison's *The Gowk Storm* (1933) in its poetic portrayal of privileged loneliness. Critic Liz Heron's first impressive novella and short stories, *A Red River* (1996), has Conradian echoes, giving her a voice which is paradoxically humanist and post-modern; and the crime fiction of Val McDermid is discussed below. The movement of writers is not always south, as the work of Scottish resident writers from Anne Fine to J. K. Rowling, creator of the phenomenally successful *Harry Potter* novels, demonstrates; Kate Atkinson is outstanding amongst those who have come north. Since her prize-winning *Behind the Scenes at the British Museum* (1995), her unique blend of tragi-comedy and romantic post-modernism has presented itself increasingly in Scottish terms. This is seen in *Human Croquet* (1997), her moving account of the idiosyncratic ways in which a sister and brother come to terms with the death of their mother, and in *Emotionally Weird* (2000), which has echoes of *The Wasp Factory* (1984) in its Scottish island setting, and of *O Caledonia* (1991) in its mouldering ancestral home – but then goes its unique Atkinson way in its mingling of many stories and past times to show the strange interiors of human mind and emotion, and their weird ways of dealing with painful experience and memory.

Nor, though predominantly so, is it all women who go south; so too, for example, did William Boyd and Stuart Hood. And since 1985 Martin Millar has focused to hilarious effect on alternative cultures in, for example, *The Good Fairies of New York* (1992) and *Love and Peace with Melody Paradise* (1998), while Andrew Cowan's *Pig* (1994), set in post-industrial Corby, is an unsentimental juxtapositioning of old and new Britain, rural and suburbanised, with its great decaying pig-in-the-middle as symbol of something rotten in the state. It won the first book award of the Saltire Book of the Year Awards in 1994; *Common Ground* (1997), his second, again focused on the rottenness at the heart of middle Britain, in its clash of new roads and old woods, bored kids and weary teachers.

New fiction in the '90s

In ending with the most significant and promising of the writers of the last few years, only a few broad categories and brief descriptive listings can be given.

NEW WRITERS, OLD CITIES

One of the strongest (and perhaps most indulged) lines of Scottish fiction has been that in which the extremes of city life have been melodramatised, celebrated, and satirised. Writers like Margaret Thomson Davis, John Burrowes, and Jessica Stirling, continued the tradition of harsh yet vital realism; John McGill's *That Rubens Guy* (1990) and *Giraffes* (1993) arguably stand as the best of this strand, with Meg Henderson's *The Holy City* (1997), with its memories of the bombing of Clydebank and its anger at the effects of war and the exploitation by employers. Des Dillon's evocations of urban twilight range from his ferocious post-Welsh treatments in *The Big Empty* (1997) and *Duck* (1998) to delightful yet grim re-creations of childhood in *Me and my Gal* (1995), and *Itchycooblue* (1999); while Robbie Kydd evoked urban old age sensitively in *Auld Zimmery* (1987). A raw energy and a sometimes hilarious combination of comedy and anger drives Jimmy Boyle's first novel about recovery from institutionalisation, *A Hero of the Underworld* (1999). The best new writing here, however, comes from poet John Burnside in *The Mercy Boys* (1997), Laura Hird's study of a dysfunctional city family in *Born Free* (1999) and Alex Benzie's perceptive story of a Glasgow-Irish woman's recovery from tragedies in *The Angle of Incidence* (1999) – and, of course, this city fiction transcends simplistic generic allocation and includes the work of writers discussed earlier, including the work of Gordon Legge, Galloway, Gray, Kelman, Kennedy, MacDougall, McLean and Welsh.

NEW MAGIC REALISM AND SURREALISM

As always, allocating categories is suspect; the work of Dolan and Hird, effectively set in the city, might well have been discussed in the previous paragraph, while Wallace and Crumey could well represent the new internationalism. What places writers here is their striking departure from realism, although their strategies and narrative techniques are often very different. Arguably the area with the best and most intriguing new writing, some of the

974

major figures here, such as Gray, Hayton and Elphinstone have been discussed earlier; the newer writers include (alphabetically): Chris Dolan with his richly varied short stories in *Poor Angels* (1995), and his account of strange destinies for city misfits in *Ascension Day* (1999); marvellously imaginative short stories from Michel Faber in *Some Rain Must Fall* (1998), and his astonishingly nasty story of aliens abducting hitchhikers for food in *Under the Skin* (2000), the reality behind the Hamlyn piper's legend, and its world war aftermath, in Christopher Wallace's *The Pied Piper's Poison* (1998), and a modern devil story set in the Edinburgh Festival, *The Resurrection Club* (1999); stunning feminist allegories in the tradition of Fell, Maitland and Tennant, drawing on Scottish doppelgänger traditions in Alice Thompson's *Justine* (1996) and *Pandora's Box* (1998); some of the most sophisticated of postmodern storytelling and fantasy, interlinking from novel to novel, in Andrew Crumey's wonderfully developing series, *Music in a Foreign Language* (1994), *Pfitz* (1995), *D'Alembert's Principle* (1996), and *Mr Mee* (2000); Laura Hird's disturbingly grotesque stories in *Nail* (1997); and Christopher Whyte's *Euphemia McFarrigle and the Laughing Virgin* (1995) and *The Warlock of Strathearn* (1997) (discussed earlier).

EXPERIMENTAL NARRATOLOGY; ALTERNATIVE AND SPECULATIVE FICTION
The work of most of the major writers discussed earlier qualifies for this heading, since almost by definition the most ambitious modern writing experiments with narrative, and surveys society and character from unusual angles. Some of the striking newer writers and work include John Burnside in his terrifyingly cold account of a modern justified sinner in *The Dumb House* (1997); James Meek, whose *McFarlane Boils the Sea* (1989) began much of this new surrealism, with its contemporary Edinburgh grotesques (the short stories of *Last Orders*, 1992, and *The Museum of Doubt*, 2000, showed him fusing the worlds of writers like Kelman and Duncan McLean with his own strange Kafkaesque logic, while *Drivetime*, 1995, is a dark account of Euro-nightmare for its claustrophobiac car travellers); Alan Jamieson's *A Day at the Office* (1991), a stream-of-consciousness through a working day which links fragmented lives; David Deans and *The Peatman* (1995), an exhaustive inner monologue of a modern rural recluse; Toni Davidson's searingly innovative study of abuse, incest and ultimate loneliness, *Scar Culture* (1999); and Andrew Murray Scott's *Tumulus* (1999), with its strange searches for lost Dundees. Writers already mentioned who could be considered under this heading include the new science fiction satirists like Terry Houston and Paul Johnston.

GENDER AND SEXUALITY

Challenging gender boundaries has already been discussed as a feature of the work of writers like Galloway, Gray and Hayton. The most significant challenges include Iain Crichton Smith's *An Honourable Death* (1992), discussed previously; Carl MacDougall's *The Casanova Papers* (1996), which, while not exactly challenging gender boundaries, explores a legend of hypersexuality in terms which reveal humanity's need to make scapegoats for its own deficiencies; Christopher Whyte's *The Warlock of Strathearn* (1997), with its eighteenth-century protagonist's change of identities and sexuality opening up areas of modern gender debate, while *The Gay Decameron* (1998) exploits Boccaccio to explore a range of issues for a group of contemporary Edinburgh gay friends; Jackie Kay's *Trumpet* (1998) which showed a mother and son coming to terms with the death of the musician husband, who turns out to have been a woman, disguised through her life; Graham Lironi's *Candyfloss Martyrs* (1999), with its endless mirror-imaging of contemporary *doppelgangers*; Joseph Mills's *Towards the End* (1989) with its intense account of Scottish small-town reactions to a homosexual love affair; Simon Taylor's *Mortimer's Deep* (1992); and Manda Scott's psychological thrillers, *Hen's Teeth* (1996), *Night Mares* (1998) and *Stronger than Death* (1999), with the quiet normality of her lesbian psychologist Kellen Stewart making her challenge to convention all the more effective.

NEW HISTORICAL

If true historical fiction involves the convincing recreation of a past age, the number of genuine writers of historical fiction decreases dramatically. We have noted some of the outstanding practitioners earlier; additionally, we should include a few older writers in the '70s who re-created the past on a wide canvas, historical and international – for example, William Watson in his grim account of a Scottish Knight Templar in *Beltran in Exile* (1979), or his comic medieval romance set in Italy, *The Knight on the Bridge* (1982). Ambitious in its effort to recreate the mindset and nightmare confusions of the sixteenth-century wars of religion in Scotland is Harry Tait's *The Ballad of Sawney Bain* (1990); even more ambitious is surely Dorothy Dunnett's *House of Niccolo* series, an enormous eight-volume project triumphantly concluded in *Gemini* (2000). Outstanding amongst new historical writers is Ross Leckie – his accounts of *Hannibal* (1995), *Scipio* (1998), and the final obsessive destruction of Rome's old enemy in *Carthage* (2000), are told in an economical style of laconic intensity which captures older mindsets, with their savagery and obsessive ambitions. In this period and mode Leckie's only rival is Alan Massie.

Another more subtle distinction must be made between historical fiction's interpretation of the past, and historical fiction's message for the present, using the past as comparison, or as allegory for the present. But the best historical fiction does both, relating the interpreted past to the present, so that our modern minds do not just compare themselves with the past, but exist in a continuum which constantly relives change along the timeline – as in the work of Mitchison or in Elphinstone's *Islanders* (1994). In this respect one of the most promising writers is James Robertson, whose *The Fanatic* (2000) tries with real success to perform the difficult tasks of simultaneously discovering the sixteenth-century motivations of religious rebels (including the legendary Major Weir) and linking them with contemporary Edinburgh characters.

Andrew Greig's *When They Lay Bare* (discussed above) could be considered here, for its linking of older *mores* to the present; while Hunter Steele's *The Lords of Montplaisir* (1989) is a witty and history-mocking post-modern treatment of sixteenth-century France. Also great fun is the audacious blending of genres by David Wishart (*I, Virgil*, 1994, *Ovid*, 1995, *Nero*, 1996, *Germanicus*, 1997, *Sejanus*, 1998), resulting in a fiction which frequently crosses Alan Massie with Raymond Chandler, illustrating that it is the essence of good creative writing to avoid neat classification.

CRIME AND DETECTIVE FICTION AS SERIOUS LITERATURE?
The claims of this genre to be considered as serious literature were discussed in the previous chapter. Arguably, the recurrent narrowness of character delineation in their detectives (lonely, misunderstood, determined, and successful), together with the limitations of the genre's plots and perspectives, must usually argue against their being accepted as literature of high quality; but since McIlvanney's *Laidlaw* series it is recognised that exceptions exist, wherein crime is used as metaphor for modern society. Undeniably the most successful in this more ambitious vein is Ian Rankin, who started with an impressive study of a decaying mining willage and its strange wasteland happenings in *The Flood* (1986), but who quickly settled into thrillers, beginning the immensely successful Inspector Rebus series with *Knots and Crosses* in 1987; there are now over fourteen Rebus novels. With McIlvanney, Frederic Lindsay in his study of evil in *Brond* (1983) arguably inaugurated a new wave of Scottish crime fiction; and this, followed by *Jill Rips* (1987), *A Charm against Drowning* (1988) and *After the Stranger Came* (1992) showed a unique talent for probing darker places of the mind. Lindsay has been successful in his creation of Inspector Jim Meldrum, a recent production being *Death Knock* (2000). And recent successes in the vein include Quintin

Jardine with his Inspector Skinner series beginning with *Skinner's Rules* (1993); Chris Brookmyre with his endearing nosy journalist Jack Parlabain in *Quite Ugly One Morning* (1996) to *Boiling a Frog* (2000); Ron Mackay's bleak-ending modern versions of *No Mean City* in *Mean City* (1995), and *The Leper Colony* (1997); and Paul Johnston's sci-fi thrillers from *Body Politic* (1997) to *The Blood Tree* (2000). Four women seem a cut above the rest in their unconventional presentations of women in men's worlds, and their unwillingness to follow the predictable rules of detective and thriller fiction. They are Ajay Close in her intelligent and subtle *Official and Doubtful* (1996) and *Forspoken* (1998); Denise Mina in one of the darkest of psychological dramas, *Garnethill* (1998); Manda Scott with her lesbian psychologist amidst grotesque horrors in *Hen's Teeth* (1996), *Nightmares* (1998) and *Stronger than Death* (1999); and quite simply the outstanding example of an apparent detective story which really does prove that the genre can overcome its limitations, Val McDermid in *A Place of Execution* (1999), a haunting account of a north of England moorland community's way of dealing with its evil-doers, full of atmosphere of place and reversing expectations in a way which reduces its central policeman to pleasingly human scale. This is probably the best so far of her distinguished novels. Finally, completely different in tone and perspective, Alexander McCall Smith's delightful series beginning with *The No 1 Ladies Detective Agency* is warmly recommended.

SHORT STORIES

As the annual volume of *Scottish Short Stories* from the Scottish Arts Council showed for twenty-five years (1973–97), Scottish short story writing is a distinguished genre. Only a few of the outstanding contemporary practitioners can be mentioned here. Spark is of course one of the greatest of short story writers, and this work was collected in a single volume in 2001 as *The Complete Short Stories*. We have noted the work here of writers like Brown, Crichton Smith, Dunn, Galloway, Gray, Kelman, Kennedy, McIlvanney, McLean, McCabe, Rose, Spence and newer writers like Michel Faber and Chris Dolan. Some newcomers deserve mention: poet and novelist John Burnside's first short stories, *Burning Elvis* (2000); Regi Claire in *Inside-Outside* (1998); Janet Paisley in *Wildfire* (1993); Bridget Penney in *Honeymoon with Death* (1991); James Robertson in *The Ragged Man's Complaint* (1993); Ali Smith in *Free Love* (1995) and *Other Stories and Other Stories* (1999); Alexander McCall Smith in *Heavenly Date* (1995); and Ruth Thomas with *Sea Monster Tattoo* (1997), and *The Dance Settee* (1999). Finally, the interested reader is referred to the Macallan/*Scotland on Sunday* annual volume *Shorts* for the best of contemporary short fiction.

978

Conclusion: the wind shifts again – towards millennial affirmation?

It is impossible to account for all that is going on today in the astonishingly rich and varied world of Scottish fiction. This essay has argued that the overriding characteristic of Scottish fiction in the last two decades has been towards a more positive – if questioning – relationship with self and society in Scotland – and beyond. Writers like Crichton Smith, Spence, and Gray seemed to have found a kind of grace and hope, and it also seemed that hitherto stern 'realist' writers were mellowing. Beyond the positivity of Gray's fictions, writers like Kelman in later work like *How Late It Was, How Late* (1994), Galloway in *Foreign Parts* (1994), and others including Greig, Kennedy and MacDougall allowed a new mood of human acceptance, qualified optimism, and reconciliation. Even Robin Jenkins seemed to be following this mood in *Poverty Castle* (1991), with its hints of reconciliation between classes and different values – though such is Jenkins's mastery of ambiguity in tone and situation that the reader is never sure; and in some of the most recent fiction, *Willie Hogg* (1993) and *Poor Angus* (2000), he returns to his dark ambiguities with a vengeance.

And as the millennium approached, something of the old grimness reappeared, Crichton Smith's last novel, *An Honourable Death* (1992), expressed continuing anger at anachronistic Imperialism and Victorian intolerance, while existential stoicism re-emerged in Kelman's *The Good Times* (1998). Along with the scepticism of Welsh's disenchanted new generation, can be set the bleakness of new writers like John Burnside, Michel Faber, Toni Davidson. The development of the fiction of Duncan McLean, one of the central figures in new Scottish fiction, whose *Bucket of Tongues* (1992) was such a notable development of the Kelman tradition, illustrates this. Deliberately playing with the ideas of a return to rural mythologies in *Blackden* (1994), and echoing Grassic Gibbon's short story title, 'Greenden', he juxtaposed the village's evolution into the new ways of bar suppers, fast cars, television chat shows with surviving older ways of life, recalled at a public roup, or in young Patrick's love of his grandparents, and their stories – and the surviving Satanism which lingered in hidden places. This seemed to allow for ghosts of an older past having some significance for today; but *Bunker Man* (1995), with its chilling and tragic exposé of suppressed male desires, suggests that the past is another country, and that present rural, as well as urban, Scottish community is gone. Is the pendulum simply swinging back to a recurrent Scottish pessimism?

Something fundamental has changed, however. Welsh, McLean, and Burnside are only a part (though a forceful and vital part) of the picture.

Scottish fiction has a huge new range, and women have transformed the scene. Kelman and Gray perhaps summarise the two main directions of Scottish writing now; on one hand, Gray's urging that his readers – and Scotland's writers – work as though they live in the early days of a better nation; on the other, Kelman's existential concern that the human condition is deeply flawed, and that in the brave new Scotland there is still much to be depressed about. For the overall mood of Scottish fiction and writing seems now to be a mixture of optimism, uncertainty and a desire to challenge what seem to most writers to be anachronistic and tired clichés of Scotland. In very different ways almost all the writers listed above challenge limits of language, gender, received history, and authority, be it in law, education, religion. Scottish fiction – and indeed Scottish writing generally – is now more varied in mood, more eclectic, and more willing to challenge Scotland's traditional beliefs and values than ever before. The results of this new eclecticism are unpredictable; the story of Scotland and Scottish culture is clearly being rewritten.

CHAPTER 42

WIDENING THE RANGE 6

PART ONE: NON-FICTION PROSE AND SHORT STORIES
Anthologies

This volume has focused primarily on the main genres of fiction, drama, and poetry – while drawing attention to non-fiction prose where appropriate, as for example that of James Boswell in the eighteenth century, that of Thomas Carlyle and Hugh Miller in the nineteenth, or work ranging from Compton Mackenzie's mammoth autobiographies to Mackay Brown's spiritual account of his islands in *An Orkney Tapestry* in the twentieth. For those wishing to explore further, the following additional suggestions comprise a brief guide to some of the most rewarding of the vivid and varied memoirs of Scots through the ages. A fuller account of twentieth-century material is given in Robert Crawford's helpful *Literature in Twentieth-Century Scotland* (1995). Several modern volumes have appeared which collect lively accounts of lives across the range of Scottish life – as in Karl Miller's collection of writers and influential cultural voices in *Memoirs of a Modern Scotland* (1970); and Trevor Royle's collection *Jock Tamson's Bairns* (1977), vivid memories of twelve Scots, from Bill Bryden to Liz Lochhead, remembering the pains and joys of adolescence. Similarly ten Scottish writers recall how writing began in Maurice Lindsay's *As I Remember* (1979). More generally, a huge range of perspectives and insights from history is to be found in T. C. Smout and Sidney Wood's *Scottish Voices 1745–1960* (1990). Billy Kay made a memorable radio series about dying working communities which he edited in two volumes as a collection of essays allowing the people to speak in *Odyssey: Voices from Scotland's Recent Past* (1980 and 1982); here are the Glasgow Irish, St Kildans, Dundee and its jute workers, Shetland whalers, Italians in Scotland, the lace-makers of Ayrshire, and many more who have vanished. More recently, Timothy Neat records the voices of a passing generation of Highland workers and Gaelic bards in his *Highland Quintet. The Summer Walkers* (1996) records the voices and memories of travelling people and pearl fishers; *The Voice of the Bard* (1999) listens to those who continue the ancient bardic traditions. *When I was Young*, which records voices from lost communities in Scotland is in two parts: *The Islands* (2000) and *The Highlands and East Coast* (2000).

Some general readers – sadly, too few – will wish to go back to medieval material. For these enthusiasts a good starting point would be *The History of Scottish Literature: Origins to 1660*, vol. 1 edited by Ronald Jack (1988), in which R. J. Lyall tackles 'Vernacular Prose before the Reformation'. For the period following the Reformation of 1560, Ronald Jack in *Scottish Prose 1550–1700* (1971) gives a stimulating selection of writers like Knox, Buchanan, Lindsay of Pitscottie, James V, William Drummond, Thomas Urquhart, and some of the vivid diarists of the age – as did J. G. Fyfe in his still valuable *Scottish Diaries and Memoirs 1746–1843* (1942), which has samples of some of the most outstanding non-fiction writers of the period like Alexander 'Jupiter' Carlyle, John Ramsay of Auchtertyre and Henry Cockburn (see the 'Widening the Range' chapters for fuller details). A richly informative and pioneering collection of Scottish women's prose writing has been collected by Dorothy McMillan in *The Scotswoman at Home and Abroad: Non-Fiction Writing 1700– 1900* (2000). Here are women's thoughts and reactions to their living conditions and repressions over two centuries, from working class to aristocracy; and from Lowlands to the far islands and abroad.

Pre-twentieth century

The letters of writers like Burns and Scott are of course primary material for their age; recently G. Ross Roy added to J. De Lancey Ferguson's *The Letters of Robert Burns* (1985) to produce the definitive edition, while H. J. C. Grierson had done so earlier for Scott, in *The Letters of Sir Walter Scott* (12 vols, 1932–7); this will be supplemented by Jane Millgate's forthcoming edition. In the period of Scott there is of course Scott's own writing across the range of Scottish history and culture, and his magnificient and sombre account of the last disaster-plagued seven years of his life, his *Journal* (first published in 1890, and available in the edition of W. E. K. Anderson, 1971). Arguably the greatest biography next to Boswell's *Johnson* is that by Scott's son-in-law, J. G. Lockhart, *Memoirs of the Life of Scott* (5 vols, 1837–8); and one of the fullest and most entertaining accounts of Scottish and Edinburgh cultural life in the time of Scott is Lockhart's intriguing blend of fiction and social history in *Peter's Letters to his Kinsfolk* (1818) – William Ruddick edited it in 1977. The non-fiction of James Hogg remains to be collected in a single volume; his essays, such as those on rural events like the wedding, funeral, and dogs of a Border shepherd bring this forgotten world to life. Already noted are the still vital, radical and provocative essays on Scottish land and landowners, and the sometimes horrific mistreatment of the poor, by Hugh Miller, the Cromarty stonemason and Free Church leader of the 1840s (George Rosie has a stimulating selection, *Outrage and Order*, 1981). The vivid memories of the liberal-minded judge, Henry Cockburn, in *Memorials of his Time* (1856), and *Circuit Journeys* (1888) bring nineteenth-century Edinburgh and Scotland to life. Jeremy Treglown selected the best of Robert Louis Stevenson's essays in *The Lantern Bearers* (1987); these show just how 'modern' and exciting a writer Stevenson could be. Recently John Walker has selected several volumes of the prose of R. B. Cunninghame Graham, the strange and many-sided genius of Scotland at the turn of the century – some of the best of Graham's prose is in *The Scottish Sketches* (1982).

Twentieth century

In the twentieth century, recommendations include Edwin Muir's wonderful *An Autobiography* (1954), which moves from some of the finest recreations of childhood scenes in literature, beginning in Orkney and island life, then lives through a nightmare experience of Glasgow just before the First World War, to move to war-time Czechoslovakia and Europe. Along with this should be read his sombre account of Depression squalor in Lowland Scotland, *Scottish Journey* (1935). G. M. Brown edited Muir's *Selected Prose* (1987). Neglected, but arguably one of the finest diaries of the twentieth century, is William Soutar's detached yet poignant record of his bed-ridden imprisonment through disease for thirteen years in *Diaries of a Dying Man*, kept till the day before his death [1954] (1988). Less detached is MacDiarmid's egotistical but still vastly impressive autobiography of his early and tormented years in *Lucky Poet* (1943). Lewis Grassic Gibbon's marvellous essays on 'The Land', 'Glasgow', 'The Antique Scene' and the like should not be forgotten – they were gathered in *A Scots Hairst* by Ian Munro in 1967; and D. M. Budge put them together with the short stories for the Longman Heritage series in 1980. MacDiarmid and Grassic Gibbon collaborated in *Scottish Scene: Or the Intelligent Man's Guide to Albyn* (1934) which stands out as an eccentric yet vital survey of Scotland in various genres. Eric Linklater's autobiography appears in *The Man on my Back* (1947) *A Year of Space* (1953) and *Fanfare for a Tin Hat* (1970). Neil Gunn's prose in *Whisky and Scotland* (1935), *Highland Pack* (1949) (the former being a spiritual history of Scotland most cleverly presented through the metaphor of Scottish drink) and *The Atom of Delight* (1956), his unusual and yet deeply revealing spiritual autobiography, is a rich part of this Renaissance non-fiction. Other major Renaissance writers who have produced intriguing prose include Sorley MacLean, whose distinguished writing on Gaelic culture appeared in *Ris a' Bhruthaich: Criticism and Prose Writings*, edited by William Gillies in 1985. More recently, poets Iain Crichton Smith and Robert Garioch have produced fine non-fiction prose – the first in his essays on his background and growth as a writer in *Towards the Human* (1986), the second in *Two Men and a Blanket* (1975), his account of how prisoners of war made it through Italian and German camps – and, even more recently, Kenneth White has searched for his unique White territory in *Travels in the Drifting Dawn* (1989); and Hamish Henderson has produced *Alias McAlias: Writings on Songs, Folk and Literature* (1992).

There are fine contributions from women, as in Catherine Carswell's revolutionary biography, her *Life of Robert Burns* (1930), which shocked conventional Burns scholars; or Willa Muir's attack on Scottish parochialism in *Mrs Grundy in Scotland* (1936). She worked on her husband's notes after his death to produce *Living with Ballads* (1965); and her account of her relationship with Edwin is in *Belonging: A Memoir* (1968). The redoubtable Naomi Mitchison has several volumes of autobiography, from *Small Talk* (1973) and *All Change Here* (1975) to *You May Well Ask* (1979) and her memories from wartime in Kintyre, *Among you Taking Notes* (1985). Other womens' memoirs include Catherine Carswell's *Lying Awake* (1950), Hannah Aitken's *In a Shaft of Sunlight* (1947), Molly Weir's *Shoes Were for Sunday* (1970), Evelyn Cowan's *Spring Remembered: A Scottish Jewish Childhood* (1974), and Janetta Bowie's trilogy of Clydeside schools in the 30s, 50s and 70s *Penny Buff, Penny Boss* and *Penny Change* (1975–7). *The Christian Watt Papers* (1983) is the fascinating and moving story of a Fraserburgh fishwife's hard life from domestic service to fishgutter to asylum for the insane – when she was totally sane; a testimony to one woman's strength and power of endurance. All these testify to the difficulties placed before independent women.

Other kinds of Scottish lives are movingly recalled in John R. Allan's account of north-east farming, *Farmer's Boy* (1935); David Daiches's *Two Worlds: An Edinburgh Jewish Childhood* (1957) – which could be read with Evelyn Cowan's *Spring Remembered* (1974) and Muriel Spark's *Curriculum Vitae* (1992), which includes her version of being a Jewish child in the capital; Ian Niall's *A Galloway Childhood* (1967) – Niall has prose 'factions' too numerous to mention here, which recall the lives of foresters, poachers, village policemen, shepherds of the south-west which give some of the richest coverage we have of any region of Scotland (see Chapter 40). David Toulmin and David Kerr Cameron achieve a similar richness in their evocations of the north-east, Toulmin in volumes like *Hard Shining Corn, Straw into Gold, Harvest Home* and *A Chiel Among Them* (1972–82), and Cameron in his wonderful trilogy *The Ballad and the Plough* (1978), *Willie Gavin, Crofter Man* (1980) and *Cornkister*

Days (1984). A bittersweet and passionate elegy for a lost West Highland way of life is given by the poet Alasdair MacLean in *Night Falls on Ardnamurchan* (1984); while Ralph Glaser reductively analyses a Highland village suspiciously like that of Glenelg, near Skye, in *Scenes from a Highland Life* (1981). Gavin Maxwell recalled the same area in the best of his several fine memoirs of a wandering naturalist's – and misfit's – life, *Ring of Bright Water* (1960), the best-selling account of his friendship with otters. David Thomson recorded his childhood and the older history of *Nairn in Darkness and Light* (1987), focusing much Scottish history and lore in the old town of Nairn on the Moray Firth. And in *On the Crofter's Trail* (1990), David Craig followed the sad movement of cleared Highlanders across to the Americas.

Understandably, childhood memories are one of the richest veins of Scottish prose. In addition to those listed, some of the finest include John Muir's *The Story of my Boyhood and Youth* (1924) and *My First Summer in the Sierra* (1911), the surprisingly little known story of the pioneering Scottish ecologist who began the National Park movement in North America. *The Early Life of James McBey: An Autobiography* (1977) is the deceptively simple story of one of Scotland finest painters, from his desperately sad youth to his maturity and fame. Christian Miller's *A Childhood in Scotland* (1981), at the other end of the social scale, is a non-fiction version of Elspeth Barker's *O Caledonia* (1991) in its picture of a lonely young aristocratic girlhood in a glum Scottish castle; in stark contrast is Ralph Glaser's *Growing up in the Gorbals* (1986).

Glasgow memoirs are many, from those of James Bridie in *One Way of Living* (1939) to the fictionalised account of Archie Hind in *The Dear Green Place* (1966). Some of the most accessible and lively memories are in Cliff Hanley's *Dancing in the Streets* (1958). Anna Blair also records a lost Glasgow vividly in *Tea at Miss Cranston's: A Century of Glasgow Memories* (1985); while a fascinating series of articles and miniature essays about the city makes up Donald Saunders's collection, *A Glasgow Diary* (1984), which can be read with interesting comparisons with Trevor Royle's *A Diary of Edinburgh* (1981).

Specialist memoirs and commentaries are often richly rewarding, from Rebecca West's monumental and disturbingly prophetic account of her Yugoslavian experiences in *Black Lamb and Grey Falcon* (1942) to Stuart Hood's *Pebbles from my Skull* (1963), vivid accounts of partisan Second World War experience, and James Cameron's *Points of Departure* (1963). These are the recollections of two of the most distinguished of Scottish journalists and broadcasters, and could be read with those of their modern counterparts, Neil Ascherson in *Games with Shadows* (1988) and *Black Sea* (1995), the latter comparable in its insights into middle Europe with Rebecca West's Yugoslavian analyses, and Ian Jack's wide-ranging commentary on post-war Scotland and Britain in *Before the Oil Ran Out: Britain in the Brutal Years* (1997). This could usefully be paired with William McIlvanney's *Surviving the Shipwreck* (1991), a similarly disenchanted view of post-1979 referendum Scotland and Britain. A sustained attack on the British Establishment is in Tom Nairn's *The Breakup of Britain* (1981), *The Enchanted Glass* (1990), and *After Britain* (2000).

Moving into the 1990s, the sheer variety of Scottish non-fiction prose continues, paralleling the new eclecticism of Scottish writing. Some outstanding examples include the work of Karl Miller, who had produced a fascinating re-creation of mid-nineteenth century Edinburgh and Scotland in *Cockburn's Millennium* (1975). His *Doubles* (1987) explored doppelgängers in Scottish and world literature, and his *Rebecca's Vest* (1993) finally came back to himself as subject, to tell how he moved from a humble Lothian background to become a distinguished academic and critic. Alastair Reid's *Whereabouts* (1987) and *Oases* (1997) are the accounts of a peripatetic poet and writer who has had homes in several countries, and is indeed at home in them all. William Dalrymple is one of the finest of modern travel writers, whose award-winning studies of India are uniquely rich in their evocations, as in *In Xanadu* (1990), *City of Djinns: A Year in Delhi* (1993), and *The Age of Kali: Indian Travels and Encounters* (1998). Novelist Duncan McLean went on a Country and Western pilgrimage in *Lone Star Swing* (1997), while likewise, but for very different and complex reasons Alison Kennedy explored a culture she was at once fascinated and repelled by, in *On Bullfighting* (1999). Poet Andrew Greig writes compellingly of his other love, mountaineering, this time in the Himalayas, in *Kingdoms of Experience: Everest, the Unclimbed Ridge* (1999) – and coming back to Scotland and Britain, Andrew O'Hagan tries to follow the trail of the forlorn figures who disappear, for various reasons, in *The Missing* (1995). All these corroborate the view that Scottish writers are restlessly moving around and out of Scotland, into new territories, personal and public.

PART TWO: A NOTE ON THE SCOTTISH SHORT STORY

This guide has included short stories as part of the overall treatment of the work of novelists and others. What follows is a short discussion of the individuating features of the Scottish short story, which attempts to identify origins of the genre.

Our modern stories have their roots in a tradition where stories were told to entertain. This imaginative pact between speaker and audience goes back to the oral tradition of the Highlands and islands and to the great store of ballads, which are essentially sung, rather than spoken, poetic narratives. Both these folk traditions are presently alive and flourishing in Scotland.

Their influence is perhaps more obvious in our earlier story writers, where the narrator takes centre stage, often presenting the story as something he, or someone known to him, either experienced or heard and almost always adding personal corroborative detail. This brings into focus an aspect of storytelling, which until it was highlighted in the ambitious modern collection edited by Carl MacDougall *The Devil and the Giro* (1989) had more or less been ignored – the role of the first person narrator.

Our beginnings in the oral tradition mean that the images have to be sharp and characters must arrive fully formed, rather than given time to develop. This precision, which is often obvious in poetry, can be ignored in short story writing where the reader may be blinded by narrative or characterisation, but it is a precision whose vitality comes from the fact that it is imposed by the form. Indeed, it is difficult to read a collection of Scottish stories without becoming aware of the spoken voice and the power of first person narration, something which is crucial to an understanding, not to mention appreciation of the Scottish short story. It establishes the tone and direction of the story by forming an immediate emotional and intellectual pact with the reader, appearing, in every instance, to take the reader into the writer's confidence. Not surprisingly, it is the first decision a writer takes and one he or she is often not aware of making, since its influence can be instinctive.

It establishes mood and narrows the focus by trapping the reader into seeing the action through the eyes of the character. It is also a wonderful way of insinuating detail. It is the one device a writer has which does more than one thing simultaneously. It establishes character, background, place, nationality and class, can tell us a range of details from mood to preferences and, most importantly, can take us inside a person's head, allowing us to walk around with him or her, to discover what they are thinking and feeling so that we can think and feel it too. Because the writer has established the reader's confidence, she has established an identity and trust to which the reader responds by accepting what she has to tell, usually without question – take, for example, the opening of 'Sunday Class' by Elspeth Davie, with the importance of the opening word, which moves the reader into the room like a camera.

Scottish culture played an important role in the coming of books and the rise of a reading public, not just here, but throughout Europe. Publications such as *The Edinburgh Review* and *Blackwood's Magazine* were early and major influences, and some of the writers from this period, such as James Hogg, Sir Walter Scott and John Galt, played important roles in establishing the mood and tone of written literature. Hogg, for example, can certainly be said to have anticipated Dostoevsky in the study of psychological division, and Galt's interest in family and social history pointed the way to the novels of Balzac and Zola. Most importantly of all, Scott was internationally famous and widely acknowledged by many European and US writers as a major influence.

Imaginative prose is a well established feature of Scottish intellectual life and could be said to be one of the few constants which both fed and was nourished by the general dissemination of ideas, certainly more so than poetry, which we tend to see in terms of individuals. This tradition lives on, and its presence is both hidden and intensified by the power of first person narration. It is difficult, not to say boring, within the scope and demands of a short story, to make a character narrated in the third person say more than the range of his action permits and to do so without implying the discreet intervention of the author. On the other hand, it is entirely legitimate for a first person character to give himself over to reflection, reasoning, philosophical meanderings and the like. But craftiest of all are those who use the intimacy of first person narration within a third person narrative, marrying insight and detachment. It is a device which is usually used to carry another, as in 'The Sailing Ship', when Edward Gaitens uses it not only to sustain anger, but to embrace what at first appears to be a contradictory notion, that far from being limited by surroundings and conditions, the working class have a capacity for dreaming; and that dreaming is something which sustains their condition. Gaitens uses it to provide a solution to Johnny Regan's unemployment and poverty, a solution which is ultimately illusory, but which fuels another dream, the dream of escape.

Gaitens is especially skilled in another of Scottish writing's tactical devices, the use of details to insinuate information, a feature which, again, is directly linked to the oral tradition. Early on, he uses it as a means of establishing the character and his surroundings. This, again, is a feature of Scottish writing which takes on a renewed importance when examined in the light of the influences and inspirations which it has offered to the USA and Europe, such as the use of the supernatural as a medium for a variety of explorations, a powerful relationship with landscape, and the instantly recognisable, though curiously defined doppelgänger search for identity, a device which makes most sense when it is seen as a symptom rather than a cause or creative impulse.

Scottish writers have become especially adept in their ways of using first person narration. Stream-of-consciousness is common, especially when dealing with the young mind or in establishing the problems of identity, as in Iain Crichton Smith's wonderful 'Murdo'. In 'Celia', George Mackay Brown interrupts a third person narrative by inserting the principal character's own voice, as does Alasdair Gray. Writers as apparently different as Sir Walter Scott and Tom Leonard use interior monologues, as do William Boyd, James Kelman, Alexander Reid, Jessie Kesson and Brian McCabe. John Buchan combines local identity, another common feature of Scottish writing, with the inquisitiveness of a young man trying to understand himself and his country. And writers as diverse as Lewis Grassic Gibbon and Ronald Frame, Robert McLellan and John Herdman use language as a means of identifying character, place and class.

Especially interesting is the way in which all the above factors combine with a peculiarly Scottish sense of irony in the works of traditional storytellers. There are two examples in *The Devil and the Giro*. Duncan Williamson's 'Death in a Nut' was transcribed orally, then adapted for the page, and Betsy Whyte's 'The Man in the Boat' is a direct oral transcription. There are a number of stories where the voice of the community can be heard, as if the writer were a sort of Everyman, speaking directly on behalf of his or her community, and addressing an issue which is particular to that community – or, more importantly, offering an insight into the community, giving an understanding of how it works. In this regard and many others, Betsy Whyte's tale is fascinating. It not only give an interesting perspective on the outsider and the traditional role the travellers have adopted, but is an intriguing view of character in Scottish fiction where a shy, somewhat repressed man literally changes sex and in the process becomes a quite different person. Not only does it raise questions of national and personal identity, but in its light John Herdman's Clapperton, Iain Crichton Smith's Murdo and the specific duality of Fred Urquhart's Robert/Hilda take on new and entirely different perspectives.

Perhaps this alteration of perspective is best seen in the work of women writers. Short stories from authors as different as Margaret Oliphant and Muriel Spark use details to build an atmosphere which they then tellingly take apart, or allow to dissipate. The façades erected by the women in Rosa Macpherson and Jessie Kesson's stories are characteristically different from men's; Kesson's child narrator appears to be speaking to a secret friend, or perhaps an older self, which creates the impression of an unspoken history which is shared with the reader (a technique also used with success by Brian McCabe).

And many Scottish writers show a fascination with the young mind, in ways which allow them to explore Scottishness. Elspeth Davie, Edward Gaitens, Muriel Spark, George Friel, Alan Spence and Ronald Frame all lay bare the nuances and crippling divisions of class and class values in Scottish society.

Spence sees life as bleak, violent and ultimately dangerous, with a faint strand of hope running through the narrative. His story and Jessie Kesson's are clearly autobiographical.

But what of Eona Macnicol's 'The Small Herdsman', which not only adopts an autobiographical approach, but combines many opposing features, rural and urban, natural and supernatural, personal and social, ancient and modern, child and adult? It takes us to the heart of an idyllic, rural Scotland with lilting accents and a curious young herdsman who could be one of the fairy folk – and is certainly thought to be so by the child narrator, until the cold facts of another, urban experience come pouring in, bringing an entirely new perspective in their wake.

These examples have been taken from *The Devil and the Giro*, a volume familiar to many readers, which offers more than fifty writers under a collective roof. But there are other short story writers not included in that collection, as well as writers whose work is lost in magazine or which has never been gathered into an individual collection. Works by Agnes Owens, Dilys Rose, Janice Galloway, Candia McWilliam, Willa Muir, Shena Mackay, Catherine Carswell, Nancy Bryson Morrison, Nan Shepherd, William McIlvanney, Ron Butlin, Jeff Torrington, Neil McCormick, William Montgomerie, Neil Paterson, Alistair MacLeod, Duncan McLean, Irvine Welsh, Carl MacDougall and many other writers take issue against the continuing baleful influence of the Kailyard, but indicate that our continuing search for identity and need for a history has deeper roots and stronger growth.

(This entry is by Carl MacDougall, novelist and editor of *The Devil and the Giro*.)

PART THREE:
SCREEN ADAPTATIONS OF THE SCOTTISH NOVEL

Since the early days of cinema, Scottish novels have been adapted often, and sometimes well, for both cinema and television. From Hollywood's early silent years, through the heydays of the studio era, to the age of television, and beyond, film-makers on both sides of the Atlantic have returned time and time again to matters Scottish, and their literary representations, for root material to transform into the specific languages of a mainly popular screen storytelling. What follows offers a general account of this process, but draws short of providing an exhaustive catalogue of what is a large and extensive body of work. This account generally avoids judgement of either the nature or extent of adaptation, working from the premise that all adaptations are essentially separate texts which might occasionally offer some parallels to a literary original.

From the point of view of film history, A. J. Cronin provides an interesting starting point for our account. Cronin is, perhaps surprisingly, the Scottish novelist whose work has provided US cinema with its most commercially fruitful source of film-making. In the years around the outbreak of the Second World War, Cronin's novels provided the major studios with a heady brew of melodrama to match the spirit of the times. Cronin's mix of heightened social realism, dogged moral purpose, small community life and family tension provided the USA with a highly palatable account of a Celtic/British culture still to be fully sugared and sentimentalised in the post-war years by such films as *Whisky Galore!* (1949) and *Brigadoon* (1954).

Hollywood's Cronin series was launched in 1938 at MGM with a British-based production of *The Citadel*, directed by the legendary King Vidor. Although Cronin's tense account of the testing of a young doctor's idealism in the slums of a Welsh mining village was given a softer ending for the movie audience, the film nevertheless caught much of the spirit of its literary original and is usually remembered for a typically sensitive and strong performance by Robert Donat. An equally lauded director, George Stevens, also turned to Cronin's fiction in 1939 with another medically-focused melodrama, *Vigil in the Night*, which was seen as a worthy vehicle by RKO for the talents of Carole Lombard.

In 1941, Paramount and director Lance Comfort exploited the success of these earlier movies with a wonderfully Gothic production of Cronin's dark family tale, *Hatter's Castle*. With a setting that seems closer to Glasgow than Cronin's native Dumbarton, *Hatter's Castle* provided an excellent vehicle for the stylised talents of Robert Newton, an actor, like Donat, who would make various appearances in films with loosely Scottish connections. *Hatter's Castle* also includes a strong performance from Deborah Kerr, providing the perfect foil for Newton's gift for melodrama.

Two generations of television viewers well acquainted with comforting series of the anodyne *Doctor Finlay's Casebook* might find the Hollywood Cronin a little strong in taste. Nevertheless his writing caught both the mood of the studios and their massive cinema audiences in the late 1930s and early 1940s and provided a fine vein of the melodrama which was the staple diet of the mass US film-goer of the period.

If Cronin provided one distinct and highly palatable image of Scottish and British culture for US audiences, another successful source has been provided by the novels of Walter Scott and Robert Louis Stevenson. With Scott

991

and Stevenson, we enter a different terrain, but another which is equally viable as a stereotype of Scottish culture to film-going audiences. While Cronin provided melodrama and a kind of realism, Scott and Stevenson's fiction contains within it the spirit of romance, history and individualism which translates effectively into the narrative of popular film.

The US silent cinema, which turned to the nineteenth-century European novels not only for many of its themes and tales, but also for much of its hoped-for legitimacy, made much of the source material provided by the great Scottish novelists. As early as 1908, Vitagraph had adapted Scott's *The Bride of Lammermoor* for brief but dramatic two-reel treatment, and this was followed by versions of *Rob Roy* (1911), *Heart of Midlothian* (1914) and Stevenson's *The Bottle Imp* (1917) and *Kidnapped* (1917). It is worth remembering that this was not only a US taste for the Celtic and exotic; many Scots, including D. W. Griffith's legendary actor and heavy, Donald Crisp, had become part of Hollywood's cultural mix and were eager to import what they might have regarded as the finer, or commercial, elements of their cultural heritage. Crisp himself was to take the lead role in a version of *Beside the Bonnie Brier Bush* (1921).

While Scott and Stevenson's tales fell out of fashion in the more austere and contemporaneous film-making of the early sound decades, they were to return to popularity with a vigour in the 1950s. Many mainstream Hollywood films of that period demanded, literally, stories for the big canvas and rich Technicolor. The western and the musical were among the decade's most successful genres, and the studios returned to the novels of Scott and Stevenson for equally powerful tales of heroism and romance. Disney studios led the way with adaptations of the historical Scots novel, and over a period of ten years provided benchmark treatments for popular adaptations of the costume adventure.

The first of these was the legendary 1950 version of *Treasure Island* with Robert Newton as a marvellous Long John Silver. This writer is one of many of his generation who tasted Stevenson first in its Disney variety and found this to be an equal, if different pleasure, from the later exposure to the literary original. The series continued with Richard Todd as Rob Roy in 1953, and Peter Finch as a plausible Alan Breck in the 1960 version of *Kidnapped*.

It is also worth mentioning Warner's swashbuckling version of *The Master of Ballantrae* made in 1953, and starring a distinctly mature Errol Flynn. Despite Warner's reputation for film realism this is cinema at its most wonderfully dramatic, and camp. It is well worth watching out for on television on a wet Saturday afternoon or bank holiday morning. Compare this to Robert Wise and Val Lewton's eerie black and white adaptation of *The Body Snatcher* from

1945 to see the range of approaches which a writer such as Stevenson can provide for an industry happy to exploit the wide freedoms of loose adaptation.

Interest in Scott and Stevenson has remained strong in more recent times. A highly entertaining *Kidnapped* was produced in 1971, with Michael Caine as a strongly ironical Alan Breck. Michael York and John Gielgud starred in a 1983 Hollywood version of *The Master of Ballantrae*. Recent cinema-goers will be familiar with the US 1994 version of *Rob Roy*. The strongly Scottish involvement in this film – directed by Michael Caton-Jones with a screenplay by Alan Sharp – ensures that it offers a strong portrayal of the mythical dimensions of the story, while keeping some recognition of Scott's source text. A much less successful adaptation of recent years was Stephen Frears's US production of *Mary Reilly* (1996). Despite a strong cast, this version of Stevenson's *Doctor Jekyll and Mr Hyde* never quite recovered from a brave Christopher Hampton adaptation which located narrative point of view in Julia Roberts's downstairs maid. The film's late release stemmed from significant post-production reworking of the ending which reduced much of the quality of Hampton's work to the level of mock-Victorian Gothic. *Mary Reilly* is an unfortunate (current) ending to Hollywood's generally successful relationship with the novels of Scott and Stevenson. It can be assumed that the relationship is durable enough to survive this particular disaster.

Apart from Cronin, Stevenson and Scott, most cinema-goers will have experienced the Scottish novel in adaptation through the works of John Buchan and Compton Mackenzie. Buchan's *The Thirty-Nine Steps* has undergone three highly popular adaptations for cinema. The 1935 version by Alfred Hitchcock is, of course, legendary, and marks one of the high points of Hitchcock's British period. His formula of extremely loose adaptation mingled with a nod to the Scottish landscape (and landmarks) was used again in 1959 with Ralph Thomas's very British version starring Kenneth More in the Hannay role. More, although a very fine actor, was no Robert Donat, as Thomas was no Hitchcock, and this version appears as a weak adaptation of the earlier film, with the literary model almost lost as an original source. Don Sharp's pacey 1978 costume drama, starring Robert Powell, enjoyed considerable success on release but can now appear empty of little more than the need to convert simple plot into hectic (and good-looking) screen narrative.

Sandy Mackendrick's 1949 Ealing version of Compton Mackenzie's *Whisky Galore!* is not only a classic of the Ealing studio style but also remains one of the strongest and fondest cinema representations of Kailyard stereotypes. *Whisky Galore*'s strong mixture of whimsy and irony, of evocative Barra settings and couthy studio interiors probably sums up much of the film industry's relationship with Scotland, and certainly paved the way for the films of Bill Forsyth, a movie-maker who has so far resisted the temptation to translate the novels of his home country for the big screen.

Other novels of the early part of the century have also been adapted for cinema, but with less artistic or popular success. Two adaptations, in 1947 and 1943 respectively, at least worthy of mention, were based on Neil Gunn's *The Silver Darlings* and George Blake's *The Shipbuilders*. Neither film offers within it either the power of the original novel or any filmic element fresh enough to challenge the imagination.

More recent adaptations have proved more successful and popular. Ronald Neame's 1968 version of Jay Presson Allen's stage version of *The Prime of Miss Jean Brodie* remains evocative of 1930s Edinburgh and the rigours and hypocrisies of a Scottish middle-class upbringing. The film may lack some of the subtleties of Muriel Spark's tale of loyalty and betrayal, but it certainly adds a richness to screen portrayals of matters Scottish. It is one of the few films dealing with Scottish subject matter to embrace an urban setting, although the gentility of Spark's Edinburgh of her childhood inspires a highly specific, strongly sentimental portrayal of Scottish city life. Spark's Edinburgh is, of course, a different animal from the view of that city presented to us in Danny Boyle's frantic and witty 1995 adaptation of Irvine Welsh's *Trainspotting*. Boyle's film utilises many of the cinematic devices of his earlier *Shallow Grave* (1994) (an original screenplay) and weaves a similar narrative thread around Welsh's quirky and disarmingly amusing tales of Muirhouse heroin culture. Morningside it isn't, but it is probably one of the most successful screen adaptations of any work of Scottish fiction. Robert Carlyle's marvellously grotesque characterisation of Begbie now probably sits, at least, as strongly in the cine-consciousness of the Scottish novel as Maggie Smith's sublime portrayal of Jean Brodie.

Glasgow has often appeared in recent years on screen, but rarely as adaptation from literature. One Glasgow novel, however, which adapted particularly well in the specific case of television was Michael Caton-Jones's haunting version of *Brond* (Channel 4, 1987). Featuring a powerful cast – a young John Hannah, Stratford Johns, James Cosmo – *Brond* offered a dark portrayal of Glaswegian settings and Scottish themes. As an adaptation it came close to grasping the mixture of political thriller and weird mystery which sat at the heart of Frederic Lindsay's prose original. Glasgow was also the setting, at least in part, for Gavin Miller's 1996 television version of *The Crow Road*. Again, a superb strong cast – Bill Paterson in particular – fleshed out Iain Banks's strong cocktail of myth and mystery. Like *Brond, The Crow Road* makes excellent use of a strong variety of Scottish locations.

Brond and *The Crow Road* indicate that much of the strongest adaptation of Scottish fiction in recent decades resides wholly or partly in television, or at least in co-production between television and film. Possibly the best of these was Mike Radford's 1983 adaptation of Jessie Kesson's *Another Time, Another Place* which powerfully evoked the sparseness of landscape and power of emotion which courses through Kesson's novel of the Black Isle in war-time. Phyllis Logan's performance brings to mind the work done by Vivien Heilbron in the BBC's 1970s version of Grassic Gibbon's *Sunset Song*. Both film and series remind us of the central role inhabited by women, and specifically women from rural cultures, in many Scottish novels of the later part of the twentieth century.

Another noteworthy Channel 4 production from recent years was *Venus Peter* (1989), adapted from his own novel *A Twelvemonth and a Day* by Christopher Rush. Wonderful Orcadian backdrops and a strong, final performance by the great Ray McAnally make *Venus Peter* one of the most moving Scottish films of recent years.

Finally, there is the question of why so many significant Scottish novels, which would seem to cry out for film treatment, have been overlooked as possibilities for adaptation, or if adopted, have failed to reach the screen.

We have the script of Bill Douglas's adaptation of Hogg's *Confessions of a Justified Sinner*, but must still wonder that Scotland's greatest film-maker could not find commercial backing for a venture to turn Hogg's most Scottish of novels into cinema. It is a particularly Scottish dilemma that, perhaps, our greatest film adaptation has never reached production. It is symptomatic that a country without a film-making industry for the whole of the twentieth century cannot look back on adaptations of *Gillespie, Docherty, Lanark* or so many others of the great Scottish novels. Clearly none of these would have enhanced in themselves either the tradition of the Scottish novel, or the recent development of a vibrant proto-Scottish film industry, but such adaptations might have added richness to the cultural awareness and sense of national self-identity which is so important to small nations.

Generally, like the rest of the world, we turn to Hollywood to see how other people see us. For the most part its viewpoint has served us well, creating for us an image that is fond, exciting and often imbued with a deep sense of social justice. We wait with eagerness at the start of a new millennium, and the anticipated Scottish film industry which might, but only might, do us greater service.

PART FOUR: FUTURE DIRECTIONS; 2000 AND BEYOND

In the first few years of a new millennium, there is a temptation to be seduced by the magic of mere numbers and see the state of the nation and its culture as being poised at a significant moment. Reason tells one that this is an illusion and has no basis in any social or psychological reality. Yet the inherited habits of a tradition die hard, and one is tempted to look for some signs of a shift from a fin-de-siècle mood to a New Age spirit.

For Scotland, the beginnings of centuries have tended to be problematic in their auspices. After 1500, the apparent Renaissance promise of James IV's court was blighted by the disaster of Flodden. A similar promise under James VI in 1600 and the hope that 1700 had brought an end to religious and civil strife were for a time negated by culturally enfeebling political union. The Enlightenment spirit of 1800 coincided with a major war and social repression by a reactionary government; while the flourishing of the arts around 1900 was all too soon overshadowed by the greatest war in history to that date. Thus in approaching the twenty-first century, the canny Scot, a restored parliament notwithstanding, may be inclined to keep the fingers crossed.

Yet there can be no denying the vigorous and expanding artistic scene in Scotland today, with literature being especially healthy, as this section has illustrated. And there is no reason to suppose that there will be any slackening of pace or drying up of the considerable loch of visible native talent. All around, the literary scene is one of great diversity and productiveness within a wide range of genres and styles. Indeed, it is possible to identify a number of important factors that tend to promote, and will continue to promote a flourishing literature at different levels within the community of Scotland.

The restoration of parliament, even with limited powers, and the creation of a permanently resident political community engaged within Scotland in the multifarious official and unofficial activities that are inescapable parts of the life of such a community, is the likeliest possible stimulus to a revived politically orientated literature. It is reasonable to expect that there will in the near future be an upsurge in the writing of political satire and polemic on the issues and personalities of Scottish politics, whether in prose fiction or drama or poetry. The shade of John Galt, if it were observing the situation, might be expected to be smiling ironically as Scottish writers take up the tradition of the political novel that he almost single-handedly started in the early years of the nineteenth century.

The Scotland of 2000 is a very different kind of community from that of

1900. In a way, Scottish writing has not yet caught up with the diverse and multi-ethnic nature of modern Scotland. Perhaps this has something to do with the fact that Scottish writers today are still, by and large, members of the traditional Scottish community and cannot speak with knowledge and insight about large tracts of the Scottish social landscape. There are signs, however, as in recent issues of *New Writing Scotland*, that writers are emerging from Scotland's newer ethnic groups to bring fresher and more exotic notes into the concert of Scottish voices. A younger generation of Scottish-Asian and Scottish-Chinese writers can be expected to comment on both their own family communities and that larger mixed community to which they are assimilating in language and cultural habits. Along with the already resident Irish and English and Italian and Jewish elements, they will be part of a newer and more eclectic Scotland, the literary 'Scotlands' already alluded to in this section.

Another factor influencing the continuing Scottish literary production, and one of the most significant because of its insistent claims on the attention of us all, is the developing revolution in the media and in electronic information storage and dissemination. The expanding network of cable and satellite and digital television already makes and will continue to make insatiable demands on writers and artists for the written and spoken word and visual imagery. It has ceased to be the case that radio and television are necessarily the enemies of local speech and culture, the literature and art of quality, and the traditions of a small nation. Yet the new media in the vast television networks, in the Internet, in the computer-generated worlds of virtual reality, in the limitless opportunities of desktop publishing, will not stand still for conservative traditions and Scottish caution. The gaps are there for Scottish literary enterprise to fill, but the ideas have to flow fast and the financial investment must be made. After a shaky start, Scottish film-making has caught on to the requirements of the market; this is a creative area allied to literature where progress may be expected to continue. The same readiness to take chances and ally creativity to confidence is required in the wider area of media production and publication. Not everything that is done will be of high quality, and a large proportion of what is broadcast is likely to be populist, as in most areas of the media, but it is necessary that the Scottish presence on the channels should be claimed and consolidated.

The days when the publishing industry and the literary scene were concentrated in one place, usually the capital, whether Edinburgh or London, are rapidly passing. Partly because of the revolution in publishing and printing techniques, partly because of the communications revolution, partly also because of the mushrooming of local community writing groups,

997

the location of the writer has become less important as a factor in the creative process. Writers now work wherever they feel best, and increasingly can publish on their own. The tendency to cease to rely on the big publishing firm is bound to gain momentum, once ways are found round the continuing difficulties of distribution and marketing. The effects that this is likely to have on the literary endeavour of Scotland are to increase the potential for publication in every part of the country, to increase the existing trend towards local and regional literature, and to make it increasingly difficult to think in terms of a single unified national tradition. Thus the role of thoughtful and wide-ranging criticism is likely to become more important. The already healthy state of Scottish literary criticism should become consolidated, with a major function of the critic being to bring to national attention what is being produced by a multitude of publishing outlets.

Varieties of writing

An unfortunate and unavoidable feature of literary guides such as this is that popular writing, that which the mass of the population actually read, tends to get ignored. Whether it is a kind of critical snobbery is debatable; the fact is that there has traditionally been a separation in the minds of academic students between 'literature' and the types of genre writing that are favourites on the library shelves. A significant sign in recent years in Scottish writing has been how 'serious' or critically respected writers have moved into genre writing, such as crime stories or science fiction. There is a flourishing school of Scottish crime thriller writing, inspired by William McIlvanney's Laidlaw stories and the STV *Taggart* series, now including Ian Rankin, Peter Turnbull, Frederic Lindsay, Christopher Brookmyre and others. The tough realistic nature of Scottish detective writing owes much to US models, but is developing a characteristic Scottish flavour in its language and concerns, so much so that it is likely to become one of the characteristic strains of Scottish popular writing in the decades to come. Science fiction has been a less significant element in Scottish writing, but in recent years the novels of Iain M. Banks (as distinct from the 'mainstream novels' of Iain Banks) have built up a powerful 'futureworld' in the 'space opera' convention, and, more recently, the novels of Ken MacLeod have contributed a more 'cyberpunk' and politically motivated note to the genre in Scotland. Where these immensely popular writers have led the way, others are bound to follow.

Historical fiction in the modern sense, of course, was invented in Scotland by that prolific genius, Walter Scott, whose achievement is discussed in Section 3. Scottish practitioners of the genre have not been lacking since the early nineteenth century. The most successful modern historical writers, like Nigel Tranter and Dorothy Dunnett, are not likely to be the last in their field. The accusation that Scots are fixated on their past has some truth, but it does not have to be a bad thing so long as the looking back is not through a mist of either anger or nostalgia. The example of Dorothy Dunnett in her most recent writing should inspire followers to look at Scottish history and personalities in the wider and more impersonal contexts of European and world history. This is part of a growing internationalism in outlook that is likely to re-examine the Scottish contribution to world history freed from neuroses about a past imperial connection, and more informed about the nature of the wandering Scot throughout European history. Resulting historical writing, whether factual or fiction, should benefit in terms of balance and depth. An associated development, connected with a greater readiness to travel and to read foreign literature in translation, is likely to be a growing awareness among Scottish writers of world literature in other languages, with an inevitable influence on their own writing.

The likely increase in the volume and quality of writing coming out of Scotland's ethnic communities has been mentioned. What of the traditional languages of Scottish writers, Scots and Gaelic? It is questionable whether the decline in the use and understanding of Gaelic can be arrested or reversed, despite the large amounts of money being made available to the cause; and likewise it is just as questionable whether Scots can again be the natural spoken or written language of Lowland Scotland in its original vigour and richness. Arguably, a decreasing minority of Scottish writers, out of a sense of cultural commitment and traditional family loyalty, will employ the full resources of Gaelic and Scots, while their natural readership in these languages will be a declining one. Most writers in Scotland will, as at the present moment, write largely in International Standard English, and employ Gaelic and Scots only for special effect, whether it be creating personality in dialogue, giving colour to description of action and setting, or as a conscious artifice in style. Of course, this may not be what happens; but if it is the future, we should recognise that nothing is being lost of what we already have in literature; the riches of Scottish literature already exist, and we are not cut off from them. Only the future is a foreign country; they will do things differently there, and writers will find it stimulating to inhabit it.

One feature of the literature to come is that it will undoubtedly be more environmentally conscious in a way that we have only begun to notice in today's writing. In the post-Cold War scenes of today's writing, there is a fashion for the doomsday thriller, the vision of disaster arising out of developments in scientific experiment and commercial exploitation of resources at the expense of nature. No doubt this will continue as a feature of popular fiction. However, at a deeper and more thoughtful level writers are likely to become in a positive manner the voices of a different way of looking at the world around us, encouraging a more responsible attitude to our planet and the life that it sustains. Perhaps a necessary part of this will be that Scottish writers become less 'Scottish' and that their writing will take on a 'post-nationalist' tone. If that is a feature that Scottish writers will share with other world writers, and if it is combined with an awareness of the past, then it is a development to be welcomed.

It has often been stated in one formulation or another that, in the centuries of the union, the Scottish middle classes (and that quaint survival, the Scottish upper class) went through a process of anglicisation, a de-Scotticising in language and thought and way of life. How deep this went is debatable; it is possibly a self-flattering working-class myth to have itself depicted as the natural inheritor and loyal preserver of authentic Scottish-ness. In literary terms, the result has been that the accurate and thoughtful presentation of the Scottish bourgeois, as distinct from a class-biased and demonised caricature, has been a rarity in twentieth-century literature. Most writers of middle-class origin, probably the majority of practising writers in all ages, have connived at this practice. Seeing themselves as being in revolt against the *mores* of their parents and their social background, they have had little incentive to observe them fairly and dispassionately. One hopeful result of a more politically identified Scotland may be that Scottish society will be seen by writers in a less highly-coloured and emotive perspective, and the middle classes, even the 'gentry', may be released from the literary ghetto to which writers have in the past confined them.

Children's writing has for long been the Cinderella of the Scottish literary world. The children and teenagers of Scotland have had in large measure to rely on the output of English or US writers and publishers of children's fiction, and Scotland rarely features in the available reading. A few honourable exceptions can be noted, but generally children's writing has been shamefully neglected, and Scottish children have only rarely been able to find themselves and their world reflected in what they choose or are given to read. The institution of incentives for Scottish children's writers, like prizes and awards, has been a fairly recent development, most recently the Scottish Arts Council Children's Book Awards, but there is much still to be done. One worthwhile area for post-2000 Scottish writers to investigate would be the provision of good imaginative literature for the young people of Scotland. They have long needed it; they deserve it. They need stories coming out of the past and traditions of Scotland, stories coming out of the real world around them, stories creating an imaginative future for their society.

So far in this discussion the emphasis has been on the writing of prose, especially fiction. Drama has ever been in a precarious position within Scotland, for all the efflorescence of plays being written and performed in the last half-century. The institutional and collective nature of the genre has much to do with this. If the national and civic institutions and private patrons could finally make a commitment to the social importance of drama, whether in the overdue foundation of a Scottish National Theatre or in some similar umbrella organisation to shade drama from the worst economic weather, then we might be able to look forward to a more secure future for the theatre in Scotland. As it is, drama could be well on its way to becoming, on the one hand, an activity supported by enthusiastic amateurs in local groups and, on the other, a packaged product for television, radio and the film screen. Much of quality could emerge from such a dichotomy; after all, the determining factor in drama, as in all creative expression, is the presence of a talented writer, the word being supreme despite the pretensions of directors and cameramen and choreographers. Yet the existence of a well-financed and popularly-supported professional theatre must be the lynchpin of a national dramatic effort. Linked with this, and demanding an urgent initiative, is a national editing and publishing venture to rescue and collect the large numbers of unprinted Scottish plays languishing in archives and thus finding neither the readers nor the potential producers that they deserve.

And what of poetry? The number of poets alive and composing in Scotland today, as they say about scientists in the modern world, probably exceeds the number of all those who have lived in all former times. Poets are a growth industry; yet, viewed dispassionately, how many of them can realistically expect, or indeed deserve, to receive public recognition? Quality is a rare element in an ocean of mediocre and self-indulgent versifying. It is debatable whether the public interest would be served by expanding the publishing outlets already available. An effective filter mechanism will always be necessary, in the interests of social sanity, although the Internet may be providing a channel for releasing bad verse upon the world. Yet Scotland has a good record for producing poets and poetry of merit. The significant number of good younger poets writing at the moment is a favourable auspice. One healthy development for post-2000 might be for those with ambitions to write poetry to consider the implications of the traditional Scottish concept of the 'makar', or maker. This implies a conscious attempt to acquire the discipline of poetry, the conscious craft of making verse, with all that this implies about learning the poetics and allying the older requirements of prosody, metrics and form to a newer consciousness of the importance of structure and rhythm in today's language. Between the extremes of uninspired formalism and undisciplined self-expression, there lies the fertile territory of the makar, a poetry rooted in awareness of the poetic tradition and in knowledgeable sensitivity to language.

Scottish literature at the millennium

Perhaps the time has come for a new attitude to the Scottish literary tradition that has been celebrated in this volume. In a new century and millennium, it should be possible to take the quality, the width and depth, of Scottish writing as proven, as no longer requiring any apology or justification. That being accepted and understood, it may be time to cast off the serious and over-respectful demeanour and become more detached, even irreverent and light-hearted in tone. A writing that uses the literature of Scotland in a conscious manner as a source of material and an inspiration for its own sake; a writing that looks at the history and institutions of Scotland without either seeking to protect them from criticism or trying to reform them by satire, seeing them as neutral entities requiring, not passionate involvement, but rather acceptance with equanimity: such a writing might be loosely described as 'post-modernist', but might more accurately be termed 'millenniarist', the tone of a new era. This volume has recognised signs of a new eclecticism and willingness to challenge traditional boundaries; the new millennium will show how far these promising signs are to be fulfilled.

SECTION 7
Reading Lists

GENERAL FURTHER READING

The following reading lists, organised to follow the six main period sections of the volume, although extensive, cannot be considered as comprehensive bibliographies, due to limitations of volume format and space. That said, these lists have been placed on the web-site maintained by the departments of Scottish Literature and STELLA (Software Teaching of Language and Literature) at **www.arts.gla.ac.uk/SESLL/ScotLit/bibliography**.

The aim is to make the lists the basis of a more inclusive bibliography of Scottish Literature, arranged in the six period sections of the present volume (Early Scottish Literature, Eighteenth Century, Age of Scott, Victorians and Edwardians, Scottish Renaissance, and Scottish Literature since 1945). This inclusive bibliography will be continuously developed; e-mail contributions and suggestions are invited, which will be incorporated bi-annually. E-mail address: enquiries@scotlit.arts.gla.ac.uk.

The presentation of the lists is unusual, in that they track and pertain to individual chapters. By no means all Scottish writers of significance, and discussion of them, are included; at the end of many chapters an alphabetical list of the names of additional Scottish writers will indicate that the web-bibliography will carry details and information not possible within the volume, which simply aims to supply helpful material regarding the fore-grounded authors and topics. In the drama sections, dates of first performance are given in the main text; publication dates only in the reading lists. Brief suggestions only are given for non-fiction prose in Chapter 42, 'Widening the Range'. For the twentieth century as a whole, covering poetry, fiction, non-fiction prose and drama, a most helpful and compact bibliography is that produced by Robert Crawford for the British Council, *Literature in Twentieth-Century Scotland: A Select Bibliography* (London: The British Council, 1995), and where appropriate, as with prolific writers, reference is made to this under 'Crawford'. *Scottish Literary Journal* and *Studies in Scottish Literature* appear as *SLJ* and *SSL*.

For access to the most up-to-date articles and criticism on modern writers a good source is via electronic databases. For example, Glasgow University students will find Worldcat [First Search], and the Annotated Bibliography of English Language and Literature [ABELL], at: http://merlin.lib.gla.ac.uk for the Glasgow University Library homepages.

Some useful catalogue web-sites are those of:

The National Library of Scotland: www.nls.uk
The British Library: http://blpc.bl.uk
The Mitchell Library, Glasgow: www.mitchelllibrary.org
Aberdeen University Library: www.abdn.ac.uk/diss/library
Edinburgh Central Reference Library:
    www.ebs.hw.ac.uk/EDC/Libraries/Reference
Edinburgh University Library: www.lib.ed.ac.uk
Glasgow University Library: http://merlin.lib.gla.ac.uk
St Andrews University Library: www-library.st-and.ac.uk
Strathclyde University Library: www.lib.strath.ac.uk
The Scottish Poetry Library: www.spl.org.uk
The Scottish Theatre Archive, Glasgow University:
    http://special.lib.gla.ac.uk/STA/index.html

Reference works and bibliographical guides

The listings below are a selection of items covering the range of Scottish literature and culture. Items relating to particular periods will be found in the following section reading lists.

Aitken, W. R., *Scottish Literature in English and Scots: A Guide* (Detroit: Gale Research Co., 1982). The most comprehensive guide so far.

Burgess, Moira, *Directory of Authors in the Scottish Fiction Reserve* (Edinburgh: National Library of Scotland, 1986). Alphabetical listing of authors and libraries holding their work.

Crawford, Robert, *Literature in Twentieth-Century Scotland: A Select Bibliography* (London: The British Council Literature Department, 1995). A useful reference guide for the modern period. Includes general reference works, anthologies, poetry, prose, drama and a list of useful addresses.

Daiches, David (ed.), *The New Companion to Scottish Culture* (Edinburgh: Polygon 1993; London: Edward Arnold, 1981). A useful guide to Scottish achievement across the range of history, literature, philosophy, law and the like.

Glen, Duncan, *The Poetry of the Scots: an introduction and bibliographical guide to poetry in Gaelic, Scots, Latin and English* (Edinburgh: Edinburgh University Press, 1991).

Menzies, David (ed.), *English Using Scottish Texts, Support Notes and Bibliographies* (Scottish Consultative Council on the Curriculum, 1999). A guide especially for teaching purposes. Includes general works, drama, prose fiction and non-fiction, poetry and also media texts, Gaelic texts in translation and Scots language texts.

Reid, Alan, and Osborne, Brian D., *Discovering Scottish Writers* (Edinburgh: Scottish Cultural Press, 1997). A short and introductory guide to Scottish writers and poets from the early to modern period.

Reid, Charlotte, *List of Plays in Scots* (Glasgow: Glasgow City Libraries, 1992).

Royle, Trevor, *The Mainstream Companion to Scottish Literature* (Edinburgh: Mainstream, 1993). Revised version of 1983 *Companion* (York: Macmillan, 1983). A comprehensive guide which provides a few paragraphs of biographical information on each writer with a list of primary and secondary reading where applicable.

Scott, Paul H. (ed.), *Scotland: A Concise Cultural History* (Edinburgh: Mainstream, 1993). An excellent introductory survey by experts of the entire range of Scottish cultural achievement.

Scottish Education Department, Scottish Central Committee on English, *Scottish Literature in the Secondary School* (Edinburgh: Her Majesty's Stationery Office, 1976). Contains bibliographical material on novels, plays, poetry, short-stories and general works of particular use for teaching in schools.

Smith, Dennis, assisted by Barnaby, Paul, and Moret, Ulrike, *Scotland: World Bibliographical Series*, vol. 34 (Oxford, Santa Barbara and Denver: Clio Press, 1998). A very general guide but useful as an initial point of reference. Includes references for bibliographies, reference works, periodicals and anthologies, a range of general critical works and specific references for the seventeenth to twentieth centuries. It gives excellent helpful short descriptions to some of the key cultural and literary texts.

From 1956 the annual supplement of the periodical *The Bibliotheck*, the *Annual Bibliography of Scottish Literature*, is useful. The National Library of Scotland has a *Bibliography of Scotland* covering the period 1976–87 in annual volumes, followed by updated databases (see internet details in previous General Further Reading).

Literary and cultural background

The first port of call here is *The History of Scottish Literature*, 4 vols, General Editor Cairns Craig (Aberdeen: Aberdeen University Press, 1987–8); the relevant volumes are listed in the appropriate reading list sections. Additional histories and general theoretical backgrounds include:

Anderson, Benedict, *Imagined Communities: Reflections on the Origin and Spread of Nationalism* (London: Verso, 1983).

Bennett, Margaret, *Scottish Customs from the Cradle to the Grave* (Edinburgh: Polygon, 1992).

Beveridge, Craig, and Turnbull, Ronald, *The Eclipse of Scottish Culture: Inferiorism and the Intellectuals* (Edinburgh: Polygon, 1989).

—, *Scotland After Enlightenment: Image and Tradition in Modern Scottish Culture* (Edinburgh: Polygon, 1997).

Bhabha, Homi K., *Nation and Narration* (London: Routledge, 1990).

Broadie, Alexander, *The Tradition of Scottish Philosophy* (Edinburgh: Polygon, 1990).

Buchan, David, *Scottish Tradition, A Collection of Scottish Folk Literature* (London: Routledge & Kegan Paul, 1984).

Calder, Angus, *Revolutionary Empire: the rise of the English-speaking empires from the 15th century to the 1780s* (London: Cape, 1981; Pimlico, 1998).

Chapman, Malcolm, *The Gaelic Vision in Scottish Culture* (London: Croom Helm, 1978).

Colley, Linda, *Britons: Forging the Nation* (New Haven: Yale University Press, 1992).

Cowan, Edward J. (ed.), *The People's Past: Scottish Folk, Scottish History* (Edinburgh: Polygon, 1980).

—, and Gifford, Douglas (eds), *The Polar Twins* (Edinburgh: John Donald Limited, 1999).

Craig, Cairns, *Out of History: Narrative Paradigms in Scottish and English Culture* (London: Polygon, 1996).

Crawford, Robert, *Devolving English Literature* (Oxford: Clarendon Press, 1992); rev. (Edinburgh: Edinburgh University Press, 2001).

D'Arcy, Julian, *Scottish Skalds and Sagamen: Old Norse Influence on Modern Scottish Literature* (East Linton: Tuckwell, 1996).

Davie, George, *The Democratic Intellect: Scotland and Her Universities in the Nineteenth Century* (Edinburgh: Edinburgh University Press, 1961; 1999).

—, *The Crisis of the Democratic Intellect* (Edinburgh: Polygon, 1986).

Devine, T. M., *The Scottish Nation 1700–2000* (London: Allen Lane, 1999).

Dick, Eddie, *From Limelight to Satellite: A Scottish Film Book* (London: BFI Publishing/Scottish Film Council, 1990).

Donachie, Ian, and Hewitt, George, *A Companion to Scottish History: From the Reformation to the Present* (London: Batsford, 1989).

Ferguson, William, *The Identity of the Scottish Nation: An Historic Quest* (Edinburgh: Edinburgh University Press, 1998).

Findlay, Bill (ed.), *A History of Scottish Theatre* (Edinburgh: Polygon, 1998).

Gellner, Ernst, *Nation and Nationalism* (Oxford: Basil Blackwell, 1983).

Gifford, Douglas, and McMillan, Dorothy (eds), *A History of Scottish Women's Writing* (Edinburgh: Edinburgh University Press, 1997).

Glendinning, Miles, MacInnes, Ranald, and MacKechnie, Aonghus, *A History of Scottish Architecture* (Edinburgh: Edinburgh University Press, 1996).

Goring, Rosemary, *Chambers Scottish Biographical Dictionary* (Edinburgh: Chambers, 1992).

Hart, Francis Russell, *The Scottish Novel: A Critical Survey* (London: John Murray, 1978).

Hardy, Forsyth, *Scotland in Film* (Edinburgh: Edinburgh University Press, 1990).

Harvie, Christopher, *Scotland and Nationalism: Scottish Society and Politics, 1707 to the Present* (1977; London: Routledge, 1998).

Henderson, T. F., *Scottish Vernacular Literature* (1898; Edinburgh: John Grant, 1910).

Hewitt, David, and Spiller, Michael (eds), *Literature of the North* (Aberdeen: Aberdeen University Press, 1983).

Hook, Andrew, *From Goosecreek to Gandercleugh: Studies in Scottish-American Literary and Cultural History* (East Linton: Tuckwell Press, 1999).

Hutchison, David, *The Modern Scottish Theatre* (Glasgow: Molendinar Press, 1977).

Jack, R. D. S., *The Italian Influence on Scottish Literature* (Edinburgh: Edinburgh University Press, 1972).

Kinsley, James (ed.), *Scottish Poetry: A Critical Survey* (London: Cassell, 1955).

Lindsay, Maurice, *A History of Scottish Literature* (London: Hale, 1991).

Lynch, Michael, *Scotland: A New History* (London: Century, 1991).

McCrone, David, Kendrick, Stephen, and Straw, Pat (eds), *The Making of Scotland: Nation, Culture and Change* (Edinburgh: Edinburgh University Press, 1989).

Macdonald, Murdo, *Scottish Art* (London: Thames & Hudson, 2000).

MacMillan, Duncan, *Scottish Art, 1460–1990* (Edinburgh: Mainstream, 1990).

Manlove, Colin, *Scottish Fantasy Literature* (Edinburgh: Canongate, 1994).

McNeill, Marion, *The Silver Bough*, 4 vols (Glasgow: MacLellan, 1957–68).

Millar, J. H., *A Literary History of Scotland* (London: T. Fisher Unwin, 1903).

Mitchison, Rosalind, *A History of Scotland* (London: Methuen, 1970).

Muir, Edwin, *Scott and Scotland: The Predicament of the Scottish Writer* (London: Routledge, 1936).

Nairn, Tom, *The Breakup of Britain* (revised edition, London: NLB and Verso, 1981).

O'Driscoll, Robert (ed.), *The Celtic Consciousness* (Edinburgh: The Dolmen Press and Canongate, 1992).

Petrie, Duncan, *Screening Scotland* (London: British Film Institute, 2000).

Pittock, Murray, *The Invention of Scotland: The Stuart Myth and Scottish Identity, 1638 to the Present* (London: Routledge, 1991).

Power, William, *Literature and Oatmeal: What Literature has Meant to Scotland* (London: Routledge, 1935).

Purser, John, *Scotland's Music, A History* (Edinburgh: Mainstream, 1992).

Robinson, Mairi (ed.), *The Concise Scots Dictionary* (Aberdeen: Aberdeen University Press, 1985)

Royle, Trevor, *Precipitous City: The Story of Literary Edinburgh* (Edinburgh: Mainstream; New York: Taplinger, 1980).

Said, Edward, *Orientalism* (London: Routledge, 1978).

Smith, G. Gregory, *Scottish Literature: Character and Influence* (London: Macmillan and co., 1919).

Smout, T. C., *A History of the Scottish People 1560–1830* (London: Collins, 1969).

—, *A Century of the Scottish People 1830–1950* (London: Collins, 1986).

Speirs, John, *The Scots Literary Tradition* (London: Chatto & Windus, 1940; Faber, 1962, revised edition).

Thomson, Derick, *An Introduction to Gaelic Poetry* (London: Gollancz, 1974).

Trumpener, Katie, *Bardic Nationalism* (Princeton, NJ: Princeton University Press, 1997).

Walker, Marshall, *Scottish Literature Since 1707* (London and New York: Longman, 1996).

Watson, Roderick, *The Literature of Scotland* (Basingstoke: Macmillan, 1984).

Wittig, Kurt, *The Scottish Tradition in Literature* (Edinburgh: Oliver & Boyd, 1958).

Womack, Peter, *Improvement and Romance: Constructing the Myth of the Highlands* (Basingstoke: Macmillan, 1988).

Wood, Harvey H., et al., *Edinburgh Essays on Scots Literature* (Edinburgh: Oliver & Boyd, 1933).

Period literary and historical studies are located in the appropriate section reading lists.

Anthologies

McCordrick, David (ed.), *Scottish Literature: An Anthology*, vol. 1 Early Middle Ages to c1775 (New York: Peter Lang, 1996). The most impressive general anthology available, covering all Scottish literature.

—, Volume 2 [1775 to Robert Louis Stevenson] (New York: Peter Lang, 1996).

—, Volume 3 [RLS to the present] (Edinburgh: Scottish Cultural Press, 2002).

Poetry

Bateman, Meg, Crawford, Robert, and McGonigal, James (eds), *Scottish Religious Poetry: An Anthology* (Edinburgh: St Andrews Press, 2000).

Crawford, Robert and Imlah, Mick *The New Penguin Book of Scottish Verse* (London: Allen Lane, 2000).

Dunn, Douglas, *The Faber Book of Twentieth-Century Scottish Poetry* (London: Faber, 1993).

Kerrigan, Catherine (ed.), *An Anthology of Scottish Women Poets* [with translations from the Gaelic by Meg Bateman] (Edinburgh: Edinburgh University Press, 1991).

Lindsay, Maurice (ed.), *Scottish Comic Verse: An Anthology* (London: Hale, 1981).

MacDiarmid, Hugh (ed.), *The Golden Treasury of Scottish Poetry* (London: Macmillan, 1940).

McQueen, Jack, and Scott, Tom (eds), *The Oxford Book of Scottish Verse* (Oxford: Clarendon, 1966).

Morgan, Edwin (ed.), *Scottish Satirical Verse* (Manchester: Carcanet, 1980).

McGonigal, James, O'Rourke, Daniel, and Whyte, Hamish (eds), *Across the Water: Irishness in Modern Scottish Writing* (Glendaruel: Argyll, 2000).

Scott, Alexander (ed.), *Scotch Passion: an Anthology of Scottish Erotic Verse* (London: Hale, 1982).

Scott, Tom (ed.), *The Penguin Book of Scottish Verse* (Harmondsworth: Penguin, 1970).

Watson, Roderick, *The Poetry of Scotland: Gaelic, Scots and English, 1380–1980* (Edinburgh: Edinburgh University Press, 1995).

Short stories

Bradford, Alan, and MacDonald, Donald (eds), *Scottish Traditional Tales* (Edinburgh: Polygon, 1994).

Dunn, Douglas (ed.), *The Oxford Book of Scottish Short Stories* (Oxford: Oxford University Press, 1995).

MacDougall, Carl (ed.), *The Devil and the Giro: Two Centuries of Scottish Short Stories* (Edinburgh: Canongate, 1989).

Murray, Ian (ed.), *The New Penguin Book of Scottish Short Stories* (Harmondsworth: Penguin, 1983).

Philip, Neil (ed.), *The Penguin Book of Scottish Folktales* (London: Penguin, 1995).

Reid, J. M. (ed.), *Scottish Short Stories* (London: Oxford University Press, 1963).

Williamson, Duncan and Linda, *A Thorn in the King's Foot: Stories of the Scottish Travelling People* (Harmondsworth: Penguin, 1987).

SECTION 1: EARLY SCOTTISH LITERATURE

Introductory reading

As with each section the reader is reminded of the websites listed at the beginning of the Further Reading section, especially the developing website maintained by the Departments of Scottish Literature and STELLA at the University of Glasgow at **www.arts.gla.ac.uk/SESLL/ScotLit/bibliography** where more information can be given than is possible here.

The areas of Medieval and Renaissance Scottish literature still lack accessible and comprehensive book-length introductions for the general reader, while remaining relatively marginalised within traditional histories of Scottish literature. Those *Literary histories* listed in the opening to this section contain general discussion of the period; see particularly W. R. Aitken, Buchan, Glen, Kinsley, Lindsay, Millar and Watson. The first volume, edited by R. D. S. Jack, of *The History of Scottish Literature* (4 vols, General Editor Cairns Craig, Aberdeen: Aberdeen University Press, 1988), is the standard history, particularly recommended for the range and depth of its essays which cover the early medieval to late seventeenth-century period; there are also excellent chapters on Scottish Latin literature and classical Gaelic. Other collections of essays are those which stem from the International Conferences on Medieval and Renaissance Scottish Language and Literature from Aitken et al. (eds) (1977), Blanchot and Graf (eds) (1979), Lyall and Riddy (eds) (1981), Strauss and Drescher (eds) (1986), McClure and Spiller (eds) (1989) to the collection edited by Ross Roy and published as volume 26 of *Studies in Scottish Literature* (1991); the 1993, 1996 and 1999 *Proceedings* are now appearing. Henryson and Dunbar are individually well-served (there are *Scotnotes* by Gerald Baird and R. D. S. Jack on each respectively). *The Mercat Anthology of Early Scottish Literature* edited by R. D. S. Jack and P. A. T. Rozendaal (Edinburgh: Mercat Press, 1997, 2000) is recommended as the most recent, comprehensive and critically helpful edition for most of the texts discussed in this section; extensive reference is made to it in Chapter 4, 'Renaissance Poetry'. See also the excellent edition entitled *The Makars: The Poems of Henryson, Dunbar and Douglas* edited by J. A. Tasioulas (Edinburgh: Canongate, 1999) and Douglas Gray's *Henryson and Dunbar* (London: Penguin, 1997). Priscilla Bawcutt and Felicity Riddy's anthology, *Longer Scottish Poems vol. 1, 1375–1650* (Edinburgh: Scottish Academic Press, 1987) is a valuable anthology, though out of print. Thomas Owen Clancy's recent anthology, *The Triumph Tree: Scotland's Earliest Poetry AD 550–1250* (Edinburgh: Canongate, 1998), has redrawn the literary, cultural and linguistic map of Scotland 'pre-Barbour': this precious collection of Gaelic, Latin, Norse, and Old English texts, which contains translations, will enrich any understanding of the identity of later Medieval and Renaissance literatures, and complement other recent collections such as *Iona: The Earliest Poetry of a Celtic Monastery* edited by Thomas Owen Clancy and Gilbert Markus (Edinburgh: Edinburgh University Press, 1995), the medieval selection in *The Penguin Book of Scottish Verse* edited by Robert Crawford and Mick Imlah (London: Allen Lane, 2000), and *Scottish Religious Poetry from the sixth century to the present: an anthology* edited by Meg Bateman, Robert Crawford and James McGonigal (Edinburgh: Saint Andrew Press, 2000). R. D. S. Jack's *Scottish Prose* (London: Calder & Boyars, 1971), while regrettably out of print, provides a useful edited selection of prose works, critical, religious and historiographical in nature, from the early modern period.

An outstanding account of cultural and intellectual relationships in Renaissance Scotland can be found in John Durkan's article, 'The Cultural Background in Sixteenth-Century Scotland', *Essays on the Scottish Reformation 1513–1625*, ed. David McRoberts (Glasgow: J. S. Burns, 1962), pp. 274–331. European literary connections have been amply traced by R. D. S. Jack in *The Italian Influence on Scottish Literature* (Edinburgh: Edinburgh University Press,

1972) and *Scottish Literature's Debt to Italy* (Edinburgh: Edinburgh University Press, 1986), and in Janet M. Smith's much earlier study, *The French Background of Middle Scots Literature* (Edinburgh: Oliver & Boyd, 1934). Excellent surveys of other arts in Medieval and Renaissance Scotland are offered by Duncan Macmillan's *Scottish Art 1460–1990* (Edinburgh: Mainstream, 1990) [chapters II and III], John Purser's *Scotland's Music* (Edinburgh: Mainstream, 1992) [chapter X] and D. James Ross's *Musick Fyne. Robert Carver and the Art of Music in Sixteenth-Century Scotland* (Edinburgh: Mercat Press, 1993). For help with issues of *language* see Aitken, A. J. and McArthur, Tom, *Languages of Scotland* (Edinburgh: Chambers, 1979); John Corbett's *Language and Scottish Literature* (Edinburgh: Edinburgh University Press, 1997); *The Edinburgh History of the Scots Language* edited by Charles Jones (Edinburgh: Edinburgh University Press, 1997); Billy Kay's *Scots: The Mither Tongue* (Edinburgh: Mainstream, 1986); and David Murison's *The Guid Scots Tongue* (Edinburgh: Blackwood, 1977). The standard dictionary of Older and Middle Scots, almost near completion, is the multivolume *Dictionary of the Older Scottish Tongue (DOST)*. Mairi Robinson's *The Concise Scots Dictionary* (Aberdeen: Aberdeen University Press, 1985) is an excellent compact dictionary. For specifically bibliographical help, the following are particularly useful: W. R. Aitken's *Scottish Literature in English and Scots. A Guide to Information Sources* (Detroit: Gale, 1982); William Geddie's *A Bibliography of Middle Scots Poets* (Edinburgh and London: Scottish Text Society, 1912); Duncan Glen's *The Poetry of the Scots. An Introduction and Bibliographical Guide to Poetry in Gaelic, Scots, Latin and English* (Edinburgh: Edinburgh University Press, 1991); Walter Scheps and Anna J. Looney's *Middle Scots Poets. A Reference Guide to James I of Scotland, Robert Henryson, William Dunbar and Gavin Douglas* (Boston, MA: G. K. Hall, 1986). See also *The Annual Bibliography of Scottish Literature*, issued annually as a supplement to *The Bibliotheck* (Aberdeen: Aberdeen University Library) from 1969 onwards, and *The Year's Work in Scottish Literary Studies* (1969–1973), after 1973 called *The Year's Work in Scottish Literary and Linguistic Studies* published annually as supplement to *Scottish Literary News* and then as supplement to its successor, the *Scottish Literary Journal* (Aberdeen: Association for Scottish Literary Studies).

For ease of reference, the recommended editions for writers and texts in this section are the most recently published, currently in print, or most readily available in libraries. Where such editions do not exist, reference is made to the earliest standard edition. As explained in the introduction to these bibliographical sections, the reading suggestions offered here cannot be wholly comprehensive; for example, there is no scope to refer to general works on the Medieval and Renaissance periods in their wider European contexts, or to include citation of doctoral theses. Instead, the aim is to provide the reader with certain useful primary tools of reference.

General historical and cultural background

Allan, David, *Philosophy and politics in later Stuart Scotland: neo Stoicism, culture and ideology in an age of crisis, 1540–1690* (East Linton: Tuckwell, 2000).

—, *Virtue, learning and the Scottish Enlightenment: ideas of scholarship in early modern history* (Edinburgh: Edinburgh University Press, 1993).

Barrow, G. W. S., *Kingship and Unity: Scotland 1000–1306* (London: Edward Arnold, 1981).

Broun, Dauvit, Finlay, R. J., and Lynch, Michael (eds), *Image and Identity: the making and remaking of Scotland through the ages* (Edinburgh: John Donald, 1998).

Cowan, Ian B., and Shaw, Duncan (eds), *The Renaissance and Reformation in Scotland: Essays in Honour of Gordon Donaldson* (Edinburgh: Scottish Academic Press, 1983).

Crawford, Barbara E. (ed.), *Church, chronicle and learning in Medieval and early Renaissance Scotland: essays presented to Donald Watt on the occasion of the completion of the publication of Bower's Scotchronicon* (Edinburgh: Mercat Press, 1999).

Donaldson, Gordon, *Scotland: James V to James VII* (Edinburgh: Oliver & Boyd, 1965).

—, *All the Queen's men: Power and politics in Mary Stewart's Scotland* (London: Batsford Academic and Educational Ltd., 1983).

Duncan, A. A. M., *Scotland: The Making of the Kingdom* (Edinburgh: Oliver & Boyd, 1975).

Dwyer, J., Mason, R. A., and Murdoch, A. (eds), *New perspectives on the politics and culture of early modern Scotland* (Edinburgh: Donald, 1982).

Ewan, Elizabeth, 'A Realm of One's Own? Women in the History of Medieval and Early Modern Scotland', *Gendering History: Scottish and international approaches*, eds T. Brotherstone and D. Symonds (Glasgow: Cruithne Press, 1999), pp. 19–36.

Ewan, E., and Meikle, M. M. (eds), *Women in Scotland c1100–c1750* (East Linton: Tuckwell Press, 1999).

Goodare, J., and Lynch, M. (eds), *The Reign of James VI* (East Linton: Tuckwell Press, 2000).

Grant, Alexander, *Independence and Nationhood: Scotland 1306–1469* (London: Arnold, 1992).

Kidd, Colin, *British identities before nationalism: ethnicity and nationhood in the Atlantic world, 1600–1800* (Cambridge: Cambridge University Press, 1999).

Kinghorn, A. M., *The Chorus of History: Literary–Historical Relations in Renaissance Britain, 1485–1558* (London: Blanford Press, 1971).

Lyall, R. J., 'The Court as a Cultural Centre', *History Today* 34 (London, 1984), pp. 27–33.

Lynch, Michael, *Scotland. A New History* (Edinburgh: Century, 1991; revised edition, 1992).

— (ed.), *Mary Stewart: Queen of Three Kingdoms* (Oxford: Basil Blackwell, 1988).

Mason, R. A., *Scots and Britons: Scottish political thought and the union of 1603* (Cambridge: Cambridge University Press, 1994).

Mitchison, Rosalind, *Lordship to Patronage: Scotland 1603–1745* (London: Edward Arnold, 1983).

Nicholson, Ranald, *Scotland: The Later Middle Ages* (Edinburgh: Oliver & Boyd, 1974).

Scott, Paul H. (ed.), *Scotland: A Concise Cultural History* (Edinburgh: Mainstream, 1993).

Sutherland, Elizabeth, *Five Euphemias: Women in Medieval Scotland 1200–1420* (London: Constable & Company Ltd., 1999).

Wormald, Jenny, *Court, Kirk and Community: Scotland 1470–1625* (Edinburgh: Edinburgh University Press, 1981).

Medieval literature

Aitken, A. J., McDiarmid, M. P., and Thomson, D. S., *Bards and Makars* (Glasgow: University of Glasgow Press, 1977).

Bawcutt, Priscilla, 'The Art of Flyting', *SLJ* 10(2) (Aberdeen: Association for Scottish Literary Studies, 1983), pp. 5–24.

Blanchot, J. J., and Graf, Claude (eds), *Actes du 2e Colloque de Langue et de Littérature Écossaises (Moyen Âge de Renaissance)* (Strasbourg: Université de Strasbourg, 1979).

Carruthers, Gerard, and Dunnigan, Sarah M., ' "A reconfused chaos now": Scottish Poetry and Nation from the Medieval Period to the Eighteenth Century', *Edinburgh Review* 100 (Edinburgh: Polygon, 1999), pp. 81–94.

Fradenburg, Louise, *City, Marriage, Tournament* (Madison, WI: University of Wisconsin Press, 1991).

Gray, Douglas, 'Some Chaucerian Themes in Scottish Writers', *Chaucer Traditions: Studies in Honour of Derek Brewer*, eds Ruth Morse and Barry Windeatt (Cambridge: Cambridge University Press, 1990), pp. 81–90.

Jack, R. D. S., *The History of Scottish Literature Vol. 1, Origins to 1660* (Aberdeen: Aberdeen University Press, 1989).

—, *The Italian Influence on Scottish Literature* (Edinburgh: Edinburgh University Press, 1972).

Kinsley, James (ed.), *Scottish Poetry: A Critical Survey* (London: Cassell, 1955).

Kratzmann, Gregory (ed.), *Anglo-Scottish Literary Relations 1430–1550* (Cambridge: Cambridge University Press, 1980).

Kinghorn, A. M. (ed.), *The Middle Scots Poets* (London: Edward Arnold, 1970).

Lyall, R. J., and Riddy, Felicity (eds), *Proceedings of the Third International Conference on Scottish Language and Literature* (Stirling and Glasgow: University of Glasgow, 1981).

Mackenzie, Agnes Mure, *An Historical Survey of Scottish Literature to 1714* (London: Maclehose, 1933).

Millar, John Hepburn, *A Literary History of Scotland* (London, 1903).

—, 'The Literature of Lowland Scotland, 1350–1700', *Scotland: A Concise Cultural History*, ed. Paul H. Scott (Edinburgh and London: Mainstream, 1993), pp. 77–98.

McClure, J. Derrick, and Spiller, Michael R. G. (eds), *Brycht Lanternis: Essays on the Language and Literature of Medieval Scotland* (Aberdeen: Aberdeen University Press, 1989).

McKenna, Stephen R. (ed.), *Selected Essays on Scottish Language and Literature: A Festschrift in Honour of Allan H. MacLaine* (Lewiston, NY: Edwin Mellen Press, 1992).

MacQueen, John and Winifred (eds), *A Choice of Scottish Verse, 1470–1570* (London: Faber & Faber, 1971).

Mill, Anna J., *Mediaeval Plays in Scotland* (Edinburgh: St Andrews University Publications, 1927).

Ross, John M., *Scottish History and Literature to the Period of the Reformation* (Glasgow: J. Maclehose, 1884).

Roy, Ross G. (ed.), *SSL* 26: *The Language and Literature of Early Scotland* (Columbia: University of South Carolina, 1991).

Scheps, Walter, and Looney, Anna J., *Middle Scots Poets: A Reference Guide to James I of Scotland, Robert Henryson, William Dunbar, and Gavin Douglas* (Boston, MA: G. K. Hall, 1986).

Scott, Tom (ed.), *Late Medieval Scots Poetry* (London: Heinemann, 1967).

Shire, Helena Mennie, *Song, Dance, and Poetry at the Court of Scotland Under King James VI* (Cambridge: Cambridge University Press, 1969).

Smith, Janet M., *The French Background of Middle Scots Literature* (Edinburgh: Oliver & Boyd, 1934).

Strauss, Dietrich, and Drescher, Horst W. (eds), *Scottish Language and Literature, Medieval and Renaissance: Fourth International Conference* (Frankfurt am Main: P. Lang, 1986).

Renaissance literature

Dunnigan, Sarah M., 'Scottish Women Writers c1560–c1650', *A History of Scottish Women's Writing*, eds Douglas Gifford and Dorothy McMillan (Edinburgh: Edinburgh University Press, 1997), pp. 15–43.

Eyre-Todd, G. (ed.), *Scottish Poetry of the Seventeenth Century* (London and Edinburgh: n. d.).

Houwen, L. A. J. R., MacDonald, A. A., and Mapstone, S. L. (eds), *A Palace in the Wild: Essays on Vernacular Culture and Humanism in Late-Medieval and Renaissance Scotland* (Leuven: Peeters, 2000).

Hughes, Joan, and Ramson, W. S., *Poetry of the Stewart Court* (Canberra, London: Australian National University Press, 1982).

Jack, R. D. S., *The Italian Influence on Scottish Literature* (Edinburgh: Edinburgh University Press, 1972).

—, 'Petrarch in English and Scottish Renaissance Literature', *Modern Language Review* 71 (Cambridge: Modern Humanities Research Association, 1976), pp. 801–11.

—, 'Scottish Literature: The English and European Dimensions', *Renaissance Culture in Context: Theory and Practice*, eds Jean R. Brink and William F. Gentrup (Aldershot: Scolar, 1993), pp. 9–17.

Kratzman, Gregory, 'Sixteenth-Century Secular Poetry', *History of Scottish Literature* Vol. I (Aberdeen: Aberdeen University Press, 1988), pp. 105–23.

Lyall, R. J., 'Politics and Poetry in Fifteenth- and Sixteenth-Century Scotland', *SLJ* 3 (Aberdeen: Association for Scottish Literary Studies, 1976), pp. 5–29.

MacDonald, Alasdair, A., 'Poetry, Politics, and Reformation Censorship in Sixteenth-Century Scotland', *English Studies* 64(5) (1983), pp. 410–21.

MacDonald, A. A., Lynch, M., and Cowan, Ian B. (eds), *The Renaissance in Scotland: Studies in Literature, Religion, History and Culture* (Leiden: Brill, 1994).

MacQueen, John (ed.), *Ballatis of Luve: The Scottish Courtly Love Lyric 1400–1570* (Edinburgh: Edinburgh University Press, 1970).

Mapstone, Sally, and Wood, Juliette (eds), *The Rose and the Thistle: Essays on the Culture of Late Medieval and Renaissance Scotland* (East Linton: Tuckwell Press, 1998).

Shire, Helena Mennie, *Song, Dance and Poetry of the Court of Scotland under King James VI* (Cambridge: Cambridge University Press, 1969).

Spiller, Michael, 'Poetry after the Union 1603–1660', *The History of Scottish Literature Vol. 1, Origins to 1660*, ed. R. D. S. Jack (Aberdeen: Aberdeen University Press, 1988), pp. 141–22.

—, *The Development of the Sonnet: An Introduction* (London: Routledge, 1992).

Waller, Gary, *English Poetry of the Sixteenth Century* (London: Longman, 1986).

Williams, Janet Hadley, *Stewart Style 1513–42: Essays on the Court of James V* (East Linton: Tuckwell Press, 1996).

For works on Scottish Medieval and Renaissance Drama, please see the bibliography for Chapter 4.

Chapter 1: Literary Roots: Medieval Poetry

BARBOUR'S BRUCE
Duncan, A. A. M. (ed.), *The Bruce* (Edinburgh: Canongate, 1997; 2000).

Secondary reading

Barrow, G. W. S., 'Robert the Bruce and Scottish Identity', *Saltire Society Pamphlet* (1984).

—, 'The Idea of Freedom in Late Medieval Scotland', *Innes Review* 30 (Glasgow, 1979), pp. 16–34.

Ebin, Lois, A., 'John Barbour's *Bruce*: Poetry, History and Propaganda', *SSL* 9 (Columbia: University of South Carolina, 1971–2), pp. 218–42.

Goldstein, R. James, *The Matter of Scotland: Historical Narrative in Medieval Scotland* (Lincoln, London: University of Nebraska Press, 1993).

Jack, R. D. S., ' "(A!) Fredome is a Noble Thing": Christian Hermeneutics and Barbour's *Bruce*', *Scottish Studies Review* 1(1) (Aberdeen: Association for Scottish Literary Studies, 2000), pp. 26–38.

Kinghorn, A. M., 'Scottish Historiography in the Fourteenth Century: A New Introduction to Barbour's *Bruce*', *SSL* 6 (Columbia: University of South Carolina, 1968–9), pp. 131–45.

Kliman, Bernice W., 'The Idea of Chivalry in Barbour's Bruce', *Medieval Studies* 35 (1973), pp. 477–508.

—, 'Speech as a Mirror of Sapientia and Fortitudo in Barbour's *Bruce*', *Medium Aevum* 44 (Oxford, 1975), pp. 151–61.

McKim, Anne M., 'James Douglas and Barbour's Ideal of Knighthood', *Forum for Modern Language Studies* 17 (Oxford: Oxford University Press for the University of St Andrews, 1981), pp. 167–80.

Schwend, Joachim, 'Religion and Religiosity in *The Bruce*', *Scottish Studies* 4 (Frankfurt am Main, 1984), pp. 207–15.

—, 'Nationalism in Scottish Medieval and Renaissance Literature', *Scottish Studies* 8 (Frankfurt am Main, 1989), pp. 29–42.

Utz, Hans, 'If Freedom Fail . . . "Freedom" in John Barbour's *The Bruce*', *English Studies* 50 (1969), pp. 151–65.

Watt, Diane, 'Nationalism in Barbour's *Bruce*', *Parergon: Bulletin of the Australia and New Zealand Association for Medieval and Renaissance Studies* 12(1) (1994), pp. 89–107.

Wilson, Grace, G., 'Barbour's *Bruce* and Harry's *Wallace*: Compliments, Compensations and Conventions', *SSL* 25 (Columbia: University of South Carolina, 1990), pp. 189–201.

JAMES I: *THE KINGIS QUAIR*

Jack, R. D. S., and Rozendaal, P. A. T. (eds), 'James I: *The Kingis Quair*', *The Mercat Anthology of Early Scottish Literature 1375–1707* (Edinburgh: Mercat Press, 1997), pp. 17–56 [most easily available edition].

McDiarmid, Matthew (ed.), *The Kingis Quair of James Stewart* (London: Heinemann, 1973).

Norton-Smith, John (ed.), *The Kingis Quair* (Leiden: E. J. Brill, 1981, 2nd edition).

Skeat, W. W. (ed.), *The Kingis Quair* (Edinburgh: Scottish Text Society, 1911, 2nd edition).

Secondary reading

Boffey, Julia, 'Chaucerian Prisoners: the Context of *The Kingis Quair*', *Chaucer and Fifteenth-Century Poetry*, eds Julia Boffey and Janet Cowan (London: King's College, 1991), pp. 84–99.

Brown, Ian, 'The Mental Traveller – A Study of the Kingis Quair', *SSL* 5 (Columbia: University of South Carolina, 1967–8), pp. 245–52.

Caretta, V., '*The Kingis Quair* and the Consolation of Philosophy', *SSL* 16 (Columbia: University of South Carolina, 1981), pp. 14–28.

Cragie, W. A., 'The Language of the *Kingis Quair*', *Essays and Studies* 25 (Oxford: Clarendon Press, 1939), pp. 22–38.

Ebin, Lois A., 'Boethius, Chaucer and the *Kingis Quair*', *Philological Quarterly* 58 (Iowa City: University of Iowa, 1974), pp. 321–41.

—, *Illuminator, Makar, Vates, Visions of Poetry in the Fifteenth Century* (Lincoln, NE: University of Nebraska Press, 1988), pp. 50–5.

James, Clair F., '*The Kingis Quair*: The Plight of the Courtly Lover', *New Readings of Late Medieval Love Poems*, ed. David Chamberlain (Lanham, MD: University Press of America, 1993), pp. 95–118.

Jeffery, C. D., 'Anglo-Scots Poetry and *The Kingis Quair*', *Actes du 2e Colloque de Langue et de Litterature Ecossaises (Moyen Age et Renaissance)*, eds J. J. Blanchot and C. Graf (Strasbourg: Université de Strasbourg, 1979), pp. 207–21.

Kratzmann, Gregory, *Anglo-Scottish Literary Relations 1430–1550* (Cambridge: Cambridge University Press, 1980), pp. 33–62.

MacColl, Alan, 'Beginning and Ending the *Kingis Quair*', *Bryght Lanternis* (Aberdeen: Aberdeen University Press, 1989), pp. 118–28.

MacQueen, John, 'Tradition and the Interpretation of the *Kingis Quair*', *Review of English Studies* 12 (1961), pp. 117–31.

Markland, M. F., 'The Structure of The *Kingis Quair*', *Research Studies of the State College of Washington* 25 (1967), pp. 273–86.

Marks, Diane R., 'Poems from Prison: James I of Scotland and Charles d'Orleans', *Fifteenth-Century Studies* 15 (Stuttgart: H.-D. Heinz, Akademischer Verlag, 1989), pp. 245–58.

Petrina, Alessandra, *The Kingis Quair of James I of Scotland* (Padua: Unipress, 1997).

Preston, John, ' "Fortunys Exiltree": A Study of *The Kingis Quair*', *Review of English Studies* 7 (1956), pp. 339–47.

Quinn, William, 'Memory and the Matrix of Unity in *The Kingis Quair*', *Chaucer Review* 15 (1980–81), pp. 332–55.

Scheps, Walter, 'Chaucerian Synthesis: The Art of *The Kingis Quair*', *SSL* 8 (Columbia: University of South Carolina, 1970–1), pp. 143–65.

Straus, Barrie Ruth, 'The Role of the Reader in *The Kingis Quair*', *Actes du 2e Colloque de Langue et de Litterature Ecossaises (Moyen Age et Renaissance)*, eds J. J. Blanchot and C. Graf (Strasbourg: Université de Strasbourg, 1979), pp. 198–206.

von Hendy, A., 'The Free Thrall: A Study of *The Kingis Quair*', *SSL* 2(2) (Columbia: University of South Carolina, 1964–65), pp. 246–52.

Chapter 2: Henryson and Dunbar

HENRYSON

Bawcutt, Priscilla, and Riddy, Felicity (eds), *Selected Poems of Henryson and Dunbar* (Edinburgh: Scottish Academic Press, The Scottish Classics Series no. 16, 1992).

Jack, R. D. S., and Rozendaal, P. A. T. (eds), *The Mercat Anthology of Early Scottish Literature* (Edinburgh: Mercat, 1997), pp. 83–126; 280–2.

Fox, Denton (ed.), *The Poems of Robert Henryson* (Oxford: Clarendon, 1980).

Gopen, George, *The Moral Fabillis of Esope the Phrygian English and Scots* (Edinburgh: Edinburgh University Press, 1987).

Gray, Douglas, *Selected poems of Robert Henryson and William Dunbar* (London: Penguin, 1998).

Tasioulas, J. A. (ed.), *The Makars: the poems of Henryson, Dunbar and Douglas* (Edinburgh: Canongate, 1999).

Secondary reading: monographs

Baird, Gerald, *The Poems of Robert Henryson* (Aberdeen: Association for Scottish Literary Studies, Scotnotes, 1996).

Gray, Douglas, *Robert Henryson* (Leiden: E. J. Brill, 1979).

Greentree, Rosemary, *Reader, Teller and Teacher: The Narrator of Robert Henryson's Moral Fables* (Frankfurt am Main: P. Lang, 1993).

Kindrick, Robert L., *Robert Henryson* (Boston: Twayne, 1979).

—, *Henryson and the Medieval Arts of Rhetoric* (New York: Garland Publishing, 1993).

McDiarmid, Matthew P., *Robert Henryson* (Edinburgh: Scottish Academic Press, 1982).

McKenna, Stephen, *Henryson's Tragic Vision* (Frankfurt am Main: P. Lang, 1994).

MacQueen, John, *Robert Henryson: A Study of the Major Narrative Poems* (Oxford: Clarendon Press, 1967).

Newlyn, Evelyn, S., 'Robert Henryson and the Fable Tradition in the Middle Ages', *Journal of Popular Culture* 14 (Special Medieval Edition) (1980), pp. 108–18.

Powell, Marianne, *Fabula Docet: Studies in the Background and Interpretation of Henryson's Morall Fabillis* (Odense: Odense University Press, 1983).

Stearns, Marshall W., *Robert Henryson* (New York: Columbia Press, 1949).

Secondary reading: general essays

Cruttwell, Patrick, 'Two Scots Poets: Dunbar and Henryson', *The Age of Chaucer* [Pelican Guide to English Literature, vol. 1], ed. Boris Ford (London: Cassell, 1961), pp. 175–87.

Fox, Denton, 'The Coherence of Henryson's Work', *Fifteenth-Century Studies: Recent Essays*, ed. Robert F. Yeager (Hamden, CT: Archon, 1984), pp. 275–81.

Hyde, I., 'Poetic Imagery: A Point of Comparison between Henryson and Dunbar', *SSL* 2 (Columbia: University of South Carolina, 1964–5), pp. 183–97.

Jamieson, I. W. A., 'Henryson's Minor Poems', *SSL* 9 (Columbia: University of South Carolina, 1971–2), pp. 125–47.

Kindrick, Robert L., 'Henryson and the Rhetoricians: The *Ars Praedicandi*', *Scottish Language and Literature, Medieval and Renaissance*, eds Dietrich Strauss and Horst W. Drescher (Frankfurt am Main: P. Lang, 1986), pp. 255–70.

Kinghorn, A. M., 'The Minor Poems of Robert Henryson', *SSL* 3 (Columbia: University of South Carolina, 1965), pp. 30–40.

Kratzmann, Gregory, *Anglo-Scots Literary Relations 1430–1550* (Cambridge: Cambridge University Press, 1980).

MacQueen, John, 'Poetry: James I to Henryson', *The History of Scottish Literature vol. 1, Origins to 1600 (Medieval and Renaissance)*, ed. R. D. S. Jack (Aberdeen: Aberdeen University Press, 1988), pp. 55–72.

Muir, Edwin, 'Robert Henryson', *Essays on Literature and Society* (London: Hogarth Press, 1965, 2nd edition).

Newlyn, E. S., 'Tradition and Transformation in the Poetry of Robert Henryson', *SSL* 18 (Columbia: University of South Carolina, 1983), pp. 33–58.

THE MORAL FABLES

Benson, C. David, ' "O Moral Henryson" ', *Fifteenth-Century Studies: Recent Essays*, ed. Robert F. Yeager (Hamden, CT: Archon, 1984).

Bright, Phillipa M., 'Medieval Concepts of the Figure and Henryson's Figurative Technique in the *Fables*', *SSL* 25 (Columbia: University of South Carolina, 1990), pp. 134–53.

Burrow, J. A., 'Henryson: "The Preiching of the Swallow" ', *Essays in Criticism* 25 (Oxford: Blackwell, 1975), pp. 25–37.

Clark, G., 'Henryson and Aesop: The Fable Transformed', *English Literary History* 43 (1976), pp. 1–18.

Ebin, Lois, 'Henryson's "Fenyeit Fabillis": A Defence of Poetry', *Actes du 2e Colloque de Langue et de Litterature Ecossaises (Moyen Age et Renaissance)*, eds J. J. Blanchot and Claude Graf (Strasbourg: Université de Strasbourg, 1979), pp. 222–38.

1018

Fox, Denton, 'Henryson's Fables', *English Literary History* 29 (1962), pp. 337–56.

Gopen, George D., 'The Essential Seriousness of Robert Henryson's *Moral Fables*: a Study in Structure', *Studies in Philology* 82 (Chapel Hill, NC: University of North Carolina Press, 1985), pp. 42–59.

Gray, Douglas, ' "The'ende is every tales strengthe": Henryson's *Fables*', *Proceedings Of the Third International Conference on Scottish Language and Literature*, eds R. J. Lyall and Felicity Riddy (Stirling and Glasgow: University of Glasgow, 1981), pp. 225–50.

Greentree, Rosemary, 'The Debate of the Paddock and the Mouse', *SSL* 26 (Columbia: University of South Carolina, 1991), pp. 481–9.

Khinoy, Stephen, 'Tale-moral Relationships in Henryson's *Moral Fables*', *SSL* 17 (Columbia: University of South Carolina, 1982), pp. 123–36.

Kratzmann, Gregory, 'Henryson's *Fables*: The Subtell Dyte of Poetry', *SSL* 20 (Columbia: University of South Carolina, 1985), pp. 49–70.

MacDonald, D., 'Narrative Art in Henryson's *Fables*', *SSL* 3 (Columbia: University of South Carolina, 1965–1966), pp. 101–13.

—, 'Chaucer's Influence on Henryson's *Fables*: The Use of Proverbs and Sententiae', *Medium Aevum* 39 (Oxford: Blackwell, 1970), pp. 21–7.

McKenna, Steven R., 'Tragedy and the Consolation of Myth in Henryson's Fables', *SSL* 26 (Columbia: University of South Carolina, 1991), pp. 490–502.

Newlyn, E. S., 'Affective Style in Middle Scots: The Education of the Reader in Three Fables by Robert Henryson', *Nottingham Medieval Studies* 26 (Nottingham: University of Nottingham, 1982), pp. 47–56.

Pope, Robert, 'A Sly Toad, Physiognomy and the Problem of Deceit: Henryson's "The paddock and the Mous" ', *Neophilogus* 63 (1979), pp. 461–8.

Pope, Robert, 'Henryson's "The Sheep and the Dog" ', *Essays in Criticism* 30 (Oxford: Blackwell, 1980), pp. 205–14.

Toliver, H. E., 'Robert Henryson: From "Moralitas" to Irony', *English Studies* 46 (1965), pp. 300–9.

THE TESTAMENT OF CRESSEID

Aronstein, Susan, 'Cresseid Reading Cresseid: Redemption and Translation in Henryson's *Testament*', *SLJ* 21 (Aberdeen: Association for Scottish Literary Studies, 1994), pp. 5–22.

Aswell, E. D., 'The Role of Fortune in *The Testament of Cresseid*', *Philological Quarterly* 46 (Iowa City: University of Iowa, 1967), pp. 471–87.

Bennett, J. A. W., 'Henryson's *Testament*: A Flawed Masterpiece', *SLJ* 1 (Aberdeen: Association for Scottish Literary Studies, 1974), pp. 5–16.

Boitani, Piero (ed.), *The European Tradition of Troilus* (Oxford: Oxford University Press, 1989).

Craik, Thomas W., 'The Substance and Structure of *The Testament of Cresseid*', *Bards and Makars: Scottish Language and Literature, Medieval and Renaissance*, eds A. J. Aitken et al. (Glasgow: Glasgow University Press, 1977), pp. 22–6.

Craun, Edwin D., 'Blaspheming Her 'Awin Gods': Cresseid's "Lamentatioun" in Henryson's *Testament*', *Studies in Philology* 82 (Chapel Hill, NC: University of North Carolina Press, 1985), pp. 25–41.

Cullen, Mairi Ann, 'Cresseid Excused: A Re-reading of Henryson's *Testament of Cresseid*' *SSL* 20 (Columbia: University of South Carolina, 1985), pp. 137–59.

Duncan, Douglas, 'Henryson's *Testament of Cresseid*', *Essays in Criticism* 11 (Oxford: Blackwell, 1961), pp. 128–35.

Godman, Peter, 'Henryson's Masterpiece', *Review of English Studies* 35 (1984), pp. 291–300.

Hanna, Ralph W., 'Cresseid's Dream and Henryson's *Testament*', *Chaucer and Middle English*

Studies in Honour of Russell Hope Robbins, ed. B. Rowland (London: Allen & Unwin, 1974), pp. 288–97.

Harth, Sydney, 'Henryson Reinterpreted', *Essays in Criticism* 11 (Oxford: Blackwell, 1961), pp. 471–80.

Harty, Kevin J., 'Cresseid and the Narrator: A Reading of Robert Henryson's "Testament of Cresseid" ', *Studi Medievali* Series 3, 23(2) (1983), pp. 753–65.

Jentoft, C. W., 'Henryson as Authentic Chaucerian: Narrator, Character and Courtly Love in *The Testament of Cresseid*', *SSL* 10(2) (Columbia: University of South Carolina, 1972–3), pp. 94–102.

McDonald, A. A., ' "Fervent Weather": A Difficulty in Robert Henryson's *Testament of Cresseid*', *Scottish Language and Literature, Medieval and Renaissance*, eds Dietrich Strauss and Horst W. Drescher (Frankfurt am Main: P. Lang, 1986), pp. 271–80.

McDonald, C., 'Venus and the Goddess Fortune in the *Testament of Cresseid*', *SLJ* 4(2) (Aberdeen: Association for Scottish Literary Studies, 1977), pp. 14–24.

McKenna, Steven R., 'Henryson's "Tragedie" of Cresseid', *SLJ* 18 (Aberdeen: Association for Scottish Literary Studies, 1990), pp. 26–36.

McNamara, John, 'Divine Justice in Henryson's *Testament of Cresseid*', *SSL* 11 (Columbia: University of South Carolina, 1973–4), pp. 99–107.

Noll, Dolores L., '*The Testament of Cresseid*: Are Christian Interpretations Valid?', *SSL* 9 (Columbia: University of South Carolina, 1971–2), pp. 16–25.

Parkinson, David J., 'Henryson's Scottish Tragedy', *Chaucer Review: A Journal of Medieval Studies and Literary Criticism* 25(4) (1991), pp. 355–62.

Patterson, Lee W., 'Christian and Pagan in *The Testament of Cresseid*', *Studies in Philology* 52 (Chapel Hill, NC: University of North Carolina Press, 1973), pp. 696–714.

Pittock, Malcolm, 'The Complexity of Henryson's the *Testament Of Cresseid*', *Essays in Criticism* 40(3) (Oxford: Blackwell, 1990), pp. 198–221.

Sklute, Larry M., 'Phebus Descending: Rhetoric and Moral Vision in Henryson's *Testament of Cresseid*', *English Literary History* 44 (1977), pp. 189–204.

Strauss, J., 'To Speak Once More of Cresseid: Henryson's *Testament* Reconsidered', *SLJ* 4 (Aberdeen: Association for Scottish Literary Studies, 1977), pp. 5–13.

Twycross-Martin, Henrietta, 'Moral Pattern in the Testament of Cresseid', *Chaucer and Fifteenth Century Poetry*, eds Julia Boffey and Janet Cowan [King's College London Medieval Studies 5] (London: King's College, 1991), pp. 30–50.

Volkbroke, S., 'Sickness and Death: Crime and Punishment in Henryson's *The Testament of Cresseid*', *Anglia* 113(2) (1995), pp. 163–83.

DUNBAR

Bawcutt, P. (ed.), *The Poetry of William Dunbar*, 2 vols (Aberdeen: Association for Scottish Literary Studies, 1999).

— (ed.), *Selected Poems; William Dunbar* (Harlow: Longman, 1996).

—, and Riddy, F. (eds), *Selected Poems of Dunbar and Henryson* (Edinburgh: Scottish Academic Press, Scottish Classics Series 16, 1992).

Secondary reading

Bawcutt, Priscilla, *William Dunbar* (Oxford: Clarendon Press, 1992).

—, 'William Dunbar and Gavin Douglas', *The History of Scottish Literature vol. 1, Origins to 1600 (Medieval and Renaissance)*, ed. R. D. S. Jack (Aberdeen: Aberdeen University Press, 1988), pp. 73–89.

Baxter, J. W., *William Dunbar: a biographical study* (Edinburgh: Oliver & Boyd, 1952).

Cunningham, J. V., 'Logic and Lyric', *Modern Philology* 51 (Chicago: University of Chicago Press, 1953), pp. 33–41.

Ebin, Lois, *Illuminator, Makar, Vates: Visions of Poetry in the Fifteenth Century* (Lincoln, NE, and London: University of Nebraska Press, 1988).

Hasler, Anthony J., 'William Dunbar: The Elusive Subject', *Bryght Lanternis: Essays on the Language and Literature of Medieval and Renaissance Scotland*, eds J. Derrick McClure and Michael R. G. Spiller (Aberdeen: Aberdeen University Press, 1989), pp. 194–208.

Jack, R. D. S., *The Poetry of William Dunbar* (Aberdeen: Association for Scottish Literary Studies, Scotnotes, 1997).

—, 'Dunbar and Lydgate', *SSL* 8 (Columbia: University of South Carolina, 1970–1), pp. 215–27.

Morgan, Edwin, 'Dunbar and the Language of Poetry', *Essays* (Manchester: Carcanet Press, 1974), pp. 81–99.

Norman, Joanne S., 'William Dunbar: Grand *Rhètoriqueur*', *Bryght Lanternis: Essays on the Language and Literature of Medieval Scotland*, eds J. Derrick McClure and Michael R. G. Spiller (Aberdeen: Aberdeen University Press, 1989), pp. 209–20.

—, 'A Postmodern Look at a Medieval Poet: the Case of William Dunbar', *SSL* 26 (Columbia: University of South Carolina, 1991), pp. 343–53.

Reiss, Edmund, 'The Ironic Art of William Dunbar', *Fifteenth-Century Studies: Recent Essays*, ed. Robert F. Yeager (Hamden, CT: Archon Books, 1984), pp. 321–31.

Ross, Ian S., *William Dunbar* (Leiden: E. J. Brill, 1981).

Scott, Tom, *Dunbar: A Critical Exposition of the Poems* (Edinburgh: Oliver & Boyd, 1966).

Speirs, John, 'William Dunbar', *Scrutiny* 7 (1938), pp. 56–68.

Dunbar's language

Burness, Edwina, 'Dunbar and the Nature of Bawdy', *Bryght Lanternis: Essays on the Language and Literature of Medieval Scotland*, eds J. Derrick McClure and Michael R. G. Spiller (Aberdeen: Aberdeen University Press, 1989), pp. 209–20.

Ebin, Lois, 'Dunbar's "Fresch Anamalit Termis Celicall" and the Art of the Occasional Poet', *Chaucer Review* 17 (1982), pp. 282–9.

— (ed.), 'Vernacular Poetics in the Middle Ages', *Studies in Medieval Culture* 16 (Kalamazoo, MI: Medieval Institute Publications, 1984).

Hyde, I., 'Primary Sources and Associations of Dunbar's Aureate Imagery', *Modern Language Review* 51 (Cambridge: Modern Humanities Research Association, 1956), pp. 481–92.

—, 'Poetic Imagery: A Point of Comparison between Henryson and Dunbar', *SSL* 2 (Columbia: University of South Carolina, 1964–5), pp. 183–97.

Morgan, Edwin, 'Dunbar and the Language of Poetry', *Essays in Criticism* 11 (Oxford: Blackwell, 1952), pp. 138–57. Also in *Essays* (Cheadle: Carcanet, 1974), pp. 81–99.

Specific poems

Bawcutt, Priscilla, 'Dunbar's Christmas Carol', *Scottish Language and Literature, Medieval and Renaissance*, eds D. Strauss and Horst W. Drescher (Frankfurt am Main: P. Lang, 1986), pp. 381–92.

Drexler, R. D., 'Dunbar's "Lament for the Makaris" and the Dance of Death Tradition', *SSL* 13 (Columbia: University of South Carolina, 1975–76), pp. 144–58.

Evans, Deanna D., 'Ambivalent Artifice in Dunbar's *The Thrissill and the Rois*', *SSL* 22 (Columbia: University of South Carolina, 1987), pp. 95–105.

—, 'Bakhtin's Literary Carnivalesque and Dunbar's "Fasternis Evin in Hell"', *SSL* 26 (Columbia: University of South Carolina, 1991), pp. 354–65.

—, 'Dunbar's *Tretis*: The Seven Deadly Sins in Carnivalesque Disguise', *Neophilologus* 73 (1989), pp. 130–41.

Fradenburg, Louise O., *City, Marriage, Tournament: Arts of Rule in Late Medieval Scotland* (Madison, WI: University of Wisconsin Press, 1991) [on 'The Thrissill and the Rois'].

READING LISTS

Gray, Douglas, 'Rough Music: Some Early Invectives and Flytings', *Yearbook of English Studies* 14 (Cambridge: Modern Humanities Research Association, 1984), pp. 21–43.

Hay, Bryan S., 'Dunbar's Flyting Abbot: Apocalypse Made to Order', *SSL* 11 (Columbia: University of South Carolina, 1973–4), pp. 217–25.

Lyall, R. J., 'William Dunbar's Beast Fable', *SLJ* 1 (Aberdeen: Association for Scottish Literary Studies, 1974), pp. 17–28.

Macafee, Caroline A., 'A Stylistic Analysis of Dunbar's "In Winter"', *Proceedings of the Third International Conference on Scottish Language and Literature, Medieval and Renaissance*, eds Roderick J. Lyall and Felicity Riddy (Stirling and Glasgow: University of Glasgow, 1981), pp. 359–69.

McKenna, Steven R., 'Drama and Invective: Traditions in Dunbar's "Fasternis Evin in Hell"', *SSL* 24 (Columbia: University of South Carolina, 1989), pp. 129–41.

Robichaud, Paul, ' "To Heir Quhat I sould Wryt" ': 'The Flyting of Dunbar and Kennedy' and 'Scots Oral Culture', *SLJ* 25(2) (Aberdeen: Association for Scottish Literary Studies, 1998), pp. 9–16.

Ting, Judith, 'A Reappraisal of Dunbar's "Dregy"', *SLJ* 41(2) (Aberdeen: Association for Scottish Literary Studies, 1987), pp. 19–36.

THE GOLDYN TARGE

Ebin, Lois A., 'The Themes of Poetry in Dunbar's *The Golden Targe*', *Chaucer Review* 7 (1972), pp. 147–59.

Fox, Denton, 'Dunbar's The Golden Targe', *English Literary History* 26 (1959), pp. 211–34.

Harrington, David V., 'The "Wofull Prisonnere" in Dunbar's *Goldyn Targe*', *SLJ* 22 (Aberdeen: Association for Scottish Literary Studies, 1987), pp. 173–82.

Lyall, R. J., 'Moral Allegory in Dunbar's Goldyn Targe', *SSL* 11 (Columbia: University of South Carolina, 1973–4), pp. 47–65.

Tilley, E. Allen, 'The Meaning of Dunbar's *The Golden Targe*', *SSL* 10 (Columbia: University of South Carolina, 1972–3), pp. 220–31.

THE TRETIS OF THE TUA MARIIT WEMEN AND THE WEDO

Bentsen, Eileen, and Sanderlin, S. L., 'The Profits of Marriage in Late Medieval Scotland', *SLJ* 12(2) (Aberdeen: Association for Scottish Literary Studies, 1985), pp. 5–18.

Bitterling, Klaus, 'The Tretis of the Tua Mariit Wemen and the Wedo: Some Comments on Words, Imagery, and Genre', *Scottish Language and Literature, Medieval and Renaissance*, eds Dietrich Strauss and Horst W. Drescher (Frankfurt am Main: P. Lang, 1986), pp. 337–58.

Butness, Edwina, 'Female Language in the *Tretis of the Tua Mariit Wemen and the Wedo*', *Scottish Language and Literature, Medieval and Renaissance*, eds Dietrich Strauss and Horst W. Drescher (Frankfurt am Main: P. Lang, 1986), pp. 359–68.

Fries, Maureen, 'Medieval Concepts of the Female and their Satire in the Poetry of William Dunbar', *Fifteenth Century Studies* 7 (Stuttgart: H.-D. Heinz, Akademischer Verlag, 1983), pp. 55–77.

Kinsley, James, 'The Tretis of the Tua Mariit Wemen and the Wedo', *Medium Aevum* 23 (Oxford, 1954), pp. 31–6.

McCarthy, Shaun, ' "Syne Maryit I a Marchand": Dunbar's *Mariit Wemen* and their Audience', *SSL* 18 (Columbia: University of South Carolina, 1983), pp. 138–56.

Moore, Arthur K., 'The Setting of *The Tua Mariit Wemen and the Wedo*', *English Studies* 32 (1951), pp. 56–62.

Pearcy, R. J., 'The Genre of William Dunbar's *Tretis of the Tua Mariit Wemen and the Wedo*', *Speculum* 55 (1980), pp. 58–74.

Roth, Elizabeth, 'Criticism and Taste: Readings of Dunbar's *Tretis*', *SLJ: Supplement* 15 (Aberdeen: Association for Scottish Literary Studies, 1981), pp. 57–90.

Chapter 3: Early Scottish Drama

SCOTTISH MEDIEVAL AND RENAISSANCE DRAMA

Billington, Sandra, 'The fool and the moral in English and Scottish Morality Plays', *Popular Drama in Northern Europe in the Later Middle Ages. A Symposium*, ed. Flemming Gotthelf Anderson (Odense: Odense University Press, 1988), pp. 113–33.

Cameron, Alisdair, 'Theatre in Scotland: 1214 to the present', *Scotland: A Concise Cultural History*, ed. Paul H. Scott (Edinburgh: Mainstream, 1993), pp. 145–58.

Carpenter, Sarah, 'Drama and Politics: Scotland in the 1530s', *Medieval English Theatre* 10(2) (1998), pp. 81–90.

Findlay, Bill, 'Beginnings to 1700', *A History of Scottish Theatre* (Edinburgh: Edinburgh University Press, 1998).

Lawson, Robb, *The Story of the Scots Stage* (Paisley, 1917).

Mill, Anna, J., *Mediaeval Plays in Scotland* (Edinburgh: Blackwood, 1927).

'The Records of Scots Medieval Plays: interpretations and misinterpretations', *Bards and Makars: Scottish Language and Literature: Medieval and Renaissance* (Glasgow: Glasgow University Press, 1977), pp. 136–42.

LYNDSAY

Lyall, R. (ed.), *Ane Satire of the Thrie Estaitis* (Edinburgh: Canongate, Canongate Classics no. 18, 1989).

Secondary reading

Cairns, Sandra, 'Sir David Lindsay's *Dreme*: Poetry, Propaganda and Encomium in the Scottish Court', *The Spirit of the Court: Selected Proceedings of the Fourth Congress of International Courtly Literature Society*, eds Glyn S. Burgess et al. (Dover, NH: Brewer, 1985), pp. 110–19.

Carpenter, Sarah, 'David Lindsay and James V: court literature as current event', *Vernacular Literature and Current Affairs in the Early Sixteenth-Century: France, England and Scotland*, eds Jennifer Britnell and Richard Britnell (Ashgate, 2000), pp. 135–52.

Edington, Carol, *Court and Culture in Renaissance Scotland: Sir David Lindsay of the Mount* (East Linton: Tuckwell Press, 1995).

Graf, Claude, 'Theatre and Politics: Lyndsay's *Satyre of the Thrie Estaitis*', *Bards and Makars: Scottish Language and Literature, Medieval and Renaissance*, eds A. J. Aitken et al. (Glasgow: Glasgow University Press, 1977), pp. 143–55.

—, 'Audience Involvement in Lindsay's *Satyre of the Thrie Estatis*', *Scottish Language and Literature, Medieval and Renaissance*, eds D. Strauss and Horst W. Drescher (Frankfurt am Main: P. Lang, 1986), pp. 423–35.

Jack, Ronald, 'Medieval Drama Lives Again? Lindsay's *Satire* and Kemp's *Satire*', *Chapman* 68 (Edinburgh: Chapman Publications, 1992), pp. 81–6.

Kantrowitz, J. S., 'Encore: Lindsay's *Thrie Estaitis*, Date and New Evidence', *SSL* 10 (Columbia: University of South Carolina, 1972–3), pp. 18–32.

—, *Dramatic Allegory: Lindsay's Ane Satyre of the Thrie Estaitis* (Lincoln, NE: University of Nebraska Press, 1975).

Reid, David, 'Rule and Misrule in Lindsay's *Thrie Estaits* and Pitcairne's *Assembly*', *SLJ* 11(2) (Aberdeen: Association for Scottish Literary Studies, 1984), pp. 5–24.

Walker, Greg, 'Sir David Lindsay's *Ane Satire of the Thrie Estaitis* and the Politics of Reformation', *SLJ* 16(2) (Aberdeen: Association for Scottish Literary Studies, 1989), pp. 5–17.

PAMPHILUS

Bawcutt, Priscilla, 'Pamphilus de Amore "in Inglish Toung"', *Medium Aevum* 64. 2 (1995), pp. 264–72

Baxter, Jamie Reid, 'Politics, Passion and Poetry in the Circle of James VI: John Burel and his Surviving Works', *A Palace in the Wild*, eds L. A. J. R. Houwen, A. A. MacDonald and S. L. Mapstone (Leuven: Peeters, 2000), pp. 199–248.

PHILOTUS

Irving, David, *Philotus* [preface] (Edinburgh: Bannatyne Club, 1835).

Jack, R. D. S., and Rozendaal, P. A. T. (eds), *The Mercat Anthology of Early Scottish Literature 1375–1707* (Edinburgh: Mercat Press, 1997), pp. 390–432.

Mill, Anna J., *Philotus Miscellany Volume* [introduction] (Edinburgh: Scottish Text Society, 1933).

Secondary reading

Baxter, Jamie Reid, 'Rich and rollicking or flat and unfocused?: Barnaby Riche's *Phylotus* contrasted with the Scottish *Philotus*', *Odd Alliances: Scottish Studies in European Contexts*, eds N. McMillan and K. Stirling (Glasgow: Cruithne Press, 1999).

Jack, R. D. S., *The Italian Influence on Scottish Literature* (Edinburgh: Edinburgh University Press, 1972), pp. 42–53.

McDiarmid, Matthew P., 'Philotus: A Play of the Scottish Renaissance', *Forum for Modern Language Studies* 3 (Oxford: Oxford University Press, 1967), pp. 223–35.

See also the section on *Philotus* in Unit 1E(2) by Jamie Reid Baxter, *William Drummond, Women's Writing and Philotus* (MPhil in Scottish Literature, Distance Teaching Unit, Glasgow University, Department of Scottish Literature), which provides an edited text and detailed critical commentary.

Chapter 4: Renaissance Poetry

GENERAL CRITICISM

Bernhart, A. Walter, 'Castalian Poetics and the "verie Twichstane musique"', *Proceedings of the Fourth International Conference on Scottish Language and Literature (Medieval and Renaissance)*, eds Dietrich Strauss and Horst W. Drescher (Frankfurt am Main: P. Lang, 1986).

Carruthers, Gerard, 'Form and Substance in the Poetry of the Castalian Band', *SLJ* 26(2) (Aberdeen: Association for Scottish Literary Studies, 1999).

Dunnigan, Sarah M., '"O venus soverane": erotic politics and poetic practice at the courts of Mary, Queen of Scots and James VI', *Terranglian Territories*, ed. Suzanne Hagemann (Frankfurt: P. Lang, 1999).

—, 'Scottish Women Writers c1560–c1650', *A History of Scottish Women Writing*, eds Douglas Gifford and Dorothy McMillan (Edinburgh: Edinburgh University Press, 1997), pp. 15–43.

Jack, R. D. S., 'Imitation in the Scottish Sonnet', *Comparative Literature XX* (Eugene, OR: University of Oregon, 1968), pp. 313–28.

—, *The Italian Influence on Scottish Literature* (Edinburgh: Edinburgh University Press, 1972).

—, 'Petrarch in English and Scottish Renaissance Literature', *Modern Language Review* 71 (Cambridge: Modern Humanities Research Association, 1976), pp. 801–11.

—, *Scottish Literature's Debt to Italy* (Edinburgh: Edinburgh University Press, 1986).

—, 'The French connection: Scottish and French Literature in the Renaissance', *Scotia* 18 (Old Dominion University, 1989), pp. 1–16.

Kastner, L. E., 'The Scottish Sonneteers and the French Poets', *Modern Language Review* 3 (Cambridge: Modern Humanities Research Association, 1907), pp. 3–15.

Kinsley, James (ed.), *Scottish Poetry: A Critical Survey* (London: Cassell, 1955).

McDiarmid, Matthew P., 'Scottish Love Poetry before 1600: A Character and Appreciation', *Proceedings of the Fourth International Conference on Scottish Language and Literature (Medieval and Renaissance)*, eds Dietrich Strauss and Horst W. Drescher (Frankfurt am Main: P. Lang, 1986).

Scott, Janet, *Les Sonnets Elizabethains* (Paris, 1929).

Shire, Helena M., *Song, Dance and Poetry of the Court of Scotland Under James VI* (Cambridge: Cambridge University Press, 1969).

Spiller, Michael R. G., *The Development of the Sonnet* (London: Routledge, 1992).

Waller, Gary, *English Poetry of the Sixteenth Century* (London: Longman, 1986).

JAMES VI

Craigie, James (ed.), *The Poems of King James VI of Scotland*, 2 vols (Edinburgh and London: Scottish Text Society, 1955–8).

Secondary reading

Akrigg, G. P. V., 'The Literary Achievement of King James I', *University of Toronto Quarterly* 44 (Toronto: University of Toronto Press, 1975), pp. 115–29.

Dunnigan, Sarah M., 'Discovering desire in the *Amatoria* of James VI', *Royal Subjects: the Writings of James VI and I*, eds Daniel Fischlin and Mark Fortier (Detroit: University of Wayne State Press, 2002).

Fischlin, Daniel, and Fortier, Mark (eds), *Royal Subjects: the Writings of James VI and I* (University of Wayne State Press, 2002).

Fleming, Morna, 'The Amatoria of James VI: Loving by the Reulis', *Royal Subjects: the Writings of James VI and I*, eds D. Fischlin and M. Fortier (University of Wayne State Press, forthcoming 2001).

Jack, R. D. S., 'James VI and Renaissance Poetic Theory', *English* XVI (London: Oxford University Press, 1967), pp. 208–11.

—, 'Poetry under King James VI', *The History of Scottish Literature Vol 1, Origins to 1660*, ed. R. D. S. Jack (Aberdeen: Aberdeen University Press, 1988).

McClure, Derrick, J., ' "O Phoenix Escossois": James VI as Poet', *A Day Estivall*, eds Alisoun Gardner-Medwin and Janet Hadley Williams (Aberdeen: Aberdeen University Press, 1990), pp. 96–111.

SIR WILLIAM ALEXANDER

Kastner, L. E. and Charlton, H. B. (eds), *The Poetical Works of Sir William Alexander, Earl of Stirling*, 2 vols (Edinburgh and London: Scottish Text Society, 1921–9).

Secondary reading

Gordon, T. Crouther, *Four Notable Scots* (Stirling: Eneas Mackay, 1960), pp. 13–39.

Jack, R. D. S., *The Italian Influence on Scottish Literature* (Edinburgh: Edinburgh University Press, 1979).

Klein, Holger M., *English and Scottish Sonnet Sequences of the Renaissance*, 2 vols (Hildesheim: Olms, 1984), pp. 150–204.

MacDiarmid, Matthew P., 'Scots Versions of Poems by Sir Robert Aytoun and Sir William Alexander', *N&Q* CCII (1957), pp. 32–5.

Spiller, Michael, 'Poetry After the Union 1603–1660', *The History of Scottish Literature*, vol. 1, ed. R. D. S. Jack (Aberdeen: Aberdeen University Press, 1988), pp. 141–62.

—, *The Development of the Sonnet* (London: Routledge, 1992).

SIR ROBERT AYTON
Gullans, C. B. (ed.), *The English and Latin Poems of Sir Robert Ayton* (Edinburgh and London: Scottish Text Society, 1963).

Secondary reading
Scott, M. J. W., 'Robert Ayton: Scottish Metaphysical', *SLJ* 2 (Aberdeen: Association for Scottish Literary Studies, 1975), pp. 5–16.

WILLIAM DRUMMOND OF HAWTHORNDEN
Kastner L. E., *The Poetical Works of William Drummond of Hawthornden*, 2 vols (Edinburgh: Scottish Text Society, 1913).

Secondary reading
Atkinson, David W., 'The Religious Voices of Drummond of Hawthornden', *SSL* 21 (Columbia: University of South Carolina, 1986), pp. 197–209.
—, 'William Drummond as a Baroque Poet', *SSL* 26 (Columbia: University of South Carolina, 1991), pp. 395–409.
Calder, Charles, '*Artificiosa Eloquentia*: Grammatical and Rhetorical Schemes in the Poetry of William Drummond', *SSL* 26 (Columbia: University of South Carolina, 1991), pp. 380–93.
Cummings, Robert, 'Drummond's *Forth Feasting*: A Panegyric for King James in Scotland', *The Seventeenth Century* 2(1) (Durham: Centre for Seventeenth-Century Studies, University of Durham, 1987), pp. 1–18.
Fogle, F. R., *A Critical Study of William Drummond of Hawthornden* (New York, 1952).
Jack, R. D. S., 'Drummond: The Major Scottish Sources', *SSL* 6 (Columbia: University of South Carolina, 1968–9), pp. 36–46.
—, *The Italian Influence on Scottish Literature* (Edinburgh: Edinburgh University Press, 1972), pp. 113–43.
MacDonald, R. H., *The Library of Drummond of Hawthornden* (Edinburgh: Edinburgh University Press, 1971).
Morgan, Edwin, 'How Good a Poet is Drummond?', *Crossing the Border* (Edinburgh, 1974; Manchester: Carcanet, 1990), pp. 56–66.
—, 'Gavin Douglas and William Drummond as Translators', *Bards and Makars*, eds A. J. Aitken et al. (Glasgow: University of Glasgow Press, 1977), pp. 149–200.
Reid, David, 'Royalty and Self-Absorption in Drummond's Poetry', *SSL* 22 (Columbia: University of South Carolina, 1987), pp. 115–31.
Severance, Sibyl Lutz, ' "Some Other Figure": The Vision of Change in Flowres of Sion, 1623', *Spenser Studies* II (New York: AMS Press), pp. 217–28.
Wallerstein, Ruth, 'The Style of Drummond of Hawthornden in its relation to his Translators', *PMLA* 48 (Modern Language Association of America, 1933), pp. 1089–107.
Weiss, Wolfgang, 'The Theme and Structure of Drummond of Hawthornden's Sonnet Sequence', *Proceedings of the Fourth International Conference on Scottish Language and Literature (Medieval and Renaissance)*, eds Dietrich Strauss and Horst W. Drescher (Frankfurt am Main: P. Lang, 1986), pp. 459–66.

WILLIAM FOWLER
Meikle, Henry W., Craigie, James and Purves, John (eds), *The Works of William Fowler*, 3 vols (Edinburgh and London: Scottish Text Society, 1912–39).

Secondary reading

Jack, R. D. S., 'William Fowler and Italian Literature', *Modern Language Review* 65 (Cambridge: Modern Humanities Research Association, 1970), pp. 481–92.

—, *The Italian Influence on Scottish Literature* (Edinburgh: Edinburgh University Press, 1972).

—, *Scottish Literature's Debt to Italy* (Edinburgh: Edinburgh University Press, 1986).

—, 'Poetry under King James VI', *The History of Scottish Literature*, vol. 1, ed. R. D. S. Jack (Aberdeen: Aberdeen University Press, 1988), pp. 125–39.

Purves, John, 'Fowler and Scoto-Italian Cultural Relations in the Sixteenth Century', *STS*, vol. 3, pp. lxxx–cl.

Smith, Janet C., *Les Sonnets Elisabéthains* (Paris, 1929).

ALEXANDER MONTGOMERIE

Cranstoun, James (ed.), *The Poems of Alexander Montgomerie* (Edinburgh and London: Scottish Text Society, 1887).

Parkinson, David J., *Poems; Alexander Montgomerie* (Edinburgh: Scottish Text Society, 2000).

Stevenson, George (ed.), *The Poems of Alexander Montgomerie* (Edinburgh and London: Scottish Text Society, 1907) [Supplementary Volume].

Secondary reading

Jack, R. D. S., *Alexander Montgomerie* (Edinburgh: Scottish Academic Press, 1985).

—, 'The Lyrics of Alexander Montgomerie', *Review of English Studies* 20 (1969), pp. 168–81.

—, 'The Theme of Fortune in the Verse of Alexander Montgomerie', *SLJ* 10(2) (Aberdeen: Association for Scottish Literary Studies, 1983), pp. 25–44.

Parkinson, David J., 'Montgomerie's Language', *Bryght Lanternis: Essays on the Language and Literature of Medieval and Renaissance Scotland*, eds J. Derrick McClure and Michael R. G. Spiller (Aberdeen: Aberdeen University Press, 1989).

Shire, H. M., 'Alexander Montgomerie: "The Oppositione of the Court to Conscience"', *SSL* 3 (Columbia: University of South Carolina, 1965–6), pp. 144–50.

—, *Song, Dance and Poetry of the Court of Scotland under King James VI* (London: Cambridge University Press, 1969).

SLJ 26(2) (Aberdeen: Association for Scottish Literary Studies, 1999): a special issue devoted to Montgomerie's writing with essays by Gerard Carruthers, Sarah M. Dunnigan, Morna J. Fleming, R. J. Lyall and Sally Mapstone.

JOHN STEWART OF BALDYNNEIS

Crockett, Thomas (ed.), *The Poems of John Stewart of Baldynneis* (Edinburgh and London: Scottish Text Society, 1913).

Secondary reading

Dunlop, Geoffrey A., 'John Stewart of Baldynneis: The Scottish Desportes', *Scottish Historical Review* 12 (Glasgow: James Maclehose, 1915), pp. 303–10.

Dunnigan, Sarah M., 'Poetic Objects of Desire: rhetorical culture and seductive arts in the lyrics of John Stewart of Baldynneis', *SLJ* 26(1) (Aberdeen: Association for Scottish Literary Studies, 1999).

MacDiarmid, Matthew P., 'John Stewart of Baldynneis', *Scottish Historical Review* 29 (Glasgow: James Maclehose, 1950), pp. 36–52.

—, 'Notes on the Poems of John Stewart of Baldynneis', *Review of English Studies* 24 (1948), pp. 12–18.

Rodger, Donna, 'John Stewart of Baldynneis: ane maist perfyt prentes', *Odd Alliances: Scottish Studies in European Contexts*, eds N. McMillan and K. Stirling (Glasgow: Cruithne Press, 1999), pp. 2–10.

Chapter 5: Ballads

BALLAD ANTHOLOGIES AND COLLECTIONS
Buchan, David (ed.), *A Scottish Ballad Book* (London and Boston: Routledge & Kegan Paul, 1973).
— (ed.), *Scottish Tradition: A Collection of Scottish Folk Literature* (London: Routledge & Kegan Paul, 1984).
Child, Francis James (ed.), *English and Scottish Popular Ballads* [5 vols, 1882–98] (Boston and New York: Dover publications, 1965, 2nd edition).
Kerrigan, Catherine (ed.), *An Anthology of Scottish Women Poets* (Edinburgh: Edinburgh University Press, 1991).
Kinsley, James, *The Oxford Book of Ballads* (Oxford: Oxford University Press, 1969).
Lyle, Emily (ed.), *Scottish Ballads* (Edinburgh: Canongate, 1994).
— (ed.), *Andrew Crawfurd's Collection of Ballads and Songs* (Edinburgh: Scottish Text Society, 1975).
Paterson, Wilma (ed.), *Songs of Scotland* (London: Mainstream, 1996).
Shuldam-Shaw, Patrick and Lyle, Emily (eds), *The Greig-Duncan Folk Song Collection* [8 vols, 1981–2001] (Edinburgh: The Mercat Press).

BALLADS IN PERFORMANCE
It Fell on A Day, Vol. 17, The Voice of the People (London: Topic Records, 1998). CD.
Folksongs of North East Scotland: Songs from the Greig-Duncan Collection (Edinburgh: Greentrax Recordings, 1995). CD.
Mary Macqueen's Ballads (Edinburgh: Scottish Text Society, no date). Audio cassette. *O'er his Grave the Grass Grew Green, Vol. 3, The Voice of the People* (London: Topic Records, 1998). CD.
Scottish Tradition 5: The Muckle Sangs (Edinburgh: Greentrax Recordings, 1992). CD.

BALLAD CRITICISM
Anderson, Flemming G., *Commonplace and Creativity* (Odense: Odense University Press, 1985).
Bold, Alan, *The Ballad* (London: Methuen, 1979).
Bronson, B. H., *The Ballad as Song* (Berkeley, CA: University of California Press, 1969).
—, *The Traditional Tunes of the Child Ballads* (Princeton: Princeton University Press, 1959–72).
—, *The Singing Tradition of Child's Popular Ballads* (Princeton: Princeton University Press, 1976).
Brown, Mary Ellen, 'Old Singing Women and the Canons of Scottish Balladry and Song', *A History of Scottish Women's Writing*, ed. Douglas Gifford and Dorothy McMillan (Edinburgh: Edinburgh University Press, 1997), pp. 44–57.
Buchan, David, *The Ballad and the Folk* (London: Routledge, 1972) [recommended].
Cowan, Edward J. (ed.), *The Ballad in Scottish History* (East Linton: Tuckwell Press, 2000).
Craig, David, *Scottish Literature and the Scottish People 1680–1830* (London: Chatto & Windus, 1961).
Crawford, Thomas, *Society and the Lyric: A Study of the Song Culture of Eighteenth-Century Scotland* (Edinburgh: Scottish Academic Press, 1979).
Elliot, F., *Further Essays on the Border Ballads* (Edinburgh, 1910).
Fergusson, Sir James, 'The Ballads', *Scottish Poetry: A Critical Survey*, ed. James Kinsley (Cassell, 1955), pp. 99–118.

Freedman, Jean R., 'With Child: Illegitimate Pregnancy in Scottish Traditional Ballads', *Folklore Forum* 24(1) (1991), pp. 3–18.

Harker, Dave, *Fakesong* (Milton Keynes: Open University Press, 1985).

Harris, Joseph (ed.), *The Ballad and Oral Literature* (Cambridge, MA, and London: Harvard University Press, 1991).

Henderson, Hamish, 'At the Foot o' Yon Excellin' Brae: the Language of Scottish Folksong', *Scotland and the Lowland Tongue*, ed. J. Derrick McClure (Aberdeen: Aberdeen University Press, 1983), pp. 100–28.

—, *Alias MacAlias: Writings on Songs, Folk, and Literature* (Edinburgh: Polygon, 1992).

—, 'The Oral Tradition', *Scotland: A Concise Cultural History*, ed. Paul H. Scott (Edinburgh: Mainstream Publishing, 1993), pp. 159–71.

Hodgart, M. J. C., *The Ballads* (Hutchinson University Library, 1950).

Marsden, John, and Barlow, Nia (eds), *The Illustrated Border Ballads: The Anglo-Scottish Frontier* (London: Macmillan, 1990).

McCarthy, William, *The Ballad Matrix: Personality, Milieu and the Oral Tradition* (Bloomington: University of Indiana Press, 1990).

MacDiarmid, M. P., 'The Scottish Ballads: Appreciation and Explication', *Proceedings of the Third International Conference on Scottish Language and Literature*, eds R. J. Lyall and Felicity Riddy (Glasgow: University of Glasgow Press, 1981), pp. 107–24.

Muir, Willa, *Living With Ballads* (London: Hogarth, 1965).

Nicolaisen, W. F. H., 'Humour in Traditional Ballads (Mainly Scottish)', *Folklore* 103(1) (Routledge, 1992), pp. 27–39.

Niles, John D., and Long, Eleanor R., 'Context and Loss in Scottish Ballad Tradition', *Western Folklore* 45(2) (1986), pp. 93–109.

Oats, Joyce Carol, 'The English and Scottish Traditional Ballads', *The Southern Review* 15 (Baton Rouge: Louisiana State University Press, 1979), pp. 560–66.

Ong, Walter, *Orality and Literacy: The Technologizing of the Word* (London: Routledge, New Accents Series, 1982).

—, *Rhetoric, Romance and Technology* (London: Cornell University Press, 1971).

Parry, Milman, *The Making of Homeric Verse*, ed. Adam Parry (Oxford: Clarendon Press, 1971).

Petrie, Elaine, 'What a Voice! Women, Repertoire and Loss in the Singing Tradition', *A History of Scottish Women's Writing*, eds Douglas Gifford and Dorothy McMillan (Edinburgh: Edinburgh University Press, 1997), pp. 262–73.

Pound, L., *Poetic Origins and the Ballad* (New York: Russell, 1962).

Purser, John, *Scotland's Music* (Edinburgh: Mainstream, 1992).

Vansina, Jan, *Oral Tradition as History* (Wisconsin: University of Wisconsin Press, 1985).

Watson, Roderick, *The Literature of Scotland* (London: Macmillan, 1984).

Wimberly, L. C., *Folklore in the English and Scottish Ballads* (New York: Dover, 1928; 2nd edition, 1965).

Wurzbach, Natascha, and Salz, Simone M., *Motif Index of the Child Corpus: The English and Scottish Popular Ballad* (Berlin: Walter de Gruyter, 1995).

Chapter 6: Widening the Range

For further bibliographical information on the writers below see relevant chapters in *The History of Scottish Literature Vol. I, Origins to 1660*, edited by R. D. S. Jack (Aberdeen: Aberdeen University Press, 1988).

THE BANNATYNE MANUSCRIPT

Bannatyne, George, *The Bannatyne Manuscript* (London: Scolar Press in association with the National Library of Scotland).

—, *The Bannatyne Manuscript Written in Tyme of Past 1568 by George Bannatyne*, 4 vols, ed. W. T. Ritchie (Edinburgh and London: Scottish Text Society, 1928–30).

Secondary reading

Brown, J. T. T., 'The Bannatyne Manuscript: a Sixteenth-Century Poetical Miscellany', *SHR* 1 (1903–4), pp. 136–58 (139).

Dunnigan, Sarah M., 'The creation and self-creation Mary Queen of Scots: rhetoric, sovereignty, and female controversies in sixteenth-century Scottish poetry', *Scotlands* 5.2 (1998), pp. 65–88.

Fox, Denton, 'Manuscripts and Prints of Scots Poetry in the Sixteenth Century', *Bards and Makars*, eds Adam J. Aitken et al. (Glasgow: University of Glasgow Press, 1977), pp. 156–71.

Heijnsbergen, Theo van, 'The Interaction between Literature and History in Queen Mary's Edinburgh: the Bannatyne Manuscript and its Prosopographical Context', *The Renaissance in Scotland: Studies in Literature, Religion, History and Culture Offered to John Durkan*, eds A. A. MacDonald et al. (Leiden: E. J. Brill, 1994), pp. 183–225.

Kratzmann, Gregory, 'Sixteenth-Century Secular Poetry', *The History of Scottish Literature*, vol. 1, ed. R. D. S. Jack (Aberdeen: Aberdeen University Press, 1989), pp. 105–24.

Lynch, Michael, 'Queen Mary's triumph: The Baptismal Celebrations at Stirling in December 1566', *SHR* 69 (1990), pp. 1–21.

MacDonald, Alasdair, 'The Bannatyne Manuscript: A Marian Anthology', *Innes Review* 37 (1986), pp. 36–47.

—, 'The printed book that never was: George Bannatyne's poetic anthology (1568)', *Boeken in de late Middeleeuwen*, eds J. M. M. Hermans and K. van der Hoek (Groningen, 1993), pp. 101–10.

Newlyn, Evelyn S., 'The Political Dimensions of Desire and Sexuality in Poems of the Bannatyne Manuscript', *Selected Essays on Scottish Language and Literature: A Festschrift in Honour of Allan H. MacLaine*, ed. Stephen R. McKenna (Lampeter: Edwin Mellen Press, 1992), pp. 75–96.

—, 'The Wryttar to the Reidaris: Editing Practices and Politics in the Bannatyne Manuscript', *SSL* 31 (Columbia: University of South Carolina, 1999), pp. 14–30.

—, '"Of Vertew Nobillest and Serpent Wrinkis": the Taxonomy of the Female in the Bannatyne Manuscript', *Scotia: Interdisciplinary Journal of Scottish Studies* 14 (199), pp. 1–12.

Ramson, William, 'On Bannatyne's Editing', *Bards and Makars*, eds Adam J. Aitken et al. (Glasgow: University of Glasgow Press, 1977), pp. 172–83.

JOHN BELLENDEN

Chambers, R. W., Batho, E. C., and Husbands, H. W. (eds), *The Chronicles of Scotland. Compiled by Hector Boece and Translated into Scots by John Bellenden*, 2 vols (Edinburgh and London: Scottish Text Society, 1936–41).

Craigie, W. A. (ed.), *Livy's History of Rome Translated into Scots by John Bellenden*, 2 vols (Edinburgh and London: Scottish Text Society, 1901–2).

Secondary reading

Royan, Nicola, 'The Relationship between the *Scotorum Historia* of Hector Boece and John Bellenden's *Chronicles of Scotland*', *The Rose and the Thistle: Essays on the Culture of Late Medieval and Renaissance Scotland*, eds Sally Mapstone and Juliette Wood (East Linton: Tuckwell, 1998).

HECTOR BOECE
Moir, J. (ed.), *Lives of the Bishops of Aberdeen, Translated from Hector Boece* (Aberdeen: New Spalding Club, 1894).
Watson, G. (ed.), *The Mar Lodge Translation of the History of Scotland by Hector Boece* (Edinburgh and London: Scottish Text Society, 1964).

Secondary reading
Royan, Nicola, 'The Relationship between Scotorum Historia of Hector Boece and John Bellenden's Chronicles of Scotland', *The Rose and the Thistle: Essays on the Culture of Late Medieval and Renaissance Scotland*, eds Sally Mapstone and Juliette Wood (East Linton: Tuckwell, 1998).

GAVIN DOUGLAS
Bawcutt, P. (ed.), *The Shorter Poems of Gavin Douglas* (Edinburgh and London: Blackwood, 1967).
Caldwell, D. F. C. (ed.), *Selections from Gavin Douglas* (Oxford: Clarendon Press, 1964).
Parkinson, David (ed.), *The Palis of Honoure* (Kalamazoo, MI: Medieval Institute Publications, 1992).
Small, J. (ed.), *The Poetical Works of Gavin Douglas*, 4 vols (Edinburgh: William Paterson, 1874).

Secondary reading
(i) *The Eneados*
Blyth, Charles R., 'Gavin Douglas's Prologues of Natural Description', *Philological Quarterly* 49 (Iowa City: University of Iowa, 1970), pp. 164–77.
Canitz, A. E. C., 'From Aeneid to *Eneados*: Theory and Practice of Gavin Douglas's Translation', *Medievalia et Humanistica: Studies in Medieval and Renaissance Culture* 17 (Lanham, MD: Rowman & Littlefield, 1991), pp. 81–99.
—, 'The Prologue to the *Eneados*: Gavin Douglas's Directions for Reading', *SSL* 25 (Columbia: University of South Carolina, 1990), pp. 1–22.
Cummings, Robert, ' "To the Cart the Fift Quheill": Gavin Douglas's Humanist Supplement to the Eneados', *Translation & Literature* 4(2) (Edinburgh: Edinburgh University Press, 1995), pp. 133–56.
Ebin, Lois, 'The Role of the Narrator in the Prologues to Gavin Douglas's Eneados', *The Chaucer Review: A Journal of Medieval Studies and Literary Criticism* 14 (Pennsylvania: Pennsylvania State University Press, 1980), pp. 353–65.
Ghosh, Kantik, ' "The Fift Quheill": Gavin Douglas's Maffeo Vegio', *SLJ* 22(1) (Aberdeen: Association for Scottish Literary Studies, 1995), pp. 5–21.
Morgan, Edwin, 'Gavin Douglas and William Drummond as Translators', *Bards and Makars: Scottish Language and Literature: Medieval and Renaissance*, eds Adam J. Aitken et al. (Glasgow: University of Glasgow Press, 1977).
Pinti, Daniel J., 'The Vernacular Gloss in Gavin Douglas's *Eneados*', *Exemplaria: A Journal of Theory in Medieval and Renaissance Studies* 7(2) (Binghamton, NY: Medieval & Renaissance Text & Studies, SUNY Binghamton, 1995), pp. 443–64.
(ii) *'The Palice of Honour'*
Miskimin, Alice, 'The Design of Douglas's "Palice of Honour" ', *Actes du 2e colloque de langue et de litterature ecossaises (Moyen Age et Renaissance)*, eds Blanchot and Graf (Strasbourg: Université de Strasbourg, 1979).

Parkinson, David, 'The Farce of Modesty in Gavin Douglas's "The Palis of Honoure"', *Philological Quarterly* 70(1) (Iowa City: University of Iowa, 1991), pp. 13–25.

THE FREIRIS OF BERWICK
Jack, R. D. S., and Rozendaal, P. A. T., *The Mercat Anthology of Early Scottish Literature, 1375–1707* (Edinburgh: Mercat, 1997), pp. 152–65.

Secondary reading
Jack, R. D. S., '*The Freiris of Berwick* and Chaucerian Fabliau', *SSL* 16 (Columbia: University of South Carolina, 1981), pp. 145–52.

RICHARD HOLLAND
Armours, F. J. (ed.), *Scottish Alliterative Poems*, 2 vols (Edinburgh and London: Scottish Text Society, 1892–9).
Bawcutt, Priscilla, and Riddy, Felicity (eds), *Longer Scottish Poems vol. 1. 1375–1650* (Edinburgh: Scottish Academic Press, 1987).
Laing, David (ed.), *The Buke of the Howlat* (Edinburgh: Bannatyne Club Publications, 1823).

Secondary reading
MacDiarmid, Matthew P., 'Richard Holland's *Buke of the Howlat*: An interpretation', *Medium Aevum* 38 (Oxford: Oxford University Press, 1969), pp. 277–90.
Parkinson, David, 'Mobbing Scenes in Middle Scots Verse: Holland, Douglas, Dunbar', *Journal of English and Germanic Philology* 85(4) (1986), pp. 494–09.
Riddy, Felicity, 'The Alliterative Revival', *The History of Scottish Literature*, vol. 1, ed. R. D. S. Jack (Aberdeen: Aberdeen University Press, 1988).
Schiebe, Regina, 'The Major Professional Skills of the Dove in The Buke of the Howlat', *Animals and the Symbolic in Medieval Art and Literature*, ed. L. A. J. R. Houwen (Groningen: Egbert Forsten, 1997).

JOHN KNOX
Laing, David (ed.), *The Works of John Knox*, 6 vols (Edinburgh: Woodrow Society, 1846–55).

Secondary reading
Farrow, Kenneth D., 'Humour, Logic, Imagery and Sources in the Prose Writings of John Knox', *SSL* 25 (Columbia: University of South Carolina, 1990), pp. 154–75.
Felch, Susan M., 'The Rhetoric of Biblical Authority: John Knox and the Question of Women', *Sixteenth Century Journal: Journal of Early Modern Studies* 26(4) (Davidson, NC: Davidson College, 1995), pp. 805–22.
Hansen, Melanie, 'The Word and the Throne: John Knox's The First Blast of the Trumpet against the Monstrous Regiment of Women', *Voicing Women: Gender and Sexuality in Early Modern Writing*, eds Kate Chedgzoy, Melanie Hansen and Suzanne Trill (Keele: Keele University Press, 1996).
Jack, R. D. S, 'The Prose of John Knox: A Re-Assessment', *Prose Studies* 4(3) (1981), pp. 239–51.
Janton, Pierre, 'John Knox and Literature', *Actes du 2e colloque de langue et de litterature ecossaises (Moyen Age et Renaissance)*, eds Blanchot and Graf (Strasbourg: Université de Strasbourg, 1979).
Lyall, R. J., 'Vernacular Prose before the Reformation', *The History of Scottish Literature*, vol. I, ed. R. D. S. Jack (Aberdeen: Aberdeen University Press, 1988).

Richards, Judith M., 'To Promote a Woman to Beare Rule': Talking of Queens in Mid-Tudor England', *Sixteenth Century Journal: Journal of Early Modern Studies* 28(1) (Davidson, NC: Davidson College, 1997), pp. 101–21.

DAVID LYNDSAY: POETRY

Burger, Glenn D., 'Poetical Invention and Ethical Wisdom in Lindsay's "Testament of Papyngo"', *SSL* 24 (Columbia: University of South Carolina, 1989), pp. 164–80.

Cairns, Sandra, 'Sir David Lindsay's *Dreme*: Poetry, Propaganda, and Encomium in the Scottish Court', *The Spirit of the Court: Selected Proceedings of the Fourth Congress of the International Courtly Literature Society* (Toronto, 1983), eds Glyn S. Burgess and Robert A. Taylor (Woodbridge: Brewer, 1985).

Kratzmann, Gregory D., 'Sixteenth-Century Secular Poetry', *The History of Scottish Literature*, vol. I, ed. R. D. S. Jack (Aberdeen: Aberdeen University Press, 1988).

Lyall, R. J., 'Complaint, Satire and Invective in Middle Scots Literature', *Church, Politics, and Society: Scotland, 1408–1929*, ed. Norman Macdougall (Edinburgh: John Donald, 1983).

Williams, Janet Hadley, 'The Lyon and the Hound: Sir David Lyndsay's Complaint and Confession of Bagsche', *Parergon* 31 (1981), pp. 3–11.

—, '"Althocht I beir nocht lyke ane baird": Sir David Lyndsay's Complaynt', *SLJ* 9(2) (Aberdeen: Association for Scottish Literary Studies, 1982), pp. 5–20.

—, '"Thus Euery Man Said for Hym Self": The Voices of Sir David Lyndsay's Poems', *Bryght Lanternis: Essays on the Language and Literature of Medieval and Renaissance Scotland*, eds J. Derrick McClure and M. R. G. Spiller (Aberdeen: Aberdeen University Press, 1989), pp. 258–72.

—, 'Sir David Lyndsay's "Antique" and "Plesand" Stories', *A Day Estivall*, eds A. Gardner-Medwin and J. Hadley Williams (Aberdeen: Aberdeen University Press, 1990), pp. 155–66.

THE MEROURE OF WYSDOME

Macpherson, Charles and Quinn, F. (eds), *The Meroure of Wysdome*, 2 vols (Edinburgh and London: Scottish Text Society, 1926–65).

Secondary reading

Broadie, Alexander, *The Tradition of Scottish Philosophy* (Edinburgh: Polygon, 1990).

—, *The Circle of John Mair: Logic and Logicians in Pre-Reformation Scotland* (Oxford: Clarendon Press, 1985).

Burns, J. H., *The True Law of Kingship: Concepts of Monarchy in Early Modern Scotland* (Oxford: Oxford University Press, 1996).

—, 'John Ireland and *The Meroure of Wysdome*', *Innes Review* 6 (Glasgow: Scottish Catholic Historical Committee, 1955), pp. 77–98.

—, 'John Ireland: Theology and political affairs in the late fifteenth century', *Innes Review* 41 (Glasgow: Scottish Catholic Historical Committee, 1990), pp. 151–81.

Lyall, R. J., 'Vernacular Prose before the Reformation', *The History of Scottish Literature*, vol. IV, ed. R. D. S. Jack (Aberdeen: Aberdeen University Press, 1987), pp. 163–82.

MacDonald, Craig, '*The Thrie Prestis of Peblis* and *The Meroure of Wysdome*: a possible relationship', *SSL* 17 (Columbia: University of South Carolina, 1982), pp. 153–64.

—, 'Mirror, Filter or Magnifying Glass: John Ireland's *Meroure of Wysdome*', *SSL* 26 (Columbia: University of South Carolina, 1991), pp. 448–55.

Mapstone, Sally, 'Was there a Court Literature in Fifteenth-Century Scotland?', *SSL* XXVI (Columbia: University of South Carolina, 1991).

Mason, Roger A., 'Kingship, tyranny and the right to resist in fifteenth-century Scotland', *SHR* 66 (Aberdeen: Aberdeen University Press, 1987), pp. 125–51.

RAUF COILYEAR
Armours, F. J. (ed.), *Scottish Alliterative Poems*, 2 vols (Edinburgh and London: Scottish Text Society, 1892–9) [includes *The Buke of the Howlat*].
Bawcutt, Priscilla, and Riddy, Felicity (eds), *Longer Scottish Poems vol. 1, 1375–1650* (Edinburgh: Scottish Academic Press, 1987).
Speed, Diane (ed.), *The Tale of Ralph the Collier* (New York: P. Lang, 1991).

Secondary reading
Craigie, Sir William, 'The Scottish Alliterative Poems', *Proceedings of the British Academy* 28 (London: Oxford University Press, 1942), pp. 217–36.
Morris, Margaret Kissam, 'Generic Oxymoron in *The Taill of Rauf Coilyear*', *Voices in Translation: the authority of 'olde books' in medieval literature*, eds Deborah M. Sinnreich-Levi et al. (New York: AMS Press, 1992), pp. 137–55.
Shepherd, S. H. A., ' "of thy glitterand gyde haue I na gle": the *Taill of Rauf Coilyear*', *Archiv fur das Studium der Neueren Sprachen und Literaturen* 228(2) (Braunschweig: Georg Westermann, 1991), pp. 284–98.
Walsh, Elizabeth, '*The Taill of Rauf Coilyear*: oral motif in literary guise', *SLJ* 6(2) (Aberdeen: Association for Scottish Literary Studies, 1979), pp. 5–19.

SATIRICAL POETRY OF THE REFORMATION
Cranstoun, James (ed.), *Satirical Poems of the Time of the Reformation*, 2 vols (Edinburgh and London: Scottish Text Society, 1890–3).

See also the selection in *The Mercat Anthology of Early Scottish Literature*, edited by R. D. S. Jack and P. A. T. Rozendaal (Edinburgh: Mercat Press, 1997).

ALEXANDER SCOTT
Cranstoun, James (ed.), *The Poems of Alexander Scott* (Edinburgh: Scottish Text Society, 1886).

Secondary reading
van Heijnsbergen, T., 'The Love Lyrics of Alexander Scott', *SSL* 26 (Columbia: University of South Carolina, 1991), pp. 336–49.

THOMAS URQUHART
Jack, R. D. S., and Lyall, R. J. (eds), *The Jewel* (Edinburgh: Scottish Academic Press, 1983).

Secondary reading
Boston, Richard, *The Admirable Urquhart: Selected Writings* (London: Gordon Fraser Gallery, 1975).
Craik, Roger, 'The Triumph of Exuberance over Inhibition: Sir Thomas Urquhart's Translation of Rabelais', *Lamar Journal of the Humanities* 22(1) (Beaumont, TX: Lamar University Press, 1996), pp. 41–64.
McClure, Derrick J., 'The "Universal Languages" of Thomas Urquhart and George Dalgarno', *Actes du 2e Colloque de langue et de litterature ecossaises (Moyen Age et Renaissance)*, eds Blanchot and Graf (Strasbourg: Université de Strasbourg, 1979).
Magan, James H., 'Verbal Excess and Sexual Abstinence', *Logophile: The Cambridge Journal of Words and Language* 3(2) (Cambridge: Logophile Press, 1979), pp. 1–7.

THE WALLACE

King, Elspeth (intro.), *Blind Harry's Wallace; William Hamilton of Gilbertfield* (Edinburgh: Luath Press, 1998) [an eighteenth-century 'translation' of the text].

MacDiarmid, Matthew P. (ed.), *Harry's Wallace*, 2 vols (Edinburgh: Blackwood, 1968–9).

Secondary reading

Goldstein, R. J., *The Matter of Scotland: Historical Narrative in Medieval Scotland* (Lincoln, NE, 1993).

—, 'Blind Hary's myth of blood: The Ideological Closure of *The Wallace*', *SSL* 25 (Columbia: University of South Carolina, 1990), pp. 70–82.

Mapstone, Sally, 'The *Scotichronicon's* First Readers', *Church Chronicle and Learning In Medieval and Early Renaissance Scotland*, ed. B. E. Crawford (Edinburgh: Mercat Press, 1999), pp. 31–55.

Walsh, Elizabeth, 'Hary's Wallace: The evolution of a Hero', *SLJ* 11 (Aberdeen: Association for Scottish Literary Studies, 1984), pp. 5–19.

JAMES WEDDERBURN

Ross, Iain (ed.), *The gude and godlie ballatis by James, John and Robert Wedderburn* (Edinburgh: Oliver & Boyd, Saltire Society, 1939).

Wedderburn, James, *A Compendious Book of Psalms and Spiritual Songs, commonly known as the Gude and Godlie Ballates* (Edinburgh: Scottish Text Society, STS First Series 39, 1897).

GAELIC LITERATURE

Baoill, Colm Ó, and Bateman, Meg (eds), *Gàir nan Clarsach: the Harp's Cry: an Anthology of Seventeenth Century Gaelic Poetry* (Edinburgh: Birlinn, 1994).

Quiggin, Edmund Crosby, and Fraser, John, *Poems from the Book of the Dean of Lismore* (Cambridge: Cambridge University Press, 1937).

Ross, Neil, *Heroic poetry from the Book of the Dean of Lismore* (Edinburgh: Oliver & Boyd, 1939).

Watson, William John, and MacGregor, James, *Scottish Verse from the Book of Dean of Lismore* (Edinburgh: Oliver & Boyd for the Scottish Gaelic Texts Society, 1978).

Secondary reading

Gillies, William, 'Courtly and Satiric Poems in the Book of the Dean of Lismore', *Scottish Studies* 21 (Edinburgh: Edinburgh University Press, 1977), pp. 35–53.

Thomson, Derick, *An Introduction to Gaelic Poetry* (Edinburgh: Edinburgh University Press, 1974; 1990), Chapters 1–4.

Women Writers: Secondary reading

Bawcutt, Priscilla, 'Women and their Books in Scotland', *Medieval Women: Texts and Contexts in Late Medieval Britain. Essays for Felicity Riddy*, eds Jocelyn Wogan-Browne et al. (Turnhout: Brepols, 2000).

Dunnigan, Sarah M., 'Scottish Women Writers c.1560–c.1650', *The History of Scottish Women's Writing*, eds Douglas Gifford and Dorothy McMillan (Edinburgh: Edinburgh University Press, 1997), pp. 15–43.

Frater, Anne, 'The Gaelic Tradition up to 1750', *A History of Scottish Women's Writing*, eds Douglas Gifford and Dorothy McMillan (Edinburgh: Edinburgh University Press, 1997), pp. 1–14.

—, 'Women of the Gàidhealtached and their Songs to 1750', *Women in Scotland c1100–c1750*, eds Elizabeth Ewan and Maureen Meikle (East Linton: Tuckwell Press, 1999), pp. 67–79.

Mullan, David, 'Mistress Rutherford's Narrative: A Scottish Puritan Autobiography', *Bunyan Studies* 7 (London: Bunyan Studies, 1997), pp. 13–37.

Newlyn, Evelyn S., 'Images of Women in Sixteenth-Century Scottish Literary Manuscripts', *Women in Scotland c1100–1750*, eds Elizabeth Ewan and Maureen Meikle (East Linton: Tuckwell Press, 1999), pp. 56–66.

ANNA HUME

The Triumphes of Love: Chastitie: Death (Edinburgh: Evan Tyler, 1644), extracted in *Kissing the Rod*, ed. Germaine Greer (London: Virago Press, 1988), pp. 101–5.

ELIZABETH MELVILLE

Excerpts of *Ane Godlie Dreme* in: Greer, Germaine et al. (eds), *Kissing the Rod: An Anthology of Seventeenth-Century Women's Verse* (London: Virago Press, 1988).

Kerrigan, Catherine (ed.), *An Anthology of Scottish Women Poets* (Edinburgh: Edinburgh University Press, 1991).

Travitsky, Betty (ed.), *The Paradise of Women, Writings by English Women of the Renaissance* (Westport, CN, and London: Greenwood Press, 1981).

The first 1603 edition of *Ane Godlie Dreme* is reproduced in:

Laing, David (ed.), *Early Popular Poetry of Scotland and the Northern Border*, 2 vols (London, 1822).

—, *Early Metrical Tales including the History of Sir Eger, Sir Gryme and Sir Greysteill* (Edinburgh, first pub. 1826), pp. 149–69.

Lawson, Alexander (ed.), *Poems of Alexander Hume* (Edinburgh and London: Blackwood, 1920), pp. 184–98.

MARY QUEEN OF SCOTS

Arbuthnot, P. Stewart-MacKenzie (ed.), *Queen Mary's Silver Book: a collection of poems and essays*, ed. P. Mackenzie Stewart Arbuthnot (London: Bell, 1907).

Bax, C. (trans.), *The Silver Casket: being love-letters and love-poems attributed to Mary Stuart, Queen of Scots*, modernised with an introduction by C. Bax (London: Home & Van Thal, 1946).

Bell, Robin (trans.), *Bittersweet within my heart: the collected poems of Mary, Queen of Scots* (London: Pavilion, 1992).

Sharman, Julian (ed.), *The Poems of Mary Queen of Scots* (London, 1873).

Secondary reading

Dunnigan, Sarah M., 'The creation and self-creation of Mary Queen of Scots: rhetoric, sovereignty and femininity in sixteenth-century Scottish poetry', *Scotlands* (Edinburgh: Edinburgh University Press, 1999).

—, 'Rewriting the Renaissance language and love and desire: the "bodily burdein" in the poetry of Mary, Queen of Scots', *Gramma* 4 (1996), pp. 183–95.

SECTION 2:
EIGHTEENTH-CENTURY SCOTTISH LITERATURE
Introductory reading

As with each section the reader is reminded of the websites listed at the beginning of the Further Reading section, especially the developing website maintained by the Departments of Scottish Literature and STELLA at the University of Glasgow at **www.arts.gla.ac.uk/SESLL/ScotLit/bibliography** where more information can be given than is possible here.

The general literary histories and bibliographies are useful first ports of call, see particularly W. R. Aitken, Daiches, Glen, Kinsley, Lindsay, Millar, Royle, Speirs, Walker, Watson, Wittig, Hewitt and Spiller. Andrew Hook's edition of *The History of Scottish Literature Vol. II, 1660–1800* (Aberdeen: Aberdeen University Press, 1987) is recommended for the range of its essays, which outline in depth many writers and related themes concerning this period. Also recommended is Kenneth Simpson's *The Protean Scot: The Crisis of Identity in Eighteenth Century Scottish Literature* (Aberdeen: Aberdeen University Press, 1988) which examines eighteenth century Scottish literature in relation to writers including Burns, Boswell, Smollett and Mackenzie; Robert Crawford's *Devolving English Literature* (Cambridge: Cambridge University Press, 1992; second edition 2001) is also useful for his discussion of Scottish writers and their relationship with 'British' and English literature. A stimulating recent coverage of the period is in chapters 1–4 of Marshall Walker's *Scottish Literature Since 1707* (London and New York: Longman, 1996). Older works which provide a useful introduction to this period are David Craig's controversial but stimulating *Scottish Literature and the Scottish People, 1680–1830* (London: Chatto & Windus, 1961); David Daiches's pioneering *The Paradox of Scottish Culture: The Eighteenth-Century Experience* (London: Oxford University Press, 1964) and his wide-ranging study, *Robert Burns* (London: G. Bell & Sons, 1952; revised, London: Deutsch, 1966) remain lucid and readable introductions to the period, as do John MacQueen's *The Enlightenment and Scottish Literature Vol. I: Progress and Poetry* (Edinburgh: Scottish Academic Press, 1982) and Thomas Crawford's *Society and the Lyric: A Study of the Song Culture of Eighteenth-Century Scotland* (Edinburgh: Scottish Academic Press, 1979). Readers wishing to sample a cross-section of longer Scottish poems of the period should go to *Longer Scottish Poems: Volume Two*, edited by Thomas Crawford, David Hewitt, and Alexander Law (Edinburgh: Scottish Academic Press, 1987). Harold Thompson's *A Scottish Man of Feeling; Henry Mackenzie and the Golden age of Burns and Scott* (London: Oxford University Press, 1931), while dated, is rich in information. See also relevant essays in *A History of Scottish Womens' Writing* edited by Douglas Gifford and Dorothy McMillan (Edinburgh: Edinburgh University Press, 1997).

For cultural background, Alexander Broadie's *The Scottish Enlightenment: An Anthology* (Edinburgh: Canongate, 1997) is a superb representative selection from all the major thinkers and strands of philosophy; see also Anand Chitnis's *The Scottish Enlightenment: A Social History* (London: Croom Helm, 1976), George Davie's *The Scottish Enlightenment and other essays* and *A Passion for Ideas: Essays on the Scottish Enlightenment* (both Edinburgh: Polygon, 1991, 1994), Jane Rendall's *The Origins of the Scottish Enlightenment 1707–1776* (London: Macmillan, 1978) and Richard Sher's *Church and University in the Scottish Enlightenment: the Moderate Literati of Edinburgh* (Edinburgh: Edinburgh University Press, 1985).

For historical background, a stimulating and popular yet reliable introduction is in *Scotland Since 1688: Struggle for a Nation* edited by Edward Cowan and Richard Finlay (London: Cima Books, 2000); while the most ambitious histories in recent years are T. M. Devine's *The Scottish Nation: 1700–2000* (London: Allen Lane, 1999) and Michael Lynch's *Scotland: A New History* (London: Century, 1991). Older but excellent is William Ferguson's *Scotland: 1689 to the Present* (Edinburgh: Oliver & Boyd, 1968); also Henry Meikle's *Scotland and the French Revolution* (Glasgow: James Maclehose, 1912); Rosalind Mitchison's *Lordship to Patronage* (London: Arnold, 1983); N. T. Phillipson and Rosalind Mitchison's *Scotland in the Age of Improvement* (Edinburgh: Edinburgh University Press, 1970; 1996); Colin Kidd's *British identities before nationalism: ethnicity and nationhood in the Atlantic world, 1600–1800* (Cambridge: Cambridge University Press, 1999) and *Subverting Scotland's past: Scottish Whig historians and the creation of an Anglo-British identity, 1689–c.1830* (Cambridge: Cambridge University Press, 1993), and the pioneering work of T. C. Smout in *A History of the Scottish People 1560–1830* (London: Collins, 1969). For a nationalist view, see Paul Scott's *The Union of Scotland and England* (Edinburgh: Mainstream, 1978).

Chapter 7: Enlightenment and Vernacular

Reading for this period includes a wider than usual range of material such as primary works of philosophy, aesthetics and literature, from writers such as Francis Hutcheson to David Hume, and from Dr Johnson to his biographer James Boswell. A selection of these primary texts will be found in 'Widening the Range' at the end of this section reading list. What follows now is contemporary critical material on the period.

BACKGROUND READING:

THE PHILOSOPHY AND CULTURE OF THE SCOTTISH ENLIGHTENMENT

Allan, David, *Virtue, Learning and The Scottish Enlightenment* (Edinburgh: Edinburgh University Press, 1993).

Beveridge, Craig, and Turnbull, Ronald, *The Eclipse of Scottish Culture* (Edinburgh: Polygon, 1989) [see chapter 6, 'Philosophical Education'].

Bryson, Gladys, *Man and Society: The Scottish Inquiry of the Eighteenth Century* (Princeton: Princeton University Press, 1945).

Buckle, Henry Thomas, *On Scotland and the Scotch Intellect*, ed. H. J. Hanham (Chicago and London: University of Chicago Press, 1970) [see chapter 5, 'An Examination of the Scotch Intellect during the Eighteenth Century'].

Camic, C., *Experience and Enlightenment: Socialization for Cultural Change in Eighteenth-Century Scotland* (Chicago: University of Chicago Press, 1983).

Campbell, R. H., and Skinner, A. S. (eds), *The Origins and Nature of the Scottish Enlightenment* (Edinburgh: John Donald, 1982).

Carruthers, Gerard, 'Culture, 1707–1850', *Modern Scottish History: 1707 to the Present*, eds A. Cooke et al. (East Linton: Tuckwell & Open University Press, 1998), pp. 253–74.

Clark, H. C., 'Women and Humanity in Scottish Enlightenment Thought: The Case of Adam Smith', *Historical Reflections – Reflections Historique* 19 (1993), pp. 363–87.

Daiches, David, *The Scottish Enlightenment: an Introduction* (Edinburgh: Saltire Society, 1986).

—, *The Paradox of Scottish Culture: The Eighteenth-Century Experience* (London: Oxford University Press, 1964).

—, Jones, Jean, and Jones, Peter (eds), *The Scottish Enlightenment, 1730–1790: a hotbed of genius* (Edinburgh: Saltire Society, 1996).

Davie, George F., *The Democratic Intellect* (Edinburgh: Edinburgh University Press, 1961).

—, 'The Social Significance of the Scottish Philosophy of Common Sense', *The Dow Lecture* (Dundee: University of Dundee, 1972).

Davis, Leith, *Acts of Union: Scotland and the literary negotiation of the British nation, 1707–1832* (Stanford, CA: Stanford University Press, 1998).

Dwyer, John, *Virtuous Discourse* (Edinburgh: J. Donald, 1987).

—, *The Age of the Passions: an interpretation of Adam Smith and Scottish enlightenment culture* (East Linton: Tuckwell Press, 1998).

—, and Sher, Richard (eds), *Sociability and society in eighteenth-century Scotland* (Edinburgh: Mercat Press, 1993).

Graham, H. G., *The Social Life of Scotland in the Eighteenth Century* (London: A. & C. Black, 1899).

Hazard, Paul, *European Thought in the Eighteenth Century: From Montesquieu to Lessing* (London: Hollis & Carter, 1954).

Hook, A. D., *Scotland and America 1750–1835* (Glasgow: Blackie, 1975).

—, and Sher, Richard, *The Glasgow Enlightenment* (East Linton: Tuckwell Press, 1997).

Kidd, Colin, *Subverting Scotland's Past: Scottish whig historians and the creation of an Anglo-British identity, 1689–c. 1830* (Cambridge: Cambridge University Press, 1993).

—, *British Identities Before Nationalism: ethnicity and nationhood in the Atlantic world, 1600–1800* (Cambridge: Cambridge University Press, 1999).

McCosh, James, *Scottish Philosophy* (London: Macmillan, 1875).

McElroy, D. D., *Scotland's Age of Improvement: A Survey of Eighteenth-Century Literary Clubs and Societies* (Pullman, Washington: Washington State University Press, 1969).

McMillan, Dorothy, *The Scotswoman at Home and Abroad: Non-Fictional Writing 1700–1900* (Glasgow: Association for Scottish Literary Studies, 1999).

McQueen, John, *Progress and Poetry* (Edinburgh: Scottish Academic Press, 1982).

—, *The Rise of The Historical Novel* (Edinburgh: Scottish Academic Press, 1989).

Mann, Alistair J., *The Scottish Book Trade 1500–1720* (East Linton: Tuckwell Press, 2000).

Mitchison, Rosalind, and Phillipson, N. T. (eds), *Scotland in the Age of Improvement* (Edinburgh: Edinburgh University Press, 1970).

Pittock, Murray G. H., *Poetry and Jacobite Politics in Eighteenth-century Britain and Ireland* (Cambridge: Cambridge University Press, 1994).

—, *Inventing and Resisting Britain: Cultural Identities in Britain and Ireland 1685–1789* (Basingstoke: Macmillan, 1997).

—, *Celtic Identity and the British Image* (Manchester: Manchester University Press, 1999).

Robinson, Daniel Sommer, *The Story of Scottish Philosophy* (New York: Exposition Press, 1961) [contains extracts from Hutcheson, Hume, Smith and Reid, highlighting their main ideas].

Sher, Richard, *Church and University in the Scottish Enlightenment: the Moderate Literati of Edinburgh* (Edinburgh: Edinburgh University Press, 1985).

Thomson, Derick S., *Gaelic Poetry in the Eighteenth century: a bilingual anthology* (Aberdeen: Association for Scottish Literary Studies, 1993).

Trevor-Roper, Hugh, 'The Scottish Enlightenment', *Studies on Voltaire* 58 (Genève: Institut et Musée Voltaire, 1967), pp. 1635–58.

Young, Douglas, 'Scotland and Edinburgh in the Eighteenth Century', *Studies on Voltaire* 58 (Genève: Institut et Musée Voltaire, 1967), pp. 1967–90.

LITERARY CRITICISM

Butt, John, 'The Revival of Scottish Vernacular Poetry in the Eighteenth Century', *From Sensibility to Romanticism: Essays presented to Frederick A. Pottle*, eds F. W. Hilles and Harold Bloom (New York: Oxford University Press, 1965), pp. 219–37.

Carruthers, Gerard, and Dunnigan, Sarah, ' "A reconfused chaos now": Scottish Poetry and Nation from the Medieval Period to the Eighteenth Century', *Edinburgh Review* 100 (Edinburgh, 1999), pp. 81–94.

Crawford, Thomas, Hewitt, David, and Law, Alexander (eds), *Longer Scottish Poems, volume 2* (Edinburgh: Scottish Academic Press, 1987).

Daiches, David, 'Eighteenth Century Vernacular Poetry', *Scottish Poetry: A Critical Survey*, ed. James Kinsley (London: Cassell & Co., 1955), pp. 150–84.

—, *Literature and Gentility* (Edinburgh: Edinburgh University Press, 1982).

Donaldson, William, *The Jacobite Song: Political Myth and National Identity* (Aberdeen: Aberdeen University Press, 1988).

Graham, H. G., *Scottish Men of Letters in the Eighteenth Century* (London: A. & C. Black, 1901).

Hook, Andrew, 'Scotland and Romanticism: The International Scene', *The History of Scottish Literature Vol. II, 1660–1800*, ed. A. D. Hook (Aberdeen: Aberdeen University Press, 1988), pp. 307–22.

Leonard, Tom (ed.), *Radical Renfrew: poetry from the French Revolution to the First World War by poets born, or sometime resident in, the County of Renfrewshire* (Edinburgh: Polygon, 1990).

MacLaine, Allan H., *The Christis Kirk Tradition: Scots Poems of Folk Festivity* (Glasgow: Association for Scottish Literary Studies, 1996).

Millar, J. H., 'Literary Revival in Scotland after the Union', *The Union of 1707: A Survey of events by various writers* (Glasgow: Outram, 1907), pp. 134–42.

Noble, Andrew, 'Versions of Scottish Pastoral: The Literati and the Tradition (1780–1830)', *Order and Space in Society: Architectural Form and its Context in the Scottish Enlightenment*, ed. Thomas Markus (Edinburgh: Mainstream, 1982).

Ross, Ian, 'Aesthetic Philosophy: Hutcheson and Hume to Alison', *The History of Scottish Literature Vol. II, 1660–1800*, ed. A. D. Hook (Aberdeen: Aberdeen University Press, 1988), pp. 239–58.

Sher, Richard, 'Literature and the Church of Scotland', pp. 259–72.

Stafford, Fiona, *The Sublime Savage: James MacPherson and the Poems of Ossian* (Edinburgh: Edinburgh University Press, 1988).

Trumpener, Katie, *Bardic Nationalism* (Princeton, NJ: Princeton University Press, 1997).

Turnbull, Gordon, 'James Boswell: Biography and the Union', *The History of Scottish Literature Vol. II, 1660–1800*, ed. A. D. Hook (Aberdeen: Aberdeen University Press, 1988), pp. 157–74.

Chapter 8: Allan Ramsay, Robert Fergusson and the Vernacular Tradition

ALLAN RAMSAY

Burns, Martin, Law, Alexander, and Kinghorn, Alexander M. (eds), *Works*, 6 vols (Edinburgh: Scottish Text Society, 1951–74).

Freeman, F. W., and Law, Alexander (eds), 'Allan Ramsay's First Published Poem: the Poem to the Memory of Dr Archibald Pitcairne', *The Bibliotheck* 9:7 (1979), pp. 153–60.

Kinghorn, Alexander M., and Law, Alexander (eds), *Poems by Allan Ramsay and Robert Fergusson* (Edinburgh: Scottish Academic Press, 1974; new edition 1985).

Wood, Henry Harvey (ed.), *Poems: epistles, fables, satires, elegies & lyrics* (Edinburgh: Oliver & Boyd, 1940).

Secondary reading

Burns, Martin, *Allan Ramsay: A Study of his Life and Works* (Cambridge, MA: Harvard University Press, 1931).

Crawford, Thomas, 'The Vernacular Revival and the Poetic Thrill: a Hedonistic Approach', *Scotland and the Lowland Tongue*, ed. J. Derrick McClure (Aberdeen: Aberdeen University Press, 1983), pp. 79–99.

Freeman, F. W., 'The Intellectual Background of the Vernacular Revival before Burns', *SSL* 16 (Columbia: University of South Carolina, 1981), pp. 168–87.

Gibson, Andrew, *New Light on Allan Ramsay* (Edinburgh: W. Brown, 1927).

Kinghorn, Alexander M., and Law, Alexander, 'Allan Ramsay and Literary Life in the First Half of the Eighteenth Century', *The History of Scottish Literature Vol. II, 1660–1800*, ed. A. D. Hook (Aberdeen: Aberdeen University Press, 1988), pp. 65–80.

McGuirk, Carol, 'Augustan Influences on Allan Ramsay', *SSL* 16 (Columbia: University of South Carolina, 1981), pp. 97–109.

MacKay, James A., 'The Hitherto Unrecorded Letters of Allan Ramsay', *SSL* 24 (Columbia: University of South Carolina, 1989), pp. 1–6.

MacLaine, Allan H., *Allan Ramsay* (New York: Twayne, 1985).

Speirs, John, 'Allan Ramsay's Scots Poems', *The Scots Literary Tradition* (London: Chatto & Windus, 1940; revised edition, Faber, 1962).

—, 'A Bibliography of the Writings of Allan Ramsay', *Records of the Glasgow Bibliographical Society* 10 (Glasgow, 1931), pp. 1–114.

Zenzinger, Peter, *My Muse is British: Allan Ramsay* (Grossen-Linden: Hoffman, 1977).

ROBERT FERGUSSON

Dickins, Bruce (ed.), *Scots Poems* (Edinburgh: Porpoise Press, 1925).

Kinghorn, Alexander M., and Law, Alexander (eds), *Poems by Allan Ramsay and Robert Fergusson* (Edinburgh: Scottish Text Society, 1974; new edition, 1985).

Law, Alexander (ed.), *Scots Poems* (Edinburgh: Oliver & Boyd, 1947).

MacDiarmid, Matthew P. (ed.), *Poems*, 2 vols. (Edinburgh: Scottish Text Society, 1954–6).

Telfer, John (ed.), *Scots Poems* (Edinburgh: Scottish Features, 1948).

— (ed.), *Works of Robert Fergusson* [1807] (Edinburgh: James Thin, 1970).

Secondary reading

Daiches, David, *Robert Fergusson* (Edinburgh: Scottish Academic Press, 1982).

Fairley, John A., 'Bibliography of Robert Fergusson', *Records of the Glasgow Bibliographical Society* 3 (Glasgow, 1915), pp. 115–55.

Freeman, F. W., *Robert Fergusson and the Scots Humanist Compromise* (Edinburgh: Edinburgh University Press, 1984).

—, 'Robert Fergusson: Pastoral and Politics at Mid-Century', *The History of Scottish Literature Vol. II, 1660–1800*, ed. A. D. Hook (Aberdeen: Aberdeen University Press, 1988), pp. 141–56.

Garioch, Robert, and Smith, Anne, *Fergusson: A Bicentenary Handsel* (Edinburgh: Reprographia, 1974).

MacDiarmid, Matthew P., 'Introduction' to Scottish Text Society Edition [see above].

MacLaine, Allan H., *Robert Fergusson* (New York: Twayne, 1965).

Morgan, Edwin, 'Robert Fergusson', *Crossing the Border: Essays on Scottish Literature* (Manchester: Carcanet, 1990), pp. 75–91.

Smith, Sydney Goodsir (ed.), *Robert Fergusson, 1750–1774: Essays by Various Hands to Commemorate the Bi-centenary of his Birth* (Edinburgh: Nelson, 1952).

Speirs, John, 'Robert Fergusson', *The Scots Literary Tradition* (London: Chatto & Windus, 1940; revised edition, Faber, 1962), pp. 110–16 [1962 edition].

—, 'Tradition and Robert Fergusson', ibid., pp. 198–206 [1962 edition].

Chapter 9: Robert Burns

Ewing, James Cameron, and Cook, Davidson (eds), *Robert Burns' Commonplace Book, 1783–1785* (Glasgow: Gowans & Gray, 1938; reproduced with introduction by David Daiches, London: Centaur Press, 1965).

Ferguson, J. De Lancey, and Roy, G. Ross, *The Letters of Robert Burns*, 2 vols (Oxford: Clarendon Press, 1985, 2nd edition).

Kinsley, James (ed.), *Poems and Songs*, 3 vols (Oxford: Clarendon Press, 1968).

O'Rourke, Donny (ed.), *Ae Fond Kiss: The Love Letters of Robert Burns and Clarinda* (Edinburgh: Mercat Press, 2000).

Roy, G. Ross (intro.), *The Merry Muses of Caledonia* (1799; Columbia: University of South Carolina, 1999).

The Mitchell Library in Glasgow holds one of the finest collections of Burns material available; see the *Catalogue of the Robert Burns Collection; The Mitchell Library, Glasgow* (Glasgow: Glasgow City Libraries and Archives, 1996).

Secondary reading

Bentman, Raymond, 'Robert Burns's use of Scottish Diction', *From Sensibility to Romanticism: Essays Presented to Frederick A. Pottle*, eds Frederick W. Hilles and Harold Bloom (New York: Oxford University Press, 1965), pp. 239–58.

—, 'Robert Burns's Declining Fame', *Studies in Romanticism* 2 (Boston: University of Boston, 1972), pp. 207–24.

Bittenbender, J. C., 'Bakhtinian Carnival in the Poetry of Robert Burns', *SLJ* 21 (Aberdeen: Association for Scottish Literary Studies, 1994), pp. 23–38.

Brown, Mary Ellen, *Burns and Tradition* (London: Macmillan, 1984).

Carruthers, Gerard, and Dunnigan, Sarah, 'Two Tales of "Tam o' Shanter"', *Southfields* 6.2 (London: Southfields Press, 2000), pp. 36–43.

Carswell, Catherine, *The Life of Robert Burns* (London: Chatto & Windus, 1930; reproduced, Edinburgh: Canongate, 1990).

Catalogue of the Robert Burns Collection in the Mitchell Library, Glasgow (Glasgow: Mitchell Library, 1959).

Crawford, Robert (ed.), *Robert Burns and Cultural Authority* (Edinburgh: Edinburgh University Press, 1997).

Crawford, Thomas, *Burns: A Study of the Poems and Songs* (London: Macmillan, 1960; reproduced, Edinburgh: Canongate Academic, 1994).

—, 'Burns since 1970', *SLJ* suppl. 3 (Aberdeen: Association for Scottish Literary Studies, 1976), pp. 4–14.

—, *Boswell, Burns and the French Revolution* (Edinburgh: Saltire Society, 1994).

—, *Robert Burns and his World* (London: Thames & Houston, 1971).

—, *Robert Burns the Poet* (Edinburgh: Saltire Society, 1994).

Daiches, David, *Robert Burns* (London, Deutsch, 1950, rev., 1966).

Damrosch, Leopold, 'Burns, Blake and the Recovery of Lyric', *Studies in Romanticism* 21 (Boston: University of Boston, 1982), pp. 637–60.

Davis, L. A., 'Bounded in a District Space: Burns, Wordsworth and the Margins of English Literature', *English Studies in Canada* 20 (1994), pp. 23–40.

Egerer, Joel Warren, *A Bibliography of Robert Burns* (Edinburgh: Oliver & Boyd, 1964).

Ferguson, J. De Lancey, *Pride and Passion: Robert Burns* (New York: Oxford University Press, 1939).

Hecht, Hans, *Robert Burns: The Man and his Work*, trans. Jane Lymbum (Edinburgh: Hodge, 1936; 2nd edition, 1950).

Jack, R. D. S., and Noble, Andrew (eds), *The Art of Robert Burns* (London: Vision Press, 1982).

Lindsay, Maurice, *Robert Burns: The Man, His Work, The Legend* (London: Macgibbon & Kee, 1954; revised edition, London: Robert Hale, 1979).

—, *The Burns Encyclopedia* (London: Robert Hale, 1980, 3rd edition).

Low, Donald A. (ed.), *Robert Burns: The Critical Heritage* (London: Routledge & Kegan Paul, 1974).

— (ed.), *Robert Burns: Critical Essays* (London: Routledge & Kegan Paul, 1975).

—, *Robert Burns* (Edinburgh: Scottish Academic Press, Scottish Writers Series, 1986).

McGuirk, Carol (ed.), *Critical Essays on Robert Burns* (New York: G. K. Hall, 1998).

—, *Robert Burns and the Sentimental Era* (Athens, GA: University of Georgia Press, 1985).

—, 'Scottish Hero, Scottish Victim: Myths of Robert Burns', *The History of Scottish Literature Vol. II, 1660–1800*, ed. A. D. Hook (Aberdeen: Aberdeen University Press, 1988), pp. 219–38.

McIntyre, Ian, *Dirt and Deity: A Life of Robert Burns* (London: Harper Collins, 1995).

Mackay, James, *Burns: A Biography of Robert Burns* (Edinburgh: Mainstream, 1992).

MacLaine, Allan H., 'Radicalism and Conservatism in Burns's The Jolly Beggars', *SSL* 13 (Columbia: University of South Carolina, 1978), pp. 125–43.

Roy, G. Ross (ed.), *SSL* 30 (Columbia: University of South Carolina, 1998).

Simpson, Kenneth G., 'The Many Voices: The Poetry of Robert Burns', *The Protean Scot* (Aberdeen: Aberdeen University Press, 1988).

— (ed.), *Burns Now* (Edinburgh: Canongate Academic, 1994).

—, *Robert Burns* (Aberdeen: Association for Scottish Literary Studies, Scotnotes, 1994).

—(ed.), *Love and Liberty: Robert Burns, A Bicentenary Celebration* (East Lothian: Tuckwell Press, 1997).

Songs of Robert Burns, sung by Ewan McColl (New York: Folkways [FW8758], 1959).

The Songs of Robert Burns, sung by Jean Redpath (Vermont: Philo, 1976).

Speirs, John, 'Burns', *The Scots Literary Tradition* (London: Chatto & Windus, 1940; revised, Faber, 1962), pp. 117–30 [1962 edition].

Strawhorn, John (ed.), *Ayrshire in the Time of Robert Burns* (Ayr: Ayrshire Archaeological and Natural History Society, 1959).

Thornton, Robert D., *James Currie, the Entire Stranger and Robert Burns* (Edinburgh: Oliver & Boyd, 1963).

—, *William Maxwell to Robert Burns* (Edinburgh: John Donald, 1979).

Chapter 10: *Tobias Smollett:* The Expedition of Humphry Clinker

Bouce, Paul Gabriel (ed.), *The Adventures of Ferdinand Count Fathom* [1753] (London: Penguin, 1990).

Bouce, Paul Gabriel (ed.), *The Adventures of Roderick Random* [1748] (Oxford: Oxford University Press, 1979).

Clifford, James L. (ed.), *The Adventures of Peregrine Pickle* [1751] (London: Oxford University Press, 1964).

Felsenstein, Frank (ed.), *Travels Through France and Italy* [1766] (Oxford: Oxford University Press, World's Classics Series, 1981).

Knapp, Lewis (ed.), *Letters* (Oxford: Oxford University Press, 1970).

Preston, Tom (ed.), *Humphry Clinker*, with an introduction and notes (Athens, GA: London: University of Georgia Press, 1990).

Ross, Angus (ed.), *Humphry Clinker* [1771] (London: Penguin, 1985).

Wanger, Peter (ed.), *The Life and Adventures of Sir Lancelot Greaves* [1762] (London: Penguin, 1988).

Secondary reading

Basker, James G., *Tobias Smollett: Critic and Journalist* (Newark and London: University of Delaware Press, 1988).

Bold, Alan (ed.), *Tobias Smollett: Author of the First Distinction* (London: Vision, 1982).

Bouce, Paul Gabriel, *The Novels of Tobias Smollett*, trans. Antonia White (London: Longman, 1976).

Giddings, Robert, *The Tradition of Smollett* (London: Methuen, 1967).

—, *Tobias Smollett* (London: Greenwich Exchange, 1995).

Goldberg, M. A., *Smollett and the Scottish School* (Albuquerque: New Mexico University Press, 1959).

Grant, Damien, *Tobias Smollett: A Study in Style* (Manchester: Manchester University Press, 1977).

Kelly, L. (ed.), *Tobias Smollett: The Critical Heritage* (London and New York: Routledge, 1987).

Knapp, Lewis M., *Tobias Smollett, Doctor of Men and Manners* (Princeton, NJ: Princeton University Press, 1949).

MacQueen, John, *The Enlightenment and Scottish Literature, Vol. I: Progress and Poetry* (Edinburgh: Scottish Academic Press, 1982) [chapters iii and v].

Martz, Louis L., *The Later Career of Tobias Smollett* (New Haven and London: Yale University Press and Oxford University Press, 1942; revised, Hamden, CT: Archon Books, 1967).

Rothstein, Eric, *Systems of Order and Inquiry in Later Eighteenth Century Fiction* (Berkeley: University of California Press, 1975).

Rousseau, G. S., *Tobias Smollett: Essays of Two Decades* (Edinburgh: T. & J. Clark, 1982).

Rousseau, G. S., and Bouce, Paul Gabriel (eds), *Tobias Smollett; Bicentennial Essays presented to Lewis M. Knapp* (New York: Oxford University Press, 1971).

Simpson, Kenneth G., 'The Scot as Novelist: Tobias Smollett', *The Protean Scot: The Crisis of Identity in the Eighteenth Century* (Aberdeen: Aberdeen University Press, 1988).

Spector, Robert D., *Tobias George Smollett* (New York: Twayne, 1968; updated edition, Boston: Twayne, 1989).

—, *Smollett's Women: A Study of Eighteenth Century Masculine Sensibility* (Westport, CT: Greenwood Press, 1994).

Warner, John M., *Joyce's Grandfathers: Myth and History in Defoe, Smollett, Sterne, and Joyce* (Athens and London: University of Georgia Press, 1993).

Chapter 11· Widening the Range

The following references are selective, providing preliminary information on writers mentioned in the main text. In this section primary and critical works are listed together. The list works in alphabetical order of eighteenth-century author, with criticism. For information on further writers of the period such as William Hamilton of Bangour or Alexander Wilson see the website bibliographies; for women writers of the period see relevant articles in Douglas Gifford and Dorothy McMillan (eds), *A History of Scottish Women's Writing* (Edinburgh: Edinburgh University Press, 1997).

SAMUEL ARNOT

Arnot, Samuel, 'Eternity: A Poem', *The Gardyne Collection* Vol. 206 (held by The Mitchell Library, Glasgow).

LADY GRIZELL BAILLIE

Baillie, G., *Recollections of a happy life begun on earth, made perfect in heaven (her brother Major Robert Baillie, of Earlston)* (Edinburgh: R&R Clark, 1890, 2nd edition).

JAMES BEATTIE

Beattie, James, and Blair, Robert, *The Poetical Works of Gray, Beattie, Blair, Collins, Thomson and Kirke White* (London: Blackwood & Co., n. d; New York: G. Routledge & sons, 1800).

King, Everard H., *James Beattie* (Boston: Twayne, 1977).

Walker, Ralph S., *James Beattie's London Diary, 1735* (Aberdeen: Aberdeen University Press, 1946).

ROBERT BLAIR

Blair, Robert, *The Grave: a poem with introduction by James A. Means* (Los Angeles: William Andrews Clark Memorial Library, University of California, 1973).

—, *The Grave: A Poem*, with Gray's celebrated elegy in a country Church-yard (Glasgow: Hutcheson, 1800).

—, *The Grave: A Poem*, illustrated by 12 etchings (executed by Louis Schiavonetti, from the original inventions of William Blake) (London, 1808).

THOMAS BLACKLOCK

Blacklock, Thomas, *Poems*, ed. Henry Mackenzie (Edinburgh, 1793).

JAMES BOSWELL

Boswell, James, *The Journal of a Tour to the Hebrides*, ed. Peter Levi (Harmondsworth: Penguin, 1984).

—, *The Life of Samuel Johnson*, 5 Vols, eds G. B. Hill and L. F. Powell (London, 1964) [Vol. V has *Tour to the Hebrides*].

Clingham, G. (ed.), *New Light on Boswell: Critical and Historical Essays* (Cambridge: Cambridge University Press, 1991).

Crawford, Thomas, *Boswell, Burns and the French Revolution* (Edinburgh: Saltire Society, 1990).

Crawford, Thomas (ed.), *Boswell in Scotland and Beyond* (Glasgow: Association for Scottish Literary Studies, 1997).

Martin, Peter, *A Life of James Boswell* (London: Weidenfled & Nicholson, 1999).

See also Frederick Pottle's *James Boswell: The Earlier Years, 1740–1769* (London: Heinemann, 1966) and the Yale series of Boswell journals from *Boswell's London Journal 1762–1763*, ed. Frederick Pottle (London, 1951) to *Boswell: The Great Biographer 1789–1795*, eds Marlies Danziger and Frank Brady (London: Heinemann, 1989), comprising thirteen volumes; and the Yale Research edition of the Letters, in seven volumes.

ALEXANDER CARLYLE

Carlyle, Alexander, *The Autobiography of Dr. Alexander Carlyle of Inveresk, 1722–1805*, ed. J. H. Burton (Edinburgh, 1860).

JAMES CRAIGS

Craigs, James, *Spiritual Life: Poems on Several Divine Subjects* (Edinburgh: Lumisden & Co., 1727; held by The Mitchell Library, Glasgow).

WILLIAM FALCONER

Falconer, William, *The Shipwreck: a poem* [with notes and a sketch of his life] (London, 1803; 1808; 1811; 1825).

ADAM FERGUSON

Ferguson, Adam, *Institutes of Moral Philosophy* (London: Routledge/Thoemmes Press, 1994).

Merolle, Vincenzo (ed.), *The Correspondence of Adam Ferguson* (London: William Pickering, 1995).

Oz-Salzberger, Fania (ed.), *An Essay on the History of Civil Society* (Cambridge: Cambridge University Press, 1995).

ANDREW FLETCHER OF SALTOUN

Daiches, D. (ed.), *Selected Political Writings and Speeches [of] Andrew Fletcher of Saltoun* (Edinburgh: Scottish Academic Press, 1979).

ALEXANDER GEDDES

Carruthers, Gerard, 'Alexander Geddes and the Burns "Lost Poems" Controversy', *SSL* XXXI (Columbia: University of South Carolina, 1999), pp. 81–5.

Geddes, A., *An Apology for Slavery* (James Johnson, 1792).

—, *Carmen Saeculare Alterum, Pro Anno Liberatus Quatro* (James Johnson, 1792).

—, 'Three Scottish Poems, with a Previous Dissertation on the Scoto-Saxon Dialect', *Transactions of the Scottish Society of Antiquaries* (Aberdeen, 1792).

WILLIAM HAMILTON OF GILBERTFIELD
Glen, D. (ed.), *Familiar Epistles between William Hamilton of Gilbertfield in Cambuslang and Allan Ramsay in Edinburgh* (Kirkcaldy: Akros Press, 2000).
Hamilton, W., *Blind Harry's Wallace* (1722; Edinburgh: Luath Press, 1998).

JOHN HOME
Home, John, *Agis: a Tragedy* (London: A. Millar, 1758 and Dublin: G. & A. Ewing et al., 1758).
—, *Alonzo: A Tragedy in Five Acts* (London: T. Beckct, 1773).
—, *Douglas: A Tragedy* (London: A. Millar, 1757 and Edinburgh: George Reid, 1798).
—, *Douglas*, ed. Gerald Parker (Edinburgh: Oliver & Boyd, 1972).

HENRY HOME (LORD KAMES)
Lehmann, William C., *Henry Home, Lord Kames and the Scottish Enlightenment: A Study in National Character and in the History of Ideas* (The Hague: Nijhoff, 1971).

DAVID HUME
Basson, Anthony Henry, *David Hume* (Harmondsworth: Penguin, 1958).
Danford, John W., *David Hume and the Problem of Reason* (New Haven, London: Yale University Press, 1990).
Green, T. H., and Grose, T. H. (eds), *Essays: moral, political and literary* (Indianapolis: Liberty Classics, 1985).
Greig, J. Y. T., *David Hume* (London: Cape, 1931).
Mossner, Ernest Campbell, *The Life of David Hume* (Oxford: Clarendon Press, 1954).
Sisson, Charles Hubert, *David Hume* (Edinburgh: Ramsay Head Press, 1970).

FRANCIS HUTCHESON
Hutcheson, Francis, *An Inquiry Concerning Beauty, Order, Harmony, Design*, ed. Peter King (The Hague: Martinus Nijhoff, 1973).
—, *Collected works of Francis Hutcheson*, facsimile editions prepared by Bernhard Fabian (Hildesheim: Olms, 1969–1990).
Scott, William Robert, *Francis Hutcheson* (Cambridge: Cambridge University Press, 1966).

CHARLES KEITH
Keith, Charles, *The har'st rig and the farmer's ha': two poems in the Scottish dialect* (Edinburgh: W. Berry, 1794).
—, *Monody to the Memory of the Rev. Dr. Charles Nisbet* (Edinburgh, 1805).

GEORGE LOCKHART
Szechi, Daniel (ed.), *'Scotland's Ruine': Lockhart of Carnwath's memoirs of the Union* (Aberdeen: Association for Scottish Literary Studies, 1995).

HENRY MACKENZIE
Barker, Gerard, *Henry Mackenzie* (New York: Twayne, 1975).
Drescher, Horst (ed.), *Literature and Literati: the literary correspondence and notebooks of Henry Mackenzie* (Frankfurt am Main: Peter Lang, 1989).
Garside, P. D., 'Henry Mackenzie, the Scottish Novel and Blackwood's Magazine', *SLJ* 15(1) (Aberdeen: Association for Scottish Literary Studies, 1988), pp. 25–48.

READING LISTS

Mackenzie, Henry, *The Man of Feeling* [1771], ed. Brian Vickers (London: Oxford University Press, 1967).
—, *The Man of the World* (Edinburgh, 1773).
Manning, Susan (ed.), *Julia de Roubigné* (East Linton: Tuckwell Press, 1999).
Thompson, Harold, *A Scottish Man of Feeling; Some Account of Henry Mackenzie and The Golden Age of Burns and Scott* (London: Oxford University Press, 1931).

JAMES MACPHERSON
Gaskill, Howard (ed.), *Ossian Revisited* (Edinburgh: Edinburgh University Press, 1991).
— (ed.), *The poems of Ossian and related works* (Edinburgh: Edinburgh University Press, 1996).
MacPherson, James, *The Poems of Ossian* (Edinburgh: John Grant, 1926).
Pittock, Murray, 'Forging North Britain in the Age of MacPherson', *Edinburgh Review* 93 (Edinburgh: Edinburgh University Press, 1995), pp. 125–39 [this issue includes other essays on MacPherson and Ossian].
Smart, J. S., *James MacPherson: an Episode in Literature* (London: Nutt, 1905).
Stafford, Fiona, *The Sublime Savage: a Study of James MacPherson and the Poems of Ossian* (Edinburgh: Edinburgh University Press, 1988).

DAVID MALLOCH
Malloch, David, *Donaides; John Ker; and A poem in imitation of Donaides*, introduction by Irma S. Lustig and a translation by Barrows Dunham (Los Angeles: William Andrews Clark Memorial Library, 1978).
—, and Thomson, James, *Alfred: a masque . . .* (London, 1747).

JOHN MAYNE
Mayne, John, *Glasgow: A Poem* (London, 1803).
—, *The siller gun; a poem, in four cantos* (Gloucester, 1808).

ARCHIBALD PITCAIRNE
Pitcarine, A., *The Assembly, or, Scotch Reformation; a comedy* (1692; Edinburgh, 1725; Lafayette, IN: Purdue University Studies, 1972).

THOMAS REID
Barker, Stephen F., and Beauchamp, Tom L., *Thomas Reid: Critical Interpretations* (Philadelphia: University City Science Centre, 1976).
Beanblossom, Ronald E., and Lehrer, Keith (eds), *Thomas Reid's Enquiry and Essays* (Indianapolis: Hakett Publishing Co., 1983).
Brookes, Derek (ed.), *Thomas Reid's An Enquiry Into the Human Mind on the Principles of Common Sense* (Edinburgh: Edinburgh University Press, 1997).
Fraser, Alexander, *Thomas Reid* (Edinburgh: Oliphant, Anderson and Ferrier, 1898).
Gallie, Roger D., *Thomas Reid and 'the way of ideas'* (Dordrecht, London: Kluwer Academic, 1989).
—, *Thomas Reid: ethics, aesthetics and the anatomy of the self* (Dordrecht, London: Kluwer Academic, 1998).
Lehrer, Keith, *Thomas Reid* (London: Routledge, 1989).
Rowe, William L., *Thomas Reid on Freedom and Morality* (Ithaca, London: Cornell University Press, 1991).

WILLIAMSON ROBERTSON

Brown, Stewart J. (ed.), *William Robertson and the Expansion of Empire* (Cambridge: Cambridge University Press, 1997).

ALEXANDER ROSS

Hewitt, David, 'The Ballad World and Alexander Ross', *Literature of the North*, eds D. Hewitt and M. Spiller (Aberdeen: Aberdeen University Press, 1983), pp. 42–54.

Ross, Alexander, *Helenore, or the fortunate Shepherdess* (Edinburgh, 1866; Dundee, 1912).

THOMAS RUDDIMAN

Ruddiman's significance lies in the important and influential eighteenth-century editions he published, which include:

Buchanan, George, *Paraphrasis Psalmorum Davidis Poetica &c.*, eds John Love and Robert Hunter (Edinburgh, 1737).

Douglas, Gavin, *Aeneid* (Edinburgh, 1710).

Drummond, William, of Hawthornden, *Works* (Edinburgh, 1711).

Johnston, Arthur (ed.), *Poetarum Scotorum musae sacrae* (Edinburgh, 1739).

Malloch, David, *A Poem in Imitation of Donaides* (Edinburgh, 1725).

Ramsay, Allan. *Poems*, quarto (Edinburgh, 1721).

— (ed.), *The Tea-Table Miscellany* (Edinburgh, 1724).

— (ed.), *The Ever-Green, being a Collection of Scots Poems, wrote by the Ingenious before 1600*, 2 vols (Edinburgh, 1724).

—, *The Gentle Shepherd: A Scots Pastoral Comedy* (Edinburgh, 1725).

—, *Poems*, vol. 2 (Edinburgh, 1728).

See also: Duncan, Douglas, *Thomas Ruddiman: a study in Scottish scholarship of the early eighteenth century* (Edinburgh and London: Oliver & Boyd, 1965).

JOHN SKINNER

Skinner, John, *An Ecclesiastical History of Scotland, from the First Appearance of Christianity in that Kingdom, to the Present Time; with Remarks on the Most Important Occurrences; in a Series of Letters to a Friend; by the Reverend John Skinner, a Presbyter of the Episcopal Church in Scotland, at Longside, Aberdeenshire* (London: Printed for T. Evans, . . .; and R. N. Cheyne, Edinburgh, 1788).

—, *Amusements of Leisure Hours: or Poetical Pieces, Chiefly in the Scottish Dialect . . .; to Which is Prefixed, a Sketch of the Author's Life, with some Remarks on Scottish Poetry* (Edinburgh: Printed by J. Moir and sold by S. Cheyne, 1809).

—, *Theological Works of the Late Rev. John Skinner, Episcopal Clergyman in Longside, Aberdeenshire: to Which is Prefixed a Biographical Memoir of the Author* (Aberdeen: Printed by J. Chalmers, 1809).

—, *Practical Sermons Selected from the Manuscripts of the Rev. John Skinner: in Two Volumes* (Salisbury: Brodie and Dowding, 1824).

ADAM SMITH

Bryce, J. C. (ed.), *Lectures on Rhetoric and Belles Lettres* (Oxford: Oxford University Press, 1983).

Farrer, J. A., *Adam Smith (1723–1790)* (London: Sampson Low, Marston, Searle & Rivington, 1881).

Franklin, Burt, *Adam Smith: a bibliographical checklist* (New York: B. Franklin, 1950).

Ross, Ian S., *The Life of Adam Smith* (Oxford: Clarendon Press, 1995) [see the bibliography pp. 434–78].

JAMES THOMSON

Carruthers, Gerard, 'James Thomson and Eighteenth-Century Scottish Literary Identity', *James Thomson: Essays for The Tercentenary*, ed. Richard Terry (Liverpool: Liverpool University Press, 2000), pp. 165–191.

Cohen, Ralph, *The Unfolding of the Seasons: A Study of Thomson's Poem* (London: Routledge, 1970).

Grant, Douglas, *James Thomson: poet of 'The Seasons'* (London: Cresset Press, 1951).

Sambrook, James, *James Thomson, 1700–1748: a life* (Oxford: Clarendon, 1991).

— (ed.), *James Thomson: The Seasons* (Oxford: Clarendon Press, 1981).

— (ed.), *James Thomson: Liberty, The Castle of Indolence and Other Poems* (Oxford: Clarendon, 1986).

—, 'James Thomson and the Anglo-Scots,' *The History of Scottish Literature*, Vol. 2, 1660–1800, ed. Andrew Hoot, (Aberdeen: Aberdeen University Press, 1987), pp. 81–100.

Scott, Mary Jane W., *James Thomson, Anglo-Scot* (Athens, GA, London: University of Georgia Press, 1988).

Terry, Richard (ed.), *James Thomson: Essays for the Tercentenary* (Liverpool: Liverpool University Press, 2000).

LADY ELIZABETH (HALKETT) WARDLAW

Wardlaw, E., *Hardyknute, a fragment of an antient Scots poem* (Glasgow: Robert Foulis, 1748).

JAMES WATSON

Wood, Harriet Harvey (ed.), *James Watson's Choice Collection of Comic and serious Scots Poems* (Aberdeen: Scottish Text Society and Aberdeen University Press, 1991).

—, 'Burns and *Watson's Choice Collection*', *SSL XXX* (Columbia: University of South Carolina, 1998), pp. 19–30.

WILLIAM WILKIE

Wilkie, William, *The Epigoniad* (Edinburgh, 1757).

SECTION 3:
SCOTTISH LITERATURE IN THE AGE OF SCOTT
Introductory reading

As always the reader is reminded of the informative websites listed at the beginning of the Further Reading section, especially the developing website maintained by the Departments of Scottish Literature and STELLA at the University of Glasgow at **www.arts.gla.ac.uk/SESLL/ScotLit/bibliography** where more information can be given than is possible here.

Again, the general literary and bibliographical works listed in General Further Reading (at the opening to the reading lists) are useful starting points, including Aitken, Daiches, Glen, Kinsley, Lindsay, Millar, Royle, Speirs, Walker, Watson and Wittig. For a recent comprehensive and critically helpful guide to the period see the collection of essays in the third volume of *The*

History of Scottish Literature series edited by Douglas Gifford (General Editor Cairns Craig, Aberdeen: Aberdeen University Press, 1988). Other useful introductions to the issues of the period are raised by G. E. Davie in *The Democratic Intellect* (Edinburgh: Edinburgh University Press, 1961); David Daiches in *Literature and Gentility in Scotland* (Edinburgh: Edinburgh University Press, 1982), and David Craig in *Scottish Literature and the Scottish People 1680–1830* (London: Chatto & Windus, 1961). Robert Crawford's *Devolving English Literature* (Oxford: Clarendon Press, 1992; rev. Edinburgh: Edinburgh University Press, 2001) challenges accepted views on the period, while John McQueen's study of Enlightenment influence on historical fiction, *The Rise of the Historical Novel: The Enlightenment and Scottish Literature* (Edinburgh: Scottish Academic Press, 1989) gives a background to Scott, Hogg, Galt and Carlyle, as does *Nineteenth-Century Scottish Fiction: A Critical Anthology* (Manchester: New Carcanet Press, 1979), essays edited by Ian Campbell. Language usage in the fiction is analysed by Emma Letley in *From Galt to Douglas Brown – Nineteenth Century Fiction and Scots Language* (Edinburgh: Scottish Academic Press, 1988), and John W. Oliver's essay entitled 'Scottish Poetry in the Earlier Nineteenth Century' in Kinsley (ed.), *Scottish Poetry: a Critical Survey* (London: Cassell, 1955), pp. 212–35, may be useful. Edwin Muir's *Scott and Scotland* (London: Routledge, 1936) raises stimulating, if controversial issues of language, identity, themes and issues. And recently the neglected achievement of women in the period has been addressed, in the essays of *A History of Scottish Women's Writing* edited by Gifford and McMillan (Edinburgh: Edinburgh University Press, 1997), in *An Anthology of Scottish Women Poets*, edited by Catherine Kerrigan (Edinburgh: Edinburgh University Press, 1991), and in McMillan's anthology *The Scotswoman Abroad: Non-Fictional Writing 1700–1900* (Glasgow: Association for Scottish Literary Studies, 1999).

For historical and cultural background there are two outstanding accounts of the period, the first from the Tory and son-in-law of Walter Scott, John Gibson Lockhart in *Peter's Letters To his Kinsfolk* (Edinburgh, 1819: William Ruddick has a modern edition, Edinburgh: Scottish Academic Press, 1977), and the Whig lawyer and Judge (Lord) Henry Cockburn in *Memorials of His Time* (Edinburgh, 1856), with a modern edition by Karl Miller (Chicago: University of Chicago Press, 1974). Margaret Oliphant's two-volume *Annals of a Publishing House: William Blackwood and His Sons* (Edinburgh: Blackwood, 1897) is still the best account of Scotland's greatest publisher. A neglected, very thorough and perceptive study of the period is Laurence Saunders's *Scottish Democracy 1825–1840: The Social and Intellectual Background* (Edinburgh: Oliver & Boyd, 1950).

Chapter 12: The Age of Scott

BACKGROUND READING

See also Background reading for Sections 2 and 4.

Anderson, Carol, and Riddell, Aileen M., 'The Other Great Unknowns: Women Fiction Writers of the Early Nineteenth Century', *A History of Scottish Women's Writing*, eds Douglas Gifford and Dorothy McMillan (Edinburgh: Edinburgh University Press, 1997), pp. 179–95.

Bell, Alan (ed.), *Lord Cockburn: A Bi-Centenary Celebration* (Edinburgh: Scottish Academic Press, 1979).

Carswell, Donald, *Sir Walter: A Four-Part Study in Biography* (London: John Murray, 1930).

Clive, John, *Scotch Reviewers: The Edinburgh Review 1802–1815* (London: Faber, 1957).

Crawford, Robert, *Devolving English Literature* (Oxford: Clarendon Press, 1992; rev. Edinburgh: Edinburgh University Press, 2001).

Daiches, David, *Sir Walter Scott and his World* (London: Thames & Hudson, 1971).

Davis, Leith, *Acts of Union: Scotland and the Literary Negotiation of the British Nation 1707–1830* (Stanford, CA: Stanford University Press, 1998).

Drescher, Horst, and Schwendt, Joachim (eds), *Studies in Scottish Fiction: Nineteenth Century* (Frankfurt: Peter Lang, 1985).

Duncan, Ian, *Modern Romance and Transformations of the Novel: the Gothic, Scott and Dickens* (Cambridge: Cambridge University Press, 1993).

Fielding, Penny, *Writing and Orality: Nationality, Culture and Nineteenth-Century Scottish Fiction* (Oxford: Clarendon, 1996).

Gifford, Douglas, *Scottish Short Stories, 1800–1900* (London: Calder & Boyars, 1971).

Hart, Francis, *Lockhart as Romantic Biographer* (Edinburgh: Edinburgh University Press, 1971).

Hook, Andrew, *From Goosecreek to Gandercleugh: studies in Scottish-American literary and cultural history* (East Linton: Tuckwell Press, 1999).

Jackson, Holbrook, *The Eighteen-Nineties: A Review of Art and Ideas at the Close of the Nineteenth Century* (London: Grant Richards, 1913; Hassocks: Harvester Press, 1976).

Kelly, Gary, *English Fiction of the Romantic Period 1789–1830* (London: Longman, 1989).

Lindsay, Maurice, *Scottish Comic Verse: An Anthology* (London: Hale, 1991).

Lukacs, Georg, *The Historical Novel*, trans. Hannah and Stanley Mitchell (London: Merlin Press, 1962).

Manning, Susan, *The Puritan-Provincial Vision; Scottish and American Literature in the Nineteenth Century* (Cambridge and New York: Cambridge University Press, 1990).

Miller, Karl, *Cockburn's Millenium* (London: Duckworth, 1975).

Morgan, Edwin (ed.), *Scottish Satirical Verse: An Anthology* (Manchester: Carcanet, 1980).

Morgan, Peter (ed.), *Jeffrey's Criticism* (Edinburgh: Scottish Academic Press, 1983).

Trumpener, Katie, *Bardic Nationalism: The Romantic Novel and the British Empire* (Princeton, NJ: Princeton University Press, 1997).

Young, Douglas, *Edinburgh in the Age of Walter Scott* (Oklahoma, 1965).

Chapters 13 and 14: Walter Scott and Scotland; and Waverley

As Scott was so prolific and as there are so many editions of his work, this bibliography makes no attempt to be exhaustive. Readers are referred to lists in Aitken and Royle and to the ambitious and informative *Edinburgh Edition of The Waverley Novels* (Edinburgh and New York: Edinburgh University Press and Columbia University Press, 1993–), presently being undertaken by international scholars under the General Editor David Hewitt; several volumes have now appeared, and are noted below, with some other good Recent editions: readers should check for the appearance of other volumes.

The Edinburgh Edition (Edinburgh and New York: Edinburgh University Press and Columbia University Press). (Dates as scheduled by Edinburgh University Press.)

The Black Dwarf, ed. P. D. Garside, 1993.
The Tale of Old Mortality, ed. Douglas S. Mack, 1993.
Kenilworth: A Romance, ed. J. H. Alexander, 1993.
The Antiquary, ed. David Hewitt, 1995.
The Bride of Lammermuir, ed. J. H. Alexander, 1995.
St. Ronan's Well, ed. Mark Weinstein, 1995.
A Legend of the Wars of Montrose, ed. J. H. Alexander, 1996.
Ivanhoe, ed. Graham Tulloch, 1997.
Redgauntlet, ed. G. A. M. Wood, 1997.
Guy Mannering, ed. P. D. Garside, 1999.
Anne of Geierstein, ed. J. H. Alexander, 2000.
The Abbot, ed. Christopher Johnson, 2000.
Chronicles of the Canongate, ed. Claire Lamont, 2000.
The Monastery, ed. Penny Fielding, 2000.
The Heart of Midlothian, eds David Hewitt and Alison Lumsden, 2001.
Quentin Durward, eds J. H. Alexander and G. A. M. Wood, 2001.
The Pirate, eds Mark Weinstein and Alison Lumsden, 2001.

Other recent editions

Waverley, ed. Andrew Hook (Harmondsworth: Penguin, 1972; reprinted, 1985).
Old Mortality, ed. Angus Calder (Harmondsworth: Penguin, 1975).
Rob Roy (London: J. M. Dent & Sons Ltd., Everyman's Library, 1986; reissued 1991, with preface by W. M. Parker).
The Heart of Midlothian, ed. Tony Inglis (Harmondsworth: Penguin Classics, 1994).
Ivanhoe, ed. Ian Duncan (Oxford: Oxford University Press, World's Classics Series, 1996).
The Two Drovers and Other Stories (Oxford: Oxford University Press, World's Classics Series, 1987).
The Waverley Novels (Oxford University Press, 1912–25); Oxford edition, 24 vols.
The Supernatural Short Stories, ed. Michael Hayes (London: John Calder, 1977).
The Prefaces to the Waverley Novels, ed. Mark A. Weinstein (Lincoln: University of Nebraska Press, 1978).
The Letters of Malachi Malagrowther, ed. Paul Scott (Edinburgh: William Blackwood, 1981).

Secondary reading

Alexander, J. H., and Hewitt, David (eds), *Scott and his Influence: The Papers of the Aberdeen Scott Conference, 1982* (Aberdeen: Association for Scottish Literary Studies, 1983).
— (eds), *Scott in Carnival: Selected Papers from the Fourth International Scott Conference, Edinburgh 1991* (Aberdeen: Association for Scottish Literary Studies, 1993).
Anderson, James, 'Sir Walter Scott as Historical Novelist', *SSL* 4 (Columbia: University of South Carolina, 1966–7), pp. 63–78; pp. 155–78; and *SSL* 5 (1967–8), pp. 14–27; pp. 83–97; pp. 143–66.

Anderson, William Eric Kinloch, 'Scott', *The English Novel: Select Biographical Guides*, ed. Anthony Edward Dyson (London: Oxford University Press, 1974), pp. 128–44.

Beiderwell, Bruce, *Power and Punishment in Scott's Novels* (Athens: University of Georgia Press, 1992).

Bell, Alan (ed.), *Scott Bicentenary Essays: Selected Papers Read at the Sir Walter Scott Bicentenary Conference, Edinburgh 1971* (Edinburgh: Scottish Academic Press, 1973).

Bradley, Philip, *An Index to the Waverley Novels* (Metuchen, NJ: Scarecrow Press, 1975).

Brown, David, *Walter Scott and the Historical Imagination* (London: Routledge & Kegan Paul, 1979).

Buchan, John, *Sir Walter Scott* (London: Cassell, 1932).

Bushnell, Nelson S., 'Walter Scott's Advent as Novelist of Manners', *SSL* 1 (Columbia: University of South Carolina, 1963–4), pp. 15–34.

—, 'Scott's Mature Achievement as Novelist of Manners', *SSL* 3 (Columbia: University of South Carolina, 1965–6), pp. 3–29.

Calder, Angus and Calder, Jenni, *Scott* (London: Evans Brothers, 1969).

Carson, James C., *A Bibliography of Sir Walter Scott: A Classified and Annotated List of Books and Articles Relating to his Life and Works, 1797–1940* (Edinburgh: Oliver & Boyd, 1943; reprinted, NY: Burt Franklin, 1969).

Chandler, Alia, 'Chivalry and Romance: Scott's Medieval Novels', *Studies in Romanticism* 14 (Boston: University of Boston, 1975), pp. 185–200.

Chandler, Bernard S., 'The motif of the journey in the eighteenth-century novel in Scott and Mazoni', *Rivista di studi italiani* 3(2) (Toronto: University of Toronto, 1985), pp. 1–10.

Clark, Arthur Melville, *Sir Walter Scott: The Formative Years* (Edinburgh: Blackwood, 1969).

Cockshut, Anthony O. J., *The Achievement of Walter Scott* (London: Collins, 1969).

Corson, James C., *Bibliography of Sir Walter Scott* (Edinburgh: Oliver & Boyd, 1943).

—, *Notes and Index to Sir Herbert Grierson's Edition of the Letters of Sir Walter Scott* (Oxford: Oxford University Press, 1979).

Cottom, David, *The Civilized Imagination* (Cambridge: Cambridge University Press, 1985).

Crawford, Thomas, *Scott* (Edinburgh: Oliver & Boyd, 1965).

—, *Walter Scott* (Edinburgh: Scottish Academic Press, Scottish Writers Series, 1982).

Crockett, William S., *The Scott Originals: An Account of Notables and Worthies, The Originals of Characters in the Waverley Novels* (Edinburgh: T. N. Foulis, 1912).

Daiches, David, 'Scott's Achievement as a Novelist', *Nineteenth-Century Fiction* 6 (California: University of California Press, 1951–2); reprinted in *Literary Essays* (Edinburgh: Oliver & Boyd, 1956), pp. 88–121; reprinted in *Walter Scott's Modern Judgements*, ed. David Douglas Devlin (London: Macmillan, 1968), pp. 33–62; reprinted in *Scott's Mind and Art*, ed. Alexander Norman Jeffares (Edinburgh: Oliver & Boyd, 1969), pp. 21–52.

—, 'Scott's Redgauntlet', *From Jane Austin to Joseph Conrad: Essays Collected in Memory of James T. Hillhouse*, eds Robert Rathburn and Martin Steinmann (Minneapolis: University of Minnosota Press, 1958), pp. 46–59; reprinted in *Walter Scott: Modern Judgements*, ed. David Douglas Devlin (London: Macmillan, 1968), pp. 148–61.

—, 'Scott's Waverley: The Presence of the Author', *Nineteenth-Century Scottish Fiction: Critical Essays*, ed. Ian Campbell (Manchester: Carcanet New Press, 1979), pp. 6–17.

Davie, Donald, *The Heyday of Sir Walter Scott* (London: Routledge & Kegan Paul, 1961).

—, 'The poetry of Sir Walter Scott', *Old Masters* (Manchester: Carcanet, 1992), pp. 276–89.

Devlin, David Douglas (ed.), *Walter Scott: Modern Judgements* (London: Macmillan, 1968).

—, *The Author of Waverley: A Critical Study of Sir Walter Scott* (London: Macmillan, 1971).

Elam, Diane, 'Delayed in the Post: Walter Scott and the Progress of Romance', *Romancing the Postmodern* (London: Routledge, 1992).

Fischer, Hermann, 'The establishment of the genre by Sir Walter Scott, its fashionable period and imitations by other poets', *Romantic Verse Narrative* (Cambridge: Cambridge University Press, 1991), pp. 86–119.

Fleishman, Avrom, *The English Historical Novel: Walter Scott to Virginia Woolf* (Baltimore: Johns Hopkins Press, 1971).

Forbes, Duncan, 'The Rationalism of Sir Walter Scott', *The Cambridge Journal* 7 (Cambridge: Cambridge University Press, 1953), pp. 20–35.

Ford, Richard, *Dramatisations of Scott's Novels: A Catalogue* (Oxford: Oxford Bibliographical Society, 1979).

Gaston, Patricia Sullivan, *Prefacing the Waverley Prefaces: A Reading of Walter Scott's Prefaces to the Waverley Novels* (New York: P. Lang, 1991).

Gordon, Jan B., '"Liquidating the sublime": Gossip in Scott's novels', *At the Limits of Romanticism*, eds Mary A. Favret and Nicola J. Watson (Bloomington: Indiana University Press, 1994), pp. 246–68.

Gordon, Robert C., *Under Which King? A Study of the Scottish Waverley Novels* (Edinburgh: Oliver & Boyd, 1969).

Goslee, Nancy Moore, 'Witch or Pawn: Women in Scott's narrative poetry', *Romanticism and Feminism*, ed. Anne K. Mellor (Bloomington: Indiana University Press, 1988), pp. 115–36.

Hart, Francis R., *Scott's Novels: The Plotting of Historic Survival* (Charlottesville: University Press of Virginia, 1966).

Hartveit, Lars, *Dream within a Dream: A Thematic Approach to Scott's Vision of Fictional Reality* (Oslo: Universitetsforlaget, 1974).

Hazlitt, William, 'Sir Walter Scott', *The Spirit of the Age* (London: H Colburn, 1825; Oxford: Oxford University Press, 1904), pp. 76–91.

Hewitt, David, *Scott on Himself* (Edinburgh: Scottish Academic Press, 1981).

Heyden, John Olin (ed.), *Scott: The Critical Heritage* (London: Routledge & Kegan Paul, 1970).

Hillhouse, James T., *The Waverley Novels and their Critics* (Minneapolis: University of Minnesota Press, 1936).

Hogg, James, 'Familiar Anecdotes of Sir Walter Scott' [1834], ed. Douglas S. Mack, with Hogg's *Memoirs of the Author's Life* (Edinburgh: Scottish Academic Press, 1972).

Husband, Margaret F., *A Dictionary of Characters in the Waverley Novels* (London: Routledge, 1910).

Jack, Ian, *Sir Walter Scott* (London: Longman for the British Council, 1958); reprinted with additions to the bibliography, 1964; 1971.

Jeffares, Alexander Norman (ed.), *Scott's Mind and Art* (Edinburgh: Oliver & Boyd, 1969).

Johnson, Edgar, *Sir Walter Scott: The Great Unknown* (New York: Macmillan and London: Hamish Hamilton, 1970) [2 vols].

Johnson, Richard E., 'The Technique of embedding in Scott's Fiction', *SSL* 13 (Columbia: University of South Carolina, 1978), pp. 63–71.

Kropf, David Glenn, *Authorship as Alchemy: Subversive Writing in Pushkin, Scott Hoffmann* (Stanford, CA: University of Stanford Press, 1994).

Lang, Andrew, *Sir Walter Scott* (London: Hodder & Stoughton, 1906).

Lascelles, Mary, *The Story-Teller Retrieves the Past* (Oxford: Oxford University Press, 1980).

Maitzen, Rohan, '"By no means an improbable fiction": Redgauntlet's novel historicism', *Studies in the Novel* 25(2) (Denton, Tex.: North Texas State University, 1993), pp. 170–83.

Mayhead, Robin, *Walter Scott* (Cambridge: Cambridge University Press, 1973).

McMaster, Graham, *Scott and Society* (Cambridge: Cambridge University Press, 1981).

Millgate, Jane, *Walter Scott: The Making of a Novelist* (Toronto: Toronto University Press, 1984).

Morgan, Peter F., 'Scott as Critc', *SSL* 7 (Columbia: University of South Carolina, 1969–70), pp. 90–1.

Muir, Edwin, *Scott and Scotland: The Predicament of the Scottish Writer* (London: Routledge, 1936).

Orel, Harold, *The Historical Novel from Scott to Sabatini: Changing Attitudes Towards a Literary Genre 1814–1920* (New York: St. Martin's Press, 1995).

Orr, Marilyn, 'Voices and text: Scott the storyteller, Scott the novelist', *SLJ* 16(2) (Aberdeen: Association for Scottish Literary Studies, 1989), pp. 41–59.

Parsons, Coleman O., *Witchcraft and Demonology in Scott's Fiction* (Edinburgh: Oliver & Boyd, 1964).

Pottle, Frederick A, 'The Power of Memory in Boswell and Scott', *Essays on the Eighteenth Century* (Oxford: Clarendon Press, 1945), pp. 168–89; reprinted in *Scott's Mind and Art*, ed. Alexander Norman Jeffares (Edinburgh: Oliver & Boyd, 1969), pp. 230–53.

Quayle, Eric, *The Ruin of Sir Walter Scott* (London: Hart-Davis, 1968).

Rignall, J. M., 'Scott and the spectacle of history', *Realist Fiction and the Strolling Spectator* (London: Routledge, 1992), pp. 20–36.

Rubenstein, Jill (ed.), *Sir Walter Scott: An Annotated Bibliography of Scholarship and Criticism 1975–1990* (Aberdeen: Association for Scottish Literary Studies, 1994).

Ruff, William, 'A Bibliography of the Poetical Works of Sir Walter Scott', *Transactions of the Edinburgh Bibliographical Society I* (1938), pp. 99–240 and pp. 277–82.

Scott, Paul, *Walter Scott and Scotland* (Edinburgh: William Blackwood, 1981).

Shaw, Harry E. (ed.), *Critical essays on Sir Walter Scott: the Waverley novels* (New York: G. K. Hall; London: Prentice Hall International, 1996).

Sutherland, John, *The Life of Sir Walter Scott, A Critical Biography* (Oxford and Cambridge, MA: Blackwell, 1995).

Tulloch, Graham, *The Language of Sir Walter Scott* (London: Andre Deutsch, 1980).

Welsh, Alexander, *The Hero of the Waverley Novels* (New Haven: Yale University Press, 1963); reissued as an expanded edition with new essays on Scott (Princeton, NJ: Princeton University Press, 1992).

Wilson, A. N., *The Laird of Abbotsford: A View of Sir Walter Scott* (Oxford: Oxford University Press, 1980).

Wilt, Judith, *Secret Leaves: The Novels of Sir Walter Scott* (Chicago: University of Chicago Press, 1985).

Worthington, Greville, *A Bibliography of the Waverley Novels* (London: Constable, 1931).

The New Cambridge Bibliography of English Literature, Vol. III (Cambridge: Cambridge University Press, 1963), columns 670–92.

Chapter 15: Susan Ferrier: Marriage

Destiny, 2 vols (London: Richard Bently, 1882) [first published as *The Chief's Daughter*, 1831].

The Inheritance, 2 vols (London: Richard Bently, 1882) [first published 1824].

Marriage, ed. Rosemary Ashton (London: Virago, 1986) [with an introduction by R. Ashton].

Marriage, ed. Herbert Foltinek (Oxford: Oxford University Press, 1977) [with an introduction by H. Foltinek].

Memoir and Correspondence of Susan Ferrier 1782–1854, ed. John A. Doyle (London: John Murray, 1898).

Secondary reading

Anderson, Carol, and Riddell, Aileen M., 'The Other Great Unknown: Women Fiction Writers of the Early Nineteenth Century', *A History of Scottish Women's Writing*, eds Douglas Gifford and Dorothy McMillan (Edinburgh: Edinburgh University Press, 1997).

Bushnell, N. S., 'Susan Ferrier's *Marriage* as a Novel of Manners', *SSL* 5 (Columbia: University of South Carolina, 1968), pp. 216–28.

Calder, Jenni, *Women and Marriage in Victorian Fiction* (London: Thames & Hudson, 1976) [especially chapters 1 and 2].

—, 'Heroes and Hero-Makers: Women in Nineteenth-Century Scottish Fiction', *The History of*

Scottish Literature Vol. III, Nineteenth Century, ed. Douglas Gifford (Aberdeen: Aberdeen University Press, 1988), pp. 261–74.

Campbell, Ian, 'The Novels of Susan Ferrier', *National Library of Scotland Exhibition Catalogue* (Edinburgh, 1982), pp. 9–16.

Craik, Wendy, 'Susan Ferrier', *Scott Bicentenary Essays*, ed. Alan Bell (Edinburgh: Scottish Academic Press, 1973), pp. 322–31.

Cullinan, Mary, *Susan Ferrier* (Boston: Twayne, 1984).

Figes, Eva, *Sex and Subterfuge: Women Writers to 1850* (London: Macmillan, 1982).

Fletcher, Loraine, 'Great Expectations: Wealth and Inheritance in the Novels of Susan Ferrier', *SLJ* 16(2) (Aberdeen: Association for Scottish Literary Studies, 1989), pp. 60–77.

Foltinek, Herbert, 'Susan Ferrier Reconsidered', *Studies in Scottish Fiction: Nineteenth Century*, eds Horst W. Drescher and Joachim Schwend (Frankfurt am Main: P. Lang, 1985), pp. 131–44.

Gifford, Douglas, 'Myth, Parody and Dissociation: Scottish Fiction 1814–1914', *The History of Scottish Literature Vol. III, Nineteenth Century*, ed. Douglas Gifford (Aberdeen: Aberdeen University Press, 1988), pp. 217–59.

Grant, Aline, *Susan Ferrier of Edinburgh: A Biography* (Denver: Alan Swallow, 1957).

Hardy, Barbara, 'The Fruits of Separation', *Times Literary Supplement* 7 (June, 1985) [A Review of the Three Rivers Books edition of *Marriage* and *The Inheritance*].

Hart, F. R., *The Scottish Novel from Smollett to Spark* (Cambridge, MA: Harvard University Press, 1978), esp. pp. 57–68.

Irvine, James E. M., 'A Glimpse of Susan Ferrier', *National Library of Scotland Exhibition Catalogue* (Edinburgh, 1982), pp. 5–8.

Kelly, Gary, *English Fiction of the Romantic Period 1789–1830* (London and New York: Longman, 1989).

Letley, Emma, *From Galt to Douglas Brown: Nineteenth Century Fiction and Scots Language* (Edinburgh: Scottish Academic Press, 1988), pp. 56–8.

Parker, W. M., *Susan Ferrier and John Galt* (London: Longman, 1965).

Paxton, Nancy L., 'Subversive Feminism: A Reassessment of Susan Ferrier's *Marriage*', *Women and Literature* 4 (New York: Holmes & Meier, 1976), pp. 18–29.

Poovey, Mary, *The Proper Lady and the Woman Writer: Ideology as Style in the Works of Mary Wollstonecraft, Mary Shelley, and Jane Austen* (Chicago and London: University of Chicago Press, 1984).

Showalter, Elaine, *A Literature of their Own: British Women Novelists from Bronte to Lessing* (London: Virago, 1973).

Spencer, Jane, *The Rise of the Woman Novelist: From Aphra Behn to Jane Austen* (London and New York: Basil Blackwell, 1986).

Williams, Ioan (ed.), *Sir Walter Scott on Novelists and Fiction* (New York: Barnes & Noble, 1968).

Chapter 16: John Galt: The Entail

All titles below published in Edinburgh by William Blackwood unless otherwise indicated.

The Battle of Largs: A Gothic Poem (1804).
Letters from the Levant (1813).
The Majolo: A Tale (1816).
The Life and Studies of Benjamin West (1816–20).
The Crusade: A Poem (1816).
The Earthquake: A Tale (1820).

The Wandering Jew (1820).
The Ayrshire Legatees, or the Pringle Family (1821).
Annals of the Parish, or the Chronicle of Dalmailing (1821).
Sir Andrew Wylie of that Ilk (1822).
The Provost (1822).
The Steamboat (1822).
The Entail, or the Lairds of Grippy (1823).
Ringan Gilhaize, or the Covenanters (1823).
Glenfell, or MacDonalds and Campbells (1823).
The Spaewife: A Tale of the Scottish Chronicles (1823).
Rotheland: A Romance of the English Histories (1824).
The Omen (1825).
The Last of the Lairds, or the Life and Opinions of Malachi Mailings Esq. of Auldbiggings (1826).
Lawrie Todd, or the Settlers in the Woods (1830).
Southennan (1830).
The Life of Lord Byron (1830).
The Lives of the Players (1831).
Bogle Corbet, or the Emigrants (1831).
The Members: An Autobiography (1832).
The Radical: An Autobiography (1832).
Stanley Buxton, or the Schoolfellows (1832).
Poems (1833).
Eben Erskine or the Traveller (1833).
The Stolen Child: A Tale of the Town (1833).
Stories of the Study (1833).
An Autobiography of John Galt (1833).
The Literary Life and Miscellanies (1834).
The Howdie and Other Tales, ed. William Roughead (Edinburgh: T. N. Foulis, 1923).
A Rich Man and Other Stories, ed. William Roughead (Edinburgh: T. N. Foulis, 1925).
Works, 10 vols, eds David S. Meldrum and William Roughead (Edinburgh: John Grant, 1936)
   [Only seven novels].

RECENT EDITIONS
Annals of the Parish, or The Chronicle of Dalmailing during the Ministry of the Rev. Micah Balwhidder, written by himself, ed. James Kinsley (London: Oxford University Press, Oxford English Novels Series, 1967).
The Ayrshire Legatees (Edinburgh: Mercat Press, 1978).
Bogle Corbet, or The Emigrants, ed. Elizabeth Waterson (Toronto: McClelland & Stewart, 1977).
The Entail, or The Lairds of Grippy, ed. Ian A. Gordon (London: Oxford University Press, Oxford English Novels Series, 1970).
'The Gudewife', *Scottish Short Stories, 1800–1900*, ed. Douglas Gifford (London: Calder & Boyars, 1971); also in *The New Penguin Book of Scottish Short Stories*, ed. Ian Murray (Harmondsworth: Penguin, 1983).
The Last of the Lairds, or The Life and Opinions of Malachi Mailings Esq. Of Auldbiggings, ed. Ian A. Gordon (Edinburgh and London: Scottish Academic Press, 1976).
The Member: An Autobiography, edited by Ian A. Gordon (Edinburgh: Scottish Academic Press, 1985).
The Provost, ed. Ian A. Gordon (Oxford: Oxford University Press, Oxford English Novels Series, 1973).
Ringan Gilhaize, ed. Patricia J. Wilson (Edinburgh: Scottish Academic Press, 1984).
Selected Short Stories, ed. Ian A. Gordon (Edinburgh: Scottish Academic Press, 1978).

Secondary reading

Aberdein, Jennie W., *John Galt* (London: Oxford University Press, 1936).

Aldrich, Ruth I., *John Galt* (Boston: Twayne, 1978).

Booth, Bradford A., 'A Bibliography of John Galt', *Bulletin of Bibliography* 16 (1936–9), pp. 7–9.

Buchan, David, 'Treatise and Fable', *Nineteenth-Century Scottish Fiction: Critical Essays*, ed. Ian Campbell (Manchester: Carcanet New Press, 1979), pp. 18–36.

Campbell, Ian, 'John Galt's Annals of his Parish', *Scotia: American Canadian Journal of Scottish Studies* 10 (Norfolk, VA: Old Dominion University, 1986), pp. 15–25.

Costain, Keith M., 'The Prince and the Provost', *SSL* 6(1) (Columbia: University of South Carolina, 1968), pp. 20–35.

—, *The Rhetoric of Realism: Art and Ideas in the Fiction of John Galt* (Ann Arbor, MI: University Microfilms International, 1969) [Microfilm available in the National Library of Scotland].

—, 'Theoretical History and the Novel: the Scottish Fiction of John Galt', *English Language History* 43 (1976), pp. 342–65.

—, 'Early Remembrances: Pastoral in the Fictional World of John Galt', *University of Toronto Quarterly* (1978), pp. 283–303.

—, 'The Spirit of the Age and the Scottish Fiction of John Galt', *The Wordsworth Circle* XI(II) (Philadelphia: Temple University, 1980), pp. 98–106.

—, 'The Scottish Fiction of John Galt', *The History of Scottish Literature vol. III*, ed. Douglas Gifford (Aberdeen: Aberdeen University Press, 1988), pp. 107–23.

Frykman, Erik, *John Galt's Scottish Stories* (Uppsala: Lundequistska, 1959).

Gibault, Henri, *Romancier Ecossais* (Grenoble: Université de Grenoble, 1979).

Gordon, Ian A., *John Galt – The Life of a Writer* (Edinburgh: Oliver & Boyd, 1972).

—, 'Three New Chapters by Galt: The Publisher', *SLJ* 3 (Aberdeen: Association for Scottish Literary Studies, 1976), pp. 23–30.

—, 'Plastic Surgery on a Nineteenth-Century Novel: John Galt, William Blackwood, Dr. D. M. Moir and *The Last of the Lairds*', *Library: A Quarterly Journal of Bibliography* 32 (Dyfed, 1977), pp. 246–55.

Gordon, R. K., *John Galt* (Toronto: University of Toronto Studies, 1920).

Graham, Robert, 'John Galt's *Bogle Corbet*: A Parable of Progress', *SLJ* 13(2) (Aberdeen: Association for Scottish Literary Studies, 1986), pp. 31–47.

Hall, L. B., 'Peripety in John Galt's *The Entail*', *SSL* 5(3) (Columbia: University of South Carolina, 1968), pp. 176–84.

Jack, Ian, *English Literature 1815–1832* (Oxford: Oxford University Press, 1963) [chapter viii].

Kelly, Gary, *English Fiction of the Romantic Period 1789–1830* (London: Longman, 1989) [especially pp. 209–12].

Letley, Emma, *From Galt to Douglas Brown – Nineteenth-Century Fiction and Scots Language* (Edinburgh: Scottish Academic Press, 1988).

Lyell, Frank H., *A Study of the Novels of John Galt* (Princeton: Princeton University Press, 1942).

Lumsden, Harry, 'The Bibliography of John Galt', *Records of the Glasgow Bibliographical Society* 9 (1931), pp. 1–41.

MacQueen, John, 'John Galt and the Analysis of Social History', *Scott Bicentenary Essays*, ed. Alan Bell (Edinburgh: Scottish Academic Press, 1973), pp. 332–42.

McClure, J. D., 'The Language of *The Entail*', *SLJ* 8(1) (Aberdeen: Association for Scottish Literary Studies, 1981), pp. 30–50.

New Cambridge Bibliography of English Literature 3 (Cambridge: Cambridge University Press, 1969).

Parker, William M., *Susan Ferrier and John Galt* (London: Longmans, Green, for the British Council, 1965), pp. 24–43.

Roughead, W., 'The Centenary of *The Entail*', *Juridical Review* (Edinburgh, 1923), pp. 1–38.

Scott, P. H., *John Galt* (Edinburgh: Scottish Academic Press, 1985).

SLJ 8(1) (Aberdeen: Association for Scottish Literary Studies, 1981) [John Galt Number: contains articles by Ian A. Gordon, K. M. Costain, J. D. McClure and Patricia J. Wilson].

Swann, Charles, 'Past into Present, Galt and the Historical Novel', *Literature and History* 3 (London: Thames Polytechnic, 1976), pp. 65–82.

Timothy, Hamilton B., *The Galts: A Canadian Odyssey: John Galt, 1779–1839* (Toronto: McClelland & Stewart, 1977).

Waterson, Elizabeth (ed.), *John Galt: Reappraisals* (Guelph: University of Guelph, 1985).

Whatley, Christopher A. (ed.), *John Galt, 1779–1979* (Edinburgh: Ramsay Head Press, 1979).

Chapter 17: James Hogg:
The Private Memoirs and Confessions of a Justified Sinner

Under the General Editorship of Douglas Mack and Gillian Hughes, Edinburgh University Press are currently producing the ambitious and informative Stirling/South Carolina Edition of Hogg's Works. So far, the following titles have appeared; readers should check for further titles.

Stirling/South Carolina Editions. (Dates as scheduled by Edinburgh University Press.)

A Queer Book, ed. Peter Garside, 1995.

The Shepherd's Calendar, ed. Douglas S. Mack, 1995.

The Three Perils of Woman, eds David Groves, Antony Hasler and Douglas S. Mack, 1995.

Tales of the Wars of Montrose, ed. Gillian Hughes, 1996.

Lay Sermons, eds Gillian Hughes and Douglas S. Mack, 1997.

Queen Hynde, eds Suzanne Gilbert and Douglas S. Mack, 1998.

Anecdotes of Scott, ed. Jill Rubenstein, 1999.

The Spy, ed. Gillian Hughes, 2000.

The Private Memoirs and Confessions of a Justified Sinner, ed. Peter Garside, 2001.

EDITIONS

Scottish Pastorals (Edinburgh: Taylor, 1801).

The Mountain Bard (Edinburgh: Constable; London: Murray, 1807).

The Shepherd's Guide (Edinburgh: Constable; London: Murray, 1807).

The Forest Minstrel (Edinburgh and London, Constable, 1810).

The Spy: A Periodical Paper of Literary Amusement and Instruction (Edinburgh: Robertson, 1810; and Aikman, 1810–11).

The Queen's Wake (Edinburgh: Goldie; London: Longman, 1813).

The Hunting of Badlewe. A Dramatic Tale (London: Colborne; Edinburgh: Goldie, 1814).

The Pilgrims of the Sun (London: Murray; Edinburgh: Blackwood, 1815).

The Poetic Mirror; or The Living Bards of Britain (London: Longman; Edinburgh: Ballantyne, 1816).

Mador of the Moor (Edinburgh: Blackwood; London: Murray, 1816).

Dramatic Tales (Edinburgh: Ballantyne; London: Longman, 1817) [2 vols].

The Brownie of Bodsbeck; and Other Tales (Edinburgh: Blackwood; London: Murray, 1818) [2 vols].

The Long Pack: A Northumbrian Tale, An Hundred Years Old (Newcastle: Quay, 1818).

No. 1 of the Border Garland (Edinburgh: Gow, 1819).

The Jacobite Relics of Scotland (Edinburgh: Blackwood; London: Cadell, 1819; 1821) [2 vols].

Winter Evening Tales, collected among the cottagers of the South of Scotland (Edinburgh: Oliver &
Boyd; London: Whittaker, 1820) [2 vols].
The Poetical Works of James Hogg (Edinburgh: Constable; London: Hurst Robinson, 1822) [4
vols].
The Royal Jubilee: A Scottish Mask (Edinburgh: Blackwood; London: Cadell, 1822).
The Three Perils of Man; or War, Women, and Witchcraft (London: Longman, 1822) [3 vols].
The Three Perils of Women; or Love, Leasing, and Jealousy (London: Longman, 1823) [3 vols]
*The Private Memoirs and Confessions of a Justified Sinner; Written by Himself: with a detail of curious
traditionary facts & other evidence by the editor* (London: Longman, 1824).
Queen Hynde: A Poem, in six books (London: Longman; Edinburgh: Blackwood, 1824).
Select and Rare Scottish Melodies: The Poetry by the Celebrated Ettrick Shepherd.
The Symphonies and Accompaniments Composed . . . *By Henry R. Bishop* (London: Goulding,
1829).
The Shepherd's Calendar (Edinburgh: Blackwood; London: Cadell, 1829) [2 vols].
Songs by the Ettrick Shepherd (Edinburgh: Blackwood; London: Cadell, 1831).
A Queer Book (Edinburgh: Blackwood; London: Cadell, 1832).
*Altrive Tales, collected among the peasantry of Scotland, and from foreign adventures, illustrated by George
Cruikshank* (London: Cochrane, 1832).
A Series of Lay Sermons on Good Principles and Good Breeding (London: Fraser, 1834).
Familiar Anecdotes of Sir Walter Scott (New York: Harper, 1834).
The Domestic Manners and Private Life of Sir Walter Scott (Glasgow: Reid; Edinburgh: Oliver &
Boyd; London: Black, 1834).
Tales of the Wars of Montrose (London: Cochrane, 1835) [3 vols] (contains *An Edinburgh Bailie*,
and other stories).

OTHER RECENT EDITIONS
Anecdotes of Sir Walter Scott, ed. and intro. Douglas S. Mack (Edinburgh and London: Scottish
Academic Press, 1976).
The Brownie of Bodsbeck, ed. and intro. Douglas S. Mack (Edinburgh and London: Scottish
Academic Press, 1976).
Highland Tours, ed. and intro. William F. Laughlan (Hawick: Byway, 1981).
James Hogg: Selected Poems, ed. and intro. Douglas S. Mack (Oxford: Clarendon, 1970).
James Hogg: Selected Poems and Songs, ed. and intro. David Groves (Edinburgh: Scottish
Academic Press, 1986).
James Hogg: Selected Stories and Sketches, ed. and intro. Douglas S. Mack (Edinburgh: Scottish
Academic Press, 1982).
James Hogg: Tales of Love and Mystery, ed. and intro. David Groves (Edinburgh: Canongate,
1985).
Memoir of the Author's Life and Familiar Anecdotes of Sir Walter Scott, ed. and intro. Douglas S. Mack
(Edinburgh and London: Scottish Academic Press, 1972).
The Private Memoirs and Confessions of a Justified Sinner, ed. and intro. Andre Gide (London:
Cresset Press, 1946).
The Private Memoirs and Confessions of a Justified Sinner, ed. and intro. Robert M. Adams (New
York: Norton, 1970).
The Private Memoirs and Confessions of a Justified Sinner, ed. and intro. John Wain (Middlesex:
Penguin, 1983).
The Private Memoirs and Confessions of a Justified Sinner, ed. and intro. Douglas Gifford (London:
Folio Society, 1978).
The Private Memoirs and Confessions of a Justified Sinner, ed. and intro. John Carey (Oxford:
Oxford University Press, Oxford World's Classics Series, 1990).
The Private Memoirs and Confessions of a Justified Sinner (Edinburgh: Canongate, 1991).

The Private Memoirs and Confessions of a Justified Sinner, ed. Adrian Hunter (Ontario: Broadview, 2001).

A Shepherd's Delight, A James Hogg Anthology, ed. and intro. Judy Steel (Edinburgh: Canongate, 1985).

The Three Perils of Man: War, Women and Witchcraft, ed. and intro. Douglas Gifford (Edinburgh and London: Scottish Academic Press, 1972).

The Three Perils of Man: War, Women and Witchcraft, ed. and intro Douglas Gifford (Edinburgh: Canongate, 1996).

Secondary reading

Batho, Edith C., *The Ettrick Shepherd* (Cambridge, 1927).

Bloede, Barbara, 'James Hogg's The Private Memoirs and Confessions of a Justified Sinner: the genesis of the double', *Etudes Anglaises* 26(2) (Paris: Didier, 1973), pp. 174–86.

Campbell, Ian, 'Hogg's Confessions and the Heart of Darkness', *SSL* 15 (Columbia: University of South Carolina, 1980), pp. 187–201.

Crawford, Thomas, 'James Hogg: The Play of Region and Nation', *The History of Scottish Literature Vol. III, Nineteenth Century*, ed. Douglas Gifford (Aberdeen: Aberdeen University Press, 1988).

— (ed.), *Scottish Literary Journal Special, James Hogg Number* (Aberdeen: Association for Scottish Literary Studies, May 1983).

Douglas, Sir George, *James Hogg* (Edinburgh: Oliphant, 1899).

Eggenschwiler, David, 'James Hogg's Confessions and the Fall into Division', *SSL* 9 (Columbia: University of South Carolina, 1971), pp. 26–39.

Garden, Mary Gray Hogg (ed.), *Memorials of James Hogg, the Ettrick Shepherd* (London and Paisley, 1885).

Gifford, Douglas, *James Hogg* (Edinburgh: Ramsay Head, 1976).

Groves, David, *James Hogg: the Growth of a Writer* (Edinburgh: Scottish Academic Press, 1988).

—, 'Myth and Structure in James Hogg's *Three Perils of Woman*', *Wordsworth Circle* (Philadelphia: Temple University, 1982), pp. 203–10.

—, 'James Hogg and "Mr W. W.": A New Parody of Wordsworth', *SSL* 23 (Columbia: University of South Carolina, 1988), pp. 186–98.

Hook, Andrew, 'Hogg, Melville, and the Scottish Enlightenment', *SSL* 4(2) (Columbia: University of South Carolina, 1977), pp. 25–39.

Kearns, M. S., 'Intuition and Narration in James Hogg's Confessions', *SSL* 13 (Columbia: University of South Carolina, 1977), pp. 81–91.

Kiely, Robert, *The Romantic Novel in England* (Cambridge: Harvard University Press, 1972).

Lee, L. L., 'The Devil's Figure: James Hogg's Justified Sinner', *SSL* 9 (Columbia: University of South Carolina, 1971–2), pp. 26–39.

Mack, Douglas, 'Lights and Shadows of Scottish Life: James Hogg's *The Three Perils of Woman*', *Studies in Scottish Fiction: Nineteenth Century*, eds Horst W. Drescher and Joachim Schwend (Frankfurt am Main: P. Lang, 1985), pp. 15–27.

Hughes, Gillian H. (ed.), *Papers given at the First Conference of the James Hogg Society* (Stirling: James Hogg Society, 1984).

Parr, Norah, *James Hogg at Home: Being the Domestic Life and Letters of the Ettrick Shepherd* (Dollar: Mack, 1980).

Parsons, Coleman, *Witchcraft and Demonology in Scott's Fiction* (Edinburgh and London, 1964) [Hogg, pp. 286–97].

Simpson, Louis, *James Hogg: A Critical Study* (Edinburgh and London: Oliver & Boyd, 1962).

Smith, Nelson C., *James Hogg* (Boston: Twayne, 1980).

Stephenson, H. T., *The Ettrick Shepherd: A Biography* (Bloomington: Indiana University, 1922).

Strout, Alan Lang, *The Life and Letters of James Hogg, the Ettrick Shepherd (1770–1825)* (Lubbock:

Texas Tech., 1946) [The unpublished second volume of this work is in manuscript in the National Library of Scotland].

Altrive Chapbooks (Stirling 1985–) [Published annually by the James Hogg Society, which also sends out to members the annual Newsletter. Enquiries to the Dept. of English Studies, University of Stirling].

Chapter 18: Widening the Range

The following references are by no means exhaustive but provide some critical information concerning those writers mentioned in relation to the main sections of this book. For considerations of space, editions and criticism are given together.

There are too many minor Scottish poets of the period to list comprehensively here; that said, important recent work is reassessing their achievement, outstandingly in William Donaldson's *Popular Literature in Victorian Scotland* (Aberdeen: Aberdeen University Press, 1986), and in Tom Leonard's groundbreaking anthology of forgotten poetic voices of the later eighteenth and nineteenth century in *Radical Renfrew* (Edinburgh: Polygon, 1990). See also the essay by William Findlay, 'Reclaiming Local Literature: William Thom and Janet Hamilton' in volume 3 of *The History of Scottish Literature: Nineteenth Century*, edited by Douglas Gifford (Aberdeen: Aberdeen University Press, 1988), pp. 353–76, and Duncan Glen's *The Poetry of the Scots: An Introduction and Bibliographical Guide to Poetry in Gaelic, Scots, Latin and English* (Edinburgh: Edinburgh University Press, 1999). The Scottish Poetry Collection for the Mitchell Library in Glasgow is probably the finest collection in the world in terms of coverage of the nineteenth century; the website address for the library is www.mitchelllibrary.org.

WILLIAM EDMONSTOUNE AYTOUN
See the bibliography, 'Widening the Range', Section 4.

GEORGE GORDON, LORD BYRON
McGann, Jerome J. (ed.), *The Complete Poetical Works* (Oxford: Clarendon Press, 1980–6).

Secondary reading
Bold, Alan (ed.), *Byron: Wrath and Rhyme* (London: Vision, 1983).
Borst, William A., *Lord Byron's First Pilgrimage* (New Haven, 1948).
Bostetter, E. E., *Twentieth-Century Interpretations of Don Juan* (Englewood Cliffs, NJ: Prentice-Hall, 1969).
Calder, Angus (ed.), *Byron and Scotland* (Edinburgh: Edinburgh University Press, 1989).
Galt, John, *The Life of Lord Byron* (London: Colburn & Bentley, 1830).
Jump, John (ed.), *Byron, Childe Harold's Pilgrimage and Don Juan: A Casebook* (London: Macmillan, 1973).

McGann, Jerome J., *Fiery Dust, Byron's Poetic Development* (Chicago and London: University of Chicago Press, 1969).

Marchand, Leslie, *Byron's Poetry: A Critical Introduction* (London: Murray, 1965).

Thorsler, Peter L., *The Byronic Hero: Types and Prototypes* (Minneapolis: Minnesota University Press, 1962).

JOANNA BAILLIE

Baillie, Joanna, *The Dramatical and Poetical Works of Joanna Baillie* (London: Longman, Brown, Green and Longmans, 1851).

Secondary reading

Cathcart, Margaret Sprague, *The Life and Work of Joanna Baillie* (New Haven, CT: Yale University Press, 1923).

Gilroy, Amanda, 'From Here to Alterity: The Geography of Femininity in the Poetry of Joanna Baillie, *A History of Scottish Women's Writing*, eds D. Gifford and D. McMillan (Edinburgh: Edinburgh University Press, 1997), pp. 145–57.

Scullion, Adrienne, 'Some Women of the Nineteenth Century Scottish Theatre: Joanna Baillie, Frances Wright and Helen MacGregor', Gifford and McMillan (eds), pp. 158–78.

MARY BRUNTON

Self-Control (Edinburgh, 1810; London: Pandora, 1986, introduced by Sara Maitland).

Emmeline: with some other pieces (Edinburgh: 1814; London: Routledge/Thoemmes Press, 1992).

Discipline (Edinburgh, 1819).

Secondary reading

Anderson, Carol, and Riddell, Aileen M., 'The Other Great Unknown: Women Fiction Writers of the Early Nineteenth Century', *A History of Scottish Women's Writing*, eds Douglas Gifford and Dorothy McMillan (Edinburgh: Edinburgh University Press, 1997), pp. 179–195.

THOMAS CARLYLE

Collected Works (London: Chapman & Hall, 1870–1).

Collected Works (Centerary Edition), 30 vols, ed. H. D. Traill (London: Chapman & Hall, 1986–99).

Secondary reading

Barfoot, C. C. (ed.), *Victorian Keats and Romantic Carlyle: The Fusions and Confusions of Literary Periods* (Amsterdam: Rodopi, 1999).

Behnken, Eloise, *Thomas Carlyle: Calvinist without the Theology* (Columbia London: University of Missouri Press, 1978).

Campbell, Ian, *Thomas Carlyle* (London: Hamish Hamilton, 1974).

Fielding, Kenneth and Tarr, Rodger, *Carlyle: Past and Present: New Essays* (London: Vision Press, 1976).

Froude, J. A., *Thomas Carlyle, A History of the First Forty Years of His Life* (London: Longmans, Green 1882–4).

Heffer, Simon, *Moral Desperado: A Life of Thomas Carlyle* (London: Weidenfeld & Nicolson, 1995).

Holloway, John, *The Victorian Sage* (London: MacMillan, 1953).

Jessop, Ralph, *Carlyle and Scottish Thought* (Houndmills: Macmillan Press, 1997).
Le Quesne, A. L., *Carlyle* (Oxford: Oxford University Press, 1982).
Le Quesne, A. L., *Victorian Thinkers: Carlyle, Ruskin, Arnold, Morris* (Oxford: Oxford University Press, 1993).
Seigel, Jules Paul (ed.), *Carlyle: The Critical Heritage* (London: Routledge & Kegan Paul, 1971).
Trela, D. J., and Tarr, Rodger L. (eds), *The Critical Response to Thomas Carlyle's Major Works* (Westport, CT, and London: Greenwood Press, 1997).
Vanden Bossche, Chris R., *Carlyle and the Search for Authority* (Columbus: Ohio State University Press, 1991).

WILLIAM FINLAYSON
Simple Scottish Rhymes (Paisley: S&A Young, 1815).

Secondary reading
Leonard, Tom (ed.), *Radical Renfrew* (Edinburgh: Polygon, 1990).

JAMES GRANT
A prolific and popular novelist of the time: a tiny selection only is given here.

The Romance of War (1846).
Adventures of a Aide-de-Camp (1848).
The Yellow Frigate (1855).

Secondary reading
Ellis, Stewart, *Mainly Victorian* (London: Hutchison, 1925).
Horsburgh, A., 'James Grant: Edinburgh's Novelist of War', *Journal of the Society for Army Historical Research* 53 (1975).

ANN GRANT OF LAGGAN
Letters from the Mountains 1773–1803, 3 vols (London: Longman & Co., 1886); ed. J. P. Grant, Longman, Brown, Green and Longmans, 1845).
Memoirs of An American Lady (London: Longman & Co., 1808).
Essays on the Superstitions of the Highlanders of Scotland (London: Longman & Co., 1811).

Secondary reading
Grant, J. P., *Memoir and Correspondence* (London: Longman, Brown, Green and Longmans, 1844).
McMillan, Dorothy, *The Scotswoman Abroad: Non-Fictional Writing 1700–1900* (Glasgow: Association for Scottish Literary Studies, 1999).

ELIZABETH GRANT
Memoirs of a Highland Lady (London: John Murray, 1898; ed. Andrew Tod, Edinburgh: Canongate, 1988).
The Highland Lady in Ireland, eds P. Pelly and A. Tod (Edinburgh: Canongate, 1991).
A Highland Lady in France, eds P. Pelly and A. Tod (East Lothian: Tuckwell, 1996).

Secondary reading

Butter, Peter, 'Elizabeth Grant', *A History of Scottish Women's Writing* eds Douglas Gifford and Dorothy McMillan (Edinburgh: Edinburgh University Press, 1997), pp. 208–15.

McMillan, Dorothy, *The Scotswoman Abroad: Non-Fictional Writing 1700–1900* (Glasgow: Association for Scottish Literary Studies, 1999).

ELIZABETH HAMILTON

Translation of the Letters of a Hindoo Rajahi (London: G. G. Robertson, 1796).

Memoirs of Modern Philosophers: A Novel (Bath: Crutwell, 1800; reprinted with an introduction by Peter Garside, London: Routledge/Thoemmes, 1992).

The Cottagers of Glenburnie: A Tale for the Farmer's Ingle-nook (Edinburgh: Manners & Millar, 1808).

JANET HAMILTON

Poems and Essays (Glasgow: Thomas Murray, 1863).

Poems of Purpose and Sketches of Scottish Peasant Life and Character (Glasgow: Thomas Murray, 1865).

Poems and Ballads (Glasgow: Thomas Murray, 1868).

Poems, Essays and Sketches (Glasgow: Maclehose, 1870).

Secondary reading

Bold, Valentina, 'Beyond the Empire of the Gentle Heart', *A History of Scottish Women's Writing*, eds Douglas Gifford and Dorothy McMillan (Edinburgh: Edinburgh University Press, 1997), pp. 246–61

Findlay, William, 'Reclaiming Local literature: William Thom and Janet Hamilton', *The History of Scottish Literature*, vol. 3 (Aberdeen: Aberdeen University Press, 1988), pp. 353–76.

THOMAS HAMILTON

The Youth and Manhood of Cyril Thornton (Edinburgh: Blackwoods, 1897; ed. Maurice Lindsay, Aberdeen: ASLS, 1990).

Secondary reading

See the introduction by Maurice Lindsay, above.

CHRISTIAN JOHNSTONE

The Saxon and the Gael: or The Northern metropolis: including a view of the Lowland and Highland Character (London: Tegg & Dick, 1814).

Clan-Albyn: A National Tale (Edinburgh: Macredie, Skelly & Muckersy, 1815).

Elizabeth de Bruce (Edinburgh: Blackwood, 1827).

The Edinburgh Tales (Edinburgh: Tate, 1845–6).

Secondary reading

Anderson, Carol, and Riddell, Aileen M., 'The Other Great Unknown: Women Fiction Writers of the Early Nineteenth Century', *A History of Scottish Women's Writing*, eds Douglas Gifford and Dorothy McMillan (Edinburgh: Edinburgh University Press, 1997), pp. 179–195.

THOMAS DICK LAUDER

Lochandhu: A Tale of the Eighteenth Century (Edinburgh: Printed for Archibald Constable and Co., 1825).

An Account of the Great Floods of August 1829, in the Province of Moray, and Adjoining Districts (Edinburgh, 1830).

The Wolf of Badenoch. A Historical Romance of the Fourteenth Century (Edinburgh: Blackwoods, 1827).

Secondary reading

Millar, J. H., *A Literary History of Scotland* (London: T. Fisher Unwin, 1903).

JOHN GIBSON LOCKHART

Peter's Letters to his Kinsfolk (Edinburgh: Blackwoods, 1819; edited version, William Ruddick, Edinburgh, 1977).

Valerius: A Roman Story (Edinburgh: Blackwood, 1821).

Some Passages in the Life of Mr Adam Blair, Minister of the Gospel at Crossmeikle (Edinburgh: Blackwoods, 1822, ed. David Craig, Edinburgh: Edinburgh University Press, 1963).

Reginald Dalton: A Story of University Life (Edinburgh: Blackwood, 1823).

The History of Matthew Wald: A Novel (Edinburgh: Blackwood, 1824).

Life of Robert Burns (Edinburgh: 1828).

Memoirs of the Life of Sir Walter Scott, 5 vols (Edinburgh: Robert Cadell, 1837–8).

Secondary reading

Carswell, Donald, 'John Gibson Lockhart', *Sir Walter: A Four Part Study in Biography* (London: John Murray, 1930).

Hart, Francis Russell, *Lockhart as a Romantic Biographer* (Edinburgh: Edinburgh University Press, 1971).

Hildyard, Margaret, *Lockhart's Literary Criticism* (London: Oxford University Press, 1919).

Lang, Andrew, *The Life and Letters of John Gibson Lockhart*, 2 vols (London: Nimmo, 1897).

Lochhead, M., *John Gibson Lockhart* (London: J. Murray, 1954).

Macbeth, G., *John Gibson Lockhart: A Critical Study* (Urbana: Illinois, 1935).

ALEX MCGILVRAY

The Town's House on the Market Day (Paisley: Caldwell & Son, 1840).

Poems and Songs, Satirical and Descriptive (Glasgow: William Gilchrist, 1850).

Secondary reading

Leonard, Tom (ed.), *Radical Renfrew* (Edinburgh: Polygon, 1990).

HUGH MILLER

(Selected editions only)

Scenes and Legends of the North of Scotland; or, the Traditional History of Cromarty (Edinburgh: A. & C. Black, 1835).

Letter from One of the Scotch People to the Right Hon. Lord Brougham & Vaux, on the Opinions Expressed by his Lordship in the Auchterarder Case (Edinburgh: John Johnstone, 1839).

The Old Red Sandstone; or, New Walks in an Old Field (Edinburgh: John Johnstone, 1841).

First Impressions of England and its People (London: John Johnstone, 1847).

Footprints of the Creator; or, the Asterolepis of Stromness (London: Johnstone and Hunter, 1849).

My Schools and Schoolmasters; or, the Story of my Education (Edinburgh: Johnstone and Hunter, 1854).

The Testimony of the Rocks; or, Geology in its Bearings on the two Theologies, Natural and Revealed (Edinburgh: Thomas Constable & Co., 1857).

The Cruise of the Betsey; or, A Summer Ramble among the Fossiliferous Deposits of the Hebrides. With Rambles of a Geologist; or, Ten Thousand Miles over the Fossiliferous Deposits of Scotland (Edinburgh: Thomas Constable & Co., 1858).

The Headship of Christ, and the Rights of the Christian People (Edinburgh: Adam and Charles Black, 1861).

Tales and Sketches (Edinburgh: W. P. Nimmo, 1863).

Secondary reading

Bayne, Peter, *The Life and Letters of Hugh Miller* (Edinburgh and London: Strachan & Co., 1871) [2 vols].

Bingham, W., *The Life and Writings of Hugh Miller* (New York, 1858).

Brown, Thomas N., *Labour and Triumph: The Life and Times of Hugh Miller* (London and Glasgow: Richard Griffin, 1859).

Geikie, A., et al., *The Centenary of Hugh Miller* (Glasgow, 1902).

Leask, W. K., *Hugh Miller* (Edinburgh and London, 1896).

Mackenzie, W. M., *Hugh Miller: A Critical Study* (London: Hodder & Stoughton, 1905).

Rosie, G., *Outrage and Order* (Edinburgh: Mainstream, 1981).

Shortland, Michael (ed.), *Hugh Miller and the controversies of Victorian Science* (Oxford: Clarendon Press, 1996).

—, *Hugh Miller's Memoir: from Stonemason to Geologist* (Edinburgh: Edinburgh University Press, 1995).

Waterston, C. D., *Hugh Miller the Cromarty Stonemason: a biography with selected writings* (Edinburgh: Mainstream, 1996).

JOHN MITCHELL

Cautious Tam (Paisley: G. Caldwell, 1847).

The Third-Class Train (Paisley: J. Mitchell, 1840).

A Braid Glower at the Clergy (Glasgow: W. & W. Miller, 1843).

Secondary reading

Leonard, Tom (ed.), *Radical Renfrew* (Edinburgh: Polygon, 1990).

D. M. MOIR

The Life of Mansie Waugh, Tailor of Dalkeith (Edinburgh: Blackwoods, 1828).

Poetical Works, ed. with a memoir, Thomas Aird (Edinburgh: Blackwoods, 1852).

Secondary reading

George, Douglas, *The Blackwood Group* (Edinburgh: Oliphant, Anderson and Ferrier, 1897).

WILLIAM NICHOLSON

The Poetical Works of William Nicholson, ed. M. M. Harper (Castle Douglas, 1878).

Secondary reading
Millar, J. H., *A Literary History of Scotland* (London: T. Fisher Unwin, 1903).

EDWARD POLIN
Councillors in their Cups, or the Reformed Transformed; A Lyrical Laughter Piece (Paisley: Caldwell & Son, 1842).

Secondary reading
Leonard, Tom (ed.), *Radical Renfrew* (Edinburgh: Polygon, 1990).

JANE PORTER
Thaddeus of Warsaw (London: Longman, 1803).
The Scottish Chiefs: A Romance (London: Longman, Hurst & Rees, 1810).

Secondary reading
Anderson, Carol, and Riddell, Aileen M., 'The Other Great Unknown: Women Fiction Writers of the Early Nineteenth Century', *A History of Scottish Women's Writing*, eds Douglas Gifford and Dorothy McMillan (Edinburgh: Edinburgh University Press, 1997).

ALEXANDER RODGER
Poems and Songs: Humorous, Serious and Satirical (Paisley, 1897).

Secondary reading
Millar, J. H., *A Literary History of Scotland* (London: T. Fisher Unwin, 1903).

ROBERT TANNAHILL
The Poems and Songs and Correspondence of Robert Tannahill, with Life and Notes, ed. David Semple (Paisley: Alex. Gardner, 1876).

Secondary reading
Leonard, Tom (ed.), *Radical Renfrew* (Edinburgh: Polygon, 1990).

WILLIAM TENNANT
The Comic Poems of William Tennant, eds Alexander Scott and Maurice Lindsay (Edinburgh: Scottish Academic Press, 1989).

Secondary reading
Conolly, M. F., *Memoir of the Life and Writings of William Tennant* (London: 1861).

WILLIAM THOM
Rhymes and Recollections of a Hand-loom Weaver, with a Biographical Sketch (Aberdeen, 1880).

Secondary reading
Bruce, R., *William Thom: The Inverurie Poet* (Aberdeen: Alex P. Reid & Son, 1970).

DAVID WEBSTER
Original Scottish Rhymes, with Humorous and Satirical Songs (Paisley: Caldwell & Son, 1835).

Secondary reading
Leonard, Tom (ed.), *Radical Renfrew* (Edinburgh: Polygon, 1990).

ALEXANDER WILSON
Hollander, or Lightweight with Other Poems and Songs (Paisley: J. Caldwell, 1829).
Lang Mills Detected (Paisley: R. Smith, 1832).
Poems Chiefly in the Scottish Dialect (London: Longman, Hurst, Rees, Orme & Brown, 1816).

Secondary reading
Hunter, Clark, *The Life and Letters of Alexander Wilson* (Philadelphia: American Philosophical Society, 1983).

JOHN WILSON ('CHRISTOPHER NORTH')
The Isle of Palms and Other Poems (Edinburgh: Blackwoods, 1812).
The City of the Plague, and Other Poems (Edinburgh: Blackwoods, 1816).
Lights and Shadows of Scottish Life (Edinburgh: Blackwoods, 1822).
The Trials of Margaret Lyndsay (Edinburgh: Blackwoods, 1823).
The Foresters (Edinburgh: Blackwoods, 1825).
The Recreations of Christopher North (Edinburgh: Blackwoods, 1842).
The Noctes Ambrosianae, ed. Robert Sheldon Mackenzie, 5 vols (New York: Redfield, 1854; Revised, 1866, 1894).
Works, 12 vols, ed. James F. Ferrier (Edinburgh: Blackwoods, 1855–8).
Tavern Sages: selections from the 'Noctes Ambrosianae', ed. J. H. Alexander (Aberdeen: Association for Scottish Literary Studies, 1992).

Secondary reading
Douglas, George, *The Blackwood Group* (Edinburgh: Oliphant and Ferrier, 1897).
Gordon, Mary, *Christopher North: A Memoir of John Wilson*, 2 vols (Edinburgh, 1862).
Noble, Andrew, 'John Wilson (Christopher North) and the Tory Hegemony', *The History of Scottish Literature*, vol. 3, ed. Douglas Gifford (Aberdeen: Aberdeen University Press, 1988), pp. 125–52.
Swann, Elsie, *Christopher North (John Wilson)* (Edinburgh: Oliver & Boyd, 1934).

SECTION 4:
VICTORIAN AND EDWARDIAN SCOTTISH LITERATURE
Introductory reading

As always the reader is reminded of the informative websites listed at the beginning of the Further Reading section, especially the developing website maintained by the Departments of Scottish Literature and STELLA at the University of Glasgow at **www.arts.gla.ac.uk/SESLL/ScotLit/bibliography** where more information can be given than is possible here.

Once again, the general histories listed at the beginning of the reading lists under General Further Reading are useful starting points, including Aitken, Daiches, Glen, Kinsley, Lindsay, Millar, Royle, Speirs, Walker, Watson and Wittig. Some useful introductory texts for this section overlap with the basic suggestions for Section 3. The third volume of the four-volume *History of Scottish Literature* series (General Editor Cairns Craig) is edited by Douglas Gifford (Aberdeen: Aberdeen University Press, 1988), and brings together essays on the major writers and on general background and issues. Other useful introductory texts include David Daiches, *Literature and Gentility: Some Late Victorian Attitudes* (Edinburgh: Edinburgh University Press, 1982); *Nineteenth-Century Scottish Fiction: A Critical Anthology*, ed. Ian Campbell (Manchester: Carcanet New Press, 1979) and *Studies in Scottish Fiction: Nineteenth Century*, eds Horst W. Drescher and Joachim Schwend (Frankfurt am Main: P. Lang, 1985). For a radical new reading of the achievements of Scottish literature in the nineteenth century see William Donaldson's pioneering and controversial *Popular Literature in Victorian Scotland: Language, Fiction and the Press* (Aberdeen: Aberdeen University Press, 1986), and its accompanying anthology, *The Language of the People: Scots Prose from the Victorian Revival* (Aberdeen: Aberdeen University Press, 1989) and Tom Leonard's ground-breaking collection of forgotten poetic voices in *Radical Renfrew* (Edinburgh: Polygon, 1990). Related language issues in the fiction are dealt with by Emma Letley in *From Galt to Douglas Brown; Nineteenth-Century fiction and Scots Language* (Edinburgh: Scottish Academic Press, 1988). Early criticism of the Kailyard tendency in writing came from George Blake in *Barrie and the Kailyard School* (London, 1921); more recently Thomas Knowles analyses the sociological background in *Ideology, Art and Commerce: Aspects of Literary Sociology in the Late Victorian Scottish Kailyard* (Göteborg: Acta Universitatis Gothoburgensis, 1983), while Ian Campbell has the most recent study in *Kailyard: A New Assessment* (Edinburgh: Ramsey Head Press, 1981). Willa Muir's *Mrs. Grundy in Scotland* (London, 1936) is a fine satirical assessment of Victorian gentility and piety, and its effect on the literature. The 'Celtic Twilight' has received less attention, but Malcolm Chapman's *The Gaelic Vision in Scottish Culture* (London and Montreal: Croom Helm, 1978) helps to bring perspective, while F. Alaya's study *William Sharp: 'Fiona MacLeod'* (Cambridge, MA: Harvard University Press, 1936), brings out the strangeness of this divided personality at the heart of the movement.

For historical and cultural background see the general works listed under General Further Reading, at the beginning of the reading lists, including Cowan and Gifford, Finlay, Devine, Fergusson, and Lynch; and additionally see Olive and Sidney Checkland's *Industry and Ethos: Scotland 1832–1914*

(London: Edward Arnold, 1984); and for a bleakly reductive view of the period, T. C. Smout's *A Century of the Scottish People 1830–1950* (London: William Collins, 1986). Specifically useful are Bruce Lenman's *Integration, Enlightenment, and Industrialisation: Scotland 1746–1832* (London: Edward Arnold, 1983), and Michael Fry's combative *Patronage and Principle: A Political History of Modern Scotland* (Aberdeen: Aberdeen University Press, 1987), which could be set against Ian Hutchison's *A Political History of Scotland* (Edinburgh: John Donald, 1985). For the beginnings of nationalism see Christopher Harvie, *Scotland and Nationalism: Scottish Society and Politics 1770–1977* (London: Allen & Unwin, 1977). For church history, A. C. Cheyne's *The Transforming of the Kirk: Victorian Scotland's Religious Revolution* (Edinburgh: Saint Andrew Press, 1983), and Callum Brown's *The Social History of Religion in Scotland Since 1730* (London: Methuen, 1987) are useful.

Chapter 19: Scottish Literature in the Victorian and Edwardian Era

The Bards of Angus and Mearns, ed. Alan Reid (Paisley: Parlane, 1879).

The Bards of Galloway, ed. M. M. Harper (Dalbeattie, 1889).

Findlay, William, 'Reclaiming Local Literature: William Thom and Janet Hamilton', *The History of Scottish Literature Vol. III, Nineteenth Century*, ed. Douglas Gifford (Aberdeen: Aberdeen University Press, 1988), pp. 353–76.

The Glasgow Poets, ed. George Eyre-Todd (Glasgow: W. Hodge, 1903).

The Harp of Perthshire, ed. R. Ford (Paisley: Alexander Gardner, 1893).

The Harp of Renfrewshire, ed. William Motherwell (Paisley: Alexander Gardner, 1873) [Second Series].

Leonard, Tom (ed.), 'On Reclaiming the Local and the Theory of the Magic Thing', *Edinburgh Review* 77 (1987), pp. 40–6; reprinted in his *Reports from the Present: Selected Work 1982–94* (London: Jonathan Cape, 1995).

—, *Radical Renfrew: Poetry from the French Revolution to the First World War* (Edinburgh: Polygon, 1990).

Manning, Susan, *The Puritan-Provincial Vision: Scottish and American Literature in the Nineteenth Century* (Cambridge and New York: Cambridge University Press, 1990).

Morgan, Edwin, 'Scottish Poetry in the Nineteenth Century', *The History of Scottish Literature Vol. III, Nineteenth Century*, ed. D. Gifford (Aberdeen: Aberdeen University Press, 1988).

One Hundred Modern Scottish Poets, ed. David Herschell Edwards (Brechin: D. H. Edwards, 1880–97) [16 vols].

Young, Douglas (ed.), *Scottish Verse 1851–1951* (London: Thomas Nelson, 1952).

—, 'Scottish Poetry in the Later Nineteenth Century', *Scottish Poetry; a Critical Survey*, ed. James Kinsley (London: Cassell, 1955), pp. 236–55.

Whistle-Binkie; or the Piper of the Party, being a Collection of Songs for the Social Circle [first published in 1832 and then in many series throughout the nineteenth century, with many additions and by various publishers. Available in central public libraries and secondhand bookshops].

See also the anthologies listed in general further reading.

Chapter 20 George MacDonald: Phantastes

David Elginbrod (London: Hurst & Blackett, 1853).

Within and Without (London: Longmans, Brown, Green, 1855).

Poems (London: Longmans, Brown, Green, 1857).

Phantastes: A Faerie Romance for Men and Women (London, 1858); reprinted (London: Everyman's, 1915); reprinted with *Lilith*, and intro. by C. S. Lewis (London, 1962); reprinted as Everyman Paperback with intro. by David Holbrook (London, 1983).

Adela Cathcart (London: Hurst & Blackett, 1864).

The Portent (London: Elder, 1864).

Alec Forbes of Howglen (London: Hurst & Blackett, 1865).

Annals of a Quiet Neighbourbood (London: Hurst & Blackett, 1867).

Dealing with the Fairies (London: Strathan, 1867).

The Disciple and Other Poems (London: Strathan, 1867).

Robert Falconer (London: Hurst & Blackett, 1868).

Guild Court (London: Hurst & Blackett, 1868).

The Seaboard Parish (Tinsley Bros., 1868).

Works of Fancy and Imagination (London: Chatto & Windus, 1871) [10 vols].

At the Back of the North Wind (Strahan, 1871); reprinted (New York, 1950).

Ronald Bannerman's Boyhood (Strahan, 1871); reprinted (London and Glasgow, 1911).

The Vicar's Daughter (Tinsley Bros., 1872).

The Princess and the Goblin (Strahan, 1872); reprinted (Harmondsworth, 1964).

Wilfrid Cumbermede (London: Hurst & Blackett, 1875).

The Marquis of Lossie (London: Hurst & Blackett, 1877).

Sir Gibbie (London: Hurst & Blackett, 1879).

Castle Warlock (London: Samson Low, 1872).

Gutta Percha Willie (Henry S. King, 1873).

Malcolm (Henry S. King, 1875).

The Wise Woman (London: Strathan, 1875) [also published as *A Double Story* (nd) and *The Lost Princess* (nd)].

Paul Faber, Surgeon (London: Hurst & Blackett, 1879).

Diary of An Old Soul (Printed Privately, 1880).

Mary Marston (Sampson Low, 1881).

Weighed and Wanted (Sampson Low, 1882).

Orts (Sampson Low, 1882).

The Princess and Curdie (London: Chatto & Windus, 1883); reprinted (Harmondsworth, 1966).

Donald Grant (London: Kegan Paul, 1883).

What's Mine's Mine (London: Kegan Paul, 1886).

The Elect Lady (London, 1888).

Cross Purposes and *The Shadows* (Reprinted, London: Blackie & Sons, 1890).

The Light Princess and Other Fairy Stories (Reprinted, London: Blackie & Sons, 1890).

There and Back (London: Kegan Paul, 1891).

A Dish of Orts (London: Sampson Low, 1893).

Poetical Works (London: Chatto & Windus, 1893) [2 vols].

Heather and Snow (London: Chatto & Windus, 1893).

Scotch Songs and Ballads (Reprints, Aberdeen: John Roe Smith, 1893).

Lilith: A Romance (London: Chatto & Windus, 1895); reprinted, with *Phantastes* and intro. by C. S. Lewis (London: Lion, 1962).

Salted with Fire (London: Hurst & Blackett, 1897).

Phantastes (London: Lion, 1982).

Secondary reading

Bulloch, John M., *A Centennial Bibliography of George MacDonald* (Aberdeen: Aberdeen University Press, 1925).

Fremantle, Anne (ed.), *The Visionary Novels of George MacDonald*, intro by W. H. Auden (New York: Noonday, 1954).

Gifford, D., 'Myth, Parody and Dissociation: Scottish Literature 1814–1914', *The History of Scottish Literature*, vol. III, ed. D. Gifford (Aberdeen: Aberdeen University Press, 1988).

Grierson, H. J. C., 'George MacDonald', *The Aberdeen University Review* 12(34) (Aberdeen: Aberdeen University Press, 1924–25), pp. 1–13.

Gunther, Adrian, 'Phantastes: The First 2 Chapters', *SLJ* 21(1) (Aberdeen: Association for Scottish Literary Studies, 1994), pp. 32–43.

Hein, Rolland, *The Harmony Within: The Spiritual Vision of George MacDonald* (Eureka, CA: Sunrise Books, 1989).

Lewis, C. S., Preface to *George MacDonald: An Anthology* (London: Bles, 1946), pp. 10–22.

—, 'The Circle of the Imagination: George MacDonald's *Phantastes* and *Lilith*', *SSL* 17 (University of South Carolina, 1982).

MacDonald, Greville, *George MacDonald and his Wife* (London: Allen & Unwin, 1924).

—, *Reminiscences of a Specialist* (London, 1932).

MacDonald, Ronald, 'George MacDonald: A Personal Note', *From a Northern Window* (London: Nisbet, 1911).

McGillis, Roderick F., 'George MacDonald – The Lilith Manuscripts', *SLJ* 4(2) (Aberdeen: Association for Scottish Literary Studies, 1977), pp. 40–57.

—, 'George MacDonald and the Lilith Legend in the Nineteenth Century', *Mythlore* 6 (Whittier, CA: Mythopoeic Society, 1979), pp. 3–11.

Manlove, Colin, *Modern Fantasy: Five Studies* (Cambridge: Cambridge University Press, 1975), pp. 55–98.

—, 'George MacDonald's Early Scottish Novels', *Nineteenth Century Scottish Fiction*, ed. Ian Campbell (Manchester: Carcanet New Press, 1979).

—, 'George MacDonald, 1824–1905', *Modern Fantasy*, ed. C. N. Manlove (Cambridge: Cambridge University Press, 1975).

—, *Scottish Fantasy Literature; A Critical Survey* (Edinburgh: Canongate, 1994).

—, 'George MacDonald's Early Scottish Novels', *Nineteenth-Century Scottish Fiction: Critical Essays*, ed. Ian Campbell (Manchester: Carcanet New Press, 1979), pp. 68–88.

—, *The Impulse of Fantasy Literature* (London: Macmillan, 1983), pp. 70–92.

Prickett, Stephen, *Romanticism and Religion: The Tradition of Coleridge and Wordsworth in the Victorian Church* (Cambridge: Cambridge University Press, 1976), pp. 211–48.

—, *Victorian Fantasy* (Hassocks: Harvester Press, 1979), pp. 150–97.

Raeper, William, *George MacDonald* (Tring: Lion, 1987).

Rankin, Jamie, 'The Genesis of George MacDonald's Scottish Novels: Edelweiss amid the Heather?', *SSL* 24 (Columbia: University of South Carolina, 1989), pp. 49–67.

Reis, Richard H., *George MacDonald* (New York: Twayne, 1972).

Robb, David S., *George MacDonald* (Edinburgh: Scottish Academic Press, 1987).

—, 'Realism and Fantasy in the Fiction of George MacDonald', *The History of Scottish Literature*, vol. III, ed. D. Gifford (Aberdeen: Aberdeen University Press, 1988).

Sadler, Glenn Edward, 'The Fantastic Imagination in George MacDonald', *Imagination and The Spirit*, ed. Charles A. Huttar (Grand Rapids, MI: Eerdmans, 1971), pp. 215–27.

Saintsbury, Elizabeth, *George MacDonald: A Short Life* (Edinburgh: Canongate, 1987).

Wolff, Robert Lee, *The Golden Key: A Study of the Fiction of George MacDonald* (New Haven: Yale University Press, 1961).

Chapter 21: James Young Geddes, John Davidson and Scottish poetry

For further details of poets mentioned in this chapter, see the following anthologies: Catherine Kerrigan's *An Anthology of Scottish Women Poets*, Maurice Lindsay's *Scottish Comic Verse*, Tom Leonard's *Radical Renfrew*, Edwin Morgan's *Scottish Satirical Verse*, Douglas Young's *Scottish Verse 1851–1951*. All these are listed in the bibliography for Chapter 19, or in General Further Reading.

WILLIAM EDMONDSTOUNE AYTOUN
Poems, ed. F. Page (Oxford: Oxford University Press, 1921).
Stories and Verse, ed. W. L. Renwick (Edinburgh: Edinburgh University Press, 1964).

Secondary reading
Frykman, E., *W. E. Aytoun: Poineer and Professor of English at Edinburgh* (Gothenburg, 1963).
Weinstein, M. A., *William Edmonstoune Aytoun and the Spasmodic Controversy* (Newhaven, CT, and London, 1968).

ROBERT WILLIAMS BUCHANAN
Poetical Works, 3 vols (London: Henry S. King, 1874) [Enlarged and published in 2 vols, 1901].
A Poet's Sketch Book (London: Chatto & Windus, 1883).
Poetical Works (London: Chatto & Windus, 1884).
Undertones (London: Alexander Strahan, 1865).
Idylls and Legends of Inverburn (London and New York: Alexander Strahan, 1866).
London Poems (London and New York: Alexander Strahan, 1866).
North Coast and Other Poems (London: George Routledge & Sons, 1867).
The Book of Orm (London: Chatto & Windus, 1870).
The City of Dream (London: Chatto & Windus, 1888).
The Outcast (London: Chatto & Windus, 1891).
The Wandering Jew (London: Chatto & Windus, 1893).
The New Rome (London: Walter Scott Ltd., 1898).
'The Fleshly School of Poetry' in *Pre-Raphaelite Writing*, ed. Derek Stanford (London: Dent, 1973) [under the pseudonym Thomas Maitland].

Secondary reading
Cassidy, John, *Robert Buchanan* (New York: Twayne, 1973).
—, 'Buchanan and the Fleshly Controversy', *Publications of the Modern Languages Association* 67 (PMLA, 1952).
Forsyth, R. A., 'Nature and the Victorian City: The Ambivalent Attitude of Robert Buchanan', *English Literary History* 36 (Baltimore: Johns Hopkins University Press, 1969).
Jay, Harriet, *Buchanan* (London: T. Fisher Unwin, 1903).
Miles, Alfred H., *The Poets and Poetry of the Century vol. 6, William Morris to Robert Buchanan* (London: Hutchinson, 1896, second edition).
Murray, Henry, *Robert Buchanan and Other Essays* (London: Philip Wellby, 1901).
Storey, G. G., 'Buchanan's Critical Principles', *Publications of the Modern Languages Association* 68 (PMLA, 1953).
Stoddart-Walker, Archibald, *Robert Buchanan: The Poet of Modern Revolt* (London: Grant Richards, 1901).

JOHN DAVIDSON

Diabolus Amans: A Dramatic Poem (Glasgow: Wilson & McCormick, 1885).

The North Wall (Glasgow: Wilson & McCormick, 1885).

Bruce: A Drama in Five Acts (Glasgow and London: Elkin Mathews and John Lane, 1886).

Smith: A Tragedy (Glasgow: F. W. Wilson & Brother, 1888).

Plays [incs. *An Unhistorical Pastoral, A Romantic Farce, Scaramouch in Naxos*] (Greenock: published by the author, 1889); reprinted, with the addition of *Bruce* and *Smith* (London and Chicago: Mathews & Lane and Stone & Kimball, 1889; 1894).

Scaramouch in Naxos: A Pantomime; and Other Plays (London: T. F. Unwin, 1890; 1893) [Reissue of the Greenock edition of *Plays*].

Perfervid: The Career of Ninian Jamieson (London: Ward & Downey, 1890) (fiction).

The Great Men, and A Practical Novelist (London: Ward & Downey, 1891) (fiction).

In A Music-Hall and Other Poems (London: Ward & Downey, 1891).

In A Music-Hall, 1891; with Ballads and Songs, 1894 (Oxford: Woodstock Books, 1993).

Persian Letters, By Charles Louis, Baron de Montesquie, trans. and intro. John Davidson, 2 vols (London: Chiswick Press, 1892); reissued as *Persian and Chinese Letters* (Washington and London: M. Walter Dunne, 1901).

Laura Ruthven's Widowhood, with Charles J. Willis (London: 1892) [3 vols, fiction].

Sentences and Paragraphs (London: Lawrence & Bullen, 1893).

Fleet Street Eclogues (London: Mathews & Lane, 1893).

A Random Itinerary (London and Boston: Mathews & Lane; Copeland & Day, 1894).

Ballads and Songs (London and Boston: Bodley Head, 1894) [reissued with *In A Music-Hall*, see above].

Baptist Lake (London: Ward & Downey, 1894) (fiction).

A Full and True Account of the Wonderful Mission of Earl Lavender, which lasted One Night and One Day: with a History of the Pursuit of Earl Lavender and Lord Brumm by Mrs Scamler and Maud Emblem (London: Ward & Downey, 1895; reprinted, New York and London: Garland, 1977) (fiction).

A Second Series of Fleet Street Eclogues (London and New York: John Lane and Dodd. Mead, 1896).

Miss Armstrong's and Other Circumstances (London: Methuen, 1896) (fiction).

For the Crown: A Romantic Play, In Four Acts, trans. into English by John Davidson from Francois Coppée, 'Pour la couronne' (London: Nassau Press, 1896).

The Pilgrimage of Strongsoul and Other Stories (London: Ward & Downey, 1896) (fiction).

New Ballads (London and New York: John Lane, 1897).

Godfrida: A Play in Four Acts (New York and London: John Lane, 1898).

The Last Ballad and Other Poems (London and New York: John Lane, 1899).

Self's the Man: A Tragi-Comedy (London: Grant Richards, 1901).

Testaments (No. I *The Testament of a Vivisector*; No. II *The Testament of a Man Forbid*; No. III *The Testament of an Empire-Builder*) (London: Grant Richards, 1901–2) [3 vols in one edition].

A Rosary (London: Grant Richards, 1903).

The Knight of the Maypole: A Comedy in Four Acts (London: Grant Richards, 1903).

The Testament of a Prime Minister (London: Grant Richards, 1904).

A Queen's Romance: A Version of Victor Hugo's 'Ruy Blas' (London: Grant Richards, 1904).

Selected Poems (London: John Lane, 1905).

The Theatrocrat: A Tragic Play of Church and Stage (London: Grant Richards, 1905).

Holiday and Other Poems, with note 'On Poetry' (London: Grant Richards, 1906).

God and Mammon: A Trilogy: The Triumph of Mammon (London: Grant Richards, 1907).

The Testament of John Davidson (London: Grant Richards, 1908).

God and Mammon: A Trilogy: Mammon and his Message (London: Grant Richards, 1909).

Fleet Street and Other Poems (London and New York: Grant Richards, 1909).

The Man Forbid and Other essays, with an introduction by Edward J. O'Brian (Boston: The Ball Publishing Co., 1910).
Poems by John Davidson, ed. R. M. Wenley (New York: Boni and Liveright Inc., 1924).
John Davidson, ed. Edward Thompson (London: E. Benn, 1925).
Poems and Ballads, ed. R. D. MacLeod (London: Unicorn Press, 1959).
John Davidson: A Selection of his Poems [incs. preface by T. S. Eliot and an essay by Hugh MacDiarmid], ed. Maurice Lindsay (London: Hutchinson, 1961).
The Poems of John Davidson, ed. Andrew Turnbull (Edinburgh and London: Scottish Academic Press, 1973) [2 vols].
Three Poets of the Rhymer's Club: Ernest Dowson, Lionel Johnson, John Davidson, ed. Derek Stanford et al. (Cheadle: Carcanet Press, 1974).
Poems (Edinburgh: Akros, Akros Pocket Classics Series No. 28, 1995).
Selected Poems and Prose of John Davidson, ed. and intro. by John Sloan (Oxford: Clarendon Press, 1995).

Secondary reading

For a list of works concerning Davidson see 'John Davidson: Annotated Bibliography of Writings about Him', *English Literature in Transition* 20 (Tempe, AZ: Arizona State University, 1977), pp. 112–74.

Bush, Douglas, *Mythology and the Romantic Tradition in English Poetry* (New York: Norton, 1963).
Colum, Padric, 'The Poet of Armageddon: John Davidson', *New Republic* 13 (New York: Republic Publishing Company, 1918), pp. 310–12.
Currie, Alexander Monteith, 'A Biographical and Critical Study of John Davidson', B. Litt. (Oxford, 1953).
Eliot, T. S., 'Preface' in *John Davidson: A Selection of His Poems*, ed. Maurice Lindsay (London: Hutchinson, 1961), pp. xi–xii.
Ferguson, Fergus (ed.), 'Biographical Sketch', *Sermons by the Late Rev. Alexander Davidson* (Edinburgh, 1893).
Fineman, Hayim, *John Davidson: A Study of the Relation of His Ideas to His Poetry* (Philadelphia: Walton Press, 1916; reprinted Folcroft, PA: Folcroft Press, 1969; 1977).
Herdman, John, 'John Davidson in Full', *Akros* 9 (Preston: Akros Publications, 1974), pp. 79–82.
Hubbard, Tom, 'John Davidson's Glasgow', *The Scottish Review* 32 (1983), pp. 13–19.
—, 'Irony and Enthusiasm: The Fiction of John Davidson', *SLJ* 11 (Aberdeen: Association for Scottish Literary Studies, 1984), pp. 71–82.
—, 'John Davidson: A Lad Apairt', *Chapman* 40 (Edinburgh: Chapman Publications, 1985), pp. 34–8.
Lester, John A. Jr., *John Davidson: A Grub Street Bibliography* (Charlottesville: University of Virginia Press, 1958).
—, 'Friedrich Nietzsche and John Davidson: A Study in Influence', *Journal of the History of Ideas* 18 (Philadelphia, 1957), pp. 411–29.
—, 'Prose-Poetry Transmutation in the Poetry of John Davidson', *Modern Philology* 56 (Chicago: University of Chicago Press, 1958), pp. 38–44.
Lindsay, Maurice, 'John Davidson – The Man Forbid', *Saltire Review* 4(11) (1957), pp. 54–61.
MacDiarmid, Hugh, *Contemporary Scottish Studies*, ed. Alan Riach (Manchester: Carcanet, 1995).
—, 'John Davidson: Influences and Influence', *John Davidson: A Selection of His Poems*, ed. Maurice Lindsay (London: Hutchison, 1961), pp. 47–54.

MacLeod, R. D., 'Introduction' to *Poems and Ballads by John Davidson* (London: Unicorn Press, 1959); first published as *John Davidson: A Study in Personality* (Glasgow: W. & R. Holmes, 1957; reprinted, Folcroft, PA: Folcroft Press, 1970).

O'Connor, Mary, 'Did Bernard Shaw Kill John Davidson? The Tragi-Comedy of a Commissioned Play', *Shaw Review* 21 (1978), pp. 108–23.

Peterson, Carroll V., *John Davidson* (New York: Twayne, 1972).

Robertson, Ritchie, 'Science and Myth in John Davidson's Testaments', *SSL* 18 (Columbia: University of South Carolina, 1983), pp. 85–109.

Sloan, John, 'New Poems by John Davidson', *Review of English Studies* 44 (Oxford: Clarendon Press, 1993), pp. 548–51.

—, *John Davidson, First of the Moderns: A Literary Biography* (Oxford: Clarendon Press, 1995).

Stoddart, Jane T., 'An Interview with Mr. John Davidson', *Bookman* 1 (New York: 1895), pp. 85–7.

Stokes, John, 'The Poet and the City: John Davidson – the 1890s', *Fin de Siècle: Fears and Fantasies of the Late Nineteenth Century*, eds John Stokes and Ian Fletcher (Basingstoke: Macmillan, 1992).

Townsend, J. Benjamin, *John Davidson: Poet of Armageddon* (New Haven: Yale University Press, 1961).

Turnbull, Andrew R., 'A Critical Edition of the Poems of John Davidson', PhD (Aberdeen, 1973).

—, ed. and intro. to *The Poems of John Davidson* (Edinburgh and London: Scottish Academic Press, 1973) [2 vols].

Turner, Paul, 'John Davidson: The Novels of a Poet', *The Cambridge Journal* 5 (1951–2), pp. 499–504.

Woolf, Virginia, 'John Davidson', *Times Literary Supplement* (16 Aug., 1917), p. 390.

—, 'The Rhymers Club', *Letters to the New Island*, 1934 (Cambridge, MA: Harvard University Press, 1970).

JAMES YOUNG GEDDES

The New Jerusalem and Other Verses (Dundee: James P. Matthew, 1879).

The Spectre Clock of Alyth and other selections (Alyth: Thomas McMurray, 1886).

In the Valhalla and Other Poems (Dundee: John Leng, 1891).

The Babes in the Wood: A Cantata for Schools and Classes [with music by John Kerr] (Paisley: J. and R. Farlane, nd).

Secondary reading

Bold, Valentina, 'James Young Geddes (1850–1913): A Re-Evaluation', *SLJ* 19(1) (Aberdeen: Association for Scottish Literary Studies, 1992), pp. 18–27.

Dryerre, Henry, 'James Young Geddes', *Blairgowrie, Stormont and Strathmore Worthies* (Blairgowrie: privately printed, 1903).

Morgan, Edwin, 'Scottish Poetry in the Nineteenth Century', *The History of Scottish Literature Vol. III, Nineteenth Century*, ed. D. Gifford (Aberdeen: Aberdeen University Press, 1988).

Young, Douglas, 'Scottish Poetry in the Late Nineteenth Century', *Scottish Poetry: A Critical Survey*, ed. J. Kinsley (London: Cassell, 1955).

JANET HAMILTON

See the bibliography, 'Widening the Range', for Section 5.

GEORGE MACDONALD
Collected Works (London: 1893).

Secondary reading
See the bibliography for Chapter 20.

ALEXANDER RODGER
See the bibliography, 'Widening the Range', Section 3.

ALEXANDER SMITH
The Poetical Works of Alexander Smith, ed. W. Sinclair (London: 1909).

Secondary reading
Messenger, Nigel Phillip and Watson, Richard (eds), *Victorian Poetry: The City of Dreadful Night and Other Poems* (London: Dent, 1974).

WILLIAM THOM
See the bibliography, 'Widening the Range', Section 3.

ALEXANDER WILSON
See the bibliography, 'Widening the Range', Section 3.

Chapter 22: *James Thomson:* The City of Dreadful Night

Messenger, Nigel Phillip, and Watson, Richard (eds), *Victorian Poetry: The City of Dreadful Night and Other Poems* (London: Dent, 1974).
Morgan, Edwin (ed.), *The City of Dreadful Night* (Edinburgh: Canongate, 1993).
Riddler, A. (ed.), *Poems and some letters of James Thomson* (Oxford: Oxford University Press, 1963).
Schefer, W. D. (ed.), *The Speedy Extinction of Evil and Misery: selected prose of James Thomson (B. V.)* (Berkeley: University of California Press, 1967).

Secondary reading
Angeletti, Gioia, 'Giacomo Leopardi and Scottish Literature: some parallels and influences', *Odd Alliances: Scottish Studies in European Contexts*, eds Neil McMillan and Kirsten Stirling (Glasgow: Cruithne Press, 1999).
Daiches, David, *Some Late Victorian Attitudes* (London: Deutsch, 1969).
Dobell, B., *The Laureate of Pessimism: a sketch of the life and character of James Thomson ('B. V.')* (London, 1910; Kennikat Press, 1970).
Leonard, Tom, *Places of the mind: The Life and Work of James Thomson* (London, 1993).
Pawley, Richard, *Secret City: The Emotional Life of Victorian Poet James Thomson (B. V.)* (Lanham, MD: University Press of America, 2001).
Salt, Henry, *The Life of James Thomson (B. V.)* (London: A. H. Bonner, 1898).

Chapter 23: Robert Louis Stevenson:
The Merry Men, Dr Jekyll and Mr Hyde *and* The Master of Ballantrae

As there are so many editions of Stevenson's work this bibliography is selective and concentrates on the most significant texts. As with Scott and Hogg, Edinburgh University Press and Catherine Kerrigan (ed.) are currently producing an ambitious Centenary Edition; to date, the following titles have appeared, or are scheduled.

Weir of Hermiston, ed. Catherine Kerrigan, 1995.
The Ebb-Tide, ed. Peter Hinchcliffe, 1996.
Treasure Island, ed. Wendy R. Katz, 1998.
The Strange Case of Dr Jekyll and Mr Hyde, ed. Richard Dury (forthcoming).

EDITIONS
The Pentland Rising (Edinburgh: Andrew Elliot, 1866).
An Inland Voyage (London: Kegan Paul & Co., 1878).
Edinburgh: Picturesque Notes (London: Seeley & Co., 1879).
Travels with a Donkey in the Cevennes (London: Kegan Paul & Co., 1879).
Deacon Brodie [with W. F. Henley] (Edinburgh: Edinburgh University Press, 1880).
Virginibus Puerisque and Other Papers (London: Kegan Paul & Co., 1881).
Familiar Studies of Men and Books (London: Chatto & Windus, 1882).
The New Arabian Nights (London: Chatto & Windus, 1882).
Penny Whistles (1883).
The Silverado Squatters: Sketches from a Californian Mountain (London: Chatto & Windus, 1883).
Treasure Island (London: Cassell & Co., 1883).
Admiral Guinea [with W. E. Henley] (1884).
Beau Austin [with W. E. Henley] (Edinburgh: R. & R. Clark, 1884).
A Child's Garden of Verses (London: Longmans, Green and Co., 1885).
Macaire [with W. E. Henley] (Edinburgh: R. & R. Clark, 1885).
Prince Otto: A Romance (London: Chatto & Windus, 1885).
More New Arabian Nights: The Dynamiter with Fanny Van De Grift Stevenson (London: Longmans, Green and Co., 1885).
The Strange Case of Dr. Jekyll and Mr Hyde (London: Longmans, Green and Co., 1886).
Kidnapped (London: J. Henderson, 1886).
The Merry Men and Other Tales and Fables (London: Chatto & Windus, 1887).
Underwoods [Poems in English and Scots] (London: Chatto & Windus, 1887).
Memories and Portraits (London: Chatto & Windus, 1887).
Memoir of Fleeming Jenkin (New York: Charles Scribner's Sons, 1887).
The Black Arrow: A Tale of the Two Roses (New York: Charles Scribner's Sons, 1888).
The Misadventures of John Nicholson (1888).
The Master of Ballantrae: A Winter's Tale (1889).
The Wrong Box [with Lloyd Osbourne] (London: Longmans, Green and Co., 1889).
In the South Seas (1890).
Ballads (1890).
Across the Plains, with Other Memories and Essays (London: Chatto & Windus, 1892).
Three Plays: Deacon Broadie, Beau Austin, Admiral Guinea [with W. E. Henley] (1892).
The Wrecker [with Lloyd Osbourne] (London: Cassell, 1892).

A Footnote to History (London: Cassell, 1892).
Island Nights' Entertainments (London: Cassell, 1893).
Catriona: A Sequel to Kidnapped (London: Cassell, 1893).
The Ebb-Tide: A Trio and a Quartette [with Lloyd Osbourne] (London: Heinemann, 1894).
Works, Edinburgh edition, edited by Sidney Colvin, 28 vols (London: Chatto & Windus, 1894–8).
Songs of Travel and Other Verses (1895).
Vailima Letters (London: Methuen, 1895).
Weir of Hermiston: An Unfinished Romance (London: Chatto & Windus, 1896).
St. Ives: Being the Adventures of a French Prisoner in England [unfinished, but completed by A. T. Quiller Couch] (London: Heinemann, 1897).
Works, Pentland edition, with bibliographical notes by Edmund Goss (1906–7).
Works, Swanson edition, with an introduction by Andrew Lang (London, 1911–12).
Works, Vailima edition, edited by Lloyd Osbourne and Fanny Van de Grift Stevenson, 26 vols. (London: Heinemann, 1922–3).
Works, Tusitala edition, 35 vols (London: Heinemann, 1923–4).
Works, Skerryvore edition, 30 vols (London: Heinemann, 1924–6).
Bell, Ian (ed.), *The Complete Short Stories* (Edinburgh: Mainstream, 1993).
Calder, Jennie (ed.), *Island Landfalls* (Edinburgh: Canongate, 1980).
Campbell, Ian (ed.), *Selected Short Stories of R. L. Stevenson* (Edinburgh: The Ramsay Head Press, 1980).
Gelder, Kenneth (ed.), *Robert Louis Stevenson's Scottish Stories and Essays* (Edinburgh: Edinburgh University Press, 1989).
Hart, James (ed.), *From Scotland to Silverado* (Cambridge, MA: Harvard University Press, 1966) [Contains complete texts of *The Amateur Emigrant* (1895), and *The Silverado Squatters* (1883), with some previously unpublished material].
Smith, Janet Adam (ed.), *Collected Poems* (London: Hart Davis, 1971, second edition).
Swearingen, Roger G. (ed.), *An Old Song and Edifying Letters of the Rutherford Family* (Paisley and Hamden, CT: Wilfion Books and Archon Books, 1982).
Treglown, Jeremy (ed.), *Robert Louis Stevenson: The Lantern Bearers and Other Essays* (London: Chatto & Windus, 1988).

BIBLIOGRAPHY
Ford, George H., *Victorian Fiction: A Second Guide to Research* (New York: Modern Language Association of America, 1978) [includes a chapter on Stevenson by Robert Kiely].
McKay, George L., *A Stevenson Library* (New Haven: Yale University Library, 1951–64) [catalogue of a collection of writings by and about R. L. Stevenson formed by Edwin J. Beinecke, 6 vols].
Prideaux, William Francis, *A Bibliography of the Works of Robert Louis Stevenson* (London: Frank Hollings, 1917).
Swearingen, Roger G., 'The Prose Writings of Robert Louis Stevenson: An Index and Finding List, 1850–1881', *SSL* 11 (Columbia: University of South Carolina, 1973–4), pp. 178–96; pp. 237–49.
—, *The Prose Writings of Robert Louis Stevenson: A Guide* (Paisley and Hamden, Connecticut: Wilfion Books and Archon Books, 1980; London: Macmillan, 1980).

Secondary reading
Balfour, Graham, *The Life of Robert Louis Stevenson* (London: Methuen, 1901).
Bell, Ian, *Robert Louis Stevenson: Dreams of Exile* (Edinburgh: Mainstream, 1992).
Bell, Gavin, *In Search of Tusitala: Travels in the Pacific after Robert Louis Stevenson* (London: Picador, 1994).

Bonds, Robert E., 'The Mystery of The Master of Ballantrae', *English Literature in Transition* (Lefayette, IN: Purdue University, 1964), pp. 8–11.

Calder, Jenni (ed.), *Stevenson and Victorian Scotland* (Edinburgh: Edinburgh University Press, 1981).

—, 'Robert Louis Stevenson: The Realist Within', *Studies in Scottish Fiction: Nineteenth Century*, eds Horst W. Drescher and Joachim Schwend (Frankfurt am Main: P. Lang, 1985), pp. 253–70.

—, *RLS: A Life Study* (Glasgow: Richard Drew, 1990) [first published, London: Hamish Hamilton, 1980].

Caldwell, Elsie N., *Last Witness for Robert Louis Stevenson* (Norman: University of Oklahoma Press, 1960).

Chesterton, G. K., *Robert Louis Stevenson* (London: Hodder & Stoughton, 1927).

Cooper, Lettice, *Robert Louis Stevenson* (London: Arthur Barker, European Novelists Series, 1947).

Daiches, David, *Robert Louis Stevenson* (Glasgow: Collins, 1947).

Daiches, David, *Robert Louis Stevenson and his World* (London: Thames & Hudson, 1973).

—, *Stevenson and the Art of Fiction* (New York: Privately Printed, 1951).

DiaKonowa, N., 'Robert Louis Stevenson in Russia', *Scottish Slavonic Review* 10 (Edinburgh, 1988), pp. 207–24.

Egan, Joseph E., 'From History to Myth: A Symbolic Reading of the *Master of Ballantrae*', *Studies in English Literature 1500–1900*, viii (Houston, TX: Rice University, 1968), pp. 699–710.

Eigner, Edwin M., *Robert Louis Stevenson and Romantic Tradition* (Princeton: Princeton University Press, 1966).

Eliott, Nathaniel, 'Robert Louis Stevenson and Scottish Literature', *English Literature in Transition* 12 (Lafayette, IN: Purdue University, 1969), pp. 79–85.

Elwin, Malcolm, *The Strange Case of Robert Louis Stevenson* (London: MacDonald, 1950).

Fiedler, Leslie, 'The Master of Ballantrae', *Victorian Literature: Modern Essays in Criticism*, ed. Austin Wright (New York: Oxford University Press, 1961), pp. 284–94.

Fowler, Alistair, 'Parables of Adventure: The Debatable Novels of Robert Louis Stevenson', *Nineteenth Century Scottish Fiction*, ed. Ian Campbell (Manchester: Carcanet Press, 1979).

—, *A History of English Literature* (Oxford: Basil Blackwell, 1987), pp. 248–9; 309–10.

Furnas, J. C., *Voyage to Winward: The Life of Robert Louis Stevenson* (London: Faber & Faber, 1952).

Gelder, Kenneth, 'Stevenson and the Covenanters: "Black Andie's Tale of Tod Lapraik" and "Thrawn Janet"', *SLJ* 11(2) (Aberdeen: Association for Scottish Literary Studies, 1984), pp. 56–70.

—, 'Robert Louis Stevenson's Revision to "The Merry Men"', *SSL* 21 (Columbia: University of South Carolina, 1986), pp. 262–87.

Gifford, Douglas, 'Stevenson and Scottish Fiction', *Stevenson and Victorian Scotland*, ed. Jenni Calder (Edinburgh: Edinburgh University Press, 1981), pp. 62–87.

—, 'Myth, Parody and Dissociation: Scottish Fiction 1814–1914', *The History of Scottish Literature Vol. III, Nineteenth Century*, ed. D. Gifford (Aberdeen: Aberdeen University Press, 1988).

Good, G., 'Rereading Robert Louis Stevenson', *Dalhousie Review* 62(1) (Halifax, Canada: University of Dalhousie, 1982), pp. 44–59.

Gwynn, Stephen, *Robert Louis Stevenson* (London: Macmillan, 1939).

Hammond, J. R., *A Robert Louis Stevenson Companion: A Guide to the Novels, Essays and Short Stories* (London: Macmillan, 1984).

Hardesty, R. W., 'Doctoring the Doctor', *SSL* 21 (Columbia: University of South Carolina, 1986), pp. 1–22.

—, 'Robert Louis Stevenson in Prose', *The History of Scottish Literature Vol. III, Nineteenth Century*, ed. D. Gifford (Aberdeen: Aberdeen University Press, 1988), pp. 291–308.

Heath, Stephen, 'Psychopathia sexualis: Stevenson's Strange Case', *Critical Quarterly* 28(1) and 28(2) (Hull: University of Hull, 1986), pp. 93–108; [reprinted in *Futures for English*, ed. Colin MacCabe (Manchester: Manchester University Press, 1988), pp. 93–108].

Hennessy, James Pope, *Robert Louis Stevenson* (London: Jonathan Cape, 1974).

Herdman, John, *The Double in Nineteenth-Century Fiction* (London: Macmillan, 1990) [see Chapter 8, 'The Double in Decline'].

Hubbard, Tom, 'The Divided Scot', *Chapman* 46 (Edinburgh: Chapman Publications, 1986), pp. 54–60.

Jefford, Andrew, 'Dr Jekyll and Professor Nabokov: Reading a Reading', *Robert Louis Stevenson*, ed. Andrew Noble (London: Vision; Totowa, NJ: Barnes & Noble, 1983), pp. 47–72.

Kiely, Robert, *Robert Louis Stevenson and the Fiction of Adventure* (Cambridge, MA: Harvard University Press, 1965).

Kilroy, James F., 'Narrative Techniques in *The Master of Ballantrae*', *SSL* (Columbia: University of South Carolina, 1969), pp. 98–106.

Letley, Emma, *From Galt to Douglas Brown: Nineteenth-Century Fiction and Scots Language* (Edinburgh: Scottish Academic Press, 1988), pp. 157–217.

Mackay, Margaret, *The Violent Friend: The Story of Mrs Robert Louis Stevenson, 1840–1914* (New York: Doubleday, 1968; abridged ed., London: Dent, 1969).

McLynn, Frank, *Robert Louis Stevenson: A Biography* (London: Random House, 1993).

Maixner, Paul (ed.), *Robert Louis Stevenson: The Critical Heritage* (London, Boston and Henley: Routledge & Kegan Paul, 1981).

Menikoff, Barry, *Robert Louis Stevenson and 'The Beach of Falesá', A Study in Victorian Publishing* (Stanford, CA: Stanford University Press, 1984).

Miller, Karl, *Doubles: Studies in Literary History* (Oxford: Oxford University Press, 1987).

Mills, Carol, '*The Master of Ballantrae*: An Experiment with Genre', *Robert Louis Stevenson*, ed. A. Noble (London: Vision; Totowa, NJ: Barnes & Noble, 1983), pp. 118–33.

Morgan, Edwin, 'The Poetry of Robert Louis Stevenson', *SLJ* 1974; also in Morgan's *Crossing the Border* (Manchester: Carcanet, 1990), pp. 141–57.

Mulholland, Honour, 'Robert Louis Stevenson and the Romantic Form', ibid., pp. 96–117.

Nabokov, Vladimir, *Lectures on Literature*, ed. Fredson Bowers (London: Weidenfeld & Nicolson, 1980).

Noble, Andrew (ed.), *From the Clyde to California: Robert Louis Stevenson's Emigrant Journey* (Aberdeen: Aberdeen University Press, 1985).

— (ed.), *Robert Louis Stevenson* (London: Vision; Totowa, NJ: Barnes & Noble, 1983).

Norquay, Glenda (ed.), *R. L. Stevenson on Fiction* (Edinburgh: Edinburgh University Press, 1999).

Oates, J. C., 'Jekyll/Hyde', *The Hudson Review* 40 (Hull: Alpha Academic, 1988), pp. 603–8.

Pavese, Cesare, 'Robert Louis Stevenson', *American Literature: Essays and Opinions*, trans. Edwin Fussell (Berkeley, Los Angeles, London: University of California Press, 1970), pp. 213–16.

Pickering, Sam, 'Stevenson's Elementary Novel of Adventure', *Research Studies* 49(2) (1981) [pp. 99–106 on *Treasure Island*].

Punter, David, *The Literature of Terror: A History of Gothic Fictions from 1765 to the Present Day* (London: Longman, 1980) [Chapter 9 concerning *Jekyll and Hyde*].

Rankin, Nicholas, *Dead Man's Chest: Travels After Robert Louis Stevenson* (London: Faber & Faber, 1987).

Rather, L. J., 'Mr Hyde and the "Damned Juggernaut"', *Synthesis* 14 (1988), pp. 49–54.

Robinson, T. M., 'In Search of Treasure Island', *London Magazine* (London: Feb., 1988), pp. 60–5.

Saposnik, Irving S., *Robert Louis Stevenson* (New York: Twayne, 1974).

Shaw, Valerie, *The Short Story: A Critical Introduction* (London: Longman, 1983) [see Chapter 2].

Smith, Janet Adam, *R. L. Stevenson* (London: Duckworth, 1937).

Stewart, John A., *Robert Louis Stevenson, Man and Writer: A Critical Biography* (London: Sampson Low, Marston, 1924) [2 vols].

Thomas, Ronald R., 'In the Company of Strangers: Absent Voices in Stevenson's Dr. Jekyll and Mr. Hyde and Beckett's Company', *Modern Fiction Studies* 32(2) (Lafayette, IN: Purdue University, 1986), pp. 157–73.

Sandison, Alan, *Robert Louis Stevenson and The Appearance of Modernism* (Basingstoke: Macmillan, 1995).

Treglown, Jeremy, 'R. L. Stevenson and the Authors-Publishers Debate', *Times Literary Supplement* (15–21 January 1988).

Veeder, William, and Hirsch, Gordon, *Dr. Jekyll and Mr. Hyde After 100 Years* (Chicago: Chicago University Press, 1988).

Chapter 24: Margaret Oliphant: Kirsteen

The following provides a brief list of key texts. For a complete list of the many works (in excess of 120) by Oliphant see *A History of Scottish Women's Writing*, edited by Gifford and McMillan, and *The Mainstream Companion to Scottish Literature*, edited by Royle. All published by William Blackwood & Sons unless otherwise listed.

Margaret Maitland (London: Henry Colburn, 1849).
Katie Stewart (Edinburgh, 1853).
Salem Chapel (Edinburgh, 1863).
The Rector and the Doctor's Family (Edinburgh, 1863) [3 vols].
The Perpetual Curate (Edinburgh, 1864).
Miss Marjoribanks (Edinburgh, 1866).
A Beleaguered City (London, 1880).
A Little Pilgrim in the Unseen (London: Macmillan & Co., 1882).
Hester (London: MacMillan & Co., 1883).
Stories of the Seen and Unseen (Edinburgh, 1885).
Effie Ogilvie (Glasgow: J. Maclehose, 1886).
The Land of Darkness (London: Macmillan & Co., 1888).
Phoebe Junior (London, 1876).
The Minister's Wife (London, 1869).
Kirsteen (London: Macmillan & Co., 1890).
The Railwayman and his Children (London: Macmillan & Co., 1891) [3 vols].

Mrs Oliphant's *Autobiography and Letters* appeared in 1899, edited by Mrs Harry Coghill (Edinburgh: Blackwood, 1899). This was edited by Queenie Leavis (Leicester: Leicester University Press, 1974), and by Elizabeth Jay (Oxford: Oxford University Press, 1990). Mrs Oliphant also wrote an invaluable account of William Blackwood, his sons, and their magazine in *Annals of a Publishing House* (Edinburgh: Blackwood, 1898); a third volume, *John Blackwood*, was added by his daughter, Mrs Gerald Porter (Edinburgh: Blackwoods, 1898); Frank Tredrey wrote a shorted account in *The House of Blackwood 1804–1954* (Edinburgh: Blackwood, 1954).

RECENT EDITIONS

The Autobiography and Letters of Mrs M. O. W. Oliphant, ed. Mrs Harry Coghill (Edinburgh and London: Blackwood, 1899) [reissued by Leicester University Press, 1974].

The Autobiography and Letters of Mrs M. O. W. Oliphant, with an introduction by Q. D. Leavis (Leicester: Leicester University Press, 1974).

The Autobiography of Mrs Oliphant, ed. Mrs Harry Coghill, with an intro. by Laurie Langbauer (Chicago and London: University of Chicago Press, 1988).

Miss Marjoribanks, intro. by Q. D. Leavis (London: Zodiac Press, 1969).

Miss Marjoribanks, intro. by Penelope Fitzgerald (London: Virago, 1988).

Kirsteen, intro. by Merryn Williams (London: Everyman, 1984).

Hester, intro. by Jennifer Uglow (London: Virago, 1984).

Salem Chapel, intro. by Penelope Fitzgerald (London: Virago, 1986).

The Rector and the Doctor's Family, intro. by Penelope Fitzgerald (London: Virago, 1986).

The Perpetual Curate, intro. by Penelope Fitzgerald (London: Virago, 1987).

Phoebe Junior, intro. by Penelope Fitzgerald (London: Virago, 1987).

Selected Short Stories of the Supernatural, ed. with intro. by Margaret K. Gray (Edinburgh: Scottish Academic Press, 1985).

A Beleaguered City and Other Stories, ed. with intro. by Merryn Williams (Oxford: Oxford University Press, 1988).

Secondary reading

Calder, Jenni, 'Heroes and Hero-makers: Women in Nineteenth-Century Scottish Fiction', *The History of Scottish Literature Vol. III, Nineteenth Century*, ed. Douglas Gifford (Aberdeen: Aberdeen University Press, 1988), pp. 261–6.

Clarke, John Stafford, 'Mrs Oliphant's Unacknowledged Social Novels', *Notes and Queries* 226 (London: George Bell, 1981), pp. 408–13.

Colby, Vineta, and Robert A., *The Equivocal Virtue: Mrs Oliphant and the Victorian Literary Marketplace* (New York: Archon Books, 1966).

—, 'Mrs Oliphant's Scotland: The Romance of Reality', *Nineteenth Century Scottish Fiction*, ed. Ian Campbell (Manchester: Carcanet New Press, 1979).

Cunningham, Valentine, *Everywhere Spoken Against: Dissent in the Victorian Novel* (Oxford: Oxford University Press, 1975).

Gilbert, Sandra, and Gubar, Susan, *No Man's Land Vol. 1: The War of the Words* (New Haven and London: Yale University Press, 1988) [see pp. 172–3 for comment on 'The Library Window'].

Haythornthwaite, J. A., 'The Wages of Success: Miss Marjoribanks, Margaret Oliphant and the House of Blackwood', *Publishing History* 15 (Cambridge: Chadwyck-Healey, 1984), pp. 97–107.

Hart, Francis Russell, *The Scottish Novel from Smollett to Spark* (Cambridge, MA: Harvard University Press, 1978), pp. 93–101.

James, Henry, 'London Notes, August 1897', *Notes on Novelists 1914*; reprinted in Literary Criticism, ed. Leon Edel (New York: Library of America, 1984), pp. 1411–13.

Jay, Elisabeth, *Mrs Oliphant: 'A Fiction to Herself': A Literary Life* (Oxford: Clarendon Press, 1995).

Stubbs, Patricia, *Women and Fiction: Feminism and the Novel 1880–1920* (London: Methuen, 1981) [esp. pp. 39–45 and pp. 141–2].

Trela, Donald, *Margaret Oliphant: Critical Essays* (London: Associated University Presses, 1995).

Williams, Merryn, *Margaret Oliphant: A Critical Biography* (London: Macmillan, 1986).

—, 'Margaret Oliphant, Novelist', *Cencrastus* 34 (Edinburgh: Cencrastus, 1989), pp. 20–2.

Wolff, Robert Lee, *Novels of Faith and Doubt in Victorian England* (London: John Murray, 1977).

Chapter 25: George Douglas Brown: The House with the Green Shutters

Love and a Sword [as 'Kennedy King'] (London: Macqueen, 1899).
Famous Fighting Regiments [as 'George Hood'] (London, 1900).
The Life of Paul Krugeras [as 'George Douglas']; serialized in *The Morning Herald* (London, Nov. 1899–Feb. 1900).
The House with the Green Shutters (London: Macqueen, 1901).
The House with the Green Shutters, ed. John T. Low (Edinburgh: Holmes McDougall, 1974) [contains useful critical material].
The House with the Green Shutters, ed. with intro. by Dorothy Porter (McMillan) (Harmondsworth: Penguin, 1985).

Secondary reading

Blake, George, *Barrie and the Kailyard School* (London: Arthur Barker, 1951).
Campbell, Ian, 'George Douglas Brown's Kailyard Novel', *SSL* 12 (Columbia: University of South Carolina, 1974–5), pp. 62–73.
—, 'George Douglas Brown: A Study in Objectivity', *Nineteenth Century Scottish Fiction: A Critical Anthology*, ed. Ian Campbell (Manchester: Carcanet Press, 1979), pp. 148–62.
Crosland, Thomas W. H., *The Unspeakable Scot* (London: Grant Richards, 1902).
Gifford, Douglas, 'Myth, Parody and Dissociation: Scottish Fiction 1814–1914', *The History of Scottish Literature Vol. III, Nineteenth Century*, ed. D. Gifford (Aberdeen: Aberdeen University Press, 1988), pp. 217–61.
Lennox, Cuthbert, *George Douglas Brown* (London: Hodder & Stoughton, 1903).
Manson, John, 'Young Gourlay', *Scottish Literature* 17 (1980), pp. 44–54.
Melrose, Andrew, 'George Douglas Brown, Reminiscences of a Friendship and a Notable Novel', *George Douglas Brown*, ed. Cuthbert Lennox (London, 1903).
Muir, Edwin, 'George Douglas', *Latitudes* (London: Melrose, 1924), pp. 31–46.
Scott, John Dick, 'R. L. Stevenson and G. D. Brown', *Horizon* 13 (1946), pp. 298–310.
Scott, Patrick, 'Questioning the Canon: The Problem of George Douglas Brown's Shorter Writings', *Studies in Scottish Fiction: Twentieth Century*, eds J. Schwend and H. W. Drescher (Frankfurt am Main: P. Lang, 1990), pp. 31–44.
Smith, Iain Crichton, '*The House with the Green Shutters*', *SSL* 7 (Columbia: University of South Carolina, 1969–70), pp. 3–10.
—, *The House with the Green Shutters* (Aberdeen: Association for Scottish Literary Studies, Scotnotes Series, 1988).
Somers, Jeffrey, '*The House with the Green Shutters*: George Douglas Brown's Perverse Bildungsroman', *SSL* 19 (Columbia: University of South Carolina, 1984), pp. 252–8.
Speirs, John, 'Nineteenth Century Scotland in Allegory', *The Scots Literary Tradition* (First published, London, 1940; second revised ed. London: Chatto & Windus, 1962), pp. 142–52.
Veitch, James, *George Douglas Brown* (London: Herbert Jenkins, 1952).

Chapter 26: J. M. Barrie and the Scottish Theatre

There are many editions of Barrie's plays; the most reliable is:

Barrie, J. M., *The Definitive Edition of the Plays of J M Barrie* (London: Hodder & Stoughton, 1942). A more accessible edition of his best known works is: Barrie, J. M., *Peter Pan and other plays*, ed. Peter Hollindale (Oxford: Oxford University Press, 1995) [includes *The Admirable Crichton, Peter Pan, When Wendy Grew Up, What Every Woman Knows*, and *Mary Rose*].

Secondary reading

Bell, Barbara, 'The National Drama', *Theatre Research International* 17(2) (Oxford: Oxford University Press, 1992), pp. 96–108.

—, 'The nineteenth century', *A History of Scottish Theatre*, ed. Bill Findlay (Edinburgh: Polygon, 1998), pp. 137–206.

Birkin, Andrew, *J M Barrie and the Lost Boys* (London: Constable, 1979).

Blake, George, *Barrie and the Kailyard School* (London: Barker, 1951).

Cameron, Alasdair, 'Scottish theatre and the shadow of Synge', *Small is Beautiful: small countries theatre conference* (Glasgow: Theatre Studies Publications, 1991), pp. 1–8.

—, 'Scottish drama in the nineteenth century', *The History of Scottish Literature vol. III, Nineteenth Century*, ed. Douglas Gifford (Aberdeen: Aberdeen University Press, 1988), pp. 429–41.

Dibdin, J. C., *The Annals of the Edinburgh Stage* (Edinburgh: Cameron, 1888).

Dunbar, Janet, *J M Barrie: The Man Behind the Image* (London: Collins, 1970).

Green, Roger Lancelyn, *Fifty Years of Peter Pan* (London: Davies, 1954).

Hutchison, David, 'Scottish drama, 1900–1950', *The History of Scottish Literature vol. IV, Twentieth Century*, ed. Cairns Craig (Aberdeen: Aberdeen University Press, 1987), pp. 163–77.

—, '1900 to 1950', *A History of Scottish Theatre*, ed. Bill Findlay (Edinburgh: Polygon, 1998), pp. 207–52.

Jack, R. D. S., *The Road to Never Land: a reassessment of J M Barrie's dramatic art* (Aberdeen: Aberdeen University Press, 1991).

—, 'Barrie and the extreme heroine', *Gendering the Nation: studies in modern Scottish literature*, ed. Christopher Whyte (Edinburgh: Edinburgh University Press, 1995), pp. 137–67.

—, *Patterns of Divine Comedy* (Cambridge: Cambridge University Press, 1989).

—, 'Barrie as journeyman dramatist: a study of Walker, London', *SSL* 22 (Columbia: University of South Carolina, 1985), pp. 60–77.

—, 'The land of myth and faery: the dramatic version of J M Barrie's *The Little Minister*', *Scotia* 9 (Norfolk, VA: Old Dominion University, 1985), pp. 1–16.

Ormond, Leonée, *J M Barrie* (Edinburgh: Scottish Academic Press, 1987).

Rose, Jacqueline, *The Case of Peter Pan: or the impossibility of children's fiction* (Basingstoke: Macmillan, 1994).

Worth, Christopher, ' "A very nice little theatre at Edinr.": Sir Walter Scott and control of the Theatre Royal', *Theatre Research International* 17(2) (Oxford: Oxford University Press, 1992), pp. 86–95.

Wright, Allen, *J M Barrie: Glamour of Twilight* (Edinburgh: Ramsay Head, 1976).

THE POPULAR THEATRE TRADITION

Bruce, Frank, 'From rough houses to swell houses: Harry Lauder, Scotch comics and mass entertainment', *Scotlands* 5(1) (Edinburgh: Edinburgh University Press, 1998), pp. 45–63.

Bruce, Frank, Foley, Archie, and Gillespie, George (eds), *Those Variety Days: Memories of Scottish Variety* (Edinburgh: Scottish Music Hall Society, 1997).

Cameron, Alasdair, 'Pantomime', *Keeping Glasgow in Stitches*, ed. Liz Arthur (Edinburgh: Mainstream, 1991), pp. 197–205.

Cameron, Alasdair, and Scullion, Adrienne, 'W F Frame and the Scottish popular theatre tradition', *Scottish Popular Theatre and Entertainment: historical and critical approaches of theatre and film in Scotland*, eds Alasdair Cameron and Adrienne Scullion (Glasgow: Glasgow University Library Studies, 1995).

Devlin, Vivien, *Kings, Queens and People's Palaces: An oral history of the Scottish variety theatre* (Edinburgh: Polygon, 1991).

Findlay, Bill, 'Scots language and popular entertainment in Victorian Scotland: the case of James Houston', *Scottish Popular Theatre and Entertainment*, eds Cameron and Scullion (Glasgow: Glasgow University Library Studies, 1995), pp. 15–38.

House, Jack, *Music Hall Memories* (Glasgow: Richard Drew, 1986).

Irving, Gordon, *The Good Auld Days: the story of Scotland's entertainers from music hall to television* (London: Jupiter, 1977).

Kift, Dagmar, *The Victorian Music Hall: culture, class and conflict* (Cambridge: Cambridge University Press, 1996).

King, Elspeth, 'Popular culture in Glasgow', *The Working Class in Glasgow, 1750–1914*, ed. R. A. Cage (London: Croom Helm, 1987), pp. 142–87.

Littlejohn, J. H., *The Scottish Music Hall, 1880–1990* (Wigtown: GC Books, 1990).

Mackie, Albert David, *The Scotch Comedians: from the music hall to television* (Edinburgh: Ramsay Head, 1973).

Maloney, Paul, 'Patriotism, Empire, and the Glasgow music hall', *Scotlands* 5(1) (Edinburgh: Edinburgh University Press, 1998), pp. 64–78.

Marshalsay, Karen, *The Waggle o' the Kilt: popular theatre and entertainment in Scotland* (Glasgow: Glasgow University Library, 1992).

Chapter 27: Widening the Range

The following references are by no means exhaustive but provide basic reading lists and critical information on writers or themes which have been mentioned in relation to the main sections of this book.

WILLIAM ALEXANDER

Sketches of Rural Life in Aberdeenshire (Aberdeen, 1853).

The Authentic History of Peter Grundie (Aberdeen, 1855).

The Laird of Drammochdyle (Aberdeen, 1865; ed. William Donaldson, Aberdeen: Aberdeen University Press, 1986).

Ravenshowe and the Residenters Therein (Aberdeen, 1868).

Johnny Gibb of Gushetneuk, in the Parish of Pyketillim; With Glimpses of the Parish Politics about A. D. 1843 (Edinburgh: Edmonston & Douglas, 1873: ed. William Donaldson, East Linton: Tuckwell Press, 1995).

Life Among My Aine Folk (Edinburgh: David Douglas, 1875).

My Uncle the Baillie (Aberdeen, 1876: ed. William Donaldson, East Linton: Tuckwell Press, 1995).

Secondary reading

Carter, Ian, ' "To Roose the Countra fae the Caul": William Alexander and *Johnny Gibb of Gushetneuk*', *Northern Scotland* 2 (1976–7), pp. 145–62.

Donaldson, William, *Popular Literature in Victorian Scotland* (Aberdeen: Aberdeen University Press, 1986).

See also Donaldson's excellent introductions to his editions of the novels above.

MARION ANGUS

See the bibliography 'Widening the Range', Section 5.

FURTHER READING SECTION 4

J. M. BARRIE (FICTION)

A selection of editions follows: for drama and criticism see also reading lists for Chapter 26.

Better Dead (London: S. Sonnenschein & Co., 1887).
Auld Licht Idylls (London: Hodder & Stoughton, 1888).
A Window in Thrums (London: Hodder & Stoughton, 1889).
The Little Minister (London: Hodder & Stoughton, 1891).
Sentimental Tommy (London: Cassell & Co., 1896).
Tommy and Grizel (Toronto: Copp, Clark, 1900).
Peter Pan (London: W. Paxton & Co., 1928).
Farewell Miss Julie Logan (London: Hodder & Stoughton, 1932; Edinburgh: Scottish Academic Press, 1989).

JOHN BUCHAN (FICTION TO 1900)
Sir Quixote of the Moors (London: T. Fisher Unwin, 1895).
John Burnet of Barns (London: John Lane, 1898).
Grey Weather (London: John Lane, 1899).
The Half-Hearted (London: Stodder & Stoughton, 1900).

Secondary reading
Buchan, William, *John Buchan: A Memoir* (London: Buchan & Enright, 1982).
Daniell, D., *The Interpreter's House: A Critical Assessment of John Buchan* (London: Nelson, 1975).
Edwards, Owen Dudley, 'John Buchan's Lost Horizon', *The Polar Twins*, eds Edward J. Cowan and Douglas Gifford (Edinburgh: John Donald, 1999), pp. 215–53.
Fitz Herbert, Margaret, *The Man Who Was Greenmantle* (London: John Murray, 1988).
Green, M., *A Biography of John Buchan and his Sister Anna* (Lewiston, NY: Lampeter: Mellen Press, 1990).
—, *Dreams of Adventure, Deeds of Empire* (London: Kegan Paul, 1980).
Harvie, Christopher, 'Second Thoughts of a Scotsman on the Make: Politics, Nationalism and Myth in John Buchan', *Nationalism in Literature, Language and National Identity*, eds Horst Drescher and Herman Völkel (Frankfurt: Peter Lang, 1989).
Kruse, J., *John Buchan and the Idea of Empire* (New York: Mellen Press, 1989).
Lownie, Andrew, *John Buchan: The Presbyterian Cavalier* (London: Constable, 1995).
—, *John Buchan: The Complete Short Stories* (London: Thistle, 1997).
Hanna, Archibald, *John Buchan 1875–1940: a Bibliography* (Hamden: Shoe String Press, 1953).
Smith, Janet Adam, *John Buchan* (London: Hart-Davis, 1965).
—, *John Buchan and his World* (London: Thames & Hudson, 1979).
Tweedsmuir, Susan Buchan, and Trevelyan, G. M., *John Buchan by his wife and friends* (London: Hodder & Stoughton, 1947).
Webb, Paul, *A Buchan Companion: A Guide to the Novels and Short Stories* (Stroud: Alan Sutton, 1994).

THOMAS CARLYLE

See the bibliography, 'Widening the Range', Section 3.

S. R. CROCKETT
The Stickit Minister (London: T. Fisher Unwin, 1893).
The Lilac Sunbonnet (London: T. Fisher Unwin, 1894).

The Raiders (London: T. Fisher Unwin, 1894).
The Men of the Moss-Hags (London: Isbister & Co., 1895).
The Grey Man (London: T. Fisher Unwin, 1896).
Cleg Kelly (London: Smith, Elder & Co., 1896).
The Black Douglas (London: Smith, Elder & Co., 1899).
The Moss Troopers (London: Hodder & Stoughton, 1912).

Secondary reading
Anderson, Eric, 'The Kailyard Revisited', *Nineteenth-Century Scottish Fiction*, ed. Ian Campbell (Manchester: Carcanet, 1979).
Donaldson, Islay Murray, *The Life and Work of Samuel Rutherford Crockett* (Aberdeen: Aberdeen University Press, 1989).
Harper, Malcolm, *Crockett and Grey Galloway: The Novelist and His Works* (London: Hodder and Stoughton, 1907).

HELEN BURNESS CRUIKSHANK
See reading lists for Chapter 36, 'Widening the Range', Section 5.

JOHN DAVIDSON (NOVELS)
See Davidson reading lists for Chapter 21.

FINDLATER SISTERS
Jane Helen Findlater
The Green Graves of Balgowrie (London: Methuen, 1896).
A Daughter of Strife (London: Methuen, 1897).
Rachel (London: Methuen, 1899).
The Story of a Mother (London: James Nisbet, 1902).
Stones from a Glasshouse (London: James Nisbet, 1904).
All that Happened in a Week (1905).
The Ladder to the Stars (London: Methuen, 1906).
Seven Scots Stories (London: John Murray, 1912).
A Green Grass Widow and Other Stories (London: John Murray, 1921).

Mary Findlater
Songs and Sonnets (London: Methuen, 1895).
Over the Hills (London: Methuen, 1897).
Betty Musgrave (London: Methuen, 1899).
A Narrow Way (London: Methuen, 1901).
The Rose of Joy (London: Methuen, 1903).
A Blind Bird's Nest (London: Smith, Elder & Co., 1907).
Tents of a Night (London: Smith, Elder & Co., 1914).

Jane and Mary Findlater
Tales That are Told (London: Methuen, 1901).
The Affair at the Inn, with Kate Douglas Wiggin and Allan McAuley (London: Smith, Elder & Co., 1904).
Crossriggs (London: Smith, Elder & Co., 1908).

Robinetta, with Kate Douglas Wiggin and Allan McAuley (London: Smith, Elder & Co., 1911).
Penny Monypenny (London: Smith, Elder & Co., 1911).
See and Heard Before and After 1914 (London: Smith, Elder & Co., 1916).
Content with Flies (London: Smith, Elder & Co., 1916).
Beneath the Visiting Moon (London: Hurst & Blackett, 1923).

Secondary reading

Gifford, Douglas, 'Caught Between Worlds: The Fiction of Jane and Mary Findlater', *A History of Scottish Women's Writing*, eds Gifford and McMillan (Edinburgh: Edinburgh University Press, 1997).
Mackenzie, Eileen, *The Findlater Sisters: Literature and Friendship* (London: John Murray, 1964).

GLASGOW NOVELS

Burgess, Moira, *Imagine a City: Glasgow in Fiction* (Glendaruel: Argyll Publishing, 1998).
—, *The Glasgow Novel 1870–1970: a bibliography* (Glasgow: Scottish Library Association, 1972).

JAMES GRANT *(a selection of this prolific novelist)*

The Romance of War (London: Smith, Elder & Co., 1846).
The Adventures of an Aide-de-camp (London: Smith, Elder & Co., 1848).
Bothwell (London: Smith, Elder & Co., 1854).
The Yellow Frigate (London: Smith, Elder & Co., 1855).

JOHN MACDOUGALL HAY

Gillespie (London: Constable, 1914; Edinburgh: Canongate, 1979, 1993, eds Bob Tait and Isobel Murray).
Barnacles (London: Constable, 1916).

Secondary reading

Murray, I., and Tait, B., *Ten Modern Scottish Novels* (Aberdeen: Aberdeen University Press, 1984).
Spring, Ian, 'Determinism in John MacDougall Hay's *Gillespie*', *SLJ* 6 (Aberdeen: Association for Scottish Literary Studies, 1979), pp. 55–68.

VIOLET JACOB (POETRY; FOR FICTION SEE READING LISTS FOR JACOB IN CHAPTER 30)

The Infant Moralist, with Lady Helena Carnegie (Edinburgh: Grant & Son, 1903).
The Golden Heart and Other Fairy Stories (London: Heinemann, 1904).
Verses (London: Heinemann, 1905).
Songs of Angus (London: John Murray, 1915).
More Songs of Angus, and Others (London: Country Life; New York: Charles Scribner's Sons, 1918).
Bonnie Joan and Other Poems (London: John Murray, 1921).
Two New Poems (Edinburgh: Porpoise Press, 1924).
The Good Child's Year Book (London: Foulis, 1928).
The Northern Lights and Other Poems (London: John Murray, 1927).
The Scottish Poems of Violet Jacob (Edinburgh: Oliver & Boyd, 1944).

Secondary reading
Caird, Janet, 'The Poetry of Violet Jacob and Helen B. Cruikshank', *Cencrastus* 19 (Edinburgh: Cencrastus Publications, 1985), p. 32.

KAILYARD FICTION
Anderson, Eric, 'The Kailyard Revisited', *Nineteenth-Century Scottish Fiction: Essays*, ed. Ian Campbell (Manchester: Carcanet, 1979).
Blake, George, *Barrie and the Kailyard School* (London: Arthur Barker, 1951).
Campbell, Ian, *The Kailyard: A New Assessment* (Edinburgh: Ramsay Head, 1981).
Drescher, Horst, and Schwend, Joachim (eds), *Studies in Scottish Fiction: Nineteenth Century* (Frankfurt: Peter lang, 1985).
Knowles, Thomas, *Ideology, Art and Commerce: Aspects of Literary Sociology in the Late Victorian Scottish Kailyard* (Gothenburg: Acta Universitatis Gothoburgensis, 1983).
Nash, Andrew, 'Re-reading the 'Lad o'Pairts': The Myth of the Kailyard Myth', *Scotlands* 3(2) (Edinburgh: Edinburgh University Press, 1996), pp. 86–102.
Shepherd, Gillian, 'The Kailyard', *The History of Scottish Literature*, vol. III, ed. Douglas Gifford (Aberdeen: Aberdeen University Press, 1988).

PATRICK MCGILL
See the reading lists for Section 5, 'Widening the Range'.

'Fiona MacLeod' (William Sharp)
Pharais (London: Frank Murray, 1894).
The Mountian Lovers (London, 1895).
The Sin-Eater (Edinburgh: Patrick Geddes, 1895).
Reissue of the Shorter Stories of Fiona Macleod, Vol. 1 Spiritual Tales; Vol. II Barbaric Tales; Vol. III Tragic Romances (Edinburgh: Patrick Geddes and Colleagues, 1895).
The Washer of the Ford (Edinburgh, 1896).
Green Fire (Westminster, 1896).
The Dominion of Dreams (London: Constable, 1899).
The Winged Destiny: Studies in the Spiritual History of the Gael (London, 1904).
The Works of Fiona Macleod, 7 Vols. Selected and Arranged by Mrs William Sharp (London: Heinemann, 1910–12).
Iona (Floris Books, 1982).

As William Sharp
The Human Inheritance, The New Hope, Motherhood (London: Elliot Stock, 1882). (ed.) *The Poems of Ossian*, translated by James Macpherson (Edinburgh: Patrick Geddes and Colleagues, 1896).
Selected Writings of William Sharp, 5 Vols. Selected and Arranged by Mrs William Sharp (London: William Heinemann, 1912).

Secondary reading
Alaya, Flavia, *William Sharp – 'Fiona Macleod', 1855–1905* (Harvard: Harvard University Press, 1970).
Hopkins, Konrad, 'Wilfion and the Green Life: A Study of William Sharp and Fiona Macleod', *Twenty-seven to One*, ed. Bradford B. Broughton (The Ryan Press, 1970), pp. 26–44.

Hopkins, Konrad, and Van Roekel, Ronald, *William Sharp/Fiona Macleod*, Renfrewshire Men of Letters Series No. 2 (Renfrew District Libraries, 1977).

Hopkins, Konrad, and Van Roekel, R. (eds), *The Wilfion Scripts transmitted through the mediumship of Margo Williams* (Wilfion Books, Publishers, 1980).

Sharp, Elizabeth A., *William Sharp (Fiona Macleod): A Memoir*, 2 vols (London: Heinemann, 1912).

NEIL MUNRO

The Lost Pibroch, and Other Sheiling Stories (Edinburgh: Blackwood, 1896).

John Splendid: the Tale of a Poor Gentleman and Little Wars of Lorn (Edinburgh: Blackwood, 1898; Edinburgh: B&W, 1994).

Gilian the Dreamer (London: Isbister, 1899; Edinburgh: B&W, 2000).

The Shoes of Fortune (London: Isbister, 1901).

Doom Castle: A Romance (Edinburgh: Blackwood, 1901; Blackwood, 1903).

Children of Tempest: A Tale of the Other Isles (Edinburgh: Blackwood, 1903).

Erchie, My Droll Friend [by H(ugh) F(oulis)] (Edinburgh: Blackwood, 1904).

The Vital Spark and her Queer Crew [by H. F.] (Edinburgh: Blackwood, 1906).

The Clyde, River and Firth (London: Black, 1907).

The Daft Days (Edinburgh: Blackwood, 1907); issued as *Bud: A Novel* (New York: Harper, 1907).

Fancy Farm (Edinburgh: Blackwood, 1910).

In Highland Harbours with Para Handy, s. s., Vital Spark [by H. F.] (Edinburgh: Blackwood, 1911).

Ayrshire Idylls (London: Black, 1912).

The New Road (Edinburgh: Blackwood, 1914; Edinburgh: B&W, 1994).

Jaunty Jock and Other Stories (Edinburgh: Blackwood, 1918).

Jimmy Swan, the Joy Traveller [by H. F.] (Edinburgh: Blackwood, 1923).

Hurricane Jack of the Vital Spark [by H. F.] (Edinburgh: Blackwood, 1923).

The Poetry of Neil Munro, introduced by John Buchan (Edinburgh: Blackwood, 1931).

The Brave Days: A Chronicle from the North, ed. George Blake (Edinburgh: Porpoise Press, 1931).

The Looker-On, ed. George Blake (Edinburgh: Porpoise Press, 1933) (essays).

Para Handy Tales (Edinburgh: Blackwood, 1958).

Para Handy, First complete edition, eds Brian D. Osborne and Ronald Armstrong (Edinburgh: Birlinn, 1991).

Erchie and Jimmy Swan, First complete edition, eds Brian D. Osborne and Ronald Armstrong (Edinburgh: Birlinn, 1993).

Secondary reading

Hart, Francis, *The Scottish Novel* (London: John Murray, 1978).

Völkel, Herman, *Das Literarische Werk Neil Munros* (Frankfurt: Peter Lang, 1994).

See also lengthy introductions to recent editions, above.

ROBERT LOUIS STEVENSON (POETRY)

See reading lists for Chapter 23.

WAR POETS

Royle, Trevor (ed.), *In Flanders Fields; Scottish Poetry and Prose of the First World War* (Edinburgh: Mainstream, 1990); an excellent survey/anthology of writers in prose (such as Lewis Grassic Gibbon and Eric Linklater) and poets, including, W. D. Cocker, Roderick Watson Kerr, Joseph Lee, Ewart MacKintosh, Charles Hamilton Sorley, John Buchan, Violet Jacob, Charles Murray, Neil Munro and Hugh MacDiarmid.

SECTION 5:
THE TWENTIETH-CENTURY SCOTTISH RENAISSANCE

Introductory reading

As always the reader is reminded of the informative websites listed at the beginning of the Further Reading section, especially the developing website maintained by the Departments of Scottish Literature and STELLA at the University of Glasgow at **www.arts.gla.ac.uk/SESLL/ScotLit/bibliography** where more information can be given than is possible here.

Readers will find good introductory material in the general histories and bibliographies given in the very beginning of the reading lists under Further General Reading (including Aitken, Daiches, Glen, Kinsley, Lindsay, Royle, Scott, Walker, Watson and Wittig). Particularly useful for the twentieth century is Robert Crawford's *Literature in twentieth-century Scotland: A Select Bibliography* (London: British Council, 1995). It is still the case that the only comprehensive (if subjective) single-volume overview is Alan Bold's *Modern Scottish Literature* (London: Longman, 1983). For those wishing to sample the poetry and fiction of the modern Scottish Literary Renaissance, there are several anthologies (contemporaneous and recent) available. Particularly focused on the Renaissance, although somewhat limited in its scope, is Maurice Lindsay's 1946 anthology *Modern Scottish Poetry* (London: Faber, 1946). There are rich modern collections in Douglas Dunn's *The Faber Book of Twentieth-Century Scottish Poetry* (London: Faber, 1993), Roderick Watson's huge *The Poetry of Scotland* (Edinburgh: Edinburgh University Press, 1995) and Robert Crawford and Mick Imlah's *The New Penguin Book of Scottish Verse* (London: Allen Lane, 2000). Leslie Wheeler's *Ten Northeast Poets* (Aberdeen: Aberdeen University Press, 1985) provides brief (but useful) biographies of the poets he highlights (including Violet Jacob, Helen Cruickshank and Marion Angus), and includes excerpts from their work. Those who want contemporaneous collections and commentary upon the Scottish Renaissance should consult issues of C. M. Grieve's *Northern Numbers* and *Scottish Chapbook* (Foulis, 1920; C. M. Grieve, 1922–3) or Hugh MacDiarmid's *The Golden Treasury of Scottish Poetry* (London: Macmillan, 1940). MacDiarmid's *Selected Prose*, ed. Alan Riach (Manchester: Carcanet, 1992), includes seminal essays, 'A Theory of Scots Letters' (1923), 'English Ascendency in British

Literature' (1931), and 'Scottish Arts and Letters: the Present Position and Post-War Prospects' (1942). See also *Albyn* (Manchester: Carcanet, 1996), and *The Raucle Tongue*, vols 1–3 (Manchester: Carcanet, 1996–8). For fiction, there are some excellent collections of short stories; some of the best include *Scottish Short Stories*, ed. J. M. Reid (Oxford: Oxford University Press, 1963); *Modern Scottish Short Stories*, eds Fred Urquhart and Giles Gordon (London: Faber & Faber, 1978); *The New Penguin Book of Scottish Short Stories*, ed. Ian Murray (Harmondsworth: Penguin, 1983), the bumper collection, *The Devil and the Giro: Two Centuries of Scottish Stories*, ed. Carl MacDougall (Edinburgh: Canongate, 1989), and *The Oxford Book of Scottish Short Stories*, ed. Douglas Dunn (Oxford: Oxford University Press, 1995). Moira Burgess's collection *The Other Voice: Scottish Women's Writing Since 1808* (Edinburgh: Polygon, 1987), introduces women's writing. To capture the vital atmosphere of the Renaissance, in prose and poetry, the reader is recommended to Grieve/MacDiarmid's anthologies (above) and (as C. M. Grieve), *Contemporary Scottish Studies* (1926; Carcanet, 1995), together with the stimulating colloboration between Lewis Grassic Gibbon and Hugh MacDiarmid in *Scottish Scene; or, The Intelligent Man's Guide to Albyn* (London: Hutchinson & Co., 1934). MacDiarmid and Gibbon (as Leslie Mitchell) in 1934 planned the provocative *Voice of Scotland* series (for Routledge); eminent Scottish writers of the day (including Gunn, Linklater, Mackenzie, Power, and the Muirs) wrote on literature, history, culture and religion, as well as food and drink; see the reading lists below, for much fuller material on cultural and social history, such as can be found in the numerous contemporary literary periodicals of the period. An outstanding example is *Hugh MacDiarmid: The Raucle Tongue (Hitherto Uncollected Prose)*, vols 1–3 (Manchester: Carcanet, 1996–8). For drama, see Cairns Craig and Randall Stevenson's *Twentieth-Century Scottish Drama: An Anthology* (Edinburgh: Canongate, 2001), Randall Stevenson and Gavin Wallace's *Scottish Theatre Since the Seventies* (Edinburgh: Edinburgh University Press, 1996) and Bill Findlay's *A History of Scottish Theatre* (Edinburgh: Polygon, 1998).

Influential ideas regarding Scottish character which MacDiarmid and others took up came from Gregory Smith's idiosyncratic study *Scottish Literature: Character and Influence* (London: Macmillan, 1919). For an early critical assessment of the whole movement, Duncan Glen's *Hugh MacDiarmid (Christopher Murray Grieve) and the Scottish Renaissance* (Edinburgh: Chambers, 1964) is useful, if angled towards poetry; later critics like Francis Russell Hart in *The Scottish Novel: A Critical Survey* (London: J. Murray, 1978) and Wittig were to restore the place of fiction. Modern criticism takes a balanced view; Edwin Morgan's *Crossing the Border: Essays on Scottish Literature*

(Manchester: Carcanet, 1990) and *Essay 1952–1973* (Manchester: Carcanet, 1974), and *The History of Scottish Literature Volume IV, Twentieth Century*, edited by Cairns Craig (Edinburgh: Edinburgh University Press, 1987), Marshall Walker's *Scottish Literature Since 1707* (London and New York: Longman, 1996), and Angus Calder's *Revolving Culture: Notes from the Scottish Republic* (London and New York: I. B. Taurus, 1994). For a stimulating discussion of the issues and themes in twentieth-century Scottish fiction, see Cairns Craig's *The Modern Scottish Novel* (Edinburgh: Edinburgh University Press, 1999). Canongate Classics have published over ninety modern fiction titles in their Classics series: these have excellent introductions, and readers are advised to check. Attention is now being paid to cross-national relations – for example in *Across the Water: Irishness in Modern Scottish Writing* eds James McGonigal, Daniel O'Rourke and Hamish Whyte (Glendaruel: Argyll, 2000).

Issues of gender have recently been foregounded, particularly in the stimulating essays of *Gendering the Nation* (Edinburgh: Edinburgh University Press, 1995), edited by Christopher Whyte. *Scottish Women's Fiction 1920s to 1960s: Journeys Into Being* (East Linton: Tuckwell Press, 2000) edited by Carol Anderson and Aileen Christianson looks at the emergence of women's fiction in the period, and there are many relevant essays in Gifford and McMillan's *A History of Scottish Women's Writing* (Edinburgh: Edinburgh University Press, 1997), and also (by Carol Anderson, Margaret Elphinstone, and Dorothy McMillan) in *Tea and Leg-Irons: New Feminist Readings From Scotland*, ed. Caroline Gonda (London: Open Letters, 1992).

For historical and cultural background, see the general histories (Cowan, Findlay, Devine and Lynch), T. C. Smout's *A Century of the Scottish People, 1830–1950* (London: Collins, 1986), Christopher Harvie's *No Gods and Precious Few Heroes* (Edinburgh: Edinburgh University Press, 1998), *Scotland: A Concise Cultural History*, edited by Paul H. Scott (Edinburgh: Mainstream, 1993), and George Davie's very influential *The Democratic Intellect* (Edinburgh: Edinburgh University Press, 1961) and *The Crisis of the Democratic Intellect* (Edinburgh: Polygon, 1986). Economic history is well covered in Bruce Lenman's *An Economic History of Modern Scotland* (London: Batsford, 1977), and R. H. Campbell's *Scotland since 1707: The Rise of an Industrial Society* (Edinburgh: John Donald, 1986). For a look at Scottish historiography contemporary with the Scottish Renaissance, see G. P. Insh's *Scotland and the Modern World* (Edinburgh, 1932). For a stimulating discussion of the marginalisation of Scottish culture, see Craig Beveridge and Ronald Turnbull's *The Eclipse of Scottish Culture* (Edinburgh: Polygon, 1989) and Cairns Craig's *Out of History: Narrative Paradigms in Scottish and English Culture* (Edinburgh:

Polygon, 1996). Language issues are treated in *Languages of Scotland* (Edinburgh: Chambers, 1979), edited by A. Aitken and T. McArthur.

Chapter 28: A Twentieth-Century Scottish Renaissance?

Aitken, W. R., 'The Scottish Literary Renaissance Movement', *SLJ* 4(2) (Aberdeen: Association for Scottish Literary Studies, 1977), pp. 58–61.

Blake, George, *Barrie and the Kailyard School* (London: Barker, 1951).

Bold, Alan, 'After the Renaissance: The Reckoning', *Chapman* 23–24 (5–6) (Edinburgh: Chapman Publications, 1979), pp. 12–21.

Bradbury, Malcolm, and Macfarlane, James (eds), *Modernism* (London: Penguin, 1976).

Bruce, George, and Munro, Ian, *Two Essays* (Edinburgh: National Library of Scotland, 1971).

Burgess, Moira, *Imagine a City: Glasgow in Fiction* (Glendaruel: Argyll Publishing, 1998).

Campbell, Ian, *Kailyard: A New Assessment* (Edinburgh: Ramsay Head, 1981).

Carswell, Catherine, *Lying Awake: An Unfinished Autobiography*, ed. John Carswell (London: Secker & Warburg, 1950).

Carswell, John, *Lives and letters: A. R. Orage, Beatrice Hastings, Katherine Mansfield, John Middleton Murry, S. S. Koteliansky, 1906–1957* (London: Faber, 1978).

Cruickshank, Helen, *Octobiography* (Montrose: The Standard Press, 1976).

D'Arcy, Julian, *Scottish Skalds and Sagamen: Old Norse Influence on Modern Scottish Literature* (East Linton: Tuckwell, 1996).

Fraser, G. S., *The Modern Writer and His World* (London: Deutsch, 1964).

Glen, Duncan (ed.), *Whither Scotland?: a prejudiced look at the future of a nation* (London: Gollancz, 1971).

—, *Hugh MacDiarmid and the Scottish Renaissance* (Edinburgh: Chambers, 1964).

Gunn, Neil M., *Whisky and Scotland: A Practical and Spiritual Enquiry* (London: Routledge, Voice of Scotland Series, 1935).

Hagemann, Susanne, ' "Bidin Naitural": Identity Questions in Scottish Twentieth Century Renaissance Literature', *SLJ* 21(1) (Aberdeen: Association for Scottish Literary Studies, 1994), pp. 44–55.

—, 'Translating Twentieth-Century Scottish Renaissance Literature: The National Element in Cross-National Communication', *Nationalism in Literature–Literarischer Nationalismus: Literature, Language, and National Identity*, eds Horst W. Drescher and Hermann Volkel (Frankfurt am Main: P. Lang, 1989), pp. 155–80.

Kincaid, John, 'The Scottish Dilemma', *Chapman* 23–24 (Edinburgh: Chapman Publications, 1979), pp. 23–31.

Kirk, John M., 'The Heteronomy of Scots with Standard English', *The Nuttis Schell: Essays on the Scots Language*, ed. Iseabail Macleod (Aberdeen: Aberdeen University Press, 1987), pp. 166–81.

Lindsay, Maurice, *Francis George Scott and the Scottish Renaissance* (Edinburgh: Paul Harris, 1980).

Linklater, Eric, *The Lion and the Unicorn: What England Has Meant to Scotland* (London: Routledge, Voice of Scotland Series, 1935).

MacDiarmid, Hugh, *At the Sign of the Thistle: A Collection of Essays* (London: Stanley Nott, n. d.).

—, *Lucky Poet: a self-study in literature and political ideas: being the autobiography of Hugh MacDiarmid (Christopher Murray Grieve)* (London: Methuen, 1943; Cape, 1972).

—, *The Letters of Hugh MacDiarmid*, ed. Alan Bold (London: Hamish Hamilton, 1984).

—, *Selected Prose* ed. Alan Riach (Manchester: Carcanet, 1992).

—, *Albyn: Shorter Books and Monographs* (Manchester: Carcanet, 1996).

—, *Annals of the Five Senses and Other Stories, Sketches and Plays*, eds Alan Riach and Roderick Watson (Manchester: Carcanet, 1999).

McCulloch, Margery Palmer, 'Women and Love: Some Thoughts on Women's Love Poetry', *Chapman* 74–75: Women's Forum (Edinburgh: Chapman Publications, 1993), pp. 46–52.

Miller, Karl (ed.), *Memoirs of a Modern Scotland* (London: Faber, 1970).

Milton, Colin, 'A Sough o' War: The Great War in the Poetry of the North East of Scotland', *Northern Visions: The Literary Identity of Northern Scotland in the Twentieth Century*, ed. David Hewitt (East Lothian: Tuckwell Press, 1995), pp. 1–38.

Muir, Edwin, *Scottish Journey* (London: Heinemann, 1935).

—, *An Autobiography* (London: Hogarth, 1954).

—, *Scott and Scotland: The Predicament of the Scottish Writer* (London: Routledge, Voice of Scotland Series, 1936).

Muir, Willa, *Belonging: A Memoir* (London: Hogarth, 1968).

—, *Mrs Grundy in Scotland* (London: Routledge, Voice of Scotland Series, 1936).

Pick, J. B., *The Great Shadow House: Essays on the Metaphysical Tradition in Scottish Fiction* (Edinburgh: Polygon, 1993).

Power, William, *Literature and Oatmeal: What Literature Has Meant to Scotland* (London: Routledge, Voice of Scotland Series, 1935).

Royle, Trevor (ed.), *In Flanders Fields: Scottish Poetry and Prose of the First World War* (Edinburgh: Mainstream, 1990).

Skelton, Robin, *Poetry of the Thirties* (London: Penguin, 1964).

Soutar, William, *Diaries of a Dying Man* (Edinburgh: Chambers, 1954).

Watson, Roderick, *The Literature of Scotland* (London: Macmillan, 1984).

Young, Douglas (ed.), *Scottish Verse, 1851–1951* (London: Thomas Nelson, 1952).

—, *The Use of Scots for Prose* (Greenock: Scots Philosophical Society, 1949).

Chapter 29: Hugh MacDiarmid, Edwin Muir and poetry in the Inter-War period

HUGH MACDIARMID/C. M. GRIEVE

This list is a selection only; see Aitken, and especially Alan Bold's *MacDiarmid: A Critical Biography* (London: John Murray, 1988), pp. 466–70, and *The Raucle Tongue* vol. III, ed. Alan Riach (Manchester: Carcanet, 1996), pp. 642–57 for a fuller bibliography. Under the general editorship of Alan Riach, the Carcanet MacDiarmid 2000 series collects the complete poems and a fully comprehensive selection of MacDiarmid's prose. It is published by Carcanet Press (Manchester) in the following volumes: *Selected Poetry*, eds Riach and Grieve (1992); *Scottish Eccentrics*, ed. Riach (1993); *Lucky Poet: The Autobiography*, ed. Riach (1994); *The Complete Poems 1920–1976*, 2 vols, eds Grieve and Aitken (1978); *Contemporary Scottish Studies*, ed. Riach (1995), the crucial series of articles which attacked the literary and cultural establishment of the 1920s; *Albyn: Shorter Books and Monographs*, ed. Riach (1996) including socio-political studies as well as literary and cultural criticism; *The Raucle Tongue: Hitherto Uncollected Prose*, 3 vols, eds Calder, Murray and Riach (1996–8) collecting a vast amount of MacDiarmid's political, literary and cultural journalism and critical writing from 1911 to 1978; *Annals of the Five Senses: Short Stories, Sketches and Plays*, ed. Watson and Riach (1999), which includes

MacDiarmid's output of fiction from the 1920s to the 1950s; and *New Selected Letters*, eds Grieve, Edwards and Riach (2001), which gives an intimate understanding of the man Christopher Murray Grieve, his life and contacts; a three volume annotated *Complete Poems* is also underway.

Scottish Chapbook (Montrose: C. M. Grieve, 1922–3) [as C. M. Grieve].
Annals of the Five Senses (Montrose: C. M. Grieve, 1923) [as C. M. Grieve].
Sangschaw (Edinburgh: Blackwood, 1925).
Penny Wheep (Edinburgh: Blackwood, 1926).
A Drunk Man Looks at the Thistle (Edinburgh: Blackwood, 1926) [see also Kenneth Buthlay's fine annotated edition, Edinburgh: Scottish Academic Press, 1987].
Contemporary Scottish Studies, First Series (London: Leonard Parsons, 1926).
To Circumjack/Cencrastus, or The Curly Snake (Edinburgh: Blackwood, 1930).
First Hymn to Lenin and Other Poems (London: Unicorn Press, 1931).
Scots Unbound, and Other Poems (Stirling: Aeneas Mackay, 1932).
At the Sign of the Thistle: A Collection of Essays (London: Stanley Nott, 1934).
Scottish Scene: Or, The Intelligent Man's Guide to Albyn [with Lewis Grassic Gibbon] (London: Jarrolds, 1934).
Stony Limits and Other Poems (London: Gollancz, 1934).
Second Hymn to Lenin and Other Poems (London: Stanley Nott, 1935).
Scottish Eccentrics (London: Routledge, 1936).
Lucky Poet: A Self-Study in Literature and Political Ideas (London: Methuen, 1943).
A Kist of Whistles (Glasgow: Mclellan, 1947).
In Memoriam James Joyce: From A Vision of World Language (Glasgow: Maclellan, 1955).
Three Hymns to Lenin (Edinburgh: Castle Wynd Printers, 1957).
The Battle Continues (Edinburgh: Castle Wynd Printers, 1957).
The Kind of Poetry I Want (Edinburgh: Duval, 1961).
A Lap of Honour (London: McGibbon & Kee, 1967).
The Uncanny Scot: A Selection of Prose, ed. Kenneth Buthlay (London: McGibbon & Kee, 1967).
The Complete Poems of Hugh MacDiarmid: 1920–1976, eds Michael Grieve and W. R. Aitken (London: Martin Brian & O'Keeffe, 1978) [2 vols].
Selected Essays of Hugh MacDiarmid, ed. Duncan Glen (London: Jonathan Cape, 1969).
The Letters of Hugh MacDiarmid, ed. Alan Bold (London: Hamish Hamilton, 1984).
Selected Poems of Hugh MacDiarmid, eds Alan Riach and Michael Grieve (London: Penguin, 1994).

Secondary reading

Akros 12(34–35) (Preston: Akros Publications, 1977) [Special Double Hugh MacDiarmid Issue].
Bell, Robin, 'All That Glitters', *Books in Scotland* 48 (Edinburgh: Ramsay Head Press, 1994), pp. 21–2.
Bold, Alan, *MacDiarmid* (London: John Murray, 1988).
Boutelle, Anne Edwards, *Thistle and Rose: A Study of Hugh MacDiarmid's Poetry* (Midlothian: Macdonald Publishers, 1981).
Brown, Dennis, Introduction to *The Modernist Self in Twentieth-Century English Literature: A Study in Self-Fragmentation* (London: Macmillan, 1989), pp. 1–13.
Buthlay, Kenneth, 'The Ablach in the Cold Pavilion', *SLJ* 16(2) (Aberdeen: Association for Scottish Literary Studies, 1988), pp. 39–57.

—, *Hugh MacDiarmid (C. M. Grieve)* (Edinburgh: Oliver & Boyd, 1964; Edinburgh: Scottish Academic Press, 1982).

—, 'A Note on a Manuscript of *A Drunk Man Looks at the Thistle*', *SLJ* 17(2) (Aberdeen: Association for Scottish Literary Studies, 1990), pp. 36–42.

Chapman 69–70 (Edinburgh: Chapman Publications, 1992) [MacDiarmid Centenary Issue].

Crawford, Robert, 'A Drunk Man Looks at the Waste Land', *SLJ* 14(2) (Aberdeen: Association for Scottish Literary Studies, 1987), pp. 62–78.

Cribb, T. J., 'The Cheka's Horrors and *On a Raised Beach*', *SSL* 20 (Columbia: University of South Carolina, 1985), pp. 88–100.

Crotty, Patrick, 'From Genesis to Revelation: Patterns and Continuities in Hugh MacDiarmid's Poetry in the Early Thirties', *SLJ* 15(2) (Aberdeen: Association for Scottish Literary Studies, 1988), pp. 5–23.

Davie, George, 'On Hugh MacDiarmid', *Cencrastus* 25 (Edinburgh: Cencrastus Publications, 1987), pp. 15–20.

Gish, Nancy K. (ed.), *Hugh MacDiarmid: Man and Poet* (Edinburgh: Edinburgh University Press, 1993).

Glen, Duncan (ed.), *Hugh MacDiarmid: a Critical Survey* (Edinburgh: Scottish Academic Press, 1972).

Herbert, W. N., 'MacDiarmid: Mature Art', *SLJ* 15(2) (Aberdeen: Association for Scottish Literary Studies, 1988), pp. 24–38.

Kerrigan, Catherine, 'MacDiarmid's Early Poetry', *The History of Scottish Literature Vol. IV, Twentieth Century*, ed. Cairns Craig (Aberdeen: Aberdeen University Press, 1987), pp. 75–86.

—, 'The Ugsome Thistle; Hugh MacDiarmid and the Nationalism of the Modern Literary Revival', *Nationalism in Literature: Literarischer Nationalismus: Literature, Language, and National Identity*, eds Horst W. Drescher and Hermann Völkel (Frankfurt am Main: P. Lang, 1989), pp. 181–7.

—, '*Whaur Extremes Meet': The Poetry of Hugh MacDiarmid, 1920–1934* (Edinburgh: Mercat Press, 1983).

— (ed.), *Hugh MacDiarmid – George Ogilvie Letters* (Aberdeen: Aberdeen University Press, 1988).

McCulloch, Margery, 'Modernism and the Scottish Tradition: The Duality of *A Drunk Man Looks at the Thistle*', *Chapman* 25 (Edinburgh: Chapman Publications, 1979), pp. 50–6.

—, 'The Undeservedly Broukit Bairn: Hugh MacDiarmid's "To Circumjack Cencrastus"', *SSL* 17 (Columbia: University of South Carolina, 1982), pp. 165–85.

Milton, C., 'Hugh MacDiarmid and North-East Scots', *Scottish Language* 5 (Aberdeen: University of Aberdeen, 1986), pp. 1–14.

—, 'Modern Poetry in Scots before MacDiarmid', *The History of Scottish Literature Vol. IV Twentieth Century*, ed. Cairns Craig (Aberdeen: Aberdeen University Press, 1987), pp. 11–36.

Montague, John, 'Hugh MacDiarmid: A Parting Gloss', *The Celtic Consciousness*, ed. Robert O' Driscoll (Toronto: McClelland & Stewart, 1987), pp. 467–70.

Morgan, Edwin, 'James Joyce and Hugh MacDiarmid', *James Joyce and Modern Literature*, eds W. J. McCormack and Alastair Stead (London: Routledge, 1982), pp. 202–17.

—, 'Jujitsu for the Educated: Reflections on Hugh MacDiarmid's Poem "In Memorium James Joyce"', *Twentieth Century* 160 (1956), pp. 223–31.

—, 'MacDiarmid Embattled', *Essays* (Manchester: Carcanet, 1974), pp. 194–202.

—, 'Poetry and Knowledge in MacDiarmid's Later Work', *Essays* (Manchester: Carcanet, 1974), pp. 203–13.

—, 'MacDiarmid at Seventy-Five', *Essays* (Manchester: Carcanet, 1974), pp. 214–21.

Murphy, Hayden, 'An Irish View of MacDiarmid', *Books in Scotland* 4 (Edinburgh: Ramsay Head Press, 1979), pp. 9–10.

Oxenhorn, Harvey, *Elemental Things: The Poetry of Hugh MacDiarmid* (Edinburgh: Edinburgh University Press, 1984).

Riach, Alan, *Hugh MacDiarmid's Epic Poetry* (Edinburgh: Edinburgh University Press, 1991).

—, 'The Idea of Order in *On a Raised Beach*', *Terranglian Territories: Proceedings of the Seventh International Conference on the Literature of Region and Nation*, ed. Suzanne Hagemann (Frankfurt am Main: Peter Lang, 2000), pp. 613–29.

—, *The Poetry of Hugh MacDiarmid*, Scotnotes (Glasgow: Association for Scottish Literary Studies, 1999).

Scott, Paul, and Davis, A. C. (eds), *The Age of MacDiarmid* (Edinburgh: Mainstream, 1980).

Speirs, John, 'The Present and C. M. Grieve', *The Scots Literary Tradition: An Essay in Criticism* (London: Chatto & Windus, 1940).

Stanforth, Susan M., 'New Light on the Text of MacDiarmid's "The Nature of a Bird's World"', SLJ 22(1) (Aberdeen: Association for Scottish Literary Studies, 1995), pp. 92–3.

Watson, Roderick, *MacDiarmid* (Milton Keynes: Open University Press, 1985).

Whyte, Christopher, 'The Construction of Meaning in MacDiarmid's *Drunk Man*', *SSL* 23 (Columbia: University of South Carolina, 1988), pp. 199–238.

Whyte, Hamish, 'MacDiarmid and the Beatniks', *SLJ* 13(2) (Aberdeen: Association for Scottish Literary Studies, 1986), pp. 87–90.

EDWIN MUIR

This list is not inclusive; see Aitken, and especially Peter Butter's *Edwin Muir: Man and Poet* (Edinburgh: Oliver & Boyd, 1966), pp. 302–8, for a fuller bibliography; see also works listed above in the introduction and under 'General'; and in Fiction lists in Chapter 36.

We Moderns: Enigmas and Guesses (London; Allen & Unwin, 1918) [as 'Edward Moore'].

Latitudes: Essays (London: Melrose, 1924).

First Poems (London: Hogarth Press, 1925).

Transitions: Essays on Contemporary Literature (London: Hogarth Press, 1925).

The Structure of the Novel (London: Hogarth Press, 1928).

Variations on a Time Theme (London: Dent, 1934).

Scott and Scotland (London: Routledge, 1936).

Journeys and Places (London: Faber, 1937).

The Story and The Fable (London: Harrap, 1940); revised as *An Autobiography* (London: Hogarth, 1954; Edinburgh: Canongate, 1993).

The Narrow Place (London: Faber, 1943).

The Voyage and Other Poems (London: Faber, 1946).

The Labyrinth (London: Faber, 1949).

One Foot in Eden (London: Faber, 1956).

The Complete Poems of Edwin Muir, ed. Peter Butter (Aberdeen: Association for Scottish Literary Studies, 1991).

Secondary reading

Aitchison, James, *The Golden Harvester: The Vision of Edwin Muir* (Aberdeen: Aberdeen University Press, 1988).

Butter, Peter, 'The Evolution of Some Late Poems of Edwin Muir', *SLJ* 24(2) (Aberdeen: Association for Scottish Literary Studies, 1997), pp. 79–84.

Calder, Robert, 'Muir and the Problem of Exclusion', *Chapman* 49 (Edinburgh: Chapman Publications, 1987), pp. 15–20.

Daly, MacDonald, 'Scottish Poetry and the Great War', *SLJ* 21(2) (Aberdeen: Association for Scottish Literary Studies, 1994), pp. 79–96.

Di Piero, Simone, 'On Edwin Muir', *Chicago Review* 37(1) (Chicago: University of Chicago Press, 1990), pp. 80–8.

Gilbert, Sandra M., 'Soldier's Heart: Literary Men, Literary Women, and the Great War', *Speaking of Gender*, ed. Elaine Showalter (London: Routledge, 1989).

Hearn, Sheila G., 'Edwin Muir: Selected Reading', *Books in Scotland* 4 (Edinburgh: Ramsay Head Head Press, 1979), p. 16.

—, 'Edwin Muir: The Man and His Work', *Books in Scotland* 9 (Edinburgh: Ramsay Head Press, 1981/1982), pp. 6–7.

Huberman, Elizabeth, *The Poetry of Edwin Muir: The Field of Good and Ill* (New York: Oxford University Press, 1971).

Knight, Robert, *Edwin Muir: An Introduction to His Work* (London: Longman, 1980).

McCulloch, Margery Palmer, *Edwin Muir: Poet, Critic, and Novelist* (Edinburgh: Edinburgh University Press, 1993).

Marshall, George, *In a Distant Isle: The Orkney Background of Edwin Muir* (Aberdeen: Aberdeen University Press, 1988).

Morgan, Edwin, 'Edwin Muir', *Essays* (Manchester: Carcanet, 1974), pp. 186–93.

Noble, Andrew (ed.), *Edwin Muir: Uncollected Scottish Criticism* (London: Vision Press, 1982).

Pittock, Murray G. H., 'Armorial Weed: The Landscape of Edwin Muir', *Northern Visions: The Literary Identity of Northern Scotland in the Twentieth Century*, ed. David Hewitt (East Lothian: Tuckwell Press, 1995), pp. 70–81.

—, ' "This is the Place": Edwin Muir and Scotland', *SLJ* 14(1) (Aberdeen: Association for Scottish Literary Studies, 1987), pp. 53–72.

Taylor, Nancy Dew, 'Edwin Muir's Penelope Poems', *SSL* 24 (Columbia: University of South Carolina, 1989), pp. 212–20.

Wiseman, Christopher, *Beyond the Labyrinth: A Study of Edwin Muir's Poetry* (Victoria, BC: Sono Nis Press, 1978).

Young, James D., 'A Socialist's-Eye View of Edwin Muir', *Chapman* 49 (Edinburgh: Chapman Publications, 1987), pp. 21–5.

Chapter 30: Opening the Doors: Fiction by Women 1911–47

Since twentieth-century Scottish fiction is intermittently in and out of print, the bibliographies to this section cite publisher and date of the first British edition of a work. For currently available modern editions, readers should check catalogues of publishers who specialise in Scottish fiction reprints, such as Canongate, B&W Publishing, Mainstream and House of Lochar. It may also be useful to consult *BookFind*, an online database of books in print, available through the Glasgow University Library website at: http://merlin.lib.gla.ac.uk.

BACKGROUND READING

Anderson, Carol and Christianson, Aileen, *Scottish Women's Fiction 1920s to 1960s: Journeys into Being* (East Linton: Tuckwell Press, 2000).

Chapman 74–75 (Edinburgh: Chapman Publications, 1993) [Issue dedicated to Scottish women writers].

Christianson, Aileen, 'Imagined Corners to Debatable Land: Passable Boundaries', *Scottish Affairs* 17 (Edinburgh: Unit for the Study of Government in Scotland, 1996), pp. 120–34.

Dunn, Douglas, 'The Representation of Women in Scottish Literature', *Scotlands* 2 (Edinburgh: Edinburgh University Press, 1994), pp. 1–23.

Gifford, Douglas, 'Contemporary Fiction I', *A History of Scottish Women's Writing*, eds Douglas Gifford and Dorothy McMillan (Edinburgh: Edinburgh University Press, 1997), pp. 577–603.

Gonda, Caroline (ed.), *Tea and Leg-Irons: Feminist Readings from Scotland* (London: Open Letters, 1992).

CATHERINE CARSWELL

Open the Door! (London: Andrew Melrose, 1920).

The Camomile: An Invention (London: Chatto & Windus, 1922).

The Life of Robert Burns (London: Chatto & Windus, 1930).

The Savage Pilgrimage: A Narrative of D. H. Lawrence (London: Chatto & Windus, 1932).

A National Gallery: being a collection of English character [with Daniel George Bunting] (London: Martin Secker, 1933).

The English in Love: a museum of illustrative verse and prose pieces from the 14th to the 20th century [with Daniel George Bunting] (London: Martin Secker, 1934).

The Fays of the Abbey Theatre: an autobiographical record [with William Fay] (London: Rich & Cowan, 1935).

The Scots Week-end and Caledonian Vade-Mecum [with Donald Carswell] (London: Routledge, 1936).

The Tranquil Heart: Portrait of Giovanni Boccaccio (London: Lawrence & Wishart, 1937).

Lying Awake: an unfinished autobiography, and other posthumous papers, ed. John Carswell (London: Secker & Warburg, 1950).

Secondary reading

Anderson, Carol, ' "Behold I make all things new": Catherine Carswell and the visual arts', *Scottish Women's Fiction, 1920s to 1960s: Journeys into Being*, eds Carol Anderson and Aileen Christianson (East Linton: Tuckwell Press, 2000), pp. 20–31.

— (ed.), *Opening the Doors: The Achievement of Catherine Carswell* (Ramsay Head: Edinburgh, 2001).

McCulloch, Margery Palmer, 'Opening the door: women, Carswell and the Scottish Renaissance', *Scottish Studies/Etudes Ecossaises: Proceedings of the Scottish workshop of the ESSE conference, Bordeaux 1993*, eds Horst W. Drescher and Pierre Morere (Grenoble: Universite Stendhal and Germersheim: Johannes Gutenberg Universitat Mainz, 1994), pp. 93–104.

Norquay, Glenda, 'Catherine Carswell: Open the Door!', *A History of Scottish Women's Writing*, eds Douglas Gifford and Dorothy McMillan (Edinburgh: Edinburgh University Press, 1997), pp. 389–99.

Pilditch, Jan, 'Opening the door on Catherine Carswell', *Scotlands* 2 (Edinburgh: Edinburgh University Press, 1994; 1995), pp. 53–65.

See also the Introduction to *Open the Door!* by John Carswell (Virago, 1986; Canongate, 1996), and to *The Camomile* by Ianthe Carswell (Virago, 1987).

WILLA MUIR

Women: an inquiry (London: Hogarth Press, 1925).

Imagined Corners (London: Martin Secker, 1931).

Mrs Ritchie (London: Martin Secker, 1933).

Mrs Grundy in Scotland (London: Routledge, 1936).

Living with Ballads (London: Hogarth Press, 1965).

Belonging (London: Hogarth Press, 1968).
Imagined Selves: Willa Muir, ed. Kirsty Allen (Edinburgh: Canongate, 1996).

Secondary reading
Butter, P. H., 'Willa Muir: Writer', *Edwin Muir: Centenary Assessments*, eds C. J. M. MacLachlan and D. S. Robb (Aberdeen: Association for Scottish Literary Studies, 1988), pp. 58–74.
Christianson, Aileen, 'Dreaming realities: Willa Muir's Imagined Corners', *Scottish Women's Fiction, 1920s to 1960s: Journeys into Being*, eds Carol Anderson and Aileen Christianson (East Linton: Tuckwell Press, 2000), pp. 84–96.
Dickson, Beth, ' "An ordinary little girl": Willa Muir's Mrs Ritchie', Anderson and Christianson eds, pp. 97–106.
Elphinstone, Margaret, 'Willa Muir: Crossing the Genres', *A History of Scottish Women's Writing*, eds Douglas Gifford and Dorothy McMillan (Edinburgh: Edinburgh University Press, 1997), pp. 400–15.
Manning, Susan, ' "Belonging with Edwin": Writing the History of Scottish Women Writers', *SLJ Supplement* 48 (Aberdeen: Association for Scottish Literary Studies, 1998), pp. 3–9.
Mudge, Patricia Rowland, 'A Quorum of Willas', *Chapman* 71 (Edinburgh: Chapman Publications, 1992–3), pp. 1–7.
Murray, Isobel, 'Selves, Names and Roles: Willa Muir's *Imagined Corners* offers some inspiration for *A Scots Quair*', *SLJ* (21) (Aberdeen: Association for Scottish Literary Studies, 1994), pp. 56–64.
Robb, David S., 'The published novels of Willa Muir', *Studies in Scottish Fiction: Twentieth Century*, eds Joachim Schwend and Horst W. Drescher (Frankfurt am Main: P. Lang, 1990), pp. 149–61.

NANCY BRYSSON MORRISON

Breakers (London: John Murray, 1930).
Solitaire (London: John Murray, 1932).
The Gowk Storm (London: Collins, 1933).
The Keeper of Time (Edinburgh: Church of Scotland, 1933).
The Strangers (London: Collins, 1935).
When the Wind Blows (London: Collins, 1937).
These Are My Friends (London: Geoffrey Bles, 1946).
The Winnowing Years (London: Hogarth Press, 1949).
The Hidden Fairing (London: Hogarth Press, 1951).
The Following Wind (London: Hogarth Press, 1954).
The Other Traveller (London: Hogarth Press, 1957).
They Need No Candle: the men who built the Scottish Kirk (London: Epworth Press, 1957).
Mary Queen of Scots (London: Vista Books, 1960).
Thea (London: Robert Hale, 1963).
The Private Life of Henry VII (London: Robert Hale, 1964).
Haworth Harvest: the lives of the Brontes (London: Dent, 1969).
King's Quiver: the last three Tudors (London: Dent, 1972).
True Minds: the marriage of Thomas and Jane Carlyle (London: Dent, 1974).

Also twenty-eight romantic novels under the name of Christine Strathern.

Secondary reading
Hunter, Stewart, 'The Morrisons', *Scots Magazine* 59(3) (1953), pp. 187–92.

McCulloch, Margery Palmer, 'Poetic Narrative in Nancy Brysson Morrison's *The Gowk Storm*', *Scottish Women's Fiction, 1920s to 1960s: Journeys into Being*, eds Carol Anderson and Aileen Christianson (East Linton: Tuckwell Press, 2000), pp. 109–19.

NAN SHEPHERD
The Quarry Wood (London: Constable, 1928).
The Weatherhouse (London: Constable, 1930).
A Pass in the Grampians (London: Constable, 1933).
The Living Mountain: a celebration of the Cairngorm Mountains (Aberdeen: Aberdeen University Press, 1977).

Secondary reading
Carter, Gillian, 'Boundaries and transgression in Nan Shepherd's The Quarry Wood', *Scottish Women's Fiction, 1920s to 1960s: Journeys into Being*, eds Carol Anderson and Aileen Christianson (East Linton: Tuckwell Press, 2000), pp. 47–57.
Kesson, Jessie, 'Nan Shepherd: In Recollection', *Aberdeen University Review* LII, 3(183) (Aberdeen: Aberdeen University Press, 1990), pp. 187–91.
Lumsden, Alison, '"Journey into Being": Nan Shepherd's The Weatherhouse', *Scottish Women's Fiction, 1920s to 1960s: Journeys into Being*, eds Carol Anderson and Aileen Christiansen (East Linton: Tuckwell Press, 2000), pp. 59–71.
Watson, Roderick, '". . . to get leave to live": patterns of identity, freedom and defeat in the fiction of Nan Shepherd', *Studies in Scottish Fiction: Twentieth Century*, eds Joachim Schwend and Horst W. Drescher (Frankfurt am Main: P. Lang, 1990), pp. 207–18.
—, ' "To know Being": substance and spirit in the work of Nan Shepherd', *A History of Scottish Women's Writing*, eds Douglas Gifford and Dorothy McMillan (Edinburgh: Edinburgh University Press, 1997), pp. 416–27.

VIOLET JACOB
The Sheep Stealers (London: Heinemann, 1902).
The Interloper (London: Heinemann, 1904).
Irresolute Catherine (London: John Murray, 1908).
The History of Aythan Waring (London: Heinemann, 1908).
Stories Told by the Miller (London: John Murray, 1909).
The Fortune Hunters and other stories (London: John Murray, 1910).
Flemington (London: John Murray, 1911).
Tales of My Own Country (London: John Murray, 1922).
The Lairds of Dun (London: John Murray, 1931).
The Lum Hat and other stories, ed. Ronald Garden (Aberdeen: Aberdeen University Press, 1982).
Flemington: and Tales from Angus, ed. Carol Anderson (Edinburgh: Canongate, 1998).
Diaries and Letters from India, ed. Carol Anderson (Edinburgh: Canongate, 1990).

Secondary reading
Anderson, Carol, 'Debatable land: the prose work of Violet Jacob', *Tea and Leg Irons: New Feminist Readings from Scotland*, ed. Caroline Gonda (London: Open Letters, 1992), pp. 31–44.
—, 'Flemington and its portraits', *ScotLit* 11 (Aberdeen: Association for Scottish Literary Studies, 1994), pp. 1–2.
—, 'Tales of her own countries: Violet Jacob', *A History of Scottish Women's Writing*, eds Douglas Gifford and Dorothy McMillan (Edinburgh: Edinburgh University Press, 1997), pp. 347–59.

READING LISTS

Bing, Sarah, 'Autobiography in the work of Violet Jacob', *Chapman* 74–75 (Edinburgh: Chapman Publications, 1993), pp. 98–109.
Garden, Ronald, 'Violet Jacob in India', *SLJ* 13(2) (Aberdeen: Association for Scottish Literary Studies, 1986), pp. 48–64.

NAOMI MITCHISON

Publications to 1947. For later titles see the bibliography to Section 6. This listing is necessarily selective. A full bibliography will be found in *A History of Scottish Women's Writing*, eds Douglas Gifford and Dorothy McMillan (Edinburgh: Edinburgh University Press, 1997), pp. 702–3.

The Conquered (Cape, 1923).
When the Bough Breaks and other stories (London: Cape, 1924).
Cloud Cuckoo Land (London: Cape, 1925).
Black Sparta: Greek Stories (London: Cape, 1928).
Barbarian Stories (London: Cape, 1929).
The Corn King and the Spring Queen (London: Cape, 1931; Edinburgh: Canongate, 1990).
The Delicate Fire: Short Stories and Poems (London: Cape, 1933).
Vienna Diary (London: Gollancz, 1934).
Beyond This Limit (London: Cape, 1935).
We Have Been Warned (London: Constable, 1935).
The Fourth Pig: Stories and Verses (London: Constable, 1936).
Blood of the Martyrs (London: Constable, 1939; Edinburgh: Canongate, 1988).
The Bull Calves (London: Cape, 1947; Glasgow: Drew, 1985).

Secondary reading

Mitchison's autobiographical works are listed in the bibliography to Section 6.

Benton, Jill, *Naomi Mitchison: a century of experiment in life and letters* (London: Pandora, 1990).
Calder, Jenni, 'Men, women and comrades', *Gendering the Nation*, ed. Christopher Whyte (Edinburgh: Edinburgh University Press, 1995).
—, 'More than merely ourselves: Naomi Mitchison', *A History of Scottish Women's Writing*, eds Douglas Gifford and Dorothy McMillan (Edinburgh: Edinburgh University Press, 1997), pp. 444–55.
—, *The Nine Lives of Naomi Mitchison* (London: Virago, 1997).
Dickson, Beth, 'From personal to global: the fiction of Naomi Mitchison', *Chapman* 50–51 (Edinburgh: Chapman Publications, 1987), pp. 34–40.
Elphinstone, Margaret, 'The location of magic in Naomi Mitchison's *The Corn King and the Spring Queen*', *Scottish Women's Fiction, 1920s to 1960s: Journeys into Being*, eds Carol Anderson and Aileen Christianson (East Linton: Tuckwell Press, 2000), pp. 72–83.
Gifford, Douglas, 'Forgiving the past: Naomi Mitchison's The Bull Calves', *Studies in Scottish Fiction: Twentieth Century*, eds Joachim Schwend and Horst Drescher (Frankfurt am Main: P. Lang, 1990), pp. 219–41.
Henegan, Alison, 'Alison Henegan talking with Naomi Mitchison', *Writing Lives: conversations between women writers*, ed. Mary Chamberlain (London: Virago, 1988), pp. 170–80.

Murray, Isobel, 'Human relations: an outline of some major themes in Naomi Mitchison's adult fiction', *Studies in Scottish Fiction: Twentieth Century*, eds Joachim Schwend and Horst Drescher (Frankfurt am Main: P. Lang, 1990), pp. 243–56.
Smith, Alison, 'The Woman From the Big House: the autobiographical writings of Naomi Mitchison', *Chapman* 50–51 (Edinburgh: Chapman Publications, 1987), pp. 10–17.

LORNA MOON
Doorways in Drumorty (London: Cape, 1926).
Dark Star (London: Gollancz, 1929).
Too Gay! (Lipstick Lady) (Newcastle-under-Lyme: Clifford Lewis, 1945).

Secondary reading
See the *Introductions* by David Toulmin to Gourdas House (Aberdeen) editions of *Dark Star* (1980) and *Doorways in Drumorty* (1981).

Chapter 31: The Poetry of William Soutar

See also Aitken, and Alexander Scott's biography, *Still Life: William Soutar (1898–1943)* (London and Edinburgh: Chambers, 1958).

Gleanings by an Undergraduate (Paisley: Alexander Gardner, 1923).
Conflict (London: Chapman & Hall, 1931).
The Solitary Way (Edinburgh: The Moray Press, 1935).
Brief Words: One Hundred Epigrams (Edinburgh: Moray Press, 1935).
Poems in Scots (Edinburgh: Moray, 1935).
A Handful of Earth (Edinburgh: Moray Press, 1936).
Riddles in Scots (Edinburgh: Moray, 1937).
In the Time of Tyrants (Perth: privately printed, 1939).
Seeds in the Wind: Poems in Scots for Children (London: A. Dakers, 1943).
But the Earth Abideth (London: A. Dakers, 1943).
The Solitary Way (London: A. Dakers, 1943).
The Expectant Silence (London: A. Dakers, 1945).
Collected Poems, ed. Hugh MacDiarmid (London: A. Dakers, 1948) [Incomplete].
Poems of William Soutar: A New Selection, ed. William Aitken (Edinburgh: Scottish Academic Press, 1988).
Diaries of a Dying Man, ed. Alexander Scott (Edinburgh: Chambers, 1988; Edinburgh: Canongate, 1991).
Into a Room: Selected Poems of William Soutar, eds Carl MacDougall and Douglas Gifford (Glendaruel: Argyll, 2000).

Secondary reading
Aitken, W. R., ' "I'll Mind Ye in a Sang": William Soutar's Whigmaleeries', *Chapman* 10(4) (Edinburgh: Chapman Publications, 1988), pp. 48–50.
—, 'The Soutar Archives in the National Library of Scotland', *Chapman* 10(4) (Edinburgh: Chapman Publications, 1988), pp. 46–7.
Glen, Duncan, 'William Soutar's Prose Writings', *Chapman* 10(53) (Edinburgh: Chapman Publications, 1989), pp. 2–9.

Goodwin, K. L., 'William Soutar, Adelaide Crapsey, and Imagism', *SSL* 3 (Columbia: University of South Carolina, 1965), pp. 96–100.

McGregor, Forbes, 'A Chiel Called Soutar', *Chapman* 10(4) (Edinburgh: Chapman Publications, 1988), pp. 21–6.

Chapter 32: Lewis Grassic Gibbon and Eric Linklater

LEWIS GRASSIC GIBBON

Some of Gibbon's novels were originally published under his real name, James Leslie Mitchell. They are listed accordingly here, but readers should note that the modern editions currently appearing from publishers such as Polygon may be published as by Gibbon, or may bear both names.

As Lewis Grassic Gibbon:
Sunset Song (London: Jarrolds, 1932).
Cloud Howe (London: Jarrolds, 1933).
Grey Granite (London: Jarrolds, 1934).
[These novels published together as *A Scots Quair* (London: Jarrolds, 1946).]
Scottish Scene [essays; with Hugh MacDiarmid] (London: Jarrolds, 1934).
A Scots Hairst: essays and short stories, ed. Ian S. Munro (London: Hutchinson, 1967).
The Speak of the Mearns [unfinished novel], ed. Ian Campbell (Edinburgh: Ramsay Head Press, 1982).
Smeddum: A Lewis Grassic Gibbon Anthology, ed. Valentina Bold (Edinburgh: Canongate, 2001).

As James Leslie Mitchell:
Stained Radiance (London: Jarrolds, 1930).
The Thirteenth Disciple (London: Jarrolds, 1931).
The Calends of Cairo (London: Jarrolds, 1931).
Three Go Back (London: Jarrolds, 1932).
Spartacus (London: Jarrolds, 1933).
Nine against the Unknown (London: Jarrolds, 1934).
Gay Hunter (London: Heinemann, 1934).

Secondary reading
Campbell, Ian, 'Chris Caledonia: the search for an identity', *SLJ* 1(2) (Aberdeen: Association for Scottish Literary Studies, 1974), pp. 45–57.

—, *Lewis Grassic Gibbon* (Edinburgh: Scottish Academic Press, 1985).

—, 'Lewis Grassic Gibbon and the Mearns', *A Sense of Place: Studies in Scottish Local History*, ed. Graeme Cruikshank (Edinburgh: Scotland's Cultural Heritage, 1988), pp. 15–26.

Gifford, Douglas, *Neil M. Gunn and Lewis Grassic Gibbon* (Edinburgh: Oliver & Boyd, 1983).

Malcolm, William, *A Blasphemer and Reformer: a study of James Leslie Mitchell/Lewis Grassic Gibbon* (Aberdeen: Aberdeen University Press, 1984).

Munro, Ian S., *Leslie Mitchell: Lewis Grassic Gibbon* (Edinburgh and London: Oliver & Boyd, 1966).

Murray, Isobel, 'Action and narrative stance in *A Scots Quair*', *Literature of the North*, eds David Hewitt and Michael Spiller (Aberdeen: Aberdeen University Press, 1983), pp. 109–20.

Murray, Isobel, and Tait, Bob, 'Lewis Grassic Gibbon: *A Scots Quair*', *Ten Modern Scottish Novels* (Aberdeen: Aberdeen University Press, 1984), pp. 10–31.

Tange, Hanne, ' "Scotland Improper"? How the nationalist landscape failed Grassic Gibbon', *Odd Alliances: Scottish Studies in European Contexts*, eds Neil McMillan and Kirsten Stirling (Glasgow: Cruithne Press, 1999).

Young, Douglas F., *Beyond the Sunset: a study of James Leslie Mitchell* (Aberdeen: Impulse Publications, 1973).

—, *Lewis Grassic Gibbon's 'Sunset Song'* (Aberdeen: Association for Scottish Literary Studies, 1986).

ERIC LINKLATER
Publications to 1945. For later titles see the bibliography to Section 6.

White Maa's Saga (London: Cape, 1929).
Poet's Pub (London: Cape, 1929).
Juan in America (London: Cape, 1931).
The Men of Ness (London: Cape, 1932).
Magnus Merriman (London: Cape, 1934).
Ripeness is All (London: Cape, 1935).
God Likes them Plain: short stories (London: Cape, 1935).
Juan in China (London: Cape, 1937).
The Sailor's Holiday (London: Cape, 1937).
The Impregnable Women (London: Cape, 1938).
Judas: a novel (London: Cape, 1939).
The Man on my Back: an autobiography (London: Macmillan, 1941).
The Wind on the Moon: a story for children (London: Macmillan, 1944).

Secondary reading
Linklater's autobiographies are listed above and in the bibliography to Section 6.

Parnell, Michael, *Eric Linklater: a Critical Biography* (London: Murray, 1984).

Ruben Valdes Miyares, ' "The Returning Sun": Eric Linklater's metafiction of the Scottish literary renaissance', *Odd Alliances: Scottish Studies in European Contexts*, eds Neil McMillan and Kirsten Stirling (Glasgow: Cruithne Press, 1999).

Rutherford, Andrew, 'Eric Linklater as comic novelist', *Literature of the North*, eds David Hewitt and Michael Spiller (Aberdeen: Aberdeen University Press, 1983), pp. 149–61.

Chapter 33: James Bridie and the Scottish theatre

There is a lack of published drama for this period, which explains why dramatists with many performed plays to their credit seem under-represented here. Some additional listings are placed here, rather than in Chapter 36, 'Widening the Range'. A useful starting point is *Twentieth-Century Scottish Drama: An Anthology*, eds Cairns Craig and Randall Stevenson (Edinburgh: Canongate, 2001), which contains the following plays; Barrie's *Mary Rose*, Corrie's *In Time o' Strife*, McLellan's *The Saxt*, Bridie's *Mr Bolfry*, Lamont Stewart's *Men Should Weep*, McMillan's *The Bevellers*, Campbell's *The Jesuit*,

Lochhead's *Mary Queen of Scots Got her Head Chopped Off*, Byrne's *Your Cheating Heart*, Glover's *Bondagers* and Hannan's *Shining Souls*.

BACKGROUND READING

Bannister, Winifred, *James Bridie and His Theatre: A Study of James Bridie's Personality, His Stage Plays and His Work for the Foundation of a Scottish National Theatre* (London: Rockliff, 1955).

Barlow, Priscilla, *Wise Enough to Play the Fool: a biography of Duncan Macrae* (Edinburgh: John Donald, 1996).

Bennet, Susan, 'Debts and Directions: The Place of Robert McLellan's *The Changeling*', *SLJ* 19(1) (Aberdeen: Association for Scottish Literary Studies, 1992), pp. 28–34.

Bold, Alan, *Modern Scottish Literature* (London: Longman, 1983).

Booth, Michael R., and Kaplan, Joel H. (eds), *Edwardian Theatre: Essays on Performance and the Stage* (Cambridge: Cambridge University Press, 1996).

Campbell, Donald, *Playing for Scotland: A History of the Scottish Stage, 1715–1965* (Edinburgh: Mercat Press, 1996).

—, 'A Sense of Community: Robert McLellan: An Appreciation', *Chapman* 8–9 (43–44) (Edinburgh: Chapman Publications, 1986), pp. 35–41.

—, *A Brighter Sunshine: A Hundred Years of the Edinburgh Royal Lyceum* (Edinburgh: Polygon, 1983).

Demastes, William, and Kelly, Katherine E. (eds), *British Playwrights, 1860–1956: A Research and Production Sourcebook* (Westport, CT: Greenwood, 1996).

Findlay, Bill (ed.), *A History of Scottish Theatre* (Edinburgh: Polygon, 1998).

Holledge, Julie, *Innocent Flowers: Women in the Edwardian Theatre* (London: Virago, 1981).

Hutchison, David, *The Modern Scottish Theatre* (Glasgow: Molendinar Press, 1977).

—, 'Scottish drama, 1900–1950', *The History of Scottish Literature vol. IV, Twentieth Century*, ed. Cairns Craig (Aberdeen: Aberdeen University Press, 1987), pp. 163–77.

—, '1900 to 1950', *A History of Scottish Theatre*, ed. Bill Findlay (Edinburgh: Polygon, 1998), pp. 207–52.

Jack, R. D. S., 'Barrie as Journey-Dramatist: A Study of "Walker London"', *SSL* 22 (Columbia: University of South Carolina, 1987), pp. 60–77.

Low, John Thomas, 'Mid Twentieth Century Drama in Lowland Scots', *Scotland and the Lowland Tongue: Studies in the Language and Literature of Lowland Scotland* (Aberdeen: Aberdeen University Press, 1983), pp. 170–94.

Michie, James, 'A Question of Success', *English* 17 (London: Oxford University Press, 1968), pp. 48–52.

Osborn, Margaret, 'The Concept of Imagination in Edwardian Drama', *Dissertation Abstracts* 28 (1967), p. 1443A.

Smith, Donald, '1950–1995', *A History of Scottish Theatre*, ed. Bill Findlay (Edinburgh: Polygon, 1998), pp. 253–308.

Stevenson, Randall, 'Scottish theatre, 1950–1980', *The History of Scottish Literature vol. IV, Twentieth Century*, ed. Cairns Craig (Aberdeen: Aberdeen University Press, 1987), pp. 349–67.

Trewin, J. C., *The Edwardian Theatre* (Oxford: Blackwell, 1976).

Wilson, A. E., *Edwardian Theatre* (London: Barker, 1951).

Wright, Allen, 'Kelvinside, Kirriemuir, and the Kailyard', *Chapman* 55–56 (Edinburgh: Chapman Publications, 1989), pp. 134–7.

SOME INDIVIDUAL PLAYWRIGHTS

Since the publication of dramatic works is sporadic, the following listings include a selection of the published work of dramatists additional to those mentioned in the text.

WILLIAM ARCHER
The Green Goddess: A Play in Four Acts (New York: Knopf, 1921).
Three Plays (London: Constable, 1927).

ROBERT BAIN
James the First of Scotland (Glasgow: Maclehose, Jackson, 1921).
Finela: A Tragedy of the Mearns (Glasgow: Brown, Son & Ferguson, 1940).

GEORGE BLAKE
The Mother: A Play in Two Scenes (Glasgow: Walter Wilson, 1921).
Clyde Built: A Play in Three Acts (Glasgow: Wilson, 1922).
The Weaker Vessel: A Play in One Act (Edinburgh: Porpoise Press, 1923).

JOHN H. BONE
The Crystal Set (London and Glasgow: Gowans & Gray, 1924).
The Loudspeaker: A Comedy in One Act (London and Glasgow: Gowans & Gray, 1927).
The Aerial: A Comedy in One Act (Glasgow: Wilson, 1932).
The Wholesale: A Scottish Comedy (Glasgow: Bone & Hulley, 1934).

GORDON BOTTOMLEY
Gruach (1923), in *Britain's Daughter: Two Plays* (London: Constable, 1925).
Lyric Plays (London: Constable, 1932)

JOHN BRANDANE
Glenforsa: A Play in One Act, with A. W. Yuill (Glasgow: Gowans & Gray, 1921).
The Change-House: A Play in One Act (Glasgow: Gowans & Gray, 1921).
The Glen is Mine and The Lifting: Two Plays of the Hebrides (London: Constable, 1925).
The Treasure Ship, Rory Aforesaid, The Happy War: Three Plays (London: Constable, 1928).
The Inn of Adventure, Heather Gentry: Two Comedies (London: Constable, 1933).
Man of Uz (London: Muller, 1938).

JAMES BRIDIE
The list below is a selection from the work of this prolific writer; see Crawford's *Literature in twentieth-century Scotland* for fuller lists, and also fiction lists.

The Sunlight Sonata (London: Constable, 1928).
The Anatomist and Other Plays (London: Constable, 1930).
Jonah and the Whale (London: Constable, 1932).
The Pardoner's Tale, in *The Switchback, The Pardoner's Tale, The Sunlight Sonata* (London: Constable, 1932).
A Sleeping Clergyman (London: Constable, 1933).
Tobias and the Angel (London: Constable, 1934).
Colonel Wotherspoon and Other Plays (London: Constable, 1934).
Marriage is No Joke (London: Constable, 1934).
The Black Eye (London: Constable, 1935).
Storm in a Tea-Cup (London: Constable, 1936).

The King of Nowhere and Other Plays (London: Constable, 1938).
Susannah and the Elders and Other Plays (London: Constable, 1940).
Mr. Bolfry (London: Constable, 1943).
Plays for Plain People (London: Constable, 1944).
Daphne Laureola (London: Constable, 1949).
John Knox and Other Plays (London: Constable, 1949).
Mr. Gillie (London: Constable, 1950).

Secondary reading

Cameron, Alasdair, 'Bridie: The Scottish Playwright', *Chapman* 55–56 (Edinburgh: Chapman Publications, 1989), pp. 124–32.
Greene, Anne D., 'Bridie's Concept of the Master Experimenter', *SSL* 2 (Columbia: University of South Carolina, 1964), pp. 96–110.
Low, John Thomas, *Doctors, Devils, Saints and Sinners: A Critical Study of the Major Plays of James Bridie* (Edinburgh: Ramsay Head Press, 1991).
Luyben, Helen L., 'Bridie's Last Play', *Modern Drama* 5 (1963), pp. 400–14.
—, 'The Dramatic Method of James Bridie', *Education Theatre Journal* 15 (1963), pp. 332–42.
—, 'James Bridie and the Prodigal Son Story', *Modern Drama* 7 (1964), pp. 35–45.
—, *James Bridie: Clown and Philosopher* (Philadelphia: University of Pennsylvania Press, 1965).
Mavor, Ronald, 'Bridie Revisited', *Chapman* 55–56 (Edinburgh: Chapman Publications, 1989), pp. 146–51.
—, *Dr. Mavor and Mr. Bridie* (Edinburgh: Canongate, 1988).
Morgan, Edwin, 'James Bridie's *The Anatomist* and John Byrne's *The Slab Boys*', *Crossing the Border: Essays on Scottish Literature* (Manchester: Carcanet, 1990).
Paterson, Tony, 'James Bridie: Playwright as Impressario', *Chapman* 11 (Edinburgh: Chapman Publications, 1989), pp. 139–45.

DONALD COLQUHOUN
Jean (Glasgow: Gowans & Gray, 1914).

STEWART CONN
The Burning (London: Calder & Boyars, 1973).
The Aquarium; The Man in the Green Muffler; I Didn't Always Live Here (London: John Calder, 1976).
Thistlewood (Todmorden: Woodhouse, 1979).

JOE CORRIE
See Crawford's *Literature in Twentieth Century Scotland* for fuller lists.

In Time o' Strife (1927).
The Shillin'-a-Week Man: A Domestic Comedy (Glasgow: Brown, Son & Ferguson, 1927).
The Home-Coming: A Play in One Act (London: French, 1931).
The Darkness (Glasgow: Brown, Son & Ferguson, 1932).
Robert Burns: A Play (Glasgow: Brown, Son & Ferguson, 1943).
Plays, Poems and Theatre Writings, ed. Linda MacKenny (Edinburgh: 7:84 Publications, 1985).

ARCHIBALD JOSEPH CRONIN
Jupiter Laughs (Boston: Little, Brown, 1940).

'GORDON DAVIOT' (ELIZABETH MACKINTOSH)
Richard of Bordeaux (London: Gollancz, 1933).
Queen of Scots (London: Gollancz, 1934).
The Laughing Woman (London: Gollancz, 1934).
The Stars Bow Down (London: Duckworth, 1939).
Leith Sands, and Other Short Plays (London: Duckworth, 1946).
Plays, 3 vols (London: Peter Davies, 1953–4).

JOHN ALEXANDER FERGUSON
Campbell of Kilmhor: a Play in One Act (Glasgow: Gowans & Gray, 1915).
The Scarecrow: A Hallowe'en Fantasy in One Act (London and Glasgow: Gowans & Gray, 1922).

MORLAND GRAHAM
C'est la Guerre: A Play in One Act (Glasgow: Scots Magazine, 1927).
A Maitter o' Money: A Farcical Comedy in One Act (Glasgow: Brown, Son & Ferguson, 1928).
The Hoose wi' the Golden Windies: A Play in One Act (Glasgow: Brown, Son & Ferguson, 1931).

NEIL MILLER GUNN
Back Home (Glasgow: Wilson, 1932).
Choosing a Play (Edinburgh: Porpoise Press, 1938).
Old Music (London: Nelson, 1939).
Net Results (London: Nelson, 1939).

IAN HAY
A Safety Match (London: French, 1927).
The Happy Ending: A Play in Three Acts (London: French, 1927).
A Blank Cartridge: A Farce (London: French, 1928).
Housemaster: A Comedy in Three Acts (London: French, 1938).
The Fourpenny Box: A Play in One Act (London: French, 1947).

ERIC LINKLATER
The Devil's in the News (London: Cape, 1934).
Crisis in Heaven: An Elysian Comedy (London: Macmillan, 1944).
Two Comedies (London: Macmillan, 1950).
The Mortimer Touch (London: French, 1952).
Breakspear in Gascony (London: Macmillan, 1958).

ROBERT MCLEISH
The Gorbals Story, ed. Linda MacKenny (Edinburgh: 7:84 Publications, 1985).

ROBERT MCLELLAN
Jeddart Justice: A Border Comedy (Glasgow: Bone & Hulley, 1934).
The Changeling: A Border Comedy in One Act (Edinburgh: Porpoise Press, 1938).
Toom Byres: A Comedy of the Scottish Borders in Three Acts (Glasgow: Maclellan, 1947).
The Cailleach: A Play in One Act (Glasgow: Donaldson, 1948).
Torwatletie, or the Apothecary: A Comedy of the Scottish Borders in Three Acts (Glasgow: Maclellan, 1950).

The Hypocrite (London: Calder & Boyars, 1970).
Jamie the Saxt: A Historical Comedy, eds Ian Campbell and Ronald D. S. Jack (London: Calder & Boyars, 1970).
Collected Plays (London: Calder, 1981).

Secondary reading
Hutchison, David, '1900–1950', *A History of Scottish Theatre*, ed. Bill Findlay (Edinburgh: Polygon, 1998), pp. 207–52.

GEORGE RESTON MALLOCH
Arabella: A Play in Three Acts (London: Stephen Swift, 1912).
The House of the Queen (Montrose: Scottish Poetry Bookship, 1923).
Thomas the Rhymer (Monstrose: Scottish Poetry Bookship, 1924).
Soutarness Water: A Play in Three Acts (Glasgow: Gowans & Gray, 1927).
Prologue to Flodden (Stirling: Eneas Mackay, 1936).

RONALD MAVOR
Roger-Not So Jolly: A Drama in One Act, with James Bridie (London: French, 1937).

ROBINS MILLAR
The Shawlie: A Play in Three Acts (London & Glasgow: Gowans & Gray, 1924).
Thunder in the Air: A Play in Three Acts (London: French, 1928).
Colossus: A Play in One Act (Edinburgh: Porpoise Press, 1938).

NAOMI MITCHISON
The Price of Freedom, with Lewis E. Gielgud (London: Cape, 1931).
As It Was in the Beginning, with Lewis E. Gielgud (London: Cape, 1939).
Spindrift, with Denis Macintosh (London: French, 1951).

GRAHAM MOFFAT
Bunty Pulls the Strings (1911).

LEFT THEATRES AND GLASGOW UNITY THEATRE
Barke, James, *Major Operation: the play of the novel* (Glasgow: Maclellan, 1943).
Carroll, Paul Vincent, *Three Plays: The White Steed; Things that are Caesar's; The Strings My Lord are False* (London: Macmillan, 1944).
Corrie, Joe, *Plays, Poems and Theatre Writings*, ed. Linda Mackenney (Edinburgh: 7:84, 1985).
McLeish, Robert, *The Gorbals Story*, ed. Linda Mackenney (Edinburgh: 7:84, 1985).
McLellan, Robert, *Jamie the Saxt*, eds Ian Campbell and R. D. S. Jack (London: Calder & Boyers, 1970).
Stewart, Ena Lamont, *Men Should Weep*, ed. Linda Mackenney (Edinburgh: 7:84, 1986).

Secondary reading
Allen, Douglas, 'Culture and the Scottish labour movement', *Journal of Scottish Labour History Society* 14 (Edinburgh: Scottish Labour Historical Society, 1980), pp. 30–9.
—, 'Glasgow Workers' Theatre Group and the methodology of theatre studies', *Theatre Quarterly* 7(27) (1980), pp. 45–54.

Caesar, Adrian, *Dividing Lines: poetry, class and ideology* (Manchester: Manchester University Press, 1991).

Chambers, Colin, *Unity* (London: Lawrence & Wishart, 1989).

Clark, Jon, et al. (eds), *Culture and Crisis in Britain in the 1930s* (London: Lawrence & Wishart, 1979).

Findlay, Bill, '7:84's Scottish popular plays series', *Radical Scotland* (Edinburgh: Radical Scotland Publications, 1985), pp. 30–1.

—, 'Fun in the Gorbals', *Radical Scotland* (Edinburgh: Radical Scotland Publications, 1986), p. 31.

Hill, John, 'Towards a Scottish People's Theatre: the rise and fall of Glasgow Unity', *Theatre Quarterly* 7(27) (1977), pp. 61–70.

—, 'Glasgow Unity Theatre: the search for a "Scottish People's Theatre"', *New Edinburgh Review* 40 (Edinburgh, 1978), pp. 27–31.

—, '"Scotland doesnae mean much tae Glesca": some notes on *The Gorbals Story*', *Scotch Reels*, ed. Colin McArthur (London: BFI, 1982), pp. 100–11.

Hutchison, David, 'Scottish drama, 1900–1950', *The History of Scottish Literature vol. IV, Twentieth Century*, ed. Cairns Craig (Aberdeen: Aberdeen University Press, 1992), pp. 163–77.

Mackenney, Linda, *The Activities of Popular Dramatists and Drama Groups in Scotland, 1900–1952* (Lewiston, NY: Edwin Mellen Press, 2000).

Scullion, Adrienne, 'Feminine pleasures and masculine indignities: gender and community in Scottish drama', *Gendering the Nation*, ed. Christopher Whyte (Edinburgh: Edinburgh University Press, 1995), pp. 169–204.

—, 'Men Should Weep – a production history'; 'Men Should Weep – the social context' and 'Men Should Weep – gender', *A Study Guide to Men Should Weep* (Glasgow: TAG, 1996).

Chapter 34: The Poetry of Sorley Maclean

Dàin do Eimhir agus Dàin Eile (Glasgow: Maclellan, 1943).

Four Points of a Saltire: The Poetry of Sorley MacLean, George Campbell Hay, William Neill, Stuart MacGregor (Edinburgh: Reprographia, 1970).

Reothairt is Contraigh: Taghadh de Dhàin 1932–72/Spring Tide and Neap Tide: Selected Poems 1932–72 (Edinburgh: Canongate, 1977).

O Choille gu Bearradh/From Wood to Ridge: Collected Poems in Gaelic and English (Manchester: Carcanet, 1989).

Ris a' Bhruthaich: The Criticism and Prose Writings of Somhairle MacGill-eain, ed. William Gillies (Stornoway: Acair, 1985).

Secondary reading

Gillies, William (ed.), *Ris a' Bhruthaich: The Criticism and Prose Writings of Somhairle MacGill-eain* (Stornoway: Acair, 1985).

Hendry, Joy, 'An Interview with Sorley MacLean', *Chapman* 66 (Edinburgh: Chapman Publications, 1991), pp. 1–8.

MacLean, Sorley, 'Par Lui Meme', *PN Review* 16(3) (17) (1989), pp. 15–18.

McCaughey, Terence, 'Somhairle MacGill-eain', *The History of Scottish Literature Vol. IV, Twentieth Century*, ed. Cairns Craig (Aberdeen: Aberdeen University Press, 1987), pp. 147–61.

McClure, J. Derrick (ed.), 'Douglas Young and Sorley MacLean', *Gaelic and Scots in Harmony* (Glasgow: University of Glasgow Press, 1988), pp. 136–48.

Montague, John, 'A Northern Vision', *The Pleasures of Gaelic Poetry*, ed. Sean MacReamoinn (London: Allen Lane (Penguin), 1982), pp. 163–74.

READING LISTS

Nicholson, Angus, 'An Interview with Sorley MacLean', *SSL* 14 (Columbia: University of South Carolina, 1980), pp. 23–36.

Nicholson, Colin, 'Poetry of Displacement: Sorley MacLean and His Writing', *SSL* 22 (Columbia: University of South Carolina, 1987), pp. 1–9.

Ross, R. J., and Hendry, J. (eds), *Sorley MacLean: Critical Essays* (Edinburgh: Scottish Academic Press, 1986).

Stoddart, John, 'Sorley MacLean a'r 'Farddonaieth Aeleg Newydd', *Y Traethodydd* 133 (1978), pp. 191–203.

Van Eerde, John, and Williamson, Robert, 'Sorley MacLean: A Bard and Scottish Gaelic', *World Literature Today* 52 (Norman: University of Oklahoma Press, 1978), pp. 229–32.

ANTHOLOGIES

Black, Ronald I. M. (ed.), *An Tuil: Anthology of 20th Century Scottish Gaelic Verse* (Edinburgh: Polygon, 1999).

Davitt, Michael, and MacDhòmhnaill, Iain (eds), *Sruth na Maoile: Modern Gaelic Poetry from Scotland and Ireland* (Edinburgh: Canongate; Dublin: Coiscéim, 1993).

MacAulay, Donald (ed.), *Nua-bhàrdachd Ghàidhlig/Modern Scottish Gaelic Poems: A Bilingual Anthology* (Edinburgh: Southside, 1976).

Macleod, Mary, *The Gaelic Songs of Mary MacLeod*, ed. J. Carmichael Watson (London: Blackie, 1934; Edinburgh: Scottish Gaelic Texts Society, 1965).

MacThòmais, Ruaraidh (ed.), *Bàrdachd na Roinn-Eòrpa an Gàidhlig* (Glasgow: Gairm, 1990).

Whyte, Christopher (ed.), *An Aghaidh na Sìorraidheachd: Ochdnar Bhàrd Gàidhlig/In the Face of Eternity: Eight Gaelic Poets* (Edinburgh: Polygon, 1991).

CRITICISM

Bateman, Meg, 'Women's Writing in Scottish Gaelic Since 1750', *A History of Scottish Women's Writing*, eds Douglas Gifford and Dorothy McMillan (Edinburgh: Edinburgh University Press, 1997), pp. 659–76.

Black, Ronald, 'Thunder, Renaissance and Flowers: Gaelic Poetry in the Twentieth Century', *The History of Scottish Literature Vol. IV, Twentieth Century*, ed. Cairns Craig (Aberdeen: Aberdeen University Press, 1987), pp. 195–215.

Douglas, S., 'Links with Gaelic Tradition Found in the Story Traditions of Perthshire Travelling People', *Scottish Language* 5 (Aberdeen: Association for Scottish Literary Studies, 1986), pp. 15–22.

Gow, Carol, 'An Interview with Iain Crichton Smith', *SLJ* 17(2) (Aberdeen: Association for Scottish Literary Studies, 1990), pp. 43–57.

MacDonald, Kenneth D., 'Glasgow and Gaelic Writing', *Transactions of the Gaelic Society of Inverness* 57 (1993), pp. 395–428.

MacDonald, Roderick, 'Some Present-Day Trends in Gaelic Writing in Scotland', *Scando-Slavica* 29 (1996), pp. 85–94.

Mackinnon, K., 'The Scottish Gaelic Speech-Community: Some Social Perspectives', *Scottish Language* 5 (Aberdeen: Association for Scottish Literary Studies, 1986), pp. 65–84.

Smith, Iain Crichton, 'The Internationalism of Twentieth-Century Gaelic Poetry', *SLJ* 18(1) (Aberdeen: Association for Scottish Literary Studies, 1991), pp. 82–6.

—, 'Recent Gaelic Poetry', *Scottish Language* 8 (Aberdeen: Association for Scottish Literary Studies, 1989), pp. 21–33.

Thomson, Derick S., *The Companion to Gaelic Scotland* (Oxford: Blackwell, 1983).

—, *Gaelic and Scots in Harmony* (Glasgow: Glasgow University Press, 1988).

— (ed.), *Gaelic in Scotland=Gaidhlig ann an Albainn: A Blueprint for Official and Private Initiatives* (Glasgow: Gairm, 1976).

—, 'Gaelic Literary Interactions with Scots and English Work: A Survey', *Scottish Language* 5 (Aberdeen: Association for Scottish Literary Studies, 1986), pp. 1–14.

—, 'The Gaelic Poetry', *Iain Crichton Smith: Critical Essays*, ed. Colin Nicholson (Edinburgh: Edinburgh University Press, 1992), pp. 1–10.

—, *An Introduction to Gaelic Poetry* (Edinburgh: Edinburgh University Press, 1990).

—, *The New Verse in Scottish Gaelic: A Structural Analysis* (Dublin: University College, Dublin, 1974).

—, 'Poetry in Scottish Gaelic, 1945–1992', *Poetry in the British Isles: Non-Metropolitan Perspectives*, eds Hans-Werner Ludwig and Lothar Fietz (Cardiff: University of Wales Press, 1995), pp. 157–72.

—, 'Scottish Gaelic Poetry: A Many-Faceted Tradition', *SLJ* 18(2) (Aberdeen: Association for Scottish Literary Studies, 1991), pp. 5–26.

Whyte, Christopher, 'The Cohesion of 'Dàin do Eimhir', *SLJ* 17(1) (Aberdeen: Association for Scottish Literary Studies, 1990), pp. 46–70.

Withers, Charles W. J., 'Gaelic in Glasgow, c. 1723–1981', *Scottish Language* 8 (Aberdeen: Association for Scottish Literary Studies, 1989), pp. 1–20.

—, *Gaelic in Scotland, 1698–1981: The Geographical History of a Language* (Edinburgh: J. Donald, 1984).

Chapter 35: The Epic Fiction of Neil Gunn

Publications to 1945. For later titles see the bibliography to Section 6.

The Grey Coast (London: Cape, 1926).
Hidden Doors (Edinburgh: Porpoise Press, 1929).
Morning Tide (Edinburgh: Porpoise Press, 1930).
The Lost Glen (Edinburgh: Porpoise Press, 1932).
Sun Circle (Edinburgh: Porpoise Press, 1933).
Butcher's Broom (Edinburgh: Porpoise Press, 1934).
Highland River (Edinburgh: Porpoise Press, 1937).
Wild Geese Overhead (London: Faber, 1939).
Second Sight (London: Faber, 1940).
The Silver Darlings (London: Faber, 1941).
Young Art and Old Hector (London: Faber, 1942).
The Serpent (London: Faber, 1943).
The Green Isle of the Great Deep (London: Faber, 1944).
The Key of the Chest (London: Faber, 1945).

Secondary reading

Gunn's autobiography and *Selected Letters* are listed in the bibliography to Section 6.

Burns, J., *A Celebration of the Light: Zen in the Novels of Neil Gunn* (Edinburgh: Canongate, 1988).
Gifford, Douglas, *Neil M. Gunn and Lewis Grassic Gibbon* (Edinburgh: Oliver & Boyd, 1983).
Gunn, Diarmid, and Murray, Isobel (eds), *Neil Gunn's Country: Essays in Celebration of Neil Gunn* (Edinburgh: Chambers, 1991).
Hart, F. R., and Pick, J. B., *Neil M. Gunn: A Highland Life* (London: John Murray, 1981).
Herbert, W. N., and Price, R. (eds), *The Anarchy of Light: Neil Gunn, a celebration* (Dundee: Gairfish, 1991).

McCulloch, Margery, *The Novels of Neil M. Gunn: A Critical Study* (Edinburgh: Scottish Academic Press, 1987).

Morrison, David (ed.), *Essays on Neil M. Gunn* (Thurso: Caithness Books, 1971).

Murray, Isobel, and Tait, Bob, 'Neil Gunn: *The Silver Darlings*', *Ten Modern Scottish Novels* (Aberdeen: Aberdeen University Press, 1984).

Price, Richard, *The Fabulous Matter of Fact: The Poetics of Neil M. Gunn* (Edinburgh: Edinburgh University Press, 1991).

Scott, Alexander, and Gifford, Douglas (eds), *Neil M. Gunn: The Man and the Writer* (Edinburgh: Blackwood, 1973).

Stokoe, C. J. L., *A Bibliography of the Works of Neil M. Gunn* (Aberdeen: Aberdeen University Press, 1987).

Chapter 36: Widening the Range: Fiction

The following lists give only major works by the authors highlighted in the text. Authors listed elsewhere in the bibliography are indicated.

DOT ALLAN
The Syrens (London: Heinemann, 1921).
Makeshift (Andrew Melrose, 1928).
The Deans (London: Jarrolds, 1929).
Deepening River (London: Jarrolds, 1932).
Hunger March (London: Hutchinson, 1934).
Mother of Millions (London: Hale, 1953).

JAMES BARKE
The World his Pillow (London: Collins, 1933).
The Wild Macraes (London: Collins, 1934).
The End of the High Bridge (London: Collins, 1935).
Major Operation (London: Collins, 1936).
The Land of the Leal (London: Collins, 1939).
The Green Hills Far Away [autobiography] (London: Collins, 1940).
Immortal Memory [five novels on the life of Burns] (London: Collins, 1946–54).
Bonnie Jean (London: Collins, 1959).

J. M. BARRIE
See reading list for Chapter 27, 'Widening the Range', Section 4.

GEORGE BLAKE
Mince Collop Close (Grant Richards, 1923).
The Wild Men (Grant Richards, 1925).
The Path of Glory (London: Constable, 1929).
The Shipbuilders (London: Faber & Faber, 1935).
Down to the Sea [autobiography] (1937).
The Valiant Heart (London: Collins, 1940).
The Constant Star (London: Collins, 1945).
The Westering Sun (London: Collins, 1946).

And many other novels, most set in Glasgow or Greenock.

JOHN BUCHAN

Publications from 1900. For earlier titles, and for criticism, see the bibliography to Section 4.

The Watcher by the Threshold, and other tales (Edinburgh: Blackwood, 1902).
A Lodge in the Wilderness (Edinburgh: Blackwood, 1906).
Prester John (Nelson, 1910).
The Thirty-Nine Steps (Edinburgh: Blackwood, 1915).
The Power-House (Edinburgh: Blackwood, 1916).
Greenmantle (London: Hodder & Stoughton, 1916).
Mr Standfast (London: Hodder & Stoughton, 1919).
Huntingtower (London: Hodder & Stoughton, 1922).
Midwinter (London: Hodder & Stoughton, 1923).
The Three Hostages (London: Hodder & Stoughton, 1924).
John Macnab (London: Hodder & Stoughton, 1925).
The Dancing Floor (London: Hodder & Stoughton, 1926).
Witch Wood (London: Hodder & Stoughton, 1927).
The Runagates Club (London: Hodder & Stoughton, 1928).
The Courts of the Morning (London: Hodder & Stoughton, 1929).
Castle Gay (London: Hodder & Stoughton, 1930).
The Blanket of the Dark (London: Hodder & Stoughton, 1931).
The Gap in the Curtain (London: Hodder & Stoughton, 1932).
The Free Fishers (London: Hodder & Stoughton, 1934).
The House of the Four Winds (London: Hodder & Stoughton, 1935).
The Island of Sheep (London: Hodder & Stoughton, 1936).
Memory Hold the Door [autobiography] (London: Hodder & Stoughton, 1940).
Sick Heart River (London: Hodder & Stoughton, 1941).

JOHN COCKBURN
Tenement: a novel of Glasgow life (Edinburgh: Blackwood, 1925).

ROBERT CRAIG
Lucy Flockhart (London: John Murray, 1931).
O People! (London: John Murray, 1932).
Campbell of Duisk (London: John Murray, 1933).

A. J. CRONIN
Hatter's Castle (London: Gollancz, 1931).
Three Loves (London: Gollancz, 1932).
The Stars Look Down (London: Gollancz, 1935).
The Citadel (London: Gollancz, 1937).
The Keys of the Kingdom (London: Gollancz, 1942).
The Green Years (London: Gollancz, 1945).
Shannon's Way (London: Gollancz, 1948).
Adventures in Two Worlds [autobiography] (London: Gollancz, 1952).
A Song of Sixpence (London: Gollancz, 1964).

Secondary reading
Salwar, D., *A. J. Cronin* (Boston: G. K. Hall, 1985).

CATHERINE GAVIN
Clyde Valley (Arthur Barker, 1938).
The Hostile Shore (London: Methuen, 1940).
The Black Milestone (London: Methuen, 1941).
The Mountain of Light (London: Methuen, 1944).

Also historical novels, a World War I quartet and a French Resistance trilogy.

Secondary reading
Alexander, Flora, 'The novels of Catherine Gavin', *Northern Visions*, ed. David Hewitt (East Linton: Tuckwell Press, 1995), pp. 166–79.

R. B. CUNNINGHAME GRAHAM
Thirteen Stories (London: Heinemann, 1900).
Scottish Stories (London: Duckworth, 1914).
Selected Writings of Cunninghame Graham, ed. C. Watts (Cambridge: Cambridge University Press, 1981).
The Scottish Sketches of Cunninghame Graham, ed. J. Walker (Edinburgh: Scottish Academic Press, 1982).

Secondary reading
MacDiarmid, Hugh, *Cunninghame Graham: A Centenary Study* (Glasgow: Caledonian Press, 1952).
Maitland, A., *Robert and Gabriela Cunningham Graham* (Edinburgh: Blackwood, 1983).
Tschiffely, A. F., *Don Roberto* (London and Toronto: Heinemann, 1937).
Watts, C., and Davies, L., *Cunninghame Graham: A Critical Biography* (Cambridge: Cambridge University Press, 1979).

TOM HANLIN
Once in Every Lifetime (Nicholson & Watson, 1945).
Yesterday Will Return (Nicholson & Watson, 1946).
Miracle at Cardenrigg (London: Gollancz, 1949).

Secondary reading
Macpherson, Hugh, 'Tom Hanlin', *Scottish Book Collector* (Edinburgh, 1989), pp. 19–20.
Malzahn, Manfred, 'Pithead metaphysics: Tom Hanlin's *Once in Every Lifetime*', *ScotLit* (Aberdeen: Association for Scottish Literary Studies, 1992), pp. 3–4.

JOHN MACDOUGALL HAY
Gillespie (London: Constable, 1914).
Barnacles (London: Constable, 1916).

Secondary reading
Spring, Ian, 'Determinism in John MacDougall Hay's *Gillespie*', *SLJ* 6 (Aberdeen: Association for Scottish Literary Studies, 1979), pp. 55–68.
Tait, Bob, and Murray, Isobel, 'Introduction' to *Gillespie* (Edinburgh: Canongate, 1979).

DAVID LINDSAY
A Voyage to Arcturus (London: Methuen, 1920).
The Haunted Woman (London: Methuen, 1922).
Sphinx (John Long, 1923).
Adventures of Monsieur de Mailly (Andrew Melrose, 1926).
Devil's Tor (London: Putnam, 1932).
The Violet Apple and *The Witch* (Chicago: Chicago Review Press, 1976).

Secondary reading
Sellin, Bernard, *The Life and Works of David Lindsay* (Cambridge: Cambridge University Press, 1981).
Wilson, Colin, et al., *The Strange Genius of David Lindsay* (London: John Baker, 1970).

'FIONN MACCOLLA' (TOM MACDONALD)
See also Section 6.

The Albannach (London: John Heritage, 1932).
And the Cock Crew (Glasgow: William Maclellan, 1945).
At the Sign of the Clenched Fist (Edinburgh, 1967).
Too Long in this Condition [autobiography] (Thurso: Caithness Books, 1975).
The Ministers (London: Souvenir Press, 1979).
Move Up, John (Edinburgh: Canongate, 1994).

Secondary reading
Morrison, David (ed.), *Essays on Fionn MacColla* (Thurso: Caithness Books, 1973).
Murray, Isobel and Tait, Bob, 'Fionn MacColla: *And the Cock Crew*', *Ten Modern Scottish Novels* (Aberdeen: Aberdeen University Press, 1984), pp. 55–77.

PATRICK MACGILL
Children of the Dead End (London: Herbert Jenkins, 1914).
The Rat-Pit (London: Herbert Jenkins, 1915).

COMPTON MACKENZIE
Sinister Street (London: Secker, 1913).
Water on the Brain (London: Cassell, 1933).
The Four Winds of Love [6 vols] (London: Rich & Cowan, Chatto & Windus, 1937–45).
The Monarch of the Glen (London: Chatto & Windus, 1941).
Keep the Home Guard Turning (London: Chatto & Windus, 1943).
Whisky Galore (London: Chatto & Windus, 1947).
Hunting the Fairies (London: Chatto & Windus, 1949).
Thin Ice (London: Chatto & Windus, 1956).
My Life and Times [autobiography; 10 vols] (London: Chatto & Windus, 1963–71).

Secondary reading
Linklater, Andro, *Compton Mackenzie: a Life* (London: Chatto & Windus, 1987).
Robertson, L., *Compton Mackenzie: an appraisal of his literary work* (London: Richards Press, 1954).

JOHN MCNEILLIE
Publications to 1945. For later titles, written as Ian Niall, see the bibliography to Section 6.

The Wigtown Ploughman (1939).

IAN MACPHERSON
Shepherd's Calendar (London: Cape, 1931).
Land of our Fathers (London: Cape, 1933).
Pride in the Valley (London: Cape, 1936).
Wild Harbour (London: Methuen, 1936).

BRUCE MARSHALL
Teacup Terrace (London: Hurst & Blackett, 1926).
Father Malachy's Miracle (London: Heinemann, 1931).
The Uncertain Glory (London: Constable, 1935).
Yellow Tapers for Paris (London: Constable, 1943).
All Glorious Within (London: Constable, 1944).
George Brown's Schooldays (London: Constable, 1946).
The Red Danube (London: Constable, 1947).
The Fair Bride (London: Constable, 1953).
The Black Oxen (London: Constable, 1972).

EDWIN MUIR
See the bibliography for Chapter 29 and *Secondary reading*.
The Marionette (London: Hogarth Press, 1927).
The Three Brothers (London: Heinemann, 1931).
Poor Tom (London: Dent, 1932).

FREDERICK NIVEN
Ellen Adair (Eveleigh Nash, 1913).
The Justice of the Peace (Eveleigh Nash, 1914).
A Tale that is Told (London: Collins, 1920).
The Three Marys (London: Collins, 1930).
Mrs Barry (London: Collins, 1933).
The Flying Years (London: Collins, 1935).
Old Soldier (London: Collins, 1936).
The Staff at Simson's (London: Collins, 1937).
Coloured Spectacles [autobiography] (London: Collins, 1938).
Mine Inheritance (London: Collins, 1940).
The Transplanted (London: Collins, 1944).

Secondary reading

New, W. H., 'Frederick John Niven', *Dictionary of Literary Biography*, vol. 92 (Detroit: Gale, 1990), pp. 271–5.

Walker, John, ' "Scotland is a Kingdom of the Mind": the novels of Frederick Niven', *SSL* 24 (Columbia: University of South Carolina, 1989), pp. 92–106.

JOHN MACNAIR REID

Homeward Journey (Porpoise Press, 1934; Edinburgh: Canongate, 1988).
Tobias the Rod (Ilfracombe: Stockwell, 1968).
Judy from Crown Street (Ilfracombe: Stockwell, 1970).

EDWARD SHIELS

Gael over Glasgow (Sheed & Ward, 1937).

GEORGE WODEN

Mungo (London: Hutchinson, 1932).
Othersmith (London: Hutchinson, 1936).

And many other novels, most set in Glasgow.

Poetry

The following lists give only major works by the authors highlighted in the text. Authors listed elsewhere in the bibliography are indicated.

MARION ANGUS

The Lilt and Other Poems (Aberdeen: Wylie, 1922).
The Tinker's Road and Other Verses (London and Glasgow: Gowans & Gray, 1924).
Sun and Candlight (Edinburgh: Porpoise, 1927).
The Singing Lass (Edinburgh: Porpoise, 1929).
The Turn of the Day (Edinburgh: Porpoise, 1931).
Lost Country and Other Verses (Glasgow: Gowans & Gray, 1937).
Selected Poems, ed. Maurice Lindsay (Edinburgh: Serif Books, 1950).

Secondary reading

Caird, Janet, 'The Poetry of Marion Angus', *Cencrastus* 25 (Edinburgh: Cencrastus, 1987), pp. 45–7.

Whyte, Christopher, 'Marion Angus and the Boundaries of Self', *A History of Scottish Women's Writing* (Edinburgh: Edinburgh University Press, 1997).

HELEN BURNESS CRUICKSHANK

Up the Noran Water and Other Scots Poems (London: Methuen, 1934).
The Ponnage Pool (Edinburgh: M. MacDonald, 1968).
Collected Poems (Edinburgh: Reprographia, 1971).
Octobiography (Montrose: Standard Press, 1976).
More Collected Poems (Edinburgh: Gordon Wright, 1978).

READING LISTS

Secondary reading

Caird, Janet, 'The Poetry of Violet Jacob and Helen B. Cruikshank', *Cencrastus* 19 (Edinburgh: Cencrastus Publications, 1985), p. 32.

Lochhead, Marion, 'Feminine Quartet', *Chapman* 27/8 (Edinburgh: Macdonald, 1980).

Porter, Dorothy, 'Scotland's Songstresses', *Cencrastus* 25, 1987.

'ADAM DRINAN' (JOSEPH MACLEOD)

The Ecliptic [A Poem] (London, 1930).

Women of the Happy Island (Glasgow: McLellan, 1944).

ALEXANDER GRAY

Any Man's Life (Oxford: Blackwell, 1924).

Poems (Edinburgh: Porpoise Press, 1925).

Gossip (Edinburgh: Porpoise Press, 1928).

Songs from Heine (Edinburgh: Porpoise Press, 1928).

Arrows: A Book of German Ballads and Folk-Songs Attempted in Scots (Edinburgh: Grant & Murray, 1932).

Robert Burns: Man and Poet (Edinburgh: J. Wilson, 1944).

Selected Poems of Alexander Gray, ed. Maurice Lindsay (Glasgow: Maclellan, 1948).

Four and Forty: A Selection of Danish Ballads Presented in Scots (Edinburgh: Edinburgh University Press, 1954).

A Timorous Civility: A Scots Miscellany (Glasgow: Collins, 1966).

GEORGE CAMPBELL HAY

Fuaran Sleibh (Glasgow: MacGill' Phaglain, 1947).

The Wind on Loch Fyne (Edinburgh: Oliver & Boyd, 1948).

O Na Ceithir Airdean (Edinburgh: Oliver & Boyd, 1952).

Seeker, Reaper (Edinburgh: Saltire Society, 1988).

Collected Poems and Songs of George Campbell Hay (Deòrsa Mac Iain Dheòrsa), ed. Michel Byrne (Edinburgh: Edinburgh University Press, 2000).

VIOLET JACOB

See also fiction lists.

Bonnie Joann and Other Poems (London: John Murray, 1921).

More Songs of Angus (London: Country Life, 1918).

Northern Lights and Other Poems (London: John Murray, 1927).

Songs of Angus (London: John Murray, 1915).

Secondary reading

Caird, Janet, 'The Poetry of Violet Jacob and Helen B. Cruickshank', *Cencrastus* 19 (Edinburgh: Cencrastus, 1984), pp. 32–4.

Hendry, Joy, 'Twentieth-Century Women's Writing: The Nest of Singing Birds', *The History of Scottish Literature Vol. IV, Twentieth Century*, ed. Cairns Craig (Aberdeen: Aberdeen University Press, 1987), pp. 291–310.

WILLIAM JEFFREY

Prometheus Returns, and Other Poems (London: MacDonald, 1921).
The Wise Men Come to Town, and Other Poems (Glasgow: Gowans & Gray, 1923).
The Nymph (Edinburgh: Porpoise Press, 1924).
The Doom of Atlas (London: Gowans & Gray, 1926).
The Lamb of Lomond (Edinburgh: Porpoise Press, 1926).
Mountain Songs (Edinburgh: Porpoise Press, 1928).
The Golden Stag (Oxford: Blackwell, 1932).
Eagle of Coruisk (Oxford: Blackwell, 1933).
Fantasia Written in an Industrial Town (London: Cranley & Day, 1933).
Sea Glimmer (Glasgow: Maclellan, 1947).
Selected poems of William Jeffrey, ed. Alexander Scott (Edinburgh: Serif, 1951).

RODERICK WATSON KERR

Style of Me: Letters of Eula from the U. S. A. (London: Muller, 1945).

JOSEPH LEE

Ballads of Battle (London: J. Murray, 1916).
Work-A-Day Warriors (London: J. Murray, 1917).

CHARLES MURRAY

Hamewith (London: Collins, 1909).
Loch Carron: Sparks from the Peat (London: Murray, 1924).
A Sough o' War (London: Constable, 1917).

Secondary reading

Milton, Colin, 'Modern Poetry in Scotland Before MacDiarmid', *The History of Scottish Literature Vol. IV, Twentieth Century*, ed. Cairns Craig (Aberdeen: Aberdeen University Press, 1992), pp. 1–36.

WILLIAM OGILVIE

Fair Girls and Gray Horses (Sydney: The Bulletin Newspaper Co., 1905).
Whaups o' the Rede: A Ballad of the Border Raiders (Dalbeattie: Fraser, 1909).
The Land We Love (Glasgow: Fraser, 1910).
The Overlander, and Other Verses (Glasgow: Fraser & Asher, 1913).
Hearts of Gold and Other Verses (London: Angus & Robertson, 1913).
Gray Horses (Sydney: Angus & Robertson, 1914).
The Australian, and Other Verses (Sydney: Angus & Robertson, 1916; second edition).
Galloping Shoes (London: Constable, 1922).
My Mither's Aunt and Other Verses (Edinburgh: Porpoise Press, 1926).
A Clean Wind Blowing: Songs of the Out-of-Doors (New York: Smith, 1930).
The Border Poems of Will H. Ogilvie (Hawick: John Murray Hood, 1959).

LEWIS SPENCE

Plumes of Time (London: Allen & Unwin, 1926).
Weirds and Vanities (Edinburgh: Porpoise Press, 1927).

MARY SYMON
Deveron Days (Aberdeen: Wyllie, 1933).

ANDREW YOUNG
The Poetical Works of Andrew Young, eds Edward Lowbury and Alison Young (London: Secker & Warburg, 1985).

SECTION 6: SCOTTISH LITERATURE SINCE 1945

Introductory reading (including reading for Chapter 37)

As always the reader is reminded of the informative websites listed at the beginning of the Further Reading section, especially the developing website maintained by the Departments of Scottish Literature and STELLA at the University of Glasgow at **www.arts.gla.ac.uk/SESLL/ScotLit/bibliography** where more information can be given than is possible here.

For the twentieth century overall, but particularly for the modern period, Robert Crawford's very comprehensive bibliography, *Literature in Twentieth-Century Scotland* (London: British Council, 1995) is probably the most inclusive and helpful single guide to reference works, anthologies, poetry, prose, and drama, and will supplement the introductory listings given below. The following recommendations for further reading are frequently similar to those given in the introduction to reading for Section 5, with the same general histories and main critical and historical texts, especially Cairns Craig's edition of *The History of Scottish Literature Volume IV, Twentieth Century* (Aberdeen: Aberdeen University Press, 1987), Marshall Walker's *Scottish Literature since 1707* (London: Longman, 1998) and Gifford and McMillan's *A History of Scottish Women's Writing* (Edinburgh: Edinburgh University Press, 1997). The major anthologies of poetry (often with very substantial introductions) include those cited in Further General Reading such as Crawford and Imlah, Dunn, Kerrigan and Watson. Scottish poets are put in wider contexts in the stimulating *The Penguin Book of Contemporary British Poetry*, edited by Blake Morrison and Andrew Motion (Harmondsworth: Penguin, 1982).

Daniel O'Rourke's collection *Dream State: The New Scottish Poets* (Edinburgh: Polygon, 1994; new edition, 2001) presents some of the most interesting new voices. The first in-depth study of Scots poetry from Stevenson to the present and from a linguistic perspective is J. Derrick McClure's *Language, Poetry and Nationhood* (East Linton: Tuckwell Press, 2000). Robin Fulton's *Contemporary Scottish Poetry: Individuals and Contexts* (Loanhead: Macdonald, 1974) is still very useful, and Colin Nicholson's *Poem, Purpose and Place: Shaping Identity in Contemporary Scottish Verse* (Edinburgh: Polygon, 1992), provides fourteen interviews with poets from Sorley MacLean to Ron Butlin and Liz Lochhead. *Seven Poets*, edited by Christopher Carrell (Glasgow: Third Eye Centre, 1981), has discussions of major Scottish poets from writers like Neal Ascherson with interviews by Marshall Walker. Gillian Somerville-Arjat and Rebecca Wilson provide similar help in *Sleeping with Monsters: Conversations with Scottish and Irish Women Poets* (Dublin: Wolfhound, 1990) and, straddling poetry and fiction, Bob Tait and Isobel Murray's *Scottish Writers Talking* (East Linton: Tuckwell Press, 1996), with the poets interviewed being MacCaig and Mackay Brown, and the novelists Kesson, McIlvanney and Toulmin. Particularly useful for recent writing is Aileen Christianson and Alison Lumsden's *Contemporary Scottish Women Writers* (Edinburgh: Edinburgh University Press, 2000). A recent valuable collection of essays is edited by Tómas Monterrey in *Contemporary Scottish Literature 1970–2000 (Revista Canaria de Estudios Ingleses)* (Servicio de Publicaciones: Universidad de la Laguna, 2000).

In fiction, the Scottish Arts Council annually published a collection of *Scottish Short Stories* via publisher William Collins/Harper Collins from 1973 to 1994, and from 1995–97 published by Flamingo. A survey of the volumes of these twenty-five years reveals some of the best of Scottish short story writing. An up-to-date introductory anthology of short stories and substantial excerpts from novels is *The Picador Book of Contemporary Fiction*, edited by Peter Kravitz (London: Picador, 1997). Other useful anthologies of poetry and prose include the major anthologies of short stories from Dunn and MacDougall (previously listed); *And Thus Will I Freely Sing: an Anthology of Gay and Lesbian Writing From Scotland*, edited by Toni Davidson (Edinburgh: Polygon, 1989); *Behind the Lines: An Anthology of New Scottish Poetry and Prose* (Glasgow: Third Eye Centre, 1989), and *Undercover: An Anthology of Contemporary Scottish Writers* (Edinburgh: Mainstream, 1993) edited by Colin E. Nicholson and Jane Ogden Smith. For the most recent prose and poetry, readers should consult annual volumes of *New Writing Scotland*, published by the Association for Scottish Literary Studies. In critical work, Manfred Malzahn's *The Contemporary Scottish Novel 1978–81* (Frankfurt: Peter Lang, 1984) focuses on fiction of the period as national self-expression; Cairns Craig's *The Modern Scottish Novel; Narrative and the National Imagination* (Edinburgh: Edinburgh University Press, 1999) is a stimulating attempt to identify the main characteristics of contemporary writers. From 1975 to 1999 *Books in Scotland* (Edinburgh: Ramsay Head Press) carried quarterly very extensive and comprehensive reviews of current fiction; its successor, *In Scotland*, continues to do so.

Those interested in the use of varieties of Scots language and language issues in literature will find, in addition to McLure's *Language, Poetry and Nationhood*, John Corbett's *Language and Scottish Literature* (Edinburgh: Edinburgh University Press, 1997) essential reading, with much of its content especially relevant to the stylistics of contemporary Scottish writing of all kinds. The same author's *Written in the Language of the Scottish Nation* (Clevedon Multilingual Matters Ltd., 1999) is a history of Scottish literature in translation.

For teachers of literature especially, *Teaching Scottish Literature: Curriculum and Classroom Applications*, edited by Alan MacGillivray (Edinburgh: Edinburgh University Press, 1997), will prove invaluable in its discussions of the place of Scottish literature in English courses, new theoretical approaches, varieties of language in use, and topics such as running workshops on contemporary writers.

Given the different style of coverage in the chapters of this section, whereby the three major genres of poetry, drama and fiction are treated in a more general discussion than previously, the lists below are grouped similarly under poetry, drama and fiction. With the very high number of writers mentioned in this part, it is only possible to give substantial listings and a modicum of critical help for the most prominent. For those not listed here the reader is referred to the critical discussions listed in the introduction to this section and to the electronic databases mentioned at the start of this section.

Chapter 38: Scottish Poetry after 1945

ANTHOLOGIES AND CRITICISM

Bateman, Meg, Crawford, Robert, and McGonigal, James (eds), *Scottish Religious Poetry: From the Sixth Century to the Present: An Anthology* (Edinburgh: Saint Andrews Press, 2000).

Bell, Robin (ed.), *The Best of Scottish Poetry: An Anthology of Contemporary Verse* (Edinburgh: Chambers, 1989).

Black, Ronald (ed.), *An Tuil: Anthology of Twentieth-Century Gaelic Verse* (Edinburgh: Polygon, 1999).

Bruce, George (ed.), *The Scottish Literary Revival: An Anthology of Twentieth-Century Poetry* (London: Collier-Macmillan, 1968).

Carrell, Christopher (ed.), *Seven Poets: MacDiarmid, MacCaig, Smith, Brown, Garioch, Maclean, Morgan* (Glasgow: Third Eye, 1981).

Crawford, Robert, and Imlah, Mick (eds), *The New Penguin Book of Scottish Verse* (Harmondsworth: Penguin, 2000).

Dunn, Douglas (ed.), *The Faber Book of Twentieth-Century Scottish Poetry* (London: Faber, 1992).

Fazzini, Marco, *Crossings: Essays in Contemporary Scottish Poetry and Hybridity* (Venice: Supernova, 2000).

Hubbard, Tom (ed.), *The New Makars: The Mercat Anthology of Contemporary Poetry in Scots* (Edinburgh: Mercat Press, 1991).

Kerrigan, Catherine (ed.), *An Anthology of Scottish Women Poets* [with translations from the Gaelic by Meg Bateman] (Edinburgh: Edinburgh University Press, 1991).

King, Charles (ed.), *Twelve Modern Scottish Poets* (London: University of London Press, 1971).

King, Charles, and Smith, Iain Crichton (eds), *Twelve More Modern Scottish Poets* (London: Hodder & Stoughton, 1986).

Lindsay, Maurice (ed.), *Scottish Comic Verse: An Anthology* (London: Hale, 1981).

—, *Modern Scottish Poetry: An Anthology of the Scottish Renaissance 1925–1985* (London: Faber, 1946; London: Hale, 1986).

, *Francis George Scott and the Scottish Renaissance* (Edinburgh: Paul Harris, 1980).

MacAuley, Donald (ed.), *Nua-Bhardachd Ghaidhlig: Modern Scottish Gaelic Poems* (Edinburgh: Southside, 1976).

MacCaig, Norman, and Scott, Alexander (eds), *Contemporary Scottish Verse, 1959–1969* (Edinburgh: Calder & Boyards, 1970).

Morgan, Edwin (ed.), *Scottish Satirical Verse* (Manchester: Carcanet, 1980).

Nicholson, Colin E., and Smith, Jane Ogden (eds), *Undercover: An Anthology of Contemporary Scottish Writers* (Edinburgh: Mainstream, 1993).

Nicholson, Colin E., *Poem, Place and Purpose: Shaping Identity in Contemporary Scottish Verse* (Edinburgh: Polygon, 1992).

O'Rourke, Daniel (ed.), *Dream State: The New Scottish Poets* (Edinburgh: Polygon, 1994; new edition, 2001).

Scott, Alexander (ed.), *Modern Scots Verse 1922–1977* (Preston: Akros, 1978).

—, *Scotch Passion: an Anthology of Scottish Erotic Verse* (London: Hale, 1982).

—, *Voices of Our Kind: An Anthology of Modern Scottish Poetry from 1920 to the Present* (Edinburgh: Chambers, 1987).

Watson, Roderick (ed.), *The Poetry of Scotland: Gaelic, Scots and English 1380–1980* (Edinburgh: Edinburgh University Press, 1996).

—, 'Scottish Poetry 1979–1980', *SSL* 17 (Columbia: University of South Carolina, 1982), pp. 218–24.

Whyte, Christopher (ed.), *An Aghaidh na Siorraidhheachd: Ochdnar Bhard Gaidhlig/ In The Face of Eternity: Eight Gaelic Poets* (Edinburgh: Polygon, 1991).

Part One: Modern Poets

J. K. ANNAND

Two Voices (Edinburgh: Macdonald, 1968).

Poems and Translations (Preston: Akros, 1975).

D. M. BLACK

With Decorum: Poems (Lowestoft: Scorpion Press, 1967).

Penguin Modern Poets 11, ed. with Peter Redgrove and D. M. Thomas (Harmondsworth: Penguin, 1968).

The Educators (London: Cresset Press, 1969).

Gravitations (Loanhead: Macdonald, 1979).

Collected Poems 1964–1987 (Edinburgh: Polygon, 1991).

Secondary reading

Hamilton, Robin, 'The Poetry of David Black', *Akros* 39, 1978.

Herdman, John, 'The World of D. M. Black', *Scottish International* 13, 1971.

READING LISTS

ALAN BOLD
To Find the New (London: Chatto & Windus, 1967).
A Perpetual Motion Machine (London: Chatto & Windus: Hogarth, 1969).
This Fine Day (Dunfermline: Borderline Press, 1979).
In This Corner: Selected Poems, 1963–1983 (Edinburgh: Macdonald, 1983).

Secondary reading
Dunn, Douglas, 'The Poetry of Alan Bold', *Akros* 42, 1979.

GEORGE MACKAY BROWN
See also fiction lists.

The Storm, and Other Poems (Kirkwall: Orkney Press, 1954).
Loaves and Fishes (London: Hogarth, 1959).
The Year of the Whale (London: Chatto & Windus, 1965).
Poems New and Selected (London: Hogarth, 1971).
Fishermen with Ploughs (London: Hogarth, 1971).
An Orkney Tapestry [prose] (London: Gollancz, 1972).
Winterfold (London: Chatto & Windus, 1976).
Voyages (London: Hogarth, 1983).
Selected Poems 1954–1983 (London: John Murray, 1991).
The Wreck of the Archangel (London: John Murray, 1989).
Selected Poems 1954–1992 (London: John Murray, 1996).
For the Islands I Sing [autobiography] (London: John Murray, 1997).
Northern Lights: A Poet's Sources, eds Archie Bevan and Brian Murray (London: John Murray, 1999).

Secondary reading
Ascherson, Neal, 'George Mackay Brown', *Seven Poets*, ed. Christopher Carrell (Glasgow: Third Eye Centre, 1981), pp. 23–5, and Walker, Marshall, 'Six Poets' in same, pp. 53–6.
Bold, Alan, *George Mackay Brown* (Edinburgh: Oliver & Boyd, 1978).
—, 'George Mackay Brown: Elemental Rhythms', *Modern Scottish Literature* (Edinburgh: Longman, 1983), pp. 241–8.
Brown, George Mackay, 'An Autobiographical Essay', *As I Remember: Ten Scottish Authors Recall How Writing Began for Them*, ed. Maurice Lindsay (London: Hale, 1979), pp. 9–21.
Butter, P. H., 'George Mackay Brown and Edwin Muir', *Yearbook of English Studies* 17 (Cambridge: Modern Humanities Research Association, 1987), pp. 16–30.
Carrell, Christopher (ed.), *Seven Poets* (Glasgow: Third Eye Centre, 1981) [essays by Neal Ascherson and Marshall Walker].
Chapman 84 (Edinburgh: Chapman Publications, 1996) [Issue on George Mackay Brown].
Dickson, Neil, 'Finding a Sense of Grace', *Books in Scotland* 88 (Edinburgh: Ramsay Head Press, 1991), pp. 8–9.
Dunn, Douglas, 'Finished Fragrance: The Poetry of George Mackay Brown', *Poetry Nation* 2 (Manchester: Manchester University Press, 1974), pp. 80–92.
Garriock, N. D., 'George Mackay Brown: Juvenalia to Loaves and Fishes', *Chapman* 60 (Edinburgh: Chapman Publications, 1990), pp. 1–7.
Herbold, Tony, 'Four Imports', *Parnassus* 3 (New York: S. Lewis, 1974), pp. 65–76.
Jones, D., 'Swatches from the Weave of Time: The Work of George Mackay Brown', *Planet* 40 (Cardiff: University of Wales Press, 1977), pp. 38–44.

Nicholson, Colin, 'Unlocking Time's Labyrinth: George Mackay Brown', *Poem, Purpose and Place: Shaping Identity in Contemporary Scottish Verse* (Edinburgh: Polygon, 1992), pp. 96–113.

O'Driscoll, D., 'Poems from a Small Island: An Introduction to the Poetry of George Mackay Brown', *Poetry Australia* 68 (Sydney, 1976), pp. 49–54.

Pacey, Philip, 'The Fire of Images: The Poetry of George Mackay Brown', *Akros* 32 (Preston: Akros Publications, 1976), pp. 61–71.

Roberts, Neil, 'George Mackay Brown', *Cambridge Quarterly* 6(?) (Cambridge: Cambridge University Press, 1973), pp. 181–9.

Scott, Tom, 'Orkney as Part of an Eternal Mood', *Chapman* 60 (Edinburgh: Chapman Publications, 1990), pp. 32–8.

GEORGE BRUCE

Sea Talk (Glasgow: McLellan, 1944).

Scottish Poetry 1–6, ed. with Maurice Lindsay (Edinburgh: Edinburgh University Press, 1966–72).

Landscapes and Figures (Preston: Akros, 1967).

(ed.), *The Scottish Literary Revival; An Anthology* (London: Collier-Macmillan, 1968).

Collected Poems (Edinburgh: Edinburgh University Press, 1971).

Perspectives: Poetry 1970–1986 (Aberdeen: Aberdeen University Press, 1987).

Pursuit: Poems 1986–98 (Edinburgh: Scottish Cultural Press, 1999).

Today Tomorrow: The Collected Poems of George Bruce 1933–2000 (Edinburgh: Polygon, 2001).

Secondary reading

Alexander, J. H., 'Make Marble the Moment: The Poetry of George Bruce', *Northern Visions: The Literary Identity of Northern Scotland in the 20th Century*, ed. David Hewitt (East Lothian: Tuckwell Press, 1995), pp. 82–98.

Lindsay, Maurice, *As I Remember: Ten Scottish Authors Remember How Writing Began For Them* (London: Hale, 1979), pp. 23–45.

Scott, Alexander, 'Myth Maker: The Poetry of George Bruce', *Akros* 29 (Preston: Akros Publications, 1975), pp. 25–40.

Smith, Iain Crichton, '*Sea Talk* by George Bruce', *Towards the Human* (Edinburgh: Macdonald, 1986), pp. 154–8.

TOM BUCHAN

Dolphins at Cochin (London: Cresset Press, 1969).

Poems 1969–1972 (Edinburgh: Poni Press, 1972).

Forewords (Glasgow: Print Studio, 1977).

DONALD CAMPBELL

See also drama lists.

Rhymes 'n' Reasons (Edinburgh: Reprographia, 1972).

Blether (Nottingham: Akros Publications, 1979).

Selected Poems 1970–1990 (Edinburgh: Galliard, 1990).

Secondary reading

Lindsay, Frederic, 'The Poetry of Donald Campbell', *Akros* 15(43) (Preston: Akros Publications, 1980), pp. 71–89.

Mason, Leonard, *Two Younger Poets: Duncan Glen and Donald Campbell: A Study of their Scots Poetry* (Preston: Akros, 1976).

STEWART CONN
See reading list, Part 2, 'Contemporary Poets'.

DOUGLAS DUNN
Terry Street (London: Faber & Faber, 1969).
The Happier Life (London: Faber & Faber, 1972).
Love or Nothing (London: Faber & Faber, 1974).
Barbarians (London: Faber & Faber, 1979).
(ed.), *The Poetry of Scotland* (London: Faber & Faber, 1979).
St Kilda's Parliament (London: Faber & Faber, 1981).
Europa's Lover (Newcastle: Bloodaxe, 1982).
Elegies (London: Faber & Faber, 1985).
Selected Poems 1964–1983 (London: Faber & Faber, 1986).
Northlight (London: Faber & Faber, 1988).
Dante's Drum-Kit (London: Faber & Faber, 1993).
The Donkey's Ears (London: Faber & Faber, 2000).

Secondary reading
Corcoran, Neil, 'Barbarians and Rhubarbarians: Douglas Dunn and Tony Harrison', *English Poetry Since 1940* (London: Longman, 1993), pp. 153–64.
Crawford, Robert, and Kinloch, David, *Reading Douglas Dunn* (Edinburgh: Edinburgh University Press, 1992).
Dunn, Douglas, *Douglas Dunn* (Glasgow: National Book League, Writers In Brief: No. 18, 1982).
Fazzini, Marco, 'An Interview with Douglas Dunn in 1997', *SSL* 31 (Columbia: University of South Carolina, 1999), pp. 121–30.
Hughes, G. E. H., 'Rhetoric and Observation in the Poetry of Douglas Dunn', *Hiroshima Studies in English Language and Literature* 31 (1986), pp. 1–16.
Kennedy, David, 'What Does the Fairy DO?: The Staging of Antithetical Masculine Styles in the Poetry of Tony Harrison and Douglas Dunn', *Textual Practice* 14(1) (London: Methuen, 2000), pp. 115–36.
Lyon, J. M., 'The Art of Grief: Douglas Dunn's Elegies', *The Journal of the English Association* 40(166) (1991), pp. 47–67.
Nicholson, Colin, 'Dimensions of the Sentient: Douglas Dunn', *Poem, Purpose and Place: Shaping Identity in Contemporary Scottish Verse* (London: Polygon, 1992).
O'Brien, Sean, and Plaice, Stephen (eds), 'Douglas Dunn: Interview with the Devil', *The Printer's Devil: A Magazine of New Writing* (Tumbridge Wells: South East Arts, 1990), pp. 12–33.
Robinson, A., 'The Mastering Eye: Douglas Dunn's Social Perceptions', *Instabilities in Contemporary British Poetry* (Basingstoke: Macmillan, 1988), pp. 82–99.
Smalley, Rebecca, 'The Englishman's Scottishman or Radical Scotsman?: Reading Douglas Dunn in the Light of Recent Re-appraisals of Philip Larkin', *SLJ* 22(1) (Aberdeen: Association for Scottish Literary Studies, 1995), pp. 74–83.
Stoneman, Patsy, 'Douglas Dunn', *Bete Noire* 12–13 (1991–2), p. 103.
Williams, D., ' "They will not leave me, the lives of other people": The Poetry of Douglas Dunn', *SSL* 23 (Columbia: University of South Carolina, 1989), pp. 1–24.

IAIN HAMILTON FINLAY
Glasgow Beasts and a Burd (Edinburgh: Flounder Press, 1961).
The Dancers Inherit the Party (Worcester: Migrant Press, 1960).
Poems to Hear and See (London: Collier-Macmillan, 1971).

Secondary reading

Abrioux, Yves, *Iain Hamilton Finlay: A Visual Primer* (London: Reaktion Books, 1992) [contains much of Finlay's small-press work].
Chapman 78–79 (Edinburgh: Chapman Publications, 1994) [Special Issue on Finlay].
Davidson, Peter, 'Iain Hamilton Finlay: (De)Signing the Landscape', *In Black and Gold: Contiguous Traditions in Post-War British and Irish Poetry*, ed. C. C. Barfoot (Amsterdam: Rodopi, 1994), pp. 169–78.
Finlay, Alec (ed.), *Wood Notes Wild: Essays on the Poetry and Art of Iain Hamilton Finlay* (Edinburgh: Polygon, 1995).
'Iain Hamilton Findlay: Retrospective', *Cencrastus* 20 (Edinburgh: Cencrastus Publications, 1985), pp. 20–43.
Keeney, Gavin, 'A Revolutionary Arcadia: Reading Iain Hamilton Finlay's Un Jardin Revolutionnaire', *Word and Image: a Journal of Verbal/Visual Enquiry* 11(3) (London: Taylor & Francis, 1995), pp. 237–55.
MacDiarmid, Hugh, *the ugly birds without wings* (Edinburgh: Allan Donaldson, 1962) [a reply to the attacks of Ian Hamilton Finlay and others and a criticism of the position they adopted in a poetry broadsheet which Finlay was editing at the time].
Milne, Drew, 'Adorno's Hut: Iain Hamilton Findlay's Neoclassical Rearmament Programme', *SLJ* 23(2) (Aberdeen: Association for Scottish Literary Studies, 1996), pp. 69–79.
Morgan, Edwin, 'Early Finlay', *Crossing the Border: Essays on Scottish Literature* (Manchester: Carcanet, 1990).
Scobie, Stephen, 'The Side-Road to Dunsyre: Some Comments on Hugh MacDiarmid and Iain Hamilton Finlay', *Akros* 15 (Preston: Akros Publications, 1970), pp. 51–61.
—, 'An Homage and An Alphabet: Two Recent Works by Iain Hamilton Finlay', *Visual Literature Criticism: A New Collection*, ed. Richard Kostelanetz (Carbondale: Southern Illinois University Press, 1979), pp. 107–13.
Smith, Dennis, 'A Garden of Bright Images: Ideas in the Art of Iain Hamilton Finlay', *Edinburgh Review* 91 (Edinburgh: Polygon Books, 1994), pp. 7–19.
Tait, Robert, 'The Wild Hawthorn Press', Scottish International 5 (1969), pp. 64–6.
Young, Alan, 'Three "Neo-Moderns": Iain Hamilton Finlay, Edwin Morgan, Christopher Middleton', *British Poetry since 1970: A Critical Survey*, eds Peter Jones and Michael Schmidt (Manchester: Carcanet Press, 1980), pp. 112–24.

OLIVE FRASER
The Wrong Music: The Poems of Olive Fraser 1909–1977, ed. Helena Shire (Edinburgh: Canongate, 1989).

G. S. FRASER
Home Town Elegy (London: Nicholson & Watson, 1944).
The Fatal Landscape and Other Poems (London: Poetry London, 1941).
The Traveller Has Regrets and Other Poems (London: Harvill Press & Editions Poetry, 1948).
Conditions (Nottingham: Byron Press, 1969).
Poems of G. S. Fraser, eds Ian Fletcher and John Lucas (Leicester: Leicester University Press, 1981).

A Stranger and Afraid: Autobiography of an Intellectual (Manchester: Carcanet, 1983).
A Garioch Miscellany, ed. Robin Fulton (Edinburgh: Macdonald, 1986).

Secondary reading

Hopewell, Janet, 'G. S. Fraser, Scottish Fugitive', *Lines Review* 123 (Loanhead: Macdonald Publishers, 1992), pp. 27–32.

Scott, Patrick, 'G. S. Fraser', *Cencrastus* 16 (Edinburgh: Cencrastus Publications, 1984), pp. 31–3.

ROBIN FULTON

See reading lists, Part 2, 'Contemporary Poets'.

ROBERT GARIOCH

Seventeen Poems for 6d with Somhairle MacGill-Eain (Edinburgh: Chalmers Press, 1940).
Chuckies on the Cairn (Hayes: Chalmers Press, 1949).
The Masque of Edinburgh (Edinburgh: Macdonald, 1954).
The Big Music (Thurso: Caithness Books, 1971).
Doktor Faust in Rose Street (Loanhead: Macdonald, 1973).
Two Men and a Blanket: Memoirs of Captivity (Edinburgh: Southside, 1975).
Complete Poetical Works, ed. Robin Fulton (Edinburgh: Macdonald, 1983).

Secondary reading

Bold, Alan, 'Three Post-MacDiarmid Makars: Soutar, Garioch, Smith', *Akros* 15(44) (Preston: Akros Publications, 1980), pp. 44–61.

Caird, James B., 'Robert Garioch: A Personal Appreciation', *SLJ* 10(2) (Aberdeen: Association for Scottish Literary Studies, 1983), pp. 68–78.

Campbell, Donald, 'Another side to Garioch, or a Glisk of Near-forgotten Hell', *Akros* 33 (Preston: Akros Publications, 1977), pp. 47–52.

—, 'Robert Garioch 1909–1981', *Lines Review* 77 (Loanhead: Macdonald Publishers, 1981), pp. 6–9.

Carrell, Christopher (ed.), *Seven Poets* (Glasgow: Third Eye Centre, 1981) [essays by Neal Ascherson and Marshall Walker].

Chapman 31 (Edinburgh: Chapman Publications, 1981–2) [Special Issue, 'In Memoriam Robert Garioch'].

Findlay, Bill, 'Robert Garioch's *Jephthah and the Baptist*: Why he considered it "my favourite work"', *SLJ* 25(2) (Aberdeen: Association for Scottish Literary Studies, 1998), pp. 45–66.

Fulton, Robin (ed.), *A Garioch Miscellany* (Edinburgh: Macdonald, 1986).

Glen, Duncan, 'In Memorian Robert Garioch 1909–1981', *Akros* 16(47) (Preston: Akros Publications, 1981), pp. 107–10.

Morgan, Edwin, 'Robert Garioch 1909–1981', *Lines Review* 77 (Loanhead: Macdonald Publishers, 1981), pp. 13–15.

Nichol, Don W., 'Belli up to date: Scots and English Sonnet Translations by Robert Garioch and Anthony Burgess', *Chapman* 39 (Edinburgh: Chapman Publications, 1984), pp. 34–41.

Relich, Mario, 'Scottish Tradition and Robert Garioch's Individual Talent', *Lines Review* 136 (Loanhead: Macdonald Publishers, 1996), pp. 5–17.

Smith, Iain Crichton, 'The Power of Craftmanship: The Poetry of Robert Garioch', *Towards the Human* (Edinburgh: Macdonald, 1986), pp. 167–70.

Tremayne, Sydney, 'Robert Garioch', *Akros* 16(47) (Preston: Akros Publications, 1981), pp. 110–13.

Tulloch, Graham, 'Robert Garioch', *Lines Review* 88 (Loanhead: Macdonald Publishers, 1984), pp. 11–15.

—, 'Robert Garioch's Different Styles of Scots', *SLJ* 12(1) (Aberdeen: Association for Scottish Literary Studies, 1985), pp. 53–69.

Watson, Roderick, 'The Speaker in the Gairdens: The Poetry of Robert Garioch', *Akros* 16 (Preston: Akros Publications, 1971), pp. 69–76.

VALERIE GILLIES

See reading lists, Part 2, 'Contemporary Poets'.

DUNCAN GLEN

In Appearances (Preston: Akros Publications, 1971).

Mr And Mrs JL Stoddart at Home (Preston: Akros Publications, 1975).

Gaitherings: Poems in Scots (Preston: Akros Publications, 1977).

Realities Poems (Nottingham: Akros, 1980).

The Stones of Time (Nottingham: D. Glen, 1984).

The Turn of the Earth: A Sequence of Poems (Nottingham: Akros, 1985).

The Autobiography of a Poet (Edinburgh: Ramsay Head Press, 1986).

Selected Poems 1965–1990 (Edinburgh: Galliard, 1991).

Selected New Poems 1987–1986 (Kircaldy: Akros, 1998).

Secondary reading

Mason, L., *Two Younger Scots Poets: Duncan Glen and Donald Campbell* (Preston: Akros, 1976).

Pacey, Philip, 'The Poetry of Duncan Glen', *Akros* 33, 1977.

W. S. GRAHAM

Cage without Grievance (Glasgow: Parton Press, 1942).

The Seven Journeys (Glasgow: Mclellan, 1944).

2nd Poems (London: Poetry London, 1945).

The White Threshhold (London: Faber & Faber, 1949).

The Nightfishing (London: Faber & Faber, 1955).

Malcolm Mooney's Land (London: Faber & Faber, 1970).

Implements in their Places (London: Faber & Faber, 1977).

Collected Poems 1942–77 (London: Faber & Faber, 1979).

Aimed at Nobody (London: Faber & Faber, 1993).

Secondary reading

Bedient, Calvin, 'W. S. Graham', *Eight Contemporary Poets* (London: Oxford University Press, 1974).

Cockburn, Ken, 'Notebooks, Canons and Damp Dustbins: W. S. Graham's *Aimed at Nobody* and Basil Bunting's *Uncollected Poems*', *Lines Review* 128 (Loanhead: Macdonald Publishing, 1994), pp. 14–18.

Corcoran, Neil, 'A New Romanticism: Apocalypse and Dylan Thomas, W. S. Graham, George Barker', *English Poetry since 1940* (London: Longman, 1993), pp. 39–58.

Duncan, Ronnie, and Davidson, Jonathan (eds), *The Constructed Space: A Celebration of W. S. Graham* (Lincoln: Jackson's Arm, 1994).

Duxbery, Robert, 'The Poetry of W. S. Graham', *Akros* 38 (Preston: Akros Publications, 1978), pp. 62–71.

READING LISTS

Edinburgh Review 75 (Edinburgh, 1987) [issue devoted to W. S. Graham, with articles by Tony Lopez, Edwin Morgan, Tom Scott, Robert Calder, Tom Leonard and others].

Grant, Damian, 'Walls of Glass: the Poetry of W. S. Graham', *British Poetry Since 1970: A Critical Survey*, eds Peter Jones and Michael Schmidt (Manchester: Carcanet Press, 1980).

Haffenden, John, ' "I Would Say I Was A Happy Man"; interview with W. S. Graham', *Poetry Review* 76(1/2) (London: Poetry Society, 1986).

Hamburger, Michael, 'W. S. Graham', *Agenda* 16(2) (1972), pp. 75–7.

Kessler, J., 'Coming Down', *Parnassus* 6 (1978), pp. 205–12.

Lopez, Tony, *The Poetry of W. S. Graham* (Edinburgh: Edinburgh University Press, 1989).

Morgan, Edwin, 'The Poetry of W. S. Graham' and 'W. S. Graham: A Poet's Letters', *Crossing the Border* (Manchester: Carcanet, 1990).

—, 'The Sea, the Desert and the City': environment and language in Graham, Henderson and Leonard', *Crossing the Border* (Manchester: Carcanet, 1990).

—, 'The Poetry of W. S. Graham', *Cencrastus* 5 (Edinburgh: Cencrastus Publications), pp. 8–10.

Passavant, Elise, 'The Nightfishing: By W. S. Graham', *Contemporary Review* 231 (1977), pp. 270–2.

Silverberg, Mark Andrew, 'A Readership of None: The Later Poetry of W. S. Graham', *English Studies in Canada* 24(2) (Fredericton: Association of Canadian University Teachers of English, 1988), pp. 139–55.

STANLEY ROGER GREEN
Waiting for the mechanic (Edinburgh: Scottish Cultural Press, 1998).
A Suburb of Belsen (Edinburgh: Paul Harris, 1977).
Advice to Travellers: Selected Poems (Aberdeen: Aberdeen University Press, 1990).

GEORGE CAMPBELL HAY
Seeker-Reaper (Edinburgh: Saltire Society, 1988).
The Collected Poems and Songs of George Campbell Hay, ed. Michel Byrne (Edinburgh: Edinburgh University Press, 2000) [2 vols].

Secondary reading
Burns, John, 'Generous Hearted Spirit: The Poetry of George Campbell Hay', *Cencrastus* 18 (Edinburgh: Cencrastus Publications, 1985), pp. 28–30.

Meek, Donald E., 'Land and Loyalty: The Gaelic Verse of George Campbell Hay', *Chapman* 39 (Edinburgh: Chapman Publications, 1984), pp. 2–8.

Rankin, Robert A., 'George Campbell Hay as I knew Him', *Chapman* 40 (Edinburgh: Chapman Publications, 1985), pp. 1–12.

HAMISH HENDERSON
Ballads of World War II (Glasgow, 1947).
Elegies for the Dead in Cyrenaica (London: John Lehman, 1948; revised, Edinburgh: Polygon, 1990).
Alias MacAlias: Writings on Songs, Folk and Literature (Edinburgh: Polygon, 1992).
Collected Poems and Songs (Edinburgh: Curly Snake Publishing, 2000).

Secondary reading
Hunter, Andrew R., 'Hamish Henderson: the Odyssey of a Wanderer, *Cencrastus* 47 (Edinburgh: Cencrastus, 1994), pp. 3–6.

McNaughton, Adam, 'Hamish Henderson – Folk Hero', *Chapman* 42 (Edinburgh: Chapman Publications, 1985), pp. 22–9.

Morgan, Edwin, 'The Sea, the Desert and the City: Environment and Language in Graham. Henderson and Leonard', *Crossing the Border* (Manchester: Carcanet, 1990), pp. 273–91.

Ross, Raymond, 'Hamish Henderson: In the Midst of Things', *Chapman* 42 (Edinburgh: Chapman Publications, 1985), pp. 11–18.

J. F. HENDRY

The Bombed Happiness (London: Routledge, 1942).
The Orchestral Mountain (London: Routledge, 1943).
A World Alien (Dunfermline: Borderline Press, 1980).

Secondary reading

Salmon, A., *Poets of the Apocalypse* (Boston: Twayne Publishers, 1983).

T. S. LAW

Whit Tyme in the Day: and Ither Poems, with a foreword by Hugh MacDiarmid (Glasgow: Caledonian Press, 1948).
Referendum (Blackford: Fingerpost Publications, 1989).

ALAN JACKSON

The Grim Wayfarer (London: Fulcrum Press, 1969).
Heart of the Sun (Hebden Bridge: Open Township, 1986).
Light Hearts (London: Sel de Mer, 1987).
Salutations: Collected Poems 1960–1989 (Edinburgh: Polygon, 1990).

TOM LEONARD

Intimate Voices: Selected Work, 1965–1983 (Newcastle-upon-Tyne: Galloping Dog Press, 1984).
Situations Theoretical and Contemporary (Newcastle-upon-Tyne: Galloping Dog Press, 1986).
Nora's Place (Newcastle-upon-Tyne: Galloping Dog Press, 1990).
(ed.), *Radical Renfrew: Poetry from the French Revolution to the First World War* (Edinburgh: Polygon, 1990).
Leonard's Shorter Catechism (Stirling: AK Press, 1991).
Places of the Mind: The Life and Work of James Thomson (B. V.) (London: Cape, 1993).
Reports from the Present: Selected Work, 1982–1994 (London: Cape, 1995).

Secondary reading

Boddy, Kasia, and Wood, Barry, 'Interview with Tom Leonard', *Edinburgh Review* 77 (Edinburgh, 1987), pp. 59–71.
Hamilton, Robin, 'The Speak of the City', *New Edinburgh Review* 65 (Edinburgh, 1984), pp. 39–40.
Kirkwood, Colin, 'Vulgar Eloquence', *Cencrastus* 20 (Edinburgh: Cencrastus, 1981), pp. 21–3.
Macafee, Caroline, 'Glasgow Dialect in Literature', *Scottish Language* 1 (Aberdeen: Association for Scottish Literary Studies, 1982), pp. 45–53.
Macauley, Ronald K. S., 'Urbanity in an Urban Dialect', *SSL* 23 (Columbia: University of South Carolina, 1988), pp. 150–63.
McGrath, Tom, 'Tom Leonard: Man With Two Heads', *Akros* 8(24) (Preston: Akros Publications, 1974), pp. 40–9.
Milton, Colin, ' "Ma Language is Disgraceful": Tom Leonard's Glasgow Dialect Poems', *Englishes Around the World, Volume I*, ed. Edgar W. Schneider (Amsterdam: Benjamin, 1997), pp. 185–210.

Morgan, Edwin, 'Glasgow Speech in Recent Scottish Literature', *Scotland and the Lowland Tongue*, ed. J. Derrick McClure (Aberdeen: Aberdeen University Press, 1983), pp. 195–208.

—, 'The Sea, the Desert, the City: Environment and Language in W. S. Graham, Hamish Henderson, and Tom Leonard', *Crossing the Border* (Manchester: Carcanet, 1990), pp. 273–91.

Mulrine, Stephen, 'Tom Leonard's "The Good Thief"', *Akros* 17(51) (Preston: Akros Publications, 1983), pp. 54–5.

Watson, Roderick, 'Alien Voices from the Street: Demotic Modernism in Modern Scots Writing', *Yearbook of English Studies* 25 (Cambridge: Modern Humanities Research Association, 1995), pp. 141–55.

MAURICE LINDSAY

Lindsay is an influential and prolific poet, critic and editor, whose output is too extensive to cite more than a selection of recent work here. For a full list see Crawford's bibliography: Lindsay's critical work (especially his *History of Scottish Literature* and his work on Burns) will be found in the appropriate section lists. Lindsay's critical histories are listed at the beginning of these sections.

The Enemies of Love: Poems 1941–1945 (Glasgow: Maclellan, 1946).

Selected Poems (Edinburgh: Oliver & Boyd, 1947).

Hurlygush: Poems in Scots (Edinburgh: Serif, 1948).

Snow Warning and Other Poems (Arundel: Linden Press, 1962).

The Business of Living (Penwortham: Akros, 1969).

Collected Poems (Edinburgh: Paul Harris, 1979).

A Net to Catch the Winds and Other Poems (London: Hale, 1981).

Thank You For Having Me: A Personal Memoir (London: Hale, 1983).

The French Mosquitoes' Woman and Other Diversions and Poems (London: Hale, 1985).

Collected Poems, 1940–1990 (Aberdeen: Aberdeen University Press, 1990).

Speaking Likesnesses: A Postscript (Edinburgh: Scottish Cultural Press, 1992).

On the Face of It: Collected Poems (London: Hale, 1993).

News of the World: Last Poems (Aberdeen: Scottish Cultural Press, 1995).

Secondary reading

Campbell, Donald, 'A Different Way of Being Right: The Poetry of Maurice Lindsay', *Akros* 24 (Preston: Akros Publications, 1974), pp. 22–6.

Jack, R. D. S., 'The First Since Millar', *Scottish Literary Journal* Supplement 5 (1977), pp. 12–20.

Macintyre, Lorn M., 'The Poetry of Maurice Lindsay', *Akros* 42 (Preston: Akros Publications, 1979), pp. 44–53.

DOUGLAS LIPTON

The Stone Sleeping-bag (Glasgow: Mariscat, 1993).

LIZ LOCHHEAD

See also drama lists.

Memo for Spring (Edinburgh: Reprographia, 1972).

Islands (Glasgow: Glasgow Print Studio, 1978).

The Grimm Sisters (London: Next Editions, 1981).

Silver Service (Edinburgh: Salamander, 1984).
Dreaming Frankenstein and Collected Poems (Edinburgh: Polygon, 1984).
True Confessions and New Cliches (Edinburgh: Polygon, 1985).
Bagpipe Muzak (Harmondsworth: Penguin, 1991).

Secondary reading

Baxter, Judith, *Four Women Poets* (Cambridge: Cambridge University Press, 1995).
Crawford, Robert, and Varty, Anne (eds), *Liz Lochhead's Voices* (Edinburgh: Edinburgh University Press, 1993).
Lochhead, Liz, 'A Protestant Girlhood', *Jock Tamson's Bairns: Essays on a Scots Childhood*, ed. Trevor Royle (London: Hamish Hamilton, 1977), pp. 112–25.
Nicholson, Colin, 'Liz Lochhead: The Knucklebones of Irony', *Poems, Purpose and Place: Shaping Identity in Contemporary Scottish Verse* (Edinburgh: Polygon, 1992), pp. 203–23.
Riach, Alan, 'A Growing End For Scottish Verse?', *Chapman* 40 (Edinburgh: Chapman Publications, 1985), pp. 75–6.
Somerville-Arjat, Gillean, and Wilson, Rebecca (eds), *Sleeping with Monsters: Conversations with Scottish and Irish Women Poets* (Edinburgh: Polygon, 1990), pp. 8–18.
Todd, Emily, 'Liz Lochhead interviewed', *Verse* 8(3); 9(1) (1992), p. 87.
Varty, Anne, 'The Mirror and the Vamp: Liz Lochhead', *A History of Scottish Women's Writing*, eds Douglas Gifford and Dorothy McMillan (Edinburgh: Edinburgh University Press, 1997), pp. 641–58.
Watson, Roderick (ed.), *MacCaig, Morgan, Lochhead: Three Scottish Poets* (Edinburgh: Canongate, 1992).

GEORGE MACBETH

My Scotland (London: Macmillan, 1973).
The Clever Garden (London: Secker & Warburg, 1986).
A Child of the War (London: Cape, 1987).
Collected Poems 1958–1982 (London: Hutchison, 1989).
Trespassing: Poems From Ireland (London: Hutchison, 1991).
The Patient (London: Hutchison, 1992).

Secondary reading

Black, D. M., 'The Poetry of George Macbeth', *Scottish International* 3 (1968), pp. 40–7.

Part Two: Five Modern Scottish Poets

NORMAN MACCAIG

Far Cry (London: Routledge, 1943).
The Inward Eye (London: Routledge, 1946).
Riding Lights (London: Hogarth Press, 1955).
The Sinai Sort (London: Hogarth Press, 1957).
A Common Grace (London: Chatto & Windus, 1960).
A Round of Applause (London: Chatto & Windus, 1962).
Measures (London: Chatto & Windus, 1965).
Surroundings (London: Chatto & Windus, 1966).
Rings on a Tree (London: Chatto & Windus, 1968).
A Man in My Position (London: Chatto & Windus, 1969).
The White Bird (London: Chatto & Windus, 1973).

READING LISTS

The World's Room (London: Chatto & Windus, 1974).
Tree of Strings (London: Chatto & Windus, 1977).
Old Maps and New (London: Chatto & Windus, 1978).
The Equal Skies (London: Chatto & Windus, 1980).
A World of Difference (London: Chatto & Windus, 1983).
Voice-Over (London: Chatto & Windus, 1983).
The Honey of Memory (London: Chatto & Windus, 1987).
Voice-Over (London: Chatto & Windus, 1988).
Collected Poems (London: Chatto & Windus, 1985; 1990).

Secondary reading

Akros 7 (Preston: Akros Publications, 1968) [Special Norman MacCaig issue].
Carrell, Christopher (ed.), *Seven Poets* (Glasgow: Third Eye Centre, 1981) [essays by Neal Ascherson and Marshall Walker].
Crawford, Thomas, 'Norman MacCaig: Makar Compleit', *Chapman* 45 (Edinburgh: Chapman Publications, 1986), pp. 4–14.
Dunn, Antony, 'The Space between Words: The Poetry of Norman MacCaig', *Lines Review* 139 (Loanhead: Macdonald Publishers, 1996), pp. 5–14.
Frykman, Erik, '*Unemphatic Marvels': A Study of Norman MacCaig's Poetry* (Gothenburg: Gothenburg University Press, 1977).
Henderson, Hamish, et al., 'At Langholm, September 13, 1992', *Chapman* 69–70 (Edinburgh: Chapman Publications, 1992), pp. 181–90.
Hendry, Joy, and Ross, Raymond, *Norman MacCaig: Critical Essays* (Edinburgh: Edinburgh University Press, 1990).
MacCaig, Norman, 'My Way of It', *As I Remember: Ten Scottish Authors Recall How Writing Began for Them*, ed. Maurice Lindsay (London: Hale, 1979), pp. 79–88.
—, 'Poetry in Scotland', *Poetry Review* 56 (London: Poetry Society, 1965), pp. 148–60.
Morgan, Edwin, 'The Poetry of Norman MacCaig', *Crossing the Border* (Manchester: Carcanet, 1990), pp. 240–8.
—, 'The Poetry of Norman MacCaig', *Books in Scotland* 16 (Edinburgh: Ramsay Head Press, 1984), pp. 4–6.
Murray, Isobel, and Tait, Bob, 'A Metaphorical Way of Seeing Things: Norman MacCaig', *Scottish Writers Talking*, eds Isobel Murray and Bob Tait (East Linton: Tuckwell Press, 1996), pp. 84–131.
Nicholson, Colin, 'Such Clarity of Seeming: Norman MacCaig', *Poem, Purpose and Place: Shaping Identity in Contemporary Scottish Verse* (Edinburgh: Polygon, 1992), pp. 37–56.
Porter, W. S., 'The Poetry of Norman MacCaig', *Akros* 32 (Preston: Akros Publications, 1976), pp. 37–53.
Riach, Alan, 'Norman MacCaig in Conversation', *P. M. Review* 120, 24:4 (1998), pp. 19–27.
—, 'Thinking of Norman MacCaig', *Quadrant* 370, 44:10 (2000), pp. 56–60.
Rillie, Jack, 'Net of Kins, Web of Ilks: MacCaig's Phantasmagoria', *Chapman* 66 (Edinburgh: Chapman Publications, 1991), pp. 46–51.
Ross, Raymond J., 'Interview with Norman MacCaig', *Cencrastus* 8 (Edinburgh: Cencrastus Publications, 1982), pp. 15–16.
Scott, Mary J. W., 'Neo-Classical MacCaig', *SSL* 10 (Columbia: University of South Carolina, 1973), pp. 135–44.
Smith, Iain Crichton, 'The Poetry of Norman MacCaig', *Saltire Review* 19 (1958), pp. 20–3.
—, 'A Lust for the Particular: Norman MacCaig's Poetry', *Chapman* 45 (Edinburgh: Chapman Publications, 1986), pp. 20–4.
Watson, Roderick, *The Poetry of Norman MacCaig* (Aberdeen: Association for Scottish Literary Studies, Scotnotes Series, 1989).

STUART MCGREGOR
Poems and Songs (Loanhead: Midlothian, 1974).

WILLIAM MCILVANNEY
The Longships in Harbour (London: Eyre & Spottiswoode, 1970).
These Words: Weddings and After (Edinburgh: Mainstream, 1984).
In Through the Head (Edinburgh: Mainstream, 1988).

Secondary reading
Gifford, Douglas, 'William McIlvanney talks to Douglas Gifford', *Books in Scotland* 30 (Edinburgh: Ramsay Head Press, 1989), pp. 1–4.
Murray, Isobel (ed.), ' "Plato in a Boiler Suit": William McIlvanney Interviewed', *Scottish Writers Talking* (East Linton: Tuckwell Press, 1996), pp. 132–54.

ALASTAIR MACKIE
Back-Green Odyssey and Other Poems (Aberdeen: Rainbow Books, 1980).
Ingaitherings: Selected Poems (Aberdeen: Aberdeen University Press, 1987).

ALASDAIR MACLEAN
From the Wilderness (London: Gollancz, 1973).
Waking the Dead (London: Gollancz, 1976).

ROBERT MCLELLAN
Sweet Largie Bay; and Arran burn: two poems in Scots (Preston: Akros Publications, 1977).

AONGHAS MACNEACAIL
Imaginary Wounds (Glasgow: Glasgow Print Studio, 1980).
Sireadh Bradain Sicir / Seeking Wise Salmon (Nairn: Balnain Books, 1983).
An Cathadh Mor / The Great Snowbattle (Nairn: Balnain Books, 1984).
An Seachnadh agus Dain Eile / The Avoiding and Other Poems (Loanhead: Macdonald, 1986).
Rock and Water: Poems in English (Edinburgh: Polygon, 1990).
A Proper Schooling and Other Poems (Edinburgh: Polygon, 1996).

NAOMI MITCHISON
The Laburnum Branch (London: Cape, 1926).
The Delicate Fire (London: Cape, 1933).
The Cleansing of the Knife (Edinburgh: Canongate, 1978).

Secondary reading
Dickson, Beth, 'A Tribute to Naomi Mitchison who celebrated her 90th birthday in November', *Books in Scotland* 26 (Edinburgh: Ramsay Head Press, 1987), pp. 1–2.
Nicholson, Colin, 'For the Sake of Alba: Naomi Mitchison', *Poem, Purpose and Place: Shaping Identity in Contemporary Scottish Verse* (Edinburgh: Polygon, 1992), 19–36.

WILLIAM MONTGOMERIE
From Time to Time: Selected Poems (Edinburgh: Canongate, 1985).

Secondary reading
Morgan, Edwin, 'A Note on William Montgomerie', *Chapman* 46 (Edinburgh: Chapman Publications, 1986/7), pp. 1–3.

EDWIN MORGAN

Selected works only – see Crawford and Royle's *Companion to Scottish Literature* (Edinburgh: Mainstream, 1993) for details of this prolific poet.

The Vision of Cathkin Braes and Other Poems (Glasgow: Maclellan, 1952).
The Second Life (Edinburgh: Edinburgh University Press, 1968).
Instamatic Poems (London: Ian McKelvie, 1972).
From Glasgow to Saturn (Cheadle: Carcanet, 1973).
Rites of Passage: Selected Translations (Manchester: Carcanet, 1976).
The New Divan (Manchester: Carcanet, 1977).
Poems of Thirty Years (Manchester: Carcanet, 1982).
Sonnets from Scotland (Glasgow: Mariscat, 1984).
Themes on a Variation (Manchester: Carcanet, 1988).
Collected Poems (Manchester: Carcanet, 1990).
Hold Hands Among the Atoms (Glasgow: Mariscat, 1991).
Sweeping Out the Dark (Manchester: Carcanet, 1994).
Collected Translations (Manchester: Carcanet, 1996).
Demon (Glasgow: Mariscat Press, 1999).

Secondary reading
Bradham, Jo Allen, 'Baleful Greetings from Morgan's "Christmas Card"', *College Literature* 14(1) (1987), pp. 49–53.
Calder, Angus, 'Morganmania', *Chapman* 64 (Edinburgh: Chapman Publications, 1991), pp. 41–5.
Campbell, Ian, 'Happy Birthday Dr Morgan', *Books in Scotland* 39 (Edinburgh: Ramsay Head Press, 1991), pp. 2–3.
Carrell, Christopher (ed.), *Six Poets* (Glasgow: Third Eye Centre, 1981) [essays on Morgan by Neal Ascherson and Marshall Walker].
Chapman 64 (Edinburgh: Chapman Publications, 1991) [Special Issue: 'Edwin Morgan: A Celebration'].
Crawford, Robert, 'Morgan's Critical Position', *Chapman* 64 (Edinburgh: Chapman Publications, 1991), pp. 32–6.
—, and Whyte, Hamish (eds), *About Edwin Morgan* (Edinburgh: Edinburgh University Press, 1990).
Edgecombe, R. S., 'The Poetry of Edwin Morgan', *Dalhousie Review* 62(4) (1982 / 1983), pp. 668–79.
Fazzini, Marco, 'Edwin Morgan: Two Interviews', *Scando-Slavica* 29 (1996), pp. 45–57.
Fulton, Robin, *Contemporary Scottish Poetry* (Edinburgh: Macdonald, 1974), pp. 13–40.
Gregson, Ian, 'Edwin Morgan's Metamorphoses', *English* 39(164) (London: Oxford University Press, 1990), pp. 149–64.
Hamilton, Robin, *Poetry and Psychodrama* (London: Bran's Head, 1982).
—, 'The Poetry of Edwin Morgan: Translator of Reality', *Akros* 15(43) (Preston: Akros Publications, 1980), pp. 23–39.
Houston, Amy, 'New Lang Syne: *Sonnets from Scotland* and Restructured Time', *SLJ* 22(1) (Aberdeen: Association for Scottish Literary Studies, 1995), pp. 66–73.

McCarra, Kevin, 'Edwin Morgan's "Cinquevalli"', *SLJ* 12(2) (Aberdeen: Association for Scottish Literary Studies, 1985), pp. 69–75.

Morgan, Edwin, 'The Poet's Voice and Craft', *The Poet's Voice and Craft*, ed. C. B. McCully (Manchester: Carcanet, 1994), pp. 54–67.

Nicholson, Colin, ' "Living in the Utterance": Edwin Morgan', *Poem, Purpose and Place: Shaping Identity in Contemporary Scottish Verse* (Edinburgh: Polygon, 1992), pp. 57–79.

Schmidt, Michael, 'Edwin Morgan', *An Introduction to Fifty Modern British Poets* (London: Pan Books, 1979), pp. 314–20.

Thomson, Geddes, *The Poetry of Edwin Morgan* (Aberdeen: Association for Scottish Literary Studies, 1986).

Watson, Roderick, ' "An Island in the City": Edwin Morgan's Urban Poetry', *Chapman* 64 (Edinburgh: Chapman Publications, 1991), pp. 12–22.

Whyte, Christopher, 'Now You See It, Now You Don't: The Love Poetry of Edwin Morgan', *The Glasgow Review* 2 (Glasgow: University of Glasgow, 1993), pp. 82–93.

Whyte, Hamish (ed.), *Nothing Not Giving Messages: Reflections on Work and Life* (Edinburgh: Polygon, 1990).

Wood, Barry, 'Scots, Poets and the City', *The History of Scottish Literature Vol. IV, Twentieth Century*, ed. Cairns Craig (Aberdeen: Aberdeen University Press, 1987), pp. 337–48.

Young, Alan, 'Edwin Morgan', *Poets of Great Britain and Ireland 1945–1960*, ed. Vincent B. Sherry, Jr. [*Dictionary of Literary Biography*, vol. 27] (Detroit: Gale Research Company, 1984), pp. 247–53.

—, 'Three "Neo-Moderns": Ian Hamilton Finlay, Edwin Morgan, Christopher Middleton', *British Poetry Since 1970: A Critical Survey*, eds Peter Jones and Michael Schmidt (New York: Persea, 1980), pp. 112–24.

DAVID MORRISON
The Saxon Toon (Edinburgh: Macdonald, 1966).
The White Hind: and Other Poems (Thurso: Caithness, 1968).
White Witch, White Woman (Reaster: Scotia, 1972).
The Constant Tide (Wick: Pulteney Press, 1986).
Grape and Grain (Wick: Pulteney Press, 1988).

STEPHEN MULRINE
Poems (Preston: Akros, 1971).

WILLIAM NEILL
Scotland's Castle (Edinburgh: Reprographia, 1969).
Despatches Home (Edinburgh: Reprographia, 1972).
Galloway Landscape and Other Poems (Haugh of Urr: Urr Publications, 1981).
Wild Places; Poems in Three Leids (Barr: Luath Press, 1985).
Blossom, Berry, Fall (Galloway: Heart Boox, 1986).
Making Tracks and other Poems (Edinburgh: Gordon Wright, 1988).
Straight Lines (Belfast: Blackstaff, 1992).
Tales frae the Odyssey (Edinburgh: Saltire Society, 1992).
Selected Poems 1969–1992 (Edinburgh: Canongate Press, 1992).
Tidsler (Arhus: Husets Forlag, 1998).

TOM POW
See reading lists, Part 2, 'Contemporary Poets'.

READING LISTS

KATHLEEN RAINE
The Pythoness: and Other Poems (London: Hamish Hamilton, 1949).
The Hollow Hill and Other Poems, 1960–1964 (London: Hamilton, 1965).
Defending Ancient Springs (London: Oxford University Press, 1967).
Death-in-Life and Life-in-Death: Cuchulain Comforted and News for the Delphic Oracle (Dublin: Dolmen Press London, 1974).
Collected Poems 1935–1980 (London: Allen & Unwin, 1981).
Autobiographies (London: Skoob Books, 1991).
Living with Mystery: Poems 1987–91 (Ipswich: Golgonooza Press, 1992).

TESSA RANSFORD
Light of the Mind (Edinburgh: Ramsay Head Press, 1980).
Fools and Angels (Edinburgh: Ramsay Head Press, 1984).
Shadows From the Greater Hill (Edinburgh: Ramsay Head Press, 1987).
A Dancing Innocence (Edinburgh: Macdonald, 1988).
Seven Valleys (Edinburgh: Ramsay Head Press, 1991).
Medusa Dozen and Other Poems (Edinburgh: Ramsay Head, 1994).
When It works It Feels Like Play (Edinburgh: Ramsay Head Press, 1998).

Secondary reading
Nairn, Thom, 'A Profile of Tessa Ransford', *Cencrastus* 25, 1987.

DILYS ROSE
Madame Doubtfire's Dilemma (Blackford: Chapman, 1989).

Secondary reading
Somerville-Arjat, Gillean, and Wilson, Rebecca E. (eds), 'Dilys Rose', *Sleeping with Monsters: Conversations with Scottish and Irish Women Poets* (Edinburgh: Polygon, 1990), pp. 208–15.

ALEXANDER SCOTT
The Latest in Elegies (Glasgow: Caledonian Press, 1948).
Selected Poems (Edinburgh: Oliver & Boyd, 1950).
Mouth Music (Edinburgh: Macdonald, 1954).
(ed.), *Diaries of a Dying Man by William Soutar* (Edinburgh: Chambers, 1954).
Still Life: William Soutar 1898–1943 (Edinburgh: Chambers, 1958).
Cantrips (Preston: Akros, 1968).
Selected Poems 1943–74 (Preston: Akros, 1975).

See also under Robb, secondary heading (below), for additional poems.

Secondary reading
Annand, James King, 'Alexander Scott: An Introduction', *Akros* 16 (Preston: Akros Publications, 1971), pp. 43–9.
Bruce, George, 'The Poetry of Alexander Scott', *Akros* 19 (Preston: Akros Publications, 1972), pp. 30–3.
Buchan, David, 'New Dimensions' [Review of *Selected Poems*], *Library Review* 25 (1975–76), pp. 85–6.

Crawford, Thomas, 'Alexander Scott', *Scottish Literature* 3 (1990), p. 2.

Farrow, Kenneth D., 'Waement the Deid': The Poetic Achievement of Alexander Scott (1920–89)', *SLJ* 27:1 (Aberdeen: Association for Scottish Literary Studies, 2000), pp. 39–64.

Lennox, Ruth, 'The Poetry of Alexander Scott', *Akros* 33 (Preston: Akros Publications, 1977), pp. 60–8.

Lindsay, Maurice, *As I Remember: Ten Scottish Authors Remember How Writing Began For Them* (London: Hale, 1979), pp. 89–107.

McCaig, Norman, 'Review of *Cantrips*', *Akros* 9 (Preston: Akros Publications, 1969), pp. 67–9.

McClure, J. D., 'The Poetic Language of Alexander Scott', *Northern Visions: The Literary Identity of Northern Scotland in the Twentieth Century*, ed. David Hewitt (East Lothian: Tuckwell Press, 1995), pp. 110–29.

McCulloch, Margery Palmer, '"I'd Sing my Sang": The Significance of Song in the Early Poetry of Alexander Scott', *SLJ* 27:1 (Aberdeen: Association for Scottish Literary Studies, 2000), pp. 77–90.

McIntyre, Lorn, 'Alexander Scott: Makar Extraordinary', *Akros* 25 (Preston: Akros Publications, 1974), pp. 71–8.

Mason, Leonard, *Two North-East Makars: Alexander Scott and Alastair Mackie: A Study of their Scots Poetry* (Preston: Akros Publications, 1975).

Robb, David S., 'Alexander Scott's Other Poems on Aberdeen', *SSL* 31 (Columbia: University of South Carolina, 1999), pp. 46–80 [Robb's appendix to this essay includes twenty-four unpublished poems].

—, '"A Teuch Toun": Alexander Scott's "Heart of Stone"', *SLJ* 27:1 (Aberdeen: Association for Scottish Literary Studies, 2000), pp. 65–76.

TOM SCOTT

The Ship and Ither Poems (Oxford: Oxford University Press, 1963).

At the Shrine o' the Unkent Sodger (Preston: Akros, 1968).

Brand the Builder (Epping: Ember Press, 1975).

The Tree (Dunfermline: Borderline Press, 1977).

The Dirty Business (Barr: Luath Press, 1980).

Collected Shorter Poems (Edinburgh and London: Chapman and Agenda, 1993).

Pervigilium Scotiae = Scotland's vigil, with Somhairle MacGill-Eain and Hamish Henderson (Buckfastleigh: Etruscan, 1997).

Secondary reading

Agenda 30(4)/31(1): Tom Scott Special Issue (Winter/Spring, 1993).

Calder, Robert, 'An Overview of Tom Scott's Poetry', *Chapman* 47/8 (Edinburgh: Chapman Publications, 1987), pp. 28–34.

Chapman 47–48 (Edinburgh: Chapman Publications, 1987) [Special Feature on Tom Scott].

Crawford, Thomas, 'Tom Scott: From Apocalypse to Brand', *Akros* 31 (Preston: Akros Publications, 1976), pp. 57–69.

Harris, T. J. G., 'The Creature's Love of Creation', *P. N. Review* 95, 20(3) (1994), pp. 63–5.

Herdman, John, 'Towards New Jerusalem: The Poetry of Tom Scott', *Akros* 16 (Preston: Akros Publications, 1971), pp. 43–9.

McClure, J. D., 'The Versification of Tom Scott's *The Tree*', *SLJ* Supplement 10 (Aberdeen: Association for Scottish Literary Studies, 1979), pp. 17–32.

Moessner, Lilo, 'A Critical Assessment of Tom Scott's Poem "The Seavaiger" as an Exercise in Translation', *Scottish Language* 7 (Aberdeen: Association for Scottish Literary Studies, 1988), pp. 9–21.

Ross, Raymond J., 'Tom Scott and the Dirty Business: An Interview', *Cencrastus* 26 (Edinburgh: Cencrastus, 1987), pp. 12–17.
Scotia Review 13–14 (1976) [A double issue devoted to Tom Scott with articles by Alan Bold and John Herdman, among others, and autobiographical contributions from Scott].

BURNS SINGER
The Collected Poems, ed. W. A. S. Keir (London: Secker & Warburg, 1970).
Selected Poems, ed. Anne Cluysennar (Manchester: Carcanet, 1977).

IAIN CRICHTON SMITH

Selected: for fuller details of this prolific poet, fiction writer and critic, see Crawford, and Royle's *Companion to Scottish Literature* (Edinburgh: Mainstream, 1993), and especially Grant F. Wilson's *A Bibliography of Iain Crichton Smith* (Aberdeen: Aberdeen University Press, 1990).

Thistles and Roses (London: Eyre & Spottiswoode, 1961).
Deer on the High Hills (Edinburgh: Giles Gordon, 1962).
The Law and the Grace (London: Eyre & Spottiswoode, 1965).
From Bourgeois Land (London: Gollancz, 1969).
Hamlet in Autumn (Loanhead: Macdonald, 1972).
Love Poems and Elegies (London: Gollancz, 1972).
The Notebooks of Robinson Crusoe (London: Gollancz, 1975).
In the Middle (London: Gollancz, 1977).
The Exiles (Manchester: Carcanet, 1984).
Selected Poems (Manchester: Carcanet, 1985).
A Life (Manchester: Carcanet, 1986).
The Village and Other Poems (Manchester: Carcanet, 1989).
Collected Poems (Manchester: Carcanet, 1992).
The Leaf and the Marble (Manchester: Carcanet, 1998).

Secondary reading

Alexander, J. A., 'The English Poetry of Iain Crichton Smith', *Literature of the North*, eds David Hewitt and Michael Spiller (Aberdeen: Aberdeen University Press, 1983), pp. 189–203.
Ascherson, Neal, 'Iain Crichton Smith', *Seven Poets*, ed. Christopher Carrell (Glasgow: Third Eye Centre, 1981), pp. 23, and Walker, Marshall, 'Six Poets', in same, pp. 43–51.
Blackburn, John, *A Writer's Journey: A Study of the Poetry of Iain Crichton Smith* (Edinburgh: SCET [for the Scottish Curriculum Development Service], 1981) [includes 5 cassettes].
—, *The Poetry of Iain Crichton Smith* (Aberdeen: Association for Scottish Literary Studies, Scotnotes Series, 1993).
Bold, Alan, 'A Thematic Note on the Poetry of Iain Crichton Smith', *Malahat Review* 62 (Victoria, BC: University of Victoria, 1982), pp. 215–22.
Daude, Gerald, 'From Different Premises, The Same Landscapes: On the Poetry of Iain Crichton Smith', *New Edinburgh Review* 66 (Edinburgh, 1984), pp. 30–1.
Duncan, Bill, 'Iain Crichton Smith in Conversation', *Chapman* 73 (Edinburgh: Chapman Publications, 1993), pp. 19–27.
Fulton, Robin, 'The Poetry of Iain Crichton Smith', *Lines Review* 42–43 (Edinburgh: Macdonald, 1972), pp. 92–116.
Gifford, Douglas, 'Bleeding from All That's Best: The Fiction of Iain Crichton Smith', *The*

Scottish Novel Since the Seventies, eds Gavin Wallace and Randall Stevenson (Edinburgh: Edinburgh University Press, 1993), pp. 25–40.

—, '*Deer on the High Hills*: The Elusiveness of Language in the Poetry of Iain Crichton Smith', *Gaelic and Scots in Harmony*, ed. Derick Thomson (Glasgow: Glasgow University Press, 1988), pp. 149–63.

—, 'The True Dialectic: The Fiction and Poetry of Iain Crichton Smith', *Chapman* 34 (Edinburgh: Chapman Publications, 1983), pp. 39–46.

Götte, Michaela, 'A Confessional Writer: Michaela Götte meets Iain Crichton Smith', *Books in Scotland* 46 (Edinburgh: Ramsay Head Press, 1993), pp. 1–6.

Gow, Carol, *Mirror and Marble: The Poetry of Iain Crichton Smith* (Edinburgh: Saltire Society, 1992).

Lindsay, Frederic, 'Disputed Angels: The Poetry of Iain Crichton Smith', *Akros* 36 (Preston: Akros Publications, 1977), pp. 15–26.

Lines Review 29 (Edinburgh: Macdonald, 1969) [Issue dedicated to Iain Crichton Smith].

Macintyre, Lorn, 'Poet in Bourgeois Land: Interview with Iain Crichton Smith', *Scottish International* (1971), pp. 22–7.

Morgan, Edwin, 'The Raging and the Grace: Some Notes on the Poetry of Iain Crichton Smith', *Essays* (Manchester: Carcanet, 1974), pp. 222–31.

—, 'The Contribution of Ian Crichton Smith', *ScotLit* 23 (Aberdeen: Association of Scottish Literary Studies, 2001).

Nicholson, Colin (ed.), *Iain Crichton Smith: Critical Essays* (Edinburgh: Edinburgh University Press, 1992).

—, 'To have Found One's Country: Iain Crichton Smith', *Poem, Purpose and Place: Shaping Identity in Contemporary Scottish Verse* (London: Polygon, 1992), pp. 114–32.

Relich, Mario, 'To hold the darkness at bay: A Conversation with Iain Crichton Smith, Taynuilt, Spring 1998', *Edinburgh Review* 99 (Edinburgh: Edinburgh University Press, 1998), pp. 108–21.

Riach, Alan, 'Ian Crichton Smith: An Appreciation', *P. M. Review* 126, 25:4 (1999), pp. 6–8.

Smith, Iain Crichton, 'Structure in My Poetry', *The Poet's Voice and Craft*, ed. C. B. McCully (Manchester: Carcanet, 1994), pp. 104–22.

Smith, Stan, 'A Double Man in a Double Place: Scotland Between the Symbolic and Imaginary in the Poetry of Iain Crichton Smith', *SLJ* 20(2) (Aberdeen: Association for Scottish Literary Studies, 1993), pp. 63–74.

Tait, Bob, 'Love and Death in Space', *Scottish International* 5 (1972), pp. 28–9.

SYDNEY GOODSIR SMITH

Skail Wind (Edinburgh: Chalmers Press, 1941).

The Wanderer and Other Poems (Edinburgh: Oliver & Boyd, 1943).

The Deevil's Waltz (Glasgow: MacLellan, 1946).

Under the Eildon Tree (Edinburgh: Serif Books, 1948).

Figs and Thistles (Edinburgh: Oliver & Boyd, 1959).

Kynd Kittock's Land (Edinburgh: Macdonald, 1965).

Collected Poems (London: John Calder, 1975).

Secondary reading

Buthlay, Kenneth, 'Sydney Goodsir Smith: Makar Macironical', *Akros* 31 (Preston: Akros Publications, 1986), pp. 46–56.

Crawford, Thomas, 'The Poetry of Sydney Goodsir Smith', *SSL* 7 (Columbia: University of South Carolina, 1970), pp. 40–59.

Gold, Eric, *Sydney Goodsir Smith's Under the Eildon Tree: An Essay* (Preston: Akros, 1975).

READING LISTS

Hall, John C., 'Sydney Goodsir Smith', *Lines Review* 88 (Loanhead: Macdonald Publishers, 1984), pp. 15–9.

—, 'Sydney Goodsir Smith', *Books in Scotland* 12 (Edinburgh: Ramsay Head Press, 1983), pp. 8–10.

Lindsay, Maurice, 'Sydney Goodsir Smith: An Appreciation', *Pembroke Magazine* 7 (Pembroke, NC: Pembroke State University, 1976), pp. 173–4.

MacDiarmid, Hugh, *Sydney Goodsir Smith* (Edinburgh, 1963).

—, *For Sydney Goodsir Smith* (Loanhead: Macdonald, 1975).

Morgan, Edwin, 'On Goodsir Smith's "perpetual opposition" and "deviation tactics"', *Crossing the Border* (Manchester: Carcanet, 1990), pp. 248–51.

Smith, Iain Crichton, 'Sydney Goodsir Smith', *Pembroke Magazine* 7 (Pembroke, NC: Pembroke State University, 1976), pp. 166–72.

DERICK THOMSON (RUARAIDH MACTHOMAIS)

Creachadh na Clàrsaich/Plundering the Harp: Collected Poems 1940–1980 (Edinburgh: Macdonald, 1980).

Bardachd Na Roinn-eorpa An Gaidhlig (Glaschu: Gairm, 1990).

Smeur An Dòchais/Bramble of Hope (Edinburgh: Canongate, 1991).

The Rugged Mountain (Glaschu: Garim, 1995).

Secondary reading

Smith, Iain Crichton, 'The Poetry of Derick Thomson', *Towards the Human* (Edinburgh: Macdonald, 1986), pp. 136–43.

Whyte, Christopher, 'Derick Thomson: Reluctant Symbolist', *Chapman* 38 (Edinburgh: Chapman Publications, 1984), pp. 1–6.

SYDNEY TREMAYNE

Selected and New Poems (London: Chatto & Windus, 1973).

Secondary reading

Bruce, George, 'The Poetry of Sydney Tremayne', *Akros* 38, 1978.

WILLIAM PRICE TURNER

Fables from Life (Newcastle: Northern House, 1966).

The Moral Rocking-Horse: Poems (London: Barrie & Jenkins, 1970).

GAEL TURNBULL

A Gathering of Poems 1950–1980 (London: Anvil Press Poetry, 1983).

From the Language of the Heart (Glasgow: Mariscat, 1983).

For Whose Delight (Glasgow: Mariscat, 1985).

RAYMOND VETTESE

The Richt Noise and Ither Poems (Edinburgh: Macdonald, 1988).

A Keen New Air (Edinburgh: Saltire, 1995).

Secondary reading

Vettese, Raymond, 'Myself and Poetry', *Akros* 16(48) (Preston: Akros Publications, 1981), pp. 42–5.

KENNETH WHITE
The Cold Wind of Dawn (London: Cape, 1966).
The Most Difficult Area (London: Caoe Goliard, 1968).
The Bird Path: Collected Longer Poems (Edinburgh: Mainstream, 1989).
Handbook for the Diamond Country: Collected Shorter Poems 1960–1990 (Edinburgh: Mainstream, 1990).

Secondary reading
Bowd, Gavin, 'Poetry after God: The Reinvention of the Sacred in the Work of Eugene Guillevic and Kenneth White', *Dalhousie French Studies* 39–40 (Halifax, NS: Dalhousie University, 1997), pp. 159–80.
Chapman 59 (Edinburgh: Chapman Publications, 1990) [issue devoted to Kenneth White including: Martin, Graham Dunstan '*A Pict in Roman Gaul: Kenneth White and France*' pp. 8–17; and McManus, Tony '*Kenneth White: A Re-Sourcing of Western Culture*', pp. 23–9].
Delbard, Olivier, *Le Lieux de Kenneth White: Paysage, Pensée, Poetique* (Paris: L'Harmattan, 1999).
Duclos, M., *Le monde ouvert de Kenneth White: essais et témoignages réunis par Michèle Duclos; ouvrage publié avec le concours du Groupe d'Études et de Recherches Britanniques et du Conseil Régional d'Aquitaine* (Bordeaux: Universitaires de Bordeaux, 1995).
Fawkner, H. W., 'Roots of the Geo-Poetic: Going beyond the Linguistic Man', *Moderna Sprak* 91(1) (Goteborg, Sweden, 1997).
McManus, Tony, 'From the Centred Complex: An Interview with Kenneth White, July 1993', *Edinburgh Review* 92 (Edinburgh, 1994), pp. 122–31.
Morgan, Edwin, 'Kenneth White: a Scottish Transnationalist', *Books in Scotland* 31 (Edinburgh: Ramsay Head Press, 1990), pp. 1–2.
Press, John, 'Ted Walker, Seamus Heaney and Kenneth White: Three New Poets', *The Southern Review* 5 (Baton Rouge, LA: Lousiana State University Press, 1969), pp. 673–88.

DOUGLAS YOUNG
Auntrin Blads (Glasgow: McLellan, 1943).
The Puddocks: A Verse Play in Scots frae the Old Greek o Aristophanes (Tayport: the author, 1957).
The Burdies: a Comedy in Scots Verse by Aristophanes and Douglas Young (Tayport: the author, 1959).

Secondary reading
Young, Clara, and Murison, David (eds), *A Clear Voice: Douglas Young Poet, and Polymath: a Selection from his Writing with a Memoir* (Loanhead: Macdonald, 1977).

Part Three: Contemporary Poets

IAN BAMFORTH
Sons and Pioneers (Manchester: Carcanet, 1992).
The Modern Copernicus (Edinburgh: Salamander, 1974).

MEG BATEMAN
Orain Ghaoi / Amhrain Ghra (Dublin: Coisceim, 1990).
Lightness and Other Poems (Edinburgh: Polygon, 1997).

READING LISTS

JOHN BURNSIDE
The Hoop (Manchester: Carcanet, 1988).
Common Knowledge (London: Secker & Warburg, 1991).
Feast Days (London: Secker & Warburg, 1992).
The Myth of the Twin (London: Cape, 1994).
Swimming in the Flood (London: Cape, 1995).
A Normal Skin (London: Cape, 1997).
The Asylum Dance (London: Cape, 2000).

RON BUTLIN
See also fiction lists.
Creatures Tamed by Cruelty: Poems in English and Scots and Translations (Edinburgh: Edinburgh
    University Press, 1979).
The Exquisite Instrument (Edinburgh: Salamander Press, 1982).
Ragtime in Unfamiliar Bars (London: Secker & Warburg, 1985).
Histories of Desire (Newcastle-upon-Tyne: Bloodaxe Books, 1995).

Secondary reading
Nicholson, Colin, 'Widdershins this Life o Mine', *Cencrastus* 24 (Edinburgh: Cencrastus
    Publications, 1987), pp. 34–40.

GERRY CAMBRIDGE
The Shell House (Aberdeen: Scottish Cultural Press, 1995).
Nothing But Heather (Edinburgh: Luath, 1999).

KATE CLANCHY
Slattern (London: Chatto & Windus, 1995).

STEWART CONN
Thunder in the Air (Preston: Akros, 1967).
The Chinese Tower (Edinburgh: Macdonald, 1967).
Stoats in the Sunlight (London: Hutchinson, 1968).
An Ear to the Ground (London: Hutchinson, 1972).
Under the Ice (London: Hutchinson, 1978).
In the Kibble Palace (Newcastle-Upon-Tyne: Bloodaxe, 1987).
The Luncheon of the Boating Party (Newcastle-Upon-Tyne: Bloodaxe, 1992).
In the Blood (Newcastle: Bloodaxe, 1995).
At the Aviary (Plumstead: Snailpress, 1995).
Stolen Light: Selected Poems (Newcastle-Upon-Tyne: Bloodaxe, 1999).

Secondary reading
Bruce, George, 'Stewart Conn', *Contemporary Poets*, ed. Thomas Riggs (Detroit, MI, London: St.
    James Press, 1996), pp. 179–81.
Smith, Iain Crichton, 'The Poetry of Stewart Conn', *Towards the Human* (Edinburgh: Mac-
    donald, 1986), pp. 159–66.

ROBERT CRAWFORD
A Scottish Assembly (London: Chatto & Windus, 1990).
Sharawaggi [with A. N. Herbert] (Edinburgh: Polygon, 1990).
Talkies (London: Chatto & Windus, 1992).
Masculinity (London: Cape, 1996).
Spirit Machines (London: Cape, 1999).

Secondary reading
Crawford, Robert, 'Myself and Poetry', *Akros* 16(48) (Preston: Akros Publications, 1981), pp. 65–8.
O'Neill, Michael, 'Robert Crawford', *Contemporary Poets*, ed. Thomas Riggs (Detroit, MI, and London: St. James Press, 1996), pp. 198–9.
O'Rourke, Daniel, *Dream State: The New Scottish Poets* (Edinburgh: Polygon, 1994), pp. xxiii–vi, 59–69.
Robertson, James, 'Robert Crawford and *Verse*: An International Flavour', *SLJ* Supplement 28 (Aberdeen: Association for Scottish Literary Studies, 1988), pp. 25–8.
Skoblow, Jeffrey, '*Sharawaggi*: Crawford and Herbert meet the incubus', *SLJ* 25(2) (Aberdeen: Association for Scottish Literary Studies, 1998), pp. 67–85.

IVOR CUTLER
A Flat Man (London: Trigram Press, 1977).
Life in a Scotch Sitting Room (London: Methuen, 1984).
Gruts (London: Methuen, 1986).
Fremsley (London: Methuen, 1987).
Glasgow Dreamer (London: Methuen, 1990).

CAROL ANN DUFFY
Beauty and the Beast (Liverpool: Carol Ann Duffy and A. Henri, 1977).
Fifth Last Song: Twenty-One Love Poems (West Kirby: Headland, 1982).
Standing Female Nude (London: Anvil Press, 1985).
Thrown Voices (London: Turret, 1986).
Selling Manhattan (London: Anvil Press, 1987).
The Other Country (London: Anvil Press, 1990).
Mean Time (London: Anvil Press, 1993).
Selected Poems (London: Penguin, 1994).
Carol Ann Duffy, Vicki Feaver, Eavan Boland (London: Penguin, 1995).
The World's Wife (London: Macmillan, 1999).

Secondary reading
Donaghy, Michael, 'Carol Ann Duffy', *Contemporary Poets*, ed. Thomas Riggs (Detroit, MI, and London: St. James Press, 1996), pp. 279–80.
O'Rourke, Daniel, *Dream State: The New Scottish Poets* (Edinburgh: Polygon, 1994), pp. xix–xx, 1–10.

ALISON FELL
Kisses for Mayakovsky (London: Virago, 1984).
The Crystal Owl (London: Methuen, 1988).

VERONICA FORREST-THOMSON
Language Games (Leeds: University of Leeds, School of English Press, 1971).
Cordelia, or, 'A Poem Should Not Mean But Be' (Leicester: Omens, 1974).
On the Periphery (Cambridge: Street Editions, 1976) [includes a personal memoir by J. H. Prynne].
Collected Poems and Translations (London: Agneau 2, 1990).

ROBIN FULTON
Instances (Edinburgh: Macdonald, 1967).
The Man With the Surbahar (Loanhead: Macdonald, 1971).
The Spaces Between the Stones (New York: New Rivers Press, 1971).
Between Flights: Eighteen Poems (Egham: Interim Press, 1976).
Selected Poems, 1963–1978 (Loanhead: Macdonald, 1980).
Fields of Focus (London: Anvil Press, 1982).
The Way the Words are Taken: Selected Essays (Edinburgh: Macdonald, 1989).
Coming Down to Earth and Spring is Soon (London: Oasis, 1990).

Secondary reading
Price, Brian, 'What to do with the word "Home"': Absence and Elegy in Robin Fulton's Poetry',
    Lines Review 131 (Loanhead: Macdonald Publishers, 1994), pp. 5–13.

VALERIE GILLIES
Bed of Stone (Edinburgh: Canongate, 1984).
Chanters Tune (Edinburgh: Canongate, 1990).
Each Bright Eye: Selected Poems, 1971–1976 (Edinburgh: Canongate, 1977).
Ringing Rock (Aberdeen: Scottish Cultural Press, 1995).

JOHN GLENDAY
The Apple Ghost (Calstock, Cornwall: Peterloo Poets, 1989).
Undark (Calstock, Cornwall: Peterloo Poets, 1995).

RODY GORMAN
Fax and Other Poems (Edinburgh: Polygon, 1996).
On the Underground (Edinburgh: Polygon, 2000).

ALASDAIR GRAY
Old Negatives: Four Verse Sequences (London: Cape, 1989).

ANDREW GREIG
Men on Ice (Edinburgh: Canongate, 1977).
Surviving Passages (Edinburgh: Canongate, 1982).
A Flame in Your Heart [with Kathleen Jamie] (Newcastle-Upon-Tyne: Bloodaxe, 1990).
The Order of the Day (Newcastle-Upon-Tyne: Bloodaxe, 1990).
Western Swing (Newcastle-Upon-Tyne: Bloodaxe, 1994).

Secondary reading
Greig, Andrew, 'Myself and Poetry', *Akros* 16(48) (Preston: Akros Publications, 1981), pp. 3–5.

W. N. HERBERT
Sharawaggi [with Robert Crawford] (Edinburgh: Polygon, 1990).
Dundee Doldrums (Edinburgh: Galliard, 1991).
Anither Music (London: Vennel Press, 1991).
The Testament of the Reverend Thomas Dick (Todmorden: Arc, 1994).
Forked Tongue (Newcastle-Upon-Tyne: Bloodaxe, 1994).
Cabaret McGonagall (Newcastle Upon Tyne: Bloodaxe, 1996).
The Laurelude (Newcastle-Upon-Tyne: Bloodaxe, 1998).

MICK IMLAH
The Zoologist's Bath and the Other Adventures (Oxford: Oxford Sycamore Press, 1982).
Birthmarks (London: Chatto & Windus, 1988).

ALAN JACKSON
See reading lists, Part 1, 'Modern Poets'.

KATHLEEN JAMIE
Black Spiders (Edinburgh: Salamander Press, 1982).
A Flame in Your Heart [with Andrew Greig] (Newcastle-Upon-Tyne: Bloodaxe, 1986).
The Way We Live (Newcastle-Upon-Tyne: Bloodaxe, 1987).
The Golden Peak (London: Virago, 1992).
The Autonomous Region (Newcastle: Bloodaxe, 1993).
The Queen of Sheba (Newcastle-Upon-Tyne: Bloodaxe, 1994).
John Burnside, Robert Crawford, Kathleen Jamie (London: Penguin, 1996).
Jizzen (London: Picador, 1999).

Secondary reading
Boden, Helen, 'Kathleen Jamie's Semiotic of Scotlands', *Contemporary Scottish Women Writers*, eds Aileen Christianson and Alison Lumsden (Edinburgh: Edinburgh University Press, 2000), pp. 27–40.
Freil, Raymond, 'Women Beware Gravity: Kathleen Jamie's Poetry', *Southfields 1* (London: Southfields Press, 1995), pp. 29–48.
Monnickendam, Andrew, 'Changing Places with What Goes Before: The Poetry of Kathleen Jamie', *Contemporary Scottish Literature, 1970–2000 (Revista Canaria de Estudios Ingleses)*, ed. T. Monterrey (Servicio de Publicaciones: Universidad de la Laguna, 2000), pp. 77–86.
Price, Richard, 'Kathleen Jamie interviewed by Richard Price', *Verse* 8:3 / 9:1 (1992), pp. 103–6; reprinted in *Talking Verse*, eds R. Crawford et al. (St Andrews and Williamsburg, VA: Verse, 1995), pp. 99–102.

ROBERT ALAN JAMIESON
Shoormal (Edinburgh: Polygon, 1986).

JACKIE KAY
The Adoption Papers (Newcastle-Upon-Tyne: Bloodaxe, 1991).
That Distance Apart (London: Turret, 1991).
Other Lovers (Newcastle-Upon-Tyne: Bloodaxe, 1993).
Off-Colour (Manchester: Bloodaxe, 1998).

READING LISTS

Secondary reading

Calder, Angus, 'Jackie Kay's Adoption Papers', *Revolving Culture: Notes from the Scottish Republic* (London: I. B. Tauris, 1994), pp. 209–16.

Lumsden, Alison, 'Jackie Kay's Poetry and Prose: Constructing Identity', *Contemporary Scottish Women Writers*, eds Aileen Christianson and Alison Lumsden (Edinburgh: Edinburgh University Press, 2000), pp. 79–94.

DAVID KINLOCH

Dustie-Fute (London: Vennel Press, 1992).
Severe Burns (Oxford: Obog Books, 1986).
Paris-Forfar (Edinburgh: Polygon, 1994).

FRANK KUPPNER

A Bad Day for the Sung Dynasty (Manchester: Carcanet, 1984).
The Intelligent Observation of Naked Women (Manchester: Carcanet, 1987).
Ridiculous! Absurd! Disgusting! (Manchester: Carcanet, 1989).
Everything is Strange (Manchester: Carcanet, 1994).
Second Best Moments in Chinese History (Manchester: Carcanet, 1997).

RODY LUMSDEN

Yeah Yeah Yeah (Newcastle-Upon-Tyne: Bloodaxe, 1997).
The Book of Love (Newcastle-Upon-Tyne: Bloodaxe, 2000).

BRIAN MCCABE

Spring's Witch (Glasgow: Mariscat, 1984).
One Atom to Another (Edinburgh: Polygon, 1987).
Body Parts (Edinburgh: Canongate, 1999).

PETER MCCAREY

Town Shanties (Glasgow: Broch, 1991).
Devil in the Driving Mirror (London: Vennel Press, 1995).
Double-Click (Kirkcaldy: Akros, 1997).
In the Meta-Forest (London: Vennel, 2000).

FEARGHAS MACFHIONNLAIGH

Bogha-Frois San Oidhche: Rainbow in the Night (Carberry: Hansel Press, 1997).

HUGH MCMILLAN

Tramontana (Glasgow: Dog & Bone, 1990).

KEVIN MCNEIL

Love and Zen in the Outer Hebrides (Edinburgh: Canongate, 1998).

ANGELA MCSEVENEY

Coming Out With It (Edinburgh: Polygon, 1992).

ELMA MITCHELL
The Poor Man in the Flesh (Calstock, Cornwall: Peterloo Poets, 1976).
The Human Cage (Calstock, Cornwall: Peterloo Poets, 1979).
Furnished Rooms (Calstock, Cornwall: Peterloo Poets, 1983).
People Et Cetera: Poems New and Selected (Calstock, Cornwall: Peterloo Poets, 1987).

DONNY O'ROURKE
Second Cities (London: Vennel Press, 1991).
The Waistband (Edinburgh: Polygon, 1997).

DON PATERSON
Nil Nil (London: Faber, 1993).
God's Gift to Women (London: Faber, 1997).
The Eyes (London: Faber, 1999).

TOM POW
Rough Seas (Edinburgh: Canongate, 1987).
The Moth Trap (Edinburgh: Canongate, 1990).
Red Letter Day (Newcastle-upon-Tyne: Bloodaxe, 1996).

RICHARD PRICE
Sense and a Minor Fever (London: Vennel Press, 1993).
Contraflow: An Informationist Primer, ed. with W. N. Herbert (London: Smithfields Press, 1994).
Perfume and Petrol Fumes (Edinburgh: Diehard, 1999).

ALAN RIACH
This Folding Map (Auckland: Auckland University Press, 1990).
An Open Return (Wellington: Untold Books, 1991).
First and Last Songs (Edinburgh: Chapman, 1995).
Clearances (Edinburgh: Scottish Cultural Press, 2001).

Secondary reading
Morgan, Edwin, 'This Folding Map', *Landfall* 179 (Christchurch: Caxton Press, 1991), pp. 382–4.
O'Rourke, Daniel, *Dream State: The New Scottish Poets* (Edinburgh: Polygon, 1994), xxix–xxx, 31–8.
Smith, Anna, 'Alan (Scott) Riach', *Contemporary Poets*, ed. Thomas Riggs (Detroit, MI, London: St. James Press, 1996), pp. 908–9.

ROBIN ROBERTSON
A Painted Field (London: Picador, 1997).

DILYS ROSE
See reading lists, Part 1, 'Modern Poets'.

KENNETH WHITE
See reading lists, Part 1, 'Modern Poets'.

BRIAN WHITTINGHAM
Ergonomic Workstations and Spinning Teacans (Edinburgh: Taranis Books, 1992).
Swiss Watches and the Ballroom Dancer (Edinburgh: Taranis Books, 1996).
Premier Results (with Magi Gibson) (Glasgow: Neruda, 1997).

CHRISTOPHER WHYTE ('CRISDEAN WHYTE')
Uirsgeul: Myth (Gaelic poems with English translations) (Glasgow: Gairm, 1991).

The poets listed above represent only a sample of the vigorous current scene in Scottish poetry. Readers should check for stimulating new work from poets such as Ian Abbot, Derek Bowman, Elizabeth Burns, Thomas A. Clark, John Dixon, G. F. Dutton, Gerrie Fellowes, Graham Fulton, George Gunn, Alexander Hutchison, Alison Kermack, Denis O'Donnell, Anne McLeod, Robin Munro, Ken Morrice, Douglas Oliver, Janet Paisley, Walter Perrie, Alistair Reid, Alan Riddell, Christopher Salvesen, Donald Saunders, Harry Smart, Ian Stephen Roderick Watson. Details of these poets and many others can be found at the developing website at **www.arts.gla.ac.uk/SESLL/ScotLit/bibliography/**, and in the various bibliographies listed throughout this section.

Chapter 39: Modern Scottish Drama

ANTHOLOGIES
A Decade's Drama (Todmorden: Woodhouse, 1980) [plays of the 1970s].
Scot-Free, ed. Alasdair Cameron (London: Nick Hern, 1990) [plays of the 1980s].
Made In Scotland, eds Ian Brown and Mark Fisher (London: Methuen, 1994) [plays of the 1990s].
Plays of the Seventies, ed. Bill Findlay (Edinburgh: Scottish Cultural Press, 1998).
Scotland Plays, ed. Philip Howard (London: Nick Hern, 1998) [Traverse plays of the 1990s].
Twentieth-century Scottish Drama: an anthology, eds Cairns Craig and Randall Stevenson (Edinburgh: Canongate, 2001).

WILLIAM BOYD
School Ties (London: Hamilton, 1985).

GEORGE MACKAY BROWN
A Spell for Green Corn (London: Hogarth Press, 1970).
Three Plays (London: Chatto & Windus, 1984).
The Loom of Light (Nairn: Balnain, 1986).
A Celebration for Magnus (Nairn: Balnain, 1987).

BILL BRYDEN
Willie Rough (Edinburgh: Southside, 1972).
Benny Lynch: Scenes from a Short Life (Edinburgh: Southside, 1975).
Old Movies (London: Heinemann, 1976).
Il Campiello: A Venetian Comedy by Carlo Goldoni, with Susanna Graham-Jones (London: Heinemann, 1976).
The Big Picnic, Theatre Scotland 3(10) (Edinburgh: Theatre Scotland, 1994)

JOHN BYRNE
The Government Inspector (London: Oberon Books, 1997).
Colquhoun and MacBryde (London: Faber & Faber, 1992).
Tutti Frutti (London: BBC, 1987).
The Slab Boys Trilogy (Harmondsworth: Penguin, 1987).
Cutting a Rug (Edinburgh: Salamander Press, 1982).
Still Life (Edinburgh: Salamander Press, 1982).

ALISDAIR CAMPBELL
Tri Dealbhan Cluiche (Skye: Clò Ostaig, 1990).

DONALD CAMPBELL
See also poetry lists.
The Jesuit (Edinburgh: Paul Harris, 1976).
Somerville the Soldier (Edinburgh: Paul Harris, 1978).
The Widows of Clyth (Edinburgh: Paul Harris, 1979).

JOHN CLIFFORD
Night in the Village (London: Nick Hern, 1991).
Losing Venice in *Scot-free: new Scottish plays*, ed. Alasdair Cameron (London: Nick Hern Books, 1990).
Innes de Castro in *First Run: new plays by new writers*, ed. Kate Harwood (London: Nick Hern, 1989).

STEWART CONN
The Burning (London: Calder & Boyars, 1973).
Thistlewood (Todmorden: Woodhouse, 1979).
Play Donkey in *A Decade's Drama* (Todmorden: Woodhouse, 1980) [plays of the 1970s].

MIKE CULLEN
Anna Weiss (London: Nick Hern, 1997).

CATHERINE LUCY CZERKAWSKA
Wormwood in *Scotland Plays: new Scottish drama*, ed. Philip Howard (London: Nick Hern Books in association with Traverse Theatre, 1998).

ANDREW DALLMEYER
The Boys in the Backroom (Edinburgh: Salamander, 1982).

READING LISTS

ANNE MARIE DI MAMBRO
Brothers of Thunder in *Scotland Plays: new Scottish drama*, ed. Philip Howard (London: Nick Hern Books in association with Traverse Theatre, 1998).

CHRIS DOLAN
Sabina! (London: Faber & Faber, 1998).
The Angel's Share (Ayr: Borderline, 2000).

SIMON DONALD
The Life of Stuff in *Theatre Scotland* 1(2) (Edinburgh: Theatre Scotland, 1992).
Prickly Heat in *First Run: new plays by new writers*, ed. Kate Harwood (London: Nick Hern, 1989).

BILL DOUGLAS
Comrades (London: Faber, 1987).

BILL DUNLOP
Female Wits (Belfast: Canto, 1990).

DOUGLAS DUNN
Andromaque by Racine (London: Faber, 1990).

JAMES DUTHIE
Donal and Sally (London: Eyre-Methuen, 1978).

MARCELLA EVARISTI
Mouthpieces (St. Andrews: Crawford Centre for the Arts, 1980).
Commedia (Edinburgh: Salamander, 1983).

RONALD FRAME
Paris; with *Privateers* (London: Faber, 1987).

TOM GALLACHER
Revival!; and *Shellenbrack* (Glasgow: Molendinar, 1978).
Natural Causes: A Mystery Thriller in Two Acts (London: Dr Jan Loewen Ltd., 1980).
Jenny (London: French, 1980).
The Only Street: A Play in Two Acts (London: Dr Jan Loewen Ltd., 1981).
Our Kindness to Five Persons (London: Dr Jan Loewen Ltd., 1981).
The Sea Change (London: Dr Jan Loewen Ltd., 1981).

ROBERT GARIOCH
The Masque of Edinburgh (Edinburgh: Macdonald, 1954).
George Buchanan: Jephthah and the Baptist, Translatit frae Latin in Scots (Edinburgh: Oliver & Boyd, 1959).

SUE GLOVER
Shetland Saga (London: Nick Hern, 2000).
Bondagers and *The Straw Chair* (London: Methuen, 1997).

STEPHEN GREENHORN
Passing Places in *Scotland Plays: New Scottish Drama*, ed. Philip Howard (London: Nick Hern Books in association with Traverse Theatre, 1998).

DAVID GREIG
Victoria (London: Methuen, 2000).
The Cosmonaut's Last Message to the Woman He Once Loved in the Former Soviet Union (London: Methuen, 1999).
Danny 306 + Me (4 Ever) (Edinburgh: Traverse, 1999).
The Speculator and *The Meeting* (London: Methuen, 1999).
Europe and *The Architect* (London: Methuen, 1996).
One Way Street in *Scotland Plays: New Scottish Drama*, ed. Philip Howard (London: Nick Hern Books in association with Traverse Theatre, 1998).

GEORGE GUNN
Songs of the Grey Coast; The Gold of Kildonan (Edinburgh: Chapman, 1992).
Whins (Edinburgh: Chapman, 1996).

CHRIS HANNAN
Shinning Souls (London: Nick Hern, 1996).
The Evil Doers and The Baby (London: Nick Hern, 1991).
Elizabeth Gordon Quinn in *Scot-Free: New Scottish Plays*, ed. Alasdair Cameron (London: Nick Hern Books, 1990).

DAVID HARROWER
Kill the Old Torture Their Young (London: Methuen, 1998).
Knives in Hens (London: Methuen, 1995).

IAIN HEGGIE
An Experienced Woman Gives Advice (London: Methuen, 1995).
A Wholly Healthy Glasgow (London: Methuen, 1988).
American Bagpipes (Harmondsworth: Penguin, 1989).

JAMES KELMAN
Hardie and Baird, and Other Plays (London: Secker & Warburg, 1991).

ROBERT KEMP
A Trump for Jerico (Edinburgh: St Giles Press, 1948).
The Satire of the Three Estates, Adapted from the play by Sir David Lindsay (Edinburgh: Scots Review, 1949).
The Saxon Saint (Edinburgh: St Giles Press, 1950).
The King of Scots (Edinburgh: St Giles Press, 1951).

READING LISTS

The Asset (London: Heinemann, 1956).
The Other Dear Charmer (London: Duckworth, 1957).
Master John Knox (Edinburgh: St Andrew Press, 1960).
Off a Duck's Back (London: French, 1961).
Let Wives Tak Tent: A Free Translation into Scots of Moliere's 'L'École de Femmes' (Glasgow: Brown & Ferguson, 1983).
Rob Roy (Glasgow: Brown & Ferguson, 1983).

TOM LEONARD
If Only Bunty Was Here: A Drama Sequence of Totally Undramatic Non-Sequiturs (Glasgow: Print Studio Press, 1979).

LIZ LOCHHEAD
Perfect Days (London: Nick Hern, 1998).
Mary Queen of Scots got her head chopped off and *Dracula* (Harmondsworth: Penguin, 1989).
Blood and Ice, Plays by Women 4, ed. Michelene Wandor (London: Methuen, 1985).
Blood and Ice (Edinburgh: Salamander Press, 1982).
Quelques Fleurs in *Scotland Plays: New Scottish Drama*, ed. Philip Howard (London: Nick Hern Books in association with Traverse Theatre, 1998).
Tartuffe, A Translation Into Scots (Edinburgh: Polygon, 1985).

Secondary reading
Christianson, Aileen, 'Liz Lochhead's Poetry and Drama: Forging Ironies', *Contemporary Scottish Women Writers*, eds Aileen Christianson and Alison Lumsden (Edinburgh: Edinburgh University Press, 2000), pp. 41–52.
Crawford, Robert and Varty, Anne (eds), *Liz Lochhead's Voices* (Edinburgh: Edinburgh University Press, 1993).
Fischer-Seidel, Therese, 'Biography in Drama: Genre and Gender in Tom Stoppard's *Travesties* and Liz Lochhead's *Blood and Ice*', *Why Literature Matters: Theories and Functions of Literature* eds Rudiger Ahrens and Laurenz Volkmann (Heidelberg: Winter, 1996), pp. 197–210.
Harvie, Jennifer, 'Desire and Difference in Liz Lochhead's *Dracula*', *Essays in Theatre / Etudes Theatrales* 11(2) (1993), pp. 133–43.
Koren-Deutsch, Ilona S., 'Feminist Nationalism in Scotland: *Mary Queen of Scots Got Her Head Chopped Off*, *Modern Drama* 35(3) (1992), pp. 424–32.
McDonald, Jan, ' "The Devil is Beautiful": *Dracula*: Freudian Novel and Feminist Drama', *Novel Images: Literature in Performance*, ed. Peter Reynolds (London: Routledge, 1993), pp. 80–104.
Neumeier, Beate, 'Past Lives in Present Drama: Feminist Theatre and Intertextuality', *Frauen und Frauenarstellung in der Englischen und Amerikanischen Literatur*, ed. Therese Fischer-Seidel (Tubingen: Narr, 1991), pp. 181–98.
Scullion, Adrienne, 'Liz Lochhead', *Contemporary Dramatists*, ed. Thomas Rigg (New York: St. James Press, 1999; sixth edition), pp. 403–5.
Varty, Anne, 'The Mirror and the Vamp: Liz Lochhead', *A History of Scottish Women's Writing*, eds Douglas Gifford and Dorothy McMillan (Edinburgh: Edinburgh University Press, 1997), pp. 641–58.

NICOLA MCCARTNEY
Heritage (Edinburgh: Traverse, 1998).

EWAN MCCOLL
Uranium 235: A Documentary Play (Glasgow: Maclellan, 1948).

ARCHIBALD MACCULLOCH
Mairead (Glasgow: An Comunn Gaidhealach, 1924).

ROBERT DAVID MACDONALD
School for Wives by Moliere (Birmingham: Oberon, 1987).
Mary Stuart by Schiller (Birmingham: Oberon, 1987).
Faust by Goethe (Birmingham: Oberon, 1988).
No Orchids for Miss Blandish (Birmingham: Oberon, 1988).
The Ice House (London: Oberon Books, 1998).
Three Plays – Chinchilla, Webster and Summit Conference (London: Oberon Books, 1991).

SHARMAN MACDONALD
Sea Urchins (London: Faber & Faber, 1998).
All Things Nice (London: Faber, 1991).
Shades (London: Faber, 1992).
*Plays: One – When I was a girl I used to scream and shout; When We Were Women; The Winter Guest;
    Borders of Paradise* (London: Faber & Faber, 1995).

STEPHEN MACDONALD
Not about Heroes: The Friendship of Siegfried Sassoon and Wilfred Owen (London: Faber, 1983).

JOHN MCGRATH
Events While Guarding the Bofors Gun (London: Methuen, 1966).
Random Happenings in the Hebrides (London: Davis-Poynter, 1972).
The Cheviot, the Stag and the Black, Black Oil (Breakish: West Highland Publishing Co., 1974).
Fish in the Sea (London: Pluto Press, 1977).
Little Red Hen (London: Pluto Press, 1977).
Yobbo Nowt (London: Pluto Press, 1978).
Joe's Drum (Aberdeen: Aberdeen People's Press, 1979).
Two Plays for the Eighties: Blood Red Roses, and Swings and Roundabouts (Aberdeen: Aberdeen
    People's Press, 1981).
Six-Pack: The Scottish Plays (Edinburgh: Polygon, 1995).

TOM MCGRATH *with* Jimmy Boyle
The Hard Man (Edinburgh: Canongate, 1977).

ROBERT MCLELLAN
The Changeling: a Border comedy in one act (Edinburgh: Porpoise Press, 1938).
Collected plays Vol. 1 (London: John Calder, 1981).
The Hypocrite (London: Calder & Boyars, 1970).
Jamie the Saxt: a Historical Comedy, edited by Ian Campbell and Ronald D. S. Jack (London:
    Calder & Boyars, 1970).

READING LISTS

HECTOR MACMILLAN
The Rising, Plays of the Seventies, ed. Bill Findlay (Edinburgh: Scottish Cultural Press, 1998).
The Sash My Father Wore (Glasgow: Molendinar Press, 1974).

RODDY MCMILLAN
All in Good Faith (Glasgow: Scottish Society of Playwrights, 1979).
The Bevellers (Edinburgh: Southside Press, 1973).

EDWIN MORGAN
Cyrano de Bergerac (Edinburgh: Carcanet Press, 1992).

JOHN MORRIS
How Mad Tulloch Was Taken Away (London: Faber, 1976).

RONA MUNRO
The Maiden Stone (London: Nick Hern, 1995).
Your Turn to Clean the Stair and Fugue (London: Nick Hern, 1995).
Bold Girls (London: Samuel French, 1991).

ANTHONY NEILSON
Plays: One – Normal; Penetrator; Year of the Family; The Night Before Christmas; The Censor (London: Methuen, 1998).

ALEXANDER REID
The Lass wi' the Muckle Mou', or Once Upon a Rhyme: A Comedy (London: Collins, 1958).
The Warld's Wonder. A Phantasy (London: Collins, 1958).

TONY ROPER
The Steamie in *Scot-free: new Scottish plays*, ed. Alasdair Cameron (London: Nick Hern, 1990).

GEORGE ROSIE
Carlucco and *The Queen of Hearts*, and *Blasphemer* (Edinburgh: Chapman, 1992).

JAMES SCOTLAND
The Burning Question: A Black-Edged Comedy (Glasgow: Brown & Ferguson, 1975).
The Holy Terror: A Scots Comedy, freely adapted from Moliere's 'Tartuffe' (Glasgow: Brown & Ferguson, 1978).
A Hundred Thousand Welcomes: A Comedy in Three Acts (Glasgow: Brown & Ferguson, 1982).

ALEXANDER SCOTT
Prometheus 48 (Aberdeen: SRC, 1948).
Untrue Thomas (Glasgow: Caledonian Press, 1952).
Shetland Yarn (London: Evans Brothers, 1954).

R. S. SILVER
The Bruce (Edinburgh: Saltire Society, 1986).

IAIN CRICHTON SMITH
A' Chuirt (Glasgow: An Comunn Gaidhealach, 1966).
An Coileach (Glasgow: An Comunn Gaidhealach, 1966).

SYDNEY GOODSIR SMITH
The Wallace: A Triumph in Five Acts (Edinburgh: Oliver & Boyd, 1960).
Fifteen Poems and a Play (Edinburgh: Southside, 1969).

W. GORDON SMITH
Jock (Edinburgh: Cacciatore Fabbro, 1977).

MURIEL SPARK
Voices at Play (London: Macmillan, 1961).
Doctors of Philosophy (London: Macmillan, 1963).

ALAN SPENCE
Sailmaker (Edinburgh: Salamander, 1982).
Space Invaders (Edinburgh: Salamander, 1983).
Changed Days: Memories of an Edinburgh Community (London: Hodder & Stoughton, 1991).

ENA LAMONT STEWART
Men Should Weep, ed. Linda Mackenney (Edinburgh: 7:84 Publications, 1986).

CECIL PHILIP TAYLOR
The Ballachulish Beat: A Play with Songs (London: Rapp & Carroll, 1967).
Bandits! (Cullercoats: Iron Press, 1977).
And a Nightingale Sang (London: Eyre-Methuen, 1979).
Good: A Tragedy (London: Methuen, 1979).
Live Theatre: Four Plays for Young People (London: Methuen, 1983).
North: Six Plays (London: Methuen/Iron Press, 1987).
Bring Me Sunshine & Other Plays (London: Methuen/Iron Press, 1988).
The Plays (Edinburgh: Edinburgh Festival Society, 1992).

MICHEL TREMBLAY
The Guid Sisters, trans. Bill Findlay and Martin Bowman (London: Nick Hern, 1992).

JOAN URE
Five Short Plays (Glasgow: Scottish Society of Playwrights, 1979).

WILLIAM WATSON
Sawney Bean, with Robert Nye (London: Calder & Boyars, 1970).

READING LISTS

BACKGROUND READING

Brown, Ian, 'Plugged into history: the sense of the past in Scottish theatre', *Scottish Theatre since the Seventies*, eds Stevenson and Wallace (Edinburgh: Edinburgh University Press, 1996), pp. 84–99.

Brown, Ian (director), 'Directing for the Scottish stage', *Scottish Theatre since the Seventies*, eds Stevenson and Wallace (Edinburgh: Edinburgh University Press, 1996), pp. 199–205.

Calder, R. (ed.), 'Scottish theatre I and II', *Chapman* 3(1) (Edinburgh: Chapman Publications, 1974).

Cameron, Alasdair, 'Glasgow's Tramway: little Diaghilevs and large ambitions', *Theatre Research International* 17(2) (Oxford: Oxford University Press, 1992), pp. 146–55.

—, 'Experimental theatre in Scotland', *Contemporary British Theatre*, ed. Theodore Shank (Basingstoke: Macmillan, 1994), pp. 123–38.

—, *Study Guide to Scottish Theatre* (Glasgow: Department of Scottish Literature: University of Glasgow, 1988).

—, and Scullion, Adrienne (eds), *Scottish Popular Theatre and Entertainment* (Glasgow: Glasgow University Library Studies, 1996).

Campbell, Donald, 'Theatre in the Community: A Playwright's View', *Chapman* 10(52) (Edinburgh: Chapman Publications, 1988), pp. 51–6.

—, *A Brighter Sunshine: A Hundred Years of the Edinburgh Royal Lyceum Theatre* (Edinburgh: Southside, 1983).

Chapman 3(1) (Edinburgh: Chapman Publications, 1974) [Issue on Scottish Theatre].

Chapman 43–44 (Edinburgh: Chapman Publications, 1974) [a special edition focusing on theatre and drama].

Clifford, John, 'New Playwriting in Scotland', *Chapman* 8–9(43–44) (Edinburgh: Chapman Publications, 1986), pp. 93–7.

Craig, Sandy, *Dreams and Deconstructions: Alternative Theatre in Britain* (Ambergate, Derbyshire: Amberlane Press, 1980).

Crawford, Tom, *Scottish Writing Today: Poetry, Fiction, Drama* (Aberdeen: Aberdeen University Press, 1972).

Di Cenzo, Maria, *The Politics of Alternative Theatre in Britain 1968–1990: The Case of 7:84 (Scotland)* (Cambridge: Cambridge University Press, 1996).

Farrell, Joseph, 'Recent Political Theatre', *Chapman* 8/9 (Edinburgh: Chapman Publications, 1986), pp. 48–54.

Findlay, B., *A History of Scottish Theatre* (Edinburgh: Polygon, 1998).

—, 'Translating Tremblay into Scots', *Theatre Research International* 17(2) (Oxford: Oxford University Press, 1992), pp. 138–45.

—, 'Talking in tongues: Scottish translations, 1970–1995', *Scottish Theatre since the Seventies*, eds Stevenson and Wallace (Edinburgh: Edinburgh University Press, 1996), pp. 186–97.

—, 'Translating into dialect', *Stages in Translation: essays and interviews on translating for the stage*, ed. David Johnston (Bath: Absolute Classics, 1996), pp. 199–217.

Fisher, Mark, 'From Traverse to Tramway: Scottish theatres old and new', *Scottish Theatre since the Seventies*, eds Stevenson and Wallace (Edinburgh: Edinburgh University Press, 1996), pp. 49–56.

Folorunso, Femi, 'Scottish drama and the popular tradition', *Scottish Theatre since the Seventies*, eds Stevenson and Wallace (Edinburgh: Edinburgh University Press, 1996), pp. 176–85.

Giesekam, Greg, 'Connections with the audience: writing for a Scottish theatre: Interview with Peter Arnott', *New Theatre Quarterly* 6(24) (Cambridge: Cambridge University Press, 1990), pp. 318–34.

Hebert, Hugh, 'Tutti Frutti (John Byrne)', *British Television Drama in the 1980s*, ed. George W. Brandt (Cambridge: Cambridge University Press, 1993), pp. 178–95.

1164

Hutchison, David, 'Economics, culture and play writing', *Scottish Theatre since the Seventies*, eds Stevenson and Wallace (Edinburgh: Edinburgh University Press, 1996), pp. 206–14.

—, *The Modern Scottish Theatre* (Glasgow: Molendinar Press, 1977).

International Journal of Scottish Theatre – an e-journal: arts.qmuc.ac.uk/ijost/.

Itzen, Catherine, *Stages in the Revolution: Political Theatre in Britain Since 1968* (London: Eyre Methuen, 1980).

Kennedy, A. L., 'Edging Close to the Bone', *Sight and Sound* 6(12) (London: British Institute of Adult Education, 1996), pp. 23–5.

Kinloch, David, ' "Lazarus at the feast of love". [Edwin] Morgan's Cyrano de Bergerac', *Scotlands* 5(2) (Edinburgh: Edinburgh University Press, 1998), pp. 34–54.

Lloyd, Matthew, 'Chris Hannan', *Contemporary Dramatists*, ed. K. A. Berney (London and Chicago: St James Press, 1993; fifth edition), pp. 275–6.

Lofton, R., 'The Idea of Scottish Drama', *Chapman* 3(3) (Edinburgh: Chapman Publications, 1975), pp. 18–24.

Low, John Thomas, 'Mid-Twentieth-Century Drama in Lowland Scots', *Scotland and the Lowland Tongue*, ed. J. Derrick McClure (Aberdeen: Aberdeen University Press, 1983), pp. 170–94.

McArthur, Colin (ed.), *Scotch Reels* (London: British Film Institute, 1982).

Macdonald, Gus, 'Fiction Friction', *From Limelight to Satellite: A Scottish Film Book*, ed. Eddie Dick (London: British Film Institute, 1990), pp. 193–206.

MacDonald, Jan, 'Scottish Women Dramatists Since 1945', *A History of Scottish Women's Writing*, eds Douglas Gifford and Dorothy McMillan (Edinburgh: Edinburgh University Press, 1997), pp. 494–513.

McGrath, John, *A Good Night Out: Popular Theatre, Class and Form* (London: Eyre Methuen, 1981).

—, *The Bone Won't Break: On Theatre and Hope in Hard Times* (London: Methuen, 1990).

—, 'When the Cutting Edge Cuts Both Ways: Contemporary Scottish Drama', *Modern Drama* 38(1) (1995), pp. 87–96.

MacKenney, Linda, *The Directory of the Scottish Theatre Archive Collection* (Glasgow: Scottish Theatre Archive, 1982).

McLennan, Elizabeth, *The Moon Belongs to Everyone: Making Popular Theatre with 7:84* (London: Methuen, 1990).

McMillan, Joyce, *The Traverse Theatre Story* (London: Methuen, 1988).

—, 'Women Playwrights in Contemporary Scottish Theatre', *Chapman* 8–9(43–44) (Edinburgh: Chapman Publications, 1986), pp. 69–75.

Maguire, Tom, 'Under New Management: The Changing Direction of 7:84 (Scotland)', *Theatre Research International* 17(2) (Oxford: Oxford University Press, 1992), pp. 132–7.

Maley, Willy, 'Borders Welfare: the state of Scottish theatre', *Scot Lit* 16 (Aberdeen: Association for Scottish Literary Studies, 1997), pp. 1–2.

Moffat, Alasdair, *The Edinburgh Fringe* (London: Johnston & Bacon, 1988).

Neilson, Sandy, 'Theatre Revival: A Director's View', *Chapman* 8–9(43–44) (Edinburgh: Chapman Publications, 1986), pp. 16–19.

Paterson, Lindsay, 'Language and identity on the stage', *Scottish Theatre since the Seventies*, eds Stevenson and Wallace (Edinburgh: Edinburgh University Press, 1996), pp. 76–83.

Peacock, D. Keith, 'Fact Versus History: Two Attempts to Change the Audience's Political Perspective', *Theatre Studies* 31–32 (Columbus: Ohio State University Theatre Research Institute, 1984–85/1985–86), pp. 15–31.

Peoples, Robin, 'Youth Theatre in Scotland', *Chapman* 8–9(43–44) (Edinburgh: Chapman Publications, 1986), pp. 85–7.

Purdie, Howard, 'Alba's Highland Charge', *Chapman* 8–9(43–44) (Edinburgh: Chapman Publications, 1986), pp. 60–2.

—, 'Starve a Rep, Feed a Theatre', *Chapman* 8–9(43–44) (Edinburgh: Chapman Publications, 1986), pp. 56–60.

Rutherford, Sarah C., 'Fantasists and philosophers', *Scottish Theatre since the Seventies*, eds Stevenson and Wallace (Edinburgh: Edinburgh University Press, 1996), pp. 112–24.

Savage, Roger, 'A Scottish National Theatre?', *Scottish Theatre since the Seventies*, eds Stevenson and Wallace (Edinburgh: Edinburgh University Press, 1996), pp. 23–33.

Scullion, Adrienne, 'Chris Hannan', *Contemporary Dramatists*, ed. Thomas Rigg (Detroit & New York: St James Press, 1999; sixth edition), pp. 280–1.

—, 'Feminine pleasures and masculine indignities: gender and community in Scottish drama', *Gendering the Nation*, ed. Christopher Whyte (Edinburgh: Edinburgh University Press, 1995), pp. 169–204.

Smith, Donald, '1950 to 1995', *A History of Scottish Theatre*, ed. Bill Findlay (Edinburgh: Polygon, 1998), pp. 253–308.

— (ed.), *The Scottish Stage: a National Theatre Company for Scotland* (Edinburgh: Candlemaker, 1994).

Stevenson, Randall, and Wallace, Gavin (eds), *Scottish Theatre since the Seventies* (Edinburgh: Edinburgh University Press, 1996).

Stevenson, Randall, 'Scottish theatre, 1950–1980', *The History of Scottish Literature vol. IV, Twentieth Century*, ed. Cairns Craig (Aberdeen: Aberdeen University Press, 1987), pp. 349–67.

—, 'Scottish Theatre Company: first days, first nights', *Cencrastus* 7 (Edinburgh: Cencrastus, 1981–2), pp. 10–3.

—, 'Snakes and ladders, snakes and owls: charting Scottish theatre', *Scottish Theatre since the Seventies*, eds Stevenson and Wallace (Edinburgh: Edinburgh University Press, 1996), pp. 1–20.

—, 'In the jungle of the cities', *Scottish Theatre since the Seventies*, eds Stevenson and Wallace (Edinburgh: Edinburgh University Press, 1996), pp. 100–11.

Theatre Scotland [a magazine with useful articles and commentary: also published a play in each edition].

Unwin, Steven, Killick, Jenny, and Pollock, A. (eds), *The Traverse Theatre, 1963–1988* (Edinburgh: Traverse, 1988).

Wells, Patricia Ann, 'Scottish Drama Comes of Age: An Examination of Three Scottish Plays', *Dissertation Abstracts International* 45(2) (1984), pp. 394A–350A.

Wright, Allen, 'Writers and the Theatre', *Scottish Writing and Writers*, ed. Norman Wilson (Edinburgh: Ramsay Head, 1977), pp. 49–52.

Zenzinger, Peter, 'The new wave', *Scottish Theatre since the Seventies*, eds Stevenson and Wallace (Edinburgh: Edinburgh University Press, 1996), pp. 125–37.

THE CITIZENS' THEATRE, GLASGOW

Coveney, Michael, *The Citizens': 21 years of the Glasgow Citizens' Theatre* (London: Nick Hern, 1990).

Eddershaw, Margaret, 'Echt Brecht? *Mother Courage* at the Citizens', 1990', *New Theatre Quarterly* 8(28) (Cambridge: Cambridge University Press, 1991), pp. 303–14.

Havergal, Giles, 'Choosing plays: the conditions of artistic choice at the Citizens' Theatre, Glasgow, 1969–85' [J. F. Arnott Memorial Lecture], *Tenth World Congress of the International Federation of Theatre Research* (1985).

Hutchison, David, 'Glasgow and its Citizens', *Scottish Theatre since the Seventies*, eds Stevenson and Wallace (Edinburgh: Edinburgh University Press, 1996), pp. 57–64.

McDonald, Jan, *What is the Citizens' Theatre?* (Proceedings of the Royal Philosophical Society of Glasgow, New Series 1, 1984).

—, ' "A house of illusions": The Citizens' Theatre Glasgow, 1969–1979', *Maske und Kothurn* (Wien: H. Böhlaus Nachf., 29 January, 1983), p. 199.

—, and Claude Schumacher (eds), *The Citizens' Theatre Season: Glasgow 1990* (Glasgow: Theatre Studies Publications, 1991).

Oliver, Cordelia, *Glasgow Citizens' Theatre: Robert David MacDonald and German drama* (Glasgow: Third Eye, 1984).
Schumacher, Claude, and Fogg, Derek (eds), *Hochhuth's The Representative at the Glasgow Citizens', 1986* (Glasgow: Theatre Studies Publications/Goethe Institute, 1988).

7:84 THEATRE COMPANY (SCOTLAND)

Di Cenzo, Maria, *The Politics of Alternative Theatre in Britain, 1968–1990: the case of 7:84 (Scotland)* (Cambridge: Cambridge University Press, 1996).
Farrell, Joseph, 'Recent Political Theatre', *Chapman* 8–9(43–44) (Edinburgh: Chapman Publications, 1986), pp. 48–54.
Itzin, Catherine, 'John McGrath and 7:84 Theatre Company', *Stages in the Revolution: political theatre in Britain since 1968* (London: Eyre Methuen, 1980).
McGrath, John, *A Good Night Out: popular theatre, audience, class and form* (London: Eyre Methuen, 1981).
—, *The Bone Won't Break: on theatre and hope in hard times* (London: Methuen, 1990).
McGrath, John, interviewed by Olga Taxidou, 'From cheviots to silver darlings', *Scottish Theatre since the Seventies*, eds Stevenson and Wallace (Edinburgh: Edinburgh University Press, 1996), pp. 149–63.
Mackenney, Linda, 'The people's story: 7:84 Scotland', *Scottish Theatre since the Seventies*, eds Stevenson and Wallace (Edinburgh: Edinburgh University Press, 1996), pp. 63–72.
McLennan, Elizabeth, *The Moon Belongs to Everyone: making popular theatre with 7:84* (London: Methuen, 1981).
Maguire, Tom, 'Still cool for cats? The life and times of Wildcat Stage Productions', *International Journal of Scottish Theatre* 1(1) (2000) [http://arts.qmuc.ac.uk/ijost/Volume1_no1/T_Maguire.htm].
—, 'Under New Management: the changing direction of 7:84 (Scotland)', *Theatre Research International* 17(2) (Oxford: Oxford University Press, 1992), pp. 132–7.
Taxidou, Olga, 'Epic theatre in Scotland', *Scottish Theatre since the Seventies*, eds Stevenson and Wallace (Edinburgh: Edinburgh University Press, 1996), pp. 164–75.
—, 'Where exactly is Scotland' local cultures, popular theatre and national television', *Boxed Sets: television representations of theatre*, ed. Jeremy Ridgman (Luton: University of Luton Press/Arts Council of England, 1998), pp. 89–105.
Thomsen, Christopher W., 'Three socialist playwrights: John McGrath, Caryl Churchill, Trevor Griffiths', *Contemporary English Drama*, ed. C. W. E. Bigsby (New York: Holmes and Meier, Stratford Upon Avon Studies 19, 1981), pp. 157–76.

WOMEN IN THEATRE

Bain, Audrey, 'Loose canons: identifying a women's tradition in play writing', *Scottish Theatre since the Seventies*, eds Stevenson and Wallace (Edinburgh: Edinburgh University Press, 1996), pp. 138–45.
Gifford, Douglas, 'Making them bold and breaking the mould: Rona Munro's *Bold Girls*', *Laverock* 2 (Aberdeen: Association for Scottish Literary Studies, 1996), pp. 2–8.
Goodman, Lizbeth, 'Rona Munro', *Contemporary Dramatists*, ed. K. A. Berney (London: St James, 1993; fifth edition), pp. 172–3.
—, *Contemporary Feminist Theatres: to each her own* (London: Routledge, 1993).
Harvie, Jennifer, 'Desire and difference in Liz Lochhead's *Dracula*', *Essays in Theatre/Etudes Theatrales* 11(2) (Guelph: University of Guelph, 1993), pp. 133–43.
Koren-Deutsch, Ilona, 'Feminist nationalism in Scotland: Mary Queen of Scots got her head chopped off', *Modern Drama* 35(3) (1992), pp. 424–32.
McDonald, Jan, 'Scottish women dramatists since 1945', *A History of Scottish Women's Writing*,

eds Douglas Gifford and Dorothy McMillan (Edinburgh: Edinburgh University Press, 1997), pp. 494–513.

—, 'The devil is beautiful: *Dracula*, Freudian novel and feminist drama', *Novel Images: literature in performance* (London: Routledge, 1993), pp. 80–104.

McDonald, Jan, and Harvie, Jennifer, 'Putting new twists to old stories: feminism and Lochhead's drama', *Liz Lochhead's Voices*, eds Robert Crawford and Anne Varty (Edinburgh: Edinburgh University Press, 1993), pp. 124–47.

Munro, Rona, 'Sex and food', *Theatre Scotland* 1(3) (Edinburgh: Theatre Scotland, 1992), pp. 15–21.

Scullion, Adrienne, 'Contemporary Scottish women playwrights', *The Cambridge Companion to Modern British Women Playwrights*, eds Janelle Reinelt and Elaine Aston (Cambridge: Cambridge University Press, 2000), pp. 94–118.

—, 'Liz Lochhead'; 'Sharman Macdonald', *Contemporary Dramatists*, ed. Thomas Rigg (Detroit & New York: St James Press, 1999; sixth edition), pp. 403–5, 419–20.

—, 'Feminine pleasures and masculine indignities: gender and community in Scottish drama', *Gendering the Nation*, ed. Cristopher Whyte (Edinburgh: Edinburgh University Press, 1995), pp. 169–204.

Stephenson, Heidi, and Langridge, Natasha (eds), 'Sharman Macdonald', *Rage and Reason: playwrights on play writing* (London: Methuen, 1997), pp. 61–70.

Strachan, Alan, 'Sharman Macdonald', *Contemporary Dramatists*, ed. K. A. Berney (London & Chicago: St James Press, 1993; fifth edition), pp. 404–5.

Varty, Anne, 'The Mirror and the Vamp: Liz Lochhead', *A History of Scottish Women's Writing*, eds Douglas Gifford and Dorothy McMillan (Edinburgh: Edinburgh University Press, 1997), pp. 641–58.

Chapter 40: Scottish Fiction since 1945 I: Continuity, Despair and Change

Since twentieth-century Scottish fiction is intermittently in and out of print, the bibliographies to this section cite publisher and date of the first British edition of a work. For currently available modern editions, readers should consult *Books in print* and catalogues of publishers who specialise in Scottish fiction reprints, such as Canongate, B&W Publishing, Mainstream, and House of Lochar. It may also be useful to consult *BookFind*, an online database of books in print, available through the Glasgow University Library website at: www.merlin.lib.gla.ac.uk.

BACKGROUND READING

In addition to histories and discussions of the Scottish novel (such as Hart: *The Scottish Novel*) and Scottish writing generally cited in the lists for Section 5 and elsewhere, the following are particularly helpful:

Anderson, Carol, and Christianson, Aileen (eds), *Scottish Women's Fiction: 1920s to 1960s: Journeys Into Being* (East Linton: Tuckwell Press, 2000).

Bold, Alan, *Modern Scottish Literature* (Harlow: Longman, 1983).

Burgess, Moira, *The Glasgow Novel: A Survey and a Bibliography* (Hamilton: The Scottish Library Association, 1999; third edition).

—, *Imagine a City: Glasgow in Fiction* (Glendaruel: Argyll, 1998).

—, *The Other Voice: Scottish Women's Writing Since 1808* (Edinburgh: Polygon, 1987).

Christianson, Aileen, and Lumsden, Alison, *Contemporary Scottish Women Writers* (Edinburgh: Edinburgh University Press, 2000).

Craig, Cairns, *The Modern Scottish Novel; Narrative and the National Imagination* (Edinburgh: Edinburgh University Press, 1999).

—, *Out of History* (Edinburgh: Polygon, 1996).

Gifford, Douglas, *The Dear Green Place: The Novel in the West of Scotland* (Glasgow: Third Eye Centre, 1985).

Hagemann, Susanne (ed.), *Studies in Scottish Fiction: 1945 to the Present* (Frankfurt am Main: P. Lang, 1996).

Hart, Francis Russell, *The Scottish Novel* (London: Murray, 1978).

Malzahn, Manfred, *Aspects of Identity: The Contemporary Scottish Novel (1798–1981) as National Self-Expression* (Frankfurt am Main: P. Lang, 1984).

Murray, Isobel, and Tait, Bob, *Ten Modern Scottish Novels* (Aberdeen: Aberdeen University Press, 1984).

Walker, Marshall, *Scottish Literature Since 1707* (Harlow: Longman, 1996).

Wallace, Gavin, and Stevenson, Randall, *The Scottish Novel Since the Seventies: New Visions, Old Dreams* (Edinburgh: Edinburgh University Press, 1993) [contains a bibliography of Scottish fiction 1970 onwards by Alison Lumsden].

Whyte, Christopher, *Gendering the Nation: Studies in Modern Scottish Literature* (Edinburgh: Edinburgh University Press, 1995).

ANTHOLOGIES
See also introduction to Section 6.

Burgess, Moira, and Whyte, Hamish (eds), *Streets of Stone: An Anthology of Glasgow Short Stories* (Edinburgh: Salamander Press, 1985).

—, *Streets of Gold: Contemporary Glasgow Short Stories* (Edinburgh: Mainstream, 1989).

Dunn, Douglas (ed.), *The Oxford Book of Scottish Short Stories* (Oxford: Oxford University Press, 1995).

Kravitz, Peter (ed.), *The Picador Book of Contemporary Scottish Fiction* (London: Picador, 1997).

MacDougall, Carl (ed.), *The Devil and the Giro: Two Centuries of Scottish Short Stories* (Edinburgh: Canongate, 1989).

McLean, Duncan, *Ahead of Its Time: A Clocktower Press Anthology* (London: Cape, 1997).

Murray, Ian (ed.), *The New Penguin Book of Scottish Short Stories* (Harmondsworth: Penguin, 1983).

Urqhart, Fred, and Gordon, Giles (eds), *Modern Scottish Short Stories* (London: Hamish Hamilton, 1978).

See also the annual *Scottish Short Stories* (London: Collins) series, sponsored by the Scottish Arts Council which ran from 1973–1997; and the annual volumes currently from The Association for Scottish Literary Studies, *New Writing Scotland*.

READING LISTS

HANNAH AITKEN
In a Shaft of Sunlight (London: Hodder & Stoughton, 1947).
Seven Napier Place (London: Hodder & Stoughton, 1952).
Whittans (London: Hodder & Stoughton, 1951).
Music for the Journey (London: Hodder & Stoughton, 1957).

ALAN BOLD
East is West (Tillydrone, Aberdeen: Keith Murray, 1991).

CHRISTOPHER BROOKMYRE
Quite Ugly One Morning (London: Little, Brown, 1996).
Country of the Blind (London: Little, Brown, 1997).
Not the End of the World (London: Little, Brown, 1998).
Boiling a Frog (London: Little, Brown, 2000).

Secondary reading
Brookmyre, Christopher, 'Plots are for Cemetaries': An Interview with Christopher Brookmyre', *Edinburgh Review* 102 (Edinburgh: Edinburgh University Press, 1999), pp. 48–52.

GEORGE MACKAY BROWN
See also poetry lists.

A Calendar of Love, and Other Stories (London: Hogarth Press, 1967).
A Time to Keep, and Other Stories (London: Hogarth Press, 1969).
An Orkney Tapestry (London: Gollancz, 1969).
Greenvoe (London: Hogarth Press, 1972).
Magnus (London: Hogarth Press, 1973).
Hawkfall, and Other Stories (London: Hogarth Press, 1974).
The Sun's Net: Stories (London: Hogarth Press, 1976).
Andrina, and Other Stories (London: Chatto & Windus, 1983).
Time in a Red Coat (London: Chatto & Windus, 1984).
The Golden Bird: Two Orkney Stories (London: John Murray, 1987).
The Masked Fisherman, and Other Stories (London: John Murray, 1989).
The Sea-King's Daughter (Nairn: Balnain, 1991).
Rockpools and Daffodils (Edinburgh: Gordon Wright, 1992).
Vinland (London: John Murray, 1992).
Beside the Ocean of Time (London: John Murray, 1994).
Winter Tales (London: John Murray, 1995).
For the Islands I Sing: An Autobiography (London: John Murray, 1997).
The Island of the Women, and Other Stories (London: John Murray, 1998).
Northern Lights: a Poet's Sources (London: John Murray, 1999).

Secondary reading
Bold, Alan, *George Mackay Brown* (Edinburgh: Oliver & Boyd, 1978).
Brown, George Mackay, 'A Sequence of Images' [interview recorded 1984], *Scottish Writers Talking*, ed. Isobel Murray (East Linton: Tuckwell Press, 1996), pp. 1–54.
Burns, John, 'Myths and Marvels', *The Scottish Novel since the Seventies: New Visions, Old Dreams* (Edinburgh: Edinburgh University Press, 1993), pp. 71–81.

Campbell, Ian, 'Beside Brown's Ocean of Time', *Studies in Scottish Fiction: 1945 to the Present*, ed. Susanne Hagemann (Frankfurt am Main: P. Lang, 1996), pp. 263–74.

D'Arcy, Julian, *Scottish Skalds and Saga Men: Old Norse Influence in Modern Scottish Literature* (East Linton: Tuckwell Press, 1996).

Fulton, Robin, 'Argus: A Scottish Survey', *New Edinburgh Review* 4 (Edinburgh, 1969), pp. 6–7.

Huberman, Elizabeth, 'Mackay Brown's "Greenvoe": rediscovering a novel of the Orkneys', *Critique: Studies in Modern Fiction* (Atlanta: Georgia Inst. of Technology, 1977), pp. 33–43.

—, 'George Mackay Brown's "Magnus"', *SSL* 16 (Columbia: University of South Carolina, 1981), pp. 122–34.

MacGillivray, Alan, *George Mackay Brown's 'Greenvoe'* (Aberdeen: Association for Scottish Literary Studies, 1989).

Murray, Rowena, 'The Influence of Norse Literature on the Twentieth Century writer George Mackay Brown', *Scottish Language and Literature, Medieval and Renaissance: Fourth International Conference, 1984: Proceedings* (Frankfurt am Main: P. Lang, 1986), pp. 547–57.

Murray, Isobel, and Tait, Bob, 'George Mackay Brown: *Greenvoe*', *Ten Modern Scottish Novels* (Aberdeen: Aberdeen University Press, 1984), pp. 144–67.

Robb, David, '*Greenvoe*: A Poet's Novel', *SLJ* 19/1 (Aberdeen: Association for Scottish Literary Studies, 1992), pp. 47–60.

Roberts, J. Graeme, 'Tradition and pattern in the short stories of George Mackay Brown', *Literature of the North*, eds David Hewitt and Michael Spiller (Aberdeen: Aberdeen University Press, 1983).

Schmid, Sabina, 'George Mackay Brown: European Poet?', *Chapman* 93 (Edinburgh: Chapman Publications, 1999), pp. 10–17.

Schoene, Berthold, '"I imagined nine centuries . . .": narrative fragmentation and mythic closure in the shorter historical fiction of George Mackay Brown', *SLJ* 22/2 (Aberdeen: Association for Scottish Literary Studies, 1995), pp. 41–59.

—, *The Making of Orcadia: Narrative identity in the prose work of George Mackay Brown* (Frankfurt am Main: P. Lang, 1995).

Watson, Roderick, 'Internationalising Scottish Poetry', *History of Scottish Literature Vol. 4* (Aberdeen: Aberdeen University Press, 1987), pp. 311–30.

JANET CAIRD

Some Walk a Narrow Path (Edinburgh: Ramsay Head Press, 1977).
A Distant Urn (Edinburgh: Ramsay Head Press, 1983).

DAVID KERR CAMERON

A Kist of Sorrows (London: Gollancz, 1987).

AJAY CLOSE

Official and Doubtful (London: Secker & Warburg, 1996).
Forspoken (London: Secker & Warburg, 1998).

DOMINIC COOPER

The Dead of Winter (London: Chatto & Windus, 1975).
Sunrise (London: Chatto & Windus, 1977).
Men at Axlir (London: Chatto & Windus, 1978).

READING LISTS

GEORGE FRIEL
The Bank of Time (London: Hutchinson, 1959).
The Boy who Wanted Peace (London: John Calder, 1964).
Grace and Miss Partridge (London: Calder & Boyars, 1969).
Mr Alfred M. A. (London: Calder & Boyars, 1972).
An Empty House (London: Calder & Boyars, 1974).
A Friend of Humanity: selected short stories, ed. Gordon Jarvie (Edinburgh: Polygon, 1992).

Secondary reading
Gardner, Raymond, 'A walk on the wild side' [interview], *The Guardian* (24 March, 1972), p. 12.
Gillespie, James, 'Friel in the thirties', *Edinburgh Review* 71 (Edinburgh, 1985), pp. 46–55.

EDWARD GAITENS
Growing Up, and other stories (London: Jonathan Cape, 1942).
Dance of the Apprentices (Glasgow: William Maclellan, 1948).

JOHN GRAHAM
Shadowed Valley (Lerwick: Shetland Publishing Company, 1987).
Strife in the Valley (Lerwick: Shetland Publishing Company, 1992).

NEIL M. GUNN
Publications from 1946. For earlier titles see the bibliography to Section 5.

The Drinking Well (London: Faber, 1946).
The Shadow (London: Faber, 1948).
The Silver Bough (London: Faber, 1948).
The Lost Chart (London: Faber, 1949).
The White Hour, and Other Stories (London: Faber, 1950).
The Well at the World's End (London: Faber, 1951).
Bloodhunt (London: Faber, 1952).
The Other Landscape (London: Faber, 1954).
The Atom of Delight [autobiography] (London: Faber, 1956).
Selected Letters, ed. J. B. Pick (Edinburgh: Polygon, 1987).
Landscape and Light: essays, ed. Alistair McCleery (Aberdeen: Aberdeen University Press, 1987).
The Man Who Came Back: Essays and Short Stories, ed. Margery McCulloch (Edinburgh: Polygon, 1991).

Secondary reading
See the bibliography to Section 5.

DOROTHY K. HAYNES
Winter's Traces (London: Methuen, 1947).
Thou Shalt Not Suffer a Witch, and other stories (London: Methuen, 1949).
Robin Ritchie (London: Methuen, 1949).
Haste Ye Back [autobiography] (London: Jarrolds, 1973).
Peacocks and Pagodas, and the Best of Dorothy K. Haynes (Edinburgh: Paul Harris, 1981).

J. F. HENDRY
Fernie Brae: A Scottish Childhood (Glasgow: William Maclellan, 1947).

Secondary reading
MacNaughton, Alistair, 'Jim Hendry Remembered', *Chapman* 52 (Edinburgh: Chapman Publications, 1988), pp. 15–16.
Withers, Jack, 'Jim Hendry Remembered', *Chapman* 52 (Edinburgh: Chapman Publications, 1988), pp. 13–15.

ARCHIE HIND
The Dear Green Place (London: Hutchinson New Authors, 1966).

Secondary reading
Bold, Alan, *Modern Scottish Literature* (London: Longman, 1983), pp. 236–9.

TERRY HOUSTON
The Wounded Stone (Glendaruel: Argyll, 1998).

QUINTIN JARDINE
Skinner's Rules (London: Headline, 1993).

And other Skinner crime novels, series continuing.

ROBIN JENKINS
So Gaily Sings the Lark (Glasgow: William Maclellan, 1950).
Happy for the Child (London: John Lehmann, 1953).
The Thistle and the Grail (Edinburgh: Macdonald, 1954).
The Cone-Gatherers (Edinburgh: Macdonald, 1955).
Guests of War (Edinburgh: Macdonald, 1956).
The Missionaries (Edinburgh: Macdonald, 1957).
The Changeling (Edinburgh: Macdonald, 1958).
Love is a Fervent Fire (Edinburgh: Macdonald, 1959).
Some Kind of Grace (Edinburgh: Macdonald, 1960).
Dust on the Paw (Edinburgh: Macdonald, 1961).
The Tiger of Gold (Edinburgh: Macdonald, 1962).
A Love of Innocence (London: Cape, 1963).
The Sardana Dancers (London: Cape, 1964).
A Very Scotch Affair (London: Gollancz, 1968).
The Holy Tree (London: Gollancz, 1969).
The Expatriates (London: Gollancz, 1971).
A Toast to the Lord (London: Gollancz, 1972).
A Far Cry from Bowmore, and other stories (London: Gollancz, 1973).
A Figure of Fun (London: Gollancz, 1974).
A Would-Be Saint (London: Gollancz, 1978).
Fergus Lamont (Edinburgh: Waterfront, 1985).
The Awakening of George Darroch (Edinburgh: Waterfront, 1985).
Just Duffy (Edinburgh: Canongate, 1988).
Poverty Castle (Nairn: Balnain, 1991).

Willie Hogg (Edinburgh: Polygon, 1993).
Leila (Edinburgh: Polygon, 1995).
Lunderston Tales (Edinburgh: Polygon, 1996).
Matthew and Sheila (Edinburgh: Polygon, 1998).
Poor Angus (Edinburgh: Canongate, 2000).
Childish Things (Edinburgh: Canongate, 2001).

Secondary reading

Ágústsdóttir, Ingibjörg, 'Chaos and Dissolution?: Deconstruction and Scotland in the Later Fiction of Robin Jenkins', *Contemporary Scottish Literature, 1970–2000* (*Revista Canaria de Estudios Ingleses)*, ed. Tomás Monterrey (Servicio de Publicaciones: Universidad de la Laguna, 2000), pp. 103–16.

—, 'A Truthful Scot', *In Scotland* 1 (Edinburgh: Ramsay Head Press, 1999), pp. 13–22.

Binding, Paul, 'Ambivalent Patriot: The Fiction of Robin Jenkins', *New Edinburgh Review* 53 (Edinburgh, 1981), pp. 20–2.

Gifford, Douglas, ' "God's colossal irony": Robin Jenkins and *Guests of War'*, *Cencrastus* 24 (Edinburgh: Cencrastus, 1986), pp. 13–17 [and other articles, pp. 3–9].

Malzahn, Manfred, ' "Yet at the start of every season hope springs up": Robin Jenkin's *The Thistle and the Grail* (1945)', *Studies in Scottish Fiction: 1945 to the Present* (Frankfurt: Peter Lang, 1996).

Morgan, Edwin, 'The novels of Robin Jenkins', *Essays* (Cheadle: Carcanet, 1974), pp. 242–5.

Murray, Isobel, and Tait, Bob, 'Robin Jenkins: *Fergus Lamont'*, *Ten Modern Scottish Novels* (Aberdeen: Aberdeen University Press, 1984), pp. 194–218.

Norquay, Glenda, 'Disruptions: the later fiction of Robin Jenkins', *The Scottish Novel since the Seventies*, ed. Gavin Wallace and Randall Stevenson (Edinburgh: Edinburgh University Press, 1993), pp. 11–24.

—, 'Against Compromise: The Fiction of Robin Jenkins', *Cencrastus* 24 (Edinburgh: Cencrastus Publications, 1987), pp. 3–6.

Sellin, Bernard, 'Robin Jenkins: The Making of the Novelist', *Cencrastus* 24 (Edinburgh: Cencrastus Publications, 1987), pp. 7–9.

—, 'Histoire personnelle et histoire collective dans les romans de Robin Jenkins', *Études Écossaises* 1 (Grenoble: University Stendhal, 1992), pp. 315–22.

—, 'Commitment and Betrayal: Robin Jenkins' *A Very Scotch Affair'*, *Studies in Scottish Fiction: 1945 to the Present* (Frankfurt: Peter Lang, 1996).

Smith, Iain Crichton, *Robin Jenkins's 'The Cone-Gatherers'* (Aberdeen: Association for Scottish Literary Studies, 1995).

Thompson, Alistair R., 'Faith and love: an examination of some themes in the novels of Robin Jenkins', *New Saltire* 3 (Edinburgh: Saltire Society, 1962), pp. 57–64.

PAUL JOHNSTON
Body Politic (London: Hodder & Stoughton, 1997).
The Boneyard (London: Hodder & Stoughton, 1998).
Water of Death (London: Hodder & Stoughton, 1999).
The Blood Tree (London: Hodder & Stoughton, 2000).

JAMES KELMAN
An Old Pub Near the Angel, and other stories (Orono, Me.: Puckerbush Press, 1973).
Short Tales from the Night Shift (Glasgow: Print Studio, 1978).
Not Not While the Giro, and other stories (Edinburgh: Polygon, 1983).
The Busconductor Hines (Edinburgh: Polygon, 1984).

A Chancer (Edinburgh: Polygon, 1985).
Lean Tales (London: Cape, 1985).
Greyhound for Breakfast (London: Secker & Warburg, 1987).
A Disaffection (London: Secker & Warburg, 1989).
The Burn (London: Secker & Warburg, 1991).
Some Recent Attacks: essays cultural and political (Stirling: AK Press, 1992).
How Late it Was, How Late (London: Secker & Warburg, 1994).
The Good Times (London: Secker & Warburg, 1998).
Translated Accounts (London: Secker and Warburg, 2001).

Secondary reading

This is a selective list. For other references see Moira Burgess: *The Glasgow Novel* (Hamilton: Scottish Library Association, 1999).

Baker, Simon, ' "Wee stories with a working-class theme": The Reimagining of Urban Realism in the Fiction of James Kelman', *Studies in Scottish Fiction: 1945 to the Present* (Frankfurt: Peter Lang, 1996).

Bohnke, Dietmar, *Kelman Writes Back: literary politics of a Scottish writer* (Glienicke/Berlin: Galda & Wilch Verlag, 1999).

Chapman 57 (Edinburgh: Chapman Publications, 1989), Special Feature on James Kelman.

Craig, Cairns, 'Resisting arrest: James Kelman', *The Scottish Novel since the Seventies*, eds Gavin Wallace and Randall Stevenson (Edinburgh: Edinburgh University Press, 1993), pp. 99–114.

Gifford, Douglas, 'Discovering Lost Voices', *Books in Scotland* 38 (Edinburgh: Ramsay Head Press, 1991), pp. 1–6.

Kelman, James, 'The importance of Glasgow in my work', *Some Recent Attacks* (Stirling: AK Press, 1992), pp. 78–84.

Klaus, H. Gustav, 'James Kelman: a voice from the lower depths', *London Magazine* 29(5/6) (London, 1989), pp. 39–48.

McLean, Duncan, 'James Kelman interviewed', *Edinburgh Review* 71 (Edinburgh, 1985), pp. 64–80.

McNeill, Kirsty, 'Interview with James Kelman', *Chapman* 57 (Edinburgh: Chapman Publications, 1989), pp. 1–9.

Malley, Willy, 'Swearing Blind: Kelman and the Curse of the Working Classes', *Edinburgh Review* 95 (Edinburgh: Edinburgh University Press, 1996), pp. 105–12.

Nicoll, Laurence, ' "This is not a nationalist position": James Kelman's existential voice', *Edinburgh Review* 103 (Edinburgh: Edinburgh University Press, 2000), pp. 79–84.

Zagratzki, Uwe, ' "Blues fell this morning' – James Kelman's Scottish Literature and Afro-American Music', *SLJ* 27(1) (Aberdeen: Association for Scottish Literary Studies, 2000), pp. 105–17.

JAMES KENNAWAY

Tunes of Glory (London: Putnam, 1956).
Household Ghosts (London: Longmans, 1961).
The Mind Benders (London: Heinemann, 1963).
The Bells of Shoreditch (London: Longmans, 1963).
Some Gorgeous Accident (London: Longmans, 1967).
The Cost of Living Like This (London: Longmans, 1969).
Silence (London: Cape, 1972).

READING LISTS

Secondary reading
Kennaway, James and Susan, *The Kennaway Papers* (London: Cape, 1981).
Massie, Allan, 'The Artful Art of James Kennaway', *New Edinburgh Review* 52 (Edinburgh, 1980), pp. 13–16.
Murray, Isobel and Tait, Bob, 'James Kennaway: *Tunes of Glory'*, *Ten Modern Scottish Novels* (Aberdeen: Aberdeen University Press, 1984), pp. 78–99.
Royle, Trevor, *James and Jim: A Biography of James Kennaway* (Edinburgh: Mainstream, 1983).
Tait, Bob, 'Scots Apart: The Novels of James Kennaway and Gordon Williams', *Cencrastus* 5 (Edinburgh: Cencrastus Publications, 1981), pp. 20–2.

J. J. LAVIN
Compass of Youth (London: Museum Press, 1953).

FREDERIC LINDSAY
Brond (Edinburgh: Macdonald, 1983).
Jil Rips (London: Deutsch, 1987).
A Charm Against Drowning (London: Deutsch, 1988).
After the Stranger Came (London: Deutsch, 1992).

See also Lindsay's Inspector Meldrum series:
Kissing Judas (London: Hodder & Stoughton, 1997), and other titles, series continuing.

Secondary reading
Hendry, Joy, 'After the Stranger Came', *SLJ* Supplement 37 (Aberdeen: Association for Scottish Literary Studies, 1992), pp. 36–8.

ERIC LINKLATER
Publications from 1946. For earlier titles see the bibliography to Section 5.

Private Angelo (London: Cape, 1946).
Sealskin Trousers, and other stories (London: Hart Davis, 1947).
A Spell for Old Bones (London: Cape, 1949).
Mr Byculla (London: Hart Davis, 1950).
Laxdale Hall (London: Cape, 1951).
A Year of Space [autobiography] (London: Macmillan, 1953).
The House of Gair (London: Cape, 1953).
The Faithful Ally (London: Cape, 1954).
The Dark of Summer (London: Cape, 1956).
A Sociable Plover, and Other Stories (London: Hart Davis, 1957).
Position at Noon (London: Cape, 1958).
The Merry Muse (London: Cape, 1959).
Husband of Delilah (London: Macmillan, 1962).
A Man Over Forty (London: Macmillan, 1963).
A Terrible Freedom (London: Macmillan, 1966).
Fanfare for a Tin Hat [autobiography] (London: Macmillan, 1970).

Secondary reading
See the bibliography to Section 5.

'FIONN MACCOLLA' (TOM MACDONALD)
Publications from 1946. For earlier titles see the bibliography to Section 5.

Too Long in This Condition [autobiography] (Thurso: Caithness Books, 1975).
The Ministers (London: Souvenir Press, 1979).
Move Up, John (Edinburgh: Canongate, 1994).

Secondary reading
See the bibliography to Section 5.

GUY MCCRONE
The Striped Umbrella (London: Constable, 1937).
Duet for Two Merklands (London: Hodder & Stoughton, 1939).
Wax Fruit: the story of the Moorhouse family (London: Constable, 1947).
Aunt Bel (London: Constable, 1949).
The Hayburn Family (London: Constable, 1952).
James and Charlotte (London: Constable, 1955).
An Independent Young Man (London: Constable, 1961).

NORMAN MACDONALD
Calum Tod (Inverness: Club Leabhar, 1976).
An Sgàineadh (Stornaway: Acair, 1993).
Portrona (Edinburgh: Birlin, 2000).

IAN MCGINNESS
Inner City (Edinburgh: Polygon, 1987).
Bannock (Edinburgh: Polygon, 1990).

WILLIAM MCILVANNEY
Remedy is None (London: Eyre & Spottiswoode, 1966).
A Gift from Nessus (London: Eyre & Spottiswoode, 1968).
Docherty (London: Allen & Unwin, 1975).
Laidlaw (London: Hodder & Stoughton, 1977).
The Papers of Tony Veitch (London: Hodder & Stoughton, 1983).
The Big Man (London: Hodder & Stoughton, 1985).
Walking Wounded [Short Stories] (London: Hodder & Stoughton, 1989).
Strange Loyalties (London: Hodder & Stoughton, 1991).
Surviving the Shipwreck [essays] (Edinburgh: Mainstream Publishing, 1991).
The Kiln (London: Hodder & Stoughton, 1996).

Secondary reading
Craig, Carol, 'On Men and Women in McIlvanney's Fiction', *Edinburgh Review* 73 (Edinburgh: Edinburgh University Press, 1986), pp. 42–9.

Dickson, Beth, 'Class and being in the novels of William McIlvanney', *The Scottish Novel since the Seventies*, eds Gavin Wallace and Randall Stevenson (Edinburgh: Edinburgh University Press, 1993), pp. 54–70.

—, *William McIlvanney's 'Laidlaw'* (Aberdeen: Association for Scottish Literary Studies, 1998).

Dixon, Keith, 'Writing on the borderline: the works of William McIlvanney', *SSL* 24 (Columbia: University of South Carolina, 1989), pp. 142–57.

—, ' "No Fairies. No Monsters. Just People." Resituating the Work of William McIlvanney', *Studies in Scottish Fiction: 1945 to the Present* (Frankfurt: Peter Lang, 1996).

McIlvanney, William, 'Growing up in the west', *Memoirs of a Modern Scotland*, ed. Karl Miller (London: Faber & Faber, 1970), pp. 168–78.

—, 'Plato in a boiler suit' [interview recorded 1984], *Scottish Writers Talking*, ed. Isobel Murray (East Linton: Tuckwell Press, 1996), pp. 132–54.

McLuckie, Craig W., 'William McIlvanney and the Provocative Witness: Resistance in the 'Laidlaw' Trilogy', *Contemporary Scottish Literature, 1970–2000 (Revista Canaria de Estudios Ingleses)*, ed. T. Monterrey (Servicio de Publicaciones: Universidad de la Laguna, 2000), pp. 87–101.

Murray, Isobel, and Tait, Bob, 'William McIlvanney: *Docherty*', *Ten Modern Scottish Novels* (Aberdeen: Aberdeen University Press, 1984), pp. 168–193.

LORN MACINTYRE

Blood and the Moon (Inverness: Club Leabhar, 1974).
Cruel in the Shadow (London: Collins, 1979).
The Blind Bend (London: Collins, 1981).
From Port Vendres (St Andrews: Priormuir Press, 1989).
Empty Footsteps (Duns: Black Ace, 1996).

Secondary reading
Thompson, Frank, 'Lorn MacIntyre talks to Frank Thompson', *Books in Scotland* 11 (Edinburgh: Ramsay Head Press, 1982–3), pp. 3–6.

COLIN MACKAY

The Song of the Forest (Edinburgh: Canongate, 1986).
The Sound of the Sea (Edinburgh: Canongate, 1989).
House of Lies (Duns: Black Ace Books, 1995).

JOHN MACKENZIE

City Whitelight (Edinburgh: Mainstream, 1986).

ROBERT MCLELLAN

Linmill stories (Edinburgh: Canongate, 1990).

DENISE MINA

Garnethill (London: Bantam Press, 1998).
Exile (London: Bantam Press, 2000).

TOM MORTON

Red Guitars in Heaven (Edinburgh: Mainstream, 1994).
Guttered (Edinburgh: Mainstream, 1999).

IAN NIALL

Publications from 1945. For earlier work as John McNeillie see the bibliography to Section 5.

Foxhollow (London: Heinemann, 1949).
No Resting Place (London: Heinemann, 1949).
The Deluge (London: Heinemann, 1951).
The Country Blacksmith (London: Heinemann, 1966).
A Galloway Childhood [autobiography] (London: Heinemann, 1967).
The Galloway Shepherd (London: Heinemann, 1970).
The Village Policeman (London: Heinemann, 1971).
The Forester (London: Heinemann, 1972).

AGNES OWENS
Gentlemen of the West (Edinburgh: Polygon, 1984).
Lean Tales (London: Cape, 1985).
Like Birds in the Wilderness (London: Fourth Estate, 1987).
A Working Mother (London: Bloomsbury, 1994).
People Like That (London: Bloomsbury, 1996).
For the Love of Willie (London: Bloomsbury, 1998).

Secondary reading
Gray, Alisdair, 'Thoughts suggested by Agnes Owen's "Gentlemen of the West" and an appreciation of it', *Edinburgh Review* 71 (Edinburgh: Edinburgh University Press, 1985), pp. 27–32.
Stark, Lynne, 'Agnes Owen's Fiction: Untold Stories', *Contemporary Scottish Women Writers*, eds Aileen Christianson and Alison Lumsden (Edinburgh: Edinburgh University Press, 2000), pp. 111–16.

NEIL PATERSON
The China Run (London: Hodder & Stoughton, 1948).
Behold Thy Daughter (London: Hodder & Stoughton, 1950).
And Delilah: Nine Stories (London: Hodder & Stoughton, 1951).

HUGH C. RAE
Skinner (London: Blond, 1965).
Night Pillow (London: Blond, 1967).
A Few Small Bones (London: Blond, 1968).
The Saturday Epic (London: Blond, 1970).
The Marksman (London: Constable, 1971).
The Shooting Gallery (London: Constable, 1972).
The Rookery (London: Constable, 1973).

For titles published under the name Jessica Stirling see the bibliography to the next chapter.

READING LISTS

Secondary reading
Bold, Alan, *Modern Scottish Literature* (London: Longman, 1983), pp. 248–9.
Henderson, Lesley (ed.), *Twentieth-century Crime and Mystery Writers* (1991, third edition), pp. 987–8.

IAN RANKIN
The Flood (Edinburgh: Polygon, 1986).
Watchman (London: Bodley Head, 1988).
Westwind (London: Barrie & Jenkins, 1990).

The Inspector Rebus series
Knots and Crosses (London: Bodley Head, 1987).

And twelve further titles, series continuing.

CHRISTOPHER RUSH
Peace Comes Dropping Slow (Edinburgh: Ramsay Head, 1983).
A Resurrection of a Kind (Aberdeen: Aberdeen University Press, 1984).
A Twelvemonth and a Day (Aberdeen: Aberdeen University Press, 1985).
Two Christmas Stories (Aberdeen: Aberdeen University Press, 1988).
Into the Ebb (Aberdeen: Aberdeen University Press, 1989).
Last Lesson of the Afternoon (Edinburgh: Canongate, 1994).

J. D. SCOTT
The Cellar (London: Pilot Press, 1947).
The Margin (London: Pilot Press, 1949).
The Way to Glory (London: Eyre & Spottiswoode, 1952).
The End of an Old Song (London: Eyre & Spottiswoode, 1954).
The Pretty Penny (London: Eyre & Spottiswoode, 1963).

MANDA SCOTT
Hen's Teeth (London: Women's Press, 1996).
Night Mares (London: Headline, 1998).
Stronger than Death (London: Headline, 1999).

ALAN SHARP
A Green Tree in Gedde (London: Michael Joseph, 1965).
The Wind Shifts (London: Michael Joseph, 1967).

IAIN CRICHTON SMITH
Consider the Lilies (London: Gollancz, 1968).
The Last Summer (London: Gollancz, 1969).
Survival Without Error (London: Gollancz, 1970).
My Last Duchess (London: Gollancz, 1971).
The Black and the Red, and other stories (London: Gollancz, 1973).
Goodbye, Mr Dixon (London: Gollancz, 1974).

1180

The Village (Inverness: Club Leabhar, 1976).
The Hermit, and other stories (London: Gollancz, 1977).
An End to Autumn (London: Gollancz, 1978).
On the Island (London: Gollancz, 1979).
Murdo, and Other Stories (London: Gollancz, 1981).
A Field Full of Folk (London: Gollancz, 1982).
The Search (London: Gollancz, 1983).
Mr Trill in Hades, and Other Stories (London: Gollancz, 1984).
The Tenement (London: Gollancz, 1985).
Towards the Human: Selected Essays (Edinburgh: Macdonald, 1986).
In the Middle of the Wood (London: Gollancz, 1987).
Na Speuclairean Dubha (Glasgow: Gairm, 1989).
The Dream (London: Macmillan, 1990).
An Honourable Death (London: Macmillan, 1992).
Thoughts of Murdo (Nairn: Balnain, 1993).

Secondary reading

Berton, Jean, 'Le degré d'historicité dans *Consider the Lillies* de Iain Crichton Smith', *Études Écossaises* 1 (Grenoble: University Stendhal, 1992), pp. 323–31.
Craig, Cairns, 'The necessity of accident: the English fiction', *Iain Crichton Smith: Critical Essays*, ed. Colin Nicholson (Edinburgh: Edinburgh University Press, 1992), pp. 11–25.
Gifford, Douglas, 'Bleeding from all that's best: the fiction of Iain Crichton Smith', *The Scottish Novel since the Seventies*, eds Gavin Wallace and Randall Stevenson (Edinburgh: Edinburgh University Press, 1993), pp. 25–40.

MURIEL SPARK

Publications to 1965. For later titles see the bibliography to the next chapter.

The Comforters (London: Macmillan, 1957).
The Go-Away Bird, and other stories (London: Macmillan, 1958).
Robinson (London: Macmillan, 1958).
Memento Mori (London: Macmillan, 1959).
The Ballad of Peckham Rye (London: Macmillan, 1960).
The Bachelors (London: Macmillan, 1960).
Voices at Play (London: Macmillan, 1961).
The Prime of Miss Jean Brodie (London: Macmillan, 1961).
The Girls of Slender Means (London: Macmillan, 1963).
The Mandelbaum Gate (London: Macmillan, 1965).

Secondary reading

Spark's autobiography is listed in the bibliography to the next chapter.

Bold, Alan (ed.), *Muriel Spark: an Odd Capacity for Vision* (London: Vision Press, 1984).
—, *Muriel Spark* (London: Methuen, 1986).
Carruthers, Gerard, 'The remarkable fictions of Muriel Spark', *A History of Scottish Women's Writing*, eds Douglas Gifford and Dorothy McMillan (Edinburgh: Edinburgh University Press, 1997), pp. 514–25.

READING LISTS

Christianson, Aileen, 'Muriel Spark and Candia McWilliam: Continuities', *Contemporary Scottish Women Writers*, eds Aileen Christianson and Alison Lumsden (Edinburgh: Edinburgh University Press, 2000), pp. 95–110.

—, 'Elspeth Barker, Candia McWilliam and Murial Spark: Writers in Exile', *Terranglian Territories: Proceedings of Seventh International Conference on the Literature of Region and Nation*, ed. Susanne Hagemann (Frankfurt am Main: Peter Lang, 2000), pp. 339–47.

Hynes, Joseph (ed.), *Critical Essays on Muriel Spark* (New York: G. K. Hall, 1992).

McCulloch, Margery Palmer, 'Nasty surprises and a kind of truth: Calvinism and narrative discourse in three novels by Muriel Spark', *Odd Alliances: Scottish Studies in European Contexts*, eds Neil McMillan and Kirsten Stirling (Glasgow: Cruithne Press, 1999).

MacLachlan, Christopher, 'Murial Spark and Gothic', *Studies in Scottish Fiction: 1945 to the Present* (Frankfurt: Peter Lang, 1996).

Mall, G. Zambardi, 'Self-violence in the art of Muriel Spark', *Odd Alliances: Scottish Studies in European Contexts*, eds Neil McMillan and Kirsten Stirling (Glasgow: Cruithne Press, 1999).

Massie, Allan, *Muriel Spark: a new assessment* (Edinburgh: Ramsay Head Press, 1979).

Murray, Isobel, and Tait, Bob, 'Muriel Spark: *The Prime of Miss Jean Brodie*', *Ten Scottish Novels* (Aberdeen: Aberdeen University Press, 1984), pp. 100–22.

Rankin, Ian, 'The deliberate cunning of Muriel Spark', *The Scottish Novel since the Seventies*, eds Gavin Wallace and Randall Stevenson (Edinburgh: Edinburgh University Press, 1993), pp. 41–53.

Robb, David S., *Muriel Spark's 'The Prime of Miss Jean Brodie'* (Aberdeen: Association for Scottish Literary Studies, 1992).

Whittaker, Ruth, ' "Angels Dining at the Ritz": the faith and fiction of Muriel Spark', *The Contemporary English Novel*, eds M. Bradbury and D. Palmer (London: E. Arnold, 1979), pp. 157–69.

DAVID STEPHEN
Alba: The Last Wolf (London: Century Press, 1985).

JEFF TORRINGTON
Swing Hammer Swing! (London: Secker & Warburg, 1992).
The Devil's Carousel (London: Secker & Warburg, 1996).

DAVID TOULMIN
Hard Shining Corn (Aberdeen: Impulse Books, 1972).
Straw Into Gold (Aberdeen: Gourdas House, 1973).
Blown Seed (Edinburgh: Paul Harris, 1976).
Harvest Home (Edinburgh: Paul Harris, 1978).
A Chiel Among Them (Aberdeen: Gourdas House, 1982).

Secondary reading
Campbell, Ian, 'The Novels of David Toulmin', *Books in Scotland* 13 (Edinburgh: Ramsay Head Press, 1983), pp. 4–5.

ALEXANDER TROCCHI
A selection only: Trocchi wrote several erotic novels such as *Helen and Desire* (Paris: Olympia Press, 1954), and *White Thighs* (Paris: Olympia Press, 1955), as well as *Frank Harris: My Life and Loves*, vol. 5 (Paris: Olympia Press, 1954).
Young Adam (Paris: Olympia Press, 1954; London: Heinemann, 1961).

Sappho of Lesbos (New York: Castle Books, 1960).
Writers Revolt, ed. with Terry Southern and Richard Seaver (New York: Fell, 1960).
Cain's Book (New York: Grove Press, 1961; London: John Calder, 1963).
New Writers 3 (short stories) (London: John Calder, 1965).
Man At Leisure (poems) (London: Calder & Boyars, 1972).

Secondary reading

Campbell, Allan, and Niel, Tim, *A Life in Pieces: Reflections on Alexander Trocchi* (Edinburgh: Rebel Inc., 1997).
Morgan, Edwin, 'Alexander Trocchi: A Survey', *Crossing the Border* (Manchester: Carcanet, 1990), pp. 300–11.
Scott, Andrew Murray, *Alexander Trocchi: The Making of the Monster* (Edinburgh: Polygon, 1991).
— (ed.), *Invisible Insurrection of a Million minds: A Trocchi Reader* (Edinburgh: Polygon, 1991).

FRED URQUHART

Time Will Knit (London: Duckworth, 1938).
I Fell for a Sailor, and other stories (London: Duckworth, 1940).
The Last G. I. Bride Wore Tartan (Edinburgh: Serif Books, 1948).
The Ferret Was Abraham's Daughter (London: Methuen, 1949).
Jezebel's Dust (London: Methuen, 1951).
Palace of Green Days (London: Quartet, 1979).
Proud Lady in a Cage (Edinburgh: Paul Harris, 1980).
A Diver in China Seas (London: Quartet, 1980).
Seven Ghosts in Search (London: William Kimber, 1983).
Full Score: Short Stories (Aberdeen: Aberdeen University Press, 1989).

IRVINE WELSH

Trainspotting (London: Secker, 1993).
The Acid House (London: Cape, 1994).
Marabou Stork Nightmares (London: Cape, 1995).
Ecstasy (London: Cape, 1996).
Filth (London: Cape, 1998).
Give (London: Cape, 2001).

Secondary reading

Freeman, Alan, 'Ourselves as Others: *Marabou Stork Nightmares*', *Edinburgh Review* 95 (Edinburgh: Edinburgh University Press, 1996), pp. 135–41.
—, 'Ghosts in Sunny Leith: Irvine Welsh's *Trainspotting*', *Studies in Scottish Fiction: 1945 to the Present* (Frankfurt: Peter Lang, 1996).
Galbraith, Iain, 'Finding Fucking Words: A German Stage Milieu for Irvine Welsh's *Trainspotting*', *Southfields* 5. 1 (London: Southfields Press, 1998), pp. 53–68.
Jackson, Ellen-Raisa and Maley, Willy, 'Birds of a Feather?: A Postcolonial Reading of Irvine Welsh's *Marabou Stork Nightmares*', *Contemporary Scottish Literature, 1970–2000 (Revista Canaria de Estudios Ingleses)*, ed. Tomás Monterrey (Servicio de Publicaciones: Universidad de la Laguna, 2000), pp. 187–196.

GORDON WILLIAMS

The Last Days of Lincoln Charles (London: Secker & Warburg, 1965).
The Camp (London: Secker & Warburg, 1966).
The Man who had Power Over Women (London: Secker & Warburg, 1967).

From Scenes Like These (London: Secker & Warburg, 1968).
The Siege of Trencher's Farm (London: Secker & Warburg, 1969).
The Upper Pleasure Garden (London: Secker & Warburg, 1970).
Walk, Don't Walk (London: Allison & Busby, 1972).
Big Morning Blues (London: Hodder & Stoughton, 1974).
The Duellists (London: Collins, 1977).
Pomeroy (London: Michael Joseph, 1983).

Secondary reading
Tait, Bob, 'Scots Apart: The Novels of James Kennaway and Gordon Williams', *Cencrastus* 5
   (Edinburgh: Cencrastus Publications, 1981), pp. 20–2.

Chapter 41: Scottish Fiction since 1945 II: Despair, Change and Hope

LEILA ABOULELA
The Translator (Edinburgh: Polygon, 1999).
Coloured Lights (Edinburgh: Polygon, 2001).

KATE ATKINSON
Behind the Scenes at the Museum (Wantage, Oxon.: Black Swan, 1995).
Human Croquet (London: Doubleday, 1997).
Emotionally Weird (London: Doubleday, 2000).

IAIN BANKS
The Wasp Factory (London: Macmillan, 1984).
Walking on Glass (London: Macmillan, 1985).
The Bridge (London: Macmillan, 1986).
Espedair Street (London: Macmillan, 1987).
The Player of Games (London: Macmillan, 1988).
Canal Dreams (London: Macmillan, 1989).
The Crow Road (London: Scribners, 1992).
Complicity (London: Little, Brown, 1995).
Whit (London: Little, Brown, 1993).
A Song of Stone (London: Little, Brown, 1997).
The Business (London: Little, Brown, 1999).
Also several science fiction novels under the name Iain M. Banks.

Secondary reading
Alegre, Sara Martin, 'Consider Banks: Iain (M.) Bank's *The Wasp Factory* and *Consider Phlebas*',
   Contemporary Scottish Literature, 1970–2000 (Revista Canaria de Estudios Ingleses), ed. Tomás
   Monterrey (Servicio de Publicaciones: Universidad de la Laguna, 2000), pp. 197–205.
MacGillivray, Alan, 'The worlds of Iain Banks', *Laverock* 2 (Aberdeen: Association for Scottish
   Literary Studies, 1996), pp. 22–7.
Nairn, Thom, 'Iain Banks and the fiction factory', *The Scottish Novel since the Seventies*, eds Gavin
   Wallace and Randall Stevenson (Edinburgh: Edinburgh University Press, 1993), pp. 127–35.
Sage, Victor, 'The Politics of Petrifaction: Culture, Religion, History in the Fiction of Iain
   Banks and John Banville', *Modern Gothic*, eds Sage and Smith (Manchester: Manchester
   University Press, 1996), pp. 20–37.

ELSPETH BARKER
O Caledonia (London: Hamish Hamilton, 1991).

Secondary reading
Anderson, Carol, 'Emma Tennant, Elspeth Barker, Alice Thompson: Gothic Revisited', *Contemporary Scottish Women Writers*, eds Aileen Christianson and Alison Lumsden (Edinburgh: Edinburgh University Press, 2000), pp. 117–30.
Christianson, Aileen, 'Elspeth Barker, Candia McWilliam and Murial Spark. Writers in Exile', *Terranglian Territories: Proceedings of Seventh International Conference on the Literature of Region and Nation*, ed. Susanne Hagemann (Frankfurt am Main: Peter Lang, 2000), pp. 339–47.

ALEX BENZIE
The Year's Midnight (London: Viking, 1995).
The Angle of Incidence (London: Viking, 1999).

CHAIM BERMANT
Jericho Sleep Alone (London: Chapman & Hall, 1964).
Ben Preserve Us (London: Chapman & Hall, 1965).
Diary of an Old Man (London: Allen & Unwin, 1966).
The Second Mrs Whitberg (London: Allen & Unwin, 1976).
The Patriarch (London: Weidenfeld, 1981).

WILLIAM BOYD
A Good Man in Africa (London: Hamish Hamilton, 1981).
On the Yankee Station, and other stories (London: Hamish Hamilton, 1981).
An Ice-Cream War (London: Hamish Hamilton, 1982).
Stars and Bars (London: Hamish Hamilton, 1984).
The New Confessions (London: Hamish Hamilton, 1987).
Brazzaville Beach (London: Sinclair-Stevenson, 1990).
The Blue Afternoon (London: Sinclair-Stevenson, 1993).
The Destiny of Nathalie 'X', and other stories (London: Sinclair-Stevenson, 1995).
Armadillo (London: Hamish Hamilton, 1998).

Secondary reading
Dunn, Douglas, 'Divergent Scottishness: William Boyd, Allan Massie, Ronald Frame', *The Scottish Novel Since the Seventies*, eds G. Wallace and R. Stevenson (Edinburgh: Edinburgh University Press, 1994), pp. 149–69.
Gifford, Douglas, 'Making Art from Despair', *Books in Scotland* 35 (Edinburgh: Ramsay Head Press, 1991), pp. 1–3.

JIMMY BOYLE
A Hero of the Underworld (London: Serpent's Tail, 1999).

FORBES BRAMBLE
Stone (London: Hamish Hamilton, 1973).

READING LISTS

JOHN BURNSIDE
The Dumb House (London: Cape, 1997).
A Normal Skin (London: Cape, 1997).
The Mercy Boys (London: Cape, 1999).
Burning Elvis (London: Cape, 2000).
The Asylum Dance (London: Cape, 2000).
The Locust Room (London: Cape, 2000).

JOHN BURROWES
Jamesie's People (Edinburgh: Mainstream, 1984).
Incomers (Edinburgh: Mainstream, 1987).
Gulf (Edinburgh: Mainstream, 1989).
Mother Glasgow (Edinburgh: Mainstream, 1991).

RON BUTLIN
The Tilting Room (Edinburgh: Canongate, 1983).
The Sound of My Voice (Edinburgh: Canongate, 1987).
Night Visits (Edinburgh: Scottish Cultural Press, 1997).

ALASDAIR CAMPSIE
By Law Protected (Edinburgh: Canongate, 1976).
The Clarinda Conspiracy (Edinburgh: Mainstream, 1989).

REGI CLAIRE
Inside-Outside (Edinburgh: Scottish Cultural Press, 1999).

ALAN CLEWS
A Child of Air (London: Review, 1995).

ANDREW COWAN
Pig (London: Michael Joseph, 1994).
Common Ground (London: Michael Joseph, 1997).

DAVID CRAIG
King Cameron (Manchester: Carcanet, 1991).

ANDREW CRUMEY
Music in a Foreign Language (Sawtry, Cambs: Dedalus, 1994).
Pfitz (Sawtry, Cambs: Dedalus, 1995).
D'Alembert's Principle (Sawtry, Cambs: Dedalus, 1996).
Mr Mee (London: Picador, 2000).

TONI DAVIDSON
Scar Culture (Edinburgh: Rebel Inc., 1999).

Secondary reading

Miller, Gavin, '"Pure dead mental": Toni Davidson's *Scar Culture*', *Edinburgh Review* 103 (Edinburgh: Edinburgh University Press, 2000), pp. 133–40.

ELSPETH DAVIE

Providings (London: John Calder, 1965).
The Spark, and other stories (London: Calder & Boyars, 1968).
Creating a Scene (London: Calder & Boyars, 1971).
The High Tide Talker, and Other Stories (London: Hamilton, 1976).
Climbers on a Stair (London: Hamilton, 1978).
The Night of the Funny Hats (London: Hamilton, 1980).
A Traveller's Room (London: Hamilton, 1985).
Coming to Light (London: Hamilton, 1989).
Death of a Doctor, and Other Stories (London: Sinclair-Stevenson, 1992).

Secondary reading

Poggi, Valentina, 'Vision and space in Elspeth Davie's fiction', *A History of Scottish Women's Writing*, eds Douglas Gifford and Dorothy McMillan (Edinburgh: Edinburgh University Press, 1997), pp. 526–36.
Spunta, Marina, 'A Universe of one's own? Elspeth Davie and the narrative of the "gap"', *Chapman* 81 (Edinburgh: Chapman Publications, 1995), pp. 19–26.

MARGARET THOMSON DAVIS

A selective list of titles by this prolific writer.

The Breadmakers (London: Allison & Busby, 1972).
A Baby Might be Crying (London: Allison & Busby, 1973).
A Sort of Peace (London: Allison & Busby, 1973).
The Prisoner (London: Allison & Busby, 1974).
A Very Civilised Man (London: Allison & Busby, 1982).
Rag Woman, Rich Woman (London: Century Hutchinson, 1987).
A Woman of Property (London: Century, 1991).
Hold Me Forever (London: Century, 1994).
Gallachers (London: Century, 1998).
The Clydesiders (Edinburgh: B & W Publishing, 1999).

DAVID DEANS

The Peatman (Edinburgh: Polygon, 1995).

DES DILLON

Me and My Gal (Glendarvel: Argyll, 1995).
The Big Empty (Glendarvel: Argyll, 1997).
Duck (Glendarvel: Argyll, 1998).
Itchycooblue (London: Review, 1999).

CHRIS DOLAN

Poor Angels, and Other Stories (Edinburgh: Polygon, 1995).
Ascension Day (London: Review, 1999).

READING LISTS

COLIN DOUGLAS
The Houseman's Tale (Edinburgh: Canongate, 1975).
The Greatest Breakthrough since Lunchtime (Edinburgh: Canongate, 1977).
Bleeders Come First (Edinburgh: Canongate, 1979).
A Cure for Living (London: Hutchinson, 1983).
Hazards of the Profession (Edinburgh: Mainstream, 1987).
Sickness and Health (London: Heinemann, 1991).

DOUGLAS DUNN
Secret Villages (London: Faber, 1985).
Boyfriends and Girlfriends (London: Faber, 1994).

Secondary reading
Dòsa, Attila, 'Love, or Nothing?: Dimensions of Scottish Identity in Douglas Dunn's *Love or Nothing*', *SLJ* 27(1) (Aberdeen: Association for Scottish Literary Studies, 2000), pp. 91–104.
Dunn, Douglas, 'Exile and Unexile', *Cencrastus* 16 (Edinburgh: Cencrastus Publications, 1984), pp. 4–6.

DOROTHY DUNNETT
The Game of Kings (London: Cassell, 1961), and further titles in the 'Lymond' series.
King Hereafter (London: Michael Joseph, 1982).
Niccolo Rising (London: Michael Joseph, 1986) and further titles in the 'Nicolo' series.

Also the 'Johnson Johnson' series of thrillers, originally published under the name Dorothy Halliday, now republished under new titles as by Dorothy Dunnett.

NIALL DUTHIE
The Duchess's Dragonfly (London: Phoenix, 1993).
Natterjack (London: Faber, 1996).
Lobster Moth (London: Fourth Estate, 1999).

MARGARET ELPHINSTONE
The Incomer (London: Women's Press, 1987).
A Sparrow's Flight (Edinburgh: Polygon, 1990).
An Apple from a Tree (London: Women's Press, 1991).
Islanders (Edinburgh: Polygon, 1994).
The Sea Road (Edinburgh: Canongate, 2000).

Secondary reading
Babinec, Lisa, ' "Between the boundaries": An Interview with Margaret Elphinstone', *Edinburgh Review* 93 (Edinburgh: Edinburgh University Press, 1995), pp. 51–60.
McLeod, Amanda J., 'Re-dressing the Boundaries: The Challenge to Gender Identity in Two Fictional Twelfth-century Communities', *Contemporary Scottish Literature, 1970–2000 (Revista Canaria de Estudios Ingleses)*, ed. Tomás Monterrey (Servicio de Publicaciones: Universidad de la Laguna, 2000), pp. 155–67.

MICHEL FABER
Some Rain Must Fall (Edinburgh: Canongate, 1999).
Under the Skin (Edinburgh: Canongate, 2000).
The Hundred and Ninety-Nine Steps (Edinburgh: Canongate, 2001).

ALISON FELL
The Grey Dancer (London: Collins, 1981).
Every Move You Make (London: Virago, 1984).
The Bad Box (London: Virago, 1987).
The Crystal Owl (London: Virago, 1988).
Mer de Glace (London: Methuen, 1991).
Mistress of Lilliput (London: Doubleday, 1999).

Secondary reading
Gifford, D., and McMillan, D. (eds), 'Contemporary Fiction III: The Anglo-Scots', *A History of Scottish Women's Writing* (Edinburgh: Edinburgh University Press, 1997), pp. 630–40.

UNA FLETT
Revisiting Empty Houses (Edinburgh: Canongate, 1988).

RONALD FRAME
Winter Journey (London: Bodley Head, 1984).
Watching Mrs Gordon, and other stories (London: Bodley Head, 1985).
A Long Weekend with Marcel Proust (London: Bodley Head, 1986).
Sandmouth People (London: Bodley Head, 1987).
A Woman of Judah (London: Bodley Head, 1987).
Penelope's Hat (London: Bodley Head, 1989).
Bluette (London: Bodley Head, 1990).
Underwood and After (London: Bodley Head, 1991).
Walking My Mistress in Deauville (London: Hodder & Stoughton, 1992).
The Sun on the Wall (London: Hodder & Stoughton, 1994).
The Lantern Bearers (London: Duckworth, 1999).

Secondary reading
Dunn, Douglas, 'Divergent Scottishness: William Boyd, Allan Massie, Ronald Frame', *The Scottish Novel Since the Seventies*, eds G. Wallace and R. Stevenson (Edinburgh: Edinburgh University Press, 1994), pp. 149–69.

GEORGE MACDONALD FRASER
Flashman (London: Barrie & Jenkins, 1969), and other Flashman novels.
The General Danced at Dawn (London: Barrie & Jenkins, 1970).
McAuslan in the Rough, and other stories (London: Barrie & Jenkins, 1974).
Mr American (London: Collins, 1980).
The Pyrates (London: Collins, 1983).
The Candlemass Road (London: Harvill, 1993).

ELLEN GALFORD
Moll Cutpurse: her true history (Edinburgh: Stramullion, 1984).
The Fires of Bride (London: Women's Press, 1986).

Queendom Come (London: Virago, 1990).
The Dyke and the Dybbuk (London: Virago, 1993).

TOM GALLACHER
Apprentice (London: Hamish Hamilton, 1983).
Journeyman (London: Hamish Hamilton, 1984).
Survivor (London: Hamish Hamilton, 1985).
The Jewel Maker (London: Hamish Hamilton, 1986).
The Wind on the Heath (London: Hamish Hamilton, 1987).

JANICE GALLOWAY
The Trick is to Keep Breathing (Edinburgh: Polygon, 1989).
Blood (London: Secker & Warburg, 1991).
Foreign Parts (London: Cape, 1994).
Where You Find It (London: Cape, 1996).

Secondary reading

Christianson, Aileen, 'Lies, Notable Silences and Plastering the Cracks: The Fiction of A. L. Kennedy and Janice Galloway', *Gender and Scottish Society: Politics, Policies and Participation* (Edinburgh: Unit for the Study of Government in Scotland, University of Edinburgh, 1998), pp. 136–40.

Coombe, Stella, 'Things Galloway' [interview], *Harpies and Quines* 1 (May/June 1992), pp. 26–9.

Galloway, Janice, 'Objective truth and the grinding machine or don't let the bastards etc. etc.', *Writers writing*, eds Jenny Brown and Shona Munro (Edinburgh: Mainstream, 1993), pp. 73–7.

Marsh, Cristie Leigh, 'Interview with Janice Galloway, Glasgow, March 21, 1999' *Edinburgh Review* 101 (Edinburgh: Edinburgh University Press, 1999), pp. 85–98.

Metzstein, Margery, 'Of myths and men: aspects of gender in the fiction of Janice Galloway', *The Scottish Novel since the Seventies*, eds Gavin Wallace and Randall Stevenson (Edinburgh: Edinburgh University Press, 1993), pp. 136–46.

Norquay, Glenda, 'Janice Galloway's Novels: Fraudulent Mooching', *Contemporary Scottish Women Writers*, eds Aileen Christianson and Alison Lumsden (Edinburgh: Edinburgh University Press, 2000), pp. 131–43.

—, 'The Fiction of Janice Galloway: Weaving a route through Chaos', *Space & Place: The Geographies of Literature*, eds G. Norquay and G. Smyth (Liverpool: John Moores University Press, 1997), pp. 323–30.

Paccaud-Huguet, Josiane, 'Breaking through Cracked Mirrors: The Short Stories of Janice Galloway', *Études Écossaises* 2 (Grenoble: Université Stendhal, 1993), pp. 5–29.

JAMES SHAW GRANT
Their Children Will See (London: Hale, 1979).

ALASDAIR GRAY
Lanark: a life in four books (Edinburgh: Canongate, 1981).
Unlikely Stories, Mostly (Edinburgh: Canongate, 1983).
1982, Janine (London: Cape, 1984).
Lean Tales (London: Cape, 1985).
The Fall of Kelvin Walker (Edinburgh: Canongate, 1985).

Saltire Self-Portrait (Edinburgh: Saltire Society, 1988).
McGrotty and Ludmilla (Glasgow: Dog and Bone, 1990).
Something Leather (London: Cape, 1990).
Poor Things (London: Bloomsbury, 1992).
Ten Tales Tall and True (London: Bloomsbury, 1993).
The History Maker (London: Bloomsbury, 1994).
Mavis Belfrage (London: Bloomsbury, 1996).
The Book of Prefaces (London: Bloomsbury, 2000).

Secondary reading

This list is necessarily selective. Many other references will be found in Crawford and Nairn: *The Arts of Alasdair Gray* (see below), and in Moira Burgess: *The Glasgow Novel* (Hamilton: Scottish Library Association, 1999; 3rd edition).

Acker, Kathy, 'Alasdair Gray interviewed', *Edinburgh Review* 74 (Edinburgh, 1986), pp. 83–90.

Calder, Angus, 'Alasdair Gray's *The Book of Prefaces*', *Chapman* 97 (Edinburgh: Chapman Publications, 2000), pp. 3–11.

Crawford, Robert, and Nairn, Thom (eds), *The Arts of Alasdair Gray* (Edinburgh: Edinburgh University Press, 1991).

Gifford, Douglas, 'Private Confession and Public Satire: The Fiction of Alasdair Gray', *Chapman* 52 (Edinburgh: Chapman Publications, 1987), pp. 101–16.

—, and Gray, Alasdair, 'Author's Postscript Completed by Douglas Gifford', *Unlikely Stories Mostly* (Edinburgh: Canongate, 1997; revised edition), pp. 278–90.

—, 'Scottish Fiction 1980–81: The Importance of Alisdair Gray's *Lanark*', *SSL* 18 (Columbia: University of South Carolina Press, 1983), pp. 210–52.

Gray, Alasdair, *Alasdair Gray* (Edinburgh: Saltire Society, 1988).

Lumsden, Alison, 'Innovation and reaction in the fiction of Alasdair Gray', *The Scottish Novel since the Seventies*, eds Gavin Wallace and Randall Stevenson (Edinburgh: Edinburgh University Press, 1993), pp. 115–26.

Manderson, Dave, 'A Letter from a Western Empire: Post-Colonial – (and other Isms) in Alisdair Gray's Early Work', *Chapman* 97 (Edinburgh: Chapman Publications, 2000), pp. 51–3.

Martínez, Mario Díaz, 'Dissecting Glasgow: Alisdair Gray's *Poor Things*', *Contemporary Scottish Literature, 1970–2000 (Revista Canaria de Estudios Ingleses)*, ed. Tomás Monterrey (Servicio de Publicaciones: Universidad de la Laguna, 2000), pp. 117–31.

Murray, Isobel, and Tait, Bob, 'Alasdair Gray: *Lanark*', *Ten Modern Scottish Novels* (Aberdeen: Aberdeen University Press, 1984), pp. 219–39.

Pittin, Marie Odile, 'Alisdair Gray: A Strategy of Ambiguity', *Studies in Scottish Fiction: 1945 to the Present* (Frankfurt: Peter Lang, 1996).

Stenhouse, David, 'A Wholly Healthy Scotland: A Reichian Reading of *1982, Janine*', *Edinburgh Review* 95 (Edinburgh: Edinburgh University Press, 1996), pp. 113–22.

Stirling, Kirsten, '"The comparative anatomy of the eye": James Bridie's *The Anatomist* and Alisdair Gray's *Poor Things*', *Odd Alliances: Scottish Studies in European Contexts*, eds Neil McMillan and Kirsten Stirling (Glasgow: Cruithne Press, 1999).

Szamosi, Gertrud, 'Post-modernist manipulation in *1982, Janine* and *Something Leather*', *Odd Alliances: Scottish Studies in European Contexts*, eds Neil McMillan and Kirsten Stirling (Glasgow: Cruithne Press, 1999).

Tiitenin, Johanna, 'Between Fiction and History', *In Scotland* 1 (Edinburgh: Ramsay Head Press, 1999), pp. 81–9.

Whyte, Christopher, 'Alisdair Gray: Not a mirror but a portrait', *Books in Scotland* 28 (Edinburgh: Ramsay Head Press, 1988), pp. 1–2.
Witschi, Beat, 'Defining a Scottish Identity', *Books in Scotland* 34 (Edinburgh: Ramsay Head Press, 1990), pp. 5–6.

ANDREW GREIG

The Order of the Day (Newcastle: Bloodaxe, 1990).
Electric Brae: a modern romance (Edinburgh: Canongate, 1992).
The Return of John Macnab (London: Headline, 1996).
When They Lay Bare (London: Faber & Faber, 1999).
That Summer (London: Faber and Faber, 2000).

CLIFF HANLEY

Dancing in the Streets [autobiography] (London: Hutchinson, 1958).
Love from Everybody (London: Hutchinson, 1959).
The Taste of Too Much (London: Hutchinson, 1960).
Nothing But the Best (London: Hutchinson, 1964).
The Hot Month (London: Hutchinson, 1967).
The Red Haired Bitch (London: Hutchinson, 1969).
Prissy (London: Collins, 1978).
Another Street, Another Dance (Edinburgh: Mainstream, 1983).

Also thrillers under the name of Henry Calvin.

SIAN HAYTON

Cells of Knowledge (Edinburgh: Polygon, 1989).
Hidden Daughters (Edinburgh: Polygon, 1992).
The Governors (Nairn: Balnain, 1992).
The Last Flight (Edinburgh: Polygon, 1993).

Secondary reading

McLeod, Amanda J., 'Fact, fiction, and gender identities: the manipulation of history and legend in Sian Hayton's *Cells of Knowledge* trilogy', *Odd Alliances: Scottish Studies in European Contexts*, eds Neil McMillan and Kirsten Stirling (Glasgow: Cruithne Press, 1999).

THOMAS HEALY

It Might Have Been Jerusalem (Edinburgh: Polygon, 1991).
Rolling (Edinburgh: Polygon, 1992).
A Hurting Business [autobiography] (London: Picador, 1996).

MEG HENDERSON

Finding Peggy [autobiography] (London: Corgi, 1994).
The Holy City (London: Flamingo, 1997).
Bloody Mary (London: Flamingo, 1999).

JOHN HERDMAN

Pagan's Pilgrimage (Preston: Akros, 1978).
Three Novellas (Edinburgh: Polygon, 1987).

Imelda, and other stories (Edinburgh: Polygon, 1993).
Ghostwriting (Edinburgh: Polygon, 1996).

Secondary reading
Daly, Macdonald, 'An Interview with John Herdman', *Southfields* 6. 1 (London: Southfields Press, 1999), pp. 85–101.

LIZ HERON
A Red River (London: Virago, 1997).

LAURA HIRD
Nail (Edinburgh: Rebel Inc., 1997).
Born Free (Edinburgh: Rebel Inc., 1999).

STUART HOOD
Pebbles from My Skull [autobiography] (London: Hutchinson, 1963; revised edition, *Carlino*, Manchester: Carcanet, 1985).
In and Out the Window (London: Davis Poynter, 1974).
A Storm from Paradise (Manchester: Carcanet, 1985).
The Upper Hand (Manchester: Carcanet, 1987).
The Brutal Heart (Manchester: Carcanet, 1989).
A Den of Foxes (London: Methuen, 1991).
The Book of Judith (Manchester: Carcanet, 1995).

Secondary reading
Lumley, Bob, 'Keeping Faith: an interview with Stuart Hood', *Edinburgh Review* 78–9 (Edinburgh: Edinburgh University Press, 1988), pp. 172–206.
Wilson, Conrad, 'Out of the den of foxes', *Books in Scotland* 39 (Edinburgh: Ramsay Head Press, 1991), p. 4 (cont. p. 13).

STUART HUTCHISON
Scully's Lugs (Edinburgh: Chambers, 1979).

ROBERT ALAN JAMIESON
Soor Hearts (Edinburgh: Paul Harris, 1983).
Thin Wealth: a novel from an oil decade (Edinburgh: Polygon, 1986).
A Day at the Office (Edinburgh: Polygon, 1991).

JACKIE KAY
Trumpet (London: Picador, 1998).

Secondary reading
Monterrey, Tomás, 'A Scottish Metamorphosis: Jackie Kay's '*Trumpet*', *Contemporary Scottish Literature, 1970–2000 (Revista Canaria de Estudios Ingleses)*, ed. Tomás Monterrey (Servicio de Publicaciones: Universidad de la Laguna, 2000), pp. 169–83.

READING LISTS

A. L. KENNEDY
Night Geometry and the Garscadden Trains (Edinburgh: Polygon, 1990).
Looking for the Possible Dance (London: Secker & Warburg, 1993).
Now That You're Back (London: Cape, 1994).
So I Am Glad (London: Cape, 1995).
Original Bliss (London: Cape, 1997).
Everything You Need (London: Cape, 1999).

Secondary reading
Adair, Tom, 'Danger woman', *Scotland on Sunday: Spectrum* (19 January 1997), p. 11.
Bell, Eleanor Stewart, 'Scotland and Ethics in the Work of A. L. Kennedy', *Scotlands* 5(1) (Edinburgh: Edinburgh University Press, 1998), pp. 105–13.
Christianson, Aileen, 'Lies, Notable Silences and Plastering the Cracks: The Fiction of A. L. Kennedy and Janice Galloway', *Gender and Scottish Society: Polities, Policies and Participation* (Edinburgh: Unit for the Study of Government in Scotland, University of Edinburgh, 1998), pp. 136–40.
Close, Ajay, 'AL right now', *Scotland on Sunday: Spectrum* (23 January 1994), p. 3.
Dickson, Beth, 'Intimacy, Violence and Identity: The Fiction of A. L. Kennedy', *Contemporary Scottish Literature, 1970–2000 (Revista Canaria de Estudios Ingleses)*, ed. Tomás Monterrey (Servicio de Publicaciones: Universidad de la Laguna, 2000), pp. 133–44.
Dunnigan, Sarah M., 'A. L. Kennedy's Longer Fiction: Articulate Grace', *Contemporary Scottish Women Writers*, eds Aileen Christianson and Alison Lumsden (Edinburgh: Edinburgh University Press, 2000), pp. 144–55.
Marsh, Cristie Leigh, 'Interview with A. L. Kennedy, Glasgow, March 17, 1999', *Edinburgh Review* 101 (Edinburgh: Edinburgh University Press, 1999), pp. 99–119.
Smith, Sarah, 'A Nose for Injustice', *New Statesman and Society* (26 May 1995), p. 25.
Thomas, Ruth, 'A. L. Kennedy' [interview], *Scottish Book Collector* 3(12) (Edinburgh, 1993), pp. 2–4.

JESSIE KESSON
The White Bird Passes (London: Chatto & Windus, 1958).
Glitter of Mica (London: Chatto & Windus, 1963).
Another Time, Another Place (London: Chatto & Windus, 1983).
Where the Apple Ripens, and other stories (London: Chatto & Windus, 1985).
Somewhere Beyond: A Jessie Kesson Companion, ed. Isobel Murray (Edinburgh: B&W Publishing, 2000).

Secondary reading
Anderson, Carol, 'Listening to the Women Talk', *The Scottish Novel Since the Seventies*, eds G. Wallace and R. Stevenson (Edinburgh: Edinburgh University Press, 1994), pp. 170–86.
Bold, Alan, *Modern Scottish Literature* (London: Longman, 1983), pp. 213–15.
Hendry, Joy, 'Jessie Kesson Country', *Scots Magazine* (Edinburgh, 1989), pp. 11–22.
Kesson, Jessie, 'My Scotland', *Scottish Review* 35 (Edinburgh: Saltire Society, 1984), pp. 39–41.
—, 'The Sma' Perfect' [interview recorded 1985], *Scottish Writers Talking*, ed. Isobel Murray (East Linton: Tuckwell Press, 1996), pp. 55–83.
Monnickendam, Andrew, 'Beauty or Beast? Landscape in the Fiction of Jessie Kesson', *Studies in Scottish Fiction: 1945 to the Present* (Frankfurt: Peter Lang, 1996).
Murray, Isobel, 'Jessie Kesson', *A History of Scottish Women's Writing*, eds Douglas Gifford and Dorothy McMillan (Edinburgh: Edinburgh University Press, 1997), pp. 481–93.
—, *Jessie Kesson: Writing her Life* (Edinburgh: Canongate, 2000).

—, 'A Far Cry from the Kailyard: Jessie Kesson's *Glitter of Mica*', *Scottish Women's Fiction 1920s to 1960s: Journeys into Being*, eds Carol Anderson and Aileen Christianson (East Linton: Tuckwell Press, 2000), pp. 147–57.

Norquay, Glenda, 'Borderlines: Jessie Kesson's *The White Bird Passes*', *Scottish Women's Fiction 1920s to 1960s: Journeys into Being*, eds Carol Anderson and Aileen Christianson (East Linton: Tuckwell Press, 2000), pp. 122–33.

ALANNA KNIGHT

A Stranger Came By (London: Hurst & Blackett, 1974).
Colla's Children (Edinburgh: Macdonald, 1982).
Enter Second Murderer (London: Macmillan, 1988).
The Bull Slayers (London: Macmillan, 1995).

And many other historical novels.

FRANK KUPPNER

A Very Quiet Street (Edinburgh: Polygon, 1989).
A Concussed History of Scotland (Edinburgh: Polygon, 1991).
Something Very Like Murder (Edinburgh: Polygon, 1994).
Life on a Dead Planet (Edinburgh: Polygon, 1996).
In the Beginning There Was Physics (Edinburgh: Polygon, 1999).

Secondary reading

Thomson, A. J. P., 'Spaces Between: Frank Kuppner's crime writing', *Edinburgh Review* 102 (Edinburgh: Edinburgh University Press, 1999), pp. 64–70.

ROBBIE KYDD

Auld Zimmery (Glasgow: Mariscat, 1987).
The Quiet Stranger (Edinburgh: Mainstream, 1991).

ROSS LAIDLAW

The Linton Porcupine (Edinburgh: Canongate, 1984).
Aphra Benn – Dispatch'd from Athole (Nairn: Balnain, 1992).

GREGOR LAMB

Langskaill (Orkney: Byrgisey, 1999).

ROSS LECKIE

Hannibal (Edinburgh: Canongate, 1995).
Scipio (Edinburgh: Canongate, 1998).
Carthage (Edinburgh: Canongate, 2000).

GORDON LEGGE

The Shoe (Edinburgh: Polygon, 1989).
In Between Talking about the Football (Edinburgh: Polygon, 1991).
I Love Me: Who do You Love? (Edinburgh: Polygon, 1994).
Near Neighbours (London: Cape, 1998).

READING LISTS

JOAN LINGARD
Liam's Daughter (London: Hodder & Stoughton, 1963).
The Prevailing Wind (London: Hodder & Stoughton, 1964).
The Tide Comes In (London: Hodder & Stoughton, 1966).
The Headmaster (London: Hodder & Stoughton, 1967).
A Sort of Freedom (London: Hodder & Stoughton, 1969).
The Second Flowering of Emily Mountjoy (Edinburgh: Paul Harris, 1979).
Greenyards (London: Hamish Hamilton, 1981).
Sisters by Rite (London: Hamish Hamilton, 1984).
Reasonable Doubts (London: Hamish Hamilton, 1986).
The Women's House (London: Hamish Hamilton, 1989).
Between Two Worlds (London: Hamish Hamilton, 1991).
After Colette (London: Sinclair-Stevenson, 1993).
Dreams of Love and Modest Glory (London: Sinclair-Stevenson, 1995).

Secondary reading
Bold, Alan, *Modern Scottish Literature* (London: Longman, 1983), pp. 229–30.
Taylor, Alan, 'The Teenage Novels of Joan Lingard', *Books in Scotland* 13 (Edinburgh: Ramsay Head Press, 1983), pp. 6–7.

BRIAN MCCABE
The Lipstick Circus (Edinburgh: Mainstream, 1985).
The Other McCoy (Edinburgh: Mainstream, 1990).
In a Dark Room with a Stranger (London: Hamish Hamilton, 1993).
A Date with My Wife (Edinburgh: Canongate, 2001).

VAL MCDERMID
The Mermaids Singing (London: HarperCollins, 1995).
The Wire in the Blood (London: HarperCollins, 1997).
A Place of Execution (London: HarperCollins, 1999).
And other crime stories.

CARL MACDOUGALL
Prosepiece (Markinch Pavement Press, 1979).
Elvis is Dead (Glasgow: Mariscat, 1986).
Stone Over Water (London: Secker & Warburg, 1989).
The Lights Below (London: Secker & Warburg, 1993).
The Casanova Papers (London: Secker & Warburg, 1996).

Secondary reading
Gifford, Douglas, 'MacDougall's Glasgow discussed with Douglas Gifford', *Books in Scotland* 33 (Edinburgh: Ramsay Head Press, 1990), pp. 1–4.

HELENA MCEWEN
The Big House (London: Bloomsbury, 2000).

TODD MCEWAN
McX (London: Secker & Warburg, 1990).

JOHN MCGILL
That Rubens Guy: stories from a Glasgow tenement (Edinburgh: Mainstream, 1990).
Giraffes (Edinburgh: Mainstream, 1993).

MATT MCGINN
Fry the Little Fishes (London: Calder & Boyars, 1975).

ERIC MCGOLDRICK
The Paradise Motel (London: Bloomsbury, 1989).

SHENA MACKAY
Dust Falls on Eugene Schlumburger and Toddler on the Run (London: Deutsch, 1964).
Music Upstairs (London: Deutsch, 1965).
Old Crow (London: Cape, 1967).
An Advent Calendar (London: Cape, 1971).
Babies in Rhinestones, and Other Stories (London: Heinemann, 1983).
A Bowl of Cherries (Brighton: Harvester, 1984).
Redhill Rococo (London: Heinemann, 1986).
Dreams of Dead Women's Handbags (London: Heinemann, 1987).
Dunedin (London: Heinemann, 1992).
Laughing Academy (London: Heinemann, 1993).
The Orchard on Fire (London: Heinemann, 1995).
The Artist's Widow (London: Cape, 1998).
The Worlds Smallest Unicorn, and Other Stories (London: Cape, 1999).

RON MACKAY
The Prophet (London: New English Library, 1992).
Mean City (London: Hodder & Stoughton, 1995).
The Leper Colony (London: Gollancz, 1997).

DAVID MACKENZIE
The Truth of Stone (Edinburgh: Mainstream, 1991).

BERNARD MACLAVERTY
Secrets (Belfast: Blackstaff, 1977).
Lamb (London: Cape, 1980).
A Time to Dance, and Other Stories (London: Cape, 1982).
Cal (London: Cape, 1983).
The Great Profundo (London: Cape, 1987).
Walking the Dog, and other stories (London: Cape, 1994).
Grace Notes (London: Cape, 1997).
The Anatomy School (London: Cape, 2001).

DUNCAN MCLEAN
Bucket of Tongues (London: Secker & Warburg, 1992).
Blackden (London: Secker & Warburg, 1992).
Bunker Man (London: Cape, 1995).

READING LISTS

CHARLES MACLEOD
Devil in the Wind (Edinburgh: Gordon Wright, 1976).

CANDIA MCWILLIAM
A Case of Knives (London: Bloomsbury, 1988).
A Little Stranger (London: Bloomsbury, 1989).
Debatable Land (London: Bloomsbury, 1994).
Wait Till I Tell You (London: Bloomsbury, 1997).

Secondary reading

Christianson, Aileen, 'Muriel Spark and Candia McWilliam: Continuities', *Contemporary Scottish Women Writers*, eds Aileen Christianson and Alison Lumsden (Edinburgh: Edinburgh University Press, 2000), pp. 95–110.

—, 'Elspeth Barker, Candia McWilliam and Murial Spark: Writers in Exile', *Terranglian Territories: Proceedings of Seventh International Conference on the Literature of Region and Nation*, ed. Susanne Hagemann (Frankfurt am Main: Peter Lang, 2000), pp. 339–47.

Gifford, D., and McMillan, D. (eds), 'Contemporary Fiction III: The Anglo-Scots', *A History of Scottish Women's Writing* (Edinburgh: Edinburgh University Press, 1997), pp. 630–40.

SARA MAITLAND
Daughter of Jerusalem (London: Blond & Briggs, 1978).
Telling Tales (London: Journeyman, 1983).
Virgin Territory (London: Michael Joseph, 1984).
A Book of Spells (London: Michael Joseph, 1987).
Arky Types (London: Michael Joseph, 1987).
Three Times Table (London: Chatto & Windus, 1990).
Home Truths (London: Chatto & Windus, 1993).
Women Fly When Men Aren't Watching (London: Virago, 1993).

ALLAN MASSIE
Change and Decay In All Around I See (London: Bodley Head, 1978).
The Last Peacock (London: Bodley Head, 1980).
The Death of Men (London: Bodley Head, 1981).
One Night in Winter (London: Bodley Head, 1984).
Augustus (London: Bodley Head, 1986).
A Question of Loyalties (London: Hutchinson, 1989).
Tiberius (London: Hodder & Stoughton, 1990).
The Hanging Tree (London: Hodder & Stoughton, 1990).
The Sins of the Father (London: Hutchinson, 1991).
These Enchanted Woods (London: Hutchinson, 1993).
Caesar (London: Hodder & Stoughton, 1993).
The Ragged Lion (London: Century Hutchinson, 1994).
King David (London: Sceptre, 1995).
Shadows of Empire (London: Sinclair-Stevenson, 1997).
Antony (London: Sceptre, 1997).
Nero's Heirs (London: Sceptre, 1999).
The Evening of the World (London: Weidenfeld and Nicholson, 2001).

Secondary reading

Dunn, Douglas, 'Divergent Scottishness: William Boyd, Allan Massie, Ronald Frame', *The Scottish Novel Since the Seventies*, eds G. Wallace and R. Stevenson (Edinburgh: Edinburgh University Press, 1994), pp. 149–69.

Wilson, Conrad, 'Awards and Aftermaths: Conrad Wilson meets Allan Massie', *Books in Scotland* 41 (Edinburgh: Ramsay Head Press, 1992), pp. 1–3.

JAMES MEEK

McFarlane Boils the Sea (Edinburgh: Polygon, 1989).
Last Orders, and other stories (Edinburgh: Polygon, 1992).
Drivetime (Edinburgh: Polygon, 1995).
The Museum of Doubt (Edinburgh: Rebel Inc., 2000).

MARTIN MILLAR

Milk, Sulphate, and Alby Starvation (London: Fourth Estate, 1987).
Lux the Poet (London: Fourth Estate, 1988).
Ruby and the Stone Age Diet (London: Fourth Estate, 1989).
Graphic Novel (London: Fourth Estate, 1992).
The Good Fairies of New York (London: Fourth Estate, 1992).
Dreams of Sex and Stagediving (London: Fourth Estate, 1994).
Love and Peace with Melody Paradise (London: IMP Fiction, 1998).

JOSEPH MILLS

Towards the End (Edinburgh: Polygon, 1989).
Obsessions (Brighton: Millivres Books, 1998).

NAOMI MITCHISON

Publications from 1948. For earlier titles see the bibliography to Section 5. The list of this prolific writer is necessarily selective. A full bibliography will be found in *A History of Scottish Women's Writing*, eds Douglas Gifford and Dorothy McMillan (Edinburgh: Edinburgh University Press, 1997), pp. 702–3.

The Big House (London: Faber, 1950).
Lobsters on the Agenda (London: Gollancz, 1952).
Travel Light (London: Faber, 1952).
To the Chapel Perilous (London: Allen & Unwin, 1955).
Behold Your King (London: Muller, 1957).
Five Men and a Swan (London: Allen & Unwin, 1958).
Memoirs of a Spacewoman (London: Gollancz, 1962).
When We Become Men (London: Collins, 1965).
Small Talk: Memories of an Edwardian Childhood [autobiography] (London: Bodley Head, 1973).
All Change Here: girlhood and marriage [autobiography] (London: Bodley Head, 1975).
Solution Three (London: Dobson, 1975).
You May Well Ask: a memoir 1920–1940 [autobiography] (London: Gollancz, 1979).
Images of Africa (Edinburgh: Canongate, 1980).
What Do You Think Yourself? Scottish Short Stories (Edinburgh: Paul Harris, 1982).
Not by Bread Alone (London: Marion Boyars, 1983).
Among You Taking Notes: wartime diary 1939–45 [autobiography] (London: Gollancz, 1985).
Early in Orcadia (Glasgow: Richard Drew, 1990).
The Oath-Takers (Nairn: Balnain Books, 1991).
Sea-Green Ribbons (Nairn: Balnain Books, 1991).

READING LISTS

Secondary reading
See the bibliography to Section 5.

CAROL MORIN
Lampshades (London: Secker & Warburg, 1991).
Dead Glamorous (London: Gollancz, 1996).

ANDREW O'HAGAN
The Missing (London: Picador, 1995).
Our Fathers (London: Faber, 1999).

JANET PAISLEY
Wildfire (Edinburgh: Taranis, 1993).

BRIDGET PENNEY
Honeymoon with Death, and Other Stories (Edinburgh: Polygon, 1991).

ALISON PRINCE
The Witching Tree (London: Allison & Busby, 1996).

SIRI REYNOLDS
House of Rooms (Edinburgh: Polygon, 1998).

JAMES ROBERTSON
Close, and Other Stories (Edinburgh: B&W Publishing, 1991).
The Ragged Man's Complaint (Edinburgh: B&W Publishing, 1993).
The Fanatic (London: Fourth Estate, 2000).

DILYS ROSE
Our Lady of the Pickpockets (London: Secker & Warburg, 1989).
Red Tides (London: Secker & Warburg, 1993).
War Dolls (London: Review, 1998).
Pest Maiden (London: Review, 1999).

BESS ROSS
A Bit of Crack and Car Culture, and Other Stories (Nairn: Balnain Books, 1990).
Those Other Times (Nairn: Balnain Books, 1991).
Dangerous Gifts (Nairn: Balnain Books, 1994).

ANDREW MURRAY SCOTT
Tumulus (Edinburgh: Polygon, 1999).

AGNES SHORT
The Heritors (London: Constable, 1977).

The Dragon Seas (London: Constable, 1988).
Willowbrae (London: Constable, 1992).

And many other historical novels.

ALEXANDER MCCALL SMITH
Heavenly Date, and Other Stories (Edinburgh: Canongate, 1995).
The No. 1 Ladies Detective Agency (Edinburgh: Polygon, 1999).
Tears of the Giraffe (Edinburgh: Polygon, 2000).
Morality for Beautiful Girls (Edinburgh: Polygon, 2001).

ALI SMITH
Free Love (London: Virago, 1995).
Like (London: Virago, 1997).
Other Stories, and Other Stories (London: Granta Books, 1999).
Hotel World (London: Hamish Hamilton, 2001).

ANNE SMITH
The Magic Glass (London: Michael Joseph, 1981).

MURIEL SPARK
Publications from 1966. For earlier titles see the bibliography in previous chapter.

The Public Image (London: Macmillan, 1968).
The Driver's Seat (London: Macmillan, 1970).
Not to Disturb (London: Macmillan, 1971).
The Hothouse by the East River (London: Macmillan, 1973).
The Abbess of Crewe (London: Macmillan, 1974).
The Takeover (London: Macmillan, 1976).
Territorial Rights (London: Macmillan, 1979).
Loitering with Intent (London: Bodley Head, 1981).
The Only Problem (London: Bodley Head, 1984).
A Far Cry from Kensington (London: Constable, 1988).
Symposium (London: Constable, 1990).
Curriculum Vitae [autobiography] (London: Constable, 1992).
Reality and Dreams (London: Constable, 1996).
Aiding and Abetting (London: Constable, 2000).

Secondary reading
See the bibliography to previous chapter.

ALAN SPENCE
Its Colours They Are Fine (London: Collins, 1977).
The Magic Flute (Edinburgh: Canongate, 1990).
Stone Garden, and other stories (London: Phoenix House, 1995).
Way to Go (London: Phoenix House, 1998).

Secondary reading

Burns, John, 'Mastering the Magic Flute', *Cencrastus* 38 (Edinburgh: Cencrastus, 1990–91), pp. 41–2.

Spence, Alan, 'Boom baby', *Jock Tamson's Bairns*, ed. Trevor Royle (London: Hamish Hamilton, 1977), pp. 14–28.

HUNTER STEELE

McCandy (London: John Murray, 1981).
The Wishdoctor's Song (Edinburgh: Macdonald, 1984).
Chasing the Gilded Shadow (London: Deutsch, 1986).
Lord Hamlet's Castle (London: Deutsch, 1987).
The Lords of Montplaisir (London: Macmillan, 1989).

IAN STEPHEN

Living at the Edge (Newmarket, Lewis: Machair, 1983).
Varying States of Grace (Edinburgh: Polygon, 1989).

JESSICA STIRLING

For titles published under the name Hugh Rae, see the bibliography to the previous chapter.

The Dark Pasture (London: Hodder & Stoughton, 1977).
The Deep Well at Noon (London: Hodder & Stoughton, 1979).
The Good Provider (London: Hodder & Stoughton, 1988).
Lantern for the Dark (London: Hodder & Stoughton, 1992).
The Penny Wedding (London: Hodder & Stoughton, 1994).

And many other historical novels.

ELIZABETH SUTHERLAND

Lent Term (London: Constable, 1973).
The Seer of Kintail (London: Constable, 1974).
Hannah Hereafter (London: Constable, 1976).
The Weeping Tree (London: Constable, 1980).

HARRY TAIT

The Ballad of Sawney Bain (Edinburgh: Polygon, 1990).

SIMON TAYLOR

Mortimer's Deep (Nairn: Balnain, 1992).

EMMA TENNANT

The Time of the Crack (London: Cape, 1973).
The Last of the Country House Murders (London: Cape, 1974).
Hotel de Dream (London: Gollancz, 1976).
The Bad Sister (London: Gollancz, 1978).
Wild Nights (London: Cape, 1979).

Alice Fell (London: Cape, 1980).
Queen of Stones (London: Cape, 1982).
Woman Beware Woman (London: Cape, 1983).
Black Marina (London: Faber, 1985).
The House of Hospitalities (London: Viking, 1987).
A Wedding of Cousins (London: Viking, 1988).
Two Women of London: the Strange case of Ms Jekyll and Mrs Hyde (London: Faber, 1988).
Sister and Strangers (London: Grafton, 1990).
Strangers (London: Cape, 1998).
Girlitude (London: Cape, 1999).
Burnt Diaries (London: Cape, 2000).

Secondary reading

Anderson, Carol, 'Emma Tennant, Elspeth Barker, Alice Thompson: Gothic Revisited', *Contemporary Scottish Women Writers*, eds Aileen Christianson and Alison Lumsden (Edinburgh: Edinburgh University Press, 2000), pp. 117–30.

Gifford, D. and McMillan, D. (eds), 'Contemporary Fiction III: The Anglo-Scots', *A History of Scottish Women's Writing* (Edinburgh: Edinburgh University Press, 1997), pp. 630–40.

Haffenden, John (ed.), 'Emma Tennant', *Novelists in Interview* (London: Methuen, 1985), pp. 281–304.

Kenyon, Olga (ed.), 'Emma Tennant', *Women Writers Talk: Interviews with 10 Women Writers* (Oxford: Lennard, 1989), pp. 173–87.

RUTH THOMAS

Sea Monster Tattoo, and other stories (Edinburgh: Polygon, 1997).
The Dance Settee (Edinburgh: Polygon, 1999).

ALICE THOMPSON

Killing Time (Harmondsworth: Penguin, 1991).
Justine (Edinburgh: Canongate, 1996).
Pandora's Box (London: Little, Brown, 1998).

Secondary reading

Anderson, Carol, 'Emma Tennant, Elspeth Barker, Alice Thompson: Gothic Revisited', *Contemporary Scottish Women Writers*, eds Aileen Christianson and Alison Lumsden (Edinburgh: Edinburgh University Press, 2000), pp. 117–30.

NIGEL TRANTER

The Master of Gray (London: Hodder & Stoughton, 1961).
Robert the Bruce trilogy (London: Hodder & Stoughton, 1969–71).
The Wallace (London: Hodder & Stoughton, 1975).
Macbeth (London: Hodder & Stoughton, 1978).
Columba (London: Hodder & Stoughton, 1986).

And many other historical novels.

READING LISTS

CHRISTOPHER WALLACE
The Pied Piper's Poison (London: Flamingo, 1998).
The Resurrection Club (London: Flamingo, 1999).

ALAN WARNER
Morvern Callar (London: Cape, 1994).
These Demented Lands (London: Cape, 1997).
The Sopranos (London: Cape, 1998).

Secondary reading
Dale, Sophy, 'An interview with Alan Warner', *Edinburgh Review* 103 (Edinburgh, 2000), pp. 121–32.
LeBlanc, John, 'Return of the Goddess: Contemporary Music and Celtic Mythology in Alan Warner's *Morvern Callar*', *Contemporary Scottish Literature, 1970–2000 (Revista Canaria de Estudios Ingleses)*, ed. Tomás Monterrey (Servicio Publicaciones: Universidad de la Laguna, 2000), pp. 145–54.

WILLIAM WATSON
Better than One (London: Barrie & Rockliff, 1969).
Beltran in Exile (London: Chatto & Windus, 1979).
The Knight on the Bridge (London: Chatto & Windus, 1982).

JAN WEBSTER
Collier's Row (London: Collins, 1977).
Saturday City (London: Collins, 1978).
Beggarman's Country (London: Collins, 1979).
Lowland Reels (London: Hale, 1992).
Tallie's War (London: Hale, 1994).

CHRISTOPHER WHYTE
Euphemia McFarrigle and the Laughing Virgin (London: Gollancz, 1995).
The Warlock of Strathearn (London: Gollancz, 1997).
The Gay Decameron (London: Gollancz, 1998).
The Cloud Machinery (London: Gollancz, 2000).

DAVID WISHART
I, Virgil (London: Sceptre, 1994).
Ovid (London: Sceptre, 1995).
Nero (London: Sceptre, 1996).
Germanicus (London: Hodder & Stoughton, 1997).
Sejanus (London: Hodder & Stoughton, 1998).
The Lydian Baker (London: Hodder & Stoughton, 1998).
The Horse Coin (London: Hodder & Stoughton, 1999).
Old Bones (London: Hodder & Stoughton, 2000).

Chapter 42: Widening the Range: Non-Fiction Prose

The following are very general suggestions for non-fiction prose; additional material can be gathered from the reading lists for other sections.

Pre-Twentieth Century

ROBERT BURNS
Ferguson, J. De Lancey (ed.), *The Letters of Robert Burns* (1931; Oxford: Clarendon Press, 1985, 2nd edition, ed. G. Roy Ross).

HENRY COCKBURN
Memorials of His Time (Edinburgh: Black, 1856; Chicago, London: University of Chicago Press, 1974, edited by Karl F. C. Miller).
Circuit Journeys (Edinburgh: David Douglas, 1888; Hawick, Roxburghshire: Byways, 1983).

R. B. CUNNINGHAME GRAHAM
Walker, John (ed.), *The Scottish Sketches* (Edinburgh: Scottish Academic Press, 1982).

JOHN GIBSON LOCKHART
Peter's Letters to His Kinsfolk (Edinburgh, 1818; Edinburgh: Scottish Academic Press, 1977, edited by William Ruddick).
Memoirs of the Life of Sir Walter Scott, Bart (Edinburgh: Robert Cadell, 1837–8).

HUGH MILLER
Rosie, George (ed.), *Hugh Miller: Outrage and Order: a biography and selected writings* (Edinburgh: Mainstream, 1981).

SIR WALTER SCOTT
Anderson, W. E. K. (ed.), *Journal* (1890; Edinburgh: Canongate, 1998).
Greirson, H. J. C. (ed.), *The Letters of Sir Walter Scott*, 12 volumes (London: Constable, 1932–37).

ROBERT LOUIS STEVENSON
Treglown, J. (ed.), *The Lantern Bearers* (London: Chatto & Windus, 1988).

Twentieth Century

HANNAH AITKEN
In a Shaft of Sunlight (London: Hodder & Stoughton, 1947).

JOHN R. ALLAN
Farmer's Boy (London: Methuen, 1935).

READING LISTS

NEIL ASCHERON
Games with Shadows (London: Radius, 1988).
Black Sea (London: Jonathan Cape, 1995).

ANNA BLAIR
Tea at Miss Cranston's: A Century of Glasgow Memories (London: Shepheard-Walwyn, 1985).

JANETTA BOWIE
Penny Buff: a Clydeside school in the 'thirties (London: Constable, 1975).
Penny Boss: a Clydeside school in the 'fifties (London: Constable, 1976).
Penny Change: Clydeside schools in the 'seventies (London: Constable, 1977).

JAMES BRIDIE
One Way of Living (London: Constable, 1939).

DAVID KERR CAMERON
The Ballad and the Plough: a portrait of the life of the old Scottish farmtouns (London: Victor Gollancz, 1978).
Willie Gavin: Crofter Man: a portrait of a land and its rituals (London: Gollancz, 1980).
Cornkister Days (London: Victor Gollancz, 1984).

JAMES CAMERON
Point of Departure: An Experiment in Biography (London: Barker, 1967).

CATHERINE CARSWELL
Life of Robert Burns (London: Chatto & Windus, 1930; Edinburgh: Canongate, 1990).
Lying Awake (London: Secker & Warburg, 1950; Edinburgh: Canongate Books, 1997).

EVELYN COWAN
Spring Remembered: A Scottish Jewish Childhood (Edinburgh: Southside, 1974).

DAVID CRAIG
On the Crofter's Trail: in search of the Clearance Highlanders (London: Cape, 1990; 1992).

WILLIAM DALRYMPLE
In Xanadu: A Quest (London: Collins, 1989).
City of Djinns: A Year in Delhi (London: Harper Collins, 1993).
The Age of Kali: Indian Travels and Encounters (London: HarperCollins, 1998).

DAVID DAICHES
Two Worlds: An Edinburgh Jewish Childhood (New York: Harcourt Brace, 1956).

ROBERT GARIOCH
Two Men and a Blanket: Memoirs of Captivity (Edinburgh: Southside, 1975).

LEWIS GRASSIC GIBBON
Bold, Valentina (ed.), *Smeddum: A Lewis Grassic Gibbon Anthology* (Edinburgh: Canongate, 2001).
Munro, I. (ed.), *A Scots Hairst: Essays and Short Stories* (London: Hutchinson, 1967).
Grassic Gibbon, L. and MacDiarmid, H., *Scottish Scene, or, The Intelligent Man's Guide to Albyn* (London Melbourne: National Book Association: Hutchinson, 1934; Bath: Chivers, 1074).

RALPH GLASER
Scenes From a Highland Life (London: Hodder & Stoughton, 1981).
Growing Up in the Gorbals (London: Chatto & Windus, 1986).

ANDREW GREIG
Kingdoms of Experience: Everest, the Unclimbed Ridge (Edinburgh: Canongate, 1999).

NEIL GUNN
Whisky and Scotland: A Practical and Spiritual Survey (London: Routledge, 1935; London: Souvenir Press, 1977).
Highland Pack (London: Faber & Faber, 1949).
The Atom of Delight (Edinburgh: Polygon, 1956, 1993).

CLIFF HANLEY
Dancing in the Streets (London: Hutchinson, 1958; London: Corgi, 1984).

HAMISH HENDERSON
Alias McAlias: Writings on Song, Folk and Literature (Edinburgh: Polygon, 1992).

STUART HOOD
Pebbles from My Skull (London: Hutchinson, 1963).

IAN JACK
Before the Oil Ran Out: Britain, 1977–86 (London: Secker & Warburg, 1987).

ALISON KENNEDY
On Bullfighting (London: Yellow Jersey, 1999).

ERIC LINKLATER
The Man on my Back (London: Macmillan, 1941).
A Year of Space (London: Macmillan, 1953).
Fanfare for a Tin Hat (London: Macmillan, 1970).

TOM LEONARD
Reports from the Present: Selected Work, 1982–94 (London: Cape, 1995).

READING LISTS

HUGH MACDIARMID
Lucky Poet: a self-study in literature and political ideas: being the autobiography of Hugh MacDiarmid (Christopher Murray Grieve) (London: Methuen, 1943; Manchester: Carcanet, 1994).
—, and Grassic Gibbon, L., *Scottish scene, or, The Intelligent Man's Guide to Albyn* (London Melbourne: National Book Association: Hutchinson, 1934; Bath: Chivers, 1974).

CARL MACDOUGALL
Painting the Forth Road Bridge (London: Aurora Press, 2001).

WILLIAM MCILVANNEY
Surviving the Shipwreck (Edinburgh: Mainstream, 1991).

ALISDAIR MACLEAN
Night Falls on Ardnamurchan: The Twilight of a Crofting Family (London: Gollancz, 1984).

JOHN MCBEY
The Early Life of John McBey (Oxford: Oxford University Press, 1977; Edinburgh: Canongate, 1993).

DUNCAN MCLEAN
Lone Star Swing: on the Trail of Bob Wills and his Texas Playboys (London: Jonathan Cape, 1997).

SORLEY MCLEAN
Gillies, W. (ed.), *Ris a Bhruthaich: Criticism and Prose Writings* (Stornoway: Acair, 1985).

GAVIN MAXWELL
Ring of Bright Water (London: Longmans, 1960).

CHRISTIAN MILLER
A Childhood in Scotland (London: John Murray, 1981; Edinburgh: Canongate, 1989).

KARL MILLER
Cockburn's Millenium (London: Duckworth, 1975).
Doubles: Studies in Literary History (Oxford: Oxford University Press, 1985).
Rebecca's Vest: a Memoir (London: Hamish Hamilton, 1993).

NAOMI MITCHISON
Small Talk: Memoirs of an Edwardian Childhood (London: Bodley Head, 1973).
All Change Here: Girlhood and Marriage (London: Bodley Head, 1975).
You May Well Ask: A Memoir 1920–1940 (London: Gollancz, 1979).
Among You Taking Notes (London: Gollancz, 1985).

EDWIN MUIR
An Autobiography (London: Hogarth Press, 1954; Edinburgh: Canongate, 1993). [An Extended version of *The Story and the Fable* (London: George G. Harrap, 1940)].

Scottish Journey (London: Heinemann, 1935; Edinburgh: Mainstream, 1979).
Brown, G. M. (ed.), *Edwin Muir: Selected Prose* (London: Murray, 1987).

JOHN MUIR
My First Summer in the Sierra (Boston, MA: Houghton Mifflin, 1916).
The Story of My Boyhood and Youth (Boston & New York: Houghton Mifflin Co., 1924).

WILLA MUIR
Mrs Grundy in Scotland (G. Routledge & Sons: London, 1936).
Living With Ballads (London: Hogarth Press, 1965).
Belonging: A Memoir (London: Hogarth Press, 1968).

TOM NAIRN
The Break-up of Britain: Crisis and Neo-nationalism (London: Verso, 1981).
The Enchanted Glass: Britain and its Monarchy (London: Radius, 1988).
After Britain: New Labour and the Return of Scotland (London: Granta, 2000).

IAN NIALL
A Galloway Childhood (London: Heinemann, 1967).

ANDREW O'HAGAN
The Missing (London: Picador, 1995).

ALISTAIR REID
Whereabouts: Notes on being a Foreigner (Edinburgh: Canongate, 1987).
Oases: Poems and Prose (Edinburgh: Canongate, 1997).

TREVOR ROYLE
A Diary of Edinburgh (Edinburgh: Polygon Books, 1981).

DONALD SAUNDERS
A Glasgow Diary (Edinburgh: Polygon Books, 1984).

IAIN CRICHTON SMITH
Towards the Human: Selected Essays (Edinburgh: Macdonald, 1986).

WILLIAM SOUTAR
Scott, A. (ed.), *Diaries of a Dying Man* (Edinburgh: W. & K. Chambers, 1954; Edinburgh: Chambers, 1988).

MURIEL SPARK
Curriculum Vitae (London: Constable, 1992).

DAVID THOMSON
Nairn in Darkness and Light (London: Hutchinson, 1987).

READING LISTS

DAVID TOULMIN
Hard Shining Corn (Aberdeen: Impulse Books, 1972).
Straw into Gold: a Scots miscellany (Aberdeen: Impulse Books, 1973).
Harvest Home (Edinburgh: P. Harris, 1978).
A Chiel Among Them (Aberdeen: Gourdas House, 1982).

CHRISTIAN WATT
Fraser, D. (ed.), *The Christian Watt Papers* (Edinburgh: Paul Harris, 1983).

MOLLY WEIR
Shoes were for Sunday (London: Hutchinson, 1970).

REBECCA WEST
Black Lamb and Grey Falcon: the Record of a Journey through Yugoslavia in 1937 (London: Macmillan, 1942; Edinburgh: Canongate, 1993).

KENNETH WHITE
Travels in the Drifting Dawn (Edinburgh: Mainstream, 1989).

SECTION 8
Resources and Connections

The following headings and contacts may be useful in support of the material in this volume.

PUBLICATIONS

Association for Scottish Literary Studies (ASLS)

c/o Dept of Scottish History
9 University Gardens
University of Glasgow
Glasgow G12 8QH
Phone: 0141 330 5309

ASLS publishes a wide variety of texts in the field of Scottish Studies, for example *Scottish Literary Journal* and its sequel, The *Review of Scottish Studies*, and *Scottish Language*, and *New Writing Scotland*, an annual volume publishing poems and prose from both emerging and established writers. Moreover, ASLS publishes the *Scotnotes* series, which are comprised of valuable and comprehensive study guides to a large number of the Scottish Classics. ASLS also publishes an *Annual Volume*, each year a different work of major importance written by a leading expert in the field. By joining the ASLS, the reader will receive each of these and more over the year of subscription (except *Scotnotes*, which are priced individually).

Scotnotes publications include the following titles:
Lewis Grassic Gibbon's Sunset Song by Douglas Young
The Poetry of Edwin Morgan by Geddes Thomson
George Douglas Brown's The House with the Green Shutters by Iain Crichton Smith
James Hogg's The Private Memoirs & Confessions of a Justified Sinner by Elaine Petrie
The Poetry of Norman MacCaig by Roderick Watson
George Mackay Brown's Greenvoe by Alan MacGillivray
Muriel Spark's The Prime of Miss Jean Brodie by David S. Robb
The Poetry of Iain Crichton Smith by John Blackburn
Robert Burns by Kenneth Simpson

RESOURCES AND CONNECTIONS

Robin Jenkins's The Cone-Gatherers by Iain Crichton Smith
The Poems of Robert Henryson by Gerald Baird
The Poetry of William Dunbar by R. D. S. Jack
John Buchan's Witch Wood, Huntingtower & The Thirty-Nine Steps by C. MacLachlan
William McIlvanney's Laidlaw by Beth Dickson
The Poetry of Hugh MacDiarmid by Alan Riach
Liz Lochhead's Mary Queen of Scots Got Her Head Chopped Off by Margery McCulloch

ASLS *Annual Volumes* include the following titles amongst many others:
Boswell in Scotland and Beyond, ed. Thomas Crawford
The Christis Kirk Tradition: Scots Poems of Folk Festivity, ed. Allan H. MacLaine
The Complete Poems of Edwin Muir, ed. Peter Butter
A Galloway Glossary by Alastair Riach
Minority Languages in Central Scotland, ed. J. D. McClure
Sir Walter Scott: An Annotated Bibliography of Scholarship and Criticism, ed. Jill Rubenstein
Margaret Oliphant: Selected Short Stories of the Supernatural, ed. Margaret Gray

ASLS Conferences

ASLS Annual Schools Conference
Dept of Scottish History
University of Glasgow
9 University Gardens
Glasgow G12 8QH
Phone: 0141 330 5309

Annual Burns Conference
Centre for Scottish Cultural Studies
University of Strathclyde
Glasgow G1 1XH
Phone: 0141 548 3518

Arts and Literary Associations

Gaelic Books Council
Department of Celtic
University of Glasgow
Glasgow G12 8QQ
Phone: 0141 339 8853
or
22 Mansfield Street
Glasgow G11 5QP

1214

Poetry Association of Scotland
38 Dovecot Road
Edinburgh EH12 7LE
Phone: 0131 334 5241

The Saltire Society
Fountain Close
22 High Street
Edinburgh EH1 1TF

The Scots Language Society
Scots Language Resource Centre
A. K. Bell Library
York Place
Perth PH2 8EP
Phone: 01738 440 199

Scottish Arts Council
12 Manor Place
Edinburgh EH3 7DD
Phone: 0131 243 2444

Scottish Book Trust
Scottish Book Centre
137 Dundee Street
Edinburgh EH11 1BG
Phone: 0131 229 3663

Scottish National Dictionary Association
27 George Square
Edinburgh EH8 9LD
Phone: 0131 650 4149

Scottish Poetry Library
5 Crichton's Close
Canongate
Edinburgh EH8 8DT
Phone: 0131 557 2876

Scottish Publishers Association
Scottish Book Centre
137 Dundee Street
Edinburgh EH11 1BG
Phone: 0131 228 6866

The Scottish Storytelling Forum
The Netherbow
45 High Street
Edinburgh EH1 1SR
Phone: 0131 556 9579/2647

Scottish Publishers Association (information re publishers)
Scottish Book Centre
137 Dundee Street
Edinburgh EH11 1BG
Phone: 0131 228 6866

Literary Journals and Publications

Books in Scotland/In Scotland
9 Glenisla Gardens
Edinburgh EH2 2HR
Phone: 0131 662 1915

The Broken Fiddle
Editorial Committee
1 Church Street
Macduff AB44 1UR

The Burns Chronicle
28 Stranka Avenue
Paisley PA2 9DW

Cencrastus
Unit 1
Abbeymount Techbase
8 Easter Road
Edinburgh EH8 8EJ
Phone: 0131 661 5687

Chapman
4 Broughton Place
Edinburgh EH1 3RX
Phone: 0131 557 2207

Cutting Teeth
The Arts and Cultural Development Office
17 Castlemilk Arcade
Glasgow G45 9AA

The Dark Horse
c/o Gerry Cambridge
Brownsbank Cottages
Candymill
Biggar
South Lanarkshire ML12 6QY

Edinburgh Review
22 George Square
Edinburgh EH8 9LF

Gairfish
71 Long Lane
Broughty Ferry
Dundee DD5 2AS

Gairm (Gaelic quarterly)
29 Waterloo Street
Glasgow G2 6BZ
Phone: 0141 221 1971

Lallans
c/o The Scots Language Society
A.K. Bell Library
York Place
Perth PH2 8AP
Phone: 01738 440199

RESOURCES AND CONNECTIONS

Lines Review
Edgefield Road
Loanhead
Midlothian EH20 9SY

Nerve Magazine
PO Box 3848
Glasgow G46 6AS

New Writing Scotland
Dept of Scottish History
University of Glasgow
9 University Gardens
Glasgow G12 8QH
Phone: 0141 330 5309

Nomad
Survivors Poetry Scotland
The Tryst
Cresswell Street
Glasgow G12

Northwords
68 Strathkanaird
Ullapool
Wester Ross IV26 2TW

Poetry Scotland
Diehard
3 Spittal Street
Edinburgh EH3 9DY
Phone: 0131 229 7252

Scotlands
School of English
University of St Andrews
St Andrews KY16 9AL

Scottish Film and Television Archive
1 Bowmont Gardens
Glasgow G12
Phone: 0141 337 7400

Scottish Studies
School of Scottish Studies
27 George Square
Edinburgh EH8 9LD
Phone: 0131 650 3056/4167

Southfields
David Kinloch
Dept of Modern Languages
University of Strathclyde
26 Richmond Street
Glasgow G1 1XH

Tocher
School of Scottish Studies
27 George Square
Edinburgh EH8 9LD
Phone: 0131 650 3056/4167

Zed 2 0
AKROS Publications
33 Lady Nairn Avenue
Kirkcaldy
Fife KY1 2AW
Phone: 01592 651 522

TELEVISION AND AUDIO RESOURCES

The reader might find some of the following useful for resources such as interviews with writers, adaptations of fiction and drama, literature readings, literary discussions, and the like.

RESOURCES AND CONNECTIONS

Television and Radio Contacts

BBC Scotland
Queen Margaret Drive
Glasgow G12 8DG
Phone: 0141 339 8844/338 2000
or John Russell
Education Officer
Edinburgh
Phone: 0131 248 4243

Channel Four
124 Horseferry Road
London SW1P 2TX
Phone: 0171 396 4444 (Switchboard)
or 0171 306 8333 (General Enquiries)

Scottish Television
Cowcaddens
Glasgow G2 3PR
Phone: 0141 300 3000

Audio Recordings

Scotsoun
Dr George Philp
5 Bogton Avenue
Muirend
Glasgow G44 3JJ

There are also a number of recordings of medieval and Renaissance music available, such as those by Coronach.

Other Media/Teaching Support

Scottish Cultural Resources Access Network (SCRAN)
Abden House
1 Marchhall Crescent
Edinburgh EH16 5HW
Phone: 0131 662 1211

1220

SCRAN is a public organisation with Millennium Commission funding to digitise Scotland's rich human history and influential material culture. The SCRAN database has information on Scottish history, landscapes, work, people, play, sport, music, and literature. SCRAN is currently working on a project called 'Sounds of Scots', an archive of spoken material by Scottish writers to be made available through the Web.

Scottish Council for Education and Technology (SCET)
74 Victoria Crescent Road
Dowanhill
Glasgow G12 9JN
Phone: 0141 337 5000
SCET's main focus is to support and promote learning through technology, and it is committed to promoting state-of-the-art educational resources to schools, further education establishments and the business community. SCET also provides advice, guidance, training, technological solutions, and consultancy.

Software for Teaching English and Scottish Language and Literature and its Assessment (STELLA)
University of Glasgow
6 University Gardens
Glasgow G12 8QQ
Phone: 0141 330 4980
The aim of the STELLA project is to examine the applications of computers in tertiary level of the teaching of English and Scots, and to develop software in the broad area of English and Scottish Studies. Three departments of the University of Glasgow are involved in STELLA: English Language, English Literature, and Scottish Literature.
   Software provided by STELLA includes:

A *Guide to Scottish Literature*, an electronic course in Scottish Literature, divided into three units: *Medieval and Renaissance Literature 1375–1700; Poetry and Fiction 1700–1900; Poetry, Fiction and Drama since 1920*. The essays are followed by notes, questions, and topics for discussion, and are suitable for use in courses from sixth-year studies upwards.

Older Scots, a software package containing information on the development of the Scots language from 1100 to modern times and is designed to help the beginning student appreciate Older Scots literature.

The Basics of Scots Metre (1, 2 & 3), a self-access software package which introduces students to the main conventional metres used in Scottish verse, especially iambic pentameter. It can be used both with students who require a straightforward grounding in the subject and with those who study it in greater depth. Unit 3 of the package deals with verse of greater metrical variety.

RESOURCES AND CONNECTIONS

Scots Teaching And Research Network (STARN)
Web site: www.arts.gla.ac.uk/www/english/comet/level2.htm

STARN has been set up by the STELLA project. It collects and makes available through the World Wide Web a selection of Scottish literary and non-literary materials: prose, poetry, drama, criticism and commentary. These materials are usually difficult to access by other means. They are primarily intended for use by educationalists and researchers into aspects of Scottish culture, particularly Scottish literature, and varieties of Scots language.

PLACES OF LITERARY INTEREST

Abbotsford (Sir Walter Scott's Home and Library)
Melrose
Roxburghshire TD6 9BQ
Phone: 01896 752 043

Burns House Museum
Castle Street
Mauchline
Ayrshire KA5 5BZ
Phone: 01290 550 045

Grassic Gibbon Centre
Arbuthnott
Laurencekirk AB30 1LX
Phone: 01561 361 668

MacDiarmid's Cottage
Biggar Museum Trust
Brownsbank Committee
Kirkstyle
Biggar, Lanarkshire ML12 6QY
Phone: 01899 221 050

The Scottish Literary Tour Company
(Tours for Edinburgh and Glasgow)
Suite 2
97B West Bow
Edinburgh EH1 2JP
Phone: 0131 226 6665

The Writer's Museum
(dedicated to Robert Burns, Sir Walter Scott and Robert Louis Stevenson)
Lady Stairs House
Lady Stairs Close
Lawnmarket
Edinburgh EH1 2PA
Phone: 0131 529 4901

FESTIVALS AND EVENTS

Edinburgh Book Festival
Scottish Book Centre
137 Dundee Street
Edinburgh E11 1BG
Phone: 0131 228 5444
Contact: Catherine Lockerbie, Director

Glasgow Book Festival
Literature Development Officer for Glasgow
Mitchell Library
North Street
Glasgow G3 7DN
Contact: 0141 287 2838

National Poetry Day
Annually, on first or second Thursday of October
Contact Scottish Book Trust
Phone: 0131 229 3663

The PEN-Glasgow University Naomi Mitchison Lecture
(Annually in November)
University of Glasgow
Dept. of Scottish Literature
6 University Gardens
Glasgow G12 8QQ
Phone: 0141–330 5093

LIBRARIES AND ARCHIVE MATERIALS

Scottish Library Association (local libraries)
1 John Street
Hamilton ML3 7EU
Phone: 01698 458 888

Mitchell Library
North Street
Glasgow G3 7DN
Phone: 0141 221 9600

The National Library of Scotland
George IV Bridge
Edinburgh EH1 1EW
Phone: 0131 226 4531

Scottish Poetry Library
5 Crichton's Close
Canongate
Edinburgh EH8 ADT
Phone: 0131 557 2876

Scottish Theatre Archive
Glasgow University Library
Hillhead Street
Glasgow G12 8QE
Phone: 0141 330 6758

LITERARY SOCIETIES

There are a number of literary societies in Scotland which are concerned
with the promotion and reading of major Scottish literary figures. For further
information on
Robert Henryson Society
James Hogg Society
Walter Scott Society

Robert Louis Stevenson Society
Neil Munro Society and others, consult *A Directory of Publishing in Scotland 2001* (Edinburgh: Scottish Publishers Association, 2001); or, *Writers' & Artists' Yearbook 2001* (London: A&C Black, 2001).

WRITERS' GROUPS

There are a vast number of active writers' groups in Scotland. The reader is advised to contact the Scottish Arts Council Helpline for information about these (e-mail: help.desk.sac@artsfb.org.uk). Information on writers' groups in Glasgow can be obtained from Catherine McInerney, Literature Development Officer for Glasgow, Mitchell Library, North Street, Glasgow G3 7DN. Phone: 0141 287 2838. The Literature Development Officer's chief objective is to raise the profile of literature in Glasgow. The Officer holds extensive information on Glasgow writers, literary organisations and writers' groups.

AUTHORIAL AND EDITORIAL CREDITS

This volume grew out of the very extensive materials (eighteen book-length volumes) which accompany the three-year distance-taught MPhil degree course offered by the Department of Scottish Literature of the University of Glasgow. As work progressed it became apparent that such extensive materials would have to be considerably edited and rewritten for the more general purposes of the book. As general editor of the Scottish Language and Literature Series, with my co-editors Sarah Dunnigan and Alan MacGillivray, I am greatly indebted to a large number of colleagues who helped in the tasks of editing, rewriting, and generally checking and piecing together the jigsaw. Such a variety of contributors and helpers makes accreditation difficult; what follows acknowledges the authors of MPhil or new material and bibliographies, and those who helped build reading lists and resource suggestions.

SECTION 1

1 Literary Roots: Medieval Poetry   *Gerald Baird*
2 Henryson and Dunbar   *Gerald Baird*
3 Early Scottish Drama: *Ane Satyre* and *Philotus*   *Morna Fleming (Ane Satyre)*,
   Maureen Farrell (Philotus)
4 Renaissance Poetry: The Jacobean Period   *Morna Fleming*
5 The Ballads   *James Alison*
6 Widening the Range 1   *Sarah Dunnigan, Nicola Royan*

SECTION 2

7 Enlightenment and Vernacular   *Gerard Carruthers, Christopher Whyte*
8 Ramsay and Fergusson   *Douglas Gifford, Alan MacGillivray*

TITLES INDEX

1229

TITLES INDEX

Names Index